Youth and skills:
Putting education to work

Youth and skills:
Putting education to work

UNESCO
Publishing

United Nations
Educational, Scientific and
Cultural Organization

Education for All Global Monitoring Report 2012

This Report is an independent publication commissioned by UNESCO on behalf of the international community. It is the product of a collaborative effort involving members of the Report Team and many other people, agencies, institutions and governments.

The designations employed and the presentation of the material in this publication do not imply the expression of any opinion whatsoever on the part of UNESCO concerning the legal status of any country, territory, city or area, or of its authorities, or concerning the delimitation of its frontiers or boundaries.

The EFA Global Monitoring Report team is responsible for the choice and the presentation of the facts contained in this book and for the opinions expressed therein, which are not necessarily those of UNESCO and do not commit the Organization. Overall responsibility for the views and opinions expressed in the Report is taken by its Director.

© UNESCO, 2012
All rights reserved
Second edition
Published in 2012 by the United Nations Educational,
Scientific and Cultural Organization
7, Place de Fontenoy, 75352 Paris 07 SP, France

Graphic design by FHI 360
Layout by FHI 360

Library of Congress Cataloging in Publication Data
Data available
Typeset by UNESCO
ISBN 978-92-3-104240-9

Cover illustration
© UNESCO/Sarah Wilkins

Foreword

This 10th edition of the *EFA Global Monitoring Report* could not be better timed. The third goal of Education for All is to ensure that all young people have the opportunity to acquire skills. The urgency of reaching this goal has sharpened acutely since 2000.

The global economic downturn is impacting on unemployment. One young person in eight across the world is looking for work. Youth populations are large and growing. The wellbeing and prosperity of young people depend more than ever on the skills that education and training can provide. Failing to meet this need is a waste of human potential and economic power. Youth skills have never been so vital.

This *Global Monitoring Report* reminds us that education is not only about making sure all children can attend school. It is about setting young people up for life, by giving them opportunities to find decent work, earn a living, contribute to their communities and societies, and fulfil their potential. At the wider level, it is about helping countries nurture the workforce they need to grow in the global economy.

There has been undeniable progress towards the six EFA goals — including an expansion of early childhood care and education and improvements in gender parity at primary level. However, with three years to go until the 2015 deadline, the world is still not on track. Progress towards some goals is faltering. The number of children out of school has stagnated for the first time since 2000. Adult literacy and quality of education still demand faster progress.

Recent developments ascribe ever greater urgency to ensuring equitable access to appropriate skills development programmes. As urban populations grow rapidly, especially in low income countries, young people need skills to work their way out of poverty. In rural areas, young people require new coping mechanisms to deal with climate change and shrinking farm sizes, and to exploit opportunities for off-farm work. This Report reveals that around 200 million young people need a second chance to acquire the basic literacy and numeracy skills, which are essential to learning further skills for work. In all of this, women and the poor face particular hardship.

We must see the growing numbers of young people who are unemployed or trapped in poverty as a call to action — to meet their needs by 2015 and to keep momentum after then. We can achieve universal lower secondary education by 2030, and we must.

Donors' commitment to education may be waning, and this is deeply worrying. Government budgets are under pressure today, but we must not risk the gains made since 2000 by reducing engagement now. Evidence in this Report shows that funds spent on education generate ten to fifteen times as much in economic growth over a person's lifetime. Now is the time to invest for the future.

We must think creatively and use all the resources at our disposal. Governments and donors must continue to prioritize education. Countries should look to their own resources, which could be giving millions of children and young people skills for life. Whatever the source of funding, the needs of the disadvantaged must be a high priority in every strategy.

Young people everywhere have great potential — this must be developed. I hope this Report will catalyse renewed efforts worldwide to educate children and young people so they can greet the world with confidence, follow their ambitions and live the lives they choose.

Irina Bokova
Director-General of UNESCO

Acknowledgements

This Report was made possible thanks to the support and advice of many individuals and organizations. The EFA Global Monitoring Report team would like to thank everyone who contributed to this endeavour.

The *EFA Global Monitoring Report*'s Advisory Board plays a key role in providing guidance and support at all stages of the Report's cycle. We would like to thank each of its members for their time, energy and enthusiasm. Particular thanks go to the chair of the Advisory Board, Amina J. Mohammed. The publication was made possible by the generous financial support of a group of funders.

We are very grateful for the advice and support of individuals, divisions and units within UNESCO, both at headquarters and in the field. The UNESCO Institute for Statistics (UIS) plays a key role in the development of the Report. We warmly thank its director and staff, including Redouane Assad, Sheena Bell, Manuel Cardoso, Cesar Guadalupe, Friedrich Huebler, Alison Kennedy, Albert Motivans, Simon Normandeau, Saïd Ould Ahmedou Voffal, Pascale Ratovondrahona and Wendy Xiaodan Weng.

We would also like to acknowledge the support from colleagues at the International Institute for Educational Planning (IIEP), the International Bureau of Education (IBE), the UNESCO Institute for Lifelong Learning (UIL), and the International Centre for Technical and Vocational Education and Training (UNEVOC).

Special thanks to colleagues in UNESCO's Education Sector as well as colleagues in the Sector for External Relations and Public Information who play a vital role in supporting the *Global Monitoring Report*. We are also grateful to our colleagues in the Knowledge Management Service and the Sections for Finance and Budget Administration and for Human Resources for facilitating our work daily.

Sincere gratitude goes to Kevin Watkins, the previous director of the *Global Monitoring Report*, who participated in the initial development of this Report.

A number of experts generously gave their time to prepare think pieces, participate in meetings and provide comments on the drafts of the Report. Special thanks go to members of the expert panel, including Arvil Van Adams, Borhene Chakroun, Christopher Colclough, Kenneth King and Furio Rosati. We would also like to thank Ragui Assaad, David Atchoarena, Roland Baecker, Michaela Baur, Laura Brewer, Gareth Conyard, Marta Encinas-Martin, Mary-Luce Fiaux Niada, Michael Härtel, Maria Hartl, Claudia Jacinto, Emmanuel Jimenez, Simon Junker, Mark Keese, Matthias Pilz, Bianca Rohrbach, Katja Römer, Roland Schwartz, Law Song Seng, Kate Shoesmith, Madhu Singh, Birgit Thomann, Richard Walther and Michael Ward.

The Report would not have been possible without the advice and support of numerous researchers who prepared background papers and other commissioned inputs to inform the analysis. We would like to thank them for sharing their expertise and time: Andrés Mejia Acosta, Peter Aggleton, Subhash Agrawal, Nadir Altinok, Monika Aring, Shubhashansha Bakshi, Farzana Bardai, Paul Bennell, Gabrielle D. Blumberg, Hong-Min Chun, Yekaterina Chzhen, David Clarke, Ute Clement, Arne H. Eide, Jakob Engel, Kyu Cheol Eo, Ernesto Martins Faria, Ningwakwe George, Ursula Grant, Lorenzo Guarcello, Eric A. Hanushek, Kenneth Harttgen, Jo Hawley, Frances Hunt, Zoe James, Kate Jere, Jyotsna Jha, Hiromichi Katayama, Maria Kett, HyeJin Kim, Irena Kovarova, Scott Lyon,

Anna McCord, Scott Murray, Maurice Mutisya, Anne-Mari Nevala, Landon Newby, Nicole Nikolaidis, Christophe Nordman, Lee E. Nordstrum, Moses Oketch, Laure Pasquier-Doumer, Francesco Pastore, Maro Ranzani, Caine Rolleston, Fiona Samuels, Roland Schwartz, Lucio Severo, Kate Shoesmith, Ratna Sudarshan, Daniela Ulicna, Justin van Fleet, Nermine Wally, Karin Wedig, Ludger Woessmann, Shoko Yamada and Kazuhiro Yoshida.

We are also grateful to the Institute of Development Studies, GHK Consulting Ltd, the City & Guilds Centre for Skills Development, the Organisation for Economic Co-operation and Development, the Overseas Development Institute, the United Nations Girls' Education Initiative, Understanding Children's Work, Young Lives Programme and the World Bank for their support in providing research and analysis.

We would like to extend our thanks to Interactive Things for the development of the World Inequalities Database on Education (WIDE) and Globescan for facilitating focus group discussions with young people around the world. We are also very grateful to Sarah Wilkins for the design of the cover and the illustration included in this Report. Warm thanks go to the young people who participated in the youth blog and took part in the art contest on youth, skills and work. Our congratulations in particular go to the winner, Khalid Mohamed Hammad Elkhateem from Sudan.

Special thanks to all those who worked tirelessly to support the production of the Report, including Sylvaine Baeyens, Rebecca Brite, Laura Chan Aramendi, FHI 360, Jana Gough, David McDonald, Max McMaster, Cathy Nolan and Stefanie Schnell. Many colleagues within and outside UNESCO were involved in the translation and production of the Report and we would like to thank them all.

The EFA Global Monitoring Report team

Director: Pauline Rose

Kwame Akyeampong, Manos Antoninis, Madeleine Barry, Nicole Bella, Stuart Cameron, Erin Chemery, Diederick de Jongh, Marcos Delprato, Hans Botnen Eide, Joanna Härmä, Andrew Johnston, Léna Krichewsky, François Leclercq, Elise Legault, Leila Loupis, Alasdair McWilliam, Patrick Montjourides, Karen Moore, Claudine Mukizwa, Judith Randrianatoavina, Kate Redman, Maria Rojnov-Petit, Marisol Sanjines, Martina Simeti, Asma Zubairi.

The *Education for All Global Monitoring Report* is an independent annual publication. It is facilitated and supported by UNESCO.

For more information, please contact:
EFA Global Monitoring Report team
c/o UNESCO, 7, place de Fontenoy
75352 Paris 07 SP, France
Email: efareport@unesco.org
Tel.: +33 1 45 68 07 41
www.efareport.unesco.org
efareport.wordpress.com

Previous *EFA Global Monitoring Reports*
2011. The hidden crisis: Armed conflict and education
2010. Reaching the marginalized
2009. Overcoming inequality: why governance matters
2008. Education for All by 2015 — Will we make it?
2007. Strong foundations — Early childhood care and education
2006. Literacy for life
2005. Education for All — The quality imperative
2003/4. Gender and Education for All — The leap to equality
2002. Education for All — Is the world on track?

Any errors or omissions found subsequent to printing will be corrected in the online version at www.efareport.unesco.org.

Contents

2012

Education for All Global Monitoring Report

List of figures, tables and text boxes

Figures

Tables

Text boxes

Overview

With just three years to go until the deadline for the Education for All goals that were set in Dakar, Senegal, it is vitally urgent to ensure that the collective commitments made by 164 countries in 2000 are met. Lessons also need to be drawn to inform the definition of future international education goals and the design of mechanisms to make sure that all partners live up to their promises.

Unfortunately, this year's *EFA Global Monitoring Report* shows that progress towards many of the goals is slowing down, and that most EFA goals are unlikely to be met. Despite the gloomy outlook overall, progress in some of the world's poorest countries shows what can be achieved with the commitment of national governments and aid donors, including greater numbers of children attending pre-school, completing primary school and making the transition to secondary education.

The 2012 *EFA Global Monitoring Report* is divided into two parts. Part I provides a snapshot of progress towards the six EFA goals, and towards spending on education to finance the goals. Part II turns to the third EFA goal, paying particular attention to the skills needs of young people.

Monitoring the Education for All goals

The six Education for All goals

Expand early childhood care and education
Early childhood is the critical period in which to lay the foundations for success in education and beyond, so early childhood care and education should be at the centre of EFA and broader development agendas.

Children who are hungry, malnourished or ill are not in a position to gain the skills needed for later learning and employment. There are signs that early childhood health is improving, but from a very low base in some countries and not fast enough to meet international development goals. The annual rate of decline in child mortality accelerated from 1.9% in 1990–2000 to 2.5% in 2000–2010. Recent estimates suggest that just over half the decline in child deaths can be attributed to more education among women of reproductive age.

While it is encouraging that today 3 more children survive for every 100 born than in 1990,

© Giacomo Pirozzi/PANOS

there are still 28 countries, 25 of which are in sub-Saharan Africa, where more than 10 in 100 children die before the age of 5.

An important factor behind child deaths is malnutrition, which also hinders children's cognitive development and capacity to learn. Stunting, or being short for one's age, is the clearest sign of malnutrition. Globally, 171 million children under age 5 were affected by moderate or severe stunting in 2010. By 2015, on current trends, the number of children suffering from stunting will still be as high as 157 million, or around one in four children under 5.

Children in rural areas and from poor households suffer more because nutrition is not just a matter of general availability of food. Rather it is also a matter of access to food, good health care, water and sanitation services, from which the poorest are often denied. For example, in Nepal, the stunting rate was 26% among the richest children and 56% among the poorest, with corresponding rates of 27% in urban and 42% in rural areas. Ongoing food price instability, climate change and conflict make improving nutrition a challenge in many parts of the world.

But the contrasting experience of many countries shows that political commitment can markedly improve nutrition. Within less than two decades, Brazil managed to eliminate an urban-rural gap in malnutrition thanks to a combination of improved education of mothers, access to maternal and child health services, provision of water and sanitation, and targeted social transfers. Over the same period, rates of malnutrition, particularly in rural areas, in countries such as the Plurinational State of Bolivia, Guatemala and Peru, remained higher than expected for their income level.

Good quality pre-school programmes are also vital to prepare young children for school. Evidence from places as diverse as Australia, India, Mozambique, Turkey and Uruguay demonstrates the short- and long-term benefits of pre-primary education. These range from a head-start in literacy and numeracy skills to improved attention, effort and initiative – all of which lead to better education and employment outcomes.

Recent evidence based on the 2009 survey in the OECD Programme for International Student Assessment (PISA) shows that in fifty-eight out of sixty-five countries, 15-year-old students who had attended at least a year of pre-primary school outperformed students who had not, even after accounting for socio-economic background. In Australia, Brazil and Germany, the average benefit after controlling for socio-economic background was equivalent to one year of schooling.

Since 1999, the number of children enrolled in pre-school has risen by almost half. However, this still leaves more than one in two children not attending, rising to five out of six in the poorest countries. The groups that would benefit the most from pre-school are missing out the most. In Nigeria, about two out of three children from the richest 20% of households attend pre-school, compared with less than one in ten from the poorest 20% of households.

Underinvestment is a key reason for low coverage of pre-schooling. This level accounts for less than 10% of the education budget in most countries, and its share tends to be particularly low in poor countries. Nepal and the Niger spend under 0.1% of GNP on pre-school, and Madagascar and Senegal less than 0.02%.

One consequence of low government investment is that the average share of enrolment in private pre-school is 33%. In the Syrian Arab Republic, with a pre-primary gross enrolment ratio of 10%, the share of private provision was 72%. This indicates demand that is not met by the public sector.

It seems unlikely that expanding fee-charging private pre-schools will reach more of the poorest households, whose children are those least likely to be enrolled. In India's Andhra Pradesh state, pre-school enrolment in rural areas is highest among the richest 20% of households, where almost one-third of children attend private institutions. Almost all children in pre-school from the poorest households are served by government providers.

Where children live can also determine the quality of the service. In rural areas of China,

Peru and the United Republic of Tanzania, children who make it to pre-school are more likely than urban children to be in an overcrowded class with fewer qualified teachers and fewer learning resources.

To ensure that all children reap the benefits of pre-school, reforms are needed, including expanding facilities and making sure they are affordable, identifying appropriate ways to link pre-schools with primary schools, and coordinating pre-school activities with wider early childhood interventions.

The importance of making balanced efforts to improve conditions for young children is further highlighted by a new index developed for this year's Report, which evaluates progress on this goal and its three main components: health, nutrition and education.

Some countries score almost equally well on all three indicators (such as Chile) or equally poorly (such as the Niger). Others have a very high or very low score for one dimension relative to their overall standing in the index scale, which reveals specific challenges. For example, Jamaica and the Philippines both have a child mortality rate of about 30 per thousand live births but have very different education records. Only 38% of children aged 3 to 7 were enrolled in a pre-primary or primary school programme in the Philippines, compared with 90% in Jamaica. This highlights the need to invest in integrated approaches that give equal importance to all aspects of early childhood development.

Achieve universal primary education
On current trends, the goal of universal primary education (UPE) will be missed by a large margin. The major push towards getting more children into school that was kick-started at the World Education Forum in Dakar in 2000 is grinding to a halt. The number of primary school age children out of school has fallen from 108 million to 61 million since 1999, but three-quarters of this reduction was achieved between 1999 and 2004. Between 2008 and 2010, progress stalled altogether.

South and West Asia and sub-Saharan Africa started from similar positions in 1999 with around 40 million children of primary school age out of school, but have subsequently progressed at very different speeds. Between 1999 and 2008, the number of out-of-school children in South and West Asia fell by 26 million, while the reduction in sub-Saharan Africa was a more modest 13 million. Between 2008 and 2010, out-of-school numbers increased in sub-Saharan Africa by 1.6 million, but declined by 0.6 million in South and West Asia. Sub-Saharan Africa now accounts for half of the world's out-of-school children.

Among countries with data, twelve account for almost half of the global out-of-school population. Nigeria heads the list with one in six of the world's out-of-school children, a total of 10.5 million. It had 3.6 million more children out of school in 2010 than in 2000. By contrast, Ethiopia and India managed to reduce their numbers of out-of-school children dramatically. In India, there were 18 million fewer children out of school in 2008 than in 2001.

Among those out of school, some may enter late, while others may have dropped out and many may never enrol. In 2010, 47% of children out of school were likely never to enrol. The proportion was highest in low income countries, where 57% of out-of-school children could expect never to enrol. Girls were more likely than boys to belong to this group.

Just five years before 2015, twenty-nine countries had a net enrolment ratio of less than 85%. These countries are very unlikely to achieve the goal of UPE by the deadline.

Children of official school starting age who did not enter school by 2010 will not be able to complete the primary cycle by 2015. In 2010, there were seventy countries with a net intake rate below 80%.

The challenge of UPE is to get children into school at the correct age and to ensure that they progress through the system and complete the education cycle. Analysis for this Report shows that, across twenty-two countries with household survey data between 2005 and 2010, 38% of students entering school were two or more years older than the official age. In the sub-Saharan African countries included in the analysis, 41% of the children starting primary school were two or more years older than the official school entry age.

More children from poor households start late, usually because they live too far from school, their health and nutritional status is worse and/or their parents may be less aware of the importance of sending children to school on time. In Colombia, 42% from the poorest households started two or more years late, compared with 11% from the richest households.

Late entry influences whether children complete the education cycle. By grade 3, children who have entered late can be four times as likely to drop out as children who started school at the correct age.

Poverty also has a negative effect on children's likelihood of leaving school early. In Uganda, 97 out of every 100 children from the richest quintile entered primary school and 80 reached the last grade in 2006; of children from the bottom quintile, 90 out of 100 entered school but only 49 reached the last grade.

To tackle the barriers that prevent disadvantaged children from entering on time and progressing through school, system-wide reforms are needed. In many countries, cost is the primary reason parents do not enrol their children in school or take them out of school. Even after school fees have been formally abolished, official or unofficial fees still accounted for almost 15% of such spending in eight countries analysed for this Report.

Richer households are able to spend significantly more on their children's education, improving their opportunities for better quality schooling. This includes spending more on private schooling or private tuition. In Nigeria, the richest 20% of households spend more than ten times as much as the poorest 20% for children to attend primary school. Even low fee private schooling is out of reach for the poorest households. Sending three children to a school in a Lagos slum costs the equivalent of 46% of the minimum wage. In Bangladesh and Egypt, the richest households spend four times as much as the poorest households on supplementary tuition, and are more likely to invest in such tuition in the first place.

Abolishing formal school fees has been a fundamental step towards realizing UPE. But it is also important for governments to take complementary measures, such as grants for schools to help them cover their costs so that they do not informally impose other charges on parents. Social protection measures, such as cash transfers, are vital to ensure that poor households have the financial means to cover all school costs without compromising their spending on other basic needs. Steps also need to be taken to ensure that the ability of richer households to spend more on private schooling and private tuition does not lead to widening of inequality.

Promote learning and life skills for young people and adults

The social and economic challenges of recent years have focused attention on the availability of skills and learning opportunities for the young. As the thematic part of this Report details, these challenges are bringing a sense of urgency to an important goal that has not been given the attention it deserves because of the ambiguity of the commitments made when the EFA goals were established in 2000.

Formal secondary schooling is the most effective way to develop the skills needed for work and life. Despite a global increase in the number of children enrolling in secondary school, the gross enrolment ratio for lower secondary school was just 52% in low income countries in 2010, leaving millions of young people to face life without the foundation skills they need to earn a decent living. Worldwide, 71 million adolescents of lower secondary school age were out of school in 2010. The number has stagnated since 2007. Three out of four out-of-school adolescents live in South and West Asia and sub-Saharan Africa.

There are 25% more children in secondary school today than in 1999. Sub-Saharan Africa has doubled the number of students enrolling over the period, yet has the world's lowest total secondary enrolment ratio, at 40% in 2010.

Some young people develop skills through technical and vocational education. The proportion of secondary school pupils enrolled in such programmes has remained at 11% since 1999.

Skills are not only developed in school. International organizations have a range of frameworks for categorizing skills and skills development programmes. But twelve years after the EFA goals were established in Dakar, the international community is still a long way from agreeing what constitutes progress in 'equitable access to appropriate learning and life skills programmes' (the core of goal 3), agreeing on a coherent set of internationally comparable indicators and assessing whether progress is being made. There are promising signs that the situation may be changing, but recent developments will not produce sufficient data in time to measure goal 3 adequately before the deadline has passed.

Any post-2015 international goals for skills development need to be more precisely defined and to set out clearly how progress can be measured. This should be based on a realistic assessment of information that can be collected, in order to avoid the problems that have plagued efforts to monitor goal 3.

The Dakar Framework for Action specified some risks from which young people need to be protected by developing the relevant life skills. One of those risks was HIV and AIDS. HIV-related knowledge remains low. Recent global estimates based on 119 countries show only 24% of young women and 36% of young men aged 15 to 24 being able to identify ways of preventing the sexual transmission of HIV and to reject major misconceptions about its transmission.

Knowledge of HIV and AIDS is low even in countries with high prevalence rates. In 2007, about 60,000 grade 6 students (aged around 13, on average) in 15 countries of southern and eastern Africa were assessed on their knowledge of HIV and AIDS. The test focused on the official curriculum frameworks for HIV education adopted by ministries of education in the participating countries. The results suggest ineffective implementation and possibly poor design of the official curriculum. On average, only 36% of students reached the minimum required knowledge levels and just 7% reached the desirable level.

It is not enough to ensure that youth know how to protect their own health and the health of others

if, for example, they do not feel empowered to take the right action at the right time.

Life skills education with a focus on HIV and AIDS encourages young people to adopt attitudes and behaviour that protect their health, for example by empowering them to negotiate sexual relations. It does this by addressing psychosocial and interpersonal skills such as assertive communication, self-esteem, decision-making and negotiation. Life skills programmes that approach sensitive issues in ways that allow student engagement should be introduced to complement topics in the curriculum such as health education and broader HIV and AIDS education.

Reduce adult illiteracy by 50%

Literacy is crucial for adults' social and economic well-being – and that of their children. Yet progress on this goal has been very limited, largely as a result of government and donor indifference. There were still 775 million adults who could not read or write in 2010. Half were in South and West Asia, and over a fifth in sub-Saharan Africa.

In 81 out of the 146 countries with data for 2005–2010, more women than men are illiterate. Of these countries, twenty-one display extreme gender disparity, with fewer than seven literate women for every ten literate men.

Globally the adult literacy rate has increased over the past two decades, from 76% in 1985–1994 to 84% in 2005–2010. But among forty-three countries with an adult literacy rate below 90% in 1998–2001 only three will reach the target of reducing illiteracy by 50% by 2015. Some countries are likely to miss the target by a very wide margin. And while some in the latter group have made significant gains – such as Mali, which doubled its literacy rate – others, like Madagascar, have experienced a decline in the last decade.

Almost three-quarters of adults who are illiterate live in just ten countries. Of the global total, 37% live in India. In Nigeria, the number of illiterate adults has increased by 10 million over the past two decades, to reach 35 million. An important question is whether these data present the full extent of the problem. Adults are asked whether they can read and write rather than having their abilities put to the test. Direct approaches to assessing adult skills provide richer profiles of literacy skills.

It is commonly assumed that it takes four or five years of school for children to use reading, writing and calculation with ease. New analysis of household surveys for this Report shows, however, that far more children than expected in low and lower middle income countries are completing primary school without becoming literate. In Ghana, for example, over half of women and over one-third of men aged 15 to 29 who had completed six years of school could not read a sentence at all in 2008. A further 28% of the young women and 33% of the young men could only read part of a sentence.

The environment in which people live can affect their ability to acquire and maintain literacy skills. Preliminary findings of the Literacy Assessment and Monitoring Programme in Jordan, Mongolia, Palestine and Paraguay show that literacy rates can mask large differences in the range of practices and in the environments that shape the literacy skills of adults.

In high income countries, the universal spread of schooling has consigned high levels of illiteracy to the distant past. Yet direct assessments indicate that as many as one in five adults in these countries, equivalent to around 160 million adults, have very poor literacy skills – unable to use reading, writing and calculation effectively in their day to day lives, for example to apply for jobs or interpret information on a medicine bottle. Those facing social disadvantage, including the poor, migrants and ethnic minorities, are particularly affected.

People with poor reading and writing skills are often stigmatized and suffer from low confidence. This poses a major challenge for adult literacy initiatives. Programmes that help participants benefit from using literacy skills in daily life encourages adults to participate while avoiding the stigma that can be associated with their involvement. High level political commitment and a long-term, coherent policy vision, backed by sufficient resources, are needed to tackle the problem.

Achieve gender parity and equality

Gender parity and equality in education constitute a basic human right, as well as an important means of improving other social and economic outcomes. Narrowing the gender gap in primary enrolment is one of the biggest EFA successes since 2000. Even so, many countries are still in danger of not achieving gender parity in primary and secondary education by 2015. And more needs to be done to ensure that education opportunities and outcomes are equitable.

Sixty-eight countries have still not achieved gender parity in primary education, and girls are disadvantaged in sixty of them. While countries like Ethiopia and Senegal have made tremendous progress, others, including Angola and Eritrea, have gone backwards.

The number of countries where girls face extreme disadvantage, or a gender parity index below 0.70, fell from sixteen in 1990 to eleven in 2000, and to just one in 2010 – Afghanistan. Despite its place at the bottom of the rankings, however, Afghanistan has made great progress in recent years.

Severe disadvantage – measured by a gender parity index below 0.90 – is also lower than ten years ago. Of the 167 countries with data for both 1999 and 2010, thirty-three had a gender parity index below 0.90 in 1999, including twenty-one in sub-Saharan Africa. By 2010, there were only seventeen countries in this group, including twelve in sub-Saharan Africa.

Countries that have made sufficient progress to have now achieved gender parity, such as Burundi, India and Uganda, show what can be done when strategies are put in place to improve girls' participation in school, such as mobilizing communities, targeting financial support for girls, ensuring that gender-sensitive teaching methods and materials are used, and providing safe, healthy school environments. Understanding the reasons for girls' lower enrolment is necessary to achieve gender parity. Analysis for this Report of household survey data in nine countries shows that girls face larger obstacles to entering primary school than boys, but once in school they tend to have an equal chance of completing it. In Guinea, for example, only 40 out of 100 girls from the poorest households reach the end of primary school, compared with 52 boys. This is largely due to fewer girls starting in the first place: 44 out of 100 girls from poor households enter school, compared with 57 boys.

In over half of the ninety-seven countries with gender disparity at secondary level, fewer boys than girls are in school. These countries tend to be richer and to have higher enrolment overall. They are concentrated in Latin America and the Caribbean, and East Asia and the Pacific. But there are also three low income countries where boys are disadvantaged: Bangladesh, Myanmar and Rwanda.

The main factor driving boys out of secondary school appears to be poverty and the pull of the labour market, as can be seen in Latin America and the Caribbean. For example, in Honduras six out of ten boys aged 15 to 17 were in paid work, of whom only two were in school. By contrast, only two in ten girls were in paid work.

Boys may also drop out because of the school environment, including teachers' attitudes. Although differences in learning styles between boys and girls are less significant than the similarities, teachers need to be aware of such differences where they exist, and be prepared to adjust their teaching and assessment methods accordingly. Two methods that have been tried but shown to be inappropriate in some contexts are single-sex schools and streaming classes by performance.

Boys also face disadvantages in learning outcomes, notably in reading. Over time, this gender gap has been widening in favour of girls. Boys continue to have an advantage in mathematics, but there is some evidence that the gap may be narrowing.

There is no inherent difference in the capacities of girls or boys to perform equally well in school. To close the gap in reading, parents, teachers and policy-makers should find creative ways to entice boys to read more, including harnessing their interest in digital texts. To close the gap in mathematics, progress in gender equity outside the classroom, notably in employment opportunities, could play a major role in reducing disparities.

Improve the quality of education

Among the world's 650 million children of primary school age, it is time for emphasis to fall not only on the 120 million who do not reach grade 4 but also on the additional 130 million who are in school but failing to learn the basics.

Analysing patterns of inequality in learning outcomes, and what is driving them, can help shape policies that enable children from poor backgrounds to beat the odds. In the seventy-four countries and economies that participated in the 2009 PISA survey, the higher the quartile of the socio-economic index to which a student belonged, the better the performance, with a similar pattern for boys and girls.

In middle income countries participating in the assessment, student performance was very low: on average, at least half scored below level 2 in mathematics. Even so, over time, some middle income countries have been able to increase mean scores and reduce inequality in learning outcomes. The percentage of low performers in each quartile of socio-economic status in Brazil and Mexico fell between 2003 and 2009. This is particularly impressive given that participation in secondary education increased significantly over the period. Targeted social protection policies that have been implemented in these countries since the late 1990s are a likely source of the gains made by disadvantaged students.

Teachers are the most important resource for improving learning. In many regions, a lack of teachers, and especially of trained teachers, presents a major obstacle to achieving the EFA goals. The latest estimates suggest that 112 countries need to expand their workforce by a total of 5.4 million primary school teachers by 2015. New recruits are needed to cover both the 2 million additional posts required to reach universal primary education and the 3.4 million posts of those leaving the profession. Sub-Saharan African countries alone need to recruit more than 2 million teachers to achieve UPE.

The number of primary school teachers per pupil is one measure of the quality of education. There was a small decline in the global pupil/teacher ratio, from 26:1 in 1999 to 24:1 in 2010. In sub-Saharan Africa, despite the recruitment of more than 1.1 million teachers, the pupil/teacher ratio rose slightly, from 42:1 to 43:1, as a result of enrolment increasing at a faster pace.

Of 100 countries with data on primary education, in thirty-three less than 75% of teachers were trained to the national standard. Teachers need to be trained appropriately to ensure they are able to carry out their tasks effectively. Assessments have shown that children in many of the world's poorest countries can spend several years in school without learning to read a word. In Mali, for instance, at least eight out of ten grade 2 students could not read a single word in a national language. Shocking results such as this have turned the spotlight on how teachers are trained, and the support they receive once they are in the classroom.

Teachers themselves may lack the necessary subject knowledge when they are admitted to teaching colleges, so courses often focus on helping teachers develop basic subject knowledge rather than learn how to teach effectively. In addition, professional develop-ment tends to stop once teachers step into the classroom.

Governments should take active steps to strengthen teaching in early grades. Pre-service training programmes need to increase the emphasis on effective classroom techniques. In-service training programmes, in turn, can engage teachers interactively to ensure that knowledge is converted into better classroom practice. Benefits are likely to be most noticeable when training is combined with other interventions, such as improvement of instructional materials.

Education for All Development Index

The EFA Development Index provides a snapshot of overall progress of national education systems towards Education for All. For a subset of fifty-two countries, it is possible to observe the evolution of the EDI since the World Education Forum in Dakar. The EDI improved in forty-one of the fifty-two countries between 1999 and 2010. A particularly large increase took place in the twelve sub-Saharan African countries in this group, with Ethiopia and Mozambique recording the greatest increases.

Similar scores may mask differences in the effort a country is putting into EFA. Colombia and Tunisia, for example, have the same EDI score. Tunisia has high primary enrolment and survival rates but a low adult literacy rate. Colombia has a much higher adult literacy rate but a low primary adjusted net enrolment ratio and an especially low survival rate. Tunisia's low adult literacy may reflect in part a historical legacy and not necessarily its current effort, while Colombia's lower scores on indicators associated with primary school age children suggest that it could face lower adult literacy rates in the future.

Extending the EDI to include the ECCE Index developed for this Report reveals which countries have put more emphasis on early childhood. Some countries – notably in Central Asia, such as Kyrgyzstan and Uzbekistan, and in East Asia, such as Indonesia and the Philippines – drop in ranking, while countries such as Jamaica and Mexico improve their ranking.

EFA will not be achieved unless equal attention is paid to all goals. This requires particular attention to those considered the most neglected, including ECCE and adult literacy. Breaking the intergenerational cycle of education deprivation by providing quality education to all children, including in their early life years, and to their parents, is key.

Financing EFA: shortfalls and opportunities

The experience of the last decade shows that increasing the financing of education can go a long way towards meeting the Education for All goals. But just as the numbers of children out of school are stagnating, there are worrying signs that donor contributions may also be slowing down. More money alone will not ensure that the EFA goals are reached, but less money will certainly be harmful. A renewed and concerted effort by aid donors is urgently needed. At the same time, it is vital to explore the potential of new sources to fill financing gaps and to strengthen the way in which aid money is spent.

Spending more matters

Total government spending on education has been rising steadily since Dakar. The greatest increase in spending has been in low income countries, where it grew by 7.2% a year, on average, since 1999. In sub-Saharan Africa, the annual increase was 5%. Among low and middle income countries with comparable data, 63% increased the share of national income spent on education in the past decade.

Most countries that accelerated progress towards EFA over the last decade did so by increasing spending on education substantially or maintaining it at already high levels. For example, in the United Republic of Tanzania, the share of national income spent on education more than tripled, and the primary net enrolment ratio doubled. In Senegal, an increase in spending from 3.2% of GNP to 5.7% allowed impressive growth in primary enrolment and the elimination of the gender gap.

Despite this promising global trend, some countries that are a long way from achieving EFA, such as the Central African Republic, Guinea and Pakistan, have maintained a low level of spending, allocating less than 3% of GNP to education. Pakistan has the second largest number of children out of school – 5.1 million – yet reduced its spending on education from 2.6% to 2.3% of GNP over the decade.

Fears that the recent food and financial crises could counter the generally positive trend in education spending do not seem to have been realized, although the longer-term impact needs to be monitored. Two-thirds of low and lower middle income countries with available data continued to expand their education budget through the crises. But some countries that are furthest from EFA, such as Chad and the Niger, made cuts in 2010 following negative economic growth in 2009.

New analysis for this Report identifies the extent to which some of the poorest countries have benefited from aid. In nine countries, all in sub-Saharan Africa, donors fund more than a quarter of public spending on education. For example, in Mozambique, numbers out of school declined from 1.6 million in 1999 to less than 0.5 million in 2010. During much of this period, aid made up 42% of the total education budget.

Has aid to education reached its peak?

The largest increase in aid to education since 2002 was recorded in 2009. It was to a large extent driven by the World Bank and International Monetary Fund's early disbursement of pledged funds to help vulnerable countries cope with possible consequences of the financial crisis. However, aid to education stagnated at US$13.5 billion in 2010. Of that amount, US$5.8 billion was for basic education. While that was almost double the 2002–2003 level, just US$1.9 billion was allocated to basic education in low income countries. This is insufficient to fill the US$16 billion financing gap these countries face. Aid for basic education to low income countries grew by just US$16 million in 2010. Not all countries benefited equally. The increase between 2009 and 2010 was mainly concentrated in Afghanistan and Bangladesh, which received 55% of the additional funding for the sixteen low income countries that experienced an increase. By contrast, funding to nineteen low income countries fell.

Despite the increases in aid over the last decade, donors failed to fulfil the promise they made at the Group of 8 Gleneagles Summit in 2005 to increase aid by US$50 billion by 2010. Sub-Saharan Africa received only around half the increase it was promised. Assuming a similar share going to education as in previous years, this failure was equivalent to US$1.9 billion less for schools that year, or around one-third of current aid to basic education.

Of even greater concern, the outlook for aid for the years to 2015 is not positive. In 2011, total aid decreased in real terms by 3%. This is the first time aid has fallen since 1997. Aid budgets have been singled out for cuts as part of austerity packages primarily as a consequence of continuing economic downturn in rich countries. From 2010 to 2011, aid as a share of national income decreased in fourteen out of twenty-three countries that belong to the OECD's Development Assistance Committee (DAC).

Some key donors are not only reducing their overall aid budgets, but may also be making education a lower priority, which would result in education aid falling faster than overall aid levels. The Netherlands, one of the top three

donors to basic education in the past decade, no longer considers education one of its priority areas and is expected to cut aid to education by 60% between 2010 and 2015. This could have serious implications in some of the poorest countries. The Netherlands is set to withdraw from Burkina Faso, for example, at the same time as four other donors have said they also intend to pull out of education in the country.

New donors, such as Brazil, China and India, are receiving greater attention. But they are not yet providing large volumes of aid, nor are they prioritizing aid to basic education for low income countries.

Spending aid effectively

Figures on aid to education tell only part of the story. Ensuring that money is spent effectively is just as vital. Of the thirteen targets on aid effectiveness established by the OECD-DAC in Paris in 2005, just one was reached by the agreed 2010 deadline.

The education sector has been at the forefront of the aid effectiveness agenda. In Kenya, Mozambique, Rwanda and Uganda, for example, significant amounts of aid deployed in conjunction with government plans contributed to unprecedented increases in access to primary education.

Despite this positive experience, there is still a need for more and better spending of aid to many of the poorest countries. One potential vehicle for aid effectiveness principles, the Global Partnership for Education (formerly the EFA Fast Track Initiative), remains underused. It is the only global pooled fund mechanism for aid to education, but it disbursed only US$1.5 billion between 2003 and 2011, equivalent to 6% of the share of total aid to basic education in low and lower middle income countries. This compares poorly with corresponding funds in the health sector. The partnership was established not only to increase aid volumes, but also to fill gaps left by national governments and aid donors. The potential of the partnership to ensure that aid is better coordinated and more effective needs to be monitored closely in coming years in order to inform a post-2015 financing framework.

More broadly, donors are calling for more tangible results from their aid investments as budgets tighten and the pressure for accountability increases. A new approach that aims to provide aid based on results gives recipient country governments more responsibility for achieving their education policy objectives. For example, the United Kingdom has piloted a complementary aid mechanism rewarding the Ethiopian Government for each extra student passing a secondary school examination. This approach carries risks, however, especially for poor countries that cannot cover the cost of achieving these results if external factors prevent a given plan from running smoothly.

Turning the 'resource curse' into a blessing for education

One of the most striking paradoxes of development is the 'resource curse': countries well endowed with non-renewable natural resources, such as oil and minerals, have experienced slower economic growth than resource-poor countries. Many are far from reaching the EFA goals and other development targets. But the curse is escapable, provided resources are invested in future generations.

Nigeria, one of the largest exporters of oil and gas, also has the largest number of children out of school. Chad redirected its newfound wealth away from priority sectors such as education and towards military purposes. In Liberia and Sierra Leone, competition for natural resources was at the centre of armed conflict. Mismanagement of natural resource revenue can reach grave proportions. In the Democratic Republic of the Congo, for example, it is estimated to have led to a loss equivalent to US$450 million in 2008, a sum larger than the country's entire education budget and enough to send 7.2 million children to primary school.

Natural resources, if turned into government revenue and utilized efficiently, could help many countries reach the EFA goals. Botswana has financed education over the past few decades thanks to diamond wealth that has made it one of the richest countries in sub-Saharan Africa. Not only has it achieved

universal primary education but its secondary gross enrolment ratio stands at 82%, double the average for the continent. Ghana has built political consensus around ensuring that its wealth is used effectively, including in investment in education.

An analysis for this Report demonstrates the potential to increase spending on education in seventeen countries that are either already resource-rich or about to begin exporting oil, gas and minerals. If revenue generated from their non-renewable natural resources were maximized and 20% of the extra resources were devoted to education, more than US$5 billion a year could be generated for the sector. This could fund schooling for 86% of these countries' 12 million out-of-school children and 42% of their 9 million out-of-school adolescents. Several countries, including Ghana, Guinea, the Lao People's Democratic Republic, Malawi, Uganda and Zambia, could reach universal primary education without needing any more aid from donors.

To encourage fair and productive use of natural resource revenue, education advocates should support measures aimed at ensuring that governments comply with high standards of transparency and fair taxation. They should also get involved in national debates on the use of natural resource revenue, and make the case for education as a long-term investment essential to diversify the economy and avoid the resource curse.

Harnessing the potential of private organizations

Given the acute need for resources to support EFA and the gloomy outlook for international aid filling this gap, private organizations are increasingly being seen as a potential alternative source of finance. One estimate suggests that total private contributions to developing countries were over US$50 billion on average between 2008 and 2010, compared with around US$120 billion of official aid. However, most of this went to the health sector. For example, of the total amount of grants made by US foundations in the period, about 53% went to health and only 8% to education.

New analysis conducted for this Report, based on publicly available information, shows that private foundations and corporations have been contributing about US$683 million per year to education in developing countries, equivalent to just 5% of education aid from DAC donors.

Around 20% of these resources were provided by foundations, whose aims are most closely aligned with those of traditional aid donors. Only five of the foundations reviewed contributed more than US$5 million a year, which is equal to aid to education by some of the smallest bilateral donors, such as Luxembourg or New Zealand.

Similarly, 71% of the contributions from corporations came from just five companies, each giving more than US$20 million a year. Most corporations that contribute the largest amounts to education are information and communication technology (ICT) or energy companies.

Only a small share of these contributions is being spent on EFA objectives or on the countries that are furthest from achieving the EFA goals. In terms of funding, higher education receives the most attention. In geographical terms, corporations – notably those in the ICT industry – focus their programmes on middle income countries, such as Brazil, India and China, that are often of strategic interest to them. Frequently, moreover, their interventions are short term and fragmented.

Several foundations and corporations have made genuinely successful and often innovative education interventions in areas including early childhood care and education, primary schooling, skills development for young people and measurement of learning outcomes. In general, however, their success is hard to gauge: private organizations tend to make bold statements about the effectiveness of their programmes without providing sufficient information or adequate impact evaluations.

The engagement of some corporations in EFA activities gives them an opportunity to influence public policy in ways that may benefit their business interests. While this can be beneficial to education, their interventions should be scrutinized as closely as those of aid donors.

As a crucial first step, all private organizations seeking to contribute to EFA should provide information on their commitments, including the amounts allocated and how they are spent. This would allow scrutiny to ensure that business interests do not override collective goals, while also giving information on the amount of resources available to fill the EFA financing gap.

Their contributions would also be more effective if they were coordinated with governments and driven by countries' needs. The Global Business Coalition for Education is a particularly promising way forward since it operates within the framework of EFA goals.

Another way private organizations could support government education efforts would be to channel some of their funding through a pooled mechanism. Global health funds, such as the Global Fund to Fight AIDS, Tuberculosis and Malaria, have been successful in this regard. But the main existing mechanism in the education sector, the Global Partnership for Education, has not yet played this role effectively. At present, the private sector has a say in the partnership's policy direction via a seat on its board, yet pledges made by foundations and corporations at the partnership's replenishment meeting will not be disbursed through the pooled funding mechanism.

Bridging the gap

After a period of expanding education budgets, which have contributed to some spectacular outcomes, a period of uncertainty looms. The economic downturn has hit richer countries, with repercussions for aid to the poorest countries that are furthest from achieving the EFA goals.

The decline in aid is likely to widen the education financing gap, so innovative solutions will be required to make up the shortfall. Aid from emerging donors such as Brazil, China and India is one possible resource, but is currently not sufficiently targeted at those countries most in need, so other sources of funding need to be found. Natural resource revenues and private organizations are two possible sources, but for such contributions to be effective, more attention must be paid to transparency and alignment with EFA objectives.

Youth and skills: Putting education to work

If someone can give me the skills and the opportunity to work, I know I can achieve my goals.

– young woman, Ethiopia

The need to develop young people's skills for work has become urgent. Governments around the world are grappling with the long-term consequences of the financial crisis and the challenges posed by increasingly knowledge-based economies. If countries are to grow and prosper in a rapidly changing world, they need to pay even greater attention to developing a skilled workforce. And all young people, wherever they live and whatever their background, require skills that prepare them for decent jobs so they can thrive and participate fully in society.

The essential need for skills development for youth was recognized in the third EFA goal, focusing on 'the learning needs of all young people and adults'. Because of the vagueness of the goal and uncertainty over how it should be measured, however, it has not received the attention it deserves from governments, aid donors, the education community or the private sector – and it is now more critical than ever.

Young people are more numerous than ever, and their numbers are increasing rapidly in some parts of the world. In developing countries alone, the population aged 15 to 24 reached over 1 billion in 2010. But jobs are not being created fast enough to meet the needs of this large youth population. Around one in eight people aged 15 to 24 are unemployed. Young people are about three times as likely as adults to be unemployed. With youth unemployment threatening to rise still higher, many young people face the prospect of remaining without secure work for years to come.

Youth unemployment is rightly rising up the agenda, leading policy-makers to prioritize job creation in private enterprises. While this focus is warranted, the needs of millions of young people who lack basic literacy and numeracy skills continue to be ignored. These young people are often working but earning wages below the poverty line in the urban informal sector, or farming smallholdings in a context of ever-decreasing access to land. Their voices are seldom heard in protests. Providing them with opportunities to escape from low skilled, low paid work should be at the core of every skills development strategy.

All too often, access to skills is unequal, perpetuating and exacerbating the disadvantage that attends being poor, female or a member of a marginalized social group. Young people who have grown up in poverty and exclusion are more likely to have had little education or to have dropped out of school. As a result, they have

© G.M.B. Akash/PANOS

fewer opportunities to develop skills for decent jobs and hence risk further marginalization in the labour market. That is why this Report takes a special interest in identifying and understanding the access disadvantaged young people have to skills development that can lead to better jobs – secure work that pays enough to buy food and put money in their pockets, jobs that can lift them out of poverty.

This Report identifies three main types of skills that all young people need – foundation, transferable, and technical and vocational skills – and the contexts in which they may be acquired:

Foundation skills: At their most elemental, foundation skills include the literacy and numeracy skills necessary for getting work that can pay enough to meet daily needs. These skills are also a prerequisite for continuing in education and training, and for acquiring transferable and technical and vocational skills that enhance the prospect of getting good jobs.

Transferable skills: Transferable skills include the ability to solve problems, communicate ideas and information effectively, be creative, show leadership and conscientiousness, and demonstrate entrepreneurial capabilities. People need these skills to be able to adapt to different work environments and so improve their chances of staying in gainful employment.

Technical and vocational skills: Many jobs require specific technical know-how, from growing vegetables to using a sewing machine, laying bricks or using a computer.

The 'Pathways to Skills' illustrated in the Report can act as a tool for understanding skills development needs and the areas where policy action should be targeted. Young people can acquire the three types of skills through formal general education and its extension, technical and vocational education. Alternatively, those who have missed out on formal schooling can benefit from skills training opportunities ranging from a second chance to acquire foundation skills to work-based training, including apprenticeships and farm-based training.

Youth, skills and work – building stronger foundations

In many countries, the youth generation is among the largest ever. These young people will become an engine of growth if countries can provide them with opportunities. But many are not being adequately prepared for this role. Unequal access to education locks many young people, particularly young women from poor households, into a life of disadvantage.

Providing equal opportunities in schooling, while strengthening the quality of education, is an important first step to ensure that young people have the wide range of skills needed to improve their job prospects. Yet many young people have not had access to such opportunities. These young people are the most likely to be consigned to unemployment or working for low pay.

A large youth population presents challenges

Every year the number of unemployed youth is increasing, not decreasing. Many students are coming out of school every year and this increases the number of unemployed youth while the job opportunities are the same.
– young man, Ethiopia

Around one in six of the world's people are aged 15 to 24. They are disproportionately concentrated in some of the poorest countries. The youth population is particularly large and fast-growing in sub-Saharan Africa. Around two-thirds of Africans are under 25, compared with less than one-third in rich countries such as France, Japan, the United Kingdom and the United States. By 2030, there will be three and a half times as many young people in sub-Saharan Africa as there were in 1980. There are also large numbers of young people living in the Arab States and South and West Asia, where around half are under the age of 25.

To accommodate the growing youth population in the Arab States, South and West Asia, and sub-Saharan Africa, an additional 57 million jobs need to be created by 2020 just to prevent unemployment rates from rising above current levels.

First, however, governments must address the enormous skills deficit that leaves young people unemployable or trapped in subsistence work. Creating more jobs will not fix the problem if a sizeable proportion of young people do not have the skills needed to fill them.

Wide inequalities leave many young people lacking foundation skills

If I want to be someone high up I would have to keep studying but, for economic reasons, I can't keep studying. I thought that I would drop out to stop being a burden and pay for my things, but I can't find a job – how am I supposed to keep studying?

– young man, Mexico

To be prepared for employment, all young people need foundation skills acquired through education that continues at least as far as lower secondary school. But in thirty of the fifty-nine countries covered by analysis carried out for this Report, at least half of 15- to 19-year-olds lack foundation skills. This is the case for twenty-three of the thirty sub-Saharan African countries in the data set.

Reasons for not achieving foundation skills vary, requiring different policy responses. In Burkina Faso, Mali and the Niger, around three in five young people have never been to school by the time they reach age 15 to 19, and so are highly unlikely to ever have the opportunity. In many sub-Saharan African countries, those who make it to school often drop out before completing primary school. In Rwanda, while most have some experience of primary schooling, almost half drop out before the end of the primary cycle.

In many low income countries, large numbers are still in primary school at 15 to 19, an age by which they should have at least completed lower secondary education. For the 35% still in primary school in Uganda at this age, for example, the chances of getting beyond this level are limited.

Even in countries where half of those aged 15 to 19 have completed lower secondary, such as India, Indonesia and the Syrian Arab Republic, there are many who have never been to school, who dropped out before completing secondary school, or who are still only in primary school.

Poverty is a barrier to education and skills. In Egypt, one in five of the poorest do not make it into primary school at all, while almost all rich children get through to upper secondary.

Many children and adolescents not in school because of poverty are working instead. In 2008, an estimated 115 million 5- to 17-year-olds were in hazardous work worldwide. Without the ability to acquire skills, they are trapped in low paid, insecure jobs for life.

Gaps between rich and poor tend to widen as children get older, as those from disadvantaged backgrounds increasingly need to contribute to household income. In Colombia and Viet Nam, almost all children go to primary school. But while most young people from rich households make it to lower secondary school, only around two-thirds from poor households do in Viet Nam, and around half in Colombia.

In most poor countries, girls are less likely than boys to achieve foundation skills. In low income countries, larger gender gaps appear for richer families while opportunities are extremely limited for both boys and girls from poor households. In Burkina Faso, almost 60% of boys from richer households reach lower secondary school, compared with 40% of girls. Among the poorest households, only 5% of children reach lower secondary, but the same proportion of poor girls and boys enrol.

The reverse is true in middle income countries, where gender discrimination occurs among the poorest households but most young people from rich households, whether boys or girls, are able to acquire foundation skills. In Turkey, there is gender parity among rich families, but for poor households, 64% of boys attain foundation skills compared with 30% of girls.

Where young people live can further determine their education opportunities, with rural/urban or regional divisions reinforced by gender. Young women living in rural areas are least likely to acquire foundation skills. In Pakistan, the share of 15- to 19-year-olds who have made it to upper secondary is roughly twice as high in urban areas as in rural areas. Nearly half of rural females in the country have never been to school, while this is true for only 14% of urban males. In Kerala, India, there is almost universal coverage to foundation skills level but only 45% get the same chance in Bihar: 57% of boys and 37% of girls.

Such differences in opportunities are no doubt partly due to patterns of poverty, but they also reflect unequal distribution of government resources. In slums in Kenya, for example, many children cannot hope to acquire foundation skills for the simple reason that schools are not available where they live. This highlights the need to redistribute resources so that young people are not denied access to the job market because of their wealth status, gender and where they live.

Young people need a second chance to acquire basic literacy and numeracy

Currently, my education and skill level is not sufficient, but if I could go to training in the future, I believe I could achieve them [basic skills].

– young woman, Ethiopia

The scale of the challenge of providing second chances to all young people lacking foundation skills is far greater than many governments recognize. This year's *EFA Global Monitoring Report* has calculated that in 123 low and middle income countries, around 200 million of those aged 15 to 24 have not even completed primary school. This is equivalent to one in five young people. Of these, 58% are female.

Regionally, almost one in three in sub-Saharan Africa, and one in five in the Arab States, lack the most basic skills. Over half of the 200 million live in just five countries: Bangladesh, Ethiopia, India, Nigeria and Pakistan. The majority of those who lack foundation skills live in South and West Asia (91 million) and sub-Saharan Africa (57 million).

Although there are numerous innovative second-chance programmes around the world, many of which are provided by non-governmental organizations (NGOs), the number of young people they reach only scratches the surface. An assessment of some of the largest programmes in seven countries indicates that they reach around 2.1 million children and young people. Yet this Report estimates that 15 million young

people in those seven countries need a second chance to get the most basic skills.

It remains the case that the most cost-effective way to provide basic skills is to make sure all children can complete good quality primary schooling and proceed to lower secondary school. As long as this is still not a reality for many, however, there is an urgent need to ensure that all young people who miss out have a second chance to achieve this goal.

Transferable skills: preparing for the world of work

[School] teaches you how to communicate with people and how a working environment would be, in a way.

– young woman, United Kingdom

Employers want assurances that young people applying for jobs have at least strong foundation skills and can deploy their knowledge to solve problems, take the initiative and communicate with team members, rather than just follow prescribed routines. These 'transferable skills' are not taught from a textbook, but can be acquired through good quality education. Yet employers often indicate that these skills are lacking in new recruits to the labour market.

Evidence from rich countries shows that staying in school longer helps assure the acquisition of problem-solving skills. In Canada, around 45% of those leaving before completing upper secondary lack these skills, compared with 20% who complete the cycle.

A good quality education will also boost confidence and motivation. Transferable skills, which could help many young people working in the informal sector in poor countries become successful in their jobs, can be developed through formal education. More needs to be done for disadvantaged youth to develop these skills. Recognizing this, Akanksha, an NGO in India, has introduced programmes in the slums of Mumbai to improve disadvantaged children's self-esteem. The impact has been positive and far-reaching – children who take part show noticeable improvements in their school performance and earnings.

A hazardous transition from school to work

*You look for a job and they ask that you
have a high school diploma but you don't.*
— young woman, Mexico

Many young people face a difficult transition from school to work. The disadvantage that youth often experience in the labour market is reflected in both a lack of jobs and the low quality of jobs – including insecure, low paid work. Factors linked to disadvantage in education, such as poverty, gender and disability, are often also associated with disadvantage in the labour market. This is not a coincidence – unequal skills development, social norms and labour market discrimination combine to lead to this outcome.

Some young people, particularly in rich countries, face long spells of unemployment after leaving school. Around 13% of the world's youth were counted as unemployed in 2011 – 75 million young people, almost 4 million more than before the economic crisis took hold in 2007. Unemployment rates are two to three times higher for young people than for adults, on average. They are six times as high for young people in Egypt, two and a half times in South Africa, four times in Italy.

While it might be expected that younger people are more likely to be out of work than older people as they wait to get their first step on the ladder, in many countries the barriers to a good job are almost insurmountable for the majority of young people. In the mid-2000s, even before the economic downturn took hold, 17% of 15- to 29-year-olds in Italy were unemployed five years after leaving education.

Since the economic downturn set in, opportunities for young people have diminished, and those with lower levels of education have been particularly affected. There were about 29 million fewer jobs globally in 2011 than before the economic crisis. For example, unemployment rates in Spain rose significantly between 2007 and 2009, particularly for those who had not completed secondary education.

Unemployment figures, however, do not give the full picture of the predicament facing many young people. They hide the fact that some young people stop looking for work because they do not believe they will find any. People who are neither in education or employment nor actively seeking work are often classified as 'inactive', even though their inactivity reflects the labour market more than their own motivation. If those feeling discouraged from finding work were to be counted, unemployment rates of young people would increase substantially, doubling in Cameroon, for example.

Women are often a majority of those classified as inactive. The gender gap is often very large among young people who have dropped out of the education system after completing only primary school. In Jordan, over 80% of young women with only primary education were not actively seeking employment, compared with 20% of young men.

Young women also often work long hours in household and informal work that is less visible to policy-makers. Analysis for this Report of recent labour force surveys in nine countries found that more young women than men were classed as inactive in all nine, often significantly so. Fewer women than men try to find work, often because of the unequal division of domestic work and discrimination in recruitment practices.

Women who do find work are often paid less than men. In India and Pakistan, men earn 60% more than women, on average. The wage gap is widest for those with low levels of literacy and numeracy. Yet education can make a big difference to women's earnings. In Pakistan, women with a high level of literacy earned 95% more than women with no literacy skills, whereas the differential was only 33% among men.

Young people with disabilities have particular difficulty gaining access to both education and work. Very few young people in Kenya living with disabilities study beyond primary level. They face constraints in employment because of their low level of education, little or no adaptation of their workplaces, and limited expectations among families and employers.

Many young people do not have the luxury of remaining unemployed and are obliged to take poor quality jobs that are insecure, low paid and often require long hours. For some, this may be a stepping stone to more stable and fulfilling employment. But for many, such work is a trap that is difficult to escape.

Globally, an estimated 152 million young people – 28% of all young workers – are paid less than US$1.25 per day. In countries such as Burkina Faso, Cambodia, Ethiopia and Uganda, working below the poverty line is a much more widespread phenomenon than not working at all.

Young people are more likely than adults to be earning very low wages. In Ouagadougou, Burkina Faso, older adults earn almost two and a half times as much as young adults, on average. While young people can usually expect their pay to increase as they get older, earning less than the minimum wage leaves them with insufficient money to meet their daily needs.

In low income countries, less educated young people, who cannot afford to wait for the right kind of job, are at greatest risk of being in low paid work. While this may be partly because education levels tend to be low where there are other barriers to finding work that pays well, it is also likely that low levels of education are often the main reason young people are in poorly paid jobs. In Cambodia, for instance, 91% of young people with no education work below the poverty line, compared with less than 67% of those with secondary education.

Young people living in rural areas in poor countries are more likely to have left school early, and to be in low paid work rather than unemployed. In rural areas of Cameroon, for example, the unemployment rate is only around 1%. Agriculture provides jobs for large numbers of young people with lower levels of education, but many are poorly paid. Two-thirds of rural youth with no education work for less than US$1.25 per day, with rural, uneducated women the worst off.

The effects of completing secondary education on young people's ability to find adequately paid work vary by gender. In Nepal, young men who have not completed secondary education are more likely to earn an adequate wage than better-educated young women – over 40% earn above the poverty line, compared with fewer than 30% of young women who have completed secondary schooling.

Investing in skills for prosperity

There is a lack of education so we don't get jobs and can't improve our life. There is no growth for us.

– young man, India

Skills development is vital in reducing unemployment, inequality and poverty, and promoting growth. It is also a wise investment – for every US$1 spent on education, as much as US$10 to US$15 can be generated in economic growth. If 75% more 15-year-olds in forty-six of the world's poorest countries were to reach the lowest OECD benchmark for mathematics, economic growth could improve by 2.1% from its baseline and 104 million people could be lifted out of extreme poverty.

The Republic of Korea went from being poor to wealthy in just thirty years, partly by emphasizing and planning for skills development. The state upgraded the skills of the whole population by achieving universal primary, then secondary, education. It then focused on supporting industries with skills training. In short, the state played a key role in matching skills supply to demand.

After decades of low or no growth, sub-Saharan African countries experienced strong growth in the 2000s. Over a third of countries in the region have achieved growth rates of at least 6%, and some hope to achieve middle income status in the first half of the twenty-first century. Experience from the Republic of Korea and the other East Asian 'tigers' suggests that sustained growth in sub-Saharan Africa will depend on sound economic policies coordinated with government investment in education and skills training that meets the needs of the labour market.

Many governments neglect skills and the disadvantaged lose out most

Despite clear evidence of the value of investing in skills development, it is still not getting the priority attention it merits. In an analysis of forty-six countries with large youth populations, most of them low and lower middle income, just over half had, or were developing, some form of policy document focusing on skills development – either a technical and vocational education

and training strategy, or a broader skills development strategy.

Where there are skills development plans, many are fragmentary, poorly coordinated, and inadequately aligned with labour market demands and countries' development priorities. Responsibility for skills development is split between several agencies and accountability is lost.

The lack of strategic planning for skills development, including targets for reaching the disadvantaged, shows the short-sightedness of many development strategies. Of forty-six countries reviewed for this Report, fewer than half address skills development among youth in the informal sector. A few, however, recognize the need and are attempting to address it.

Ethiopia, for example, is making skills development a cornerstone of its ambitious and inclusive growth strategy, with the hope of attaining middle income country status by 2025. It aims to achieve universal secondary school enrolment by 2020 while emphasizing skills in the agricultural and industrial sectors. There is also substantial emphasis on increasing

productivity of micro- and small enterprises, where many disadvantaged young people work.

Only around a quarter of country strategies analysed seek to re-engage young people who have dropped out of primary school in education or training. Sierra Leone, for example, developed a well-intentioned youth employment strategy aimed at training in entrepreneurial skills. In a context where about 57% of 15- to 19-year-olds dropped out before completing lower secondary education, the strategy did not give sufficient attention to youth who lack foundation skills and therefore need second-chance education programmes.

Young people are rarely able to contribute to policy-making, but it is important for their voices to be heard. Those aged 15 to 24 constitute almost a sixth of the global population, and often form the most dynamic section of society, as well as its most vulnerable and most powerless. They have a deeper understanding than policy-makers do of the realities of their own lives, including the experience of education and training and the challenge of finding a good job. Even where youth are invited to participate, the voices of the disadvantaged are unlikely to be heard. Youth consultations tend to be dominated by educated and privileged urban youth, while the voices of the poor majority are rarely included.

Boosting finance to bring skills to disadvantaged youth

There is an urgent need for donors to commit to skills development in three ways: by supporting country programmes to ensure that all young people can stay in school at least until lower secondary level, by supporting second-chance programmes for young people who have not had the opportunity to gain basic literacy and numeracy skills, and by giving disadvantaged youth training to improve their chances of earning a decent wage.

This approach requires more and better-targeted funding. Simply enrolling all young people in education up to lower secondary level would cost US$8 billion annually, in addition to the US$16 billion needed to achieve universal basic education by 2015. Those needing education and training are mainly from the poorest households, so they cannot bear the cost themselves. Governments, with the support of aid donors, need to extend their support to make sure all young people get a chance to acquire foundation skills either through formal schooling or second-chance education.

Although there is undoubtedly more that can be done, many poor countries have increased their support for education over the past decade. Even so, spending on secondary education is often squeezed in favour of higher education. In addition, some donors provide significant support to the development of foundation skills. An estimated US$3 billion was spent last year by all donors on skills development, around 40% of which was on formal secondary general education and vocational training.

Some donors prioritize spending in this area, with Germany being the biggest, followed by the World Bank, France and Japan. Some smaller donors, including Luxembourg and Switzerland, have also concentrated their education support on skills development. Countries such as Japan have built on their own experience of achieving impressive growth through skills development.

Much of France's funding does not reach developing countries, however: over 60% of the US$248 million that France disbursed for secondary general education and vocational training in 2010 went to two overseas French territories.

There are two potential avenues for increasing external financing for education: redistributing funds currently spent on scholarships that bring young people from developing countries to study at tertiary level in developed countries, and encouraging emerging donors to engage more effectively in skills development, with a greater focus on disadvantaged youth.

While aid to higher education can in some circumstances play an important role in supporting capacity development, it unfortunately rarely reaches developing countries. In 2012, for the first time, the OECD-DAC required donors to report the share of aid disbursed for post-secondary education that was allocated to scholarships and imputed student costs (costs incurred by donor-country institutions when they receive students from developing countries). Around three-quarters of direct aid to post-secondary education – equivalent to about US$3.1 billion – disbursed in 2010 fell into those categories.

In 2010, almost 40% of Japan's direct aid to education went to scholarships for students studying in Japan. For the amount it costs for one Nepalese student to study on scholarship in Japan, as many as 229 young people could have access to secondary education in Nepal. Germany's aid disbursements to scholarships and imputed student costs were almost eleven times the amount it spent on direct aid to secondary general education and vocational training in 2010. France's aid disbursements to scholarships and imputed student costs were four times the amount it spent on direct aid to secondary general education and vocational training in 2010. If some of the US$3.1 billion currently being spent by donors on students to study in their countries were redirected back to developing countries, it could help address the huge gap in foundation skills.

Emerging donors such as Brazil, China and India could become important players in aid to skills development. To do so, they will need to focus more on education and target their financing at disadvantaged young people, learning from their own experience of linking investment in skills development with labour market reforms and poverty reduction. Just 2% of India's commitment of around US$950 million annually to other developing countries from 2008 to 2010 was directed at education. As with other emerging donors, much of this will focus on higher levels of education that are not within the reach of disadvantaged young people.

The private sector also needs to invest more in skills training, particularly as it stands to gain from a skilled workforce capable of boosting productivity and competitiveness, as industries in Germany and Switzerland that have engaged youth in apprenticeships have found. Private foundations are supporting innovative projects. Notably, the MasterCard Foundation provides funding for programmes that help youth gain the skills they need to find employment. However, the amount foundations currently provide is very small compared with the scale of the challenge.

With funds coming from several different sources, governments must coordinate to maximize the impact of these resources and ensure that disadvantaged youth receive due attention. One way of streamlining spending is through well-managed training funds that pool financing from different sources – including earmarked taxes and levies on companies, as well as funds from aid donors – for governments to manage and disburse, while the private sector provides training. Nepal's Employment Fund is one example of such an approach to extending training to disadvantaged young people. Where training funds have been well-managed, the impact has been positive. Tunisia set up a training fund in 1999 and has reached over a quarter of all unemployed young people with skills development.

Secondary education: paving the way to work

Secondary school is a crucial way for young people to acquire skills that improve their opportunities for good jobs. High quality secondary education that caters for the widest possible range of abilities, interests and backgrounds is vital not just to set young people on the path to the world of work, but also to give countries the educated workforce they need to compete in today's technologically driven world.

Worldwide, 71 million adolescents are not enrolled in school. Even in countries where overall enrolment is high, significant numbers leave school early. On average, 14% of young people in European Union countries reach no further than lower secondary education. In Spain, as many as one in three drop out of secondary school, which is a cause for concern given the severity of the economic crisis and an unemployment level among young people of 51% in March 2012. Attention is needed in all countries to assure the relevance of secondary education to the world of work.

Removing the barriers to secondary education

I had no money for books and uniform. The financial situation of the family was bad. I had to supplement family income by working for daily wages, for the very survival of the family. Earning money was more important for me than going to school.

— young man, India

In many poor countries that need to expand secondary enrolment from a low level, the immediate problem is still ensuring that children complete the primary cycle. In the Niger, where only one in five are enrolled in lower secondary school, the primary net enrolment ratio is just 62%.

For children who do complete primary school, the costs of secondary schooling can be prohibitive. Secondary schools are often located in urban areas, limiting access for those from rural poor households who cannot afford the cost of transport. Social and cultural barriers can prevent girls from continuing with schooling once they reach adolescence. Governments need to carry out reforms to specifically address these barriers, and so enable young people to consolidate foundation skills.

Some sub-Saharan African countries have boosted lower secondary enrolment by linking primary and lower secondary education. In Rwanda, for instance, the introduction of a nine-year basic education cycle and the elimination of fees for lower secondary school in 2009 boosted the number of lower secondary students by 25% within a year. In addition, the curriculum was redesigned to focus on fewer core subjects, and a new assessment system was introduced.

Fees, whether official or unofficial, dispropor-tionately affect youth from poor families, preventing them from enrolling and continuing with secondary education. If measures to remove fees are not targeted to reach the disadvantaged, they can favour the non-poor. Kenya abolished fees for secondary school, for example, increasing enrolment from 1.2 million

in 2007 to 1.4 million in 2008. Governments compensated schools with US$164 per student – ten times the amount received per pupil for primary school. Because fewer poor children make it to secondary school, they stand to benefit least from this policy.

Deeply engrained social, cultural and economic barriers, such as early marriage, often prevent young women from continuing education. Becoming a mother cuts education short for many, and they face considerable obstacles against returning to school. More than one in ten women aged 15 to 19 are pregnant or mothers in sub-Saharan Africa, Latin America, and South Asia, and the proportion rises to 30% or more in Bangladesh, Liberia and Mozambique.

Even where the law assures the right to education of young mothers, more has to be done to empower them to take advantage of that right. In Jamaica, a foundation provides support, including food and transport costs, to help mostly poor pregnant girls and mothers under age 16 to re-enter school after giving birth. The programmes have increased the

© Stefan Erber/UNESCO

likelihood of young mothers completing high school from 20% to 32%.

Making secondary education more relevant to the world of work

Secondary education should build on foundation skills and provide equal opportunities for all youth to develop transferable and technical and vocational skills to find a good job or for further education. A common curriculum in lower secondary school helps give all children an equal chance of consolidating foundation skills. When students at greater risk of school failure are grouped together, lower expectations, a less stimulating learning environment and peer effects often diminish their learning achievement. For this reason, some low and middle income countries, such as Botswana, Ghana, South Africa and Uganda, have developed a common curriculum framework, together with new assessment practices, learning materials and teacher training activities.

At upper secondary level, young people need to learn transferable skills to smooth the transition from school to work, and technical and vocational skills for specific trades or sectors of work. Combining all these skills equally and tailoring them to the needs of the local market provides a good curriculum balance that can benefit all.

Pushing low performing students into technical and vocational training can cement social inequality and result in employers devaluing these programmes. In eighteen of twenty-two countries in the 2009 PISA survey, students streamed into vocational schools had lower socio-economic status, on average, than their peers in general education. The four countries where performance gaps were widest between those in secondary general education and technical and vocational education were ones where the proportion of those from disadvantaged backgrounds in technical and vocational education was greatest.

Experience from OECD countries suggests that when technical and vocational subjects are introduced alongside general subjects and made more relevant to the labour market, enrolment and completion rates can increase.

Making the curriculum more flexible in upper secondary schools in terms of subject choices and allowing a route back to further education can result in benefits for all students, as Singapore's experience has shown. There are some impediments to this approach, however. Many developing countries lack the resources, materials and qualified teachers to offer such flexibility effectively. After Ghana introduced a diversified secondary curriculum, numbers in vocational courses rose by about 50% but the cost of delivering the new courses was as much as twenty times more in rural schools than in urban schools even though quality in rural areas was poor. If it is not possible to train and supply teachers for technical and vocational subjects and distribute resources equitably, students in rural areas may end up with low quality training.

Strengthening the links between school and work

In colleges and in schools as well, they should do more, not just a day release where you go off and do a bit of work experience; they should do it like if they have two days in school, three days in placement, just balance it out. That way you're in school, you're learning what you need to learn and you're out there trying to get some experience.
– young woman, United Kingdom

School leavers are often told they are not suitable for a job because they have no work experience. Linking schooling with work-based programmes through internships and apprenticeships has the potential to help young people learn practical problem-solving skills and practise crucial workplace skills. Apprenticeships have proven particularly successful in some contexts. The German dual model, for example, combines structured training within a company and part-time classroom tuition. It works well in Germany because of strong regulation and partnerships between government, employers and employees.

Because apprenticeships often lead to employment, they can also motivate young people to stay in school and complete their education. In France, going through an apprenticeship increases the likelihood of being employed three years after completion.

Apprenticeships can be of particular benefit to the disadvantaged, but apprenticeship programmes can be discriminatory. In the United Kingdom, 32% of black and other ethnic minority youth enter apprenticeships, compared with 44% of young white people. Women are less likely to find apprenticeships, and those who do earn 21% less from these opportunities than men. Career counselling can help more disadvantaged young people find and stay in apprenticeships, or ease the transition to work as experience from Japan has shown.

Formal apprenticeships are much more difficult to implement in poorer countries, but can work under appropriate conditions. Egypt adapted the German model to its own context, with business associations playing a key role in providing training places. A third of graduates from the programme were able to find work immediately and about 40% continued in further education. Such systems, however, rely strongly on trust between government and employers, which is not easy to find in many low income countries that have a large informal sector.

Transferable skills for all: a desirable but challenging goal

Skills learned at school need to extend beyond subject knowledge. Applying knowledge to real work situations, analysing and solving problems, and communicating effectively with colleagues are all crucial elements of skills development that young people need if they are to obtain good jobs in a global economy increasingly driven by technology. Recognizing this, some countries are striving to incorporate transferable skills into their curricula. Denmark, New Zealand and Hong Kong (China), for example, all specify problem solving as a key curriculum feature.

The use of ICT in education is gathering momentum across the world. It not only improves the learning experience and reduces dropout, but also prepares young people for work. Computers may be too expensive or scarce for some schools, especially in poorer countries, but radio and mobile phones have wide reach in remote areas. Interactive radio instruction, as used in Honduras and South Sudan, for example, offers opportunities to improve learning for disadvantaged groups at low cost. Its use has enhanced performance by up to 20%.

Providing alternative routes for early school leavers

Large numbers of young people drop out before completing secondary school, even in middle and high income countries. Those leaving school early are more likely to be from poor and disadvantaged households. Targeted support is required to enable them to continue with their learning so that they acquire the qualifications and skills needed to benefit from employment opportunities.

In the Netherlands and the Philippines, schools have adopted flexible approaches to support those at risk of dropping out, including allowing re-entry at any point in the school year. In New York City, where one in five of those aged 17 to 24 is neither in school nor in work, two programmes targeted vulnerable youth in neighbourhoods with paid internships, individual counselling and workshops. This approach resulted in over half finding work within nine months, and around a fifth re-entering courses to learn foundation skills.

Alternative approaches to learning skills outside secondary school, such as open and distance learning and community training centres, need to be carefully attuned to local labour market needs and backed by long-term financial commitment. Moreover, the skills acquired need to be ones that are formally recognized by employers.

National qualification frameworks can provide employers with information on the learning attained by youth who follow alternative learning pathways. If carefully designed, they can bring greater clarity to otherwise fragmented standards and qualifications systems operating outside formal secondary education. Implementing them effectively, however, is not easy. It requires close cooperation between interested parties, including government, training institutions, employers and trade unions.

Skills for urban youth:
A chance for a better future

Today's urban youth population, the largest in history and still growing, is better educated than previous generations and represents a powerful force for political and social change, as well as economic growth. As a result of natural increase and migration from rural areas, it is estimated that virtually all the world's population growth will be concentrated in urban areas over the next thirty years, with more people living in urban than in rural areas in all developing regions by 2040.

Many urban poor lack foundation skills

Rapid urbanization has led to substantial urban poverty, manifested in the growth of slums and informal settlements. One in three people living in today's cities are slum dwellers, rising to two in three in sub-Saharan Africa. In all, latest counts show more than 800 million people living in slums, a figure that is expected to rise to 889 million by 2020. Young people make up a disproportionate share of those living in these settlements. Skills training and work can offer them an alternative to the poor conditions in which they live and struggle to find decent jobs.

The extent of education deprivation among the urban poor is often overlooked. Inequalities within urban areas are often extreme – implying that slum dwellers do not necessarily live better than the rural poor – and the extent and depth of urban poverty are underestimated.

While education opportunities are more widespread in urban areas than rural ones in many developing countries, the difference in acquisition of foundation skills between the urban poor and rural poor is not large. Across forty-five low and middle income countries, the urban rich are far more likely than the urban poor to have continued at least until the end of lower secondary school. In ten of these countries, the proportion of those aged 15 to 24 lacking foundation skills is even higher among the urban poor than among the rural poor.

In Cambodia, for example, 90% of urban poor youth have not completed lower secondary education, compared with 82% of the rural poor and 31% of the urban rich. In Kenya, where 60% of Nairobi's inhabitants live in slums, low levels of formal education for youth due to a lack of secondary schools in slums limit their opportunities of finding decent jobs.

© Sven Torfinn/PANOS

Employment for poor urban youth is mostly informal

It is difficult to find a job that lasts long. The longest period of work is not more than a week. And for my work I earn 30 birr [US$1.70] per day.

– young man, Ethiopia

A lack of skills and education for the urban poor leaves the vast majority working in small and microbusinesses operating informally with no business records, legal status or regulations. Such informal work includes subsistence activities, such as waste-picking and street vending, as well as sewing and garment-making, car repair, construction, farm work and craft-making. Informal and unregulated, these jobs are often low paid and fragile, with bad working conditions.

While the number of people worldwide trapped in vulnerable, unregulated work is hard to measure accurately, the International Labour Organization (ILO) estimates it at 1.53 billion. The informal sector accounts for as much as 70% of non-agricultural employment in some sub-Saharan African countries, and more than half in poorer countries of Latin America. It is also the main employer for many workers in South and West Asia.

Discrimination both in education and in labour markets denies opportunities to certain groups. Young women in many contexts face limited mobility and access to education and training, as well as to paid work, while experiencing a heavy burden of unpaid, domestic work. More women than men are employed either in the informal sector or informally in the formal sector in twenty-five out of thirty-nine countries in a recent ILO survey. The range of activities women engage in is constrained: many are confined to home-based work, and women are overrepresented in the most informal and insecure activities, such as waste-picking and street vending. Once in work, they are also likely to earn less than men. In greater Buenos Aires, for example, women in informal companies earned 20% less than men.

The informal sector can become a more attractive option when young people have the appropriate skills. Informal sector workers in seven West African capitals who had completed primary or lower secondary education could earn 20% to 50% more than those without qualifications, in most cases. But many enter the informal sector lacking foundation skills. In Rwanda in 2006, only 12% of those working in the informal sector had studied beyond lower secondary level, compared with 40% in the formal sector.

Expanding skills training opportunities for disadvantaged youth

As the effects of the economic downturn continue, the sheer number of young people earning wages below the poverty line in low skilled informal jobs is growing. They should be a key concern in national skills development strategies, yet this is rarely the case. The review of forty-six developing countries conducted for this Report shows that most do not have a national skills development strategy that explicitly addresses the urban informal sector.

India, one of the few countries targeting this issue, has developed a strategy on informal workers. It has also developed a National Policy on Street Vendors which states that, as India's 10 million street vendors run microenterprises, they should receive training to upgrade their technical and business skills so they can increase their income and look for alternative work.

Second-chance programmes are vital to equip the urban poor with literacy and numeracy skills. Although there are many innovative approaches run by NGOs, second-chance opportunities in the parts of the world where they are needed the most are often small in scale. They also tend to be poorly coordinated, and governments often have little information about their activities.

Extending foundation skills to those aged 15 to 24, and combining that with vocational training, can help them find secure work. The Training for Employment project in Nepal for out-of-school young people is one such programme. It has been successful in reaching marginalized groups – 66% of its students belonged to disadvantaged castes or ethnic minorities. A tracer study covering 206 project graduates reported that 73% had found employment.

A potentially effective way of delivering skills training is to combine it with microfinance or social protection programmes that help beneficiaries overcome poverty constraints in the short term. Chile Solidario, introduced in 2002, provides cash transfers together with other forms of support, including preferential access to training aimed at increasing employability, with a focus on poor women with low educational attainment and little or no professional experience. Employment grew by up to four to six percentage points among women who entered the programme in 2005, partly through increased participation in the training programmes.

Programmes that offer classroom training and work experience in basic and specific trades, alongside life skills, job search assistance, counselling and information to enhance employability, have been successful in some parts of the world, notably Latin America and the Caribbean. These programmes target disadvantaged urban youth, especially young women, with particular success. In Colombia, the wages of women who had completed the Jóvenes en Acción programme rose by an average of almost 20%. Their chances of formal employment also increased as a result of the combination of classroom training and on-the-job training in a wide range of activities that were closely linked to demand in the labour market. In Peru, the PROJoven programme improved men's chances of finding work by up to 13%, and women's by up to 21%.

Most Jóvenes programmes in Latin American countries have been integrated into national public training institutions or replaced by other similar interventions, notably Entra 21. They provide useful models for other ountries, including in the Arab States, showing that well-targeted programmes can improve the employment fortunes of many disadvantaged young people. They can be costly, however, and require enough companies able to participate, which may not be possible in parts of sub-Saharan Africa, for example, where the numbers employed in the formal sector are small.

Beyond foundation skills for disadvantaged youth

Where young urban people already have foundation skills, governments need to target and support training in transferable and technical skills, especially in small and medium-sized informal businesses with growth potential. Traditional apprenticeships are one approach that can reach large numbers of young people employed in the informal sector. They can be cost effective, have immediate practical relevance and often lead to employment.

It is important, however, to ensure that access to apprenticeship training is equitable. In Ghana, only 11% of the poorest quintile of young people had been through an apprenticeship as opposed to 47% of the wealthiest. Similarly, apprenticeships are often in trades more accessible to male workers and so disadvantage women.

Reforms aiming to transform traditional apprenticeship into a dual apprenticeship system were developed in the 1990s and 2000s in several countries, including Benin and Togo. They combine theoretical learning with practical training. This approach requires agreement between the government, groups representing informal workers and craftspeople willing to take apprentices. If successfully implemented, dual apprenticeship can become an effective and sustainable part of national technical and vocational education and training systems. In Burkina Faso, the costs of reformed apprenticeships were about one-third as much as formal training courses, for example.

Gradually recognizing traditional apprenticeships formally may be an easier policy option than transforming them completely into dual apprenticeships for countries with limited institutional capacity, as experience in Cameroon and Senegal illustrates. Such initiatives may be particularly efficient if designed and implemented in cooperation with informal sector associations or other professional organizations.

Gradual adoption of formal status can include regulations to protect apprentices from exploitation, a common concern in traditional systems. They include limits on daily and weekly working hours, a ceiling on the number of years of training for each type of occupation, and safety measures. Certifying apprentices' skills and work experience through a national qualification framework can further enhance the value of this training and boost their employability.

Another route out of subsistence work is self-employment. Many young people in urban centres in the Arab States and sub-Saharan Africa see this as a viable option. In 2008, a survey in Egypt revealed that about 73% of young people would be happy to become entrepreneurs. Entrepreneurial skills, however, are lacking among poor urban youth.

Experience from Bosnia and Herzegovina and Ghana shows that the impact of entrepreneurship training is reduced where participants lack foundation skills and do not have access to other forms of support, including the assets required to set up a business, enabling them to apply their newly acquired skills.

Curriculum design of entrepreneurship training targeting disadvantaged urban youth, therefore, needs to factor in training in basic literacy and numeracy skills and combine this with resources to start a business to give young people a better chance of succeeding.

Skills for rural youth – an escape route from poverty

I am from the countryside. It is known that education is not given that much attention in rural areas; families do not encourage their children to go to school. I started learning all by myself as I had the desire. But to be a student you need educational materials and I couldn't afford those.

– young man, Ethiopia

The majority of the poor – 70%, or about 1 billion people – live in rural areas, predominantly in low and some middle income countries. They are heavily concentrated in sub-Saharan Africa and South Asia, where most are dependent on a combination of small-scale farming, seasonal casual labour and microentrepreneurial activities with low earnings potential. As the world population continues to grow and demand for food rises while land becomes more scarce, skills development is vital so that young people in rural areas can learn to adopt new technologies in agriculture, and have greater opportunities for non-farm work.

© Tim Dirven/PANOS

In rural areas, young women are more disadvantaged than young men

In rural areas many poor young people, especially young women, lack foundation skills, locking young generations into subsistence work. The gender gap is most pronounced in countries where the majority of rural people do not make it to the end of lower secondary school. In Benin, Cameroon, Liberia and Sierra Leone, around 85% of young rural women lack foundation skills, compared with less than 70% of young men. Even in Turkey, a middle income country, the rural gender gap is wide – 65% of young women do not complete lower secondary school, compared with 36% of young men.

Women not only have lower levels of education, but also fewer assets, and are less able to migrate. They are often left behind to do low skilled tasks that others are unwilling to undertake.

Enhancing the education and skills of young people in rural areas, and young women in particular, would not only expand their opportunities, but could also increase their productivity, with gains for their families as well as the wider economy. In rural China, wages are significantly higher for those involved in non-farm work who have at least some post-primary education.

Rural youth with foundation skills have a better chance of non-farm work. Across eight countries analyzed for this Report, the higher the level of education, the more likely it is that a young person is involved in non-agricultural employment, with similar patterns for women and men. In Turkey, 23% of those with no education are involved in non-farm activities, compared with 40% of those with primary education and 64% of those with at least secondary education.

Addressing rural training needs

Of the national plans of forty-six countries analysed for this Report, only about half acknowledged the specific training and skills needs of the rural poor in their national plans. Countries that do prioritize the needs of the rural poor, however, can reap rewards. In China, from the 1970s, focusing on productivity for smallholder farmers and non-farm self-employment reduced the number of those living below the poverty line.

Ensuring that all young people have access to foundation skills is an immense challenge in rural areas because of the dispersion of populations and the numbers involved. However, youth in rural areas will not benefit from training programmes if they lack basic skills that would allow them to understand and apply new technology in business and farming. Extending coverage of formal primary and secondary schooling and improving its relevance to rural environments are key priorities. Emphasis should also be given to second-chance programmes that provide basic skills combined with skills training related to agricultural and non-farm activities of rural people.

In Malawi, where 85% of the population live in rural areas, and around half of children starting primary school drop out, a second-chance skills training programme has produced remarkable success. Targeting those living in rural areas who have never been to school or dropped out, it resulted in over half the learners either completing the course or returning to primary school. Participants also achieved better results in literacy and numeracy than those in formal schooling. Similar initiatives are needed in many poor countries with large numbers of rural people who have little or no education.

Programmes also need to tackle the specific difficulties faced by young women. In Egypt in 2008, 20% of rural women aged 17 to 22 had less than two years of schooling. Many are likely to marry young. Ishraq, a programme in Egypt, tackles social stereotypes directly, working with rural families, local leaders and communities to include them in determining the rationale behind literacy and numeracy skills programmes for girls. Over nine out of ten of the first graduates of the Ishraq programme passed their final exams.

Including literacy, numeracy and other skills training in microfinance and social protection programmes for poor rural women increases their chances of moving out of poverty. Two pioneers are BRAC in Bangladesh and Camfed in Africa. BRAC provides poor rural families with an asset, such as a cow, from which to earn a living. It also provides training in microfinance and marketing to improve the profitability of the investment. As a result, income per household member has almost tripled. Camfed targets poor rural adolescent girls, providing business management skills, a grant, microloans and peer mentoring. Its approach has resulted in over 90% of the businesses created by the young women turning a profit.

Bringing additional skills to rural youth

To make sure work in rural areas is attractive for young people, it is vital to provide training beyond the foundations so that smallholders can strengthen agricultural productivity and non-farm workers can enhance their business and finance skills.

Forming associations can help smallholders gain skills while strengthening their common voice. Farmer field schools and cooperatives are two approaches that have proved successful. In Kenya, Uganda and the United Republic of Tanzania, farmer field schools have led to significant improvements. The approach has been particularly beneficial for those with low levels of literacy. Crop value per acre increased by 32% on average across the three countries, and by 253% for those who had not had any formal schooling. Income increased by 61% on average, and by 224% for households whose heads had no previous schooling.

An effective way to promote productive learning and practical use of new skills is to demonstrate them using radio and video. Experiments in Burkina Faso, India and the Niger have shown the potential benefits of augmenting training with ICT, especially radio, which can reach large numbers of disadvantaged farmers.

Innovative training programmes for non-farm work can be beneficial in encouraging young people to remain in rural areas. Several programmes aimed at providing entrepreneurship and microbusiness skills for disadvantaged young people, including indigenous youth, have been developed on a large scale in rural areas of Latin America. Many of these have shown impressive results.

© Sven Torfinn/PANOS

In Mexico, the JERFT programme (Young Rural Entrepreneur Programme and Land Fund) began in 2004 to address young people's lack of access to land and the need for a new generation of young rural entrepreneurs. The programme, which targeted indigenous groups, aimed to enable beneficiaries to start sustainable, profitable agribusinesses. Within a year, participants had increased their income by one-fifth.

Whether in agriculture or not, it is essential for training to be adapted to each local context, filling clear gaps in the skills base in the local area. Training for Rural Economic Empowerment (TREE), designed by the ILO, takes this approach, helping match supply with labour market demand, resulting in strong successes in very varied contexts on different continents. In Bangladesh, it has helped women enter non-traditional trades such as appliance and computer repair. The approach combines technical and business training with training in gender issues and gender sensitization sessions for trainees' families, communities and partner organizations.

Youth skills: pathways to a better future

The need to take action in support of skills development for young people has become urgent. This Report identifies the ten most important steps that should be taken. These can be tailored to fit country-specific circumstances and needs.

1 Provide second-chance education for those with low or no foundation skills

Providing second-chance education to the 200 million young people in low and lower middle income countries who did not complete primary school requires well-coordinated and adequately funded programmes on a much greater scale. With the support of aid donors, governments should make this a policy priority, including it in education sector strategic planning that sets targets to reduce significantly the large number of young people without foundation skills. Budgetary allocations based on the number of disadvantaged youth requiring a second-chance education should be identified and included in the national budget forecast.

© Jun Yamamoto/UNESCO

2 Tackle the barriers that limit access to lower secondary school

Countries with large numbers of young people who lack foundation skills need to start by tackling the barriers that exclude many disadvantaged children and adolescents from participating and progressing in education through to at least lower secondary level. Abolishing school fees and providing targeted financial support, linking lower secondary to primary schools, providing a common core curriculum to equip all children with core skills, ensuring that there are enough government school places and assuring accessibility in rural areas are key measures that can improve access to lower secondary school.

A global target should be set to ensure all young people benefit from lower secondary school, with the aim of achieving universal lower secondary education of acceptable quality by 2030. Long-term education plans should identify strategies and financial resources required to meet this goal.

3 Make upper secondary education more accessible to the disadvantaged and improve its relevance to work

Upper secondary education must be in tune with the skills needs of the labour market. First, it has to strike a balance between technical and vocational and general subjects by providing flexibility in subject choices and links with the workplace.

Second, secondary school curriculum reforms should focus much more on developing in learners the capacity to solve problems, and tap into the potential of ICT to help learners develop the skills required in a labour market that is increasingly dependent on technology.

Third, flexible opportunities should be offered to students who are at risk of dropping out of secondary education. Distance education centres can be set up to cater for the learning needs of disadvantaged youth. Appropriate recognition should be given to skills gained through alternative learning pathways that offer a route back into education or provide similar secondary qualifications that are recognized in the workplace.

4 *Give poor urban youth access to skills training for better jobs*

Public interventions building on traditional apprenticeship systems should strengthen training by master craftspeople, improve working conditions of apprentices and ensure that skills can be certified through national qualification frameworks. As well as enhancing the legitimacy of traditional apprenticeships, such measures will ensure that they meet business and industry standards, and will improve apprentices' access to a wider range of better-paid jobs.

Strategies should provide skills training to young people who aspire to be entrepreneurs, but must not stop there. Providing young people with access to funds to start businesses can help them use their skills successfully.

5 *Aim policies and programmes at youth in deprived rural areas*

Many rural young people need to be given a second chance to acquire foundation skills, together with training in agricultural techniques that can help enhance their productivity. Farmer field schools and training via cooperatives, which are attuned to the local needs of farmers, are particularly successful. Since many rural youth also work off the farm, training in entrepreneurship and financial management can widen their opportunities. This is important where farmland is becoming scarce, and to provide opportunities to encourage young people to remain in rural areas.

6 *Link skills training with social protection for the poorest youth*

Combining microfinance or social protection, such as productive asset transfers, with training in basic literacy and numeracy as well as livelihood skills has been shown to be successful in helping counter the multiple forms of disadvantage that can lock youth into poverty.

7 *Prioritize the training needs of disadvantaged young women*

Targeted programmes that address the multiple causes of disadvantage that young women face have proved effective. Providing young women with microfinance and livelihood assets, and stipends until assets start to yield income, together with the skills needed to make the most out of these assets, gives them greater control over their own resources in ways that benefit them and their families.

8 *Harness the potential of technology to enhance opportunities for young people*

ICT can be used to bring skills training to a larger number of youth. Even basic technology such as radio can play an important role in skills training, particularly for people in remote rural areas. Such methods should be exploited further to enhance training opportunities for young people.

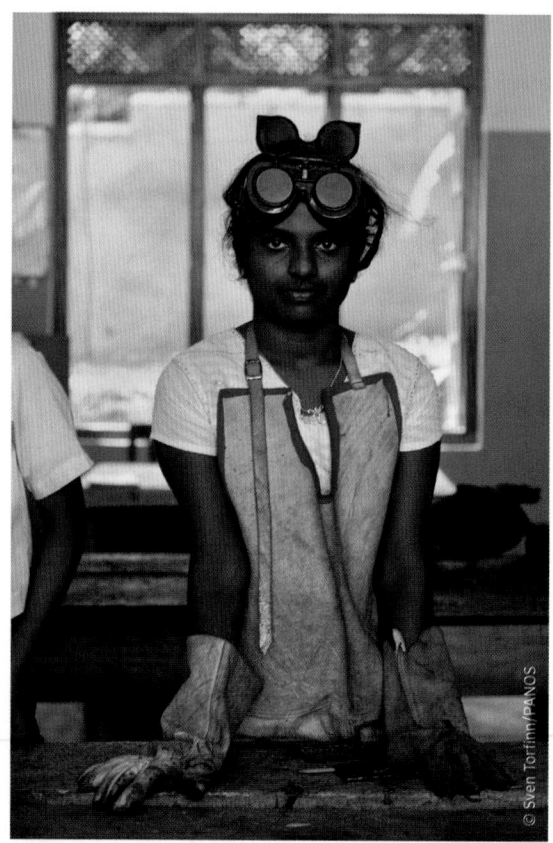

© Sven Torfinn/PANOS

Education for All Global Monitoring Report

2 0 1 2

9 *Improve planning by strengthening data collection and coordination of skills programmes*

Government leadership is important in coordinating the diverse range of actors involved in skills training and associated programmes to ensure that they reflect national priorities targeting the most disadvantaged youth. Doing so will reduce fragmentation and duplication of effort, and assure equitable access.

More and better data are needed for national governments and the international community to monitor accessibility of skills development programmes and so to plan more effectively. For reporting to the UNESCO Institute for Statistics, better information on lower and upper secondary education is needed. This should include more information on dropout and completion, and on subjects taken, including details on academic as well as technical and vocational areas, enabling analysis of choice of subject by gender.

Better data are also needed on skills development programmes beyond the formal school system, such as second-chance programmes and traditional apprenticeships, linking these data with labour market information. Given its expertise in this area, the ILO could take on the responsibility for gathering and disseminating such data from national governments. The international community should also build on recent developments to measure a range of skills of youth and adult populations more systematically.

Involving young people, especially those facing disadvantage, in planning is vital to identify constraints and appropriate solutions. Governments also need to work more closely with businesses and trade unions to improve the relevance of skills training efforts in the workplace.

10 *Mobilize additional funding from diverse sources dedicated to the training needs of disadvantaged youth*

There is an urgent need, especially in poor countries, for resources to make sure all young people have a good foundation in education, extending at least through to lower secondary school. National governments and aid donors should prioritize finding additional funds to support second-chance opportunities on a much larger scale. Reallocating some of the US$3.1 billion that aid donors currently spend on scholarships and imputed costs for developing country students to study in donor countries would go a long way towards helping provide the US$8 billion needed to ensure that all youth complete lower secondary school.

The private sector could extend its support to skills development programmes for disadvantaged young people through their foundations. But such support needs to be available on a much larger scale and more closely coordinated with national priorities.

Training funds that bring together resources from governments, aid donors and the private sector have had some success in reaching disadvantaged youth, including those in the informal sector. There is even greater potential for these funds to raise additional finance while improving coordination among governments, enterprises, donors, trade unions, youth groups and other interested parties.

Part 1 Monitoring progress

With just three years to go until the deadline for the Education for All goals that were set in Dakar, Senegal, it is vitally urgent to ensure that the collective commitments made by 164 countries in 2000 are met. Lessons also need to be drawn to inform the definition of future international education goals and the design of mechanisms to make sure that all partners live up to their promises.

Unfortunately, this year's *EFA Global Monitoring Report* shows that progress towards many of the targets is slowing down, and that most EFA goals are unlikely to be met. After remarkable progress in the initial years after Dakar, the global number of children out of school stagnated at 61 million in 2010, the latest year for which data are available. In 28 countries, fewer than 85 out of 100 children were in school in 2010, excluding a number of conflict-affected countries for which data are not available. It is clear that the target of universal primary education will be missed by a considerable margin.

Of particular concern is that the number of out-of-school children in sub-Saharan Africa – the region already furthest from achieving EFA – increased by 1.6 million between 2008 and 2010. Governments and their partners urgently need to increase their support to education in countries with large numbers of out-of-school children, paying particular attention to marginalized groups.

Despite the gloomy outlook overall, progress in some of the world's poorest countries shows what can be achieved with the commitment of national governments and aid donors, including greater numbers of children attending pre-school, completing primary school and making the transition to secondary education. The goal closest to being achieved is gender parity.

A more detailed assessment of each of the EFA goals helps identify where efforts should be concentrated to make up for lost ground in the short time remaining until 2015:

■ *Progress on early childhood care and education has been too slow.* The early years are critical for child development. As this Report shows, pre-primary education is the key to improving learning in subsequent years. Yet in many countries with low pre-primary enrolment, a large proportion of places are at private pre-schools that cost too much for those who need them most. Even in countries with higher enrolment, children in poorer areas are more likely to lack access or to have access only to pre-schools that are less well resourced. Policy-makers must act urgently to improve access to pre-school. Moreover, while progress on child health and nutrition appears to be speeding up, it is coming too late to achieve the Millennium Development Goals on child mortality and malnutrition.

■ *Many children do not complete primary school.* To improve universal primary enrolment, governments must renew efforts to prevent dropout. Of 100 children out of school, 47 are never expected to enter school at all. While this is shocking, within a period of six years the share has come down from 61. However, the share of out-of-school children who have dropped out has increased from 9 out of 100 to 26 out of 100. Whether they live in low income or middle income countries, children from marginalized households are more likely to enter late and to drop out early. Despite the abolition of school fees in many countries, costs associated with schooling still prevent many children from attending school.

■ *Adult literacy remains an elusive goal.* The world will miss the target of halving adult illiteracy between 1990 and 2015. Over 400 million of the global total of 775 million illiterate adults live in South and West Asia. The number of illiterate adults has risen over the period by 27% in sub-Saharan Africa. And around two-thirds of the world's illiterate adults are women. Direct measurements of literacy skills reveal large percentages of illiterate adults even among those who have

towards the EFA goals

completed primary education, and show that being literate is not a clear-cut matter of yes or no. In richer countries, this more nuanced picture has revealed that as many as one in five are likely to have very poor literacy skills.

- *Gender disparities take a variety of forms.* Global averages suggesting that gender parity in access to school has almost been attained can be deceptive. Many countries continue to struggle with ensuring that gender is not an obstacle to education. Despite progress in reducing severe disparity in access to primary school, there are still seventeen countries with fewer than nine girls for every ten boys in primary school. In secondary education, a majority of upper middle and high income countries experience disparity at the expense of boys. Regional and international assessments of learning outcomes show that across the world there is a large and increasing gender gap in reading, with boys, especially from poorer backgrounds, falling behind.

- *Global inequality in learning outcomes remains stark.* While inequality in access to school is of great concern, there is a greater gulf in learning between rich and poor. As many as 250 million children could be failing to read or write by the time they should reach grade 4. It is time to focus on improving data availability to have a better look at this estimate, and on ensuring that learning is more central to efforts to improve educational development. Many middle and high income countries have benefited from using the results of learning assessments as a basis to improve outcomes and reduce inequality. The world as a whole needs to do the same.

The Dakar Framework for Action included a commitment that no country should be left behind due to lack of resources. Increased spending on education has been a common ingredient of positive educational outcomes over the past ten years, with expanding education budgets in low income countries contributing to remarkable success. However, there are clouds on the horizon. Many of the countries furthest behind on the EFA goals have benefited from aid. Even if the economic downturn has not yet hit the education budgets of low and middle income countries as much as had been feared, it has hit the aid budgets of richer countries. Some have reacted by reducing the emphasis on education in their aid portfolio.

How will the widening financing gaps be filled? Aid from Brazil, China and India is expected to increase but is unlikely to be a strong complement to what is already available in the short term. Contributions from private foundations and corporations appear too small to make a significant difference and are not focused on the countries that most need support. The role of the Global Partnership for Education, as a coordinating mechanism channelling resources where they are likely to have the biggest impact, needs to be strengthened.

Governments need to continue prioritizing education and improving revenue collection. One option in countries endowed with natural resources is to use this revenue to invest in education as a way to overcome the ´resource curse´. Not only must resource-rich countries ensure that they are getting a fair share of the profits generated, but they and their partners must also adhere to revenue transparency standards. The EFA community should get involved in national debates on the use of natural resource revenue to make the case for investment in education. ☐

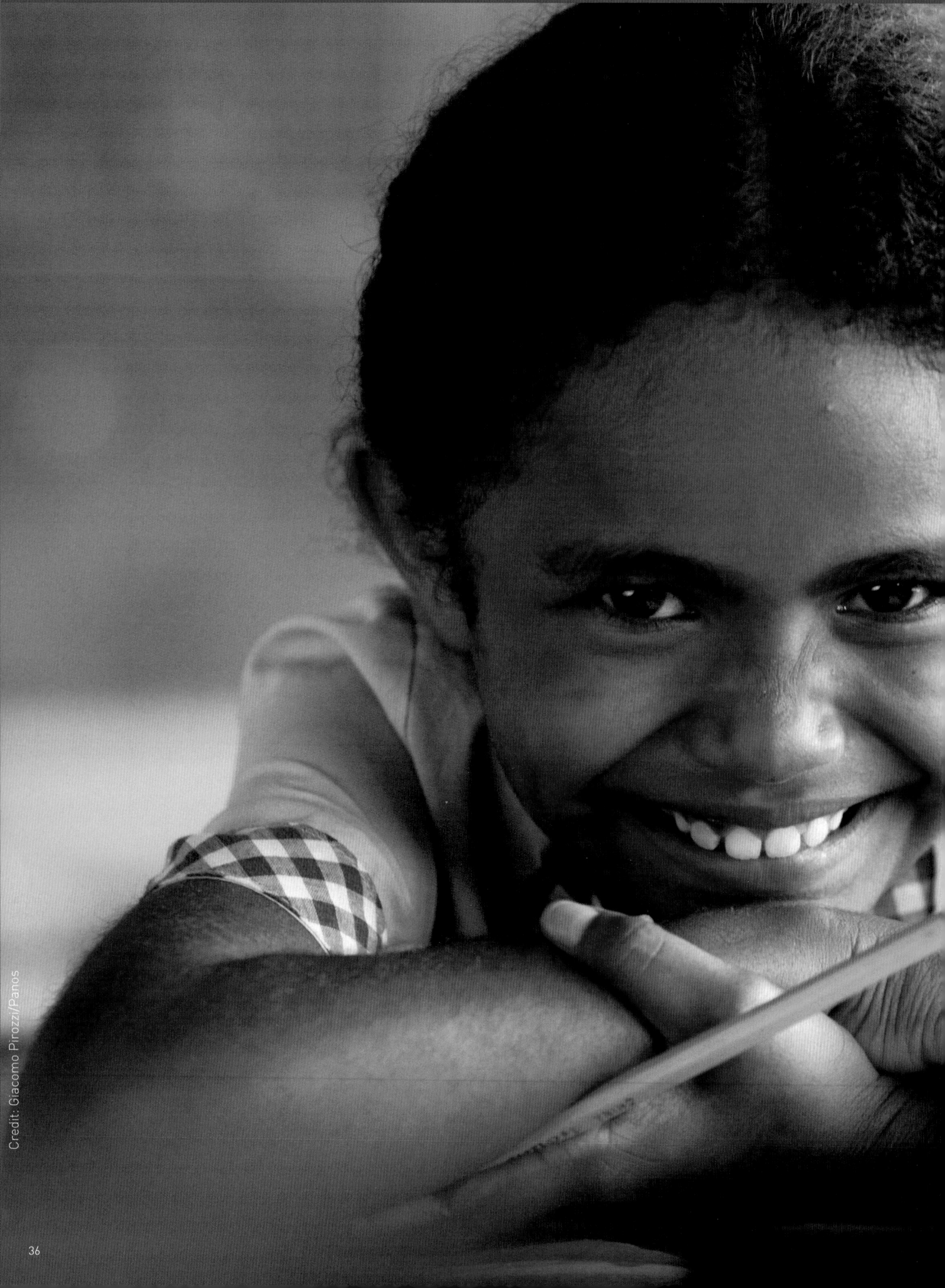

Credit: Giacomo Pirozzi/Panos

Chapter 1
The six EFA goals

A girl in grade 2 at St John Primary School in Honiara, Solomon Islands. Progress in reducing the number of children who are not enrolled in primary school has stalled since 2008.

It is ten years since the *EFA Global Monitoring Report* began following progress towards the international education goals. Over this time, many more children have had the opportunity to go to school. On current trends, however, the promise made in Dakar will be broken for millions of children, young people and adults unless governments act with greater urgency.

Goal 1 | Early childhood care and education

Expanding and improving comprehensive early childhood care and education, especially for the most vulnerable and disadvantaged children.

Highlights

■ Early childhood care and education (ECCE) is improving, but from a low base in some regions.

■ The child mortality rate fell from 88 per 1,000 live births in 1990 to 60 in 2010, but current rates of decline are insufficient to achieve the target of 29 by 2015. In 2010, there were still 28 countries where the child mortality rate exceeded 100 per 1,000 live births.

■ It is projected that around one in four children globally will suffer from moderate or extreme stunting by 2015. In half of low income countries with data, the stunting rate was 40% or higher in 2010.

■ Despite a 46% increase in the number of children enrolled in pre-school between 1999 and 2010, less than half the world's children receive pre-primary education. Progress has been slowest in low income countries, where only 15% of children received pre-primary education in 2010.

Table 1.1: Key indicators for goal 1

	Care			Pre-primary education					
	Under-5 mortality rate		Moderate and severe stunting (children under age 5)	Total enrolment		Gross enrolment ratio (GER)		Gender parity index of GER	
	2000–2005 (‰)	2010–2015 (‰)	2005–2010 (%)	2010 (000)	Change since 1999 (%)	1999 (%)	2010 (%)	1999 (F/M)	2010 (F/M)
World	74	60	29	163 525	46	32	48	0.97	1.00
Low income countries	138	111	40	9 357	63	11	15	0.98	1.00
Lower middle income countries	87	70	29	65 552	110	22	45	0.93	1.01
Upper middle income countries	31	23	14	59 206	20	43	62	1.01	1.02
High income countries	8	7	...	29 411	16	72	82	0.99	1.01
Sub-Saharan Africa	155	123	39	11 887	119	10	17	0.95	1.01
Arab States	54	41	21	3 904	62	15	22	0.77	0.94
Central Asia	57	46	19	1 591	25	19	30	0.95	1.00
East Asia and the Pacific	33	25	...	44 502	21	39	57	1.00	1.01
South and West Asia	88	69	38	48 144	125	21	48	0.93	1.02
Latin America and the Caribbean	32	24	...	20 541	28	54	70	1.02	1.01
North America and Western Europe	7	6	...	22 050	15	76	85	0.98	1.01
Central and Eastern Europe	22	16	...	10 906	15	51	69	0.96	0.98

Sources: Annex, Statistical Tables 3A and 3B (print) and Statistical Table 3A (website); UIS database.

CHAPTER 1

Early childhood is widely recognized as the critical period in which to lay the foundations for success in education and beyond. Thus early childhood care and education should be at the centre of both the Education for All (EFA) and broader development agendas. National and international policy-makers are more convinced than ever that early childhood well-being is not only a right but also a cost-effective investment.

The health of young children continues to improve, a fact demonstrated by substantial progress in the reduction of child mortality. The global number of deaths of children under 5 declined from 12 million in 1990 to 9.6 million in 2000 and 7.6 million in 2010 (IGME, 2011). This translates to a drop in the child mortality rate from 88 deaths per 1,000 live births in 1990 to 73 in 2000 and 60 in 2010.

The annual rate of decline of the child mortality rate accelerated from 1.9% in 1990–2000 to 2.5% in 2000–2010 (UNICEF, 2012). But progress is insufficient to meet the fourth Millennium Development Goal (MDG) of reducing child mortality by two-thirds by 2015. The advance towards reducing child mortality rates has been slowest in South and West Asia and sub-Saharan Africa, the regions with the highest mortality rates. Recent estimates suggest that just over half the decline in child deaths can be attributed to increased education attainment in women of reproductive age (Gakidou et al., 2010).

Of the 28 countries where child mortality rates were above 100 per 1,000 live births in 2010, 25 were in sub-Saharan Africa (the other three being Afghanistan, Djibouti and Mauritania). Chad is the country with the highest child mortality rate, 195 deaths per 1,000 live births. Of the 65 countries with more than 40 child deaths per 1,000 live births, only 11 are expected to reach the MDG target (IGME, 2011). Children marginalized by poverty, rural location and other factors have benefited least from progress (UNICEF, 2010b).

Good nutrition *in utero* and in early childhood is crucial for children's health, well-being, growth and survival. It is also required for cognitive development. Progress is being made on nutrition, but not fast enough, especially in the poorest countries and for the most marginalized children. While global rates of moderate and severe stunting were 29% in 2010, they remained high in low income countries and were over 50% in four of the countries with data: Burundi, Ethiopia, the Niger and Timor-Leste.

In many countries, there is large inequality between urban and rural areas. In Peru, for example, the stunting rate in rural areas in 2007/08 was almost triple that in urban areas. When there is a clear political commitment to increasing investment in a country's youngest citizens, however, meeting young children's right to adequate nutrition is possible [Panel 1.1].

Health and nutrition are of paramount importance for child development. In addition, equitable access to good quality pre-schools prepares young children for primary education, improves their prospects for learning and builds the foundations for positive social and economic outcomes in adulthood [goal 1, policy focus].

There has been significant progress across the world in extending access to pre-primary education since 1999, with the gross enrolment ratio increasing from 32% in 1999 to 48% in 2010. However, progress was larger in middle income countries than in low income countries, where only 15% of children attend pre-school. Globally more than half of young children remain excluded from pre-primary education.

Gender parity in pre-primary education has been met everywhere but the Arab States region, which has nonetheless made significant progress since 1999. But enrolment rates differ widely by location and wealth. Children in remote, underserved areas and children of poorer households have fewer opportunities to attend even though they are the ones who stand to benefit most from pre-school. In Nigeria, for example, the attendance rate among children of the richest quintile was seven times as high as that for children from the poorest quintile in 2007.

Greater levels of investment and better coordination among stakeholders are required if goal 1 is to be met. This edition of the *EFA Global Monitoring Report* introduces a new ECCE index that aims to capture the three main dimensions of child well-being encompassed by the early childhood care and education goal [Panel 1.2].

Panel 1.1: Early childhood nutrition is improving globally, but progress is too slow and uneven

Early childhood nutrition is crucial for children's health, well-being, growth and survival. Child malnutrition underlies more than half of all deaths among young children (Blössner and de Onis, 2005; Fishman et al., 2004). Insufficient food and poor quality food, with too few micronutrients, weaken children's immune systems, making them more vulnerable to disease. Malnutrition also hinders cognitive development and the capacity to learn, limiting progress towards the Education for All goals.

According to the World Health Organization, stunting (low height for age) is the most appropriate measure of chronic child malnutrition (de Onis and Blössner, 1997). Globally, 171 million children under 5 were affected by moderate or severe stunting in 2010. On current trends, the number of children suffering from stunting will still be as high as 157 million in 2015, or around one in four children under the age of 5 (de Onis et al., 2012).

Progress in reducing stunting has not been even across the world. Improvements over the past two decades are apparent in all regions except sub-Saharan Africa, where, in the context of slow progress and rapid population growth, the number of stunted children increased from 38 million in 1990 to 55 million in 2010. The share of sub-Saharan Africa in the global population of stunted children therefore increased dramatically in this period, from 15% to 32%, and is projected to reach 42% by 2020 (de Onis et al., 2012). As of 2010, sixteen of the twenty-four countries where the stunting rate is 40% or higher were in sub-Saharan Africa.

Moreover, looking at twenty-two countries with data from around 1990, progress has not been the same even within regions over the course of these two decades (Figure 1.1). For example, in the Arab States, the stunting rate in Mauritania fell from 55% to 23%, while it increased in Djibouti from 28% to 33%. In sub-Saharan Africa, the stunting rate in Nigeria fell from 51% to 41%, while it remained stagnant in Cameroon at 36%.

Figure 1.1: There has been considerable progress in reducing stunting, but it has been uneven

Moderate or severe stunting rate, selected countries, from about 1990 to 2005–2010

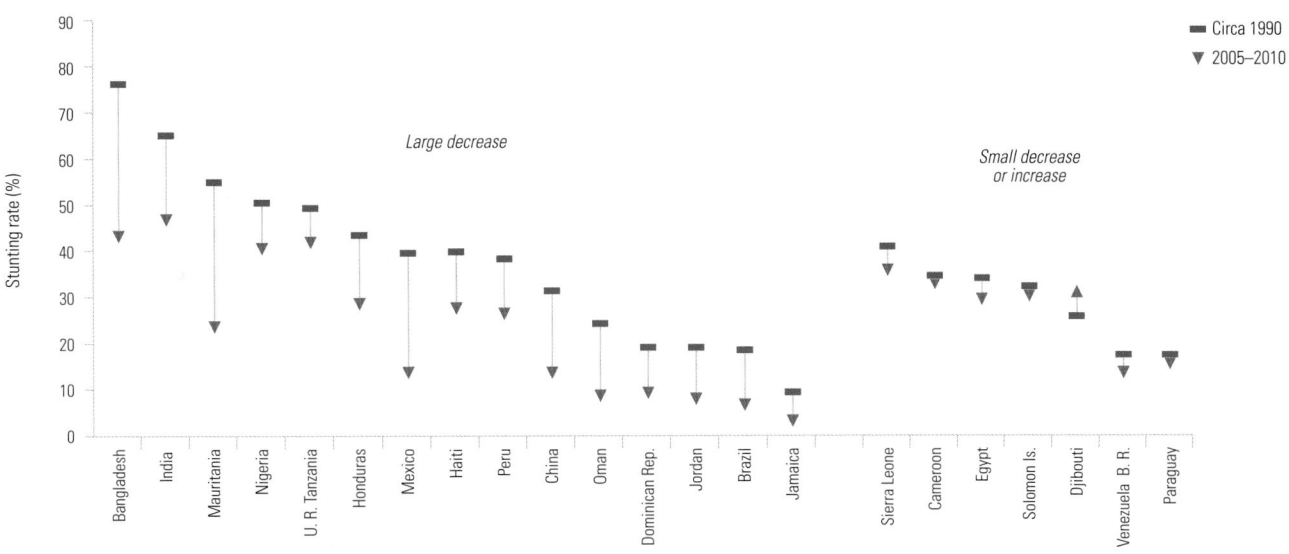

Note: A child is moderately or severely stunted if its height for age is less than two standard deviations from the median of the reference population.
Source: WHO (2012).

CHAPTER 1

Good nutrition is not just about whether a country produces enough food. It is also about whether children are healthy enough to benefit from the food they receive. This status depends on good water and sanitation, access to clinics, and good health and nutrition practices at home. As a result, rural areas have higher stunting rates even though they are food producing.

An analysis of thirty-six countries found that rural areas had lower access to public services and, crucially, lower levels of maternal education, which is correlated with health-seeking and care-giving practices (Smith et al., 2005). In more than two-fifths of the eighty-eight countries with data available for 2005–2010, the difference in stunting rates between rural and urban children was more than ten percentage points (Figure 1.2). In several countries, such as the Democratic People's Republic of Korea, Honduras and Papua New Guinea, the rural-urban gap in stunting rates exceeds twenty percentage points.

Malnutrition is deeply rooted in poverty and deprivation. The poor cannot purchase food even when it is available in local markets. In most countries, malnutrition differences between the richest and the poorest exceed those between urban and rural inhabitants (Figure 1.3). For example, in Nepal, the stunting rate was 26% among the richest children and 56% among the poorest compared with corresponding rates of 27% in urban and 42% in rural areas.

The poor are also vulnerable to price hikes, whether temporary or permanent, seasonal or unexpected. The substantial increase in staple food prices between 2007 and 2008 was correlated with an 8% increase in undernutrition in sub-Saharan Africa (FAO, 2011). In the Horn of Africa, as of December 2011, it was estimated that about 850,000 children under 5 and 120,000 pregnant and lactating women were suffering from acute malnutrition in Kenya and Somalia alone because of the combined impact of drought-induced crop failure, conflict and displacement,

Figure 1.2: Malnutrition is a greater problem in rural areas

Moderate or severe stunting rate by location, selected countries, 2005–2010

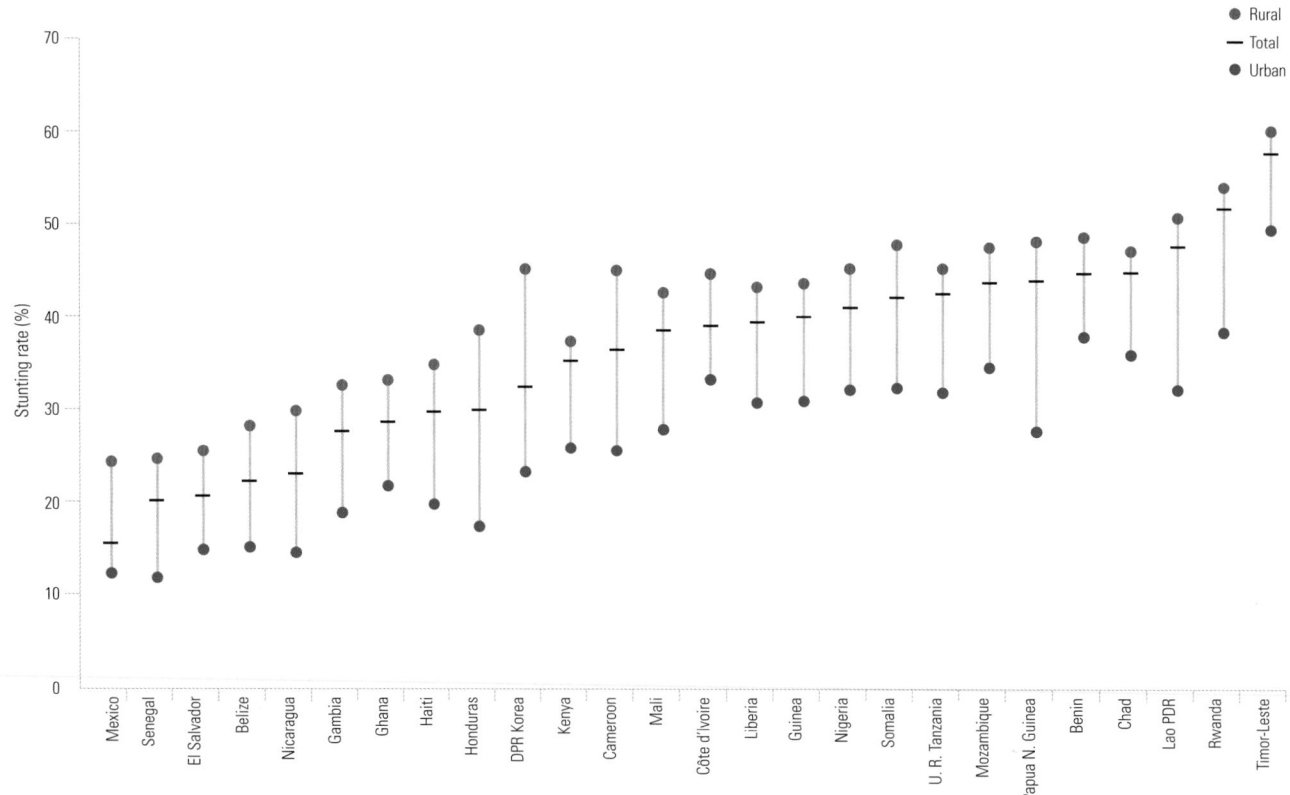

Source: WHO (2012).

Figure 1.3: In most countries, the gap in nutrition between the richest and the poorest exceeds the gap between urban and rural areas

Moderate or severe stunting rate by location and wealth, selected countries

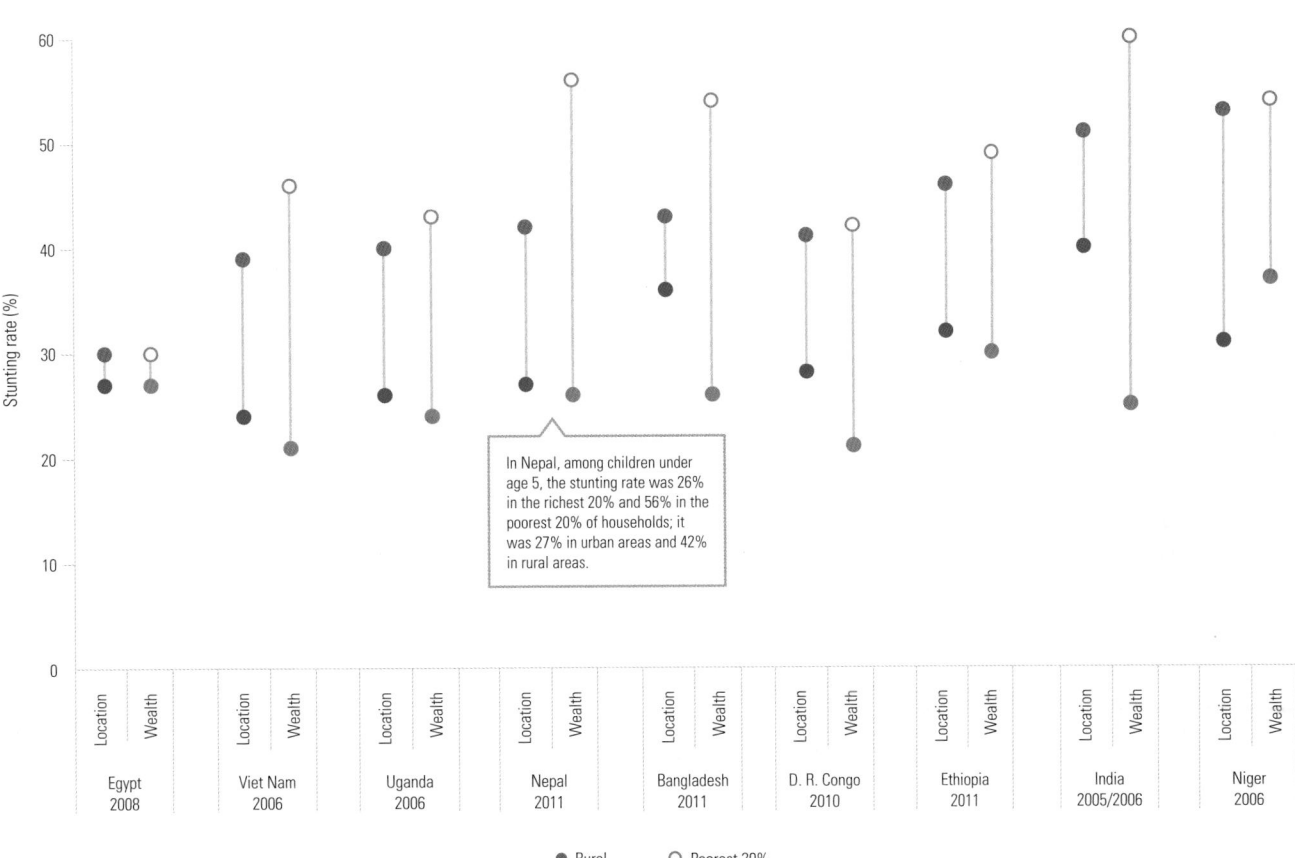

In Nepal, among children under age 5, the stunting rate was 26% in the richest 20% and 56% in the poorest 20% of households; it was 27% in urban areas and 42% in rural areas.

● Rural   ○ Poorest 20%
● Urban   ● Richest 20%

Sources: Bangladesh NIPORT et al. (2012); D. R. Congo National Institute of Statistics and UNICEF (2011); El-Zanaty and Way (2009); Ethiopia Central Statistical Agency and ICF International (2012); International Institute for Population Sciences and Macro International Inc. (2007); Nepal Ministry of Health and Population et al. (2012); Niger National Institute of Statistics and Macro International Inc. (2007); Uganda Bureau of Statistics and Macro International Inc. (2007); Viet Nam General Statistics Office (2007).

and the earlier food price rise (OCHA, 2011a, 2011b). The governments of Burkina Faso, Mauritania and the Niger have declared 2012 a crisis year. In the Niger, acute malnutrition affects 12% of children aged 6 to 59 months (IASC, 2012).

Success in tackling child malnutrition varies widely among regions and countries. There are notable differences in progress between three of the five most populous countries, Brazil, India and China, which have all achieved impressive levels of economic growth in the past decade. Stunting rates in India have remained persistently high because of poor maternal nutrition, low birth weight, high levels of poverty and low levels of maternal education (Svedberg, 2009). Many Indians still struggle to meet their most basic needs, including access to sufficient food and health care. The fact that almost half of children under 5 are

malnourished is a 'national shame', Prime Minister Manmohan Singh has said. Yet the main policy tool for tackling malnutrition, the network of Anganwadi centres, which cater for children under 6, pregnant women and lactating mothers, is not fulfilling its potential. A survey of more than 74,000 mothers found that only 19% of them reported receiving nutrition counselling (Naandi Foundation, 2011).

By contrast, in Brazil and China, child malnutrition began declining dramatically around the mid-1990s, which led to the elimination of the urban-rural gap in Brazil and its reduction by more than two-thirds in China (Figure 1.4A). In Brazil, the expansion of primary schooling (leading to improved maternal education), maternal and child health services, and — to a lesser extent — the improvement of water supply and sanitation systems are considered the main determinants of this impressive outcome, alongside equitable growth (Monteiro et al., 2009; Victora et al., 2011).

Mexico has emulated Brazil's success. The gap between urban and rural areas halved between 1998/99 and 2006, at least in part because of the Progresa programme and its successor, Oportunidades. As well as a cash transfer, the programmes provided food fortified with micronutrients to children aged 6 months to 23 months, to underweight children aged 2 to 4 and to pregnant and lactating women (Rivera et al., 2009).

In some other Latin American countries, however, rates of malnutrition are higher than expected for their income level, and inequality rates in malnutrition are among the world's highest. The very limited progress in the last two decades in the Plurinational State of Bolivia,

Guatemala and Peru has mainly benefited children in urban areas (Figure 1.4B). In Peru, early evaluations of the national conditional cash transfer programme, Juntos, did not show any effect on malnutrition (Perova and Vakis, 2009). More recently, the government aligned Juntos with Crecer, the national nutrition strategy, by making the cash transfer conditional on regular monitoring of children's growth (Acosta, 2011).

Fighting childhood malnutrition requires tackling poverty and building equitable access to health care, both of which require a clear political commitment to increase expenditure. Attention should be focused on interventions for pregnant women and children under 3, as it is difficult to reverse stunting after that age (Bhutta et al., 2008).

Figure 1.4: Country experiences in tackling malnutrition in rural areas vary enormously

Moderate or severe stunting rate by location, selected countries, from about 1990 to 2010

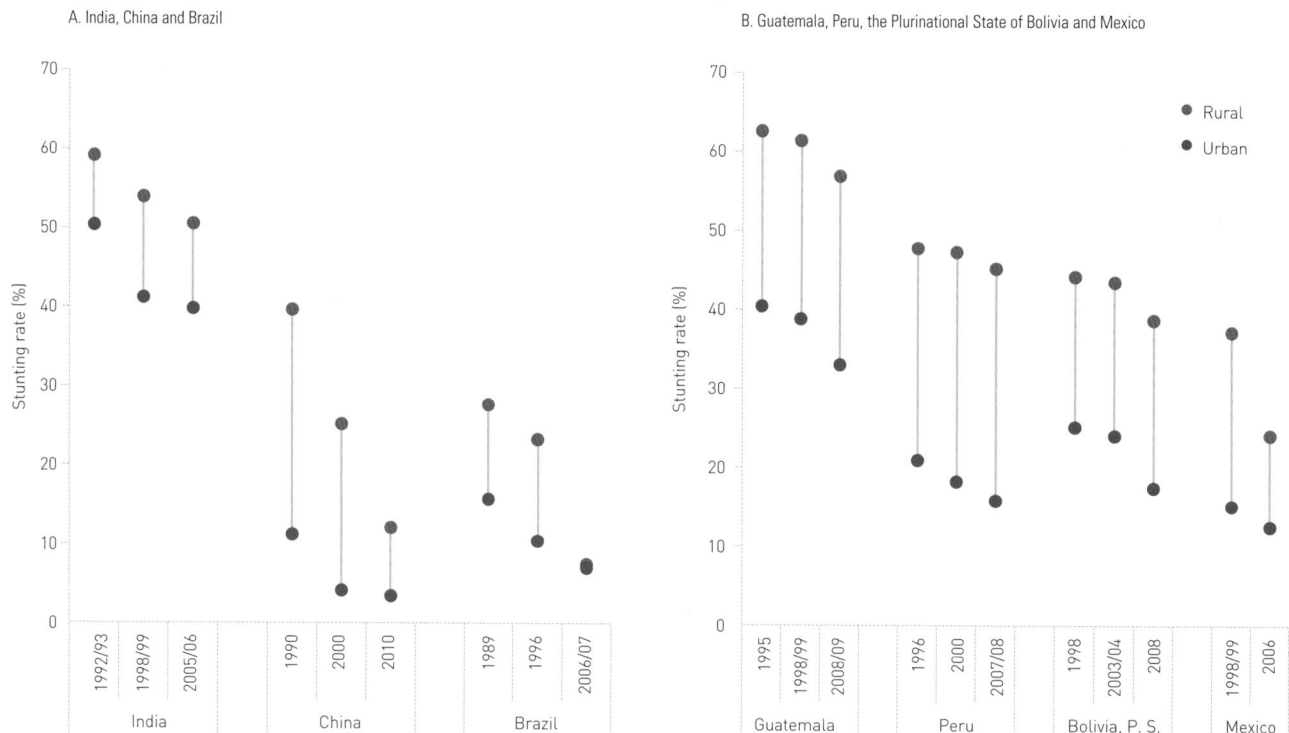

Note: In India, the rate is calculated for the 0–4 age group in the 1992/93 survey and the 0–3 age group in the 1998/99 survey. As a result, the stunting rate is underestimated in those years.
Source: WHO (2012).

Panel 1.2: The ECCE index, a new instrument for monitoring goal 1

Each of the three key dimensions of early childhood development – child health, nutrition and education – is often considered as a separate goal. They are interrelated in many ways, however, so to understand progress towards goal 1 it is vital to pay attention to all of them simultaneously. This panel proposes a simple index that provides benchmarks to enable countries' performance to be measured.[1]

The ECCE index summarizes the results of early childhood development policies on:

- health, measured by the percentage of children who will survive beyond their fifth birthday; this ranges, among countries with a full set of data, from a low of 82% in Guinea-Bissau to a high of 99% in Chile;

- nutrition, measured by the percentage of children under 5 who do not suffer from moderate or severe stunting, which ranges from 45% in the Niger to 98% in Chile;

- education, measured by the percentage of children aged 3 to 7 who are enrolled either in pre-primary or in primary school, which ranges from 20% in Ethiopia to 95% in Belarus.[2]

The value of the ECCE index is the mean of these three indicators.[3] Since each indicator is expressed in percentages, the value ranges from 0 to 1. Only 68 out of 205 countries had a full set of information on all these indicators in 2010 (or the most recent year for which data are available). The lack of data on stunting for most high income countries accounts largely for the gaps (Table 1.2). While this prevents a broader assessment of progress, it nevertheless provides useful insights into the global state of early childhood development.

It is clear that most countries are far from assuring the minimum conditions for the youngest children. Of the sixty-eight countries, only Belarus achieved a score over 0.95. The twenty-five countries with an index score between 0.80 and 0.95, viewed as achieving a middle ranking, are mostly middle income countries in Central Asia, Central and Eastern Europe, and Latin America and the Caribbean. Many have good health and nutrition indicators but have made limited progress in early childhood education. Among countries in this group, enrolment ratios are below 60% in Brazil, the Dominican Republic and The former Yugoslav Republic of Macedonia. The remaining forty-two countries, with an index score below 0.80, are mostly low and lower middle income countries, and a majority are in sub-Saharan Africa.

There is also uneven development across the three dimensions, as a comparison of the country rank for each of the three component indicators shows (Figure 1.5). Some countries score almost equally well (such as Belarus and Chile) or equally poorly (such as the Niger) on all three. Others have a very high or very low score

Figure 1.5: Progress towards early childhood goals varies widely across key dimensions

Country rank, ECCE index and its three components, selected countries, 2010

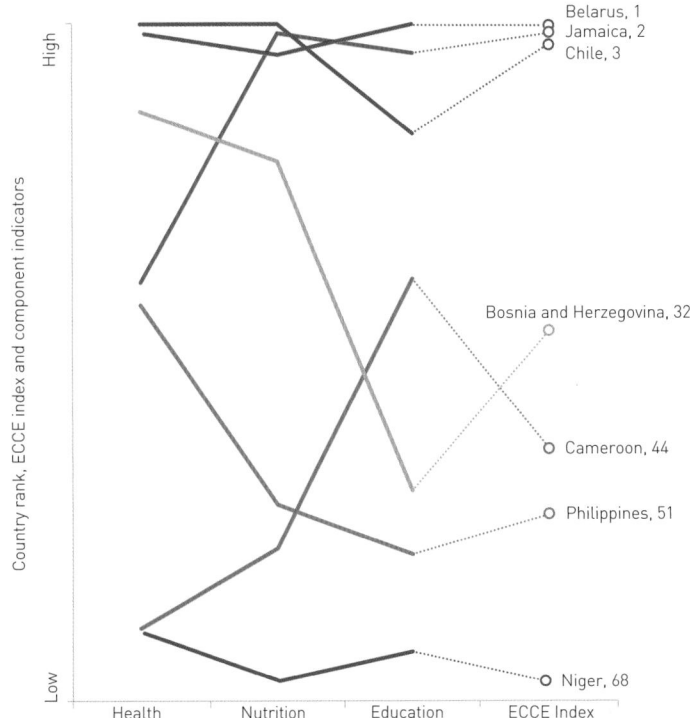

Note: The ECCE index country rank is indicated next to the country name.
Source: EFA Global Monitoring Report team calculations (2012).

---

1. Among attempts to develop indices of early childhood development, a notable example is the Child Development Index (Save the Children, 2008) and the child component of the Mothers' Index (Save the Children, 2012). UNESCO is developing a Holistic Early Childhood Development Index, which was proposed at the World Conference on ECCE in September 2010. This process has been informed by the publication of five background papers, which reviewed the relevance and availability of indicators in the fields of care, education and child development; policy and planning; social protection; legal protection; and health and nutrition (UNESCO, 2012a).
2. The age-specific enrolment ratio is used instead of the pre-primary or primary net enrolment ratio to be consistent with the common definition of early childhood as the period from birth until at least the age of primary school entry.
3. Using different weighting for the three indicators does not significantly change the ranking of countries. Additional information on the ECCE index is available on this Report's website.

CHAPTER 1

for one dimension relative to their overall standing in the index scale, which reveals specific challenges.

For example, Jamaica and the Philippines both have a child mortality rate of 3% but are ranked at opposite ends of the overall ECCE index because of their nutrition and education records. Almost one in three children in the Philippines suffer from moderate or extreme stunting, compared with only one in twenty-seven in Jamaica. Only 38% of children aged 3 to 7 were enrolled in a pre-primary or primary school programme in the Philippines, compared with 89% in Jamaica.

Despite great differences in child health and nutrition indicators between Bosnia and Herzegovina and Cameroon, related to the large difference in living standards, only 45% of 3- to 7-year-olds were enrolled

in some form of education in Bosnia and Herzegovina, compared with 60% in Cameroon.

Although the poorest countries are also the ones with the lowest values on the ECCE index, the relationship between income and early childhood development outcomes weakens among middle income countries. For example, Botswana had an annual per capita income of US$13,700 (in purchasing power parity terms) in 2010, yet was ranked just above two countries with less than a fifth of its per capita income — the Lao People's Democratic Republic (which had a higher enrolment ratio) and Senegal (which had a lower stunting rate).

The ECCE index highlights the need for all countries, regardless of income, to invest in integrated approaches that give equal importance to all aspects of early childhood development.

Table 1.2: The ECCE index and its components, 2010

Rank	Countries	ECCE index	Under 5 survival rate	Children under 5 not suffering from moderate or severe stunting	Age-specific enrolment ratio of children aged 3 to 7
High ECCE index (0.95–1.00)					
1	Belarus	0.967	0.991	0.955	0.955
Medium ECCE index (0.80–0.94)					
2	Jamaica	0.944	0.974	0.963	0.894
3	Chile	0.914	0.992	0.980	0.769
4	Kuwait	0.914	0.990	0.962	0.789
5	Thailand	0.911	0.987	0.843	0.902
6	Mexico	0.901	0.983	0.845	0.874
7	Maldives	0.900	0.988	0.797	0.914
8	Republic of Moldova	0.892	0.981	0.887	0.807
9	Venezuela, B. R.	0.881	0.980	0.844	0.818
10	Belize	0.879	0.979	0.784	0.873
11	Suriname	0.852	0.973	0.893	0.690
12	Peru	0.849	0.972	0.702	0.874
13	Montenegro	0.849	0.991	0.921	0.634
14	Serbia	0.843	0.987	0.919	0.622
15	Oman	0.841	0.989	0.902	0.632
16	Colombia	0.835	0.977	0.873	0.654
17	Brazil	0.832	0.976	0.929	0.592
18	Viet Nam	0.830	0.977	0.695	0.817
19	Dominican Republic	0.823	0.972	0.899	0.598
20	Guyana	0.819	0.954	0.818	0.685
21	Nicaragua	0.811	0.978	0.783	0.673
22	TFYR Macedonia	0.809	0.985	0.889	0.554
23	Mongolia	0.807	0.963	0.725	0.734
24	Kazakhstan	0.805	0.971	0.825	0.620
25	Panama	0.805	0.979	0.809	0.626
26	Albania	0.803	0.981	0.807	0.622

Table 1.2: The ECCE index and its components, 2010 (continued)

Rank	Countries	ECCE index	Under 5 survival rate	Children under 5 not suffering from moderate or severe stunting	Age-specific enrolment ratio of children aged 3 to 7
Low ECCE index (<0.80)					
27	Jordan	0.796	0.978	0.917	0.495
28	Palestine	0.795	0.978	0.882	0.526
29	Algeria	0.794	0.973	0.851	0.559
30	Turkey	0.794	0.977	0.897	0.506
31	Paraguay	0.774	0.967	0.825	0.529
32	Bosnia and Herzegovina	0.771	0.984	0.882	0.447
33	El Salvador	0.769	0.977	0.794	0.537
34	Sao Tome and Principe	0.768	0.931	0.684	0.690
35	Ghana	0.765	0.937	0.714	0.644
36	Honduras	0.755	0.967	0.706	0.592
37	Syrian Arab Republic	0.754	0.984	0.725	0.554
38	Bolivia, P. S.	0.740	0.946	0.728	0.545
39	Azerbaijan	0.733	0.957	0.749	0.494
40	Kyrgyzstan	0.728	0.958	0.825	0.400
41	Egypt	0.724	0.975	0.711	0.486
42	Uzbekistan	0.716	0.947	0.810	0.392
43	Indonesia	0.706	0.969	0.632	0.516
44	Cameroon	0.700	0.864	0.642	0.595
45	Kenya	0.700	0.911	0.648	0.542
46	Swaziland	0.689	0.908	0.596	0.563
47	Angola	0.685	0.844	0.708	0.503
48	Gambia	0.684	0.907	0.756	0.390
49	Congo	0.682	0.896	0.688	0.461
50	Iraq	0.681	0.959	0.736	0.347
51	Philippines	0.678	0.973	0.677	0.384
52	Botswana	0.677	0.954	0.686	0.392
53	Senegal	0.673	0.915	0.799	0.306
54	Lao PDR	0.671	0.954	0.524	0.533
55	Guatemala	0.657	0.966	0.520	0.485
56	Cambodia	0.654	0.931	0.591	0.440
57	Uganda	0.646	0.886	0.619	0.432
58	Tajikistan	0.601	0.935	0.608	0.259
59	Rwanda	0.597	0.886	0.558	0.346
60	Djibouti	0.593	0.896	0.674	0.208
61	Côte d'Ivoire	0.588	0.893	0.610	0.260
62	Guinea-Bissau	0.585	0.819	0.719	0.218
63	Mali	0.575	0.827	0.623	0.274
64	Guinea	0.573	0.866	0.600	0.252
65	Burkina Faso	0.569	0.853	0.650	0.203
66	Central African Republic	0.564	0.845	0.574	0.272
67	Ethiopia	0.531	0.904	0.493	0.196
68	Niger	0.508	0.856	0.452	0.217

Note: The age-specific enrolment ratio of children aged 3 to 7 years measures the proportion of children in the corresponding age group who are enrolled in either pre-primary or primary school.
Sources: EFA Global Monitoring Report team calculations (2012); Annex, Statistical Table 3A; UIS database.

Policy focus: Preparing children for school by expanding pre-primary education

Good quality pre-school programmes are vital to prepare young children for primary school. As the goal of universal primary education moves closer, concern has been rising over whether schoolchildren are actually acquiring the basic knowledge and skills that primary schools are meant to impart. This has focused attention not only on the quality of primary education but also on whether young children are being adequately prepared to benefit from primary school.

This section shows that, as part of a comprehensive package of early childhood care and education interventions, equitable access to good quality pre-school programmes markedly improves young children's readiness to succeed in school. This can have particular advantages for those who are marginalized due to poverty or other factors.

Yet participation in pre-school remains low in many countries, especially among children who need it most, and quality remains a concern. Action is needed to expand access to good quality pre-school programmes, particularly for the disadvantaged, and to better coordinate pre-school education with early childhood care and with primary school.

Pre-primary education plays a key role in preparing children for school and beyond

Young children are ready to learn, but their early experiences are crucial in facilitating their learning. Attending a good quality pre-school can lay the foundations for learning and help children make a smooth transition to primary school. Extending access to the poorest and most vulnerable children can boost their education and livelihood opportunities later in life.

The more time children spend in pre-school, the better their performance in school. Recent evidence based on the 2009 survey in the Programme for International Student Assessment (PISA) shows that in fifty-eight of sixty-five countries, 15-year-old students who had attended at least a year of pre-primary school outperformed students who had not, even after accounting for socio-economic background. In countries including Australia, Brazil and Germany, the average benefit after controlling for socio-economic background was equivalent to one year of schooling (Figure 1.6).

Overall, PISA results suggest that the school systems that combine high performance and equitable learning opportunities for all students are also those that offer pre-primary education to a larger proportion of pupils, have smaller pupil/teacher ratios in pre-primary school, invest more per child at the pre-primary level and, especially, provide longer periods of pre-primary education (OECD, 2011b).

Long-term studies from high income countries show that pre-school contributes to school readiness and later academic achievement

Figure 1.6: Pre-primary education has a positive impact on learning outcomes in school

Score point difference between 15-year-old students who attended pre-primary school for more than one year and those who had not, after accounting for socio-economic background, selected countries, PISA 2009

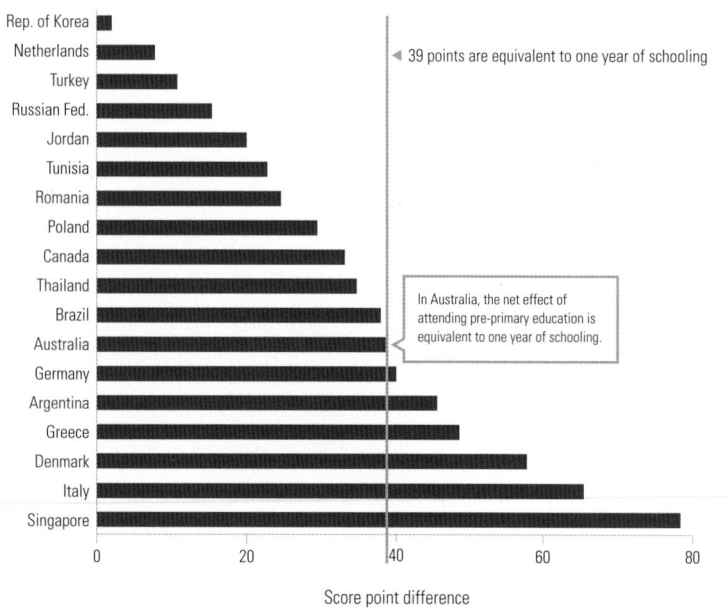

Source: OECD (2010b).

through the development of non-cognitive skills, such as attention, effort, initiative and behaviour, as well as cognitive skills in reading and mathematics (Duncan et al., 2007; Reynolds et al., 2010; Romano et al., 2010). An evaluation of Head Start, the publicly funded national early childhood programme in the United States that focuses on poor children, has shown that it had significant positive long-term effects. For example, those who had participated in the programme were 9% more likely to have graduated from secondary school and 7% less likely not to be in school and to be reporting zero wages in their early twenties (Deming, 2009).

There is now a growing body of evaluations from developing countries highlighting the benefits of pre-schooling (Box 1.1).

The short- to medium-term effects of pre-school attendance on cognitive and non-cognitive skills and school performance provide the foundation for the basic skills that young people require to do well in schooling. It also leads to higher earnings and better employment outcomes in adulthood. The Early Enrichment Project in Turkey in the 1980s — which included a pre-schooling intervention — targeted children of low income families whose mothers had little education. Two decades later, participants were found to have better educational attainment and occupational status than those who had not participated (Kagitcibasi et al., 2009).

Higher pre-primary enrolment is expected to increase primary school enrolment in poor countries. A recent simulation of potential

Box 1.1: Pre-schooling has striking benefits for school performance

Studies in developing countries on the benefits of pre-school vary in scope, but paint a similar picture overall, demonstrating positive effects on subsequent school performance. Participation is found to be particularly beneficial for those from poor and disadvantaged backgrounds.

The benefits of pre-school for non-cognitive skills are demonstrated by a study in Argentina. As well as having higher test scores, third graders who had one year of public pre-primary school in an urban area showed improved attention, effort, class participation and discipline. In rural Gansu, Shaanxi and Henan, China, 4- and 5-year-olds who had attended pre-primary education scored 20% higher on a school readiness scale, which included non-cognitive skills such as independence and motor skills, than those who had not.

Studies from many countries, including Chile, India and Madagascar, show the contribution of pre-school to cognitive abilities. In Chile, children entering primary school who had enrolled in public pre-schools or child care centres had higher cognitive skill scores. In rural Maharashtra, India, a project that improved the pre-school component of the Integrated Child Development Services had significant positive effects on the developmental and cognitive outcomes of 4- to 6-year-olds. In Madagascar, primary school children who had attended pre-school showed a 2.7 month benefit in terms of cognitive development and a 1.6 month benefit in terms of language.

Pre-school attendance can be particularly beneficial in addressing disadvantage. In a study in Argentina, the effect

of having attended pre-school on third grade test scores was twice as large for students from poor backgrounds as for students from non-poor backgrounds. A rare evaluation in a low income country found that children who had attended pre-school in rural Mozambique scored, on average, 12.1 percentage points above the other students on a cognitive development test in the first grade of primary school, including classifying objects and counting to twenty.

Fourth grade primary school children in Brazil who had attended day care and/or kindergarten scored higher in mathematics. In rural Bangladesh, a project run by local non-governmental organizations (NGOs) set up 1,800 pre-schools and provided them with better materials. Participating children performed better in speaking, reading, writing and mathematics by the second grade of primary school than those who did not attend pre-school. In rural Guizhou, China, first-grade children who had attended kindergarten had literacy and mathematics scores significantly better than other children.

Attending pre-school also tends to increase the years of education that children eventually attain. In Uruguay, 15-year-olds who had attended a public or private pre-school accumulated 0.8 years more education, were 27% more likely to still be in school and were less likely to repeat a grade than siblings who had not attended. In Mozambique, attending pre-school increased the probability of enrolling in primary school by 24%.

Sources: Aboud and Hossain (2011); Ade et al. (2010); Berlinski et al. (2008); Berlinski et al. (2009); Luo et al. (2011); Martinez et al. (2012); Mingat and Seurat (2011); Rao et al. (2012); Rodrigues et al. (2011); Urzúa and Veramandi (2011).

long-term economic effects in seventy-three low and middle income countries showed potentially high benefits. For example, it was estimated that raising the pre-primary gross enrolment ratio to 25% in countries such as Ethiopia and Yemen would lead to increased school attendance. Those who increase their school attendance can later be expected to increase their income by an amount around six times as high as the per capita cost of providing access to pre-school (Engle et al., 2011).

Participation in pre-primary education is low and inequitable

The number of children enrolled in pre-school has increased substantially over the past decade. Despite this increase, participation in pre-school remains extremely low in many countries, with children from poor households least likely to attend.

Between 1999 and 2010, the number of children enrolled in pre-school worldwide rose by 46% to a total of 164 million. The pre-primary gross enrolment ratio increased from 32% in 1999 to a still-low 48% in 2010. In low income countries, however, the pre-primary gross enrolment ratio increased from 11% in 1999 to only 15% in 2010.

On average, national education systems allow for 2.9 years of pre-primary education. But in practice, children can expect to attend pre-school for less than half that long.[4] The gap between intentions and outcomes is widest in low income countries, particularly in the Arab States, Central Asia and sub-Saharan Africa (Figure 1.7).

Pre-primary gross enrolment ratios vary widely between and within regions. The lowest levels are in sub-Saharan Africa (17%) and the Arab States (22%). The gap between these regions

Figure 1.7: Participation in pre-primary education is lower than the system allows
Duration of pre-primary education ('official') and pre-primary school life expectancy ('actual'), number of years, weighted average, 2010

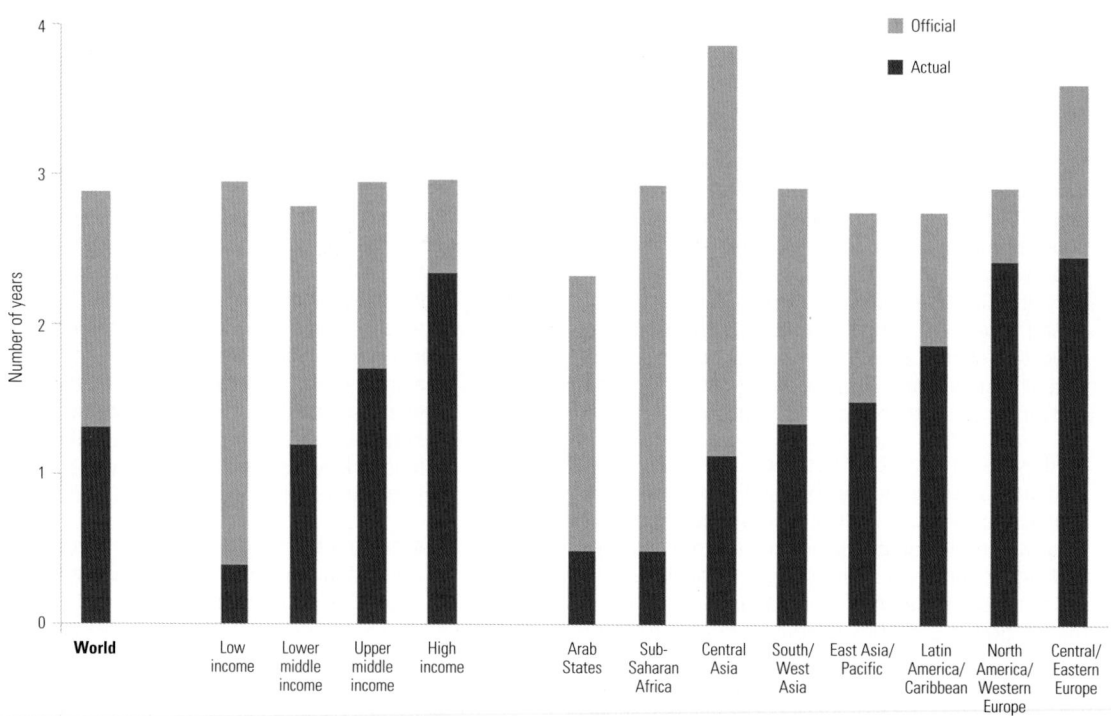

Source: Annex, Statistical Table 3B (website).

4. Comparisons among countries and over time are hindered by differences in pre-school and primary school start age; differences in the way that pre-school relates to day care and primary school, including whether kindergarten is considered part of primary; and the large numbers of private providers, often under-reported, in many countries.

and the rest of the world widened during the last decade as these two regions also recorded the slowest progress of all regions except North America and Western Europe, where enrolment is already high.

Some countries with low enrolment have made very slow progress or even worsened. In the Niger and the Syrian Arab Republic, enrolment has stagnated at a very low level, below the regional average. Of the 150 countries that reported data for both the beginning of the period (1999–2001) and the end (2008–2011), seventeen countries recorded a lower gross enrolment ratio in the more recent year, including Bangladesh, where enrolment was already very low (Figure 1.8).

All regions except the Arab States have achieved gender parity in pre-primary enrolment, and even this region has made large improvements since 1999. Even so, of the 162 countries with data, 69 had not reached gender parity in 2010. In about 60% of these countries, girls were more likely to be enrolled.

Patterns of disadvantage vary among countries. A child in Bangladesh has very little chance of attending pre-school: whether urban or rural, rich or poor, male or female, only around one in six attend. By contrast, 61% of 3- to 4-year-olds attend pre-school in Thailand, although there is a distinct wealth bias, with 74% of children from rich households enrolled compared with 54% of poor children. In Nigeria, disparities

17 countries had fewer children enrolling in pre-school in 2011 than a decade ago

Figure 1.8: Enrolment in pre-primary education varies widely between and within regions

Pre-primary gross enrolment ratio, selected countries, 1999 and 2010 or nearest year

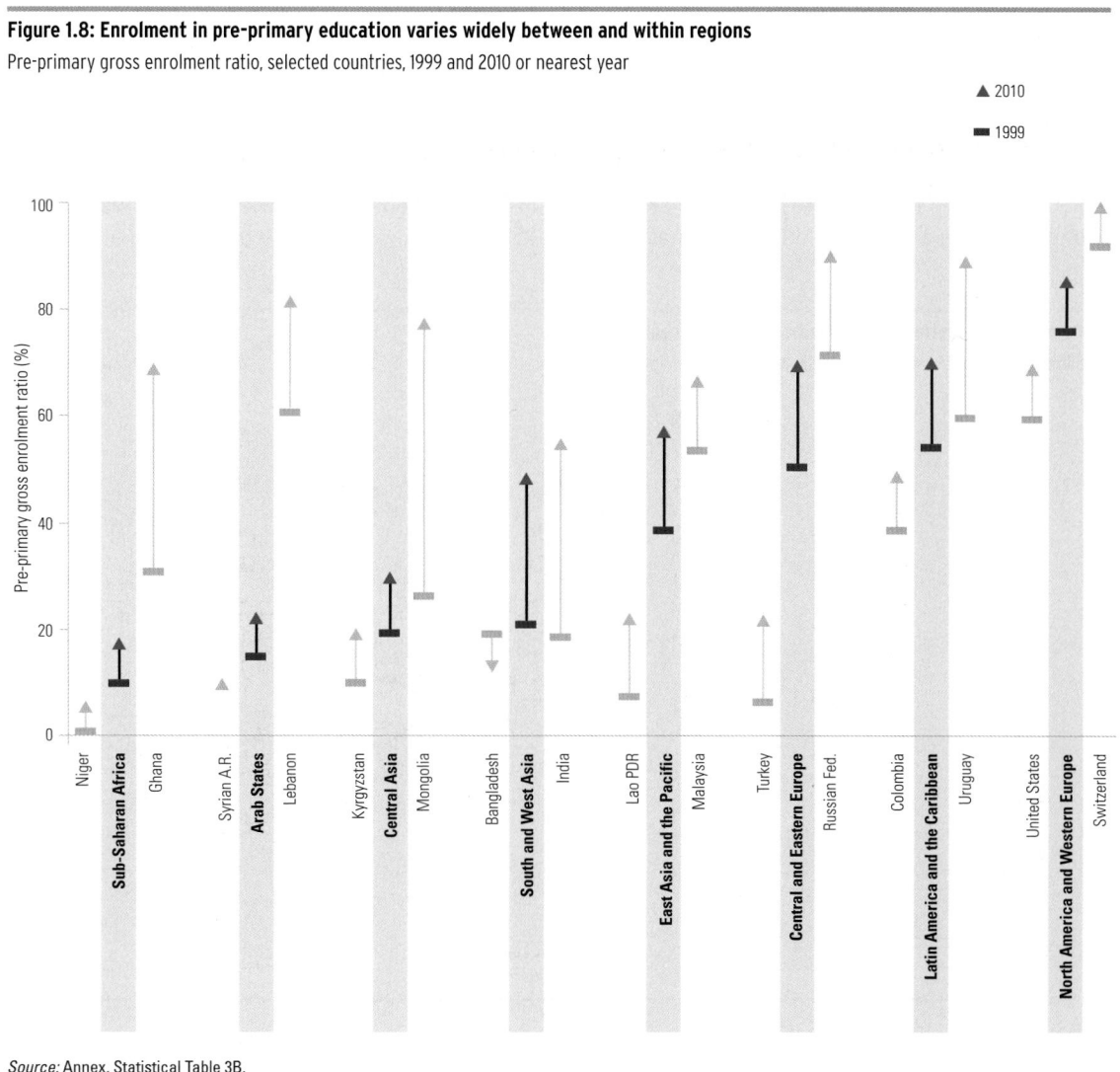

Source: Annex, Statistical Table 3B.

Where children live, and their family's wealth, affect pre-school attendance

are particularly wide. Girls and boys from rich households, whether living in urban or rural areas of Nigeria, have a similar chance of going to school as a child in Thailand. By contrast, girls and boys from poor Nigerian households are on a par with children in Bangladesh. In all three countries, there is very little gender difference amongst those in rich and poor households living in either rural or urban areas (Figure 1.9).

Where children live can determine their chances of attending pre-school, as well as the quality of the service. In China, urban children are more likely than rural children to attend two or three years of kindergarten before entering primary school. If rural children have access at all, they are more likely to attend for just one year. Moreover, the pre-school pupil/teacher ratio is 10:1 in cities and 19:1 in towns, but 34:1 in rural areas (World Bank, 2011).

Other factors that lead to disadvantage can also make it less likely that a child enters pre-school, including belonging to a minority ethnic group, speaking a language other than that used

in school and having a less educated mother (Nonoyama-Tarumi and Ota, 2010; Woodhead, 2009). Yet such marginalized children may be the ones who would benefit most from early education opportunities, as they are least likely to receive adequate support at home.

One reason children from urban areas and wealthier households are more likely to participate in pre-primary education is that they have greater access to private pre-schools some of which charge fees. In many countries and regions a large proportion of pre-schools are private. Globally, the average share of enrolment in private pre-school is 33% — and this may well be an underestimate, as data from private providers are not collected systematically in many countries. In the Arab States it is 76%.

A large share of pre-school enrolment in many low and lower middle income countries is in private institutions. For example, in Ethiopia, where the gross enrolment ratio was only 5% in 2010, the share of private provision was 95%. In the Syrian Arab Republic, with a gross

Figure 1.9: Participation in pre-primary education varies significantly within countries
Pre-school attendance rate of children aged 36 to 59 months, by wealth, location and gender

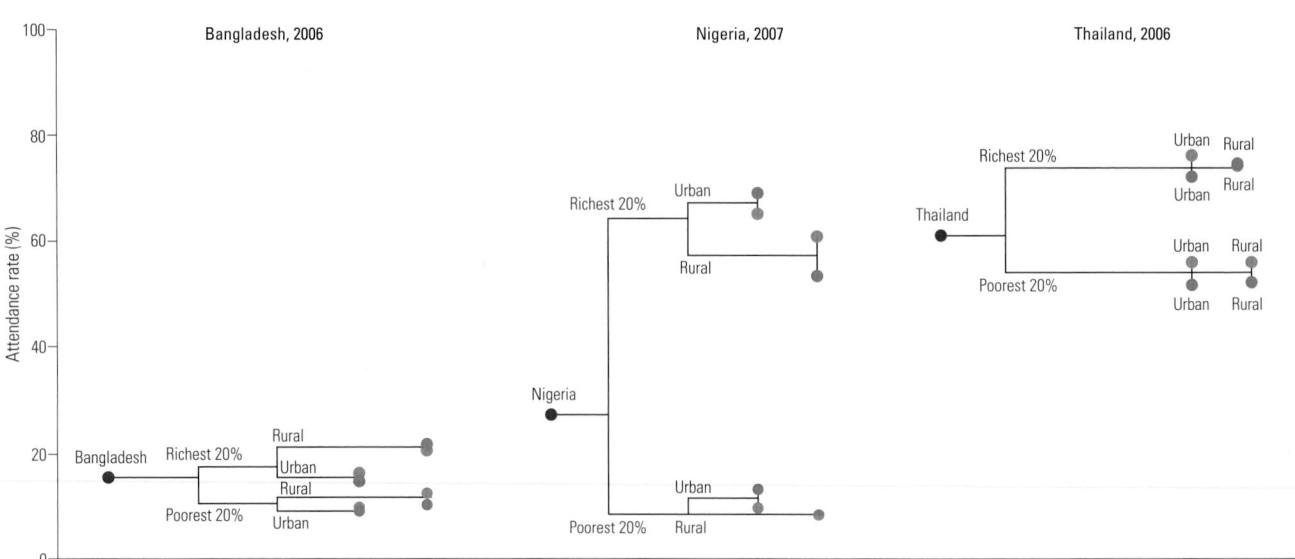

Notes: The official age for pre-primary education is 3 to 5 in the three countries. In Nigeria, the poorest 40% are shown for urban areas.
Source: EFA Global Monitoring Report team calculations (2012) based on Multiple Indicators Cluster Survey data.

enrolment ratio of 10%, the share of private provision was 72%. This indicates demand that is not met by the public sector.

Given that overall enrolment remains low, with gross enrolment ratios below 20% in thirty-two countries (including twenty-one in sub-Saharan Africa), could expansion occur through the private sector? It seems unlikely. Private pre-schools are often priced out of reach of the poorest households, whose children are those least likely to be enrolled.

In India's Andhra Pradesh state, for example, pre-school enrolment in rural areas is highest among the richest 20% of households, where almost one-third of children attend private institutions. Almost all children in pre-school from the poorest households attend government providers. There are also marked differences in urban areas, with almost all children from rich households attending private pre-schools, compared with around one-third among the poorest households (Streuli et al., 2011). Girls are more likely to be enrolled in government pre-schools. Where private provision is of better quality, this could further reinforce inequality between the rich and poor and between boys and girls.

One survey in rural China found that costs of private pre-school were prohibitive for poor households. Only 44% of sampled children aged 4 to 6 were attending pre-school or kindergarten. While primary schools are free, pre-schools and kindergartens are predominantly private and charge fees. The average yearly tuition fee is US$50, and yearly fees for in-school lunches are even higher, around US$55 (Luo et al., 2011). Comparing the total of US$105 with the average per capita income of US$130 for Chinese families at the poverty line, it is clear that poor rural families cannot afford these costs.

Action is needed to increase equitable access to good quality pre-school

Increasing equitable access to pre-school programmes of good quality can play a significant role in supporting children's success in primary school and help them overcome early disadvantage. Reforms are needed to ensure that all children reap the benefits of pre-school, including expanding facilities and making sure they are affordable, coordinating pre-school activities with wider early childhood interventions and identifying appropriate ways to link pre-schools with primary schools.

Make pre-primary education compulsory

Legislation that makes pre-school compulsory can increase enrolment if it is complemented with measures that expand supply. Pre-primary education is compulsory in very few countries. The 2007 *EFA Global Monitoring Report* counted thirty countries with some form of compulsory pre-primary education (UNESCO, 2006). Since then, available evidence suggests that only five more countries have taken this step (UNESCO-IBE, 2011).[5]

Complementing legislation with other reforms to support expansion has had positive results. Compulsory pre-school was introduced in Mexico in 2001 for children aged 3 to 5 (Vegas and Santibáñez, 2010), and the gross enrolment ratio expanded from 73% in 1999 to 101% in 2010. This growth was accomplished by increasing the numbers of classrooms and teachers. Ghana, the first sub-Saharan African country with compulsory pre-primary education, passed legislation in 2007/08 to include two years of kindergarten in compulsory basic education starting from age 4. Capitation grants were extended from primary school to kindergartens and teacher training programmes expanded (UNESCO, 2011c). The gross enrolment ratio, which was 31% in 1999, had reached 69% by 2009.

Other countries making moves towards compulsory pre-school include the Philippines, where implementation will begin in the 2012/13 school year (Philippines Presidential Communications Operations Office, 2012), and South Africa, which intends to make grade R (reception) for 5-year-olds compulsory by 2014 (Biersteker, 2010). In India, the government is considering whether to extend the Right to Education Act, which currently covers classes one to eight, to include pre-school for children aged 4 to 6. The logistical and financial

Private pre-schools are often priced out of reach of the poorest households

5. The five are Bosnia and Herzegovina, Ecuador, Ghana, Guatemala and Nicaragua (UNESCO-IBE, 2011).

implications are significant, involving hiring 1 million trained pre-school teachers to serve 40 million children (Goswami, 2011).

Legislation making pre-school compulsory, however, is rarely enforced. In the thirteen Latin American countries with compulsory pre-primary education, the average gross enrolment ratio in 2008–10 was 71%; only in Ecuador, Mexico and Uruguay did it surpass 80%. And it was below 50% in Colombia, the Dominican Republic and Honduras.

While making pre-school compulsory gives a strong political signal that it is valued, and can provide the impetus to expand infrastructure and invest in teachers, widely accessible pre-school can emerge without legislation. Few high income countries have compulsory pre-primary education, yet more children from these countries are expected to enrol in pre-school and to stay longer. In France, 99% of 3- to 5-year-olds attended pre-primary school in 2010, even though pre-primary education is not compulsory.

Link pre-primary and primary education

A common way to expand pre-primary education is to attach pre-school classrooms to existing primary schools. The Gambia is attaching early childhood development centres to primary schools in deprived communities (UNESCO, 2010a). In Armenia, primary school classrooms have been converted into pre-school playroom-classrooms in rural areas (Armenia Government, 2008). According to Bangladesh's national education strategy, one teacher in each government primary school will be recruited to teach a new pre-primary class (Bangladesh Ministry of Education, 2010).

This approach has clear advantages. There is potential for more efficient use of existing facilities, including classrooms, and of administrative support. It can also foster continuity for schoolchildren and make it possible for older siblings to take young children to pre-school.

Where pre-schools and primary schools use the same facilities, however, there is a danger that pre-school children will be taught using primary school approaches for which they are not developmentally ready, in terms of pupil/teacher ratios, classroom organization, curriculum and teaching methods – a phenomenon described as 'schoolification' (Kaga et al., 2010).

Private pre-schools in India have been seen largely as a downward extension of the primary education curriculum. This tendency also imposes academic pressure on children from an early age (Streuli et al., 2011). In Kenya, while 70% of public primary schools have a pre-primary class, their teachers are only trained in primary school methods (Biersteker et al., 2008). A more appropriate approach is being adopted in South Africa, where the plan is for most reception classes to be based in primary schools, but financed and staffed differently (Biersteker, 2010).

Pre-school needs to be made affordable for the poor

Pre-schooling accounts for less than 10% of the education budget in most countries, and its share tends to be particularly low in poor countries. Nepal and the Niger spend under 0.1% of gross national product (GNP) on pre-school, and Madagascar and Senegal less than 0.02%. One consequence is that the cost of pre-school is transferred to households, making it less likely that poor children will attend, even though they are the ones who stand to gain the most.

Governments need to ensure that pre-school is affordable for poor families, either by providing more public pre-school places or through conditional cash transfers. Where pre-schools are provided by non-state bodies, governments need to play a strong regulatory role to assure quality.

In Hong Kong, pre-schools are private but access is almost universal. In 2007, the government introduced a voucher programme, which covers about half the tuition costs for half-day kindergarten programmes, with families continuing to pay the balance. The voucher can be spent at the school of the parent's choice as long as it is non-profit (about 80% of pre-schools in Hong Kong). The programme is designed to enhance access and affordability, while improving quality. Three-quarters of parents have reported that the vouchers have helped reduce their

Senegal spends less than 0.02% of GNP on pre-school

Education for All Global Monitoring Report

2 0 1 2

financial burden. A proportion of the funding is earmarked for upgrading school staff qualifications. Schools have to pass inspections and publish information to help parents choose (Li et al., 2010; Rao and Li, 2009). But principals and teachers have found it difficult to administer the programme. Such difficulties are likely to be even more pronounced in poorer countries, which would need to overcome considerable administrative constraints to ensure that access to pre-school is increased among poor households.

Short pre-school programmes can help smooth the transition to primary school

As an interim measure to a full public pre-school service, there have been experiments with shorter programmes. In Cambodia, not attending pre-school has been linked to high repetition rates in grade 1 of primary school. To overcome this problem, a special programme in the first two months of primary school uses a modified curriculum to focus on skills that children need to succeed in school, such as basic language skills; the concepts of number, time and space; and working in groups (Kagan et al., 2010). An evaluation showed that the listening and speaking skills of children who took part in the programme were significantly higher by the end of the school year (Nonoyama-Tarumi and Bredenberg, 2009).

A similar programme is being introduced in Malawi to help children make the transition from home and from community-based child care centres to primary school (Kholowa, 2011). In China and Mongolia, mobile 'ger kindergartens' (each housed in a *ger*, a traditional felt tent) enrol children from pastoralist families for three or four weeks before moving on to the next site (Whitman, 2011).

Another approach is for older schoolchildren to help young children make the transition to primary school. UNICEF has adopted a child-to-child approach within its Getting Ready for School programme, which has been piloted in Bangladesh, China, the Democratic Republic of the Congo, Ethiopia, Tajikistan and Yemen. With far fewer hours of direct support than most formal pre-school programmes, this lower cost intervention had a positive impact on children's school readiness in all countries and on literacy

and mathematics in four of the six countries (UNICEF, 2010a).

Attention to improving quality is needed

Pre-school models that effectively prepare children for success in primary school develop literacy and mathematics skills through play, child-generated projects, collaborative activities and everyday experiences. Such characteristics require classes small enough for frequent interaction with teachers, as well as teacher training appropriate to young children's level of development.

For the seventy-four countries reporting the percentage of trained pre-primary teachers, data from the UNESCO Institute of Statistics (UIS) indicate that more than two in three teachers are trained. The quality of training, and of pre-schools more broadly, however, is often very low. In poor areas of rural China, one teacher is responsible for twenty-nine 4- to 6-year-olds, on average — far higher than the government requirement of seven children per teacher. And only 27% of these teachers had training in early childhood pedagogy (Luo et al., 2011).

In the United Republic of Tanzania, although national educational policy specifies the same standards for pre-primary education regardless of location, there are also considerable differences between urban and rural schools. Rural classes have less space, larger group sizes, fewer instructional resources and less qualified teachers (Mtahabwa and Rao, 2010). In Peru, the two main publicly funded pre-school programmes are highly differentiated, with disadvantaged children attending pre-schools of poorer quality (Box 1.2).

National programmes can help increase the quality of pre-schools. Maldives' inclusion of a comprehensive early childhood care and development programme in national development and education sector plans has helped strengthen access (Rao and Sun, 2010). Despite challenges associated with the country's island geography and post-tsunami reconstruction, the pre-primary gross enrolment ratio rose from 56% in 1999 to 114% in 2011. Teachers and parents have noted that teacher training, parent education and play-based, child-friendly teaching have

In the United Republic of Tanzania, rural classes have larger group sizes and less qualified teachers

Box 1.2: Variations in pre-school in Peru widen inequality

Pre-schooling has expanded over the past decade in Peru. The gross enrolment ratio reached 79% in 2010, above average for the region, with gender parity achieved. The expansion has benefited children from disadvantaged backgrounds as well as the more privileged, but there are distinct differences in quality depending on where children live. Given the importance of pre-schooling in preparing young children for learning in school, this disparity is likely to lead to a widening of inequality as they get older.

There are two main kinds of publicly funded pre-school in Peru. The Centros de Educación Inicial (CEIs) are formal early education centres for children aged 3 to 5. They tend to serve richer urban communities, have a qualified teacher paid by the Ministry of Education and follow a standard pre-school curriculum. The Programa No Escolarizada de Educación Inicial (PRONOEIs) are non-formal, community-based programmes that enable the government to expand coverage and enrolment at lower cost, since the community provides the building and furniture, and the volunteer 'facilitators' receive minimal training and earn about one-third as much as CEI teachers.

PRONOEIs usually serve children in socially and economically marginal areas, including rural areas, informal settlements and shanty towns. Limited funding for PRONOEIs has been linked to low attendance and high dropout.

The differences between CEIs and PRONOEIs translate into different outcomes for children as they enter school. While attending either programme boosts writing and mathematics achievement, CEIs have a greater impact. For example, 8-year-olds who had attended a CEI for three years were about 11% more likely to attend school at the correct age, 20% more likely to spell correctly and 24% more likely to do a simple calculation than children who had not. Those who had attended a PRONOEI for three years were more likely to perform well on the spelling task only, and even then by just 12%.

While community involvement in pre-schooling brings advantages, such outcomes draw attention to the need to ensure that government support is targeted at those who need it most.

Sources: Beltrán and Seinfeld (2010); Diaz (2006); Woodhead et al. (2009)

Play-based teaching can increase confidence and learning

increased pre-schoolers' confidence, sociability and engagement in learning (McBride, 2005; UNICEF, n.d.).

Innovative programmes have been found to be particularly successful, even at relatively low cost. In Kenya, Uganda and Zanzibar (the United Republic of Tanzania), Madrasa Resource Centre pre-schools, developed by the Aga Khan Foundation, provide training and support that help staff use locally available, low cost materials for children to select, explore and experiment with. Staff are also trained to use appropriate language to stimulate children's curiosity in a sensitive and supportive way. After one year of pre-school, participating children were found to have better school readiness outcomes, with higher verbal, non-verbal and numeric cognitive skills, than those who attended public, community or other NGO-run pre-schools (Malmberg et al., 2011). In addition to the minimum eight years of schooling plus one year of teacher training required for pre-

school teachers in each country, the Madrasa Resource Centre teachers received six months of early childhood development training, plus professional development and support after graduation.

While it makes good sense to prepare children for school, primary schools must also be ready for young children. Without trained and motivated teachers employing good quality, developmentally appropriate methods and materials in a safe, non-violent and inclusive environment, the chances of a smooth transition to and success in primary school are radically reduced, particularly for children with few learning opportunities outside school (Arnold et al., 2006).

Coordinate and integrate pre-school with early childhood care
Early childhood care and education programmes often suffer from fragmented planning, reducing their effectiveness. Analysis of thirty programmes in twenty-three developed and

developing countries has shown that those that combined care with education boosted cognitive abilities the most (Nores and Barnett, 2010). However, early childhood care (including maternal and child health and nutrition for pregnant women and young children) and pre-school education have traditionally developed as separate systems, with separate policies, programmes and administrative responsibility. Split systems tend to lead to differences in funding, access, regulation and workforce, and a lack of coordination between care and education.

Countries have tackled these challenges either through interministerial mechanisms or by integrating early childhood programmes under a single ministry, such as education or social welfare. Integrating care and education under one organization can be particularly beneficial in promoting a coherent overall policy, administrative and funding framework (Kaga et al., 2010).

In Chile, presidential commitment to early childhood well-being led to the introduction of a programme called Chile Crece Contigo (Chile is Growing with You). The programme has been coordinated by the Ministry of Planning and implemented by lower tier government. A network of professionals supports low income families: health institutions monitor mothers and children to identify risk factors that call for referral to specific services, educational institutions assure access to crèches and nurseries, and municipalities support access to other social services and conditional cash transfers. A public awareness strategy increased the visibility of the system and recognition that everybody has a right to early childhood care and education. Effective integration has been aided by a unified information system that supports marginalized children across social sectors (Delpiano and Vega, 2011). The programme has been supported by the expansion of childcare provision. Between 2005 and 2007 the two main public providers of child care centres more than doubled their enrolment, from 15,000 to 33,000 (Noboa-Hidalgo and Urzúa, 2012).

Conclusion

As part of a comprehensive package of early childhood care and education, equitable access to good quality pre-schooling plays a vital role in improving young children's readiness to succeed in school. Pre-school education that helps smooth the transition to primary school must be affordable and of good quality. Even in poorer countries, political commitment and adequate funding can extend access to greater numbers of children. To reduce inequality, governments need to pay particular attention to children from poor households who already face disadvantages — and who stand to benefit most.

Equitable access to good quality pre-school improves success in school

CHAPTER 1

Goal 2 Universal primary education

Ensuring that by 2015 all children, particularly girls, children in difficult circumstances and those belonging to ethnic minorities, have access to and complete, free and compulsory primary education of good quality.

Highlights

- On current trends the target of universal primary education will be missed. The number of out-of-school children of primary school age fell from 108 million in 1999 to 61 million in 2010.

- The rate of decline was rapid between 1999 and 2004, but then started slowing, and progress has stalled since 2008. Sub-Saharan Africa, where the number of children out of school increased by 1.6 million between 2008 and 2010, accounts for half of the world's total.

- The number of countries with a primary net enrolment ratio of over 97% increased from 37 to 55 out of 124 countries between 1999 and 2010. Just five years before 2015, twenty-nine countries have a net enrolment ratio of less than 85%, and so are very unlikely to achieve the goal by the deadline.

- Children of official school starting age who did not enter school by 2010 will not be able to complete the primary cycle by 2015. In 2010, out of 98 countries with data there were 16 countries with a net intake rate below 50% and 71 countries below 80%.

- Dropout remains a problem in low income countries, where on average 59% of those starting school reached the last grade in 2009. The problem is particularly acute for those children starting late.

Table 1.3: Key indicators for goal 2

	Total primary enrolment		Primary gross intake rate		Survival rate to last grade of primary education		Primary adjusted net enrolment ratio		Out-of-school children	
	2010 (000)	Change since 1999 (%)	1999 (%)	2010 (%)	1999 (%)	2009 (%)	1999 (%)	2010 (%)	2010 (000)	Change since 1999 (%)
World	690 665	6	105	110	87	91	84	91	60 684	-44
Low income countries	122 465	64	100	123	55	59	59	81	22 244	-43
Lower middle income countries	293 373	19	111	112	71	78	79	90	29 362	-47
Upper middle income countries	202 165	-20	101	103	90	95	95	96	7 230	-31
High income countries	72 663	-5	103	100	...	98	97	97	1 848	-18
Sub-Saharan Africa	132 809	62	92	115	62	62	59	77	30 641	-27
Arab States	41 741	19	89	101	88	93	79	88	5 036	-40
Central Asia	5 461	-20	100	100	96	98	94	94	317	-28
East Asia and the Pacific	185 304	-17	101	106	...	...	95	96	6 579	-36
South and West Asia	188 366	21	116	115	...	66	77	93	13 261	-67
Latin America and the Caribbean	66 413	-5	120	119	83	89	94	95	2 652	-26
North America and Western Europe	51 140	-3	104	100	98	...	98	97	1 267	41
Central and Eastern Europe	19 433	-22	97	99	97	98	93	95	931	-43

Sources: Annex, Statistical Tables 4, 5 and 6 (print) and Statistical Table 5 (website); UIS database.

Education for All Global Monitoring Report 2012

The push towards universal primary education (UPE) that was kick-started in Dakar is grinding to a halt. Early signs of a slowdown, identified in previous editions of the *EFA Global Monitoring Report*, have been corroborated by the latest data, which show that the number of out-of-school children of primary school age stagnated at 61 million between 2008 and 2010 (Panel 1.3).[6] Most of the decrease observed since 1999 was achieved in the first five years after Dakar, and the momentum has since been lost. The consequence is that the EFA target, which captured the world's attention, will be missed.

This is not to deny that major progress has been made in many parts of the world. Total enrolment rose by nearly two-thirds in low income countries. Some countries achieved remarkable increases: in Afghanistan there were fewer than 1 million primary school students in 1999 but more than 5 million in 2010, including over 2 million girls. In the same period, nearly 8.5 million more children were enrolled in primary schools in Ethiopia.

The challenge of achieving UPE consists not only of getting children into school at the correct age, but also ensuring that they progress through the system and complete the education cycle. Entry into school has increased substantially in many countries that were lagging well behind in 1999. Gross intake rates increased rapidly in countries such as Congo, Senegal and Yemen. Many countries in sub-Saharan Africa are absorbing more than twice as many new entrants to the first grade as they were a decade ago. In the Niger, the number of new entrants increased by more than three and a half times between 1999 and 2011.

These positive trends have contributed to an increase in the global primary net enrolment ratio from 84% in 1999 to 91% in 2010, with the greatest increases observed in the Arab States, South and West Asia, and sub-Saharan Africa. Even so, in sub-Saharan Africa, only 77% of children of primary school age were in school in 2010.

Countries that have achieved noticeable improvements include Guatemala (from 84% to 99% in 2010), the Lao People's Democratic Republic (from 77% to 97% in

2010), Morocco (from 71% to 96% in 2011) and Zambia (from 71% to 91% in 2010).

But effort has been insufficient in other countries. According to the most recent data (2008–2011), there were still 29 countries with fewer than 85 out of 100 children of primary school age in school. These countries are consequently at serious risk of not achieving UPE by 2015. Of these, sixteen were in sub-Saharan Africa. The primary net enrolment ratio in many countries in western sub-Saharan Africa, including Burkina Faso, Côte d'Ivoire and Mali, is below 70%. In Pakistan, despite an increase, the net enrolment ratio is still only 74%.

What is keeping the world from meeting its commitments on UPE? There is no doubt that the challenge becomes harder as the final target approaches. It is the most marginalized who remain out of reach and who face considerable disadvantage in overcoming the two main hurdles to UPE: entering school and progressing through the cycle.

In terms of entry, the issue is not just getting children into school, but also getting them there at the right age. Household surveys have helped draw attention to the problem of late entry, which appears to be pervasive in countries with high UPE challenges. Children who are above the official entry age when they enter school do not benefit from their schooling experience in equal terms and are more likely to drop out than their younger peers (Panel 1.4). This happens because they face greater pressures to work and because the school environment is often not suitable for the needs of older children.

In terms of progression, the global survival rate to the last grade of primary school increased from 87% in 1999 to 91% in 2009. In sub-Saharan Africa, where the rate was 62%, survival to the last grade was as low as 28% in Chad and 32% in Angola.

Among the global population of out-of-school children, the share of those who have been to school but have left before completing the cycle has increased. In other words, the drive towards higher enrolment levels may not be complemented by higher numbers of children reaching the last grade. For example, in Burundi the gross intake rate increased from 70% to 160% between

---

6. While this is a smaller number than reported in the *EFA Global Monitoring Report 2011*, it reflects an adjustment resulting from updating global population figures. There has been no improvement in enrolment in the last two years.

1999 and 2010, but the survival rate to the last grade hardly changed (going from 54% to 56%). In Ethiopia, where the gross intake rate increased from 81% to 137% between 1999 and 2010, the survival rate to the last grade fell from 51% to 47%.

There are multiple reasons for low survival and completion rates. Analysis undertaken for this Report shows that in some countries poverty has a greater effect on progression than on entry (Panel 1.5). In Madagascar and Rwanda, for example, children may have an almost equal chance of entering school,

regardless of wealth. But children from richer households are about 30% more likely to reach the last grade. In Uganda, the difference is about 60%.

For poor households, costs of schooling have a strong bearing on whether children attend school. Officially sanctioned school fees no longer play a major role in deterring families from sending their children to school thanks to the abolition of fees after 2000 in many countries, but other costs remain a real obstacle to UPE (goal 2, policy focus).

Panel 1.3: Progress in reducing numbers of children out of school has stalled

The potential for achieving UPE depends on the speed with which countries succeed in reducing overall numbers of children out of school. The number of out-of-school children of primary school age fell from 108 million in 1999 to 61 million in 2010, but three-quarters of this reduction was achieved between 1999 and 2004, when the number of out-of-school children fell at an average annual rate of 6.8 million. The rate of

decline slowed considerably between 2004 and 2008, to just 3.3 million per year. There are now worrying signs that progress has stalled altogether.

These overall changes mask important differences between regions. South and West Asia and sub-Saharan Africa started from similar positions in 1999, but have subsequently progressed at very different speeds.

Figure 1.10: The number of out-of-school children decreased in the initial years after Dakar, but this has been followed by stagnation

A. Number of out-of-school children of primary school age, 1999–2010

B. Percentage of out-of-school children of primary school age, 1999–2010

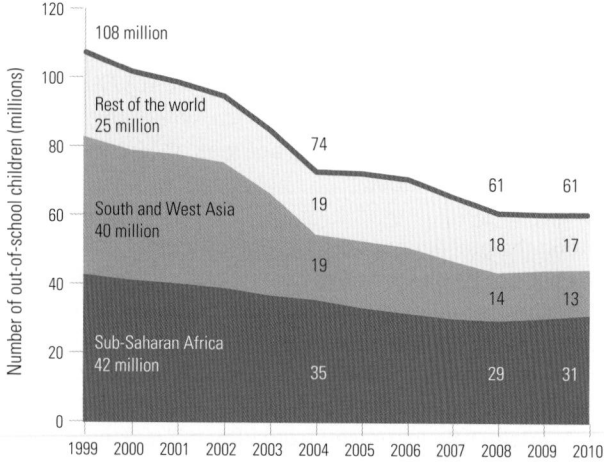
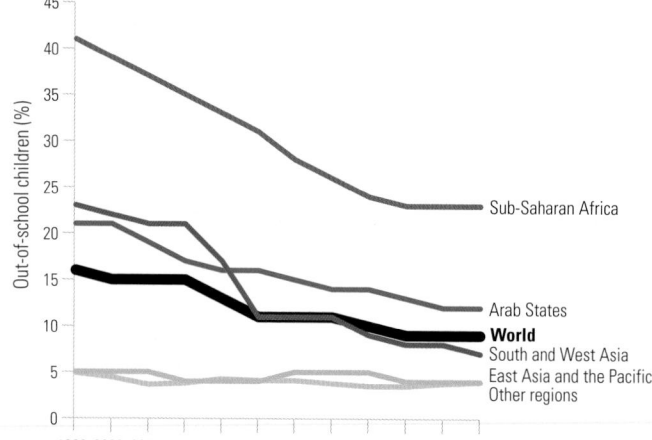

Sources: Annex Statistical Table 5; UIS database.

Education for All Global Monitoring Report

Between 1999 and 2008, the number of out-of-school children in South and West Asia fell by 26 million. India alone is responsible for two-thirds of this decline. The corresponding reduction in sub-Saharan Africa was 13 million. Between 2008 and 2010, the regions went in different directions: the number of out-of-school children in sub-Saharan Africa increased by 1.6 million, but declined by 0.6 million in South and West Asia (Figure 1.10A). Half of those out of school now live in sub-Saharan Africa. In percentage terms, the proportion of primary school age children out of school fell from 16% in 1999 to 9% in 2010, but has levelled off since 2008 (Figure 1.10B).

With the deadline for the EFA goals fast approaching, prospects of achieving UPE by 2015 have now been missed for those children who did not enter school by 2010. While some of those out of school may have dropped out or may enter later, many may never enrol.

Analysis conducted by the UNESCO Institute for Statistics infers the likelihood of children currently out of school entering education, based on past trends (UIS, 2008). Globally, 47% of children out of school in 2010 were likely never to enrol. The proportion is highest in low income countries, where 57% of children are expected never to enrol. A sizeable proportion are also expected never to enrol in lower middle income countries, where the majority of out-of-school children live, suggesting that income alone is insufficient to combat the problem (Figure 1.11).

Compared with 2004, when these estimates were first made, the proportion of out-of-school children expected never to enrol has fallen from 61% to 47% (UNESCO, 2006). In contrast, the proportion of children who were out of school because they dropped out increased during the same period from 9% to 26%. This suggests that while more of the hardest-to-reach children enter school, they find it more difficult to complete the cycle. Within this group of hard-to-reach children, girls are more likely than boys never to enrol, with the difference particularly large in lower middle income countries.

Twelve countries account for 47% of the global out-of-school population (Figure 1.12). Nigeria, which heads the list with 10.5 million out-of-school children, has experienced the highest increase since 1999. It is one of only four among these twelve countries where the number increased in absolute terms. It now accounts for almost one in five out-of-school children in the world.

Figure 1.11: Almost one in two out-of-school children are expected never to enrol

Distribution of out-of-school children, by school exposure and country income group, 2010

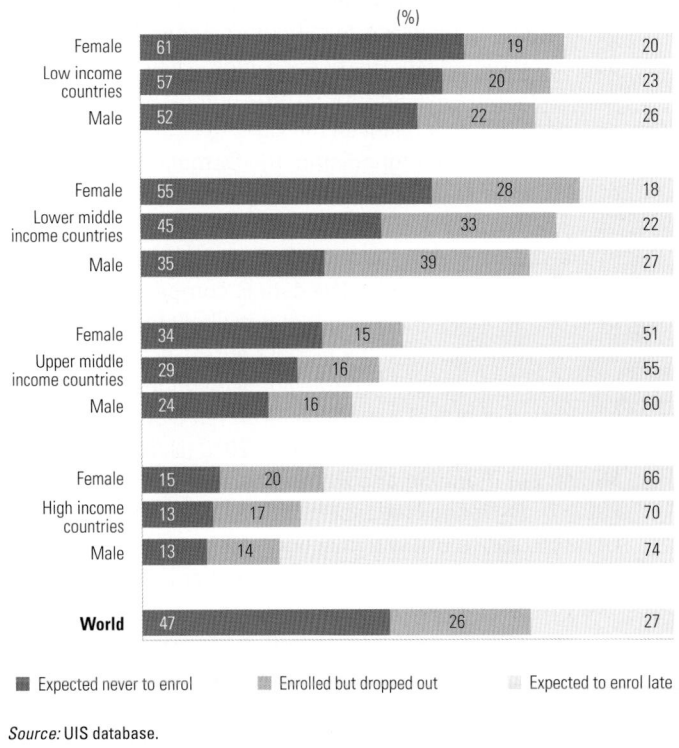

Source: UIS database.

Figure 1.12: Almost half the world's out-of-school children live in just twelve countries

Number of children of primary school age who were out of school in 2010 or nearest year

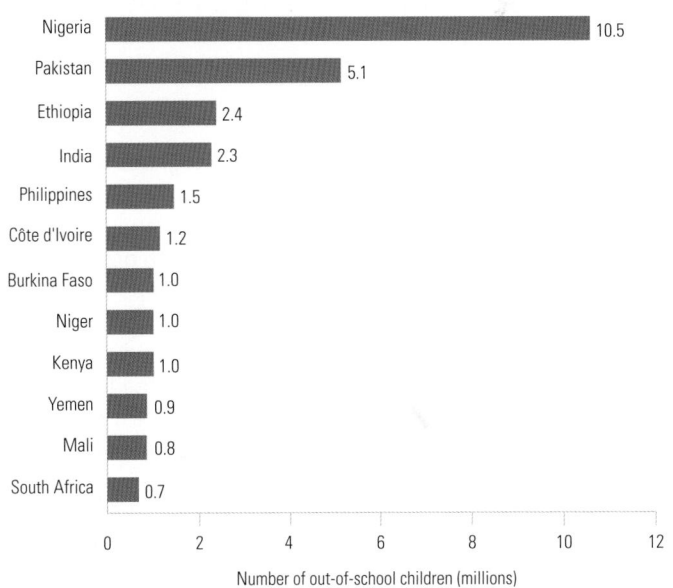

Source: Annex, Statistical Table 5.

This ranking may omit some countries that are likely to be among the worst performing but do not appear due to lack of data. They include countries with large populations but lower rates of out-of-school children, such as Bangladesh, Brazil and China. They also include countries that have suffered from conflict, which has denied millions of children the right to education; examples include Afghanistan, the Democratic Republic of the Congo, Iraq, Somalia and the former Sudan.

In the case of the Democratic Republic of the Congo, lack of recent administrative data is compensated for by other sources indicating that it is likely to be among the five countries with the highest out-of-school numbers. Household survey evidence suggests that the proportion of out-of-school children fell from around one-half in 2001 to one-quarter in 2010 (D. R. Congo Ministry of Planning and Reconstruction and UNICEF, 2002; D. R. Congo National Institute of Statistics and UNICEF, 2011). But with a cohort of 11 million primary school age children, the out-of-school population is likely to be still well above 2 million.

The four countries with the largest reported numbers of out-of-school children have experienced different trajectories over the last decade. Between 2001 and 2008, the proportion of children who were out of school in India decreased from 17% to 2%. Ethiopia also achieved spectacular progress, reducing the number of out-of-school children by more than 60% over this period. Pakistan made slower progress, while in Nigeria the number of out-of-school children increased by more than 50%, leaving 3.6 million more out of school in 2010 than in 2000 (Figure 1.13).

Contrasting patterns of progress and stagnation can also be identified across four pairs of countries with a smaller yet sizeable out-of-school population in 1999 (Figure 1.14). Morocco and Yemen have both achieved significant reductions in their out-of-school population. But Morocco's progress has been faster. It has benefited from relative political stability and a lower population growth rate. In addition, Yemen was one of the few countries to reduce education spending since 1999, albeit from a relatively high initial level. Côte d'Ivoire's progress could not match that of Ghana. The conflict that seriously affected Côte d'Ivoire over the past decade led to internal displacement and insecurity that has harmed school enrolment.

In the Philippines, education spending fell as a share of national income and conflict continued to affect a large

Figure 1.13: In Nigeria, the number of children out of school is large and has increased

Rate and number of out-of-school children of primary school age, 2001 to 2010

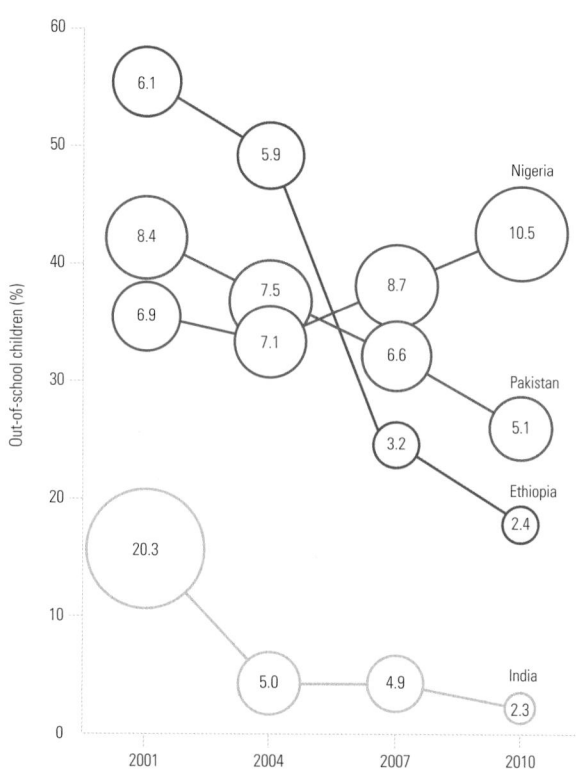

Notes: The size of the bubble is proportional to the number of out-of-school children. The numbers in the bubbles show the number of out-of-school children. The 2001 figures for Nigeria are from 2000. The 2010 figures for India are from 2008.
Source: UIS database.

part of the country, whereas Indonesia has improved security. Finally, while both Kenya and the United Republic of Tanzania achieved major breakthroughs, it can be argued that the significantly higher expansion of education spending in the latter contributed to achieving almost universal school enrolment.

Even in countries that have made good progress towards UPE, some groups continue to get left behind, and so targeted policies are needed to reach them. In 2011, poor rural girls in Ethiopia were more likely to have never attended school. Rich boys and girls in rural Ethiopia have a chance of attending similar to that of their rich urban counterparts, with only around one in ten not having the opportunity. But 43% of poor rural females aged 7 to 16 have never been to school (Figure 1.15).

Figure 1.14: Countries with large numbers of out-of-school children have followed different trajectories

Number of out-of-school children of primary school age, selected countries, 1999 to 2011

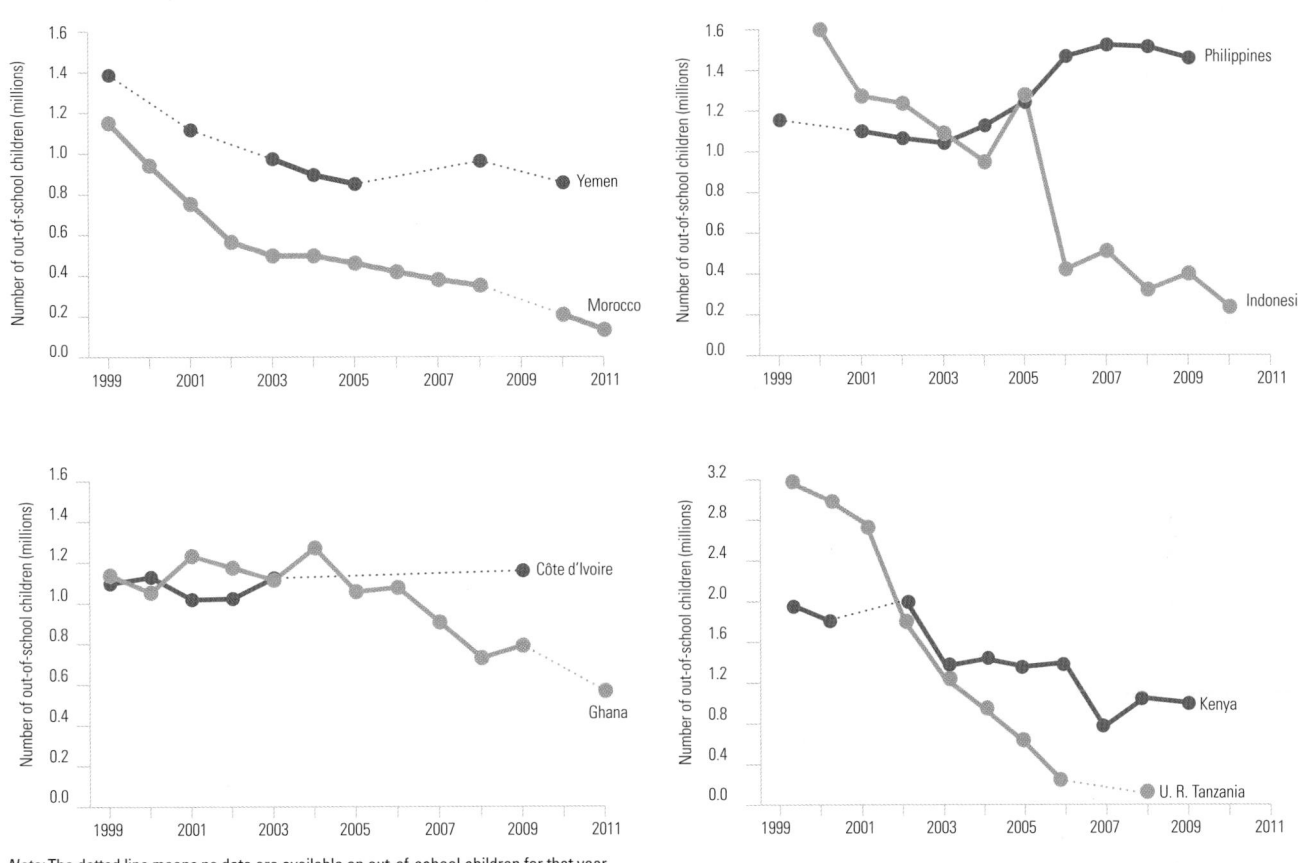

Note: The dotted line means no data are available on out-of-school children for that year.
Source: UIS database.

Figure 1.15: In Ethiopia poor rural females are least likely to go to in school

Percentage of 7- to 16-year-olds who have never attended school by location, wealth and gender, Ethiopia, 2011

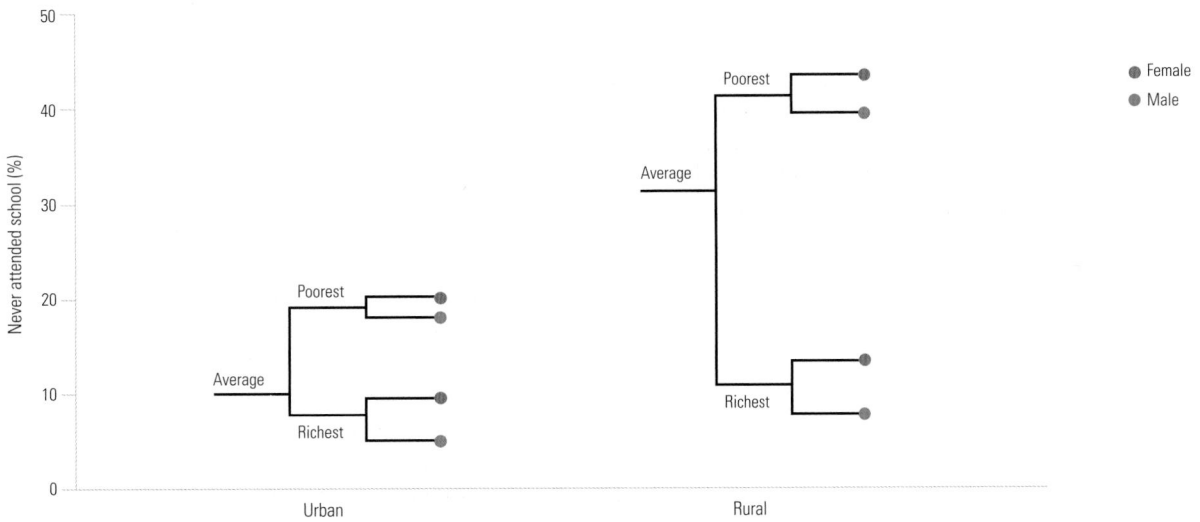

Note: The terms 'poorest' and 'richest' refer to the households in the bottom and top 20%, respectively, in terms of a wealth index except for urban 'poorest', which refers to the bottom 40%.
Source: UNESCO (2012c).

Panel 1.4: Entering school on time is critical

Late entry into the first grade of primary school is a major barrier to achieving universal primary education, as children who start school late are more likely to drop out before they complete the cycle.

In 2010, in fifty-nine countries that provided information on the distribution of new entrants by age, about 8% of new first grade pupils were at least two years older than the official age. The average was significantly higher in the twenty-three sub-Saharan African countries reporting these data, where 20% of children started at least two years after the official age (UIS database). But administrative data may underestimate the extent of the problem, as school registers in low and middle income countries often do not provide an accurate picture of pupil age (UNESCO, 2010b).

This tendency to underestimate is reflected in a new analysis for this Report of Demographic and Health Survey data from twenty-two countries for the period from 2005 to 2010. On average, 38% of students who entered primary school were two years or more above the official school entry age. Among the sixteen

sub-Saharan African countries analysed, the average was 41%, or twice the estimates based on school records (Delprato, 2012). In Liberia, for example, about 87% of new first grade pupils were two years older than the official age and 77% were at least three years older (Figure 1.16). This is in part a legacy of conflict, with many older children now wanting an opportunity to attend school. But late entry is also an issue in countries that have not experienced such problems. In Ghana, 53% were at least two years older than the official age.

Data from household surveys provide further information on the characteristics of pupils entering late, showing that late entry is more common among poor households. In Madagascar, 62% of pupils from the poorest fifth of households entered primary school at least two years later than the official school entrance age in 2008, compared with 32% of pupils from the richest fifth of households. Richer countries show a similar pattern. In Colombia, 42% from the poorest households started two years late, compared with 11% of those from the richest households (Figure 1.17).

Poverty and late school entry are linked in various ways. Poor children are more likely to live further from school, and often cannot afford the costs of transport. Some may not go to school until they are able to walk long distances. Parents are also likely to be concerned about safety on long trips to school, particularly for girls. Poor parents may also be less aware of the importance of enrolling at the right age, particularly if they have not had much experience of schooling themselves. Finally, the nutritional and health status of poor children is worse, which makes them less able to enrol in school on time.

Starting late influences whether children complete the education cycle. Evidence from the countries analysed for this Report shows that those who are the right age for their grade are less likely to drop out than those who are two or more years older, with the difference widening throughout the primary cycle (Delprato, 2012). In Zambia, for example, among children who were of the official age for their grade, about 2% dropped out of grade 1 and grade 3 in 2007. In contrast, of those who were at least two years older than their grade age, 5% dropped out of grade 1 and 8% dropped out of grade 3 (Figure 1.18).

Figure 1.16: Late entry into primary school is widespread in low and middle income countries

Distribution of new entrants relative to official school entrance age, selected countries, 2005 to 2010

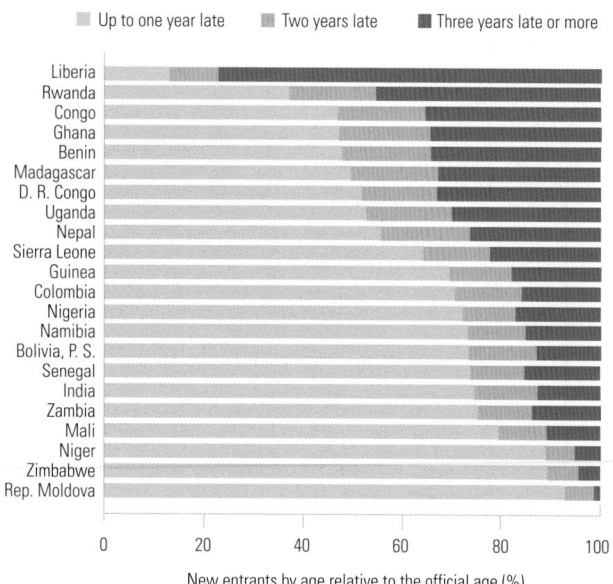

Note: The category 'up to one year late' includes children who enrol on time or before the official school entrance age.
Source: Delprato (2012), based on Demographic and Health Survey data.

2012

Education for All Global Monitoring Report

Figure 1.17: Late entry is more common among disadvantaged children

Percentage of children attending the first grade of primary school who are two or more years older than the official school entrance age, by wealth, selected countries

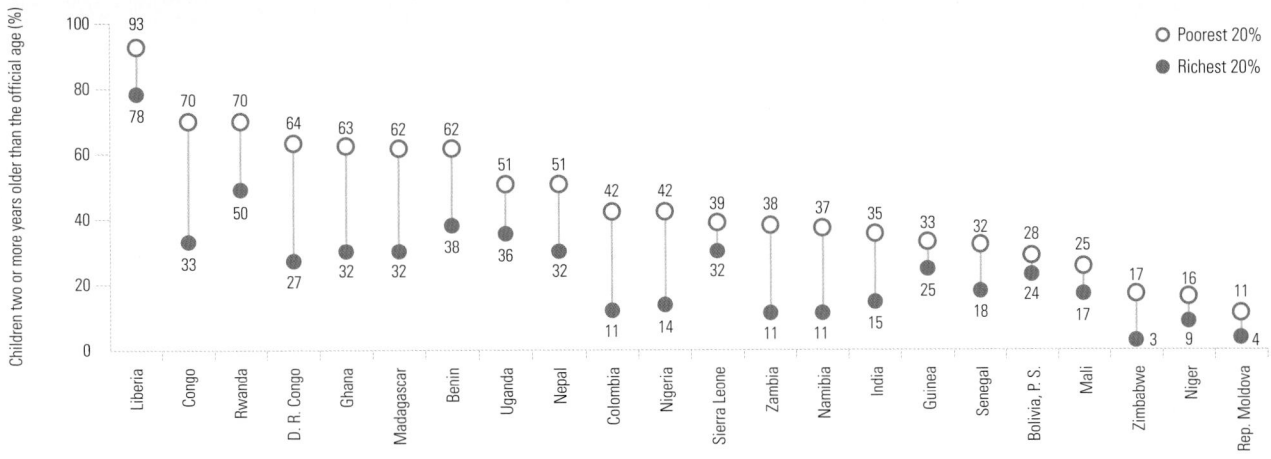

Source: Delprato (2012), based on Demographic and Health Survey data.

Figure 1.18: Pupils who are older than the official age for their grade are more likely to drop out

Dropout rate by grade, pupils of official age for their grade compared with pupils who are at least two years older, selected countries, 2005 to 2010

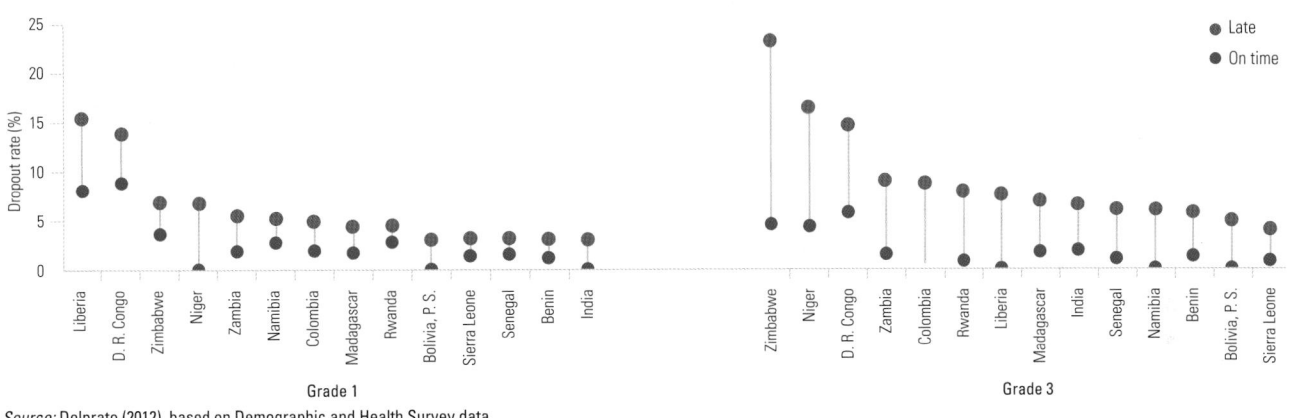

Source: Delprato (2012), based on Demographic and Health Survey data.

Late entry increases the likelihood of dropout in several ways. First, a wide age range in a particular grade disadvantages older children because the pedagogical approach, curriculum and learning materials are suited to younger children who progress at a slower pace (Lewin, 2007). Second, large differences in age frustrate older children, who may feel that they cannot integrate well socially in the classroom. Third, older children from poor households are more likely to need to work. Fourth, in the case of girls, those who start late reach the average age of marriage before completing the basic education cycle in some countries (Brown, 2012). In Nigeria, about one in six young women aged 20 to 24 were married or in a union before the age of 15. Among girls aged 15 to 19, only 2% of those married were in school, compared with 69% of those unmarried (UNICEF, 2011c).

Among countries for which there were administrative data for both 1999 and 2010, there is some evidence that the percentage of over-age children has declined in recent years. For example, in Ethiopia it fell from 50% to 19%.

Household survey data do not show that the poor are the first to benefit, however. For example, between 2003 and 2008 the decline in the number of over-age new entrants in Ghana and Madagascar was twice as large among the richest quintile compared with the poorest quintile (Delprato, 2012).

Late entry poses major challenges to policy-makers and requires action on two fronts. To prevent late entry, governments need to raise awareness among parents by mounting publicity campaigns, and to build schools closer to homes. To moderate the impact of late entry, teachers need to be trained to take into account the learning needs of older students.

Panel 1.5: Progression through primary school varies between and within countries

As 2015 approaches, it is critical to monitor trends in progression to the last grade of primary school. Many children who have the opportunity to enter school are still not able to complete the primary cycle. Tracking cohorts of children provides an integrated perspective on the chances of not only entering school, but also staying until the end of the primary cycle.

Household survey data on attendance can offer valuable insights into the characteristics of children who are unable to enter or complete primary education. Starting from a cohort of 100 children, these data track their entry into school and progression through the cycle until completion. For a country to achieve UPE, the expected cohort completion rate would be 100. Many countries are far from this ideal and the poorest are furthest behind.

In Uganda, for example, 97 out of 100 children from the richest households enter school, compared with 90 out of 100 children from the poorest households. By the end of the cycle, the gap has widened further, with 80 of the richest 100 completing, compared with 49 of the poorest 100 (Figure 1.19).

The inequality between the poorest and richest children — in access, progression or both — takes different forms. The Democratic Republic of the Congo, India and Kenya exhibit patterns similar to Uganda's, where inequality is evident throughout the cycle, from access through to completion. Some West African countries follow a pattern of unequal access, but once in school, children demonstrate similar progression through the cycle.

In Nigeria, most children from rich households start school. In contrast, only 30 out of 100 of those from the poorest households start school. But once in school they are likely to remain until the end of the cycle. In Colombia, Congo, Rwanda and Zambia, most children, whether rich or poor, enter primary school. But those from rich households have a better chance of staying in school. In Rwanda, only 58 out of the initial 100 of the poorest reach the last grade, compared with 76 of the richest.

Figure 1.19: Inequality in primary education access and completion between the
Expected cohort net intake rate to first grade and survival rate to last grade of primary school,

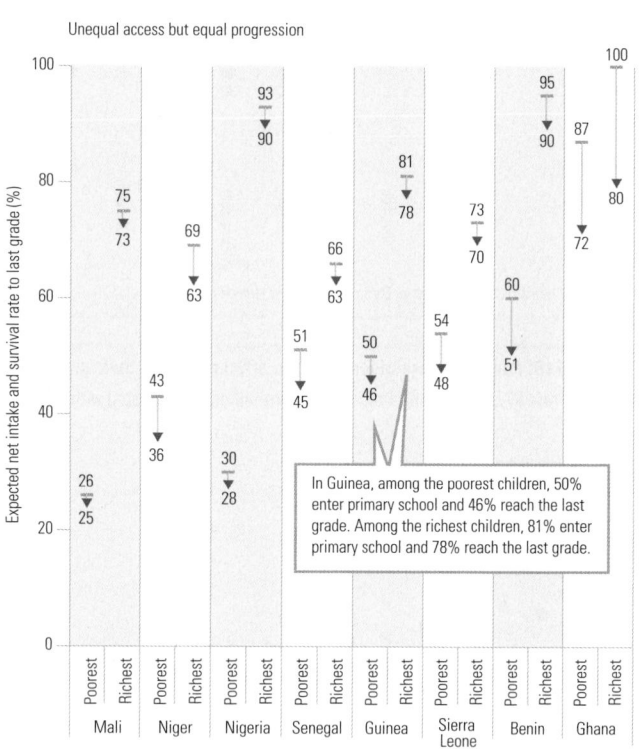

Source: Delprato (2012), based on Demographic and Health Survey data.

Other characteristics, such as where a child lives, can also play a role in whether a child starts school and completes. In India, intake and progression vary between states, from high intake and high retention in Tamil Nadu to low intake and low retention in Gujarat (Figure 1.20).

Comparing changes in access and progression over a period of five to six years shows that countries can make large gains in a short time, but also that progress has

poorest and the richest is very large

by wealth, selected countries, 2005 to 2010

— Grade 1
▼ Last grade

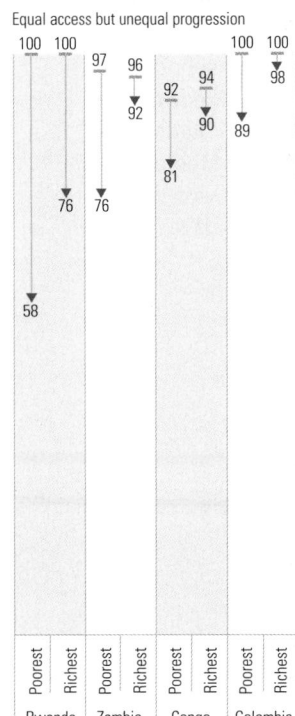

Equal access but unequal progression

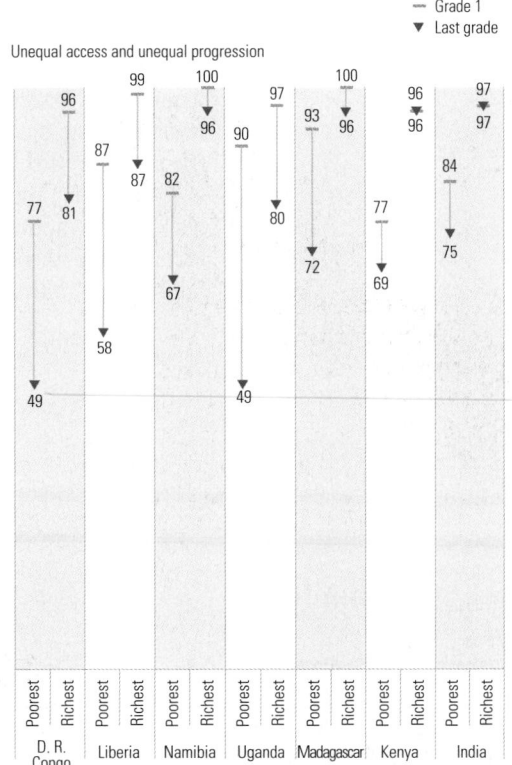

Unequal access and unequal progression

been slower than is required to achieve UPE, especially in the countries furthest from the goal (Figure 1.21).

In Nepal, for example, entry into grade 1 improved from 88 out of 100 in 2001 to 98 in 2006. Once in school, children are also more likely to stay: over the five-year period, the survival rate to the last grade of primary school increased from 78 to 91 out of every 100. Zambia also experienced improvements in both entry and survival to the end of the cycle. Ghana made major gains

in access, but only four in five children in each cohort were reaching the end of the cycle by 2008 – the same as in 2003.

Zimbabwe experienced a reversal of fortunes. In 1999, most children entered school; by 2005, the numbers entering had fallen to 89 out of 100. There was an even bigger drop in the numbers completing, from 85 in 1999 to 71 in 2005. In Mali, where the UPE challenge is one of entry rather than retention, there was no progress

Education for All Global Monitoring Report

2 0 1 2

Figure 1.20: Different patterns of access and progression can exist in the same country

Expected cohort net intake rate to first grade and survival rate to last grade of primary school, selected states, India, 2005/06

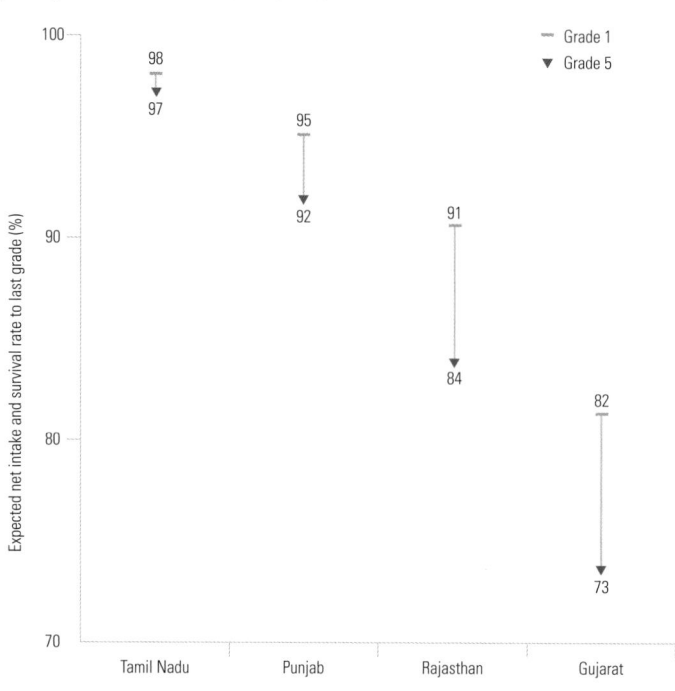

Source: Delprato (2012), based on Demographic and Health Survey data.

between 2001 and 2006, with still only 40 out of 100 entering or completing by 2006.

In the limited time that remains before the EFA deadline in 2015, system-wide interventions that can lower barriers to school entry and progression for disadvantaged children are likely to be the most effective way of getting closer to UPE. In countries where initial entry is the biggest barrier, constraints such as school costs or distance to school need to be tackled. Where the problem is more one of keeping children in school once they have started, strategies also need to address the learning environment, including ensuring that all students have appropriate learning materials.

Figure 1.21: Countries can make progress over a short period, but can also lose ground

Expected cohort net intake to first grade and survival rate to the last grade of primary school, selected countries, 1999 to 2008

Countries that have stagnated or regressed

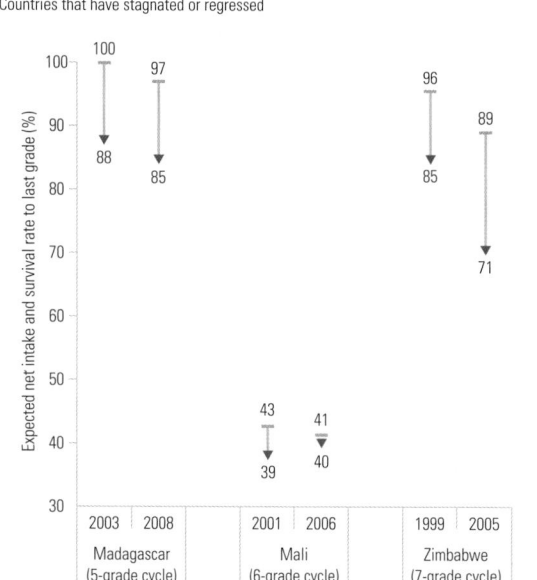

Countries that have progressed

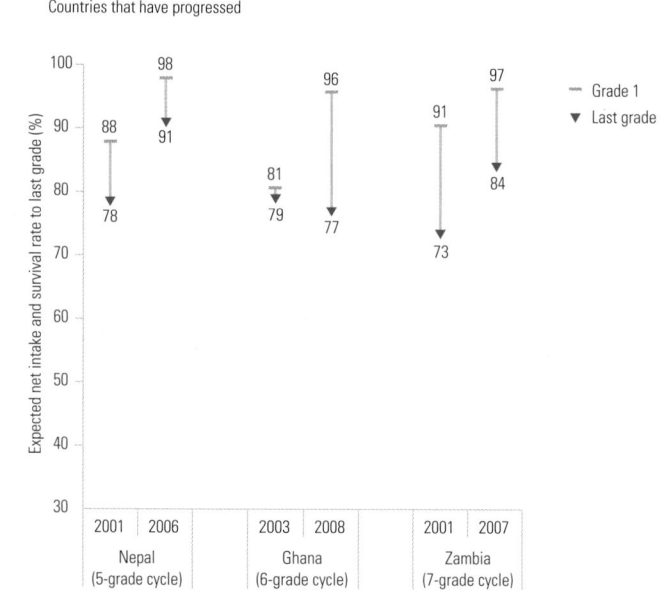

Source: Delprato (2012), based on Demographic and Health Survey data.

Policy focus: Reducing costs of primary schools for the poorest

With progress towards universal primary education stagnating, reaching out to the poorest families has become an urgent priority, as their children are most likely to be denied access to education. Such households have very meagre incomes to draw on for basic needs in food and health as well as education.

This section demonstrates that abolishing school fees is a key approach to increasing access to primary schooling for poor households, but emphasizes that it is not sufficient by itself. Many other costs remain that prove prohibitive for the poorest households. In contrast, rich households can afford supplementary tuition or private schooling.[7]

Financial constraints matter in schooling decisions

Parents and caregivers take into account economic, social and cultural considerations when assessing the costs and benefits of sending their daughter or son to primary school. In addition to direct costs of education, such as school fees, uniforms or transport, families also face indirect opportunity costs. These include costs associated with a loss of income that could have been earned by the child if sent to work.

Analysis of household surveys in eight countries shows that parents regard the financial burden of education as the most important factor when deciding whether to send their children to school (Table 1.4).[8] In Indonesia, for example, 47% of

Improving access to primary schools for the poorest is not achieved just by abolishing school fees

Table 1.4: Financial constraints matter when a household decides not to send a child to school

Reason given by parents or guardians for primary school age child being out of school (%)

Reason for not attending school	Never attended primary school[1]					Dropped out of primary school					Number of out-of-school children (000)
	Cost	Work	Distance	Not necessary	Other	Cost	Work	Distance	Not necessary	Other	
Single response											
Bangladesh[2], 2008	...	...	...	...	...	25	5	10	24	36	...
Indonesia, 2009	44	3	2	0	52	52	5	5	2	36	236
Iraq, 2007	5	0	6	41	48	11	4	11	49	25	...
South Africa, 2007	26	6	9	1	57	10	0	11	5	74	679
U. R. Tanzania, 2007	5	8	10	12	64	6	15	4	43	32	137
Uganda, 2007	15	21	13	25	25	47	4	1	21	27	623
Multiple response[3]											
Egypt[4], 2005-06	61	34	6	38	—	33	20	11	61	—	368
Nigeria, 2010	27	34	34	9	—	33	17	8	27	—	10 542

Notes: 1. For children who have never attended primary school, cases where parents claimed that their child was too young to go to school have been excluded, assuming that these children will eventually attend school. 2. Results for Bangladesh are for all out-of-school children (never enrolled and dropped out). 3. In multiple response surveys, the responses do not add up to 100%, and the 'other' category is not applicable. 4. Results for Egypt refer to dropouts from lower secondary school.

Sources: EFA Global Monitoring Report team calculations (2012) based on data from the following household surveys: 2009 Indonesia National Socio-Economic Survey, 2007 Iraq Household Socio-Economic Survey, 2008 South Africa National Income Dynamics Study, 2007 Tanzania Household Budget Survey, and 2005/06 Uganda National Household Survey; data was extracted from survey reports for Bangladesh (Nath and Chowdhury, 2009), Egypt (El-Zanaty and Gorin, 2007) and Nigeria (Nigeria National Population Commission and RTI International, 2011); Annex, Statistical Table 5.

7. This section draws in part on Nordstrum (2012b).

8. There are several challenges in interpreting such responses from household surveys. Response categories are fixed, and in some cases, when parents are asked to identify a single reason, this may not capture situations where more than one factor may be at play. A particular response may mask the real reason. Parents may be embarrassed to admit that certain issues were decisive. Where multiple responses are permitted, it becomes difficult to identify the most important factor. Comparing responses across countries is also challenging, as response categories may not be fully compatible.

In Indonesia, half of parents whose children never attended school or dropped out said this was because of cost or work

parents whose children had never attended primary school and 57% of parents whose children had dropped out identified either cost or work as the primary cause. In Nigeria, the country with the largest number of children out of school, a third of children who had never attended school stayed away because they were working, while a third of children who had dropped out did so because of direct costs.

Even where the importance of financial factors is not immediately apparent, they are still likely to have an impact. For example, in Iraq 41% of parents whose children were never enrolled and 49% of those whose children dropped out reported that the decision was made because they believed education was not necessary. This view is most likely based on a perception that the costs of education outweigh the benefits, such as expected higher wages in the future.

Another obstacle cited by parents was long distances to school, resulting in transport costs. Such major expenses may be prohibitive to all but the richer households.

Parental identification of cost as a major reason for their children not being in school is supported by analysis from the same surveys which show that children from the poorest households are significantly more likely to be out of school in all eight countries. For example, in Nigeria 62% of children from the poorest quintile did not attend school in 2010, compared with just 2% from the richest quintile (Figure 1.22).

Household spending on education varies widely

Even if a poor family is able to send all its children to school, it must make a decision regarding the amount of resources to be dedicated to improving their chances of completing and succeeding in school. This decision is influenced by the immediate availability of money, and the trade-off between spending on education or on other basic needs.

A study of household spending in fifteen sub-Saharan African countries for 2001–2007 showed that households spent on average 4.2% of their

Figure 1.22: Children from the poorest families are more likely to be out of school

Percentage of primary school age children who are out of school, by wealth/expenditure quintile and gender, selected countries

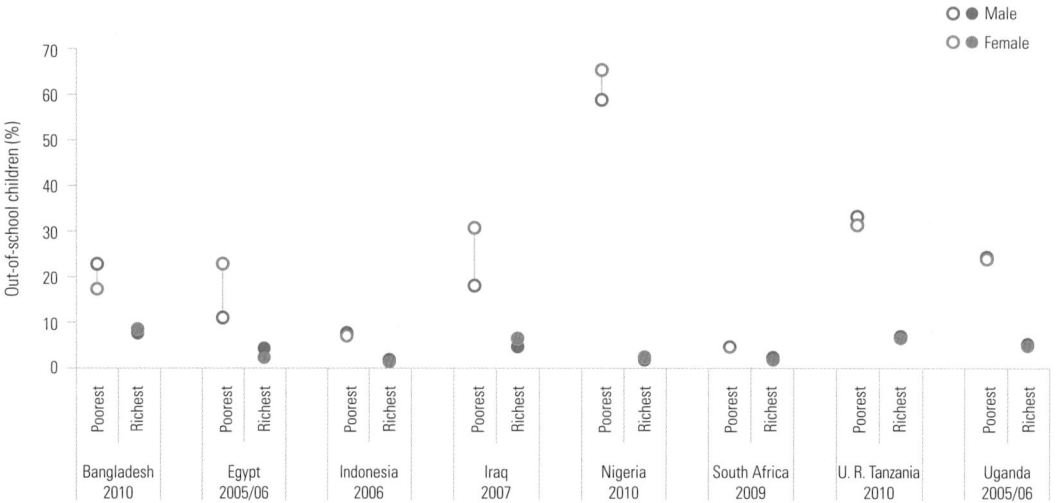

Sources: EFA Global Monitoring Report team calculations (2012) based on data from the following household surveys: 2010 Bangladesh Household Income and Expenditure, 2005/06 Egypt Household Education Survey, 2006 Indonesia National Socio-Economic Survey, 2007 Iraq Household Socio-Economic Survey, 2010 Nigeria Education Data Survey, 2009 South Africa General Household Survey, 2010 Tanzania Demographic and Health Survey, and 2005/06 Uganda National Household Survey.

total expenditure on education, with the richest quintile spending 5.4% and the poorest quintile spending 2.6% (Foko et al., 2012).

Direct costs incurred generally involve obligatory payments to schools, including tuition and other types of fees, some of which may not be legally sanctioned. They also involve necessary spending on other schooling costs whose level may be more or less fixed, such as uniforms and textbooks. Other costs may vary depending on family circumstances (for example, transport) or involve optional expenses to improve the quality of the schooling experience (for example, private supplementary tuition).

Seven of the eight countries reviewed for this Report have in principle abolished primary school fees.[9] Nevertheless, on average across the eight countries, tuition and other fees account for almost 15% of household spending on education among households with children in public primary schools. In South Africa and Uganda, the share of fees is as high as one-third of total household primary education expenditure per child. Among other common direct costs, books and stationery account for about one-quarter, uniforms for another quarter, and private supplementary tuition for about one-eighth, on average for the eight countries (Figure 1.23).

Richer households spend considerably more per child than poorer households. Among

Figure 1.23: Across eight countries, school fees make up almost 15% of household spending on education

Distribution of primary education costs per child across types of expenditure among households with children in public primary schools, selected countries

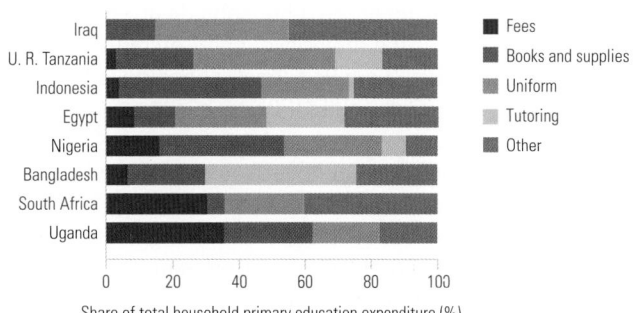

Share of total household primary education expenditure (%)

Sources: EFA Global Monitoring Report team calculations (2012) based on data from the following household surveys: 2010 Bangladesh Household Income and Expenditure, 2005/06 Egypt Household Education Survey, 2006 Indonesia National Socio-Economic Survey, 2007 Iraq Household Socio-Economic Survey, 2010 Nigeria Education Data Survey, 2009 South Africa General Household Survey, 2008/09 Tanzania National Panel Survey, and 2005/06 Uganda National Household Survey.

households with children in public primary schools, the range varies from about two and a half times in Iraq and the United Republic of Tanzania to almost eight times in South Africa. The range increases significantly if widened to include households whose children attend private schools. In Nigeria, average spending per child by the richest 20% of households is more than three times as much as that by the poorest 20% in public primary schools, and more than ten times as much for those in both

In Uganda, fees make up one-third of household spending on education

Figure 1.24: In Nigeria, rich households spend more to improve the quality of schooling for their children

A. Primary education costs per child, by wealth quintile, in US$, Nigeria 2010

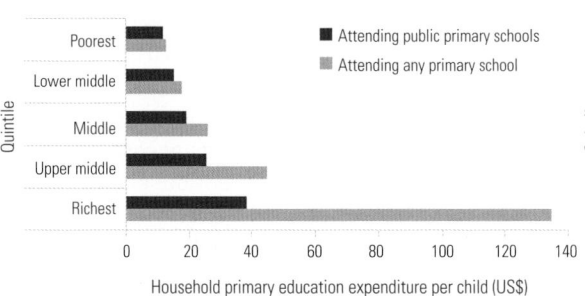

Household primary education expenditure per child (US$)

B. Distribution of primary education costs per child across types of expenditure among households with children in public primary schools, by wealth quintile, Nigeria 2010

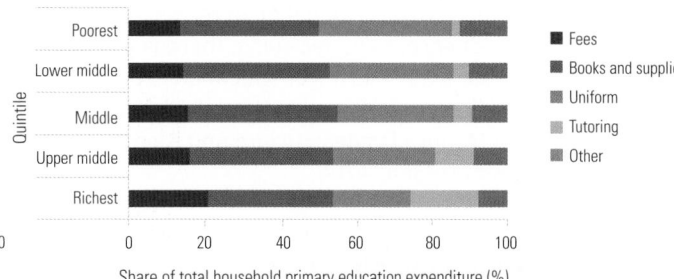

Share of total household primary education expenditure (%)

Sources: EFA Global Monitoring Report team calculations (2012) based on the 2010 Nigeria Education Data Survey; Nigeria National Population Commission and RTI International (2011).

9. South Africa is the only one of the eight countries that has not entirely abolished fees, although it has done so for the poorest 60% of communities

public and private primary schools. About 66% of children from the richest households attend private schools. Spending per pupil from a rich household is US$135 on average but only US$39 in a public school. By comparison, just 6% of children from poorest households attend private school. For the majority of children in these households in public school, spending is less than US$12 per child (Figure 1.24A).

The composition of household primary education expenditure also differs between poorer and richer households, even among those households that send children to public schools only. Richer households either spend more on discretionary items that improve the education experience of their children, such as more and better quality school supplies, or are able to afford to pay for supplementary tuition. Spending on public schooling in Nigeria demonstrates some of these characteristics (Figure 1.24B). The richest households allocate a much higher share of their primary education expenditure to private supplementary tuition (18%) than the poorest households (2%).

The amount spent on schooling per child may also vary within households. Gender discrimination may mean that children in the household do not benefit equally. Such discrimination can operate through different channels. In some countries girls are more likely to be out of school and therefore incur zero education expenditure, especially among poorer households, as shown in the cases of Egypt, Iraq and Nigeria (Figure 1.22). Once girls are in school, less may also be spent on them. In India, for example, while there is little evidence of discrimination in terms of primary school enrolment decisions, there is evidence of a male bias in terms of education expenditure decisions in states such as Andhra Pradesh and Madhya Pradesh (Azam and Kingdon, 2011; Zimmermann, 2012).

Removing direct costs can help poor households send children to primary school

Abolishing formal school fees is a fundamental step towards realizing UPE, but it is not sufficient by itself. Implementation needs to be monitored closely to ensure that fees are not reintroduced

in indirect ways as schools seek to make up for lost funds. Measures are also needed to ensure that the abolition of fees does not reinforce inequalities between those who can pay for better quality education and those who cannot. Given that fees represent only part of schooling costs with other direct and indirect costs often keeping children out of school, additional strategies are needed to help poor households.

Abolishing school fees

Many countries have eliminated official school fees in line with the Dakar Framework commitment that primary education should be 'free of tuition and other fees'. Fee abolition had a strong positive impact on enrolment either during the year of abolition or in subsequent years (Figure 1.25). In Burundi, for example, the gross enrolment ratio was 83% in 2004, the year preceding fee abolition; it increased to 88% in the year that fees were abolished as part of the post-conflict election promise and by 2009 stood at 147%.

Countries generally introduce fee exemptions across the board. For example, the Right to Education Act in India applies to all children aged 6 to 14 (Box 1.3). Fee abolition is akin to transferring resources from the government back to families of children of primary school age. This transfer disproportionately benefits poorer households for two reasons: they are more likely to have been excluded from education due to inability to pay fees, and they tend to have more children of primary school age. In rural Kenya, the poorest quintile of households reaped a larger share of the benefit of fee abolition (from 21% in 2004 to 30% in 2007), as new entrants to school were mainly poorer children (Muyanga et al., 2010).

South Africa adopted a different approach, staggering the abolition of fees according to income, and targeting poorer households first. However, even when the information necessary for effective targeting is available, some poor children are still excluded. The No Fee Schools policy eliminated tuition fees initially in schools serving the poorest 40% of children in 2007, extending to schools serving the poorest 60% two years later. Schools were generally ranked according to the poverty level of their catchment area, although each province refined this ranking

In Nigeria, 66% of rich children attend private school compared with just 6% of the poor

Figure 1.25: Fee abolition has boosted primary school participation

Primary gross enrolment ratio before and after abolition of tuition fees, selected countries

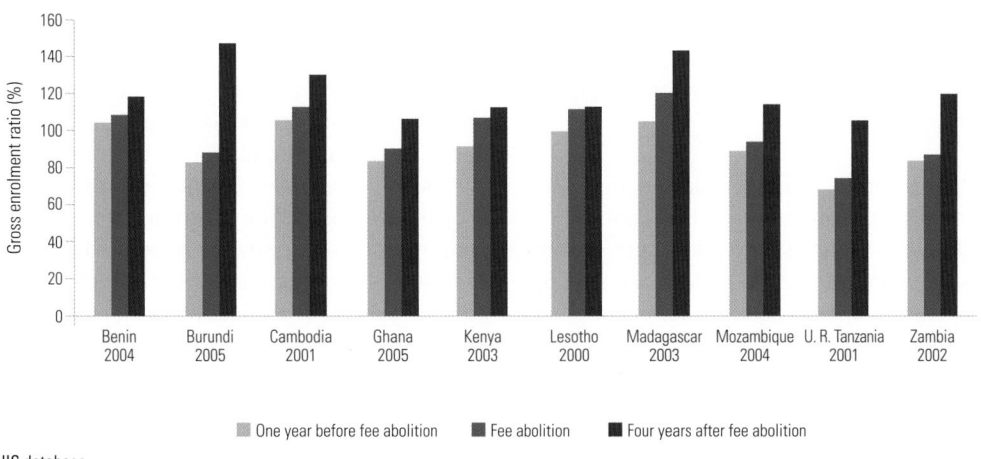

Source: UIS database.

Box 1.3: The Right to Education Act in India

India has made tremendous progress in reducing the number of out-of-school children, from 20 million in 2000 to 2 million in 2008. An effort to enshrine the right to education for all children in legislation began in 1993 with a Supreme Court decision, which was based on the principle that no one can live with dignity without education, and that education should therefore be a fundamental right. In 2002, the 86th Amendment to the Constitution provided for an Act mandating free and compulsory education. It took the government seven more years before it passed the Right of Children to Free and Compulsory Education Act. The law came into effect in April 2010 and consolidated existing compulsory education acts of individual states.

Implementing the legislation has not been straightforward. There has been disagreement among central, state and local governments over the sharing of financial responsibilities for meeting the education standards stipulated by the law. Monitoring has also proven difficult. The law made

it possible to prosecute institutions or individuals who may have violated children's right to education. The National Commission for Protection of Child Rights, the government body responsible for monitoring the implementation of the law, received 2,850 complaints related, among others, to admission procedures, discrimination, teacher attendance, reserved places in private schools, charging of fees and inadequate infrastructure. However, as of March 2012 the Commission had only resolved about one in four complaints.

The experience of India demonstrates that guaranteeing the right of all children to free compulsory education is a major step forward, but underlines the need to reinforce the right with clear rules and adequate financing for its implementation. Moreover, organizational challenges must be overcome to ensure that possible violations are investigated and brought to justice.

Sources: Economic Times (2010); Gazette of India (2009); Isaac (2012); Little (2010); Mehrotra (2012); Taneja et al. (2012).

In Uganda, despite abolishing fees, the gap in spending between rich and poor has widened

based on even more detailed, locally available information (Wildeman, 2008). However, poor children also live in catchment areas of schools that continue to charge fees: according to household survey data, only 65% of children from the bottom quintile benefited from fee exemption in 2009 (Nordstrum, 2012a).

Despite the generally positive experience with fee abolition, many children from poor households are still not able to complete primary school, suggesting that other factors are leading to their exclusion, including other financial costs. In many cases, fee abolition only covers tuition fees. This means that households still have to pay other charges. For example, Nigeria announced a universal basic education initiative in 1999 and passed a corresponding Act in 2004 (Obanya, 2011). Tuition fees were abolished, but 10% of parents reported paying some form of fee in 2010. Around 57% of parents also reported paying a compulsory parent–teacher association fee and a further 40% had to pay exam fees (Nigeria National Population Commission and RTI International, 2011).

Even though fee abolition has helped expand access for poor children, the ability of the rich to pay other costs can perpetuate inequality in

the schooling experience. The case of Uganda provides useful insights. The 1997 fee abolition led to a large increase in enrolment, particularly among the poorest children (Deininger, 2003). But this meant that the poorest households whose children were previously out of school had to spend some of their meagre income on non-fee costs of education. Rich households whose children were already in school could reallocate the money saved to cover other costs that maintained, or even further widened, their children's schooling advantage. Evidence from three rounds of the Uganda National Household Survey shows that richer households with children in public primary schools increased their allocation to education, widening the gap in spending between rich and poor: between 1999 and 2006 expenditure per child increased from US$4 to just US$6 among the poorest households, but from US$46 to US$82 among the richest (Figure 1.26).

Fee abolition needs to be accompanied by capitation grants to compensate schools for loss of income

Where official fees have been abolished schools need to be compensated for their loss of income, otherwise they may charge unofficial fees that can place a similar burden

Figure 1.26: In Uganda the education expenditure gap between poorer and richer households widened after fee abolition
Education expenditure per child among households with children in public primary schools, Uganda, 1999 to 2006

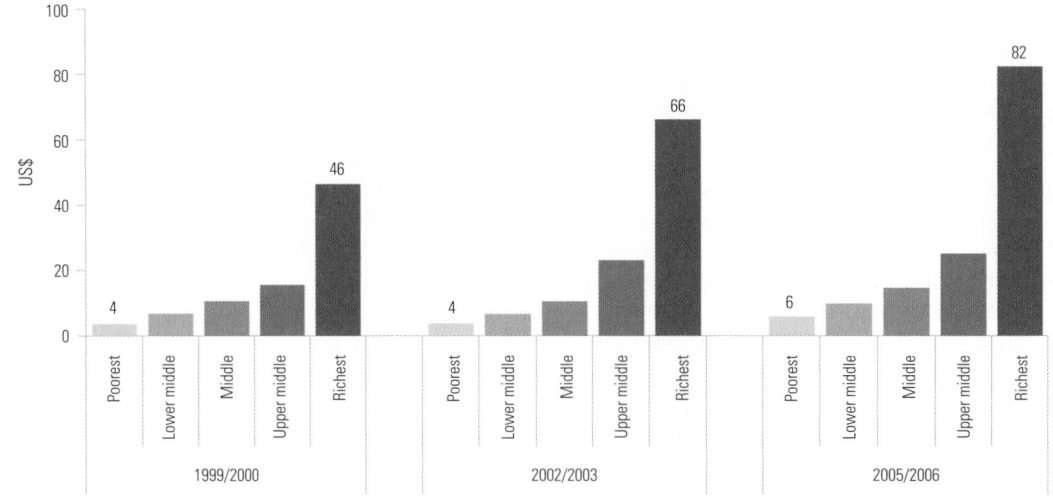

Source: EFA Global Monitoring Report team analysis (2012) based on three rounds of the Uganda National Household Survey.

on households. Alternatively, they may let quality deteriorate — for example, by letting infrastructure go unrepaired or buying fewer textbooks. Capitation grants, which provide funds to schools based on enrolment, are a common way of addressing this need.

In Ghana, tuition fees were abolished in 1995, but households were still expected to pay other fees. A capitation grant programme was rolled out in 2005 to address this problem. The grant was equivalent initially to approximately US$3 per student and was raised to US$4.5 in 2008 (Akyeampong, 2011). Households still have to pay fees related to exams or parent–teacher associations, but these represent only 6% of their total education expenditure (Akaguri and Akyeampong, 2010).

Governments need to demonstrate commitment to ensure that capitation grants are set at an appropriate level, maintain their value and benefit the poor. For example:

- In Mozambique, the Direct Support to Schools (Apoio Directo às Escolas) programme provides primary schools with grants to purchase learning materials, including items for which households would previously have paid, such as books and stationery (UNICEF, 2011a). As of 2005, the grant was equivalent to about US$1 per primary school student and, of that, only 71% was spent on items that would reduce costs for households, such as books, stationery and other learning materials (World Bank and UNICEF, 2009). This suggests that the size of the grant is very small relative to need.

- In the United Republic of Tanzania, a capitation grant was introduced alongside fee abolition in 2001. But between 2002 and 2009, the real value of the capitation grant declined by more than 30% to about US$7 per student, and was not even sufficient to finance a full set of textbooks (Uwazi, 2010). A public expenditure tracking survey further showed that the amount actually budgeted was only equivalent to US$5 and the amount received by schools was US$4.5 (Claussen and Assad, 2010).

- In Indonesia, fees were abolished in 2005 under the Free Basic Education policy. The School Operational Assistance (Bantuan Operasional Sekolah) programme of block grants (equivalent to about US$43 per student) was introduced at this time to guarantee the ability of schools to finance their operational costs without shifting the burden back to households. According to the guidelines, the funds can also be utilized to directly support poor children, notably by paying for transportation costs. However, only one-third of 1,250 schools surveyed had actually done so (Widyanti and Suryahadi, 2008).

Costs of uniforms can be prohibitive for poor households

Some governments have introduced measures to stop the cost of school uniforms inhibiting access to school. Before India abolished fees, subsidies were provided via the District Primary Education Programme to households that could not afford uniforms (Ayyar and Bashir, 2004).

Another option adopted by some countries is to remove the requirement to wear a uniform. However, the success of such interventions has sometimes been limited. Timor-Leste removed uniform requirements during the tuition fee abolition process in 2000 (World Bank, 2003). Yet an analysis by the EFA Global Monitoring Report team, based on the 2007 Survey of Living Standards, shows that even seven years after official abolition, school uniforms accounted for 52% of total household primary education expenditure per child among the poorest 20% of households. In Uganda, which also removed the requirement in 2003 (Avenstrup et al., 2004), analysis by the EFA Global Monitoring Report team shows that school uniforms accounted for 28% of total household primary education expenditure per child among the poorest 20% of households in 2006.

Where wearing a uniform has been compulsory for a long time, abolishing the obligation is not always sufficient to remove the social barrier associated with not wearing one. Stigma attached to not wearing a uniform or wearing one of lower quality can affect girls' attendance in particular (South Africa Department of Education, 2003).

Although uniforms are voluntary in Timor-Leste, they account for half of the poorest families' education expenditure

In Bangladesh and Egypt, the richest spend four times more than the poorest on private tuition

The potential benefits of removing this burden from households are considerable. In Kenya, as part of an NGO-sponsored project, students were randomly assigned to receive school uniforms, whose cost ranged between US$4 and US$7. An evaluation found that students who received a uniform reduced their absenteeism rate from 15% to 9%. The study also looked at long-term effects, but found no significant effect on the likelihood of completing primary school and on the number of years of education completed (Evans et al., 2011). This could suggest that while relieving poor households of high costs is helpful, achieving positive long-term outcomes also requires measures that focus on quality.

Supplementary tuition is only affordable to some

In some countries a parallel education system has emerged, often because the quality of public schools is low. After school hours, children buy the services of tutors to increase their chances of passing exams and progressing through the grades. The costs can be substantial, implying that poorer children are less likely to benefit.

In Bangladesh, about 43% of children from the poorest quintile of households attending public primary school received supplementary tuition, compared with 67% of children from the richest quintile in 2010. In Egypt the corresponding figures were 25% and 47% in 2005/06.

Richer households are not only more likely to receive supplementary tuition, but also to spend more. Higher costs may be the result of richer households recruiting more experienced tutors, selecting individual rather than group-tutoring, and purchasing more hours. In both Bangladesh and Egypt, the richest households spend four times more than poorest households on supplementary tuition (Figure 1.27).

The recourse to supplementary tuition can further reinforce the gap in the quality of the education received by rich and poor children. Teachers may also see an opportunity to increase their incomes. In some countries, including Cambodia and Egypt, it has been reported that teachers withhold curriculum content during the school day, forcing students to attend tutorials where the omitted areas are covered (Dawson, 2011; Hartmann, 2008).

Once such practice becomes widespread it is very difficult to reverse with punitive measures. However, measures can be taken to ease the burden for poor households. Governments can reduce the demand for supplementary tutoring, for example, by avoiding high stakes examinations. Alternatively, they can improve inspection to ensure that teachers cover the curriculum as expected (Bray, 2009).

Figure 1.27: Richer households are more likely to spend more on supplementary tuition for their children
Supplementary tuition among households with children attending public primary schools, Bangladesh 2010 and Egypt 2005/06

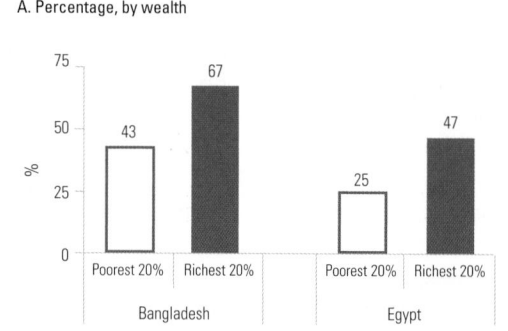

A. Percentage, by wealth

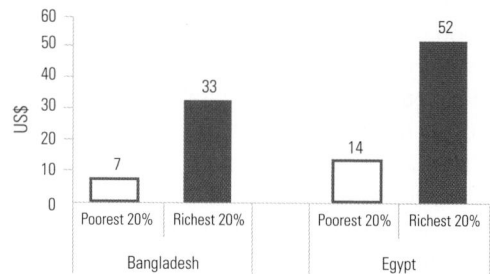

B. Mean expenditure per child, by wealth

Sources: EFA Global Monitoring Report team analysis (2012) based on the 2010 Bangladesh Household Income and Expenditure Survey and the 2005/06 Egypt Household Education Survey.

Are low fee private schools affordable for the poor?

Low fee private primary schooling has expanded in some countries, especially where a rapid increase in enrolment following fee abolition has led to a perceived decline in the quality of public primary schooling. Advocates maintain that the growth of low fee private schooling helps expand access where there are insufficient public schools, and improves quality (Tooley and Dixon, 2006).

There is some evidence that these schools are reaching some poor households (UNESCO, 2009). But even though their fees are low, their overall costs for households are considerably more than those of government schools. As a result, the poorest families are unable to afford them. Recent survey data for eight countries show per capita household spending on children in private primary school is US$220 compared with US$36 on their public school counterparts (Foko et al., 2012).

The average cost of educating a child in a private school in Makoko slum in Lagos, Nigeria, was estimated to be around US$217 per annum, equivalent to about four 50 kg bags of rice, which would feed the average family of six members for approximately seventy days. Sending three children to a slum school equates to 46% of the Lagos minimum wage (Härmä, 2011a). In rural Uttar Pradesh, India, around 41% of children in one survey were enrolled in private schools. Children in these schools were predominantly from richer households in the villages, with almost all children from the poorest households in government schools. These households could not afford private schools, which were more than eight times as expensive as government schools. These costs were prohibitive for the poorest 40% of households, which would have to pay up to 30% of total household income to send their children to private primary schools (Härmä, 2010).

With the costs of low fee private schools out of reach, vouchers are one approach to extending access to the poorest households. The regular and predictable payment of fees from a voucher could also benefit schools that suffer from irregular payments from poor parents who mostly rely on precarious employment.

Vouchers are not an easy solution, however. Many low fee private schools are not registered. This is the case for three-quarters of the private schools in Lagos, for example (Härmä, 2011b). These unregistered schools would not be able to participate in an official, government-backed voucher programme. A raft of administrative requirements also accompanies effective implementation. Effective and efficient targeting of potential beneficiaries is a major challenge, as is government capacity to implement a programme on a larger scale. Even in countries where such capacity exists, public opposition can make vouchers a politically unpopular choice. In Chile, for example, students protested over the perceived inequitable outcomes of the country's well-established voucher programme (UNESCO, 2009).

There is also the question of ensuring that vouchers can be carried out at the scale required to reach the most disadvantaged. In Pakistan, the Punjab Education Foundation has been implementing a programme since 2006 that provides vouchers to children from disadvantaged backgrounds that allow them to choose from among more than 1,000 low fee private schools (Punjab Education Foundation, 2012a). In a country of 5.1 million out-of-school children, the programme is reaching a small number: 267 schools and 80,000 pupils (Punjab Education Foundation, 2012b). Punjab is also the part of Pakistan where enrolment is already highest; consequently, the voucher programme is not helping extend access to the parts of the country where it is most needed.

Governments have a choice between investing their scarce resources to arrest the decline in public school quality or subsidizing households to send children to private schools through voucher programmes. Vouchers may appear to be a quick fix, but investing in public schools is likely to be the best way to reach the poorest.

The annual cost of a private school in a Lagos slum could feed a family of six for 70 days

CHAPTER 1

Strengthening social protection policies to help households send children to primary school

The cost of schooling can be eased by helping households meet specific education expenses, as well as through measures that increase and stabilize their income – freeing resources they can invest in education. The impact on education depends on the size of the intervention, the design of the programme and the targeting of the beneficiaries, as well as whether there is an adequate supply of education providers of appropriate quality.

Scholarships. Some countries implement targeted scholarship programmes to offset education costs. Indonesia first put in place a scholarship programme targeting poor children in the aftermath of the 1997–1998 financial crisis, as part of the Social Safety Net Programme (Jaring Pengaman Sosial). The central government allocated a scholarship budget to districts according to household budget survey estimates of poverty; districts allocated budgets to schools based on their knowledge of community characteristics; and school committees decided on individual recipients. The sizeable amount of the scholarship (equivalent to twice the average household expenditure on education for a primary school child from the bottom wealth quintile) and the reasonable effectiveness of the targeting (seven in ten beneficiaries belonged to the two lowest quintiles) enabled it to prevent enrolment declines at the primary school level (Cameron, 2009; Sparrow, 2007).

Conditional and unconditional cash transfers. These programmes provide cash grants to poor households that meet criteria such as school attendance or use of a health centre, or unconditionally for certain population groups. Cash transfers are prevalent in Latin American countries; many have been rigorously evaluated, showing a positive impact on education (UNESCO, 2009, 2010b). In contrast, there are few large programmes — and even fewer evaluations — in the three regions with the largest numbers of out-of-school children: East Asia and the Pacific, South and West Asia and sub-Saharan Africa (Fiszbein et al., 2009; Garcia and Moore, 2012).

In Kenya, an unconditional monthly transfer of US$20 has improved school attendance

One of the most ambitious programmes, the Cash Transfer for Orphans and Vulnerable Children in Kenya, provides ultra-poor beneficiary families with an unconditional monthly transfer worth US$20. Early reviews point to relatively small effects on primary school attendance, age-for-grade and progression, which is not surprising given that initial average levels were already generally high. But the effects are larger for the subset of children who face steeper costs, including those who live more than 2 km from the primary school or those attending schools that informally charge fees (Kenya CT-OVC Evaluation Team, 2012).

A project developed by BRAC in Bangladesh, Challenging the Frontiers of Poverty Reduction — Targeting the Ultra Poor, provides an unconditional package of support to protect the ultra-poor and promote their livelihoods, including asset transfers, stipends and skills training. Between 2007 and 2011, 300,000 households received a full package and 500,000 households a reduced package, helping to increase household income. Although education outcomes are not the main focus, they have been followed closely. A randomized trial based on a survey of about 7,000 households found that there was no impact on primary school attendance and repetition, even though the programme used volunteers and local committees to encourage enrolment (Das and Shams, 2011).

Bangladesh's experience suggests that unconditional transfers in the form of assets may not increase the income of ultra-poor families immediately and, if the transfer is not large enough, could even increase demand for child labour in the short term. This further suggests that the type and size of the transfer needs to be carefully considered, and that an element of conditionality may be necessary in some contexts if positive education results are to be achieved.

The potential of social protection programmes may be considerable in middle income countries that continue to lag in terms of education outcomes, such as the Philippines, where 1.5 million children were out of school in 2009. In response to the lack of progress in social indicators, the government launched the Pantawid Pamilyang Pilipino programme in 2008. Beneficiary households receive an average monthly cash transfer of US$19 if they have one school-age child, increasing to US$33 for families with three school-age children, equivalent to about 20% of household income. In 2011 the programme was scaled up to reach 2.3 million poor households and further expansion to 4.8 million households by 2014 is planned. Eligible households must live in targeted poor areas, be classified as poor, have a pregnant woman or at least one child aged up to 14 years as a member, and meet certain conditions, including an 85% attendance record in school (Fernandez and Olfindo, 2011; Velunta, 2012). Results from a pilot phase showed that primary school completion rates increased from 68% to 73% (ADB, 2010). Evidence from administrative data also shows that public primary school enrolment growth was faster in targeted areas than other areas between 2008 and 2010 (Manasan, 2011).

Conclusion

Abolishing primary school fees has helped reduce costs, but has not removed the cost barrier to enrolment for the poorest. Non-fee costs, such as school uniforms and supplies, can be substantial, particularly for poor households, and require additional solutions. Strategies are needed to compensate poor families for the direct costs of schooling and the indirect costs of the child being in school rather than working. Formal fee elimination is unlikely to be successful unless it is integrated into a larger educational finance framework that addresses these issues.

The Philippines gives the poorest the equivalent of 20% of their income in cash transfers

Goal 3   **Youth and adult learning needs**

Ensuring that the learning needs of all young people and adults are met through equitable access to appropriate learning and life skills programmes.

Highlights

■ Despite a global increase in the number of children enrolling in secondary school, the lower secondary gross enrolment ratio was just 52% in low income countries in 2010, leaving millions of young people to face life without the foundation skills they need to earn a decent living.

■ Although the number of out-of-school adolescents of lower secondary school age fell from 101 million in 1999 to 71 million in 2010, it has stagnated since 2007. Three out of four out-of-school adolescents live in South and West Asia and sub-Saharan Africa.

■ Twelve years after the EFA goals were established, the international community is only now coming closer to agreeing on a coherent set of internationally comparable indicators of skills development and the means to measure them. But recent developments will not produce sufficient data in time to measure goal 3 adequately before 2015.

Table 1.5: Key indicators for goal 3

	Total secondary enrolment		Total secondary gross enrolment ratio		Lower secondary gross enrolment ratio		Upper secondary gross enrolment ratio		Technical and vocational education as a share of secondary enrolment		Out-of-school adolescents of lower secondary school age	
	2010 (000)	Change since 1999 (%)	1999 (%)	2010 (%)	1999 (%)	2010 (%)	1999 (%)	2010 (%)	1999 (%)	2010 (%)	2010 (000)	Change since 1999 (%)
World	542 684	25	59	70	72	82	45	59	11	11	70 570	-30
Low income countries	46 333	78	29	42	36	52	21	29	4	5	17 666	-19
Lower middle income countries	204 343	47	46	61	61	76	31	48	5	5	43 214	-24
Upper middle income countries	205 788	12	72	85	89	97	52	74	13	16	8 790	-58
High income countries	86 221	-1	99	102	102	104	97	99	17	14	899	-46
Sub-Saharan Africa	43 653	110	25	40	29	47	20	31	7	8	21 676	-4
Arab States	29 722	33	59	69	75	87	43	49	14	8	3 732	-29
Central Asia	10 443	13	84	95	85	97	81	92	6	19	315	-65
East Asia and the Pacific	163 268	24	63	80	78	90	44	70	14	17	10 317	-59
South and West Asia	143 351	47	44	59	61	75	30	47	1	2	30 946	-22
Latin America and the Caribbean	60 074	14	81	91	95	102	62	75	10	10	1 749	-48
North America and Western Europe	61 828	2	100	102	102	105	97	99	14	13	554	-53
Central and Eastern Europe	30 347	-25	88	88	92	95	81	81	18	20	1 281	-56

Sources: Annex, Statistical Table 7 (print) and Statistical Table 8 (website); UIS database.

In recent years, heightened social and economic challenges have placed skills development at the centre of the global education debate. As the thematic part of this Report details, this has introduced urgency to a vital EFA goal that has not been given the attention it deserves because of the ambiguity of the commitments made when the EFA goals were established in 2000.

Formal secondary schooling is the most effective way to develop the skills needed for work and life. The expansion of primary schooling over the past decade is now being reflected in higher enrolments at the next level of education. Total enrolment at secondary level rose by 25% globally between 1999 and 2010, with growth in low income countries by 78% and lower middle income countries by 47%.

Most of the growth has taken place in regions with low initial participation levels. Enrolment more than doubled in sub-Saharan Africa, resulting in the gross enrolment ratio reaching 40%. The gross enrolment ratio increased from 44% to 59% in South and West Asia and from 59% to 69% in the Arab States. In absolute terms, the fastest progress was achieved in East Asia and the Pacific, with an increase of seventeen percentage points to 80%.

Yet not all young people have benefited from the expansion. There are still 71 million adolescents of lower secondary school age who are not in school. Half of the total reduction in their numbers since 1999 is accounted for by progress in East Asia and the Pacific. As with the number of out-of-school children of primary school age, progress was fastest in the first half of the decade after the EFA goals were established, from 2000 to 2005. Worryingly, the number of out-of-school adolescents has stagnated since 2007.

This stagnation is particularly apparent in some regions. The number of out-of-school adolescents has remained at 22 million in sub-Saharan Africa since 1999, in part due to high population growth. In South and West Asia, there was a 18% decline between 2002 and 2005 but there has been no progress since. As a result, the regional distribution of out-of-school adolescents has shifted towards these two regions, which accounted for three out of every four out-of-school adolescents in 2010, up from three out of five in 1999.

Some young people develop skills through technical and vocational education. The proportion of secondary school pupils enrolled in these programmes has remained at 11% since 1999. However, there are regional variations, with the percentage having increased significantly in Central Asia from 6% in 1999 to 19% in 2010 and having decreased in the Arab States from 14% to 8%.

Formal general education and technical and vocational secondary education only capture part of the skills picture, however. Information on enrolment in these types of institutions does not tell us what kinds of skills young people are acquiring. There has been intense debate as to which learning needs should be met – and how to determine whether they have been met. The Dakar Framework of Action considered knowledge, values, attitudes and skills as enabling individuals to succeed across a continuum of life domains, including employment, civic participation, personal relations and lifelong learning (UNESCO, 2000).

The thematic part of this Report is dedicated to understanding how skills development can improve young people's job opportunities. As a prelude, this section looks at recent developments in measuring skills development. Although there are some promising signs, adequate data will become available too late to enable the goal to be measured before 2015 (Panel 1.6). The section also examines how life skills education can help young people deal with one of the risks identified in the Dakar Framework of Action: HIV and AIDS (goal 3, policy focus).

Panel 1.6: Promising progress towards measuring skills development

Twelve years after the EFA goals were established in Dakar, the international community is still a long way from defining what constitutes progress in 'equitable access to appropriate learning and life skills programmes' (the core of goal 3), agreeing on a coherent set of internationally comparable indicators and assessing whether progress is being made. There are promising signs that the situation may be changing, but recent developments will not produce sufficient data in time to measure goal 3 adequately before the deadline has passed.[10]

Monitoring access to appropriate learning and life skills programmes has been difficult for several reasons. First, skills can be gained in many ways, but existing systems do not sufficiently record who is providing which skills to whom. Skills programmes involve numerous agencies and providers apart from the schools and other education and training institutions supported by ministries of education.

Some programmes take place within the workplace, ranging from traditional apprenticeships in the informal sector to more formal on-the-job training programmes. In developing countries, second-chance programmes offering basic literacy and numeracy together with vocational skills are provided by non-governmental organizations, often with limited government oversight. Governments often lack the capacity to collect information across this wide range of providers, and many countries have even struggled to present data on formal technical and vocational education programmes.[11]

Second, the challenges of a rapidly changing world have led to a major reconsideration of what skills are and how they are acquired. It is now recognized that the set of qualities that individuals need to become 'active agents in shaping their future', in the words of the Dakar Framework for Action (UNESCO, 2000, p. 16), is much broader than the occupation-specific skills on which technical and vocational education and training systems have so far tended to focus.

The economic crisis affecting developed countries and widespread high levels of youth unemployment have underlined the urgency of identifying skills needs and measuring skills levels. The Group of 20 (G20) Multi-Year Action Plan on Development, adopted at the Seoul Summit in November 2010, called on the International Labour Organization (ILO), the OECD, UNESCO and the World Bank to create internationally comparable skills indicators by 2012, with particular reference to low income countries (G20, 2010). The organizations involved have proposed a set of indicators, including on skills acquisition (Table 1.6) (OECD and World Bank, forthcoming). These are largely based on indicators that are readily available, many of which are already monitored in the context of other goals within the EFA framework.

Three distinctive indicators in the set proposed by the G20 partly capture the essence of goal 3. The first is cognitive skills of youth and adults. Some surveys hold promise of gauging this indicator. The OECD has

Table 1.6: G20 Multi-Year Action Plan on Development proposed indicators on skills acquisition

Indicator	Rationale
Stock of human capital	
Educational attainment of adult population	Proxy measure of stock of skills
Literacy of youth and adult population	Prerequisite for many types of further learning
Cognitive skills (literacy/numeracy) of youth and adults*	Direct measure of competence in key skills
Skills formation	
Primary school enrolment ratio	Basic skills
Primary school completion rate	Basic skills
Secondary school enrolment ratio	Basic skills
Tertiary level enrolment ratio	Higher-level skills
Share of tertiary graduates/students in science and technology	Skills which drive economic growth
Participation of youth in apprenticeships*	Alternative source of skill formation
Participation of adults in education and training*	Lifelong learning

Note: * These indicators are ones that have potential for measuring goal 3.
Source: OECD and World Bank (forthcoming).

10. This section draws on material provided by UNESCO's Technical and Vocational Education and Training section.
11. The Inter-Agency Group on Technical and Vocational Education and Training, bringing together the European Commission, the European Training Foundation, the ILO, the OECD, UNESCO, the World Bank and the regional development banks was established in 2009 to coordinate monitoring activities with particular reference to developing countries (IAG-TVET, 2012).

developed skills measurement surveys for young people and adults.[12] Both surveys are underpinned by a common framework with three key competence categories: the ability to use language, symbols, information and technology interactively; the ability to interact in heterogeneous groups; and the ability to act autonomously and exercise control over one's living and working conditions (OECD, 2005).

Working in cooperation with the OECD, the World Bank's Skills Toward Employment and Productivity (STEP) measurement survey is also relevant for measuring progress towards goal 3. The approach takes a lifelong learning perspective in linking skills to productivity and growth. It consists of a household survey and an employer survey.

The STEP household survey assesses the supply of skills among those aged 15 to 64, whether working or not, based on a random sample of households in the urban areas of participating countries. Three types of skills are assessed:

■ *Cognitive skills:* The survey administers a subset of the OECD PIAAC assessment of literacy skills, and includes reading components fine-tuned to assess the abilities of adults with very poor skills.

■ *Non-cognitive skills:* The survey includes questions to capture traits, behaviours and preferences, and tries to distinguish more stable personality traits from more malleable non-cognitive skills.

■ *Technical skills:* Respondents are asked to describe the competences needed to perform their job, such as use of technology and machinery, autonomy and repetitiveness, time management, and physical tasks.

The STEP employer survey assesses demand for skills. Questions include workforce characteristics, hiring practices, training and remuneration.

As of July 2012, fieldwork had been completed in the Plurinational State of Bolivia, the Lao People's

Democratic Republic and Yunnan province in China. It was being rolled out in Colombia, Sri Lanka and Viet Nam, and was expected to begin in Ghana and Ukraine. Armenia, El Salvador, Kenya and Morocco are expected to follow in 2013 (Sanchez Puerta and Valerio, 2012; World Bank, forthcoming).

For the other two indicators in the G20 initiative that are relevant to goal 3 – participation of youth in apprenticeships, and that of adults in education and training – it has been difficult in practice to collect comparative data, particularly in non-OECD countries. With respect to adult participation in education and training, the European Union has developed a systematic approach to measuring skills development. Its reference framework of eight competences[13] combines knowledge, skills and attitudes that all individuals require for employment and other needs (European Parliament and European Council, 2006). Five targets have been set for 2020, of which one is directly related to goal 3: an average of at least 15% of adults should participate in lifelong learning (European Commission, 2011b). This is monitored via the annual Labour Force Survey and two surveys done every five years, the Adult Education Survey and the Continuing Vocational Training Survey (Eurostat, 2011).

Because of the time it has taken to agree on indicators for monitoring goal 3, and complexities in collecting information, useful data are unlikely to be available before the 2015 deadline. Even if a consensus is reached, countries still need to build their capacity so that recent initiatives do not prove to be one-off experiments.

Any post-2015 international goals for skills development need to be more precisely defined and to set out clearly how they can be measured, based on a realistic assessment of information that can be collected, to avoid the problems that have plagued efforts to monitor goal 3. In addition, one body will need to act as the depository for data on skills collected by various agencies. Given the responsibility and expertise of the ILO in this area, it could play such a role.

---

12. The OECD's Programme for the International Assessment of Adult Competencies (PIAAC) is the most comprehensive international survey of adult cognitive skills. It builds on a previous measurement programme, the Adult Literacy and Lifeskills (ALL) survey, by expanding the skills domains assessed from literacy and numeracy to include problem-solving in technology-rich environments (OECD, 2012a). The survey was administered in twenty-five countries in 2011/12 and results will be published in late 2013.

13. Communication in the mother tongue; communication in foreign languages; mathematical competence and basic competences in science and technology; digital competence; learning to learn; social and civic competences; sense of initiative and entrepreneurship; and cultural awareness and expression.

Policy focus: Life skills education can help tackle HIV and AIDS

In 119 countries, only 24% of young women knew how to prevent transmission of HIV

By 2000, AIDS had become a full-blown development crisis presenting 'a grim picture with glimmers of hope' (UNAIDS, 2000). Its social and economic consequences were being felt widely not only in health but also in education and other areas. A decade later, hope appears to have triumphed over despair. The overall growth of the global AIDS pandemic has been stabilized by HIV prevention efforts and the natural course of HIV epidemics, with young people leading the change in adopting safer sexual behaviour.

Despite this success, there is no room for complacency. Many countries still have high rates of HIV prevalence (Box 1.4). Education has a crucial role in maintaining and reinforcing the positive trend, not only by increasing knowledge about HIV transmission and prevention, but also through life skills programmes that help young people use that knowledge to reduce their vulnerability to infection.[14]

Life skills education with a focus on HIV and AIDS encourages young people to adopt attitudes and behaviours that protect their health, for example by empowering them to negotiate

sexual relations and condom use. It does this by addressing psychosocial and interpersonal skills such as assertive communication, self-esteem, decision-making and negotiation. Life skills programmes that approach sensitive issues in ways that allow student engagement should be introduced to complement topics in the curriculum such as health education, sexuality education and broader HIV and AIDS education.

While it is difficult to analyse the results of life skills elements of wider HIV programmes, life skills education is likely to have played an important part in cases where HIV education coverage in schools has been high, where implementation has been generally effective and where life skills education has been combined with other prevention measures.

Despite education's key role in HIV prevention, knowledge remains low

Schooling can reduce the risk of HIV infection in various ways. It can help empower young women to assert their sexual and reproductive rights. Curriculum-based interventions also provide essential knowledge on HIV and AIDS, which is critical for young people before they become sexually active.

HIV prevalence remains high in some parts of the world. Yet HIV-related knowledge remains low. According to recent global estimates based on 119 countries that provided information, only 24% of young women and 36% of young men aged 15 to 24 were able to identify ways of preventing the sexual transmission of HIV and to reject major misconceptions about HIV transmission (UNAIDS, 2011a).

Young people who have stayed in school longer tend to be more aware of HIV and AIDS, and more inclined to take protective measures such as using condoms, seeking counselling and testing, and discussing AIDS with their partners, according to data from Demographic and Health Surveys in five sub-Saharan African countries (de Walque, 2009). Educated women are more

---

Box 1.4: HIV and AIDS remain prevalent in some countries

Efforts to control HIV prevalence and the AIDS epidemic have led to some recent successes. The number of new HIV infections fell by a fifth from 1999 to 2009. HIV prevalence fell by more than a quarter from 2001 to 2009 in thirty-three countries, including twenty-two in sub-Saharan Africa. Nevertheless, many countries still have high HIV prevalence rates. It is estimated that 34 million people globally were living with HIV in 2010 and that 2.7 million people became infected with HIV that year. And young people aged 15 to 24 accounted for 41% of all new HIV infections among adults in 2009.

Young women are particularly vulnerable, accounting for more than 60% of all young people living with HIV, and 71% of all young people living with HIV in sub-Saharan Africa. That region still bears the largest share of the global HIV burden, accounting for 68% of all people living with HIV and 70% of new HIV infections in 2010. Within the region, prevalence rates are much higher in southern and eastern Africa.

Sources: UNAIDS (2010, 2011b); UNICEF (2011b).

---

14. This section draws on Clarke and Aggleton (2012) and Samuels (2012).

likely to know that HIV cannot be transmitted by supernatural means and that using condoms can reduce the risk of transmission. They are also more likely to seek HIV testing during pregnancy, to know that HIV can be transmitted to an infant by breastfeeding and to know that this risk can be reduced by taking anti-retroviral drugs during pregnancy (UNESCO, 2011c).

Children need to be informed about the risks of HIV before they become sexually active. In southern and eastern Africa, where prevalence rates remain high, younger students' knowledge of HIV and AIDS is extremely low. This raises a concern that education is not reducing the risk of infection in societies where such intervention is most needed (Box 1.5).

Monitoring the availability of life skills programmes

Even where young people know about HIV and AIDS, this knowledge is not enough to ensure that they adopt behaviour that protects their own health and the health of others. Information about condom use and access to services, such as HIV testing, may not be applied if people are not empowered to say no to sex or negotiate condom use. Life skills education needs to be a key part of HIV- and AIDS-related health and sexuality education to ensure that increased knowledge translates into a change in attitudes and behaviour.

Many countries report that such programmes exist. There is also evidence of some having been successfully implemented. But far more needs to be done if these programmes are to reach the large numbers of young people still at risk of HIV infection.

The Dakar Framework for Action on Education for All included HIV and AIDS as a learning need under goal 3, stating that '[y]outh-friendly programmes must be made available to provide the information, skills, counselling and services needed to protect them from' the risk of HIV, and that '[c]urricula based on life-skills approaches should include all aspects of HIV/AIDS care and prevention' (UNESCO, 2000, pp. 16, 20). The importance of life skills education in the context of HIV and AIDS was also recognized in the Declaration of Commitment on HIV and AIDS, agreed at the first United Nations General Assembly Special Session (UNGASS), the annual high-level meeting bringing together all Member States to discuss responses to HIV and AIDS and make political commitments (United Nations, 2001).

The UNGASS Declaration set the ambitious target of ensuring that, by 2010, at least 95% of those aged 15 to 24 would have access to the information, education and services needed to develop the life skills required to reduce their vulnerability to HIV infection. Monitoring progress in this area has proved difficult given the broadness of the definition, which is difficult to translate into a time-bound, quantifiable target.

One of the twenty-five UNGASS core indicators attempts to monitor progress by identifying the percentage of schools that provided life skills-based HIV education for at least thirty hours in the last academic year. Unfortunately, there are no standard guidelines for what constitutes life skills education in response to HIV and AIDS, and the information is self-reported, making it difficult to establish its quality. Many countries do not differentiate between provision in primary and secondary schools. The response rate by ministries of education is also low: only 99 out of 192 countries reported on this indicator in either 2007 or 2009 (UNAIDS, 2011b). This result may be due in part to the fact that many ministries of education still view HIV and AIDS as the responsibility of health ministries.

Despite these problems, available data suggest that many countries are now providing life skills-based HIV education (Clarke and Aggleton, 2012). Twenty-three countries reported that all schools provided such education in the last academic year, including high-prevalence countries such as Kenya, South Africa and Zimbabwe (UNAIDS, 2010).

Effective life skills education can change attitudes and behaviour

Monitoring coverage is just a first step towards evaluating programme outcomes. It is not easy to identify whether life skills education programmes have had an impact on reducing HIV incidence. But it is possible to identify whether these programmes have an effect on skills, attitudes and behaviour. A review of twenty-five rigorous evaluations of life skills programmes for HIV prevention among

In 2009, only 99 out of 192 countries had monitored progress in providing life skills HIV education

Box 1.5: Schoolchildren are not learning enough about HIV and AIDS in southern and eastern Africa

Despite the widespread gains in HIV prevention, many school-children in southern and eastern Africa do not have adequate knowledge about HIV and AIDS. This is likely to hamper progress in further reducing new infections among youth.

In 2007, about 60,000 grade 6 students (aged around 13, on average) and 8,000 of their teachers in fourteen countries of southern and eastern Africa were assessed on their knowledge of HIV and AIDS. The test focused on the official curriculum frameworks for HIV education adopted by ministries of education in the countries participating. The results are worrying. They indicate that very few students know enough about HIV and AIDS. This is not a sound basis for behaviour that avoids risk of infection. On average, only 36% of students reached the minimum required knowledge levels and just 7% reached the desirable level.

Of particular concern is that groups that are vulnerable to HIV infection are also those with the least knowledge. In twelve of the fifteen countries, students of low socio-economic status or living in isolated rural areas scored significantly lower than those of high socio-economic status or living in urban areas. The magnitude of the difference varied among the countries. In Malawi, Uganda and Zambia, around 30% to 40% reached the minimum level, whether rich or poor. By contrast, inequality was particularly wide in Botswana and South Africa, two of the countries with the highest prevalence rates. In South Africa, more than half of students from rich households reached the minimum level, compared with just one in five of those from poor households (Figure 1.28). While socio-economic status and location are factors affecting levels of knowledge across countries, gender differences are less noticeable.

The results suggest ineffective implementation and possibly poor design of official curriculum frameworks for HIV education. Even in mainland Tanzania,

which had the best overall performance, 33% of grade 6 pupils reported that they had never attended HIV education classes during the current school year. Some teachers may not know enough about HIV and AIDS, but this does not appear to be the main constraint. Teachers fared far better in the tests than their students, with 99% at the minimum required knowledge levels and 82% at the desirable level. This result suggests that teachers are failing to pass on their knowledge adequately to their pupils.

Such evidence shows that far more needs to be done to ensure that schools play their part in communicating knowledge in countries that continue to experience high rates of new HIV infections among young people.

Sources: Clarke and Aggleton (2012); Dolata (2011); Dolata and Ross (2010); Ponera et al. (2011).

Figure 1.28: Knowledge about HIV and AIDS varies within countries

Percentage of grade 6 pupils who achieved minimal level of HIV and AIDS knowledge, by socio-economic status, 2007

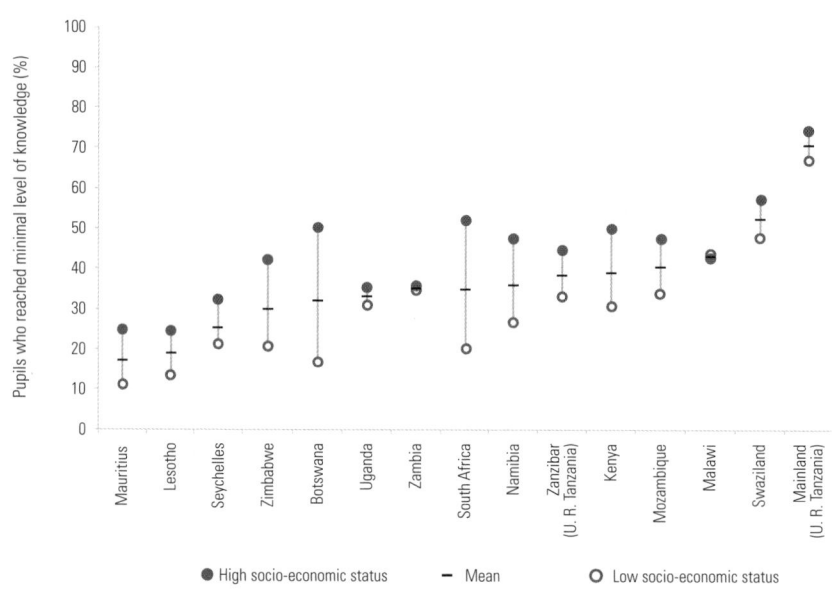

Note: Low and high socio-economic status refers to pupils in the bottom and top quarter, respectively, of the SACMEQ pupil socio-economic status scale within each country.
Source: SACMEQ team calculations based on 2007 data of the Southern and Eastern Africa Consortium for Monitoring Educational Quality.

young people from seventeen countries found that effective interventions had positive effects in these areas (Yankah and Aggleton, 2008).

Positive behavioural changes included increased delay of sexual debut, increased condom use at first sex and fewer sexual partners. For example, in rural Eastern Cape, South Africa,

the participatory Stepping Stones approach to sexual and reproductive health education was shown to be more effective than a single three-hour session on safer sex and HIV in terms of a decrease in the number of sexual partners and an increase in the correct use of condoms among men (Jewkes et al., 2007).

Life skills education in response to HIV and AIDS is delivered in a range of institutional contexts (including schools and youth drop-in centres), by teachers, facilitators and peer educators, and via the public, private and non-government sectors. The focus is sometimes on particular groups considered at risk. Successful examples bring a life skills approach to HIV and AIDS education, health education and sexuality education.

School-based programmes reach large numbers of young people

To reach a critical mass of young people, comprehensive programmes incorporating health, sexuality and HIV and AIDS education using a life skills approach need to be integrated into national curricula and be compulsory. In addition, successful programmes of this type have a planned and sequenced curriculum across primary and secondary school, incrementally adjusted to the age, stage and situation of the learner (Box 1.6) (UNESCO, 2011e).

To be successful, life skills education needs to adopt interactive, responsive and participatory methods that challenge young people to find new ways of relating to one another. In Mexico, a programme developed by a local NGO in collaboration with the Ministry of Public Education incorporated material on HIV in an existing life skills-based sexuality and contraception education programme. Through role-playing activities, students practised assertive communication and negotiation about sexual relations and the use of condoms under peer or partner pressure. Those who took part in the programme displayed positive changes in their attitude, self-efficacy, self-esteem, decision-making, communication and intentions – and these persisted for a year after the programme (Givaudan et al., 2007).

Teaching life skills education is not easy. Teachers need to be trained to adopt participatory approaches. Evaluations of the Health and Family Life Education curriculum framework initiative in five Caribbean countries showed that teachers needed more training in leading participatory activities. They usually focused on lesson content and used teaching methods that led to the life skills component being neglected and little student participation (UNESCO-IBE, 2009; UNICEF, 2009).

Teachers also need to be trained and supported to deliver life skills education on sensitive issues related to sexuality and HIV and AIDS. In Papua New Guinea, a compulsory pre-service teacher training programme on HIV and AIDS, in place since 2007, takes a participatory approach, asking student teachers to reflect on and debate controversial topics, prepare teaching plans for remote rural schools and generally connect what they have been learning with the context in which they live. This helps teachers not shy away from addressing sensitive issues (UNESCO, 2011d).

One reason for reluctance to teach these topics is the perception that doing so encourages promiscuity. It is vital to let everyone involved in such programmes know that the evidence does not support this belief. Rather, well-designed sexuality education programmes tend to delay the onset or frequency of sexual activity and increase condom use. A review of fifty-two

---

Box 1.6: Botswana curriculum boosts HIV and AIDS awareness

Botswana has made great strides in reducing the incidence of new adult HIV infections, halving the rate between 2001 and 2009. Yet the country still has the world's third highest prevalence rate among young men, and fourth highest among young women. Extending knowledge about HIV through education can be a vital way to maintain and accelerate progress.

To intensify HIV prevention efforts, the government introduced a national HIV and AIDS awareness curriculum in 2006, adopting a life skills education approach. The curriculum has been scaled up by the Ministry of Education, in close partnership with the Ministry of Health.

Sets of teacher guides and learner worksheets were designed in collaboration with teachers and other key parties. The materials are interactive, locally based, gender-balanced, culturally sensitive and adapted to learners' levels and ages. The worksheets present activities that help learners explore situations and practise appropriate responses. Teachers use stories, role-playing, poems and class discussions. Topics include self-awareness, goal-setting, stress management, social responsibility, healthy living, relationships, sexuality, risk reduction, and facts and myths about HIV and AIDS. The materials discuss HIV prevention, abstinence and delaying of sexual debut. For students 15 and older, the programme also discusses and provides referrals for condoms and other prevention methods.

Knowledge about HIV appears to be improving in the country. The percentage of young women aged 15 to 24 who correctly identified ways of preventing the sexual transmission of HIV and rejected major misconceptions increased from 28% to 45% between 2003 and 2009. Continued efforts to improve and expand life skills approaches to HIV and AIDS education could further reduce infection rates by helping young people translate their increased knowledge into safe attitudes and behaviour.

Sources: Education Development Center (2012); UNAIDS (2010).

In Estonia, schools partner with youth counselling centres to teach about HIV

studies of sex and HIV education programmes, focusing on children and young people aged 9 to 24 in both developed and developing countries, showed that only one led to significantly earlier onset of sexual activity (Kirby et al., 2007). In South Africa, a life skills education programme in KwaZulu-Natal province increased condom use at first sex by ten to twelve percentage points for 14- to 18-year-olds (Magnani et al., 2005).

Messages need to be adapted to different age groups, including young people who are already sexually active. The power structures that govern personal relationships also need to be recognized. In Kenya, the official curriculum promotes abstinence in order to completely eliminate risky behaviour. A randomized impact evaluation of an intervention with a life skills element demonstrated the strength of a more realistic approach. In the project, grade 8 students were shown a short video that highlighted the risks for adolescent girls of sexual relationships with older men. The screening was followed by a discussion supported by information on risks of infection. In schools that received the programme, the incidence of pregnancies with older partners among teenage girls declined by 61% compared with control schools (pregnancy served as a proxy for the incidence of unprotected sex). Access to information on various types of risky activity enabled girls to resist pressure from older men and reduce their exposure to risk while remaining sexually active (Duflo et al., 2011; Dupas, 2011).

Programmes outside schools are needed to reach some of those most at risk

School-based programmes do not reach some of those most at risk: those no longer in school. Also, where teaching about sexuality and HIV and AIDS in school is highly sensitive or taboo, programmes outside school may be the only means of getting knowledge and life skills education to young people.

Life skills education outside school is likely to be most effective when it complements other services targeting young people. The tailored activities, small group sizes, and voluntary and anonymous participation offered by youth drop-in centres can enhance reach and effectiveness. In Estonia, partnerships have developed between schools, which provide sexuality education,

and youth counselling centres. The centres support teachers in handling difficult topics using interactive methods. Once young people become acquainted with the centres and are assured that they are a friendly and safe social space, they are more likely to return for advice. The partnerships, together with increased availability of modern contraception and health system reforms, have contributed to significant improvements in youth sexual health indicators in Estonia (Haldre et al., 2012; Kivela et al., 2011).

Programmes run by youth organizations or using peer educators have proved an effective means of delivering life skills education, as young people are often more comfortable talking to their peers. One example is the Together We Can programme, a partnership between national Red Cross societies and ministries of health in Guyana, Haiti and the United Republic of Tanzania. Young people have been mobilized to deliver HIV-prevention messages, offer life skills training and provide education and support to other youth (American Red Cross, 2010, 2012).

Peer educators have also helped improve knowledge about HIV in the Grassroot Soccer programme, an out-of-school activity for girls and boys aged 12 to 18 in several high-prevalence countries.[15] Over 490,000 young people have participated. The curriculum uses activities and games to provide comprehensive HIV prevention and life skills education. Football stars and Grassroot Soccer graduates act as educators, community advocates and spokespeople. Teachers have become a key part of the programme in some countries, in an attempt to improve its chances of being sustained, replicated and scaled up.

Ten evaluations of the Grassroot Soccer programme in seven countries have shown positive effects on knowledge, attitudes and communication related to HIV. A study in Zimbabwe showed that the proportion of students who knew where to go for help with HIV-related problems increased from 47% to 76%, and the proportion of those who believed condoms were effective increased from 49% to 71% (Botcheva and Huffman, 2004; Grassroot Soccer, 2012; Kaufman et al., 2010).

---

15. Grassroot Soccer operates flagship sites in South Africa, Zambia and Zimbabwe, and has helped design and launch projects in Botswana, the Dominican Republic, Guatemala, Ethiopia, Kenya, Lesotho, Malawi, Namibia, Sudan and the United Republic of Tanzania.

Whether life skills programmes are offered inside or outside formal education, they need to reflect the fact that boys and girls have different needs and vulnerabilities. Single gender groups, with a teacher or facilitator of the same gender, can foster more open communication on sensitive issues. For example, recognizing the particular vulnerability of women aged 15 to 19, the Sister 2 Sister Initiative in Malawi targets young women with life skills education provided by older young women ('big sisters'). The training is extracurricular: while it supplements the long-established formal life skills curriculum, it can also be delivered to young women who are out of school. Overall, the programme has led to increased knowledge in the areas of sexuality, HIV, condom use, multiple and concurrent partners, age-disparate relationships, and health-seeking behaviours, with evidence that knowledge is sustained over time (Bakaroudis, 2011).

Strengthening and mainstreaming life skills education

Life skills education programmes are often implemented through NGOs. They tend to be extracurricular, voluntary, small-scale initiatives, and are generally not recognized by governments. They can provide useful lessons, however, and can gradually be integrated into a national curriculum, as has occurred in Indonesia, Kenya and Uganda (Leerlooijer et al., 2011; UNESCO, 2011e).

In order to replicate, scale up and incorporate such programmes into public education, it is crucial to explain the need for them to communities and others who will be involved. This is especially true in settings where talking about sex and sexuality is politically or culturally sensitive. To be effective, such advocacy needs to be budgeted and planned from the outset (Box 1.7).

In Indonesia, during the development and implementation of a secondary school-based HIV prevention programme delivered through life skills education, advocacy activities that targeted a range of interested parties – including local government and education authorities, school management and teachers, religious and community leaders, and students and parents – were found to be a key factor in their acceptance of the programme (Pohan et al., 2011).

Conclusion

Life skills programmes that focus on young people are a vital component of a comprehensive HIV prevention response. Adequate support and training for teachers and facilitators are crucial. Life skills programmes outside formal education, particularly involving youth as facilitators and mentors, can complement school-based approaches and broaden coverage to reach young people who are most at risk.

Box 1.7: Scaling up life skills and HIV education in India and Nigeria

Extending life skills education with a focus on HIV and bringing it into the mainstream can be especially challenging in contexts where this is a particularly sensitive issue. Programmes in India and Nigeria show that talking the issues through with those involved can lead to their acceptance.

In India, the Adolescent Education Programme aimed to empower young people to respond to real-life situations by adopting a life skills approach. Development began in 1998 and the programme was launched in six pilot states in 2002. However, it was shelved between 2003 and 2006 because of opposition to the content of the curriculum, which was seen as being too explicit and targeting children who were too young. Moreover, the programme's development was viewed as a top-down process with limited consultation at the state and district levels.

The programme was reintroduced in the state of Odisha in 2007 as the Adolescent Reproductive and Sexual Health curriculum, after consultation with a range of interested parties, including adolescents themselves. The consultation highlighted the need for close involvement of family and community members, and for training and support for teachers. Implemented by the state government, the compulsory curriculum targeting 13- to 16-year-olds is being scaled up to all districts. A recent evaluation in five states, including Odisha, found that knowledge of HIV and AIDS was higher, and discriminatory attitudes lower, among students and teachers in schools that had been part of the programme.

In Nigeria, the National Sexuality Education Curriculum for Upper Primary, Secondary and Tertiary Institutions was approved in 2001. In response to concerns from parents, politicians and religious leaders that the curriculum was too explicit, discussions on condoms and contraception were removed and the title was changed to Family Life and HIV Education. After being successfully scaled up in Lagos state, the programme is being extended to all primary and junior secondary schools in all states, with funding from the Global Fund to Fight AIDS, Tuberculosis and Malaria. The 2010 Nigeria Education Data Survey found that 59% of parents and guardians with a child in primary or secondary school were aware that the curriculum was being taught.

The exclusion of key topics could be a problem, particularly in a country with a generalized HIV epidemic and with a large and vulnerable population of young people. But because the concerns were taken into account, and individual states were allowed to adapt the curriculum to suit their socio-cultural characteristics, many original objectives of the curriculum continue to be met, and discussions about reintroducing key topics continue.

Sources: McManus and Dhar (2008); Nigeria Federal Ministry of Education (2011); Samuels et al. (forthcoming); TARSHI (2008); UNESCO (2011e); UNFPA (2009, 2011).

Goal 4 — Improving levels of adult literacy

Achieving a 50% improvement in levels of adult literacy by 2015, especially for women, and equitable access to basic and continuing education for all adults.

Highlights

- Most countries will miss goal 4, some by a large margin. There were still 775 million adults who could not read or write in 2010, about two-thirds of whom were women.

- Globally the adult literacy rate has increased over the past two decades, from 76% in 1985–1994 to 84% in 2005–2010 but, partly because the world's population has grown, the number of illiterate adults has fallen modestly from 881 million to 775 million.

- Of the forty countries that had an adult literacy rate below 90% in 1998–2001, only three are expected to meet the goal of reducing their illiteracy rate by 50%.

- The global youth literacy rate stood at 90% in 2005–2010, equivalent to 122 million young people. This means that the world is not in a position to eradicate illiteracy by 2015 or any time soon thereafter.

Table 1.7: Key indicators for goal 4

	Illiterate adults				Adult literacy rates				Youth literacy rates			
	Total		Women		Total		Gender parity index		Total		Gender parity index	
	2005–10	Change since 1985–94	1985–94	2005–10	1985–94	2005–10	1985–94	2005–10	1985–94	2005–10	1985–94	2005–10
	(000)	(%)	(%)	(%)	(%)	(%)	(F/M)	(F/M)	(%)	(%)	(F/M)	(F/M)
World	774 756	-12	63	64	76	84	0.85	0.90	83	90	0.90	0.95
Low income countries	174 291	17	60	60	51	63	0.69	0.81	60	74	0.79	0.93
Lower middle income countries	469 452	2	62	65	59	71	0.71	0.78	71	84	0.80	0.89
Upper middle income countries	122 305	-53	67	68	82	94	0.86	0.95	94	99	0.96	1.00
High income countries	…	…	…	…	…	…	…	…	…	…	…	…
Sub-Saharan Africa	169 313	27	62	62	53	63	0.68	0.76	66	72	0.80	0.87
Arab States	50 286	-3	63	66	55	75	0.62	0.79	74	89	0.78	0.93
Central Asia	302	-68	77	64	98	99	0.98	1.00	100	100	1.00	1.00
East Asia and the Pacific	99 156	-57	69	71	82	94	0.84	0.95	95	99	0.96	1.00
South and West Asia	406 419	1	60	64	47	63	0.57	0.70	60	81	0.70	0.86
Latin America and the Caribbean	35 805	-15	55	55	86	91	0.97	0.98	93	97	1.01	1.00
North America and Western Europe	…	…	…	…	…	…	…	…	…	…	…	…
Central and Eastern Europe	6 794	-44	79	77	96	98	0.96	0.98	98	99	0.98	1.00

Notes: Data are for the most recent year available during the period specified. Adults are those aged 15 and over; youth are those aged 15 to 24. Gender parity is reached when the gender parity index is between 0.97 and 1.03.
Sources: Annex, Statistical Tables 2 and 10; UIS database.

Goal 4: Improving levels of adult literacy

Literacy is crucial for adults' social and economic well-being – and for that of their children. Yet progress on this goal has been very limited, largely as a result of government and donor indifference [Panel 1.7].

The global adult illiteracy rate was 16% in 2010, corresponding to about 775 million adults, almost two-thirds of whom are women. Progress in reducing adult illiteracy has slowed in recent years. After a decrease of almost 100 million in the 1990s, the number of illiterate adults fell by less than 8 million between 1995–2004 and 2005–2010. It is projected that by 2015 there will still be 738 million illiterate adults, a reduction of only 16% since the 1985–1994 literacy data reference period.

Over half of all illiterate adults live in South and West Asia, and over one-fifth in sub-Saharan Africa. Literacy rates have been growing too slowly in sub-Saharan Africa to counter the effects of population growth. As a result, the number of illiterate adults in the region has actually grown by 27% over the past twenty years, reaching 169 million in 2010. In South and West Asia the illiteracy rate has fallen at a faster pace, although the number of illiterate adults has increased slightly, by 6 million.

While youth illiteracy rates are lower than rates among adults overall – reflecting improved education in recent generations – about 10% of youth remain illiterate globally. This is equivalent to around 122 million young people. At 28%, sub-Saharan Africa has replaced South and West Asia as the region with the highest youth illiteracy rate. In absolute terms, 45 million illiterate young people live in sub-Saharan Africa and 62 million in South and West Asia.

Global literacy estimates are based on national surveys and censuses, which include questions about whether the respondent or household members have been to school and are literate. This approach can overestimate actual literacy levels, in part because respondents may be reluctant to reveal that they cannot read or write. Direct assessments of literacy skills provide a much better understanding of literacy levels than either self-declarations of the ability to read and write, or the number of years of formal education.

The UNESCO Institute for Statistics Literacy Assessment and Monitoring Programme (LAMP) is an attempt to measure literacy and numeracy skills directly and draws attention to the hitherto neglected role of literacy practices and literate environments in maintaining literacy skills [Panel 1.8]. Analysis of direct literacy tests from household surveys shows that completing primary school does not ensure that such skills are acquired by all [Panel 1.9].

On a global scale, few illiterate adults live in rich countries. Even in high income OECD countries, however, large numbers of adults have very poor literacy skills. There is a strong association between poor literacy skills and marginalization, indicating a need for innovative ways to provide more and better adult literacy programmes [goal 4, policy focus].

Education for All Global Monitoring Report 2 0 1 2

Panel 1.7: Progress in reducing adult illiteracy has been slow

The majority of the world's 775 million illiterate adults are concentrated in a small group of countries. Of the countries with data, ten have more than 10 million illiterate adults each, accounting for 72% of the global population of illiterate adults (Figure 1.29A).

These countries have experienced different rates of progress over the past two decades. India alone contains 37% of the global number of illiterate adults. A large improvement in its adult literacy rate, from 48% in 1991 to 63% in 2006, has been counterbalanced by population growth, so the total number of illiterate adults in the country has remained stagnant over the period. In Nigeria, the number of illiterate adults has risen by over 10 million between 1991 and 2010. In recognition of the problem, the government announced in April 2012 an initiative to revitalize adult and youth literacy programmes, aiming to educate up to 5 million illiterate adults over the next three years.

China, by contrast, has managed to reduce the number of illiterate adults by 66%, from 183 million to 62 million. This has been achieved thanks to a rise in the literacy rate from 78% to 94%, combined with a lower population growth rate. Indonesia has seen similar success, improving its literacy rate from 82% to 93% and reducing the number of illiterate adults by almost 9 million.

Other countries have smaller numbers of illiterate adults, but they make up a large share of the population. Eleven countries have an adult literacy rate below 50%, eight of which are in the western part of sub-Saharan Africa (Figure 1.29B).

Most countries will miss goal 4, some by a large margin. Among seventy-three countries with adult literacy data for both the 1998–2001 and 2008–2011 periods, forty countries had literacy rates below 90% in the earlier period. Of these, only three are expected to meet the goal of halving their illiteracy rate by 2015: the Plurinational State of Bolivia, Equatorial Guinea and Malaysia – each of which started with a literacy rate very close to 90% (Figure 1.30).

But of the thirty-seven countries not expected to meet the goal, some will be close. In particular, fourteen countries will come within less than five percentage points of the target. These include two countries

---

Figure 1.29: Almost three-quarters of the world's illiterate adults live in just ten countries

A. Countries with more than 10 million illiterate adults, 2005 to 2010.

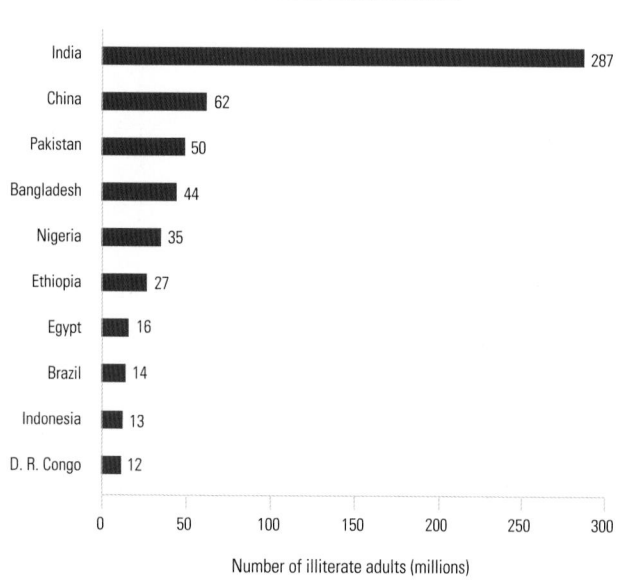

B. Countries with an adult literacy rate below 50%, 2005 to 2010.

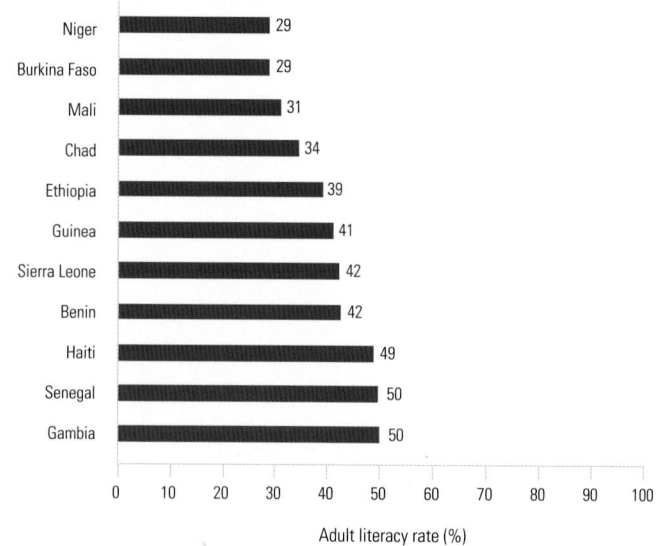

Source: Annex, Statistical Table 2.

Figure 1.30: Most countries will miss the adult literacy target, some by a wide margin

Adult illiteracy rate, 1998–2001 to 2015 (projection)

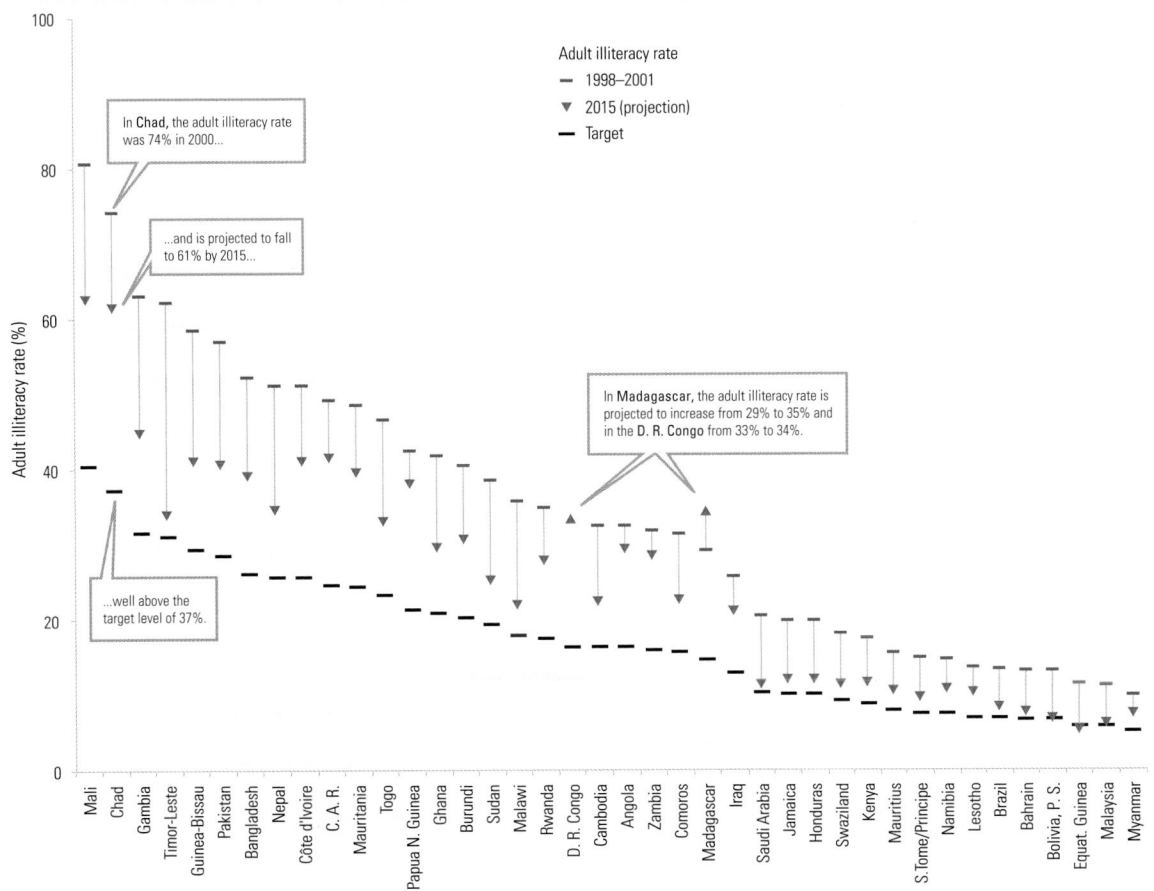

Note: The countries shown in the figure are those for which a projection to 2015 was feasible and that had an adult illiteracy rate above 10% in 1998–2001.

Sources: Annex, Statistical Table 2; UIS database.

with weak starting points that have made significant progress. Malawi increased its adult literacy rate from 64% in 1998 to 75% in 2010 and is expected to reach 79% by 2015, while the literacy rate in Timor-Leste improved from 38% in 2001 to 58% in 2010 and is expected to reach 67% by 2015.

Six countries will miss the goal by a particularly wide margin, at least fifteen percentage points. Among them, the Democratic Republic of the Congo and Madagascar will have experienced declines in the adult literacy rate over the period. The Central African Republic and Papua New Guinea recorded only small gains. By contrast, Chad and Mali experienced significant gains from very low starting points. The adult literacy rate in Mali is expected to have doubled between 1998 and 2015.

Within the group of seventy-three countries for which comparisons over time are possible, the number of countries which have achieved gender parity increased from 26 to 34. The eight countries that have made the greatest strides in women's literacy in the past decade are, in increasing order of improvement, Saudi Arabia, Nepal, Cambodia, Equatorial Guinea, Malawi, the Gambia, Timor-Leste and Chad. All countries that started with gender disparity in literacy in 1998–2001 made progress except for Zambia.

Even so, there were still 81 out of the 146 countries with data for 2005–2010 in which more women than men were illiterate. Of these, twenty-one displayed extreme gender disparity, with a gender parity index (GPI) below 0.70. The Niger's GPI was the lowest, at 0.35.

Panel 1.8: LAMP deepens understanding of literacy contexts

Information on literate environments and literacy practices is of crucial importance for understanding the presence of literacy skills (OECD and Statistics Canada, 2000; Statistics Canada and OECD, 2005). The UNESCO Institute for Statistics Literacy Assessment and Monitoring Programme (LAMP) is providing new evidence linking actual reading and numeracy skills with information on the environments in which these skills are acquired and maintained.

Most literacy skills are acquired in schools or literacy centres, but whether adults maintain or lose these skills depends on whether they engage in certain literacy practices, such as reading a newspaper, reading bills or using a computer. They also need to live in environments where these practices are encouraged or, at least, possible. This can be affected, for example, by the availability of stores in the community that sell newspapers.

To understand the processes involved in acquiring literacy skills, LAMP collects background information on a wide range of literate environments and literacy practices. This information is used to develop measures of 'literate environment density' at individual or household level and at community level (Guadalupe and Cardoso, 2011).

Adult literacy rates vary widely among countries implementing LAMP, from 29% in the Niger to 97% in Mongolia.[16] The four countries that have already carried out the LAMP main assessment – Jordan, Mongolia, Palestine and Paraguay – have all achieved a relatively high literacy rate. Their literacy practices differ, however. The percentage of adults who reported reading for pleasure ranged from 36% in Palestine to 60% in Mongolia. The use of a computer varied from 35% in Paraguay to 57% in Jordan. Reading bills, invoices or budget tables was twice as frequent in Paraguay as in Mongolia (Figure 1.31).

Figure 1.31: Even among countries with similar literacy rates, people use their literacy skills in different ways

Frequency of selected practices included in the individual literate environment density measure, Jordan, Mongolia, Palestine and Paraguay, 2010/2011

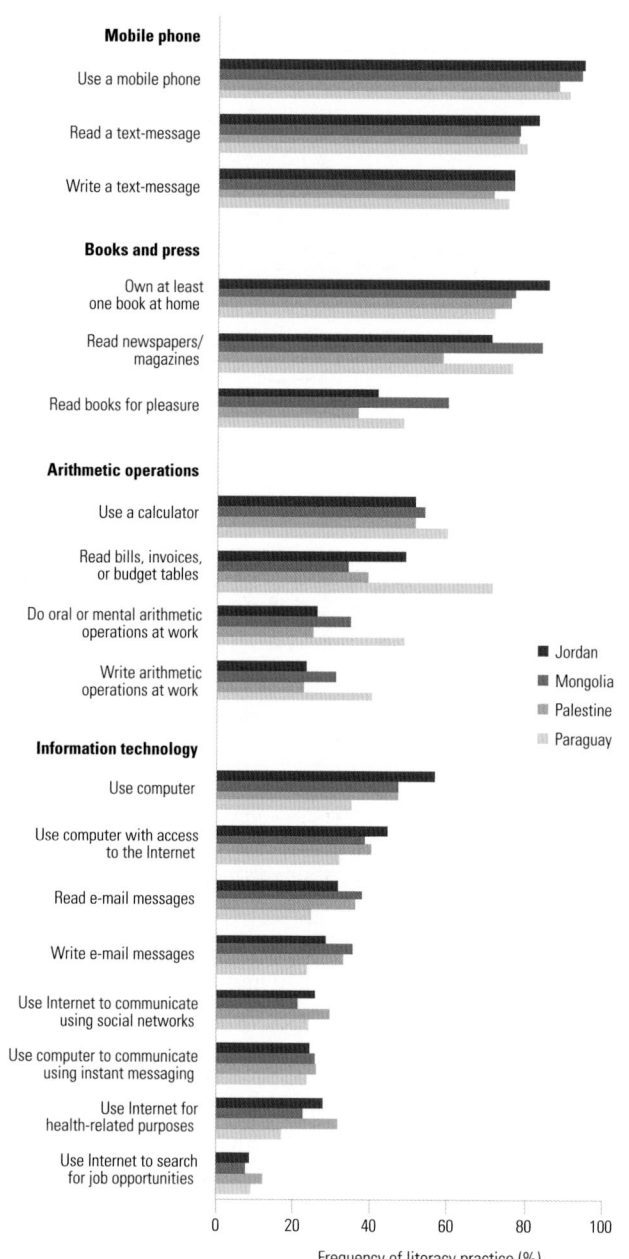

Source: UIS, preliminary analysis of LAMP data.

16. The main assessment was conducted in Jordan, Mongolia, Palestine and Paraguay in 2010–11. In addition, field trials have taken place in El Salvador, Morocco, the Niger and Viet Nam. Several other countries are going through the initial stages of the process, including Afghanistan, Jamaica, the Lao People's Democratic Republic and Namibia.

Some community characteristics of the literate environment are found to be relevant to all countries, such as the availability of public lighting, street names and dwelling numbers, newsstands, and public libraries. Other characteristics on which information has been collected are relevant only for particular countries, such as cinemas, public billboards and advertisements. Health centres are also included as an indicator of literate environment density. This is because in many developing countries they expose people to printed materials, such as posters, prescriptions and medicine labels.

Initial LAMP data show large differences in community characteristics that can help maintain literacy skills. For example, only 25% of the population in Mongolia has access to a store or kiosk that sells printed materials, compared with 85% in Palestine. While 28% of dwellings are numbered in Palestine, 91% are in Jordan (Figure 1.32).

Figure 1.32: Community characteristics that help maintain literacy differ widely by country

Population living in communities with selected services included in the community literate environment density measure, Jordan, Mongolia, Palestine and Paraguay, 2010/2011

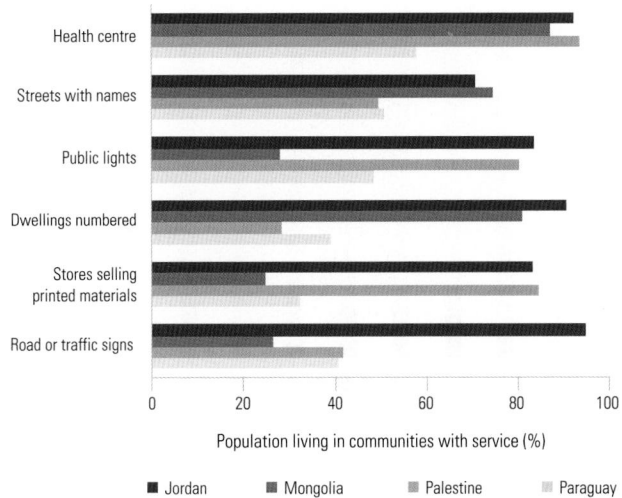

Population living in communities with service (%)

■ Jordan   ■ Mongolia   ■ Palestine   ■ Paraguay

Source: UIS, preliminary analysis of LAMP data.

Panel 1.9: Completing primary school does not guarantee literacy for all

Curricula around the world expect children to learn to read by the end of the second year of primary school (Abadzi, 2010). In practice, it is more commonly assumed that it takes four or five years of school for all children to become literate (UNESCO, 2005). New analysis of household surveys prepared for this Report reveals that many children in poor countries have not become literate even by the time they have completed primary school.

Recent Demographic and Health Surveys ask respondents who have not attended secondary school to read a short sentence from a card.[17] The interviewer records whether respondents can read all or part of the sentence, and so whether they are literate or semi-literate.

Evidence from surveys in ten low income and lower middle income countries shows that a considerable proportion of young adults are illiterate or semi-literate. One reason is that some still never make it to school or are likely to have dropped out of school early. But that is by no means the only reason. Many young people aged 15 to 29 had not become literate even after completing

six years of school. To take one example, in Ghana 51% of the young women in this category and 37% of the young men were illiterate in 2008. In addition, 28% of the young women and 33% of the young men were semi-literate (Figure 1.33).

Children who leave school after completing only six years are likely to have different characteristics from those who stay in school longer. Many of the early leavers probably struggled at school, which is often one reason for children not continuing to secondary school. Nevertheless, their experience carries important lessons. As countries strive to achieve universal primary education, more children from disadvantaged backgrounds enter school but are unlikely to progress beyond the primary level. Schools need to ensure that they are given the necessary support to learn effectively.

Comparing this cohort with an earlier cohort of students can give some insights into changes in the quality of education. For example, in Kenya many of those aged 15 to 29 in 2003 went to primary school in the early 2000s. Of those young women who left school after six years in 2008, 43% had only partial literacy skills or none

Figure 1.33: For many young people, six years of school are insufficient to build literacy skills

Literacy status, men and women aged 15 to 29 who completed only six years of school, selected countries, 2005 to 2011 (%)

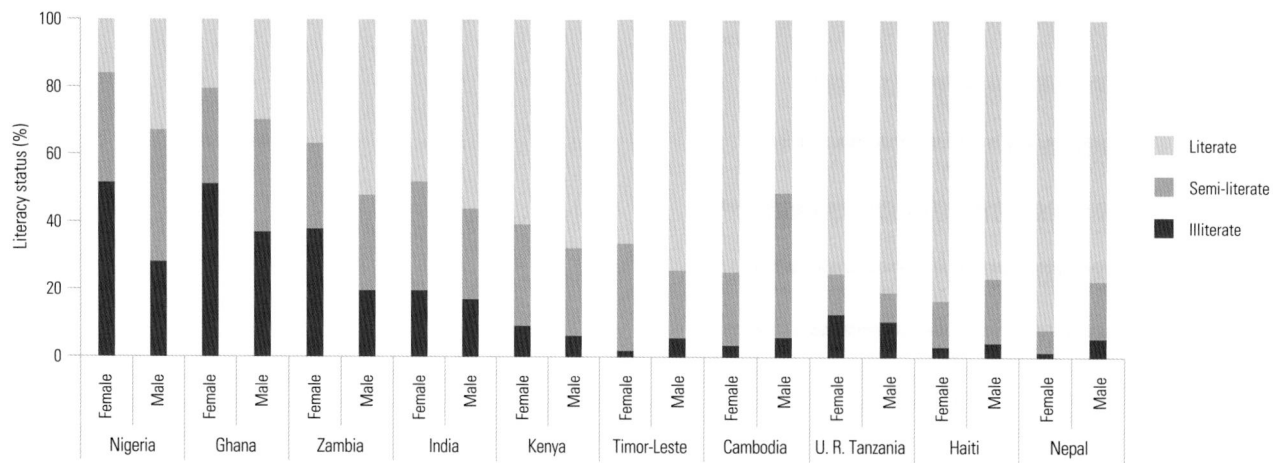

Source: EFA Global Monitoring Report team analysis (2012) based on Demographic and Health Survey data.

17. If respondents have attended secondary school, they are assumed to be literate and the question is not asked.

Figure 1.34: Literacy skills are not improving across sub-Saharan Africa

Literacy status, women aged 15 to 29 who completed only six years of school, selected countries (%)

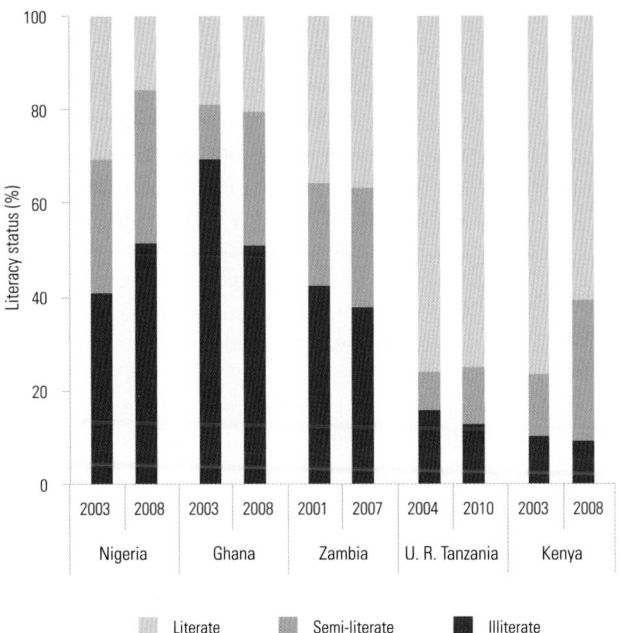

Source: EFA Global Monitoring Report team analysis (2012) based on Demographic and Health Survey data.

Figure 1.35: In Ghana, not even lower secondary school is sufficient to guarantee literacy

Literacy status, women aged 15 to 29, by highest grade completed, Ghana, 2003 and 2008 (%)

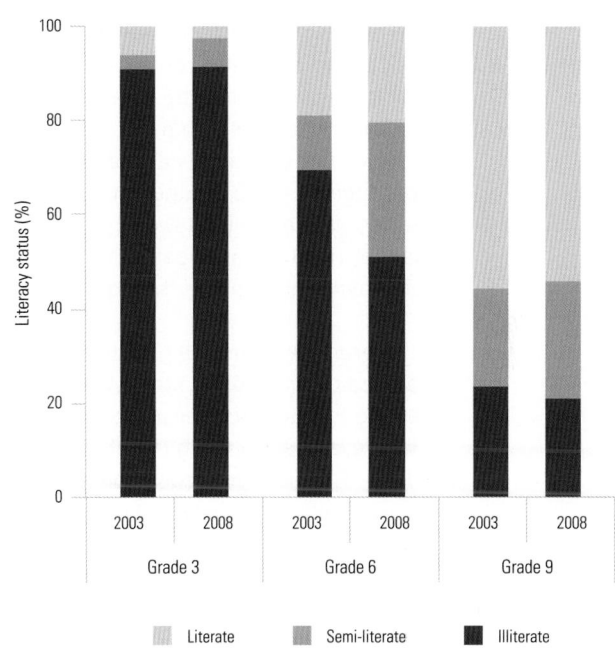

Source: EFA Global Monitoring Report team analysis (2012) based on the 2003 and 2008 Ghana Demographic and Health Surveys.

at all, compared with 20% five years earlier. In Nigeria, the percentage of young women still illiterate after six years of school increased from 41% in 2003 to 52% in 2008 (Figure 1.34). This suggests that the perceived deterioration in the quality of education in some African countries is not associated only with the more recent increase in enrolment but, rather, that there is a chronic quality problem.

How many years of school are necessary to guarantee that all children master basic literacy skills? The answer is likely to vary from country to country. In some

cases, even reaching lower secondary school may be insufficient. In Ghana, illiteracy rates decline with years in school, but even among those who had completed nine years of school in 2008, 21% were illiterate, and about a quarter were only partially literate in both 2003 and 2008 (Figure 1.35).

This evidence suggests that countries need to monitor the acquisition of literacy skills more closely, and should not assume that increasing the number of years children spend in school will soon eradicate adult illiteracy.

Policy focus:
Strengthening adult literacy in rich countries

In high income countries, the universal spread of schooling has consigned high levels of illiteracy to the distant past. Yet significant numbers of adults still have very poor literacy skills – unable to use reading, writing and calculation effectively in their day to day lives. Those facing social disadvantage, including the poor, migrants and ethnic minorities, are particularly affected. Policies do not sufficiently address the extent of poor literacy skills among adults in rich countries, leaving millions without the basic skills they need to participate fully in productive employment and improve their quality of life.

Adult literacy skills in rich countries need to be tackled on two fronts: strengthening formal schooling to assure better adult literacy skills in the future, and supporting the literacy learning of adults. This section focuses on the second strategy in high income OECD countries.

In high literacy societies, people with poor reading and writing skills are often stigmatized and suffer from low confidence, and so tend to keep their struggles with literacy under wraps. This poses a major challenge for adult literacy initiatives. Programmes that have clear benefits for using literacy skills in daily life can encourage adults to participate while avoiding the stigma that can be associated with their involvement in them.

Low adult literacy skills in rich countries are a wider problem than is often recognized

Conventional data on illiteracy, measuring those who are unable to read or write at all, vastly underestimate the share of adults who have very poor literacy skills in rich countries, which the most reliable estimates put as high as one in five.

Conventional estimates based on projections for a very few countries suggest that around

8 million adults in developed countries were unable to read or write in 2008, giving an illiteracy rate below 1% for adults and close to zero for those aged 15 to 24 (UNESCO, 2011c, Statistical Table 2).[18] But such figures tell us little about actual literacy and numeracy skills because they are derived by asking people to estimate their own skills, or those of household members, by answering a simple yes/no question. In reality, literacy is a continuum, from complete unfamiliarity with written letters and numbers to the ability to communicate via long and complex written texts quickly and with ease. And it can only be accurately measured by directly testing people's abilities.

Adult Literacy and Life Skills (ALL) surveys undertaken in nine high income OECD countries assess skill proficiency on a five-level scale (OECD and Statistics Canada, 2011).[19] A person only at level 1 in prose literacy can at most locate a single piece of information in a text that is identical or synonymous to the information in the question. Even if they can read, adults at that level may be unable to apply this skill to simple tasks, such as determining the correct amount of medicine to take from information printed on the package (OECD and Statistics Canada, 2011).

For the nine countries surveyed, the average share of respondents achieving no more than level 1 in prose literacy was about 22%, or 70 million adults; national shares ranged from 8% in Norway to 47% in Italy. The proportion at level 1 for numeracy was even higher – almost 27% on average, or 84 million adults (Figure 1.36).

47% of adults in Italy have poor literacy skills

18. As of 2012 the UNESCO Institute for Statistics is no longer providing figures on adult illiteracy for the North America and Western Europe region or the group of high income countries.

19. The ALL surveys covered Canada, Italy, Norway, Switzerland and the United States in 2003 and Australia, Hungary, the Netherlands and New Zealand in 2006–2008. They assessed prose literacy, document literacy, numeracy and problem solving. The results for prose literacy (the knowledge and skills needed to understand and use information from continuous texts) and document literacy (the knowledge and skills required to locate and use information contained in non-continuous texts such as forms, maps and charts) are very similar.

Figure 1.36: Many adults in rich countries have low literacy and numeracy skills
Distribution of population aged 16 to 65 by skill level, selected countries, 2003 to 2008

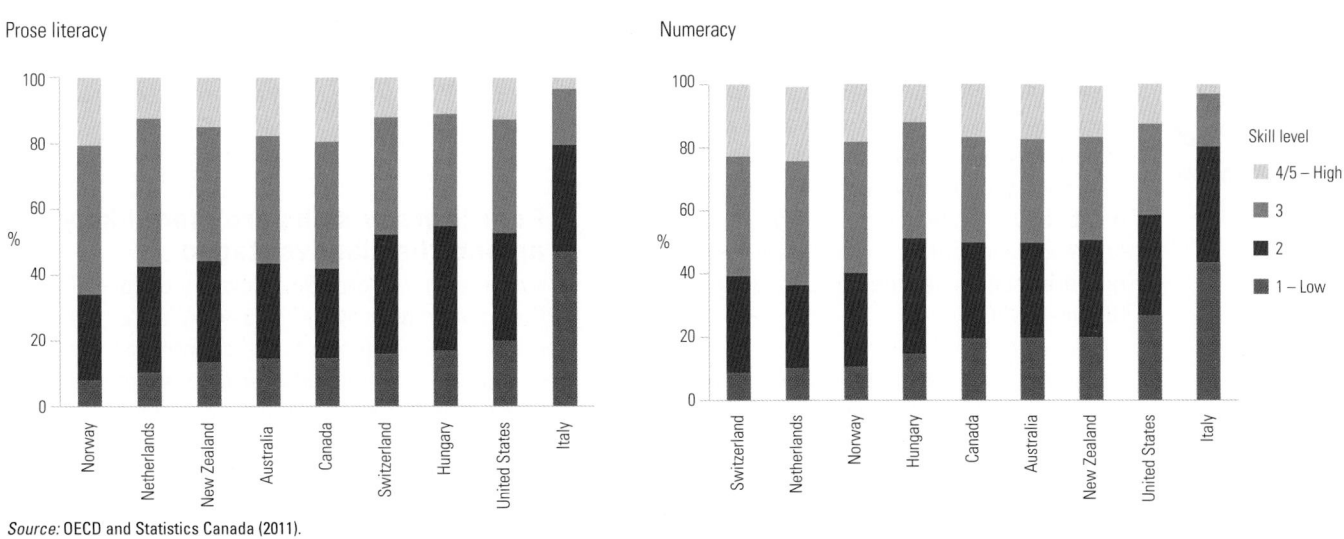

Prose literacy

Numeracy

Skill level
- 4/5 – High
- 3
- 2
- 1 – Low

Source: OECD and Statistics Canada (2011).

If it is assumed that literacy rates in the nine countries (which account for 43% of the population aged 15 to 64 in the thirty-one high income OECD countries) are representative of the total population, that means close to 160 million adults in high income OECD countries have poor literacy skills.

While national literacy assessments are not comparable from country to country, because of differences in sampling, methodology and definitions, they confirm that poor literacy skills are a significant problem. For example:

■ In Germany, a 2010 assessment estimated that 14.5% of the population aged 18 to 64, or about 7.5 million people, were functionally illiterate. Of these 0.6% could not read, understand or write single words; 3.9% could read, understand and write single words but only letter by letter; and 10% could read single sentences, but not continuous text, such as instructions (Grotlüschen and Riekmann, 2011).

■ In France, a 2004/05 survey estimated that 9% of the population aged 18 to 65, or about 3.1 million people, did not possess basic

reading, writing and arithmetic skills to write a shopping list, understand their child's school report or write a cheque (ANLCI, 2008).

■ In Scotland (United Kingdom), a 2009 survey estimated that 8% of the population aged 16 to 65 were at level 1 in prose literacy (St. Clair et al., 2010).

Low educational attainment leads to low adult literacy skills

Wide differences in educational attainment across countries are partly responsible for observed literacy levels. In Italy, which suffers from particularly low average levels of literacy skills, only 47% of those aged 16 to 65 have at least some upper secondary school, compared with 85% in Norway, where average literacy skills are the highest (OECD and Statistics Canada, 2011).

Literacy and numeracy skills tend to decline with age, partly because the expansion of secondary schooling is a phenomenon of recent decades. In the Netherlands and Norway, while 5% of those aged 16 to 25 have very poor literacy skills, for those aged 46 to 65 the share is 15% (OECD and Statistics Canada, 2011).

An estimated 160 million adults in rich countries have poor literacy skills

In the United States, 43% of adults with low literacy skills were poor

Even controlling for education and other individual characteristics, however, older adults are more likely to have very poor literacy skills, both because the quality of education has improved and because people lose skills as they age. Those with less education are more affected by skill loss as they get older. For those with post-secondary education, numeracy skills do not begin to decline before age 40, whereas for people without post-secondary schooling, numeracy skills decline throughout adulthood (Figure 1.37).

Those with less education not only have lower numeracy skills as they enter adulthood, but are also more likely to find employment in low skill occupations that do not require the use and development of numeracy skills. They are also less likely to benefit from lifelong education opportunities such as adult education courses and learning on the job.

Figure 1.37: Adults lose numeracy skills over time, but those with less education lose them faster

Average numeracy score by age and education, selected countries, 2003 to 2008

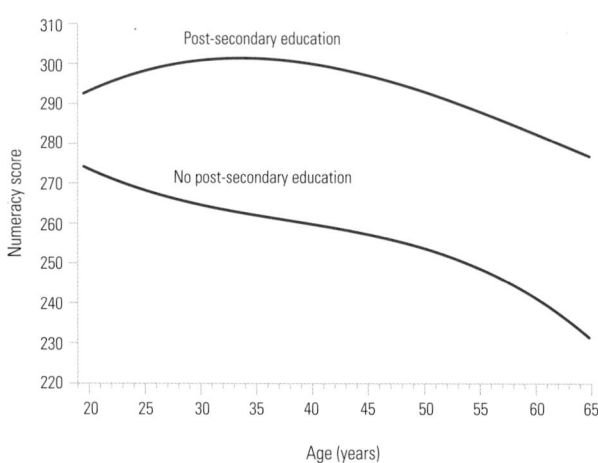

Note: The data represent averages for the countries that participated in the ALL surveys.
Source: OECD and Statistics Canada (2011).

But educational attainment is not the only determinant of adult literacy and numeracy skill levels. Even young people still in school at the age of 15 can have very poor literacy skills that may persist into adulthood. In surveys carried out in 2009 by the OECD's Programme for International Student Assessment, the proportion of young people in school who

performed below level 2, the level required to demonstrate reading ability that enables them to participate productively in life, ranged from under 10% in Finland and the Republic of Korea to over 25% in Austria, Israel and Luxembourg (OECD, 2010d).

Poor literacy skills are more likely among the disadvantaged

Average figures provide an overall picture of the scale of poor adult literacy skills. Yet they mask wide disparities within countries. Even in countries with higher overall levels of adult literacy skills, certain groups continue to face disadvantage linked to characteristics such as gender, poverty, ethnicity, language and disability:

■ *Gender:* Women scored higher in prose literacy in each of the ALL survey countries except Italy and Switzerland. Men scored higher in numeracy everywhere except Hungary, but the gap was smaller for the youngest adults, especially in Canada, Italy and New Zealand (OECD and Statistics Canada, 2011).

■ *Socio-economic status:* Poverty can have a strong effect on literacy even after controlling for education. For example, in the United States 43% of adults with very low literacy skills were poor, compared with only 4% of adults scoring at the highest literacy level (Kirsch et al., 2002). In the United Kingdom, among people born in 1970 who were in the lowest literacy category, 30% had fathers who were working in unskilled or partly skilled manual jobs when they were born compared with only 17% for those in the highest literacy category (Parsons and Bynner, 2007).

■ *Language and immigration status:* In the nine ALL surveys, immigrants were more likely to have very poor literacy skills in the assessment language than native-born people. The disadvantage was particularly severe for those whose mother tongue was different from the assessment language: this group was three to six times more likely than the native-born to score at level 1 (OECD and Statistics Canada, 2011). In the Netherlands and the United States almost half the immigrants whose native tongue was not the assessment language scored at level 1.

■ *Ethnicity:* Ethnic and other minorities may have faced marginalization in education and the labour market, reducing their chances of acquiring literacy skills. Their schooling experiences have often been marred by poor quality and culturally inappropriate education, leading to low achievement and high dropout rates. Notably, throughout much of Europe, conventional illiteracy rates among the Roma have been estimated to be very high; 11% in Poland and 35% in Greece cannot read or write at all (European Union Agency for Fundamental Rights, 2009). In Australia, Canada, New Zealand and the United States, indigenous populations have lower literacy skills (Box 1.8).

35% of Roma in Greece cannot read or write

Box 1.8: Adult literacy among indigenous populations in high income OECD countries

The legacy of discrimination and stigmatization facing indigenous people in rich countries – such as in Australia, Canada, New Zealand and the United States – has received insufficient attention but is clearly visible in literacy data:

■ First Nations, Inuit and Métis adults in Canada are more likely to lack basic literacy skills. In Nunavut, Inuit adults were over ten times as likely as non-Inuit to have very poor literacy skills in English or French (Figure 1.38).

■ In New Zealand, where around 14.6% of the population identify with Māori ethnicity, 22% of Māori adults have very poor literacy skills in English, compared with 13% of the non-indigenous population.

■ In the United States, 19% of American Indian and Native Alaskan adults scored below the basic level on prose literacy, compared with 7% of white Americans. For quantitative literacy, the gap was even higher: 32% compared with 13%.

The origins of poor literacy skills among indigenous populations vary, but often begin in school. In Australia, the 2009 PISA survey showed that the proportion of 15-year-olds who had not reached the basic level in reading was 38% among indigenous students, compared with 14% among non-indigenous students. For mathematics, the proportions were 40% and 15%. And as of 2008, only 30% of indigenous Australians aged 25 to 34 had completed twelve years of school, compared with 73% of non-indigenous Australians.

Countries are seeking ways to address the challenges indigenous populations face. The Canadian government has been attempting to redress the legacy of residential schooling that separated indigenous children from their families and aimed to assimilate them, including punishing them for speaking their own language. Following the Indian Residential Schools Settlement Agreement in 2007 and a formal apology by the government for the residential schools in 2008, the government has committed to improve the funding, quality and cultural relevance of schools on reserves.

Figure 1.38: In Canada, indigenous people have lower literacy skills

Percentage of adults aged over 16 years at level 1, prose literacy, selected provinces and territories, Canada, 2003

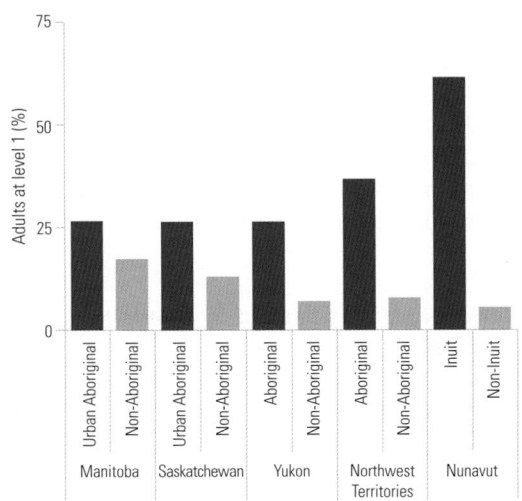

Source: Human Resources and Skills Development Canada and Statistics Canada (2005).

Sources: ABS and AIHW (2011); George and Murray (2012); Kutner et al. (2007); National Panel on First Nation Elementary and Secondary Education for Students on Reserve (2012); Satherley and Lawes (2009); Statistics New Zealand (2007); Thomson et al. (2011); Truth and Reconciliation Commission of Canada (2012).

■ *Disability:* Certain learning, vision and hearing impairments have direct implications for literacy. A lack of appropriate inclusive education opportunities means that adults with disabilities may have faced challenges during their school years with implications for their literacy skills. In the United States, an assessment found that those without basic literacy skills were more than twice as likely as an average adult to have multiple disabilities (Baer et al., 2009).

While all these factors increase the risk of having very poor literacy skills, the problem affects people of all ages and from all walks of life. Many are employed, speak the national language as a mother tongue, and have some form of educational qualification. In Germany, three out of five adults with poor literacy skills are native German speakers (Grotlüschen and Riekmann, 2011). In France, more than half are working and almost three-quarters spoke only French at home as a child (ANLCI, 2008).

Poor literacy skills have important economic and social effects for individuals and households. Lower literacy scores translate into lower employment rates and earnings in most countries – even after taking into account education, parental background, experience, gender and immigrant status. Lower levels of numeracy skills are related to higher unemployment rates in all nine countries participating in the ALL surveys (OECD and Statistics Canada, 2011). Adults with level 1 skills were eight times more likely to be unemployed than adults with level 4 or level 5 skills in the United States, ten times more in the Netherlands and sixteen in Switzerland. Workers with higher prose literacy or numeracy skills earned on average 10% to 20% more than those with low skills, even after controlling for level of education (OECD and Statistics Canada, 2011).

Low literacy hinders full participation in other ways, making it hard to carry out tasks such as helping children with homework and filling in job application forms. It can act as a barrier to further education, social mobility and civic engagement. Among older people in England,

In rich countries, workers with higher literacy earned up to 20% more

lower levels of literacy are associated with poorer self-reported physical and psychological health, and lower self-reported quality of life (Jenkins et al., 2011).

Political commitment and policy vision can strengthen adult literacy

To prevent more people from entering adulthood with poor literacy, countries must continue to improve the quality of primary and secondary schooling and increase retention rates, paying particular attention to students from disadvantaged backgrounds. For those who have left school with poor literacy and numeracy skills, the challenge for policy-makers is greater. High level political commitment and a long-term, coherent policy vision are needed – both of which are often lacking, despite the attention that international literacy assessments have helped put on the low level of literacy skills.

High level commitment puts literacy in the spotlight

Recognizing the extent of literacy challenges is a vital first step towards tackling the problem. While it is too early to assess the effectiveness of several recent high level initiatives, such commitment helps raise awareness of the issues.

In February 2011 the European Commission launched a High-Level Group on Literacy charged with giving visibility to literacy in Europe and evaluating the effectiveness of existing policies (European Commission, 2011a). The results of the OECD's Programme for the International Assessment of Adult Competencies (PIAAC), due to be released in 2013, should be another opportunity to call rich countries to action.

National policies backed by financing are vital

Some countries have developed literacy plans in recent years. The results of adult literacy surveys have often been a trigger for this commitment.

In New Zealand, there has been increased focus on literacy since the publication of the results of the 1996 International Adult Literacy Survey, which showed low levels of literacy skills (New Zealand Ministry of Education, 2008). The 2008–2012 Literacy, Language and Numeracy Action Plan prioritizes raising the literacy and numeracy skills of people at level 1 and level 2 who are in the workforce. The Ministry of Māori Affairs and the Ministry of Pacific Island Affairs are among the participating agencies, and tertiary institutions providing education in a Māori cultural context are also involved. The plan more than doubles the number of training opportunities (to almost 40,000) and the budget (to US$63 million) (New Zealand Tertiary Education Commission, 2008). Targets of participating learners have been on track, and an assessment tool has been developed that will provide initial information on literacy outcomes in 2013 (New Zealand Tertiary Education Commission, 2011).

Similarly, the United Kingdom's Skills for Life strategy was initiated in 2001 in response to a government-commissioned report recognizing that many adults lacked basic literacy and numeracy skills. About US$8 billion was spent between 2001 and 2007. Some 5.7 million adult learners were reached, and 2.25 million of them gained accredited qualifications (United Kingdom Public Accounts Committee, 2009). Learners were approached through a wide range of programmes, including family and workplace programmes, English for speakers of other languages, and literacy and numeracy embedded in vocational training. Although the target number of adults was reached, there was no progress in outcomes. Between 2003 and 2010, the proportion of adults at the three lowest literacy levels remained unchanged at around 15% (Harding et al., 2011). An emphasis on quantitative targets may have made it less attractive to focus on the hardest to reach (Bathmaker, 2007).

In the Netherlands, the national plan to combat low levels of literacy among adults (Aanvalsplan Laaggeletterdheid) was triggered by the findings of international assessments showing that one in ten adults had very poor literacy skills. Its targets were set within a longer-term goal of reducing the number of adults with very poor literacy skills by 60% to 600,000 by 2015. One aim was to increase the number of participants in literacy training from 5,000 to 12,500 annually by 2010. That target was almost reached in 2008/09, but budgetary pressures meant that there were only 10,000 beneficiaries in 2010 (CINOP, 2011).

Adult literacy programmes can lead to secondary school qualifications

One incentive for adults to attend literacy programmes is that they can lead to formal qualifications which can help them get better jobs. In Italy, there are two providers of basic skills which lead to a lower secondary school certificate: secondary schools that give evening courses, and Provincial Centres for Adult Education. While 130,000 adults attend basic education courses, they are mostly immigrants (Oliva, 2011). In light of the 19 million adults who had very poor literacy skills in Italy in 2003, this is a small effort.

The basic education programme for adults in Spain is larger. There are three levels. The first and second focus on basic literacy skills and were attended by about 95,000 students in 2009-2010. The third level leads to a compulsory secondary education certificate and was followed by almost 210,000 students in 2009-2010. In addition, about 70,000 immigrants attend language courses (Rodríguez Alvariño, 2008; Spain Ministry of Education Culture and Sport, 2012).

Family or intergenerational literacy programmes show good results

Adults often mention an inability to help their child with reading or homework as a reason for entering literacy programmes. Family or intergenerational literacy programmes, where parents and children develop their literacy skills together, take advantage of this drive. For such programmes, teachers need to be trained in both child and adult literacy learning as the methods for each are different (Kruidenier et al., 2010). The programmes have been shown to be

New Zealand plans to double the number of training opportunities over five years

effective in improving child literacy, the capacity of parents to support their children and parental motivation to engage in learning (Carpentieri et al., 2011).

In the United States, the Family and Child Education programme has served more than 12,500 American Indian families with young children since 1990. According to the programme's assessment system, there have been improvements in adult literacy levels and more than 1,000 adults have obtained a high school diploma (Yarnell et al., 2010).

Workplace-based programmes help tackle illiteracy

If workplace literacy programmes are appropriately designed, they can be convenient and relevant, reaching adults who otherwise might not have participated. Many employers do not sufficiently recognize that raising workforce skills can improve product quality, workplace communications, and health and safety. To overcome this, publicly funded, enterprise-based basic skills programmes are in place, particularly in many Nordic and anglophone countries (Keogh, 2009; National Adult Literacy Agency, 2011). The New Zealand Workplace Literacy Fund, for example, provides funding to strengthen employee literacy and numeracy skills linked to workplace requirements (New Zealand Tertiary Education Commission, 2012).

In Norway, the Basic Competences in Working Life Programme began in 2006. By 2011, it was supporting 249 projects in more than 400 companies with a budget of about US$16 million, and more than 20,000 adults had benefitted. Any enterprise in Norway, private or public, can apply for funding. Preference is given to proposals that combine work and basic skills training (reading, writing, numeracy and digital skills) with other job-relevant learning, and that are related to the competency goals of the Framework for Basic

Skills developed by the Norwegian Agency for Lifelong Learning. Special efforts are made to include small and medium-sized enterprises in the programme and to encourage applications from industries that employ people with low formal skills (Hussain, 2010; Vox, 2012).

An evaluation of the workplace literacy component of the Skills for Life programme in the United Kingdom showed that courses needed to be long enough for any gains in productivity to be achieved, and that interventions had to be sensitive to the constraints of small and medium-sized enterprises, which may not easily be able to release workers for literacy training (Wolf, 2008).

Quality and commitment of literacy teachers are key factors

Trainers need to be well prepared to adjust to the needs of the heterogeneous populations they serve. In Greece, the Second Chance School programme targets adults who do not have a lower secondary school leaving certificate. Established in 2001 as part of a European Union initiative, it was serving about 7,000 students by 2009. The schools follow an open, interdisciplinary curriculum with active learning through group work. This flexible approach is markedly different from the formal education system. Yet teachers are seconded from formal primary and secondary schools and are not well prepared to deliver such a curriculum (Koutrouba, 2008; Koutrouba et al., 2011).

This shortcoming highlights the importance of providing appropriate training and professional development opportunities to attract and motivate the best adult educators. In the US state of Massachusetts, a model for a voluntary professional licence for adult education teachers was set up and training was provided in the areas covered by the licence (Comings and Soricone, 2005).

Overcoming stigma is a key challenge

Adults with very poor literacy skills are not always willing to participate in literacy programmes, partly because of the stigma attached to being recognized as illiterate. To help adults overcome this, many successful programmes have often been based on media campaigns and free, confidential advice. In England, for example, Skills for Life has been supported by major campaigns on television and in other media, which have led to high public recognition of adult illiteracy and have encouraged uptake (National Adult Literacy Agency, 2011).

In many countries and regions, governments and private foundations have developed services via telephone that offer help and information about how to take part in literacy programmes. For example, Info-Alpha in Quebec, Canada, is a free, confidential, bilingual service that offers help and information to people with low literacy skills. The service refers callers to literacy resources and providers in each area (Canada Council of Ministers of Education, 2008).

Information technology can also offer ways to overcome reservations about participating in literacy programmes. In Germany, the website www.ich-will-schreiben-lernen.de (I want to learn to write) offers self-study courses in reading, writing, mathematics and English. The anonymous nature of the courses and the fact that learners can take them anywhere, at any time and at any pace means people are more inclined to participate. About 200,000 learners have used the portal since it opened in 2004 (UIL, 2011).

Providing literacy training alongside career counselling, advisory services or skills training can encourage individuals to participate. In Spain, the Acceder programme embedded literacy training in guidance and vocational training delivered through forty-eight Integrated Employment Centres. These have served more than 37,000 people, of whom 70% were Roma (Centre for Strategy and Evaluation Services, 2011).

Conclusion

The challenge of poor adult literacy skills has not been sufficiently addressed in rich countries. Recognizing that poor literacy skills remain a social and economic barrier to millions of adults in these countries, a comprehensive policy focus backed by sufficient resources is required.

The challenge of poor adult literacy skills has not been sufficiently addressed in rich countries

Education for All Global Monitoring Report 2012

Goal 5 | Assessing gender parity and equality in education

Eliminating gender disparities in primary and secondary education by 2005, and achieving gender equality in education by 2015, with a focus on ensuring girls' full and equal access to and achievement in basic education of good quality.

Highlights

- Convergence in enrolment between boys and girls has been one of the successes of the EFA movement since 2000, but more needs to be done to ensure that education opportunities and outcomes are equitable.

- There are still sixty-eight countries that have not achieved gender parity in primary education, and girls are disadvantaged in sixty of them.

- The incidence of severe gender disparity has become less common. Of the 167 countries with data in both 1999 and 2010, the number of countries where fewer than nine girls were in primary school for every ten boys fell from 33 to 17.

- At the secondary level, ninety-seven countries have not reached gender parity; in forty-three of them, girls are disadvantaged. In much of the Arab States, South and West Asia, and sub-Saharan Africa gender disparities are at the expense of girls, while in many countries in Latin America and the Caribbean, and in East Asia and the Pacific, disparities are at the expense of boys.

- International learning assessments indicate that girls perform better than boys in reading at both primary and secondary school level, and the gap is widening. Boys have an advantage in mathematics in most countries, although there is some evidence that the gap may be narrowing.

Table 1.8: Key indicators for goal 5

	Primary education					Secondary education				
	Gender parity achieved in 2010		Countries where the GPI is lower than 0.90	Gender parity index		Gender parity achieved in 2010		Countries where the GPI is lower than 0.90	Gender parity index	
	Total number of countries	Countries with data		1999	2010	Total number of countries	Countries with data		1999	2010
World	108	176	17	0.92	0.97	60	157	26	0.91	0.97
Low income countries	9	29	10	0.86	0.95	1	23	14	0.83	0.87
Lower middle income countries	23	49	6	0.86	0.96	12	41	10	0.80	0.93
Upper middle income countries	34	50	1	0.99	1.00	21	47	1	0.98	1.04
High income countries	42	48	0	1.00	0.99	26	46	1	1.01	1.00
Sub-Saharan Africa	16	43	12	0.85	0.93	2	30	16	0.82	0.82
Arab States	6	15	1	0.87	0.93	3	14	4	0.88	0.94
Central Asia	7	8	0	0.99	0.98	5	7	1	0.99	0.97
East Asia and the Pacific	14	23	1	0.99	1.01	6	23	1	0.94	1.03
South and West Asia	4	7	2	0.83	0.98	0	6	3	0.75	0.91
Latin America and the Caribbean	18	35	1	0.97	0.97	11	33	0	1.07	1.08
North America and Western Europe	22	24	0	1.01	0.99	16	24	1	1.02	1.00
Central and Eastern Europe	21	21	0	0.97	0.99	17	20	0	0.96	0.97

Note: Gender parity is reached when the GPI is between 0.97 and 1.03.
Source: Annex, Statistical Tables 5 and 7.

Goal 5: Assessing gender parity and equality in education

Gender parity and equality in education constitute a basic human right, as well as an important means of improving other social and economic outcomes. Narrowing the gender gap in primary enrolment is one of the biggest EFA successes since 2000. Even so, some countries are still in danger of not achieving gender parity in primary and secondary education by 2015. The goal goes beyond numbers of boys and girls in school. More needs to be done to ensure that all girls and boys have equitable access to educational opportunities and achieve equal educational outcomes.

At pre-primary level, gender parity had already been achieved, on average, in 2000 and has been maintained since, although enrolment levels remain low for both boys and girls in many parts of the world. The Arab States is the only region still falling short, even though major progress has been achieved, with the gender parity index (GPI) rising from 0.77 in 1999 to 0.94 in 2010.

At primary level, the Arab States and sub-Saharan Africa, each with a GPI of 0.93, have yet to achieve parity. These regions have, however, made significant progress since 1999, with the GPI increasing from 0.87 and 0.85, respectively. South and West Asia has made huge progress since 1999, reaching gender parity in primary education by 2010.

A key reason for fewer girls being in school is that they are less likely to start school in the first place. Once in school, their chances of progressing through the system are similar to those of boys (Panel 1.10).

At secondary level, the picture varies by region. Of particular concern is sub-Saharan Africa, whose GPI of 0.82 has not changed since 1999. Girls also remain disadvantaged in the Arab States and in South and West Asia. Latin America and the Caribbean, by contrast, faces a 'reverse gender gap', with more girls enrolled than boys (goal 5 policy focus). Yet disadvantage in secondary school – in access as well as learning outcomes – is preventable.

Gender disparities in secondary education enrolment are also narrowing. Of the 137 countries with data in both years, in 1999 there were 28 with fewer than 90 girls enrolled for every 100 boys; 16 were in sub-Saharan Africa. By 2010, this had declined to 22 countries, of which 15 were in sub-Saharan Africa.

At tertiary level, regional disparities are even greater than at secondary level, with as few as six girls for every ten boys in sub-Saharan Africa, while around eight boys for every ten girls are studying at this level in North America and Western Europe.

Reaching gender parity remains a challenge in many countries – but gender equality is about more than making sure equal numbers of boys and girls enter and progress through school. It is also about assuring their equal treatment within school – which means providing a safe, secure and supportive learning environment for all – and equal learning outcomes, which help build equitable access to social, economic and political life in adulthood.

Analysis of international and regional learning assessments shows that there are notable gender differences in learning outcomes by subject, which suggests that more needs to be done to prevent these gaps. Girls perform better than boys in reading, and there is evidence that the gap is increasing. Boys retain an advantage in mathematics in most countries, although there is some evidence that the gap may be narrowing (Panel 1.11).

With the emergence of several new initiatives – including the Global Partnership for Girls' and Women's Education and the High Level Panel on Girls' and Women's Education for Empowerment and Gender Equality, both launched by UNESCO in May 2011 – there are renewed opportunities to highlight and challenge barriers to gender parity and equality for girls. It will be important for these initiatives to tackle the root causes of gender disadvantage, ensuring that the high level initiatives translate into action leading to an equalizing of opportunities between girls and boys.

Panel 1.10: Girls face obstacles in entering school

Considerable progress has been made in reducing gender disparities in primary education over the past decade, but several countries still have a long way to go. They have not only missed the deadline that was set for 2005, but are in danger of missing an extended deadline of 2015.

The reasons for girls' disadvantage vary, but new analysis prepared for this Report indicates that the biggest obstacle for girls in the countries furthest from achieving gender parity is entering school in the first place. Once enrolled, their chance of progressing through the cycle is usually similar to that of boys.

The number of countries where girls face extreme disadvantage, or a gender parity index below 0.70, fell from sixteen in 1990 to eleven in 2000, and to just one in 2010 – Afghanistan. Despite its place at the bottom of the rankings, however, Afghanistan has overcome the biggest obstacles to girls' education any country has witnessed: from an estimated female gross enrolment ratio of less than 4% in 1999, when the ruling Taliban had banned girls' education, to 79% in 2010, resulting in an increase in the GPI from 0.08 to 0.69. With a long way still to go, the government needs to continue to address constraints on girls' schooling. Community schools that reduce the distance from home have proved to be a successful approach to address the insecurity that continues in many parts of the country and affects girls' enrolment in particular (Burde and Linden, 2009).

Severe disadvantage – measured by a GPI below 0.90 – is also lower than ten years ago. Of the 167 countries with data in both 1999 and 2010, 33 had a GPI below 0.90 in 1999, including 21 in sub-Saharan Africa. By 2010, there were only 17 countries in this group, including 12 in sub-Saharan Africa (Table 1.9).

Countries where severe gender disparities remain are more likely to have fewer children in school overall. This is the case in Afghanistan, the Central African Republic, Chad, Côte d'Ivoire, Eritrea, Mali, the Niger, Papua New Guinea and Yemen, which all have gross enrolment ratios below 80% and GPIs below 0.90.

But countries with high enrolment can also experience a wide gender gap, partly because there are more over-age boys in school than girls. This is the case for Angola, Benin, Cameroon, the Dominican Republic

and Togo. It cannot be taken for granted, therefore, that increasing enrolment will automatically lead to a narrowing of the gender gap.

Comparing countries with data for 1990, 2000 and 2010, out of thirty-eight countries where the gender parity index was below 0.90 in 1990, twenty-five had passed this threshold by 2010. But of these, only six had achieved gender parity: Burundi, the Gambia, Ghana, India, the Islamic Republic of Iran, and Uganda – and Malawi, Mauritania and Senegal made such progress getting more girls into school that there is now a slight gender disparity at the expense of boys (Figure 1.39). These nine countries show what can be achieved when countries put in place strategies to overcome gender barriers at the same time as increasing primary enrolment overall.

In some countries that have not achieved gender parity, the GPI has nonetheless improved rapidly in the last

Table 1.9: Countries where the gender parity index is below 0.90, 2010

	GER, female	GPI
Sub-Saharan Africa		
Central African Republic	79	0.725
Chad	78	0.729
Angola	124	0.813
Côte d'Ivoire	80	0.833
Niger	64	0.837
Eritrea	41	0.838
Guinea	86	0.838
Cameroon	111	0.862
Democratic Republic of the Congo	87	0.867
Benin	117	0.871
Mali	76	0.882
Togo	132	0.899
Arab States		
Yemen	78	0.817
East Asia and the Pacific		
Papua New Guinea	57	0.892
South and West Asia		
Afghanistan	79	0.694
Pakistan	85	0.818
Latin America and the Caribbean		
Dominican Republic	102	0.882

Note: Data for the Central African Republic, Côte d'Ivoire, Mali and the Niger are from 2011; data for Papua New Guinea are from 2008.
Source: Annex, Statistical Table 5.

Figure 1.39: There has been progress in reducing gender disparity but girls still face major obstacles gaining access to school

Gender parity index of the gross enrolment ratio, countries with GPI in 1990 below 0.90, 1990 to 2000 and 2000 to 2010

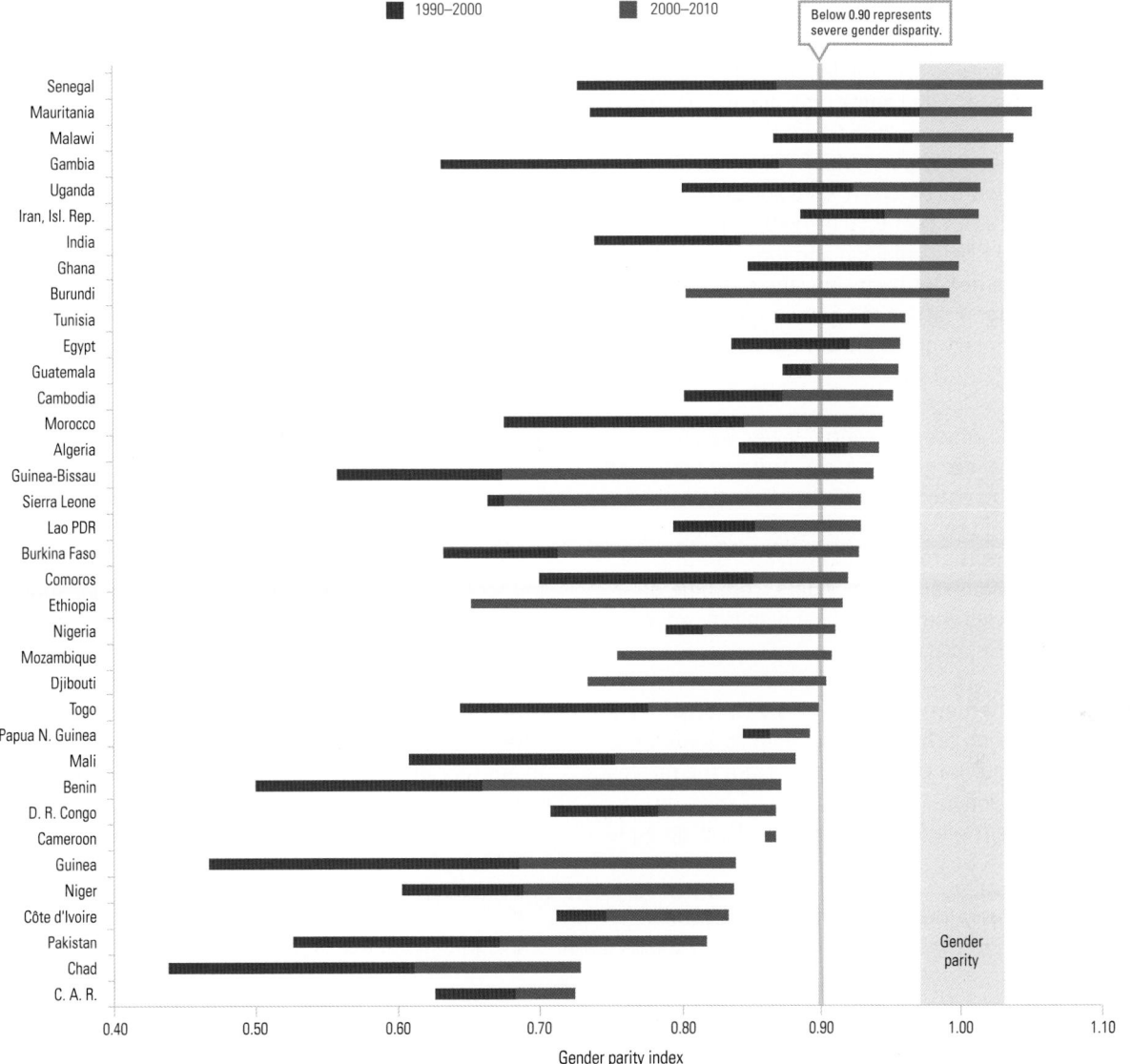

Notes: Only countries with data for 1990, 2000 and 2010 are plotted. If there was no information for a particular year, information was substituted up to two years before or after. Afghanistan and Oman are excluded because they experienced negative trends.
Source: UIS database.

ten years. In Ethiopia, for example, the index rose from 0.65 in 2000 to 0.91 in 2010. This reflects Ethiopia's commitment both to expanding access to primary schooling and to tackling gender disparities. Its speed of progress suggests there is hope of achieving gender parity by 2015, although this will require a concerted effort to address entrenched gender disadvantages in some parts of the country, particularly where early marriage remains pervasive.

By contrast, progress has been very slow in some countries. This includes some where enrolment levels were initially relatively high, such as Cameroon and Papua New Guinea, and some where they were relatively low, such as the Central African Republic and Côte d'Ivoire. The speed at which progress has been made elsewhere indicates that these countries could reach gender parity if they showed the same kind of commitment to addressing girls' disadvantage in coming years.

The move towards gender parity has slowed in some countries after good progress over the 1990s. Some are close to the goal, such as Algeria, Egypt, Morocco and Tunisia: such countries need to tackle the problems facing the most marginalized girls who still cannot attend school. Slower progress over the last decade in Chad and Guinea means they are still some distance from the goal.

Angola and Eritrea are of particular concern because they slipped backwards between 1990 and 2010. Each country recorded a GPI over 0.90 in 1990, but Angola now is at 0.81 and Eritrea at 0.84, and therefore both are unlikely to achieve gender parity in primary schooling by 2015. In Eritrea, not only has the gender gap widened, but the female primary gross enrolment ratio fell from 47% in 1999 to 41% in 2010.

Understanding the reasons for girls' lower enrolment is necessary to achieve gender parity. Is it because girls have less chance to enter school? Or is it, rather, that boys and girls have the same opportunity of entering school but girls are more likely to drop out? To answer these questions, household survey data from nine of the sixteen countries with the highest disparity were analysed for this Report.

The message that emerges is that girls face larger obstacles to entering primary school (Figure 1.40). In Guinea, for example, 44 out of 100 girls from the poorest households start school, compared with 57 boys. In most cases, once in school, girls and boys have an equal chance of progressing through the cycle. Therefore, the fact that only 40 out of 100 girls from poor households reach the end of primary school in Guinea, compared with 52 boys, is largely because fewer girls started in the first place.

While children from rich households have a better chance of starting school than those from poor households, more rich boys than rich girls enter school. In Mali, for example, 70 out of 100 girls from the richest households start school, compared with 81 boys.

Within this general pattern, there are exceptions. In Yemen, girls not only have less chance of entering school, but, once in school, are also less likely to reach grade 6. Only 49 out of 100 of poor girls enter school, compared with 72 out of 100 poor boys. And only 27 of poor girls reach grade 6, compared with 52 of poor boys.

Policy-makers need to tackle the causes of girls being out of school on multiple fronts: mobilizing communities to send girls to school by enlisting the support of media and local leaders; providing targeted financial support; providing gender-sensitive curriculum and textbooks; ensuring that teacher recruitment, deployment and training are gender-sensitive; and ensuring that school environments are healthy, safe and free of gender-based violence (Clarke, 2011). Countries that have adopted an appropriate mix of interventions have witnessed the most progress in narrowing the gender gap in primary enrolment over the past decade.

Figure 1.40: Poor girls have a lower chance of starting primary school

Expected cohort intake to grade 1 and survival rate to grade 6 by gender and wealth, selected countries with GPI in 2010 below 0.90, 2005 to 2008

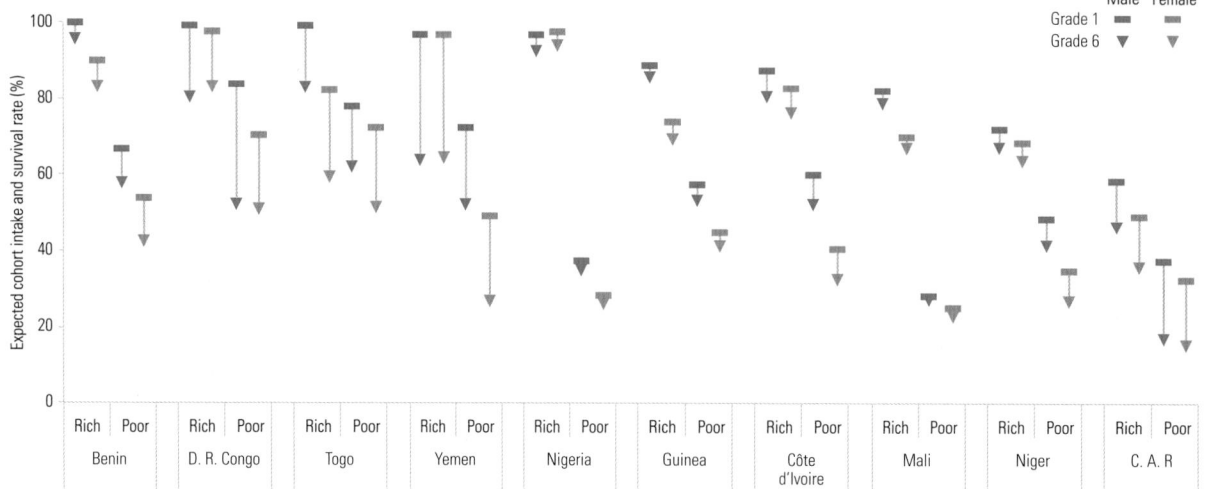

Sources: Delprato (2012) based on analysis of Demographic and Health Surveys; EFA Global Monitoring Report team estimates (2012) based on analysis of Multiple Indicator Cluster Surveys.

Panel 1.11: Gender disparities in learning outcomes persist

Achieving gender parity and gender equality in education requires not only that girls and boys have an equal chance to enter and stay in school, but also that they have equal opportunity in learning.

Regional and international learning assessments at primary and secondary level indicate distinct gender patterns that vary by subject. Girls perform better than boys in reading in all but one country,[20] while boys retain an advantage in mathematics in most countries. There is more variation in science, with many countries not showing a significant difference between boys and girls (Figure 1.41). These patterns are broadly similar across education levels, regions and country income groups.

Results from the 2009 PISA show an even stronger pattern in favour of girls in reading than earlier surveys, with girls performing significantly better than boys in all seventy-four countries or economies surveyed. In OECD countries, girls' advantage in reading was equivalent to one school year, on average. But not all girls performed well in these countries: one in eight girls and one in four boys failed to reach level 2, deemed the level at which students demonstrate reading skills that will enable them to participate effectively and productively in life (OECD, 2010d). Among non-OECD countries participating, such as Malaysia and Romania, one in three girls and one in two boys failed to reach this level, on average.

In mathematics, the difference in performance tends to favour boys, although there are countries where girls perform as well as or better than boys. Boys performed better than girls in thirty-eight countries and in twenty-eight there was no significant difference. Girls performed better than boys in eight countries.

While the general pattern for mathematics is the opposite of that for reading, the gender gap in favour of boys is narrower. In addition, there is little difference between boys and girls in those failing to reach the minimum level required to use their skills effectively: in OECD countries, around one in five of both boys and girls failed to reach level 2. Among non-OECD countries, around half of both boys and girls did not reach this level.

Figure 1.41: Girls outperform boys in reading while boys often do better in mathematics

Number of countries and economies according to the direction of the gender mean score difference, by subject and survey, 2005 to 2009

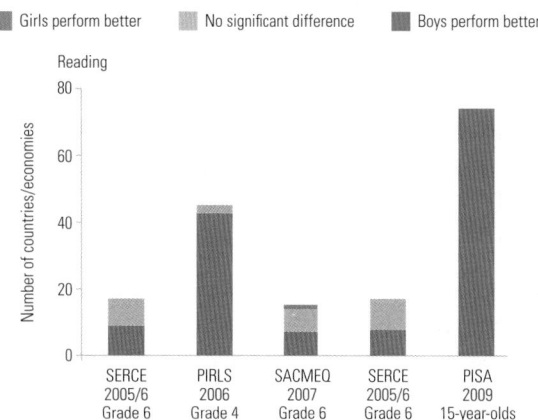

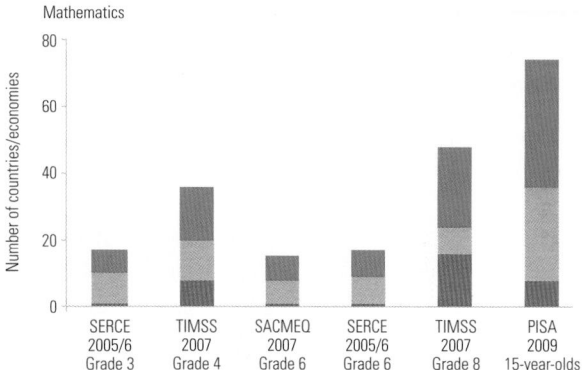

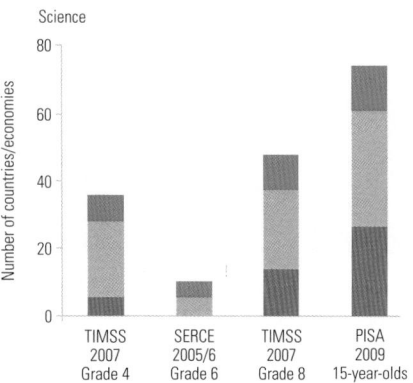

Note: The figure summarizes the results of six regional and international programmes of learning assessment: the Programme of Analysis of Education Systems of the CONFEMEN (PASEC, sub-Saharan Africa); the Progress in International Reading Literacy Study (PIRLS, international); the Programme for International Student Assessment (PISA, international); the Southern and Eastern Africa Consortium for Monitoring Educational Quality (SACMEQ, sub-Saharan Africa); the Second Regional Student Achievement Test (SERCE, Latin America); and the Trends in International Mathematics and Science Study (TIMSS, international).
Sources: Gonzales et al. (2009); Hungi et al. (2010); UNESCO-OREALC (2008); Mullis et al. (2007); Saito (2010); Walker (2011).

---

20. In the United Republic of Tanzania, boys perform better than girls in reading.

CHAPTER 1

Science presents a more mixed picture than either reading or mathematics, indicating that there are circumstances in which either boys or girls can perform better. Boys performed better than girls in thirteen countries, in thirty-four there was no significant difference, and girls performed better than boys in twenty-seven countries.

These average figures are likely to mask differences between subgroups of the population. For example, in Tunisia there was no gender gap in the mean science score. However, boys from the lowest socio-economic quartile were more likely to score above level 2 than girls in this group. By contrast, girls from the highest quartile had a better chance than boys of scoring above this level (Altinok, 2012b).

Overall, girls appear to be making greater progress in reading than boys. Comparing the subset of thirty-eight countries that took part in both the 2000 and 2009 PISA surveys, the gender gap in reading has widened in favour of girls by seven points (Figure 1.42).

The increase was significant in Brazil, France, Hong Kong (China), Indonesia, Israel, Portugal, the Republic of Korea, Romania and Sweden. In France, Romania and Sweden, the main reason behind the wider gender gap was a decline in boys' performance (OECD, 2010a). While the gender gap in favour of girls has been widening for reading, there is some evidence that improvements in girls' performance in mathematics have narrowed the gender gap.

There is no inherent difference in the capacities of girls or boys in reading, mathematics or science. Girls and boys can perform equally well in these subjects under the right conditions. To close the gap in reading, parents, teachers and policy-makers need to find creative ways to entice boys to read more, including by harnessing their interest in digital texts. To close the gap in mathematics, progress in gender equality outside the classroom, notably in employment opportunities, could play a major role in reducing disparities (Kane and Mertz, 2012).

Figure 1.42: The gender gap in reading has widened

A. Percentage of countries and economies by gender gap, countries and economies with data in both years, PISA 2000–2009

B. Gender gap by subject, countries and economies with data in both years, PISA 2000–2009

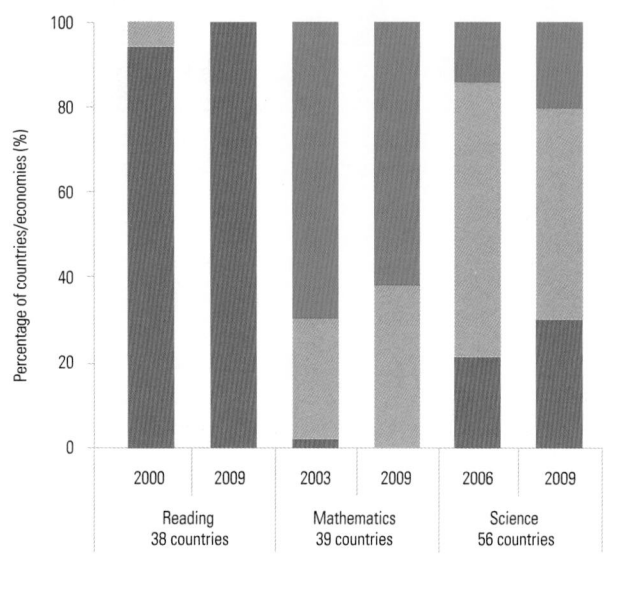

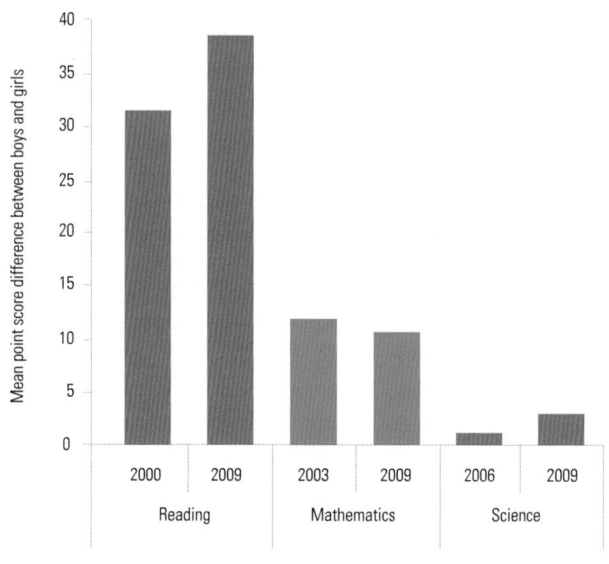

■ Girls perform better   ■ No significant difference   ■ Boys perform better

Sources: OECD (2004, 2007, 2010a, 2010d).

Policy focus: Challenging disadvantage and disengagement among boys in secondary school

As more children around the world get the chance to enter secondary school, it is vital to ensure that girls and boys benefit equitably from this progress. At primary level, girls remain much more likely to be disadvantaged in many countries, so it is imperative to maintain the international focus on supporting girls (Panel 1.10). At secondary level, however, boys are at a disadvantage in some countries.

This section describes the extent of the problem, examines why it occurs and explores possible solutions. It shows that the causes of boys' disadvantage in secondary school are different from those of girls, and that different remedies are often required. Boys' lower enrolment or learning achievement may partly result from disadvantage related to poverty, and partly from disengagement, associated with a disaffection with school and a sense of not belonging to the school community.[21]

Disparities in secondary education are sometimes at the expense of boys

Boys are less likely than girls to enrol in secondary school and to do as well once in school, particularly in many upper middle and high income countries. The experiences of these countries offer lessons for poorer countries where enrolment is rising.

Unequal participation: more girls are enrolled than boys in some countries

For more than half of the ninety-seven countries that have not achieved gender parity in secondary education participation, the problem is due to fewer boys than girls being enrolled in school:[22]

■ There are fifty-four countries where gender disparity in secondary enrolment is at the expense of boys; in fifteen of these countries, the disparity is so high that fewer than ninety boys are enrolled for every hundred girls.

■ At the lower secondary level, boys are disadvantaged in thirty-three countries; in six of these, there are fewer than ninety boys for every hundred girls enrolled.

■ At the upper secondary level, boys are disadvantaged in seventy-five countries; in forty-two of these, fewer than ninety boys are enrolled for every hundred girls.

In most countries with fewer boys than girls in lower secondary education, the disparity is due to higher dropout rates for boys rather than higher transition rates of girls from primary to secondary school. In Nicaragua, for example, similar proportions of girls and boys enter lower secondary education, but fewer boys graduated in 2010: the gross entry ratio was 88% for boys and girls, while the gross graduation ratio for lower secondary general education was 36% for boys and 50% for girls.

The situation is similar in upper secondary education, although data are available for fewer countries. In Paraguay, a two percentage point difference in favour of girls in the gross entry ratio for upper secondary general education extended to ten percentage points in the gross graduation ratio in 2008 (UIS database).

Lower enrolment for boys is more common in upper middle and high income countries with high levels of enrolment overall. Colombia, Costa Rica and Mexico have all achieved secondary gross enrolment ratios of over 80% but have fewer than 95 boys enrolled for every 100 girls (Table 1.10). But there are also poorer countries where boys are less likely to be enrolled, including fifteen lower middle income countries and three low income countries – Bangladesh, Myanmar and Rwanda (Box 1.9).

Within poor countries where girls' secondary enrolment is lower than boys' on average, there may be locations where boys face greater disadvantage. For example, 2005/06 Demographic and Health Survey data indicated the proportion of those aged 15 to 19 attending school across India

Over half of countries with gender disparity in secondary education have fewer boys than girls in school

---

21. This section draws on Jha et al. (2012).
22. As of 2010, there were relevant data for 157 out of 204 countries.

Table 1.10: Boys' disadvantage in secondary school participation is more common in richer countries

Number of boys enrolled for every 100 girls, by total secondary education gross enrolment ratio, 2010

	<90 boys enrolled	90–95 boys enrolled	95–96 boys enrolled
<80% Total secondary education GER			
Low income countries	Bangladesh	Myanmar	Rwanda
Lower middle income countries	Honduras	Nicaragua	Bhutan
	Lesotho	Viet Nam	Paraguay
	Sao Tome/Principe		
Upper middle income countries	Dominican Republic	Malaysia	Ecuador
	Suriname	Panama	
	Nauru	Thailand	
High income countries	Bermuda		
80–100% Total secondary education GER			
Lower middle income countries	Cape Verde	Fiji	
	Samoa	Guyana	
		Kiribati	
		Mongolia	
		Palestine	
		Philippines	
Upper middle income countries	Argentina	Botswana	China
	Lebanon	Colombia	Jamaica
	Cook Islands	Costa Rica	South Africa
		Dominica	
		Jordan	
		Mexico	
		Tunisia	
		Venezuela, B. R.	
High income countries	Cayman Islands	Bahamas	Andorra
	Qatar	Croatia	
		Trinidad/Tobago	

Note: Countries with total secondary education gross enrolment ratios above 100% are not included.
Source: Annex, Statistical Table 7.

Unequal achievement: girls outperform boys in many countries

International learning assessments from middle and high income countries show that girls perform better than boys in reading (Panel 1.11). The 2009 PISA survey, which covered thirty-four OECD countries and forty partner countries and economies, showed that 15-year-old girls achieved significantly higher scores in reading than boys in all countries. The gender gap had widened in some countries since 2000, largely due to a greater improvement in girls' performance.

Boys continue to outperform girls in mathematics in many countries, but the overall extent of their advantage is smaller than girls' advantage in reading. Outcomes in science are more equal, although there are more countries in which girls do significantly better than boys than countries where boys perform better.

Why some boys face disadvantage in secondary school

The common causes of girls' disadvantage in secondary education, related to discrimination, are generally not as applicable to boys. Outside the school, poverty and the nature of the labour market can affect boys more than girls. Inside the school, the classroom environment can lead to boys' disengagement.

was higher for boys (47%, compared with 36% for girls). However, the proportion was higher for girls in the state of Kerala (67%, compared with 62% for boys) and in Delhi (54% for girls and 49% for boys) (UNESCO, 2012c).

Some regions are more likely to show patterns of boys' disadvantage. Of countries with data, boys' enrolment is lower than girls' in 64% of countries in Latin America and the Caribbean and 57% of countries in East Asia and the Pacific. For most countries experiencing a reverse gender gap, it is not a new phenomenon. For example, in the Dominican Republic, South Africa and the Bolivarian Republic of Venezuela, the pattern has persisted for a decade.

Boys' disadvantage is compounded by poverty

Average indicators mask the fact that disparities at secondary school do not apply to all boys but affect those marginalized by factors such as poverty, social class, ethnicity and location. These boys experience greater economic and social pressure, with disproportionately negative outcomes for their participation and learning (Box 1.10).

In countries where secondary school-aged boys are more likely than girls to work outside the home, this can translate into education disadvantage. In Latin America and the Caribbean, there are strong links between gender and children's work. In many countries across the region, more young males enter the workforce early and hold a paying job than

Box 1.9: Boys' disadvantage in secondary school enrolment in Bangladesh

Bangladesh is one of only three low income countries where more girls are in secondary school than boys. The disparity is largely due to measures supporting girls' enrolment, suggesting a need for similar programmes that take into account the barriers that boys face in obtaining secondary education – especially poverty. The gender gap in enrolment begins as early as the first year of primary school, and continues into grades 6 to 10 of secondary school, with boys' disadvantage having grown over time (Figure 1.43). In grades 11 and 12, there is disparity in favour of boys but overall enrolment rates are extremely low for both boys and girls.

This unique pattern is mainly due to stipends introduced in the early 1990s, which provide fee-free secondary schooling and a payment

to all girls in school except in the largest urban areas. Alongside other policies and projects, the programme has been very successful in raising female secondary enrolment rates, from just 25% in 1992 to 60% in 2005.

The gender gap has not been a result of an absolute decline in the enrolment of boys – at worst, the enrolment rates of poor boys may have stagnated, and it is not clear that this is because of support to girls. As poor boys enter adolescence, they have more opportunities – and more need – to find wage work, which keeps them out of school. In order to enhance the poverty focus of the programme, stipends have been extended to poor boys since 2008 in about a quarter of the country.

Sources: Antoninis and Mia (2011); Asadullah and Chaudhury (2009); World Bank (2008).

Figure 1.43: In Bangladesh, there are increasingly more girls than boys in secondary school
Number of boys enrolled per 100 girls, by grade, 1999 and 2010

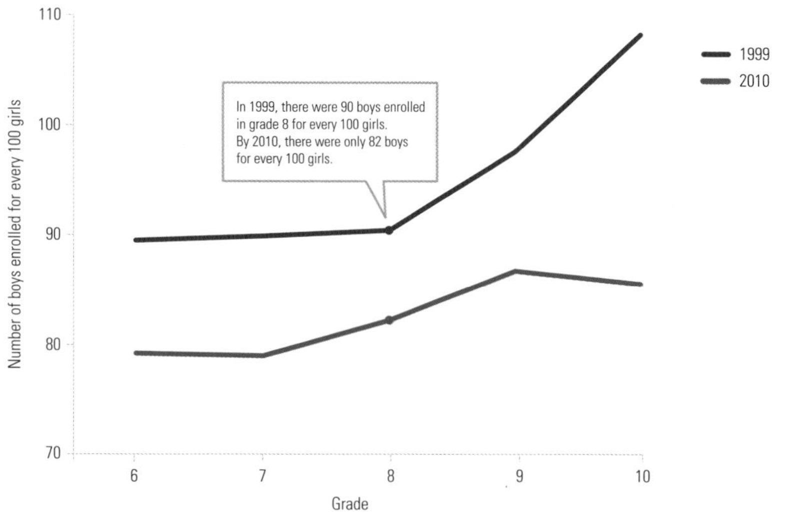

Source: UIS database.

Box 1.10: In Trinidad and Tobago, boys are at a disadvantage in secondary education

Boys in Caribbean countries are more likely to be disadvantaged in secondary education than girls. Trinidad and Tobago illustrates this pattern for both attendance and achievement in secondary school (Figure 1.44). Gender gaps in attendance are modest at the lower secondary school level, but widen for the poorest boys at the upper secondary level. While there are only small differences in achievement between urban boys and girls, living in a rural area amplifies boys' disadvantage. A rich girl living in either an urban or rural area achieves a score above the average for Germany, while a poor male living in a rural area scores close to the average for Tamil Nadu, India. A combination of two factors seems to be at work: the labour market is pulling poor rural boys out of school, and high levels of youth violence increase the chance that boys become disengaged.

Figure 1.44: In Trinidad and Tobago, boys – especially from poor and rural households – face acute disadvantage in participation and achievement

A. *Secondary education attendance rate by wealth and gender, 2006*

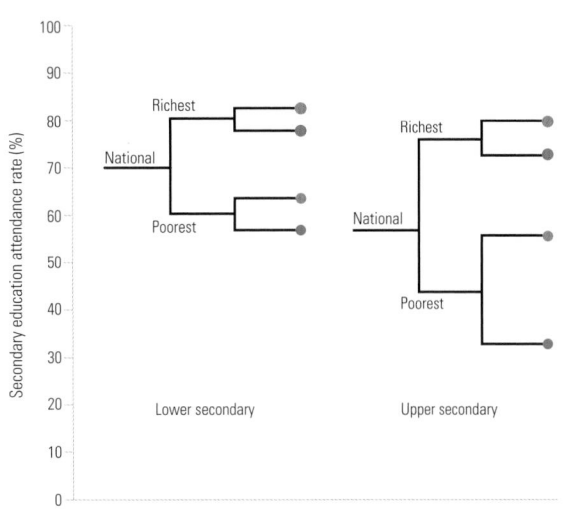

B. *Mean reading score by economic, social, and cultural status, residence and gender, 2009*

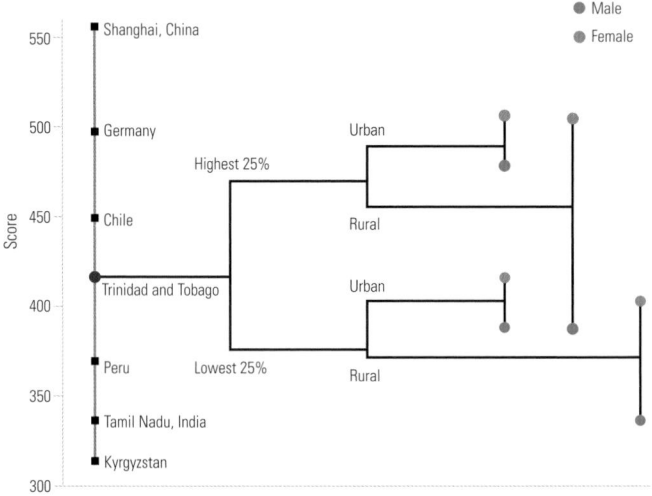

Note: Highest/Lowest 25% refers to the student ranking in terms of the PISA economic, social and cultural status index.
Source: Altinok (2012b), based on the 2009 PISA.

Source: UNESCO (2012c).

young females (Cunningham et al., 2008). Boys engaged in economic activity are also more likely not to attend school. The differences first appear among children of lower secondary school age but become even stronger among adolescents. For example, in Honduras, one of the countries with the highest gender disparities in secondary school participation, 60% of boys aged 15 to 17 were engaged in economic activity in 2002 compared with 21% of girls. About 82% of the boys engaged in economic activity were not in school, compared with 61% of the girls (Guarcello et al., 2006) (Figure 1.45).

Poverty reinforces boys' disadvantage further. When a poor household's income suddenly drops, the family may respond by withdrawing a boy from secondary school to earn money. In Brazil, adolescent boys are more likely to drop out of school because of the need to join the labour market. A sudden fall in family income has a 46% larger effect on the probability of dropout for boys in poor households compared to boys in non-poor households (Côrtes Neri et al., 2005; Duryea et al., 2007). Similarly, after Hurricane Mitch devastated rural Honduras in 1998, children from poor families were more likely to miss out on school – and boys paid a higher price because they were more likely than girls to get a job (Gitter and Barham, 2007).

Household strategies depend on the type of employment opportunities available. If parents perceive that available jobs for young men do not require secondary school completion, then investment in secondary education will seem less valuable than early entry into work. Boys and their families may consider the type or quality of education available to be irrelevant to the types of jobs on offer. In rural Lesotho, looking after livestock tends to keep poor boys out of school, while girls are able to attend for longer – though girls' enrolment rates at secondary level are also very low. Boys' herding activities may also play a role in keeping boys out of school in other southern African countries, such as Botswana and Namibia (Jha and Kelleher, 2006).

Poverty can also negatively affect boys' participation in secondary education in richer countries, but the main consequences are on learning achievement. Low socio-economic status amplifies boys' disadvantage in reading in many OECD countries (Figure 1.46). For example, almost all rich girls across seven OECD countries reach level 2 in reading (the level which, according to the OECD, will enable students to 'participate effectively and productively in life'). Within these countries, most rich boys also perform relatively well, with only between 3% and 13% not reaching level 2. There is, however, a striking gender difference among poor students. In Greece, for example, 24% of female students from the bottom quartile had not reached level 2, compared with 50% of male students in that category.

The school environment may lead to boys' disengagement

In some countries facing a reverse gender gap in enrolment or achievement, female teachers tend to outnumber male teachers in secondary schools. For example, this is the case in Brazil, Jamaica and the Philippines, where there are around six to seven male teachers for every ten female teachers. This fact has caused some to

In some southern African countries, herding keeps boys out of school

Figure 1.45: Boys are more likely than girls to be engaged in economic activity, and those who work are more likely not to attend school
Percentage of those aged 15 to 17 who are engaged in economic activity by school attendance status, selected Latin American countries, 2000 to 2002

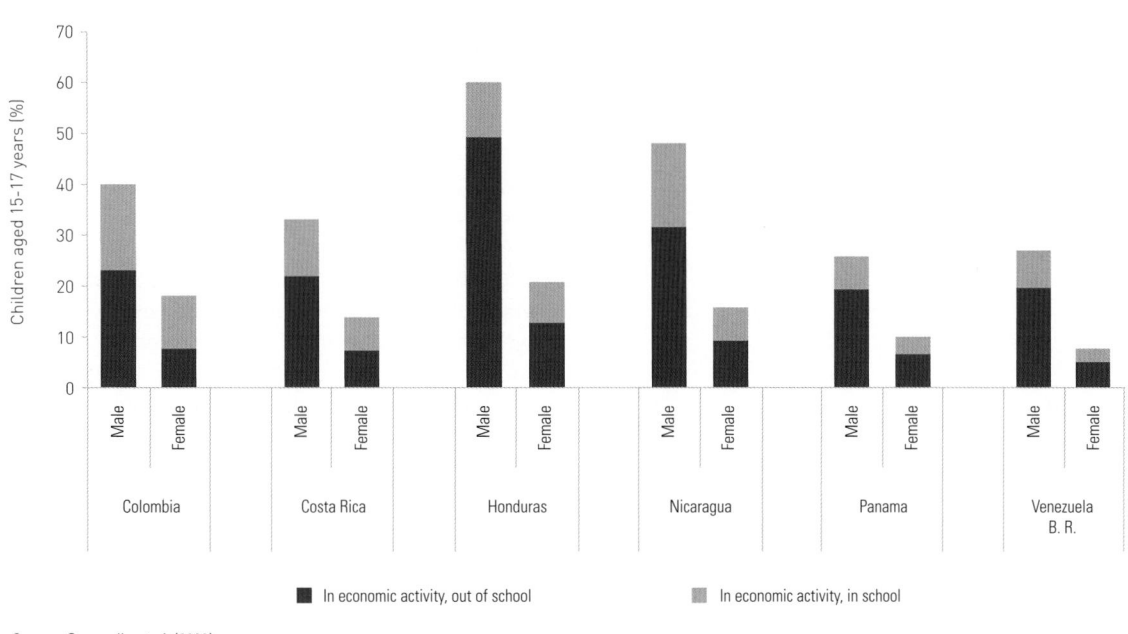

Source: Guarcello et al. (2006).

A lack of male role models in school may lead to boys' disengagement

ask whether children relate better to teachers of the same gender and whether male teachers are more likely to teach in ways best suited to boys.

A lack of male role models in education may disadvantage boys. Boys' disengagement could be more likely where there are no adult male role models in the family. While there is no solid evidence of such a link between role models and boys' engagement, teachers and principals often believe one exists, as a survey in Trinidad and Tobago has shown (George et al., 2009).

While wealthier boys in the Caribbean are more likely to see higher education and professional careers as realistic options, a vicious cycle of disengagement from education and involvement in risky behaviour has been observed for poorer boys in Jamaica and Trinidad and Tobago, where school gangs have emerged (UNDP, 2012). Female teachers may be less able to discipline boys in such contexts of high levels of crime and violence.

Teacher expectations about the capacities of male and female students may play a part in performance. One study in Jamaica found that boys were told they were lazy, leading to low self-esteem, streaming into remedial classes, and poor academic achievement and test results (MSI, 2005). Teachers have been noted as having

low academic expectations of boys in Malaysia, Samoa, Seychelles, and Trinidad and Tobago (Page and Jha, 2009).

If boys perceive that female teachers discriminate against them, they may use this to justify their negative attitude. A study of more than 200 teachers and 3,000 adolescent students in Finland showed that, while all teachers viewed boys' temperament and educational competence more negatively than girls', male teachers perceived the differences between boys and girls to be smaller than female teachers did (Mullola et al., 2012).

The gender of the teacher, however, accounts for only part of the observed differences in achievement and engagement between boys and girls. A more important factor is likely to be teacher attitudes towards boys' and girls' learning processes, behaviour and academic success. Some commentators argue that, while there may be differences in learning styles between the genders, they are minor compared with the similarities, and can be shaped through the schooling experience (Eliot, 2011; Hyde, 2005). Teachers need to be aware of differences in learning styles where they exist, and be prepared to adjust their teaching and assessment methods accordingly (Younger et al., 2005).

Challenging boys' disadvantage and disengagement

Gender disparities and inequality in education are not inevitable. In countries where boys are disadvantaged, there are ways that schools and society can help improve their participation, attainment and learning outcomes.

Policy-makers have begun to show greater awareness of problems associated with boys' disadvantage and disengagement in education. In some contexts, this focus has emerged due to a perceived relationship between adolescent boys' educational underachievement and rising levels of gang involvement, violence, crime, access to guns and drug-related activity, as in the Caribbean (Figueroa, 2010; Jha et al., 2012). In other situations, a combination of increased media focus on educational league tables and rising levels of youth unemployment has brought

Figure 1.46: In several countries, socio-economic status amplifies the gender difference in learning achievement

Percentage of 15-year-old boys and girls who scored below level 2 in reading, by economic, social and cultural status, selected countries, 2009 PISA

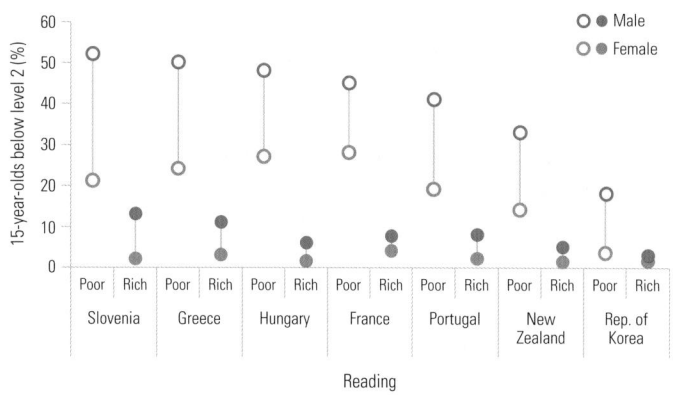

Note: Poor/Rich = bottom/top quartile in PISA economic, social and cultural status index.
Source: EFA Global Monitoring Report team analysis of Altinok (2012b), based on the 2009 PISA.

the issue to the fore, as in the United Kingdom (Cassen and Kingdon, 2007).

Increased awareness is not yet being sufficiently translated into effective action, however. A lack of consensus about the causes of boys' educational disadvantage is one reason; another is the justified focus on the range of challenges girls still face.

Tackling boys' lower enrolment and performance requires a comprehensive approach that addresses their disadvantage due to labour market demands as well as their disengagement due to classroom practices and gender attitudes. A focus on three areas, each of which can also benefit girls' education, is required:

■ reducing the effects of poverty on educational participation and achievement;

■ improving the quality and inclusive nature of schools; and

■ offering second chances to those who have dropped out.

Reducing poverty can boost boys' enrolment and achievement
Social protection programmes can support school participation for boys and girls, and in some cases improve learning outcomes (UNESCO, 2010b). Such programmes need to take gender into account. In Jamaica, the Programme of Advancement through Health and Education (PATH) is a government-funded conditional cash transfer programme supporting poor families, which includes waivers for secondary school fees and textbooks. The programme had a significant positive effect on school attendance but the effect on boys aged 13 to 17 was not stronger than that for girls, even though the policy was concerned with the lower attendance rates of teenage boys (Levy and Ohls, 2007). Since 2008, the transfer has been higher for boys than for girls and for secondary school than for primary school students to address the pressure on poor boys to get a job (Fiszbein et al., 2009).

Evaluations of cash transfer programmes show that boys do not always stand to benefit more in countries where they are at a greater disadvantage. In Brazil, the Bolsa Família programme has sizeable positive effects on school outcomes but girls in lower secondary schools have benefited significantly more, with lower dropout and higher promotion rates (Glewwe and Kassouf, 2012). In Mexico, the grant provided to households by the Progresa programme (later renamed Oportunidades) was larger for girls of secondary school age. It increased school attendance by 7.5% for boys aged 14 to 17, slightly less than for girls (Attanasio et al., 2012; Barrera-Osorio et al., 2011). Such outcomes point to the need to consider the barriers to boys' participation when designing programmes.

High quality, inclusive schools can create the right environment
A range of approaches can help raise boys' engagement and achievement by promoting a school ethos of cooperation, respect for students and action against gender stereotypes. Some countries have encouraged individual schools to come up with their own approaches to improving outcomes for boys.

In England, the Raising Boys' Achievement Project worked with primary and secondary schools that had succeeded in narrowing the gender gap to identify strategies that improve boys' learning and engagement with schooling. Some schools emphasized individual strategies to stimulate boys' interest and engagement, for example through setting realistic targets to bolster their belief in themselves. Other schools responded to the range of learning styles exhibited by both girls and boys by adapting their pedagogy. For example, they emphasized creative approaches to literacy and interactive classroom activities. There were also school-wide organizational approaches. Some schools developed a team ethic so that underachieving students would feel included (Younger et al., 2005).

Cash transfer programmes need to include the most disadvantaged boys

A similar programme in Australia, Boys' Education Lighthouse Schools, documented best practice in boys' education from about 350 schools. A compendium of resources based on the programme was developed for teachers. A follow-up project, Success for Boys, provided grants for up to 1,600 schools to improve boys' education. The professional learning programme included a focus on effective literacy teaching and on the use of information technology to improve boys' engagement with active learning (Munns et al., 2006).

This is a rare example where lessons learned have fed into a teacher training programme. Few countries appear to have given sufficient attention to professional development aimed at reducing the gender gap in achievement and male disaffection with school. When it comes to learning outcomes, it is the capacity of teachers to engage and support the learning of both boys and girls that matters. That fact underlines the need for high quality teacher education that includes appropriate training in gender issues.

In some countries, achievement-based streaming is practised in secondary schools with the intention of helping underperforming students. However, findings from a large number of studies in high income countries have failed to demonstrate consistently positive effects of streaming on student performance (Meier and Schütz, 2007; OECD, 2010c). Moreover, where boys are underperforming and perceived as hard to discipline, this practice can result in higher proportions of boys in the lower streams. Streaming students can reinforce negative perceptions of their ability by teachers, peers and themselves.

Single-sex schools are another response to boys' disengagement from education. If such schools sometimes improve the learning outcomes of girls or boys, however, it may be because they tend to be particularly well funded and well managed, with high achieving students who have supportive parents (ACCES, 2011; Halpern et al., 2011). Trinidad and Tobago converted many schools to single-sex environments on the assumption that this would make it easier for teachers to cater to boys' learning styles and reduce peer pressure (Jones-Parry and Green, 2010). However, a recent study showed that most students performed no better at single-sex schools in Trinidad and Tobago, the exception being students (particularly girls) who had expressed a strong preference for attending a single-sex school (Jackson, 2011).

Mentoring programmes can help boys – especially the most disadvantaged – become more self-confident, improve their behaviour and prevent them from disengaging from school (DuBois et al., 2002). In the United States, the century-old Big Brothers Big Sisters programme, which requires volunteer mentors to spend three to five hours per week with a child for at least a year, has been credited with improved behaviour. This result led to the introduction of a school-based variant of the programme. For this type of intervention to succeed, mentors need to be trained, interactions monitored and parents closely involved (Smith and Stormont, 2011).

One of the most difficult aspects of tackling boys' disadvantage in education is how to foster positive gender attitudes, helping boys respect themselves and take pride in responsible, socially acceptable, non-violent behaviour. While this needs to happen in households and communities, schools are a key place where action can be taken. In the Caribbean, a regional contest among non-government projects highlighted the best ways of helping boys at risk, including developing a sense of achievement by valuing each boy's contributions and creating a non-threatening and non-judgemental environment (Orlando and Lundwall, 2010; World Bank, 2011b).

Offering second chances can help boys make progress

In some countries, boys have been the focus of policies and programmes that bring young

In Trinidad and Tobago, most children performed no better at single-sex schools

people who had dropped out back into school. Second-chance programmes, often run outside the formal education system, can offer boys an opportunity to complete their secondary schooling and gain social and economic skills:

- In Jamaica, the Male Awareness Now (MAN) project, managed by the NGO Children First, works with out-of-school males aged 14 to 24 and their parents in Spanish Town, a poor and crime-ridden urban area. The project provides vocational and life skills, health forums, guidance, and cultural and sporting activities to help boys and young men move into school, training or employment and away from drugs and guns. The project has improved self-esteem, behaviour and attitudes among most participants, and two-thirds of participants successfully completed and received certification in a specific basic skill (Christian Aid, 2010; World Bank and Commonwealth Secretariat, 2009).

- In Samoa, the government and religious bodies run second-chance schools offering basic, vocational and life skills for early school leavers, primarily boys (Jha et al., 2012; UIS, 2012).

- In Lesotho, an NGO runs night schools where English, Sesotho and mathematics are taught, and a hot meal is provided, for young male herders who are otherwise unable to go to school because of their livestock rearing responsibilities (Sentebale, 2011).

Conclusion

Policymakers must not lose sight of the goal of bringing all school-age girls into primary and secondary school. At the same time, it is vital to address the fact that some boys are falling behind in secondary school. Focusing on education quality and inclusiveness, while tackling the effects of poverty and offering second chances, can reduce boys' disadvantage and disengagement, and so improve participation and outcomes for all children.

Policy-makers must address the fact that some boys are falling behind in secondary school

CHAPTER 1

Goal 6 The quality of education

Improving all aspects of the quality of education and ensuring excellence of all so that recognized and measurable learning outcomes are achieved by all, especially in literacy, numeracy and essential life skills.

Highlights

■ Millions of children who go to school do not learn the basics. Out of around 650 million children of primary school age, as many as 250 million either do not reach grade 4 or, if they do, fail to attain minimum learning standards.

■ Pupil/teacher ratios at primary level improved globally between 1999 and 2010, especially in East Asia and Latin America. But they worsened in sub-Saharan Africa and South and West Asia, the regions that already had the highest pupil/teacher ratios.

■ A significant proportion of teachers remain untrained at both primary and secondary level. Of 100 countries with data at the primary level, in 33 less than 75% of teachers were trained to the national standard. Even those who have received training are not always well-prepared to teach in early grades.

Table 1.11: Key indicators for goal 6

	Pre-primary education				Primary education				Secondary education			
	Teaching staff		Pupil/teacher ratio		Teaching staff		Pupil/teacher ratio		Teaching staff		Pupil/teacher ratio	
	2010 (000)	Change since 1999 (%)	1999	2010	2010 (000)	Change since 1999 (%)	1999	2010	2010 (000)	Change since 1999 (%)	1999	2010
World	7 787	45	21	21	28 483	15	26	24	31 951	31	18	17
Low income countries	384	80	27	24	2 830	64	43	43	1 787	84	27	26
Lower middle income countries	...	...	26	...	9 576	22	31	31	9 680	67	24	21
Upper middle income countries	3 152	21	19	19	10 885	4	24	19	13 269	18	16	16
High income countries	1 899	37	18	15	5 193	9	16	14	7 215	14	14	12
Sub-Saharan Africa	444	126	28	27	3 103	59	42	43	1 722	107	25	25
Arab States	193	63	20	20	1 954	29	23	21	1 992	46	16	15
Central Asia	152	18	10	11	323	-2	21	17	920	8	11	11
East Asia and the Pacific	2 096	49	26	21	10 376	13	24	18	10 459	38	17	16
South and West Asia	...	...	37	...	4 853	12	36	39	5 376	84	33	27
Latin America and the Caribbean	1 028	35	21	20	3 020	11	26	22	3 635	31	19	17
North America and Western Europe	1 545	45	18	14	3 741	9	15	14	5 204	16	14	12
Central and Eastern Europe	1 086	-3	8	10	1 113	-18	18	17	2 643	-24	12	11

Sources: Annex, Statistical Tables 4 and 8.

Making sure that children learn should be at the heart of any education system. National, regional and international assessments have contributed to a growing realization that, despite international convergence in terms of access to primary school, inequality in learning achievement between countries remains wide. The scale of learning deficits shows that there is far more to be done to ensure not only that more children get into school, but also that they achieve expected learning outcomes. For each child who does not reach grade 4, estimates for this Report suggest, another child who reaches this grade may be failing to learn the basics (Panel 1.12).

To achieve good learning outcomes for all, extreme disadvantage within countries needs to be overcome (Panel 1.13). Some education systems are better prepared than others to narrow the gap between an average child and a child marginalized by poverty, location, ethnicity or other factors.

Teachers are the most important resource for improving learning. A lack of teachers, and especially of trained teachers, presents a major obstacle to achieving the EFA goals.

The latest estimates suggest that 112 countries need to expand their teacher workforce by a total of 5.4 million primary school teachers by 2015 (UIS, 2011). New recruits are needed to cover both the 2 million additional posts required to reach universal primary education and the 3.4 million posts of those leaving the profession. Sub-Saharan African countries alone need to recruit more than 2 million teachers to achieve universal primary education.

The total number of primary school teachers grew by 15% between 1999 and 2010, resulting in a small decline in the global pupil/teacher ratio from 26:1 to 24:1. However, the number of teachers did not keep pace with the increasing number of pupils in the two regions facing the largest challenges. The pupil/teacher ratio increased in South and West Asia from 36:1 to 39:1. In sub-Saharan Africa, despite the recruitment of more than 1.1 million teachers, equivalent to a 59% increase, the pupil/teacher ratio rose slightly, from 42:1 to 43:1 – the highest in the world.

Overall, of 165 countries with data, there were 26 in which the pupil/teacher ratio was above 40:1 in 2010, including 22 in sub-Saharan Africa. Seven countries

saw their ratios grow by more than five pupils for every teacher over the decade: the Democratic Republic of the Congo, Guinea-Bissau, Kenya, Pakistan, Samoa, the former Sudan and Yemen. Each experienced a significant rise in the gross enrolment ratio, far outstripping any increase in teacher numbers. This raises serious concerns for the quality of education in these countries.

Yet some countries with growing primary enrolment were able to improve their pupil/teacher ratio significantly. In Senegal, for example, the gross enrolment ratio rose from 68% in 1999 to 87% in 2010, while the pupil/teacher ratio fell from 49:1 to 34:1.

In many countries, the percentage of teachers trained according to national standards is low. Of 100 countries with data, 33 have less than 75% of their primary school teachers trained, and in 12 the share is less than 50%; among them are Benin, Ethiopia, Honduras, Liberia, Mali and Sierra Leone.

In secondary education, the global teaching force has grown by 31% – much more than at the primary level. Growth was particularly strong in South and West Asia, with an 84% rise, and sub-Saharan Africa, where the number more than doubled. The secondary pupil/teacher ratio stayed constant or decreased in every region, markedly so in South and West Asia (from 33:1 to 27:1). Overall, out of 110 countries with data, only 11 had pupil/teacher ratios in lower secondary education above 35:1 in 2010.

Data on the percentage of trained teachers are more sporadic at secondary level, but it is clear that many countries are not training enough secondary school teachers to the minimal level prescribed. Of fifty-nine countries with data, twenty-six have less than 75% of their secondary school teachers trained, and eleven have less than 50% of their teachers trained. The latter include Bangladesh, Burkina Faso, the Democratic Republic of the Congo, and the Niger.

Overcrowded classrooms and poorly trained teachers are resulting in children struggling to learn the basics in many parts of the world, particularly in low income countries. While many factors contribute to poor learning outcomes, lack of teacher preparedness in early grades leaves a legacy that is difficult to overcome later in the education cycle. This is a constraint that policy-makers must rectify (goal 6, policy focus).

Panel 1.12: Millions of primary school-age children are failing to learn the basics

Concerning the world's 650 million children of primary school age, it is time for the emphasis to fall not only on the 120 million who do not reach grade 4 but also on the additional 130 million who are in school but failing to learn the basics.

Getting more children into school has been one of the successes of the EFA movement since 2000. There were 50 million more children in classrooms in sub-Saharan Africa and 33 million more in South and West Asia in 2010 than in 1999. This inevitably places a strain on the limited resources available for teaching and learning in the regions that have been furthest from the EFA goals. Many of the new students may enter school with disadvantages that make their learning more difficult: they may have poorer health, they are less likely to have had the opportunity to attend pre-school, and their parents are less likely to be educated and so are unable to support their learning.

Should getting more children into primary school really be considered a success if they are not acquiring the necessary skills? Concern about this question has led to a call for steps to tackle the problem, such as improving measurement of learning outcomes (Center for Universal Education, 2011). This urgent call for action is amply justified.

Four recent regional and international surveys provide a basis for comparing learning outcomes at the primary education level across countries.[23] New analysis for this Report attempts to provide a snapshot of the extent to which children are both staying in school until grade 4 and learning the basics. The focus for this purpose is on mathematics.

In some countries, a large proportion do not reach grade 4: either they have not had the chance to enter school, or they have dropped out before reaching that level (Figure 1.47). In Burundi, Congo, Mozambique,

23. The surveys are PASEC, SACMEQ, SERCE and TIMSS.

Nicaragua and Senegal, at least one in three children do not reach grade 4. For these children who have dropped out before grade 4, it can be assumed that they would be unlikely to achieve minimum learning outcomes.

For those children who make it to grade 4, many do not achieve what the four surveys define as the minimum level in mathematics. According to the benchmarks set by the studies, one in six children in Latin America who took part in SERCE and almost two in three children in southern and eastern Africa who took part in SACMEQ failed to acquire basic numeracy skills.

In Nicaragua, for example, only 61% of children have reached grade 4, of whom 74% achieved the expected minimum learning level in SERCE; in other words, only 46% of the cohort is expected to achieve the minimum learning level. By contrast, almost all children reached grade 4 in Cuba and achieved the minimum learning level in SERCE.

Not only do few children reach grade 4 in southern Africa, but many do not achieve the minimum benchmark set by SACMEQ. The experience of Malawi is of particular concern. Despite great strides in increasing enrolment and narrowing the gender gap in recent years, 34% of children do not reach grade 4. Due to high levels of dropout and poor quality of schooling, only 5% of the cohort achieves the minimum learning level.

There is no inevitable trade-off between quantity and quality of education; increasing enrolment does not necessarily lead to lower learning achievement. Comparing countries participating in a given survey highlights the relative ability of education systems to help children acquire basic skills. Among countries that participated in the third SACMEQ study, almost four in five children make it to grade 4 in Kenya and Zambia, but schools in Kenya are more than twice as effective in ensuring that they learn basic mathematics skills. Among participating countries in TIMSS, both Algeria and Tunisia saw 98 of 100 children make it to grade 4.

Figure 1.47: Even if they progress through the grades, many primary school children do not acquire basic knowledge and skills

Percentage of cohort who reach grade 4 and achieve minimum learning level in mathematics, four regional and international learning assessments

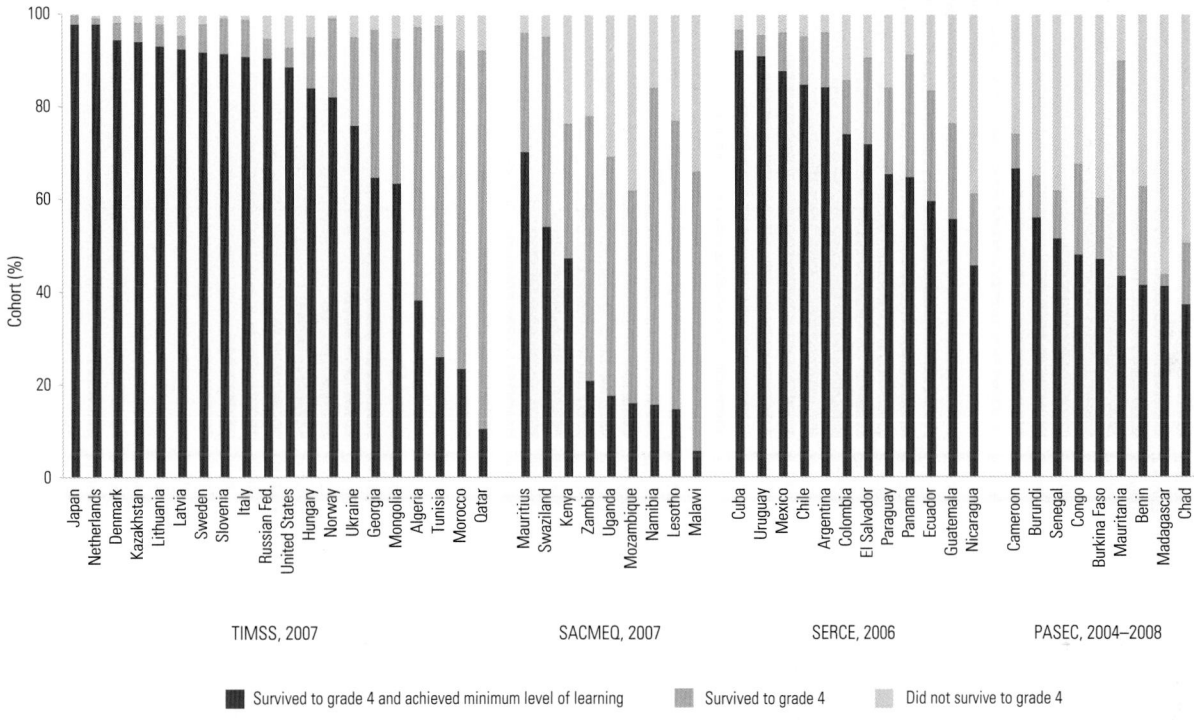

TIMSS, 2007   SACMEQ, 2007   SERCE, 2006   PASEC, 2004–2008

■ Survived to grade 4 and achieved minimum level of learning   ■ Survived to grade 4   ▢ Did not survive to grade 4

Notes: The percentage of children who reached grade 4 is based on the expected cohort completion rate methodology. The definition of achievement of a minimum learning level depends on the benchmark specified in a given survey: low international benchmark (TIMSS); level 1 (SERCE); level 3 (SACMEQ); and level 1 (PASEC).
Sources: Altinok (2012a); UIS database; and EFA Global Monitoring Report team calculations (2012).

Yet the percentage achieving basic numeracy skills was 50% higher in Algeria than in Tunisia.

The learning assessments do not provide a global picture of achievement at primary level, as each is designed with different objectives and for different contexts. They measure reading and mathematics in different ways and test students in different grades.

A proper comparison would require students from all countries to take the same test in the same grade or at the same age. However, even though they are not strictly comparable, the lack of a full set of rigorously comparable data should not prevent recognition of the full extent of the learning deficit – and the inequalities in learning between countries.

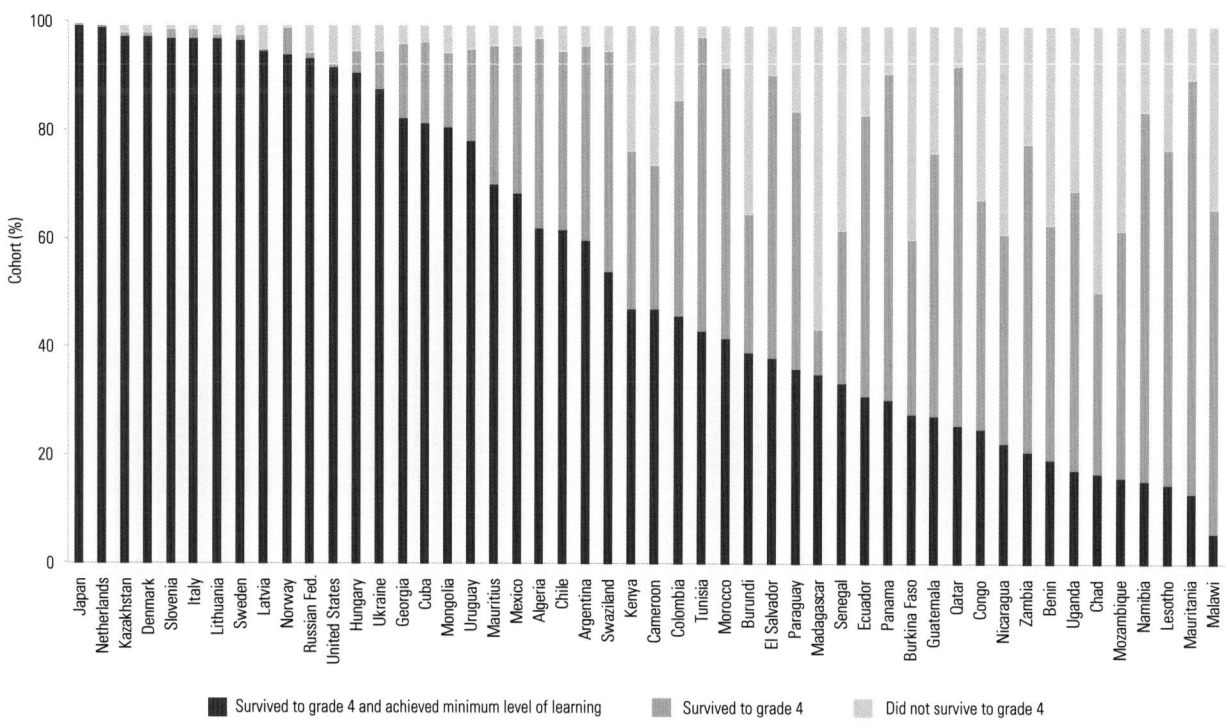

Figure 1.48: Cross-country inequality in primary school participation is much smaller than inequality in learning outcomes
Percentage of cohort who reach grade 4 and achieve minimum learning level in mathematics in four regional and international learning assessments

■ Survived to grade 4 and achieved minimum level of learning   ■ Survived to grade 4   ■ Did not survive to grade 4

Notes: The percentage of childen who reached grade 4 is based on the expected cohort completion rate methodology. The ranking of countries is based on an anchoring process that linearly transforms the score of each country in relation to the scores of countries that have participated in two learning achievement surveys.
Sources: Altinok (2012a); UIS database; and EFA Global Monitoring Report team calculations (2012).

Analysis for this Report places all countries on a rough common scale of learning (Altinok, 2012a) (Figure 1.48).[24] The comparisons show that, inevitably, children in rich countries, such as Japan and the Netherlands, are not only more likely to stay in school until grade 4 but also to achieve the minimum learning benchmark. At the other end of the spectrum, children in poorer countries – notably in Africa but also some Latin American countries, including Guatemala and Nicaragua – are more likely to drop out and, for those who make it to grade 4, not to achieve the basics.

The scale of the variation provides a stark illustration of the vast difference in opportunity to learn that children face by virtue of where they are born. Just 16 in 100 children in a poor country like Mozambique are able to learn the basics, compared with 79 in Uruguay and 100 in Japan.

What can this information tell us about the global learning deficit? The average rate of achievement of basic learning outcomes for the four assessments was used to estimate the extent of basic learning in countries lacking data. There are additional challenges because China and countries in South and West Asia, which together make up 41% of the population of primary school age children, have not participated in any international or regional assessment at primary level. Using further assumptions for these countries,[25] estimates by the EFA Global Monitoring Report team suggest that around 250 million children either fail to make it to grade 4 or do not reach the minimum level of learning.[26]

24. This is achieved by anchoring the results of all international and regional assessments (carried out over 2004–2008) at upper primary level (grades 4 to 6) using countries that at some point took part in more than one survey (such as Colombia and El Salvador in TIMSS and SERCE; Botswana in TIMSS and SACMEQ; and Mauritius in SACMEQ and PASEC).

25. For China, an estimate close to the TIMMS average was used. For South and West Asia, the average used was around ten percentage points lower than SERCE.
26. A similar figure is estimated based on analysis of the same learning assessments using data on reading.

Panel 1.13: Learning achievement within countries varies with socio-economic status

International and regional learning assessments can show the extent to which factors of disadvantage, such as low socio-economic status, determine individual achievement in each country.

Of the international assessments, the 2009 PISA has the most comprehensive coverage. PISA surveyed seventy-four countries and economies: all the OECD countries and forty other countries and economies. This includes less affluent non-OECD countries, although no sub-Saharan African countries participated and, in South and West Asia, only two states in India were included.

The survey assessed the performance of 15-year-olds, and in addition collected data on parental occupation and education and on selected home characteristics, such as the availability of books. With this information, an index

of economic, social and cultural status was constructed. It can be used to identify the relationship between students' performance in school and the disadvantages they face because of their home background.

In every country, the higher the quartile of the socio-economic index to which a student belongs, the better the performance, with a similar pattern for boys and girls (Figure 1.49). At one end of the spectrum, most 15-year-olds in richer countries such as Canada, Finland, the Republic of Korea and Singapore reach level 2, and the gap between students from households with higher and lower socio-economic status is narrow. At the other end, in less wealthy countries such as Argentina, Chile, Colombia and Jordan, the gap is much wider. The achievement gap can, however, only partially be explained by a country's overall income level.

Figure 1.49: Learning achievement varies by socio-economic status

Percentage of students at or above level 2 in mathematics, by economic, social and cultural status and gender, 2009 PISA

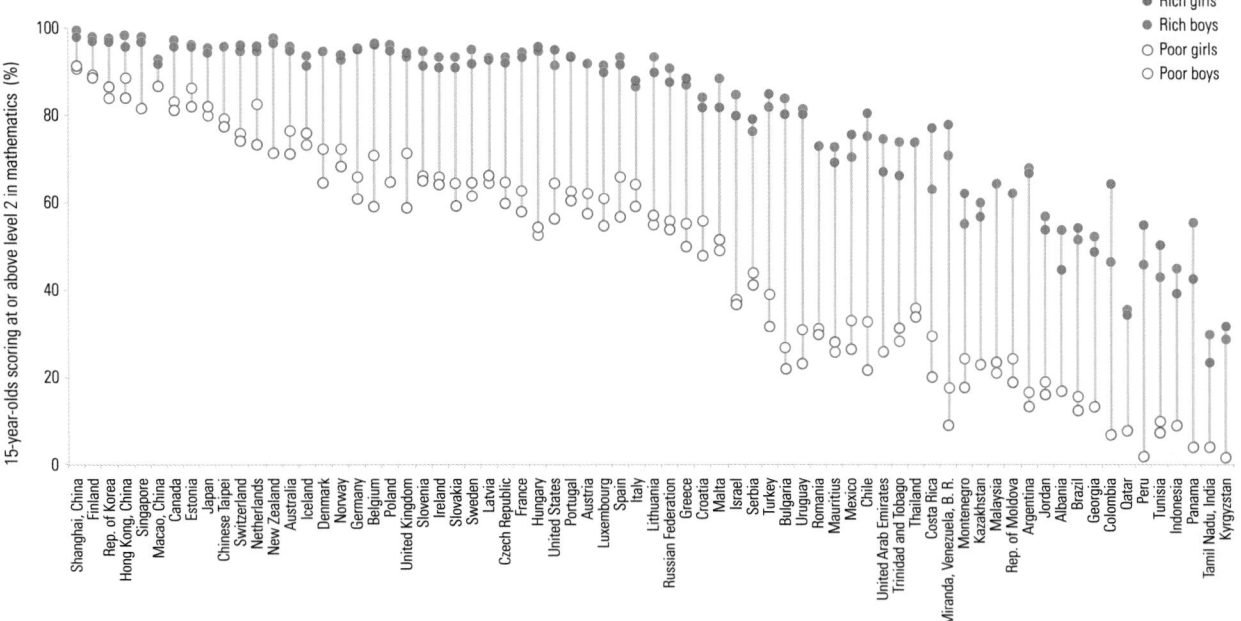

Notes: Of countries and economies that participated in the 2009 PISA, Azerbaijan, Himachal Pradesh (India) and Liechtenstein are not included. Poor/Rich refers to the bottom/top quartile in the PISA economic, social and cultural status index.

Sources: Altinok (2012b), based on 2009 PISA data; Walker (2011).

In high income and upper middle income countries, even among countries with the same mean score, some education systems are better in ensuring that disadvantaged students are not left too far behind. For example, although Finland and Switzerland have a similar mean score, the difference in performance between rich and poor is much wider in Switzerland. In particular, there is a very large gap in the proportion of students from the bottom quartile performing below level 2, with 11% in Finland scoring below this level compared to 25% in Switzerland.

The role of socio-economic status and other background characteristics in explaining variation in learning achievement differs from country to country. For example, individual background explains a higher share of variation in reading performance in Austria, France and Hungary (between 28% and 36%) than in Croatia, Greece and Norway (between 18% and 21%) (OECD, 2010b). Where the relationship between background and learning is strong, disadvantaged students are denied one of the key routes to social mobility.

In middle income countries, student performance is very low: on average, at least half scored below level 2 in mathematics. In Brazil, seven out of ten are below this benchmark. In addition, the distribution of student performance is heavily skewed towards richer households: students in the top quartile do much better than those in the three bottom quartiles. In Thailand, for example, the percentage of students from the bottom three quartiles who scored below level 2 ranged between 56% and 65%. By comparison, only 26% of students from the top quartile performed so poorly (Figure 1.50).

Over time, some middle income countries have been able to reduce inequality in learning outcomes. The percentage of low performers in each quartile of socio-economic status in Brazil and Mexico fell between 2003 and 2009. This is particularly impressive given that participation in secondary education increased significantly over the period. Targeted social protection policies since the late 1990s in these countries are a likely source of the gains made by disadvantaged students. By contrast, in Indonesia and Thailand the gap between the top and bottom quartiles widened.

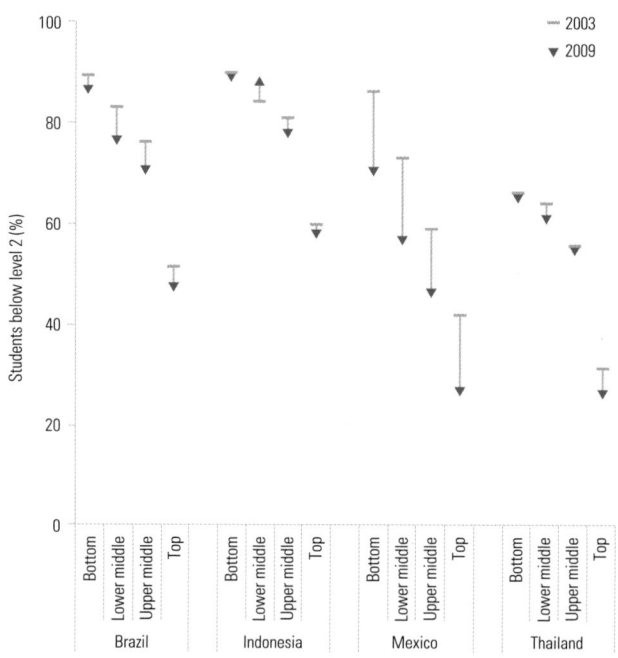

Figure 1.50: Learning outcomes are very low for disadvantaged students in middle income countries – but can improve rapidly

Percentage of students below level 2 in mathematics, by economic, social, and cultural status, selected middle income countries, 2003 and 2009 PISA

Source: Altinok (2012b), based on 2003 and 2009 PISA data.

Middle income countries see more children drop out of school before age 15 than do high income countries. Since surveys like PISA only test those in school, they exclude the poorest performing children who have already dropped out of school and tend to be from disadvantaged backgrounds – so the achievement gap could be even wider than the surveys show (Ferreira and Gignoux, 2011). In Indonesia, for example, the proportion of 15-year-olds included in the 2009 survey was 53%, but the OECD average was 88%.

To reduce inequality in learning achievement, middle income countries need to surmount several obstacles. First, they have wider income inequality (reflected in the larger range of the PISA index of economic, social and cultural status). Second, their schools are less diverse –

Table 1.12: Characteristics of sampled populations in PISA, selected middle income countries relative to the OECD average

	Coverage rate of population of 15-year olds (%)		Range of index of economic, social and cultural status	Social inclusion index
	2003	2009	2009	2009
Brazil	54	63	3.94	65
Indonesia	46	53	3.55	61
Mexico	49	61	4.18	56
Thailand	69	73	3.72	49
OECD average	89	88	2.92	75

Source: OECD (2010b).

or more segregated along socio-economic lines – than in OECD countries: students from a low socio-economic background are more likely to be grouped in the same schools (a fact reflected in the lower value of the PISA social inclusion index) (Table 1.12). Such segregation can have adverse consequences for learning, as it means weaker students do not receive stimulation from stronger-performing students. Without redistributive measures, there is also a risk of fewer resources being allocated to schools with weaker students, since they tend to be in poorer areas.

In low income countries, socio-economic status has a very strong effect on both education attainment and learning outcomes. This fact may not be as apparent if these countries are compared on the same scale of learning outcomes as richer countries. The vast majority score below the minimum level, and so differences

between wealth groups tend to be smaller. For example, in Kyrgyzstan, the only low income country that took part in the 2009 PISA, 88% of students scored below level 2 in mathematics, with 70% of those from the highest quartile scoring below this level, compared with 98% from the lowest quartile.

The role of socio-economic status becomes clearer in assessments which are able to identify differences at the lower end of the learning outcome distribution. For example, in 2009/10, Uwezo household surveys in three East African countries assessed whether children aged 6 to 16 had mastered the rudimentary literacy and numeracy skills expected of children at the end of grade 2. Among grade 3 students in Kenya, only 28% of students from the poorest fifth of households had attained the expected numeracy skills, compared with 48% of children from the richest fifth of households (Uwezo, 2011).

Analysing these patterns of inequality in learning outcomes, and what is driving them, can help shape policies that enable children from poor backgrounds to beat the odds (OECD, 2011a). Policy-makers can target additional resources for disadvantaged students to prevent low performance or to help low-performing schools bridge gaps. Where individual background accounts for a large share of differences in performance, authorities can offer incentives to good teachers to encourage them to teach in poor neighbourhoods. In middle income countries, where income inequality can thwart the effectiveness of education-specific measures, cash transfers can mitigate the multiple disadvantages that students from poorer backgrounds face.

Policy focus:
Addressing the crisis in early grade teaching

Teachers' knowledge and abilities are at the heart of children's learning in school. Yet, all too often, teachers are insufficiently prepared to teach. This is leading to a crisis in learning, with many children completing early grades of primary school unable to read a single word.

The expansion of primary enrolment in many countries has led to chronic shortages of teachers. With an estimated 2 million additional teachers needed by 2015, this is a key concern (UIS, 2011). But it is not the only one. Low levels of education and poor training are leaving teachers without the core subject knowledge and pedagogical skills they need to ensure that children develop strong foundations in basic literacy and numeracy. Nowhere is this more of a concern than in the initial years of primary school. If children are unable to learn the basics early on, their chances of acquiring other skills in later grades are slim. Evidence is increasing that early grade education is failing children, especially in poor countries.

The learning crisis is leading policy-makers to turn their attention to the role of teachers in early grades and the contributions made by pre-service and in-service training. This section identifies challenges in teacher training and explores effective solutions.

Assessments in the early grades highlight a chronic learning problem

Very poor levels of learning at lower grades of primary school are resulting in millions of children leaving education before acquiring basic skills. Children who have not learned to read a text or do basic calculations have little chance of benefiting from higher primary school grades. Moreover, their commitment to education is likely to diminish and they are more likely to drop out (Glick and Sahn, 2010; Liddell and Rae, 2001).

Early grade reading assessments in several countries have shown that many children spend two or three years in school without learning to

read a single word. In Mali, for instance, 94% of second graders could not read a single word in French and at least eight out of ten could not read a single word in four national languages, despite the fact that Mali is the most advanced among West African francophone countries in using national languages in education (Gove and Cvelich, 2010; Varly, 2010).

In Bauchi and Sokoto, two states of northern Nigeria, 4,000 grade 3 students were assessed in Hausa, which is the language of instruction and the lingua franca as well as the mother tongue for the vast majority of students. Just 29% of students in Bauchi and 18% in Sokoto could read full words. These students were given a reading comprehension test: less than one-fifth of them achieved a score of 80% – accounting for only 6% of all students in Bauchi and 3% in Sokoto (RTI International, 2011).

The shocking results have turned the spotlight on how teachers are trained, and the support they receive once they are in the classroom.

Well-trained teachers are key to improving children's early learning

Children cannot benefit fully from school if they live in poverty, are malnourished, suffer from ill health or live in conflict zones. Yet teachers who are effectively trained and have strong subject knowledge can make a huge difference in the educational fortunes of children from disadvantaged backgrounds, especially in the early years of schooling.

Children are more likely to develop reading and writing skills when their families encourage them by providing learning materials such as books at home (Ngorosho, 2011). In poor countries, where many children are first-generation learners, there may be no adults in their families to provide crucial support, for example by reading them stories. Pre-school can help disadvantaged children benefit from primary school, but early childhood services

In Mali, over 80% of students in grade 2 could not read a single word in four national languages

2012
Education for All Global Monitoring Report

are underdeveloped in areas where they are needed most (see goal 1 policy focus). This means that it is even more crucial to prepare early grade teachers well to teach basic skills in poor countries, and to pay particular attention to children from disadvantaged backgrounds.

Teachers themselves may lack the necessary subject knowledge and the ability to turn it into effective approaches to instruction. In a 2010 survey of primary schools in Kenya, teachers and their students in grade 6 were given a mathematics test. The average score for the teachers was 60%. Not surprisingly, students also received low scores, around 47%. Some teachers scored as low as 17% on the standardized mathematics test, which was set from the primary school syllabus. Researchers concluded that no teacher in the sample had complete mastery of the subject (Ngware et al., 2010). In Kano state of northern Nigeria, a test of some 1,200 basic education teachers found that around 78% had 'limited' knowledge in English after an assessment in which they were asked to take a reading comprehension test and correct sentences written by a 10-year-old child for form, content and punctuation (ESSPIN, 2011).

Teachers' poor scores reveal their own low levels of educational attainment. Where education systems have expanded rapidly, teachers have sometimes been recruited with few qualifications. Trainees tend to enter teacher training colleges in Kenya, Uganda and the United Republic of Tanzania, for example, having completed only basic education (Akyeampong et al., 2011).

More broadly, there is a need to attract the best people into the teaching profession. Brazil has managed to make teacher recruitment more selective by introducing a national entry exam and competitive recruitment of newly qualified teachers. It also funds places for teachers at universities, especially in subjects where they are most needed, and has created a high-speed career track for top-performing teachers (Bennell, 2011). But attracting teacher candidates with strong subject content backgrounds is difficult in many poor countries because teaching has low status and the pay is poor (Bennell and Akyeampong, 2007). In

Ghana, for example, teachers see primary school teaching as a stepping stone to jobs with higher status or better pay (Akyeampong, 2003).

Ensuring that children achieve the basic foundations in the early grades is a vital way of overcoming early disadvantage, so the best teachers should be deployed to the early grades. Unfortunately, the opposite is often true, with less experienced teachers assigned to lower classes, where the number of students can be extremely large. The pattern holds even more often in areas that are less likely to attract experienced teachers, such as slums or remote rural districts, where working and living conditions are poor (Bennell and Akyeampong, 2007). This translates into low achievement. Data collected in Malawi in 2010 show that the number of words grade 4 students could read correctly in a minute varied from 26 in classes with 75 students to just 13 in classes with 175 students (Trudell et al., 2012).

In Kenya, some teachers scored just 17% in primary school maths tests

Effective teacher education needs to combine subject knowledge with pedagogical skills

Most teachers learn to teach reading and basic mathematics during pre-service and in-service training. Where teacher trainees have inadequate subject knowledge in core subjects, teacher training colleges need to emphasize remedial measures, while paying attention to pedagogical training.

Pre-service training often does not prepare teachers adequately for early grades

For pre-service training to be effective, teachers should already have a sufficient knowledge of their subjects so that training can develop their skills in teaching children in the early grades. Too often this is not the case.

Just receiving training is not enough – the content and quality of training are crucial. Children in many East Asian countries have achieved impressive literacy results mainly because their teachers have strong backgrounds in the subjects they teach and have received effective initial training and professional support in schools (Jensen, 2012). This achievement shows what is possible, although lack of

In the Gambia, 77% of primary teacher trainees had never taught at primary school

resources and institutional capacity makes it difficult to replicate in poorer countries.

In low income countries, teachers can spend from six months to four years in pre-service training programmes. Whatever the duration, these programmes can be costly. In Ghana, for example, governments pay around forty-five times as much on training a teacher as on teaching a primary school student (Lewin and Stuart, 2003). Given this significant public investment, it is vital to ensure that trainees learn how to teach. In many developing countries, a large part of training is devoted to repeating the secondary school curriculum to improve trainees' subject knowledge. While this is necessary when trainees have left school without core knowledge, it leaves too little time for developing teaching skills.

The problem is reinforced by the limited experience of some of those who train. In anglophone African countries, instructors in many primary school teacher preparation courses tend to be former secondary school teachers with little knowledge or experience of teaching at primary level: in the Gambia, 77% of instructors had never taught primary school themselves (Mulkeen, 2010).

In some West African countries, contract teachers have been recruited to reduce the strain on education budgets while ensuring that there are sufficient teachers in the classroom (UNESCO, 2010b). In Guinea, for example, only contract teachers have been recruited since 1998. By 2003 they accounted for half the teaching force. The duration of teacher preparation has been reduced to between fifteen and eighteen months, compared with a total of three years previously. This has helped reduce large pupil/teacher ratios. Evaluations suggest that the new teachers are as able as the previous ones to teach basic skills (Pôle de Dakar, 2009).

While this helps to alleviate the immediate pressures, in other contexts there is a risk that shorter training periods offered to contract teachers do not allow trainees to develop sufficient basic teaching skills and to improve their subject knowledge where it is weak. In Mali, for instance, civil servant teachers receive more

than a year of training while 73% of contract teachers receive only a three-month course (Pôle de Dakar, 2009).

In addition to the length of training, attention is also needed to ensure teachers receive training that prepares them to teach in the early grades. A study covering Ghana, Kenya, Mali, Senegal, Uganda and the United Republic of Tanzania found that trainees received only a very basic introduction to teaching early grade reading (Akyeampong et al., 2011). The teaching of reading was often not seen as needing special attention but was treated alongside other topics in the language or literature course. In Senegal and the United Republic of Tanzania, for example, teaching reading is not a separate topic. The study also found that initial teacher education did not prepare trainee teachers for the multilingual classroom. In the francophone countries, training was given only in French, and just 8% of new teachers surveyed in Senegal and 2% in Mali expressed any confidence in teaching reading in local languages. In the anglophone countries, there was provision for teaching in local languages but 68% of new teachers in Uganda, 74% in Kenya and 79% in Ghana expressed confidence in teaching reading only in English.

Providing trainees with more practical experience is important. To be effective, this classroom time needs to be accompanied by adequate supervision and support. But time spent in the classroom as part of training programmes is often too short, and separate from what is taught in the training college. It usually offers no opportunity to learn how to teach over many lessons. Thus many new teachers start without any experience of the challenges of teaching children to read or do basic sums. Only in Ghana, Kenya and Senegal were trainees expected to teach the three early grades. In Ghana, trainees were paired and, with the support of experienced mentors, taught for stretches of time in lower grades. The rationale was to give trainees the opportunity to support each other in teaching and discuss with mentors challenges they faced (Akyeampong et al., 2011).

In summary, pre-service teacher training needs to pay attention to the particular challenges of teaching in early grades, and ensure that all trainees have some experience of teaching at this level before becoming qualified.

In-service training can help teachers teach in early grades

Properly designed and adequately supported in-service training can make a significant difference to teachers' classroom performance and hence to children's learning.

Many new primary school teachers have not had the opportunity for training, particularly in poor countries that have recruited untrained teachers. This is often because of acute shortages of trained teachers willing to serve in remote and poor rural communities. Some countries are responding by investing in special training programmes.

For example, in Ghana teacher training has not been able to supply enough trained teachers willing to serve in rural areas, a situation that has led to significant growth in numbers of untrained teachers. The government decided to invest in training specifically geared for untrained teachers who are on one-year renewable contracts and serving in some of the poorest districts. A distance learning programme begun in 2007 had trained about 25,000 teachers by 2010. An evaluation revealed striking improvements in the teachers' performance compared with an untrained control group. The trained teachers engaged pupils more actively in the development of ideas, used teaching and learning aids more effectively to demonstrate concepts and principles, and showed greater flexibility in their teaching approaches in response to pupils' learning needs (Ghana Education Service, 2010).

Professional development programmes can help teachers develop their skills in teaching reading and mathematics. They have been used to great effect in East Asian school systems (Jensen, 2012). In many low income countries, however, some teachers teach for long periods without receiving any in-service training. In the fifteen national school systems of the Southern and Eastern Africa Consortium for Monitoring Educational Quality in 2007, only 53% of grade 6 students were taught reading by teachers who

had received in-service training over the past three years (ranging from 32% in Lesotho to 79% in South Africa). Since 2000, the share had declined in four countries and improved in only seven (Hungi et al., 2011).

Good quality textbooks and other supplementary reading materials are needed to teach and generate interest in learning, but in many developing countries they tend to be in short supply, not relevant to real life situations, pitched at an inappropriate level of difficulty or characterized by poor illustrations and printing. In such situations, teachers have a key role in ensuring that limited resources are used effectively. Room to Read, an NGO that sets up and equips libraries in ten countries and supports local-language publishing industries, recognizing that teacher capacities need to be strengthened, has developed support programmes. These include teacher in-service training focusing on child-centred, interactive teaching methods coupled with one-on-one support provided regularly during the school year by literacy facilitators who help teachers use the new methods (Room to Read, 2012).

The way in-service training is delivered makes a difference. Short-term workshops can be ineffective. Recommended approaches include engaging trainees in researching their own teaching practise, preparing teaching portfolios or using book clubs. In Kenya, two Ministry of Education programmes address some of these issues. The school-based teacher development programme guides teachers to use a more problem-solving approach. It has been found that trainees are more likely to use effective mixed-ability group work, to spend time enabling children to practice reading and to encourage the use of library books. Their lessons tend to move through content more quickly and keep all pupils engaged. Reading to Learn, a pilot project introduced in 2010 in two low income districts of the Coast province with support from the Aga Khan Foundation, focuses training on how to write stories and to use them in teaching (Akyeampong et al., 2011).

Recognizing the particular challenges of teaching early grades, some countries have set up centres to improve teachers' effectiveness.

In Ghana, distance learning programmes reached 25,000 untrained teachers

In the United Kingdom, a daily literacy hour helped increase reading scores

Between 2002 and 2009, as part of a USAID project covering the Andean countries, Central America, the Dominican Republic and the English-speaking Caribbean, Centers for Excellence in Teacher Training were introduced to provide professional development to early grade teachers. In the Dominican Republic, a course consisted of three eight-hour sessions of face-to-face teacher preparation on teaching practices, eight three-hour meetings of teachers, forty hours of independent study of teachers' own practices and a monthly visit to each teacher at school. Teachers were trained to improve their teaching of reading and writing, their ability to develop curriculum and their classroom management. Children had more opportunities to read and write, interact with different types of texts and develop advanced reading skills, beyond memorization. About 3,400 teachers in grades 1 to 4 participated (Montenegro, 2011).

An evaluation of the overall programme in eight countries found that trainees had adopted a wide range of effective teaching behaviours involving grouping and feedback, classroom management and use of physical space. The trainees' knowledge did not deepen, however. This reflects weaknesses in initial teacher training and illustrates the critical need for continuous professional development (USAID, 2011a).

Experience from in-service teacher training in rich countries shows that it works better when it supports the introduction of broader interventions, including ones targeting children who fall behind or ones aimed at improving the system overall. Under the United Kingdom's broader National Literacy Strategy, which aimed to raise literacy standards among primary school children aged 5 to 11, a daily 'literacy hour' was introduced in 1998. It consisted of sessions of whole-class reading or writing, whole-class work on words and sentences, directed group activities and reviewing the objectives of the lesson. Teachers were trained to implement the programme: an initial day on class management for literacy was followed by a week of training on the activities expected in the literacy hour. An evaluation found that the programme significantly helped improve reading skills and overall achievement in English, especially for boys. At the national level, the share of children meeting targets in reading by the end of primary education rose from 67% to 80% during the first six years of implementation (Machin and McNally, 2008).

NGO interventions provide positive experience, but often do not reach most teachers

Many non-governmental organizations have recently implemented literacy projects, which tend to support teachers in targeting disadvantaged populations. Teacher training is often combined with other measures to improve learning. Governments need to monitor these efforts so that they can learn from, adopt and expand initiatives that provide useful lessons and have the potential to be scaled up. NGOs, for their part, need to consider whether their projects can be replicated and collaborate with governments to strengthen systems and sustain any gains.

In South Africa, a project providing reading materials, together with training to help teachers use them effectively, has improved learning outcomes. Learning for Living, a project initiated by the READ Educational Trust, is aimed at enhancing the learning of English as a second language in primary schools by providing teachers with books and in-service training, combined with visits to monitor results. Training covered the teaching of phonics and spelling, the use of stories for language development, and more advanced use of written material, including non-fiction books, along with reading and writing for real-life situations. The project reached almost 1,000 schools – most of them rural – and more than 13,000 teachers over five years. An evaluation comparing project and non-project schools found significant improvements in teaching practices. There was more use of teacher-made materials and an increase in lesson time spent reading. These results translated into improvements in reading and writing (Hoffman et al., 2004; Schollar, 2008).

An NGO programme in India also illustrates how in-service teacher training can be combined with other interventions to improve learning outcomes. The NGO, Pratham, has successfully implemented a large programme providing in-service training for government school teachers in the teaching of reading. The programme includes training to help teachers articulate clear learning goals and use appropriate teaching–learning activities and materials (Banerjee et al., 2012; Walton and Banerji, 2011). Initial results of a randomized experiment conducted in 2008/09 and 2009/10 in rural areas of Bihar and Uttarakhand states showed that teacher training was effective only when complemented with other interventions. In schools that received teacher training, monitoring and support, combined with supplementary learning materials for children and after-school support by Pratham volunteers for students who were lagging behind, the achievement of all children, as measured by speed of accurate reading and writing in Hindi, improved significantly. But there was no such impact in schools that received teacher training only. The impact was limited by low teacher and child attendance, a curriculum unrelated to children's initial level, and wide diversity of learning needs in the classroom (Walton and Banerji, 2011).

The biggest challenge is scaling up such innovations so they can be institutionalized as part of regular teacher development, especially in poor countries. Unfortunately, the vast majority of teachers in poor countries have few opportunities for in-service training.

Conclusion

Governments should take active steps to strengthen teaching in early grades. Teacher education systems need to be reinvigorated to assure the success of such interventions. Pre-service training programmes appear to be paying insufficient attention to the teaching of reading. Courses need to increase the emphasis on effective classroom techniques. In-service training programmes engaging teachers in an interactive way can ensure that knowledge is converted into better classroom practice. Benefits are likely to be most noticeable where training is combined with other interventions, such as improved instructional materials.

Governments should take active steps to strengthen teaching in early grades

World Inequality

To coincide with the publication of this Report, the EFA Global Monitoring Report Team has developed a new interactive website that shows the scale of education inequality within countries. The World Inequality Database on Education (WIDE) brings together the latest data from Demographic and Health Surveys and Multiple Indicator Cluster Surveys.

Wealth disparities widen for countries struggling to enrol children in school

Population aged 17 to 22 with fewer than two years of education, by wealth, (%)

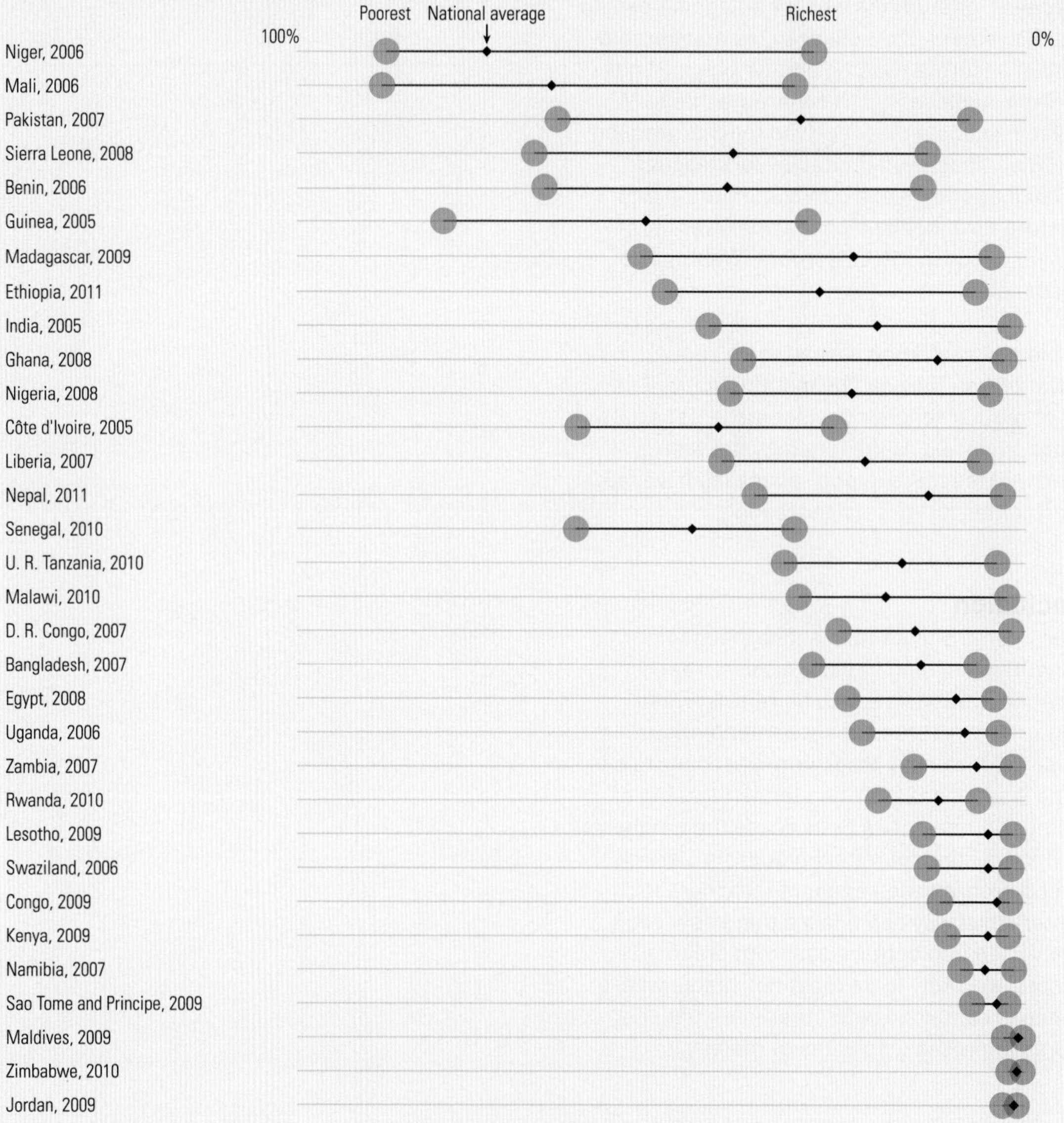

	Poorest	National average	Richest	
	100%	↓		0%

Niger, 2006
Mali, 2006
Pakistan, 2007
Sierra Leone, 2008
Benin, 2006
Guinea, 2005
Madagascar, 2009
Ethiopia, 2011
India, 2005
Ghana, 2008
Nigeria, 2008
Côte d'Ivoire, 2005
Liberia, 2007
Nepal, 2011
Senegal, 2010
U. R. Tanzania, 2010
Malawi, 2010
D. R. Congo, 2007
Bangladesh, 2007
Egypt, 2008
Uganda, 2006
Zambia, 2007
Rwanda, 2010
Lesotho, 2009
Swaziland, 2006
Congo, 2009
Kenya, 2009
Namibia, 2007
Sao Tome and Principe, 2009
Maldives, 2009
Zimbabwe, 2010
Jordan, 2009

Selecting three of the regions furthest from achieving EFA – the Arab States, sub-Saharan Africa and South and West Asia – The figure shows that disparities in wealth exist in almost every country with data. By clicking on the dots on the website, the percentages affected appear. In the Niger, the country with the widest disparities, 88% of the poorest young people have less than two years of schooling – that is, they suffer from extreme education poverty – compared with 29% of the richest. Jordan, at the other end of the figure, has the narrowest disparities. Whether rich or poor, only 1% of 17 to 22 year olds are affected by extreme education poverty.

Database on Education (WIDE)

Visitors to the website can compare groups within countries according to various education indicators, and according to the factors that are associated with inequality, including wealth, gender, ethnicity, religion and location. Users can create maps, charts and tables from the data, and download, print or share them online. The site was designed by InteractiveThings.

Wealth disparities are further aggravated by gender disparities

Population aged 17 to 22 with fewer than two years of education, by wealth and gender, the Niger, Pakistan and Egypt, (%)

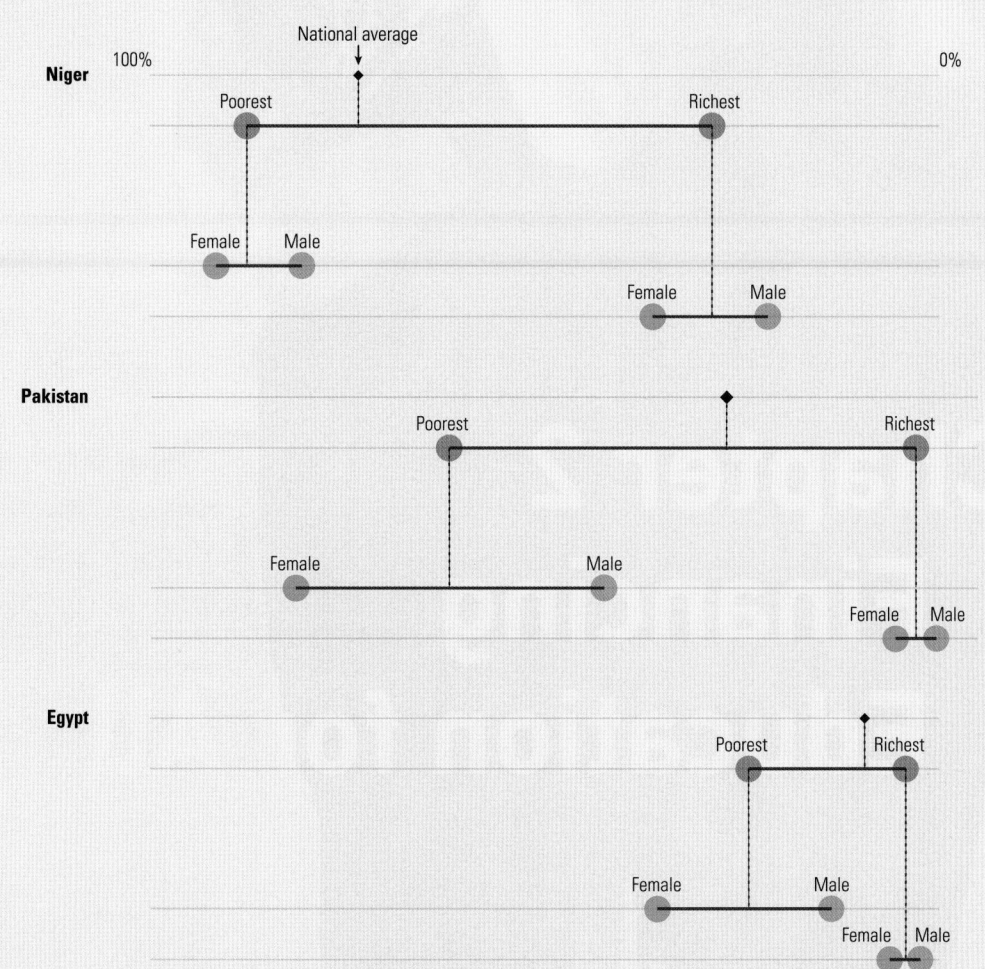

On the WIDE site, the user can look in detail at intersecting patterns of disadvantage within selected countries. In the Niger, not only are wealth disparities wide, but they are further aggravated by gender. The poorest young women are the worst affected: 92% are likely to have spent less than two years in school, compared with 22% of richest young men. In Pakistan, a vast gender gap among the poorest leaves eight out of ten young women affected, compared with less than five out of ten young men. While the severity of the problem is not as great in Egypt overall, gender gaps are wide: 36% of poor young women are in extreme education poverty compared with just 2% of the richest young men.

www.education-inequalities.org

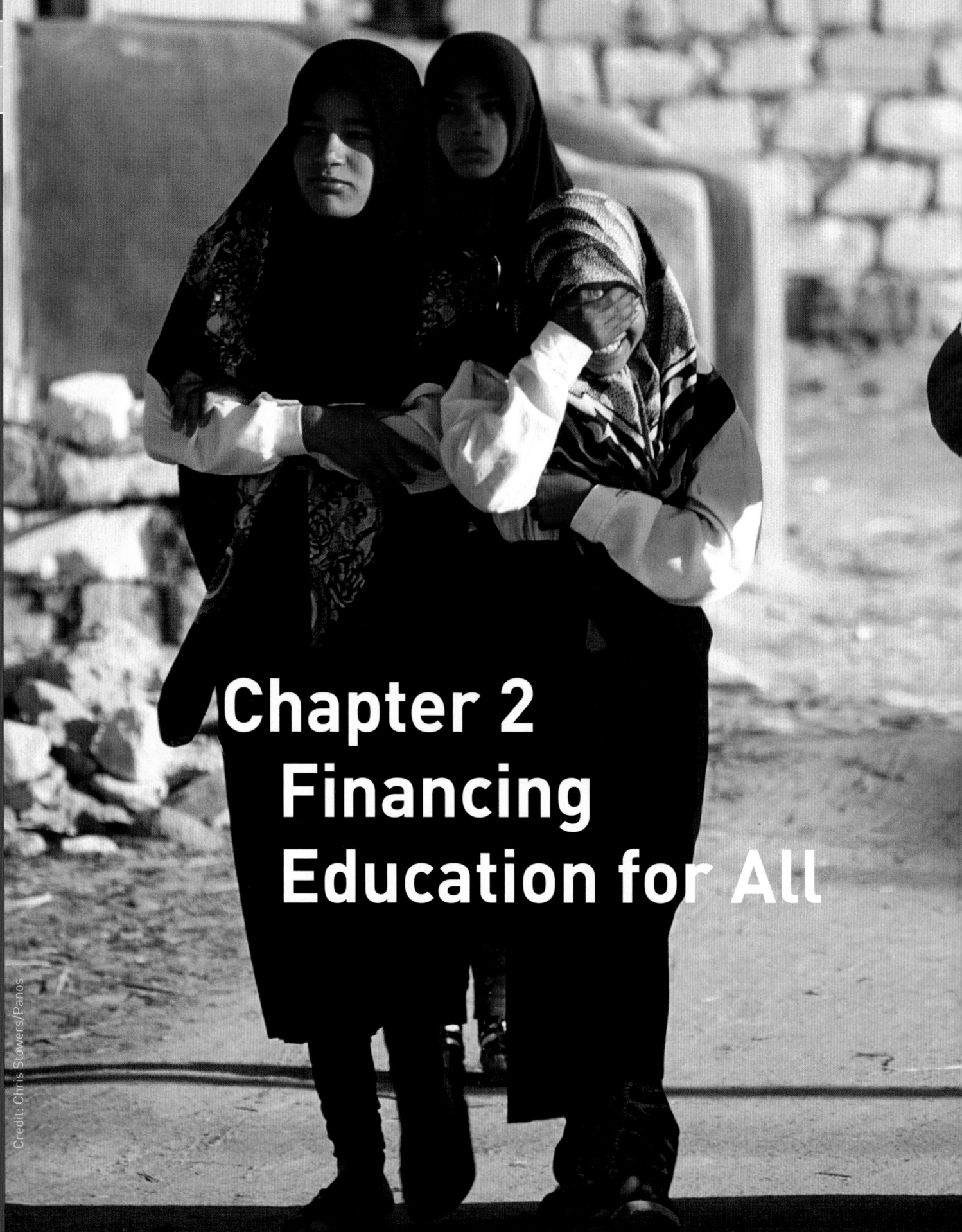

Chapter 2
Financing
Education for All

Girls walking to school on the
outskirts of Siwa, Egypt.

Just when a big push is needed to reach Education for All by 2015, there are worrying signs that donor commitment to education is stagnating. The economic downturn has tightened budgets. This chapter shows how developing countries' natural resources and contributions of the private sector hold significant potential to help reach the international education goals.

Monitoring progress on financing Education for All

Highlights

- Despite increased financial commitments of national governments towards education, many of the poorest countries face major shortfalls in resources needed to achieve Education for All.

- Faster economic growth, better revenue generation, stronger commitment to education, and increased aid levels have helped increase real spending on education in low income countries by 7.2% a year, on average, since 1999.

- A few low and middle income countries have made cuts to their education budgets during the economic downturn, but the education sector overall has so far not suffered as much as previously expected.

- Even though aid to basic education increased in 2009, it remained unchanged at US$5.8 billion in 2010. And the outlook is worrying. Total aid decreased in real terms in 2011 for the first time since 1997 and aid to the education sector is likely to stagnate until 2015.

- Some countries have the opportunity to draw on their natural resource wealth. For a group of seventeen countries, maximizing such revenue could generate enough funds to send 86% of their out-of-school children and 42% of their out-of-school adolescents to school.

- At an estimated US$683 million per year, the contributions of private foundations and corporations to education in developing countries are equivalent to just 5% of aid. Their engagement needs to be better coordinated and aligned to EFA objectives.

Table 2.1: Public spending on education, by region and income level, 1999 to 2010

	Public education spending					
	% of GNP		Real annual growth rate (%)	Per capita (constant 2009 US$)	
	1999	2010	1999–2010	1999	2010
World	4.5	4.9	2.7	528	644
Low income countries	3.1	4.6	7.2	15	22
Lower middle income countries	4.3	4.8	3.1	83	105
Upper middle income countries	4.6	4.7	5.3	250	332
High income countries	5.0	5.4	2.3	1 489	1 792
Sub-Saharan Africa	3.5	4.7	5.0	77	91
Arab States	5.5	5.5	1.4	305	266
Central Asia	4.0	3.5	7.6	48	103
East Asia and the Pacific	4.1	4.2	2.4	503	570
South and West Asia	2.9	4.4	2.3	74	122
Latin America and the Caribbean	5.0	4.9	5.3	255	306
Central and Eastern Europe	4.6	5.1	5.6	357	544
North America and Western Europe	5.5	5.7	2.3	2 086	2 532

Notes: Education spending as percentage of GNP regional and income values are medians for countries with data in both 1999 and 2010, and may therefore not match those reported in Statistical Table 9. Spending per capita data are weighted averages.
Source: EFA Global Monitoring Report team calculations (2012) based on UIS database and World Bank (2012).

Just when EFA needs a final push, there are signs that donor contributions are slowing down

Just as a final push is needed to reach the Education for All goals by 2015, particularly as the numbers of children out of school are stagnating, there are worrying signs that donor contributions may be slowing down. More money alone will not ensure that the EFA goals are reached, but less money will certainly be harmful. A renewed and concerted effort by aid donors is urgently needed. At the same time, it is vital both to explore the potential of new sources to fill financing gaps and to strengthen the way in which aid money is spent.

This chapter outlines trends in funding and aid effectiveness in the education sector over the past decade. It then takes a closer look at two sources of education financing with growth potential: natural resource revenue (first policy focus) and contributions from private organizations (second policy focus).

Trends in financing Education for All, 1999-2010

Faster economic growth, improved revenue generation, greater government commitment to education and increased aid levels have combined to increase real spending on education since 1999. The increase has been greatest in low income countries. While a few countries have reduced their education budgets during the economic downturn, the education sector has not suffered as much as had been feared. Increases have not been large enough, however, to fill the financing gap, leaving many countries with insufficient resources to achieve the 2015 EFA targets.

Figure 2.1: Spending on education has increased or been maintained in most countries
Public expenditure on education as percentage of GNP, low and middle income countries, 1999 to 2010

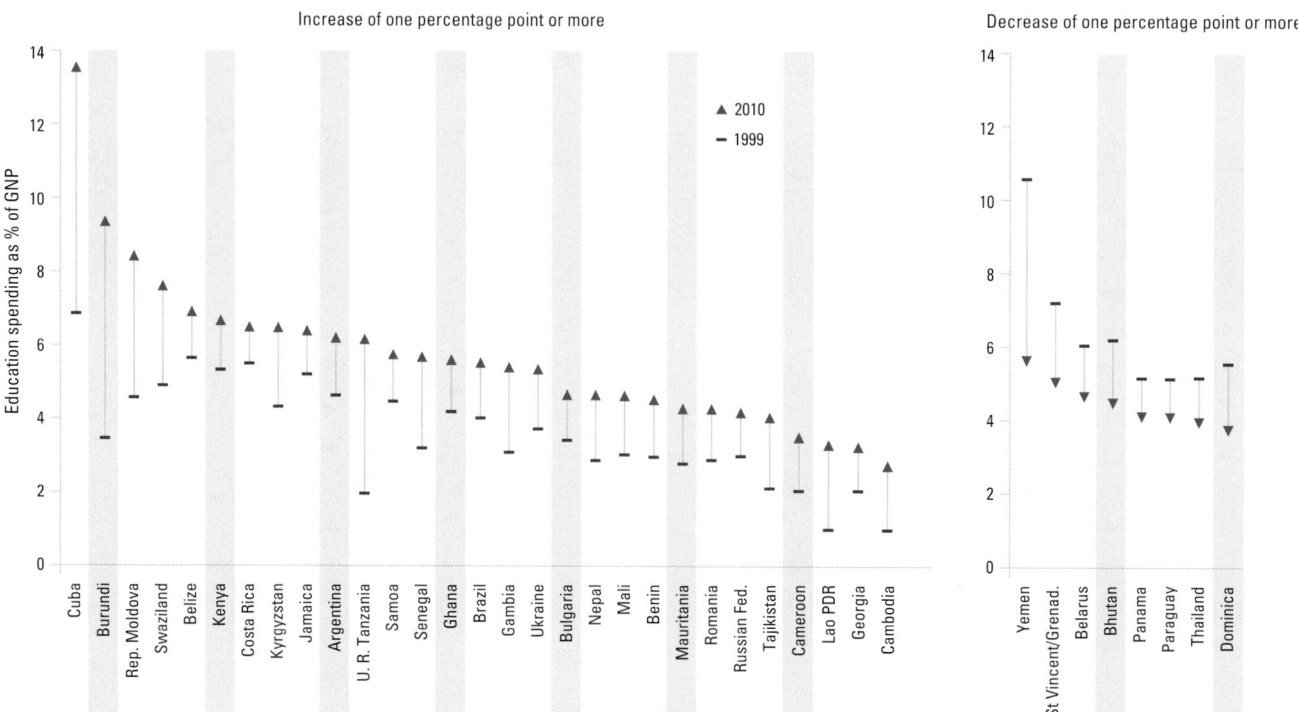

Source: Annex, Statistical Table 9.

Spending on education has increased in most countries since 1999

Spending on education increased by an average of 2.7% a year globally from 1999 to 2010. Increases were particularly notable in low income countries, where spending went up by 7.2%, and in sub-Saharan Africa, where it increased by 5% (Table 2.1).

The share of national income devoted to education is an indicator of commitment to EFA. Among low and middle income countries with comparable data, 63% have increased the share of national income spent on education in the past decade. Coupled with economic growth and greater government capacity to raise revenue, this led to significant increases in total education expenditure. In eight countries, spending decreased by more than one percentage point of gross national product (GNP), usually from relatively high initial levels (Figure 2.1).

Despite this promising global trend, some countries have maintained a low level of spending, allocating less than 3% of GNP to education over the past decade. They include countries that are still a long way from achieving EFA. With a net enrolment ratio of just 69% in 2011, the Central African Republic, for example, reduced its spending from 1.6% to 1.2% of GNP on education, the lowest proportion among all low and middle income countries with data. Guinea spent less than 3% of GNP on education, even though it still has wide gender disparities in primary and secondary school – 84 girls in primary school and 59 in secondary school for every 100 boys. Pakistan has the second largest number of children out of school – 5.1 million – yet reduced its spending on education from 2.6% to 2.3% of GNP.

Spending more matters

Most countries that accelerated progress towards EFA over the last decade did so by increasing spending on education substantially or maintaining it at already high levels.

Among poorer countries, 63% have increased the share of national income spent on education since 1999

Change of less than one percentage point

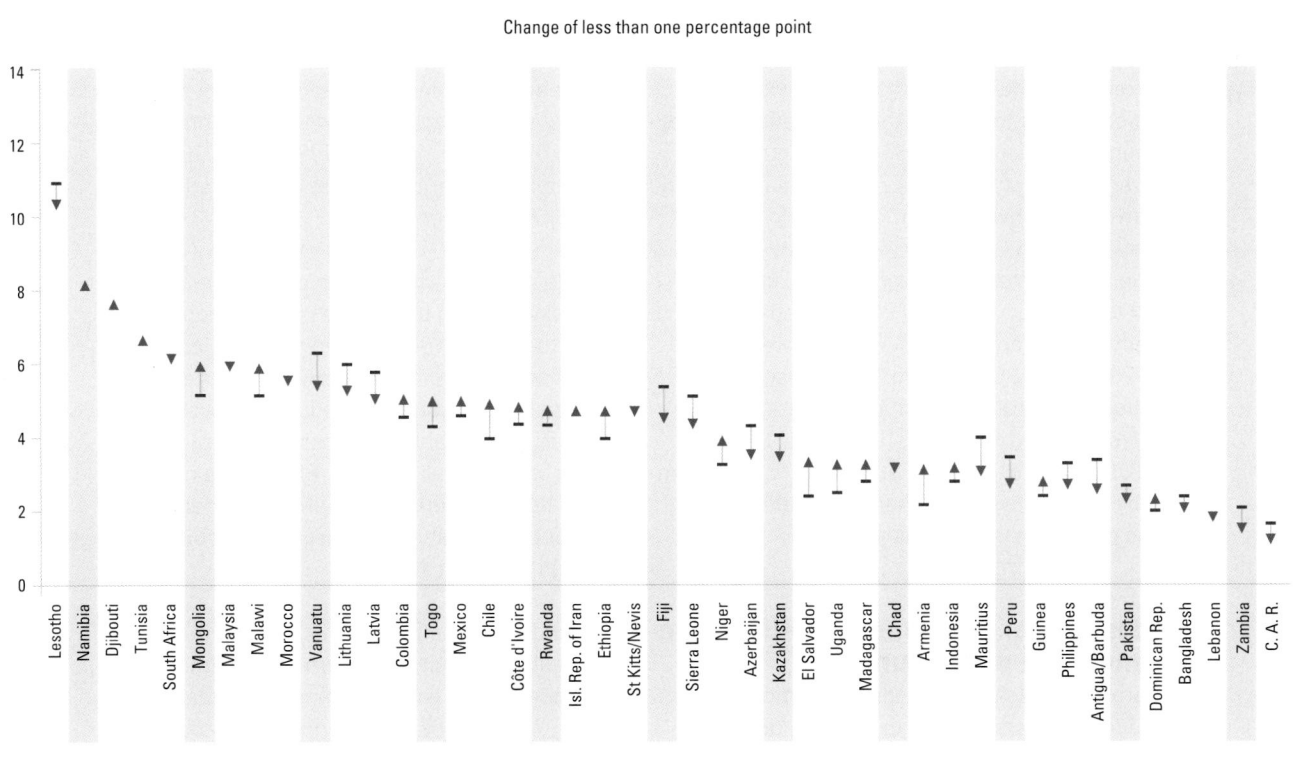

**Aid amounts
to as much
as one-fifth
of education
budgets in poor
countries**

Among countries furthest from universal primary education in 1999, the ten where the net enrolment ratio increased fastest from a starting point below 85% devoted 4.4% of GNP, on average, between 1999 and 2010. This is substantially more than in the ten countries where net enrolment ratios increased the least, in which just 3.4% of GNP went to education over the period.

Countries in sub-Saharan Africa that have shown increased financial commitment to education have witnessed impressive progress in education. In 1999, the United Republic of Tanzania spent just 2% of its GNP on education. By 2010, the share was 6.2%. Over the same period, its primary net enrolment ratio doubled. In Senegal, an increase in spending from 3.2% of GNP to 5.7% allowed impressive growth in primary enrolment and the elimination of the gender gap. In Kenya, which spent over 5% of its income on education over the decade, the net enrolment ratio rose from 62% in 1999 to 83% in 2009.

Fears that the recent food and financial crises could counter the generally positive trend in education spending do not seem to have been realized, although monitoring of the longer-term impacts will be needed. Two-thirds of low and lower middle income countries with recent data continued to expand their education budget through the crisis years. But some countries that are furthest from EFA made cuts in 2010 following negative economic growth in 2009.

In the Niger, after the food crises in 2008 and 2009 lowered government revenue, spending on education contracted by 9.9% between 2009 and 2010 (UNESCO, 2011c). As a consequence, public expenditure on primary education per pupil decreased from US$102 in 2009 to US$94 in 2010. In Chad, the total allocation to education fell by 7.2% between 2009 and 2010 after high rates of growth in previous years.

Aid is a vital component of education spending in poor countries
Figures on education spending commonly include both national and external sources. New analysis for this Report aims to disentangle

domestic financing from aid contributions (Box 2.1). While national spending provides the most important contribution, aid amounts to as much as one-fifth of education budgets in low income countries on average.

Regional or income group averages do not tell the full story. In nine countries, all in sub-Saharan Africa, donors fund more than a quarter of public spending on education (Figure 2.2). Even among similar groups of countries, there are significant differences. In Kenya, for example, around 4% of the education budget is funded by aid, a much lower proportion than in other low income sub-Saharan African countries, such as Mali, where the share is 25%. Most Latin American countries rely almost entirely on national resources, but Guatemala receives 11% of its budget from donors. And although India receives the second largest amount of aid in absolute terms globally, the share of aid is small relative to the government's own spending on education – just 1%.

The fact that donors are major funders of education in several countries means that aid matters. Donors have provided essential support to countries where access to basic education was limited just a decade ago. Mozambique, for instance, has seen spectacular increases in access to schooling, with numbers out of school declining from 1.6 million to less than 0.5 million between 1999 and 2010. During much of this period, 42% of the education budget was funded externally.

While aid has a vital role to play, depending on it is risky. Aid can be volatile or even stop suddenly due to political instability in recipient countries or changing priorities in donor countries. And, ultimately, a sustainable education system that is accountable to its citizens must be built on domestic funding. Efforts are needed, therefore, to increase the share of education expenditure that is paid through resources raised domestically.

Rwanda's education system, for example, has benefited considerably from aid, which helped support an increase in the net enrolment ratio from 76% in 2001 to 99% in 2010. Recognizing the need to avoid dependence, Rwanda's 2006

Box 2.1: Estimating the contributions of national governments and aid donors to education spending

How much do donors contribute to education funding in developing countries compared with national governments? Although this question cannot currently be answered with precision, estimates are possible.

Figures on education spending reported by governments include some aid to education, but not all. There is often a share of aid to education that is 'off budget', such as when donors implement parallel projects or fund non-governmental organizations. Because these funds are not channelled through government budgets, they are not reported as national education spending.

Even when aid to education is 'on budget', difficulties arise in trying to disentangle which portion of the budget is financed by domestic resources rather than donors. One important challenge concerns general budget support, or aid not earmarked for a specific sector. The *EFA Global Monitoring Report* has adopted a simple assumption that 20% of this aid is allocated to education. However, because this is typically channelled directly to finance ministries, it is not recorded as aid in education ministry budgets.

To get a better picture of the relative contributions of governments and aid donors towards education, new analysis for this Report has produced rough estimates based on internationally available data from two sources: the UIS for public expenditure on education as reported by developing country governments, and the OECD's Development Assistance Committee (DAC) for aid

to education as reported by donors. The new calculations attempt to reconcile these two sources and separate them into three components: funding from domestic resources, 'on-budget' aid to education and 'off-budget' aid to education (Figure 2.2). Adding the first two items roughly corresponds to total public education spending.

To get the best estimate of aid to education that appears 'on budget', three steps have been taken:

■ Following established practice, 20% of general budget support is included in aid to education, and counted in the 'on-budget' portion.

■ Of direct aid to education, only country programmable aid, a subset of total aid developed by the OECD, is included. Excluded are items that do not reach developing countries' education budgets, such as imputed student costs and donors' administrative costs.

■ Where information is available, the specific share of this aid to education that is included in each country's budget is used. Otherwise, it is assumed that 60% of aid is channelled through the national budget, and so is considered 'on budget'.

The remainder of country programmable aid to education is considered 'off budget' and added to national education spending figures to get the total expenditure on education from both domestic sources and donors.

Source: UNESCO (2012b).

Aid Policy aimed to reduce the proportion of the budget provided by aid. As a share of total government spending, aid dropped from 85% in 2000 to 45% in 2010, largely due to efforts to expand the share of tax revenue in the budget: it increased from just 16% in 1998 to over 50% in 2010 (ActionAid, 2011, 2012).

As the 2011 *EFA Global Monitoring Report* showed, most poor countries have significantly increased domestic revenue in the past decade, demonstrating their potential to rely more on their own resources to fund education. But such efforts take time, and changes are unlikely to happen as quickly as is needed to fund the ongoing expansion of access to education in the short term. Donors still have a crucial role to play.

Has aid to education reached its peak?

Increases in aid have contributed significantly to progress towards EFA over the past decade. In line with a rise in overall aid, donor contributions to education increased in 2009 and remained at their highest level for a decade in 2010. There are strong signs that these increases could be reversed in coming years, however. In 2011, total aid fell for the first time since 1997. It is expected that this drop will have a negative impact on the education sector.

In 2011, total aid fell for the first time since 1997

Aid to education stagnated in 2010
Between 2002/03 and 2010, aid to education increased by 77% to US$13.5 billion (Table 2.2).

Figure 2.2: Aid to education is an important share of resources for poor countries

Domestic and aid resources for education, selected regional and low or lower middle income country averages, 2004 to 2010

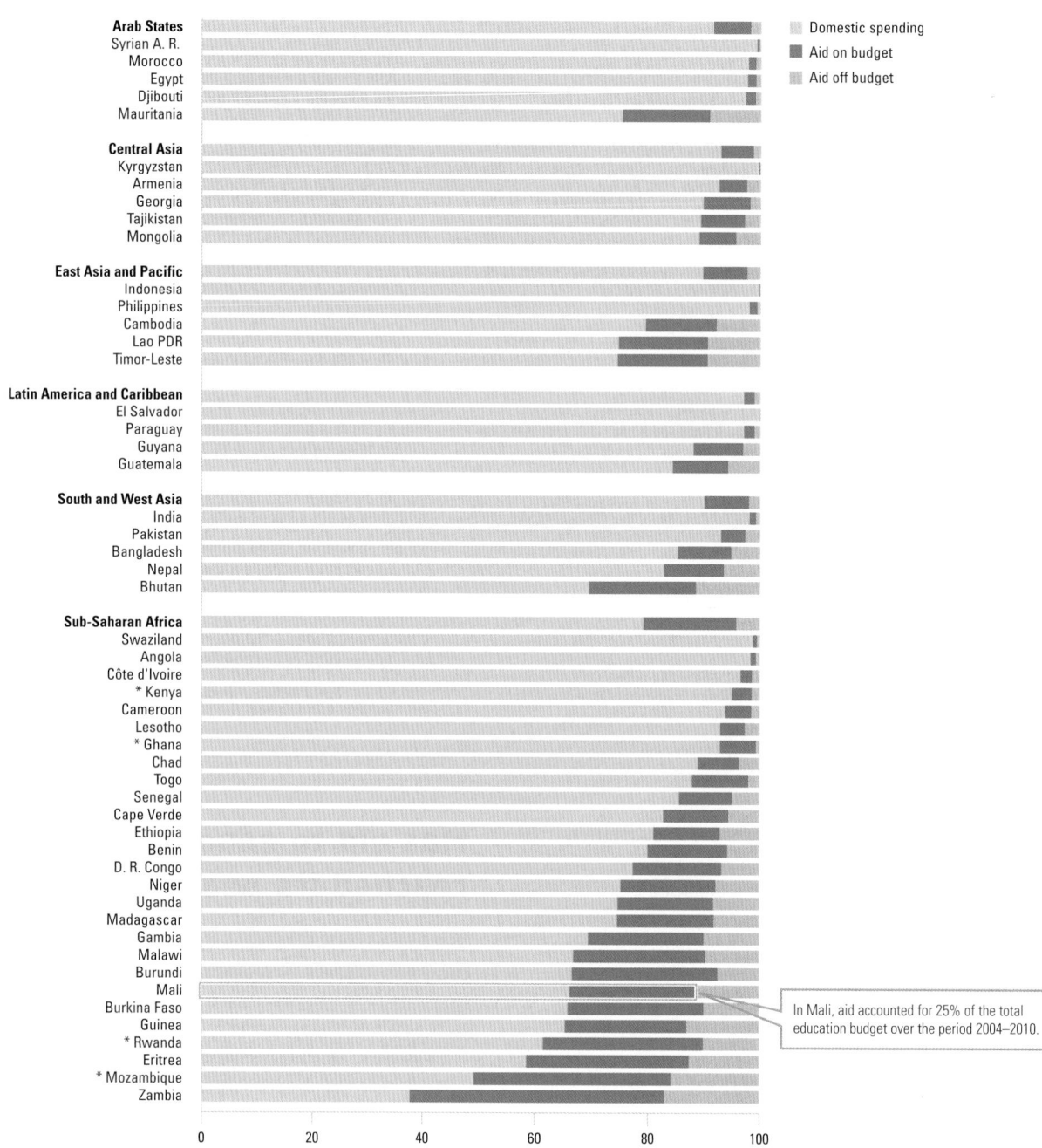

Notes: * indicates that a country-specific share of aid on budget was estimated from country documents; for the other countries, an average of 60% of aid was assumed. The regional figures are unweighted averages across all low and middle income countries.
Source: UNESCO (2012b).

Table 2.2: Total aid disbursements to education and basic education, by region and income level, 2002 to 2010

	Total aid to education					Total aid to basic education				
	Constant 2010 US$ millions			% change		Constant 2010 US$ millions			% change	
	2002	2009	2010	2002–2010	2009–2010	2002	2009	2010	2002–2010	2009–2010
World	7 616	13 425	13 468	77	0	2 939	5 791	5 789	97	0
Low income countries	2 002	3 386	3 528	76	4	1 154	1 899	1 913	66	1
Lower middle income countries	2 933	5 550	5 054	72	-9	1 205	2 704	2 315	92	-14
Upper middle income countries	1 917	3 079	3 080	61	0	381	714	759	99	6
High income countries	28	34	33	19	-2	6	7	8	41	22
Unallocated by income	735	1 377	1 773	141	29	193	467	793	310	70
Arab States	1 056	1 983	1 824	73	-8	211	853	779	269	-9
Central and Eastern Europe	325	496	537	65	8	85	60	75	-12	24
Central Asia	139	231	311	124	35	40	57	93	132	63
East Asia and the Pacific	1 147	2 305	2 140	87	-7	231	671	636	176	-5
Latin America and the Carribbean	547	983	1 039	90	6	212	385	413	95	7
South and West Asia	949	2 172	2 127	124	-2	561	1 379	1 228	119	-11
Sub-Saharan Africa	2 689	3 865	3 718	38	-4	1 400	1 890	1 781	27	-6
Overseas territories	237	402	491	107	22	118	166	229	93	38
Unallocated by region or country	525	988	1 281	144	30	81	329	556	586	69

Note: The 2002 figure is an average over the two year period 2002–2003.
Source: Annex, Aid Table 3.

Aid to basic education accounted for about 43% of this.[1] In 2010, US$5.8 billion was allocated to this level, double the amount in 2002/03. The increase was not evenly shared, however, and was not necessarily directed at the countries most in need. Although sub-Saharan Africa is the region furthest from EFA, the amount it received increased by only 27% over the period, while it increased by more than three and a half times in the Arab States.

A jump in aid between 2008 and 2009 resulted in the allocation to basic education increasing by US$0.9 billion, the largest year-to-year increase since records began in 2002 (Figure 2.3). Almost half the increase was additional lending to basic education by the World Bank and International Monetary Fund, partly to support developing countries during the financial crisis. The United Kingdom accounted for most of the rest.

This increase did not continue in 2010, however. Aid to basic education remained at the same level in 2010. The three donors that made the biggest increases in 2009 reduced their funding in 2010. This decline was offset by a significant increase from the European Union and smaller rises from other donors, such as France and Germany (Figure 2.4). However, that increase did not benefit the low income countries that are the furthest from achieving EFA. Indonesia and South Africa, both middle income countries, were among those receiving some of the largest increases in EU basic education aid in 2010.

Of the US$5.8 billion in aid to basic education in 2010, only US$1.9 billion was allocated to low income countries. Aid for basic education to low income countries grew, on aggregate, by just US$14 million in 2010. Given that forty-six low and lower middle income countries need US$16 billion a year to achieve the EFA goals by 2015, this still leaves a large deficit.[2]

Of US$5.8 billion that went to basic education, only US$1.9 billion went to low income countries

1. In the OECD-DAC classification, 'basic education' covers pre-primary, primary and basic life skills for youth and adults.

2. These forty-six countries were the focus of an EFA costing exercise in the 2010 Report (UNESCO, 2010b).

CHAPTER 2

Figure 2.3: Aid to education stagnated in 2010

Total aid to education disbursements, 2002 to 2010

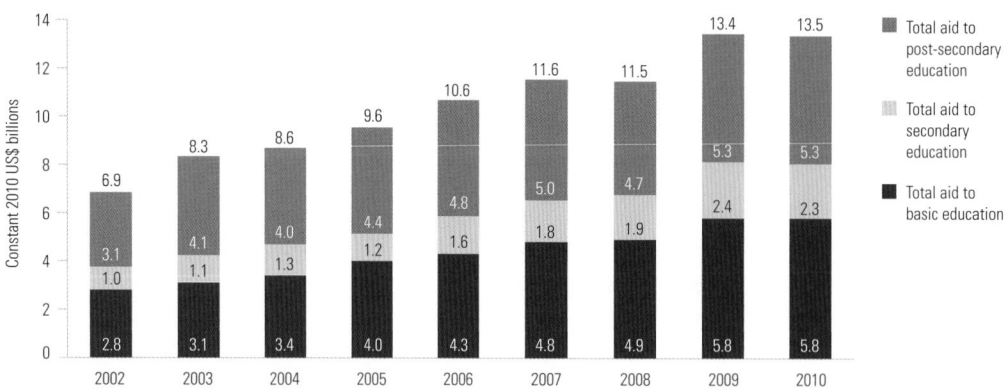

Source: OECD-DAC (2012b).

Figure 2.4: The three donors that made the largest increases in aid in 2009 made cuts in 2010

Total aid to basic education, top fifteen donors, 2008 to 2010

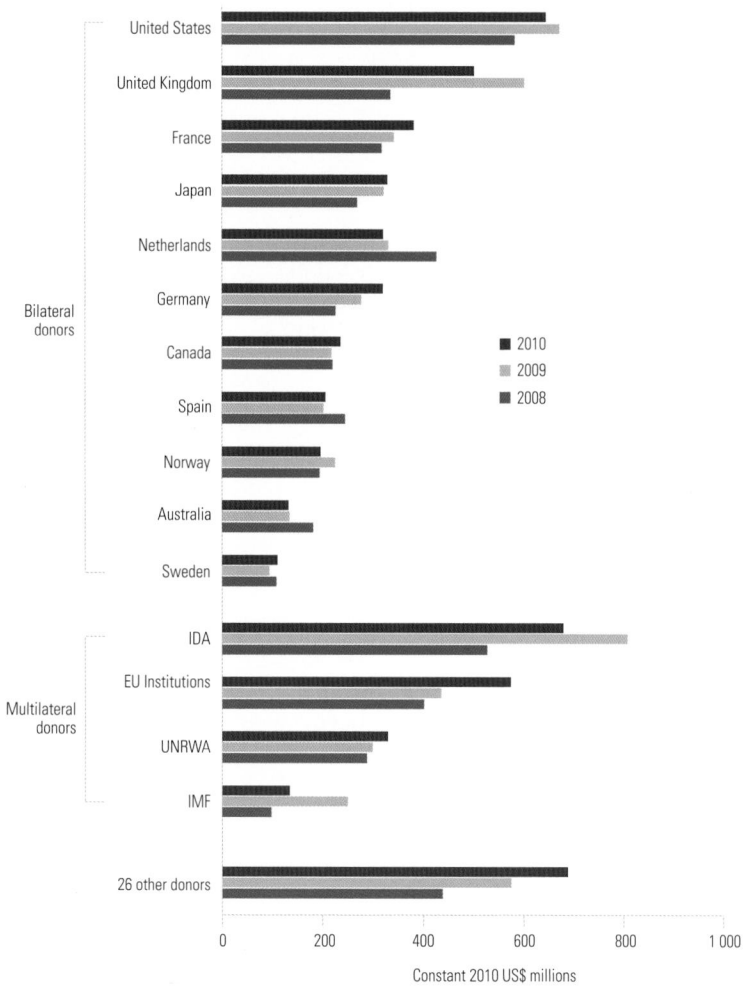

Notes: IDA = International Development Association (World Bank); UNRWA = United Nations Relief and Works Agency for Palestine Refugees in the Near East; IMF = International Monetary Fund.
Source: OECD (2012b).

The increase in aid for low income countries was mainly concentrated in Afghanistan and Bangladesh, which received 55% of the additional funding for the sixteen low income countries that experienced an increase. By contrast, funding to nineteen low income countries fell. Among them were some of those furthest from the EFA goals, such as Ethiopia, where the number of out-of-school children remains among the highest in the world.

Overall aid decreased in 2011, and future prospects are not encouraging

The outlook for aid in the years leading up to 2015 is not promising. Many governments are cutting their overall aid budgets and the education sector is likely to suffer.

Education has received a relatively constant share of total aid since 2002. Assuming this pattern continues, aid to education is likely to decline at a similar pace to overall aid. Worryingly, some key donors are not only reducing their overall aid budgets, but may also be making education a lower priority, which would lead education aid to fall faster than overall aid levels (Box 2.2).

Even before the economic crisis hit, donors were off track to fulfil the promise they made at the Group of 8 Gleneagles Summit in 2005 to increase aid by US$50 billion by 2010. The target was missed by US$24 billion (in 2010 dollars)

(Figure 2.5). Sub-Saharan Africa received only around half the increase it was promised. Assuming a similar share going to the sector as in previous years, meeting the Gleneagles targets would have meant US$1.9 billion more for schools in 2010, or around one-third of current aid to basic education. A year after the target had been missed by a large margin, the G8 leaders at their 2011 summit offered only a vague commitment to strive to maintain their efforts, with no clear plan for aid increases (G8, 2011).

Of even greater concern is that, for the first time since 1997, total official development assistance (ODA) to all sectors decreased in real terms by 3% from 2010 to 2011. The drop was primarily a consequence of the financial crisis, as aid budgets tend to lag in their reaction to changes in overall economic conditions. But the decrease was not only a consequence of lower economic growth in rich countries. Between 2010 and 2011, fourteen out of twenty-three DAC members also reduced their aid as a share of national income, suggesting that aid was more vulnerable to cuts than domestic spending (Figure 2.6).

Financial and political pressures on governments to reduce spending mean that foreign aid budgets, no matter how small their part of the overall budget, can be an easy target for cuts. Some countries made drastic cuts. Spain, which had become an important donor in the past decade, made cuts of over 30%. Japan cut its aid by 11%. Norway and France also made cuts. In the case of France, the drop was not only related to the financial crisis; it was also due to Mayotte changing its status in 2011 to a French department. Previously, as an overseas collectivity, it received half of all French aid to basic education in 2009/10. It is now ineligible for aid.

Canada cut its aid budget by 5% in 2011 despite having weathered the storm better than other donors: between 2007 and 2009, its GDP fell by 2.1%, compared with 3.8% for the United States, 5.5% for the United Kingdom and 4.2% for the euro zone (OECD, 2012b). Canada is set to reduce aid further in 2012–2015; as its economy is expected to grow, its aid will fall even more as a share of national income (OECD-DAC, 2012a)

Box 2.2: Aid cuts by the Netherlands jeopardize education gains

The Netherlands, which has been one of the top three donors to basic education over the past decade, is expected to cut its aid to education by 60% between 2010 and 2015. Assuming other donors maintain their direct aid to basic education at 2010 levels, this would mean the Netherlands would go from being the third largest donor to basic education in 2008 to twelfth in 2015.

In response to the government's 2011 development aid policy, activities are being concentrated on sectors and countries viewed as those that are most aligned with the country's foreign policy priorities and where the most impact is expected. Aid spending will be limited to four sectors: security, law and order; water; food security; and sexual and reproductive health and rights. The expectation is that education programmes not directly contributing to these priorities will be phased out.

The shift in priorities could have real implications for the well-being of children in some of the countries most in need. The Netherlands is set to withdraw support from education in Burkina Faso, for example, where it has been by far the largest donor in recent years, providing 31% of basic education funding in 2008–2010. Burkina Faso urgently needs continued, predictable support: in 2011 its net enrolment ratio was just 63%. While the Netherlands aims to reduce its support gradually, it is withdrawing just as four other donors have said they also intend to pull out of education in the country.

The Netherlands has become a specialist in aid to education over the years, as a key funder and at the forefront of policy development. As its own recent evaluation concludes, the Netherlands has been valued by its partner countries and other donors for the leading role it has played in advancing aid effectiveness. This expertise risks being lost if planned reductions in support to the education sector are fully realized.

Sources: EFA-FTI and Brookings Institution (2011); Netherlands Ministry of Foreign Affairs (2011a, 2011b, 2012).

Figure 2.5: The Gleneagles target was missed and total aid even decreased in 2011

Total net official development assistance disbursement from OECD DAC donors, 2000 to 2011

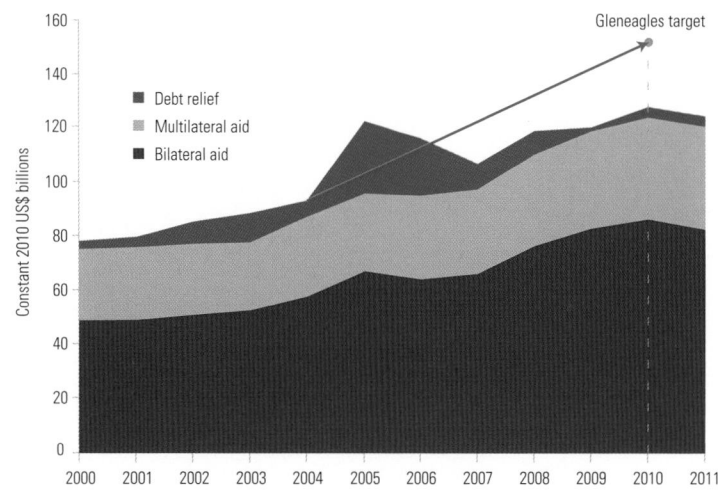

Source: OECD-DAC (2012c).

Education for All Global Monitoring Report

PART I: MONITORING PROGRESS TOWARDS THE EFA GOALS

CHAPTER 2

Table 2.3: Trends in expected aid to education from the ten largest donors to education

Donor	Share of total aid to basic education %, 2002–2010	Expected future trend on aid to basic education	Notes
World Bank	16	▼▲	Support to basic education dropped by 67% in 2011, but the World Bank projects a compensating increase in 2012.
United States	11	▼	Current budget request for 2013 implies a 28% drop in aid to basic education. Overall foreign aid budget expected to decrease from 2012 onwards.
United Kingdom	9	▲	Increase due to commitment to increase aid to 0.7% of GDP by 2013.
Netherlands	8	▼	Planned withdrawal from the education sector and overall aid reduction: 45% cuts in aid to education between 2010 and 2012, reaching 60% by 2015.
European Union	8	▲	Under the current proposals for the 2014–20 EU Multi-Annual Financial Framework, funding for the Development Cooperation Instrument is expected to increase by 19% as compared with the previous 2007–13 MFF.
Japan	6	▼	A further decrease in 2012 is expected, following 11% overall aid budget cuts in 2011.
France	5	▼	Decrease likely in the short term due to the change in status of Mayotte, medium term will depend if money is reinvested elsewhere.
Germany	4	▲	Increase in overall aid combined with commitment to education as a priority sector as stated in the BMZ Education Strategy 2010–2013.
Norway	4	▼▲	Development assistance levels maintained at 1% of GNI, with levels earmarked for the education sector being maintained at 2008 levels.
Canada	4	▼	Cuts due to reduction in overall aid budget of 7.5% by 2015.

Sources: BMZ (2011); Canada Ministry of Finance (2012); EFA-FTI and Brookings Institution (2011); Gavas (2012); Global Campaign for Education (2012); Japan Ministry of Finance (2011); Netherlands Ministry of Foreign Affairs (2012); Norway Ministry of Foreign Affairs (2011); OECD-DAC (2012c); World Bank (2011a).

Figure 2.6: Most donors reduced aid as a share of their national income in 2011

Official development assistance as percentage of gross national income, 2010-2011, OECD-DAC donors

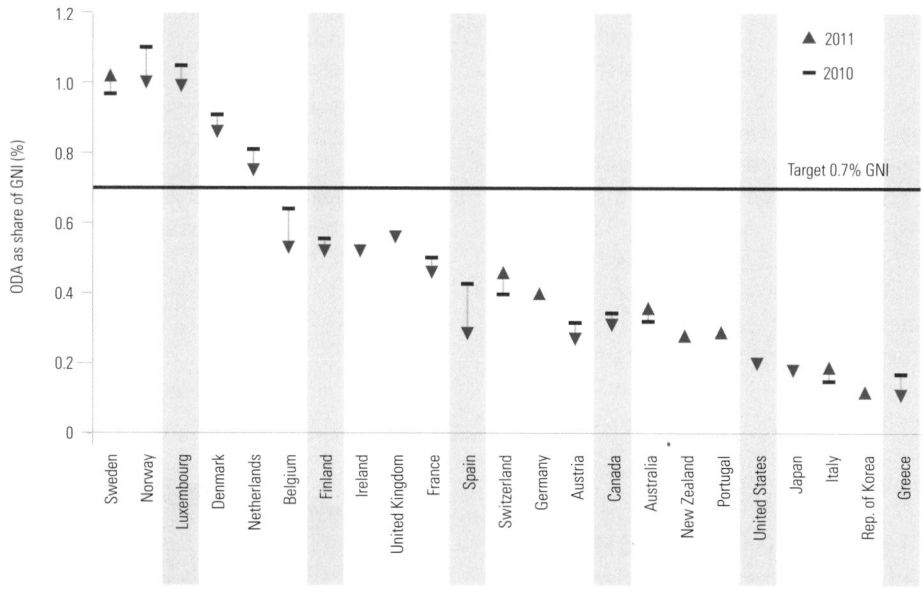

Source: OECD-DAC (2012c).

(Table 2.3). Similarly, in the United States, plans to cut the federal budget are putting foreign aid under severe pressure (Myers, 2011).

Australia, Germany, New Zealand, Sweden and Switzerland, by contrast, managed to continue increasing their aid budgets despite the crisis. The United Kingdom's aid decreased slightly in real terms in 2011 because its economy contracted at the height of the crisis in 2009, but the government remains committed to keep its pledge to bring its aid budget to 0.7% of GNI by 2013.

The 2012–2015 OECD survey on donor spending projects that country programmable aid levels will increase in 2012 but then stagnate (OECD-DAC, 2012d). If the share of education as a proportion of sector allocable aid remains at 13%, then direct aid to the education sector will remain at its current level of around US$13 billion (Figure 2.7). As a result, it will fail to bridge the financing gap to achieve the EFA goals.

Education remains a low priority in humanitarian aid

Conflict-affected countries are the most off track in efforts to achieve EFA. Many fall through the cracks in the international aid structure, with their education systems receiving neither long-term development assistance nor short-term humanitarian aid. There are promising signs that donors such as the United States are increasing their support for education in conflict-affected countries, at least through official policy statements (USAID, 2011b). The United Nations refugee agency, UNHCR, recently developed its first education strategy (UNHCR, 2012). And, after many years of difficulties in engaging with fragile states, the Global Partnership for Education now includes them as one of its three core priorities (Global Partnership for Education, 2012a).

These policy commitments have yet to translate into funding, however. Of the twenty consolidated appeals in 2012 to the United Nations Office for the Coordination of Humanitarian Affairs, just five proposed that funding to education should make up more than 5% of the total requirements of their humanitarian work plans. Within Mali's consolidated appeal, for instance,

education sector requirements made up 4.5% of total requirements. The majority, roughly 70%, was earmarked for food security and nutrition. Insufficient funding for education during the recent conflict in the country could have serious consequences on the progress Mali has made towards increasing primary enrolment and narrowing the gender gap.

There is no guarantee, moreover, that even these extremely modest requests for funding will be met. The education sector remains one of those lagging behind most in terms of requirements that actually receive funding. Education received less than half of its proposed requirements in the 2011 consolidated and flash appeals. As a result, education received just 2% of humanitarian aid in 2011, a share unchanged since 2009.

Figure 2.7: Projections show overall aid levels flattening out
Total education as a share of total sector allocable aid, 2002 to 2010, with projections, 2011 to 2015

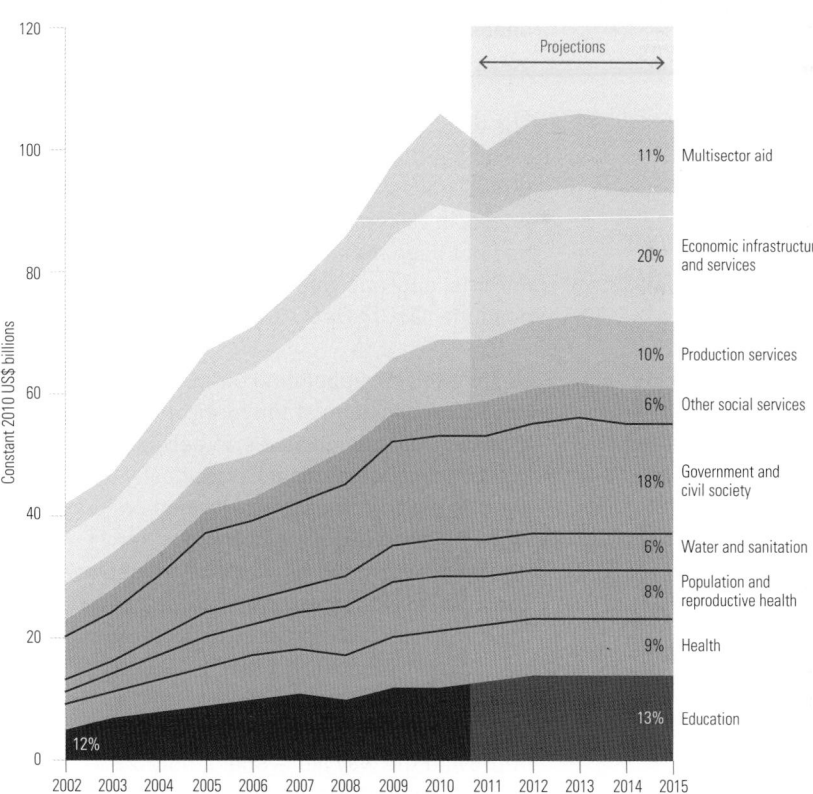

Notes: For the projections by sector, the same growth rates are applied to sector allocable aid disbursements for 2011–2015 as those for country programmable aid which the OECD-DAC released in April 2012. The average share going to education directly (excluding the 20% proportion of general budget support) for 2002–2010 has been applied to sector allocable ODA for 2011–2015.
Source: OECD-DAC (2012b, 2012d).

Aid to education: the challenge of effectiveness

Figures on aid to education tell only part of the story. Ensuring that money is spent effectively – that it reaches classrooms, is directed to those most in need and has a lasting impact – is just as vital.

Education has been at the forefront of aid effectiveness initiatives

The 'Paris targets' on aid effectiveness were not met

To improve aid effectiveness, OECD-DAC members developed a set of common goals to strengthen ownership, alignment, harmonization, mutual accountability and management for results (OECD-DAC, 2011). Donors and recipient countries were expected to adhere to these principles, established in Paris in 2005 and reiterated in Accra, Ghana, in 2008, with the aim of reaching a set of quantitative targets by 2010. The principles have particular relevance for education, which needs long-term, sustainable investment in schools, teacher recruitment and training.

The deadline has now passed, and the overall verdict at the fourth High-Level Forum on Aid Effectiveness, held in Busan, the Republic of Korea, in December 2011, was that the targets had not been met. Of the thirteen targets agreed in Paris, only one was achieved by the 2010 deadline (OECD-DAC, 2011; Wood et al., 2011).

Despite this disappointing outcome, however, education has been at the forefront of aid effectiveness initiatives, in particular in terms of aligning donor priorities with country programmes and priorities. In Kenya, Mozambique, Rwanda and Uganda, for example, significant amounts of aid deployed in conjunction with government plans contributed to unprecedented increases in access to primary education (UNESCO, 2011a).

Mobilizing resources for education and improving the way aid is spent, notably through support for national plans, were the explicit goals of the Global Partnership for Education (formerly the EFA Fast Track Initiative) when it was established in 2002 as the only global pooled fund mechanism for aid to education. In the few years left before the EFA deadline in 2015, the partnership has a crucial role to play in accelerating progress by mobilizing additional resources for education (Box 2.3).

New donors and the post-Busan aid effectiveness agenda

A key feature of the Busan aid effectiveness forum was the prominence given to donors that are not members of the OECD-DAC (Busan Partnership for Effective Development Co-operation, 2011). These countries contributed about US$11 billion of development financing in 2010, equivalent to 8% of global aid (OECD-DAC, 2012c).

Among the non-DAC countries, the so-called BRICS grouping (Brazil, the Russian Federation, India, China and South Africa) has received increased attention as donors because their economies are playing a greater role on the world stage and because aid from traditional donors is unlikely to increase in the current economic climate.

How will these donors change the aid landscape? This question cannot be answered with precision, partly because of a lack of transparency in their reporting on the aid they provide. At the meeting in Busan there was a failure to reach agreement on their adherence to DAC standards. The BRICS countries are currently under no obligation to report to the OECD. As a result, their data are patchy and, to the extent that they report, they do not necessarily adhere to the ODA definition (Smith el al., 2010). There is no way to clearly separate aid from other financial flows towards developing countries. In 2011, the DAC attempted to identify the component of their funding that is most consistent with its definition of ODA. It has estimated that BRICS accounted for US$3.6 billion of the US$11 billion contributed by non-DAC donors in 2010 (OECD-DAC, 2012c).

China is by far the largest BRICS donor: it contributed US$2 billion in 2010, and plans to increase and diversify its development assistance, particularly to Africa. But China does not distinguish its commercial and diplomatic activities from its aid. Some observers have argued that many of the

Box 2.3: Aid effectiveness and the Global Partnership for Education

When the Global Partnership for Education was established in 2002 as the EFA Fast Track Initiative, its goals were to accelerate progress towards primary education by promoting sustained increases to aid and more efficient spending, together with sound sector policies and adequate and sustainable domestic financing. How far has it achieved these goals?

One way is to assess how much it has spent. Between 2003 and 2011, it disbursed US$1.5 billion, corresponding to 13% of total aid to basic education in the forty countries whose plans it had endorsed and 6% of aid to basic education in low and middle income countries. The disbursement corresponded to 69% of the US$2.2 billion allocated over the period. At a pledging conference in Copenhagen in 2011, donors promised an additional US$1.5 billion between 2011 and 2015 – US$1 billion less than was initially sought.

Another way of gauging how successful the partnership has been is to compare its performance with resource mobilization for global health funds. Between 2001 and 2011, donor contributions to the Global Fund to Fight AIDS, Tuberculosis and Malaria totalled US$22 billion – around ten times as much as those made to the Global Partnership for Education over a comparable time frame. In addition, global health funds receive contributions directly from foundations and corporations, as well as through innovative financing mechanisms such as the International Finance Facility for Immunisation,

Debt2Health and Advanced Market Commitments. While these sources contribute only about 5% of total pledges to global health funds, no such contribution from private organizations is made to the Global Partnership for Education.

The initiative's performance should also be weighed against the original intentions. It was established to provide additional resources aligned with those of other donors – for example, stepping in to fill temporary gaps and reduce volatility. While the success of this is difficult to assess, more needs to be done to evaluate whether the partnership has been meeting the goal of 'additionality' – that is, bringing additional resources to fill gaps left by national governments and aid donors.

The Global Partnership for Education has recently developed a new framework, which states that it works in two important ways: 'by mobilizing resources, both domestic and external, and by helping donors and developing countries work together to ensure that aid is better coordinated and more effective, based on countries' own education strategies' (Global Partnership for Education, 2012c, p. 11). Any assessment of the partnership will need to continue to focus on these roles, ensuring that independent monitoring is undertaken to make sure lessons can be learned for the design of any post-2015 financing framework.

Sources: Cambridge Education et al. (2010); EFA-FTI (2004); Global Fund (2012); Global Partnership for Education (2011a, 2011c, 2012b, 2012d); UNESCO (2009, 2011c).

loans it extends to developing countries would not qualify as aid, as their interest rates, if properly assessed, are not below market rates (Bräutigam, 2011).

The same is true for India, whose contribution was estimated to be US$639 million in 2010 (OECD-DAC, 2012c). Infrastructure development features prominently within the technical cooperation budget. Around 60% of Indian technical cooperation in 2011–12 was a mix of grants and loans to build hydroelectric dams in Bhutan, which could generate electricity that would in part benefit India (India Ministry of External Affairs, 2012). Similarly, its recent announcement that it planned US$5 billion in aid to Africa concerns the extension of loans

(NEPAD, 2011). It is unclear whether these loans would be offered at interest rates lower than market rates.

The evidence to date suggests the impact of BRICS on aid to education could be limited. Their contributions are small compared with those of DAC donors and the information available indicates that education in low income countries is not high among their priorities (see Chapter 4). Nevertheless, there are signs that these countries are engaging to some extent with EFA. For example, the Russia Education Aid for Development, a trust fund launched in collaboration with the World Bank, focuses on institutional capacity-building to carry out and use data from student assessments. The fund is

Evidence suggests the impact of the BRICS on aid to education could be weak

providing US$32 million over 2008–2014, offering an example of how new donors can engage with the education sector (READ Trust Fund, 2012).

Results-based approaches entail risks

Taxpayers funding aid budgets understandably want to see where their money is going and whether aid is achieving its stated aims. Donors therefore are increasingly turning to 'results-based' aid, linking their funding to specific outcomes. The World Bank, for example, is launching the Program-for-Results financing instrument, under which loans will be disbursed to countries once results have been achieved (World Bank, 2011d).

In the education sector, the United Kingdom's Department for International Development (DFID) is testing this approach as part of its partnership with the Government of Ethiopia in 2012–2014. DFID will make a grant to the Ministry of Education for the additional students, above a baseline, who sit or pass the national grade 10 examination. To address gender disparities, the unit grant for each girl sitting or passing the examination will be higher than the amount for each boy. Similarly, grants for each additional student sitting the exam are higher for the poorest regions in Ethiopia (Birdsall and Perakis, 2012). Putting more emphasis on outcomes such as children's learning is welcome and necessary. Results-based aid could also increase country ownership over policies because governments would take responsibility for their own decisions.

Nonetheless, results-based aid involves considerable risks. First, if circumstances beyond recipients' control prevent them from reaching agreed outcomes, withholding the promised funds could be unfair and put governments in a difficult financial situation. Proposals for paying for results usually allow for some extenuating circumstances, but the reality of the development process is that such circumstances are unlikely to be an exception, as many external factors could prevent a given plan from running smoothly.

Second, there is a danger that results-based aid will create perverse incentives. While a greater emphasis on measuring children's learning is necessary to reach the sixth EFA goal of education quality, a system where funding is contingent on standardized test results would drastically raise the stakes of the test. Such high-stakes testing has been common in some richer countries, such as the United States, where it has been used as a criterion to assess performance and has increased pressure on teachers and administrators to meet the standards. In some cases, teachers are reported to have changed answer sheets after students took the test to guarantee high pass rates (Georgia State Office of the Governor, 2011; Jacob and Levitt, 2003). In other situations, including in Chile and Mexico, paying teachers by results has led them to focus on the best performing students, raising a problem of widening inequality (UNESCO, 2009).

In linking payments to verified results, there is also a risk of giving governments an incentive to overreport. Experience from the health sector, where programmes under the GAVI Alliance include a payment for every vaccinated child above a certain baseline, found that in Bangladesh, Indonesia and Mali official data had systematically understated the baseline and therefore overstated subsequent coverage of vaccinated children (Lim et al., 2008).

Third, poor countries need aid because they have insufficient funds to finance their own development and need up-front money to deliver programmes. In addition, education outcomes cannot be achieved within an annual budget cycle. If aid is only disbursed once children have graduated, who will pay for school buildings and teacher salaries to improve the conditions that would allow them to graduate?

Current results-based aid proposals, such as the one being piloted in Ethiopia, are avoiding this problem by introducing the approach gradually alongside more traditional aid delivery mechanisms. But this raises the question of whether the donor–recipient relationship would change as fundamentally as hoped if results-based aid only amounts to a small bonus at the end of a programme and were dwarfed in size by more traditional aid.

Taxpayers funding aid budgets want to see proof that aid has achieved its aims

Conclusion

After a period of expanding education budgets, which have contributed to some spectacular outcomes, a period of uncertainty looms. The economic downturn has hit richer countries, with repercussions for aid to the poorest countries, which are furthest behind in achieving the EFA goals.

The decline in aid is likely to result in a widening of the education financing gap, which will necessitate innovative solutions. Aid from emerging donors such as Brazil, China and India is one possible resource, but is currently not sufficiently targeted at those countries most in need. It is therefore necessary to identify other sources of funding. Natural resource revenue and private organizations are two possible additional sources that are explored in the following sections.

The decline in aid will require innovative solutions to fill the EFA financing gap

Policy focus: Turning the 'resource curse' into a blessing for education

17 countries could use natural resource revenues to send 86% of their out-of-school children to school

One of the most striking paradoxes of development is the 'resource curse': countries well endowed with non-renewable natural resources, such as oil and minerals, have experienced slower economic growth than resource-poor countries. Many are far from reaching the Education for All goals and other development targets.

But the curse is escapable. This section shows that there is considerable potential for resource-rich countries to close their EFA financing gap. In seventeen countries already rich in resources or with recently discovered deposits, including Ghana, the Niger and Uganda, revenue from natural resources could finance access to primary school for 86% of out-of-school children if their governments maximized the revenue generated and dedicated a significant share to education. About 42% of out-of-school adolescents in these countries could also have access to school. In a context where donors are cutting back spending and turning away from education, this would be an important development. Ensuring that resource-rich countries embark on a path towards efficient, transparent and fair management of natural resources should therefore be a central concern of the EFA community.

The risks of natural resource wealth

Most low and middle income resource-dependent countries[3] have struggled to harness their riches in ways that assure sustained development for future generations (Sachs and Warner, 1997; Sala-i-Martin and Subramanian, 2003). Many of these countries have been unprepared to deal with the sudden discovery of an oil field or ore deposits.

Governments have often struck poor deals with multinational companies. Others have been unable to maintain a steady flow of revenue through good and lean years. Many countries have mismanaged the income, either through

corruption or inadvertently through misguided spending choices.

Natural resource revenue has also often been used to finance armed conflict. 'Blood diamonds' in Liberia and Sierra Leone were used to pay for civil wars (UNESCO, 2011c). In the Democratic Republic of the Congo, high-value minerals such as coltan and tin ore, used in mobile phones, have provided armed militias responsible for human rights violations with a lucrative source of revenue (Global Witness, 2009).

Resource discovery can also create macroeconomic disruptions through 'Dutch disease', a term coined by economists to describe the experience of the Netherlands after a significant natural gas discovery in the 1960s. Because natural resources are mostly paid for outside a country, for example from oil sales in foreign markets, they can increase the value of the local currency and make exported products less competitive (Corden, 1984; Heuty and Aristi, 2010).

To transform natural resources into a blessing, governments must maximize their revenue from extractive activities, manage them transparently and invest the wealth in sectors that will generate higher, equitable benefits for the population. Education is a sector that has delivered such benefits: resource-rich countries such as Botswana have used their economic success to expand schooling. Using natural resource wealth to fund education today can be a way to escape the resource curse tomorrow.

Striking a good deal

The current high prices for non-renewable commodities mean that potential revenue for governments from these resources is greater than ever. In the region furthest from reaching the EFA goals, sub-Saharan Africa, potential profit per capita from non-renewable natural resources tripled between 1998 and 2008 (World Bank, 2012). While commodity prices are vulnerable to economic crises such as that of

---

3. Resource-dependent countries are those that derive at least a quarter of government revenue or exports from natural resources (IMF, 2007).

2008–2009, they have been following an overall upward trend (IMF, 2012b).

A first step towards translating natural resource wealth into development outcomes is for governments to obtain a fair share of the profit. One key decision in this regard is who will extract and sell the resources. Three options are generally available. First, some countries, such as Malaysia and the Bolivarian Republic of Venezuela, choose to manage extraction directly through a state institution, which means they take all the risk but earn all the profit (Victor et al., 2012).

Second, governments may enter into agreement with a firm to share the risk and cost of extraction, which can be considerable. Third, governments can grant concessions to private companies for exploration and extraction, then raise revenue by imposing royalties on production or taxes on profit, including windfall taxes. The last approach is preferred when there is major uncertainty or when exploitation requires technology and capital that the country lacks (Auty, 2006; Boadway and Keen, 2010).

Botswana is an example of a country that has chosen the second option and entered into an agreement with a private company. Diamonds are mined through a 50-50 arrangement with De Beers (Kojo, 2010). Around half of diamond exports translated into government revenue in 2007/08, compared with 20% on average for other mineral-rich countries. This positive experience is underpinned by good governance, a competent civil service and political stability (Transparency International, 2007). Returns to investment in foreign financial assets, managed by a special fund, have been directed towards social services. Botswana has consistently spent over 5% of its GNP on education since the mid-1970s, reaching 8.2% in 2010. Today, it is one of the richest countries in sub-Saharan Africa and not only has it achieved universal primary education but its secondary gross enrolment ratio stands at 82%, double the average for the continent.

Whether governments enter into partnerships or grant concessions, considerable capacity is needed to manage the relationship. Many governments are in a weak bargaining position vis-à-vis private mining and oil companies (Stiglitz, 2007). As a result, they are not getting

nearly as much as they could, as the example of Zambia shows (Box 2.4). These countries are missing an opportunity to finance their own development.

In the Democratic Republic of the Congo, a parliamentary investigation estimated that in 2008, the government lost US$450 million in revenue through a mix of bad management, corruption and insufficient taxation (Smith and Rosenblum, 2011). This is a sum larger than the country's entire education budget, and enough to send 7.2 million children to primary school. Even in the United Republic of Tanzania, which is closer to achieving EFA, if royalties paid by gold mining companies rose from the current 3% of production to the 5% recommended by a presidential commission, it would generate an additional US$12 million a year in government revenue (OSISA et al., 2009). That could cover the cost of sending more than 132,000 children to primary school.

Transparency is a precondition for maximizing government revenue

The natural resources extracting industry has been characterized by opacity, with details of contracts between states and companies often shrouded in secrecy (Karl, 2007). Recently, however, the international community has been pushing for norms of transparency for resource extraction and revenue generation. The Publish What You Pay campaign, launched in 2002, brought more than 230 NGOs together to put pressure on governments and companies to make their transactions fully transparent and publicly available (Karl, 2007). A year later, the Extractive Industries Transparency Initiative (EITI) was launched. Today fourteen countries fully comply with its standard for 'companies to publish what they pay and for governments to disclose what they receive', and a further twenty-two countries have taken steps to adhere to them (EITI, 2012).

In 2010, in another landmark development in resource revenue transparency, the Dodd-Frank Wall Street Reform and Consumer Protection Act required mining companies based in the United States to disclose their tax and revenue payments publicly. While details have yet to be worked out and resistance

In 2008, the Democratic Republic of the Congo lost resource revenue that would be enough to send 7.2 million children to school

Box 2.4: Getting a better deal for Zambia's mineral resources

Zambia has some of the world's largest reserves of copper and cobalt, but after initial success in using this wealth towards economic and social development it has suffered a severe case of the resource curse. In 1970, Chile, another leading copper producer, was four times as rich as Zambia in terms of GDP per capita. By 2010, the gap had widened to fifteen times.

Copper prices were high during the first ten years of Zambia's independence. The mines were owned by the state and generated two-thirds of government revenue. However, a sharp drop in prices in the mid-1970s unleashed a severe debt crisis, leading to the privatization of mines under advice from the IMF and World Bank.

Largely secret agreements offered mining companies favourable terms, such as royalties at 0.6% of production instead of the 3% set in the 1995 Mines and Minerals Act, and profit taxes at 25%, compared with 35% for other sectors. As a result, government revenue fell and spending on social sectors could not be sustained. While the primary net enrolment ratio was as high as

85% in 1986, it had dropped to 70% by 1999. It was estimated that Zambia lost US$63 million in revenue between 2002 and 2004, when copper prices began rising again, because it taxed mining activities insufficiently.

The situation in Zambia could turn around, however. After pressure from civil society, a new Mines and Minerals Development Act promulgated in 2008 has helped ensure that the full royalty payments are made. Revenue from mining taxes more than tripled between 2009 and 2011 to reach 3.2% of GDP. Moreover, the new government doubled royalty rates to 6% in late 2011. Some of this new income will be used for education, where many challenges remain. While the primary net enrolment ratio had bounced back to 91% by 2010, there are still considerable challenges with progression and learning. The government also needs to show greater commitment towards education: Zambia spent only 1.5% of its GNP on education in 2010, one of the lowest shares in the world.

Sources: IMF (2011c); OSISA et al. (2009); England (2011); Hart Nurse Ltd. (2011).

Liberia's natural resources were at the heart of its 14 years of civil war

from affected industries is strong, the Act could set a precedent (Ayogu and Lewis, 2011). The European Commission recently followed suit, issuing a draft directive that would require listed companies involved in natural resource extraction to disclose their payments to governments (Revenue Watch Institute, 2011).

Transparency has considerable power to help turn the resource curse into a blessing. Liberia's natural resources, including iron ore, diamonds, gold, timber and rubber, were at the centre of the country's fourteen years of civil war, which left it with some of the lowest education indicators in the world. By the end of the war in 2003, the net enrolment ratio in primary school was just 35% (UNESCO, 2011c). After elections in 2005, one of the first actions of the new government was to vow to assure transparency in how revenue from natural resources was managed, as a means to promote national growth, development and reconciliation (EITI, 2009). The country has participated in EITI since 2006. Transparency is not only helping build government legitimacy but also ensuring that funds from natural

resources are used to strengthen education and other social sectors.

Invest natural resource revenue for future generations

There is broad agreement that natural resource revenue should be used wisely, either by saving it or investing it for the benefit of future generations. Education is a key ingredient of long-term equitable economic and social development; therefore natural resource revenue should be also used to fund education – whether to build infrastructure or to pay teachers' salaries.

For countries still in the initial stages of economic development, targeted investments in sectors that promote long-term growth and development, including education, yield high returns. Investing in a skilled workforce, for example, can help diversify the economy (Collier et al., 2009; Sachs, 2007).

Legal or institutional mechanisms may be needed to prevent corruption and to ensure that an important share of natural resource revenue is spent on education. Natural resource revenue may be channelled into a special fund and earmarked for specific purposes. Ghana's legal framework for its new oil revenue management includes a provision that 70% of spending must go to priority sectors (Ghana Ministry of Finance and Economic Planning, 2010).

Governments also need to demonstrate a commitment to education more broadly. Botswana, for example, adopted in 1994 a Sustainable Budget Index, a formula which directs some of its mineral revenue to health and education (Lange and Wright, 2002). The existence of an institutional mechanism does not in itself guarantee that revenue will be used for education however, as Chad's experience shows (Box 2.5).

As an alternative approach to minimizing opportunities for corruption, some commentators recommend that countries distribute new resource wealth directly to citizens in the form of cash transfers instead of spending it via government budgets to build schools, hospitals or roads. This 'oil-to-cash' concept has many attractions, as it is based on the positive experience of cash transfers in addressing poverty, together with the possibility that it could help mitigate the resource curse. Transferring resources directly to citizens, it is argued, gives them

greater incentives to hold their governments to account. Alaska, the United States, is an example of such an approach: its government sends an annual cheque based on oil revenue to every person living in the state. The payments amount to 3% to 6% of household income (Moss, 2011; Segal, 2010).

However, there are drawbacks to this approach. Unlike conditional cash transfers in countries like Brazil and Mexico that target poor households and have been successful in improving education outcomes, the oil-to-cash idea does not incorporate the redistributive element of approaches that have been successful in targeting poverty. In addition, where the supply of public services is inadequate, transferring most or all natural resource revenue directly to citizens may not improve education outcomes for those most in need. In many countries, strengthening the education system as a whole is required: schools need to be built and teachers properly trained and paid. Cash transfers are more likely to be effective when accompanied by improvements in education provision. Brazil's impressive results in increasing access to education and improving learning illustrate this. Its success has been made possible by a combination of conditional cash transfers and equitable distribution of government resources:

Botswana adopted a formula directing mineral revenue to health and education

---

Box 2.5: Chad's unsuccessful Oil Revenue Management Law

Originally intended to guarantee that oil revenue would be used to improve social services, Chad's Oil Revenue Management Law has effectively been dismantled by the government. The law, promulgated in January 1999, was a condition for the country to receive World Bank finance for the construction of a pipeline to Cameroon.

The initial version of the law stipulated that, of the total revenue, 10% would be saved and, out of the remainder, 5% would go to the oil producing region, 15% to general government expenditure and 80% to 'priority sectors', including education. However, an amendment in 2006 redirected the savings component to 'priority sectors', whose definition was extended to include security. The government, which was under pressure from a rebel force insurgency,

redirected public expenditure for military purposes. Military expenditure as a percentage of non-oil GDP increased from 2% in 2005 to more than 14% in 2009. Education had been scheduled in the National Poverty Reduction Strategy to receive 21% of the budget in 2004-2007 but only received 13%.

Chad's oil wealth could have supported an education system that is failing: only one pupil in three reaches the last grade of primary, and only 45% of men and 24% of women were literate in 2010. Chad's experience shows that even legal provisions requiring spending of natural resource revenue on priority sectors cannot guarantee that education receives a large enough share.

Sources: Frank and Guesnet (2009); IMF (2011a); Independent Evaluation Group (2009); World Bank (2011e).

Several countries could reach UPE with income from natural resources

the Bolsa Familia programme transfers 1% to 2% of the gross national income to 12 million of the poorest households, while education budget reforms distribute a larger share of government spending to the poorest states, allowing for greater public investment in building schools and paying teachers (Bruns et al., 2012; UNESCO, 2010b).

Seizing the opportunity: natural resource revenue can fund education

Several of the countries that are furthest away from achieving the EFA goals are endowed with natural resource wealth but have failed to generate enough revenue, have not managed it efficiently or have not invested it in productive sectors like education. Meanwhile, natural resource discovery is expected to grow significantly in coming decades in some regions, including sub-Saharan Africa (Barma et al., 2012). Several countries that have recently made oil or mineral discoveries are set to join the list of resource-rich countries.

Table 2.4 lists low and middle income countries with youth literacy rates below 90% that are either dependent on natural resources or have recently discovered oil, gas or minerals. It shows the considerable potential for natural resource revenue to fund education and increase access to primary and lower secondary schooling. The scenario is based on two assumptions.

First, it is assumed that governments would maximize the amount of revenue raised from natural resources (measured by the ratio of natural resource revenue to export receipts). Thus, mineral-rich countries would convert 30% of their mining export receipts into government revenue. On average, mineral-rich countries currently retain around 20%, though Mauritania has reached 30% and Botswana and Mongolia have passed 50%. For oil-rich countries, the scenario would bring all countries up to the current average of 75% of oil exports being converted to government revenue.[4] Government revenue from oil tends to be higher because it is easier to quantify and tax than minerals, it involves lower up-front investment and a good share of world oil production is done through

nationally owned companies (Barma et al., 2012). Second, the scenario assumes that countries will channel 20% of these new resources to education. Low and middle income countries currently spend, on average, 16% of their budget on education.

The potential gains for education are enormous. Several countries, including Ghana, Guinea, the Lao People's Democratic Republic, Malawi, Uganda and Zambia, could reach universal primary education without needing any more aid from donors. In a group of seventeen countries where extra revenue could be raised, natural resources could fund schooling for 86% of the 12 million out-of-school children and 42% of the 9 million out-of-school adolescents.

While the potential is considerable, so are the challenges. Some mineral-rich countries, such as the Democratic Republic of the Congo, Sierra Leone and Zambia, currently receive less than 10% of export income as government revenue. They are still struggling with the first step: bargaining with extracting companies. Nigeria, on the other hand, already retains 72% of oil exports as government revenue, meaning that the extra funding for education from the scenario presented here could only send 23% of the country's 10.5 million out-of-school children to primary school. In this case the challenge is to manage, distribute and use the revenue better and to ensure that education is a top priority for the government.

In other countries, oil wealth holds great potential for building an education system, but capacity constraints may act as a barrier. South Sudan became independent in 2011 and is already resource-rich, since it possesses most of the oil of the former Sudan. Capacity is weak, however, and the education system has been largely destroyed by decades of war. There are more than 1 million out-of-school children and massive shortages of qualified teachers, and a major school building drive is needed (UNESCO, 2011b). As part of the Comprehensive Peace Agreement reached in 2005, oil revenue was shared 50-50 between north and south, but it is unclear how it will be split now that the south is an independent state, as terms are still being negotiated (IMF, 2011b).

If the agreed share were to hold, South Sudan could in principle derive enough income

4. These shares are an average for 2007–2008. They are based on natural resource export data from IMF Article IV reviews, revenue data from IMF Article IV reviews and/or EITI reports.

Turning the 'resource curse' into a blessing for education

Table 2.4: Many resource-rich countries could reach Education for All if they raised more revenue and increased focus on education

Country		Current situation					Potential	
	Conflict-affected[1]	Youth literacy rate (%)	Education as share of total public spending (%)	Natural resource revenue		Potential extra education funding from natural resource revenue[2]	Out-of-school children who could be funded by natural resource revenue[3]	
				% natural resource exports	% total public revenue		Number (thousand)[4]	%
		2005–2010	2010	2007–08	2007–08	US$ million		
Resource dependent								
Oil and gas								
Iraq	Yes	83	. . .	111	89	. . .	. . .	. . .
Angola	Yes	73	9	54	81	2 245	493	100
Yemen	Yes	85	16	77	72	. . .	. . .	. . .
Nigeria	Yes	72	. . .	72	79	457	2 374	23
Congo	No	80	. . .	54	83	271	56	100
Chad	Yes	47	10	41	72	247	1 895	. . .
Cameroon	No	83	18	39	34	203	179	100
Minerals								
D. R. Congo	Yes	65	9	8	20	223	3 620	. . .
Zambia	No	74	. . .	8	10	159	184	100
Papua New Guinea	No	68	. . .	24	37	49	334	. . .
Guinea	Yes	63	19	11	22	45	355	100
Mauritania	No	68	15	30	25	. . .	. . .	. . .
Sierra Leone	Yes	59	18	4	2	11	97	. . .
Liberia	Yes	77	12	. . .	15	. . .	. . .	. . .
Recently discovered deposits[5]								
Oil and gas								
South Sudan	Yes	37	. . .	. . .	. . .	762	3 876	. . .
Uganda	Yes	87	15	. . .	. . .	450	623	100
Minerals								
Afghanistan	Yes	. . .	. . .	. . .	. . .	120	1 786	. . .
U. R. Tanzania	No	77	18	. . .	. . .	130	137	100
Lao PDR	No	84	13	. . .	. . .	95	23	100
Burkina Faso	No	39	21	. . .	. . .	82	596	58
Malawi	No	87	15	. . .	. . .	12	62	100
Both								
Ghana	No	81	24	. . .	. . .	692	567	100
Niger	No	37	17	. . .	. . .	92	916	91

Notes: The countries included in the table are those with youth literacy rates below 90%. Cambodia, Côte d'Ivoire, Madagascar and Mali are also set to increase extraction of natural resources in coming years, but the potential quantity of exports is not yet known. Countries in italics are the seventeen included in the aggregate figure used in the text.
1. According to the list of conflict-affected countries compiled for the 2011 EFA Global Monitoring Report.
2. 'Potential extra education funding from natural resource revenue' is based on assumptions that (a) governments increase the share of revenue raised from natural resource exports to 30% for mineral-rich countries and 75% for oil- and gas-rich countries and (b) governments spend 20% of the extra revenue (i.e. above what is already being raised) on education. Because Iraq and Yemen already raise more than 75% from oil exports, and Mauritania 30% of minerals exports, there is no extra education funding available.
3. Pupil unit costs were calculated for primary school and lower secondary school using either EPDC and UNESCO (2009) costings (therefore including improvements in quality) or actual unit costs as reported in the statistical tables of this Report. For countries where data were unavailable, an income group average was used.
4. For countries with available data, the potential number of pupils that could be funded was capped at the number of current out-of-school children, with funds remaining in many cases. For countries without out-of-school figures, the total number of pupils that could be funded is shown in italics. The inclusion of this number does not mean that there are necessarily that many children out of school.
5. For countries with recently discovered deposits, an annual average over 2010–2015 of current IMF projections on exports for natural resource revenue was used to calculate potential education funding.
Sources: EFA Global Monitoring Report team calculations (2012) based on IMF Article IV reviews and EPDC and UNESCO (2009); Annex, Statistical Tables 2 and 9.

98% of South Sudan's revenue has been from oil, badly exposing it to price changes

to send all primary school-aged children to school. The challenge will be to gradually increase the capacity of the education system, manage oil funds efficiently and work towards a more diverse economy with less dependence on oil. The government has derived 98% of its revenue from oil, which leaves it badly exposed to drops in world prices such as those witnessed during the world financial crisis of 2008–2009 (IMF, 2011b).

Countries that have recently discovered natural resource riches are in a unique position to tackle these challenges, as they can learn from the experience of others, and vastly extend access to primary and secondary schooling. In countries such as Ghana, new oil discoveries could complement mineral wealth to provide additional

development spending (Box 2.6). The extractive industries boom is reaching all corners of the world, and the opportunities are significant (Figure 2.9):

■ In the Lao People's Democratic Republic, revenue from copper and gold mining in 2012 will be worth more than double its value in 2008, which could double the education budget.

■ In the Niger, oil and uranium extraction is set to increase massively between 2011 and 2016. Maximizing government revenue could send nine out of ten out-of-school children to primary school.

Box 2.6: Ghana's natural wealth: a new source of education financing

Ghana's strong record on governance and development allows for cautious optimism about how it will manage its newly discovered oil riches to reduce poverty. In coming years, oil revenue is expected to make up a larger proportion of government income than aid.

Oil revenue started to flow into government coffers in 2011, and the Petroleum Revenue Management Act was passed in April of that year. The Act stipulates that 50% to 70% of oil revenue will be spent through the regular budget, with a minimum of 70% going to twelve priority sectors, including human resources development and education. The remaining 30% to 50% will be put into a heritage fund (a savings fund) and a stabilization fund. Transparency is to be guaranteed by following EITI principles and adhering to a strong framework of public accountability. Reports on revenue are to be published in national newspapers and the oil funds are to undergo annual external audits.

Ghana is set to use both oil and non-oil revenue to double expenditure on reducing poverty between 2009 and 2013, which is likely to benefit education and other social sectors. The new oil wealth will be supplemented by greater revenue collection on the country's existing gold riches, with corporate taxes on mining set to increase from 25% to 35% and a new windfall profit tax of 10% to be introduced.

Figure 2.8: Ghana's increased revenue is set to boost expenditure on reducing poverty

Actual and projected government revenue and poverty-reducing expenditure, 2008 to 2013

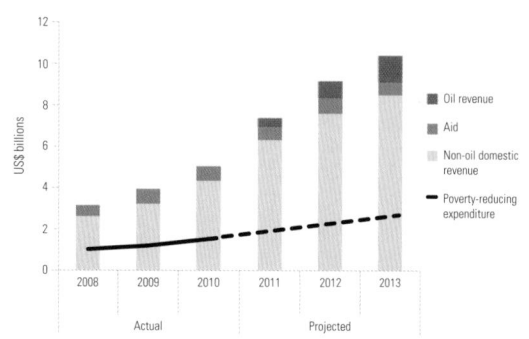

Source: IMF (2012a).

If Ghana were to maximize revenue from oil and mineral wealth as outlined in Table 2.4, the education budget could increase by 43%, and all children and adolescents currently out of school could have access to primary and lower secondary education.

Sources: IMF (2012a); Ghana Ministry of Finance and Economic Planning (2010).

Figure 2.9: Natural resource revenue could significantly increase education budgets

Potential extra funding from maximizing natural resource revenue relative to 2010 total education budget, selected countries, in billion US dollars

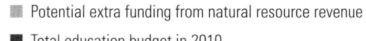
■ Potential extra funding from natural resource revenue
■ Total education budget in 2010

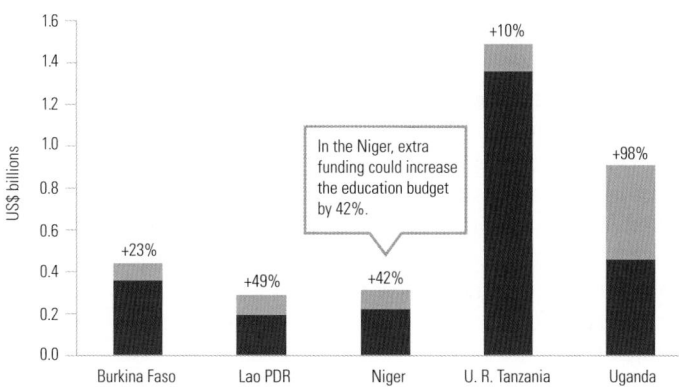

Note: Maximizing natural resource revenue is assumed to take place in two steps: (i) an increase in the share of revenue from natural resource exports to 30% for minerals and to 75% for oil; and (ii) the allocation of 20% of this additional revenue to education.
Source: EFA Global Monitoring Report team calculations (2012) based on UIS database and IMF Article IV reviews.

■ In Uganda, following recent oil discoveries, the government's total budget is set to almost double by 2016. This could lead to a doubling of the education budget and send all primary and lower secondary school-aged children to school.

Conclusion

The potential for natural resource revenue to finance the achievement of EFA and other development goals is enormous. With commodity prices increasing and new exploration and extraction opportunities arising, developing countries – with those in sub-Saharan Africa at the forefront – could raise sums vastly surpassing what they currently receive from aid donors.

For the seventeen countries with available data, total extra funding for education from natural resource revenue could reach US$5 billion a year. This is equivalent to two and a half times the amount that these countries received in aid

to education in 2010. Ensuring that 'old' and 'new' resource-rich countries maximize the revenue they get from extractive activities, that funds are managed efficiently and transparently, and that a good share is spent on education should be central concerns for EFA actors: international organizations, national and international civil society groups, donors and governments.

To encourage fair and productive use of natural resource revenue, education advocates should concentrate on three fronts. First, they should support EITI and other transparency and fair taxation measures, pushing all governments to comply with their standards. Second, they should get involved in national debates on the use of natural resource revenue, and make the case for education as a long-term investment essential to diversify the economy and avoid the resource curse. Third, each country should explore options to ensure that this income is spent on education.

Education advocates should make the case for natural resource wealth to be spent on education

2 0 1 2

Education for All Global Monitoring Report

Policy focus: Harnessing the potential of private organizations

Given the acute need for resources to support Education for All and the gloomy outlook for international aid in filling this gap, private organizations are increasingly seen as a potential source of finance. Private foundations and corporations engage in education in many different ways and with very different motivations, ranging from altruistic philanthropy to self-interested investment. They channel hundreds of millions of dollars to education in developing countries annually, but a lack of transparency and accountability limits the evidence available about the magnitude and effectiveness of this support to education.

According to analysis for this Report drawing on publicly available information from the largest private foundations and corporations based in rich countries, such organizations provide an estimated US$683 million per year to support education in developing countries.[5] While this is a drop in the ocean compared with national education budgets, and equivalent to just 5% of aid from donor countries that belong to the OECD-DAC, private contributions have the potential to catalyse innovation, advance policy reform and address the education needs of marginalized populations.

Private organizations could do much more to realize this potential, not only by dramatically increasing their funding, but also by aligning their activities better with EFA objectives and building more effective partnerships with the EFA community – national governments, civil society groups and other donors.

Mapping contributions of private organizations to global education

The two broad types of private organizations that support activities related to EFA, foundations and corporations, are influenced by different objectives and operate in different ways (Box 2.7).

Contributions from private organizations amount to 5% of aid to education

A lack of comparable information makes it difficult to measure their total contribution.

On one estimate, private contributions to all sectors originating from OECD-DAC countries amounted to over US$50 billion in 2008–2010,[6] compared with around US$120 billion for official development assistance (ODA) from governments (Center for Global Prosperity, 2012). While these figures look impressive, education benefits very little. US foundations, for example, give around 8% of their grants to education, compared with 53% to health. As much as 90% of corporate contributions are from pharmaceutical companies (Center for Global Prosperity, 2012).

Contributions to education come in a variety of shapes and sizes. A review for this Report identified spending of around US$683 million a year by key foundations and corporations based in DAC-member countries, on activities specifically related to education in developing countries.

Funding from foundations is low compared with official aid

Among thirty philanthropic foundations surveyed, nineteen provide publicly available financial information on their programmes in ways that allow their funding for education in developing countries to be identified. Their contributions total around US$135 million a year. This is likely to be an underestimate because information on some key foundations, such as the Aga Khan Foundation, is either not available or not sufficiently detailed.

Among foundations with data, only five provide more than US$5 million a year. These five account for 87% of the total amount from foundations (Table 2.5). Their contributions are comparable with aid to education from some of the smallest government donors, such as Luxembourg and New Zealand (Figure 2.11).

---

5. This section draws heavily on van Fleet (2012), which includes the full list of organizations reviewed.

6. This estimate covers contributions from foundations, corporations, voluntary organizations, religious organizations and academic institutions.

Box 2.7: The many faces of private contributions to education

Discussions about contributions by private organizations to global education often mix very different types of involvement. The motivation for engagement of foundations and corporations can be placed on a continuum between philanthropy and corporate interest, with corporate social responsibility falling somewhere in between (Figure 2.10).

Foundations. The activities of philanthropic foundations are generally the most comparable to aid from DAC donors. Some of the foundations that contribute to education, such as the William and Flora Hewlett Foundation, are supported by personal wealth. Their activities are commonly not directly related to corporate goals. Others, such as the MasterCard Foundation, are established by a corporation but operate independent of corporate oversight and have their own programmes, separate from any business interests. They rarely run their own projects but instead channel their funds to other organizations, usually local or international NGOs. Some also engage in advocacy aimed at influencing policy.

Corporations. The involvement of corporations differs widely in terms of how closely it is tied to core business activities. It can be divided into three broad subcategories. First, some corporations make contributions towards education in developing countries through grants to NGOs or international organizations, which is classified here as 'corporate giving'. This is the subcategory most closely aligned to philanthropic motives. About 78% of the surveyed US Fortune 500 corporations that made contributions to education channelled at least some of them through international NGOs. All of ING's US$13 million contribution to global education since 2005 has been spent on a partnership with UNICEF. Other corporations, such as Nike, channel their contributions through a foundation or trust housed within the company, with corporate executives serving on the governing board.

Second, companies with activities in developing countries undertake 'social investments' in sectors such as education as a form of corporate social responsibility. Some corporations, typically oil and mining companies, are contractually obliged by governments to invest in social sectors. For example, the Hess Corporation, which operates oilfields in Equatorial Guinea, has contributed US$20 million over five years towards reform of the education system, including building model schools and providing teacher training.

Third, companies may supply products or expertise, sometimes through a partnership with a government. Companies in the field of information and communication technology (ICT) have been particularly active in providing training for teachers or students. For example, the Cisco Networking Academy is a global programme that trains students to create and maintain computer networks.

Sources: van Fleet (2011, 2012); ING (2012).

Figure 2.10: The motivation of private engagement in education ranges from philanthropy to corporate interest

Figure 2.11: Education funding from the largest foundations is dwarfed by donor aid

Contributions towards education from the five largest foundations and total aid to education from selected government donors, 2009-2010 or closest available year

Notes: Around two-thirds of the US$15 million annual average from the William and Flora Hewlett Foundation originally came from the Bill & Melinda Gates Foundation. In most cases, the amount of support to education in developing countries had to be estimated using aggregate data from foundations.
Sources: Annex, Aid Table 2; Carnegie Corporation of New York (2011); Ford Foundation (2011); MasterCard Foundation (2010); William and Flora Hewlett Foundation (2010); van Fleet (2012).

Table 2.5: Funding provided by foundations identified as supporting education in developing countries

Annual average funding	Foundations	Share
More than US$5 million	Ford Foundation, William and Flora Hewlett Foundation, MasterCard Foundation, Open Society Foundations, Carnegie Corporation of New York	87%
Between US$1 and US$5 million	Michael and Susan Dell Foundation, Kellogg Foundation, MacArthur Foundation, Bernard van Leer Foundation	10%
Less than US$1 million	Jacob and Hilda Blaustein Foundation, Global Fund for Children, Global Fund for Women, International Community Foundation, Unbound Philanthropy, d.o.b. foundation, International Development Exchange, Voxtra, Roger Federer Foundation	3%
Total		US$135 million

Source: van Fleet (2012).

The largest corporate contributors are ICT and energy companies

Through publicly available information for the world's 100 top revenue generating companies and a survey of Fortune 500 companies in the United States, 103 were identified for the analysis in this Report as contributing to education in developing countries. However, only fifty-six provided financial information on the size of their contributions, most of them confidentially.[7]

Contributions towards education in developing countries from these corporations amount to

an estimated US$548 million a year. This is four times the amount identified as coming from foundations. It is concentrated among just a few contributors: around 71% comes from five corporations that each report giving more than $20 million a year.

Most corporations that contribute over US$5 million a year to education are ICT or energy companies, and their activities fall into the 'social investment' or 'supply of goods and services' category. For example, Cisco Systems and Intel each report spending over US$100 million a year on education in developing countries, much of which is in-kind contributions (Table 2.6).

Private contributions are seldom aligned with EFA goals

The contributions of most foundations and corporations are not strategically coordinated with the broader global EFA framework. In terms of recipients, middle income countries tend to attract these donors' interest more than low income countries.

In terms of the EFA goals, about 75% of the foundations and 70% of the corporations surveyed reported supporting primary education. Nearly half contribute to youth and adult skills, including a large programme of the MasterCard Foundation. The skills focus generally includes science, technology, financial literacy and entrepreneurship (van Fleet, 2012). Corporations that pay attention to activities associated with goal 3 are likely to do so because a skilled workforce is of direct interest to their needs. Some, such as the Nike Foundation, pay attention to gender equity and girls'

---

7. For 14 of the 103 identified corporations it was possible to estimate annual funding for education in developing countries using publicly available data. A further 42 provided this information confidentially; it has been used to estimate the aggregate amount but the donors cannot be listed individually.

Table 2.6: Corporations spending above US$5 million a year on education (2010 or closest available year)

Corporation	Industry	Annual (US$ million)	Corporate giving	Social investment	Supply of goods and expertise	Examples	Where?
Aviva	Insurance	7	X			Street to School (urban youth programme)	China, India
Banco Santander	Banking	124	X		X	University networks and scholarships (83%); other scholarships; youth programmes	Latin America
Cisco Systems	ICT	120	X		X	Cisco Networking Academies (93%); grants to organizations	World
Citigroup	Banking	5	X			Secondary education; youth training	Africa, Brazil, India
Coca-Cola	Food	24	X	X		Grants to organizations	World
ExxonMobil	Oil	24		X		Technology; vocational training for women	Oil-producing countries
Intel	ICT	100	X		X	Teacher training in ICT; ICT access in classrooms	World
Repsol YPF	Oil	8		X		Primary and secondary education; youth training	Oil-producing countries

Note: In most cases, the amount of support to education in developing countries had to be estimated using aggregate data from corporate social responsibility reports.
Sources: Aviva (2011); Banco Santander (2012); Citigroup (2011); ExxonMobil (2011); Intel (2011); van Fleet (2012).

education. A few place a special focus on early childhood education, such as the Open Society Foundations and the Bernard van Leer Foundation. Others, notably the William and Flora Hewlett Foundation, pay particular attention to improving the quality of education (Box 2.8). Adult literacy, the goal that is probably most neglected in the EFA agenda, also appears to receive the least attention from private organizations. Only 18% of surveyed foundations indicate support in this area.

It is difficult to translate this information into the amount of money available for each goal, since the reporting of foundations and corporations is not broken down in this way. However, in terms of the volume of funding, higher education appears to receive more attention than the EFA goals as a whole. Two of the foundations giving the most to education (Carnegie Corporation of New York and Ford Foundation) and the corporation giving the most (Banco Santander) directed over 80% of their grants to developing countries in 2010 towards scholarships and support for higher education institutions. While higher education certainly needs more funding, the fact that many poor children and young people do not even complete primary school means that such investment is not sufficiently targeted at the disadvantaged.

Foundations tend to focus their efforts on countries most in need, whereas corporations typically disburse to regions of strategic importance to them. The most frequent recipients of the ICT sector's education contributions are Argentina, Brazil, Chile, China, India and Mexico (van Fleet, 2011).

Private interests and public policy: too close for comfort?

Over the past decade aid donors have improved aid effectiveness by working to strengthen government systems. But this approach is not common among private organizations, particularly corporations, which contribute the largest amount of resources.

The work of some domestic foundations shows that they can support broader government efforts in education in ways that can have a large impact. In India, Azim Premji, chairman of Wipro, one of the largest ICT corporations in India, transferred US$2 billion worth of shares from his company to found the Azim Premji Foundation, which aims to improve the quality of the public education system. Over the past ten years, the foundation reports, it has reached over 2.5 million children in 20,000 schools across thirteen states in India (Azim Premji Foundation, 2012; Bajaj, 2011; The Times of India, 2010; van Fleet, 2012).

The private sector gives least attention to adult literacy, the most neglected EFA goal

Box 2.8: Leveraging private resources to improve the quality of education

Through strategically focused grants, foundations can achieve a broader influence in education policy debates.

Since 2008, the William and Flora Hewlett Foundation, with support from the Bill & Melinda Gates Foundation, has developed the Quality Education in Developing Countries initiative, focused on Ghana, India, Kenya, Mali, Senegal, the United Republic of Tanzania and Uganda.

One of the initiative's areas of emphasis has been generating data on learning outcomes in developing countries. For example, in India it gives funding to Pratham to assist the NGO in conducting its Annual Status of Education Report, the world's largest non-government household survey collecting data on learning outcomes of primary school children. In East Africa, the initiative supports Uwezo, which has adapted Pratham's survey to the region.

Reporting of the results of these assessments has been instrumental in promoting national debate on the quality of education in the countries concerned. While the initiative's investment is modest, it highlights the potentially innovative role of philanthropy in improving learning and catalysing policy dialogue.

Source: van Fleet (2012).

Some corporations may provide genuine value to education systems even if this directly benefits their business strategies. This is particularly true for ICT companies. One example concerns the Assessment & Teaching of 21st-Century Skills research project. As part of this initiative, Cisco, Intel and Microsoft contributed ideas on how to develop the assessment of ICT skills in the Programme for International Student Assessment (PISA) (van Fleet, 2012). Intel recognizes that its corporate success depends on 'young people having access to a quality education and technology' (Intel, 2011, p. 16). Yet even if such activities add value, they need to be subject to scrutiny. In Egypt, where the Intel Teach programme works with the Ministry of Education, teachers must take Intel Teach or an equivalent computer course to receive a promotion (Intel, 2011).

Such scrutiny is not easy, because private organizations do not face the same level of accountability as governments or aid donors. And there is a risk that they may exercise unwarranted influence over education policy. Pearson announced in July 2012 that it was launching the Pearson Affordable Learning Fund with US$15 million to invest in private companies seeking to identify affordable ways to improve learning outcomes. The first investment of the fund is a stake in Omega Schools, a privately held chain of for-profit schools in Ghana. This follows Pearson's investment in 2010 in Bridge International Academies, a chain of low fee private schools in Kenya. Promoting private schooling is closely associated with Pearson's business interests. Since these schools commonly operate independently of governments, it is not clear, however, how such an approach will help achieve Pearson's commitment at the Global Partnership for Education replenishment meeting to strengthen and improve national education systems (Global Partnership for Education, 2011b; Pearson, 2012).

Towards more productive engagement

The greater involvement of private organizations is a welcome move towards increasing funding and raising the visibility of education needs in poor countries. For their engagement to support EFA effectively, however, there is still a long way to go.

Transparency on funding and impact is vital

As a crucial first step, all private organizations should provide information on their commitments, including the amounts allocated and how they are spent. This would allow scrutiny to ensure that business interests do not override collective goals, while also giving information on the amount of resources available to fill the EFA financing gap.

At present, few report such information. Private organizations made a joint statement outlining their commitments at the Global Partnership for Education replenishment meeting in Copenhagen in 2011. But many private organizations were unwilling to reveal details of their commitments publicly. As a result, there is no way of knowing whether they keep their promises. It is also not possible to tell whether the pledge to spend on education in developing countries made by the private sector at the replenishment conference referred to previously planned investment

Education for All Global Monitoring Report

or additional commitments. If private organizations want to make a genuine contribution to collective education goals, they should make public their current and future spending plans, in the same way expected of national governments and aid donors.

By the same token, to have a lasting impact on EFA, private organizations need to provide sufficient funding over several years to assure the sustainability of initiatives, because education is a long-term endeavour. Some philanthropic foundations, such as the MasterCard Foundation, the Firelight Foundation and the Roger Federer Foundation, make multi-year commitments to their grantees. However, most contributions, particularly from corporations, tend to be short term (van Fleet, 2012).

Private organizations often publicize the details of their interventions. According to their brochures, IKEA will support the education needs of 10 million children between 2009 and 2015, Intel trained 10 million teachers in more than seventy countries in the last twelve years, and the UBS Foundation aims to spend five years improving the lives of 200 million children under the age of 5 (IKEA, 2012; Intel, 2012; UBS, 2009). But how these results are substantiated remains unclear. Impact evaluations seldom exist or are not easily accessible, especially in the case of corporations.

Private organizations should align their support with government priorities

The contributions from private organizations would be more effective if they were coordinated with governments and driven by countries' needs. The Global Business Coalition for Education is one promising way forward since it operates within the framework of EFA goals (van Fleet, 2012).

Another way private organizations could support government education efforts would be to channel some of their funding through a pooled mechanism. Global health funds, such as the Global Fund to Fight AIDS, Tuberculosis and Malaria, have been successful in this regard. But the main existing mechanism in the education sector, the Global Partnership for Education, has not yet played this role effectively.

At present, the private sector has a say in the partnership's policy direction via a seat on its board, yet pledges made by foundations and corporations at the partnership's replenishment meeting will not be disbursed through the pooled funding mechanism.

There is no administrative or legal reason for private organizations not to channel resources through the Global Partnership for Education, so why does the partnership seem to be less attractive than global health funds? First, the partnership may not yet be sufficiently recognized as an effective mechanism for funding education, capable of disbursing resources quickly and linking results to funding. Second, activities may need to be identified that are both consistent with the partnership's priorities and sufficiently attractive to private organizations. Third, education needs private sector champions that will lead by example. The drive of the Bill & Melinda Gates Foundation has given visibility and credibility to the Global Fund to Fight AIDS, Tuberculosis and Malaria, encouraging the involvement of other private organizations.

Conclusion

Private organizations contribute to EFA in several ways, but the limited data available on the size of their contributions suggest that the education sector is not a prime destination of their resources. Their support is equivalent to 5% of what was spent by official donors on education in 2010 – and of that only a small share is spent on EFA priorities.

Calls for the increased involvement and funding of the private sector in education need to be accompanied by measures to ensure that partnerships are more balanced. Foundations and corporations keen to support EFA should be much more transparent about how much they are investing, where, and what the results are. And governments, donors and non-governmental and multilateral organizations that want to bring private organizations into EFA partnerships should specify more clearly how the private sector can contribute to collective efforts.

The private sector should be transparent about its investments in EFA

Part 2 | Putting education

If someone can give me the skills and opportunity to work, I know I can achieve my goals.
— young woman, Ethiopia

The need to develop young people's skills has become urgent. Governments around the world are grappling with the long-term consequences of the financial crisis and the challenges posed by increasingly knowledge-based economies. If countries are to grow and prosper in a rapidly changing world, they need to pay even greater attention to developing a skilled workforce. And all young people, wherever they live and whatever their background, require skills that prepare them for decent jobs so they can thrive and participate fully in society.

These needs were recognized when the third Education for All goal – which focuses on 'the learning needs of all young people and adults' – was formulated in 2000. But they have not received enough attention from governments, aid donors, the education community or the private sector – and now they are even more critical.

Young people are more numerous than ever. Globally, the population aged 15 to 24 reached over 1.2 billion in 2010. Jobs are not being created fast enough to meet the needs of this large youth population. Around one in eight people aged 15 to 24 are unemployed. Young people are about three times as likely as adults to be unemployed. With youth unemployment threatening to rise still higher, many young people face the prospect of remaining without secure work for years to come.

If governments and the private sector fail to educate and train young people and employ them in decent jobs, they risk disappointing young people's aspirations and wasting their potential. This limits opportunities for sustainable growth, and jeopardizes gains from policy interventions in other areas, such as poverty reduction, health and agriculture.

Alongside the risks, growing youth populations represent a window of opportunity for development. The rising ratio of working-age people to dependants could give economic growth a boost: a demographic dividend.

Education and skills are not the only part of this puzzle – growth also requires balanced policies that favour investment and job creation – but they are an essential part. To a very large extent, skills will determine whether growing numbers of young people, and their communities, societies and countries, realize their potential. Youth are also a positive force for political change and freedom, as the Arab Spring and youth unrest in several European countries have shown. But social movements will fail if new governments do not address the problems in education, training and employment opportunities for youth that have fuelled broader protests.

Youth unemployment is rightly rising up the agenda, leading policy-makers to prioritize job creation in private enterprises. While this focus is warranted, the needs of millions of young people who lack basic literacy and numeracy continue to be ignored. Often earning wages below the poverty line in the urban informal sector, or farming smallholdings in a context of ever-decreasing access to land, these young people are seldom heard in protests. Providing them with opportunities to escape from low skilled, low paid work should be at the core of every skills development strategy.

All too often, access to skills is unequal, perpetuating and exacerbating the disadvantage that attends being poor, female or a member of a marginalized social group. Young people who have grown up in poverty and exclusion are more likely to have had little education or to have dropped out of school. As a result they have fewer opportunities to develop skills for decent

to work

jobs and hence risk further marginalization in the labour market. That is why this Report takes a special interest in identifying and understanding what access disadvantaged young people have to skills development that can lead to better jobs – secure work that pays enough to buy food and put money in their pockets, jobs that can lift them out of poverty.

Young people's learning needs are very broad, involving not only skills for earning a living but also personal development that lays the foundations for a fulfilling life. Those needs start with early childhood care and education – the crucial preparation for a life of learning. The scale and urgency of the problem demand that this Report take a pragmatic approach, focusing on skills that can offer all young people, including the disadvantaged, a chance of obtaining better jobs.

As previous editions of the *EFA Global Monitoring Report* have noted, the third EFA goal that governments signed up to in 2000 amounted to a vague aspiration, with no quantifiable benchmarks against which progress could be measured. Goal 3 is 'ensuring that the learning needs of all young people and adults are met through equitable access to appropriate learning and life-skills programmes'.

One consequence of the vagueness of the third EFA goal is that it has suffered from neglect in comparison with the other EFA goals. Another consequence is that the attention it has received has largely been confined to technical and vocational education and training, offered in formal contexts. As this Report shows, skills development initiatives need to cast a much wider net – making up for deficits of foundation skills, ensuring that more young people enter and complete at least lower secondary school, increasing opportunities to learn skills in the informal sector, and focusing on the specific needs of urban and rural youth. While skills development extends to higher education, those who make it to tertiary level tend not to be among the disadvantaged, who are the focus of this Report.

Although considerable progress has been made in improving access to primary school globally, a large proportion of young people still leave school without the skills necessary to avoid some of the worst forms of disadvantage in the labour market. Early unemployment, or employment in low skilled work with no prospect of advancement, wastes young people's potential to forge better lives for themselves and to contribute to their economies and societies. And those with the worst educational outcomes – the urban poor and those in rural areas – are consigned to activities with very low pay, or none at all. Young women, in particular, face discrimination that limits their opportunities in both education and the labour market.

To provide a concrete framework for discussing skills development for decent jobs, this Report identifies three categories of skills and the contexts in which they may be acquired: foundation skills, associated with literacy and numeracy; transferable skills, including problem-solving and the ability to transform and adapt knowledge and skills in varying work contexts; and technical and vocational skills, associated with specific occupations (see Pathways to Skills illustration on next page).

Foundation skills

At their most elemental, foundation skills are the literacy and numeracy skills necessary for getting work that pays enough to meet daily needs. These foundations are also a prerequisite for engaging in further education and training, and for acquiring transferable skills and technical and vocational skills. For those unable to read, write and understand basic texts and to do basic sums and apply them, the possibilities of gainful employment or entrepreneurial activity are greatly reduced. That is why completing primary and lower secondary education of good quality is vital.

Where disadvantaged young people have not acquired foundation skills – because they did not enrol in school, dropped out, or completed school without achieving the expected proficiency – second-chance and social protection programmes that include basic literacy and numeracy components can bridge the gap. As Chapters 6 and 7 show, the need for such programmes is huge and has largely gone unfulfilled.

Transferable skills

Finding and keeping work require a broad range of skills that can be transferred and adapted to different work needs and environments. Transferable skills include analyzing problems and reaching appropriate solutions, communicating ideas and information effectively, being creative, showing leadership and conscientiousness, and demonstrating entrepreneurial capabilities.

Such skills are nurtured to some extent outside the school environment. They can, however, be further developed through education and training – especially through secondary schooling and work-based programmes – in ways that are particularly beneficial for young people whose home environments do not foster the self-confidence needed in most workplace settings.

Technical and vocational skills

Many jobs require specific technical know-how, whether related to growing vegetables, using a sewing machine, engaging in bricklaying or carpentry, or working on a computer in an office. Technical and vocational skills can be acquired through work placement programmes linked to secondary schooling and formal technical and vocational education, or through work-based training, including traditional apprenticeships and agricultural cooperatives.

If young people are to maximize the benefits of technical and vocational training, foundation and transferable skills are essential – even more so in today's dynamic global economy, where labour market demands and the skills for specific occupations are constantly evolving.

Countries with large numbers of young people who lack foundation skills require a focus on improving access to primary and lower secondary education, as well as expanding second-chance programmes for those who have missed out. Where the main skills gap

is the result of low participation in secondary education, improving access to that level, along with career guidance and job placement programmes, is an appropriate policy and investment response. For those at risk of dropping out of upper secondary school, opportunities for work-based training are needed. For young people who have already left school and are working in the urban informal sector, traditional apprenticeships provide a route to skills development. Farm-based and entrepreneurship training allows those living in remote rural areas to make the most of available resources.

The urgency of the need for skills development is detailed in Chapter 3, which identifies the way discrimination in education systems and discrimination in the labour market reinforce each other, pushing up the numbers of young people who are unemployed or in very low paid work. Chapter 4 shows how education and skills can contribute to economic growth if appropriate national strategies are in place, and considers the roles of national governments, the private sector and international agencies in financing skills development programmes.

Chapters 5 to 7 identify approaches that can help bridge global skills deficits. Chapter 5 examines the contribution made by formal secondary education to skills development, and focuses on extending access to the disadvantaged, increasing retention and improving relevance to the world of work. Chapter 6 looks at the need to extend skills training to urban youth working in the informal sector, many of whom live in poverty and lack foundation skills. Chapter 7 explores the way skills can offer rural youth an escape route from poverty. It emphasizes the foundation skills needs of smallholders as well as the need to extend entrepreneurial and financial skills so that some of the most disadvantaged rural young people, particularly young women, can engage more productively in non-farm work.

The Report concludes by identifying the ten most important steps that need to be taken to meet the skills needs of disadvantaged young people around the world.

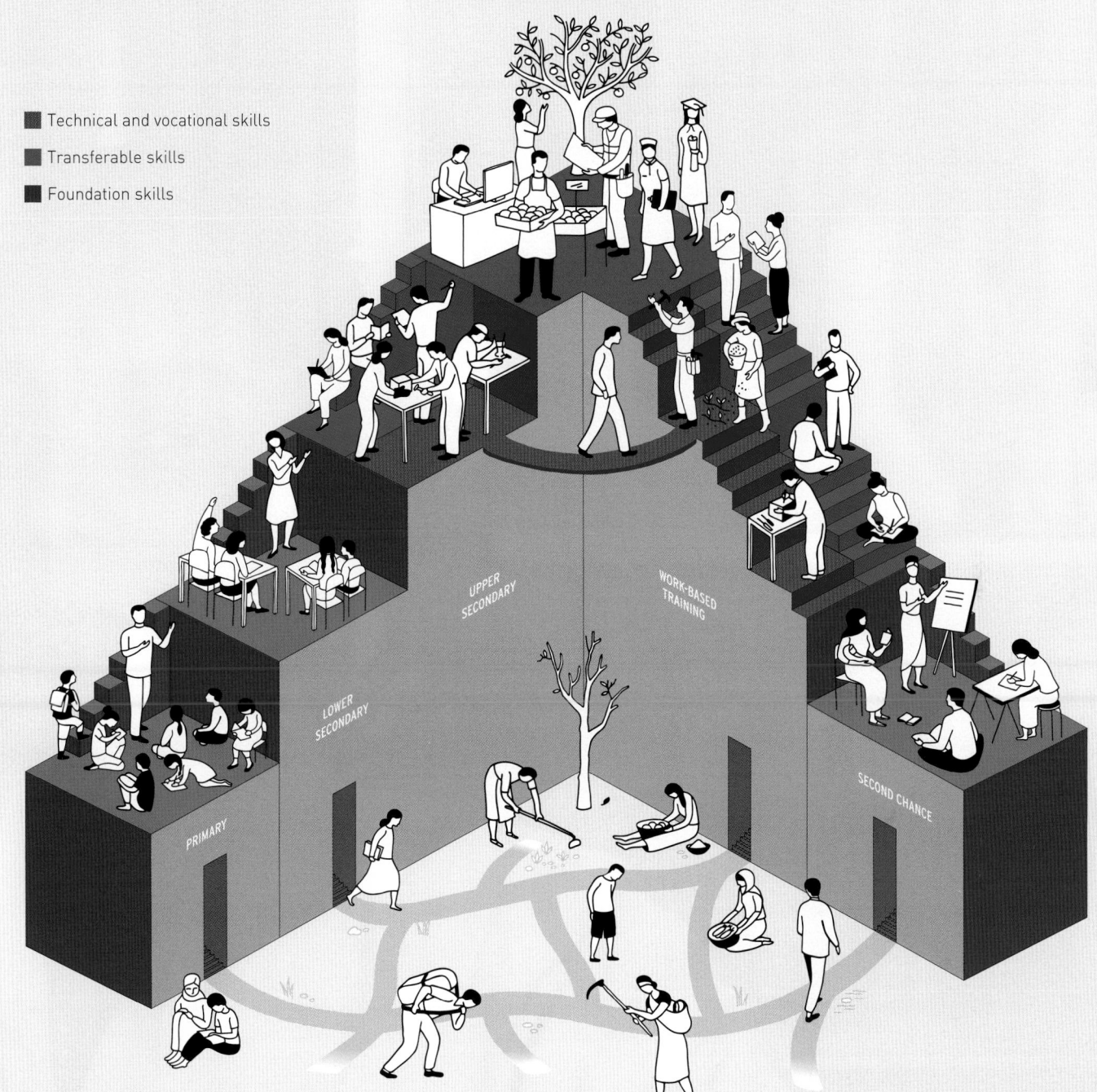

Technical and vocational skills

Transferable skills

Foundation skills

UPPER SECONDARY

WORK-BASED TRAINING

LOWER SECONDARY

SECOND CHANCE

PRIMARY

Pathways to Skills

The Pathways to Skills illustrated here can act as a tool for understanding skills development needs and the areas where policy action should be targeted. The illustration shows the three main types of skills that all young people need – foundation, transferable, and technical and vocational skills – and the contexts in which they may be acquired. One side shows formal general education and its extension, technical and vocational education. The other side shows skills training opportunities for those who have missed out on formal schooling, ranging from a second chance to acquire foundation skills to work-based training, including apprenticeships and farm-based training. Those lacking even foundation skills, represented at the base of the illustration, often have to make do with subsistence-level work, for wages that trap them in poverty. The uppermost level represents those whose accumulated skills enable them to advance to better-paid work, including entrepreneurial opportunities, and to higher education.

Education for All Global Monitoring Report

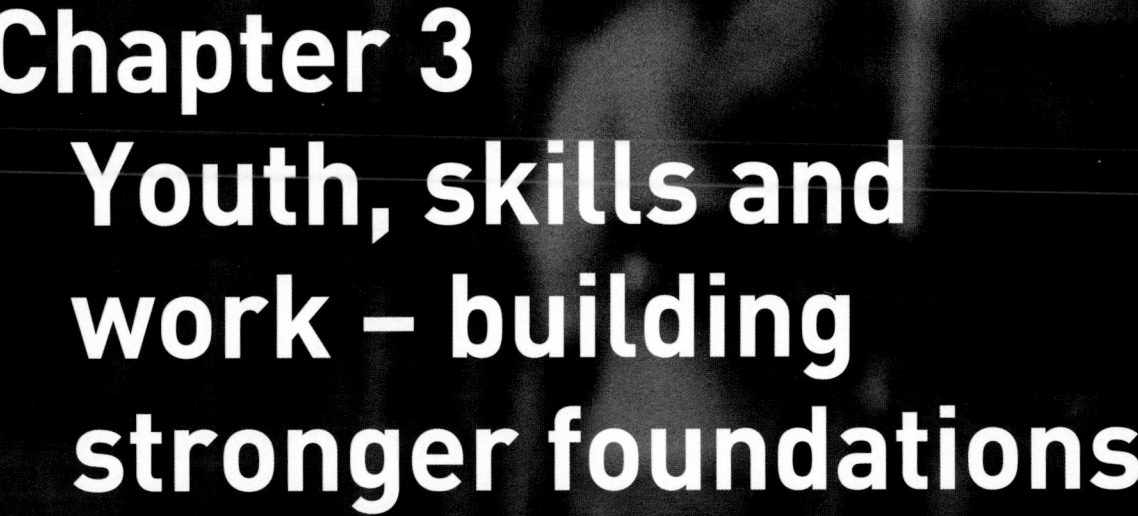

Chapter 3
Youth, skills and work – building stronger foundations

A former child labourer learning how to work in the garment industry at a vocational training school in Dhaka, Bangladesh.

175

2012

Education for All Global Monitoring Report

Many young people do not have the skills they need for decent jobs. This chapter outlines the urgency of making sure young people are given a second chance to acquire skills for work. It shows the regions in the world with the largest numbers of young people in need of foundation skills to find decent jobs. Left unassisted, unskilled youth either add to the increasing number of unemployed or are trapped working for very low pay.

Introduction

In many countries, the youth generation is among the largest ever. These young people will become an engine of growth if countries can provide them with opportunities. But many are not being adequately prepared for this role. Unequal access to education locks many young people, particularly young women from poor households, into a life of disadvantage.

This chapter shows how discrimination in education interacts with discrimination in labour markets to reinforce disadvantage. As a result, many young people are in a weak position when they enter the world of work because they lack foundation skills that they should acquire through primary and lower secondary school, including literacy and numeracy. These skills are not only crucial in themselves but are also needed to build other skills in demand in the workplace, such as communication skills, problem-solving and critical thinking.

Providing equal opportunities in schooling, while strengthening the quality of education, is an important first step to ensure that young people have the range of skills needed to improve their prospects. Yet many young people have not had access to such opportunities. They need a second chance in education, as well as skills training beyond the formal school system.

A large youth population presents challenges

Every year the number of unemployed youth is increasing not decreasing. Many students are coming out of school every year and this increases the number of unemployed youth while the job opportunities are the same.
— young man, Ethiopia[1]

Around one in six of the world's people are aged between 15 and 24. They are disproportionately concentrated in some of the poorest countries. The 170 million young people in low income countries represent both an opportunity and a challenge. As the ratio of working-age people to dependants rises, economic growth could get a boost. But if youth of the current generation enter adulthood without the education and skills they need to realize their potential, unemployment, poverty and social dislocation could rise.

The youth population is particularly large in sub-Saharan Africa, numbering around 163 million. Around two-thirds of Africans are under 25, compared with less than one-third in rich countries such as France, Japan, the United Kingdom and the United States (Figure 3.1). Youth populations in the Arab States and South and West Asia are also large, with one in two under 25. Investing in the skills of these young people could ensure that countries benefit from the massive potential they offer.

Such investment currently remains too limited to meet future challenges. Even countries with declining mortality and fertility will continue to have high proportions of young people for some time. The youth population in sub-Saharan Africa is expected to rise steeply for decades to come, with more than three and half times more young people in 2030 than in 1980 (Figure 3.2).

Many factors that are beyond young people's control affect their chances of finding good work. One is whether opportunities in the labour market change at the same rate as the size of the youth population. Over the last ten years, the number of 15- to 24-year-olds in the Arab States, South and West Asia, and sub-Saharan Africa has increased from 474 million to 566 million. By 2020 it will reach 623 million. An additional 57 million jobs will therefore need to be created for new entrants into the labour market just to prevent unemployment rates from rising above current levels.

At the same time, a larger population can generate higher demand for goods and services, which in turn can lead to more jobs. Whether young people can benefit will depend to a large extent on whether they have acquired education and skills that match those in demand in the workplace.

By 2020, 57 million jobs need to be created in these regions to prevent unemployment rising

---

1. This, and all similar quotes, are taken from focus groups carried out with young people exclusively for this Report through GlobeScan in Egypt, India, Mexico, the United Kingdom and Viet Nam.

Figure 3.1: In many countries, more than half the population is younger than 25

Percentage of population by age group, EFA regions and selected countries, 2010

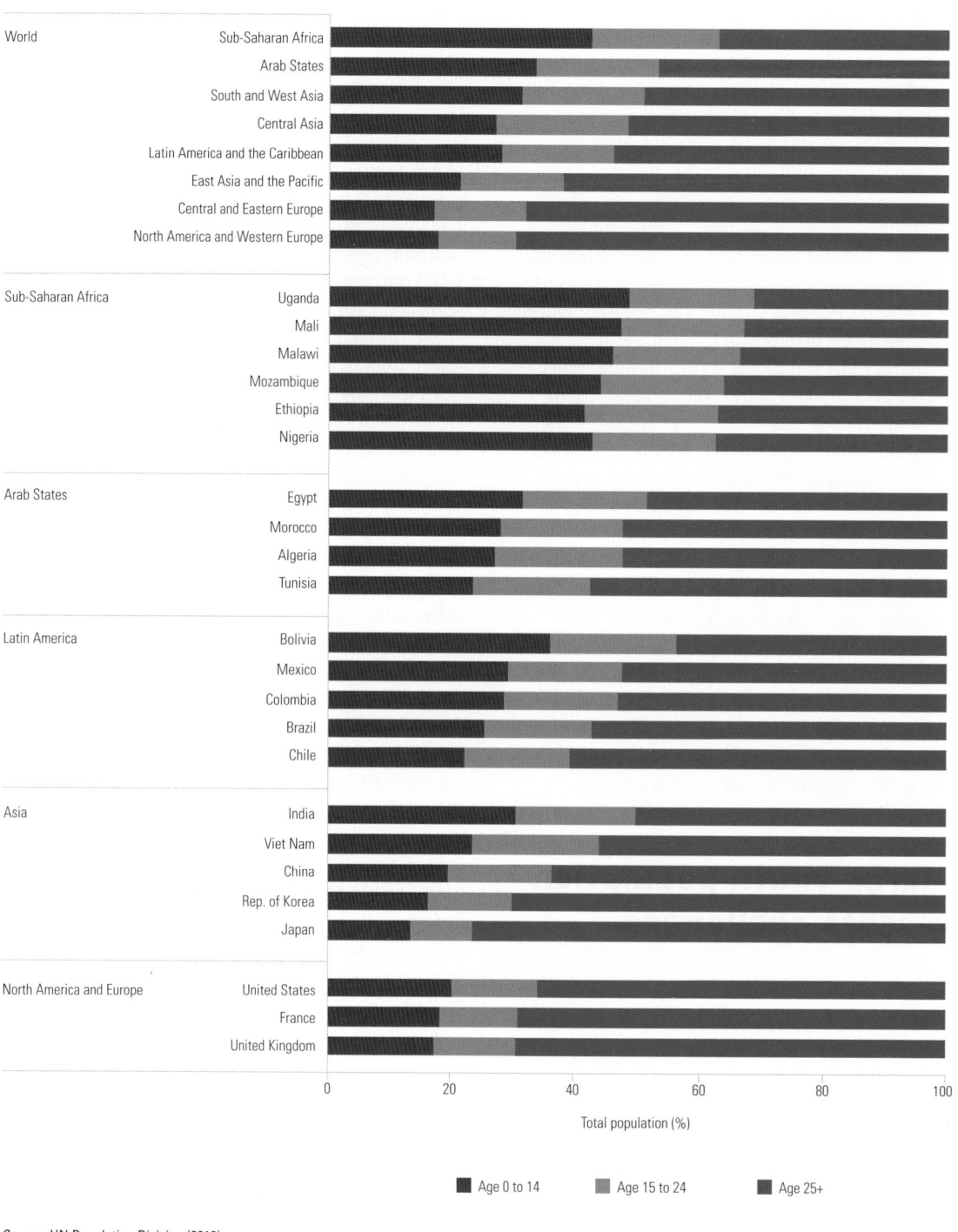

Source: UN Population Division (2010).

Figure 3.2: The youth population in sub-Saharan Africa will continue to grow at a fast pace
Youth population (age 15 to 24) in five geographic regions, 1980 to 2030

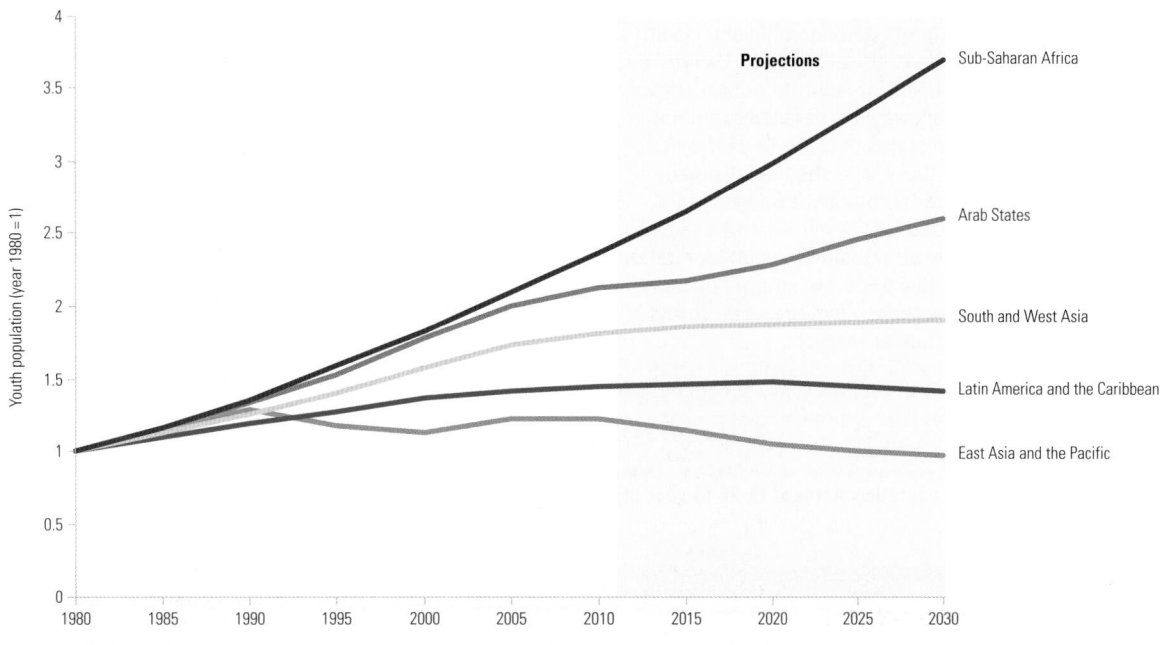

Note: The youth population data for 1980–2030 based on the medium fertility variant projections are converted to be normalized at 1 in 1980.
Source: UN Population Division (2010).

Many young people lack foundation skills

If you don't have your basic maths and English, there's no hope for you really.
— young woman, United Kingdom

People need foundation skills to stand a chance of getting jobs that pay decent wages and becoming a productive force in the economy. These skills are best acquired through formal education. But many people enter adult life without these skills.

A new data set prepared for this Report, drawing on household surveys in fifty-nine countries, shows the extent to which education systems are failing young people and limiting their chances of securing jobs that pay decent wages (Box 3.1).

Some young people never make it to school

In richer countries, most of those aged 15 to 19 reach upper secondary education and make the transition to work or higher education. In many Central Asian and Central and East European countries, such as Armenia and Kazakhstan, and some Latin American countries, including Plurinational State of Bolivia, Brazil and Colombia, the majority reach upper secondary school. This is not yet the case for many low income and some middle income countries (Figure 3.3).

In thirty of the fifty-nine countries included in the analysis, at least half of 15- to 19-year-olds lack foundation skills. This is the case for twenty-three of the thirty sub-Saharan African countries in the data set. Reasons for not achieving foundation skills vary, requiring different policy responses. In Burkina Faso, Mali and the Niger, around three in five young people have never even been to school by the time they reach age 15 to 19, and so are highly unlikely to ever have the opportunity. In many sub-Saharan African countries, many of those who have made it to school drop out before completing primary school. In Rwanda, while most have some experience of primary

In the Niger, around three in five aged 15-19 years have never been to school

179

Box 3.1: Measuring foundation skills of young people

Drawing on the latest Demographic and Health Survey and Multiple Indicator Cluster Survey data, analysis by the UNESCO Institute of Statistics for this Report allows for a detailed examination of the education status of 15- to 19-year-olds to assess whether those who should have made it to at least lower secondary level were able to do so (UIS, 2012a). By lower secondary level they should have attained the crucial foundation skills enabling them to develop more advanced skills and helping them avoid the worst forms of disadvantage in labour markets.

If young people are still in primary school by age 15 to 19, their chances of completing and continuing to secondary are slim. If they have never been to school, or dropped out before completing primary or lower secondary school, they are unlikely ever to acquire foundation skills. In Ghana, for example, in 2008 around half of young women aged 15 to 29 who had left school after completing six years of primary school could not even read or write; a further 28% were only partially literate (see Panel 1.9).

Table 3.1 explains how education status is used in the analysis to assess whether young people have attained foundation skills.

Table 3.1: Current education status of 15- to 19-year-olds

	Level	Explanation	Examples
Lacking foundation skills	No education	Never attended school	In Mali and the Niger, more than 60% never attended school.
	Dropped out (primary)	Entered primary but dropped out before completing	In the Central African Republic and Mozambique, almost one-third dropped out before completing primary; in Rwanda, 45%.
	In primary	Still attending primary but older than the official age	In Haiti and Liberia, over 40% are still in primary school.
	Dropped out (lower secondary)	Completed primary but not lower secondary	In the Syrian Arab Republic, 44% complete primary school but stop before completing lower secondary school.
Acquired foundation skills	In lower secondary	Attending lower secondary but may be older than the official age	In Ghana, Namibia and Timor-Leste, one in three are still in lower secondary despite being officially of upper secondary age.
	Dropped out (upper secondary)	Completed lower secondary but not upper secondary	One in three in Zimbabwe and one in five in Bangladesh complete lower secondary but drop out before completing upper secondary school.
	In upper secondary or higher	In upper secondary or higher education	Plurinational State of Bolivia, Egypt and Ukraine have more than 70% in upper secondary or higher.

schooling, almost half dropped out before the end of the primary cycle.

In many low income countries, large numbers are still in primary school at 15 to 19, an age by which they should have at least completed lower secondary education. For the 35% still in primary school in Uganda, for example, and the 27% in Mozambique, the chances of getting beyond this level is limited. The proportion in Haiti is even higher, reaching 44%. In general, those still in primary school by this age are less likely to complete (see Panel 1.4).

Even in countries where half of those aged 15 to 19 have completed lower secondary, such as India, Indonesia and the Syrian Arab Republic,

there are many who have never been to school, who dropped out before completing secondary school, or who are still only in primary school.

The consequences of such low levels of education are grim for the young people concerned and for the countries in which they live. Many youth will be consigned to poorly paid, insecure and often risky work, and their countries will be deprived of the kind of skills that can drive economic growth. Ensuring that all young people achieve at least a good primary and lower secondary education is vital to give countries the skilled workforce they need to realize the demographic dividend for development.

Figure 3.3: Many young people are unable to acquire foundation skills

Education status of 15- to 19-year-olds, by country, latest available year

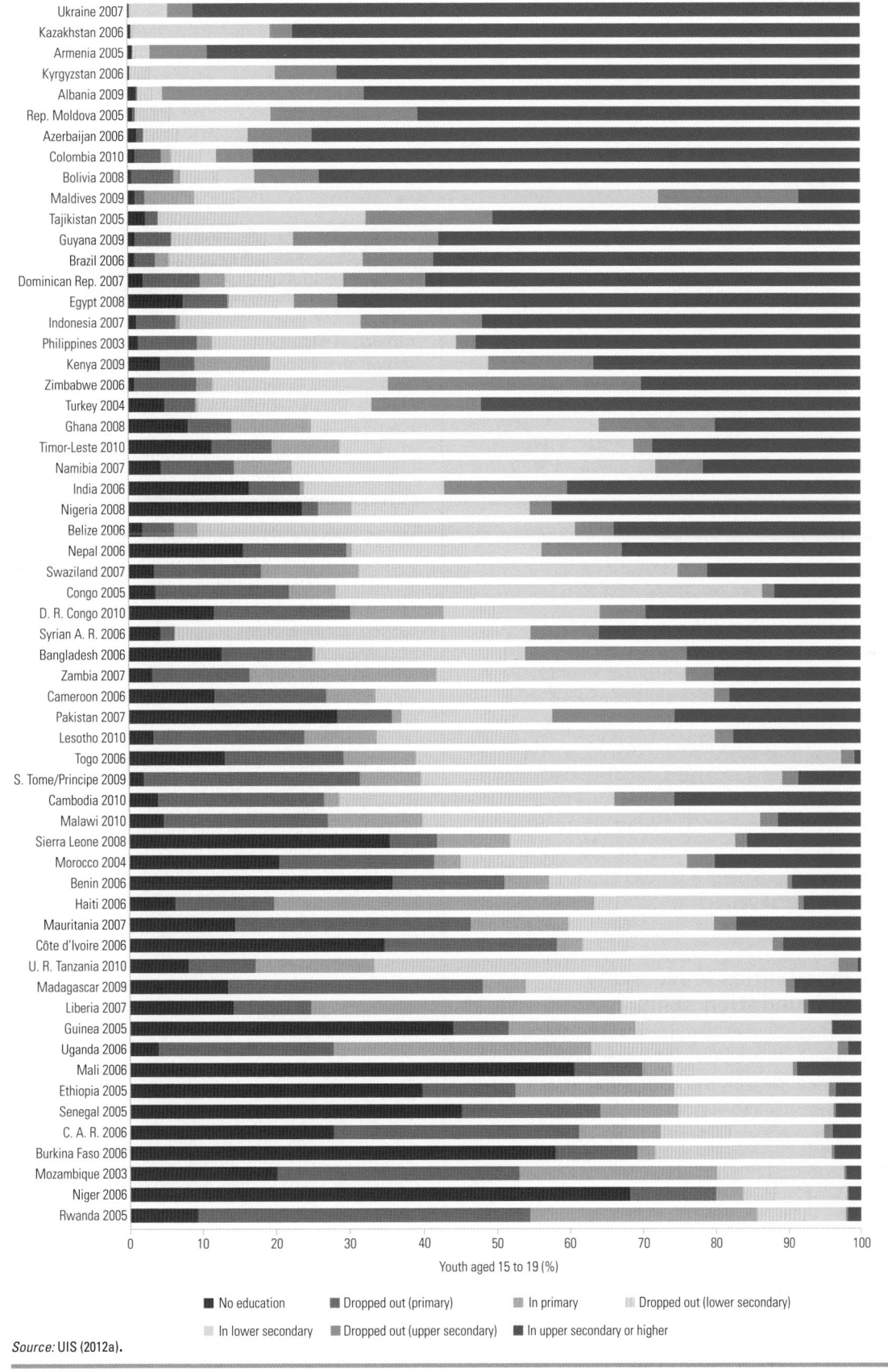

Source: UIS (2012a).

Young people need a second chance to acquire basic literacy and numeracy

Currently, my education and skill level is not sufficient enough, but if I could go to training in the future, I believe I could achieve them [basic skills].

– young woman, Ethiopia

In countries where many young people have never had the chance to go to school or have dropped out before completing primary school, skills development strategies need to focus first on providing all young people with the most basic literacy and numeracy skills through second-chance programmes. Yet they rarely do.

The scale of the challenge of providing second chances to all young people lacking foundation skills is far greater than many governments recognize. EFA Global Monitoring Report team estimates indicate that at least 200 million 15- to 24-year-olds have not managed to complete primary school in 123 low and middle income countries (Box 3.2).

Although there are many innovative second-chance programmes around the world, many of which are provided by non-governmental organizations (NGOs), the number of young people they reach only scratches the surface. An assessment of some of the largest programmes in seven countries[2] indicates that they reach around 2.1 million people (DeStefano et al., 2007). Yet according to this Report's estimates, in those seven countries there are 15 million young people who need a second chance to get the most basic skills.

Wide inequalities leave many lacking foundation skills

While average figures like those above are useful, they hide wide disparities between rich and poor, women and men, rural and urban residents, and various ethnic, religious and language groups. Targeted approaches will be needed to reach those most likely to be missing out.

Around 200 million youth need a second chance in 123 low and middle income countries

Poverty prevents many young people from achieving their potential

If I want to be someone high up I would have to keep studying but, for economic reasons, I can't keep studying. I thought that I would drop out to stop being a burden and pay for my things, but I can't find a job — how am I supposed to keep studying?

– young man, Mexico

Box 3.2: How many young people need a second chance?

Arriving at robust estimates of the numbers that second-chance programmes need to reach is not easy. The EFA Global Monitoring Report team drew on data from Demographic and Health Surveys and Multiple Indicator Cluster Surveys in fifty-nine low and middle income countries to calculate the number of 15- to 24-year-olds who have not completed primary school.

The percentage of the youth population that has not completed primary education is strongly correlated with the youth illiteracy rate. Building on this relationship, the team carried out an analysis suggesting that around 200 million youth need a second chance in 123 low and middle income countries.[3] This is equivalent to around one in five young people. Of these, 58% are female.

The challenges for some regions and countries in providing a second-chance education for these young people are enormous. Of those in the 123 countries, the vast majority live in South and West Asia (91 million) and sub-Saharan Africa (57 million). Almost one in three Africans have not had the opportunity to acquire even the most basic skills. Even in the Arab States, around one in five have not completed primary school. Over half of young people requiring a second chance reside in just five countries: Bangladesh, Ethiopia, India, Nigeria and Pakistan.

The most cost-effective way to provide basic skills is to ensure that all children have access to good quality primary schooling in the first place. As long as this is still not a reality, there is an urgent need to ensure that all young people today have a second chance to achieve this goal.

---

2. Bangladesh, Egypt, Ghana, Guatemala, Honduras, Mali and Zambia.

3. Around 20 countries did not have data on which to make estimates, including Afghanistan, Somalia, the former Sudan and the Bolivarian Republic of Venezuela. This suggests that the estimate could, if anything, be an underestimate.

The contrast between rich and poor households is stark, regardless of a given country's overall economic status. In Ethiopia, almost two in three young people in the poorest households never had a chance to go to school, compared with around one in seven in the richest households (Figure 3.4). Even in a richer country like Indonesia, where most children go to school, almost 80% of 15- to 19-year-olds from the poorest households are not in upper secondary school or higher education, compared with less than 20% from the richest households.

In Egypt, one in five of the poorest do not make it into primary school at all, while upper secondary school is almost universal among the richest. But even for the richest, a high level of education does not necessarily guarantee a good job.

Many factors, including the macroeconomic and investment climate, determine job availability. While several factors led to the revolution in Egypt in January 2011, a combination of high unemployment and corruption was key among them for educated young urban people. As well as the sheer lack of jobs for an ever increasing youth population, the education system was

failing to prepare them adequately for the world of work. Rote learning dominates teaching in poor communities, which often lack basic resources required for effective learning (Assaad and Barsoum, 2007). In the 2007 Trends in International Mathematics and Science Study, 53% of Egyptian Grade 8 students failed to achieve even the lowest international benchmark in mathematics. Those who can afford it pay for private tuition to compensate, but many cannot. Meanwhile, employers complain that workers lack the skills they need.

Gaps between rich and poor tend to widen as children get older, often because those from disadvantaged backgrounds increasingly need to contribute to household income. In some countries, including Colombia and Viet Nam, almost all children go to primary school. But while most young people from rich households make it to lower secondary school, only around two-thirds from poor households do in Viet Nam, and around half in Colombia. The gap widens even further at upper secondary level. In Ethiopia, however, the gap is wider in primary than in upper secondary, simply because so few, rich or poor, make it to upper secondary (Figure 3.5).

In Colombia, only around half of young people from poor households make it to lower secondary school

---

Figure 3.4: Youth from wealthy households are more likely to have foundation skills

Education status of 15- to 19-year-olds by wealth in Egypt, Indonesia, Nepal and Ethiopia latest available year

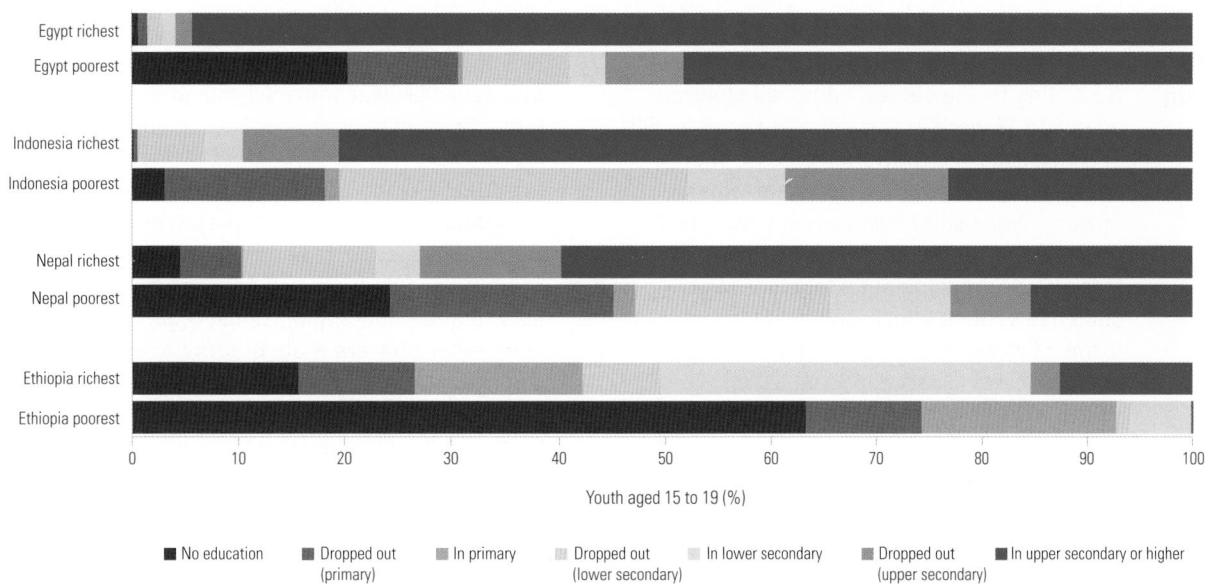

Youth aged 15 to 19 (%)

■ No education ■ Dropped out (primary) ■ In primary ▨ Dropped out (lower secondary) ▨ In lower secondary ▨ Dropped out (upper secondary) ■ In upper secondary or higher

Note: The richest are the top 20% and the poorest the bottom 20% of the wealth distribution.
Source: UIS (2012a).

Figure 3.5: Wealth gaps widen as education levels increase

Net attendance rate by school level and wealth, selected countries, latest available year

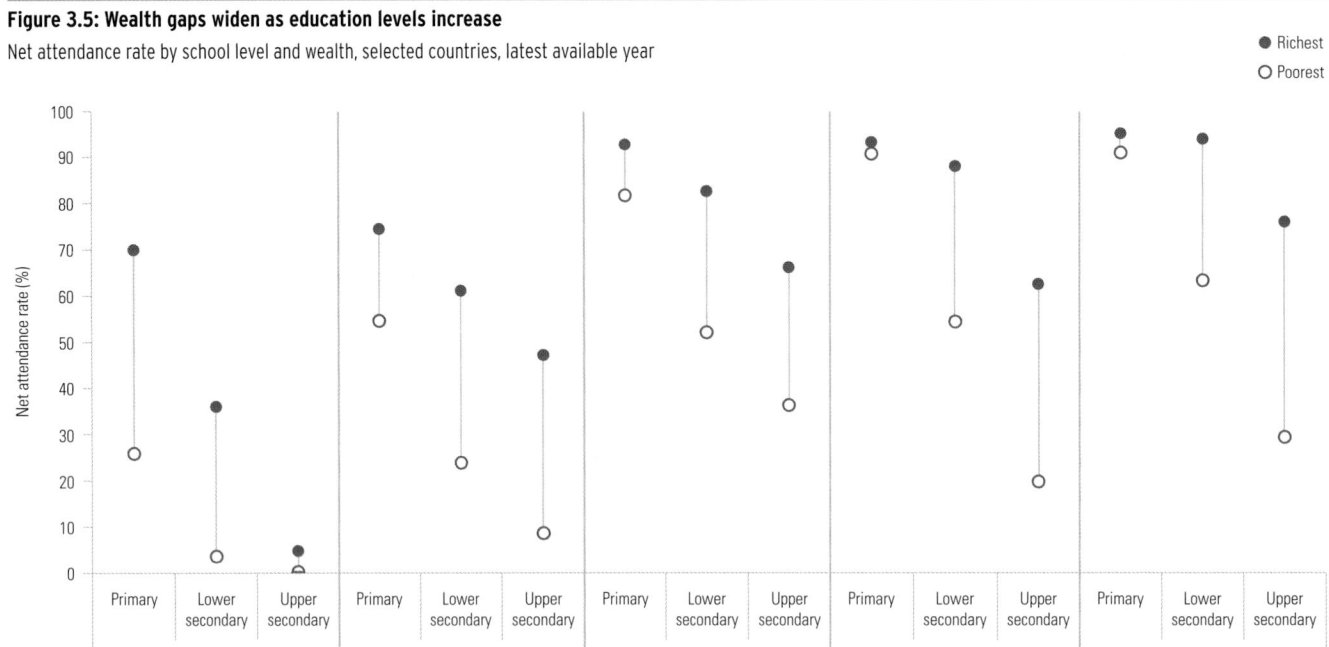

● Richest
○ Poorest

Note: The richest are the top 20% and the poorest the bottom 20% of the wealth distribution.
Source: EFA Global Monitoring Report team calculations (2012) based on Demographic and Health Survey data (Measure DHS, 2012) except for Viet Nam, Multiple Indicator Cluster Survey data (UNICEF, 2011b).

Only 30% of the poorest young women in Turkey attain foundation skills

Many children not in school because of poverty are working instead. In 2008, an estimated 115 million 5- to 17-year-olds were in hazardous work worldwide (ILO, 2010a). Children who work, rather than study, from an early age are likely to be consigned to low paid work throughout their lives. Ethiopia has one of the highest rates of child labour in the world. According to one survey, half of all children aged 5 to 14 were in some form of work in 2001. The incidence of child work increases with age, but even around 40% of 5- to 9-year-olds were in work. While some can combine work with schooling, work can contribute to their performing less well or dropping out altogether. Working as a child has serious knock-on effects for later life in terms of patterns of employment, unemployment and pay levels (Guarcello et al., 2006).

Gender disparities are aggravated by wealth disparities

In most poor countries, girls are less likely than boys to achieve foundation skills. The interaction between gender and wealth depends in part on how far a country has progressed, on average, in providing foundation skills to those aged 15 to 19.

In Burkina Faso, Ethiopia and Mozambique, where only around one in six are in or complete lower secondary school, very few of the poorest, male or female, reach this level. In these low income countries, even among richer households decisions have to be made about who to send to school. The decisions are most often in favour of boys. In Burkina Faso, almost 60% of rich boys attain foundation skills, compared with 40% of rich girls, but only 5% of poor girls or boys (Figure 3.6).

In countries that fare better on average, including India, Morocco, Pakistan and Turkey, the opposite is the case. Large proportions of young people from rich households are able to attain foundation skills, regardless of whether they are male or female. Gender discrimination occurs among the poorest households. In Turkey, almost all young people from rich households, male and female, achieve foundation skills. The proportion of boys from poor households who do so is 64%, compared with only about 30% for the poorest girls.

The gender gap is not always at the expense of girls (see goal 5 policy focus). In a smaller number of middle income countries, such as Brazil and

Figure 3.6: Gender gaps are often larger among the poorest

Percentage of 15- to 19-year-olds in lower secondary school, or having completed at least lower secondary, by wealth and gender, selected countries, latest available year

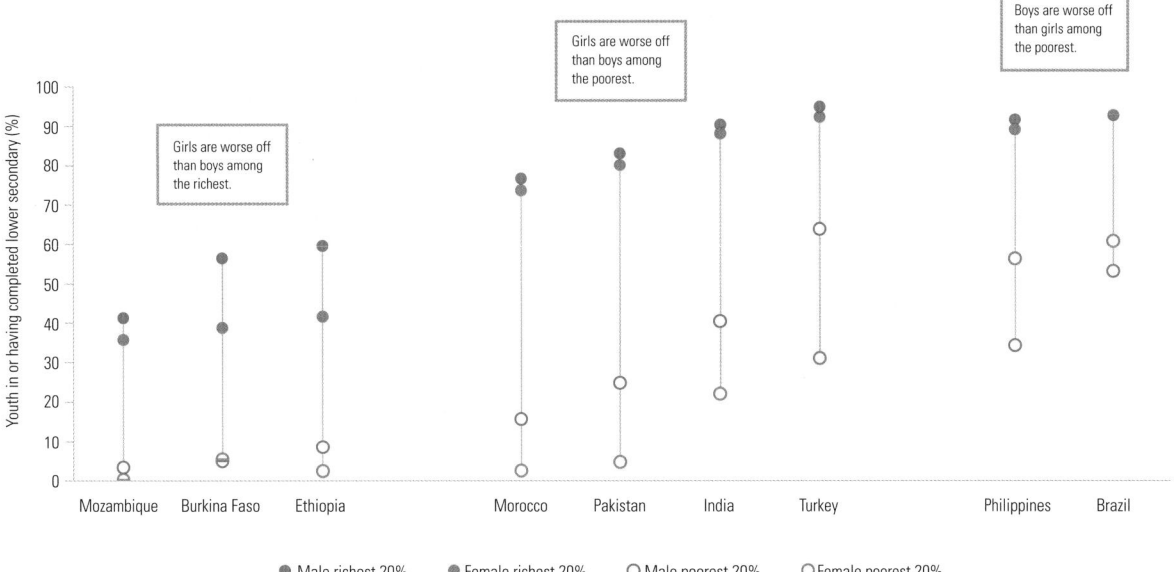

Note: The richest are the top 20% and the poorest the bottom 20% of the wealth distribution.
Source: UIS (2012a).

the Philippines, almost all boys and girls from rich households attain foundation skills. But boys from the poorest households are getting left behind. In the Philippines, around 56% of girls acquire foundation skills, compared with just 35% of boys.

Such variations in gender disadvantage call for different targeted strategies. In countries such as Burkina Faso, Ethiopia and Mozambique, the approach needs to raise the levels for all children. In countries such as India, Morocco, Pakistan and Turkey, strategies need to target young women from the poorest households, while in Brazil and the Philippines, attention has to be paid to poor young men.

Location affects the acquisition of foundation skills

Where young people live can further determine their education opportunities, with rural/urban or regional divisions reinforced by gender. Young women living in rural areas are least likely to acquire foundation skills. In Pakistan, the share of 15- to 19-year-olds who have made it to upper secondary is roughly twice as high in urban areas as in rural areas. Nearly half of rural females

have never been to school, while this is true for only 14% of urban males (Figure 3.7).

The differences in opportunities between rural and urban areas are no doubt partly due to poverty, but they also reflect unequal distribution of government resources, with secondary schools often not available in rural areas (see Chapter 7). Within urban areas, opportunities can also vary widely. In slums in Kenya, for example, many children cannot go to secondary school for the simple reason that schools are not available (Oketch and Mutisya, 2012) (see Chapter 6).

Differences in achieving foundation skills also vary from region to region within countries. Even in a rapidly growing economy like India's, opportunities for acquiring foundation skills can be very unequal, with some states doing much better than others (Figure 3.8). In Kerala, almost all of those aged 15 to 19 acquire foundation skills – boys and girls alike. In Bihar, by contrast, only around 45% do so overall: 57% of boys and 37% of girls. This highlights the need for more redistributive approaches if young people are not to suffer the effects of labour market marginalization because of their gender and where they live.

In slums in Kenya, children rarely go to secondary school because schools are not available

185

CHAPTER 3

Figure 3.7: Youth from urban areas are more likely to acquire foundation skills

Education status of 15- to 19-year-olds by area of residence and gender in Nigeria and Pakistan, latest available year

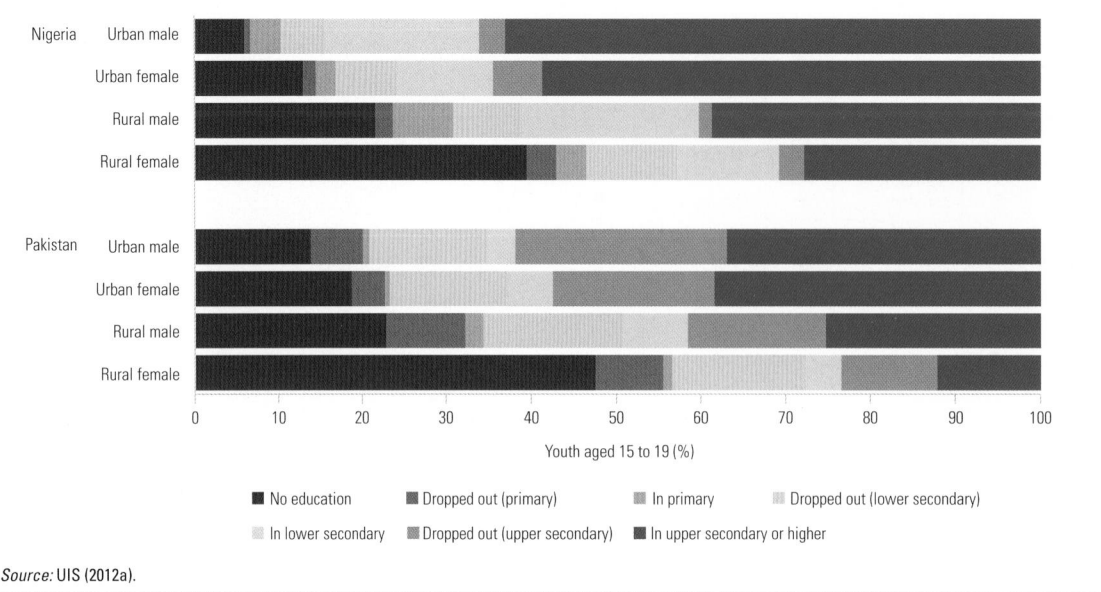

Source: UIS (2012a).

Figure 3.8: Gender gaps in foundation skills are wide in some states in India

Percentage of 15- to 19-year-olds in lower secondary or having completed at least lower secondary in India, selected regions, by gender, 2006

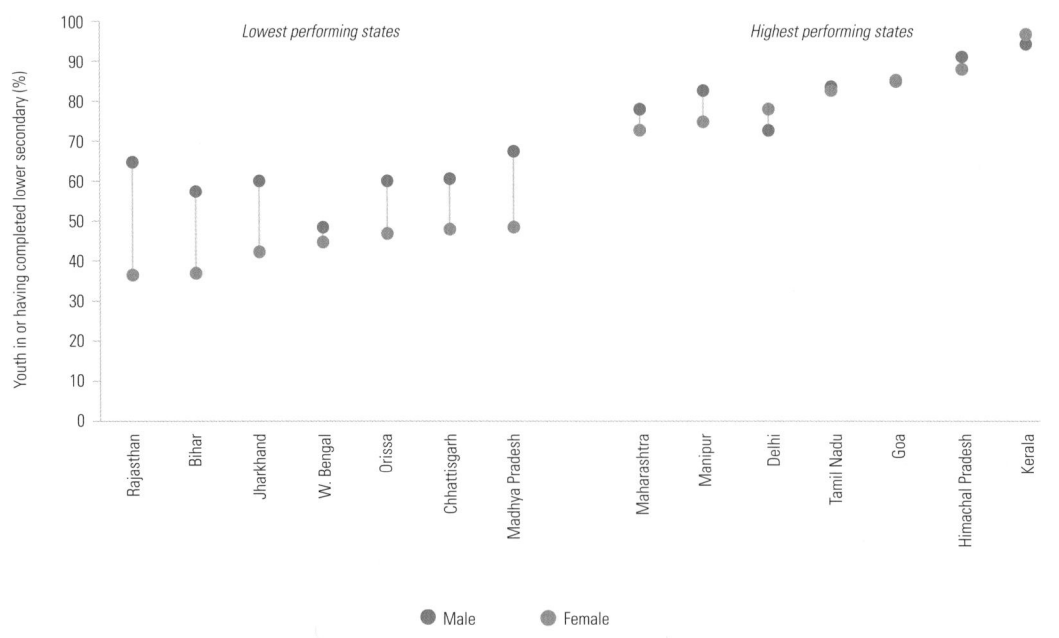

Note: The figure shows the seven top and seven bottom performing states in terms of percentage of 15- to 19-year-olds in lower secondary or having completed at least lower secondary in India.
Source: UIS (2012a).

Transferable skills: preparing for the world of work

Understanding how education influences people's futures is not straightforward. For several decades, economists have measured the effects of skills on work opportunities mainly by looking at the difference in earnings between people with different levels of education. These studies originally analysed the apparently simple relationship between wages, years of schooling and years of experience, controlling for basic demographic characteristics such as gender and age, to estimate the rate of return to education – the percentage increase in wages for each year of school.

The most recent compilation of studies from around the world suggests that not only are returns to education high in general, but the return to post-primary education is higher than for primary schooling (Colclough et al., 2010). Yet there are wide variations in these patterns among countries.

One reason for the mixed evidence is that the number of years of education is an imperfect measure of what young people learn. Simply completing primary and lower secondary education does not necessarily mean obtaining foundation skills. And acquiring basic literacy and numeracy alone is not enough to get good jobs.

Information is needed on how particular skills can lead to various outcomes. For employers, education credentials may only be a signal about a prospective worker's potential or capability rather than indicating something about actual productivity. Employers want assurances that young people applying for jobs have at least strong foundation skills and can deploy their knowledge to solve problems, take the initiative and communicate with team members, rather than just follow prescribed routines.

These 'transferable skills' are not taught from a textbook, but can be acquired through good quality education. Yet employers often indicate that they are lacking in new recruits to the labour market. In Peru, socio-emotional skills were found to be strongly in demand by employers, especially in certain low skill occupations, and particularly in the service sector (World Bank, 2011e). In the Philippines, employers similarly reported strong demand but lack of supply for attributes such as creativity, initiative, leadership and ability to work independently (di Gropello et al., 2010).

Such skills help young people adapt to labour market changes, including new technologies and the demands of a 'green economy'. They can also help many young people working in the informal sector in poor countries to become successful entrepreneurs.

There is limited evidence on how education shapes transferable skills, such as problem-solving, teamwork or motivation, mainly because measuring such skills is difficult, particularly across countries (see Panel 1.6). The limited information available does suggest, however, that schooling can make a difference.

Acquiring basic literacy and numeracy alone is not enough to get good jobs

Schools need to teach IT skills

The world we are living in is getting modernized day by day, but here some of us don't even know how to operate computers.
— young woman, Ethiopia

New technologies are increasingly important for the employment prospects of young people. However, the 2009 Programme for International Student Assessment (PISA) found that significant numbers of 15-year-old students had low digital literacy. For the forty-five countries surveyed, almost one-fifth of participating students performed below the basic level of competence on the digital reading scale (OECD, 2011).[4] Large variations between countries exist. For example, in Colombia nearly 70% of students were identified as lacking digital literacy skills, compared with less than 10% in Australia and Japan.

In all the countries, the gender gap is significantly narrower in digital literacy than in print literacy: girls outperform boys by an

---

4. The measure used in PISA is for those scoring below level 2. At this level, students can scroll and navigate across web pages, as long as explicit directions are provided, and can locate simple pieces of information in a short block of hypertext. Although these students have some digital reading skills, according to PISA, they are performing below levels that would allow them full access to educational, employment and social opportunities in the 21st century.

average of twenty-four score points in digital literacy, but by an average of thirty-nine points in print literacy (OECD, 2011).

Staying in school longer can enhance problem-solving skills

One of the few surveys that has collected comparative data attempting to show problem-solving skills in addition to basic literacy and numeracy skills[5] shows that, even in rich countries, not only have some young people failed to acquire basic literacy and numeracy skills, but a larger proportion have not yet succeeded in gaining problem-solving skills.

At one extreme, around half the youth surveyed in Italy reached the lowest level of competence in problem-solving skills, compared with around one-third having basic literacy and numeracy skills (Figure 3.9). In Canada, around 28% of young people had not reached the desired level in problem-solving skills, compared with around

12% whose level of literacy was not sufficient to be able to interpret information on a medicine bottle, and 19% who lacked basic numeracy skills.

Staying in school longer helps ensure not only that young people improve their literacy and numeracy skills, but also that they acquire problem-solving skills, as evidence from Canada illustrates (Figure 3.10). Around 30% of those leaving school before completing upper secondary have poor numeracy skills, compared with 13% who complete upper secondary. Higher levels of education are even more important for improving the ability to solve problems: around 45% of those leaving before completing upper secondary lack these skills, compared with 20% who complete the cycle.

Good quality education boosts confidence and motivation

We do not have self-confidence. We think that unless we have some relatives in that place … we can never get hired. So we will be discouraged to go there and apply.

– young man, Ethiopia

Transferable skills that are less tangible but crucial for employability and other life outcomes, such as self-esteem, motivation and aspiration, are in part shaped outside the school environment. Yet good quality education can play a role in promoting such skills in ways that could be particularly beneficial to students who lack a supportive home environment. Where socio-cultural environments result in young women lacking self-esteem, for example, good quality education can help enhance their confidence. These skills can improve young people's readiness to learn, as well as enabling them to meet the demands of the labour market.

Pioneering analysis in the United States by the Nobel economics laureate James Heckman shows that self-esteem and self-control measured at age 14 to 21 have strong effects on employment status, occupational choice and wages at age 30. Moving from 25% to 75% on a measure of these non-cognitive skills improved wages at age 30 by about 10% for males and more than 30% for females. The probability of employment by age 30 increased by fifteen percentage points for males and forty percentage points for females (Heckman et al., 2006).

Figure 3.9: In rich countries, young people struggle with problem-solving skills

Percentage of youth (age 16 to 25) at level 1 in literacy, numeracy and problem-solving in seven OECD countries, latest available year

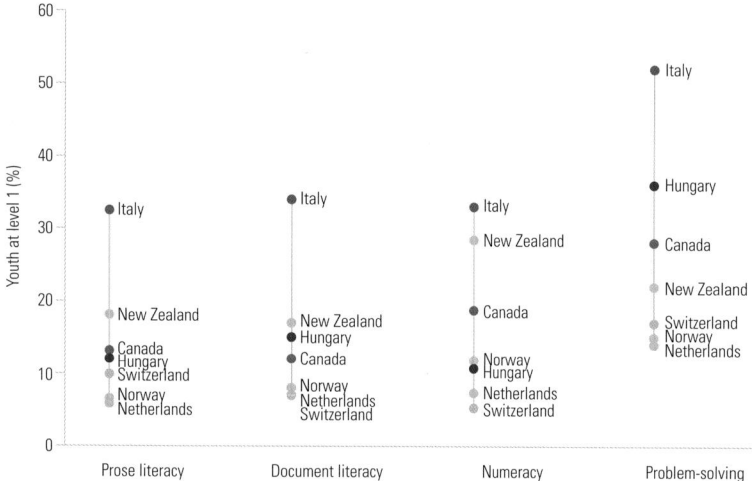

Note: Level 1 is the lowest level of skills.
Source: OECD calculations based on 2003–2008 ALL survey data (OECD and Statistics Canada, 2011).

5. In the Adult Literacy and Life Skills (ALL) survey, 'prose' literacy refers to the reading of 'continuous text' such as newspaper and magazine articles. Literacy is defined as understanding, evaluating, using and engaging with written texts to participate in society, to achieve one's goals and to develop one's knowledge and potential. Problem-solving is measured in the survey by questions aimed at identifying the respondent's ability to clarify the nature of a problem and develop and apply appropriate solution strategies (OECD and Statistics Canada, 2011).

Education for All Global Monitoring Report

2 0 1 2

Figure 3.10: Education can improve problem-solving skills

Percentage of youth (age 16 to 25) by skill level in prose literacy, document literacy, numeracy and problem-solving in Canada, 2003

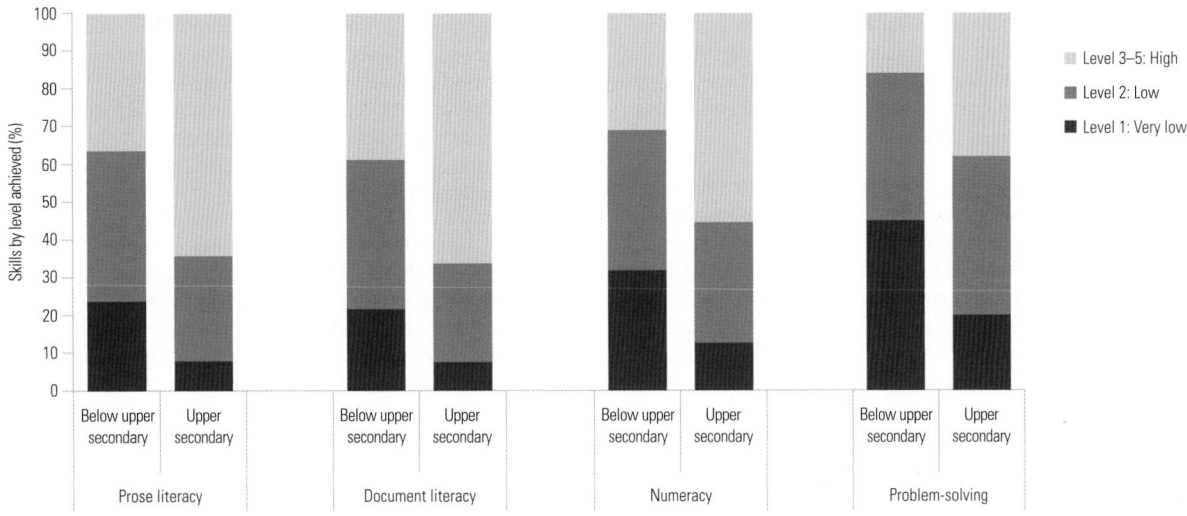

Source: OECD calculations based on 2003 ALL survey data (OECD and Statistics Canada, 2011).

Evidence from a survey on school-aged children in Ethiopia, India, Peru and Viet Nam found that the degree of self-esteem at age 12 was positively associated with higher levels of schooling at age 15 in all four countries. Self-esteem was also found to be associated both with occupational aspirations and educational attainment (Rolleston and James, 2012).

In Peru, a recent national skills survey measured cognitive and socio-emotional skills in the working-age urban population. In addition to basic cognitive skills, the survey captured self-reported personality traits important for labour market outcomes. Results indicated that members of lower socio-economic groups had significantly lower basic cognitive and socio-emotional skills than their counterparts from more affluent backgrounds. This in turn has implications for social mobility. For example, socio-emotional skills were found to be significantly correlated with earnings (World Bank, 2011e).

These surveys show that transferable skills matter, but less evidence exists on how they can be cultivated through targeted interventions. Non-cognitive skills are conventionally viewed as more difficult to impart than cognitive skills. Yet studies show that they can have particular benefits for disadvantaged young people.

In Portugal, the innovative Entrepreneurs for Social Inclusion (Empresários Pela Inclusão Social) programme has been adopted on a large scale to raise at-risk students' achievement by strengthening their non-cognitive skills, including motivation, discipline, self-esteem and confidence, which enables them to better focus on their studies. By 2010, 15,000 students, half of them female, had been reached in 85 schools. The programme resulted in improved academic achievement and hence reduced repetition rates, which fell by at least ten percentage points. This programme shows that non-cognitive skills that may not be fully developed through the home environment for certain at-risk youth may have a major effect on how well those youth can apply themselves to their studies and develop their cognitive capabilities (Martins, 2010).

New evidence from a pioneering NGO programme in slums in India highlights the ways that education can actively foster attitudes, aspirations and self-esteem to help disadvantaged young people improve their chances in work, even in one of the most challenging environments (Box 3.3).

Schools can foster aspirations and self-esteem

Box 3.3: Building self-esteem through education: evidence from Mumbai

A long-term programme for children and adolescents in slums in Mumbai shows that targeted interventions can substantially improve non-cognitive skills among children and young people from deprived families.

Akanksha (which means aspiration in Hindi) is an Indian NGO focusing on imparting non-cognitive skills such as self-esteem and positive aspirations through the use of workshops, mentoring, drama, art, sport and story-telling. It admits primary school pupils from deprived neighbourhoods to an after-school programme in which children are tutored for about three hours every day.

Using carefully selected comparison groups to control for differences in home and school

environments, a study of the programme found that those involved in the Akanksha initiative in childhood and adolescence had substantially higher non-cognitive skills as young adults. An increase in these skills was found to be accompanied by higher earnings and better school performance, even after controlling for cognitive ability.

While the initiative is relatively small in scale, the implications of these findings are important. They suggest that where education extends beyond teaching the basics, it can provide young people from disadvantaged backgrounds with the broader range of skills needed to improve their life chances.

Source: Krishnan and Krutikova (2012).

A hazardous transition from school to work

[A good job] is one that helps me to live honourably, not the one that would be spent on transportation and lunch at work and that is all.
— young woman, Egypt

Many young people face a difficult transition from school to work. The disadvantage that youth often experience in the labour market is reflected in both a lack of jobs and the low quality of jobs – including insecure, low paid work. Factors linked to disadvantage in education, such as poverty, gender and disability, are often also associated with disadvantage in the labour market. This is not a coincidence – unequal skills development, social norms and labour market discrimination combine to lead to this outcome.

For some, particularly in rich countries, these hazards are associated with long spells of unemployment. Leaving young people unemployed or underemployed for long periods not only wastes a precious resource in the short term but also risks damaging their long-term careers.

In countries with high rates of poverty and little state support for the unemployed, young people from disadvantaged backgrounds – those who tend also to have lower levels of skills – have no option but to take whatever work they can find,

often under undesirable conditions. A policy focus on creating more jobs is likely to overlook the fact that the problem for most disadvantaged young people in these countries is not a lack of jobs, but that they are trapped in low paid work.

A lack of skills is not the only reason many young people cannot get work that pays a decent wage. Stagnant economies, corrupt politics and nepotism can also play a role, as was starkly evident in pre-revolution Egypt. In a 2009 survey, 90% of youth complained about nepotism in job markets and 84% felt that corruption was growing in Egypt. Youth felt that their future depended to a large extent on their connections with the government (Wardany, 2012).

Despite increasing policy attention to young people's working conditions, there is insufficient data to measure the extent of skills-work mismatches across countries. In addition, the same indicators may not capture in full the nature of young people's labour market challenges in different contexts. While youth unemployment may be a good indicator in rich countries, precarious jobs or very low paid employment may be more relevant in middle and low income countries – but are also more difficult to measure in a systematic way. Some attempts have been made to address these problems in recent years in the context of the Millennium Development Goals, but challenges remain (Box 3.4).

In Egypt, youth surveyed in 2009 felt their future depended on connections with the government

Many young people face difficulties obtaining work

You look for a job and they ask that you have a high school diploma but you don't.

– young woman, Mexico

Unemployment figures give a first impression of how many people who are actively looking for jobs are not getting the work opportunities they would like, especially in richer countries. Some 13% of the world's youth were counted as unemployed in 2011 – equivalent to 75 million young people, almost 4 million more than before the economic crisis took hold in 2007 (ILO, 2012a).

Most young people want to work but many face problems obtaining their first job. For some, the difficulty is finding work that best suits their

---

Box 3.4: Decent and productive work for all: employment in the MDGs

The importance of work to the international development agenda is enshrined in the first Millennium Development Goal, which aims to eradicate extreme poverty and hunger, and includes as one of its three targets full and productive employment and decent work for all.

The International Labour Organization (ILO) has developed a definition of 'decent work' that attempts to move beyond a focus on simply getting people into jobs regardless of how good they are. It defines decent work as 'work that gives people the opportunity to earn enough for themselves and their families to escape poverty, not just temporarily but permanently. ... A decent job provides social security and ensures protection by labour laws, and a voice at work through freely chosen workers' organizations' (Schmidt, 2007, p. 4).

Measuring progress towards this target is fraught with technical difficulties. Unemployment rates – the proportion of the workforce made up of those who do not have a job but are available and actively looking for one – are not up to the task, despite being the staple of media headlines. People who are not searching for a job simply because they have no prospect of finding one are left out of unemployment statistics in most countries, and coverage of rural and informal sectors is inconsistent. Moreover, the most disadvantaged young people in developing countries are often not the unemployed but those with jobs that are variously low paid, part time, insecure and with difficult working conditions.

The ILO has therefore developed four inter-connected indicators to measure progress towards the MDG target of decent and productive work:

■ The employment to population ratio compares the number in work with the total population. Unlike the unemployment rate, it does not try to distinguish those actively searching for work from those who are not. But the indicator has shortcomings. It is particularly low in South Asia and the Arab States as a result of low female participation in the labour force. A drop in this ratio can be positive if it results from young people staying longer in education, as has happened in East Asia. But a drop without a commensurate rise in school enrolment suggests that the job market is shrinking.

■ Working poverty is the proportion of employed people who live below the poverty line. People's work is not classed as decent if it does not provide an income high enough to lift them and their families out of poverty.

■ Vulnerable work is defined statistically as the proportion of workers who are self-employed with no employees, or who work for their families. Though not all are necessarily vulnerable, they are less likely to have formal work arrangements, and therefore more likely to lack decent working conditions, adequate social security and 'voice' through representation by trade unions and similar organizations. Changes in the share of vulnerable work are correlated with changes in working poverty.

■ Labour productivity growth – growth in gross domestic product (GDP) per person employed, a measure of the capacity of a country's economic environment to create and sustain economic opportunities.

Each of these indicators has imperfections and ambiguities. Given these challenges, this Report primarily uses measures that distinguish job quantity – whether young people can find work and how long it takes to get on the job ladder; and job quality – whether they are in work that pays above the poverty line.

Sources: ILO (2009a, 2010b, 2011b); Schmidt (2007); United Nations (2011b).

The first Millennium Development Goal includes a target of full and productive employment and decent work for all

aspirations, particularly for those with higher levels of education whose expectations have been raised. Others are in a more desperate situation.

Young people are more likely to be out of work than adults

While it might be expected that younger people are more likely to be out of work than older people as they wait to get their first step on the ladder, in many countries the barriers to a good job are almost insurmountable for the majority of young people.

Worldwide, unemployment rates are about two to three times higher for young people than for adults, with vast disparities in some regions and countries. In the Middle East, youth unemployment stands at around 25%, compared with 6% for adults. Youth unemployment is six times as high as unemployment of older people in Egypt, two and a half times in South Africa, four times in Italy (Figure 3.11). In some countries, this gap translates into sizeable numbers of young people unemployed – almost one in two young people in South Africa. Moreover, these are only official unemployment rates, hiding potentially much larger numbers of young people who have part-time work, work for very low pay or have opted to stay out of the labour market altogether.

Many young people face a long wait for work

Youth unemployment rates are high partly because the time taken to find work has become even longer as a result of the economic downturn. Long-term unemployment can be particularly damaging for young people, leaving them with little hope of earning a decent wage throughout their lives.

In European countries, those with low educational attainment are the most likely to face barriers preventing them from getting their first step on the employment ladder. In the mid-2000s, over 40% of 15- to 29-year-olds in Greece and Italy were unemployed even five years after leaving education. Better-educated youth had a quicker transition to employment: there were large gaps in employment rates between those who did not complete upper secondary and those who did, with gaps persisting ten years after

leaving school (OECD, 2008). The dire economic circumstances in these countries are likely to accentuate the difference between those with differing levels of education.

Young people are also waiting a long time to obtain work in other parts of the world. In an ILO study in eight countries,[6] over 40% of the unemployed youth in each country had been unemployed for more than one year. In the Syrian Arab Republic, more than 70% fell into this category. In Egypt, 25% had been unemployed for more than two years. Most said they were willing to take a job regardless of whether it matched their education (Matsumoto and Elder, 2010). A review of thirteen African countries found that in eight of them, young people face a wait between school and work of more than five years; in Mozambique it was closer to seven years (Garcia and Fares, 2008).

Some young people do not wait for work, but take jobs deemed below their level of qualification. The news media have focused recently on the apparent 'over education' of young people who have made it to higher levels of education. In countries such as Australia, Belgium, Canada and the United States, around one in five young people are identified as being overqualified for their work. For some, the mismatch is temporary while they wait for a better job, but others can remain in jobs not suited to their qualifications for several years (Quintini, 2011). In many regions of the world, however, the reality is that the vast majority of young people do not make it to the end of secondary school, and face far more severe problems in finding work that pays enough for them to feed themselves and their families.

Young people with less education are most vulnerable to unemployment

In some rich countries, the term 'not in employment, education or training' (NEET) is used to describe a group of young people that governments are particularly concerned about helping to get back into education or into work. Youth in this category, who may or may not be actively seeking work, have increased risk of

---

6. Azerbaijan, China, Egypt, the Islamic Republic of Iran, Kosovo, Mongolia, Nepal and the Syrian Arab Republic.

Unemployment rates are two to three times higher for young people than for adults

Figure 3.11: Youth unemployment is more than double adult unemployment in many countries

Youth (age 15 to 24) and adult (age 25+) unemployment rates, by region and selected countries, latest available year (2006-2010)

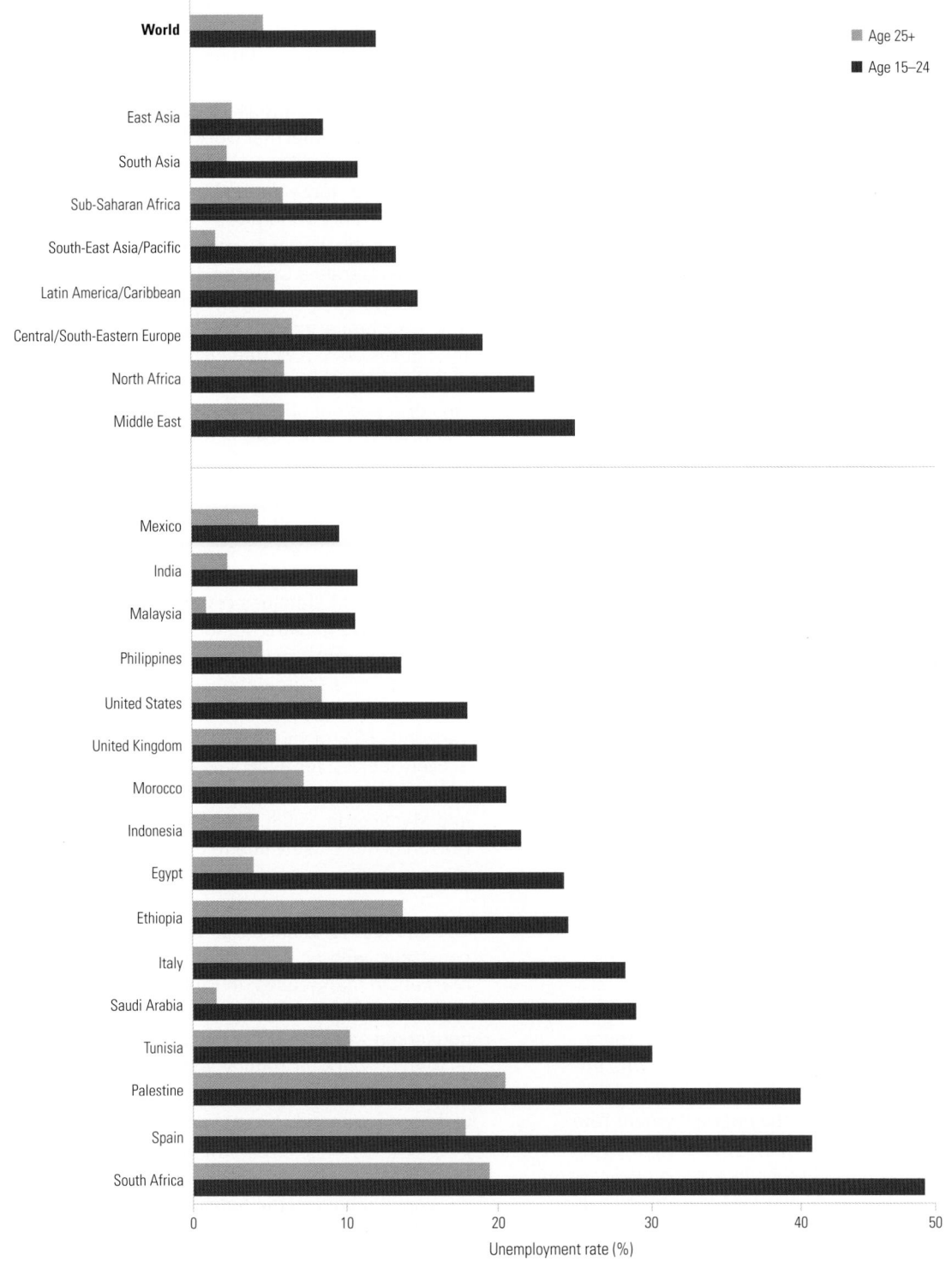

Source: ILO (2012a).

unemployment or lower wages later in life, and are likely to end up with health and psychological problems if they continue to be unemployed for a long time. The scale of the problem in OECD countries is large, especially for those with lower levels of education.

There were an estimated 29 million fewer people in the labour force globally in 2011 than before the economic crisis hit, with young people most affected (ILO, 2012a). Among youth in Europe, those with lower levels of education have been hardest hit. While the effects have been slight in Germany, unemployment rates in Spain rose significantly between 2007 and 2009, particularly for those who had not completed secondary education (Figure 3.12).

Many young women are invisible in the labour force

Usually the work environment [as a daily labourer] is not comfortable for females. Usually it is men who can work at this because a lot of labour is demanded. As a result of this, females usually do not get the type of job they want. And to get hired in an office they always require paper [qualifications] and more skills. Otherwise no one will hire you and it will be very difficult. And youth like us, who have dropped out of school, can never get any papers. So we don't even try.

– young woman, Ethiopia

Unemployment figures hide the fact that some young people stop looking for work because they do not believe they will find any. People who are neither in education or employment nor actively seeking work are often classified as 'inactive', even though their inactivity reflects the labour market more than their own motivation. If those who are discouraged from participating in the labour force are included, the unemployment rate increases substantially – doubling in Cameroon, for example, and rising by around one-quarter in Jordan, Mexico and Turkey (Understanding Children's Work, 2012).

Women are often a majority of those classified as 'inactive'. Yet the way they see their life chances depends on realistic opportunities in the workplace. In China's urban areas, young women and men have very similar aspirations overall, but in Egypt and Nepal where women's work opportunities are limited, young women stress the importance of family life while young men focus more on jobs and money (Pastore, 2012).

Young women often work long hours in household and informal work that is less visible to policy-makers. Analysis for this Report of recent labour force surveys in nine countries found that more young women than men were classed as inactive in all nine, often significantly so (Understanding Children's Work, 2012). In Jordan, 37% of females were identified as inactive, compared with 10% of males. In Turkey, the figures were 52% and 16%. The gender gap was often very large among young people who dropped out of the education system after completing only primary school. In Jordan, over 80% of young women with only primary education were not actively seeking employment, compared with 20% of young men (Figure 3.13).

By excluding youth not actively seeking work, unemployment statistics reveal nothing about why young women are not in paid work. Is it because of family responsibilities, cultural pressures or discrimination in the job market? In Dar es Salaam, the United Republic of Tanzania, 68% of young women who were not actively looking for a job said it was because they did not think they would find one (Kondylis and Manacorda, 2008). This suggests that the reason is more likely due to discrimination than other factors.

The unequally divided burden of domestic work constrains women's participation in labour markets in many cases. In Ethiopia, women spent six times as much time as men on household work, and roughly half as much time as men on work for money. 43% of women were unpaid family workers, and female employees were predominantly temporary. Women, particularly younger women, earned less than men. Women were disadvantaged both by the division of labour in the household and within the labour market (Kolev and Robles, 2010; Robles, 2010).

Women who are looking for work are more likely than young men to face a long wait. In Jordan,

2012
Education for All Global Monitoring Report

There were 29 million fewer jobs in 2011 than before the economic downturn

Figure 3.12: Young people with low levels of education have been hit harder by the economic crisis in Europe

Unemployment rates among 16- to 35-year-olds by level of education, selected countries, 2007 and 2009

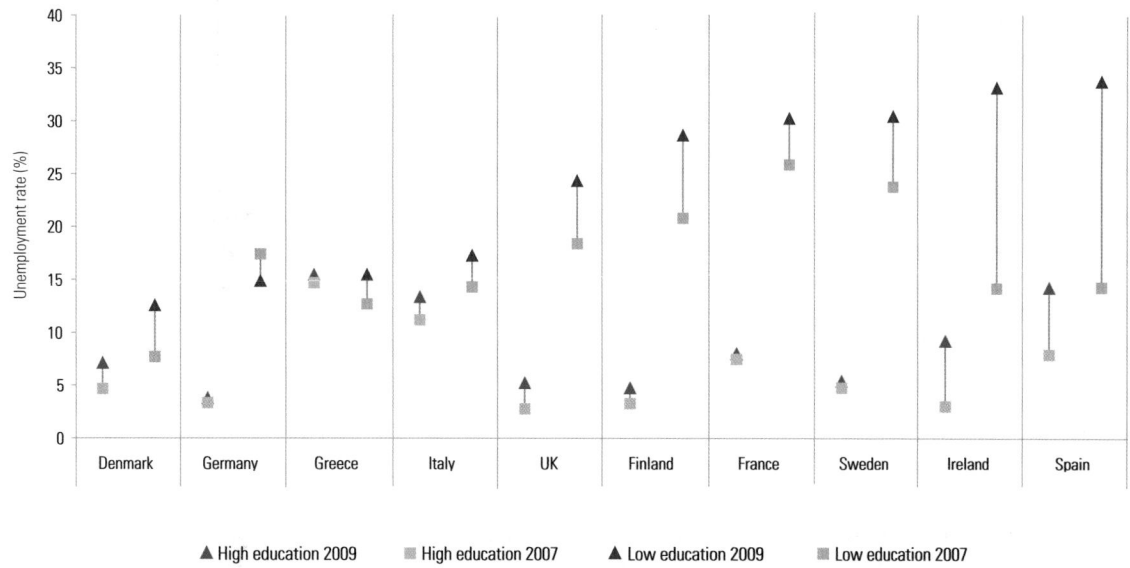

Note: 'Low education' refers to completed lower secondary education or less. 'High education' refers to completed tertiary education.
Source: Livanos and Núñez (2012).

Figure 3.13: In Jordan and Turkey, many young women are not seeking work

Percentage of 15- to 24-year-olds classified as 'inactive' by gender and education level in Jordan and Turkey, latest available year

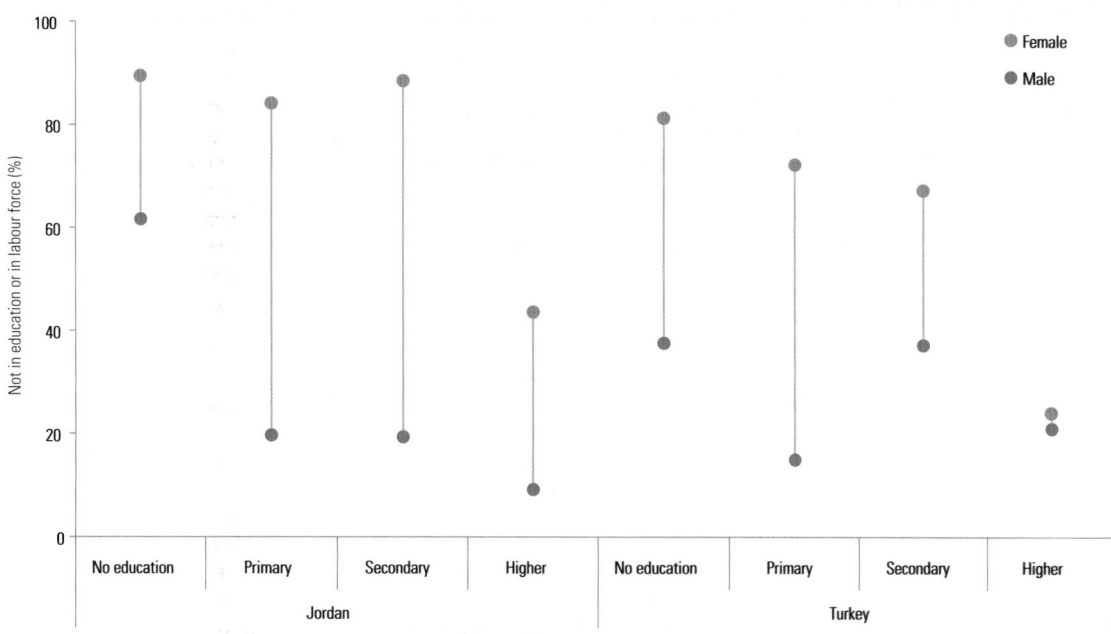

Source: Understanding Children's Work (2012).

Discriminatory practices make it more difficult for women to find work

two-thirds of young women are available for work. Of these, as many as one in three are unemployed. By contrast, of the 90% of young men available for work, 16% were unemployed in 2007 (Understanding Children's Work, 2012). The increase in female education in Jordan in recent years, to the extent that their enrolment is higher than for males particularly in urban areas, does not therefore appear to be translating into improvements in their opportunities for work (Amer, 2012). In Egypt, less than one-quarter of 15- to 29-year old women are economically active, one-third of the male rate. Those women who do make it into the labour force face a longer wait, with three-quarters still looking for work after five years in 2006 (Assaad and Barsoum, 2007).

These findings suggest that not only do cultural factors keep young women out of the labour market, but discriminatory practices also make it more difficult for them to find work. Those who do work can expect to receive lower pay, although more education can make a difference, as experience in India and Pakistan illustrates (Box 3.5).

Young people with disabilities face discrimination in education and work

Young people with disabilities have particular difficulty gaining access to both education and work. In Malawi and Swaziland, less than half of those aged 15 to 29 with disabilities had ever been to school, and employment rates among 15- to 29-year-olds were under 3% in Swaziland and 28% in Malawi (Eide, 2012).

Kenya's 2008 National Survey on Persons with Disabilities found that 3.6% of youth aged 15 to 24 had disabilities, with visual and physical impairments being the most reported (1.1% each). Over 90% of those youth found their disability to be a 'big problem' in their lives, and in the week preceding the survey, only 8% had worked for pay, and 14% had worked on the family business. Over 50% had not worked (Kenya NCADP, 2008; Kett, 2012). Very few young people in Kenya living with disabilities study beyond primary level. Constraints they face regarding employment include a lack of suitable jobs, little or no adaptation of workplaces, limited expectations among families and employers, and a lack of networks (Mugo et al., 2010). Not only are they

Box 3.5: In India and Pakistan, working women with more education reap benefits

In India and Pakistan, as in many developing countries, regular wage employment is a small and even shrinking part of the labour market. In both countries, women are more likely than men to be out of the labour force.

In India, 39% of women are not counted as being in the labour force, compared with 12% of men. For uneducated urban women the share is as much as 70%. Many women, often those with lower levels of education, are obliged to work in undesirable jobs. Uneducated rural Indian women have around a 55% chance of being unpaid family workers, and almost a 25% chance of being in casual work of some kind.

In Pakistan, while men have an 8% chance of being out of the labour force, the figure for women is 69%, and it drops only for the few women with more than ten years of schooling. Such women are rare in Pakistan: only 18% reached that stage in 2007.

For those who do find work in India and Pakistan, men earn 60% more than women, on average. The wage gap is widest for those with low levels of literacy and numeracy. Yet education can make a big difference to women's earnings. In Pakistan, women with a high level of literacy earned 95% more than women with no literacy skills, whereas the differential was only 33% among men.

From these patterns in India and Pakistan it appears that the cultural expectation is for women, including more educated women, to stay in the home to care for the family. Years of education, therefore, have a very limited effect on labour market participation for women in general. Yet education can have a strong effect on their earnings, suggesting that investing in women's education can pay dividends, provided they can participate in the labour force and find work.

Source: Aslam et al. (2010).

unable to find work, but only 1.8% of all people living with disabilities in urban areas were receiving any form of social benefit, disability grant or other financial support (Kenya NCADP, 2008).

Leaving school early consigns youth to poorly paid work

An upholsterer like me will make 30 [Egyptian] pounds per day. 15 of them will be spent on transport and 15 on food and then I return home with nothing in my pockets.

– young man, Ethiopia

Many young people do not have the luxury of remaining unemployed and are obliged to take poor quality jobs that are insecure, low paid and often require long hours. For some, this may be a stepping stone to more stable and fulfilling employment. But for many, such work is a trap that is difficult to escape.

Globally, an estimated 152 million young people, 28% of all young workers, are paid less than US$1.25 per day, an amount that is unlikely to lift them and their families out of poverty (Understanding Children's Work, 2012). In countries such as Burkina Faso, Cambodia, Ethiopia and Uganda, working below the poverty line is a much more widespread phenomenon than not working at all (ILO, 2011b).

In low income countries, less educated young people, who cannot afford the wait for the right kind of job, are at greatest risk of being in low paid work. In some middle income countries such as Brazil, by contrast, unemployment plays a larger role (Box 3.6).

Young people are more likely than adults to be earning very low wages. In Ouagadougou, Burkina Faso, about 90% of 15- to 19-year-olds and 80% of 20- to 24-year-olds earn less than the official minimum wage, and older adults earn almost two and a half times as much as young adults, on average (Nordman and Pasquier-Doumer, 2012). While young people can usually expect their pay to increase as they get older, earning less than the minimum wage leaves them with insufficient money to meet their daily needs.

There is a strong relationship between low education and working poverty in many countries (Figure 3.14). While this in part may be because education levels tend to be low where there are other barriers to finding work that pays well, it is also likely that low levels of education are often the main reason young people are in poorly paid jobs. In Cambodia, for instance, 91% of young people with no education work below the poverty line, compared with less than 67% of those with secondary education and 15% of those with tertiary education. In Zambia, around three-quarters of young people with primary education or less are working below the poverty line; youth with secondary education fare somewhat better, while for the minority who reach higher levels of education, poverty rates are very low.

The effects of completing secondary education on ensuring that young people have the skills needed to find adequately paid work vary by location and gender. For both rural and urban women in Nepal who have completed secondary education, less than 30% earn above the poverty line (Figure 3.16). By contrast, young men who

Over one-quarter of all young workers are paid less than US$1.25 per day

---

Figure 3.14: Low levels of education lead to working poverty

Percentage of employed young people (age 15 to 24) earning less than US$1.25 per day, by educational attainment, selected countries, latest available year

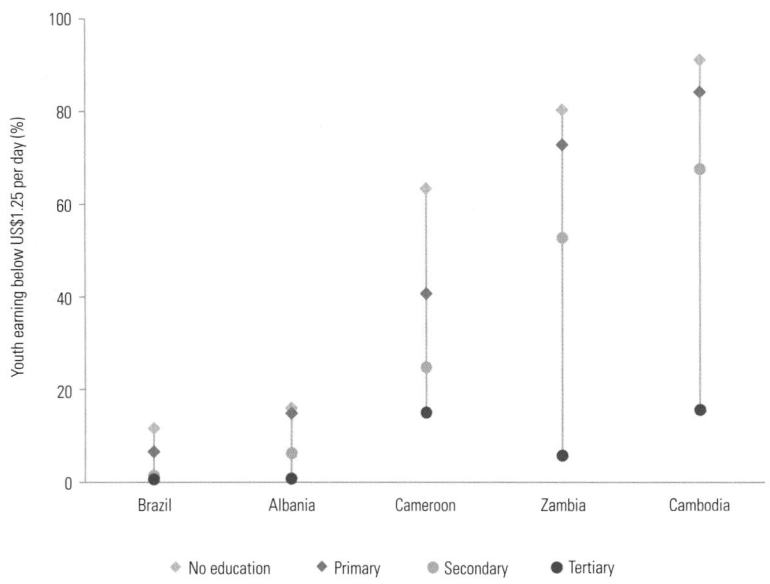

Source: Understanding Children's Work (2012).

In Cameroon, two thirds of rural youth with no education work for less than US$1.25 a day

Box 3.6: High unemployment in Brazil, low paid work in Cameroon

Comparing a middle income country such as Brazil with a low income one such as Cameroon illuminates how youth disadvantage in the world of work can take different forms.

In Brazil, youth unemployment is a big problem. Of the 63% of youth who participate in the labour market, nearly one in five is unemployed. Youth unemployment is around three times that of adult unemployment. Female and urban youth are particularly affected, as are those with less education (Figure 3.15).

In Cameroon the story is quite different. Most young people are working, including many who are still in education. In rural areas the unemployment rate is only around 1%, although it rises to 9% for urban males and 14% for urban females. It is particularly high among youth with higher levels of education. Those who are unemployed are generally among the better off in Cameroon. While they face real difficulty in finding work, they can afford to wait for what they consider acceptable work. For survival reasons, the poor can rarely choose to wait.

The bigger issue in Cameroon is working poverty, as it is for many youth in low income settings. Agriculture provides jobs for large numbers of young people with lower levels of education, but many are poorly paid. Two-thirds of rural youth with no education work for less than US$1.25 per day, with rural, uneducated young women worst off. Even though education makes a difference, around 40% of those with secondary education in rural areas are in working poverty. Urban residents do better, whether they have education or not – one in five of those with no education are in working poverty, compared with one in ten of those with secondary schooling.

In Brazil, by contrast, working poverty is much less of a problem. Very few youth with at least secondary education work for less than US$1.25 per day. But here, too, there are around one-third of rural youth with no more than primary education, mostly working on farms, whose earnings are not enough to take them out of poverty.

Source: Understanding Children's Work (2012).

Figure 3.15: Unemployment versus working poverty in Brazil and Cameroon

Youth (age 15 to 24) unemployment rate and youth earning less than US$1.25 per day, Brazil and Cameroon

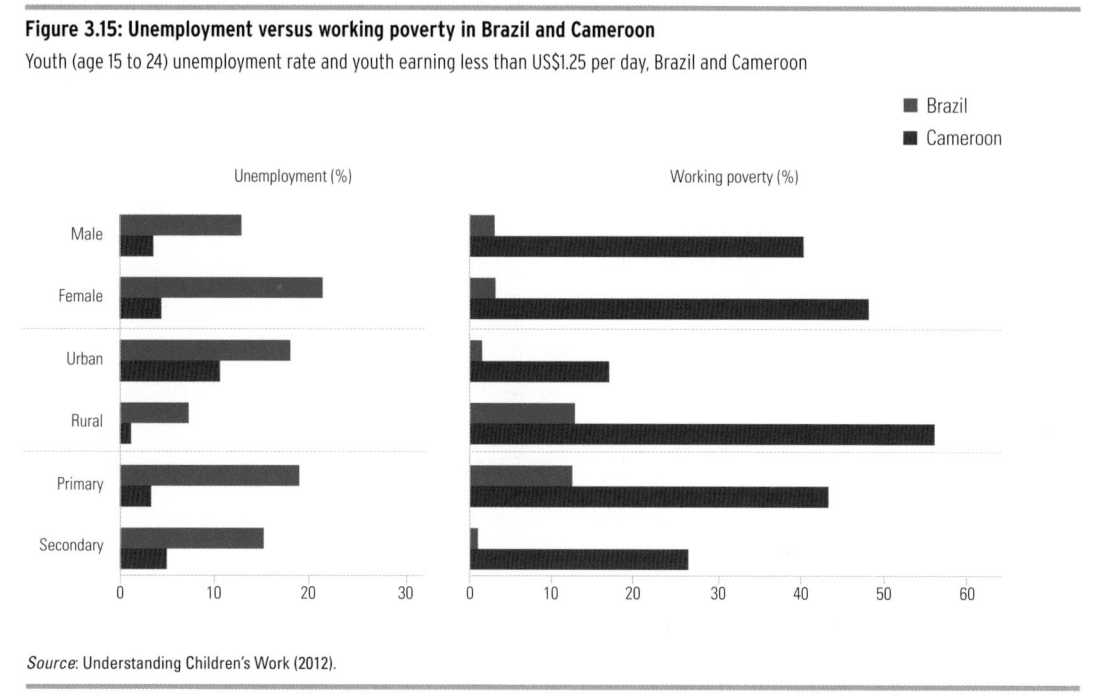

Source: Understanding Children's Work (2012).

Figure 3.16: Young women are often confined to low paid work

Percentage of youth (age 15 to 29) working above poverty line (>US$2/day), by gender, educational attainment and area in Mongolia, Azerbaijan, Nepal, the Islamic Republic of Iran and Egypt, latest available year

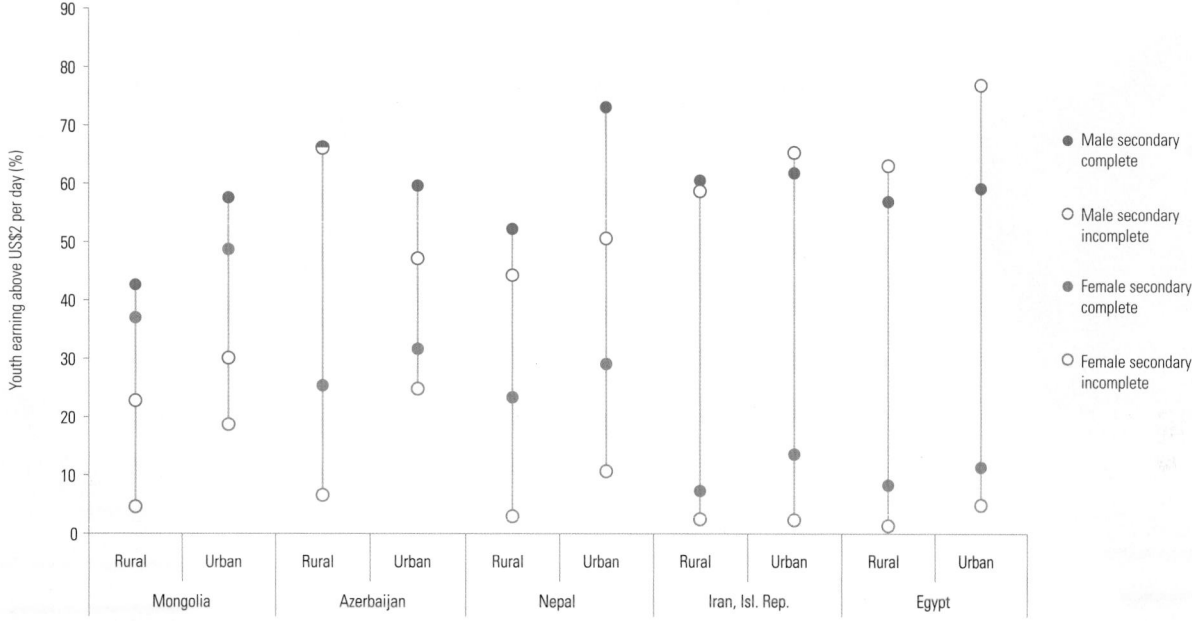

Source: EFA Global Monitoring Report team calculations (2012) based on School to Work Transition Survey data (ILO, 2011c).

have not even completed secondary education are more likely to earn an adequate wage than better educated young women – over 40% earn above the poverty line.

A similarly wide gender gap is evident in Azerbaijan, Egypt, the Islamic Republic of Iran and Mongolia. The reasons are likely to differ by country, and may in part have to do with the fact that young women who do domestic work at home are not paid. But given that young women, like young men, from disadvantaged backgrounds often need resources for their own and their families' survival, and that such gender gaps are likely to persist as they get older, the reasons behind these differences deserve greater attention from policy-makers.

Conclusion

Pressure is mounting on governments to ensure that young people have skills that allow them to find good jobs. Young people could face even more difficult times as demand grows for skills

to keep up with structural changes brought about by urbanization, technological advances and moves towards a green economy.

Unfortunately, large numbers of young people are leaving school without even the foundations necessary to avoid some of the worst forms of disadvantage in the labour market. These young people are unlikely to possess the skills needed to adapt flexibly in the changing workplace. In richer countries, those with low education, who face unemployment early in their lives, will have a higher risk of being out of work for long periods, with negative effects on their future earnings.

The problems for many young people in poor countries are even more acute. Those lacking foundation skills face the prospect of extremely low pay – barely enough for their own survival, let alone to support their families. Addressing the deficit in foundation skills is now more urgent than ever.

Addressing the deficit in foundation skills is now more urgent than ever

Chapter 4
Investing in skills
for prosperity

A computer training course at
Green Hill Academy in Kampala, Uganda,
financed by Denmark's aid agency.

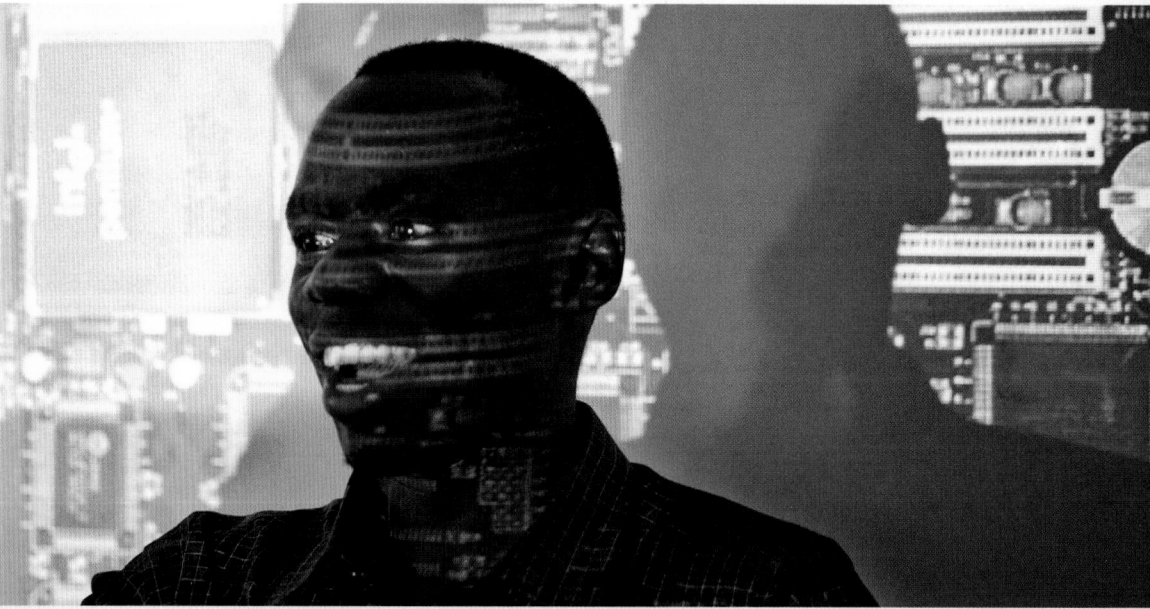

Skills development is a wise investment because it is vital in order to reduce unemployment, inequality and poverty, and to promote economic growth. This chapter lays out the economic argument for investing in education and skills. It provides guidance on the importance of investing in equitable skills strategies and identifies areas where additional funds could be found to bring skills to disadvantaged youth.

Introduction

*When the youth is affected, so is the country.
When the life of the youth is improved, so is
the country's status. They go hand in hand.
If one person opens a business, that person
gives a job opportunity to a lot of people. So,
if there are 10 business owners and they hire
100 people each, that would have a big positive
effect on unemployment.*

– young man, Ethiopia

The key role of skills in fostering prosperity is
evident worldwide: countries that have invested
wisely in skills training have made considerable
progress in equitable development. Such
investment could also help to protect countries
from the impact of economic downturns and lift
large numbers of people out of poverty.

While countries require a skilled workforce to
thrive, skills do not automatically lead to jobs
and growth. Skills development needs to be
part of a comprehensive, integrated strategy for
growth that improves the lives of all. But there
should be no question of whether creating jobs
or developing skills comes first; both need to be
pursued in a coherent, integrated manner.

Many countries are still drawing up national
development plans that pay insufficient
attention to the vital role of skills. Planning and
provision of skills are often fragmentary, poorly
coordinated and inadequately aligned with labour
market demands and national development
priorities. These failures contribute to a serious
neglect of the need to improve the skills of
disadvantaged youth, which is reflected in a
general lack of attention to developing skills
in the informal sector and a failure to include
marginalized youth in the planning process.

Governments are the most important funders of
skills development programmes. Their support
can be most effective when complemented by
funding from the private sector and aid donors.
It is vital for governments and donors to ensure
that all young people achieve foundation skills
first and foremost, ideally by focusing on good
quality education until lower secondary level and
providing a second chance for those who have
already missed out. The private sector can play
a further role in supporting work-based learning
beyond the classroom.

Skills development is vital to reduce poverty and promote growth

*Although I haven't completed my education
I need a chance. We want to work and give
something good to the country.*

– young woman, Egypt

To a large degree, young people's ability to
find good jobs depends on the growth of the
economy and the distribution of wealth. But
without the right skills, young people are much
less likely to obtain work that pays them enough
to live and support their families. The rate of
economic growth, and the way the benefits of
growth are shared, is intimately connected with
skills development.

Rather than economic growth, the current reality
for many countries is economic slowdown. In this
context, youth unemployment has increasingly
become a global and national policy priority, a fact
that has sometimes focused attention on the need
to develop young people's skills (Box 4.1).

The crucial next step is to put effective skills
development policies in motion that give a
central place to the needs of the disadvantaged.
The interaction between education, skills and
growth is not straightforward, not least because
it can operate in both directions: a better skilled
workforce can contribute to a country's growth,
while growing economies can invest more in
education and training. Even so, the evidence is
clear that investing in skills pays dividends.

New analysis carried out for this Report
looks at the relationship between learning
outcomes and growth in forty-six of the
world's poorest countries. Two-thirds of all
out-of-school children live in these countries,
where the average annual income is only
about US$500. If an additional 75% of 15-year-
olds reached the lowest benchmark on the
OECD's Programme for International Student
Assessment (PISA) test score for mathematics
at the end of a ten-year period, long-run
economic growth would receive a major boost,
increasing above the baseline trend by 2.1
percentage points. In addition, 104 million more
people living on less than US$1.25 per day would
be lifted out of extreme poverty.

**Investing in
skills pays
dividends**

Box 4.1: Prioritizing skills development as a response to youth unemployment

In the light of the economic downturn, combating youth unemployment has taken on added urgency in debates over global and country strategies, and the need for skills development has been part of the focus. It does not always receive the attention it merits, however. While the Group of 20 has focused over the past two years on youth joblessness, for example, it has not sufficiently acknowledged the extent to which skills development can contribute to helping young people find good jobs.

Among multilateral agencies, the Organisation for Economic Co-operation and Development (OECD) recently released a skills development strategy recognizing that the global economic downturn and high rates of youth unemployment have added urgency to the need to foster better skills. The strategy promotes lifelong development of skills as the most promising solution to the challenges of unemployment and inequality. The World Bank's 2013 *World Development Report* aims to explain and analyse the connections between jobs and dimensions of economic and social development, while identifying policies for the creation of good jobs. The multi-agency *African Economic Outlook 2012* recognizes the importance of education and appropriate skills in mitigating unemployment and vulnerable employment.

The International Labour Organization goes further than most in focusing on disadvantaged youth. Its 2012 *World of Work Report* examines the labour market implications of the economic downturn, observing that imbalances are becoming more structural, particularly in advanced economies, where youth and the long-term unemployed are at risk of exclusion from the labour market. The report states that this has huge economic costs in terms of loss of skills and motivation, requiring an emphasis on skills training through active labour market programmes – with a focus on youth, for whom skills erosion is a particular challenge.

UNESCO's Third International Congress on Technical and Vocational Education and Training in Shanghai, China, in May 2012 defined a

seven-point action plan and proposed recommendations relevant to tackling the skills development needs of disadvantaged youth, including targeted funding schemes. Recommendations included adopting innovative measures to improve the quality and inclusiveness of technical and vocational education and training, targeting disadvantaged groups including learners with disabilities, marginalized and rural populations, migrants and those in situations affected by conflict and disaster; and promoting equal access of females and males to technical and vocational education and training programmes, particularly in fields where there is strong labour market demand.

Some governments have also recently highlighted in policy proposals and political statements the need for enhanced investment in education and training. In February 2011, President Jacob Zuma announced a 'year of job creation' for South Africa, focusing on infrastructure development, agriculture, extractive industries, manufacturing, tourism and the 'green economy'. The country's Industrial Development Corporation agreed to provide finance to support these key sectors, which promised to create around 20,000 jobs directly, as well as 8,100 jobs in the informal sector.

The electoral programme on which François Hollande was elected as France's new president in May 2012 includes a focus on supporting weaker students, with the goal of halving within five years the number of young people leaving the formal education system without any qualifications. He further promised a strengthening of the technical and vocational education and training track and the opening of training opportunities, for example through apprenticeships or civic service, to all out-of-school youth aged 16 to 18. This is intended to be part of broader efforts to target the funding of vocational training at those with the lowest education and training levels and at the unemployed.

Sources: Hollande (2012); ILO (2012b, 2012c); OECD (2012a); OECD Development Centre (2012); SouthAfrica.info (2011); UNESCO (2012a); World Bank (2011f).

Education for All Global Monitoring Report

2 0 1 2

The investment in education would pay off handsomely: for every US$1 spent on education, between US$10 and US$15 would be generated through the economic growth premium over a working lifetime of eighteen to twenty-two years (Hanushek and Woessmann, 2011).

Making sure that education contributes to economic growth is not just about increasing enrolment, but also about ensuring that the skills required for the workplace are equitably distributed. Take five countries that had similar per capita incomes in 1970: Colombia, the Democratic Republic of the Congo, Ghana, the Republic of Korea and Tunisia. In the early 1970s the gross enrolment ratio for secondary education was around or below 40% in all of them. By 2010, however, they had reached very different positions (Figure 4.1).

Uniquely among these countries, the Republic of Korea rapidly expanded its education system early on, reaching a gross secondary education enrolment ratio of 70% by the 1980s and nearly universal secondary schooling by the late 1990s. Colombia and Tunisia started from a lower base and are only now catching up with the Republic of Korea. Forty years on, the Republic of Korea has a per capita income level more than one hundred and fifty-eight times that of the Democratic Republic of the Congo, forty-six times that of Ghana, five times that of Colombia and six times that of Tunisia.

Several factors have affected growth and education trajectories in each of these countries. But it is clear that the key to the Republic of Korea's success has been its linking of skills development with broader strategies aimed at stimulating the economy. To understand how skills development has made such a difference for the Republic of Korea, it helps to examine trends in the other four countries.

At one extreme, the Democratic Republic of the Congo has been held back by ongoing conflict. But the country's economic and social progress has also been hindered by poor organization and meagre funding of education, as well as severe regional inequality. In North Kivu province, one of the regions worst affected by conflict, 61% of 15- to 19-year-olds did not make it to lower secondary school in 2010, while 10% in the capital, Kinshasa, were unable to reach secondary school (UIS, 2012a).

Figure 4.1: The Republic of Korea's investment in skills development has contributed to its impressive economic growth
Economic and education growth in five countries with similar incomes in 1970

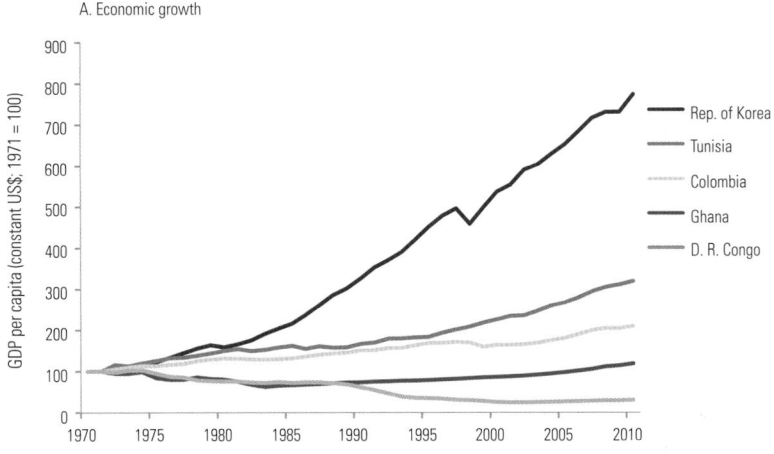

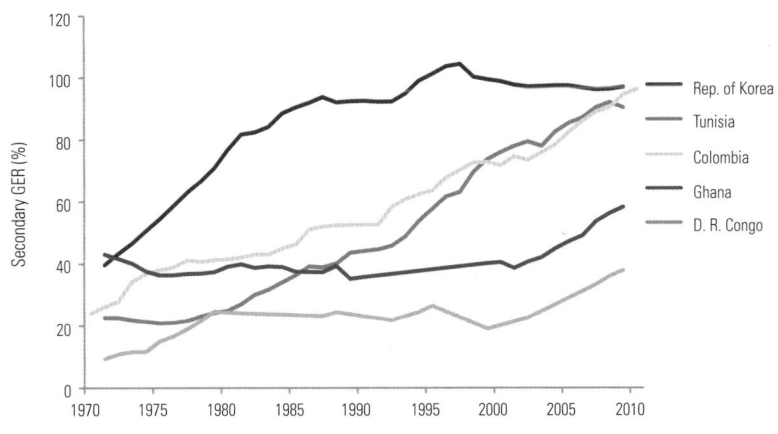

Note: The top figure is normalized with the year 1971 set to 100.
Sources: UIS database and World Bank (2012c).

For every US$1 spent on education, $10-$15 is generated in economic growth

More young people in sub-Saharan Africa need skills for their countries to achieve middle income status

Colombia, for its part, has been one of the faster growing economies in Latin America. But its growth has been volatile, affected by recessions and stagnation as well as conflict and violence, and the poorest part of the population has not enjoyed much of this growth. As in other countries in Latin America, unequal access to good quality education is one of the main factors behind inequality, along with segmented labour markets and ethnic and gender discrimination (Lustig et al., 2011). In 2010, around one-quarter of young people from the poorest quintile had not completed primary or lower secondary school, compared with almost 100% of the richest (UIS, 2012a).

Tunisia has fared better in terms of economic growth and education expansion. Education has been a high policy priority, receiving 6.6% of GDP in 2010. The higher education system produces graduates in massive numbers; in 2008, 57% of new entrants to the labour market had a university degree. Although primary and lower secondary enrolment has been almost universal for some time, substantial numbers of children still do not finish upper secondary. With an economy that continues to be dominated by low skill industries such as textiles, clothing and agro-industry, Tunisia has problems at both ends of the spectrum: finding decent-paying work for young people with little education, and diversifying the economy into high skill industries that provide the kind of jobs university graduates expect (Diop, 2010).

Comparing Ghana and the Republic of Korea brings the effects of skills policies into particularly stark perspective. While the Republic of Korea is now a high income country and member of the OECD, Ghana, like many other countries in sub-Saharan Africa, has struggled to become a significant player in the global economy (Box 4.2).

After decades of low or no growth, Ghana and other sub-Saharan African countries enjoyed relatively strong growth in the 2000s. Over a third of countries in the region have achieved growth rates of at least 6% (World Bank, 2012a). Some hope to achieve middle income status in the first half of the twenty-first century.

Experience from the Republic of Korea and the other East Asian 'tigers' suggests that sustained growth in sub-Saharan Africa depends on sound economic policies coordinated with government investment in education and training that meets the needs of the labour market. However, many African countries remain reliant on exports of oil or minerals, or specialize in exporting one or two agricultural products, and much of their growth has resulted from high global demand for these commodities. Between 1995 and 2008, 73% of Africa's export growth came from mining, leaving countries vulnerable to price changes (World Economic Forum et al., 2011). If the growth surge is to be sustained or accelerated, African countries need to diversify their economies and move up the technological ladder (World Bank, 2011a). For this to take place, all young people need foundation skills, as well as transferable and technical skills that enable them to adapt flexibly to new areas of work.

African countries may be tempted to try to emulate emerging economies such as India by spurning manufacturing growth in favour of high skilled, high value added service industries such as information and communication technology (ICT). This strategy could lead to rapid growth, but there is a risk of leaving a large swathe of the population behind. In Rwanda, for instance, the government has ambitious goals to reduce poverty by improving education and building a knowledge economy, with an emphasis on ICT. While this is laudable as a medium-term goal, it is not clear that ICT and other services, which tend not to create as many jobs as other types of industry, can help children of poor parents escape from poverty in a country where 90% of the population is engaged in agricultural production and the secondary gross enrolment ratio is only 36% (Education Development Center, 2009).

Countries have difficult choices to make about what types of development to prioritize. Concentrating public resources on privileged groups that are already highly skilled is unlikely to deliver prosperity equally. What is needed is a concentrated effort to upgrade the skills of the whole population and a focus on industries that can provide better job opportunities for most young people once they have these skills.

Box 4.2: Skills and growth – comparing Ghana and the Republic of Korea

After the Republic of Korea became independent in 1945, it began an early push to ensure that its education and growth were inclusive. It reached universal primary education in the 1960s, then rapidly extended access for all children to lower secondary school. This expansion was achieved in a country where 30% were aged below 25 years in 1980.

A planned rapid rise in labour-intensive, export-oriented industries led to growing demand for foundation skills. In addition, the government extended vocational and technical secondary education to develop skills for industries whose growth it planned to encourage, including technology-intensive heavy and chemical industries. At the same time, the government provided incentives to small and medium-sized enterprises to upgrade the skills of their workforce as the economy became more sophisticated and technology-driven.

The Republic of Korea's approach has been similar to that of the other East Asian 'tiger' economies (including Hong Kong, Singapore and Taiwan). First, the state developed trade and industrial policies directing the economy towards higher value added industries such as electronics. Second, it deployed a range of mechanisms to develop the necessary skills in advance, with flexibility between technical and vocational and general education, and learning from mistakes. Third, education and training policies were linked to the formation of economic policies. Finally, attention was paid to sequencing: the development of education and training is linked to the stage of economic growth. Throughout all stages, attempts have been made to strike a balance between labour intensive, lower skill industries that provide jobs for many, and more knowledge intensive industries that require higher levels of skills.

Given how extensively and rapidly skills needed to be transformed as East Asian economies moved from the early stages of industrialization to higher value added goods and services, it is doubtful that market forces could have done the job. The state played a key role in matching skills supply to demand.

Although Ghana had a similar starting point to the Republic of Korea in the early 1970s, it has lagged far behind since then. The Republic of

Korea began to expand its secondary system rapidly in the 1970s, but in Ghana the secondary education gross enrolment ratio stagnated at around 40% for another thirty years.

Ghana's lack of progress in education was partly the result of economic problems. But it was also because of insufficient investment in education or linking of economic planning with skills development policies. In the early 1980s, Ghana's spending on education was less than 2% of GDP per capita, compared with around 4% in the Republic of Korea at the time.

Even though Ghana embarked on education reforms from 1987, the quality of education and its relevance to the labour market have remained poor. Technical and vocational education has not been well enough linked with the economy. And although access to education has expanded, by 2008 almost one-third of 15- to 19-year-olds were still not making it through lower secondary school, with some not even completing primary school.

Since the 1990s, Ghana's economy has started to grow faster. By 2010, it had achieved a growth rate of 7.7%, and it acquired lower middle income status in 2011. Some workers have moved from agriculture into the urban informal economy where they can earn more, even if they still lack the security or benefits associated with the formal sector. Most employment is now in small enterprises that pay low wages. But unlike in the Republic of Korea, these companies have only recently begun to benefit from government support to foster skills development.

There are many reasons why Ghana's economic success has not matched that of the East Asian 'miracle' economies since the 1960s. But the short-sightedness of economic reforms that failed to invest in skills for the future economy must take some share of the blame. The kind of rapid industrial development that can turn a country like the Republic of Korea from a poor one to a wealthy one in the space of thirty years cannot happen without widespread basic education and well-coordinated systems for providing skills, including to workers in small and medium-sized enterprises.

Sources: Addae-Mensah et al. (1973); Akyeampong (2010); Ashton et al. (1999; 2002); Lee (2006); Nsowah-Nuamah et al. (2012); Sang-Duk (2010); UIS (2012a); World Bank (2011c).

The Republic of Korea matched skills supply to demand to become wealthy in 30 years

Many governments neglect skills and the disadvantaged lose out most

The major problem of the youth is unemployment. They cannot get jobs because they did not complete school and move to the next level of education to help them get skills for employment.

– young woman, Ethiopia

Despite the economic benefits it can bring, skills development has often been neglected in national plans. Even where its importance is recognized, skills development is frequently given low priority, with no clear line of responsibility for action, poor coordination among agencies and providers, and limited attention to the needs of disadvantaged young people.

Skills development requires much better national coordination

Responsibility for skills development planning is generally divided among several ministries or government agencies, so there is a danger that those who need skills training the most are likely to fall through the cracks.

Although education ministries are the core institutions responsible for formal education and accreditation, ministries of labour and youth are also likely to focus on skills to improve young people's job chances, particularly outside the formal system. Some countries have specific ministries with responsibilities for technical and vocational education and training. In Uruguay, for example, outside the formal primary and secondary school system there are at least eight major public and semi-public providers of training programmes (UIS, 2012b).

As a result, many countries have several different skills development policies. Responsibility for defining and addressing skills development requirements is often unclear, and the needs of disadvantaged youth are often overlooked.

There are notable exceptions. In Bangladesh, where as many as twenty-two ministries and

agencies are involved in skills development, a National Skills Development Council was set up in 2008 to bring them all under the leadership of the prime minister. The council includes representatives of government, employers, workers, civil society and industry, and is responsible for approving and implementing all governance, regulatory and legislative provisions (Engel, 2012).

A study commissioned for this Report examined the objectives and prioritization of skills development in national development strategies and relevant sector policies in forty-six countries with large youth populations, most of them low and lower middle income countries. Just over half of the countries had, or were developing, some form of policy document focusing on skills development – either a technical and vocational education and training strategy or a broader skills development strategy. These were frequently vague, however. The split in responsibility among various government agencies is often reflected in national development strategies that address skills development only in relation to broad objectives, with little outlining of sequenced reforms and targets. Objectives tend to be dispersed among several pillars (for example, growth and competitiveness, social and basic services), while skills development is rarely specifically addressed as a cross-cutting issue (Engel, 2012).

Among the forty-six countries, South Africa has one of the most comprehensive sets of policies and programmes addressing youth skills development. At least eight policies present priorities for skills development. They include the National Development Plan, the Accelerated and Shared Growth Initiative, the New Growth Path, the National Skills Development Strategy, the National Youth policy, and strategic plans for the Departments of Labour, Basic Education, and Higher Education and Training (South Africa Government, 2007, 2009a, 2009b, 2010a, 2010b, 2011a, 2011b).

The institutional complexity makes it vital for policies to be well aligned and the needs of the disadvantaged clearly integrated. South Africa has made progress in this regard through its 2010 Human Resource Development Strategy.

South Africa has one of the most comprehensive sets of policies addressing youth skills

The strategy is explicitly based on education and training frameworks, each of which broadly addresses the needs of the disadvantaged, such as rural unemployed youth or women. Many departments and entities have clearly defined roles in relation to the strategy, with indicators and activities related to each line department or subsystem coordinated via governmental forums – including a Human Resources Development Council – to ensure that planning is integrated and targets are reached (South Africa Government, 2009a).

Around 60% of the countries reviewed had some form of measurable target or objective regarding skills development – an indication of the extent of the priority given to skills development in national strategies and sector policies. India is committed to increase training opportunities from 2.5 million to 10 million over the course of its eleventh five-year plan (2007–2012) and Ethiopia's fourth Education Sector Development Plan (2010/11–2014/15) aims to increase enrolment in technical and vocational education and training by 40% by 2014/15. Even fewer countries explicitly link targets to increased expenditure on skills training. Exceptions include Malawi and Senegal, which have targets to increase the share of technical and vocational expenditure in the education budget, while in Pakistan there are targets for local governments to allocate a minimum of 4% of education budgets for literacy and non-formal basic education (Engel, 2012).

Skills strategies need to cover the full range of providers

Just as there are numerous government agencies engaged in developing skills plans, a large number of providers need to be covered in these plans. The diversity is particularly broad among programmes that aim to reach the disadvantaged, which need to adopt innovative, flexible approaches.

Governments and the private sector are the most prominent providers of formal general and vocational education. While some private providers are registered and follow official curricula, a large number operate informally, are unregistered and provide short courses with no guarantee of teaching standards.

These institutions depend entirely on fees, and thus are not accessible to the poorest (Adams et al., forthcoming).

Beyond the formal system, second-chance programmes and work-based training draw on a range of providers in addition to government, including non-governmental organizations (NGOs) and industry. International NGOs, along with national and community-based organizations, are important providers of second-chance training, mostly for disadvantaged youth, including in slums and remote rural areas where skills deficits are often greatest. Some, such as BRAC, provide other support services for small businesses, including microcredit (see Chapter 7). The ability of non-government providers to offer regular, continuous training over long periods can be constrained because their financial base is often limited and insecure (Adams, 2008; Adams et al., forthcoming).

In many poor countries, disadvantaged young people predominantly receive skills training through traditional apprenticeships in small enterprises (see Chapter 6). But some businesses are too small and fragile to invest in structured training (Adams et al., forthcoming). The institutional framework for skills development in many countries cannot cope with the diversity of providers. As a result, the wide array of skills programmes is not adequately aligned with labour market demands or national development priorities.

In Jordan, for example, many NGOs providing skills training outside the formal system, notably to disadvantaged young people, fall under the jurisdiction of the Employment Technical and Vocational Education and Training Council. But NGOs are generally overseen by a number of agencies and ministries, including the Higher Council for Youth and four ministries responsible for registering NGOs. And while the Higher Council for Youth is responsible for implementing the National Youth Policy, in which skills development figures prominently, it is deemed to lack capacity for the task (Gorak-Sosnowska, 2009).

India's five-year plan aims to increase training opportunities from 2.5 million to 10 million

Disadvantaged youth suffer the most

There is a lack of education so we don't get jobs and can't improve our life. There is no growth for us.

– young man, India

Even where national strategies do refer to skills development, the overarching objective is commonly to improve productivity and growth, rather than the employment conditions of the poor. Very few of the forty-six countries have specific strategies to meet the needs of vulnerable groups, which are rarely explicitly addressed in detail in separate youth, employment and skills development policies. Ethiopia is a notable exception, having adopted a more comprehensive national and sectoral education strategy aimed at tackling disadvantage as well as achieving growth (Box 4.3).

While many skills strategies emphasize the importance of equity, particularly gender equality, as an objective in broader discussions of access to skills development, training and

Ethiopia aims to achieve universal secondary schooling by 2020 to achieve middle income status

---

Box 4.3: Ethiopia aims for growth through comprehensive skills planning

With the aim of becoming a middle income country by 2025, Ethiopia has developed ambitious strategies for boosting growth and reducing poverty, which include enhanced investment in education and training.

Over the past five years Ethiopia has achieved high rates of growth, averaging over 10% annually. Yet it remains one of the world's poorest countries. Around 85% of the population is rural and agriculture provides about 80% of employment. The formal private sector is small. Aside from state-owned enterprises, very small companies with limited productivity predominate. They cannot absorb a growing labour force, so urban unemployment is high.

In education, too, there has been rapid progress but significant challenges remain. According to official figures, the primary net enrolment ratio rose from 36% in 1999 – then one of the world's lowest levels – to 81% in 2010. Gross enrolment in secondary school rose from 13% in 1999 to 36% in 2010. Enrolment in technical and vocational training also expanded rapidly over the decade, from an estimated 106,336 in 2003/04 to 717,603 in 2009/10, according to government data.

Despite these gains, 81% of 15- to 19-year-old men and 92% of young women lack foundation skills in rural areas, where only 20% of secondary schools are situated.

Recognizing the need to address these challenges, Ethiopia's 2010/11-2014/15 Growth and Transformation Plan gives skills development high priority. Although smallholder agriculture is projected to continue to be the predominant, if declining, source of economic activity, there is substantial emphasis within the plan on increasing productivity of micro and small enterprises primarily within urban areas, acknowledging their considerable potential to create jobs and reduce poverty.

For Ethiopia to achieve its ambitious objectives, including annual GDP growth rates in excess of 11%, a substantial proportion of growth will have to come from increases in productivity, requiring greater use of technology and a more skilled labour force. To meet that need, a five-year Education Sector Development Plan, running in conjunction with the Growth and Transformation Plan, aims to achieve universal secondary schooling by 2020.

The education plan aims to provide technical and vocational skills to create a competent and adaptable workforce in agriculture and industry. To assure balanced growth across rural and urban areas, the plan includes a doubling of the number of institutions providing technical and vocational skills in rural areas. Special focus is also given to adult literacy, alternative basic education for out-of-school and disadvantaged children, and expanded education in rural areas, along with preferential access for students from disadvantaged regions. Technical and vocational training is intended to better meet demand and support strategic sectors, with enterprises participating in most training.

Ethiopia's plans for education expansion and growth are ambitious. Its remarkable achievements in expanding primary education in a short time and its recent impressive economic growth give reason to hope that the government's commitments can be translated into action, provided appropriate investment is made to support its plans.

Sources: Brixiova and Asaminew (2010); Engel (2012); Ethiopia Ministry of Education (2005, 2008); Ethiopia MoFED (2010); UIS (2012a).

employability, few countries set explicit targets. Exceptions include Bangladesh and Ethiopia. Bangladesh aims to increase female enrolment in technical and vocational education by 60% by 2020, and Ethiopia expects a 50% share of female enrolment in technical and vocational programmes by 2014/15 (Engel, 2012; Ethiopia MoFED, 2010). India and Malawi have introduced affirmative action programmes aimed at increasing the share of women in training, but in the absence of other strategies addressing the multiple challenges young women face in gaining access to training, they may not achieve the desired outcomes (Engel, 2012).

Even fewer countries include strategies to help marginalized young people overcome barriers to skills training. Bangladesh is again an exception, having instituted a skills development strategy that strongly targets marginalized groups. Closely linked with other policies, including the second National Strategy for Accelerated Poverty Reduction, it emphasizes varied types of training needs and recognizes the importance of linking microfinance and skills development for those in rural communities (Bangladesh Planning Commission, 2008).

Only around a quarter of the countries reviewed explicitly acknowledge the need to provide better access to education or training for youth who have dropped out of primary school. Nepal has formulated a non-formal education policy outlining objectives to provide alternative basic and vocational education to school dropouts. Under Malawi's National Education Sector Plan, 90% of out-of-school youth are expected to have access to education and training by 2017. The plan includes a goal of more than tripling the number of facilitators offering second-chance education, from 700 to 2,380. The plan is laudable in allocating a government budget for this purpose, even though it is likely to be too limited to reach all youth needing a second chance; the aim is to ensure that at least 2% of the education budget is spent on out-of-school youth by 2017 (Engel, 2012).

In the majority of the countries, skills development policies focus on expanding the scope and quality of formal technical and vocational education and training – including enhancing the role of the private sector – often

with the explicit aim of addressing the mismatch between supply and demand in the labour market. Yet such measures do not reach the vast majority of disadvantaged young people, who do not get a chance to benefit from upper secondary school – whether general or technical and vocational – let alone from higher education.

Skills development strategies often overlook the informal sector

Most government policies, particularly overarching national development strategies, largely view skills development in relation to the demands of formal sector employment. Although many policies encourage entrepreneurial and management skills to promote self-employment, it is not always clear whether such objectives are explicitly targeted at the informal sector, so they may not reach disadvantaged young people. Even where they do, they often do not extend sufficiently to the large numbers of disadvantaged young people in low and middle income countries who lack foundation skills, as Sierra Leone's youth employment strategy shows (Box 4.4).

Of the forty-six countries reviewed for this Report, fewer than half addressed skills development among youth in the informal sector, and very few had detailed policies in this regard (Engel, 2012). South Africa's National Skills Development Strategy is a notable exception. It aimed to transform its vocational education and training system to provide youth with jobs in the informal labour market. Financed almost exclusively by a vocational education levy paid by enterprises, it has been able to train more than 320,000 youth for employment in the informal sector. About 66% were able to find work in informal public work infrastructure programmes in rural areas. Information about informal sector job opportunities was provided by job centres under the Ministry of Labour (Heitmann and Schröter, 2009).

Ghana's medium-term national development strategy, the Ghana Shared Growth and Development Agenda 2010–2013, is an example of a plan that extends to the informal sector. It outlines objectives for expanding technical and vocational education and training to promote productivity, employment creation and improved working conditions in the formal and informal sectors. These objectives are complemented by

Only one country in four acknowledges the need for second-chance programmes

> ## Box 4.4: Sierra Leone's youth employment strategy needs to reach all those lacking foundation skills
>
> Improving young people's chances of acquiring skills and obtaining jobs has become a policy priority in Sierra Leone, which recently emerged from a civil war that was in part fuelled by the large number of young people with limited education and work opportunities. Its youth employment strategy for 2009-2011, the government's most concerted effort to date to address youth unemployment, aimed to help 300,000 young people find jobs.
>
> The strategy is intended to provide a range of skills development opportunities linked to jobs in the informal and formal sectors. Since few young people get their first jobs in the formal sector (less than 1% of those under age 19, 3% of those aged 20 to 24, and 8% of 25- to 35-year-olds hold formal sector jobs), the strategy focuses on linking training to business and entrepreneurial development.
>
> Over the last three years, with assistance from donor agencies, the government has supported 40 projects reaching 20,000 youth. About 5,600 young people have also been trained for two to three months in establishing and managing private
>
> sector enterprises. Others have received training for six months to one year in skills relevant to the wider labour market through apprenticeship and job training. Of these youth, 75% are in some form of paid employment (including self-employment), 22% are in apprenticeship programmes with artisans and 2% have a micro franchise business.
>
> These programmes have made some progress in providing skills and facilitating employment, but they are still a long way from reaching the strategy's target of 300,000, let alone the one in four young men and one in five young women who are neither working nor in school. Given that 57% of 15- to 19-year-olds drop out before completing lower secondary school, the government needs to go much further in providing second-chance programmes in conjunction with other job-related skills programmes that would put many more young people in a better position to obtain gainful employment.
>
> *Sources:* Engel (2012); Peeters et al. (2009); UIS (2012a); United Nations et al. (2010).

Voices of disadvantaged youth are rarely heard in planning processes

the National Technical and Vocational Education and Training Policy Framework, which proposes a large-scale intervention to improve productivity in the informal sector. It includes an ambitious plan to provide competency-based training and assessment for the traditional apprenticeship system, and to facilitate the formation of trade associations as a means of delivering training (Engel, 2012).

Zambia's sixth National Development Plan, in contrast, contains no reference to skills development in the informal sector (Zambia MoFNP, 2011), and a historical emphasis on training for formal sector employment has effectively excluded many young people from poor backgrounds (Johanson and Adams, 2004).

Disadvantaged youth should participate in planning

Young people are rarely able to contribute to policy-making, but it is important for their voices to be heard. Those aged 15 to 24 constitute around a sixth of the global population, and often form the most dynamic section of society, as well

as its most vulnerable and most powerless. They have a deeper understanding than policy-makers do of the realities of their own lives, including the experience of education and training and the challenge of finding a good job.

Few planning processes include the voices of youth, however, even though their right to contribute is supported by a number of United Nations General Assembly resolutions.[1] Where their views are sought, structures facilitating their input into policy-making include youth and school councils, youth forums and youth parliaments, as well as one-off activities such as youth hearings and workshops. Even where youth participate, the voices of the disadvantaged are unlikely to be heard. Youth consultations tend to be dominated by educated and privileged urban youth, while the voices of the poor majority (both urban and rural) are rarely included (te Lintelo, 2011).

---

1. These include the World Programme of Action for Youth to the Year 2000 and Beyond (A/RES/50/81), UN General Assembly Resolution A/RES/57/165, the Commission for Social Development Resolution 2006/15 on Youth Employment and UN General Assembly Resolutions A/RES/60/2 (2005) and A/RES/58/133 (2003) on Policies and Programmes involving Youth (Youth Employment Network, 2009).

Fairly successful examples of youth participation in policy-making can be found in Brazil and Sri Lanka. Brazil's National Youth Council is an advisory body, two-thirds of whose members come from youth civil society groups. Working in partnership with the National Youth Secretariat to formulate and implement a national youth policy, the council has been involved in establishing a 'special commission for youth public policies' within the Brazilian Congress, underscoring the strong national focus on youth. The council has coordinated a national discussion leading to the development of a youth statute and a national youth plan to help ensure that the rights of youth are emphasized in future legislation.

In Sri Lanka, a National Youth Employment Task Force was created to develop and implement the National Action Plan on Youth Employment. Both the Sri Lankan Youth Parliament and the Secretary General of the Junior Chamber of Sri Lanka played a key role on the task force in managing the consultation process for the action plan. Youth of different social and ethnic backgrounds – rural, urban and conflict-affected – contributed to the process. Following the consultations, concrete inputs and amendments based on youth feedback were incorporated in the draft National Action Plan (Youth Employment Network, 2009).

South Sudan provides a notable recent example of inviting young people to contribute to education planning processes. Emerging from decades of conflict, the country has a young population, with 68% under 30. Many youth have missed education opportunities, and only 40% of those aged 15 to 24 are literate (South Sudan National Bureau of Statistics, 2010). Consultative processes have helped ensure that youth concerns are reflected in the new country's forthcoming Education Sector Strategic Plan. Young people expressed huge demand for education and training, but also recognized the lack of schools and qualified teachers, as well as the limited relevance of the education system to the labour market (South Sudan Ministry of Education, 2012).

Boosting finance to bring skills to disadvantaged youth

Given the scale of training required to help disadvantaged young people get work that pays a decent wage, more and better-targeted funding is needed. Decisions about who pays for each aspect of education and training are complex because of the wide range of skills programmes and providers. Governments and donors need to ensure that all young people acquire at least foundation skills, so the first priorities for education spending are early childhood care and education, and primary and lower secondary schooling.

In low and middle income countries, however, around 200 million 15- to 24-year-olds have not even completed primary school – including 57 million in sub-Saharan Africa alone – and they need a second chance to acquire foundation skills. They are mainly from the poorest households, so they cannot bear the costs of training themselves. Governments in these countries, with the support of aid donors, need to extend their support further to make sure all young people get a chance to acquire foundation skills.

The private sector also has a role to play, particularly as employers are the beneficiaries of a skilled workforce. Training funds made up of contributions from industries and aid donors have helped extend skills development to some vulnerable young people, but far more could be done. The private sector can also help fill training gaps by using foundations to finance programmes that are beyond the reach of governments and aid donors. Governments need to take responsibility for coordinating finance from the various sources, including donors and the private sector, and ensuring that it is directed at achieving national goals for equitable development through a more coherent approach to tackling the different dimensions of disadvantage.

Government efforts on foundation skills need to be complemented by donors

Many poor countries have increased their support for education over the past decade (see Chapter 2). Some could further increase the

68% of South Sudan's population is under 30 years old

Primary and secondary education is being squeezed in government budgets

proportion of national spending allocated to the sector. Each country's commitment to the most vulnerable is reflected in the share of its education budget allocated to the levels that benefit the disadvantaged most.

Around half of the education budget in countries such as the Central African Republic and Chad is spent on primary schooling, and a further one-fifth to one-quarter on general secondary. Spending on vocational training is just 3% and 7%, respectively (World Bank, 2007a, 2008c). Yet these countries still have extremely low enrolment in primary and lower secondary school. For example, the gross enrolment ratio in lower secondary school was only 24% in the Central African Republic in 2011 and 29% in Chad in 2010.

If more of their young people are to enrol in primary and lower secondary school, these countries need not only to increase education's share of the national budget from the current levels of around 10%, but also to use resources more efficiently and to redistribute them to parts of the country where disadvantaged young people live, including remote rural areas, slums, and regions with low enrolment. In addition, there is scope for redistributing to secondary schooling some government resources currently devoted to higher education, which is extremely costly and benefits a small privileged class.

Despite vast needs for primary and secondary schooling, Burundi spends around one-fifth of its education budget on higher education, and the Central African Republic more than one-quarter (World Bank, 2006a, 2008c). It remains important, however, for these countries to strengthen the capacity of higher education, and even if some of the resources available are reallocated, this will only go part of the way to addressing the vast financing needs for expanding secondary schooling, let alone providing a second chance to young people who have missed out.

Unfortunately, it seems that primary and secondary education is being squeezed in government budgets. Of the seventeen low and low middle income countries for which there are comparable national expenditure data for primary, secondary and tertiary

education for 1999 and 2010, ten countries decreased the share of public education expenditure going to primary and secondary education overall over this period. In many cases this has been accompanied by a concurrent rise in the share of the education budget earmarked for tertiary education.

In Malawi, for example, the share of the government education budget going to tertiary education rose from just under 20% in 1999 to 26% in 2011, while primary education's share fell from 61% to 37% over the same period, even though primary education in Malawi is in urgent need of greater investment to improve its quality. Ghana has similarly increased the share of the education budget earmarked for tertiary education. By 2010 it made up 23% of public expenditure on education; the shares for both primary and secondary education, on the other hand, have decreased since 1999.

Donors have a key role to play

Donors already provide important support to the development of foundation skills by funding primary and secondary schooling (see Chapter 2). Some also support skills training outside the formal education system. Part of this funding has helped extend opportunities to disadvantaged young people, including through support to local and international NGOs to deliver targeted aid to marginalized groups. But such assistance has tended to be uncoordinated, small-scale and fragmented, partly because numerous agencies are involved in delivery. More rigorous evaluation of aid programmes would enable lessons to be learnt, ensuring that resources are allocated in ways that bring more benefits to disadvantaged young people.

Identifying aid donors' policy priorities that are specifically aimed at skills development for disadvantaged youth is not straightforward. A review of twenty-four donor strategies for this Report shows that skills development is often found in more than one sector – not only education but also areas such as economic growth, employment generation, poverty reduction and the Millennium Development Goals (MDGs). The skills development programmes range from vocational training for disadvantaged women, skills for economic integration of youth into the labour market and life skills for marginalized communities to training for civil servants, lawyers and business managers. Most donors also include scholarship programmes for postgraduate students under the heading of skills development (Hunt, 2012).

The EFA and MDG movements have helped ensure that poorer and more marginalized sections of society are targeted by skills strategies and programmes, notably those of key skills development donors, such as Germany, Japan, Switzerland and the World Bank. German aid for skills development, for example, has shifted towards reducing poverty, introducing appropriate technology and providing non-formal training to cater for the needs of more disadvantaged sections of the population such as women, and the rural and urban poor (Clement, 2012).

Since the early 2000s, Japan has expanded the scope of its aid for skills development towards disadvantaged groups. In South Sudan, the Japanese International Cooperation Agency has supported a formal vocational training centre and non-formal training programmes to improve the skills of unemployed youth, including internally displaced people and school dropouts (Yoshida and Yamada, 2012). Switzerland's skills development strategy focuses on women, youth and the rural poor, targeting the poorest and most vulnerable, and World Bank support for increased employability and income generation for the disadvantaged has become more pronounced in recent years (Hunt, 2012).

As well as funding formal primary and secondary schooling, some aid donors support skills development outside the education sector, for example as part of agricultural or microfinance programmes. Many of these reach disadvantaged young people, and some target the disadvantaged explicitly. Indeed, many of these programmes tend to rely on aid donors for funding (Hunt, 2012).

Skills training funded by donors is a highly diverse field in which the informal, private and non-government sectors are important – and sometimes the main providers. Supporting non-government providers may be the best way to provide skills training to the disadvantaged, as NGOs may have better

capacity than government agencies to reach marginalized groups and adapt training to their needs. Working through a multitude of small organizations can, however, lead to fragmentation and a lack of coordination with wider government policies on labour or economic growth. It can also be difficult for non-government providers to sustain their programmes, especially if they are time-bound and not included in national budgets. Many NGO projects reach very few trainees compared with the scale needed.

Providing skills training for disadvantaged groups and working with government are by no means mutually exclusive. Training by NGOs or private providers can be part of a national strategy, planned in cooperation with the government. The Franchising-SKILL programme in Nepal, funded by Switzerland, the United Kingdom, the United States and other donors, provides training in trades for 16- to 30-year-olds from scheduled-caste, indigenous and conflict-affected backgrounds who have been unable to complete secondary school. It works alongside the government, but the training itself is franchised to private providers (Hunt, 2012).

Donors can also support the public training system. In Viet Nam, the Training for Employment programme, funded by Australia, caters for ethnic minorities via the formal state system, with training taking place in a range of industry areas depending on perceived labour market needs (Hunt, 2012).

How much do donors spend on skills development?

Given the diversity of activities that are included under the umbrella of skills development, assessing how much aid donors spend specifically on disadvantaged young people is extremely difficult. It is also virtually impossible to determine how much needs to be allocated to different types of support, for example to reach the 200 million young people needing a second chance to achieve basic literacy and numeracy, or to support training for informal sector workers.

Estimates by the EFA Global Monitoring Report team indicate that the total amount spent on skills development, including all spending on

German aid for skills development aims to reduce poverty

secondary education, vocational training and basic skills training, together with other forms of training that can be identified outside the education sector, reached US$3 billion per year on average over 2009–2010, or 2.1% of total official aid (Figure 4.2 and Box 4.5). There is not enough information available to determine what proportion of this amount is spent on disadvantaged young people specifically.

Over 60% of France's aid to secondary education went to two of its own territories

Direct aid to general secondary education and vocational training, one component of the amount spent on skills development for young people, has grown since the 2000 Dakar World Education Forum (Figure 4.3), despite fears that the emphasis on basic education at Dakar could come at the expense of post-primary skills development. Between 2002 and 2010, the share of direct aid spending on education that went to general secondary education and vocational training remained relatively stable, at around 10%. Vocational training made up at least half this amount.

One reason for the continued emphasis on post-primary skills development since Dakar is that some key donors have remained steadfast in making it a high priority. There is, in effect, a division of labour among donors, with some that have a historical commitment maintaining their support in these areas.

Germany emerges as the most important bilateral donor to vocational training and to skills development (Figure 4.4). Vocational training has been a key component of the country's aid strategy for decades, and has received on average US$98 million annually since 2002. By the broader definition of skills development, the amount increases to US$213 million. France is the second largest bilateral aid donor, but much of its funding does not reach developing countries: over 60% of the US$248 million that France disbursed to general secondary education and vocational training in 2010 went to Mayotte and to Wallis and Futuna, two overseas territories officially part of France.[2]

The analysis also shows that Spain is an important donor to skills development, which may be linked to the Latin American focus of its aid spending. Countries in this region are closer to achieving universal primary education, and so are more likely to receive support for vocational training and other aspects of skills development.

Being a large aid donor, the World Bank also provides significant funding to skills development, particularly for general secondary education. A review of World Bank lending between 2000 and 2010 shows that support for formal training systems remained steady despite shifting priorities in education (Hunt, 2012). The European Union is also an important source of funds for skills development, although programmes are concentrated in the neighbouring Mediterranean region, with Morocco, Tunisia and Turkey receiving more than US$5 million a year on average since 2002.

The only Asian members of the OECD Development Assistance Committee, Japan and the Republic of Korea, have both been strong supporters of skills and training, building on

Figure 4.2: Donors spend around US$3 billion on skills development
Aid for skills development in relation to aid to education, 2009 to 2010

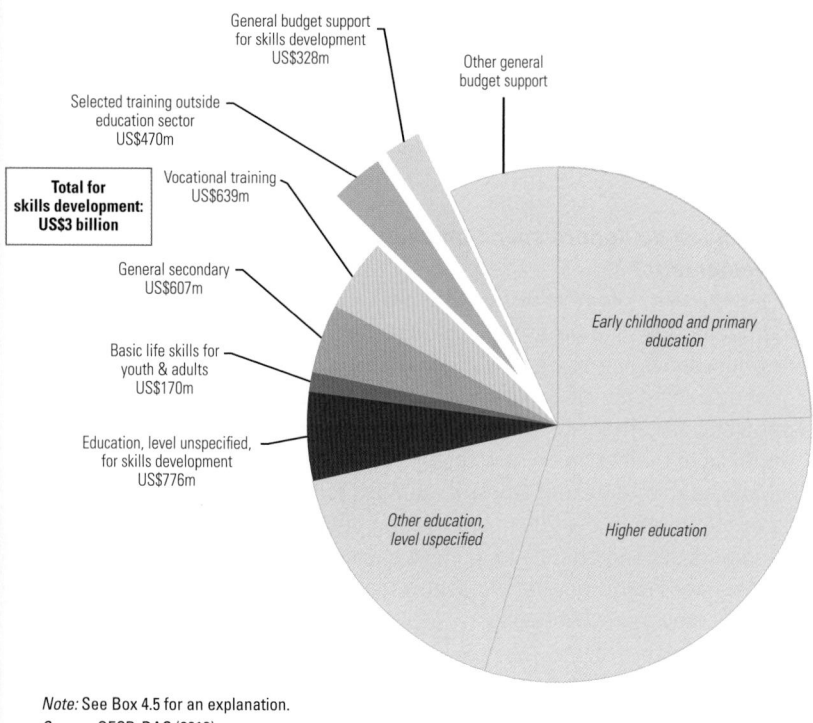

Note: See Box 4.5 for an explanation.
Source: OECD-DAC (2012).

2. In 2011, Mayotte became an overseas department and so is no longer classed as an eligible aid recipient under OECD-DAC reporting rules.

Box 4.5: Measuring aid for skills development

Identifying how much aid goes to skills development is not easy. Reporting by donors cuts across different codes in the OECD's Creditor Reporting System (CRS) classification, making it difficult to disentangle. The analysis of spending in Figure 4.2 includes the following as areas where aid is most likely to be allocated to programmes that reach young people:

- secondary general education;

- vocational secondary training;[3]

- basic life skills for youth and adults (including literacy programmes);

- training outside the education sector.[4]

In addition, it is assumed that 25% of aid to education that is not specified by level[5] and

5% of general budget support are allocated to skills development.[6]

The resulting figure represents a subset of spending that contributes to skills development more widely. Spending on early childhood care and education and on primary schooling is important to ensure that young people enter secondary school with the necessary basic skills, and higher education is vital to provide the higher level skills needed for the economy.

Aid for all these aspects of education and skills training amounts to US$13.9 billion a year on average for 2009-10, of which around one-quarter is spent on skills development according to the definition used for the purposes of this Report.

Sources: Reporting system of the OECD Development Assistance Committee (DAC).

Figure 4.3: Aid to general secondary education and vocational training has increased over the past decade

Direct aid disbursements to general secondary education and vocational training, 2002 to 2010

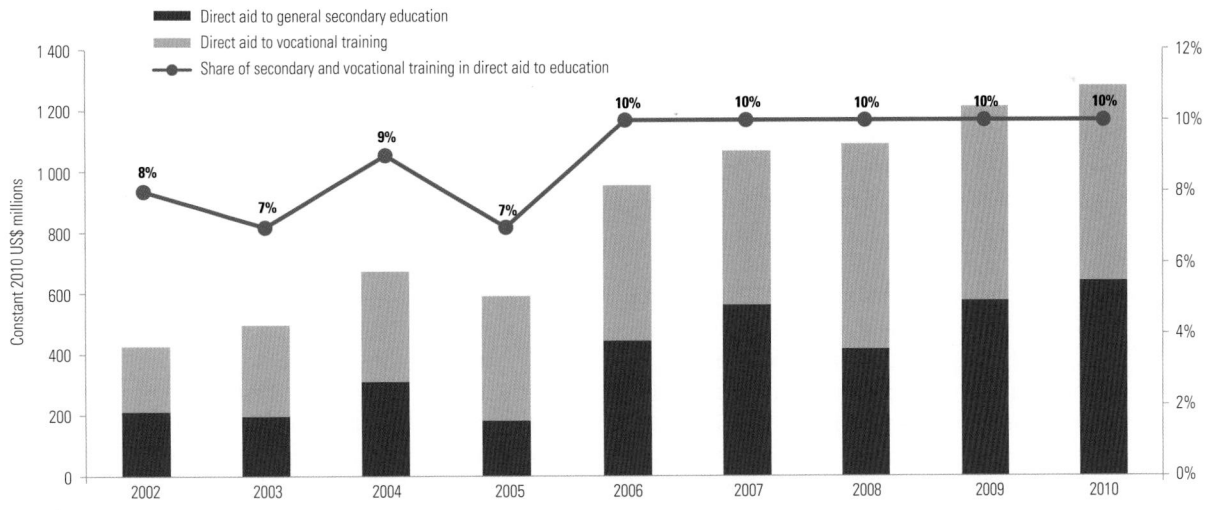

Note: This figure shows only direct aid to secondary general education and vocation training; it excludes aid to the sub-sectors from general budget support and from 'education, unspecified'.
Source: OECD-DAC (2012).

3. Together vocational training and secondary general education are classed as secondary education in the reporting system of the OECD Development Assistance Committee (DAC) OECD-DAC (2012).
4. This category refers to eleven CRS codes: medical education and training; health personnel development; population and reproductive health personnel development; training for water supply and sanitation; training in transport and storage; training in energy; training in agricultural education; training in forestry education; training in fishery education; training in trade education; and training in environment education. Other types of training are excluded as being either defined too broadly (for example, multisector training) or likely to be primarily targeted at government officials (such as statistical training).

5. This concerns aid related to an activity that cannot be attributed to a single level of education. In the DAC reporting systems it falls under four codes: education policy and administrative management; education facilities and training; educational research; and teacher training.
6 The *EFA Global Monitoring Report* includes 20% of general budget support in its aid to education figures. It is assumed that 5% is attributed to skills development.

Figure 4.4: Skills development is a prominent part of aid spending for some donors
Top fifteen donors' disbursements on direct aid for skills development, 2002 to 2010, annual average

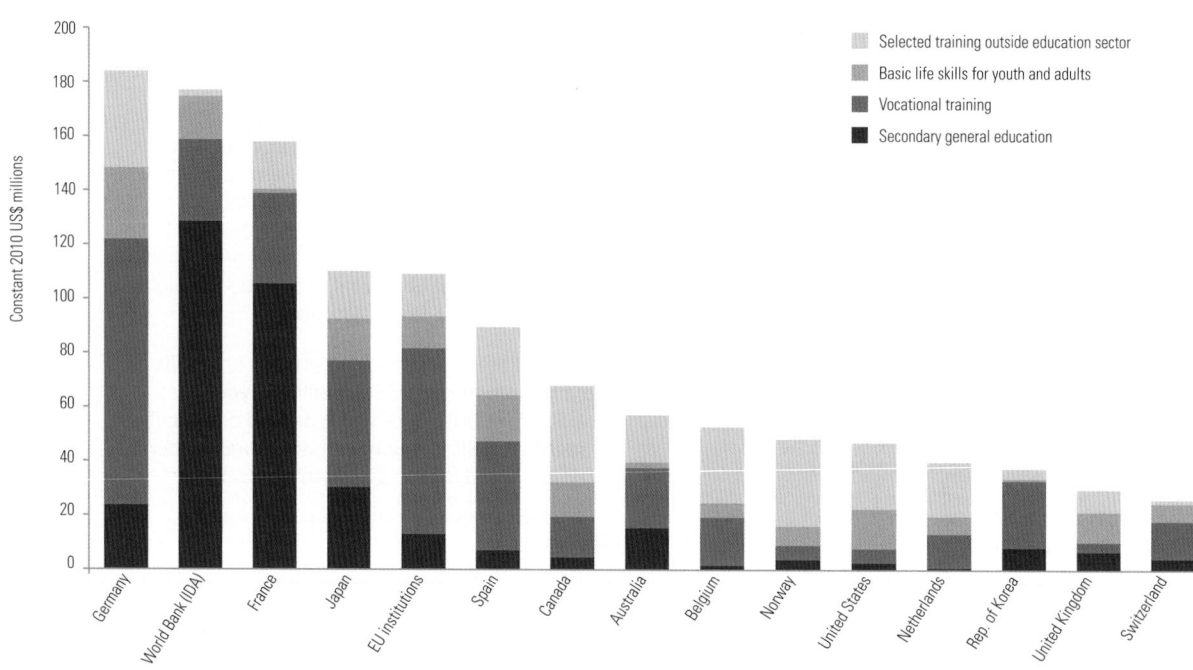

Notes: Data for the Republic of Korea shows the average for 2006–2010 due to lack of reporting in previous years. This figure shows only direct aid to skills development; it excludes aid to skills development from general budget support and from 'education, unspecified'.
Source: OECD-DAC (2012).

US$3 billion was spent on skills development in 2010

their experience of achieving impressive growth through skills development. Since 2002, Japan has spent on average US$47 million a year on vocational training, or US$147 million using the broader definition. The Republic of Korea became a member of the DAC in 2010, spending 0.1% of its gross national income on aid (Chun et al., 2010). Despite being a newcomer and having a relatively small and fragmented aid programme compared with other DAC members, the country has already established itself as a key supporter of skills development, spending on average 28% of its aid to education on vocational training alone since 2006.

Some smaller donors, including Luxembourg and Switzerland, have also concentrated their education support on skills development (Hunt, 2012). Luxembourg's share of vocational training within aid to education is by far the highest, at 44%. Switzerland spends around one-quarter of its aid to education on vocational training.

What are the prospects for increasing aid to skills development?

The US$3 billion per year spent, on average, on skills development primarily for young people in 2009–2010 compares favourably with the US$5.8 billion of total aid to basic education. The fact that more is spent on basic education does not mean funds should shift away from that level. Universal primary education has yet to be reached in many countries, and aid levels to the poorest countries remain vastly insufficient. Moreover, increasing the provision and quality of early childhood care and education and of primary education is essential to build the basic skills that are necessary for further skills development.

At the same time, there is an urgent need for donors to commit to skills development in three ways: by supporting country programmes to ensure that all young people can stay in school at least until lower secondary level; by supporting second-chance programmes for young people who have not had the opportunity to gain basic

Education for All Global Monitoring Report   2 0 1 2

literacy and numeracy skills; and by giving disadvantaged youth training to ensure that they can earn a decent wage.

It is difficult to estimate how much these priorities would cost. This Report estimates that achieving the target of all young people entering lower secondary school would add US$8 billion to the US$16 billion needed to attain universal basic education by 2015 (EPDC and UNESCO, 2009).[7] And significant additional resources are needed for large-scale second-chance programmes.

Given the vast financing needs for skills training, the first step is to ensure that the US$3 billion already available for skills development is directed at those most in need. But this still leaves a considerable funding gap at a time when aid donor budgets are constrained. Could more external support for young people in developing countries be found elsewhere?

There are two potential avenues: redistributing funds currently spent on scholarships for young people from developing countries to study at tertiary level in developed countries, and encouraging emerging donors to engage more effectively in skills development.

Reallocating some aid from higher education
The focus on skills development used in this Report is on pre-tertiary levels of education. This does not imply that higher education is not important, but recognizes that most disadvantaged young people have little hope of reaching that level. The first priorities remain ensuring that everyone has the opportunity to acquire foundation skills – through primary and lower secondary education, or second-chance opportunities for those who have missed out – and providing work-based training for vulnerable young people. Aid to education needs to maintain a focus on countries and subsectors where those marginalized in education face the biggest problems.

While aid to higher education can in some circumstances play an important role in

supporting capacity development, unfortunately aid to this level rarely reaches developing countries. In 2012, for the first time, the OECD-DAC required donors to report the share of aid disbursed for post-secondary education allocated to scholarships and imputed student costs (the costs incurred by donor country institutions when they receive students from developing countries). Around three-quarters of direct aid to post-secondary education that was disbursed in 2010 fell into those categories (Figure 4.5).

Some of the important donors to skills development, including Canada, France, Germany and Japan, also spend a significant portion of aid resources on higher education. But as the figures reveal, a large proportion of these funds never leaves donor countries.

Spending on higher education within donor countries swamps the contribution of prominent donors to skills development. In 2010, almost 40% of Japan's direct aid to education went to scholarships for students studying in Japan; the equivalent for Canada was 22%. Germany's aid disbursements to scholarships and imputed student costs were almost eleven times the amount it spent on direct aid to general secondary education

It would cost US$8 billion for all young people to enrol in lower secondary school

---

Figure 4.5: For some donors, a large proportion of 'aid' never leaves the country

Top four donors that disbursed the most direct aid to education as scholarships and imputed student costs, 2010

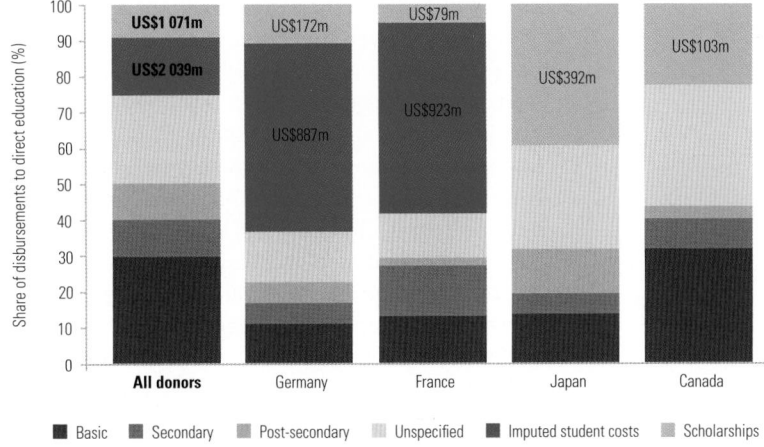

Note: This figure shows only direct aid to education; it excludes aid to education from general budget support.
Source: OECD-DAC (2012).

2012

Education for All Global Monitoring Report

and vocational training in 2010. France's aid disbursements to scholarships and imputed student costs were four times as much as was spent on direct aid to general secondary education and vocational training in 2010.

Reallocating some of this funding from higher education spent within donor countries to programmes that reach disadvantaged young people in developing countries would further position these aid donors as important contributors to skills development for poverty reduction, and accelerate progress towards EFA. In total, in 2010 one-quarter of direct aid to the education sector was in the form of scholarships and imputed student costs. If invested directly in developing countries' education systems, some of this US$3.1 billion could provide an important contribution to the US$8 billion needed to attain schooling for all at the lower secondary level, and so to reducing the figure of 71 million adolescents currently out of school.

To give one example, Japan spends between US$20,000 and US$25,000 a year per foreign student on stipends for higher education (JASSO, 2011).[8] In Nepal, by contrast, US$406 a year is spent on one post-secondary student and US$109 per secondary school student. This means that for what it costs for one Nepalese student to study on scholarship in Japan, as many as 229 young people could have access to secondary education in Nepal.[9]

Whether scholarships and imputed student costs should qualify as official development assistance is debatable, given that these funds are spent entirely in donor countries, with little or no input from 'recipient' governments, and they fail to build institutional capacity locally. This type of financial assistance is an example of 'tied aid', where the line between aid and donors' economic self-interest is blurred. The OECD-DAC, as part of its definition of 'real aid' – better known as country programmable aid – excludes aid earmarked for imputed student costs in order to better monitor the levels of aid that are actually transferred to developing countries. But imputed

In 2010, one-quarter of aid to education was spent on scholarships and imputed student costs

student costs and scholarships are still counted as aid in the broader DAC reporting practices. Until this changes, confusion over whether they should be counted as aid is likely to continue.

Emerging donors could engage in skills development more effectively

Another potential source of additional funding is emerging economies such as Brazil, China and India, which already support skills development. Despite high expectations of the assistance these donors could provide, their funding is modest, and does not appear to be sufficiently aimed at disadvantaged young people. Much of it is also not directly comparable with DAC donors' aid (see chapter 2).

To take one example, estimates suggest India committed around US$950 million annually to other developing countries from 2008 to 2010. Just 2% of this was allocated to education, compared with 25% for energy projects and 15% for transport infrastructure projects (Findley et al., 2009). India's commitment of around US$15 million to education is less than half the amount provided by Luxembourg, the smallest DAC donor to education. Around a third of India's US$15 million for education went to vocational training projects, concentrated in the ICT sector, where India sees it has an advantage (Agrawal, 2012). In May 2011, India pledged to spend US$700 million on training in Africa over the next three years (Chaudhury, 2011). This would bring it into the premier league of aid donors for skills development. But much of this aid will focus on higher levels of education that are not within the reach of disadvantaged young people.

There are exceptions. Following success in assisting women towards employment in India, in 2006 the government invited the Self-Employed Women's Association to set up a vocational training centre in Kabul. In coordination with the Afghan Ministry of Women's Affairs, the Indian government funded the construction of the centre, provided equipment, covered training fees for poor and often illiterate Afghan women to be trained in skills such as sewing and food processing, and helped them set up livelihood groups, marketing networks and bank accounts (Agrawal, 2012; SEWA, 2008; UN ECOSOC, 2008). India needs to give the disadvantaged much

8. Although scholarships in Japan are administered by the Ministry of Education, Culture, Sports, Science and Technology, those for foreign students from developing countries are reported as official aid to the DAC.
9. This assumes the upper-end estimate of US$25,000 on Japan stipends for higher education students.

greater attention, however, if it is to have an international influence on reducing poverty through skills development.

Skills development is similarly high on Brazil's list of development financing priorities, but the amounts spent are very small. Around one-quarter of development finance from Brazil as compiled in the AidData database went to education-related projects in 2008–2009. Nearly all of it would fit this Report's broader definition of skills development.[10] The sum amounts to just US$2.1 million a year, however – considerably less even than the amount spent by India (Findley et al., 2009).

As with India, some of Brazil's support is based on successful experience tackling disadvantage within its own country. Its government-industry body overseeing vocational training, Serviço Nacional de Aprendizagem Industrial (SENAI), has provided technical assistance for vocational training to other countries, helping set up training institutions in several Portuguese-speaking African countries, including Cape Verde, Guinea-Bissau, Mozambique, and Sao Tome and Principe, as well as to Soweto in South Africa (Costa Vaz and Aoki Inoue, 2007; World Bank and IPEA, 2012). By expanding its aid to poor countries, Brazil could replicate its remarkable success in lifting many of its people out of poverty through skills development with a focus on support to unemployed youth, apprentices in the informal sector and smallholders.

China's investment in education and skills in developing countries appears to be dwarfed by that for infrastructure projects, which make up over 60% of its total development finance. Where education and training projects exist, they tend to centre on providing scholarships, sending Chinese teachers abroad, training workers in Chinese companies and building limited numbers of schools (China Information Office of the State Council, 2011). Through the Forum on China-Africa Cooperation, China has proposed putting more emphasis on human resource development by training 15,000 African professionals (FOCAC, 2009). This is unlikely to have a significant impact on those with low skills.

For emerging economies, as for some DAC donors, scholarships are an important component of support to education. Almost half of India's aid to education is allocated to higher education, mostly for scholarships to study in India (AidData, 2012). Around 6,000 scholarships a year are offered to developing country students (Agrawal, 2012). Brazil also offers scholarships for young people to study in Brazil, often in science and technology (Costa Vaz and Aoki Inoue, 2007). Scholarships for Africans to study in China are expected to expand significantly, as China pledged to double them from 2,000 to 4,000 a year between 2006 and 2009 (King, 2010).

For emerging donors such as Brazil, China and India to become important players in aid to skills development, they will need to ensure that their aid is targeted at disadvantaged young people, learning from their own experience of linking investment in skills development with labour market reforms and poverty reduction.

Extending private sector support to disadvantaged youth

Governments and aid donors can only go so far in fulfilling the wide range of training needs required. This leaves a gap that the private sector, as a key beneficiary of skills, should fill. To some extent it is already playing this role by providing on-the-job training. But this is likely to reach only a very small share of the disadvantaged young people who mainly work in the urban informal sector or in smallholder agriculture and non-farm small enterprises in rural areas.

There are other ways that private companies can help extend skills training for disadvantaged youth. This is not only a social responsibility but also a route to longer-term gains by creating a better skilled workforce, strengthening the economy and improving the climate for business.

Some multinational companies allocate part of their profits to programmes that reach young people with low skills outside the formal job market, through either corporate social responsibility activities or autonomous private foundations (see chapter 2). Skills development is one of the most popular aspects of the EFA agenda for companies and foundations to support, no doubt in part because they can

Brazil could replicate its success in skills for growth through its aid to poor countries

---

10. AidData does not provide a full picture of development assistance from non-DAC donors.

contribute their expertise and also directly see the benefits (van Fleet, 2012).

The International Youth Foundation, which was established in 1990 with funding from the Kellogg Foundation and now has multiple public and private sector funders, focuses on addressing the challenges and needs of out-of-school and at-risk youth through its Education and Employment Alliance programme. The programme has had activities in Egypt, Indonesia, Morocco, Pakistan and the Philippines, and 56% of its graduates have secured jobs (International Youth Foundation, 2012). The MasterCard Foundation is another notable example (Box 4.6).

In addition to global initiatives, regional and national philanthropists sometimes focus support on disadvantaged young people. Youth in the Arab States have particularly poor prospects of finding good jobs. Recognizing this, several foundations in the region seek to provide youth with the skills needed for the workplace. The Sawiris Foundation, one such initiative, has been active in Egypt since 2001. Its Yalla Neshtaghal in Ready-Made Garment programme is training 900 youths over 18 months, with graduates receiving a recognized qualification. The foundation works with national and regional companies; NGOs; all relevant government ministries, departments and agencies; and educational institutions (Sawiris Foundation for Social Development, 2012).

Elsewhere in the Arab States, Education for Employment is a network of affiliated foundations working in many countries. In Morocco, for example, the network aims to reach 15,500 unemployed and disadvantaged

The MasterCard Foundation gives US$20.5 million a year to youth skills training

---

Box 4.6: Private foundations can reach disadvantaged youth through productive partnerships

Some private foundations support innovation in ways that bridge the gap between skills and work. The MasterCard Foundation, for example, provides funding for programmes that help youth gain the skills they need to find employment. It adopts a three-pronged approach: extending secondary school provision, providing skills opportunities to out-of-school youth and linking youth with jobs. Some of this support is targeted at disadvantaged young people. With an annual budget of US$20.5 million, providing commitments over four to ten years, it is one of the largest international foundations working on these issues.

In partnership with the MacArthur Foundation and the Douglas B. Marshall, Jr. Family Foundation, the MasterCard Foundation intends to promote innovation for girls' secondary schooling in India, Kenya, Nigeria, Rwanda, Uganda and the United Republic of Tanzania. The programme budget amounts to US$5 million. While it is a significant programme for a private foundation and has important benefits in terms of coordination, it is small relative to the scale needed. Based on an estimated unit cost of US$163 for lower secondary school, it would reach around 30,000 young people – a small number in comparison to the 650,000 out-of-school adolescents in Uganda alone.

Programmes that enhance the relevance of formal technical and vocational education and training have been supported by the MasterCard Foundation in partnership with national foundations. Support to the CAP Foundation in India has helped improve technical and vocational education and training through market scans and advice on demand-side training needs, as well as the establishment of structures for mentoring, internships and placements for trainees, focusing on disadvantaged youth. A reported 79% of completers have found jobs.

The foundation also supports successful second-chance initiatives, including those run by NGOs such as Camfed, an international NGO working for girls' education in Africa. Another programme, in which the foundation is partnered with Swisscontact, a private sector organization for development cooperation, aims to reach 16- to 25-year-olds in rural areas of Uganda and the United Republic of Tanzania who have never attended secondary school, with a particular focus on females.

Support from the MasterCard Foundation goes some way towards addressing disadvantages that young people face. Given the large numbers of people in such situations, there is far more that foundations need to do. In global terms, their contributions are a drop in the ocean compared with the amount provided by even the smallest aid donor, and the impact of their programmes has not yet been sufficiently evaluated.

Sources: CAP Foundation (2011); EPDC and UNESCO (2009); MasterCard Foundation (2012a, 2012b, 2012c); Van Fleet (2012).

youth by providing employability training. The programme draws on the expertise of several large corporations. Cooperating employers have pledged to hire a large proportion of the trainees. Although this programme is in its infancy, it illustrates the potential for partnerships that draw on partners' expertise in particular areas (MasterCard Foundation, 2011).

These examples show that the private sector can play an innovative role when foundations work strategically in partnership with other organizations to reach disadvantaged young people. To make an impact on the scale required, however, they need to put in place mechanisms for independent evaluation of their work, and drastically increase their funding to ensure that it goes beyond limited support to individual projects.

Training funds offer a way to channel skills finance

Given the budgetary constraints most governments face and the importance of maintaining their focus on foundation skills through formal primary and lower secondary education, countries need to identify alternative sources of funding for skills development targeting disadvantaged youth, beyond the formal education system. Training funds have emerged as a way to leverage financing for skills development outside normal government budgetary channels, including by raising funds from enterprises to finance public training institutions (Johanson, 2009).[11] Experience shows that such funds have the potential to reach disadvantaged young people, including those working in the urban informal sector, but need to operate on a much larger scale (Johanson, 2009; Ziderman, 2003).

Training funds bring together finance from various sources, including governments, enterprises and donors, which can be allocated according to national policies and priorities. This institutional framework can prevent the fragmentation often apparent in skills training programmes and target those most in need. Training funds also facilitate coordination among interested parties, including those involved in funding as well as groups such as trade unions, to ensure that training meets labour market demands.

A study commissioned for this Report identified fifty-three national training funds in upper middle to low income countries (Aboagye et al., 2012). A more detailed review of training funds in five countries[12] showed how they could be used to extend training to disadvantaged people. Cambodia's training funds, for example, delivered short-term employment for disadvantaged groups, including school dropouts, primarily in rural areas (ADB, 2005). Côte d'Ivoire's training funds traditionally focused on the formal sector, but a seven-year contribution from the World Bank was used to target women, high school graduates and early school leavers who lacked skills to join the workforce. Papua New Guinea's funds also targeted a range of disadvantaged groups, including the unemployed and underemployed, with specific targets for training women and young people aged 16 to 28 (ADB, 2008; World Bank, 2003).

Training funds can be used to mobilize resources from the formal sector to support skills development for disadvantaged workers in the informal sector, where those who are self-employed in subsistence activities, as well as most micro and small enterprises, are seldom able to finance training themselves (Almeida and Aterido, 2010). Benin's Fund for the Development of Vocational Training and Apprenticeship, Burkina Faso's Support Fund for Vocational Training and Apprenticeship and Mali's Promotion of Employment and Vocational Training Fund were established in the late 1990s and early 2000s with support from France, the World Bank and other donors. Funded by payroll levies on formal businesses, they have provided training to both formal and informal enterprises, supporting the introduction of dual apprenticeships based on traditional apprenticeship systems.

These funds have succeeded in pooling different types of resources, with formal sector employers supporting the funding of training for informal sector workers. A lack of involvement by employers, weakness on the part of some unions and rigid administrative procedures have prevented full use of the funds, which in some cases were appropriated for other government expenditure. They have also suffered from a lack

Training funds can mobilize resources from the private sector for disadvantaged youth

---

11. This section draws on Aboagye et al. (2012).

12. Cambodia, Côte d'Ivoire, Papua New Guinea, Togo and Tunisia.

79% found employment three months after completing Nepal's training fund programmes

of the expertise necessary to design training programmes adapted to the needs of specific sectors; moreover, the demand for training was sometimes too weak for providers to invest in costly equipment when it was needed (Johanson, 2009; Walther and Gauron, 2006).

Brazil's SENAI, the national apprenticeship agency created in 1942, has been more successful, influencing the design of funds in other Latin American countries. It draws on resources raised through several sector levies: on industrial companies (1% of monthly payroll, plus 0.5% on companies with more than 500 employees), commercial and sector service enterprises (1%), land transport companies, including self-employed taxi and truck owners (1%), and agricultural companies (2.5% on the sale of agricultural products). An additional 0.3% payroll levy is imposed on all companies to finance technical assistance for small and micro enterprises (Johanson, 2009). In 2010, SENAI had 2.4 million registered trainees, up by 59% from the previous year, making it one of the largest industrial apprenticeship services in the developing world (World Bank and IPEA, 2012).

Mobilizing funds from the private sector can be difficult. Some formal sector companies may be successful in opposing levies or otherwise avoid paying. In Cambodia, employers rejected a proposal to introduce a levy on payrolls, partly because of concerns about the government's capacity to collect and disburse funds (Johanson, 2009). The experience in Tunisia shows, however, that it is possible to operate a training fund sustainably on a large scale by drawing on resources raised nationally (Box 4.7).

Raising funds through payroll taxes can only be effective if there is a significant formal sector to be taxed, and if the government has the capacity to tax it. In many poor countries, this is not the case. Many rely, therefore, on a diversified funding base. Of the fifty-three training funds reviewed, most drew on a range of sources, including multi-donor funding. Donors can play a key role by working with governments to coordinate their funds to offer training using private sector providers with direct links to the labour market. This ensures that training meets labour market needs.

Nepal's Employment Fund is an example. It is a multi-donor basket fund established in 2008 by the government and three donors: Switzerland, the United Kingdom and the World Bank (under its Adolescent Girls Employment Initiative). Through private sector training and employment service providers, the fund provides short-term, market-oriented skills training, and business and life skills training, for unemployed youth – with a particular focus on disadvantaged 16- to 35-year-olds, notably women and those of low caste status – in order to link them to gainful employment. Thirty-two private sector providers offer training and employment services for 13,500 youths throughout the country in sixty-five occupations. In 2010, nearly all trainees took examinations set by the National Skills Testing Board, with an 87% pass rate. Of the 11,418 youths who had completed training by the end of the year, 79% had found gainful employment within three months of completion (Helvetas, 2011).

Some training funds depend on donor financing, which poses a risk that they will have to cease operations once the donor funds run out. Togo's National Training Fund, supporting apprentices in the informal sector, ceased when World Bank funding ended. In Cambodia, a training fund established in 1997 to reach marginalized groups drastically reduced operations once funding from the Asian Development Bank expired (Ziderman, 2003).

Training funds have not generally succeeded in reaching the large numbers needing support, in part because of bottlenecks in disbursement. Papua New Guinea's Skills Development Trust Fund, established as part of an Asian Development Bank programme, aimed to provide training in the informal sector. The funding application process took between two and ten months to be approved, rather than the expected two weeks. Conflict among stakeholders on how the funds were to be disbursed led to failure in meeting training objectives (ADB, 2008). Although it aimed to train at least 40,000 young people by 2005 in computer skills, bookkeeping, tourism and welding, the programme managed to train only 2,500 (Boeha et al., 2007). Training funds in Cambodia suffered similar problems: inefficiencies in the Ministry of Labour and Vocational Training's procedures led to slow

Box 4.7: Tunisia's training fund reaches large numbers of unemployed youth

Tunisia's National Employment Fund (Fonds National de l'Emploi) was established in 1999. Its aim was to reduce unemployment – then running at 16% – by preparing the most vulnerable young jobseekers for the labour market and closing skills gaps. Reaching 100,000 beneficiaries annually, the fund has three main sources of finance: private, tax-deductible gifts from individuals and corporations; a proportion of the benefits from privatizing state assets; and earmarked tax revenue. Funding, provided through allocations in the annual budget, amounted to around US$143 million in 2010, or 0.42% of GDP, making this more sustainable than some other training funds.

The fund adopted three methods to increase the job chances of those who lacked primary education or had not completed secondary education:

■ *On-site training programmes* offer nine months within a participating institution (public or private), carrying out labour such as construction, landscaping or cleaning. Beneficiaries receive a daily stipend of US$3.50 and acquire a marketable skill in addition to securing a guaranteed limited income for a certain period of time.

■ *Vocational apprenticeships* offer a chance for those aged 15 to 20 with no qualifications to work with a qualified instructor at a public or private institution to develop basic manual skills. Instructors are paid US$8 to US$13 per student per month. Students receive US$8 to US$22 per month, depending on the location, type and duration of the apprenticeship.

■ *Microenterprise and self-employment development* offer individuals with no qualifications a chance to receive a loan of up to US$13,000 for approved small business projects from the Banque Tunisienne de Solidarité.

The annual number of beneficiaries rose steadily from 41,500 in 2000 to nearly 111,000 in 2010. Even at the outset, the number of beneficiaries was equivalent to 27% of the official total of unemployed. Several factors contributed to this success, notably effective management of the funds and a commitment to yearly allocation in the national budget through taxes and levies. The revolution in Tunisia, driven in part by high unemployment, showed that there is far more to be done, however, to ensure that all young people have the skills needed for good jobs.

Sources: AfDB (2011); ODI (2006); Paciello (2011).

Tunisia's training fund reached over one-quarter of its unemployed

financial transfers and delays in disbursement, limiting the numbers of those who were willing to engage with the fund (ADB, 2009b).

Training funds offer the opportunity to mobilize finance outside constrained national budgets to reach disadvantaged youth. Scaling them up can be challenging, although the example of Tunisia suggests that it is not impossible. The full range of interested parties, including government, employers, labour and training providers, should play a part in administering the funds. Ensuring that training providers receive finance on time is important if programmes are to be sustainable and reach disadvantaged groups. Funds must have sufficient administrative capacity to collect revenue, process applications for funding and handle disbursement quickly and efficiently in order to reach disadvantaged young people.

Conclusion

National development strategies need to identify and set targets for meeting the youth skills gap, including programmes aimed at the most disadvantaged in urban and rural areas. Governments and aid donors are making considerable contributions towards skills development, but need to reallocate funds to ensure that all young people have foundation skills. Aid resources currently spent on educating students in higher education in donor countries should be redirected towards skills development programmes within developing countries. Training funds are a promising approach to boost funding from the private sector for informal sector workers. Taken together, these measures could make a significant contribution to youth well-being and economic prosperity. ☐

Chapter 5
Secondary education – paving the way to work

Students attending practical mechanical training at a technical college in Viet Nam.

This picture was selected from the winners of the UNESCO-UNEVOC Photo Competition 2012: Work has many faces.

2 0 1 2

Education for All Global Monitoring Report

To be able to adapt to the workplace and fast-evolving technologies in competitive economies, all young people need to acquire the skills that a good quality primary and secondary education can offer. This chapter looks at ways to increase enrolment and reduce the numbers dropping out of secondary school. It identifies successful ways to link schools with work, and shows how flexible learning options for acquiring skills outside of school can complement a formal general education.

Introduction

Secondary school is an important channel through which young people acquire skills that improve opportunities for good jobs. High quality secondary education that caters for the widest possible range of abilities, interests and backgrounds is vital not just to set young people on the path to the world of work, but also to give countries the educated workforce they need to compete in today's technologically driven world.

Lower secondary school extends and consolidates the basic skills learned in primary school; upper secondary school deepens general education and adds technical and vocational skills. Neither is possible, however, without ensuring that all children complete a good quality primary education as the first priority in building the skills that individuals, societies and economies need.

Beyond the challenge of universal primary education, in the world's poorest countries there are still significant barriers preventing many young people from entering secondary education; worldwide, 71 million adolescents are not in school. In countries where secondary enrolment is already high, the priority is to assure the quality and relevance of secondary education, which continues to require improvement.

It is not enough, however, simply to increase access, quality and relevance across the board. In secondary education, the risk of reproducing or reinforcing inequalities is high, because it has a dual function: providing skills for early employment for some, selecting and preparing others for further education, based on their interests and academic ability.

If disadvantaged youth are to have similar chances as youth from rich backgrounds to gain access to good jobs on the basis of merit and not privilege, secondary education has to be made more equitable and more inclusive, offering the widest possible range of opportunities in order to meet young people's differing abilities, interests and backgrounds. Achieving equity and inclusiveness

is important not only because education is a universal right, but also because countries need an educated workforce to compete in the modern global economy.

In examining the contribution made by formal education systems to skills development at secondary level, this chapter focuses in particular on disadvantaged youth. It identifies the patterns of secondary enrolment and the dynamics of inequality and marginalization operating within education systems that have tended to limit access for disadvantaged youth. It explores how some countries have structured and delivered secondary education to achieve more equitable access to skills development. Finally, it discusses policies – both within secondary education and alongside it – that have facilitated young people's access to good jobs.

Global inequalities in secondary education

The government needs to increase the number of government training schools in technical and vocational fields to create chances for many to get skills and education. Opportunities to be hired will come next.
– young man, Ethiopia

Formal secondary education is divided into two stages – a lower secondary level that aims at consolidating and expanding the basic skills acquired in primary school, and an upper secondary level that builds on these foundations to prepare young people for the world of work or further education and training.

Enrolment rates in secondary education have been increasing in the last decade, although huge differences remain between regions and countries (see Chapter 1). Disparities in access also persist within countries, driven by factors such as wealth, location and gender.

One way of gauging the progress that countries have made in offering young people skills beyond the foundations is to compare enrolment ratios in lower secondary school with those in upper secondary school. Some countries have very low

71 million adolescents of lower secondary school age are not in school

Figure 5.1: Some young people do not even enter secondary school, and many do not complete it
Lower secondary gross enrolment ratio and proxy for progression from lower to upper secondary school, by country, 2010

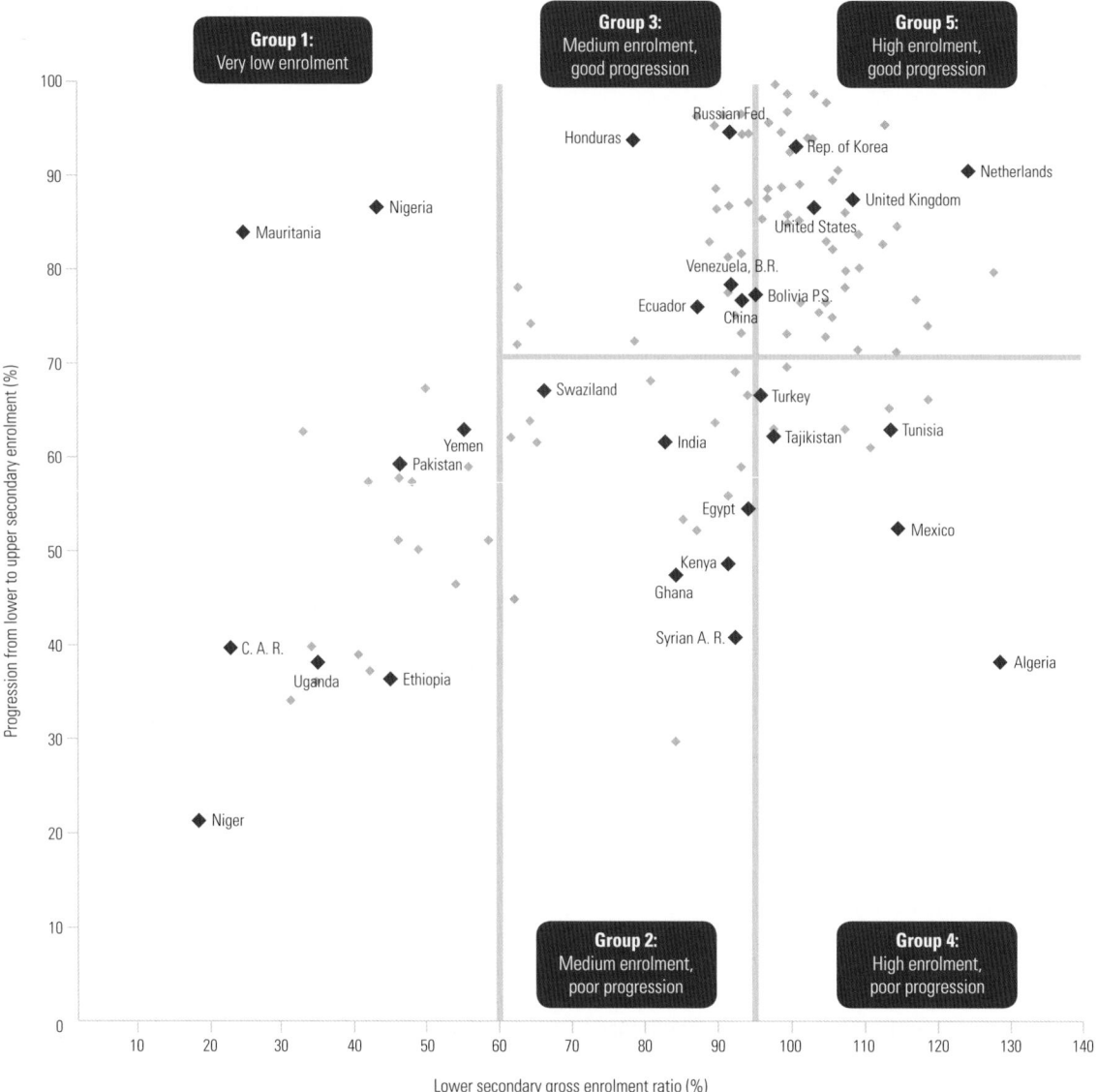

Notes: The rate of progression to upper secondary school is a proxy indicator for progression from lower secondary to upper secondary. It is measured by the proportion of upper secondary to lower secondary gross enrolment ratios. In an ideal system where all lower secondary students continue to upper secondary, the ratio equals 1. Honduras has a lower secondary gross enrolment ratio of 75% and an upper secondary gross enrolment ratio of 71%. The rate of progression is calculated to be 95%, indicating that most of those who have the chance to go to lower secondary are likely to continue to upper secondary. In Egypt, the gross enrolment ratio at lower secondary level is 94%. With a gross enrolment ratio of 51% at the upper secondary level, Egypt's progression rate from lower to upper secondary is estimated to be about 0.54 (51/94). This suggests that, while most young people have the opportunity to participate in lower secondary education, only around half are able to continue to upper secondary.
Source: Annex, Statistical Table 7.

enrolment ratios in lower secondary education, while others have achieved near universal enrolment at that level (Figure 5.1). Even in countries that have achieved high levels of lower secondary enrolment, many young people are not able to continue into upper secondary school. Improving the transition to upper secondary is

a challenge not just for poorer countries; some rich countries are still struggling to make upper secondary near universal.[1]

---

1. Data from official sources on the transition rate to upper secondary school, and on upper secondary school completion, are difficult to obtain across countries. The proxy measure on progression between these levels, therefore, has been calculated as a proxy for transition.

Countries with the relevant data on the transition to upper secondary can be divided into five groups according to enrolment at each level.

■ *Group 1: Very low enrolment – a problem faced by many low income countries.* Many young people in poor countries, including many of those affected by conflict, have little chance of entering lower secondary school. The gross enrolment ratio at lower secondary level is below 60% in nineteen sub-Saharan African countries with data, as well as some countries in the Arab States and South and West Asia. In the Central African Republic, Mauritania and the Niger, lower secondary gross enrolment ratios rose from 19% to 26%.

For many countries in this group, participation in secondary education is severely limited by the low numbers completing primary school. In the Niger, the reason for such low participation in secondary school is because the primary net enrolment ratio is just 62%.

The lower secondary gross enrolment ratio in Nigeria is similar to that of poorer countries such as Ethiopia, although the rate of progression to upper secondary is higher than in emerging economies such as China, India or Turkey. This suggests that secondary education in Nigeria is highly inequitable, with only a minority having access to lower secondary but most of those who do enter being able to continue to upper secondary.

Girls are less likely than boys to make it to lower secondary school in most countries where overall enrolment is low. For example, in the Central African Republic in 2011 only one girl was in lower secondary school for every two boys.

While some young people unable to make it into secondary school in these countries have opportunities outside the formal education system (see Chapters 6 and 7), it is alarming that many of them are entering the world of work without even foundation skills.

■ *Group 2: Medium enrolment, but poor progression – the problem of early school leaving.* In the second group of countries, gross enrolment ratios in lower secondary

education are higher, ranging from 60% to 95%, but progression to upper secondary is limited. This is the case in some countries where the benefits of recent growth have not been evenly spread, such as Egypt and India.

Some sub-Saharan African countries that are beginning to experience strong growth, including Ghana and Kenya, are also in this group. An expansion in primary enrolment together with good economic prospects are helping to increase lower secondary enrolment, which could feed through to upper secondary enrolment in the coming years

■ *Group 3: Medium enrolment and good progression – balancing access across levels of education.* A small number of countries have achieved a more balanced pattern of access between lower secondary and upper secondary education, even though they have not yet reached universal provision. Among them are several Latin American countries, including the Plurinational State of Bolivia, Ecuador, Honduras and the Bolivarian Republic of Venezuela.

■ *Group 4: High enrolment but poor progression – the challenge of persistent inequalities.* Around one-third of the world's countries that have data already offer lower secondary education to the vast majority of adolescents, with gross enrolment ratios exceeding 95%, but many of those adolescents do not continue to upper secondary education. Some countries in the Arab States, such as Algeria and Tunisia, have low gross enrolment ratios at upper secondary level despite high lower secondary enrolment.

■ *Group 5: High enrolment and good progression – even in rich countries, some students leave school early.* High participation in upper secondary education is the norm in many rich countries. In some of these countries, however, early school leaving remains a problem. In some European countries, as many as one young person in five does not complete upper secondary school (Box 5.1).

Secondary education should equalize young people's life chances by developing their transferable and technical and vocational

In some European countries, one young person in five does not complete upper secondary school

Box 5.1: Early school leaving is a challenge in Europe

Early school leaving has been recognized by member states of the European Union as a major problem for societies and for individuals. European Union countries have set themselves a target of reducing the proportion of those who only have lower secondary education to less than 10% by 2020. On average, 14% of young people in European Union countries have lower secondary education, at most (Figure 5.2).

South European countries are particularly affected. In Spain, as many as one in three do not complete upper secondary education, which is a cause for concern given the severity of the economic crisis and an unemployment level among young people of 51% in March 2012. The country's education system reproduces existing patterns of disadvantage. Having a mother with less than secondary education increases the risk of being out of school at ages 16 and 17 by roughly 14%, with a slightly larger impact for male teenagers. Other aspects of family context also have a significant influence: the absence of the mother from the household increases the probability of being an early school leaver by 22%.

A study in Germany, where around 12% of students leave school early, showed that performance at school had an impact. Mathematics and language skills, as well as

attitudes towards school and life in general, had a considerable influence on the probability of dropping out, with an increase of school grades, for instance, reducing the risk of dropout by up to nine percentage points.

Among Europe's minorities, Roma children have particularly low chances of completing secondary education in Central and Eastern Europe: only 6% of Roma aged 14 to 18 are enrolled in secondary education in Bulgaria, and less than 7.3% in Romania.

In most EU countries, boys are more at risk of leaving school early than girls. In Greece, for example, 15% of boys do not complete secondary school, compared with 10% of girls. In some circumstances, however, girls are more likely to drop out. Teenage mothers are particularly vulnerable. Most already have a history of poor educational achievement and come from disadvantaged backgrounds. In the United Kingdom, for instance, around 3.6% of those aged 15 to 17 become pregnant. Pregnancy decreases the probability of post-16 schooling by as much as 24%.

Sources: Coneus et al. (2009); Dawson and Hosie (2005); European Commission (2010); Fernández-Macías et al. (forthcoming); GHK (2005); Lamb (2011); Lyche (2010); OECD (2012b); UK Office for National Statistics (2012); World Bank (2008b).

Figure 5.2: Many European Union countries are not on target to reduce early school leaving

Percentage of the population aged 18 to 24 with at most lower secondary education and not in further education or training, by gender, 2010

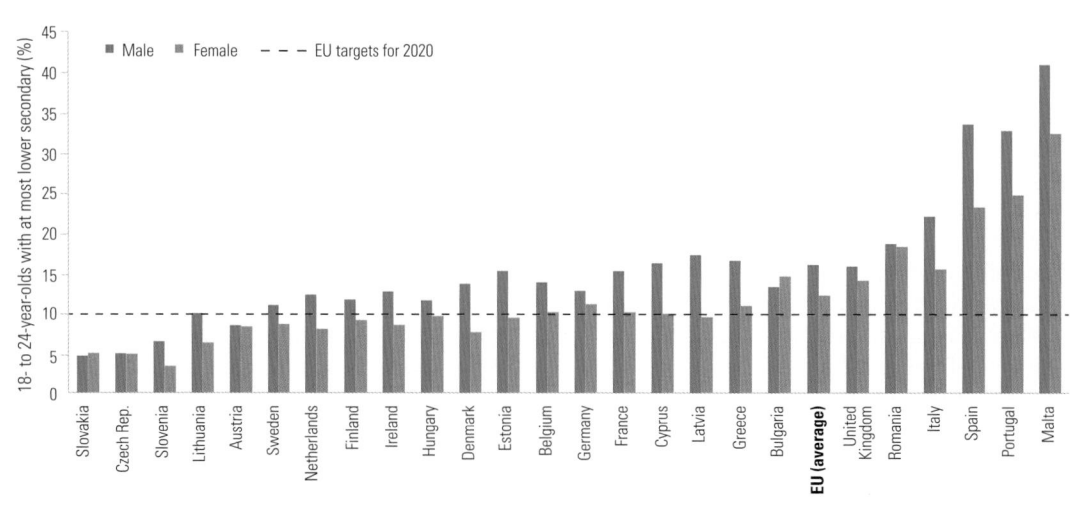

Source: Eurostat (2010).

skills so that they can secure good jobs. Depending on countries' starting points, however, they face very different challenges in reaching this goal. Poor countries need to overcome barriers to access in order to get more children into lower secondary school. All countries need to ensure that the education provided is relevant to the skills needs of young people, many of whom are likely to leave school to start work rather than go on to further education. Rich countries that have succeeded in getting most children through the secondary system still need to support the sizeable minority who leave early.

Removing the barriers to secondary education

The problem in this area is that while there is only one high school, there are a lot of students. There are no government technical and vocational schools in the area except private ones. We cannot afford to pay [for those].

— young woman, Ethiopia

In many poor countries that need to expand secondary enrolment from a low level (group 1, Figure 5.1), the immediate problem is still ensuring that children complete the primary cycle. For children who do complete primary school, the costs of secondary schooling can be prohibitive. More secondary schools are located in urban areas, limiting access to those from rural poor households who cannot afford the cost of transport. Social and cultural barriers can prevent girls from continuing with schooling once they reach adolescence. Governments need to carry out reforms to specifically address these barriers, and so ensure that young people consolidate foundation skills.

Linking lower secondary to primary education

Primary education is no longer enough to give young people a chance for decent work. Technological change is demanding stronger foundation skills. But for children in poor countries, the transition from primary to secondary education is not smooth. Only around

one in three children in the last grade of primary school enter secondary general education in Angola and Burundi, for example. Some sub-Saharan African countries have boosted lower secondary enrolment by introducing universal basic education that links primary and lower secondary education. Countries that have followed this path include Botswana, the Gambia, Ghana, Kenya, Namibia, Rwanda, South Africa and Zambia. Delivering lower secondary education at the same site as primary schooling can pose problems if expanding infrastructure is not adequately factored into planning, as the example of Zambia shows (Box 5.2).

These reforms can be undermined by assessment practices at the end of the primary cycle that are designed to select a small minority for lower secondary education. In the United Republic of Tanzania, for example, fewer than

In Burundi, only one in three in the last grade of primary school enter secondary general education

---

Box 5.2: Challenges of linking primary and secondary schooling in Zambia

With a longstanding commitment to providing all children with a basic education of nine years, Zambia has made progress on many fronts. Participation in primary education has reached 91%. The gross enrolment ratio in lower secondary school rose from 27% in 1999 to 72% in 2010. Even so, Zambia remains some distance from achieving its ambitions.

After the basic education goals were adopted, primary and lower secondary grades were merged within the same 'basic schools' starting in 1996, with upper secondary schools phasing out the lower secondary grades. This put additional pressure on primary schools already coping with rising enrolment – pressure that grew further after 2002 as the withdrawal of fees contributed to a sharp increase in school participation. One symptom of the difficulty schools and teachers face in managing the surge in enrolment is that the transition from grade 7 – the last year of primary, when pupils sit a leaving examination – continues to be a bottleneck, with one in three still not making it to grade 8, the first year of lower secondary.

Progress has also been held back by major shortages of schools and classrooms; by 2006, only 30% of basic schools were offering grades 8 and 9. In addition, many of those teaching lower secondary school classes had only been trained to teach primary grades.

Zambia's experience does not present a case against universalizing lower secondary education. It does, however, underline the importance of sequencing reform and putting in place a structure that facilitates progression through the full cycle.

Sources: Bennell et al. (2005); UNESCO-IBE (2011); World Bank (2006c).

Rwanda is aiming to achieve 12 years of free education for all within seven years

half of grade 7 children passed the Primary School Leaving Examination in 2010. Only 41% of those who reached the last grade of primary school in 2009 made the transition to secondary education (Sumra and Rajani, 2006; UNICEF, 2011a).

In general, however, this strategy has succeeded in improving accessibility, provided it has been linked with wider reforms. In Rwanda, for instance, the introduction of a nine-year basic education cycle and the elimination of fees for lower secondary school in 2009 boosted the number of lower secondary students by 27% within a year, leading to an increase in the gross enrolment ratio to 47% by 2011, compared with 28% in 2008. In addition, the curriculum was redesigned to focus on fewer core subjects and a new assessment system was introduced. The difficulty of accommodating the growing number of children put the quality of education at risk, however. This was partially addressed by introducing a double-shift system and building over 3,000 new classrooms between September 2009 and January 2010 (Global Partnership for Education, 2011; Lynd, 2010; World Bank, 2011d).

To smooth the transition from primary school, some countries have abolished examinations at the end of the primary cycle that had limited access to lower secondary. The Gambia increased lower secondary enrolment in part by phasing out such an examination in 2002. Enrolment in lower secondary education increased from 44% in 2002 to 57% in 2003 and 63% in 2004.

Making secondary education affordable

I had no money for books or a uniform. The financial situation of the family was bad. I had to supplement family income by working for daily wages, for the very survival of the family. Earning money was more important for me than going to school.

— young man, India

Many countries continue to charge secondary school fees, which are sometimes substantial and can be a major barrier for the poorest households. Abolishing fees can be a key way of improving access for children from

disadvantaged groups, as evidence from some Asian and African countries that have expanded secondary education suggests. Cambodia, the Lao People's Democratic Republic, Malaysia, Mongolia and Thailand have abolished lower secondary fees (Caillods, 2010) as have some sub-Saharan African countries, including Ghana and Uganda in 2007. In Uganda, abolishing lower secondary school fees particularly increased the enrolment of girls from poor households, who had been more likely to be out of school. Girls were about 49% more likely to enrol in secondary education in 2009 than in 2005 (Asankha and Takashi, 2011).

Kenya went a step further, with an ambitious programme abolishing fees for all secondary school grades. Enrolment rose immediately, but not for everyone; the government needs to make sure its increased investment is geared to give poor rural children and girls just as much chance as others (Box 5.3). Rwanda is also taking this path from 2012, aiming to achieve twelve years of free education for all within seven years (Mugisha, 2012; Rwanda Ministry of Education, 2012).

Instead of abolishing tuition fees for all, some countries have opted to reduce or eliminate fees only for specific groups, such as girls, rural dwellers or members of ethnic minorities. Under Nepal's Tenth Plan (2002–2007), children from the Dalit community, the Janajati ethnic groups and households living below the poverty line are exempt from fees (ILO Nepal, 2005; Panta and Pokhrel, 2011). In Bangladesh, stipends for secondary school girls have been so successful that there are now more girls than boys in secondary school (see goal 5 policy focus).

Even when fees are abolished, other costs can far exceed family incomes. When there are no secondary schools nearby, for example, transport or boarding costs can be prohibitive, as Kenya's experience illustrates (Box 5.3). Measures that aim to reduce the wider costs of education can be effective in increasing access for disadvantaged youth.

Conditional cash transfer programmes have become popular following early successes in some Latin American countries. On average, such programmes have been found to raise

Box 5.3: Abolishing secondary school fees in Kenya

Some countries in sub-Saharan Africa are considering making secondary education free. Kenya has already moved in this direction, abolishing fees for upper secondary school in 2008. The initial response was impressive. Enrolments rose from 1.2 million in 2007 to nearly 1.4 million in 2008, reflecting the large cost barriers that parents had been facing, especially in rural areas. Kenya continues to have serious problems in making sure that all children benefit, however - problems that will require fixing at primary level.

Fee abolition is part of a broader strategy to triple secondary enrolments by 2015. What are the prospects of Kenya achieving this target? Much will depend on progress at primary level. Many from the poorest households do not make it beyond primary school: one in three of poor young women had dropped out before reaching lower secondary in 2009. Moreover, while the abolition of secondary school fees reduced the costs for households by 58% for day schools and

31% for boarding schools, indirect costs are still twelve to twenty times as much as the monthly income of parents in rural areas, meaning secondary school remains out of reach for the poorest households.

Abolishing fees has required allocating the equivalent of US$164 per pupil annually to compensate secondary schools for the loss in income – ten times the amount per pupil annually received by primary schools. But only a minority of children from poor rural households or urban slums – who still have to pay for uniforms and books – get to secondary school, so public spending on secondary education still heavily favours the non-poor. The increased investment in secondary education would be more equitably distributed if it were geared towards remote rural areas, slum settlements and pastoralist communities.

Sources: Mawathe (2008); Kenya Ministry of Education (2005); Njoroge and Kerei (2012); Ohba (2009); Onsomu et al. (2006); Oyaro (2008); Somerset (2009); (UIS, 2012a).

enrolment at secondary level by three to twelve percentage points in developing countries (Slavin, 2009). The success of these Latin American programmes is encouraging some sub-Saharan African countries to emulate it, sometimes with strong positive effects. In Malawi, cash transfers to teenage girls and young women reduced dropout rates from 11% to 6% and multiplied by 2.5 the share of re-enrolment of girls who had dropped out before the launch of the programme (Baird et al., 2009). Scholarships granted to poor girls at the end of primary school in Cambodia were also found to lower the barrier to secondary education, increasing attendance by 30% (Caillods, 2010).

The most disadvantaged youth are not always aware that they may be eligible for such programmes and application processes may present barriers for poor households. In Kenya, for example, the need to photocopy an application form has sometimes prevented poor families in rural areas from applying for government scholarships (Ohba, 2009). Where properly implemented, however, grants and scholarships are powerful ways of giving young

people from poor families a better chance of getting to secondary school.

Young mothers need support to return to school

I was engaged to someone and he refused to let me complete my education, so I stopped.
– young woman, Egypt

For young women in low income countries, it is not only poverty that leads some to drop out. Deeply engrained social, cultural and economic barriers, such as early marriage, may also prevent them from continuing education. More than one in ten young women aged 15 to 19 are pregnant or mothers in sub-Saharan Africa, Latin America and South Asia, with as many as 30% or more in some countries, such as Bangladesh, Liberia and Mozambique (World Bank, 2010c).

In the Plurinational State of Bolivia, Colombia, the Dominican Republic, Haiti, Nicaragua and Peru, teenage mothers have an average of 1.8 to 2.8 fewer years of education than other girls and are fourteen times as likely to drop out of school. Even if they had attended school before they

More than 1 in 10 Latin American young women aged 15 to 19 are pregnant or mothers

became pregnant, up to 89% are out of school, compared with 35% of girls who did not have children in their teenage years (Näslund-Hadley and Binstock, 2010).

Education is good protection against early marriage

Education itself is good protection against early marriage for teenage girls. The median age for marriage among women with a secondary education, compared with those who have no education or only a primary school education, is over two years higher in Bangladesh and Nigeria, three years higher in Ethiopia and Mali, and four years higher in Chad (Brown, 2012).

Including basic life skills for sexual and reproductive health and HIV prevention has proved effective in preventing early pregnancy and reducing the risk of sexually transmissible diseases. The Better Life Options Programme for adolescent girls in India offers a combination of skills: literacy and vocational training, support to enter and stay in formal school, family life education and leadership training. An impact assessment found significant benefits. The share of those married at age 18 or above was 37% among graduates but only 26% in a control group, and more graduates were reported to use contraception. Among unmarried girls, graduates were 65% more likely to be aware of AIDS and 17% more likely to know how to prevent HIV and AIDS. These differences were even greater among married respondents (CEDPA, 2001).

In some developing countries, including Botswana, Malawi, Namibia, Swaziland and Zambia, pregnant girls are excluded from school after giving birth, for a period that ranges from at least six months to eighteen months. These girls are often not allowed to return to the same school after giving birth. In countries where schools are legally obliged to readmit young mothers, such as Cameroon, South Africa and most countries in Latin America, social stigma and the absence of educational, financial and psychological support make it difficult to return (Hubbard, 2008).

Even where the law has changed to assure the right to education of young mothers, more has to be done to empower them to take advantage of that right. Recognizing this need, since 1978 the Women's Centre of Jamaica

Foundation has provided all-round support to help mostly poor pregnant girls and mothers under age 16, including food and transport costs, so they can re-enter school after giving birth. The programme has been partly funded by the government since 1991, although recent budgetary cuts have forced the foundation to reduce its activities. Over 1,000 young mothers take part in life skills and school re-entry programmes each year. Evaluations in the late 1990s showed that the programmes increased the likelihood of young mothers completing high school from 20% to 32% (Advocates for Youth, 2012; Barnett et al., 1996; Drayton et al., 2000; ECLAC, 2007; Tomlinson, 2011).

A survey conducted by the Forum for African Women Educationalists in Zambia shows how a combination of communication activities, legislative change and local training for teachers and students can change attitudes towards school re-entry. While 69% of teachers were against school re-entry for pregnant girls in 2001, 84% expressed a positive attitude after receiving training in 2004. Opposition also decreased among parents, from 53% to 25% (FAWE, 2004).

Making secondary education more relevant to the world of work

Lessons like history, you sit there, like, 'why am I here?' It didn't interest me. Why do I need to know about Henry VIII? It's never going to come up in the workplace, is it? Writing reports and letters – that's important, and ICT … you're always going to use a computer.
　　　　　　　　　　 – young woman, United Kingdom

If adolescents feel that secondary education lacks meaning or is not preparing them adequately for life and work, a gradual process of disengagement can set in that undermines their learning or leads them to drop out. Making secondary education more inclusive reduces the risk that they will join the millions of young people in the world who leave school without the skills required for good jobs or further training.

Some countries have made secondary education more equitable and more relevant to the world of work by diversifying the curriculum to cater for a wider range of interests and abilities. They have also struck a good balance between technical, vocational and general subjects, ensured that these subjects build on foundation skills, and smoothed the school-to-work transition by emphasizing transferable skills.

Many countries that have achieved high upper secondary enrolment, such as the Netherlands, the Republic of Korea and the United States, have made great strides in these areas. Some middle income countries, including Brazil, China and India, are using similar measures to expand secondary education.

Lower secondary: a common curriculum to equip all with core skills

A vital first step in making sure that secondary education offers the most opportunities to the widest range of students, including those from disadvantaged backgrounds, is to provide a common core curriculum that consolidates foundation skills.

Providing a common curriculum for all learners up to age 15, rather than sorting students into streams according to academic performance, is a better way of ensuring that all students acquire core skills. International and national comparisons in OECD countries show that the earlier such selection occurs, the more learning achievement is correlated with students' socio-economic background (Field et al., 2007; Woessmann, 2009).

When students at greater risk of school failure are grouped together, lower expectations, a less stimulating learning environment and peer effects often diminish their learning achievement. Inequalities in reading performance are wider in systems that group students early according to ability, as in the Czech Republic, Germany and Greece, whereas they decrease most in countries with a comprehensive system, such as Canada, New Zealand and Turkey (Hanushek and Woessmann, 2005; Hattie, 2009; OECD, 2010b). In Poland, delaying grouping of students by ability by one year before the age of 15 led to an increase in students' performance and

a significant decrease in the share of low performing students who were typically enrolled in vocational schools, from 21.4% in 2000 to 15% in 2003 (Wiśniewski 2007).

Some low and middle income countries, such as Botswana, Ghana, South Africa and Uganda, have developed a common curriculum framework together with new assessment practices, learning materials and teacher training activities (Hoppers, 2008). This has allowed schools to concentrate on core skills, including literacy and numeracy, while offering extracurricular activities to meet the wider needs and interests of their students. Botswana, for example, reformed its basic education system in 1995 to offer a core curriculum for all learners at lower secondary level. Core subjects undertaken by all students, irrespective of ability, include languages, sciences, social studies and practical subjects such as agriculture and technology. Practical subjects are aimed not only at mastering a particular trade, but also at fostering transferable skills for employability (Tabulawa, 2009; UNESCO-IBE, 2010; World Bank, 2008a).

Upper secondary: striking a balance between technical, vocational and general subjects

After lower secondary education, some students enter general secondary school and follow an academic or vocational route, while others enter technical and vocational institutions. There is a vast array of public and private institutions at this level, but the numbers of those entering the different types of institutions are notoriously difficult to obtain.

Upper secondary enrolment is increasing, but varies between countries

From 1999 to 2010, as overall upper secondary enrolment increased, enrolment in technical and vocational education also increased, but with wide variations between and within regions. The proportion of secondary students in technical and vocational education is low, on average, in sub-Saharan Africa, South and West Asia, and the Arab States (Figure 5.3). This is an indication that countries where overall enrolment in secondary school is low are less likely to offer

Botswana reformed its education system to offer a core lower secondary curriculum to all learners

Figure 5.3: Low secondary enrolment, a smaller share in technical and vocational education

Upper secondary gross enrolment ratio by type of programme, by country, latest year available (2009–2011)

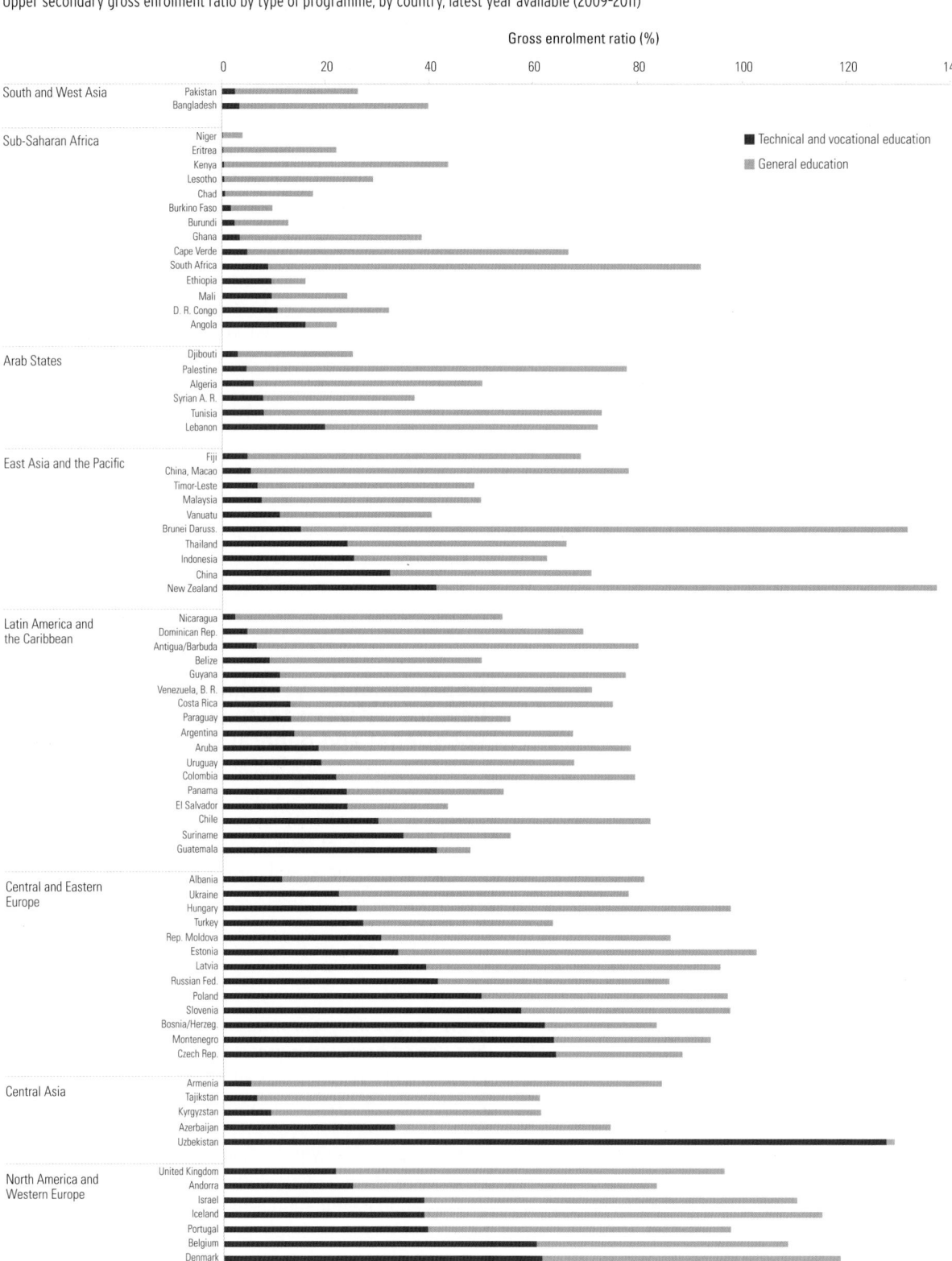

Gross enrolment ratio (%)

■ Technical and vocational education

■ General education

Sources: Annex, Statistical Table 7; UIS database.

a vocationalized curriculum for most students. There are exceptions, however. In Angola, where only 22% are in upper secondary school, around three out of four are in technical and vocational education.

Gender disparities are often wider in technical and vocational education than in general education. In Bangladesh, girls accounted for only 21% of technical and vocational enrolment, compared with 51% of general secondary enrolment. Girls who are enrolled in technical and vocational education tend by and large to be in areas that lead to traditionally female occupations, often characterized by low pay, such as hairdressing, sewing and tailoring, sales and service occupations, and care professions (European Commission, 2006; Gaidzanwa, 2008; Solotaroff et al., 2009).

The benefits of technical and vocational education depend on labour market demand

Technical and vocational education may be most effective when it builds on solid foundation skills and meets labour market demand for skills, as in China and the Republic of Korea, which have experienced economic growth and expanded primary education.

The importance of linking the content of technical and vocational education to labour market needs is illustrated by evidence from several countries. In Cambodia, Indonesia, Thailand and Turkey, for example, where labour market returns to secondary education – the effect on earnings of additional schooling – are generally high, they are higher for vocational education than for secondary general education. In Cambodia, returns to male vocational secondary school graduates in wage employment are 39%, relative to primary school graduates, compared with 32% for secondary general school graduates (Patrinos et al., 2006). This reflects recent developments in the Cambodian labour market, where scarce skills are increasingly being rewarded (Lall and Sakellariou, 2010).

In other countries, such as Egypt, the Islamic Republic of Iran, Rwanda and the United Republic of Tanzania, returns to vocational secondary are lower than to secondary general education, sometimes considerably so

(Kahyarara and Teal, 2008; Lassibille and Tan, 2005). In Egypt, where returns to secondary schooling are low overall, the returns to graduates of vocational secondary schools are 4%, compared with 7% for graduates from upper general secondary schools (Salehi-Isfahani et al., 2009). This may in part reflect the fact that students who join secondary general schools are more likely to be from wealthier backgrounds. According to analysis by the EFA Global Monitoring Report team based on the 2005–2006 Egypt Household Education Survey, around one in two of adolescents aged 14 to 17 from the wealthiest quintile were in secondary general education, while fewer than one in ten from the poorest quintile were. For the wealthiest and the poorest households, around 20% were in vocational school.

Although technical and vocational education can improve the transition from school to work in the short term, it can limit students' ability to adapt to long-term structural and technological change in the economy. Analysis of eighteen OECD countries found that those with more general education had better long-term employment prospects (Hanushek et al., 2011).

In rich countries, diversifying the curriculum enables upper secondary school to cater for all students

A diversified secondary curriculum that balances technical, vocational and general education is crucial in order to offer students from all backgrounds more choice, and to avoid perceptions of the vocational track as second best and a dead end that does not lead to further education.

Technical and vocational education tends to be dominated by young people from disadvantaged backgrounds, and so is often seen as second rate. Among sixty-five countries and territories that took part in the 2009 Programme for International Student Assessment survey, at least one in seven 15-year-olds attended vocational education in twenty-two of them.[2] A comparison of these twenty-two countries and

Technical and vocational education is often dominated by disadvantaged young people

---

2. Austria, Belgium (Flemish), Bulgaria, Colombia, the Czech Republic, Croatia, Hungary, Indonesia, Italy, Japan, Luxembourg, Mexico, Montenegro, Shanghai, the Republic of Korea, Romania, Serbia, Slovakia, Slovenia, Chinese Taipei, Thailand and Turkey.

territories shows that, in eighteen, students streamed into vocational schools have lower socio-economic status on average than their peers in general education.

In Hungary, for example, 19% of students in secondary general education were in the bottom socio-economic quartile, compared with 54% of students in vocational schools. In the Republic of Korea, the figures were 17% and 52%, respectively. In countries where disadvantaged students are streamed into vocational schools, average scores in mathematics were lower than in secondary general education. The four countries with the widest performance gaps were ones where the proportion of those from disadvantaged backgrounds was greatest. By contrast, where students in vocational secondary schools tended to be of higher socio-economic status (including Colombia, Indonesia, Japan and Mexico), the average mathematics score was higher in these schools than in secondary general education schools. This suggests that vocational secondary education school is not necessarily second rate, but that streaming of disadvantaged students into these schools is a key reason for differences in performance (Altinok, 2012).

Pushing lower performing students into parallel technical and vocational streams therefore risks cementing social inequalities. In the United Kingdom, for instance, low level vocational qualifications have attracted criticism for bringing no returns in the labour market, and for sometimes even being harmful because they send poor signals to employers (Wolf, 2011). As the skills upon which these low qualifications are based do not reflect those required in most jobs, some employers prefer students with strong general education qualifications and more transferable skills. High performing students with such qualifications are more able to adapt and learn on the job. The result is that low performing students tracked into low level vocational qualifications face further social and economic disadvantage.

If the technical and vocational education offered is of high quality however, and relevant to the world of work, combining vocational subjects with work-based learning opportunities can help re-engage students who might otherwise leave school early. Experience from OECD countries suggests

Australia reduced dropout by introducing vocational courses in its general curriculum

that when technical and vocational subjects are introduced alongside general subjects and made more relevant to the labour market, enrolment and completion rates can increase. One study found that a 10 percentage point increase in the share of upper secondary students in vocational and pre-vocational programmes was associated with a 2.6 percentage point increase in completion rates. In Australia, the introduction of vocational courses in the general curriculum helped reduce early school leaving significantly (Markussen and Sandberg, 2011).

If weaker students are tracked into technical and vocational subjects, they need to be offered a route back into general education, or given options to include relevant general education subjects, as a rigid separation of these pathways can reinforce inequality of opportunity, increase dropout rates and damage career prospects. Recognizing this, some rich countries have striven to offer more flexible approaches.

Switzerland has created a special one-year programme so that technical and vocational graduates who want to enter university can catch up on academic subjects. In 2010, about 13% of 21-year-olds were taking additional academic subjects under the programme. Participating in the programme improved the prospects of girls from low socio-economic backgrounds who wanted to study at post-secondary level in particular. Girls with well-educated parents were 15% less likely to take these additional subjects than those with less educated parents, suggesting that the opportunity corrects to some extent for the socio-economic bias operating at the entry to vocational school (Falter and Wendelspiess Chávez Juárez, 2011).

Singapore's flexible approach is a particularly strong example (Law, 2011). The system allows students to move among five different streams, according to their abilities and interests (OECD, 2012b). Regardless of the stream they take, their qualifications can be a route into tertiary education. This approach has been successful thanks to features not necessarily found in poorer countries, such as strong links between government and industry, large investments in teacher training, adequate teaching and learning resources, and efficient monitoring of student capacities and interests.

Singapore's experience raises a question that many low income countries have had to address: at what stage should countries aim to develop a diversified curriculum with a flexible approach? Or, where upper secondary enrolment remains low, as in Burkina Faso, Ethiopia and Mozambique, for example, should countries first expand the general secondary system, or embark immediately on a diversified curriculum? The former, it would appear, can reduce social inequalities, as it allows more students to acquire and consolidate strong foundations for further learning or work.

Diversifying the curriculum in poorer countries depends on funding

Many developing countries are moving quickly to make technical and vocational subjects a key component of secondary education, often with a focus on expanding access for disadvantaged young people.

The African Union has advocated the development of vocational skills, provided both in formal and non-formal settings, as part of Africa's economic growth strategy, calling for stronger integration between post-primary education and training systems (African Union, 2006, 2007). Bangladesh is aiming at a massive expansion of the vocational track in public and private secondary schools, from 3% to between 20% and 25% of total secondary enrolment,

targeting the poor and women in particular (Engel, 2012). China has set a target of 50% technical and vocational enrolments by 2020 (China Ministry of Education, 2009). Pakistan, in its Vision 2030 plan, aims to increase secondary technical and vocational enrolment from 4.2% in 2010 to 15% in 2015 and 40% in 2030. It also envisages reserving places at technical and vocational institutions for disadvantaged youth (Engel, 2012).

Are these goals realistic? The answer depends partly on cost. For low income countries, gains from diversifying the curriculum by introducing technical and vocational education need to be weighed against what could be gained by investing the same limited resources in raising the quality of teaching in core curriculum subjects. In Benin, Chad, Guinea, Mauritania and Togo, the cost of technical and vocational education and training is more than three times that of upper secondary general education (Kamano et al., 2010).

Integrating technical, vocational and general secondary subjects in one curriculum framework requires sufficient resources and trained teachers in all subject areas. In Ghana, wide disparities in school facilities and equipment and in the trained teacher supply meant that some secondary schools, particularly in rural areas, offered fewer subjects and of lower quality (Box 5.4).

In Benin, technical and vocational education is three times as expensive as general education

---

Box 5.4: In Ghana, technical and vocational subjects are better resourced in urban schools than in rural ones

Technical and vocational subjects were introduced into Ghana's secondary school curriculum from the mid-1960s, but not until 1987 was a comprehensive plan launched to make vocational education an integral part of the secondary education system. Education reformers maintained that this step would provide youth with skills for salaried work and self-employment and for post-secondary general, technical and vocational education. The move increased the proportion of students studying vocational subjects by about 50%.

Although the reforms made vocational and technical subjects more available, the high costs involved meant that schools in urban areas,

with higher enrolment and students from rich backgrounds, benefited most. Because of their high enrolment and better resources, urban schools made more intensive use of equipment and facilities than those in rural areas. The cost of providing some technical subjects was twenty times as much in rural areas as in urban ones, yet the quality was poorer due to lack of equipment and trained teachers.

Ghana's experience suggests that when resources are scarce, expanding technical and vocational education can further widen inequalities, benefiting those in urban areas.

Source: Akyeampong (2005).

Internships often replicate discrimination in the labour market

To be successful, an integrated curriculum needs to offer a wide enough range of subjects. Studies in Botswana, Ghana, Kenya and Mozambique show that adding only a few vocational subjects to the curriculum of secondary general education brought no benefits in the labour market. In Mozambique, it was only when vocational subjects made up at least 30% to 40% of the curriculum that tangible benefits became apparent (Lauglo, 2005).

As countries seek to expand access to secondary education, some have adapted the content of traditional subjects, such as mathematics and science, to incorporate vocational relevance. The Tutorial Learning System or SAT (Sistema de Aprendizaje Tutorial), developed by FUNDAEC, the Foundation for the Application and Teaching of Science (Fundación para la Aplicación y Enseñanza de las Ciencias), in Colombia, provides a good example of this approach. SAT is a rural education programme based on a revised secondary school curriculum integrating practical skills through conventional subjects in ways that make sense to rural youth. They can gain knowledge in agriculture, animal husbandry and other rural activities through subjects such as mathematics and science. SAT's success has led several other countries in Latin America to adopt it, and some NGOs are experimenting with it in Zambia and other African countries (IFAD, 2010; Murphy-Graham et al., 2002).

Strengthening the links between school and work

In colleges and in schools as well, they should do more, not just a day release where you go off and do a bit of work experience, they should do it like if they have two days in school, three days in placement, just balance it out. That way you're in school, you're learning what you need to learn and you're out there trying to get some experience.
— young woman, United Kingdom

School leavers often face a conundrum: they cannot get a job because they lack work experience, but they cannot get work experience unless they get a job. In Egypt, for instance, employers consider work experience the most important criterion for recruitment (El Zanety and Associates, 2007). For those who are able to remain in upper secondary education, connecting schools to the workplace is a way to solve the conundrum, smoothing the transition to work.

Internships and apprenticeships are ways young people can acquire transferable and vocational skills through direct work experience. While formal apprenticeships can last several years, internships sometimes last only weeks or months. Internships are not structured on the basis of a curriculum and the learning outcomes are seldom assessed. By contrast, formal apprenticeships are geared towards learning a trade, with the workplace as the site for acquiring the skills recognized in a qualification. Internships are generally either unpaid or offer a small stipend, while apprentices are usually paid a minimum wage or stipend during their training. In both cases, companies bear the costs of training and governments pay the costs of schooling.

Internships are not reaching the disadvantaged

The only thing that I haven't got every single time I've gone to an interview is experience, and you can't get that unless you work for free. I've been to interviews and they've said, 'Oh, we can't offer you a place but we can offer you an internship for six months for free,' and sometimes they don't even pay your travel. I have done internships but it gets to the stage, like, 'if you're not going to employ me then you can't take advantage.'
— young woman, United Kingdom

Short-term internships can help students discover the world of work, provide career ideas, improve motivation at school and develop students' transferable skills. To provide good quality training, they require a high level commitment from employers and well-developed legal and institutional frameworks.

In poorer countries, where small, informal enterprises often dominate and youth populations are large, internships may be available only to a minority. Even in rich countries, the availability of internships often replicates discrimination in the labour market, making it difficult for disadvantaged youth to secure contracts because of gender, disabilities or ethnic background (ECOTEC, 2009). A German survey found that young people with German-sounding names applying for internships were 14% more likely, on average, to receive a call for an interview than those with Turkish-sounding names (Kaas and Manger, 2010). Similar discriminatory practices have been reported in the United Kingdom and Greece (Drydakis and Vlassis, 2007; Woods et al., 2009).

Interns often receive low or no remuneration, often no more than enough to cover basic living expenses. Around one-half of interns surveyed in Europe in 2011 received no compensation. As a consequence, the majority relied on parental funds to enable them to benefit from this form of work experience, effectively excluding those whose parents cannot afford to provide such support (European Youth Forum, 2011).

Formal apprenticeships can provide skills for good jobs

[In my apprenticeship], I will go to the centre to learn computer repair. When I study in the centre I can practise there and after getting a certificate, I can work right away. I don't only learn theory. They allow me to practise assembling or repairing computers.
— young man, Viet Nam

Experience in most regions of the world shows that formal apprenticeships can be beneficial in building bridges between school and the workplace. Formal apprenticeships linked with the school system are most common in developed countries.[3] They can increase the attractiveness of staying in education while benefiting employers by ensuring that young people enter the labour market with relevant skills and experience.

In France, apprentices alternate between general and theoretical instruction at an apprenticeship training centre (Centre de Formation d'Apprentis) and practical training at the workplace. They receive 25% to 78% of the minimum wage, depending on their age and the

length of their contract (France DARES, 2011). Apprenticeships lead to the same qualifications as education in the classroom-based technical and vocational education and training track (Abriac et al., 2009).

Public policy initiatives, including financial incentives for employers, have led to a large increase in the number of apprentices. The number of new contracts signed each year rose from about 130,000 in the early 1990s to 287,000 in 2010. That year, 57% of the new apprentices were aged 15 to 18, two-thirds were males, and two-thirds had either no qualification or secondary-level vocational certificates (France DARES, 2011). Even so, the French apprenticeship system operates on a much smaller scale than the better-established German system, and tends to contract during recessions, as was observed in 2009 and 2010 (Lefresne, 2011) (see Box 5.5).

Apprenticeships succeed in bridging the schooling system and the labour market: they facilitate the acquisition of skills relevant to employer needs, and provide youth with workplace experience. In France in 2007, three years after completing their training, 84% of former apprentices were employed; 95% of those had full-time jobs, and 74% permanent contracts. The corresponding figures for youth from the classroom-based technical and vocational education and training track were 78%, 89% and 64%. After taking into account initial education and other socio-economic characteristics, going through an apprenticeship increased the likelihood of being employed three years after completion by 6.5 percentage points, and salaries were 2.9% higher (Abriac et al., 2009). One limitation is dropout: one-quarter of apprenticeship contracts are terminated early, either because apprentices lacked necessary foundation skills, or did not receive enough attention at the workplace, or faced financial, housing or transportation difficulties (Lefresne, 2011).

Apprentices are often more likely to be men because of discrimination in the labour market and the types of occupations for which apprenticeships are available. In 2010 only 13% of graduates of Egypt's dual system, for instance, were women because of the focus on traditional industrial

In France, 84% of trainees were employed three years after an apprenticeship

---

3. Traditional apprenticeships, which are particularly taken up by disadvantaged youth in low income countries, are usually offered by small business owners who teach a skill or trade to young people, but with no direct links to school (see Chapter 6).

occupations (Adams, 2010). Young women who have taken apprenticeships get paid less in them, find it harder to get a job and receive lower pay once they are in work (Adams, 2007). In the United Kingdom, female apprentices earn 21% less, on average, while undertaking their training. The wage benefit of a woman who has undertaken an apprenticeship was just 4%, compared with 20% for a man undertaking the same apprenticeship (TUC and YWCA, 2010).

Formal apprenticeships can achieve different outcomes for students depending on how they are organized. Japan has a long history of apprenticeships in which schools and employers cooperate in placing school graduates directly into jobs. Schools play an active role in the selection process by recommending students for particular apprenticeship positions. Evidence suggests that this creates an incentive for less academically oriented students to work harder in order to gain higher marks to improve their chances of being recommended for larger, more prestigious companies (Genda and Kurosawa, 2001). One disadvantage of this approach is that there are incentives for teachers to support better performing students to ensure that their schools maintain links with more prestigious companies.

In the United Kingdom, schools play a less active role. About 42% of secondary school graduates who enter apprenticeships do so by applying directly to an employer. About 10% find their apprenticeships through connections, and only 10% secure an apprenticeship through a careers adviser or teacher. The share of black and other ethnic minority youth already employed who enter apprenticeships is 32%, compared with 44% for white youth (Learning and Skills Council, 2008) – a situation that reflects the general difficulties that socially disadvantaged groups face in securing jobs in the United Kingdom.

In other contexts, combining school and work can benefit disadvantaged students, especially if they are specifically targeted, as Career Academies in the United States have shown. About 2,500 of these offer academic and technical curricula related to career themes and establish partnerships with local companies to offer work-based learning opportunities.

In the United Kingdom, female apprentices earn 21% less than men

Evaluations have shown that young men at the greatest risk of dropping out who attend Career Academies benefit in particular. They are more likely to complete school and get a job, and those least likely to do well academically become more engaged with school (Kemple, 2004).

Apprenticeships link the school curriculum with the workplace in a variety of ways. The German dual model, combining structured training within a company and part-time classroom tuition, works well in Germany because of strong regulation and partnerships between government, employers and employees. Its success in other settings would depend on matching the conditions that have enabled it to work well in Germany (Box 5.5).

Switzerland, with a long tradition of employer engagement in technical and vocational education, has a slightly different model from the German dual system, described as a triple system. It involves three learning sites: the factory or business place for three or four days a week, the vocational school for one or two days a week and a special centre or workshop where introductory courses are given, usually for three months (Gonon, 2004). The Swiss experience shows that investment in such training can be very beneficial to companies. One study estimated that in 2004 Swiss companies invested US$3.8 billion in apprenticeship training while obtaining a productive output of US$4.2 billion (OECD, 2010a). The willingness of companies to offer a wide range of apprenticeships depends partly on the economic climate. In the early 2000s, for example, the share of companies offering apprenticeships fell (Gonon, 2004).

Combining work experience and schooling can help address inequality, but a large modern sector is necessary for this approach to work well. In many low income countries, including those in sub-Saharan Africa where employment in the informal sector is prevalent, it is difficult to provide youth in school with well-structured work experience in small enterprises that are often household based. In such countries, the limited opportunities for work-based learning are likely to be rationed to the privileged few who make it to upper secondary school, thus widening inequality.

Box 5.5: How does Germany's successful dual model work?

Germany has managed to maintain low levels of youth unemployment, even as other countries in Europe have experienced an economic downturn. In January 2012, youth unemployment stood at 8%, compared with 23% in France and 22% in the United Kingdom. The German dual model of structured training within a company combined with part-time classroom tuition in vocational and general subjects is often cited as a reason for this achievement.

The model has been successful in providing young people with skills for a smooth transition to the labour market. Open to all students who have completed lower secondary education at age 15, it lasts two to three and a half years. Around 60% of German youth enrol in the dual system, and 57% of those who complete an apprenticeship are immediately employed by their training company.

Apprentices are considered employees and paid by the training company. They can choose from about 340 occupations, from hairdressing and car repair to insurance and financial services.

Regulation and partnership are the principles that make the system so successful. Representatives of the federal government, the states, employers and employees work together by consensus to develop curricula, provide training and carry out assessment, certification and quality assurance.

Mutual trust and a long-term commitment to developing human resources are the key ingredients that enable the dual system to deliver the skills that employers need while guaranteeing employees sufficient skills to change jobs and move up the career ladder. They are also the aspects of the dual system that make it so difficult to replicate elsewhere.

Germany's economy has a broad industrial base, with many small and medium-sized companies involved in export-oriented activities and requiring a highly skilled workforce. Companies thus see apprenticeships as a vital investment to guarantee their long-term competitiveness.

While the dual system has often been cited as one reason youth unemployment is lower in Germany than elsewhere in Europe, economic growth and an ageing population are also key factors. Given the economic downturn and demographic growth in many other OECD countries, it remains to be seen to what extent elements of the dual system could help to solve the problem of unemployment on a large scale.

Sources: BIBB (2011); Eurostat (2010); Hippach-Schneider and Toth (2009); Germany Ministry of Education (2011).

Germany's dual system has helped maintain its youth unemployment at 8%

Implementing programmes of formal apprenticeships linked with schooling is even more challenging. Compared with richer countries, low and lower middle income countries have fewer formal firms and industries that can be partners and they lack the necessary regulatory capacity. In addition, the benefits of formal apprenticeships for government, employers and students are sometimes not clear and the level of mutual trust is low. Such apprenticeships benefit only those students fortunate enough to reach upper secondary school, moreover, as many leave school before this stage with even more limited opportunities to gain skills for good jobs. Despite the difficulties involved, Egypt has successfully experimented with formal apprenticeships linked to schools (Box 5.6).

Career counselling should aim to help disadvantaged youth secure apprenticeships

I think it would make a big difference if I could find someone well-educated to guide and give me a better understanding of my vocation of interest. If someone can give me the skills and the possibility to start work, I know I can achieve my goals.

– young woman, Ethiopia

Although some schools offer career counselling, it tends to focus more on education decisions than on occupation choices (Watts and Fretwell, 2004). In Japan, however, teachers take a more active role in counselling apprenticeship-bound students about the appropriateness of specific companies and jobs. This tends to ensure that students are fully informed and that the jobs match their interests, hence reducing dropout from the apprenticeships (Brinton, 1998; Hori, 2010).

Box 5.6: Egypt adopts the German model with success

Confronted with high youth unemployment and a skill mismatch, in 1994 the Egyptian Government set up a dual system of school- and work-based technical education, known as the Mubarak-Kohl initiative, with the support of Germany.

Students spent two days a week at school and four days in a company. The Ministry of Education paid the cost of schooling, including classrooms and teachers, while the private sector paid for training in factories and provided a stipend for trainees throughout the three-year programme. By 2009, the initiative included 76 technical secondary schools and 1,900 companies providing training in 32 trades to 13,000 students.

The programme has continued to expand. In 2010, 10,200 new students enrolled, almost doubling the intake. About 30% of graduates immediately found a job, while 40% continued further studies in higher education. Rather than copying the German dual system, the project adapted its basic principles to the local context. For example, business associations play a key role in providing training places, while in Germany the link is made with companies directly.

Source: Adams (2010).

Employers value problem-solving and communication skills

Even in countries where career guidance in schools is difficult, initiatives such as career fairs, school visits to workplaces and partnerships with local employers have shown some positive results. The INJAZ Al-Arab programme, for instance, offers a framework for local partnerships between schools and enterprises in twelve countries in the Middle East and North Africa. In Lebanon, volunteers from leading companies go to secondary schools to share their professional experience and teach courses on job-seeking skills and business ethics, as well as advanced programmes on economics and entrepreneurship. More than 600,000 beneficiaries have been reached through INJAZ Al-Arab since 2004.

In Jordan, during the 2010/11 school year over 100,000 students benefited from various activities conducted by INJAZ volunteers in secondary schools, such as careers guidance, job shadowing (or work readiness), and life skills training (INJAZ Jordan, 2012). In Lebanon, the programme is being scaled up to reach all secondary school students (ETF, 2012). It increased by 33% the share of students who felt confident about their ability to manage a job interview successfully, compared with students who had not attended the programme (Angel-Urdinola et al., 2010).

Transferable skills for all: a desirable but challenging goal

Skills learned at school need to extend beyond subject knowledge. Employers repeatedly indicate that they value transferable skills such as applying knowledge in real work situations, solving unexpected problems and communicating effectively with colleagues.

Denmark, Hong Kong (China), New Zealand and Queensland (Australia) all specify problem solving as part of their curricula. The New Zealand Ministry of Education, for example, identifies problem-solving skills such as thinking critically, creatively, reflectively and logically; exercising imagination, initiative and flexibility; analysing problems from a variety of perspectives; trying out innovative and original ideas; and making decisions on the basis of experience and evidence (World Bank, 2008a).

Teaching practices that aim to develop skills such as problem solving have been popular mostly in developed countries and require a special commitment. Teachers need to be trained to devise learning programmes based on specific skill requirements, to promote these skills in students and to help students take a more active role in learning (Roegiers, 2008; Tehio, 2009).

Some Asian and Latin American countries have adopted ideas and practices that emphasize problem solving and reflective learning rather than mechanical training in routine tasks (Tippelt, 2010). Applying them in these settings has sometimes been difficult, even where political will is strong, teachers are well trained and financial means are adequate.

Singapore's initiative Thinking Schools, Learning Nation, launched in 2004, is an example of just how challenging it can be to implement an approach to learning based on problem solving. The initiative has sought to develop creativity, problem-solving ability and a passion for lifelong learning, which tend not to be encouraged by rote learning of factual knowledge and performance on standardized tests. It focuses on problem-based learning, collaborative learning and project work. Not all students and teachers are ready to accept such fundamental changes; some schools are reluctant to move away from existing practices, especially as these led to good results in examinations (Ng, 2008).

Analysis of international evidence suggests that problem-solving and creative-thinking skills can be developed when reforms align curriculum objectives with examination practices, and are not constrained by resources at the school level (Schweisfurth, 2011). In reality, however, such alignment and the conditions required to make programmes effective are hard to achieve in many education systems, particularly in developing countries.

Many secondary level curricula in sub-Saharan Africa retain a traditional focus on theoretical knowledge. Far too often, learning is still limited to memorizing and recalling facts, and geared towards passing paper-and-pencil tests in order to progress to the next level of schooling (World Bank, 2008a). Students often lack the capacity to make sense of their knowledge and use it for effective problem solving in real-life situations.

Information and communication technology can improve learning

I know a bit about computers, but if I got proper training I could do well. I gained computer knowledge by going to cybercafés, but no one teaches computers.

— young man, India

The use of information and communication technology (ICT) in education is gathering momentum across the world, even in some of the most challenging environments in developing countries. Much of the interest centres on making learning more attractive, especially for students at risk of leaving school early. It also

aims to ensure that all students develop the ICT-based skills required by the twenty-first century workplace.

Businesses in the formal and informal sectors alike increasingly use mobile phones, computers and the Internet for trade and commerce, even in some of the world's poorest regions. While this has prompted governments to introduce ICT in education, most schools teach computer use as a technical or vocational skill, or simply a research tool, rather than a way to develop transferable skills (Trucano, 2005).

There is evidence from some developed countries that ICT can be used to improve the learning experience of students, including those at risk of dropping out of secondary school. When ICT is used to connect students to information and resources in ways which make learning more interesting, intellectually challenging and engaging, the results have been positive (OECD, 2006).

But much depends on how teachers use ICT in teaching. It is important to ensure that teachers have the skills necessary to use ICT effectively, and to align examinations. A five-year study on teachers' practices using ICT in the United States revealed that some found it difficult to help students develop critical thinking and literacy skills, partly because national examinations did not focus enough on the skills that ICT was supposed to promote. Teachers also found that their heavy workloads limited the time they could spend using ICT in teaching. Examinations and demands on teachers' time need to change to support the introduction of ICT in schools, the study concluded (Orlando, 2011).

Many poor countries with constrained education budgets cannot afford computers and Internet connections. But there are more affordable options (Box 5.7).

The operation of the international One Laptop per Child programme in Peru is an example of how access to computers can improve learning. As well as increasing the use of ICT at school and home, the distribution of laptops to primary school children has helped improve their verbal fluency, abstract reasoning and processing speed (Cristia et al., 2012). Evaluators, however,

'One Laptop per Child' in Peru helped improve verbal fluency

Box 5.7: Affordable new and old technology can improve learning for disadvantaged groups

The prevalence of ICT in some parts of the world does not mean that this is the cheapest or even most effective type of technology for educational purposes. In the developing world, the radio – so-called old technology – has a powerful reach, particularly in rural areas or sparsely populated regions. Radios are everywhere, with at least 75% of households in developing countries having access to a radio.

An example is South Sudan Interactive Radio Instruction. It offers daily half-hour lessons in English, local language, mathematics and life skills. More generally, such programmes have improved student learning by 10% to 20% over control groups that did not use interactive radio instruction. This type of instruction is also extremely cost effective. In one project in Honduras, such instruction cost US$2.94 per student in the first year and US$1.01 per year thereafter.

Tablet computers and e-readers, although currently expensive, are expected to fall in price, allowing for their use in expanding access to information resources for all learners. In India, with government subsidies, such devices could be provided to students for as little as US$10. Multimedia educational resources, such as videos, are also being used to enhance the learning experience and reach students in remote areas. The Khan Academy, for example, produces short educational videos that serve as self-learning tools. There have been over 60 million downloads of its videos to supplement teaching in many classrooms in developing countries.

Policy-makers seldom adequately address how new technology will affect the inclusion of marginalized youth. Cost is a key factor. But some forms of technology can be affordable, and could be used to provide a wide range of information resources for disadvantaged learners.

Source: Winthrop and Smith (2012).

At least 75% of households in developing countries have access to a radio

recommended first improving teacher skills in using ICT in teaching and learning, rather than taking technology as the starting point for devising new means of improving learning (Sánchez and Salinas, 2008).

One large-scale government-led initiative to help schools use ICT for teaching and learning is the Enlaces programme in Chile, which started in 1992. The programme, which has reached all secondary schools and half of primary schools, was implemented over 15 years with a budget of US$250 million. The government systematically equipped secondary schools with computers and Internet connections, and trained teachers in educational uses of digital technology. The programme has helped many students improve their information and communication skills. But ICT has not been sufficiently well integrated into the curriculum, with teachers notably failing to use such technology to encourage effective problem-solving skills in students (Sánchez and Salinas, 2008).

In many low income countries, Internet connections and computers are often scarce, so relying on ICT could exacerbate inequality, for example where access is concentrated in rich urban areas. Mobile phones are widely available, however, offering opportunities to use new technology even in more challenging environments.

In the United Republic of Tanzania, the BridgeIT programme allows teachers to download videos on subjects such as science and mathematics on a mobile phone and transfer them to a television in the classroom. With the support of Nokia, Vodafone and other partners, about 80,000 lower secondary children and 3,000 teachers in 150 schools have used this service, which is available even in remote areas without Internet connections. The project has led to an improvement in test results (Kasumuni, 2011). In developing countries, while less than 20% of the population can access the Internet, mobile phones are accessible to over 70%, offering hope that new ideas in teaching and learning can reach those even in rural areas of low income countries who might otherwise be left behind (Newby, 2012).

Providing alternative routes for early school leavers

Large numbers of young people drop out before completing secondary school, even in middle and high income countries. Those leaving school early are more likely to be from poor and disadvantaged households, requiring targeted support to enable them to continue with their learning to ensure that they acquire the qualifications and skills needed to benefit from employment opportunities.

Reaching those at risk of dropping out

Some rich countries offer alternative routes to learning for those at risk of dropping out. The Dutch Ministry of Education spent US$451 million in 2008 on measures aimed at preventing dropout and giving young people a second chance, with an expectation that funding would increase to US$556 million by 2011 (De Witte and Cabus, 2010).

Part of the Dutch approach to preventing early school leaving is allowing dropouts to re-enter school at any point during the school year. This can help learners who performed well academically but chose to leave school to take a job or because of a change in circumstances, such as pregnancy. It may not work so well, however, for low achieving students who have been alienated from school for long periods and whose motivation for learning is low. Thus the government has also supported the creation of alternative learning opportunities, for instance in adult education centres or through distance education, that can cater for the learning needs of low achievers who have dropped out. Thanks to the government's attention to supporting some of those at risk of dropping out, the share of early school leavers in the population aged 18 to 24 decreased from 17.6% in 1996 to 10.1% in 2010 (Eurostat, 2010).

The Philippine Government's Dropout Reduction Programme, a nationwide module-based approach allowing students to study at home, has also reduced the number of early school leavers (Box 5.8).

The Netherlands spent US$451 million to prevent dropout and provide second chances

---

Box 5.8: Reducing dropout in secondary education in the Philippines through flexible provision

The Dropout Reduction Programme, launched in 1998, has achieved considerable success thanks to high-level government commitment.

The programme has three main components, which are part of a comprehensive strategy for improving the quality of education and making sure all students complete compulsory education up to the age of 15:

■ The Open High School Programme is a formal, structured distance learning programme for upper secondary education.

■ Effective Alternative Secondary Education consists of modularized courses and learning materials for students who intermittently miss classes.

■ School-Initiated Interventions are implemented by schools at their own initiative to retain students in school or reintegrate dropouts.

The programme targets students who intermittently miss classes for reasons such as illness, family responsibilities or farm work. The content of the learning modules is not very different from that of textbooks but allows students to develop understanding with minimum guidance. The formal structured distance learning programme uses media beyond traditional textbooks to aid learners who lack parental support. Additional flexible classes are organized at times that suit both student and teacher.

By combining modularized courses and school-initiated interventions, some provinces have achieved very low dropout rates. Overall, the programme was successful in reducing school dropout from 13% in 2005 to 8% in 2009/10.

Source: ADB (2009a)

In New York City, one in five aged 17-24 is neither in school nor in work

In New York City, one in five of those aged 17 to 24 – an estimated 173,000 young people – is neither in school nor in work. Amongst these, about a third lack a high school diploma. The secondary school dropout rate stands at some 12%. Those who did not complete secondary education and who have not had a stable job by age 25 face sharply diminished chances of enjoying financial stability over their lifetime (Treschan et al. 2011; NYC Department of Education 2011). Recognizing the scale of this problem, Mayor Michael Bloomberg has initiated a programme aimed at re-engaging into education and work dropouts or those at risk of leaving school early (Box 5.9).

Providing opportunities through alternative vocational pathways

In developing countries where few young people are enrolled in secondary school, community training centres or private vocational institutions can provide a viable alternative, but they need to be carefully attuned to local labour market needs and backed by long-term financial commitment.

One example is the 600 or so youth polytechnics in Kenya. They account for more than half of total vocational and technical enrolment. About twice as many women are enrolled as men (Nyerere, 2009). They deliver module-based general and vocational courses developed in partnership with local industry, flexibly organized to allow for entry and re-entry into the formal education system or the local labour market. After completion, students receive a National Vocational Education and Training Certificate (Mwinzi and Kelemba, 2010).

A core aim of the youth polytechnics is to provide training in skills directly related to local income-generating opportunities, but it has not yet been achieved because of excessive formalization of the programme and orientation to certification (Nyerere, 2009). Equipment in the institutions soon became outdated, denting their image in the public eye. To revive the youth polytechnics, the government has proposed introducing an even more flexible programme and revising the curriculum in areas such as fashion design and garment making, ICT, hairdressing, building/construction, and electrical/electronics technology. Like other programmes of its kind in Africa, it is costly, and sustainable funding remains a challenge.

In Ethiopia, where formal secondary education is accessible only to a minority, alternative training programmes have been initiated by the private sector, civil society organizations or the government. At least 400 institutions offer skills training to early school leavers who are

---

Box 5.9: Reconnecting young people with school and work in New York City

The Summer Youth Employment Program (SYEP) and Young Adult Internship Program (YAIP) were set up by New York City to provide real-world work experience and equip young people at risk of dropping out of school with employability skills. Both combine a paid internship (participants receive the New York State minimum wage of US$7.25 per hour) with workshops and individual counselling.

The programmes target vulnerable youth – the 'court involved', disabled, runaway and homeless, as well as youth from poor households. It is expected that more than 26,500 will have participated in the 2012 SYEP, which takes adolescents from age 14 on. The YAIP, open to ages 16 to 24, serves around 1,360 youth per year; most are aged 18 to 20 and about 44% have not

completed secondary education. About 60% of YAIP participants are African-American and 32% Hispanic/Latino, and about 49% are female.

Nine months after completing the YAIP, at least half the participants are in employment, in education or in a training programme. While few return to secondary schools after the internship, 18% enter a programme of basic reading, mathematics, writing and livelihood skills in preparation for the General Educational Development test, which leads to a qualification equivalent to a high school diploma; 49% enter for the General Educational Development test directly.

Sources: Annie E. Casey Foundation (2012); Holder (2010); New York City DYCD (2012a, 2012b); Treschan et al. (2011); WESTAT (2009).

not eligible for formal education programmes that require the completion of ten years of basic general education. The quality of training is very diverse; recruitment of skilled trainers is difficult. Although NGOs have a role to play in filling the gap when public institutions are insufficient or inequitable, there are concerns over the relevance of training received by disadvantaged youth. In an attempt to address these concerns, Ethiopia has been undertaking a comprehensive reform of technical education and training at all levels, with a focus on training the trainers and setting national occupational standards to link training more closely to labour market demand (Atchoarena and Esquieu, 2002; Edukans Foundation, 2009; Walther, 2006a).

Open and distance learning can extend access to secondary schooling

Given how many young people lack secondary education and how much it would cost to reach them through traditional means, some suggest that governments should use technology to reach large numbers of youth at low cost via distance and open learning (Daniels, 2010).

India, Mexico, Namibia and Turkey are among countries that have established innovative learning approaches operating parallel to the formal education system, sometimes with considerable reach. These open and distance learning programmes combine tuition via different forms of technology with conventional face-to-face learning.

India's National Institute of Open Schooling is one of the largest of its kind, targeting out-of-school learners, women, lower castes, scheduled tribes and those with little or no income. Over 300,000 are enrolled annually in a network of accredited study institutions (Haughey et al., 2008; Rumble and Koul, 2007). That number is low, however, given that 39% of 15- to 19-year-olds drop out before completing lower secondary schooling in India. Cost may limit its accessibility; depending on the level of subsidy, a student pays between half and all of the actual cost. Though this is considerably less than the cost of conventional secondary schools, it is still likely to be out of reach for students from the poorest households.

In Mexico, the Telesecundaria programme, in existence since 1968, has significantly increased access to secondary education by providing direct television teaching to rural learners. Television programmes covering the same secondary school curriculum offered in schools in the formal system are transmitted daily to Telesecundaria schools. Programming is integrated with book and teacher-led activities, with one teacher within the school responsible for all subjects in each grade. In 2010, 1.26 million students were enrolled in the Telesecundaria programme, equivalent to around 20% of total secondary enrolment. Enrolment is higher in poorer and rural parts of the country (Creed and Perraton, 2001; Coneval, 2011).

Some programmes of this type target disadvantaged groups specifically. Turkey's Open High School programme, which started in 1992, and Open Vocational High School programme, begun in 1995, use ICT and face-to-face instruction. The programmes offer greatly reduced tuition fees, free textbooks and online training materials. They aim to reach youth with physical disabilities; prisoners; children (especially girls) living in isolated rural areas; and youth who drop out to work. Graduation rates of 27% for the Open High School and 19% for the Open Vocational High School – for a total of 835,000 graduates – are an achievement for youth who would otherwise not have been able to receive a post-primary education, but still leave many young people lacking such opportunities (CEDEFOP, 2011).

Demonstrating that open learning is feasible in poorer countries, the Namibian College of Open Learning is the largest provider of open schooling at secondary level in sub-Saharan Africa. The vast majority of learners are aged 18 to 24, and almost seven out of ten are women. The college caters for over 30,000 students annually. Nearly half of all places at upper secondary level are offered through this institution, which provides a second chance to youth who completed school with poor grades or never had a chance to attend secondary school. The college provides access to printed self-study materials, study premises, weekly tutorials and periodic workshops (Rumble and Koul, 2007).

In Mexico, distance learning reached 1.26 million secondary students in 2010

2 0 1 2

Education for All Global Monitoring Report

In terms of cost per student per subject,[4] the Namibian distance system is roughly as cost-effective as traditional schooling at lower secondary level, and much cheaper for upper secondary: about one-third of conventional costs. In Mexico, by contrast, annual costs per student were about 16% higher in the Telesecundaria programme than in regular schools, including costs of TV programme production, supplementary materials, teacher salaries and infrastructure (De Moura Castro et al., 1999).

Experience from Mexico highlights the importance of ensuring that distance programmes are sufficiently resourced. Students in the Telesecundaria programme performed worse on average than students in other schools, even after controlling for socio-economic status. In earlier years, the programme faced problems such as inadequate infrastructure and lack of equipment. Reforms have since been adopted to introduce technological equipment, enhance teacher training and provide more teaching materials (Cortés and Giacometti, 2010).

Countries where open and distance secondary education has been used successfully to reach disadvantaged groups and students needing an alternative route to education tend to have good infrastructure and technology, and a wide network of institutions for programme delivery.

Formally recognizing learning and skills acquired outside of school

A widespread concern for employers and students alike is the lack of information on what skills have actually been acquired through various learning and qualification pathways, especially in countries where most youth acquire working skills informally, on the job or in training programmes that do not deliver nationally recognized certificates. Setting nationally recognized competence standards, against which learners' performance can be assessed, is one approach to addressing this concern.

In many countries, representatives of businesses, trade unions and training institutions

National qualification frameworks can recognize general and vocational skills

have helped develop national standards defining the skills and knowledge required for a range of jobs. The standards are registered in a national qualification framework, which training providers use to develop learning programmes; in some countries, individuals can have their skills assessed against the standards and be awarded a recognized qualification, independent of where and when they acquired their skills. This approach helps overcome the fragmentation of technical and vocational qualifications and establish equivalences between general and vocational qualifications.

Although more than seventy countries are developing or implementing national qualification frameworks, there is as yet little evidence on their impact (Allais et al., 2009). Experience from Australia, England and Scotland (United Kingdom) and South Africa shows that it is crucial to provide good quality training and maintain a high level of trust among employers and education institutions so that qualifications are valued in the labour market. Some countries have frequently revised the levels of skills and competencies within their national qualification frameworks, causing confusion and ultimately undermining the value of qualifications in the eyes of some employers and students (Allais, 2010; Heitmann, 2010).

There is debate over whether national qualification frameworks are appropriate for low income countries (Allais, 2010; Heitmann, 2010). Lessons from developed countries suggest that unrealistic expectations of frameworks and failure to adapt them to labour market demands can lessen their usefulness (Chakroun, 2010).

Setting standards too low or making them too general can diminish their value on the labour market. In the United Kingdom, for instance, frameworks have been accused of setting low standards for low achieving students, lowering qualifications' market value and limiting career progression and pay. Employers look for applicants with academic qualifications showing strong literacy and numeracy capabilities; those with low national vocational qualifications can find themselves severely disadvantaged in the labour market (Wolf, 2011).

---

4. Students in the programme generally take fewer courses than their counterparts in the formal system.

South Africa's mixed experience illustrates the challenges involved. Its national qualification framework for vocational and technical skills helped improve training and became important for job recruitment. Some providers cited the ability to develop learning and assessment tools that focus on the skill needs of industry as a major benefit of the framework, and some employers felt the qualifications had become more relevant to the needs of industry. Others, though, felt that some skill specifications were not clear enough to enable easy judgements on what had been achieved (Granville, 2005; McGrath, 2009). Giving employers a say in specifying skills, and providing guidance on how specifications are to be interpreted and applied, could address such concerns.

Sri Lanka provides an example of the advantages of clearly defined standards and qualifications. Its national qualification framework brought clarity to highly fragmented technical and vocational education outside formal secondary education. The design of competence standards and qualifications, accreditation of providers, development of curricula and creation of a network of guidance centres contributed to a system of provision and certification that is used by almost 20% of learners and well recognized by the labour market. About 81% of those with a vocational qualification based on the national framework found employment without a long wait. One reason the framework has been successful is the establishment of fifty career guidance and counselling centres providing support to trainees. By 2008, the centres had provided information about training opportunities to nearly 40,000 young people and helped place more than 4,400 directly into jobs (GHK, 2012).

Many young people with low initial qualifications or little formal schooling prefer to re-enter formal education. Non-formal alternative learning programmes help them develop at least basic skills and receive a certificate of recognition of prior learning for re-entry into formal education. A transcript of competencies certifies their levels of achievement. Australia, France and the Philippines offer such alternative learning programmes for out-of-school youth.

The Philippine Alternative Learning System, funded by the Department of Education, runs in parallel to elementary and secondary schooling. Out-of-school youth using this system can upgrade their competencies to primary or secondary school level outside the formal system. After testing, successful participants receive a Department of Education certificate recognized as the equivalent of elementary or secondary qualifications. The certificate allows them to be mainstreamed back into formal basic or higher education, or a technical and vocational school, after passing the entrance examinations. The programme began in 2004 and by 2008 had reached about 43,347 young people aged 15 to 24, or 61% of learners (GHK, 2012).

National qualification frameworks and programmes for recognition of prior learning can become good tools for ensuring that youth with low education who follow alternative learning pathways are not condemned to a dead-end stream but can either re-enter formal education or get a job. They are difficult to implement, however, and require close cooperation between interested parties, including government, training institutions, industry and trade unions.

Secondary education gives youth the best hope to develop skills for a good job

Conclusion

Secondary education offers the best hope for youth to develop skills that would put them in a strong position to get good jobs. Many countries have made good progress in improving access to primary education, but in the developing world many youth are still not making the transition to secondary education that would enable them to consolidate and build on basic skills. Promoting the kind of skills that employers repeatedly ask to see in new recruits from school will be more successful if students have exposure to work through apprenticeships and other innovative approaches to learning, such as the use of ICT to develop problem-solving skills. But unless more disadvantaged youth actually complete lower secondary school, they are unlikely to benefit.

Chapter 6
Skills for urban youth – A chance for a better future

Credit: Sven Torfinn/Panos

A street vendor in Juba, South Sudan, selling plastic Christmas trees and inflatable balls made in China. Training can help street vendors improve their business skills, their income and their chances of finding alternative work.

Increasing numbers of young people are trapped in urban poverty, without the skills they need to build themselves a better life. This chapter examines ways of providing skills training as part of a package of measures to help the urban poor overcome the disadvantages they face. It shows how combining work experience in specific trades with training to improve basic literacy and numeracy skills can help the urban poor find better work.

Introduction

The urban population is growing rapidly in many parts of the world, most notably in developing countries. Large numbers of young people are migrating away from rural deprivation towards towns and cities that hold the promise of greater freedom, better living conditions and improved work opportunities. Population growth is also contributing to rapid urbanization. Today's urban youth population, the largest in history, is better educated than previous generations and represents a powerful force for political and social change as well as for economic growth.

Urbanization has been accompanied by a rise in urban poverty, however. Young people tend to make up a disproportionate share of those living in squalid conditions in unplanned urban settlements. Many are trapped in insecure, subsistence activities. Women are at particular disadvantage in urban labour markets. Many of these young people left school before mastering basic skills such as literacy and numeracy.

Urbanization can broaden opportunities if policies not only promote economic development and job creation but also allow disadvantaged youth to take advantage of opportunities by acquiring relevant skills. Unless they are offered a second chance at education, young people are unlikely to be able to develop skills through workplace training, including traditional apprenticeships.

Urban poverty is widespread and increasing

It is estimated that virtually all the world's population growth will be concentrated in urban areas over the next thirty years, and that by 2040 more people will be living in urban areas than in rural areas in all developing regions (UN-HABITAT, 2008).

Although the economy and infrastructure of urban areas are expected to improve, they are unlikely to keep pace with growth in the youth population. Urbanization has led to significant urban poverty, manifested in the growth of slums and informal settlements. More than 800 million people are estimated to live in slums

in developing countries – equivalent to one in three city dwellers (UN-HABITAT, 2008). In sub-Saharan Africa, almost two-thirds of the urban population live in slums, and in South Asia more than one-third. This population is expected to reach 889 million by 2020 (UN-HABITAT, 2008), making it even more crucial to pay attention to skills and work in these environments.

Whether in regions where urbanization is increasing, or others that have long been urbanized – such as Latin America, where around one-quarter live in slums – many young people live in extremely poor environments that offer little prospect of finding decent jobs. Slum dwellers and other urban poor suffer from inadequate housing, overcrowding, lack of access to sanitation and water, and inadequate basic services. They are vulnerable to natural disasters and environmental hazards, experience high levels of crime and violence, and lack legal protection. Under these conditions, a growing number of disadvantaged youth are struggling to find good jobs that will give them a secure future. But the odds are against them. Many are trapped in informal, insecure, low paid work.

Young people migrate to urban areas in the hope of better lives

Most urban growth is driven by natural increase, but rural to urban migration also plays a part, especially where countries are urbanizing from a predominantly rural context, such as in East and South Asia, sub-Saharan Africa and the Arab States. Migrants made up more than 40% of the population of seven West African capitals in the early 2000s (Brilleau et al., 2004).[1] Many are young: in Egypt, those aged 15 to 29 were 40% more likely to migrate than those aged 30 to 39, and 80% more than those aged 40 to 59 (Kabbani and Kothari, 2005).

The reasons for migration to urban areas vary. For young men in particular, migration to cities offers the prospect of work and income opportunities that do not exist in rural areas. In some places, male and female migration patterns are converging. In China, rural to urban migration is taking place on a massive scale, with 145 million migrant workers living in urban

By 2040, more people will live in urban areas than in rural areas

---

1. The seven cities are Abidjan, Bamako, Cotonou, Dakar, Lomé, Niamey and Ouagadougou.

In one-fifth of countries, urban poor youth have less education than rural poor

areas in 2009. More than half were born after 1980; among these younger migrants, 41% were women. Among rural youth with low education or unable to afford higher education, moving to a city is an alternative to continuing with studies: more than 70% of migrants had not completed upper secondary education (Chiang et al., 2011).

Young women, like young men, are increasingly responding to economic incentives to migrate, which include escaping rural unemployment or working to save money to start a business. In Viet Nam, growth in manufacturing increased rural to urban labour mobility. But young women unable to obtain manufacturing jobs often seek work in low skilled, low paying occupations, including domestic work. They cannot compete equally with men in the private sector, partly because of discrimination in recruitment and partly because they tend to have less education and fewer skills (Kabeer et al., 2005). Elsewhere, young women migrate from rural areas in hopes of escaping restrictions imposed by discriminatory cultural practices. In slum areas of Addis Ababa, Ethiopia, 25% of girls had migrated to escape forced marriage (Tacoli and Mabala, 2010).

Many young people are displaced to cities by a range of other factors, including rapid population growth in rural areas, effects of climate change on agricultural productivity and livelihoods, and internal conflict (Grant, 2012). In Sudan and South Sudan, conflict has led to forced displacement of large rural populations to a small number of urban centres, whose population has grown exponentially (Pantuliano et al., 2011).

Many arriving in urban areas have fewer chances of getting jobs than other urban residents because they have less education and lack contacts and job information. This is reflected in differences in employment and earnings. In China, 80% of short-term or seasonal migrants aged 15 to 18 have dropped out of school, compared with 34% of permanent residents in urban areas. They lack access to education, health and other public services, which are primarily restricted to those with residence permits: 40% of children of migrants (aged 11 to 14) are out of school, compared with 15% of children of permanent residents (Grant, 2012; World Bank, 2007b). Consequently, they

end up filling the least skilled jobs available, without health insurance or pension benefits, and with lower pay – often half of what similarly skilled urban residents are paid, although still above rural income levels (Grant, 2012).

Many urban poor lack foundation skills

The extent of education deprivation among the urban poor is often overlooked. Inequalities within urban areas are often extreme – implying that slum dwellers do not necessarily live better than the rural poor – and the extent and depth of urban poverty are underestimated (Grant, 2012). For instance, in greater Cairo a large share of the population live in informal settlements. Not only do they lack a decent income, but they also face costs that are often higher than in more prosperous areas of the city due to the lack of infrastructure for education, health, water, sanitation, electricity and transport (Sabry, 2010).

While education opportunities are more widespread in urban areas than rural ones in many developing countries, the difference in acquisition of foundation skills between the urban poor and rural poor is not large. Across forty-five countries, the urban rich are far more likely than the urban poor to have continued at least until the end of lower secondary school (Figure 6.1). In ten of these countries, the proportion of those aged 15 to 24 lacking foundation skills is even higher among the urban poor than among the rural poor.

In Cambodia, 90% of poor urban youth do not have the chance to complete lower secondary education, compared with 82% of the rural poor and 31% of the urban rich. In Nigeria, there is a vast gulf in education opportunities between the rich and poor in urban areas. Almost all the urban rich get at least as far as lower secondary, compared with less than half of the urban poor. In Kenya, low levels of formal education for youth living in slums limit their opportunities of finding decent jobs (Box 6.1).

Policy-makers often neglect to provide education and training alongside economic strategies that promote job creation, confining many young people to low skilled, low paid work. The Kazi Kwa Vijana (Jobs for Youth) programme in Kenya, for example, offers manual jobs to young people but lacks systematic skills training (Oketch and Mutisya, 2012).

A review of poverty reduction strategies in nine countries[2] found that they tended to view poverty as a rural issue, and that seven failed to provide an adequate discussion of education in

urban areas, if they mentioned it at all (Baker and Reichardt, 2007). Some countries have recognized the need to improve living conditions in slums, but tend to focus on housing, sanitation and health. While these are crucial, without better opportunities for education and skills training, many young people will remain trapped in subsistence living.

Figure 6.1: Wide disparities between urban rich and poor

Percentage of 15-to-24 year-olds leaving before completing lower secondary school, by wealth and location, selected countries, latest available year

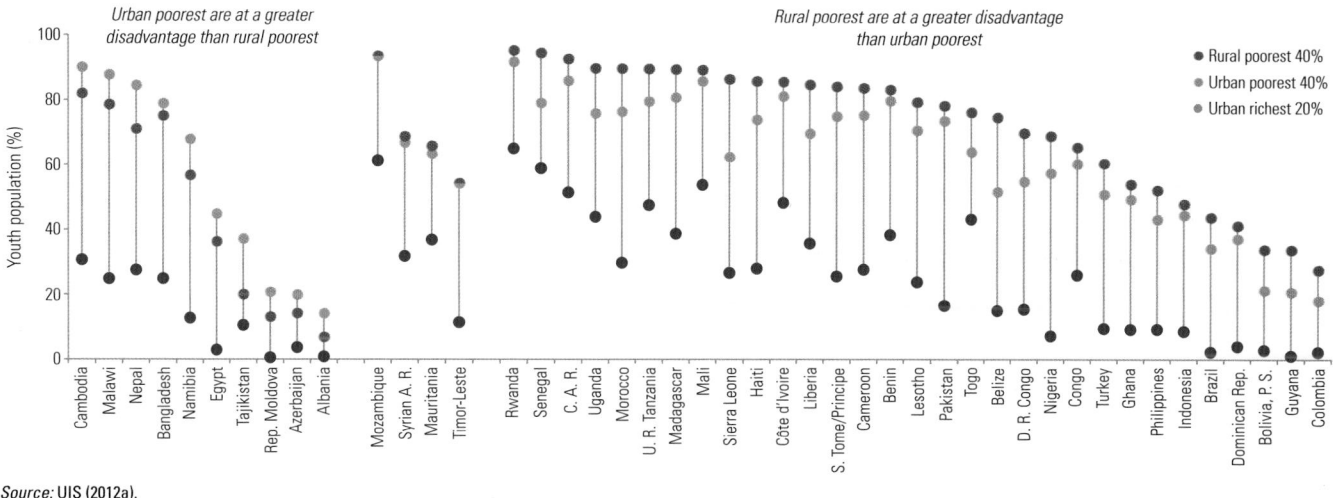

Source: UIS (2012a).

Box 6.1: Many young people in Nairobi slums lack education and training opportunities

About 60% of Nairobi's 3 million inhabitants live in slums. Occupying public land along two rivers, Korogocho and Viwandani are two of the poorest, with a combined population of around 66,000 in 2010. Young people aged 20 to 29 comprise a large share of this population – 31%, compared with around 18% in Kenya overall. Kenya's prospects of reducing poverty depend to a large extent on expanding secondary education and training opportunities for these young people, while improving their working conditions.

Inhabitants of the two slums live in extremely poor conditions: river pollution and proximity to industrial areas and dump sites create major health hazards. There are no secondary schools in either slum. Viwandani attracts more educated migrants from rural Kenya, many of whom then manage to move to non-slum settlements: about half of men and more than one-third of women living there have attended secondary school.

In Korogocho, only around 19% of men and 12% of women have attended secondary school. Training opportunities are sparse. Only around one in five of those aged 19 and 20 report having received any training in a trade or skill, and just half of these can use their training to help them earn an income.

About 50% of men and 80% of women aged 15 to 24 have no income-generating activities. Some, particularly young men, are still in school, but the rest are having trouble finding work. Many young women are confined to household work. Most of the employed (about 60% of men and 40% of women) are in petty trading or casual employment for survival. Around one-third work in the formal sector, but seldom in formal, salaried jobs. Most are in casual jobs with daily or short-term engagement.

Source: Oketch and Mutisya (2012).

---

2. Albania, Burkina Faso, Cambodia, Djibouti, Georgia, Honduras, Kenya, Pakistan and Yemen.

Employment for poor urban youth is mostly informal

Usually for the uneducated they find hard, labour work – for instance in construction. For the educated, they can be hired in offices that demand skills.

– young man, Ethiopia

In urban areas of developing countries, a large share of employment is in medium-sized, small and micro enterprises that operate informally – that is, they do not keep formal business records, have no legal status and are not regulated. Informal enterprises are typically fragile because they operate in markets that are limited geographically and often saturated with other informal businesses, as entry is relatively easy. In many cases, low levels of technology are used, output prices are low and customers are poor (Adams et al., forthcoming; Charmes, 2009; Palmer, 2007). The diversity of the informal sector makes its size and scope difficult to grasp (Box 6.2).

The informal sector is here to stay

It is difficult to find a job that lasts long. The longest period of work is not more than a week. And for my work I earn 30 birr (US$1.70) per day.

– young man, Ethiopia

Many young people around the world are employed in the informal sector. In sub-Saharan African countries including Côte d'Ivoire, Mali and Zambia, the informal sector accounts for

The ILO estimates that there are 1.53 billion in vulnerable employment

---

Box 6.2: Defining the urban informal sector

The informal sector is heterogeneous. It includes self-employed workers and family enterprises that do not regularly employ workers, as well as small and medium-sized enterprises that do. It covers a wide range of economic activities, from subsistence activities, such as waste-picking and street vending, to sewing and garment-making, car repair, construction and various crafts.

For many young people, particularly those with low levels of education, informal sector work is a necessity for survival. They receive very low pay and face poor and insecure working conditions. Others, with higher levels of education, may choose informal entrepreneurship rather than wait for a formal sector job – and for them it can be a pathway to prosperity.

Given the diversity of the informal sector, determining its size is problematic. The International Labour Organization (ILO) measures what it terms 'vulnerable employment', including own-account workers and unpaid family workers, aiming to indicate numbers in informal work arrangements characterized by low pay and difficult working conditions. The global vulnerable employment rate is put at around 50%, equivalent to 1.53 billion people worldwide. An alternative ILO measure of informal sector employment is the share of non-agricultural employment (Figure 6.2).

A further complication to measuring the informal sector arises when considering work in the sector in urban and rural areas together, without recognizing the distinctiveness of their labour markets. Since most agricultural employment and rural off-farm work is considered part of the informal sector, almost all work in some developing countries could be viewed as informal. Combining rural and urban sectors makes it difficult to establish a differentiated policy response.

The ILO and the Organisation for Economic Co-operation and Development (OECD) have attempted to bring together the definition of the informal sector with the broader concept of informal employment. Informal employment includes not just the informal sector but also workers in formal businesses who are employed without a contract, job security or benefits, and without labour regulations being enforced. This is likely to be a growing phenomenon in the economic downturn.

Distinguishing between the informal sector and informal employment, and between the informal sector in urban areas and that in rural areas, matters for policy formation. This chapter focuses primarily on the informal sector in urban areas of developing countries. Chapter 7 examines smallholder farming and non-farm work in rural areas.

Sources: Adams et al. (forthcoming); Charmes (2009); ILO (2011a); Palmer (2007); Walther (2006b); Walther and Filipiak (2007b).

---

around 70% of non-agricultural employment. In some countries in the region, women are much more likely than men to be working in the informal sector (Figure 6.2).

Large numbers are also in informal sector work in Latin American and the Caribbean. The informal sector accounts for more than half of total non-agricultural employment in poorer countries of the region, including the Plurinational State of Bolivia, Honduras, Nicaragua, Paraguay, and Peru – and one-quarter to one-third in more advanced economies such as Argentina or

Brazil. In some of these countries, a sizeable proportion is also in informal employment.

In South and West Asia, the informal sector is the main 'employer'. In India, 41% of both men and women in urban areas were self-employed in 2009/10, and 17% of men and 20% of women were casual labourers (Chowdhury, 2011). Informal employment represented about 70% of non-agricultural employment during the 2000s in East Asian countries, whether in the informal sector or the formal sector (Charmes, 2009; World Bank, 2010a). The share of informal

Figure 6.2: The urban informal sector employs large numbers in low and middle income countries

Share of employment in the informal sector, and of informal employment outside the informal sector, in non-agricultural employment, selected countries, late 2000s.

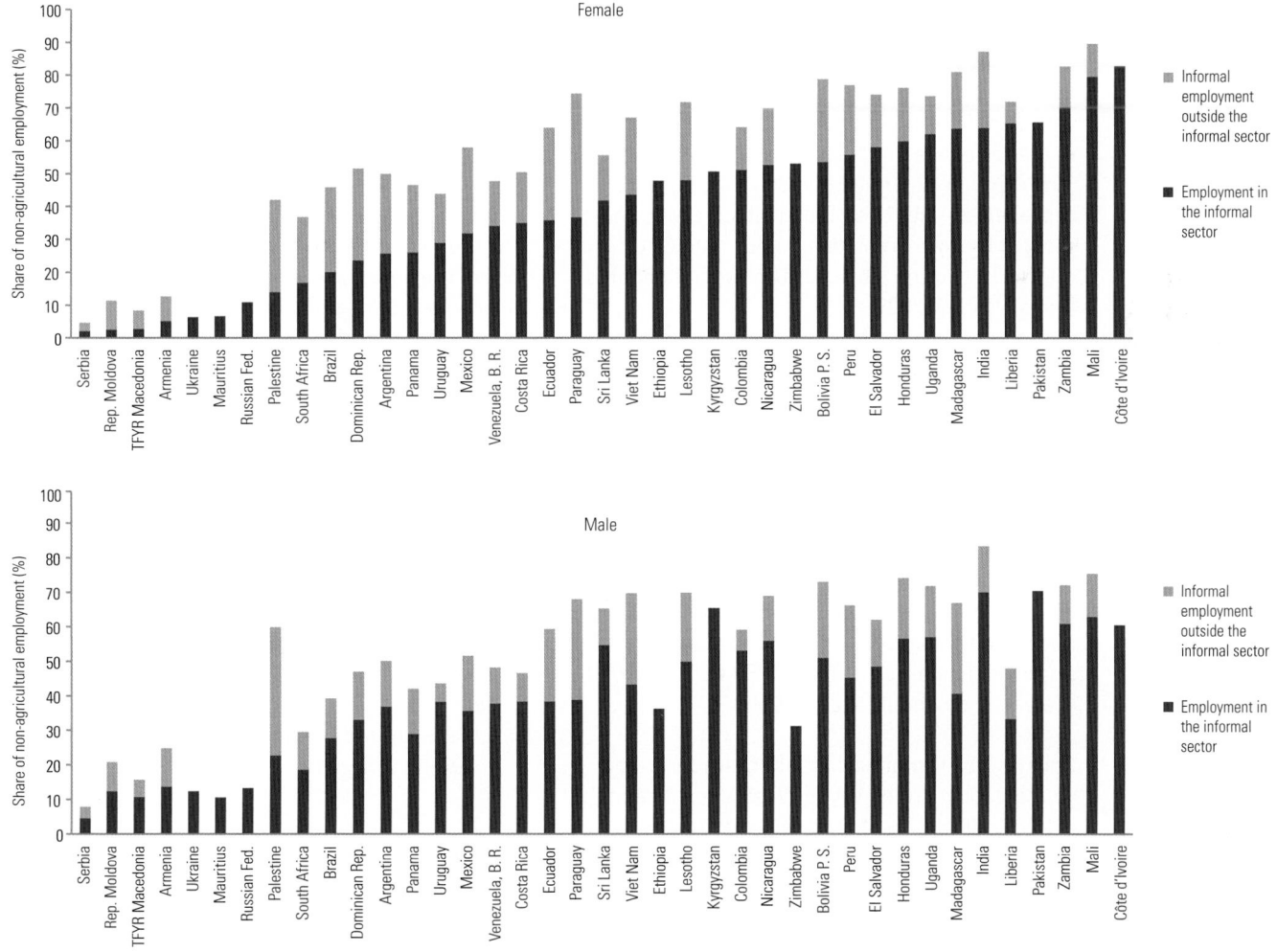

Note: Data pertain to the latest year available, between 2008 and 2010 for most countries.
Source: ILO (2011d).

employment in non-agricultural employment varied widely across the Arab States during the 2000s, from 31% in the Syrian Arab Republic to 67% in Morocco (Charmes, 2009).

After the ILO recognized the existence of the informal sector in the early 1970s, it was expected to be a temporary phenomenon, providing work opportunities until the formal sector created more jobs. In the 1980s, however, structural adjustment programmes and slow economic growth led to a reduction in public sector jobs that was not offset by job creation in the formal private sector. Rapid economic growth in the 2000s did not reverse these trends, so the informal sector has persisted and, in the current economic downturn, is likely to grow.

The decline in public sector jobs and the persistence of the informal sector has increased job insecurity for disadvantaged youth. In India, the number of workers employed in the formal sector rose from 54.1 million in 1999/2000 to 62.6 million in 2004/05, but this represented only 14% of total job creation, and most of the jobs created in the formal sector offered little or no job security or social benefits (India NCEUS, 2009).

Formal jobs remain a distant dream for many young people

While over 80% of employed men and over 90% of employed women aged 15 to 24 worked in the informal private sector in West African capitals in the early 2000s, employment in the public sector was rare (Nordman and Pasquier-Doumer, 2012). In 1980 in urban Burkina Faso, 13% of men aged 15 to 24 had obtained their first job in the formal public sector, but the share fell to 8% in 1990 and 3% in 2000. The same trend was observed for the formal private sector, with the share declining from 10% in 1980 to 5% in 2000 (Calvès and Schoumaker, 2004).

Formal jobs remain a distant dream for many young people. In the seven West African capitals, in 2001–2002, 27% of youth aged 15 to 24 expressed a wish to join the public sector, even though it accounted for only 4% of jobs created the previous two years, as opposed to 82% for the informal sector (Brilleau et al., 2004)
.

Education can enhance earnings in the informal sector

Evidence suggests that returns to education and skills in the informal sector can be strong. A study of informal sector workers in seven West African capitals found that those who had completed primary or lower secondary education could earn 20% to 50% more than those without qualifications, in most cases. Informal sector workers holding a vocational secondary school certificate rather than the secondary general education diploma received earnings premiums of between 80% and 110% in four of the seven cities (Kuepie et al., 2006).

High returns in some situations show that the informal sector can become a more attractive option when young people have the appropriate skills, but many enter the informal sector lacking foundation skills. In Rwanda in 2006, only 12% of those working in the informal sector had studied beyond the lower secondary level, compared with 40% in the formal sector (Adams et al., forthcoming).

But conditions do not always enable microentrepreneurs to raise their earnings above the poverty level, for example where they operate in saturated markets in which most consumers are poor as well. In Kingston, Jamaica, market stalls, street vendors, grocery shops and taxis provide an illusion of prosperity, but most make little if any profit. Many youth in such settings are 'necessity entrepreneurs' lacking marketing skills and other business skills (Grant, 2012; Rakodi, 2004).

Discrimination excludes many from good jobs

Employers prefer boys to work for them. They don't want girls to work for them. They turn girls away and feel there could be problems by employing girls.

– young woman, India

Even if the challenges facing young people living in poor urban areas can be solved, discrimination both in education and in labour markets denies opportunities to certain groups, notably young women and people with disabilities. This requires special attention in policy.

Discriminatory social norms (such as early marriage) and institutional practices limit young women's mobility and access to education and training, as well as to paid work, while imposing a heavy burden of unpaid, domestic work. More women than men are employed either in the informal sector or informally in the formal sector in twenty-five of thirty-nine countries in a recent ILO survey (Figure 6.2). The range of activities women engage in is constrained: many are confined to home-based work, and women are overrepresented in the most informal and insecure activities, such as waste-picking and street vending.

In urban Bolivia, where female labour force participation is high by Latin American standards, women are much more likely than men to be self-employed in the informal sector, and have much lower earnings (World Bank, 2009b). Women also face discrimination in pay in informal work. In greater Buenos Aires, controlling for education, qualifications, industry and personal characteristics, wages were 20% higher for men working in informal firms than women (Esquivel, 2010).

Young disabled people also face discrimination in education and labour markets. The limited evidence available points to their lower activity rates and higher unemployment in urban areas, even where legislation is meant to protect against discrimination in the labour market (Freedman, 2008). The lack of access to employment of youth living with disabilities is compounded by discriminatory attitudes, inaccessible environments, and physical and communication barriers. Among young people living with disabilities, young women are further disadvantaged (Kett, 2012; UNDESA, 2012).

A pilot survey conducted in 2009 in five urban areas of Sierra Leone found that 69% of people living with disabilities had no income at all, and 28% were living in households with no income. Youth aged 15 to 25 with disabilities were 8.5 times less likely to work than those without disabilities (Kett, 2012).

Expanding skills training opportunities for disadvantaged youth

Public policies fostering skills development for young people are crucial to the development of urban economies. Because of the diversity of the informal sector, training needs are wide-ranging. For some youth, the most immediate need is a second chance to develop foundation skills. Approaches that combine basic literacy and numeracy with social protection can be particularly effective. Those who have already achieved foundation skills need equitable opportunities to develop further skills in a trade, as well as transferable skills to enable them to become more successful entrepreneurs.

National skills strategies need to include disadvantaged urban youth

Given their share in the employment and output of urban areas, informal enterprises should be a key concern in national skills development strategies, yet this is not the case (Fluitman, 2009, 2010; Walther and Filipiak, 2007b). A review of forty-six developing countries in the Arab States, South and West Asia, and sub-Saharan Africa conducted for this Report shows that most do not have a national skills development strategy that explicitly addresses the urban informal sector (Engel, 2012). Reforms of formal technical and vocational education and training are seen as the main policy option, and training for those who have left the formal system is rarely mentioned. India's ambitious strategy is a notable exception, but faces challenges in reaching disadvantaged young people (Box 6.3).

Combining skills training with broader protection of informal sector workers

Given the precarious circumstances of many informal sector workers, a vital first step towards enabling them to participate in skills training programmes is offering them broader social support, including legal protection, to help them move out of high risk environments.

The situation of street vendors, who make up a large number of informal sector workers in many countries, illustrates this need. India's urban

In greater Buenos Aires, men in informal firms earned 20% more than women

2
0
1
2

Education for All Global Monitoring Report

Box 6.3: India's skills strategy recognizes training needs for the urban informal sector

India's training policy historically focused on the formal sector and operated on a small scale. By the mid-2000s, the overwhelming majority of urban youth had received no training. Resulting skills shortages risk hampering India's rapid economic growth and reinforcing inequality.

Since 2008, India has embarked on an ambitious strategy to raise the number of skilled workers to 500 million by 2022. The National Council on Skill Development formulates principles and provides policy advice, while strategy design is entrusted to national and state boards. A non-profit partnership between the government and the private sector, the National Skill Development Corporation (NSDC), is in charge of implementation, for which a National Skill Development Fund has been created. The overall approach is to finance short-term courses (no more than six months) delivered by either public or private providers, including apprenticeships, and to assure the relevance of training to rapidly changing market and technological conditions through cooperation with the private sector and non-governmental organizations (NGOs). A National Vocational Education Qualifications Framework is also being proposed.

Skills development in informal businesses is vital, as they employ most workers and are linked to formal companies via outsourcing and contract work. The NSDC has identified the 'unorganized sector' as a priority area and proposed a framework for a Labour Market Information System that would cover that sector. Detailed analysis was conducted of labour demand and skills gaps in activities where employment is mostly or entirely informal, such as construction, textiles, transportation, tourism, jewellery, domestic work and private security. A proposal by the Self-Employed Women's Association was one of the first proposals funded by the National Skill Development Fund.

A comprehensive Action Programme for the Unorganized Sector proposed by the National Commission on Enterprises in the Unorganized Sector, appointed in 2004, was not fully implemented, however. For the time being, India's principal focus remains on formal institutions such as (public) Industrial Training Institutes and (private) Industrial Training Centres, working with high growth sectors such as automobiles, textiles, food processing, tourism and banking. Access to such training and employment remains difficult for marginalized urban youth, who lack foundation skills, who cannot take time off even for free training and whose mobility is constrained by gender- or caste-based discrimination.

Sources: India NCEUS (2009); India NSDC (2011, n.d.); Sudarshan (2012).

India's national policy recognizes technical and business training for street vendors

areas were estimated to have 10 million street vendors in the mid-2000s (Bhowmik, 2005), and South Africa's some 445,000 around 2000 (Mitullah, 2004). Women are overrepresented. A study in Uganda found that those who turned to street vending tended to do so because they could not engage in other activities due to poverty, orphanhood, widowhood and low levels of education. Studies across Africa show that vendors face long working hours and poor working and living conditions, characterized by lack of shelter, roads, water, toilets, sewerage and garbage collection (Mitullah, 2004).

Street vendors, like others working in particularly insecure work, are sometimes harassed by police or other officials because they lack legal protection. This increases their economic uncertainty and hampers any training effort. Mohammed Bouazizi, the street vendor whose self-immolation is said to have been a catalyst for the revolution in Tunisia and the wider Arab Spring in 2011, set himself on fire in protest against the ongoing harassment that he reported was inflicted on him by police and a municipal official.

Some national and local governments have taken measures to facilitate training of subsistence workers. India's National Policy on Street Vendors states that, as street vendors run microenterprises, they should receive training to upgrade their technical and business skills so they can increase their income and look for alternative work (India MHUPA, 2006). In Malaysia, the economic crisis of the late 1990s led to large losses of jobs in the formal sector through mergers, downsizing of production units and outsourcing of work to the informal sector. Many laid-off workers became street vendors, whose numbers increased sharply between 1990 and 2000. The Department of Hawkers and Petty Traders regulates and controls their activities while funding credit and training programmes in areas such as business skills, accounting, health and hygiene, as food stalls account for a large share of street shops (Bhowmik, 2005).

NGOs, trade unions and other social movements are often more active than governments or donors in improving conditions for subsistence workers. India's Self-Employed Women's

Association (SEWA), a trade union registered in 1972, provides a variety of services: banking, insurance, legal aid, health care and child care, together with training in literacy, vocational skills and political mobilization (Chen et al., 2006; Jhabvala et al., n.d.). Negative perceptions about women's skills and capabilities among male builders, engineers, supervisors and clients have made it difficult for women to access new work opportunities. SEWA's answer has been the promotion of a cooperative of women that provides technical training and links up with employers to facilitate placement (Sudarshan, 2012).

SEWA inspired the creation of the Self-Employed Women's Union (SEWU) in South Africa. It has helped training providers adapt their courses to the needs of its members and has subsidized members' participation. This has allowed women to receive training in vocational skills such as baking, fashion design and sewing as well as in more general management skills and in English. SEWU has encouraged its members to receive training in male-dominated areas such as construction and wire fencing (Devenish and Skinner, 2004).

Giving disadvantaged youth a second chance

A huge number of young people living in urban poverty need a second chance to learn basic skills. Existing programmes are mainly provided by NGOs, largely because they are perceived as too expensive by many low income countries that are already struggling to strengthen primary schooling (Garcia and Fares, 2008).

Although there are many innovative approaches, second-chance opportunities in the parts of the world where they are needed the most are often small in scale. They also tend to be poorly coordinated, and governments often have little information about their activities.

Second-chance programmes aim to provide basic skills corresponding to the primary education curriculum so as to improve young people's employability. Practical curricula that offer technical skills, together with flexible schedules and less formal instruction methods, are the most attractive to young people. Programmes are more likely to be successful if they are part of a package that also offers other forms of

social protection to address the multiple disadvantages that young people often face.

Many second-chance opportunities focus on children who have just missed the opportunity for schooling. It is vital for these to be extended to 15- to 24-year-olds, who also need the chance to catch up. Accelerated learning programmes that have been developed in conflict-affected countries, including Afghanistan, Liberia, Sierra Leone, South Sudan and Uganda, offer some positive experience. The programmes focus on promoting re-entry into primary and secondary education for out-of-school youth. In addition to basic literacy and numeracy, the curriculum incorporates life skill subjects and sometimes includes vocational education and microenterprise activities (Nicholson, 2007).

Even where second-chance programmes are successful in extending basic literacy and numeracy skills, one problem they can face is ensuring that these translate into improved work opportunities for young people. In Liberia, the government has run an accelerated learning programme since 1998 with UNICEF support, providing ex-combatants and older youth with three years of education covering the primary school curriculum. Successful students are then qualified to continue in the formal education system, but some use their new skills as the basis for engaging in small businesses to improve their lives. By 2009, the programme had reached around 75,820 students, almost half of them female. In 2008, 93% of graduates passed national exams allowing them to progress further with their education (Nicholson, 2007; Nkutu et al., 2010). Participants were, however, critical of the lack of technical and vocational teaching in the programme and of the absence of links with the labour market (Williams and Bentrovato, 2010).

Addressing the need to combine a second chance in basic literacy and numeracy with vocational skills to improve work opportunities, the Training for Employment project in Nepal was implemented between 2000 and 2008 by a local organization, the Alliance for Social Mobilization. The project aimed to provide access to technical and vocational education and training to out-of-school young people. Training packages of six to fifteen months were developed

Second-chance programmes need to be scaled up

2012

Education for All Global Monitoring Report

Second-chance programmes need to be well aligned with the labour market

for a broad range of activities, such as car repair, computer hardware maintenance, construction and cooking. They were open to youth with five to eight years of schooling. All packages included on-the-job training, and employers were consulted during their design. The number participating in the project was small: 854, 37% of whom were women. But it was successful in reaching marginalized groups – 66% of students belonged to disadvantaged castes or ethnic minorities. A tracer study covering 206 project graduates reported that 73% had found employment (Paudyal, 2008).

Similarly, in Jordan, where overall enrolment is relatively high, large numbers of young people are still missing out on education. Questscope, an international NGO, has run a second-chance education programme since 2000, targeting youths who missed out on education or dropped out. The aim is to provide twenty-four months of accelerated learning towards grade 10 requirements, together with tutoring, so that programme graduates may re-enter the formal education system or have access to loans to start a microenterprise. According to Questscope, more than 7,000 youth have participated (Questscope, 2012). About 98% of those who sat the 10th grade proficiency test at the end of the programme passed and were able to continue with formal education (Angel-Urdinola et al., 2010).

It is vital to strengthen and expand second-chance programmes to give disadvantaged young people better work opportunities. To be successful, such programmes need to be well targeted and geared towards labour market needs, and provide the opportunity for young people to re-enter the education system.

Packaging skills training with pro-poor programmes

If young people engaged in subsistence activities are to move on to more profitable informal sector activities, they need to improve their literacy and numeracy skills as well as to acquire technical and vocational skills. To set up a profitable small business, for example, young people need not only credit but also financial skills to invest the money wisely. They also need

help to overcome disadvantages such as poor health, insufficient assets and lack of networks. Since young women face even greater adversity, they require particular attention.

Microfinance and social protection programmes have been successful in alleviating the immediate financial constraints that disadvantaged young people face but have tended to pay insufficient attention to transforming their lives in the longer term. Providing skills training as part of the package can change this.

Microfinance seeks to alleviate financial constraints on self-employment and entrepreneurship. Initially it offered only small loans, but it now includes savings and insurance services. In 2010, 82% of all microcredit clients lived in Asia; 7% were in Latin America and the Caribbean, 6% in sub-Saharan Africa and 2% in the Middle East and North Africa (Maes and Reed, 2012). Microfinance started in rural areas, but has recently expanded to urban areas.

Often targeted at women, microfinance has been hailed as promoting women's empowerment and gender equality and improving children's health and education, but evaluations find a significant impact only on access to credit and business outcomes. In slums in Hyderabad, India, the introduction of group-based lending resulted in an increase in the number of new businesses and in the purchase of business durables but had no impact on consumption or human development indicators (Banerjee et al., 2010).

Social protection programmes organized by governments and aid donors, including cash transfers and public works programmes, aim to protect the poor from economic crises and other income shocks. These programmes, which usually have national coverage, have outcomes that contrast markedly with those of microfinance. Cash transfers, which are often small, are mostly used by households to meet basic consumption needs. Nutrition improves, access to health care or education may also improve, but there is rarely productive investment (McCord, 2012).

Incorporating skills development into microfinance or social protection measures can make them 'transformative', allowing their beneficiaries to improve their livelihoods permanently and to move out of poverty. Some programmes have begun to include skills training, but evidence on them is limited so far.

Microfinance institutions could become an effective vehicle for skills training

Microfinance institutions could be a good platform for training, as they already reach large numbers of the poor. At the end of 2010, 3,652 microfinance institutions reported having more than 205 million clients with a current loan, 55% of whom were women living below the international poverty line of US$1.25 a day when they took up the loan (Banerjee et al., 2010; Maes and Reed, 2012). Recent studies show that beneficiaries lack technical, entrepreneurial and financial skills that microfinance institutions assumed they had (Karlan and Valdivia, 2006).

Microfinance programmes offering entrepreneurial training are rare, but some experience indicates they can be very effective. In 2002–2003, the Foundation for International Community Assistance, which provides credit and savings services to young, poor, largely female microentrepreneurs, introduced entrepreneurial training in mandatory weekly meetings with its clients in Lima and Ayacucho, Peru. A randomized evaluation found that participants were more likely to maintain records of sales and expenses, reinvest profits in the business and plan for future expansion, resulting in higher, less volatile income (Karlan and Valdivia, 2006).

One reason for the programme's success is that credit officers received training. More generally, though, NGOs specialized in microfinance may not be efficient in skills development. Where credit officers are asked to double as trainers, they need teaching skills and training in subjects such as health education, entrepreneurship and financial literacy.

Skills training is necessary to sustain the benefits of social protection

Adding skills development to social protection programmes may help their beneficiaries gain greater autonomy; by the same token, complementing training programmes with cash transfers, to help learners meet their basic

consumption needs during the training period, can improve retention and completion. Training may also be associated with public works jobs, either by making initial life skills or vocational training a condition for receiving work or by emphasizing on-the-job training and work experience (McCord, 2012).

Social protection programmes help young people move into the labour market who would not otherwise be employed, particularly women (McCord, 2012). The programme Chile Solidario, introduced in 2002, provides cash transfers for twenty-four months to extremely poor families in Chile, as long as they cooperate with a social worker who helps them identify and solve their main problems and raises their awareness and use of social services. Participants are then given preferential access to other programmes, including training aimed at increasing employability. After 2004, specific programmes focused on women with low educational attainment and little or no professional experience. The programme now reaches 40,000 to 50,000 families every year, 60% of which belong to the poorest fifth of the population and more than 80% of which live in urban areas. Employment grew by up to four to six percentage points among women who entered the programme in 2005, partly through increased participation in the training programmes (Carneiro et al., 2009).

Experience from South Africa's Expanded Public Works Programme, initiated in 2004, highlights the importance of ensuring that training is sufficiently long and of appropriate quality to be transformative (Box 6.4).

Overall, transformative microfinance and social protection programmes are promising, but they are harder to design and implement than individual interventions, and may therefore be more difficult in contexts where institutional capacity is weak, as in many low income countries.

Scaling up the programmes is also difficult, even for governments and aid donors. In Afghanistan, the World Food Programme's Food for Training provided poor urban widows (including, though not targeting, youth) with food rations as well as training in functional literacy, health, and vocational skills such as handicrafts, tailoring

Cash transfers and training in Chile increased employment for women

2012

Education for All Global Monitoring Report

Box 6.4: Enhancing outcomes of South Africa's Expanded Public Works Programme through skills training

South Africa's Expanded Public Works Programme aims to extend job opportunities in a context of extremely high unemployment. By December 2010, only 12.5% of youth aged 15-24 were employed. The recession that hit South Africa resulted in a contraction of youth employment – youth accounted for 40% of jobs lost over the period. Unemployment rates were higher for youth aged 18-24 who had at most some secondary education compared with those with tertiary education.

The first phase of the public works programme (2004-2009) aimed to provide 100,000 to 200,000 short-term work opportunities each year for four to six months in total. A second phase (2009-2014) aims at even broader coverage; in 2014 the programme expects to offer 1.5 million work opportunities lasting 100 days each. Work is in areas such as road construction and maintenance, home care for elderly people,

child care and providing school meals. For every month worked, participants take two days of training, including life skills (HIV awareness, job search skills), on-the-job learning and formal training.

An evaluation of the first phase found that the number of work opportunities created had far exceeded targets but that only 46% of the target number of days of training had been reached. Difficulties defining relevant training content and a scarcity of good quality training providers sometimes posed problems. The benefits of the training received were further affected by the limited duration of public works and the low wage paid: at best workers could invest in survivalist microenterprise activities. Investing more in training could help ensure that the programme has a more sustainable impact.

Sources: McCord (2005, 2012); Meth (2011); South Africa National Treasury (2011); Walther et al. (2006a).

and embroidery. Shortages of implementing organizations and trainers prevented the programme from reaching the poorest women and those most in need of food, however, and it proved difficult to expand to rural areas (WFP, 2004).

Despite these challenges, when social protection and microfinance programmes are carefully designed and implemented to incorporate relevant skills training, they can enhance the opportunities for disadvantaged youth to work in improved conditions.

In Latin America, work experience along with classroom training has reduced unemployment

Programmes targeting unemployed youth are successful, but need resources

Programmes that combine basic literacy and numeracy, vocational skills training and other forms of support to enhance employability have been successful in some parts of the world, notably in Latin America and the Caribbean. Innovative programmes in the region offer classroom training and work experience in basic and specific trades, alongside life skills, job search assistance, counselling and information. Participants receive stipends and their employers receive wage subsidies. The programmes have played a key role in countries where large

numbers of young people living in poor urban conditions lack opportunities for good jobs.

Several programmes have been found to raise rates of employment, formality of employment and earnings, particularly for women and youth from poorer households (Betcherman et al., 2007). For instance, the Inter-American Development Bank has run programmes in Argentina, Chile, Colombia, the Dominican Republic, Mexico, Panama and Peru that provide short training covering both basic job readiness skills and specific vocational skills. These have increased participants' employment rates and job quality, defined by wages, social benefits and formality (Card et al., 2011; Ibarrarán and Rosas Shady, 2009).

In Mexico, PROBECAT (Programa de Becas de Capacitación para Trabajadores Desempleados/ Unemployed Workers' Training Grants Program), which began in 1984, relies on companies rather than training institutions. Beneficiaries receive a stipend equivalent to the minimum wage. They are trained in private sector businesses, which cover the training costs and have to offer them an internship of at least three months. Companies have to agree to keep at least 70% of the trainees for one year (Ibarrarán and Rosas Shady, 2009).

Jóvenes is another successful programme in Latin America. It was introduced in Chile in 1991, targeting unemployed or underemployed youth aged 16 to 29, with eligibility tied to income, educational attainment (below secondary education), gender and region of residence. It has been successfully replicated in Argentina, Colombia, the Dominican Republic, Panama, Paraguay, Peru and the Bolivarian Republic of Venezuela. While governments have coordinated and funded Jóvenes programmes, they are delivered by private providers selected through competitive bidding. This helps assure the quality of the training and its relevance to labour market demand. Evaluations indicate that the programmes have improved labour market outcomes, particularly for younger participants and women (Box 6.5).

In Colombia, between 2001 and 2005, Jóvenes en Acción targeted poor youth aged 18 to 25 who were unemployed or working informally. Participants received three months of classroom training and three months of on-the-job training in the country's seven largest cities. Courses covered a wide range of activities aimed at the needs of the formal sector. Random selection of participants from a larger group of applicants found a strong positive impact on women: their probability of being in paid employment rose by 7% and their wages by almost 20%. The likelihood of being in formal employment also increased significantly, by 7% for women and 5% for men (Attanasio et al., 2011).

The drawback is that these programmes tend to be expensive. The cost per participant ranges from US$700 to US$2,000 – clearly unaffordable for many of the low income countries (Betcherman et al., 2007). In addition, for the programmes to be successful, a country has to have enough companies able to participate, and parts of sub-Saharan Africa may not meet this criterion.

Most Jóvenes programmes have been integrated into national public training institutions or replaced by smaller interventions. Since 2002, a new model has emerged in Latin America: Entra 21, conceived by the International Youth Foundation and funded by the Inter-American Development Bank, local organizations, multinational companies and other partners. Like the Jóvenes programmes, Entra 21 targets

In Colombia, three months of training increased women's wages by 20%

Box 6.5: Peru's PROJoven programme helps young people find better jobs

In Peru, as in other Latin American countries, large numbers of young people work in the informal sector. While access to primary schooling is high, many still leave school lacking foundation skills. In 2009, around one-quarter of young people were neither in employment nor education or training, and 76% of women and 66% of men were working in the informal sector.

When PROJoven (Programa de Capacitación Laboral Juvenil/Youth Labour Training Programme) was introduced in 1996 following the Jóvenes model, poor youth in particular were less likely to receive any training and only had access to institutions of lower quality. The programme was funded by a variety of national and donor sources, including the Inter-American Development Bank, and run by the Ministry of Labour. It targeted youth aged 16 to 24 who had low educational attainment, lacked work experience and were unemployed, underemployed or inactive. Almost all belonged to poor households. The focus was on basic or semi-skilled training to improve employability in the short term. Between 1996 and 2003, about 42,000 youths participated. Courses, financed by PROJoven, were offered in training centres for three months, followed by a three-month internship in private firms that had to pay trainees at least the minimum wage.

Participation in the programme significantly improved young people's chances of securing a paid job, and increased their monthly earnings. The impact was larger for younger participants (aged 16 to 20) and for women. For instance, the likelihood of gaining access to formal employment increased by between seven and thirteen percentage points among men and by seventeen to twenty-one percentage points for females. Close links between training centres and participating companies may have contributed to the positive outcomes.

Sources: Cárdenas et al. (2011); Díaz and Jaramillo (2006); ILO (2011d).

unemployed youth aged 16 to 29, providing them with short-term training[3] in technical skills, life skills and job-search skills, combined with internships with local employers. One innovation of Entra 21 is that almost half of training focuses on information and communication technology skills, responding to growing employer demand. A second innovation is the inclusion of job placement services in close association with local employers (Pezzullo, 2006).

The first phase of Entra 21 projects operated between 2001 and 2007 through thirty-five local projects in eighteen countries.[4] They attracted almost 20,000 young people, well beyond the initial target of 12,000. Of these, 54% were female. The vast majority were from poor urban families. But unlike Jóvenes, Entra 21 mainly benefited youth who had completed upper secondary school rather than very poor youth with low educational attainment (Lasida and Rodriguez, 2006; Pezzullo, 2009). Some projects did include basic literacy and numeracy training for youth with lower initial achievement, but this accounted for only 5% of training time on average (Pezzullo, 2009).

Evaluations of twenty-eight projects between 2005 and 2007 show several positive outcomes on employment and wages six months after participants had graduated. A shortcoming of the first phase of Entra 21, however, in addition to the lack of targeting of poorly educated young people, was that women did not benefit to the same degree as men in most countries, in contrast to the Jóvenes programme. On average, controlling for age and education, a female graduate was only 59% as likely as a male to get a job. Men earned 32% more than the minimum wage and women only 19% more (Pezzullo, 2009).

In response, the second phase of Entra 21, starting in 2007, targeted young people who were more disadvantaged than those in the first phase, including those with less than ten years of formal education, people living with disabilities, and youth living in rural areas. By early 2011,

In Indonesia, a second-chance programme costs US$300 per student

more than 51,500 had enrolled, exceeding the target of 50,000 (Pezzullo, 2011).

Entra 21's evaluation of programmes in four countries[5] indicated that vulnerable youth in the second phase found it harder to keep up with classes or internships, mainly because of lack of formal education or personal circumstances such as child care and family problems. To retain trainees, projects had to provide tutoring, basic literacy and numeracy training and personalized attention to respond to special needs. About 40% of employers in Ecuador said the youth lacked sufficient technical, mathematic or literacy skills. This led employers to allot more time to upgrading trainees' basic skills so they could acquire sufficiently high levels of work skills.

Another difficulty was that employers were sometimes reluctant to recruit disadvantaged youth into the programmes. In Nicaragua, some employers were initially unwilling to hire youth who lived in high crime neighbourhoods. However, once businesses overcame their resistance, they reported being satisfied with the trainees' performance (International Youth Foundation, 2011). To overcome potential prejudice and negative stereotypes, it is important to establish strong relationships with businesses, NGOs and the public sector.

The Latin American experience formed the basis for programmes targeting unemployed youth in other emerging economies. Indonesia's Education for Youth Employment programme was an example. Although Indonesia is a middle income country that has experienced relatively high levels of growth, income-related and regional disparities in education are strong. Education for Youth Employment targeted poor, unemployed youth aged 16 to 24 with low educational attainment. It sought to improve 'equivalency education' at secondary level. The programme included training in life skills and had a job placement component using a network of companies. A 2006 evaluation found that 82% of participants were employed after three to four months of training, at a cost per participant of US$300. After three years, 80% of those were still employed and receiving at least the local minimum wage (di Gropello et al., 2011).

---

3. The duration ranged from 270 hours to 1,210 hours over 4 to 12 months.
4. Argentina, Belize, the Plurinational State of Bolivia, Brazil, Chile, Colombia, the Dominican Republic, Ecuador, El Salvador, Guatemala, Honduras, Mexico, Nicaragua, Panama, Paraguay, Peru, Uruguay and the Bolivarian Republic of Venezuela.

5. Ecuador, Nicaragua, Paraguay and Peru.

If programmes for unemployed youth are well targeted and offer a comprehensive range of skills development training, as the Jóvenes programmes have done, this increases their chances of reaching the most vulnerable young people and improving their earnings and employment. The successes of these Latin American programmes in targeting disadvantaged young people hold lessons for the Arab States, where government and private training programmes tend to focus on highly educated youth (Subrahmanyam, 2011).

In Morocco, for example, where around 30% of the population is aged 15 to 29, about 90% of females and 40% of males not in school are either unemployed or not in the labour force. Among the unemployed, 80% have less than secondary education. Yet policy interventions tackling unemployment have tended to focus on the 5% who have benefited from tertiary education, in part because these young people have been better able to exert media and sociopolitical influence (World Bank, 2012b).

Beyond foundation skills for disadvantaged youth

To improve the employability of young people who already possess foundation skills, policies need to foster the development of transferable and technical skills, especially in small and medium-sized informal businesses with growth potential. Governments need to identify activity sectors to be targeted and organize training in the relevant skills. Two promising avenues for such efforts are traditional apprenticeships, which are already a major provider of skills development for informal sector workers, and training to enhance entrepreneurship.

Expanding access to traditional apprenticeships

In many countries, more youth are trained in the urban informal sector through traditional apprenticeships than in formal training institutions: costs for their families are usually lower, as are educational entry requirements. The poorest may still be disadvantaged, though, especially where apprentices are recruited through family or community networks, and young women are largely excluded from

male-dominated activities. Making access to traditional apprenticeships more equitable and improving their quality are key priorities for skills development policy.

In sub-Saharan Africa, traditional apprenticeship is the main type of skills training in the informal sector (Johanson and Adams, 2004). In the mid-2000s, Senegal had just 10,000 young people in formal technical and vocational education training compared with 440,000 traditional apprentices in the motor repair business alone (Walther, 2011). In Ghana, according to various sources, apprenticeship training is responsible for 80% to 90% of all skills training, compared with no more than 5% to 10% for public training institutions and 10% to 15% for NGOs (both for-profit and non-profit) (Palmer, 2007).

Traditional apprenticeships are also found in other regions. In Pakistan, where official statistics estimate that 79% of youth aged 15 to 24 working outside of agriculture are employed in the informal sector, traditional apprenticeships are the most prevalent mode of skills acquisition (Bhatti et al., 2011; Janjua and Naveed, 2009).

Traditional apprenticeship has several advantages over formal training. It is more flexible, cheaper, and has immediate practical relevance. Many apprentices are hired in the workshop where they were trained. In Punjab and Khyber Pakhtunkhwa provinces of Pakistan in 2006–2007, the average length of apprenticeship was longer than formal technical and vocational education and training courses, yet the average cost for households was less than one-tenth as much (Bhatti et al., 2011).

For many young people, therefore, traditional apprenticeships are the preferred way to acquire skills. In Kenya, in the early 2000s, the World Bank-financed Micro and Small Enterprise Training and Technology Project distributed vouchers to 24,000 informal sector manufacturing workers, letting them choose what kind of training they wanted to receive, and from whom. Only 15% of participants opted for public or private training institutions, while 85% chose to train with master craftspeople. A strong preference was thus revealed for traditional

In sub-Saharan Africa, most skills training in the informal sector is in apprenticeships

Access to apprenticeships is broad but not equitable

apprenticeships, a type of provision that had hitherto been 'invisible' to policy-makers (Johanson, 2002; Johanson and Adams, 2004; Riley and Steel, 2000).

There are disadvantages, however, with this form of training. Access may be broader than in formal training, but it is not equitable. In Ghana, for instance, the poorest and least educated are disadvantaged: in 2008, only 11% of the poorest 20% of 15- to 30-year-olds had done an apprenticeship, as opposed to 47% of the wealthiest. Only 9% of those with no education had been apprentices, compared with 51% of those who had completed lower secondary education (Adams et al., forthcoming).

Such differences in access are compounded by differences in employment status and earnings once the apprenticeship is completed. According to 2005/06 data from the Ghanaian Living Standards Survey, less than 20% of former apprentices with no formal education were working and had earnings placing them above the poverty line, compared with about 30% of those who had attained lower or upper secondary school. In urban areas, the mean earnings of former apprentices who had attended lower secondary school were almost triple those of former apprentices with only primary education (Baradai, 2012).

Traditional apprenticeship systems may also reflect gender segregation in the local labour market. A survey in the towns of Lindi and Mtwara in the United Republic of Tanzania found that 95% of apprentices in tailoring were women, but that there were hardly any female apprentices in the other trades surveyed, including carpentry, car mechanics, electrical service, food processing, local arts and plumbing (Nübler et al., 2009). Since most apprenticeships are in trades that women are less likely to take up, this limits their opportunity for training.

Lack of organization can lead to exploitation of sometimes very young apprentices in poor learning and working conditions (Johanson and Adams, 2004). In Lindi and Mtwara, apprentices worked 60 hours per week on average. While more than 90% of master craftspeople taught their apprentices technical skills specific to their occupation, and 65% gave theoretical background information, few masters also taught managerial

skills (Nübler et al., 2009). In Senegal, a study on motor repair found that young apprentices worked from 8 a.m. till 9 p.m. (Senegal METFP, 2007).

Public interventions building on traditional apprenticeship systems need to provide access to those usually excluded, improve skills of master craftspeople, improve working conditions of apprentices and ensure that skills are certified (Johanson and Adams, 2004; Walther, 2011; Walther and Filipiak, 2007b).

The size and potential of traditional apprenticeship systems have led several sub-Saharan African countries to pass laws on apprenticeship in recent years (Hofmann, 2011). Two distinct directions have been explored (Walther, 2011):

■ transforming traditional apprenticeships into a dual system that combines theoretical learning with practical training;

■ gradually recognizing traditional apprenticeships formally and providing them with support, including by training master craftspeople to improve their vocational and teaching skills and by introducing regulations, assessment and certification.

Both approaches face practical difficulties. For example, cooperation between formal training institutions and master craftspeople is often limited, and the state may lack the capacity to enforce regulations where there are no trade unions.

Reforms aiming to transform traditional apprenticeship into a dual apprenticeship system were developed in the 1990s and 2000s in several countries, starting with projects in Benin and Togo run by the Hans Seidel Foundation, a German development organization. Côte d'Ivoire, Mali, Senegal and the United Republic of Tanzania are also taking steps to reform traditional apprenticeships (Walther, 2011). The ILO has made the development of dual apprenticeship one of its priorities for action in these countries (ILO, 2008).

Evolution towards dual apprenticeship requires an agreement between the government and organizations representing informal sector employers and master craftspeople. It is therefore possible only to the extent such organizations exist. The agreement needs to define a model contract for apprenticeships and training structures. At the same time, formal training institutions need to be reformed to accommodate apprentices, to whom they provide theoretical training covering general education as well as technical and vocational skills. Apprentices are then awarded a diploma recognized by the national authorities and included in the national qualifications system (Walther, 2011).

If successfully implemented, dual apprenticeship can become an effective and sustainable part of national technical and vocational education and training systems. A study on the costs of training and job programmes in Burkina Faso showed that reformed apprenticeships cost about one-third as much as formal training courses (Walther and Savadogo, 2010).

In Benin, an experimental project in the city of Abomey in the 1990s led to a decision in 2001 to include dual apprenticeship as part of the country's technical and vocational education and training system. Political consensus and cooperation with unions and informal sector associations such as the Fédération Nationale des Artisans du Bénin (Benin National Craftspeople's Federation) allowed a relatively quick elaboration of the legal and regulatory framework by 2005/06. Dual apprenticeships last two to three years, with a day of theoretical training in a technical and vocational training institution and five days of practical training in a workshop every week. Master craftspeople are assisted by a local trainer, who acts as a link between the workshop and the training centre and facilitates the exchange between local languages spoken at the workshop and official languages used as the medium of instruction in training centres. Apprentices are awarded a professional qualification certificate after passing a national examination covering theory and practice. The number of youth entering dual apprenticeships progressed quickly, from 700 in 2006 to 1,740 in 2007. Barriers to further expansion included low levels of education among prospective apprentices, requiring pre-apprenticeship courses that were lacking. There was also a lack of ownership by informal sector associations, as funding remained dependent on aid donors (Walther and Filipiak, 2007a).

Reforms aiming to create dual apprenticeships require institutional capacity from the state and strong informal sector associations. Those initiated by aid donors may prove unsustainable once donor support is withdrawn. In Mali, interviews with masters and apprentices in five cities suggested that dual apprenticeships introduced in the late 1990s improved skills levels. Masters reported that apprentices were quicker, better at using materials and maintaining equipment, more autonomous and able to take on more responsibilities in the workshop. By the mid-2000s, however, traditional apprenticeships were still much more common than dual apprenticeships, the development of which was hampered by the institutional weakness of the country's training fund and of informal sector associations, which lacked capacity to train employers as trainers. The system remained dependent on donors, in this case the Swisscontact foundation (Thiéba and Ndiaye, 2004).

Gradually recognizing traditional apprenticeships formally may be an easier policy option than transforming them completely into dual apprenticeships. Such initiatives may be particularly efficient if designed and implemented in cooperation with informal sector associations or other professional organizations.

Gradual adoption of formal status can include regulations to protect apprentices from exploitation, a common issue in traditional systems. They include limits on daily and weekly working hours, a ceiling on the number of years of training for each type of occupation, and safety measures. In Senegal, PROMECABILE, a professional association in metalwork, mechanics and automobile maintenance, has set rules for apprenticeships conducted by its members regarding the age of apprentices, the duration of their training (linked to their initial education level) and availability of literacy classes. Training covers health and safety issues along with technical skills and apprentices can take nationally recognized diplomas. Further support is given for youth to start their own workshop or be employed by companies partnering with PROMECABILE (Walther, 2011; Walther and Filipiak, 2007b).

In Senegal, a professional association has set rules for apprenticeships

2012

Education for All Global Monitoring Report

In Egypt, 73% consider becoming an entrepreneur a desirable career choice

Gradual formal recognition of traditional apprenticeships also involves improvements in teaching practices and the introduction of certification, which are best promoted by informal sector associations. In Cameroon, the Interprofessional Association of Craftspeople (Groupement Interprofessionnel des Artisans, GIPA) comprises about 100 companies in Yaoundé. Member companies have, on average, three workers and two apprentices, and represent eleven trades, including joinery, tailoring, hairdressing, pottery and construction. Training at these companies used to be based on repetition and did not lead apprentices towards greater autonomy. GIPA has developed a pedagogy involving progression through several stages, with an evaluation at the end of each. The length of apprenticeship depends on apprentices' initial education level and their evaluation results. Vocational training is complemented with training in management. GIPA also organizes a common final examination in which a jury evaluates an object made by the apprentice and awards a certificate recognized by the Ministry of Employment and Vocational Training (Walther et al., 2006b).

Certifying apprentices' skills and work experience through national qualification frameworks may be a good way to recognize their legitimacy. Similar certificates would also benefit master craftspeople. Such measures would provide official acknowledgement of the part played by the informal sector in skills development for young people and help build capacity in the sector. However, measures of this type are often difficult to design and implement and require strong commitment from government and the informal labour market (King and Palmer, 2010; Walther, 2011).

When appropriately implemented, traditional apprenticeships have a lot to offer young people. Given their potential benefits, attention is needed to ensure that they extend access to disadvantaged groups, including young women.

Easing the path to entrepreneurship

I want to work in my own hair salon and be an owner, you don't depend on others who may exploit you. As an owner, you can do anything you want. I don't want others to exploit me.
— young woman, Viet Nam

Some young people working in the informal sector choose self-employment to avoid the rigidities of the formal sector. They tend to have higher education levels, parents who are entrepreneurs and access to the resources needed to start a business (DIAL, 2007). In the Arab States, many young people are eager to start their own businesses. A survey in Egypt, Palestine, Saudi Arabia and Tunisia revealed that the countries have particularly high total entrepreneurial activity rates, as does sub-Saharan Africa. In Egypt in 2008, 73% of the adult population considered entrepreneurship a desirable career choice, although only 40% saw opportunities for themselves to open a business in the next six months (Wally, 2012).

The lack of managerial or entrepreneurial skills has long been neglected by policy-makers and training providers, but it is a key constraint on the profitability and growth of the informal sector (Bruhn et al., 2010; Mano et al., 2011). Skilled entrepreneurs are better able to manage workers, maintain physical capital, and market and sell their products (Bruhn et al., 2010; Mano et al., 2011).

Data from the Global Entrepreneurship Monitor on thirty-eight low, middle and high income countries suggest that training programmes can make a difference provided there is a favourable environment allowing for the use of the knowledge, skills and perceptions developed through training. In low and middle income countries, this is often lacking, reducing programme impact (Coduras Martínez et al., 2010).

The impact of entrepreneurship training is often reduced because participants lack the financial assets required to apply their newly acquired skills. Another reason is that the complex nature of some skills requires initial levels of education higher than many trainees have attained:

- In a randomized experiment conducted in 2007 in the Dominican Republic, female microentrepreneurs in urban areas were taught either a simplified curriculum based on simple 'rules of thumb' (for example, microentrepreneurs were taught to pay themselves a wage, but to take no other money out of the company) or a more standard curriculum based on fundamental accounting principles such as cash-flow analysis. Business practices, such as setting cash aside for business expenditures, improved systematically in the group that received the simplified training suiting those with lower levels of education, but not in the group that studied the standard curriculum, which was more difficult (Drexler et al., 2011).

- A training programme for microentrepreneurs in car mechanics and metalwork was run in 2007 in Kumasi, Ghana's second-largest city. Training comprised three modules of five days each, covering business planning, marketing, production and quality management, record-keeping and costing. Participants' interest in the training was reflected in high attendance, and they were more likely than non-participants to adopt recommended business practices. For instance, the share of participants keeping business records increased from 28% before the training to 64%, the share analysing business records rose from 21% to 55% and those visiting customers went from 20% to 51%. Participants with higher levels of education were more likely to start keeping records, pointing to complementarities between entrepreneurship training and formal education (Mano et al., 2011).

- In Bosnia and Herzegovina, where 47% of youth aged 15 to 24 were unemployed in 2007, vocational skills deficits have been identified in specific activity sectors (World Bank, 2009a). Nearly half of new businesses

do not survive beyond the first year, which may point to a lack of entrepreneurship skills (Bruhn and Zia, 2011). In 2009, a financial literacy programme was run as a randomized experiment with 445 clients of a microcredit institution living in the city of Tuzla. Some were already running a small company, while others planned to create one. Initial levels of financial literacy were low. Among those who received training, financial literacy improved significantly for those with the lowest initial levels, but it was the business owners who received training and had higher initial financial literacy who saw their profits increase. More financially literate business owners were able to immediately translate into practice advanced aspects of the training, covering business practices such as account-keeping or the use of bank accounts (Bruhn and Zia, 2011).

To be successful, curriculum design of entrepreneurship training, therefore, needs to take into account the low initial levels of education among many of those working in the informal sector who are most likely to benefit from such programmes.

Conclusion

Youth offer huge potential to transform urban economies in developing countries. Yet most disadvantaged young people in poor urban areas have low levels of education and skills that consign them to low paid, insecure work in the informal sector. Together with broader macroeconomic, education and employment policies, skills development strategies adapted to the realities of the informal sector can give them a chance for a better future.

Youth offer huge potential to transform urban economies in developing countries

Bichera Ntamwinsa, 23, picks berries from her coffee plants in Bukavu, Democratic Republic of the Congo. Farmer field schools and agricultural cooperatives can help smallholder farmers gain skills while strengthening their common voice.

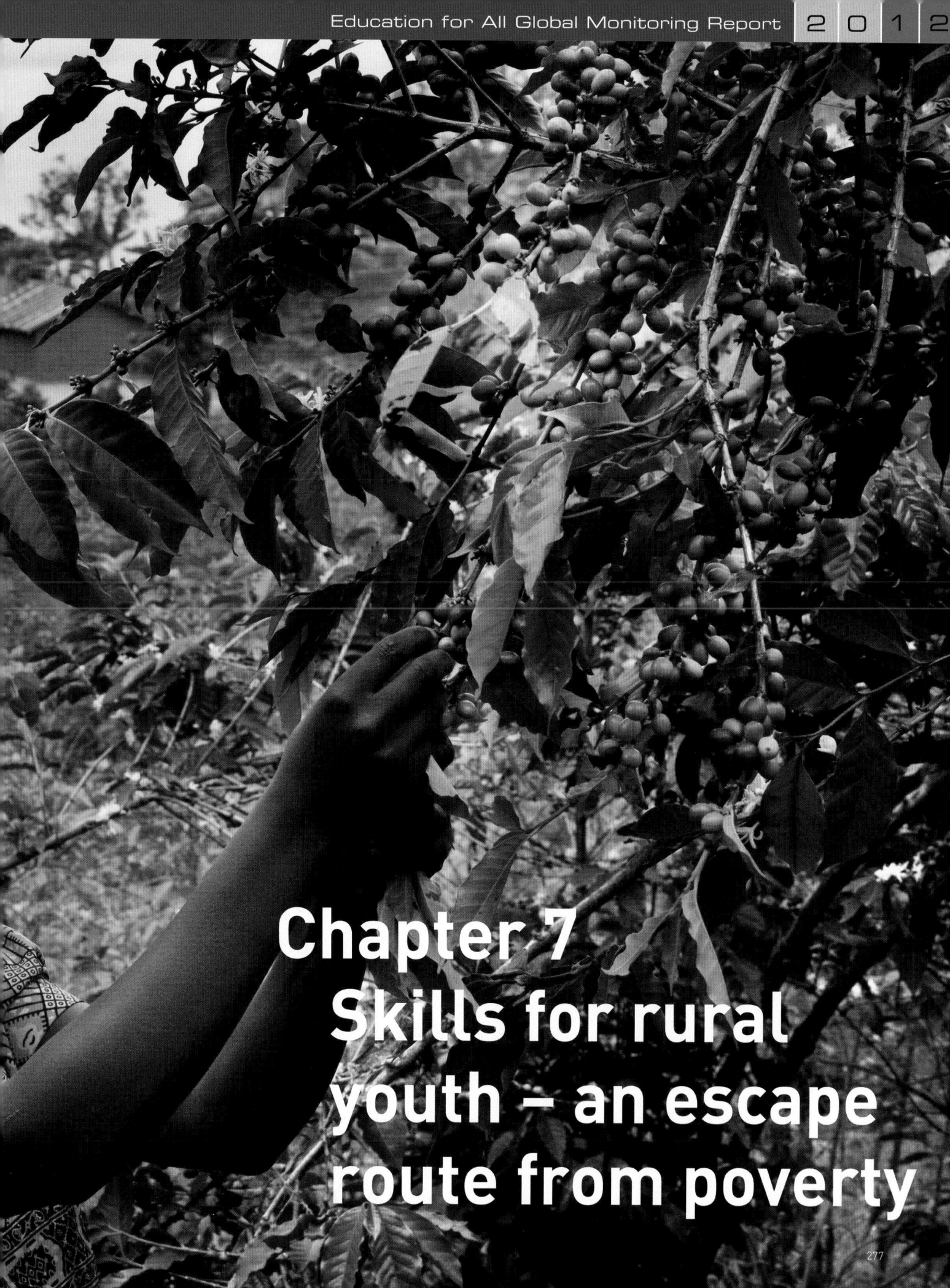

Chapter 7
Skills for rural youth – an escape route from poverty

Education for All Global Monitoring Report

2012

The majority of the world's poor live in rural areas. This chapter identifies the entrenched disadvantages faced by young people in rural areas and how skills training combined with access to assets could bring them greater prosperity. The chapter highlights the need to tailor skills training to specific needs of young people in rural areas, whether they work as smallholder farmers or in non-farm work, and shows how new technologies can help deliver skills even to the most remote communities.

Introduction

The majority of the poor worldwide live in rural areas, predominantly in low and some middle income countries. Most are dependent on a combination of small-scale farming, seasonal casual labour and microentrepreneurial activities with low earnings potential. They face challenges that threaten their ability to achieve secure livelihoods, including increasing land scarcity, insufficient non-agricultural employment opportunities, lack of capital and a relatively poor socio-economic infrastructure.

For the poorest, disadvantage is reinforced by a lack of even foundation skills. This locks them into work that makes it difficult to move out of poverty. Many migrate to urban areas in search of better jobs, but without skills adequately suited for the urban labour market, they end up at best in poorly paid, insecure jobs (see Chapter 6). Young women are particularly marginalized. They have less education and fewer assets, and are less able to migrate so are left behind to do tasks that others are unwilling to undertake.

Agricultural development is the best way for economic growth to reach the rural poor. This requires increased investment in a variety of areas, including electricity and the improved roads and transport needed to bring produce to markets (IFAD, 2010). Productivity in rural areas depends on availability of land, labour, capital, technology and skills. The first four are relatively fixed in the short term. However, with appropriate education and training, the productivity of young people can be enhanced. A key challenge is providing young people in rural areas, especially women, with appropriate skills while expanding opportunities to ensure that working in rural areas, whether in agriculture or non-farm work, is an attractive option.

As the world population continues to grow and demand for food rises, skills development is vital so that young people in rural areas can learn to adopt new technologies in agriculture, increasing the productivity of small farms and building their capacity to adapt to climate change. Young people in rural areas of poor countries are often more open to using new farming methods and engaging in innovative entrepreneurial activities than the older generation. But far more must be done to meet their training needs.

Policies and programmes for rural skills development have to focus on three key areas if rural youth are to have enhanced job opportunities. First, improve access to primary and post-primary education, paying particular attention to girls (see Chapter 5). Second, expand training for basic and vocational skills to make up for skills deficiencies or gaps within the rural labour market. Third, provide business and entrepreneurial skills training to improve young people's understanding of market opportunities and develop their management expertise. This chapter explores the second and third areas in relation to both smallholder farming and non-farm work.

Rural poverty limits opportunities for education and better livelihoods

I am from the countryside. It is known that education is not given that much attention in rural areas; families do not encourage their children to go to school. I started learning all by myself as I had the desire. But to be a student you need educational materials and I couldn't afford those.

– young man, Ethiopia

Despite widespread urbanization, around 70% of the world's 1.4 billion people living in extreme poverty inhabit rural areas (IFAD, 2010). The 1 billion rural poor are heavily concentrated in sub-Saharan Africa and South Asia, where small-scale farming and casual agricultural wage labour are their major sources of income.Even more urbanized regions, including the Arab States and Latin America and the Caribbean, have sizeable rural populations, though their numbers have been declining over the past two decades (IFAD, 2010).

Deprivation is particularly concentrated in rural areas. The likelihood of being poor is at least twice as high for the rural population in countries as diverse as Brazil, Morocco, Nepal and Uganda (United Nations, 2011a). Most poor rural youth in developing countries are likely to depend on smallholder farming and non-farm work for the foreseeable future. Greater attention needs to

70% of people in extreme poverty live in rural areas

2 0 1 2

Education for All Global Monitoring Report

In Turkey, 65% of young rural women do not complete lower secondary school

be paid to enhancing the skills of smallholders to improve their livelihoods and assure higher yields for food security, while protecting the environment. New developments in agricultural production and marketing are likely to mean that job opportunities will be scarcer and demand higher skills, so the rural non-farm sector will become more important as a source of jobs for poor rural youth, who will need improved skills to make the best of the available opportunities.

In rural areas, young women are more disadvantaged than young men

While young people living in urban poverty can suffer from low levels of education (see Chapter 6), those lacking foundation skills are far more numerous in rural areas. Even for young people who make it to lower secondary school, curricula are generally not attuned to the needs of the rural economy, and the quality of education is affected by poor infrastructure and a lack of qualified teachers (see Chapter 5).

In rural areas, young women are more disadvantaged in education than young men.

The gender gap is most pronounced in countries where the majority of rural people do not make it to the end of lower secondary school. Some women who lack foundation skills have never entered school at all, and many others have not completed primary school. In Benin, Cameroon, Liberia and Sierra Leone, about 85% of young rural women lack foundation skills, compared with less than 70% of young men. Even in Turkey, a middle income country, the rural gender gap is wide – 65% of young women do not complete lower secondary school, compared with 36% of young men. In some countries, young men in rural areas are more likely to lack foundation skills, but in these countries overall levels of education tend to be higher, and gender gaps narrower (Figure 7.1).

Young women living in rural poverty face disadvantage in education starting in the early years of schooling, even in countries that have made strong progress in expanding access to primary education. In Kenya, for example, young people from rich households, whether urban or rural, male or female, are very likely to get at least four years of schooling. But for those from

Figure 7.1: Young women in rural areas are the most likely to lack foundation skills

Percentage of youth (age 15 to 24) with less than lower secondary education, by gender, in rural areas of selected countries, latest available year

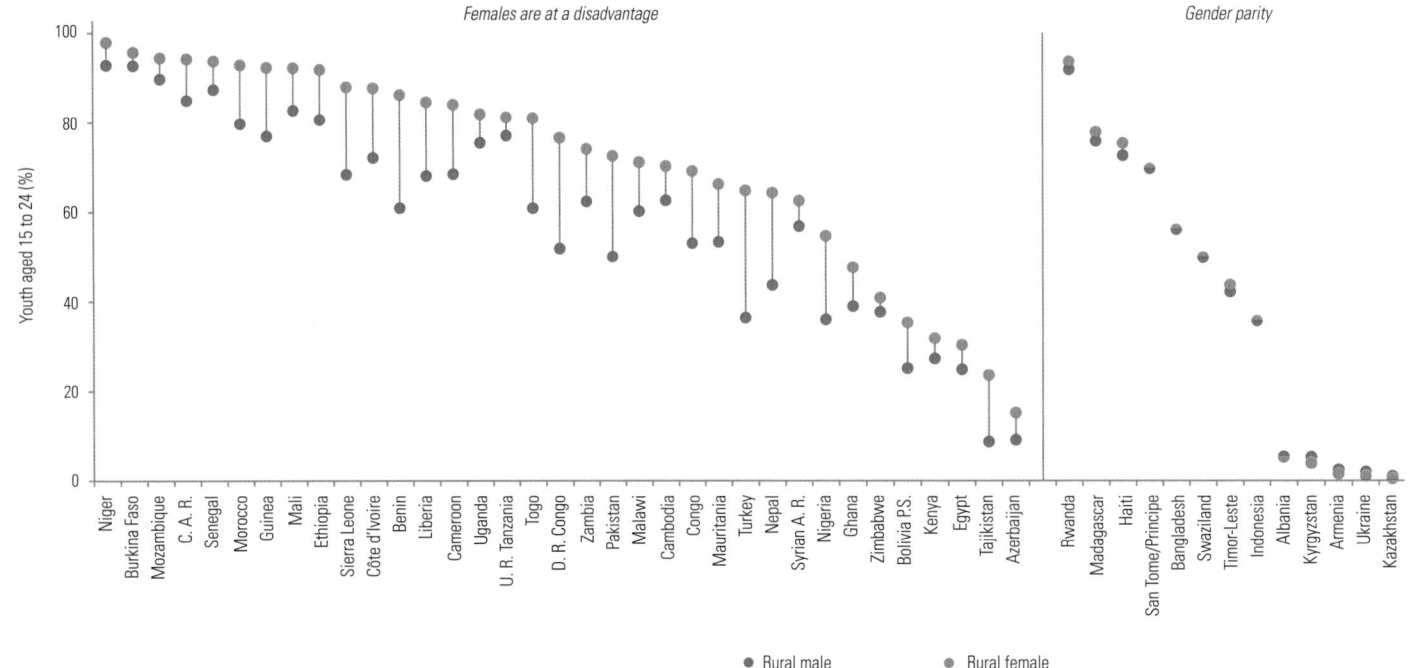

Source: UIS (2012a).

poor households living in a rural area it is a very different story, and even more so for females. Of poor rural young women in Kenya, 32% have less than four years in school, compared with 16% of poor rural males (UNESCO, 2012b). Ethnic minority and indigenous young women also fare particularly badly in rural areas.

Gender-specific social norms and practices and the gendered division of labour shape young women's expectations in ways that influence decisions over their engagement in education and training programmes. Such barriers tend to be particularly pronounced in rural areas, for several reasons.

Customary rules, threats to personal safety and lack of transport often limit women's ability to leave their villages to attend training programmes (Mujahid-Mukhtar, 2008). In Ethiopia, India and Viet Nam, the timing and location of training were identified as crucial to women's ability to participate (Barwa, 2003; Danida, 2004; Women in Development, 2003). Women's weaker bargaining position within the household can also prevent them from joining

training programmes. In Uganda, for example, the rules, norms and practices that structure the division of labour and the distribution of resources in the household are crucial to rural women's access to the time and money necessary for participation in rural agricultural training programmes (Wedig, 2012).

Young rural women are more likely not only to lack foundation skills, but also to be in the most arduous jobs, often working long hours for limited pay. In sub-Saharan Africa, South Asia, South-East Asia and the Arab States, women are overrepresented in smallholder farming and agricultural labour, indicating limited economic opportunities for rural girls and women (FAO et al., 2010).

Even if young women have the necessary skills, they face discrimination that limits the types of work they can do and their access to capital, posing significant challenges in starting businesses (World Bank, 2006b). In Uganda, women are disproportionately represented in lower paid jobs and small-scale agriculture. Within the agricultural sector, women are more likely to be engaged in marketing and selling food crops while men dominate the sales of export cash crops, such as coffee – even though women contribute a large share of the labour for coffee production (Wedig, 2012).

Skills training programmes that do not take the challenges facing young women into account are likely to fail. For example, a USAID Integrated Agriculture Training Programme in Papua New Guinea had only limited success because it did not consider women's family responsibilities. The training courses were arranged away from the village for three full days and women found it difficult to travel and arrange for child care (Cahn and Liu, 2008).

Enhancing the education and skills of young people in rural areas, and young women in particular, would not only expand their opportunities, but could also increase their productivity, with gains for their families as well as the wider economy. In rural China, wages are significantly higher for those involved in non-farm work who attended at least some post-primary education (Qiang et al., 2005).

Skills training programmes that ignore the challenges young women face are likely to fail

Males are at a disadvantage

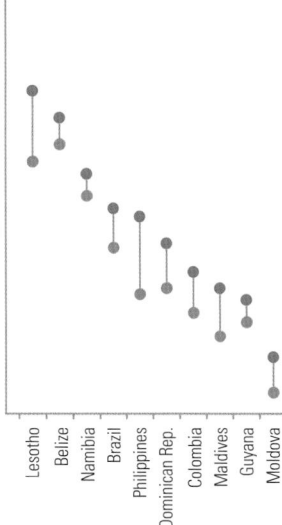

Smallholder farming is the main source of livelihood for many poor households

We do not have a very big farm. Just enough for my family to survive.

– young man, Viet Nam

Farming remains the main source of livelihood for many people in poor countries. Over 80% of rural households farm to some extent (IFAD, 2010). In Ghana, for example, agriculture accounted for around half of total employment in 2005/06, a similar proportion to fifteen years earlier. In Rwanda, farming remains the main source of employment despite a decline in the proportion working in agriculture from 90% in 2000 to 77% in 2006 (Adams et al., forthcoming).

Given that agriculture is likely to remain vital for the economy of these countries as demographic and environmental pressures increase, sustainable ways need to be found of using increasingly scarce natural resources to feed growing populations while adapting to the effects of climate change. The world's population is expected to reach around 9 billion in 2050, and food production will need to increase by 70% (IFAD et al., 2011). Yet crop yields are not keeping pace. In sub-Saharan Africa, yields have remained stagnant since the 1960s (Larsen et al., 2009).

With population growth, farms have been decreasing in size (IFAD, 2010). Over three-quarters of farms in Africa and Asia are small-holdings (Collett and Gale, 2009). In sub-Saharan Africa, 80% of all farms (33 million in total) are smaller than 2 hectares (Agriculture for Impact, 2012). Farms are often divided between male heirs, so holdings become progressively smaller (Eastwood et al., 2004). Landholdings that are already small can be severely reduced in one or two generations (Wedig, 2012).

Two of the world's largest countries have some of its smallest farm sizes: in India, average farm size decreased from 2.3 to 1.4 hectares between 1970 and 2010, and in China, average farm size was 0.6 hectares in 2010 (Chand et al., 2011). To put these sizes into context, the average Indian farm can feed six people and its counterpart in China fewer than three. Enhancing productivity of such farms while identifying other sources

The average Chinese farm can only feed three people

of income for survival is key to helping smallholders secure a sustainable livelihood.

In some contexts, such as parts of Latin America and South Asia, decreasing plot sizes and increasing land values are leading to larger farms in fewer hands, and many landless or near-landless people. In Peru, for example, disparity in land ownership is now wider than before agrarian reforms in the 1970s (IFAD, 2010). There are also moves in some parts of the world towards agricultural intensification. As a result of climate change, rapid urbanization and growing demand for natural resources, some governments are leasing or selling land to foreign companies and investors for tree plantations, biofuel crops and food crops.

India, for example, began to advertise in March 2012 for public-private partnerships in 'integrated agricultural development', in which private corporations would form agreements with up to 10,000 smallholder farmers to farm on a large scale (India Department of Agriculture and Cooperation, 2012). Technological advances in agriculture have led to very large intensive farms in some middle income countries, such as Brazil (Laabs et al., 2001). These trends are likely to reduce the number of workers needed and raise the skills level required. For those who are left landless with low levels of skills, it will be even more essential to increase their opportunities for non-farm work, including through enhancing their skills base.

Rural youth with foundation skills have a better chance of non-farm work. Many poor rural households combine work on small farms with non-farm labour to bolster their livelihoods. In sub-Saharan Africa and parts of Asia, the share of non-farm income is increasing (IFAD, 2010). In eastern Uganda, for example, approximately 30% of smallholder coffee farmers also depend on non-farm self-employment and wage labour outside agriculture (Wedig, 2012). Fostering non-agricultural employment in rural areas and improving the conditions for entrepreneurial activities outside agriculture are needed to meet the aspirations of rural youth, particularly where farm sizes are decreasing.

Evidence from fifteen countries shows that young household heads are more likely than

Figure 7.2: Better educated rural youth tend to be in non-farm work

Non-farm employment rate of youth (age 15 to 24) in rural areas, by education level, selected countries, latest available year

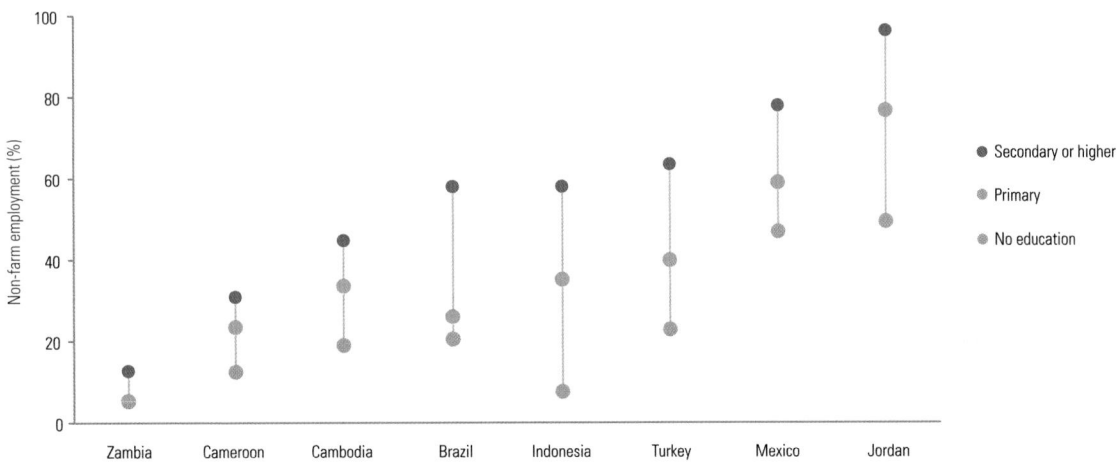

Note: Data for Mexico are for 'less urbanized' areas.
Source: Understanding Children's Work (2012).

their older counterparts to be involved in non-farm activities (Davis et al., 2007). Education is an important condition for young people to make the transition to non-farm work. Across eight countries analysed for this Report, the higher the level of education, the more likely it is that a young person is involved in non-agricultural employment, with similar patterns for women and men. In Turkey, 23% of those with no education are involved in non-farm activities, compared with 40% of those with primary education and 64% of those with at least secondary education (Figure 7.2).

Those making the transition to non-farm work can expect better pay. In Ghana and Rwanda, average earnings in the informal sector are double those in agriculture (Adams et al., forthcoming).

Addressing rural training needs

Promoting skills training as part of rural development can bring considerable benefits, as evidence from some growing economies shows. In China, a focus on productivity growth in smallholder agriculture and non-farm self-

employment from the late 1970s onwards was crucial to the fight against poverty (Ravallion, 2009). Targeted public investment in non-farm activities was accompanied by investment in better education and training in rural areas, helping marginalized rural people gain access to non-agricultural income sources.

Prioritizing skills for rural youth in national strategies

Despite the potential contribution of skills to rural development, many countries have not paid close attention to training. Among forty-six policies and strategies reviewed for this Report, only about half acknowledge the training needs of rural youth, and many lack initiatives that focus on rural areas (Engel, 2012). Efforts to provide more training for rural people are frequently part of more general commitments to expand skills development for marginalized groups and fail to recognize the specific needs of rural areas.

In many countries, there are large numbers of workers in low skilled and low paid jobs in the agricultural sector. This highlights the need not only for skills development to enhance agricultural productivity but also for increased investment in training that can lead to more and

A young rural person with more education is more likely to take up non-farm work

better employment in the rural non-farm economy. Where training plans do address rural needs, however, they tend to ignore non-farm work.

Ethiopia has recently developed an ambitious plan: the Agricultural Sector Policy and Investment Framework 2010–2020, led by the Ministry of Agriculture and Rural Development (Ethiopia MoARD, 2010). The plan aims at increasing the productivity of small farms in order to decrease rural poverty and improve food security. It envisages expanding agricultural research and training, including deploying at least 54,000 extension agents and creating 18,000 farmer training centres. The focus on breaking gender divides, including by ensuring that women receive training, is another positive aspect of the plan.

Labour market information systems are needed in rural areas to assess and respond to changing skills needs, but in many low and middle income countries, such systems are inadequate or nonexistent (Sparreboom and Powell, 2009). Analysis of rural training needs is often conducted sporadically or not at all.

Indonesia provides an example of a middle income country that is responding to this challenge. Around half the population lives in rural areas (Statistics Indonesia, 2012). Of the 82% of working poor who live in these areas, more than two-thirds are engaged in agriculture (ADB et al., 2010). As part of Indonesia's Masterplan for the Acceleration and Expansion of Economic Development 2011–2025, the Ministries of National Education and Culture and the Coordinating Ministry for Economic Affairs have started to address the need for better labour market analysis in rural as well as urban areas (Indonesia Coordinating Ministry for Economic Affairs, 2011). Furthermore, measures have been taken to improve the availability and effective use of labour market data since 2010 in two pilot regions, although the efforts need to be scaled up because the database on this huge labour market is still insufficient (Wedig, 2010a).

Providing foundation skills to all rural young people

Ensuring that all young people have access to foundation skills is an immense challenge

in rural areas because of the dispersion of populations and the numbers involved. Young people who lack foundation skills are unlikely to benefit from training programmes that require the ability to access and process information and adopt new technologies for productive work. Extending coverage of formal primary and secondary schooling and improving its relevance to rural environments are key priorities.

To maximize the impact of approaches to enhancing rural youth skills, they have to be combined with other poverty alleviation strategies. Young people in rural areas need not only second-chance programmes that address gaps in their basic literacy and numeracy skills, but also programmes that provide skills beyond the foundations, so that they have a better chance of moving out of poverty by productively engaging in agriculture and non-farm activities.

Giving young rural people a second chance

Many rural youth, particularly women, need to improve their literacy and numeracy skills as a first step to ensuring that they can benefit from other agricultural and non-farm skills development programmes. Many second-chance programmes are provided by non-governmental organizations (NGOs) in ways that are flexible and oriented towards practical skills. Designed by small, locally based organizations, these programmes often adapt training content and delivery methods to local needs.

Part-time programmes using local facilities help improve participation by accommodating local constraints on time, mobility and finances. The flexibility of locally designed programmes can be particularly beneficial for young rural women, who often have to balance training with other commitments that result in long working hours. Malawi's Complementary Basic Education programme illustrates one approach to extending basic skills to rural young people who have dropped out of primary school (Box 7.1).

Young women are likely to require more targeted forms of support to address discrimination and other challenges. The Ishraq programme in Egypt provides a positive example of increasing young women's possibilities for skills development in a particularly conservative

Flexible programmes for young rural women help balance training with other commitments

284

Box 7.1: A second chance for Malawi's primary school dropouts

Around 85% of Malawi's people live in rural areas, and government sources say 60% of the rural population is 'poor' or 'ultra-poor'. Over half the population is under 18, and most young people are involved in unpaid subsistence farming. Young people are particularly vulnerable to HIV and AIDS. It is estimated that there are 110,000 new infections annually, at least half of them among 15- to 24-year-olds.

In this context, completing primary school is a major challenge. In 2009, almost half the children starting primary school dropped out. Only a small proportion made it to secondary school. There were 319,000 out-of-school adolescents, a large number for a small country.

To give youth a chance to acquire skills, the government, initially with donor backing, set up the Complementary Basic Education programme, which has now been mainstreamed into government operations. The programme targets those aged 9 to 17 who either never enrolled in school or dropped out before completing the fifth grade.

The pilot programme was launched in 2006 in three districts. By 2011 the programme was operating in six rural districts with very high dropout rates and had reached 10,000 children and youth; by 2012 it was to be rolled out nationally. It has attracted many young people, more than half of whom in the initial phase were aged 14 or over. Marginalized groups have been successfully targeted. Almost one in five participants had never been to school. Most were from very poor households. Around half of the older learners were orphaned, and some of the young women were married with children of their own, though only around a third of older participants were female.

The programme is carried out by local NGOs, which recruit and train local facilitators under age 35 who have a secondary school qualification. Local recruitment provides jobs and role models for poor local youth. The programme has smaller class sizes than formal primary schools. Learner centres are located centrally within villages and managed by communities.

The curriculum covers basic literacy and numeracy skills, based on the primary curriculum, as well as more practical skills, including agriculture and the environment, livelihoods and entrepreneurial skills, healthy living, and citizenship. The course is designed so that graduates of the three-year programme can enter grade 6 in a formal primary school if they desire.

Older learners are most concerned with learning basic literacy and numeracy skills, with around 84% stating this as their objective. Most have said they wanted to use the skills to find work or set up a business, but this has proved difficult. The original plan was to use local artisans to provide training in livelihood skills, such as pottery, weaving, making hoe and broom handles, and repairing radios. But the craftspeople wanted payment, and it was not always possible to find and buy needed materials. As a result, demonstration of practical skills was often skipped. Some young people wanted training in technical and vocational skills (such as carpentry and metalwork) that were beyond the scope and budget of the programme. The limited practical relevance may have contributed to some older youth dropping out.

Despite these problems, the programme has been successful in ensuring that young people acquire basic skills, with participants often performing better than children in formal primary schools. Over half the learners in the first three-year cycle either completed the programme or left early to (re-)enter primary school. Of those completing three years in the programme, 40% passed at a level equivalent to grade 5 of the formal curriculum in numeracy. By contrast, a recent SACMEQ survey found that less than 1% of grade 5 school pupils attained grade level competency in mathematics.

Source: Jere (2012).

Young people in Malawi's second-chance programmes often perform better than those in primary school

setting (Box 7.2). Assuring strong local participation and adapting learning approaches to the local context contributed to the programme's success.

Despite the potential of second-chance programmes, their impact has been limited.

They are numerous, poorly coordinated and usually small, so there is often little information on their quality and on labour market outcomes. Programmes do not always offer certificates, and this can prevent participants from re-entering the education system or getting good jobs.

Box 7.2: Bringing skills to adolescent girls in rural Egypt

Egypt's current adolescent population is the country's largest ever: more than 13 million boys and girls aged 11 to 19. Despite major progress in primary schooling, many young people, particularly rural girls and women, have almost entirely missed out. In 2008, 20% of rural women aged 17 to 22 had less than two years of schooling. Many are likely to get married young.

The Ishraq programme was launched in 2001 by a coalition of international NGOs to provide skills training through a pilot project involving 277 out-of-school girls aged 13 to 15. The programme designers realized that, in this very conservative setting, parents would have to agree to the types of skills their daughters would be taught. Literacy and numeracy were among the most accepted and sought-after. A 'safe place' was provided in every community where the girls met four times a week over the thirty months of the project to receive training to become active members of their communities and to become earners.

The programme also educated boys, parents and community leaders to allow girls greater freedom to seek education and enter the world of work. In addition, Ishraq worked at the governorate and national ministry levels to gain support.

Participation in the pilot programme increased literacy and numeracy skills significantly.

Of participants who took the government literacy examination, 92% passed, and 69% of participants who completed the programme entered or re-entered the formal school system. Ingrained negative beliefs among the girls themselves and their families significantly decreased and girls were allowed greater freedom. The proportion of girls saying they wanted to be married before 18 fell from 26% before the programme to 2% among those who completed it. All in all, the girls were found to be more empowered and ready for roles as productive family and society members.

Only 18% of the initial 277 participants pursued vocational skills courses, and an evaluation of the programme acknowledged that this area would need strengthening. Some wanted training in electrical appliance repair, but most were interested in more traditionally female occupations such as hairdressing.

Overall success led to the programme being extended, and it currently reaches at least 2,500 girls in fifty villages. The challenge is ensuring that even more girls are reached, given the large numbers who still do not complete primary school in rural Egypt.

Sources: Brady et al. (2007); Ishraq (2010); UNESCO (2012b).

Combining skills training with other support to address multiple disadvantages

Combining microfinance or social protection with skills development programmes, including basic literacy and numeracy as well as livelihood skills training, is an important strategy for tackling the multiple forms of disadvantage that lock rural populations in poverty. Successful programmes have been able to transform lives by improving the asset base of the poor while providing them with skills to diversify their use of assets and improve access to markets.

The combination of skills training with microfinance services or social protection can also strengthen the capacities of rural youth for non-agricultural employment and entrepreneurship. A pioneer in this area is BRAC, the Bangladesh-based NGO. Its programmes have been successful in including support for immediate needs, skills training together with small grants and asset transfers to get small enterprises off the ground (Box 7.3).

More often, social protection programmes have not sufficiently incorporated skills training. Early experience of Ethiopia's Productive Safety Net Programme showed that its outcomes could be stronger and last longer if skills training were a more integral part of the package. The largest social protection programme in sub-Saharan Africa, reaching almost 8 million beneficiaries (around 9% of Ethiopia's population), it provides cash transfers to allow families to buy food and acquire productive assets (USAID, 2012). It was envisaged that credit would be part of the package, but training to assist those with little education to get the most out of a loan was not included in early phases of the programme (Slater et al., 2006). Learning from experience, the government decided

Having learnt from experience, Ethiopia's Safety Net Programme now includes skills training

Education for All Global Monitoring Report

2 0 1 2

Box 7.3: BRAC tackles multiple faces of poverty with training

BRAC has pioneered innovative approaches to reduce rural poverty through a variety of programmes that tackle simultaneously the multiple constraints that prevent young people from escaping rural poverty. Because of the particular disadvantage young women face, their needs have been a focus of these programmes. Building on the success of its programmes in Bangladesh, BRAC is expanding them to other parts of the world, including sub-Saharan Africa.

About 20% of rural households in Bangladesh live in extreme poverty. They suffer from persistent food insecurity, own no cultivable land or assets, and are often illiterate and prone to illness. Women often suffer from gender discrimination, limiting their opportunities for income-generating activities. A disproportionate number of the poorest households are headed by women.

A programme called Challenging the Frontiers of Poverty Reduction was born of BRAC's experience that the poorest households find it difficult to participate in and benefit from microfinance. People living on less than US$1 a day account for less than half of those obtaining microfinance, and need training to gain any benefits from assets or credit obtained through microfinance. The programme provides an income-earning asset to the poorest people (those living on less than US$0.35 per day) in rural Bangladesh, usually giving it to women in the household, and provides them with training so they can get the most out of the asset. For example, an extremely poor woman might receive a cow, and would be supported by a small weekly stipend for a short period, or until the asset starts to yield income. Training in how to market the produce and how to use microfinance is also provided. The programme has been implemented on a large scale: it was piloted in 3 districts with 5,000 households starting in 2002, increasing to 15 districts and 100,000 households over the next 4 years.

Evaluations of the programme between 2002 and 2008 found it had effected lasting change in the economic condition of beneficiary households. Initial targeting of beneficiaries has been successful, and income gains are substantial and have not eroded with time. Income per household member nearly tripled between 2002 and 2008.

Training is central to these results, ensuring that beneficiaries realize the potential of such high quality assets as Jersey cows with higher milk yields than the traditional South Asian breed to which beneficiaries are accustomed. It has also been found that entrepreneurial and marketing training helps beneficiaries maximize gains. This support is offered for up to two years to ensure that lessons are absorbed.

Another BRAC approach provides adolescent girls, particularly those who are out of school, with a range of support, including skills training. Initiated in Bangladesh, it has been adapted to poor rural contexts in sub-Saharan Africa. In Uganda, the Empowerment and Livelihoods for Adolescents programme was designed to reinforce or reintroduce literacy and numeracy, and to provide girls with a safe space. Girls received life and livelihood skills training, along with training to help them earn and manage money in occupations such as hairdressing, tailoring, information technology, agriculture, poultry rearing and small trading. There were 690 adolescents' clubs accessible to all girls and women aged 13 to 22 in the target areas.

Over the two years of the programme, the number of participants who became involved in income-earning activities doubled, compared with an increase of just 4% among non-participants. Girls took up poultry rearing, food processing and small trade. Their financial literacy increased. Their borrowing for earning activities rose considerably, as did their savings. For example, before participating in the programme, 23% of the girls reported having savings, compared with 34% after their involvement. The programme appears to have had a broadly positive effect on participants' entrepreneurialism, and some were able to lend money to their own families.

Sources: Abed (2009); Bandiera et al. (2011); BRAC (2011a, 2011b); Improving Institutions for Pro-Poor Growth (2011); Krishna et al. (2010); Rural Poverty Portal (2012a, 2012b).

In Bangladesh, the poorest get greater benefits from microfinance with skills training

to invest more in training. By 2008, two-thirds of farmers reported attending training programmes and one-third were applying new techniques to their land (World Bank, 2011b). Positive results include some environmental regeneration, increased access to water sources and expanded use of small-scale irrigation. Even more could be done through greater investment in skills training (Slater et al., 2006; World Bank, 2011b).

Combining training with microfinance can have particular benefits for women, giving them more control over resources. In Nepal, the Project for Agriculture Commercialization and Trade was initiated in the 1990s with funding from the World Bank. One of its subprojects, the Women's Empowerment Program, aimed to provide literacy training and financial literacy education to enable women in rural communities to become independent of male relatives. The project facilitated the formation of women's savings and loans groups and provided the training necessary to allow the women to operate these profitably for the members. Literacy classes formed an integral part of the support and training given. The programme was highly successful in terms of saving and borrowing for members, with only 4% of groups making loans that defaulted. The programme lasted three years; the goal was for the groups then to be self-sustaining. More than 74,000 out of 130,000 women became literate through the programme (Ashe and Parrott, 2001).

In rural Uganda, married women have been given the chance to borrow via a commercial village microfinance banking model promoted by the government that has become widespread. An in-depth study was carried out of one microfinance model: a small 'village bank' that was owned, used and controlled by members but still commercially oriented. The programme provided training in credit norms and procedures, savings discipline, and business management. As a result women were able to start their own businesses, were found to be less dependent on their husbands, and sometimes were even able to offer their husbands employment. Many women not only became familiar with micro-credit borrowing and saving, but also developed diverse saving strategies, such as buying livestock that would prove a productive asset. They also chose to invest in the education of their children, possibly as a result of their increased financial and management knowledge (Lakwo, 2006).

Bringing additional skills to rural youth

To make sure that work in rural areas is an attractive option for young people, it is vital to provide training beyond the foundations so that smallholder farmers can strengthen agricultural productivity and non-farm workers can enhance their business and finance skills.

Extending smallholders' agricultural and business skills

Smallholder farming can be productive and a viable source of decent income if farmers have the appropriate skills. Shifting towards biodiverse farming that uses the right combination of crops, trees and animals in an integrated system can make smallholder farming profitable (UNEP et al., 2008).

To succeed in farming, young people need many types of skills beyond basic literacy and numeracy. They need training in what to farm, what inputs to use and in what quantities, how to deal with environmental challenges, and how to use scarce resources such as water with the greatest efficiency (Collett and Gale, 2009).

Smallholders in low income countries also need improved business and marketing skills (Collett, 2010). While food production for the household is vital, the rural poor also sell cash crops on local, regional and national markets, so they need business skills to better represent their own interests. Forming associations can help smallholders gain skills while strengthening their common voice (Chuhan-Pole et al., 2011). Farmer field schools and cooperatives are two such approaches.

Farmer field schools promote knowledge sharing and boost productivity

Agricultural extension services, which play an important role in providing farmers with knowledge and skills, have tended to benefit richer, educated farmers. In Uganda, for example, they have focused on farmers with the potential to become larger export-crop producers, while the poorest and most risk-averse farmers obtain limited benefits (Wedig, 2010b). It is vital to ensure that extension services offer smallholders, including those with little formal schooling, a chance to improve their capacity for agricultural entrepreneurship, farm management, marketing and organization.

Farmer field schools are one successful response to the limited reach and lack of financial sustainability of many public sector extension systems. In these season-long programmes, farmers meet regularly to learn new agricultural techniques. The approach

Smallholder farmers need business and marketing skills

started in Indonesia in 1989 to help stop the use of highly toxic pesticides that were jeopardizing farmers' health and the success of their crops (Braun and Duveskog, 2008). Such programmes are now in place in at least eighty-seven countries, and have been beneficial in improving agricultural productivity. The schools bring together groups of smallholders to address topics such as animal husbandry, organic agriculture, soil and groundwater management, and marketing. Farmers are involved in the design and implementation of skills development programmes, which helps ensure that they are relevant and economically viable. Long experience of farmer field schools in Indonesia shows that when smallholders share knowledge and experience, this can maximize the benefits of the skills they acquire (Feder et al., 2004; Van den Berg and Jiggins, 2007).

Farmer field schools in sub-Saharan Africa have had strong benefits for poor farmers with little or no formal schooling. By 2003, the region had at least 1,000 such schools, with 30,000 graduates in Kenya alone. In Kenya, Uganda and the United Republic of Tanzania, it has been found that young people in particular participate in farmer field schools, showing the schools' potential to promote new agricultural technologies to youth. Around half the participants are women. In Kenya and Uganda, around 70% of those involved have only primary education. The share is 80% in the United Republic of Tanzania. Members of savings and credit groups and other farmer groups are more likely to participate, indicating the importance of connecting the schools with other rural services. The poorest households and those headed by women may be unable to take part, however, due to the need to pay a small fee and reduced flexibility to attend if they work on other people's farms.

Overall, farmer field schools have led to significant improvements in productivity and incomes. The approach has been particularly beneficial for those with low levels of literacy. Crop value per acre increased by 32% on average across the three countries, and by 253% for those who had not had any formal schooling. Income increased by 61% on average, and by 224% for households whose heads had no previous schooling (Davis et al., 2010).

Cooperatives offer farmers access to highly relevant skills and knowledge

Agricultural cooperatives are another way that agricultural and business skills can be transmitted to smallholders, along with other forms of support. Their main objective is to improve market access and prices; associated credit and savings cooperatives aim to provide members with sustainable financing mechanisms. Cooperatives bring accumulated know-how to individual farmers through strong networks (Wedig, 2012). They can provide practical training in specific agricultural subsectors, even in remote rural areas, drawing on farmers' own up-to-date knowledge. The training complements other cooperative initiatives aimed at enabling smallholders to increase their bargaining power and get better prices, including microfinance and the development of rural infrastructure.

Agricultural cooperatives are important training providers for small coffee producers in eastern Uganda. Farmer-members (usually smallholders) can get access to training through their membership. Most training available to farmers through NGOs and other providers focuses on agricultural skills, while cooperatives offer more comprehensive training covering business, organizational and other transferable skills.

The agricultural skills training provided, for example, by Gumutindo Coffee Cooperative Enterprise, a Fairtrade producer of certified organic arabica, helps small farmers achieve and maintain organic certification while increasing productivity in the long term. Farmers receive short training sessions, and some express a strong desire for more. The training is very relevant, since it takes place as part of working life. The cooperatives invest in local infrastructure such as roads, crop storage facilities, medical clinics and school repairs. They also facilitate group-based investment in technical equipment and joint marketing strategies, and help secure good market prices in return for a modest fee (Wedig, 2010b, 2012).

Farmer field schools in sub-Saharan Africa benefit poor farmers who have little education

Using information and communication technology to improve practical skills

One effective way to promote productive learning and practical use of new skills is to demonstrate them using audio and video media. In Benin, for example, a project that used videos to train female smallholders resulted in more successful adoption and use of skills than training with lectures alone (Zossou et al., 2009). Experiments in Burkina Faso, India and the Niger provide further insights into the potential benefits of augmenting training with information and communication technology, especially radio, which can reach large numbers of disadvantaged farmers.

In the Indian state of Tamil Nadu, interactive multimedia instruction is used to train sugarcane growers in new production practices. These skills, formerly taught in traditional lecture-style classes, are communicated via text, audio, video, graphics and animation. The multimedia module, which covers all stages of sugarcane production from planning to harvesting, is broken down into sections to allow the learner to go at his or her own pace. The module was designed according to a detailed qualitative needs assessment with farmers. It adopts new cultivation technologies at the appropriate stages. Standard written materials supplement the interactive module. Wherever text is used, there is voice commentary to assist weaker readers. Each class lasts one hour (Shanthy and Thiagarajan, 2011).

A sample of farmers from three villages participated in a trial. They were mostly literate, and around three-quarters had a secondary or tertiary education. A preliminary test found that all three groups had similar baseline knowledge of sugarcane farming techniques. Group I received multimedia training only, group II was given lectures as well as the multimedia module, and group III was given only lectures. Scores on tests after the training were between 19 and 29 percentage points higher than scores on the initial test. Those receiving both multimedia and traditional training benefited the most. The use of audio and video, and the interactivity of the multimedia approach, was said to be more interesting, capturing learners' imaginations (Shanthy and Thiagarajan, 2011).

This study shows that in getting farmers to learn vital new technologies, the medium matters. The farmers in the study were well educated and owned their own land and only 9% were female, which indicates that the most marginalized did not take part. In addition, most farmers lack access to the necessary equipment unless they go to a training centre (Shanthy and Thiagarajan, 2011).

By contrast, an experiment in Burkina Faso and the Niger used radio in an effort to reach more farmers, including those who might otherwise be excluded from using technology by low levels of education or access to facilities. Farmers were trained in a new type of storage that allows them to safely keep their crop to sell when it suits them, for example when prices have risen, rather than having to sell quickly before the crop becomes damaged (Moussa et al., 2011).

The study tested farmers in villages where no training was given, where only village demonstrations were used, and where demonstrations were followed up by radio broadcasts. Where demonstrations alone were conducted there was 34% more use of the new technique in the Niger and 13% more in Burkina Faso, compared with villages where no training took place. Where the messages from the demonstrations were reinforced using the radio broadcasts, adoption of the new technique was 23% higher in the Niger and 20% higher in Burkina Faso compared with villages where there were demonstrations alone. The addition of the radio reinforcement made an already effective means of extension training even more effective (Moussa et al., 2011).

Along with radios, mobile phones are one of the most accessible forms of technology, covering over 70% of the world's population (Newby, 2012). Training via such technology can be particularly beneficial for women who are restricted from attending regularly scheduled classes. In southern India an NGO programme uses mobile phones to train women with limited schooling in how to care for and get the most from their animals. Participants receive voice messages on their phones every day regarding

Burkina Faso has used radio to reach more farmers with training

livestock care, and self-help group members meet weekly to discuss and to learn from each other (Balasubramanian et al., 2010).

Entrepreneurial and microbusiness skills for non-farm rural work

Most smallholders require non-farm income to survive, especially where the size of holdings is declining. At the same time, any gains from agriculture will increase demand in other areas, such as for carpenters, electricians, plumbers and builders. There are also many microbusinesses that rural people can run. If young people acquire skills in mechanics and a small amount of capital to buy the necessary machinery, they can operate a small mill to turn grain into flour, for example (IFAD, 2010). Helping rural youth acquire entrepreneurial

skills puts them in a stronger position to benefit from such non-farm activities.

Making rural work attractive to young people. Innovative training programmes for non-farm work can be beneficial in encouraging young people to remain in rural areas. In Cambodia, the government established a professional training school in Siem Reap, capital of the province of that name, in 1992 to teach crafts-making to disadvantaged rural youth with little formal education. Each year the school provides over 100 people aged 18 to 25 with six months of residential training, giving them skills that enable them to work in their home regions rather than migrating to urban areas. Those who complete training at the school can take an internship with Artisans d'Angkor, a network established as an offshoot of the school to get

Cambodia has trained artisans in order to reduce migration

Box 7.4: Camfed provides business skills to poor young rural women

Camfed, a major international NGO, has been working for many years to help girls get into education and finish secondary school. More recently it started the Seed Money Programme for alumnae who were poor, rural and economically inactive. The goal is to help them create livelihood opportunities in villages where opportunities are scarce. By providing initial training and funds, the programme aims to make women financially independent and raise their status within their households and communities.

The Seed Money Programme provides rural young women with training in business management skills (including record keeping, market competition and marketing), a grant to help set up an enterprise, peer mentoring to support the new business, and access to micro loans at low interest once the business is up and running. The programme started in Zimbabwe in 1998 and has been replicated in Ghana, the United Republic of Tanzania and Zambia.

In 2007 in Zimbabwe, 13,614 people took part at a cost of US$6.20 each. The Zimbabwe programme was successful even in the extremely difficult circumstances of the economic crisis that started in 2008. Women have opened businesses in gardening and livestock, sales of produce and cooked food, and sewing and hairdressing. By 2010, 93% of the businesses that were started via the grants had made a profit. Nearly all the

women reinvested some of the profit into the business. Women interviewed said they felt it had made a major difference to their lives, improving their standard of living and the respect they received within their households and communities.

From 2009 to 2011, Camfed also ran Financial Education for Young Women in Rural Areas of Zambia, a very different kind of project. It provided an intense one-day course to 10,701 girls – many more than are reached through the Seed Money Programme. The training covered money management, budgeting, saving, credit risk and banking services. Trust, honesty and personal integrity were also discussed.

The programme used a cascade training model, with 20 core trainers trained intensively over two weeks, while 160 peer trainers were then trained by them. Participants raised their annual income significantly, from an average of US$74 to US$93. The training also dramatically increased participants' appreciation of their ability to save money and they became more financially independent. An evaluation found, however, that it would be preferable to extend training to two days, and that providing grants to trainees would allow them to use their new skills, as practical experience with money management was lacking.

Sources: Kasonka and Mutelo (2011); Mak et al. (2010).

newly trained craftspeople into work, produce high quality crafts and help prevent rural depopulation. Artisans d'Angkor runs workshops in thirteen villages, providing equipment and materials to the craftspeople. It employs over 700 artisans, 40% of whom can live and work in their home villages. The training methods are aimed at those who have little formal education and are unused to conventional schooling. The artisans earn between US$60 and US$80 per month, equivalent to the amount a typical farmer earns in a year, and they receive social and medical benefits (Kenyon, 2009).

Foundation skills are needed to realize benefits of entrepreneurship training. Those who already have basic literacy and numeracy are likely to benefit most from entrepreneurship skills, as is shown by an innovative programme run by Camfed, an NGO working to support education of girls and women in Africa (Box 7.4).

Several innovative programmes aimed at providing entrepreneurship and microbusiness skills for disadvantaged young people, including indigenous youth, have been developed on a large scale in rural areas of Latin America. Many of these have shown impressive results.

In Mexico, the Programa Joven Emprendedor Rural y Fondo de Tierras (Young Rural Entrepreneur Programme and Land Fund, known as JERFT) began in 2004 to address young people's lack of access to land and the need for a new generation of young rural entrepreneurs. The programme, which particularly targeted indigenous groups, aimed to enable beneficiaries to start sustainable, profitable agribusinesses. Within a year, participants had increased their income by one-fifth (Severo, 2012).

Given that young rural women are often particularly disadvantaged both in education and work, initiatives to improve their livelihoods are needed. In rural Mexico, women involved in activities such as selling food and making crafts received six weeks of practical training to improve their business and financial skills. The women already knew how to make basic calculations, but did not know how to determine profit or set prices. After the training, the

women's business accounting improved and their daily profit increased by as much as 80% (Calderon et al., 2011).

To benefit from training, young entrepreneurs need start-up funds. An important lesson from the programmes in Latin America is that skills on their own are not sufficient. Young entrepreneurs also need access to funds to start up businesses, as well as support in the early stages, as the Jóvenes Rurales Emprendedores programme in Colombia illustrates. The programme, established by the national apprenticeship agency, SENA (Servicio Nacional de Aprendizaje), began in 2003 with a pilot project in 167 municipalities, and was extended to all departments in 1,091 municipalities in 2009. As well as strengthening entrepreneurial skills, the programme provides vocational training to promote productive projects ranging from agribusiness to services and industry. Beneficiaries are rural unemployed people aged 16 to 25, with a particular focus on vulnerable groups, including displaced persons and indigenous groups.

The programme is implemented by the Vocational Training Centre of SENA through strategic partnerships with local and regional governments and with trade unions. Young entrepreneurs have access to funds from a range of sources. By 2009, the programme had trained more than 257,000 young people. It has achieved impressive results, including increasing the probability of participants starting their own business by between 75% and 88%, compared with a control group not involved in the programme (Severo, 2012).

Enhancing the relevance of training by adapting to the local context. Skills development that is tailored to the local context through an assessment of the local market and its needs is more likely to be successful. One example is Training for Rural Economic Empowerment (TREE), a programme designed by the International Labour Organization that promotes local development and income generation, targeting disadvantaged groups. The TREE methodology has worked successfully in diverse contexts, from the Niger to the Philippines. It provides vocational, entrepreneurial and

In Mexico, rural tradeswomen earned 80% more after business training

management skills for income generation, as well as basic literacy and numeracy, which are lacking in many poor rural contexts.

It begins with an assessment of why local entrepreneurs or government have not filled gaps in the skill base in the local area, then works to identify how the gaps can be filled. Involvement of the community is crucial to ensure that training meets the needs not only of local business people but also of their customers and of community leaders.

After the training, support is offered to ensure that lessons are absorbed and put into practice. It includes links with employers, access to credit, business development services, and help in formalizing microenterprises and establishing local business groups and other self-help organizations. This support can be provided by a wide range of government and non-government bodies.

Between 2002 and 2007, TREE was carried out in the Khyber Pakhtunkhwa province of Pakistan and the southern island of Mindanao in the Philippines, with positive results. These areas are among the poorest in the two countries, both having been affected by conflict. In Pakistan, over 3,072 people received training, exceeding the target of 2,400; in the Philippines, 1,897 were trained, exceeding the target of 1,220 (ILO, 2005). Women, disenfranchised young men and those living with disability were targeted, along with former combatants in central Mindanao. In both countries, nearly all trainees used their new skills productively by either finding work or setting up a microenterprise three to five months after the end of the programme. Just over a third of Pakistani trainees, the vast majority of whom were women, began earning cash income for the first time and learned new skills, allowing them to raise their self-confidence and social status (ILO, 2005).

The programme has been adopted successfully in other African and Asian countries. TREE in Bangladesh has helped women enter non-traditional trades such as appliance and computer repair. The approach combines technical and business training with training in gender issues and gender sensitization sessions

for trainees' families, communities and partner organizations (ILO, 2009b).

The programme has been successful because it builds on partnerships involving the government, local communities, and employer and worker groups. It works towards empowering community target groups and promotes strong ownership by beneficiaries and partners, which contributes to its sustainability. With this type of foundation, the programme is in touch with local needs, providing highly relevant training, as the high rate of success for trainees shows (ILO, 2009b).

Training unemployed youth to become technological entrepreneurs. For young rural entrepreneurs with relatively high levels of literacy, the spread of mobile phones offers greater access to markets by enabling them to tap into information about prices, customer demand and developments within their sector. Access to financial services via mobile phones, especially in areas with few microfinance banks, is also becoming more common (Jansen, 2010).

An example of an initiative taking advantage of mobile phone and Internet technology is the Agricultural Knowledge Management System, set up in Bangladesh in 2006 and based at the Padma Research and Development Organization, a regional non-profit youth organization working with marginalized farming communities. Many of the farmers are illiterate and many more are not computer-literate, have no Internet connection and would not know how to search for the information they need. The Agricultural Knowledge Management System provides farmers with up-to-date information through knowledge brokers — local youth, educated but unemployed, who are trained to find the relevant agricultural, economic and social information and translate it into an understandable and digestible form.

The trainee knowledge brokers start as volunteers at the centre for two weeks, then take one month of intensive training based on the Microsoft 'Unlimited Potential' Curriculum. This is followed by two weeks focusing on the use and management of information in the Agricultural Knowledge Management System. The service,

In Bangladesh, educated youth are trained to support farmers who are not computer-literate

set up with international donor support, now charges a user fee (Braun and Islam, 2012). This may make it more sustainable, as it will not depend solely on outside funding, but could put it out of reach of the poorest communities.

'Green skills' training helps protect the environment and increase productivity

To help meet growing global demand for food and nutrition, to conserve energy and to protect vulnerable groups against the effects of climate change, smallholders need knowledge and skills that enable them to increase productivity while preventing degradation and depletion of natural resources. Training in new technologies needs to be accompanied by the preservation and dissemination of traditional knowledge about biodiversity, such as appropriate combinations of crops, trees and animals in integrated agricultural systems.

The importance of building on traditional knowledge and practices is clear in Yemen's dry highlands, where much of the country's crop production takes place. Traditional methods of managing water, soil and seeds help protect against drought, erosion and diseases. Yet the adoption of high yield seed varieties has reduced agro-biodiversity, while knowledge about alternative agricultural practices is vanishing. This loss of knowledge is significant because some wild crop species are more resistant to extreme conditions than commercial varieties. A project begun in 2010 and due to end in 2014 aims to strengthen the resilience of rural communities to climate change through conservation of agro-biodiversity in rain-fed agriculture. Skills development at local level is key to building farmers' coping mechanisms by improving their knowledge of climate change and their management of natural resources, as well as diversifying their income (World Bank, 2010b).

Skills training can also enable rural people to take advantage of economic opportunities that arise with the development of renewable energy resources, because the industries related to hydroelectricity and to wind, solar and geothermal energy are often located in rural areas (World Bank, 2008d). One example is Bangladesh's Grameen Shakti, an affiliate

of the Grameen Bank group, which pioneered microfinance. Grameen Shakti was established in 1996 as a non-profit distributor of home solar systems and other renewable energy technologies. Its Grameen Technology Centers (forty-six are now in operation) were set up to train local women to be service engineers, spare part manufacturers and sales representatives for Grameen Shakti systems. The programme focuses on training young women to provide them with opportunities, since they are more likely than men not to have paid work outside the home. Some 60,000 households install solar systems every year, leading to rising demand for trained technicians to keep them running. Monthly home visits for up to three years are part of the Grameen Shakti purchase agreement, and some training is also given to the client (Barua, 2012; Grameen Creative Lab, 2011; Grameen Shakti, 2009).

Given the potential for green skills to benefit young rural people, this area requires further attention. As well as helping conserve the environment and making farming more productive, sustainable agriculture can increase the attractiveness of rural life to young people by creating jobs that offer a decent livelihood.

Conclusion

Rural youth, and young rural women in particular, are among the most disadvantaged of all young people in terms of education and work. Many have missed out on basic literacy and numeracy skills and need a second chance to acquire them in order to improve their livelihoods by enhancing the productivity of smallholder farms. To be effective, second-chance programmes need to include opportunities to learn about new techniques. Information and communication technology, including radio and mobile telephony, can help spread training even to those living in remote areas. Training to improve farming productivity is unlikely to be enough on its own to discourage young people from moving to cities, however. To enhance opportunities in non-farm work, training in financial and entrepreneurial skills is needed, along with livelihood assets that can be used to set up businesses.

To enhance opportunities in non-farm work, training in financial and entrepreneurial skills is needed

In the Middle of Nowhere, by Khalid Mohamed Hammad Elkhateem, 23, from Sudan, winner of the *EFA Global Monitoring Report*'s "Youth, Skills, Work" art contest. The artist says "I decided to give my work very uncertain shapes and quite ambiguous features to reflect how the link between youth, skills, and jobs remains 'in the middle of nowhere'."

295

Women in Bangladesh attend a literacy class
given at a BRAC support centre

Young people need a pathway along which they can acquire the skills they need to benefit from a fulfilled life. This section identifies the ten most important steps that can improve young people's job prospects by developing their skills. They should influence national policies as well as donor and private sector financing strategies. As part of broader development efforts, they can help lift disadvantaged youth out of poverty.

Youth skills: pathways to a better future

Around one in six of the world's population are aged between 15 and 24. These young people are disproportionately concentrated in some of the poorest countries, where their numbers are still rising. Sub-Saharan Africa alone will have over three and half times more young people in 2030 than it had in 1980. Large numbers of young people equipped with appropriate skills have the potential to boost their country's prosperity. Ignoring the skills needs of disadvantaged young people not only limits their chances of achieving their potential, but also threatens to slow growth and poverty reduction.

Disadvantaged youth are often below the radar of youth employment policies and programmes, or approaches aimed at creating jobs in the private sector. Many have not been able to progress to lower secondary school and urgently need support to develop foundation skills. To give them a better chance of obtaining good jobs, they must be able to build on these foundations by acquiring the transferable skills and technical and vocational skills that are required in today's ever-changing labour market.

This Report describes policies and programmes that have been successful in meeting the skills needs of disadvantaged young people – whether engaged in the formal or informal sector in urban areas, or as smallholder farmers or rural entrepreneurs. By closing the gap between rich and poor and males and females, investment in skills development can help make societies more equitable.

Several lessons from this Report should form the backbone of national policies, as well as donor and private sector investment strategies, that can improve young people's job prospects. As part of broader development efforts, they can help lift disadvantaged youth out of poverty.

One of the most important messages is that all young people need a pathway along which they can acquire strong foundation skills, starting from early childhood right through to lower secondary school and beyond. To help give all young people an equal chance in life, it is vital to ensure that they do not face discrimination in educational access, quality or relevance because of where they live or what their gender is. Those who have missed out on foundation skills need a second chance to acquire them. Otherwise they will be consigned to low paid, insecure work, and will not be able to benefit from the further training that can lead to better jobs.

The need to take action in support of skills development for young people has become urgent. This Report identifies the ten most important steps that should be taken. These can be tailored to fit country-specific circumstances and needs.

1 Provide second-chance education for those with low or no foundation skills

There are around 200 million 15- to 24-year-olds in low and middle income countries who have missed out on completing primary school. Governments need to offer them second-chance education to provide at least the basic literacy and numeracy skills they need to get back on track and escape the cycle of low paid or unpaid work that can trap them in poverty.

As well as helping young people acquire foundation skills needed for work, second-chance programmes that also include practical skills for particular trades can boost their self-confidence. Having such skills gives them more control over work and livelihood choices.

Providing second-chance education to the large number of young people who need it requires well-coordinated and adequately funded programmes on a much greater scale. With the support of donor organizations, governments should make this a policy priority, including it in education sector strategic plans that sets targets to reduce significantly the large number of young people without foundation skills. Budgetary allocations based on the number of disadvantaged youth requiring a second-chance education should be identified and included in the national budget forecast.

2 Tackle the barriers that limit access to lower secondary school

It is vital that young people get the chance to attend lower secondary school to consolidate their foundation skills. Alarmingly, around one in three of youth in low and middle income countries do not get to this level. Most of those not in lower secondary school live in rural areas or poor urban informal settlements, and a disproportionate number are young women. Large numbers do not even make it through primary school. Those who do stay in school often receive education of poor quality and relevance. Without the foundation skills that primary and lower secondary school should offer, their chances of finding secure and decently paid work are severely limited.

A global target should be set to ensure all young people benefit from lower secondary school, with the aim of achieving universal lower secondary education of acceptable quality by 2030. Long-term education plans should identify strategies and financial resources required to meet this goal.

Countries with large numbers of young people who lack access to lower secondary school need to start by tackling the barriers that exclude many disadvantaged children and adolescents from participating and progressing in education. Key measures that can improve access to lower secondary school include abolishing school fees and providing targeted financial support, linking lower secondary to primary schools, ensuring that there are enough government school places and assuring accessibility in rural areas. In addition, strategies are needed that address the cultural barriers that young women often face.

Even in countries where access is not a major problem, providing a common core curriculum is a vital way of equipping all young people with foundation skills.

3 Make upper secondary education more accessible to the disadvantaged and improve its relevance to work

Upper secondary education offers young people opportunities to develop skills that will put them in a strong position to obtain good jobs. In the developing world, however, making the transition to upper secondary school remains difficult, while some rich countries are still struggling to make upper secondary near universal. To address these shortcomings, action is urgent in three key areas.

First, upper secondary education has to strike a balance between technical and vocational and general subjects by providing flexibility in subject choices and links with the workplace. Offering students short work placements as part of the curriculum and enhancing the relevance of what they learn in school in relation to the world of work can make them better candidates for good jobs. It is important for all students, irrespective of their gender or where they live, to have this opportunity. All students should also receive career guidance that emphasizes the skills requirements of a wide range of jobs in the formal and informal sectors, helping them choose school subjects that are relevant to these jobs.

Second, secondary school curriculum reforms should focus much more on developing in learners the capacity to solve problems and to apply knowledge creatively in ways that are relevant to many different job contexts. In addition, curriculum innovations are needed to tap into the potential of information and communication technology (ICT) to help learners develop the skills required in a labour market that is increasingly dependent on technology. More emphasis should be placed on its practical use in the workplace.

Third, flexible opportunities should be offered to students who are at risk of dropping out of secondary education. Distance education centres can be set up to cater for the learning needs of disadvantaged youth. Appropriate recognition should be given to skills gained through such alternative learning pathways.

4 Give poor urban youth access to skills training for better jobs

National policies and development strategies need to provide a clearer indication of how the skills needs of young people living in urban poverty will be met and funded. Many of these young people lack foundation skills, are thus trapped in low paid and insecure informal sector work, and are often invisible in national strategies. By supporting skills development in this sector, governments can harness the potential of the part of the economy that is most likely to absorb the large numbers of young people in developing countries.

Traditional apprenticeships are an important way of acquiring transferable and job-specific skills. Attention must be paid to how they are delivered in order to avoid exploitation and improve accessibility, especially for young women. Public interventions building on traditional apprenticeship systems should strengthen training by master craftspeople, improve working conditions of apprentices and ensure that skills can be certified through national qualification frameworks. As well as enhancing the legitimacy of traditional apprenticeships, such measures will ensure that they meet business and industry standards, and improve apprentices' access to a wider range of better-paid jobs.

Governments should improve national data collection on the informal sector, and work with associations and cooperatives in the sector to target urban youth as one way of improving their access to training and jobs. Micro- and small enterprises and their umbrella organizations will require considerable outside support and guidance to help them provide training. But producing labour market information about jobs is only half the challenge – it must also be distributed through youth-friendly community associations. Such services should provide information about where good jobs can be found, the skills needed to obtain them, and the likely earnings.

Policies and strategies should provide skills training, but must not stop there. They should also include job placement or careers advice services, in close association with local employers, to ease the search for gainful employment or entrepreneurial opportunities. Providing young people with access to funds to start up businesses, as well as other forms of support in the early stages, can help them use their skills successfully.

5 Aim policies and programmes at youth in deprived rural areas

Around 70% of the world's 1.4 billion people living in extreme poverty are in rural areas, many of them involved in smallholder farming. Greater attention should be given to their skills needs. Once young people in this situation have been given a second chance to acquire foundation skills, training in agricultural techniques can help enhance their productivity. Farmer field schools and training via cooperatives, which are attuned to the local needs of farmers, are particularly successful. Since many rural youth also work off the farm, training in entrepreneurship and financial management can widen their opportunities, especially where farmland is becoming scarce.

Enhancing smallholders' access to inputs and technology for more productive and sustainable agricultural practices must be accompanied by training in how to adapt to new practices. If young people already have foundation skills, such training can not only improve farm output but also make work in rural areas more attractive, and so help curtail the flow of young people to urban areas. Youth living in rural areas, who are particularly disadvantaged by a lack of access to land, financial assets and educational opportunities, need an integrated package of support that includes training in entrepreneurial and business skills to enable them to expand their livelihood options through non-farm work.

6 Link skills training with social protection for the poorest youth

Skills training alone is unlikely to be sufficient for the most disadvantaged of the urban and rural poor, including those involved in subsistence activities, such as street vendors, waste-pickers, smallholders and home-based workers. Some need legal protection from harassment and entitlement to skills training to enhance the profitability of their small businesses.

Many low and lower middle income countries offer support to the most vulnerable via microfinance or social protection programmes that provide access to productive and financial assets. Combining such assets with training in basic literacy and numeracy as well as livelihood skills can help counter the multiple forms of disadvantage that lock youth into poverty. By providing the skills needed to use the assets effectively, the programmes can help boost productivity and income, ensuring that the impact of the programmes is long-term and transformative.

7 Make the training needs of disadvantaged young women a high priority

The training needs of young women are particularly neglected. In many regions of the world, young women work for long hours in household and informal labour that is seldom visible to policy-makers. Women carry a heavy workload and face discrimination in education and labour markets, especially in rural areas, where their mobility is often highly restricted. More should be done to help young women make productive use of their skills by giving them access to credit and assets.

Targeted programmes that address the multiple causes of this disadvantage have proved effective. Providing young women with microfinance and livelihood assets, together with the skills needed to make the most out of these assets, gives them greater control over their own resources in ways that benefit them and their families. Successful programmes take into account the restrictions that young women can face in particular settings.

8 Harness the potential of technology to enhance opportunities for young people

Young people need to develop ICT skills to ensure that they can participate fully in an increasingly knowledge-based economy. ICTs can also be used to bring skills training to a larger number of youth. Even basic technology such as radio can play an important role in skills training, particularly for those in remote rural areas. Such methods should be exploited further to enhance training opportunities for young people.

The spread of mobile phones has huge potential for improving livelihood opportunities for young people. Skills programmes, especially in rural contexts, should include training in how mobile phone and similar technologies can be used to access information and financial services that can increase productivity and earnings. This will enhance opportunities for small businesses, especially in rural areas, to grow and reach larger markets.

9 Improve planning by strengthening data collection and coordination of skills programmes

Many training programmes are not sufficiently integrated with national development strategies. Government leadership is important in coordinating the diverse range of skills training and associated programmes to ensure that they reflect national priorities targeting the most disadvantaged youth. Doing so will reduce fragmentation and duplication of effort, and assure equitable access.

More and better quality data are needed to enable national governments and the international community to monitor access to skills development programmes, and so plan more effectively. For reporting to the UNESCO Institute for Statistics, better information on lower and upper secondary education is needed. This should include more data on dropout and completion and on subjects taken, such as details on academic as well as technical and vocational areas, enabling analysis of choice of subject by gender.

Better data are also needed on skills development programmes beyond the formal school system, including second-chance programmes and traditional apprenticeships, for example, linking this with labour market information. Given its expertise in this area, the International Labour Organization could take on responsibility for gathering and disseminating such data from national governments. The international community should also build on recent developments to measure a range of youth and adult skills more systematically.

Involving young people in planning, especially those facing disadvantages, can help to identify constraints and appropriate solutions. Governments also need to collaborate more closely with businesses and trade unions so that skills training efforts are more relevant to the workplace, including through the development of national qualifications frameworks. At the same time, businesses should support skills development by expanding access to enterprise-based training, which can improve productivity by increasing their pool of skilled labour.

10 Mobilize additional funding from diverse sources to meet the training needs of disadvantaged youth

There is an urgent need for more resources to ensure that all young people have a good foundation in education, extending at least until lower secondary school. Additional funds are needed to support second-chance opportunities on a much larger scale for those who have missed out. In poor countries, where government budgets are already overstretched, many young people will simply not be reached without additional funding dedicated to ensuring that they have foundation skills. It is therefore essential to mobilize additional funding for this purpose, not only from aid donors but also from the private sector, which ultimately is the main beneficiary of a better-trained workforce.

Ensuring that all youth are enrolled in lower secondary school would cost US$8 billion, over and above the US$16 billion needed to attain universal basic education by 2015. Extending second-chance opportunities to the one in five 15- to 24-year-olds in low and middle income countries who have not completed primary school would raise this figure considerably. Resources are finite and some aid donors are already providing significant support to disadvantaged young people. But donors could do far more. The same donors that champion skills development are often those that spend large amounts of their aid to pay for students from developing countries to study in the donor countries. Reallocating some of these funds could support skills development programmes for disadvantaged young people living in developing countries.

If invested directly in developing countries' education systems, the US$3.1 billion of aid spent on scholarships and imputed student costs in donor countries could contribute significantly to the US$8 billion needed for lower secondary schooling and to providing second-chance opportunities for around 200 million young people who lack even the most basic skills.

Aid donors offering skills development programmes also need to work more closely with governments and the private sector, coordinating their funds to ensure that the training offered has direct links to the labour market. Training funds are one approach that has been used with some success in reaching disadvantaged youth, including those in the informal sector. They offer the potential both of raising additional funds from diverse sources, including through payroll taxes and levies, and of improving coordination among governments, enterprises, donors and other interested parties. To be successful, however, they need effective management and broad representation from the business sector, youth, and other groups to ensure that funds are allocated according to demand and delivered on schedule.

The private sector could also extend its support to skills development programmes for disadvantaged young people through its foundations. Some have already shown innovation in this area, but their funding needs to be available on a much larger scale, and more closely coordinated with national priorities.

Conclusion

All countries, regardless of income level, need to pay greater attention to the needs of young people who face disadvantage in education and skills development by virtue of their poverty, gender or other characteristics. The precise nature and extent of these needs vary according to where young people live, but the response should address a common set of issues. The ten steps outlined here, based on evidence of policies, programmes and strategies that have been successful in many countries, can inform the choices that governments, donors and the private sector make in addressing the skills needs of disadvantaged youth.

A girl attends an electrical repair class at the USCOD Early Learning Centre in Badulla, Sri Lanka, supported by Terre des Hommes Netherlands, an NGO.

Annex

The Education for All Development Index

Statistical tables

Aid tables

The Education for All Development Index

The EFA Development Index (EDI) is a composite index that provides a snapshot of overall progress of national education systems towards Education for All.[1] Due to data constraints, the index has until now captured only four of the six goals. The development of an ECCE index this year (see Panel 1.2) allows the EDI to be broadened to five goals.[2] The first part of this Annex assesses countries across four dimensions of the EDI. The next part extends the EDI to include the ECCE index and shows how this affects the ranking of countries for which data are available.

The value of the standard EDI for a given country is the arithmetic mean of the four components:

■ universal primary education (goal 2), measured by the primary adjusted net enrolment ratio;

■ adult literacy (goal 4), measured by the literacy rate for those aged 15 and above;

■ gender parity and equality (goal 5), measured by the gender-specific EFA index (GEI), an average of the gender parity indices (GPIs) of the primary and secondary gross enrolment ratios and the adult literacy rate;[3]

■ quality of education (goal 6), measured by the survival rate to grade 5; in the absence of comparable indicators on quality, notably on learning outcomes, the survival rate is used as a proxy because of its positive correlation with average international learning assessment scores.

The EDI value falls between 0 and 1, with 1 representing full achievement of EFA across the four goals.

The EDI in 2010

Out of 205 countries, 120 have the data on all four indicators required to calculate the standard EDI. By region, the coverage ranges from over 90% in Central and Eastern Europe and North America and Western Europe to less than 40% in East Asia and the Pacific and in South and West Asia. Given that the standard EDI excludes goals 1 and 3, the relatively low coverage means the index provides only a partial global overview of progress towards EFA. In 2010, Japan had the highest EDI score and the Niger the lowest.

Countries are grouped in three categories according to the value of the EDI (Table EDI.1). There are fifty-eight countries in the top category (EDI>0.95). About 60% of the countries in this group are in either Central and Eastern Europe or North America and Western Europe.

In the middle category, there are forty-two countries, mostly in the Arab States (70% of countries in the region included in the EDI) and Latin America and the Caribbean (60% of countries in the region included in the EDI). In many of the countries in this category, progress across its components is unbalanced: half the countries in this group had a score of over 0.95 on the gender equity component but only five reached this score on the adult literacy component.

In the low category (EDI<0.80) there are twenty low and lower middle income countries. Six out of ten countries in this category are in sub-Saharan Africa, as well as two of the three countries in South and West Asia included in the analysis (India and Pakistan). All these countries had a poor record across the EFA goals. However, a few have made great progress towards universal primary enrolment. The primary adjusted net enrolment ratio was as high as 98% in India and Rwanda.

Similar scores may reflect differences in the effort a country is putting into EFA. Colombia and Tunisia, for example, have the same EDI score in the middle category. Tunisia has high primary enrolment and survival rates but a low adult literacy rate. Colombia has a much higher adult literacy rate but a low primary adjusted net enrolment ratio and an especially low survival rate. Tunisia's low adult literacy may reflect in part a historical legacy and not necessarily its current effort, while Colombia's lower scores on indicators associated with primary school age children suggest that it could face lower adult literacy rates in the future.

---

1. Additional information on the EDI is available on the Report's website.
2. The remaining goal, learning needs of youth and adults (goal 3), is excluded because progress is still not easy to measure and monitor.
3. An additional step is sometimes required to compute the GEI. When expressed as the ratio of female to male enrolment ratio or literacy rate, the GPI can exceed unity when more females than males are enrolled or literate. For the purpose of the GEI, the standard formula (female over male) is inverted (male over female) in cases where the GPI is higher than 1. This ensures that the GEI remains below 1 while maintaining the ability of the GEI to show gender disparity. Once all necessary adjustments are made, the GEI is obtained by calculating a simple average of the three GPIs.

Changes between 1999 and 2010

For a subset of fifty-two countries, it is possible to observe the evolution of the EDI since the World Education Forum in Dakar (Figure EDI.1). The EDI improved in forty-one of the fifty-two countries between 1999 and 2010. A particularly large increase took place in the twelve sub-Saharan African countries in this group.

Mozambique, which recorded the highest increase in the EDI, achieved improvement across all four of the index's components. It caught up with Angola in terms of education development thanks to a strong government commitment to education. Ethiopia, which recorded the second highest increase in the EDI over the period, made faster progress in terms of the universal primary enrolment component but regressed on survival to grade 5.

Four countries moved from the low EDI category in 1999 to the middle category in 2010 as a result of their commitment to education: Ghana, Guatemala, Lesotho and Malawi. In Ghana and Lesotho, the main driver was an increase in primary enrolment. Nicaragua advanced due to an increase in primary school participation and survival. In Malawi, the increase in the EDI was mainly due to the improvement in survival rate. The country is also reaping the positive results of primary education expansion in the 1990s in the form of higher adult literacy rates.

Extending the EDI

Expanding the EDI to include ECCE provides insights in comparative progress towards EFA. The extended EDI is the arithmetic mean of five components, the ECCE index being the fifth component.

One effect of extending the EDI is that the absolute value of the index falls, on average, indicating that countries are farther from achieving goal 1. Among the fifty-two countries for which the extended EDI can be calculated, just three have a high score, above 0.95: Belarus, Kazakhstan and Kuwait. This is partly because high income countries are under-represented due to a lack of information on child nutrition. By contrast, thirty-four countries are in the middle group, and fifteen countries are in the low group (Table EDI.1).

Another effect of extending the EDI is that it reveals which countries have put more emphasis on early childhood. Some countries – notably in Central Asia, such as Kyrgyzstan and Uzbekistan, and in East Asia, such as Indonesia and the Philippines – drop in ranking. By contrast, other countries – notably in Central and Eastern Europe, such as Belarus and the Republic of Moldova, and in Latin America and the Caribbean,

such as Jamaica and Mexico – improve their standing considerably when the ECCE index is included.

EFA will not be achieved unless equal attention is paid to all goals. Breaking the intergenerational cycle of educational deprivation requires particular attention to those considered as the most neglected, including ECCE and adult literacy.

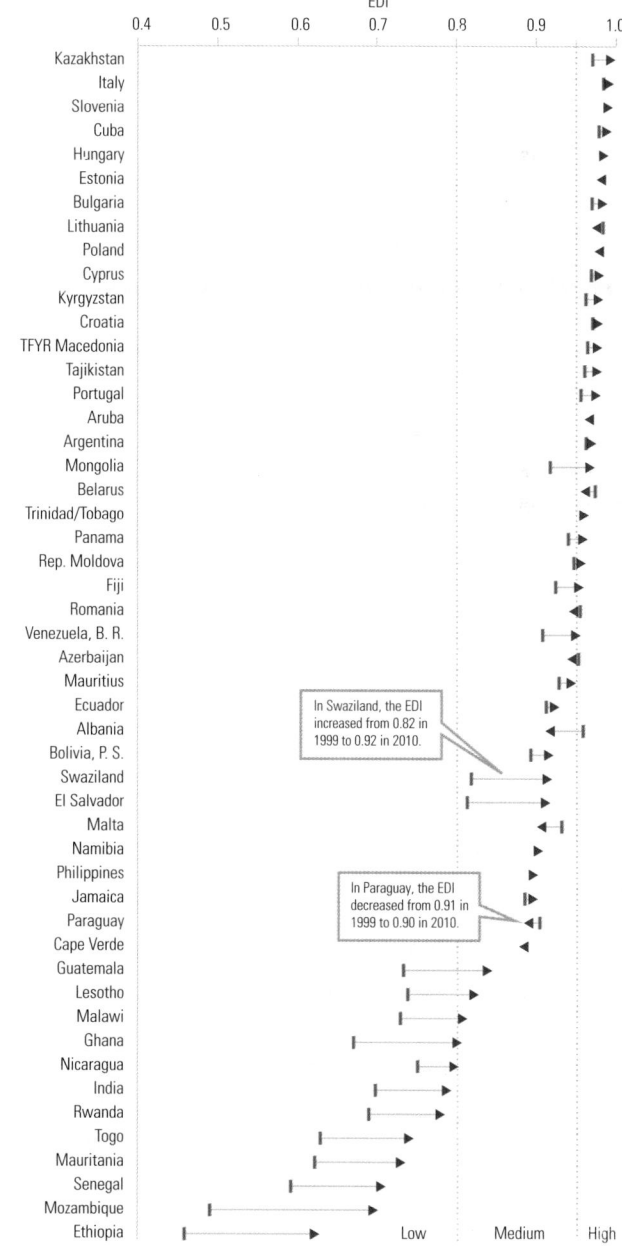

Figure EDI.1: Countries furthest from EFA have progressed, but not enough, since 1999

Change in EDI scores, 1999-2010

Source: EFA Global Monitoring Report team calculations.

Table EDI.1: The EFA Development Index and its components, 2010

Ranking	Countries	Standard EDI					Extended EDI				
		EDI	Primary adjusted net enrolment	Adult literacy rate	Gender-specific EFA index	Survival rate to grade 5	ECCE index	Extended EDI	EDI ranking (1)	Extended EDI ranking (2)	Difference between (1) and (2)
High EDI > 0.95											
1	Japan[2]	0.997	1.000	0.992	0.999	1.000	…	…	…	…	…
2	Sweden[2]	0.996	0.994	1.000	0.995	0.995	…	…	…	…	…
3	Norway[2]	0.995	0.991	1.000	0.993	0.995	…	…	…	…	…
4	United Kingdom[2]	0.994	0.998	0.998	0.992	0.990	…	…	…	…	…
5	Iceland[2]	0.994	0.994	1.000	0.990	0.990	…	…	…	…	…
6	Switzerland[2]	0.993	0.992	1.000	0.989	0.990	…	…	…	…	…
7	Kazakhstan[3]	0.992	0.997	0.997	0.988	0.988	0.805	0.955	1	2	-1
8	France[2]	0.992	0.992	0.994	0.992	0.990	…	…	…	…	…
9	Netherlands[2]	0.992	1.000	0.985	0.993	0.990	…	…	…	…	…
10	Ireland[2]	0.992	0.997	0.994	0.983	0.993	…	…	…	…	…
11	Italy	0.991	0.991	0.989	0.989	0.996	…	…	…	…	…
12	Slovenia	0.990	0.972	0.997	0.996	0.996	…	…	…	…	…
13	Finland[2]	0.990	0.978	1.000	0.984	0.997	…	…	…	…	…
14	Spain	0.989	0.998	0.977	0.985	0.997	…	…	…	…	…
15	New Zealand[2]	0.989	0.995	0.988	0.983	0.990	…	…	…	…	…
16	Cuba	0.989	0.998	0.998	0.989	0.970	…	…	…	…	…
17	Denmark[2]	0.987	0.960	1.000	0.992	0.997	…	…	…	…	…
18	Australia[2]	0.986	0.972	1.000	0.982	0.990	…	…	…	…	…
19	Belgium[2]	0.986	0.990	0.999	0.989	0.965	…	…	…	…	…
20	Hungary[2,3]	0.985	0.980	0.990	0.990	0.977	…	…	…	…	…
21	Germany[2,3]	0.985	0.998	1.000	0.981	0.962	…	…	…	…	…
22	Estonia	0.984	0.963	0.998	0.989	0.988	…	…	…	…	…
23	Georgia	0.983	1.000	0.997	0.972	0.964	…	…	…	…	…
24	Bulgaria[3]	0.983	0.995	0.984	0.981	0.974	…	…	…	…	…
25	United States[2]	0.982	0.957	0.989	0.993	0.990	…	…	…	…	…
26	Lithuania[3]	0.982	0.957	0.997	0.991	0.983	…	…	…	…	…
27	Poland[2]	0.982	0.960	0.995	0.991	0.980	…	…	…	…	…
28	Cyprus	0.979	0.990	0.983	0.990	0.954	…	…	…	…	…
29	Israel[2]	0.978	0.970	0.971	0.982	0.990	…	…	…	…	…
30	Kyrgyzstan[3]	0.978	0.953	0.992	0.991	0.976	0.728	0.928	2	11	-9
31	Croatia[3]	0.978	0.959	0.988	0.974	0.991	…	…	…	…	…
32	Luxembourg[2]	0.977	0.968	0.990	0.987	0.964	…	…	…	…	…
33	TFYR Macedonia[3]	0.977	0.982	0.973	0.983	0.970	0.809	0.944	3	7	-4
34	Tajikistan[3]	0.976	0.978	0.997	0.943	0.989	0.601	0.901	4	20	-16
35	Russian Federation[3]	0.976	0.957	0.996	0.991	0.961	…	…	…	…	…
36	Latvia	0.976	0.958	0.998	0.990	0.957	…	…	…	…	…
37	Portugal	0.975	0.994	0.952	0.965	0.990	…	…	…	…	…
38	Serbia[3]	0.973	0.945	0.979	0.983	0.986	0.843	0.947	5	5	0
39	Republic of Korea[2]	0.972	0.989	0.935	0.969	0.994	…	…	…	…	…
40	Aruba	0.971	0.997	0.968	0.987	0.930	…	…	…	…	…
41	Uzbekistan[3]	0.970	0.921	0.994	0.985	0.981	0.716	0.920	6	14	-8
42	Samoa	0.970	0.979	0.988	0.950	0.964	…	…	…	…	…
43	Argentina	0.970	0.990	0.978	0.958	0.954	…	…	…	…	…
44	Ukraine[3]	0.969	0.911	0.997	0.989	0.977	…	…	…	…	…
45	Mongolia	0.968	0.991	0.974	0.967	0.941	0.807	0.936	7	9	-2
46	Belarus[3]	0.966	0.920	0.996	0.952	0.997	0.967	0.966	8	1	7
47	Bahamas[2]	0.964	0.978	0.988	0.975	0.914	…	…	…	…	…
48	Mexico	0.962	0.996	0.931	0.963	0.960	0.901	0.950	9	4	5
49	Trinidad and Tobago	0.962	0.974	0.988	0.965	0.921	…	…	…	…	…
50	Kuwait	0.960	0.982	0.939	0.957	0.960	0.914	0.950	10	3	7
51	Panama	0.959	0.987	0.941	0.963	0.946	0.805	0.928	11	10	1
52	Armenia[3]	0.957	0.871	0.996	0.984	0.977	…	…	…	…	…
53	Republic of Moldova[3]	0.957	0.901	0.985	0.988	0.953	0.892	0.944	12	6	6
54	Fiji[2]	0.955	0.991	0.929	0.955	0.943	…	…	…	…	…
55	Qatar	0.954	0.962	0.963	0.937	0.955	…	…	…	…	…
56	Romania[3]	0.953	0.876	0.977	0.989	0.971	…	…	…	…	…
57	Bosnia and Herzegovina[3]	0.953	0.871	0.979	0.975	0.987	0.771	0.917	13	15	-2
58	Venezuela, B. R.	0.951	0.949	0.955	0.960	0.938	0.881	0.937	14	8	6

Notes: Data in blue indicate that gender disparities are at the expense of boys or men.
1. The primary adjusted net enrolment ratio measures the proportion of children of primary school age who are enrolled in either primary or secondary school.
2. Adult literacy rates are unofficial UIS estimates.
3. The survival rate to the last grade was used because the primary education cycle is less than five years.
Source: Annex, Statistical Tables 2, 5, 6 and 7 (print), Statistical Table 5 (website); UIS database; *EFA Global Monitoring Report* calculations.

		Standard EDI					Extended EDI				
Ranking	Countries	EDI	Primary adjusted net enrolment	Adult literacy rate	Gender-specific EFA index	Survival rate to grade 5	ECCE index	Extended EDI	EDI ranking (1)	Extended EDI ranking (2)	Difference betwee (1) and (2)
Medium 0.80<EDI<0.94											
59	Azerbaijan[3]	0.949	0.847	0.998	0.989	0.964	0.733	0.906	15	18	-3
60	Montenegro	0.948	0.832	0.984	0.984	0.990	0.849	0.928	16	12	4
61	Mauritius	0.945	0.934	0.885	0.980	0.980	...	...	...	...	...
62	Antigua and Barbuda	0.942	0.878	0.990	0.965	0.935	...	...	...	...	...
63	Peru	0.942	0.981	0.896	0.959	0.932	0.849	0.923	17	13	4
64	Indonesia	0.938	0.991	0.926	0.973	0.861	0.706	0.891	18	24	-6
65	Turkey	0.932	0.975	0.908	0.928	0.918	0.794	0.905	19	19	0
66	Saint Lucia[2]	0.931	0.897	0.901	0.979	0.947	...	...	...	...	...
67	Barbados[2]	0.930	0.951	0.884	0.964	0.922	...	...	...	...	...
68	Suriname	0.929	0.909	0.947	0.918	0.941	0.852	0.913	20	16	4
69	Syrian Arab Republic[3]	0.928	0.991	0.834	0.942	0.946	0.754	0.894	21	23	-2
70	Lebanon	0.927	0.932	0.896	0.928	0.953	...	...	...	...	...
71	Macao, China	0.926	0.826	0.935	0.955	0.989	...	...	...	...	...
72	Ecuador	0.924	0.985	0.919	0.975	0.817	...	...	...	...	...
73	Albania	0.923	0.799	0.959	0.980	0.952	0.803	0.899	22	21	1
74	Bolivia, P. S.	0.917	0.942	0.912	0.963	0.851	0.740	0.881	23	26	-3
75	Swaziland	0.915	0.856	0.874	0.968	0.962	0.689	0.870	24	29	-5
76	Colombia	0.914	0.915	0.934	0.963	0.845	0.835	0.898	25	22	3
77	El Salvador	0.913	0.953	0.845	0.962	0.894	0.769	0.885	26	25	1
78	Saudi Arabia	0.913	0.899	0.866	0.947	0.939	...	...	...	...	...
79	Malta	0.912	0.938	0.924	0.953	0.835	...	...	...	...	...
80	Botswana	0.912	0.873	0.845	0.965	0.966	0.677	0.865	27	32	-5
81	Tunisia	0.910	0.994	0.776	0.909	0.961	...	...	...	...	...
82	Namibia	0.903	0.864	0.888	0.945	0.915	...	...	...	...	...
83	Sao Tome and Principe	0.902	0.986	0.892	0.957	0.773	0.768	0.875	28	27	1
84	Philippines	0.898	0.887	0.954	0.964	0.787	0.678	0.854	29	35	-6
85	Jamaica	0.897	0.824	0.866	0.938	0.961	0.944	0.907	30	17	13
86	Paraguay	0.896	0.857	0.939	0.967	0.823	0.774	0.872	31	28	3
87	Egypt	0.890	0.963	0.720	0.903	0.972	0.724	0.857	32	34	-2
88	Cape Verde	0.889	0.935	0.843	0.883	0.897	...	...	...	...	...
89	Algeria	0.888	0.973	0.726	0.903	0.950	0.794	0.869	33	30	3
90	Honduras	0.884	0.972	0.848	0.938	0.778	0.755	0.858	34	33	1
91	Guyana[2]	0.877	0.841	0.849	0.952	0.867	0.819	0.865	35	31	4
92	Guatemala	0.841	0.986	0.752	0.920	0.706	0.657	0.804	36	36	0
93	Lesotho	0.824	0.737	0.896	0.857	0.804	...	...	...	...	...
94	Morocco	0.813	0.941	0.561	0.811	0.939	...	...	...	...	...
95	Cameroon	0.810	0.939	0.707	0.831	0.763	0.700	0.788	37	39	-2
96	Malawi	0.809	0.975	0.748	0.906	0.609	...	...	...	...	...
97	Ghana	0.803	0.842	0.673	0.913	0.784	0.765	0.795	38	38	0
98	Bhutan	0.803	0.899	0.528	0.854	0.930	...	...	...	...	...
99	Lao PDR	0.802	0.968	0.727	0.843	0.670	0.671	0.776	39	40	-1
100	Cambodia	0.801	0.959	0.739	0.883	0.621	0.654	0.771	40	41	-1
Low EDI <0.80											
101	Nicaragua	0.799	0.939	0.780	0.962	0.514	0.811	0.801	41	37	4
102	India	0.790	0.982	0.628	0.865	0.685	...	...	...	...	...
103	Rwanda	0.781	0.987	0.711	0.956	0.472	0.597	0.744	42	43	-1
104	Uganda	0.771	0.910	0.732	0.872	0.571	0.646	0.746	43	42	1
105	Timor-Leste	0.769	0.859	0.583	0.930	0.705	...	...	...	...	...
106	Togo	0.742	0.943	0.571	0.679	0.777	...	...	...	...	...
107	Mauritania	0.732	0.744	0.580	0.862	0.743	...	...	...	...	...
108	Nigeria	0.721	0.576	0.613	0.830	0.863	...	...	...	...	...
109	Senegal	0.707	0.780	0.497	0.815	0.737	0.673	0.701	44	44	0
110	Mozambique	0.698	0.919	0.561	0.775	0.537	...	...	...	...	...
111	Angola	0.685	0.857	0.701	0.734	0.448	0.685	0.685	45	45	0
112	Gambia	0.677	0.693	0.500	0.866	0.651	0.684	0.679	46	46	0
113	Pakistan	0.656	0.741	0.549	0.720	0.615	...	...	...	...	...
114	Guinea	0.634	0.770	0.410	0.668	0.686	0.573	0.621	47	47	0
115	Eritrea	0.623	0.349	0.678	0.777	0.690	...	...	...	...	...
116	Ethiopia	0.622	0.822	0.390	0.772	0.505	0.531	0.604	48	50	-2
117	Central African Republic	0.617	0.705	0.560	0.639	0.563	0.564	0.606	49	48	1
118	Mali	0.612	0.620	0.311	0.678	0.840	0.575	0.605	50	49	1
119	Burkina Faso	0.594	0.583	0.287	0.754	0.751	0.569	0.589	51	51	0
120	Niger	0.528	0.572	0.287	0.612	0.643	0.508	0.524	52	52	0

A young employee working at a family-owned bakery in Paris, France

This picture was selected from the winners of the
UNESCO-UNEVOC Photo Competition 2012:
Work has many faces.

Statistical tables[1]

Introduction

The most recent data on pupils, students, teachers and education expenditure presented in these statistical tables are for the school year ending in 2010.[2] They are based on survey results reported to and processed by the UNESCO Institute for Statistics (UIS) before the end of March 2012. Data received and processed after that date are published on the UIS website and will be used in the next *EFA Global Monitoring Report*. A small number of countries submitted data for the school year ending in 2011, presented in bold in the statistical tables.[3]

These statistics refer to all formal schools, both public and private, by level of education. They are supplemented by demographic and economic statistics collected or produced by other international organizations, including the United Nations Development Programme (UNDP), the United Nations Children's Fund (UNICEF), the United Nations Population Division (UNPD), the World Bank and the World Health Organization (WHO).

The statistical tables list a total of 205 countries and territories. Most of them report their data to the UIS using standard questionnaires issued by the Institute. For some countries, however, education data are collected via surveys carried out under the auspices of the World Education Indicators (WEI) programme, or jointly by the UIS, the Organisation for Economic Co-operation and Development (OECD) and the Statistical Office of the European Union (Eurostat) through the UIS/OECD/Eurostat (UOE) questionnaires. These countries are indicated with the symbols given at the end of the introduction.

Population
The indicators on school access and participation in the statistical tables are based on the 2010 revision of population estimates produced by the UNPD. Because of possible differences between national population estimates and those of the United Nations, these indicators may differ from those published by individual countries or by other organizations.[4] The UNPD does not provide data by single year of age for countries with a total population of fewer than 50,000. Where no UNPD estimates exist, national population figures, when available, or UIS estimates were used to calculate enrolment ratios.

ISCED classification
Education data reported to the UIS since 1998 are in conformity with the 1997 revision of the International Standard Classification of Education (ISCED97). Data for the school year ending in 1991, presented in Statistical Tables 12 and 13 (website), were collected according to the previous version of the classification, ISCED76. Where possible, the UIS has adjusted these data to comply with ISCED97 and to minimize any inconsistencies with data for years after 1997.[5] ISCED is used to harmonize data and introduce more international comparability across national education systems. Countries may have their own definitions of education levels that do not correspond to ISCED. Some differences between nationally and internationally reported education statistics may be due, therefore, to the use of these nationally defined education levels rather than the ISCED standard, in addition to the population issue raised above.

Adult participation in basic education
ISCED does not classify education programmes by participants' age. For example, any programme with a content equivalent to primary education, or ISCED 1, may be classed as ISCED 1 even if provided to adults. The guidance the UIS provides for respondents to its regular annual education survey asks countries to exclude 'data on programmes designed for people beyond regular school age'. As for the guidance for the UOE and WEI questionnaires, until 2005 it stated that 'activities classified as "continuing", "adult" or "non-formal" education should be included' if they 'involve studies with subject content similar to regular educational programmes' or if 'the underlying programmes lead to similar potential qualifications' as the regular programmes. Since 2005, however, the

---

1. A full set of statistics and indicators related to this introduction is posted in Excel format on the EFA Global Monitoring Report website at www.efareport.unesco.org
2. This means 2009/10 for countries with a school year that overlaps two calendar years and 2010 for those with a calendar school year.
3. Bhutan, Burkina Faso, the Central African Republic, the Cook Islands, Côte d'Ivoire, Cuba, Djibouti, Gabon, Ghana, Kazakhstan, Maldives, Mali, the Marshall Islands, Morocco, Mozambique, Nepal, the Niger, Rwanda, Sao Tome and Principe, Sierra Leone, Thailand and Uzbekistan.

4. Where obvious inconsistencies exist between enrolment reported by countries and the United Nations population data, the UIS may decide not to calculate or publish the enrolment ratios. This is the case with Bahrain, Brazil, Kuwait, Nepal, Singapore and the United Arab Emirates, where enrolment ratios at all levels of education are not published, and with Bangladesh, Belarus, Belize, the British Virgin Islands and Malaysia, where publication of enrolment ratios at some levels of education is suspended.
5. To improve comparisons over time, the UIS has begun to harmonize time-series data, adjusting data from before 1997 so that they comply with the ISCED97 classification.

countries involved in the UOE/WEI survey have been requested to report data for such programmes separately so that the UIS can exclude them when calculating internationally comparable indicators. Despite the UIS instructions, data from some countries in the annual survey may still include students (or participants) who are substantially above the official age for basic education.

Literacy data

UNESCO has long defined literacy as the ability to read and write, with understanding, a short simple statement related to one's daily life. However, a parallel definition arose with the introduction in 1978 of the notion of functional literacy, which emphasizes the use of literacy skills. That year the UNESCO General Conference approved defining as functionally literate those who can engage in all activities in which literacy is required for the effective functioning of their group and community and also for enabling them to continue to use reading, writing and calculation for their own and the community's development.

In many cases, the literacy statistics in the corresponding table rely on the first definition and are largely based on data sources that use self or third-party declaration methods, in which respondents are asked whether they and the members of their household are literate, as opposed to being asked a more comprehensive question or to demonstrate the skill. Some countries assume that persons who complete a certain level of education are literate.[6] As definitions and methodologies used for data collection differ by country, data need to be used with caution.

Literacy data in this Report cover adults aged 15 and over as well as youth aged 15 to 24. They refer to two periods, 1985–1994 and 2005–2010, and include both national observed data from censuses and household surveys, indicated with an asterisk (*), and UIS estimates. The latter are for 1994 and 2010 and are based on the most recent national observed data. They were produced using the Global Age-Specific Literacy Projections Model (GALP). The reference years and literacy definitions for each country are presented in the table posted on the EFA Global Monitoring Report website.

Estimates and missing data

Both actual and estimated education data are presented throughout the statistical tables. When data are not reported to the UIS using the standard questionnaires, estimates are often necessary. Wherever possible, the UIS encourages countries to make their own estimates, which are presented as national estimates and marked with one asterisk (*). Where this does not happen, the UIS may make its own estimates if sufficient supplementary information is available. These estimates are marked with two asterisks (**). In addition, gaps in the tables may arise where data submitted by a country are found to be inconsistent. The UIS makes every attempt to resolve such problems with the countries concerned, but reserves the final decision to omit data it regards as problematic.

To fill the gaps in the statistical tables, data for earlier school years are included when information for the school years ending in 1999 and 2010 is not available. Such cases are indicated by a footnote.

Regional and other country grouping averages

Regional figures for literacy rates, gross, net and adjusted net intake rates, gross, net and adjusted net enrolment ratios, school life expectancy and pupil/teacher ratios are weighted averages, taking into account the relative size of the relevant population of each country in each region. The figures for countries with larger populations thus have a proportionately greater influence on the regional aggregates. The averages are derived from both published data and imputed values for countries for which no recent data or reliable publishable data are available. Weighted averages marked with two asterisks (**) in the tables are UIS partial imputations due to incomplete country coverage (between 33% and 60% of the population of a given region or country grouping). Where insufficient reliable data are available to produce an overall weighted mean, a median figure is calculated based only on countries with available data accounting for at least half of those in a region or group of countries.

Capped figures

There are cases where an indicator theoretically should not exceed 100% (the net intake rates and net enrolment ratio, for example), but data inconsistencies may have resulted nonetheless in the indicator exceeding the theoretical limit. In these cases, the total male and female values of the given indicator are recalculated and

6. For reliability and consistency reasons, the UIS does not publish literacy data based on educational attainment proxies. Only data reported by countries based on self-declaration or household declaration are included in the statistical tables. However, in the absence of such data, educational attainment proxies for some countries, particularly developed ones, are used to compute regional weighted averages and the EFA Development Index.

lowered using a capping factor so that the gender parity index of the new set of values remains the same as for the uncapped values.[7]

Symbols used in the statistical tables (printed and web versions)

  *   National estimate
  **   UIS partial estimate
  ...   No data available
  -    Magnitude nil or negligible
  .   Category is not applicable or does not exist

Footnotes to the tables, along with the glossary following the statistical tables, also provide additional help in interpreting the data and information.

Composition of regions and other country groups

o   Countries whose education data are collected through UOE questionnaires
w WEI programme countries

World classification[8]

■ Countries in transition (18):
12 countries of the Commonwealth of Independent States, including 4 in Central and Eastern Europe (Belarus, Republic of Moldova, Russian Federation° and Ukraine) and the countries of Central Asia minus Mongolia; and 6 countries in Central and Eastern Europe formerly in the developed countries group: Albania, Bosnia and Herzegovina, Croatia, Montenegro, Serbia and The former Yugoslav Republic of Macedonia.

■ Developed countries (39):
North America and Western Europe (minus Cyprus°); Central and Eastern Europe (minus Albania, Belarus, Bosnia and Herzegovina, Croatia, Montenegro, Republic of Moldova, Russian Federation°, Serbia, The former Yugoslav Republic of Macedonia, Turkey° and Ukraine); Australia°, Bermuda, Japan° and New Zealand°.

■ Developing countries (148):
Arab States; East Asia and the Pacific (minus Australia°, Japan° and New Zealand°); Latin America and the Caribbean (minus Bermuda); South and West Asia; sub-Saharan Africa; Cyprus°, Mongolia and Turkey°.

EFA regions[9]

■ Arab States (20 countries/territories):
Algeria, Bahrain, Djibouti, Egypt[w], Iraq, Jordan°, Kuwait, Lebanon, Libya, Mauritania, Morocco, Oman, Palestine, Qatar, Saudi Arabia, Sudan (pre-secession), Syrian Arab Republic, Tunisia[w], United Arab Emirates and Yemen.

■ Central and Eastern Europe (21 countries):
Albania, Belarus, Bosnia and Herzegovina, Bulgaria°, Croatia, Czech Republic°, Estonia°, Hungary°, Latvia°, Lithuania°, Montenegro, Poland°, Republic of Moldova, Romania°, Russian Federation°, Serbia, Slovakia°, Slovenia°, The former Yugoslav Republic of Macedonia°, Turkey° and Ukraine.

■ Central Asia (9 countries):
Armenia, Azerbaijan, Georgia, Kazakhstan, Kyrgyzstan, Mongolia, Tajikistan, Turkmenistan and Uzbekistan.

■ East Asia and the Pacific (33 countries/territories):
Australia°, Brunei Darussalam, Cambodia, China[w], Cook Islands, Democratic People's Republic of Korea, Fiji, Indonesia[w], Japan°, Kiribati, Lao People's Democratic Republic, Macao (China), Malaysia[w], Marshall Islands, Federated States of Micronesia, Myanmar, Nauru, New Zealand°, Niue, Palau, Papua New Guinea, Philippines[w], Republic of Korea°, Samoa, Singapore, Solomon Islands, Thailand[w], Timor-Leste, Tokelau, Tonga, Tuvalu, Vanuatu and Viet Nam.

  ● East Asia (16 countries/territories):
Brunei Darussalam, Cambodia, China[w], Democratic People's Republic of Korea, Indonesia[w], Japan°, Lao People's Democratic Republic, Macao (China), Malaysia[w], Myanmar, Philippines[w], Republic of Korea°, Singapore, Thailand[w], Timor-Leste and Viet Nam.

  ● Pacific (17 countries/territories):
Australia°, Cook Islands, Fiji, Kiribati, Marshall Islands, Federated States of Micronesia, Nauru, New Zealand°, Niue, Palau, Papua New Guinea, Samoa, Solomon Islands, Tokelau, Tonga, Tuvalu and Vanuatu.

---

7. For instance, net enrolment ratios in primary education are capped using a factor that takes into account the male and female primary school-age populations and enrolment of primary school age boys and girls in pre-primary, primary and secondary education. If the total enrolment of primary school age children (whether male or female) is higher than the corresponding population, all net enrolment indicators (net enrolment ratio, adjusted net enrolment ratio, etc.) and their derivative indicators (out-of-school rate, etc.) are capped based on the same capping factor. In this case, the capping factor is calculated by taking the maximum of the male and female enrolments and dividing by the population of primary school age.
8. This is a United Nations Statistical Division world classification, in three main country groupings, as revised in September 2011.

9. These are regional classifications as defined in 1998 for the EFA 2000 assessment.

■ Latin America and the Caribbean (41 countries/
territories):
Anguilla, Antigua and Barbuda, Argentina^w, Aruba,
Bahamas, Barbados, Belize, Bermuda, Plurinational
State of Bolivia, Brazil°, British Virgin Islands, Cayman
Islands, Chile°, Colombia, Costa Rica, Cuba, Dominica,
Dominican Republic, Ecuador, El Salvador, Grenada,
Guatemala, Guyana, Haiti, Honduras, Jamaica^w,
Mexico°, Montserrat, Netherlands Antilles, Nicaragua,
Panama, Paraguay^w, Peru^w, Saint Kitts and Nevis, Saint
Lucia, Saint Vincent and the Grenadines, Suriname,
Trinidad and Tobago, Turks and Caicos Islands,
Uruguay° and Bolivarian Republic of Venezuela.

● Latin America (19 countries):
Argentina^w, Plurinational State of Bolivia, Brazil°,
Chile°, Colombia, Costa Rica, Cuba, Dominican
Republic, Ecuador, El Salvador, Guatemala,
Honduras, Mexico°, Nicaragua, Panama,
Paraguay^w, Peru^w, Uruguay° and Bolivarian
Republic of Venezuela.

● Caribbean (22 countries/territories):
Anguilla, Antigua and Barbuda, Aruba, Bahamas,
Barbados, Belize, Bermuda, British Virgin Islands,
Cayman Islands, Dominica, Grenada, Guyana,
Haiti, Jamaica^w, Montserrat, Netherlands Antilles,
Saint Kitts and Nevis, Saint Lucia, Saint Vincent
and the Grenadines, Suriname, Trinidad and
Tobago, and Turks and Caicos Islands.

■ North America and Western Europe:
(26 countries/territories)
Andorra, Austria°, Belgium°, Canada°, Cyprus°,
Denmark°, Finland°, France°, Germany°, Greece°,
Iceland°, Ireland°, Israel°, Italy°, Luxembourg°, Malta°,
Monaco, Netherlands°, Norway°,
Portugal°, San Marino, Spain°, Sweden°, Switzerland°,
United Kingdom° and United States°.

■ South and West Asia (9 countries):
Afghanistan, Bangladesh, Bhutan, India^w, Islamic
Republic of Iran, Maldives, Nepal, Pakistan and
Sri Lanka^w.

■ Sub-Saharan Africa (46 countries):
Angola, Benin, Botswana, Burkina Faso, Burundi,
Cameroon, Cape Verde, Central African Republic,
Chad, Comoros, Congo, Côte d'Ivoire, Democratic
Republic of the Congo, Equatorial Guinea, Eritrea,
Ethiopia, Gabon, Gambia, Ghana, Guinea, Guinea-
Bissau, Kenya, Lesotho, Liberia, Madagascar,

Malawi, Mali, Mauritius, Mozambique, Namibia,
Niger, Nigeria, Rwanda, Sao Tome and Principe,
Senegal, Seychelles, Sierra Leone, Somalia, South
Africa, South Sudan, Swaziland, Togo, Uganda, United
Republic of Tanzania, Zambia and Zimbabwe.

Income groups[10]
■ Low income (36 countries):
Afghanistan, Bangladesh, Benin, Burkina Faso,
Burundi, Cambodia, Central African Republic, Chad,
Comoros, Democratic People's Republic of Korea,
Democratic Republic of the Congo, Eritrea, Ethiopia,
Gambia, Guinea, Guinea-Bissau, Haiti, Kenya,
Kyrgyzstan, Liberia, Madagascar, Malawi, Mali,
Mozambique, Myanmar, Nepal, Niger, Rwanda, Sierra
Leone, Somalia, Tajikistan, Togo, Tokelau, Uganda,
United Republic of Tanzania and Zimbabwe.

■ Lower middle income (56 countries):
Angola, Armenia, Belize, Bhutan, Plurinational
State of Bolivia, Cameroon, Cape Verde, Congo, Côte
d'Ivoire, Djibouti, Egypt, El Salvador, Fiji, Georgia,
Ghana, Guatemala, Guyana, Honduras, India,
Indonesia, Iraq, Kiribati, Lao People's Democratic
Republic, Lesotho, Marshall Islands, Mauritania,
Federated States of Micronesia, Mongolia, Morocco,
Nicaragua, Nigeria, Pakistan, Palestine, Papua New
Guinea, Paraguay, Philippines, Republic of Moldova,
Samoa, Sao Tome and Principe, Senegal, Solomon
Islands, South Sudan, Sri Lanka, the former Sudan,
Swaziland, Syrian Arab Republic, Timor-Leste, Tonga,
Turkmenistan, Tuvalu, Ukraine, Uzbekistan, Vanuatu,
Viet Nam, Yemen and Zambia.

■ Upper middle income (56 countries):
Albania, Algeria, Antigua and Barbuda, Argentina,
Azerbaijan, Belarus, Bosnia and Herzegovina,
Botswana, Brazil, Bulgaria, Chile, China, Colombia,
Cook Islands, Costa Rica, Cuba, Dominica, Dominican
Republic, Ecuador, Gabon, Grenada, Islamic Republic
of Iran, Jamaica, Jordan, Kazakhstan, Latvia, Lebanon,
Libya, Lithuania, Malaysia, Maldives, Mauritius,
Mexico, Montenegro, Montserrat, Namibia, Nauru,
Niue, Palau, Panama, Peru, Romania, Russian
Federation, Saint Kitts and Nevis, Saint Lucia, Saint
Vincent and the Grenadines, Serbia, Seychelles, South
Africa, Suriname, Thailand, The former Yugoslav
Republic of Macedonia, Tunisia, Turkey, Uruguay and
Bolivarian Republic of Venezuela.

10. Country groupings by level of income presented in the statistical tables are as defined
by the World Bank but include EFA countries only. The present list of countries by income
group is that of the July 2011 revision.

■ High income (57 countries):
Andorra, Anguilla, Aruba, Australia, Austria,
Bahamas, Bahrain, Barbados, Belgium,
Bermuda, British Virgin Islands, Brunei
Darussalam, Canada, Cayman Islands,
Croatia, Cyprus, Czech Republic, Denmark,
Equatorial Guinea, Estonia, Finland, France,
Germany, Greece, Hungary, Iceland, Ireland,
Israel, Italy, Japan, Kuwait, Luxembourg,
Macao (China), Malta, Monaco, Netherlands,
Netherlands Antilles, New Zealand, Norway,
Oman, Poland, Portugal, Qatar, Republic
of Korea, San Marino, Saudi Arabia,
Singapore, Slovakia, Slovenia, Spain, Sweden,
Switzerland, Trinidad and Tobago, Turks and
Caicos Islands, United Arab Emirates, United
Kingdom and United States.

Table 1
Background statistics

Country or territory	DEMOGRAPHY[1]			GNP, AID AND POVERTY						
	Total population (000)	Average annual growth rate (%) total population	Average annual growth rate (%) age 0–4 population	GNP per capita[2]				Net official development assistance received (% of GDP)[3]	Population below income poverty line	
				Current US$		PPP US$			PPP US$1.25 a day[3] (%)	National poverty line[3] (%)
	2012	2010–2015	2010–2015	1998	2010	1998	2010	2009	2000–2009[4]	2000–2009[4]
Arab States										
Algeria	36 486	1.4	-0.1	1 570	4 450	4 860	8 180	0.2	...	...
Bahrain	1 359	2.1	4.6	10 110	...	18 780	...	0.5	...	...
Djibouti	923	1.9	1.4	730	...	1 590	...	14	19	...
Egypt	83 958	1.7	0.5	1 220	2 420	3 330	6 060	0.5	2	22
Iraq	33 703	3.1	1.7	...	2 340	...	3 370	5	4	23
Jordan	6 457	1.9	-1.8	1 590	4 340	2 920	5 800	3	0.4	13
Kuwait	2 892	2.4	-2.1	20 430	...	43 040	...	...	...	...
Lebanon	4 292	0.7	-0.5	4 250	8 880	7 570	14 080	2	...	...
Libya	6 469	0.8	-0.6	...	...	...	...	0.1	...	...
Mauritania	3 623	2.2	1.3	540	1 030	1 310	1 960	9	21	46
Morocco	32 599	1.0	-0.4	1 280	2 850	2 440	4 600	1	3	9
Oman	2 904	1.9	-1.2	6 460	...	14 760	...	0.1	...	...
Palestine	4 271	2.8	2.1	...	...	...	...	25	...	22
Qatar	1 939	2.9	4.3	...	...	...	...	...	...	...
Saudi Arabia	28 705	2.1	-0.7	8 300	...	17 710	...	-0.03	...	...
Sudan (pre-secession)	45 722	2.4	1.4	330	1 270	1 090	2 030	...	...	...
Syrian Arab Republic	21 118	1.7	-1.7	950	2 750	3 300	5 120	0.5	2	...
Tunisia	10 705	1.0	0.1	2 190	4 160	4 620	9 060	1	3	4
United Arab Emirates	8 106	2.2	3.0	...	...	...	...	...	...	...
Yemen	25 569	3.0	2.6	390	...	1 740	...	2	18	35
Central and Eastern Europe										
Albania	3 227	0.3	-0.5	890	3 960	3 550	8 740	3	1	12
Belarus	9 527	-0.3	0.4	1 550	5 950	4 480	13 590	0.2	0	5
Bosnia and Herzegovina	3 744	-0.2	-1.7	1 430	4 770	4 710	8 810	2	0.04	14
Bulgaria	7 398	-0.7	-0.6	1 240	6 270	5 350	13 290	...	1	13
Croatia	4 387	-0.2	0.4	5 360	13 870	10 020	18 860	0.3	0	11
Czech Republic	10 566	0.3	1.2	5 580	17 890	13 700	23 620	...	...	...
Estonia	1 340	-0.1	0.5	3 820	14 460	8 330	19 760	...	0	...
Hungary	9 950	-0.2	0.5	4 380	12 850	10 050	19 050	...	0	...
Latvia	2 235	-0.4	1.0	2 650	11 620	6 980	16 350	...	0	6
Lithuania	3 292	-0.4	1.1	2 850	11 390	7 810	17 870	...	0	...
Montenegro	633	0.1	-0.9	...	6 750	...	12 930	2	0	5
Poland	38 317	0.04	1.4	4 310	12 440	9 310	19 060	...	0	17
Republic of Moldova	3 519	-0.7	-0.9	...	...	...	...	4	2	29
Romania	21 388	-0.2	0.1	1 520	7 840	5 280	14 060	...	0.5	14
Russian Federation	142 703	-0.1	0.6	2 140	9 900	5 250	19 190	...	0	11
Serbia	9 847	-0.1	-1.1	...	5 630	5 910	11 020	1	0.1	7
Slovakia	5 480	0.2	1.2	5 290	16 830	10 330	23 100	...	...	...
Slovenia	2 040	0.2	0.5	10 870	23 860	15 730	26 660	...	0	...
TFYR Macedonia	2 067	0.1	-0.9	...	...	...	...	2	0.3	19
Turkey	74 509	1.1	-0.6	3 390	9 890	8 580	15 170	0.2	3	18
Ukraine	44 940	-0.5	0.3	850	3 000	2 870	6 620	0.6	0.1	8
Central Asia										
Armenia	3 109	0.3	-0.04	590	3 200	1 830	5 660	6	1	27
Azerbaijan	9 421	1.2	2.2	510	5 330	1 810	9 280	0.6	1	16
Georgia	4 304	-0.6	-1.6	820	2 690	2 120	4 990	9	15	24
Kazakhstan	16 381	1.0	0.1	1 390	7 590	3 990	10 770	0.3	0.2	15
Kyrgyzstan	5 448	1.1	1.1	350	840	1 150	2 100	7	2	43
Mongolia	2 844	1.5	1.1	520	1 870	1 850	3 670	9	22	35
Tajikistan	7 079	1.5	1.2	180	800	740	2 140	8	22	47
Turkmenistan	5 170	1.2	0.5	560	3 790	1 490	7 490	0.2	...	...
Uzbekistan	28 077	1.1	0.3	620	1 280	1 310	3 120	0.6	46	...
East Asia and the Pacific										
Australia	27 380	1.3	1.7	21 890	...	23 550	...	...	...	...
Brunei Darussalam	413	1.7	-0.2	14 740	...	40 970	...	...	...	...
Cambodia	14 478	1.2	-0.1	280	750	740	2 080	8	28	30
China	1 353 601	0.4	-0.6	790	4 270	1 960	7 640	0.02	16	3
Cook Islands	21	0.5	...	...	...	...	...	...	...	...
DPR Korea	24 554	0.4	-0.05	...	...	...	...	...	...	...
Fiji	876	0.8	-0.3	2 300	3 630	3 040	4 510	3	...	31
Indonesia	244 769	1.0	-0.8	650	2 500	2 050	4 200	0.2	19	13
Japan	126 435	-0.1	-0.3	32 990	41 850	24 310	34 640	...	...	...
Kiribati	103	1.5	...	1 530	2 010	3 270	3 530	16	...	...

Table 1 (continued)

Country or territory	DEMOGRAPHY[1] Total population (000) 2012	Average annual growth rate (%) total population 2010–2015	Average annual growth rate (%) age 0–4 population 2010–2015	GNP per capita[2] Current US$ 1998	Current US$ 2010	PPP US$ 1998	PPP US$ 2010	Net official development assistance received (% of GDP)[3] 2009	Population below income poverty line PPP US$1.25 a day (%)[3] 2000–2009[4]	National poverty line (%)[3] 2000–2009[4]
Lao PDR	6 374	1.3	-0.4	310	1 050	1 020	2 460	7	34	28
Macao, China	567	2.0	4.4	15 520	…	21 450	…	…	…	…
Malaysia	29 322	1.6	0.5	3 610	7 760	7 500	14 220	0.1	0	4
Marshall Islands	56	1.6	…	2 530	3 640	…	…	32	…	…
Micronesia, F. S.	112	0.5	-0.4	1 970	2 730	2 440	3 490	42	…	…
Myanmar	48 724	0.8	-0.4	…	…	410	1 950	…	…	…
Nauru	10	0.6	…	…	…	…	…	…	…	…
New Zealand	4 461	1.0	0.6	15 450	…	18 080	…	…	…	…
Niue	1	-2.8	…	…	…	…	…	…	…	…
Palau	21	0.8	…	6 110	6 560	11 740	11 000	28	…	…
Papua New Guinea	7 170	2.2	0.8	780	1 300	1 650	2 420	5	…	…
Philippines	96 471	1.7	0.6	1 150	2 060	2 430	3 980	0.2	23	27
Republic of Korea	48 588	0.4	0.2	9 200	19 890	13 290	29 010	…	…	…
Samoa	185	0.5	-1.1	1 380	3 000	2 440	4 270	16	…	…
Singapore	5 256	1.1	2.1	25 180	40 070	29 170	55 790	…	…	…
Solomon Islands	566	2.5	1.0	1 330	1 030	2 360	2 210	43	…	…
Thailand	69 892	0.5	-1.6	2 040	4 150	4 250	8 190	-0.03	11	8
Timor-Leste	1 187	2.9	2.0	…	2 220	…	3 600	9.5	37	50
Tokelau	1	0.3	…	…	…	…	…	…	…	…
Tonga	105	0.4	-1.3	2 210	3 280	3 240	4 580	12	…	…
Tuvalu	10	0.2	…	…	4 760	…	…	…	…	…
Vanuatu	252	2.4	1.5	1 420	2 640	3 070	4 320	17	…	…
Viet Nam	89 730	1.0	-0.5	360	1 160	1 230	3 070	4	13	15
Latin America and the Caribbean										
Anguilla	16	1.6	…	…	…	…	…	…	…	…
Antigua and Barbuda	91	1.0	…	7 730	13 170	13 360	20 240	0.6	…	…
Argentina	41 119	0.9	0.1	8 010	8 620	9 140	15 570	0.04	0.9	…
Aruba	109	0.3	-0.7	…	…	…	…	…	…	…
Bahamas	351	1.1	0.6	14 260	…	19 760	…	…	…	…
Barbados	275	0.2	0.2	8 200	…	14 540	…	-0.06	…	…
Belize	324	2.0	1.0	2 700	3 810	3 920	6 210	2.0	…	34
Bermuda	65	0.2	…	…	…	…	…	…	…	…
Bolivia, P. S.	10 248	1.6	0.5	1 000	1 810	3 030	4 640	4.4	14	60
Brazil	198 361	0.8	-0.8	4 870	9 390	6 510	11 000	0.0	4	21
British Virgin Islands	24	0.9	…	…	…	…	…	…	…	…
Cayman Islands	57	0.8	…	…	…	…	…	…	…	…
Chile	17 423	0.9	-0.03	5 260	10 120	8 630	14 590	0.1	0.8	15
Colombia	47 551	1.3	-0.3	2 560	5 510	5 750	9 060	0.5	16	46
Costa Rica	4 794	1.4	0.2	3 510	6 810	6 400	11 270	0.4	0.7	22
Cuba	11 249	0.0	-1.7	2 240	…	…	…	0.2	…	…
Dominica	68	0.0	…	3 360	6 760	6 850	11 990	10	…	…
Dominican Republic	10 183	1.2	-0.2	2 370	5 030	4 340	9 030	0.3	4	51
Ecuador	14 865	1.3	-0.3	1 820	3 850	4 680	7 880	0.4	5	36
El Salvador	6 264	0.6	-0.1	1 900	3 380	4 170	6 550	1	5	38
Grenada	105	0.4	0.4	2 990	6 930	5 870	9 890	8	…	…
Guatemala	15 138	2.5	1.6	1 670	2 740	3 270	4 650	1	17	51
Guyana	758	0.2	-1.1	880	2 870	1 900	3 450	8	…	…
Haiti	10 256	1.3	0.04	…	…	…	…	…	55	77
Honduras	7 912	2.0	0.7	750	1 870	2 380	3 770	3	23	60
Jamaica	2 761	0.4	-0.9	2 700	4 800	5 360	7 310	1	0.2	10
Mexico	116 147	1.1	-0.9	3 950	8 890	7 740	14 290	0.02	3	47
Montserrat	6	0.9	…	…	…	…	…	…	…	…
Netherlands Antilles	205	0.7	-0.7	…	…	…	…	…	…	…
Nicaragua	5 955	1.4	-0.3	670	1 110	1 610	2 790	13	16	46
Panama	3 625	1.5	-0.2	3 540	6 970	6 450	12 770	0.3	10	33
Paraguay	6 683	1.7	0.9	1 650	2 710	3 560	5 050	1	5	35
Peru	29 734	1.1	-0.4	2 230	4 700	4 610	8 930	0.4	6	35
Saint Kitts and Nevis	54	1.2	…	6 160	11 740	11 230	15 850	1	…	…
Saint Lucia	178	1.0	-0.4	3 830	6 560	6 870	10 520	5	…	…
Saint Vincent/Grenadines	109	0.0	-1.5	2 790	6 300	5 770	10 830	6	…	…
Suriname	534	0.9	-0.5	2 360	…	5 130	…	4	…	…
Trinidad and Tobago	1 351	0.3	-0.4	4 470	15 380	10 210	24 040	0.03	…	…
Turks and Caicos Islands	40	1.2	…	…	…	…	…	…	…	…
Uruguay	3 391	0.3	-0.4	7 280	10 590	8 540	13 990	0.2	0	21
Venezuela, B. R.	29 891	1.5	0.1	3 360	11 590	8 470	12 150	0.0	4	29

Table 1 (continued)

	DEMOGRAPHY[1]			GNP, AID AND POVERTY						
	Total population (000)	Average annual growth rate (%) total population	Average annual growth rate (%) age 0-4 population	GNP per capita[2] Current US$		PPP US$		Net official development assistance received [% of GDP][3]	Population below income poverty line PPP US$1.25 a day[3] [%]	National poverty line[3] [%]
Country or territory	2012	2010–2015	2010–2015	1998	2010	1998	2010	2009	2000–2009[4]	2000–2009[4]
North America and Western Europe										
Andorra	88	1.5	...	19 310	...	...	...	...	...	...
Austria	8 429	0.2	-1.0	27 260	47 060	25 850	39 790	...	...	...
Belgium	10 788	0.3	-0.02	26 030	45 910	24 810	38 260	...	...	...
Canada	34 675	0.9	1.1	20 310	43 270	24 630	38 310	...	...	...
Cyprus	1 129	1.1	0.6	14 770	29 430	18 230	30 300	...	...	...
Denmark	5 593	0.3	-0.5	32 960	59 050	25 850	40 230	...	...	...
Finland	5 403	0.3	0.5	24 860	47 720	22 050	37 290	...	...	...
France	63 458	0.5	-0.04	25 180	42 390	22 960	34 440	...	...	...
Germany	81 991	-0.2	0.4	27 060	43 110	23 900	37 950	...	...	...
Greece	11 419	0.2	-0.2	13 010	26 940	16 730	27 050	...	...	...
Iceland	328	1.2	0.8	28 400	32 710	27 200	27 680	...	...	...
Ireland	4 579	1.1	0.1	20 950	41 000	21 510	33 370	...	...	...
Israel	7 695	1.7	1.5	16 840	27 170	19 150	27 630	...	...	...
Italy	60 964	0.2	-0.4	21 230	35 150	23 560	31 130	...	...	...
Luxembourg	523	1.4	1.9	43 820	77 160	39 790	61 790	...	...	...
Malta	419	0.3	-0.02	9 750	19 270	15 690	24 840	0.3	...	...
Monaco	35	0.0	...	86 960	...	...	...	...	...	...
Netherlands	16 714	0.3	-0.7	25 830	49 050	25 220	41 900	...	...	...
Norway	4 960	0.7	0.7	35 410	84 290	27 100	56 830	...	...	...
Portugal	10 699	0.0	-2.0	12 040	21 880	15 570	24 760	...	...	...
San Marino	32	0.6	...	...	...	...	...	...	...	...
Spain	46 772	0.6	-0.1	15 220	31 750	18 700	31 640	...	...	...
Sweden	9 495	0.6	0.6	29 520	50 110	24 060	39 730	...	...	...
Switzerland	7 734	0.4	0.5	41 630	71 530	31 210	50 170	...	...	...
United Kingdom	62 798	0.6	0.5	23 450	38 370	23 520	36 410	...	...	...
United States	315 791	0.9	0.1	30 950	47 390	32 060	47 360	...	...	...
South and West Asia										
Afghanistan	33 397	3.1	2.2	...	410	...	1 060	46	...	36
Bangladesh	152 409	1.3	-0.5	360	700	800	1 810	1	50	40
Bhutan	750	1.5	-0.02	640	1 870	2 140	4 990	10	26	23
India	1 258 351	1.3	-0.1	420	1 330	1 390	3 550	0.2	42	28
Iran, Islamic Republic of	75 612	1.0	-0.6	1 700	...	6 200	...	0.03	1	...
Maldives	324	1.3	0.5	1 930	5 750	3 230	8 110	2.4	1	...
Nepal	31 011	1.7	-0.05	210	...	730	1 210	6.7	55	31
Pakistan	179 951	1.8	0.6	450	1 050	1 520	2 790	1.7	23	22
Sri Lanka	21 224	0.8	-1.2	820	2 240	2 360	5 010	1.7	7	15
Sub-Saharan Africa										
Angola	20 163	2.7	1.3	460	3 940	1 820	5 410	0.4	54	...
Benin	9 352	2.7	1.8	370	780	1 060	1 590	10	47	39
Botswana	2 053	1.1	0.1	3 300	6 790	7 770	13 700	2	...	31
Burkina Faso	17 482	3.0	2.7	230	550	720	1 250	14	57	46
Burundi	8 749	1.9	1.8	150	170	310	400	41	81	67
Cameroon	20 469	2.1	1.2	640	1 180	1 450	2 270	3	10	40
Cape Verde	505	0.9	-1.1	1 270	3 270	1 730	3 820	13	21	27
Central African Republic	4 576	2.0	1.6	290	470	630	790	12	63	62
Chad	11 831	2.6	1.8	220	620	700	1 220	9	62	55
Comoros	773	2.5	1.1	410	750	910	1 090	9	46	45
Congo	4 233	2.2	1.7	570	2 150	2 040	3 220	4	54	50
Côte d'Ivoire	20 595	2.2	1.2	740	1 160	1 550	1 810	11	24	43
D. R. Congo	69 575	2.6	1.6	110	180	250	320	24	59	71
Equatorial Guinea	740	2.7	2.3	940	14 540	4 380	23 750	0.5	...	...
Eritrea	5 581	2.9	1.4	210	340	680	540	8	...	...
Ethiopia	86 539	2.1	0.3	130	390	420	1 040	13	39	39
Gabon	1 564	1.9	1.9	3 920	7 740	11 770	13 170	0.8	5	33
Gambia	1 825	2.7	1.7	320	450	890	1 300	19	34	58
Ghana	25 546	2.3	1.0	390	1 230	870	1 660	6	30	29
Guinea	10 481	2.5	1.6	460	400	710	1 020	6	43	53
Guinea-Bissau	1 580	2.1	1.4	150	590	820	1 180	18	49	65
Kenya	42 749	2.7	2.3	440	790	1 110	1 680	6	20	46
Lesotho	2 217	1.0	0.5	580	1 040	1 210	1 960	6	43	57

Table 1 (continued)

Country or territory	DEMOGRAPHY[1]			GNP, AID AND POVERTY						
	Total population (000)	Average annual growth rate (%) total population	Average annual growth rate (%) age 0–4 population	GNP per capita[2]				Net official development assistance received (% of GDP)[3]	Population below income poverty line	
				Current US$		PPP US$			PPP US$1.25 a day[3] (%)	National poverty line[3] (%)
	2012	2010–2015	2010–2015	1998	2010	1998	2010	2009	2000–2009[4]	2000–2009[4]
Liberia	4 245	2.6	1.5	130	200	260	340	78	84	64
Madagascar	21 929	2.8	2.1	260	430	740	960	5	68	69
Malawi	15 883	3.2	3.7	200	330	560	850	17	74	52
Mali	16 319	3.0	2.2	250	600	610	1 030	11	51	47
Mauritius	1 314	0.5	-0.8	3 780	7 750	7 110	13 960	2	...	...
Mozambique	24 475	2.2	1.0	220	440	400	930	21	60	55
Namibia	2 364	1.7	0.3	2 030	4 500	3 870	6 420	4	...	38
Niger	16 644	3.5	3.1	200	370	550	720	9	43	60
Nigeria	166 629	2.5	2.2	270	1 180	1 130	2 170	1	64	55
Rwanda	11 272	2.9	3.1	270	520	560	1 150	18	77	59
Sao Tome and Principe	172	2.0	0.7	...	1 200	...	1 920	16	29	54
Senegal	13 108	2.6	1.4	550	1 090	1 240	1 910	8	34	51
Seychelles	87	0.3	...	7 320	9 760	14 590	21 210	4	0.3	...
Sierra Leone	6 126	2.1	0.3	180	340	380	830	23	53	66
Somalia	9 797	2.6	2.2	...	...	...	...	...	...	...
South Africa	50 738	0.5	-0.4	3 290	6 090	6 280	10 360	0.4	17	23
South Sudan	...	...	...	...	...	...	...	...	...	...
Swaziland	1 220	1.4	0.7	1 660	2 630	3 320	4 840	2	63	69
Togo	6 283	2.0	0.9	330	490	770	890	18	39	62
Uganda	35 621	3.1	2.3	280	500	630	1 250	11	29	25
United Republic of Tanzania	47 656	3.1	3.0	250	530	700	1 430	14	68	33
Zambia	13 884	3.0	4.2	320	1 070	820	1 380	11	64	59
Zimbabwe	13 014	2.2	1.3	590	460	...	...	14	...	72

	Sum	Weighted average		Median				Median	Median	Median
World	7 018 201	1.1	0.3	1 915	3 960	4 250	6 965	3	16	33
Countries in transition	303 585	0.1	0.4	835	4 365	2 870	8 775	2	1	15
Developed countries	1 031 728	0.5	0.2	20 950	35 150	22 050	31 640	...	...	...
Developing countries	5 682 887	1.3	0.3	1 330	2 565	2 920	4 200	4	23	38
Arab States	316 077	1.9	0.7	1 570	2 800	3 330	5 460	1	...	...
Central and Eastern Europe	401 109	0.1	0.2	2 850	9 900	7 395	16 350	...	0	12
Central Asia	81 834	1.0	0.6	560	2 690	1 810	4 990	6	8	27
East Asia and the Pacific	2 201 692	0.6	-0.5	2 040	3 000	3 070	4 235	8	...	...
East Asia	2 160 363	0.6	-0.5	2 040	3 325	3 340	4 200	0.2	19	15
Pacific	41 329	1.4	1.2	2 090	3 000	3 070	4 270	16	...	...
Latin America/Caribbean	598 268	1.1	-0.4	2 890	6 430	5 870	10 205	1	...	...
Caribbean	17 735	1.0	-0.1	3 360	6 660	6 850	10 675	3	...	...
Latin America	580 532	1.1	-0.4	2 370	5 270	5 215	9 045	0.4	5	36
N. America/W. Europe	772 512	0.6	0.1	25 180	43 110	23 900	37 290	...	...	...
South and West Asia	1 753 029	1.4	-0.0	545	1 330	1 830	3 170	2	24	28
Sub-Saharan Africa	847 958	2.4	1.8	330	685	845	1 380	10	48	53
Countries with low income	827 712	2.1	1.4	250	480	700	1 090	12	51	53
Countries with middle income	5 083 620	1.0	0.1	1 570	3 830	3 325	6 485	2	5	27
Lower middle	2 593 714	1.5	0.4	750	2 220	1 970	3 670	5	21	34
Upper middle	2 489 906	0.6	-0.5	2 745	6 760	6 055	11 270	1	1	16
Countries with high income	1 106 585	0.5	0.2	16 840	35 150	21 450	31 640	...	...	...

Note A: The country groupings by income level presented in the tables are as defined by the World Bank. They are based on the list of countries by income group as revised in July 2011.
Note B: The median values for 1998 and 2010 are not comparable since they are not necessarily based on the same number of countries.
1. The demographic indicators in this table are from the United Nations Population Division estimates, revision 2010 (United Nations, 2011). They are based on the median variant.
2. World Bank database, December 2011 update.
3. UNDP (2011); World Bank (2011).
4. Data are for the most recent year available during the period specified. For more details see UNDP (2011).
(...) No data available.

Table 2
Adult and youth literacy

Country or territory	ADULT LITERACY RATE (15 and over) (%) 1985–1994¹ Total	Male	Female	2005–2010¹ Total	Male	Female	Projected 2015 Total	Male	Female	ADULT ILLITERATES (15 and over) 1985–1994¹ Total (000)	% Female	2005–2010¹ Total (000)	% Female	Projected 2015 Total (000)	% Female
Arab States															
Algeria	50*	63*	36*	73*	81*	64*	80	87	73	6 562	64*	6 472	66*	5 588	68
Bahrain	84*	89*	77*	92	93	90	93	94	92	55	56*	82	42	78	41
Djibouti	...	...	...	...	...	...	...	...	...	...	...	...	...	...	...
Egypt	44*	57*	31*	72*	80*	64*	74	82	66	16 910	62*	15 631	65*	16 110	66
Iraq	...	...	...	78	86	71	79	86	73	...	...	3 930	68	4 438	65
Jordan	...	...	...	93*	96*	89*	94	97	92	...	...	287	71*	250	70
Kuwait	74*	78*	69*	94*	95*	92*	96	96	94	281	49*	118	50*	102	48
Lebanon	...	...	...	90*	93*	86*	94	96	92	...	...	319	70*	210	71
Libya	77	88	65	89	96	83	91	97	86	646	73	477	80	416	82
Mauritania	...	...	...	58	65	51	61	67	55	...	...	873	58	925	58
Morocco	42*	55*	29*	56*	69*	44*	62	74	51	9 603	62*	9 967	66*	9 405	67
Oman	...	...	...	87*	90*	81*	87	90	84	...	...	257	56*	281	51
Palestine	...	...	...	95*	98*	92*	96	98	94	...	...	118	76*	108	75
Qatar	76*	77*	72*	96*	97*	95*	97	97	96	68	30*	57	25*	59	24
Saudi Arabia	71*	80*	57*	87	90	81	89	92	85	2 871	59*	2 571	59	2 327	60
Sudan (pre-secession)	...	...	...	71	80	62	75	83	68	...	...	7 551	66	7 458	65
Syrian Arab Republic	...	...	...	83	90	77	86	92	81	...	...	2 132	70	2 033	70
Tunisia	59	70	48	78*	86*	71*	84	90	77	2 329	63	1 661	68*	1 400	71
United Arab Emirates	71*	72*	69*	90*	89*	91*	93	92	95	264	31*	327	24*	502	19
Yemen	37*	57*	17*	64	81	47	70	85	55	4 466	66*	4 841	74	4 734	76
Central and Eastern Europe															
Albania	...	...	...	96*	97*	95*	98	98	97	...	...	98	67*	59	63
Belarus	98*	99*	97*	100*	100*	99*	97	97	97	166	87*	31	72*	233	55
Bosnia and Herzegovina	...	...	...	98	99	96	98	100	97	...	...	68	87	49	86
Bulgaria	...	...	...	98*	99*	98*	98	99	98	...	...	106	64*	100	62
Croatia	97*	99*	95*	99	99	98	99	100	99	120	82*	44	80	34	77
Czech Republic	...	...	...	...	...	...	...	...	...	...	...	...	...	...	...
Estonia	100*	100*	100*	100	100	100	100	100	100	3	79*	2	49	2	47
Hungary	...	...	...	...	...	...	...	...	...	...	...	...	...	...	...
Latvia	99*	100*	99*	100	100	100	100	100	100	11	80*	4	52	4	49
Lithuania	98*	99*	98*	100	100	100	100	100	100	44	76*	8	51	8	51
Montenegro	...	...	...	98	99	97	99	99	98	...	...	8	81	6	77
Poland	...	...	...	...	...	...	...	...	...	...	...	...	...	...	...
Republic of Moldova	96*	99*	94*	99	99	98	99	99	99	113	82*	44	70	29	65
Romania	97*	99*	95*	98	98	97	98	98	97	586	78*	424	65	397	61
Russian Federation	98*	99*	97*	100	100	99	100	100	100	2 288	88*	515	69	432	63
Serbia	...	...	...	98	99	97	98	99	98	...	...	170	81	126	77
Slovakia	...	...	...	...	...	...	...	...	...	...	...	...	...	...	...
Slovenia	100*	100*	99*	100	100	100	100	100	100	7	60*	5	56	5	54
TFYR Macedonia	94*	97*	91*	97	99	96	98	99	97	87	77*	46	76	39	74
Turkey	79*	90*	69*	91*	96*	85*	91	97	86	7 196	76*	4 839	81*	5 035	85
Ukraine	...	...	...	100	100	100	100	100	100	...	...	114	67	88	60
Central Asia															
Armenia	99*	99*	98*	100	100	99	100	100	100	31	77*	11	71	9	66
Azerbaijan	...	...	...	100*	100*	100*	100	100	100	...	...	17	68*	14	69
Georgia	...	...	...	100	100	100	100	100	100	...	...	10	64	8	60
Kazakhstan	98*	99*	96*	100	100	100	100	100	100	278	82*	37	70	32	65
Kyrgyzstan	...	...	...	99*	100*	99*	100	100	99	...	...	28	69*	19	64
Mongolia	...	...	...	97	97	98	97	96	98	...	...	52	42	61	38
Tajikistan	98*	99*	97*	100	100	100	100	100	100	68	74*	13	69	11	66
Turkmenistan	...	...	...	100	100	99	100	100	100	...	...	15	67	12	62
Uzbekistan	...	...	...	99	100	99	100	100	99	...	...	119	69	86	66
East Asia and the Pacific															
Australia	...	...	...	...	...	...	...	...	...	...	...	...	...	...	...
Brunei Darussalam	88*	92*	82*	95	97	94	96	98	95	21	67*	14	67	12	67
Cambodia	...	...	...	74*	83*	66*	78	85	72	...	...	2 449	68*	2 312	66
China	78*	87*	68*	94	97	91	96	98	93	182 744	70*	61 882	74	50 320	74
Cook Islands	...	...	...	...	...	...	...	...	...	...	...	...	...	...	...
DPR Korea	...	...	...	100*	100*	100*	100	100	100	...	...	0.3	71*	0.2	67
Fiji	...	...	...	...	...	...	...	...	...	...	...	...	...	...	...
Indonesia	82*	88*	75*	93*	96*	90*	95	97	93	21 557	68*	12 709	71*	9 832	72
Japan	...	...	...	...	...	...	...	...	...	...	...	...	...	...	...
Kiribati	...	...	...	...	...	...	...	...	...	...	...	...	...	...	...

YOUTH LITERACY RATE (15–24) (%)									YOUTH ILLITERATES (15–24)						
1985–1994[1]			2005–2010[1]			Projected 2015			1985–1994[1]		2005–2010[1]		Projected 2015		
Total	Male	Female	Total	Male	Female	Total	Male	Female	Total (000)	% Female	Total (000)	% Female	Total (000)	% Female	Country or territory
															Arab States
74*	86*	62*	92*	94*	89*	96	96	96	1 213	73*	611	65*	288	50	Algeria
97*	97*	97*	100	100	100	100	100	100	3	52*	0.05	44	0.01	50	Bahrain
...	...	...	...	...	...	...	...	...	...	...	...	...	...	...	Djibouti
63*	71*	54*	88*	91*	84*	92	94	90	3 747	61*	2 004	62*	1 289	60	Egypt
...	...	...	83	85	81	82	82	81	...	...	1 081	54	1 346	51	Iraq
...	...	...	99*	99*	99*	99	99	99	...	...	16	48*	10	43	Jordan
87*	91*	84*	99*	99*	99*	100	100	100	38	62*	6	41*	0.04	45	Kuwait
...	...	...	99*	98*	99*	99	99	99	...	...	10	36*	7	36	Lebanon
98	99	96	100	100	100	100	100	100	22	86	1	72	0.5	66	Libya
...	...	...	68	71	65	71	73	70	...	...	219	54	218	52	Mauritania
58*	71*	46*	79*	87*	72*	83	89	78	2 234	65*	1 296	68*	1 009	67	Morocco
...	...	...	98*	98*	98*	99	99	99	...	...	15	43*	3	72	Oman
...	...	...	99*	99*	99*	99	99	99	...	...	7	47*	6	46	Palestine
90*	89*	91*	97*	96*	98*	99	99	99	6	31*	8	14*	2	17	Qatar
88*	94*	81*	98	99	97	99	99	98	345	73*	108	73	67	76	Saudi Arabia
...	...	...	87	90	84	90	91	88	...	...	1 143	60	1 014	58	Sudan (pre-secession)
...	...	...	95	96	94	96	97	96	...	...	211	60	172	59	Syrian Arab Republic
83	90	75	97*	98*	96*	99	99	98	299	72	62	69*	25	61	Tunisia
82*	81*	85*	95*	94*	97*	99	100	99	34	37*	34	24*	5	71	United Arab Emirates
60*	83*	35*	85	96	74	90	98	83	1 042	78*	787	86	572	87	Yemen
															Central and Eastern Europe
...	...	...	99*	99*	99*	100	99	100	...	...	7	37*	3	23	Albania
100*	100*	100*	100*	100*	100*	98	98	98	3	43*	3	42*	17	48	Belarus
...	...	...	100	100	100	100	100	100	...	...	2	47	2	49	Bosnia and Herzegovina
...	...	...	98*	98*	98*	98	98	98	...	...	18	54*	14	54	Bulgaria
100*	100*	100*	100	100	100	100	100	100	2	53*	2	46	2	44	Croatia
...	...	...	...	...	...	...	...	...	...	...	...	...	...	...	Czech Republic
100*	100*	100*	100	100	100	100	100	100	0.3	35*	0.4	37	0.3	36	Estonia
...	...	...	...	...	...	...	...	...	...	...	...	...	...	...	Hungary
100*	100*	100*	100	100	100	100	100	100	0.8	40*	1.0	42	0.8	42	Latvia
100*	100*	100*	100	100	100	100	100	100	2	44*	1	48	0.8	50	Lithuania
...	...	...	99	99	99	99	99	99	...	...	0.6	50	0.6	48	Montenegro
...	...	...	...	...	...	...	...	...	...	...	...	...	...	...	Poland
100*	100*	100*	99	99	100	99	99	100	2	48*	3	34	3	32	Republic of Moldova
99*	99*	99*	97	97	97	97	97	97	34	53*	78	46	74	45	Romania
100*	100*	100*	100	100	100	100	100	100	55	44*	65	39	51	37	Russian Federation
...	...	...	99	99	99	99	99	99	...	...	10	50	9	49	Serbia
...	...	...	...	...	...	...	...	...	...	...	...	...	...	...	Slovakia
100*	100*	100*	100	100	100	100	100	100	0.7	44*	0.4	34	0.3	31	Slovenia
99*	99*	99*	99	99	99	99	99	98	4	62*	4	55	4	53	TFYR Macedonia
93*	97*	88*	98*	99*	97*	98	99	96	806	77*	282	77*	319	77	Turkey
...	...	...	100	100	100	100	100	100	...	...	14	40	12	40	Ukraine
															Central Asia
100*	100*	100*	100	100	100	100	100	100	0.5	49*	1	36	1	34	Armenia
...	...	...	100*	100*	100*	100	100	100	...	...	0.9	54*	0.4	66	Azerbaijan
...	...	...	100	100	100	100	100	100	...	...	1	37	1	35	Georgia
100*	100*	100*	100	100	100	100	100	100	8	44*	6	38	5	37	Kazakhstan
...	...	...	100*	100*	100*	100	100	100	...	...	3	40*	3	38	Kyrgyzstan
...	...	...	96	94	97	95	93	97	...	...	25	32	26	31	Mongolia
100*	100*	100*	100	100	100	100	100	100	3	56*	2	46	2	44	Tajikistan
...	...	...	100	100	100	100	100	100	...	...	2	33	2	27	Turkmenistan
...	...	...	100	100	100	100	100	100	...	...	4	11	3	0.5	Uzbekistan
															East Asia and the Pacific
...	...	...	...	...	...	...	...	...	...	...	...	...	...	...	Australia
98*	98*	98*	100	100	100	100	100	100	0.9	49*	0.2	55	0.1	58	Brunei Darussalam
...	...	...	87*	88*	86*	91	91	92	...	...	410	54*	265	47	Cambodia
94*	97*	91*	99	99	99	100	100	100	14 235	73*	1 356	54	884	49	China
...	...	...	...	...	...	...	...	...	...	...	...	...	...	...	Cook Islands
...	...	...	100*	100*	100*	100	100	100	...	...	0.01	33*	0.01	23	DPR Korea
...	...	...	...	...	...	...	...	...	...	...	...	...	...	...	Fiji
96*	97*	95*	99*	100*	99*	100	100	100	1 450	65*	228	57*	109	53	Indonesia
...	...	...	...	...	...	...	...	...	...	...	...	...	...	...	Japan
...	...	...	...	...	...	...	...	...	...	...	...	...	...	...	Kiribati

Table 2 (continued)

Country or territory	ADULT LITERACY RATE (15 and over) (%)									ADULT ILLITERATES (15 and over)					
	1985–1994[1]			2005–2010[1]			Projected 2015			1985–1994[1]		2005–2010[1]		Projected 2015	
	Total	Male	Female	Total	Male	Female	Total	Male	Female	Total (000)	% Female	Total (000)	% Female	Total (000)	% Female
Lao PDR	…	…	…	73*	82*	63*	80	87	72	…	…	958	69*	934	68
Macao, China	…	…	…	93*	96*	91*	96	98	94	…	…	27	74*	21	71
Malaysia	83*	89*	77*	93*	95*	91*	94	96	93	2 013	66*	1 363	67*	1 219	65
Marshall Islands	…	…	…	…	…	…	…	…	…	…	…	…	…	…	…
Micronesia, F. S.	…	…	…	…	…	…	…	…	…	…	…	…	…	…	…
Myanmar	…	…	…	92	95	90	93	95	91	…	…	2 748	67	2 637	66
Nauru	…	…	…	…	…	…	…	…	…	…	…	…	…	…	…
New Zealand	…	…	…	…	…	…	…	…	…	…	…	…	…	…	…
Niue	…	…	…	…	…	…	…	…	…	…	…	…	…	…	…
Palau	…	…	…	…	…	…	…	…	…	…	…	…	…	…	…
Papua New Guinea	…	…	…	61	64	57	63	64	61	…	…	1 646	54	1 794	51
Philippines	94*	94*	93*	95*	95*	96*	96	96	97	2 328	53*	2 635	46*	2 495	44
Republic of Korea	…	…	…	…	…	…	…	…	…	…	…	…	…	…	…
Samoa	98*	98*	97*	99	99	99	99	99	99	2	59*	1	58	1	56
Singapore	89*	95*	83*	96*	98*	94*	97	98	95	260	78*	172	76*	147	75
Solomon Islands	…	…	…	…	…	…	…	…	…	…	…	…	…	…	…
Thailand	…	…	…	94*	96*	92*	95	97	94	…	…	3 361	67*	2 768	66
Timor-Leste	…	…	…	58*	64*	53*	67	71	62	…	…	252	56*	244	56
Tokelau	…	…	…	…	…	…	…	…	…	…	…	…	…	…	…
Tonga	…	…	…	99*	99*	99*	99	99	99	…	…	0.6	48*	0.5	46
Tuvalu	…	…	…	…	…	…	…	…	…	…	…	…	…	…	…
Vanuatu	…	…	…	…	…	…	…	…	…	…	…	…	…	…	…
Viet Nam	88*	93*	83*	93	95	91	94	96	92	5 002	73*	4 579	67	4 294	65
Latin America and the Caribbean															
Anguilla	…	…	…	…	…	…	…	…	…	…	…	…	…	…	…
Antigua and Barbuda	…	…	…	99	98	99	…	…	…	…	…	0.7	29	…	…
Argentina	96*	96*	96*	98	98	98	98	98	98	890	53*	668	51	615	50
Aruba	…	…	…	97*	97*	97*	98	99	98	…	…	3	55*	1	54
Bahamas	…	…	…	…	…	…	…	…	…	…	…	…	…	…	…
Barbados	…	…	…	…	…	…	…	…	…	…	…	…	…	…	…
Belize	70*	70*	70*	…	…	…	…	…	…	33	51*	…	…	…	…
Bermuda	…	…	…	…	…	…	…	…	…	…	…	…	…	…	…
Bolivia, P. S.	80*	88*	72*	91*	96*	87*	94	93	94	823	71*	543	76*	439	48
Brazil	…	…	…	90*	90*	90*	92	92	93	…	…	13 899	51*	11 929	50
British Virgin Islands	…	…	…	…	…	…	…	…	…	…	…	…	…	…	…
Cayman Islands	…	…	…	99*	99*	99*	…	…	…	…	…	0.5	44*	…	…
Chile	94*	95*	94*	99*	99*	98*	99	99	99	548	54*	191	53*	195	53
Colombia	81*	81*	81*	93*	93*	93*	95	95	95	4 222	52*	2 187	51*	1 911	51
Costa Rica	…	…	…	96	96	96	97	96	97	…	…	134	47	130	46
Cuba	…	…	…	100	100	100	100	100	100	…	…	16	52	15	52
Dominica	…	…	…	…	…	…	…	…	…	…	…	…	…	…	…
Dominican Republic	…	…	…	90*	89*	90*	91	91	92	…	…	716	49*	644	48
Ecuador	88*	90*	86*	92*	93*	90*	95	95	94	732	59*	818	59*	601	58
El Salvador	74*	77*	71*	84*	87*	82*	88	90	86	845	59*	653	62*	565	62
Grenada	…	…	…	…	…	…	…	…	…	…	…	…	…	…	…
Guatemala	64*	72*	57*	75	81	70	78	83	74	1 921	61*	2 089	63	2 127	63
Guyana	…	…	…	…	…	…	…	…	…	…	…	…	…	…	…
Haiti	…	…	…	49	53	45	61	64	58	…	…	3 028	55	2 748	55
Honduras	…	…	…	85*	85*	85*	89	88	89	…	…	733	51*	634	50
Jamaica	…	…	…	87	82	91	89	84	93	…	…	260	33	234	31
Mexico	88*	90*	85*	93*	94*	92*	93	95	92	6 437	62*	5 561	60*	5 714	60
Montserrat	…	…	…	…	…	…	…	…	…	…	…	…	…	…	…
Netherlands Antilles	95*	95*	95*	96	96	96	97	97	97	7	53*	6	55*	5	54
Nicaragua	…	…	…	78*	78*	78*	83	82	83	…	…	743	51*	728	50
Panama	89*	89*	88*	94*	95*	93*	95	96	94	176	52*	147	55*	139	56
Paraguay	90*	92*	89*	94*	95*	93*	96	96	95	255	59*	263	57*	212	52
Peru	87*	93*	82*	90*	95*	85*	93	96	89	1 850	72*	1 991	75*	1 573	75
Saint Kitts and Nevis	…	…	…	…	…	…	…	…	…	…	…	…	…	…	…
Saint Lucia	…	…	…	…	…	…	…	…	…	…	…	…	…	…	…
Saint Vincent/Grenadines	…	…	…	…	…	…	…	…	…	…	…	…	…	…	…
Suriname	…	…	…	95*	95*	94*	96	96	95	…	…	20	57*	18	56
Trinidad and Tobago	97*	98*	96*	99	99	98	99	99	99	26	70*	13	68	11	65
Turks and Caicos Islands	…	…	…	…	…	…	…	…	…	…	…	…	…	…	…
Uruguay	95*	95*	96*	98*	98*	98*	98	98	99	102	46*	50	41*	46	40
Venezuela, B. R.	90*	91*	89*	96*	96*	95*	96	96	96	1 240	54*	898	52*	828	52

2012 Education for All Global Monitoring Report

Table 2

YOUTH LITERACY RATE (15–24) (%)									YOUTH ILLITERATES (15–24)						
1985–1994[1]			2005–2010[1]			Projected 2015			1985–1994[1]		2005–2010[1]		Projected 2015		
Total	Male	Female	Total	Male	Female	Total	Male	Female	Total (000)	% Female	Total (000)	% Female	Total (000)	% Female	Country or territory
...	...	...	84*	89*	79*	90	93	87	...	...	196	66*	146	64	Lao PDR
...	...	...	100*	100*	100*	100	100	100	...	...	0.3	43*	0.1	34	Macao, China
96*	96*	95*	98*	98*	98*	98	98	99	158	53*	81	48*	86	46	Malaysia
...	...	...	...	...	...	...	...	...	...	...	...	...	...	...	Marshall Islands
...	...	...	...	...	...	...	...	...	...	...	...	...	...	...	Micronesia, F. S.
...	...	...	96	96	96	96	96	96	...	...	374	54	320	50	Myanmar
...	...	...	...	...	...	...	...	...	...	...	...	...	...	...	Nauru
...	...	...	...	...	...	...	...	...	...	...	...	...	...	...	New Zealand
...	...	...	...	...	...	...	...	...	...	...	...	...	...	...	Niue
...	...	...	...	...	...	...	...	...	...	...	...	...	...	...	Palau
...	...	...	68	65	72	70	64	77	...	...	412	43	453	38	Papua New Guinea
97*	96*	97*	98*	97*	98*	98	97	99	425	45*	406	33*	412	25	Philippines
...	...	...	...	...	...	...	...	...	...	...	...	...	...	...	Republic of Korea
99*	99*	99*	99	99	100	100	99	100	0.4	49*	0.2	39	0.2	36	Samoa
99*	99*	99*	100*	100*	100*	100	100	100	6	44*	2	45*	2	41	Singapore
...	...	...	...	...	...	...	...	...	...	...	...	...	...	...	Solomon Islands
...	...	...	98*	98*	98*	99	99	99	...	...	208	53*	135	50	Thailand
...	...	...	80*	80*	79*	82	81	82	...	...	47	51*	53	48	Timor-Leste
...	...	...	...	...	...	...	...	...	...	...	...	...	...	...	Tokelau
...	...	...	99*	99*	100*	100	99	100	...	...	0.1	38*	0.1	36	Tonga
...	...	...	...	...	...	...	...	...	...	...	...	...	...	...	Tuvalu
...	...	...	...	...	...	...	...	...	...	...	...	...	...	...	Vanuatu
94*	94*	93*	97	97	96	98	98	97	842	53*	549	56	384	56	Viet Nam
															Latin America and the Caribbean
...	...	...	...	...	...	...	...	...	...	...	...	...	...	...	Anguilla
...	...	...	...	...	...	...	...	...	...	...	...	...	...	...	Antigua and Barbuda
98*	98*	99*	99	99	99	99	99	99	92	43*	55	38	47	37	Argentina
...	...	...	99*	99*	99*	100	99	100	...	...	0.1	40*	0.1	40	Aruba
...	...	...	...	...	...	...	...	...	...	...	...	...	...	...	Bahamas
...	...	...	...	...	...	...	...	...	...	...	...	...	...	...	Barbados
76*	76*	77*	...	...	...	...	...	...	10	50*	...	...	...	...	Belize
...	...	...	...	...	...	...	...	...	...	...	...	...	...	...	Bermuda
94*	96*	92*	99*	100*	99*	99	98	99	83	70*	12	74*	25	30	Bolivia, P. S.
...	...	...	98*	97*	99*	99	98	99	...	...	655	33*	390	30	Brazil
...	...	...	...	...	...	...	...	...	...	...	...	...	...	...	British Virgin Islands
...	...	...	99*	99*	99*	...	...	...	...	...	0.1	62*	...	...	Cayman Islands
98*	98*	99*	99*	99*	99*	99	99	99	38	41*	33	49*	37	50	Chile
91*	89*	92*	98*	98*	99*	99	98	99	655	43*	161	38*	123	36	Colombia
...	...	...	98	98	99	98	98	99	...	...	16	37	13	35	Costa Rica
...	...	...	100	100	100	100	100	100	...	...	0.2	54	0.2	59	Cuba
...	...	...	...	...	...	...	...	...	...	...	...	...	...	...	Dominica
...	...	...	97*	96*	98*	98	97	99	...	...	59	33*	39	29	Dominican Republic
96*	97*	96*	99*	98*	99*	99	99	99	79	54*	36	42*	22	39	Ecuador
85*	85*	85*	96*	96*	96*	97	97	98	167	51*	53	46*	36	43	El Salvador
...	...	...	...	...	...	...	...	...	...	...	...	...	...	...	Grenada
76*	82*	71*	87	89	85	89	90	88	461	62*	380	58	361	56	Guatemala
...	...	...	...	...	...	...	...	...	...	...	...	...	...	...	Guyana
...	...	...	72*	74*	70*	82	83	82	...	...	570	54*	391	52	Haiti
...	...	...	95*	94*	96*	96	95	97	...	...	78	42*	64	35	Honduras
...	...	...	95	93	98	97	94	99	...	...	23	17	19	16	Jamaica
95*	96*	95*	98*	98*	98*	98	98	98	832	56*	325	49*	377	47	Mexico
...	...	...	...	...	...	...	...	...	...	...	...	...	...	...	Montserrat
97*	97*	97*	98	98	98	99	99	99	0.9	44*	0.4	50	0.2	50	Netherlands Antilles
...	...	...	87*	85*	89*	92	90	94	...	...	153	43*	107	38	Nicaragua
95*	95*	95*	98*	98*	97*	98	98	98	25	52*	14	55*	13	52	Panama
96*	96*	95*	99*	99*	99*	99	98	100	37	52*	18	45*	17	14	Paraguay
95*	97*	94*	97*	98*	97*	98	98	98	215	67*	143	62*	107	54	Peru
...	...	...	...	...	...	...	...	...	...	...	...	...	...	...	Saint Kitts and Nevis
...	...	...	...	...	...	...	...	...	...	...	...	...	...	...	Saint Lucia
...	...	...	...	...	...	...	...	...	...	...	...	...	...	...	Saint Vincent/Grenadines
...	...	...	98*	98*	99*	99	98	100	...	...	1	37*	0.9	17	Suriname
99*	99*	99*	100	100	100	100	100	100	2	50*	1	49	0.7	48	Trinidad and Tobago
...	...	...	...	...	...	...	...	...	...	...	...	...	...	...	Turks and Caicos Islands
99*	98*	99*	99*	98*	99*	99	98	99	6	37*	6	31*	7	30	Uruguay
95*	95*	96*	99*	98*	99*	99	99	99	175	39*	79	40*	60	43	Venezuela, B. R.

Table 2 (continued)

Country or territory	ADULT LITERACY RATE (15 and over) (%) 1985–1994[1] Total	Male	Female	2005–2010[1] Total	Male	Female	Projected 2015 Total	Male	Female	ADULT ILLITERATES (15 and over) 1985–1994[1] Total (000)	% Female	2005–2010[1] Total (000)	% Female	Projected 2015 Total (000)	% Female
North America and Western Europe															
Andorra	...	...	...	...	...	...	...	...	...	...	...	...	...	...	...
Austria	...	...	...	...	...	...	...	...	...	...	...	...	...	...	...
Belgium	...	...	...	...	...	...	...	...	...	...	...	...	...	...	...
Canada	...	...	...	...	...	...	...	...	...	...	...	...	...	...	...
Cyprus	94*	98*	91*	98	99	97	99	99	98	33	80*	16	76	12	75
Denmark	...	...	...	...	...	...	...	...	...	...	...	...	...	...	...
Finland	...	...	...	...	...	...	...	...	...	...	...	...	...	...	...
France	...	...	...	...	...	...	...	...	...	...	...	...	...	...	...
Germany	...	...	...	...	...	...	...	...	...	...	...	...	...	...	...
Greece	93*	96*	89*	97	98	96	98	99	97	615	74*	273	71	221	68
Iceland	...	...	...	...	...	...	...	...	...	...	...	...	...	...	...
Ireland	...	...	...	...	...	...	...	...	...	...	...	...	...	...	...
Israel	...	...	...	...	...	...	...	...	...	...	...	...	...	...	...
Italy	...	...	...	99	99	99	99	99	99	...	...	555	64	444	63
Luxembourg	...	...	...	...	...	...	...	...	...	...	...	...	...	...	...
Malta	88*	88*	88*	92*	91*	94*	94	93	96	32	50*	26	43*	20	39
Monaco	...	...	...	...	...	...	...	...	...	...	...	...	...	...	...
Netherlands	...	...	...	...	...	...	...	...	...	...	...	...	...	...	...
Norway	...	...	...	...	...	...	...	...	...	...	...	...	...	...	...
Portugal	88*	92*	85*	95	97	94	96	98	95	960	67*	437	69	328	69
San Marino	...	...	...	...	...	...	...	...	...	...	...	...	...	...	...
Spain	96*	98*	95*	98*	99*	97*	98	99	98	1 104	73*	882	68*	755	67
Sweden	...	...	...	...	...	...	...	...	...	...	...	...	...	...	...
Switzerland	...	...	...	...	...	...	...	...	...	...	...	...	...	...	...
United Kingdom	...	...	...	...	...	...	...	...	...	...	...	...	...	...	...
United States	...	...	...	...	...	...	...	...	...	...	...	...	...	...	...
South and West Asia															
Afghanistan	...	...	...	...	...	...	...	...	...	...	...	...	...	...	...
Bangladesh	35*	44*	26*	57	61	52	61	65	58	40 252	55*	44 149	55	43 876	54
Bhutan	...	...	...	53*	65*	39*	64	73	54	...	...	206	60*	205	60
India	48*	62*	34*	63*	75*	51*	71	81	61	287 272	61*	287 355	65*	266 367	67
Iran, Islamic Republic of	66*	74*	56*	85*	89*	81*	91	94	88	10 687	63*	8 256	64*	5 680	66
Maldives	96*	96*	96*	98*	98*	98*	99	99	99	5	46*	3	49*	3	49
Nepal	33*	49*	17*	60	73	48	66	77	56	7 531	62*	7 587	67	7 425	67
Pakistan	...	...	...	55*	69*	40*	60	72	47	...	...	49 507	65*	51 037	65
Sri Lanka	...	...	...	91*	93*	90*	93	94	92	...	...	1 373	59*	1 221	58
Sub-Saharan Africa															
Angola	...	...	...	70	83	58	71	82	61	...	...	3 044	72	3 491	69
Benin	27*	40*	17*	42	55	30	47	59	35	1 998	61*	2 872	62	3 093	62
Botswana	69*	65*	71*	84	84	85	87	87	88	251	47*	210	48	183	47
Burkina Faso	14*	20*	8*	29*	37*	22*	36	43	29	4 326	56*	5 806	57*	6 752	57
Burundi	37*	48*	28*	67	73	62	70	74	66	1 944	61*	1 710	60	1 747	58
Cameroon	...	...	...	71*	79*	63*	77	84	69	...	...	3 134	64*	3 057	66
Cape Verde	63*	75*	53*	84	89	79	87	91	83	70	69*	53	67	48	66
Central African Republic	34*	48*	20*	56	69	43	59	71	48	1 059	62*	1 155	66	1 213	65
Chad	11*	18*	5*	34	45	24	39	48	31	3 155	55*	4 014	59	4 313	58
Comoros	...	...	...	75	80	70	78	82	74	...	...	106	60	106	59
Congo	...	...	...	...	...	...	...	...	...	...	...	...	...	...	...
Côte d'Ivoire	34*	44*	23*	56	65	47	60	67	51	4 149	54*	5 110	59	5 399	59
D. R. Congo	...	...	...	67	77	57	66	74	59	...	...	11 765	66	14 153	66
Equatorial Guinea	...	...	...	94	97	91	95	97	93	...	...	26	75	23	71
Eritrea	...	...	...	68	79	58	73	82	65	...	...	989	68	954	68
Ethiopia	27*	36*	19*	39*	49*	29*	49	57	40	21 815	57*	26 847	59*	29 280	59
Gabon	72*	79*	65*	88	92	85	91	94	88	165	64*	113	65	97	66
Gambia	...	...	...	50	60	40	56	64	48	...	...	485	61	504	61
Ghana	...	...	...	67	73	61	71	76	66	...	...	4 903	58	4 959	57
Guinea	...	...	...	41	52	30	49	58	39	...	...	3 360	59	3 370	59
Guinea-Bissau	...	...	...	54	68	41	60	72	48	...	...	407	66	406	65
Kenya	...	...	...	87	91	84	89	91	87	...	...	2 942	63	2 950	63
Lesotho	...	...	...	90	83	96	90	84	96	...	...	141	22	142	19

YOUTH LITERACY RATE (15–24) (%)									YOUTH ILLITERATES (15–24)						
1985–1994[1]			2005–2010[1]			Projected 2015			1985–1994[1]		2005–2010[1]		Projected 2015		
Total	Male	Female	Total	Male	Female	Total	Male	Female	Total (000)	% Female	Total (000)	% Female	Total (000)	% Female	Country or territory
															North America and Western Europe
...	...	...	...	...	...	...	...	...	...	...	...	...	...	...	Andorra
...	...	...	...	...	...	...	...	...	...	...	...	...	...	...	Austria
...	...	...	...	...	...	...	...	...	...	...	...	...	...	...	Belgium
...	...	...	...	...	...	...	...	...	...	...	...	...	...	...	Canada
100*	100*	100*	100	100	100	100	100	100	0.5	42*	0.2	34	0.1	34	Cyprus
...	...	...	...	...	...	...	...	...	...	...	...	...	...	...	Denmark
...	...	...	...	...	...	...	...	...	...	...	...	...	...	...	Finland
...	...	...	...	...	...	...	...	...	...	...	...	...	...	...	France
...	...	...	...	...	...	...	...	...	...	...	...	...	...	...	Germany
99*	99*	99*	99	99	99	99	100	99	16	49*	8	53	6	56	Greece
...	...	...	...	...	...	...	...	...	...	...	...	...	...	...	Iceland
...	...	...	...	...	...	...	...	...	...	...	...	...	...	...	Ireland
...	...	...	...	...	...	...	...	...	...	...	...	...	...	...	Israel
...	...	...	100	100	100	100	100	100	...	...	6	47	4	46	Italy
...	...	...	...	...	...	...	...	...	...	...	...	...	...	...	Luxembourg
98*	97*	99*	98*	97*	99*	99	99	99	1.0	26*	1	25*	0.5	26	Malta
...	...	...	...	...	...	...	...	...	...	...	...	...	...	...	Monaco
...	...	...	...	...	...	...	...	...	...	...	...	...	...	...	Netherlands
...	...	...	...	...	...	...	...	...	...	...	...	...	...	...	Norway
99*	99*	99*	100	100	100	100	100	100	13	46*	3	43	2	42	Portugal
...	...	...	...	...	...	...	...	...	...	...	...	...	...	...	San Marino
100*	100*	100*	100*	100*	100*	100	100	100	29	47*	19	38*	11	37	Spain
...	...	...	...	...	...	...	...	...	...	...	...	...	...	...	Sweden
...	...	...	...	...	...	...	...	...	...	...	...	...	...	...	Switzerland
...	...	...	...	...	...	...	...	...	...	...	...	...	...	...	United Kingdom
...	...	...	...	...	...	...	...	...	...	...	...	...	...	...	United States
															South and West Asia
...	...	...	...	...	...	...	...	...	...	...	...	...	...	...	Afghanistan
45*	52*	38*	77	75	78	83	81	86	12 116	55*	6 951	46	5 254	41	Bangladesh
...	...	...	74*	80*	68*	89	90	87	...	...	38	59*	17	55	Bhutan
62*	74*	49*	81*	88*	74*	90	93	87	65 244	64*	41 275	67*	23 738	62	India
87*	92*	81*	99*	99*	99*	99	99	99	1 392	71*	235	54*	114	45	Iran, Islamic Republic of
98*	98*	98*	99*	99*	99*	99	99	99	0.7	46*	0.5	45*	0.4	39	Maldives
50*	68*	33*	83	88	78	88	91	86	1 862	67*	1 048	62	815	60	Nepal
...	...	...	71*	79*	61*	77	82	72	...	...	10 820	64*	9 038	59	Pakistan
...	...	...	98*	98*	99*	99	98	99	...	...	61	37*	39	33	Sri Lanka
															Sub-Saharan Africa
...	...	...	73	80	66	73	79	67	...	...	1 016	64	1 212	61	Angola
40*	55*	27*	55	66	45	60	69	51	580	63*	785	62	800	62	Benin
89*	86*	92*	95	94	97	98	96	99	31	35*	21	32	10	12	Botswana
20*	27*	14*	39*	47*	33*	45	48	43	1 518	54*	1 838	55*	2 076	51	Burkina Faso
54*	59*	48*	78	78	78	79	78	81	494	56*	427	50	393	46	Burundi
...	...	...	83*	89*	77*	87	92	82	...	...	632	68*	573	69	Cameroon
88*	90*	86*	98	97	99	99	98	100	8	57*	2	25	1	19	Cape Verde
48*	63*	35*	65	72	58	67	72	63	265	64*	317	61	323	58	Central African Republic
17*	26*	9*	47	53	41	53	55	50	1 013	56*	1 174	56	1 208	53	Chad
...	...	...	86	86	85	88	87	88	...	...	19	51	19	46	Comoros
...	...	...	80*	87*	78*	...	...	...	...	...	123	62*	...	...	Congo
49*	60*	38*	67	72	62	69	73	66	1 059	60*	1 320	58	1 372	55	Côte d'Ivoire
...	...	...	65	68	62	62	63	61	...	...	4 665	55	5 844	51	D. R. Congo
...	...	...	98	98	98	98	98	99	...	...	3	42	3	34	Equatorial Guinea
...	...	...	89	92	87	93	95	92	...	...	113	63	77	60	Eritrea
34*	39*	28*	55*	63*	47*	69	71	68	6 808	54*	7 090	59*	6 222	53	Ethiopia
93*	94*	92*	98	99	97	98	99	98	12	59*	7	70	6	73	Gabon
...	...	...	67	72	62	73	76	71	...	...	118	58	110	55	Gambia
...	...	...	81	82	80	85	84	85	...	...	934	51	813	47	Ghana
...	...	...	63	70	57	74	77	72	...	...	725	58	574	55	Guinea
...	...	...	72	79	65	77	81	74	...	...	84	62	76	58	Guinea-Bissau
...	...	...	93	92	94	93	91	95	...	...	608	42	634	35	Kenya
...	...	...	92	86	98	92	86	98	...	...	41	12	40	10	Lesotho

Table 2 (continued)

Country or territory	ADULT LITERACY RATE (15 and over) (%) 1985–1994[1] Total	Male	Female	2005–2010[1] Total	Male	Female	Projected 2015 Total	Male	Female	ADULT ILLITERATES (15 and over) 1985–1994[1] Total (000)	% Female	2005–2010[1] Total (000)	% Female	Projected 2015 Total (000)	% Female
Liberia	43	55	32	61	65	57	65	67	64	639	61	885	55	900	52
Madagascar	...	...	...	64	67	62	65	67	63	...	...	4 039	55	4 945	53
Malawi	49*	65*	34*	75	81	68	79	83	74	2 212	68*	2 037	63	2 018	61
Mali	...	...	...	31*	43*	20*	38	50	27	...	...	5 554	59*	5 891	60
Mauritius	80*	85*	75*	89	91	86	90	92	88	150	63*	117	61	106	60
Mozambique	...	...	...	56	71	43	62	74	50	...	...	5 740	68	5 746	68
Namibia	76*	78*	74*	89	89	88	90	90	90	201	56*	163	52	163	49
Niger	...	...	...	29*	43*	15*	36	49	23	...	...	4 731	61*	6 072	61
Nigeria	55*	68*	44*	61	72	50	65	74	55	24 489	64*	35 025	64	36 357	63
Rwanda	58*	...	...	71	75	68	73	75	70	1 472	...	1 764	58	1 905	56
Sao Tome and Principe	73*	85*	62*	89	94	85	91	94	88	17	73*	11	72	10	68
Senegal	27*	37*	18*	50*	62*	39*	56	67	46	2 600	57*	3 400	63*	3 539	63
Seychelles	88*	87*	89*	92	91	92	...	...	...	6	47*	5	46	...	...
Sierra Leone	...	...	...	42	54	31	48	59	38	...	...	1 936	61	1 963	62
Somalia	...	...	...	...	...	...	...	...	...	...	...	...	...	...	...
South Africa	...	...	...	89*	91*	87*	93	94	92	...	...	3 754	59*	2 615	58
South Sudan	...	...	...	...	...	...	...	...	...	...	...	...	...	...	...
Swaziland	67*	70*	65*	87	88	87	89	89	89	123	59*	92	54	86	52
Togo	...	...	...	57*	71*	44*	68	79	57	...	...	1 515	67*	1 349	67
Uganda	56*	68*	45*	73*	83*	65*	78	85	71	4 140	64*	4 560	67*	4 444	66
United Republic of Tanzania	59*	71*	48*	73	79	67	74	79	70	5 205	65*	6 642	61	7 365	59
Zambia	65*	73*	57*	71	81	62	72	81	63	1 487	62*	2 021	66	2 240	66
Zimbabwe	84*	89*	79*	92	95	90	94	96	93	979	66*	597	67	514	66

	Weighted average									Sum	% F	Sum	% F	Sum	% F
World	76	82	69	84	89	80	86	90	82	880 566	63	774 756	64	738 241	64
Countries in transition	98	99	97	99	100	99	100	100	100	4 698	85	1 389	72	974	61
Developed countries	...	...	...	...	...	...	...	...	...	...	...	...	...	...	...
Developing countries	67	76	58	80	86	74	82	87	76	865 958	63	764 919	64	728 903	64
Arab States	55	68	42	75	83	66	79	86	71	51 697	63	50 286	66	49 105	67
Central and Eastern Europe	96	98	94	98	99	97	97	98	97	12 142	79	6 794	77	8 544	65
Central Asia	98**	99**	97**	99	100	99	100	100	100	937	77**	302	64	253	59
East Asia and the Pacific	82	89	75	94	97	92	95	97	93	231 592	69	99 156	71	83 377	71
East Asia	82	89	74	94	97	92	95	97	93	230 164	69	97 300	72	81 459	72
Pacific	...	...	...	...	...	...	...	...	...	...	...	...	...	...	...
Latin America/Caribbean	86**	87**	84**	91	92	91	93	93	92	42 204	55**	35 805	55	32 523	55
Caribbean	...	...	...	69	70	68	73	74	71	...	...	3 504	54	3 478	53
Latin America	86**	88**	85**	92	93	91	93	94	93	39 300	56**	32 301	56	29 045	55
N. America/W. Europe	...	...	...	...	...	...	...	...	...	...	...	...	...	...	...
South and West Asia	47	59	34	63	74	52	70	80	61	400 974	60	406 419	64	381 810	65
Sub-Saharan Africa	53**	64**	43**	63	71	54	66	73	59	133 134	62**	169 313	62	176 170	61
Countries with low income	51**	60**	42**	63	70	56	67	73	62	148 835	60**	174 291	60	179 514	59
Countries with middle income	72	80	64	83	89	78	86	90	81	722 944	64	591 757	66	552 509	66
Lower middle	59	69	48	71	80	62	76	84	68	461 635	62	469 452	65	448 733	66
Upper middle	82	88	76	94	96	91	95	97	93	261 310	67	122 305	68	103 776	67
Countries with high income	...	...	...	...	...	...	...	...	...	...	...	...	...	...	...

Source: UNESCO Institute for Statistics database (UIS, 2012).
Note A: The country groupings by income level presented in the tables are as defined by the World Bank. They are based on the list of countries by income group as revised in July 2011.
Note B: For countries indicated with (*), national observed literacy data are used. For all others, UIS literacy estimates are used. The estimates were generated using the UIS Global Age-specific Literacy Projections model. Those in the most recent period are for 2010 and are based on the most recent observed data available for each country.
Note C: The population used to generate the number of illiterates is from the United Nations Population Division estimates, revision 2010 (United Nations, 2011). It is based on the median variant. For countries with national observed literacy data, the population corresponding to the year of the census or survey was used. For countries with UIS estimates, populations used are for 1994 and 2010.

1. Data are for the most recent year available during the period specified. See the introduction to the statistical tables and the table of metadata on literacy statistics for a broader explanation of national literacy definitions, assessment methods, and sources and years of data.
(**) For country level data: UIS partial estimate; for regional and other country-grouping sums and weighted averages: partial imputation due to incomplete country coverage (between 33% and 60% of population for the region or other country grouping).
(. . .) No data available.

Total	Male	Female	Total	Male	Female	Total	Male	Female	Total (000)	% Female	Total (000)	% Female	Total (000)	% Female	Country or territory
YOUTH LITERACY RATE (15–24) (%)									**YOUTH ILLITERATES (15–24)**						
1985–1994[1]			2005–2010[1]			Projected 2015			1985–1994[1]		2005–2010[1]		Projected 2015		
60	66	54	77	71	82	80	73	88	164	57	183	38	175	31	Liberia
…	…	…	65*	66*	64*	65	65	65	…	…	1 384	51*	1 703	50	Madagascar
59*	70*	49*	87	87	87	90	89	91	621	64*	392	50	357	45	Malawi
…	…	…	44*	56*	34*	53	62	44	…	…	1 657	59*	1 644	59	Mali
91*	91*	92*	97	96	98	97	96	98	19	47*	7	34	6	31	Mauritius
…	…	…	72	79	65	78	82	73	…	…	1 299	62	1 177	61	Mozambique
88*	86*	90*	93	91	95	94	91	96	36	40*	33	36	33	32	Namibia
…	…	…	37*	52*	23*	46	56	36	…	…	1 440	64*	1 880	60	Niger
71*	81*	62*	72	78	66	75	79	71	5 256	66*	8 617	60	8 647	57	Nigeria
75*	…	…	77	77	78	77	76	78	320	…	498	50	515	48	Rwanda
94*	96*	92*	95	95	96	95	94	97	1	65*	2	43	2	36	Sao Tome and Principe
38*	49*	28*	65*	74*	56*	73	80	67	817	59*	874	63*	769	62	Senegal
99*	98*	99*	99	99	99	…	…	…	0.2	36*	0.1	30	…	…	Seychelles
…	…	…	59	69	50	67	76	59	…	…	461	63	424	64	Sierra Leone
…	…	…	…	…	…	…	…	…	…	…	…	…	…	…	Somalia
…	…	…	98*	97*	98*	98	98	99	…	…	243	39*	157	28	South Africa
…	…	…	…	…	…	…	…	…	…	…	…	…	…	…	South Sudan
84*	83*	84*	94	92	95	94	93	96	23	51*	19	38	17	35	Swaziland
…	…	…	82*	88*	75*	88	90	86	…	…	232	67*	161	58	Togo
70*	77*	63*	87*	90*	85*	91	90	91	1 051	62*	837	59*	733	49	Uganda
82*	86*	78*	77	78	76	77	77	77	827	62*	2 013	52	2 325	50	United Republic of Tanzania
66*	67*	66*	74	82	67	74	82	66	524	51*	668	64	781	65	Zambia
95*	97*	94*	99	98	100	99	99	100	101	62*	31	23	23	15	Zimbabwe

Total	Male	Female	Total	Male	Female	Total	Male	Female	Sum	% F	Sum	% F	Sum	% F	
Weighted average															
83	88	79	90	92	87	92	93	91	167 792	62	122 160	61	96 035	56	World
100	100	100	100	100	100	100	100	100	116	46	130	40	100	38	Countries in transition
…	…	…	…	…	…	…	…	…	…	…	…	…	…	…	Developed countries
80	85	75	88	91	85	89	91	88	167 158	62	121 526	61	95 443	56	Developing countries
74	83	65	89	92	86	92	94	90	10 177	67	6 499	65	5 037	61	Arab States
98	99	98	99	99	99	99	99	98	979	72	520	62	692	58	Central and Eastern Europe
100**	100**	100**	100	100	100	100	100	100	30	47**	45	33	43	31	Central Asia
95	97	93	99	99	99	99	99	99	19 855	69	4 406	52	3 377	46	East Asia and the Pacific
95	97	93	99	99	99	99	99	99	19 463	69	3 955	53	2 899	47	East Asia
…	…	…	…	…	…	…	…	…	…	…	…	…	…	38	Pacific
93**	93**	93**	97	97	97	98	98	98	6 166	48**	2 900	46	2 316	44	Latin America/Caribbean
…	…	…	81	82	81	87	86	87	…	…	623	52	471	50	Caribbean
93	93**	94**	98**	98	98	98	98	98	5 649	47**	2 278	44	1 845	42	Latin America
…	…	…	…	…	…	…	…	…	…	…	…	…	…	…	N. America/W. Europe
60	70	49	81	87	75	88	91	86	96 043	61	62 275	64	39 921	58	South and West Asia
66**	73**	59**	72	76	67	75	77	73	34 268	60**	45 251	58	44 395	54	Sub-Saharan Africa
60**	67	53**	74	77	71	78	79	77	41 428	59**	40 848	55	38 661	51	Countries with low income
84	88	79	91	94	88	93	95	92	126 969	63	80 829	64	58 645	59	Countries with middle income
71	79	63	84	89	79	89	91	87	103 110	62	75 850	64	54 973	60	Lower middle
94	96	92	99	99	99	99	99	99	23 859	66	4 979	51	3 672	46	Upper middle
…	…	…	…	…	…	…	…	…	…	…	…	…	…	…	Countries with high income

Table 3A
Early childhood care and education (ECCE): care

	CHILD SURVIVAL[1]				CHILD WELL-BEING[2]				
				% of children under age 5 suffering from stunting moderate and severe	% of 1-year-old children immunized against				
					Tuberculosis	Diphtheria, Pertussis, Tetanus	Polio	Measles	Hepatitis B
	Infant mortality rate (‰)	Under-5 mortality rate (‰)	Infants with low birth weight (%)		Corresponding vaccines:				
					BCG	DPT3	Polio3	Measles	HepB3
Country or territory	2010–2015	2010–2015	2005–2010[3]	2005–2010[3]	2010	2010	2010	2010	2010
Arab States									
Algeria	21	27	6	15	99	95	95	95	95
Bahrain	7	9	...	...	...	99	99	99	99
Djibouti	75	104	10	33	90	88	88	85	88
Egypt	22	25	13	29	98	97	97	96	97
Iraq	33	41	15	26	80	65	69	73	64
Jordan	19	22	13	8	95	98	98	98	98
Kuwait	8	10	...	4	98	98	98	98	99
Lebanon	20	24	...	...	...	74	74	53	74
Libya	13	15	...	21	99	98	98	98	98
Mauritania	70	106	34	23	85	64	63	67	64
Morocco	29	31	15	...	99	99	99	98	98
Oman	8	11	12	10	99	99	99	97	98
Palestine	20	22	7	12	...	...	...	...	...
Qatar	8	10	...	...	99	97	98	99	97
Saudi Arabia	16	19	...	...	98	98	98	98	98
Sudan (pre-secession)	57	87	...	38	...	...	...	...	...
Syrian Arab Republic	14	16	10	28	90	80	83	82	84
Tunisia	18	23	5	9	98	98	98	97	98
United Arab Emirates	7	8	6	...	98	94	94	94	94
Yemen	44	57	...	...	65	87	88	73	87
Central and Eastern Europe									
Albania	17	19	7	19	99	99	99	99	99
Belarus	6	9	4	5	99	98	99	99	96
Bosnia and Herzegovina	13	16	5	12	97	90	90	93	90
Bulgaria	9	11	9	...	98	94	96	97	95
Croatia	6	7	5	...	99	96	96	95	97
Czech Republic	3	4	7	...	...	99	99	98	99
Estonia	4	7	4	...	97	94	94	95	94
Hungary	5	7	9	...	99	99	99	99	...
Latvia	7	8	5	...	92	89	89	93	89
Lithuania	6	9	4	...	99	95	95	96	94
Montenegro	8	9	4	8	95	94	93	90	90
Poland	6	7	6	...	94	99	96	98	98
Republic of Moldova	14	19	6	11	98	90	97	97	98
Romania	12	15	8	...	99	97	96	95	98
Russian Federation	11	16	6	...	96	97	98	98	97
Serbia	11	13	6	8	99	91	91	95	89
Slovakia	6	7	7	...	98	99	99	98	99
Slovenia	3	4	...	...	...	96	96	95	...
TFYR Macedonia	13	15	6	11	98	95	95	98	90
Turkey	20	23	11	10	96	96	96	97	94
Ukraine	12	15	4	...	95	90	91	94	84
Central Asia									
Armenia	24	27	7	18	95	94	96	97	94
Azerbaijan	38	43	10	25	81	72	78	67	49
Georgia	26	27	5	11	96	91	88	94	95
Kazakhstan	24	29	6	18	96	99	98	99	99
Kyrgyzstan	33	42	5	18	98	96	88	99	96
Mongolia	31	37	5	28	99	96	96	97	96
Tajikistan	51	65	10	39	82	93	95	94	93
Turkmenistan	49	62	4	...	99	96	96	99	96
Uzbekistan	44	53	5	19	99	99	99	98	99
East Asia and the Pacific									
Australia	4	5	...	...	...	92	92	94	92
Brunei Darussalam	5	6	...	...	95	95	99	94	96
Cambodia	53	69	9	41	94	92	92	93	92
China	20	24	3	9	99	99	99	99	99
Cook Islands	...	...	...	...	99	99	99	99	99
DPR Korea	25	32	6	32	98	93	99	99	93
Fiji	17	22	10	...	99	99	99	94	99
Indonesia	25	31	9	37	97	83	93	89	83
Japan	3	3	...	...	99	98	98	94	...
Kiribati	...	...	...	...	87	91	95	89	91

Table 3A (continued)

	CHILD SURVIVAL[1]		CHILD WELL-BEING[2]						
				% of children under age 5 suffering from stunting moderate and severe	% of 1-year-old children immunized against				
					Tuberculosis	Diphtheria, Pertussis, Tetanus	Polio	Measles	Hepatitis B
	Infant mortality rate [‰]	Under-5 mortality rate [‰]	Infants with low birth weight [%]		Corresponding vaccines:				
					BCG	DPT3	Polio3	Measles	HepB3
Country or territory	2010–2015	2010–2015	2005–2010[3]	2005–2010[3]	2010	2010	2010	2010	2010
Lao PDR	37	46	11	48	72	74	76	64	74
Macao, China	4	5	…	…	…	…	…	…	…
Malaysia	7	9	11	17	99	94	94	96	95
Marshall Islands	…	…	18	…	99	94	95	97	97
Micronesia, F. S.	31	38	…	…	70	85	85	80	88
Myanmar	45	57	9	35	93	90	90	88	90
Nauru	…	…	27	24	99	99	99	99	99
New Zealand	5	6	…	…	…	93	93	91	90
Niue	…	…	…	…	99	99	99	99	99
Palau	…	…	…	…	…	49	48	75	80
Papua New Guinea	44	58	10	44	79	56	61	55	56
Philippines	21	27	21	32	90	87	86	88	85
Republic of Korea	4	5	…	…	96	94	95	98	94
Samoa	20	24	10	…	91	87	86	61	87
Singapore	2	2	…	…	99	97	97	95	96
Solomon Islands	35	43	13	33	85	79	78	68	79
Thailand	11	13	7	16	99	99	99	98	98
Timor-Leste	56	76	12	58	71	72	72	66	72
Tokelau	…	…	…	…	…	…	…	…	…
Tonga	21	25	3	…	99	99	99	99	99
Tuvalu	…	…	…	10	99	89	89	85	89
Vanuatu	24	29	10	26	81	68	67	52	59
Viet Nam	18	23	5	31	94	93	94	98	88
Latin America and the Caribbean									
Anguilla	…	…	…	…	…	…	…	…	…
Antigua and Barbuda	…	…	5	…	…	98	99	98	98
Argentina	12	14	7	…	99	94	96	99	94
Aruba	15	17	…	…	…	…	…	…	…
Bahamas	14	18	11	…	…	99	97	94	98
Barbados	12	14	12	…	…	86	90	85	86
Belize	16	21	14	22	98	96	96	98	96
Bermuda	…	…	…	…	…	…	…	…	…
Bolivia, P. S.	41	54	6	27	90	80	80	79	80
Brazil	19	24	8	7	99	98	99	99	96
British Virgin Islands	…	…	…	…	…	…	…	…	…
Cayman Islands	…	…	…	…	…	…	…	…	…
Chile	7	8	6	2	95	92	92	93	92
Colombia	17	23	6	13	84	88	88	88	88
Costa Rica	9	11	7	6	77	88	93	83	89
Cuba	5	6	5	…	99	96	99	99	96
Dominica	…	…	10	…	99	98	99	99	98
Dominican Republic	22	28	11	10	98	88	86	79	84
Ecuador	19	23	8	…	99	99	99	98	98
El Salvador	19	23	7	21	91	92	92	92	92
Grenada	13	15	9	…	…	97	94	95	97
Guatemala	26	34	11	48	99	94	94	93	94
Guyana	37	46	19	18	98	95	95	95	95
Haiti	58	76	25	29	75	59	59	59	…
Honduras	24	33	10	29	99	98	98	99	98
Jamaica	22	26	12	4	95	99	99	88	99
Mexico	14	17	7	16	98	95	95	95	93
Montserrat	…	…	…	…	…	…	…	…	…
Netherlands Antilles	12	14	…	…	…	…	…	…	…
Nicaragua	18	22	9	22	98	98	99	99	98
Panama	16	21	10	19	97	94	94	95	94
Paraguay	27	33	6	18	92	90	88	94	98
Peru	18	28	8	30	95	93	92	94	93
Saint Kitts and Nevis	…	…	8	…	91	95	90	99	96
Saint Lucia	12	16	11	…	97	97	97	95	97
Saint Vincent/Grenadines	21	25	8	…	90	99	99	99	99
Suriname	20	27	…	11	…	88	88	89	88
Trinidad and Tobago	24	31	19	…	…	90	91	92	90
Turks and Caicos Islands	…	…	…	…	…	…	…	…	…
Uruguay	12	15	9	…	99	95	95	95	95
Venezuela, B. R.	15	20	8	16	92	78	74	79	78

Table 3A (continued)

	CHILD SURVIVAL[1]				CHILD WELL-BEING[2]				
				% of children under age 5 suffering from stunting moderate and severe	% of 1-year-old children immunized against				
					Tuberculosis	Diphtheria, Pertussis, Tetanus	Polio	Measles	Hepatitis B
	Infant mortality rate (‰)	Under-5 mortality rate (‰)	Infants with low birth weight (%)		Corresponding vaccines:				
					BCG	DPT3	Polio3	Measles	HepB3
Country or territory	2010–2015	2010–2015	2005–2010[3]	2005–2010[3]	2010	2010	2010	2010	2010
North America and Western Europe									
Andorra	...	...	...	...	...	99	99	99	96
Austria	4	5	7	...	...	83	83	76	83
Belgium	4	5	...	...	...	99	99	94	97
Canada	5	6	...	...	...	80	80	93	17
Cyprus	4	5	...	...	...	99	99	87	96
Denmark	4	5	5	...	...	90	90	85	...
Finland	3	3	4	...	...	99	99	98	...
France	3	4	...	...	...	99	99	90	42
Germany	3	4	...	...	...	93	95	96	90
Greece	4	5	...	...	91	99	99	99	95
Iceland	2	3	4	...	...	96	96	93	...
Ireland	4	4	...	...	96	94	94	90	94
Israel	3	4	8	...	...	96	94	98	96
Italy	3	4	...	...	...	96	96	90	96
Luxembourg	2	3	...	...	...	99	99	96	94
Malta	5	7	6	...	...	76	76	73	86
Monaco	...	...	...	...	89	99	99	99	99
Netherlands	4	5	...	...	...	97	97	96	...
Norway	3	4	...	...	...	93	93	93	...
Portugal	4	5	8	...	96	98	97	96	97
San Marino	...	...	...	...	...	92	92	93	92
Spain	4	4	...	...	...	97	97	95	97
Sweden	3	3	...	...	23	98	98	96	...
Switzerland	4	5	...	...	...	96	95	90	...
United Kingdom	5	6	...	...	...	96	98	93	...
United States	6	8	8	...	...	95	93	92	92
South and West Asia									
Afghanistan	125	184	...	...	68	66	66	62	66
Bangladesh	42	51	22	43	94	95	95	94	95
Bhutan	38	52	10	34	96	91	92	95	91
India	48	65	28	48	87	72	70	74	37
Iran, Islamic Republic of	23	31	7	...	99	99	99	99	99
Maldives	8	12	22	20	97	96	97	97	97
Nepal	32	39	21	49	94	82	83	86	82
Pakistan	66	86	32	...	95	88	88	86	88
Sri Lanka	11	13	17	17	99	99	99	99	99
Sub-Saharan Africa									
Angola	96	156	...	29	93	91	92	93	91
Benin	77	121	15	43	97	83	83	69	83
Botswana	35	46	13	31	99	96	96	94	93
Burkina Faso	71	147	16	35	99	95	94	94	95
Burundi	94	152	11	58	93	96	94	92	96
Cameroon	85	136	11	36	96	84	83	79	84
Cape Verde	18	22	6	...	99	99	99	96	98
Central African Republic	96	155	13	43	74	54	47	62	54
Chad	124	195	22	39	52	59	63	46	59
Comoros	63	86	...	...	76	74	82	72	81
Congo	67	104	13	31	95	90	90	76	90
Côte d'Ivoire	69	107	17	39	91	85	81	70	85
D. R. Congo	109	180	10	43	85	63	72	68	63
Equatorial Guinea	93	151	...	...	73	33	39	51	...
Eritrea	48	62	14	...	99	99	99	99	99
Ethiopia	63	96	20	51	69	86	86	81	86
Gabon	44	64	...	...	89	45	44	55	45
Gambia	66	93	11	24	95	98	96	97	94
Ghana	44	63	13	29	99	94	94	93	94
Guinea	84	134	12	40	81	57	53	51	57
Guinea-Bissau	110	181	11	28	93	76	73	61	76
Kenya	58	89	8	35	99	83	83	86	83
Lesotho	62	89	13	39	95	83	91	85	83

Table 3A (continued)

	CHILD SURVIVAL[1]		CHILD WELL-BEING[2]						
				% of children under age 5 suffering from stunting moderate and severe [%]	% of 1-year-old children immunized against				
					Tuberculosis	Diphtheria, Pertussis, Tetanus	Polio	Measles	Hepatitis B
	Infant mortality rate [‰]	Under-5 mortality rate [‰]	Infants with low birth weight [%]		Corresponding vaccines:				
Country or territory					BCG	DPT3	Polio3	Measles	HepB3
	2010–2015	2010–2015	2005–2010[3]	2005–2010[3]	2010	2010	2010	2010	2010
Liberia	77	107	14	39	80	64	71	64	64
Madagascar	41	58	16	49	67	74	72	67	74
Malawi	86	119	13	48	97	93	86	93	93
Mali	92	173	19	38	86	76	73	63	76
Mauritius	12	15	14	…	99	99	99	99	99
Mozambique	78	123	16	44	90	74	73	70	74
Namibia	30	39	16	29	88	83	83	75	83
Niger	86	144	27	55	83	70	75	71	70
Nigeria	88	141	12	41	76	69	79	71	66
Rwanda	93	114	6	44	75	80	80	82	80
Sao Tome and Principe	47	69	8	32	99	98	98	92	98
Senegal	50	85	19	20	80	70	70	60	70
Seychelles	…	…	…	…	99	99	99	99	99
Sierra Leone	103	157	14	37	99	90	89	82	90
Somalia	100	162	…	42	29	45	49	46	…
South Africa	46	64	…	24	86	63	67	65	56
South Sudan	…	…	…	…	…	…	…	…	…
Swaziland	65	92	9	40	98	89	89	94	89
Togo	67	104	11	27	94	92	92	84	92
Uganda	72	114	14	38	84	60	55	55	60
United Republic of Tanzania	54	81	10	43	99	91	94	92	91
Zambia	81	130	11	46	89	82	66	91	82
Zimbabwe	47	71	11	32	90	83	84	84	83

	Weighted average				Median				
World	42	60	10	29	96	94	94	94	93
Countries in transition	22	28	6	15	98	94	96	97	95
Developed countries	5	6	…	…	…	96	96	95	94
Developing countries	46	67	11	30	95	92	92	92	92
Arab States	31	41	11	21	98	97	98	97	97
Central and Eastern Europe	12	16	6	…	98	96	96	97	95
Central Asia	38	46	5	19	96	96	96	97	96
East Asia and the Pacific	20	25	10	…	97	93	94	94	92
East Asia	20	25	9	32	96	93	94	94	93
Pacific	19	25	…	…	99	92	93	90	91
Latin America and the Caribbean	19	24	9	…	97	95	94	95	95
Caribbean	47	61	11	…	…	97	96	95	97
Latin America	18	23	8	18	98	94	94	94	94
N. America/W. Europe	5	6	…	…	…	96	97	93	95
South and West Asia	51	69	21	38	95	91	92	94	91
Sub-Saharan Africa	77	123	13	39	91	83	83	79	83
Countries with low income	72	111	13	40	90	83	83	82	83
Countries with middle income	38	53	8.9	22	97	94	94	94.5	94
Lower middle	49	70	10	29	95	90	91	92	89
Upper middle	19	23	8	14	98	96	96	96	95
Countries with high income	6	7	…	…	…	96	97	95	96

Note: The country groupings by income level presented in the tables are as defined by the World Bank. They are based on the list of countries by income group as revised in July 2011.
1. The indicators on child survival in this table are from the United Nations Population Division estimates, revision 2010 (United Nations, 2011). They are based on the median variant.
2. UNICEF (2012); WHO Global Database on Child Growth and Malnutrition (2012).
3. Data are for the most recent year available during the period specified.
(. . .) No data available.

Table 3B
Early childhood care and education (ECCE): education

	Country or territory	Age group 2010	ENROLMENT IN PRE-PRIMARY EDUCATION				Enrolment in private institutions as % of total enrolment		GROSS ENROLMENT RATIO (GER) IN PRE-PRIMARY EDUCATION (%)							
			School year ending in				School year ending in		School year ending in							
			1999		2010		1999	2010	1999				2010			
			Total (000)	% F	Total (000)	% F			Total	Male	Female	GPI (F/M)	Total	Male	Female	GPI (F/M)
	Arab States															
1	Algeria	5-5	36	49	500	48	.	14	2	2	2	1.01	77	79	76	0.96
2	Bahrain[1]	3-5	14	48	26	49	100	100	38	39	37	0.96	...	...	...	...
3	Djibouti	4-5	0.2	60	**2**	**49**	100	**65**	0.4	0.3	0.5	1.50	**4**	**4**	**4**	**0.97**
4	Egypt	4-5	328	48	814[z]	48[z]	54	...	10	11	10	0.95	24[z]	24[z]	23[z]	0.95[z]
5	Iraq	4-5	68	48	...	...	.	...	5	5	5	1.00	...	...	...	...
6	Jordan	4-5	74	46	99	47	100	83	29	31	28	0.91	32	33	31	0.94
7	Kuwait	4-5	57	49	71[y]	49[y]	24	42[y]	85	84	87	1.03	82[y]	81[y]	83[y]	1.02[y]
8	Lebanon	3-5	143**	48**	154	48	78**	81	61**	62**	60**	0.97**	81	82	81	0.98
9	Libya	4-5	10	48**	...	...	.	...	5	5**	5**	0.98**	...	...	...	...
10	Mauritania	3-5	...	...	...	...	...	...	...	...	...	...	...	...	...	...
11	Morocco	4-5	805	34	**740**	**41**	100	**92**	62	81	42	0.53	**63**	**73**	**53**	**0.72**
12	Oman	4-5	...	...	46	49	...	...	...	...	...	...	45	45	45	0.99
13	Palestine	4-5	77	48	91	48	100	100	35	36	35	0.96	39	40	39	0.98
14	Qatar	3-5	8	48	25[z]	47[z]	...	87[z]	25	26	25	0.96	55[z]	57[z]	54[z]	0.96[z]
15	Saudi Arabia	3-5	...	...	190	...	...	51	...	...	...	...	11	...	...	...
16	Sudan (pre-secession)	4-5	366	...	632[z]	50[z]	90**	23[z]	19	...	...	...	27[z]	26[z]	27[z]	1.04[z]
17	Syrian Arab Republic	3-5	108	46	149	47	67	72	8	9	8	0.90	10	10	9	0.97
18	Tunisia	3-5	78	47	...	...	88	...	14	14	13	0.93	...	...	...	...
19	United Arab Emirates[1]	4-5	64	48	125	49	68	79	64	64	64	0.99	...	...	...	...
20	Yemen	3-5	12	45	26	46	37	52	0.7	0.7	0.6	0.86	1	1	1	0.90
	Central and Eastern Europe															
21	Albania	3-5	82	50	75	47	.	5	43	42	45	1.06	56	56	55	0.98
22	Belarus	3-5	278	47	282	48	-	4[y]	83	86	79	0.92	99	100	98	0.98
23	Bosnia and Herzegovina	3-5	...	...	17	48	...	15	...	...	...	...	17	17	17	0.99
24	Bulgaria	3-6	219	48	218	48	0.1	0.8	68	69	68	0.99	79	80	79	0.99
25	Croatia	3-6	81	48	99	48	5	14	39	40	39	0.98	61	62	61	0.98
26	Czech Republic	3-5	312	50	304[z]	48[z]	2	2[z]	89	86	91	1.07	106[z]	107[z]	105[z]	0.98[z]
27	Estonia	3-6	55	48	51[z]	49[z]	1	3[z]	93	94	92	0.99	96[z]	96[z]	96[z]	1.00[z]
28	Hungary	3-6	376	48	326[z]	48[z]	3	6[z]	80	81	79	0.98	85[z]	85[z]	84[z]	0.98[z]
29	Latvia	3-6	58	48	71	48	1	3	56	58	55	0.95	84	85	82	0.96
30	Lithuania	3-6	94	48	88	48	0.3	0.5	50	51	50	0.97	74	75	73	0.97
31	Montenegro	3-6	*11*	*48*	10	47	.	.	*34*	*34*	*33*	*0.98*	31	32	30	0.96
32	Poland	3-6	958	49	919[z]	49[z]	3	12[z]	49	49	49	1.00	66[z]	65[z]	66[z]	1.01[z]
33	Republic of Moldova[2,3]	3-6	103	48	112	48	...	0.1	48	49	48	0.96	76	76	75	0.98
34	Romania	3-6	625	49	666	49	1	2	68	67	69	1.03	79	79	79	1.01
35	Russian Federation	3-6	4 379	...	5 105[z]	48[z]	...	0.8[z]	71	...	...	...	90[z]	91[z]	89[z]	0.98[z]
36	Serbia[2]	3-6	175	46	158	49	...	1.0	54	57	51	0.90	53	53	53	1.01
37	Slovakia	3-5	169	...	143	48	0.4	4	79	...	...	...	91	92	90	0.98
38	Slovenia	3-5	59	46	46[z]	48[z]	1	2[z]	75	79	72	0.91	86[z]	87[z]	85[z]	0.98[z]
39	TFYR Macedonia	3-5	33	49	17	49	.	.[z]	27	27	27	1.01	25	25	26	1.05
40	Turkey	3-5	261	47	805[z]	48[z]	6	9[z]	7	7	6	0.94	22[z]	22[z]	21[z]	0.95[z]
41	Ukraine	3-5	1 103	48	1 214	48	0.0	1	50	51	50	0.98	97	99	96	0.97
	Central Asia															
42	Armenia	3-6	57	...	54	50	-	1	26	...	...	...	31	29	34	1.15
43	Azerbaijan[2,4]	3-5	88	46	92	46	-	0.6	18	19	17	0.89	25	26	25	0.97
44	Georgia	3-5	74	48	79[y]	51**,[y]	0.1	-[y]	35	36	35	0.98	58[y]	52**,[y]	64**,[y]	1.23**,[y]
45	Kazakhstan	3-6	165	48	**520**	**48**	10	**5**	15	15	15	0.96	**48**	**48**	**47**	**0.99**
46	Kyrgyzstan	3-6	48	43	76	50	1	3	10	11	9	0.80	19	19	19	1.02
47	Mongolia	3-5	74	54	109	50	4	6	26	24	29	1.18	77	76	79	1.03
48	Tajikistan	3-6	56	42	58	44	.	.[y]	8	9	7	0.77	9	9	8	0.84
49	Turkmenistan	3-6	...	...	...	...	...	...	...	...	...	...	...	...	...	...
50	Uzbekistan	3-6	616	47	**523**	**49**	...	1	24	24	23	0.93	**26**	**26**	**26**	**1.00**
	East Asia and the Pacific															
51	Australia	4-4	*273*	*49*	218	48	*63*	75	*103*	*103*	*104*	*1.00*	78	79	78	0.98
52	Brunei Darussalam	4-5	11	49	13	49	66	72	81	79	82	1.04	88	88	88	1.00
53	Cambodia	3-5	58**	50**	115	50	22**	33[y]	5	5**	5**	1.03**	13	13	13	1.04
54	China	4-6	24 030	46	26 578	45	...	43	37	37	37	1.00	54	54	54	1.01
55	Cook Islands[2]	4-4	0.4	47	**0.5**	**49**	25	**34**	86	87	85	0.98	**181**	**180**	**181**	**1.01**
56	DPR Korea	4-5	...	...	...	...	...	...	...	...	...	...	...	...	...	...
57	Fiji	3-5	9	49	9[z]	50[z]	...	...	15	15	15	1.01	18[z]	17[z]	19[z]	1.07[z]
58	Indonesia	5-6	1 981**	49**	3 863	50	99**	97	23**	22**	23**	1.01**	43	43	44	1.03
59	Japan	3-5	2 962	49**	2 904	...	65	70	83	83**	84**	1.02**	88	...	...	...
60	Kiribati	3-5	...	...	...	...	...	...	...	...	...	...	...	...	...	...

NET ENROLMENT RATIO (NER) IN PRE-PRIMARY EDUCATION (%)				GROSS ENROLMENT RATIO (GER) IN PRE-PRIMARY AND OTHER ECCE PROGRAMMES (%)				NEW ENTRANTS TO THE FIRST GRADE OF PRIMARY EDUCATION WITH ECCE EXPERIENCE (%)			
School year ending in 2010				School year ending in 2010				School year ending in 2010			
Total	Male	Female	GPI (F/M)	Total	Male	Female	GPI (F/M)	Total	Male	Female	
										Arab States	
70	72	67	0.94	...	...	...	...	33^z	34^z	32^z	1
...	...	...	...	...	...	...	...	83^y	83^y	84^y	2
3	**3**	**3**	**0.97**	**4**	**4**	**4**	**0.97**	...	...	...	3
21**,^{z}	22**,^{z}	20**,^{z}	0.95**,^{z}	24^z	24^z	23^z	0.95^z	...	...	...	4
...	...	...	...	...	...	...	...	...	...	...	5
32	33	31	0.94	32	33	31	0.94	52.1	53.0	51.0	6
68^y	68^y	69^y	1.02^y	...	...	...	...	...	...	...	7
79	79	78	0.98	81	82	81	0.98	100	100	100	8
...	...	...	...	...	...	...	...	...	...	...	9
...	...	...	...	...	...	...	...	...	...	...	10
55	**64**	**45**	**0.70**	**63**	**73**	**53**	**0.72**	**47**	**48**	**46**	11
33	33	33	0.99	45	45	45	0.99	...	...	...	12
32	33	32	0.98	39	40	39	0.98	...	...	...	13
49^z	51^z	48^z	0.94^z	55^z	57^z	54^z	0.96^z	...	...	...	14
10**,^{y}	11**,^{y}	10**,^{y}	0.95**,^{y}	11	...	...	...	...	...	...	15
...	...	...	...	27^z	26^z	27^z	1.04^z	65^z	61**,^{z}	70**,^{z}	16
10	10	9	0.97	10	10	9	0.97	...	...	...	17
...	...	...	...	...	...	...	...	...	...	...	18
...	...	...	...	...	...	...	...	87	87	86	19
0.4	0.3	0.4	1.02	1	1	1	0.90	2	2	2	20
								Central and Eastern Europe			
53	53	52	0.98	56	56	55	0.98	...	...	...	21
89	89	89	1.00	120	121	119	0.98	...	...	...	22
12	12	12	1.01	...	...	...	...	...	...	...	23
76	76	76	0.99	79	80	79	0.99	...	...	...	24
61	61	61	0.99	61	62	61	0.98	...	...	...	25
...	...	...	...	106^z	107^z	105^z	0.98^z	...	...	...	26
92^z	91^z	92^z	1.01^z	96^z	96^z	96^z	1.00^z	...	...	...	27
84^z	84^z	83^z	0.99^z	85^z	85^z	84^z	0.98^z	...	...	...	28
82	83	81	0.97	84	85	82	0.96	...	...	...	29
73	74	72	0.98	74	75	73	0.97	...	...	...	30
31	...	...	...	40	40	39	0.96	...	...	...	31
64^z	63^z	64^z	1.01^z	66^z	65^z	66^z	1.01^z	...	...	...	32
74	74	74	0.99	76	76	75	0.98	91	90	93	33
78	77	78	1.01	79	79	79	1.01	...	...	...	34
73^z	73^z	72^z	0.99^z	90^z	91^z	89^z	0.98^z	...	...	...	35
52	52	53	1.01	...	...	...	...	99	99	99	36
...	...	...	...	91	92	90	0.98	...	...	...	37
85^z	86^z	84^z	0.98^z	86^z	87^z	85^z	0.98^z	...	...	...	38
24	24	25	1.03	25	25	26	1.05	...	...	...	39
22^z	22^z	21^z	0.95^z	...	...	...	...	...	...	...	40
...	...	...	...	97	99	96	0.97	...	...	...	41
								Central Asia			
...	...	...	...	31	29	34	1.15	...	...	...	42
22	22	21	0.98	25	26	25	0.97	11	11	11	43
41**,^{y}	38**,^{y}	45**,^{y}	1.17**,^{y}	...	...	...	...	...	...	...	44
47	**48**	**47**	**0.99**	**48**	**48**	**47**	**0.99**	...	...	...	45
16	16	16	1.02	19	19	19	1.02	18	18	18	46
58	57	58	1.03	100	99	102	1.03	68.2	67.5	68.9	47
7	7	6	0.84	9	9	8	0.84	...	...	...	48
...	...	...	...	...	...	...	...	...	...	...	49
20	**20**	**20**	**1.01**	**26**	**26**	**26**	**1.00**	...	...	...	50
								East Asia and the Pacific			
51	52	51	0.98	78	79	78	0.98	...	...	...	51
65	64	65	1.02	...	...	...	...	...	...	...	52
13	13	13	1.04	13	13	13	1.04	23	23	24	53
...	...	...	...	54	54	54	1.01	88	...	...	54
...	...	...	...	**181**	**180**	**181**	**1.01**	...	...	...	55
...	...	...	...	...	...	...	...	...	...	...	56
...	...	...	...	18^z	17^z	19^z	1.07^z	...	...	...	57
31	31	31	1.02	43	43	44	1.03	48^z	47^z	49^z	58
88	...	...	...	106	...	...	...	...	...	...	59
...	...	...	...	...	...	...	...	...	...	...	60

Table 3B (continued)

	Age group 2010	ENROLMENT IN PRE-PRIMARY EDUCATION				Enrolment in private institutions as % of total enrolment		GROSS ENROLMENT RATIO (GER) IN PRE-PRIMARY EDUCATION (%)							
		School year ending in 1999		2010		School year ending in 1999	2010	School year ending in 1999				2010			
Country or territory		Total (000)	% F	Total (000)	% F			Total	Male	Female	GPI (F/M)	Total	Male	Female	GPI (F/M)
61 Lao PDR	3-5	37	52	91	50	18	22	8	7	8	1.11	22	22	22	1.04
62 Macao, China	3-5	17	47	10	48	94	97	91	93	88	0.95	80	83	78	0.94
63 Malaysia	4-5	572	50	786^z	50^z	49	46^z	54	53	55	1.04	67^z	64^z	69^z	1.08^z
64 Marshall Islands	4-5	2	50	1	50	19	18	57	56	59	1.05	46	45	47	1.05
65 Micronesia, F. S.	3-5	3	...	...	...	...	...	37	...	...	...	...	...	...	...
66 Myanmar	3-4	41	...	159	51	90	61	2	...	...	...	10	10	10	1.06
67 Nauru^2	3-5	0.6	45	1^y	50^y	...	...	74	79	69	0.88	94^y	96^y	93^y	0.97^y
68 New Zealand	3-4	101	49	111	50	...	98	85	85	85	1.01	93	91	95	1.04
69 Niue^2	4-4	0.1	44	...	...	.	...	154	159	147	0.93	...	...	...	...
70 Palau^2	3-5	0.7	54	...	...	24	...	63	56	69	1.23*	...	...	...	...
71 Papua New Guinea	6-6	...	...	178^y	48^y	...	...	...	...	...	...	100^y	101^y	99^y	0.98^y
72 Philippines	5-5	593	50	1 166^z	49^z	47	37^z	30	29	31	1.06	51^z	51^z	52^z	1.02^z
73 Republic of Korea	3-5	536	47	1 538	48	75	83	76	76	75	0.98	119	118	119	1.01
74 Samoa	3-4	5**	53**	4	52	100**	100	53**	49	59	1.21**	38	35	41	1.19
75 Singapore	3-5	...	...	...	...	...	...	...	...	...	...	...	...	...	...
76 Solomon Islands	3-5	13**	48**	23	49	...	...	36**	36**	36**	1.02**	49	49	50	1.03
77 Thailand	3-5	2 745	49	2 755	48	19	20	91	90	91	1.00	100	101	100	0.99
78 Timor-Leste	4-5	...	...	...	...	...	...	...	...	...	...	...	...	...	...
79 Tokelau^2	3-4	0.1	42	...	...	.	...	99	107	90	0.84	...	...	...	...
80 Tonga	3-4	2	53	...	...	...	...	29	26	31	1.22	...	...	...	...
81 Tuvalu^2	3-5	0.7	50	...	...	...	...	96	92	100	1.09	...	...	...	...
82 Vanuatu	3-5	9	49	11	49	...	...	53	52	53	1.01	59	58	59	1.01
83 Viet Nam	3-5	2 179	48	3 410	47	49	47	40	41	39	0.94	82	84	79	0.94
Latin America and the Caribbean															
84 Anguilla^5	3-4	0.5	52	0.5^y	51^y	100	100	...	...	...	...	95**^{,y}	99**^{,y}	91**^{,y}	0.92**^{,y}
85 Antigua and Barbuda	3-4	2	...	2^y	49^y	100	100^y	57	...	...	...	76^y	76^y	76^y	1.00^y
86 Argentina	3-5	1 191	50	1 462^z	50^z	28	32^z	57	56	57	1.02	74^z	73^z	75^z	1.02^z
87 Aruba	4-5	3	49	3	48	83	75	95	95	94	0.99	112	115	109	0.94
88 Bahamas	3-4	1	51	...	...	...	...	11	11	12	1.08	...	...	...	...
89 Barbados	3-4	6	49	6*	50*	...	16*	75	73	76	1.04	108*	108*	108*	1.00*
90 Belize	3-4	4	50	7	51	...	85	24	25	23	0.90	46	45	47	1.06
91 Bermuda	4-4	...	...	...	...	...	...	...	...	...	...	...	...	...	...
92 Bolivia, P. S.	4-5	208	49	222^z	49^z	...	12^z	44	44	45	1.02	45^z	45^z	45^z	1.01^z
93 Brazil^1	4-6	5 733	49	6 792	49	28	27	58	58	58	1.00	...	...	...	...
94 British Virgin Islands^2	3-4	0.5	53	0.7^z	49^z	100	100^z	62	57	66	1.16	71**^{,z}	74**^{,z}	69**^{,z}	0.92**^{,z}
95 Cayman Islands	3-4	0.5	48	1^y	54^y	88	97^y	42	43	41	0.96	91^y	82^y	101^y	1.22^y
96 Chile	3-5	450	49	414^z	50^z	45	57^z	76	77	76	0.99	56^z	55^z	58^z	1.05^z
97 Colombia	3-5	1 034	50	1 302	49	45	28	39	38	39	1.02	49	49	49	1.00
98 Costa Rica	4-5	75	49	108	49	15	13	47	48	47	1.00	71	71	72	1.01
99 Cuba	3-5	484	50	389	48	.	.	105	103	107	1.04	104	104	104	1.00
100 Dominica	3-4	3	52	2	49	100	100	82	78	86	1.10	112	111	114	1.02
101 Dominican Republic	3-5	195	49	242	49	45	59	32	31	32	1.01	38	38	38	1.00
102 Ecuador	5-5	181	50	331**^{,y}	50**^{,y}	39	37**^{,y}	65	63	66	1.04	112**^{,y}	109**^{,y}	115**^{,y}	1.05**^{,y}
103 El Salvador	4-6	194	49	227	49	22**	15	41	40	41	1.02	64	63	65	1.02
104 Grenada	3-4	4	50	4	51	...	54	90	89	91	1.02	99	95	102	1.07
105 Guatemala	5-6	308	49	585	50	22	15	46	46	45	0.97	71	70	72	1.02
106 Guyana	4-5	37	49	25	49	1	6	101	103	99	0.97	76	74	78	1.07
107 Haiti	3-5	...	...	...	...	...	...	...	...	...	...	...	...	...	...
108 Honduras	3-5	120	50	248	50	...	14	22	21	22	1.05	44	43	44	1.03
109 Jamaica	3-5	138	51	159	49	88	92	79	76	82	1.08	...	...	...	...
110 Mexico	4-5	3 361	50	4 619	49	9	14	73	72	74	1.02	101	101	102	1.02
111 Montserrat^5	3-4	0.1	52	0.1^z	53^z	-	-^{z}	137	165	119	0.72	...	...	...	...
112 Netherlands Antilles	4-5	7	50	...	...	75	...	112	113	112	1.00	...	...	...	...
113 Nicaragua	3-5	161	50	218	50	17	16	28	27	28	1.04	55	55	56	1.03
114 Panama	4-5	49	49	93	49	23	18	39	39	40	1.01	67	67	67	1.01
115 Paraguay	3-5	123	50	155^z	49^z	29	30^z	29	29	30	1.03	35^z	35^z	35^z	1.01^z
116 Peru	3-5	1 017	50	1 376	49	15	25	56	56	57	1.03	79	79	79	1.00
117 Saint Kitts and Nevis	3-4	2	54**	2	48	72	64	129	116**	142**	1.22**	90	92	88	0.96
118 Saint Lucia	3-4	4**	50**	3	48	...	100	64**	63**	65**	1.04**	60	62	59	0.95
119 Saint Vincent/Grenadines	3-4	...	...	3^z	50^z	...	100^z	...	...	...	...	80^z	79^z	80^z	1.01^z
120 Suriname	4-5	16	49	18^z	50^z	45	45^z	85	84	85	1.01	85^z	85^z	86^z	1.01^z
121 Trinidad and Tobago	3-4	23**	50**	...	...	100**	...	59**	59**	60**	1.01**	...	...	...	...
122 Turks and Caicos Islands^5	4-5	0.8	54	1^z	50^z	47	...	...	...	...	...	...	...	...	...
123 Uruguay	3-5	100	49	133^z	49^z	...	37^z	60	59	60	1.02	89^z	89^z	89^z	1.01^z
124 Venezuela, B. R.	3-5	738	50	1 269	51	20	17	45	45	46	1.03	73	71	76	1.07

NET ENROLMENT RATIO (NER) IN PRE-PRIMARY EDUCATION (%)				GROSS ENROLMENT RATIO (GER) IN PRE-PRIMARY AND OTHER ECCE PROGRAMMES (%)				NEW ENTRANTS TO THE FIRST GRADE OF PRIMARY EDUCATION WITH ECCE EXPERIENCE (%)			
School year ending in 2010				School year ending in 2010				School year ending in 2010			
Total	Male	Female	GPI (F/M)	Total	Male	Female	GPI (F/M)	Total	Male	Female	
21	21	22	1.04	22	22	22	1.04	27	26	28	61
78	80	75	0.94	80	83	78	0.94	…	…	…	62
58z	56z	60z	1.07z	67z	64z	69z	1.08z	90z	88z	92z	63
…	…	…	…	46	45	47	1.05	…	…	…	64
…	…	…	…					…	…	…	65
10	10	10	1.06	…	…	…	…	20	19	21	66
…	…	…		…	…	…					67
92	90	94	1.04	158	155	161	1.04	…	…	…	68
…	…	…		…	…	…					69
…	…	…		…	…	…					70
				100y	101y	99y	0.98y				71
39z	38z	39z	1.01z	51z	51z	52z	1.02z	70y	69y	70y	72
85	85	85	1.01	119	118	119	1.01				73
…	…	…	…	38	35	41	1.19	…	…	…	74
…	…	…	…	…	…	…					75
…	…	…	…	49	49	50	1.03	…	…	…	76
93	**92**	**93**	**1.01**	**100**	**101**	**100**	**0.99**				77
…	…	…		…	…	…					78
…	…	…		…	…	…					79
…	…	…		…	…	…					80
				…	…	…					81
41	40	42	1.05	59	58	59	1.01	70	70	71	82
65	…	…	…	82	84	79	0.94	…	…	…	83

Latin America and the Caribbean

NET ENROLMENT RATIO (NER) IN PRE-PRIMARY EDUCATION (%)				GROSS ENROLMENT RATIO (GER) IN PRE-PRIMARY AND OTHER ECCE PROGRAMMES (%)				NEW ENTRANTS TO THE FIRST GRADE OF PRIMARY EDUCATION WITH ECCE EXPERIENCE (%)			
Total	Male	Female	GPI (F/M)	Total	Male	Female	GPI (F/M)	Total	Male	Female	
95**,y	99**,y	91**,y	0.92**,y	95**,y	99**,y	91**,y	0.92	100	100	100	84
70**,y	70y	70y	0.99y	119y	120y	118y	0.99y	82	81	83	85
73z	73z	74z	1.02z	74z	73z	75z	1.02z	…	…	…	86
98z	100z	96z	0.96z	112	115	109	0.94	…	…	…	87
…	…	…	…	…	…	…		56y	55y	57y	88
96*	95*	96*	1.01*	…	…	…		100*	100*	100*	89
44	43	45	1.05	46	45	47	1.06	…	…	…	90
…	…	…		…	…	…		…	…	…	91
32z	32z	32z	1.02z	45z	45z	45z	1.01z	…	…	…	92
								…	…	…	93
58**,z	61**,z	55**,z	0.90**,z	131**,z	135**,z	128**,z	0.95	90z	90z	89z	94
82y	72y	92y	1.28y	143y	…	…	…	95y	94y	95y	95
54z	52z	55z	1.06z	56z	55z	58z	1.05z	…	…	…	96
44	44	45	1.01	59	59	59	1.00	…	…	…	97
…	…	…		76	76	77	1.01	90	89	90	98
90	**90**	**90**	**1.00**	**182**	**178**	**187**	**1.05**	**100**	**100**	**100**	99
82	77	88	1.15	112	111	114	1.02	84	82	86	100
36	36	36	1.00	38	38	38	1.00	59	57	62	101
…	…	…		…	…	…		…	…	…	102
55	54	55	1.03	65	65	66	1.02	78	77	80	103
94	90	98	1.09	99	95	102	1.07	100	100	100	104
56	56	57	1.01	71	70	72	1.02	…	…	…	105
65	64	67	1.06	76	74	78	1.07	100	100	100	106
…	…	…		…	…	…		…	…	…	107
27y	27y	27y	1.03y	…	…	…					108
84	…	…	…	…	…	…					109
84	84	85	1.01	101	101	102	1.02	…	…	…	110
…	…	…		…	…	…		100z	100z	100z	111
…	…	…		…	…	…					112
55	55	56	1.03	55	55	56	1.03	42	42	43	113
60	60	60	1.00	67	67	67	1.01	81	81	82	114
32z	32z	33z	1.02z	35z	35z	35z	1.01z	82z	81z	83z	115
78	78	78	1.00	79	79	79	1.00	80.5	80.6	80.4	116
…	…	…		149	149	148	0.99	99	100	99	117
44	44	44	0.99	60	62	59	0.95	…	…	…	118
…	…	…		80z	79z	80z	1.01z	76	73	79	119
80z	79z	80z	1.00z	85z	85z	86z	1.01z	100z	100z	100z	120
…	…	…		…	…	…		84*	82*	86*	121
				…	…	…					122
78z	78z	78z	1.01z	…	…	…		97**,z	96**,z	99**,z	123
70	68	73	1.07	90	87	94	1.08	85	82	88	124

Table 3B (continued)

		ENROLMENT IN PRE-PRIMARY EDUCATION				Enrolment in private institutions as % of total enrolment		GROSS ENROLMENT RATIO (GER) IN PRE-PRIMARY EDUCATION (%)							
		School year ending in				School year ending in		School year ending in							
		1999		2010		1999	2010	1999				2010			
	Age group	Total		Total							GPI				GPI
Country or territory	2010	(000)	% F	(000)	% F			Total	Male	Female	(F/M)	Total	Male	Female	(F/M)
North America and Western Europe															
125 Andorra	3-5	...	...	2	47	...	2	...	...	...	...	102	104	99	0.96
126 Austria	3-5	225	49	240	49	25	28	80	81	80	0.99	100	100	100	1.00
127 Belgium	3-5	399	49	425ᶻ	49ᶻ	56	53ᶻ	114	115	114	0.98	118ᶻ	118ᶻ	118ᶻ	1.00ᶻ
128 Canada	4-5	512	49	489ʸ	49ʸ	8	6ʸ	63	64	63	1.00	71ʸ	71ʸ	71ʸ	1.00ʸ
129 Cyprus²	3-5	19	49	21	49	54	51	60	59	60	1.02	81	81	81	1.01
130 Denmark	3-6	251	49	251ᶻ	49ᶻ	27	21ᶻ	90	90	90	1.00	96ᶻ	97ᶻ	96ᶻ	0.99ᶻ
131 Finland	3-6	125	49	157	49	10	9	47	48	47	0.99	68	68	68	1.00
132 France⁶	3-5	2 393	49	2 551	49	13	13	112	112	112	1.00	109	109	108	0.99
133 Germany	3-5	2 333	48	2 360	48	54	65	101	101	100	0.98	114	114	113	0.98
134 Greece	4-5	143	49	...	...	3	...	67	66	67	1.01	...	...	...	...
135 Iceland	3-5	12	48	12ᶻ	49ᶻ	5	12ᶻ	86	87	86	0.98	97ᶻ	97ᶻ	97ᶻ	1.00ᶻ
136 Ireland	4-4	...	...	62	48	...	97	...	...	...	...	98	99	97	0.98
137 Israel	3-5	294	48	428ᶻ	50ᶻ	...	9ᶻ	89	89	88	0.99	106ᶻ	103ᶻ	109ᶻ	1.05ᶻ
138 Italy	3-5	1 578	48	1 681	48	30	31	97	97	96	0.99	98	100	96	0.97
139 Luxembourg	3-5	12	49	15ʸ	48ʸ	5	8ʸ	72	72	72	1.00	87ʸ	87ʸ	86ʸ	0.99ʸ
140 Malta	3-4	10	48	9	48	37	34	100	101	99	0.99	117	119	115	0.97
141 Monaco⁵	3-5	0.9	52	0.9	50	26	20	...	...	...	...	...	...	...	...
142 Netherlands	4-5	390	49	379	49	69	...	97	98	97	0.99	93	93	93	1.00
143 Norway	3-5	139	50	174	49	40	45	75	73	77	1.06	99	100	98	0.98
144 Portugal	3-5	220	49	275ᶻ	48ᶻ	52	48ᶻ	67	67	66	1.00	82ᶻ	82ᶻ	82ᶻ	1.00ᶻ
145 San Marino⁵	3-5	1.0	47	1	46	.	.	...	...	...	...	...	...	...	...
146 Spain	3-5	1 131	49	1 822	49	32	36	99	99	99	1.00	126	126	127	1.00
147 Sweden	3-6	360	49	399	49	10	16	76	75	76	1.01	95	95	95	1.00
148 Switzerland	5-6	158	48	147	49	6	4	92	93	92	1.00	99	99	100	1.01
149 United Kingdom	3-4	1 155	49	1 122ᶻ	49ᶻ	6	28ᶻ	77	77	77	1.00	81ᶻ	81ᶻ	82ᶻ	1.01ᶻ
150 United States	3-5	7 183	48	8 840	50	34	45	59	60	58	0.97	69	68	70	1.04
South and West Asia															
151 Afghanistan	3-6	...	...	...	...	...	...	...	...	...	...	...	...	...	...
152 Bangladesh	3-5	1 825	50	1 234*	49*	...	48*	19	18	19	1.04	13*	14*	13*	0.99*
153 Bhutan	4-5	0.3	48	2	51	100	68	0.9	1.0	0.9	0.92	5	5	5	1.08
154 India	3-5	13 869	48	41 301	49	...	...	19	18	19	1.02	55	54	56	1.04
155 Iran, Islamic Republic of	5-5	220	50	463	51	16	5	14	14	15	1.03	42	41	44	1.08
156 Maldives	3-5	12	48	18	49	...	91	56	56	57	1.01	114	113	115	1.02
157 Nepal¹	3-4	216*	42*	1 019	48	...	16	10*	12*	9*	0.76*	...	...	...	...
158 Pakistan	3-4	5 160*	40*	...	...	...	...	63*	74*	51*	0.70*	...	...	...	...
159 Sri Lanka	3-4	...	...	...	...	...	...	...	...	...	...	...	...	...	...
Sub-Saharan Africa															
160 Angola	5-5	389**	40**	668	50	...	0.8	27**	33**	22**	0.66**	104	103	105	1.02
161 Benin	4-5	18	48	97	51	20	25	4	5	4	0.93	18	18	19	1.04
162 Botswana	3-5	...	...	24ᶻ	50ᶻ	...	...	...	...	...	...	19ᶻ	19ᶻ	19ᶻ	1.02ᶻ
163 Burkina Faso	3-5	20	50	49	49	34	76	2	2	2	1.03	3	3	3	1.01
164 Burundi	4-6	5	50	55	50	49	20	0.8	0.8	0.8	1.01	9	9	9	1.00
165 Cameroon	4-5	104	48	317	50	57	65	11	11	11	0.95	28	28	29	1.02
166 Cape Verde	3-5	20**	50	22	50	...	64	53**	53**	54**	1.02**	70	70	70	1.00
167 Central African Republic	3-5	...	...	21	51	...	55	...	...	...	...	6	6	6	1.02
168 Chad	3-5	...	...	21	48	...	46	...	...	...	...	2	2	2	0.91
169 Comoros	3-5	1	51	14ʸ	48ʸ	100	100ʸ	3	3	3	1.07	22ʸ	22ʸ	21ʸ	0.97ʸ
170 Congo	3-5	6	61	43	51	85	72	2	2	3	1.61	13	12	13	1.07
171 Côte d'Ivoire	3-5	36	49	75	50	46	40	2	3	2	0.96	4	4	4	1.00
172 D. R. Congo	3-5	39**	49**	219	51	93**	91ᶻ	0.7**	0.8**	0.7**	0.99**	3	3	3	1.06
173 Equatorial Guinea	3-6	17	51	40ʸ	57ʸ	37	...	27	27	28	1.04	55ʸ	47ʸ	63ʸ	1.33ʸ
174 Eritrea	5-6	12	47	41	48	97	53	5	6	5	0.89	14	14	13	0.95
175 Ethiopia	4-6	90	49	341	49	100	95	1	1	1	0.97	5	5	5	0.96
176 Gabon	3-5	15**	...	45	50	68**	74	14**	...	...	...	42	41	43	1.04
177 Gambia	3-6	29	47	65	51	...	77	18	19	17	0.91	30	30	31	1.04
178 Ghana	3-5	506	49	1 338ᶻ	50ᶻ	26**	28**·ᶻ	31	30	31	1.03	69ᶻ	68ᶻ	70ᶻ	1.04ᶻ
179 Guinea	4-6	...	...	121	49	...	72	...	...	...	...	14	14	14	0.99
180 Guinea-Bissau	4-6	4**	51**	9	51	62**	84	4**	4**	4**	1.06**	7	7	7	1.06
181 Kenya	3-5	1 188	50	1 914ᶻ	49ᶻ	10	38ᶻ	43	43	43	1.00	52ᶻ	52ᶻ	52ᶻ	0.99ᶻ
182 Lesotho	3-5	33**	52**	53	...	100**	...	20**	19**	21**	1.08**	33	...	...	...

	NET ENROLMENT RATIO (NER) IN PRE-PRIMARY EDUCATION [%]				GROSS ENROLMENT RATIO (GER) IN PRE-PRIMARY AND OTHER ECCE PROGRAMMES [%]				NEW ENTRANTS TO THE FIRST GRADE OF PRIMARY EDUCATION WITH ECCE EXPERIENCE [%]			
	School year ending in 2010				School year ending in 2010				School year ending in 2010			
	Total	Male	Female	GPI (F/M)	Total	Male	Female	GPI (F/M)	Total	Male	Female	
										North America and Western Europe		
	86	88	83	0.95	102	104	99	0.96	100	100	100	125
	...	...	...	...	100	100	100	1.00	...	...	...	126
	98^z	98^z	99^z	1.00^z	118^z	118^z	118^z	1.00^z	...	...	...	127
	71^y	71^y	71^y	1.00^y	...	...	...	...	...	...	...	128
	72	71	73	1.02	81	81	81	1.01	...	...	...	129
	92^z	91^z	93^z	1.03^z	96^z	97^z	96^z	0.99^z	...	...	...	130
	67	67	67	1.00	68	68	68	1.00	...	...	...	131
	100	100	99	1.00	109	109	108	0.99	...	...	...	132
	...	...	...	...	114	114	113	0.98	...	...	...	133
	...	...	...	...	...	...	...	...	...	...	...	134
	97^z	97^z	97^z	1.00^z	...	...	...	...	...	...	...	135
	28	30	25	0.86	98	99	97	0.98	...	...	...	136
	97^z	94^z	100^z	1.07^z	106^z	103^z	109^z	1.05^z	...	...	...	137
	93	94	91	0.97	98	100	96	0.97	...	...	...	138
	85^y	85^y	85^y	1.00^y	87^y	87^y	86^y	0.99^y	...	...	...	139
	98	100	97	0.97	117	119	115	0.97	...	...	...	140
	...	...	...	...	...	...	...	...	...	...	...	141
	93	93	93	1.00	...	...	...	...	...	...	...	142
	99	100	98	0.98	99	100	98	0.98	...	...	...	143
	81^z	81^z	81^z	1.00^z	82^z	82^z	82^z	1.00^z	...	...	...	144
	...	...	...	...	...	...	...	...	...	...	...	145
	98	98	99	1.01	126	126	127	1.00	...	...	...	146
	95	95	95	1.00	95	95	95	1.00	...	...	...	147
	76	76	76	1.00	99	99	100	1.01	...	...	...	148
	76^z	75^z	77^z	1.02^z	...	...	...	...	...	...	...	149
	64	62	65	1.05	...	...	...	...	...	...	...	150
										South and West Asia		
	...	...	...	...	...	...	...	...	...	...	...	151
	13*	13*	13*	0.99*	13*	14*	13*	0.99*	...	...	...	152
	...	...	...	...	5	5	5	1.08	...	...	...	153
	...	...	...	...	55	54	56	1.04	...	...	...	154
	...	...	...	...	42	41	44	1.08	46^z	43^z	48^z	155
	92	91	93	1.02	114	113	115	1.02	98	98	98	156
	...	...	...	...	...	...	...	...	52	52	52	157
	...	...	...	...	...	...	...	...	...	...	...	158
	...	...	...	...	...	...	...	...	91	91	92	159
										Sub-Saharan Africa		
	66*	65*	67*	1.04*	...	...	...	...	...	...	...	160
	...	...	...	...	18	18	19	1.04	...	...	...	161
	15^z	15^z	16^z	1.04^z	...	...	...	...	...	...	...	162
	3	3	3	1.01	3	3	3	1.01	6	6	6	163
	7	7	7	1.00	9	9	9	1.00	7	6	7	164
	20	...	...	...	28	28	29	1.02	...	...	...	165
	65	65	65	1.00	70	70	70	1.00	87^y	85^y	88^y	166
	6	6	6	1.02	6	6	6	1.02	...	...	...	167
	2	2	2	0.92	...	...	...	...	4	4	4	168
	...	...	...	...	...	...	...	...	...	...	...	169
	13	12	13	1.07	13	12	13	1.07	9	9	10	170
	4^z	4^z	4^z	0.98^z	4	4	4	1.00	...	...	...	171
	...	...	...	...	3	3	3	1.06	...	...	...	172
	...	...	...	...	...	...	...	...	87	86	87	173
	9	9	9	0.95	...	...	...	...	50^y	48^y	52^y	174
	4	4	4	0.96	5	5	5	0.96	5^y	5^y	6^y	175
	42	41	43	1.04	42	41	43	1.04	...	...	...	176
	27	27	28	1.04	...	...	...	...	...	...	...	177
	47**,^{z}	46**,^{z}	49**,^{z}	1.05**,^{z}	...	...	...	...	73	69	76	178
	9	9	9	0.99	14	14	14	0.99	20^y	19^y	21^y	179
	5	5	5	1.05	...	...	...	...	...	...	...	180
	29^z	27^z	30^z	1.12^z	52^z	52^z	52^z	0.99^z	...	...	...	181
	...	...	...	...	...	...	...	...	...	...	...	182

Table 3B (continued)

	Age group 2010	ENROLMENT IN PRE-PRIMARY EDUCATION				Enrolment in private institutions as % of total enrolment		GROSS ENROLMENT RATIO (GER) IN PRE-PRIMARY EDUCATION (%)							
		School year ending in				School year ending in		School year ending in							
		1999		2010		1999	2010	1999				2010			
Country or territory		Total (000)	% F	Total (000)	% F			Total	Male	Female	GPI (F/M)	Total	Male	Female	GPI (F/M)
183 Liberia	3-5	112	42	...	...	39	...	47	54	40	0.75	...	...	...	...
184 Madagascar	3-5	50**	51**	164	50	...	91	3**	3**	3**	1.02**	9	9	9	1.03
185 Malawi	3-5	...	...	...	...	...	...	...	...	...	...	...	...	...	...
186 Mali	3-6	21	51	71	50	...	73	1	1	2	1.10	3	3	3	1.05
187 Mauritius	3-4	42	50	35	49	85	82	95	94	96	1.02	96	97	96	0.99
188 Mozambique	3-5	...	...	...	...	...	...	...	...	...	...	...	...	...	...
189 Namibia	5-6	35	53	...	...	100	...	33	31	35	1.15	...	...	...	...
190 Niger	4-6	12	50	96	50	33	15	1	1	1	1.05	6	6	6	1.07
191 Nigeria	3-5	939	48	2 021	49	...	27	8	8	8	0.94	14	14	14	0.99
192 Rwanda	4-6	17**	50**	112	51	...	100	3**	3**	3**	0.98**	11	11	12	1.05
193 Sao Tome and Principe	3-5	4	52	9	51	-	7	24	23	26	1.13	62	60	63	1.05
194 Senegal	4-6	24	50	147	52	68	50	3	3	3	1.00	13	12	14	1.12
195 Seychelles	4-5	3	49	3	48	5	10	110	110	111	1.01	102	106	97	0.92
196 Sierra Leone	3-5	17	...	37	51	...	41	4	...	...	...	7	7	7	1.03
197 Somalia	3-5	...	...	...	...	...	...	...	...	...	...	...	...	...	...
198 South Africa	6-6	207	50	667^z	50^z	26	5^z	21	21	21	1.01	65^z	65^z	65^z	1.00^z
199 South Sudan		...	...	...	...	...	...	...	...	...	...	...	...	...	...
200 Swaziland	3-5	...	...	21	50	...	100	...	...	...	...	23	22	23	1.03
201 Togo	3-5	11	50	43	51	53	33	3	3	3	0.99	9	9	9	1.02
202 Uganda	3-5	...	...	499	51	...	100	...	...	...	...	14	14	14	1.05
203 United Republic of Tanzania	5-6	...	...	925	50	...	5	...	...	...	...	33	33	34	1.02
204 Zambia	3-6	...	...	...	...	...	...	...	...	...	...	...	...	...	...
205 Zimbabwe	3-5	...	...	...	...	...	...	...	...	...	...	...	...	...	...

		Sum	% F	Sum	% F	Median		Weighted average				Weighted average			
I	World	111 745	48	163 525	48	29	33	32	33	32	0.97	48	48	48	1.00
II	Countries in transition	7 456	47**	8 739**	48**	-	1	46	47**	45**	0.94**	64**	65**	64**	0.98**
III	Developed countries	25 314	49	28 106	49	9	13	75	76	75	0.99	85	84	85	1.01
IV	Developing countries	78 975	47	126 680	48	47	50	27	27	26	0.96	43	43	43	1.00
V	Arab States	2 407	42	3 904**	47**	78	76	15	17	13	0.77	22**	23**	22**	0.94**
VI	Central and Eastern Europe	9 443	48	10 906**	48**	0.6	2.1	51	52	50	0.96	69**	70**	69**	0.98**
VII	Central Asia	1 272	48	1 591	49	0.1	1.0	19	20	19	0.95	30	30	30	1.00
VIII	East Asia and the Pacific	36 704	47	44 502	47	49	54	39	39	39	1.00	57	57	58	1.01
IX	East Asia	36 251	47	43 932	47	57	47	39	39	39	1.00	57	57	57	1.01
X	Pacific	452**	49**	570	48	...	...	67**	67**	67**	1.00**	78	78	78	1.00
XI	Latin America/Caribbean	16 010	49	20 541	49	42	32	54	54	55	1.02	70	70	71	1.01
XII	Caribbean	...	...	...	...	85	88	...	...	...	...	...	...	...	...
XIII	Latin America	15 712	49	20 223	49	23	18	55	55	56	1.01	72	71	72	1.01
XIV	N. America/W. Europe	19 102	48	22 050	49	26	24	76	77	76	0.98	85	85	86	1.01
XV	South and West Asia	21 381	46	48 144	49	...	48	21	22	21	0.93	48	48	49	1.02
XVI	Sub-Saharan Africa	5 427**	48**	11 887	50	53	55	10**	10**	10**	0.95**	17	17	18	1.01

		Sum	% F	Sum	% F	Median		Weighted average				Weighted average			
XVII	Countries with low income	5 723**	49**	9 357	49	...	53	11**	11**	10**	0.98**	15	15	15	1.00
XVII	Countries with middle income	80 598	47	124 757	48	25	26	32	32	31	0.97	52	52	52	1.01
XIX	Lower middle	31 173	46	65 552	49	46	28	22	23	21	0.93	45	45	46	1.01
XX	Upper middle	49 425	48	59 206	47	20	20	43	43	44	1.01	62	61	62	1.02
XXI	Countries with high income	25 424	48	29 411	49	34	34	72	72	72	0.99	82	82	82	1.01

Source: UNESCO Institute for Statistics database (UIS, 2012). Enrolment ratios in the table are based on the United Nations Population Division estimates, revision 2010 (United Nations, 2011), median variant.
Note A: The country groupings by income level presented in the tables are as defined by the World Bank. They are based on the list of countries by income group as revised in July 2011.
Note B: The median values for 1999 and 2010 are not comparable since they are not necessarily based on the same number of countries.

1. Enrolment ratios for one or both of the two school years were not calculated due to inconsistencies in the population data.
2. National population data were used to calculate enrolment ratios.
3. Enrolment and population data exclude Transnistria.
4. Enrolment and population data exclude the Nagorno-Karabakh region.
5. Enrolment ratios for one or both of the two school years were not calculated due to lack of United Nations population data by age.

	NET ENROLMENT RATIO (NER) IN PRE-PRIMARY EDUCATION (%)				GROSS ENROLMENT RATIO (GER) IN PRE-PRIMARY AND OTHER ECCE PROGRAMMES (%)				NEW ENTRANTS TO THE FIRST GRADE OF PRIMARY EDUCATION WITH ECCE EXPERIENCE (%)			
	School year ending in 2010				School year ending in 2010				School year ending in 2010			
	Total	Male	Female	GPI (F/M)	Total	Male	Female	GPI (F/M)	Total	Male	Female	
	...	...	...		...	...	...		...	...	...	183
	8	8	8	1.03	10	10	10	1.03	...	...	...	184
	...	...	...		...	...	...		...	...	...	185
	3	**3**	**3**	**1.05**	3	3	3	1.05	16	15	16	186
	89	89	88	0.99	96	97	96	0.99	99	99	99	187
	...	...	...		...	...	...		...	...	...	188
	...	...	...		...	...	...		...	...	...	189
	5	**5**	**5**	**1.06**	**6**	**6**	**6**	**1.07**	13^z	12^z	14^z	190
	...	...	...		...	...	...		...	...	...	191
	10	**10**	**11**	**1.05**	**11**	**11**	**12**	**1.05**	...	...	...	192
	57	**55**	**58**	**1.06**	...	...	...		**42**	**38**	**45**	193
	9	8	9	1.12	13	12	14	1.12	...	...	...	194
	87	91	83	0.91	102	106	97	0.92	...	...	...	195
	...	...	...		...	...	...		...	...	...	196
	...	...	...		...	...	...		...	...	...	197
	...	...	...		88^z	88^z	88^z	1.00^z	...	...	...	198
	...	...	...		...	...	...		...	...	...	199
	23	22	23	1.03	23	22	23	1.03	...	...	...	200
	9	9	9	1.02	9	9	9	1.02	...	...	...	201
	14	14	14	1.05	...	...	...		...	...	...	202
	33	33	34	1.02	33	33	34	1.02	...	...	...	203
	...	...	...		...	...	...		16	16	17	204
	...	...	...		...	...	...		...	...	...	205
	Weighted average				Weighted average				Median			
	...	...	...	...	...	...	...	...	...	...	...	I
	...	...	...	...	...	...	...	...	...	...	...	II
	...	...	...	...	...	...	...	...	...	...	...	III
	...	...	...	...	...	...	...	...	...	...	...	IV
	...	...	...	...	...	...	...	...	...	...	...	V
	...	...	...	...	...	...	...	...	...	...	...	VI
	...	...	...	...	...	...	...	...	...	...	...	VII
	...	...	...	...	...	...	...	...	...	...	...	VIII
	...	...	...	...	...	...	...	...	...	...	...	IX
	...	...	...	...	...	...	...	...	...	...	...	X
	...	...	...	...	...	...	...	...	85	82	88	XI
	...	...	...	...	...	...	...	...	97	97	97	XII
	...	...	...	...	...	...	...	...	82	81	83	XIII
	...	...	...	...	...	...	...	...	...	...	...	XIV
	...	...	...	...	...	...	...	...	...	...	...	XV
	...	...	...	...	...	...	...	...	...	...	...	XVI
	Weighted average				Weighted average				Median			
	...	...	...	...	...	...	...	...	...	...	...	XVII
	...	...	...	...	...	...	...	...	...	...	...	XVII
	...	...	...	...	...	...	...	...	...	...	...	XIX
	...	...	...	...	...	...	...	...	...	...	...	XX
	...	...	...	...	...	...	...	...	...	...	...	XXI

6. Data include French overseas departments and territories (DOM-TOM).
Data in bold are for the school year ending in 2011, those in italics are for 2000 and those in bold italic are for 2001.
(z) Data are for the school year ending in 2009.
(y) Data are for the school year ending in 2008.
(*) National estimate.

(**) For country level data: UIS partial estimate; for regional and other country-grouping sums and weighted averages: partial imputation due to incomplete country coverage (between 33% and 60% of population for the region or other country grouping).
- Magnitude nil or negligible.
(.) The category is not applicable or does not exist.
(. . .) No data available.

Education for All Global Monitoring Report 2012

Table 4
Access to primary education

Country or territory	Compulsory education (age group)[1]	Official primary school age entry 2010	New entrants (000) School year ending in 1999	New entrants (000) School year ending in 2010	GIR 1999 Total	GIR 1999 Male	GIR 1999 Female	GIR 1999 GPI (F/M)	GIR 2010 Total	GIR 2010 Male	GIR 2010 Female	GIR 2010 GPI (F/M)
Arab States												
Algeria	6-16	6	745	662	101	102	100	0.98	106	107	105	0.98
Bahrain[2]	6-15	6	13	15^z	108	106	110	1.03	...	...	...	...
Djibouti	6-16	6	6	**13**	29	33	24	0.74	**60**	**63**	**57**	**0.90**
Egypt	6-14	6	1 451**	1 758	90**	92**	88**	0.96**	103	...	...	...
Iraq	6-12	6	709**	...	107**	113**	101**	0.89**	...	...	...	...
Jordan	6-16	6	126	146	100	100	101	1.00	96	97	96	0.99
Kuwait[2]	6-14	6	35	45	104	103	105	1.01	...	...	...	...
Lebanon	6-12	6	75**	72	99**	102**	95**	0.93**	107	108	106	0.98
Libya	6-15	6	...	...	...	...	...	...	...	...	...	...
Mauritania	6-14	6	**73**	97	**96**	**96**	**95**	**0.99**	105	104	107	1.04
Morocco	6-15	6	731	**636**	112	115	108	0.94	**110**	**110**	**109**	**0.99**
Oman	.	6	52	51^z	88	87	88	1.02	106^z	108^z	103^z	0.96^z
Palestine	6-16	6	95	103	95	95	95	1.00	91	91	91	1.00
Qatar	6-18	6	11**	16	108**	107**	109**	1.02**	107	107	107	1.00
Saudi Arabia	6-11	6	...	578	...	...	...	...	105	104	106	1.02
Sudan (pre-secession)	6-14	6	447	915^z	47	51	42	0.81	79^z	83**,z	75**,z	0.91**,z
Syrian Arab Republic	6-12	6	466	604	109	113	106	0.94	117	116	117	1.00
Tunisia	6-16	6	204	163^z	102	103	101	0.98	106^z	106^z	106^z	0.99^z
United Arab Emirates[2]	6-14	6	47	72	94	94	94	1.00	...	...	...	...
Yemen	6-15	6	440	714	76	89	63	0.71	103	109	96	0.88
Central and Eastern Europe												
Albania	6-14	6	67**	42	102**	103**	101**	0.98**	87	87	87	1.01
Belarus[2]	6-15	6	173	87	130	131	130	0.99	96	96	96	1.00
Bosnia and Herzegovina	6-14	6	...	36	...	...	...	...	99	99	100	1.01
Bulgaria	7-16	7	93	63	101	102	100	0.98	98	98	98	0.99
Croatia	6-15	7	50	39	94	95	93	0.98	92	92	92	1.00
Czech Republic	6-15	6	124	93^z	100	101	99	0.98	107^z	107^z	108^z	1.01^z
Estonia	7-17	7	18	12^z	97	98	97	0.99	100^z	100^z	100^z	1.00^z
Hungary	6-18	7	127	96^z	104	106	102	0.97	102^z	103^z	102^z	0.99^z
Latvia	7-16	7	32	20	96	96**	95**	0.99**	101	100	102	1.02
Lithuania	6-16	7	54	28	104	104	103	0.99	92	93	91	0.98
Montenegro	6-15	7	**9**	8	**104**	**106**	**103**	**0.97**	96	97	94	0.97
Poland	6-18	7	535	356^z	101	...	...	...	99^z	99^z	99^z	1.00^z
Republic of Moldova[3,4]	7-16	7	62	35	105	105**	104**	1.00**	97	98	97	0.98
Romania	6-16	7	269	202	89	90	89	0.99	94	94	94	0.99
Russian Federation	6-18	7	1 866	1 322^z	93	...	...	...	102^z	...	...	...
Serbia[3]	7-15	7	...	72	...	...	...	...	92	92	92	1.00
Slovakia	6-16	6	75	50	98	98	97	0.99	96	96	96	1.00
Slovenia	6-15	6	21	18^z	97	97	96	0.99	99^z	99^z	98^z	0.99^z
TFYR Macedonia	6-19	6	32	23	103	103	103	1.00	98	97	100	1.03
Turkey	6-14	6	...	1 234^z	...	...	...	...	98^z	99^z	97^z	0.98^z
Ukraine	6-17	6	...	...	...	...	...	...	...	...	...	...
Central Asia												
Armenia	7-16	7	...	36	...	...	...	...	92	91	93	1.02
Azerbaijan[3,5]	6-16	6	175	119	100	99	101	1.02	90	91	88	0.98
Georgia	6-12	6	74	46	96	96	96	1.00	101	100	102	1.02
Kazakhstan	7-18	7	303**	**261**	101**	100**	103**	1.02**	**111**	**112**	**111**	**1.00**
Kyrgyzstan	7-16	7	120*	101	99*	98*	99*	1.02*	105	106	104	0.99
Mongolia	6-15	6	70	50	108	110	107	0.97	114	117	111	0.95
Tajikistan	7-18	7	177	167	98	100	95	0.95	100	102	98	0.96
Turkmenistan	7-17	7	...	...	...	...	...	...	...	...	...	...
Uzbekistan	7-19	7	677	**482**	102	101**	103**	1.01**	**96**	**97**	**94**	**0.96**
East Asia and the Pacific												
Australia	6-17	5	...	...	...	...	...	...	...	...	...	...
Brunei Darussalam	6-15	6	8	7	112	113	111	0.99	96	95	97	1.03
Cambodia	6-15	6	397	416	110	113	107	0.95	143	143	144	1.01
China[6]	6-15	7	**19 598**	16 677	**93**	...	...	...	97	95	99	1.04
Cook Islands[3]	5-16	5	0.6	**0.3**	131	...	...	...	**121**	**116**	**127**	**1.09**
DPR Korea	5-16	6	...	...	...	...	...	...	...	...	...	...
Fiji	6-15	6	21	17^z	108	108	107	0.99	102^z	102^z	102^z	0.99^z
Indonesia	7-15	7	**4 818**	5 154^z	**110**	**113**	**107**	**0.95**	119^z	121^z	118^z	0.97^z
Japan	6-15	6	1 222	1 149	101	101	101	1.00	102	102	102	1.00
Kiribati	6-14	6	3	3^y	117	114	120	1.05	115^y	116^y	113^y	0.98^y

Table 4

NET INTAKE RATE (NIR) IN PRIMARY EDUCATION (%)								SCHOOL LIFE EXPECTANCY (expected number of years of formal schooling from primary to tertiary education)						
School year ending in								School year ending in						
1999				2010				1999			2010			
Total	Male	Female	GPI (F/M)	Total	Male	Female	GPI (F/M)	Total	Male	Female	Total	Male	Female	Country or territory
Arab States														
77	78	76	0.97	89	90	88	0.97	...	...	...	13.6^z	13.4^z	13.8^z	Algeria
86	84	88	1.05	...	...	...	...	13.3**	12.8**	14.0**	...	...	...	Bahrain[2]
21	24	18	0.75	41**,y	43**,y	39**,y	0.91**,y	3.0**	3.6**	2.5**	**5.7****	**6.2****	**5.3****	Djibouti
...	...	...	...	...	...	...	...	11.6**	...	...	12.1**	12.4**	11.8**	Egypt
83**	86**	79**	0.91**	...	...	...	...	8.5**	9.7**	7.3**	...	...	...	Iraq
67**	66**	68**	1.02**	64^y	64^y	65^y	1.01^y	...	...	...	12.7	12.4	12.9	Jordan
66	67	65	0.97	...	...	...	...	14.6**	13.9**	15.3**	...	...	...	Kuwait[2]
73**	74**	71**	0.96**	71	72	70	0.97	12.7**	12.6**	12.8**	13.9	13.5	14.3	Lebanon
...	...	...	...	...	...	...	...	...	...	...	...	...	...	Libya
29	*29*	*29*	*0.99*	34	34	35	1.05	6.7**	...	...	8.1**	8.1**	8.0**	Mauritania
50	52	48	0.93	**77**	**78**	**76**	**0.98**	8.0**	8.9**	7.1**	...	...	...	Morocco
71	70	72	1.03	65^z	67^z	63^z	0.95^z	...	...	...	13.5^z	13.5^z	13.6^z	Oman
...	...	...	...	77	78	76	0.98	11.6	11.6	11.5	13.5	12.9	14.1	Palestine
...	...	...	...	52**	52**	52**	1.00**	12.9**	11.9**	14.0**	12.2	11.6	13.6	Qatar
...	...	...	...	62^z	61^z	63^z	1.03^z	...	...	...	14.3**	14.3**	14.3**	Saudi Arabia
...	...	...	...	...	...	...	...	4.5**	...	...	...	...	...	Sudan (pre-secession)
62	62	61	0.98	51^y	52^y	51^y	0.99^y	...	...	...	...	...	...	Syrian Arab Republic
...	...	...	...	92^z	92^z	91^z	0.99^z	13.0**	13.3**	12.7**	14.5^z	14.1**,z	14.9**,z	Tunisia
49	48	50	1.03	...	...	...	...	11.4**	10.9**	12.4**	...	...	...	United Arab Emirates[2]
25	30	20	0.68	45**,y	48**,y	42**,y	0.87**,y	7.5**	10.2**	4.7**	...	...	...	Yemen
Central and Eastern Europe														
...	...	...	...	65	63	67	1.06	11.0**	11.0**	10.9**	...	...	...	Albania
76	76	76	0.99	...	...	...	...	13.7	13.5	13.9	...	...	...	Belarus[2]
...	...	...	...	81	80	83	1.03	...	...	...	13.4**	13.1**	13.8**	Bosnia and Herzegovina
...	...	...	...	...	...	...	...	13.0	12.6	13.4	14.0	13.8	14.2	Bulgaria
68	69	67	0.96	...	...	...	...	12.0	11.9	12.2	14.1	13.5	14.8	Croatia
...	...	...	...	52^z	48^z	56^z	1.17^z	13.2**	13.1**	13.3**	15.3**,z	14.9**,z	15.9**,z	Czech Republic
...	...	...	...	...	...	...	...	14.3	13.8	14.9	15.8^z	14.8^z	16.9^z	Estonia
...	...	...	...	...	...	...	...	13.9	13.7	14.1	15.3^z	14.9^z	15.6^z	Hungary
...	...	...	...	...	...	...	...	13.6**	12.9**	14.3**	14.8	13.9	15.6	Latvia
...	...	...	...	...	...	...	...	13.9	13.5	14.4	15.7	15.0	16.5	Lithuania
...	...	...	...	...	...	...	...	...	...	...	15.0	14.7	15.2	Montenegro
...	...	...	...	...	...	...	...	14.7	14.3	15.0	15.2^z	14.6^z	15.8^z	Poland
...	...	...	...	77	78	76	0.97	11.4	11.3	11.6	11.8	11.5	12.2	Republic of Moldova[3,4]
...	...	...	...	69^z	70^z	68^z	0.97^z	11.7	11.6	11.8	14.5	14.0	15.0	Romania
...	...	...	...	...	...	...	...	12.1**	...	...	14.3^z	13.8^z	14.8^z	Russian Federation
...	...	...	...	81	81	81	1.00	...	...	...	13.6	13.2	14.0	Serbia[3]
...	...	...	...	...	...	...	...	12.9	12.7	13.0	14.7**	14.1**	15.3**	Slovakia
...	...	...	...	...	...	...	...	14.6	14.1	15.1	16.9^z	16.1^z	17.6^z	Slovenia
...	...	...	...	85^z	85^z	86^z	1.01^z	11.8	11.8	11.8	13.4	13.2	13.6	TFYR Macedonia
...	...	...	...	...	...	...	...	10.6**	11.8**	9.3**	12.9**,z	13.4**,z	12.3**,z	Turkey
...	...	...	...	...	...	...	...	12.8**	12.6**	13.0**	14.8	14.4*	15.1*	Ukraine
Central Asia														
...	...	...	...	...	...	...	...	11.2**	...	...	12.2**	11.7**	12.6**	Armenia
...	...	...	...	68	69	66	0.95	11.0	11.2	10.8	11.7**	11.8**	11.5**	Azerbaijan[3,5]
...	...	...	...	...	...	...	...	11.4**	11.4**	11.4**	13.2^z	...	...	Georgia
66	*66*	*66*	*1.00*	52^y	54^y	51^y	0.93^y	12.1	11.9	12.3	**15.3**	**14.9**	**15.6**	Kazakhstan
58*	58*	58*	0.99*	62*	63*	60*	0.94*	11.4**	11.3**	11.6**	12.6*,z	12.3*,z	12.9*,z	Kyrgyzstan
81	82	79	0.97	90	91	89	0.98	8.9**	8.0**	9.7**	14.3**	13.6**	15.0**	Mongolia
84	87	82	0.95	95^y	97^y	93^y	0.96^y	9.7	10.5	8.8	11.5	12.5	10.6	Tajikistan
...	...	...	...	...	...	...	...	...	...	...	...	...	...	Turkmenistan
...	...	...	...	77^z	79^z	76^z	0.96^z	10.6	10.7	10.5	**11.6**	**11.8**	**11.4**	Uzbekistan
East Asia and the Pacific														
...	...	...	...	...	...	...	...	20.3**	20.0**	20.6**	19.6	19.2	20.0	Australia
...	...	...	...	67	66	68	1.03	13.7	13.5	14.0	15.0**	14.6**	15.4**	Brunei Darussalam
65	66	64	0.97	90	90	91	1.01	...	...	...	10.5**,y	11.2**,y	9.9**,y	Cambodia
...	...	...	...	...	...	...	...	**10.1**	...	...	11.7	11.5	12.0	China[6]
...	...	...	...	80	82	77	0.94	10.6*	10.5*	10.6*	**12.5**	**11.9**	**13.1**	Cook Islands[3]
...	...	...	...	...	...	...	...	...	...	...	...	...	...	DPR Korea
72	72	73	1.02	74^y	75**,y	73**,y	0.98**,y	...	...	...	...	...	...	Fiji
44	*44*	*43*	*0.98*	45^z	43^z	46^z	1.07^z	*10.3***	*10.5***	*10.1***	12.9	12.9	12.9	Indonesia
...	...	...	...	...	...	...	...	14.5**	14.6**	14.3**	15.3	15.5	15.1	Japan
...	...	...	...	...	...	...	...	10.0**	9.6**	10.4**	12.0^y	11.6^y	12.4^y	Kiribati

Table 4 (continued)

Country or territory	Compulsory education (age group)[1]	Official primary school age entry 2010	New entrants (000) School year ending in 1999	New entrants (000) School year ending in 2010	GIR 1999 Total	GIR 1999 Male	GIR 1999 Female	GIR 1999 GPI (F/M)	GIR 2010 Total	GIR 2010 Male	GIR 2010 Female	GIR 2010 GPI (F/M)
Lao PDR	6-10	6	180	189	116	122	109	0.89	134	137	131	0.96
Macao, China	5-15	6	6	...	89	87	90	1.04	...	...	...	...
Malaysia[2]	6-11	6	509	474[z]	97	98	97	0.99	...	...	...	...
Marshall Islands	6-14	6	1	**2**	100	96	103	1.07	**100**	**102**	**99**	**0.97**
Micronesia, F. S.	6-14	6	...	...	...	...	...	...	...	...	...	...
Myanmar	5-9	5	1 226	1 196	133	132	135	1.02	152	152	151	0.99
Nauru[3]	6-16	6	*0.3*	...	*118*	*124*	*111*	*0.89*	...	...	...	...
New Zealand	6-16	5	...	...	...	...	...	...	...	...	...	...
Niue[3]	5-16	5	0.05	...	105	79	137	1.73	...	...	...	...
Palau[3]	6-17	6	*0.4*	...	*117*	*116*	*118*	*1.01*	...	...	...	...
Papua New Guinea		7	...	...	...	...	...	...	...	...	...	...
Philippines	6-11	6	2 551	2 759[y]	130	133	127	0.95	125[y]	129[y]	121[y]	0.94[y]
Republic of Korea	6-15	6	720	477	105	105	105	1.00	107	107	107	0.99
Samoa	5-14	5	5	6	105	106	104	0.98	125	122	128	1.05
Singapore[2]	6-14	6	...	46[z]	...	...	...	...	...	...	...	...
Solomon Islands		6	...	...	...	...	...	...	...	...	...	...
Thailand	6-15	6	1 037**	...	101**	103**	98**	0.95**	...	...	...	...
Timor-Leste	6-15	6	...	46	...	...	...	...	141	141	141	1.00
Tokelau[3]	5-16	5	0.03	...	70	91	44	0.49	...	...	...	...
Tonga	6-14	5	3	...	102	106	97	0.92	...	...	...	...
Tuvalu[3]	6-15	6	0.2**	...	89**	94**	83**	0.89**	...	...	...	...
Vanuatu		6	6**	8	115**	115**	114**	0.99**	124	123	125	1.02
Viet Nam	6-14	6	2 035	...	109	113	106	0.93	...	...	...	...
Latin America and the Caribbean												
Anguilla[7]	5-17	5	0.2	0.2	...	...	...	...	...	...	...	...
Antigua and Barbuda	5-16	5	*2*	1	*109*	...	...	...	94	103	84	0.81
Argentina	5-18	6	781	752[z]	112	112	112	0.99	114[z]	114[z]	115[z]	1.00[z]
Aruba	4-17	6	1	1	105	108	101	0.93	106	108	104	0.96
Bahamas	5-16	5	7	5	116	122	110	0.90	118	116	120	1.04
Barbados	5-16	5	4	4*	100	98	102	1.05	130*	133*	127*	0.95*
Belize	5-14	5	8	8	116	124	109	0.88	115	115	114	0.99
Bermuda	5-16	5	*0.8*	0.7	*105*	*100*	*110*	*1.10*	90	90	90	1.00
Bolivia, P. S.	5-16	6	282	270[y]	124	124	125	1.01	112[y]	113[y]	111[y]	0.99[y]
Brazil	7-14	7	*3 876*	...	*117*	...	...	...	...	...	...	...
British Virgin Islands[3]	5-17	5	0.4	0.5	106	109	103	0.95	91	95	87	0.92
Cayman Islands	5-16	5	0.6	0.6[y]	112	109	115	1.05	88[y]	85[y]	91[y]	1.07[y]
Chile	6-21	6	284	239[z]	95	95	94	0.99	97[z]	97[z]	96[z]	0.99[z]
Colombia	5-15	6	1 267	970	143	146	140	0.96	110	113	107	0.95
Costa Rica	5-15	6	87	76	106	106	106	1.00	98	98	98	1.00
Cuba	6-16	6	164	**123**	97	99	95	0.95	**93**	**93**	**93**	**1.00**
Dominica	5-16	5	2	1	125	130	119	0.92	131	133	129	0.98
Dominican Republic	5-14	6	267	223	132	136	127	0.93	107	113	101	0.89
Ecuador	5-15	6	374	...	134	134	134	1.00	...	...	...	...
El Salvador	7-15	7	196**	141	125**	128**	122**	0.95**	113	117	110	0.94
Grenada	5-16	5	*2**	2**	*91**	*100**	*83**	*0.83**	106**	99**	113**	1.14**
Guatemala	6-15	7	425	526	132	136	128	0.94	131	131	131	1.00
Guyana	6-15	6	18	15	104	100	107	1.06	85	82	87	1.06
Haiti	6-11	6	...	...	...	...	...	...	...	...	...	...
Honduras	6-15	6	*252*	228	*140*	*140*	*140*	*1.00*	123	125	120	0.96
Jamaica	6-12	6	*56*	40	97	97	*96*	*0.99*	79	81	78	0.96
Mexico	4-16	6	2 509	2 420	110	110	110	1.00	108	108	108	1.00
Montserrat[7]	5-16	5	0.1	0.1[z]	174	218	141	0.65	...	...	...	...
Netherlands Antilles	4-18	6	4**	...	116**	113**	118**	1.05**	...	...	...	...
Nicaragua	5-12	6	203	185	143	146	139	0.95	142	146	138	0.95
Panama	4-15	6	69	70	111	112	111	0.99	102	103	101	0.98
Paraguay	6-15	6	179**	145[z]	131**	134**	128**	0.96**	100[z]	101[z]	98[z]	0.97[z]
Peru	5-17	6	731	616	123	122	123	1.01	106	106	107	1.01
Saint Kitts and Nevis	5-16	5	*1*	0.7	*120*	*121*	*119*	*0.98*	78	76	80	1.06
Saint Lucia	5-15	5	4**	3	100**	102**	98**	0.96**	92	96	87	0.90
Saint Vincent/Grenadines	5-16	5	*2**	2	*102**	*102**	*103**	*1.00**	104	107	100	0.93
Suriname	7-12	6	*9**	11[z]	*98**	*101**	*96**	*0.95**	100[z]	101[z]	99[z]	0.97[z]
Trinidad and Tobago	6-12	5	20	19	95	96	94	0.98	103	104	101	0.97
Turks and Caicos Islands[7]	4-17	6	0.3**	0.5[z]	...	...	...	...	...	...	...	...
Uruguay	4-18	6	60	53[z]	107	107	107	1.00	106[z]	106[z]	106[z]	0.99[z]
Venezuela, B. R.	5-14	6	537	564	98	99	97	0.98	99	100	98	0.97

	NET INTAKE RATE (NIR) IN PRIMARY EDUCATION [%]							SCHOOL LIFE EXPECTANCY (expected number of years of formal schooling from primary to tertiary education)						
	School year ending in							School year ending in						
	1999				2010			1999			2010			
Total	Male	Female	GPI (F/M)	Total	Male	Female	GPI (F/M)	Total	Male	Female	Total	Male	Female	Country or territory
52	53	51	0.96	90.1	...	...	...	8.2	9.2	7.2	10.1	10.7	9.4	Lao PDR
63	60	66	1.10	...	...	...	...	12.4	12.7	12.2	14.0	14.3	13.8	Macao, China
...	...	...	...	...	...	...	...	11.6	11.5	11.8	...	...	...	Malaysia[2]
...	...	...	...	**99**	**100**	**97**	**0.97**	...	...	...	...	...	...	Marshall Islands
...	...	...	...	...	...	...	...	...	...	...	...	...	...	Micronesia, F. S.
...	...	...	...	...	...	...	...	...	...	...	...	...	...	Myanmar
...	...	...	...	...	...	...	...	*8.8*	*7.8*	*9.9*	9.3**,y	8.9**,y	9.9**,y	Nauru[3]
...	...	...	...	...	...	...	...	17.2**	16.6**	17.9**	19.7	18.8	20.5	New Zealand
...	...	...	...	...	...	...	...	11.9	11.5	12.4	...	...	...	Niue[3]
...	...	...	...	...	...	...	...	13.7**	12.9**	14.6**	...	...	...	Palau[3]
...	...	...	...	...	...	...	...	...	...	...	...	...	...	Papua New Guinea
45**	46**	44**	0.95**	46y	43y	49y	1.12y	11.4	11.1	11.7	11.7*,y	11.4*,y	12.0*,y	Philippines
98	98	98	1.01	92	93	92	1.00	15.8	16.6	14.9	17.2**	18.0**	16.2**	Republic of Korea
...	...	...	...	...	...	...	...	12.3	12.1	12.5	...	...	...	Samoa
...	...	...	...	...	...	...	...	...	...	...	...	...	...	Singapore[2]
...	...	...	...	...	...	...	...	7.4**	7.9**	7.0**	...	...	...	Solomon Islands
...	...	...	...	...	...	...	...	...	...	...	12.3z	11.9z	12.7z	Thailand
...	...	...	...	53	52	53	1.02	**10.0****	...	...	11.7z	12.2*,z	11.2*,z	Timor-Leste
...	...	...	...	...	...	...	...	*11.0***	*10.6***	*11.6***	...	...	...	Tokelau[3]
48	50	45	0.92	...	...	...	...	13.7	13.4	14.1	...	...	...	Tonga
...	...	...	...	...	...	...	...	...	...	...	...	...	...	Tuvalu[3]
...	...	...	...	40	39	42	1.09	9.6**	9.9**	9.4**	...	...	...	Vanuatu
82	...	...	...	...	...	...	...	10.3**	10.8**	9.8**	11.9	11.8	11.9	Viet Nam
														Latin America and the Caribbean
...	...	...	...	...	...	...	...	...	...	...	...	...	...	Anguilla[7]
...	...	...	...	61	67	56	0.83	...	...	...	13.3	13.2	13.3	Antigua and Barbuda
...	...	...	...	97y	97y	96y	0.99y	14.3	13.6**	15.0**	16.1z	15.1z	17.1z	Argentina
85	86	83	0.97	93z	90z	96z	1.07z	13.4	13.2	13.5	12.8	12.7	13.0	Aruba
84	86	82	0.95	78z	73z	82z	1.12z	10.8**	10.9**	10.7**	...	...	...	Bahamas
78**	76**	80**	1.05**	...	...	...	...	14.0**	13.0**	15.1**	16.3*	14.7*	18.1*	Barbados
...	...	...	...	66	66	66	1.00	...	...	...	...	...	...	Belize
...	...	...	...	68	68	67	0.99	...	...	...	12.1**	11.3**	12.9**	Bermuda
69**	68**	69**	1.03**	...	...	...	...	13.4**	...	...	...	...	...	Bolivia, P. S.
...	...	...	...	...	...	...	...	14.0**	13.7**	14.2**	...	...	...	Brazil
...	...	...	...	52	57	48	0.83	15.9**	15.0**	16.8**	15.2**,z	14.9**,z	16.3**,z	British Virgin Islands[3]
60	61	58	0.94	46y	46y	47y	1.01y	13.6**	13.5**	13.6**	11.9y	11.2y	12.6y	Cayman Islands
...	...	...	...	...	...	...	...	12.8**	12.9**	12.7**	14.7z	14.7z	14.7z	Chile
62**	64**	61**	0.96**	62	63	62	0.99	11.5	11.2**	11.8**	13.6	13.3	13.9	Colombia
...	...	...	...	...	...	...	...	...	...	...	...	...	...	Costa Rica
88	89	88	1.00	**93**	**93**	**93**	**1.00**	12.0	11.9	12.2	16.2	15.2	17.3	Cuba
...	...	...	...	...	...	...	...	...	...	...	12.7y	12.5y	12.8y	Dominica
58	57	58	1.00	62	64	61	0.95	...	...	...	...	...	...	Dominican Republic
84	83	84	1.01	...	...	...	...	...	...	...	13.7**,y	13.4**,y	13.9**,y	Ecuador
...	...	...	...	62	62	62	1.00	10.5	10.5	10.4	12.0	12.1	11.9	El Salvador
...	...	...	...	83z	83z	83z	1.00z	...	...	...	15.8z	15.3z	16.3z	Grenada
56	59	54	0.92	70	71	70	0.98	...	...	...	...	...	...	Guatemala
...	...	...	...	...	...	...	...	...	...	...	10.3	9.7	10.9	Guyana
...	...	...	...	...	...	...	...	...	...	...	...	...	...	Haiti
49	*49*	*49*	*1.00*	66	65	67	1.03	...	...	...	11.4**,y	10.8**,y	12.0**,y	Honduras
79**	*77***	*81***	*1.05***	...	...	...	...	*11.0***	*10.7***	*11.2***	13.1	12.8	13.4	Jamaica
86	85	86	1.01	75	75	75	1.00	11.8**	11.9**	11.7**	13.7	13.6	13.9	Mexico
...	...	...	...	...	...	...	...	19.8	23.6	16.6	...	...	...	Montserrat[7]
...	...	...	...	...	...	...	...	14.8	14.5	15.1	...	...	...	Netherlands Antilles
40	41	39	0.95	65	64	66	1.04	...	...	...	...	...	...	Nicaragua
84**	84**	84**	1.00**	...	...	...	...	12.5**	12.0**	13.0**	13.2z	12.6z	13.7z	Panama
...	...	...	...	67z	67z	68z	1.01z	11.5**	11.5**	11.5**	12.1z	11.8z	12.4z	Paraguay
...	...	...	...	85	85	85	1.01	...	...	...	13.2	13.2	13.3	Peru
...	...	...	...	53	54	53	0.99	...	...	...	12.9**,y	12.4**,y	13.4**,y	Saint Kitts and Nevis
70**	71**	70**	0.98**	68	72	65	0.91	...	...	...	12.7**	12.4**	13.0**	Saint Lucia
...	...	...	...	59	59	59	1.00	12.8**	12.3**	13.3**	...	...	...	Saint Vincent/Grenadines
...	...	...	...	89z	89z	89z	1.00z	**12.0****	**11.6****	**12.3****	...	...	...	Suriname
67	67	68	1.01	74	74	75	1.00	11.4**	11.2**	11.6**	...	...	...	Trinidad and Tobago
...	...	...	...	...	...	...	...	...	...	...	...	...	...	Turks and Caicos Islands[7]
...	...	...	...	...	...	...	...	13.9**	13.1**	14.8**	15.5z	...	...	Uruguay
60**	60**	61**	1.01**	75	75	75	1.01	...	...	...	14.4z	...	...	Venezuela, B. R.

Table 4 (continued)

Country or territory	Compulsory education (age group)[1]	Official primary school age entry 2010	New entrants (000) School year ending in 1999	New entrants (000) School year ending in 2010	GIR 1999 Total	GIR 1999 Male	GIR 1999 Female	GIR 1999 GPI (F/M)	GIR 2010 Total	GIR 2010 Male	GIR 2010 Female	GIR 2010 GPI (F/M)
North America and Western Europe												
Andorra	6-16	6	...	0.7	...	...	...	...	85	81	88	1.08
Austria	6-15	6	100	83	107	108	105	0.97	101	103	100	0.97
Belgium	6-18	6	...	111ᶻ	...	...	...	...	95ᶻ	94ᶻ	95ᶻ	1.01ᶻ
Canada	6-16	6	416	343ʸ	102	103	102	0.99	98ʸ	99ʸ	98ʸ	1.00ʸ
Cyprus[3]	4-15	6	10	9	86	86	85	0.99	103	102	104	1.02
Denmark	6-16	7	66	67ᶻ	101	100	101	1.00	100ᶻ	100ᶻ	100ᶻ	1.00ᶻ
Finland	7-16	7	65	56	102	102	102	1.00	98	99	98	0.99
France[8]	6-16	6	736	...	101	...	...	...	...	...	...	...
Germany	6-18	6	869	744ᶻ	101	101	101	1.00	100ᶻ	100ᶻ	99ᶻ	0.99ᶻ
Greece	5-15	6	113	...	106	107	104	0.98	...	...	...	...
Iceland	6-16	6	4	4ᶻ	100	101	98	0.96	97ᶻ	97ᶻ	97ᶻ	1.00ᶻ
Ireland	6-16	5	51	64	99	100	98	0.98	103	103	103	1.00
Israel	3-15	6	*112***	131ᶻ	*101***	*100***	*103***	*1.02***	100ᶻ	98ᶻ	101ᶻ	1.03ᶻ
Italy	6-16	6	558	561	102	103	101	0.99	100	101	98	0.97
Luxembourg	4-16	6	5	6ʸ	95	88	103	1.17	96ʸ	94ʸ	99ʸ	1.06ʸ
Malta	5-16	5	5	4	98	98	97	0.99	105	105	105	1.00
Monaco[7]	6-16	6	...	0.3ᶻ	...	...	...	...	...	...	...	...
Netherlands	5-16	6	199	199	100	101	99	0.99	98	98	98	1.00
Norway	6-16	6	61	59	100	101	99	0.98	101	101	100	0.99
Portugal	6-18	6	...	114ᶻ	...	...	...	...	103ᶻ	103ᶻ	103ᶻ	1.00ᶻ
San Marino[7]	6-16	6	*0.3*	0.3	...	...	...	...	87***	89***	85***	0.97***
Spain	6-16	6	411	460	107	107	107	1.00	101	100	102	1.02
Sweden	7-16	7	127	100	105	106	104	0.98	103	103	104	1.00
Switzerland	6-16	7	82	71	97	95	99	1.04	94	92	96	1.04
United Kingdom	5-16	5	...	...	...	...	...	...	...	...	...	...
United States	5-18	6	4 322	4 138	107	110	104	0.95	100	101	98	0.97
South and West Asia												
Afghanistan	7-16	7	...	1 033	...	...	...	...	108	124	91	0.74
Bangladesh[2]	6-10	6	...	3 688*	...	...	...	...	...	...	...	...
Bhutan	.	6	12	**15**	79	83	74	0.89	**102**	**101**	**103**	**1.02**
India	6-14	6	29 639	31 584ʸ	121	130	111	0.86	127	129ʸ	125ʸ	0.96ʸ
Iran, Islamic Republic of	6-14	6	1 563	1 119ᶻ	98	99	97	0.98	107	107ᶻ	108ᶻ	1.00ᶻ
Maldives	...	6	8	**5**	103	102	104	1.02	**101**	**104**	**99**	**0.95**
Nepal[2]	.	5	879	**1 140**	133	151	114	0.76	...	...	...	...
Pakistan	5-16	5	...	4 596	...	...	...	...	118	129	108	0.84
Sri Lanka	5-14	5	*330*	345	*103*	*103*	*103*	*1.00*	94	94	95	1.00
Sub-Saharan Africa												
Angola	6-14	6	...	1 029*	...	...	...	...	165*	182*	148*	0.82*
Benin	6-11	6	*205***	391	*104***	*119***	*89***	*0.75***	153	159	147	0.92
Botswana	6-15	6	50	47**,ᶻ	113	114	112	0.99	111**,ᶻ	114**,ᶻ	108**,ᶻ	0.95**,ᶻ
Burkina Faso	6-16	6	154	**445**	44	51	36	0.72	**89**	**91**	**86**	**0.94**
Burundi	...	7	138	324	70	78	63	0.81	161	164	158	0.96
Cameroon	6-11	6	335**	706	75**	83**	67**	0.81**	134	144	123	0.86
Cape Verde	6-16	6	13**	10	105**	107**	104**	0.97**	96	96	96	1.00
Central African Republic	6-15	6	...	**116**	...	...	...	...	**96**	**108**	**85**	**0.79**
Chad	6-16	6	175	423	73	86	61	0.71	124	140	109	0.78
Comoros	6-14	6	13	16ʸ	93	102	85	0.84	80ʸ	82ʸ	77ʸ	0.94ʸ
Congo	6-16	6	32	119	39	38	39	1.03	109	109	108	0.99
Côte d'Ivoire	6-15	6	309	**458**	68	75	60	0.80	**83**	**88**	**78**	**0.88**
D. R. Congo	6-15	6	767	2 268	49	48	51	1.08	111	117	105	0.90
Equatorial Guinea	7-11	7	...	16	...	...	...	...	92	93	90	0.97
Eritrea	6--10	7	57	59	54	60	49	0.81	42	44	40	0.91
Ethiopia	.	7	1 537	3 171	81	96	66	0.69	137	145	129	0.89
Gabon	6-16	6	*33*	...	*92*	*93*	*92*	*0.99*	...	...	...	...
Gambia	...	7	36**	44**	98**	103**	93**	0.91**	88**	88**	88**	1.00**
Ghana	4-15	6	469	**703**	90	91	88	0.97	**110**	**109**	**111**	**1.02**
Guinea	7-16	7	119	287	50	56	44	0.80	104	112	96	0.86
Guinea-Bissau	7-13	7	35**	67	105**	120**	90**	0.75**	166	169	164	0.97
Kenya	...	6	892	...	99	101	98	0.97	...	...	...	...
Lesotho	.	6	51	53	95	95	96	1.01	99	103	94	0.92

NET INTAKE RATE (NIR) IN PRIMARY EDUCATION (%)								SCHOOL LIFE EXPECTANCY (expected number of years of formal schooling from primary to tertiary education)						
School year ending in								School year ending in						
1999				2010				1999			2010			
Total	Male	Female	GPI (F/M)	Total	Male	Female	GPI (F/M)	Total	Male	Female	Total	Male	Female	Country or territory
														North America and Western Europe
...	...	...	...	...	...	...	...	...	...	...	11.7y	11.1y	12.3y	Andorra
...	...	...	...	...	...	...	...	15.2**	15.3**	15.1**	15.3**,z	15.1**,z	15.6**,z	Austria
...	...	...	...	...	...	...	...	18.2**	17.7**	18.7**	16.4z	16.1z	16.7z	Belgium
...	...	...	...	...	...	...	...	15.9	15.5	16.4	...	...	...	Canada
...	...	...	...	...	...	...	...	12.5	12.4	12.7	14.9	15.1	14.7	Cyprus[3]
...	...	...	...	...	...	...	...	16.1	15.6	16.6	16.8z	16.1z	17.4z	Denmark
...	...	...	...	...	...	...	...	17.3	16.7	18.1	16.9	16.4	17.5	Finland
...	...	...	...	...	...	...	...	15.6	15.4	15.9	16.1z	15.8z	16.5z	France[8]
...	...	...	...	...	...	...	...	...	...	...	...	...	...	Germany
96	97	96	0.99	...	...	...	...	13.5	13.3	13.7	...	...	...	Greece
98	100	96	0.97	96z	97z	96z	1.00z	16.8	16.2	17.4	18.3z	17.1z	19.6z	Iceland
...	...	...	...	...	...	...	...	16.6	16.2	17.0	18.3z	18.0z	18.6z	Ireland
...	...	...	...	...	...	...	...	15.2	14.8	15.6	15.7z	15.3z	16.2z	Israel
...	...	...	...	...	...	...	...	14.9	14.7	15.1	16.2z	15.7z	16.7z	Italy
...	...	...	...	...	...	...	...	13.5	13.4	13.6	13.5y	13.4y	13.5y	Luxembourg
...	...	...	...	...	...	...	...	13.4	13.8	13.0	15.1	15.2	14.9	Malta
...	...	...	...	...	...	...	...	...	...	...	...	...	...	Monaco[7]
...	...	...	...	...	...	...	...	16.5	16.7	16.2	16.9z	16.8z	16.9z	Netherlands
...	...	...	...	...	...	...	...	17.2	16.7	17.7	17.5	16.8	18.2	Norway
...	...	...	...	96z	96z	96z	1.00z	15.4	15.0	15.7	16.0z	15.8z	16.2z	Portugal
...	...	...	...	86**	87**	84**	0.96**	...	...	...	12.5**	12.1**	12.9**	San Marino[7]
...	...	...	...	99z	98z	99z	1.01z	15.9	15.5	16.2	16.4z	16.0z	16.9z	Spain
...	...	...	...	97z	98z	96z	0.98z	18.9	17.3	20.5	16.0	15.2	16.7	Sweden
...	...	...	...	...	...	...	...	15.1	15.5	14.6	15.7	15.8	15.5	Switzerland
...	...	...	...	...	...	...	...	15.9**	15.7**	16.1**	16.4z	15.9z	16.9z	United Kingdom
...	...	...	...	75	75	75	1.00	15.7	...	...	16.8	15.9	17.6	United States
														South and West Asia
...	...	...	...	...	...	...	...	2**	...	...	8.1z	10.1z	6.1z	Afghanistan
...	...	...	...	...	...	...	...	...	...	...	...	...	...	Bangladesh[2]
20**	21**	19**	0.90**	...	...	...	...	7.2**	8.0**	6.5**	**12.4**	**12.3**	**12.4**	Bhutan
...	...	...	...	...	...	...	...	...	...	...	10.7**,y	...	...	India
...	...	...	...	...	...	...	...	11.9**	12.6**	11.2**	14.4	14.8	13.9	Iran, Islamic Republic of
...	...	...	...	70**,y	69**,y	70**,y	1.00**,y	11.6**	11.6**	11.7**	...	...	...	Maldives
...	...	...	...	...	...	...	...	...	...	...	...	...	...	Nepal[2]
...	...	...	...	95	103	86	0.84	...	...	...	7.3**,z	8.0**,z	6.5**,z	Pakistan
*95***	*95***	*95***	*1.00***	...	...	...	...	...	...	...	...	...	...	Sri Lanka
														Sub-Saharan Africa
...	...	...	...	64*	71*	57*	0.81*	...	...	...	10.2**	11.5**	9.0**	Angola
...	...	...	...	60	63	58	0.91	6.9**	8.8**	5.0**	...	...	...	Benin
22	20	24	1.20	...	...	...	...	11.5**	11.5**	11.6**	...	...	...	Botswana
19	22	15	0.71	**16**	**17**	**16**	**0.95**	3.2	3.8	2.6	**6.9**	**7.4**	**6.4**	Burkina Faso
...	...	...	...	68z	68z	67z	0.99z	...	...	...	11.3	11.8	10.9	Burundi
...	...	...	...	59z	63z	55z	0.88z	7.2**	...	...	10.9**	11.7**	9.9**	Cameroon
68**	67**	69**	1.02**	92	92	92	1.01	...	...	...	12.7	12.4	13.1	Cape Verde
...	...	...	...	41	45	37	0.84	**5.6***	...	...	6.8**	8.1**	5.5**	Central African Republic
22	26	19	0.72	...	...	...	...	4.8**	6.3**	3.2**	7.4**	9.0**	5.7**	Chad
21	24**	17**	0.70**	...	...	...	...	8.1**	8.9**	7.4**	...	...	...	Comoros
...	...	...	...	51*	52*	51*	1.00*	...	...	...	...	...	...	Congo
28	31	25	0.79	...	...	...	...	6.5**	7.8**	5.2**	...	...	...	Côte d'Ivoire
22	21	23	1.10	51	54	49	0.90	4.4**	5.0**	3.8**	8.5**,z	9.8**,z	7.2**,z	D. R. Congo
...	...	...	...	28	28	28	1.01	9.1**	11.1**	7.1**	...	...	...	Equatorial Guinea
17	18	16	0.89	16**	17**	15**	0.89**	4.1**	4.7**	3.5**	4.6	5.2	4.0	Eritrea
21	23	19	0.80	68	71	66	0.93	4.1**	5.1**	3.1**	8.7**	9.3**	8.0**	Ethiopia
...	...	...	...	...	...	...	...	12.1**	12.4**	11.7**	...	...	...	Gabon
...	...	...	...	...	...	...	...	...	...	...	8.7**,y	...	...	Gambia
30**	30**	31**	1.01**	39**,z	38**,z	39**,z	1.04**,z	7.6**	8.2**	7.0**	11.4**	11.8**	11.0**	Ghana
19	20	18	0.87	48z	50z	46z	0.93z	4.5**	5.8**	3.2**	8.8**,y	10.2**,y	7.4**,y	Guinea
...	...	...	...	42	43	41	0.96	...	...	...	...	...	...	Guinea-Bissau
28**	27**	29**	1.08**	...	...	...	...	8.0**	8.2**	7.8**	11.1**,z	11.4**,z	10.7**,z	Kenya
25	24	26	1.06	58	59	57	0.97	9.0**	8.5**	9.5**	...	...	...	Lesotho

Table 4 (continued)

Country or territory	Compulsory education (age group)[1]	Official primary school age entry 2010	New entrants (000) School year ending in 1999	New entrants (000) School year ending in 2010	GIR 1999 Total	GIR 1999 Male	GIR 1999 Female	GIR 1999 GPI (F/M)	GIR 2010 Total	GIR 2010 Male	GIR 2010 Female	GIR 2010 GPI (F/M)
Liberia	6-16	6	…	119[y]	…	…	…	…	116[y]	120[y]	112[y]	0.93[y]
Madagascar	6-10	6	495	1 095	110	111	109	0.98	184	184	184	1.00
Malawi	.	6	616	699	178	177	180	1.02	154	150	159	1.06
Mali	6-15	7	171**	374	53**	60**	46**	0.77**	79	82	76	0.92
Mauritius	5-16	5	22	18	96	94	97	1.03	97	95	99	1.04
Mozambique	6-12	6	536	1 193	102	111	94	0.84	161	165	157	0.95
Namibia	7-16	7	54	52[z]	106	105	108	1.03	94[z]	93[z]	95[z]	1.02[z]
Niger	4-16	7	133	470	42	49	35	0.71	95	100	90	0.89
Nigeria	6-15	6	3 606**	3 974	105**	116**	94**	0.81**	88	93	83	0.89
Rwanda[2]	7-12	7	295	583	137	138	135	0.98	195	200	191	0.95
Sao Tome and Principe	6-11	6	4	5	108	109	106	0.97	112	117	107	0.92
Senegal	6-16	7	190	359	70	…	…	…	103	100	106	1.06
Seychelles[2]	6-16	6	2	1	115	116	115	0.99	105	107	103	0.97
Sierra Leone	6-15	6	99	218	87	90	84	0.93	127	133	121	0.91
Somalia	…	6	…	…	…	…	…	…	…	…	…	…
South Africa	7-15	7	1 157	926[z]	115	117	114	0.97	91[z]	94[z]	88[z]	0.94[z]
South Sudan	…	…	…	…	…	…	…	…	…	…	…	…
Swaziland	.	6	31	35	94	96	93	0.97	118	123	113	0.92
Togo	6-15	6	139	247	104	111	97	0.88	154	157	150	0.96
Uganda	6-12	6	1 437	1 718	180	182	177	0.98	155	153	157	1.02
United Republic of Tanzania	7-13	7	714	1 265	73	74	73	0.99	96	96	97	1.01
Zambia	.	7	252	453	87	87	87	1.01	115	114	117	1.03
Zimbabwe	.	6	…	…	…	…	…	…	…	…	…	…

			Sum 1999	Sum 2010	Weighted average 1999 Total	Male	Female	GPI (F/M)	Weighted average 2010 Total	Male	Female	GPI (F/M)
World	…	…	131 508	134 587**	105	109**	100**	0.92**	110	112**	109**	0.98**
Countries in transition	…	…	4 721	3 409**	97	98**	97**	0.99**	100**	101**	100**	0.99**
Developed countries	…	…	12 200	11 267	103	104	102	0.98	100	100	99	0.99
Developing countries	…	…	114 586**	119 911**	105**	110**	100**	0.91**	112**	113**	110**	0.97**
Arab States	…	…	6 243	7 760	89	93	86	0.92	101	102**	99**	0.97**
Central and Eastern Europe	…	…	5 616	4 262**	97	98**	95**	0.96**	99**	100**	99**	0.99**
Central Asia	…	…	1 783	1 349	100	100	100	1.01	100	101	98	0.97
East Asia and the Pacific	…	…	37 912**	32 245	101**	101**	101**	1.00**	106	105	107	1.02
East Asia	…	…	37 426**	31 797	101**	101**	101**	1.00**	106	105	107	1.02
Pacific	…	…	486**	…	94**	95**	93**	0.97**	…	…	…	…
Latin America and the Caribbean	…	…	13 223	13 164**	120	123	117	0.95	119**	121**	117**	0.97**
Caribbean	…	…	509**	498**	137**	141**	132**	0.94**	136**	140**	131**	0.94**
Latin America	…	…	12 714	12 666**	119	122	117	0.95	119**	120**	117**	0.97**
North America and Western Europe	…	…	9 315	8 861	104	106	103	0.97	100	100	99	0.98
South and West Asia	…	…	40 901	40 666**	116	126	105	0.84	115**	117**	113**	0.97**
Sub-Saharan Africa	…	…	16 514	26 281	92	98	86	0.87	115	119	111	0.93
Countries with low income	…	…	17 650	25 798	100	106	94	0.89	123	126	120	0.95
Countries with middle income	…	…	100 585**	96 406**	106**	110**	102**	0.92**	109**	110**	107**	0.98**
Lower middle	…	…	57 041	60 162**	111	119	102	0.86	112**	115**	110**	0.96**
Upper middle	…	…	43 544**	36 245	101**	101**	101**	1.00**	103	103	104	1.01
Countries with high income	…	…	13 273	12 383	103	104	101	0.97	100	101	100	0.99

Source: UNESCO Institute for Statistics database (UIS, 2012). Intake rates in the table are based on the United Nations Population Division estimates, revision 2010 (United Nations, 2011), median variant.
Note: The country groupings by income level presented in the tables are as defined by the World Bank. They are based on the list of countries by income group as revised in July 2011.
1. Information on compulsory education comes from various sources: the International Bureau of Education's World Data on Education database (7th edition, 2010/11); national law and policies on minimum ages; National system overview on education systems in Europe (Eurydice, 2011 edition); etc.
2. Intake rates (either gross or net or both rates) for one or both of the two school years were not calculated due to inconsistencies in the population data.
3. National population data were used to calculate intake rates.
4. New entrants and population data exclude Transnistria.
5. New entrants and population data exclude the Nagorno-Karabakh region.

NET INTAKE RATE (NIR) IN PRIMARY EDUCATION (%)								SCHOOL LIFE EXPECTANCY (expected number of years of formal schooling from primary to tertiary education)						
School year ending in								School year ending in						
1999				2010				1999			2010			
Total	Male	Female	GPI (F/M)	Total	Male	Female	GPI (F/M)	Total	Male	Female	Total	Male	Female	Country or territory
...	...	...	...	...	...	...	...	8.6**	10.2**	7.0**	...	...	...	Liberia
...	...	...	...	82^y	82^y	83^y	1.02^y	...	...	...	10.4**,z	10.7**,z	10.2**,z	Madagascar
...	...	...	...	81	78	83	1.05	11.2**	11.9**	10.5**	10.4**	10.4**	10.4**	Malawi
...	...	...	...	**20**	**21**	**19**	**0.90**	4.2**	5.0**	3.4**	**7.5**	**8.3**	**6.6**	Mali
...	...	...	...	82	80	83	1.04	11.9**	12.0**	11.7**	13.6**,y	13.4**,y	13.8**,y	Mauritius
18	18	17	0.93	**66**	**66**	**65**	**0.99**	5.4**	6.3**	4.5**	...	...	...	Mozambique
60	59	62	1.06	50**,z	48**,z	52**,z	1.09**,z	11.6**	11.4**	11.7**	...	...	...	Namibia
27	31	21	0.68	**66**	**71**	**61**	**0.87**	2.4**	2.9**	1.9**	4.9**	5.5**	4.3**	Niger
...	...	...	...	...	...	...	...	7.5**	8.2**	6.8**	...	...	...	Nigeria
...	...	...	...	...	...	...	...	6.8**	6.9**	6.7**	10.9	10.9	11.0	Rwanda²
...	...	...	...	**95**	**98**	**91**	**0.93**	...	...	...	10.8**	10.8**	10.8**	Sao Tome and Principe
39	...	...	...	...	...	...	...	5.4	...	...	8.2*	8.3**	8.0**	Senegal
...	...	...	...	70	71	69	0.97	13.4	13.2	13.6	14.3^y	13.5**,y	15.2**,y	Seychelles²
...	...	...	...	...	...	...	...	...	...	...	...	...	...	Sierra Leone
...	...	...	...	...	...	...	...	...	...	...	...	...	...	Somalia
43	44	42	0.95	...	...	...	...	...	...	...	...	...	...	South Africa
...	...	...	...	...	...	...	...	...	...	...	...	...	...	South Sudan
40	38	41	1.07	49	52	47	0.90	9.4	9.7	9.2	...	...	...	Swaziland
42	45	39	0.87	...	...	...	...	10.2**	12.5**	8.0**	...	...	...	Togo
...	...	...	...	68**	66**	70**	1.06**	*10.7**	*11.3**	*10.2**	11.1**,z	11.3**,z	10.8**,z	Uganda
14	13	15	1.16	...	...	...	...	...	...	...	...	...	...	United Republic of Tanzania
39	37	40	1.07	51**	49**	52**	1.07**	...	...	...	...	...	...	Zambia
...	...	...	...	...	...	...	...	...	...	...	...	...	...	Zimbabwe
Weighted average				**Weighted average**				**Weighted average**			**Weighted average**			
...	...	...	...	70**,z	71**,z	69**,z	0.97**,z	9.7**	10.1**	9.3**	11.5**	11.6**	11.3**	World
...	...	...	...	73**,z	73**,z	72**,z	0.98**,z	11.8	11.7	12.0	13.5**	13.3**	13.8**	Countries in transition
...	...	...	...	79**	79**	79**	1.00**	15.5	15.2**	15.9**	16.3**	15.9**	16.8**	Developed countries
...	...	...	...	70**,z	71**,z	68**,z	0.97**,z	9.0**	9.5**	8.4**	10.9**	11.1**	10.7**	Developing countries
68**	69**	66**	0.96**	73**	74**	71**	0.97**	9.5	10.3**	8.7**	11.0**	11.4**	10.6**	Arab States
...	...	...	...	...	...	...	...	12.2	12.3	12.1	14.0**	13.8**	14.2**	Central and Eastern Europe
72**	74**	71**	0.96**	73**	75**	72**	0.96**	10.8	10.9	10.8	12.5**	12.5**	12.4**	Central Asia
...	...	...	...	...	...	...	...	10.4**	10.6**	10.2**	12.2	12.0	12.3	East Asia and the Pacific
...	...	...	...	...	...	...	...	10.3**	10.5**	10.1**	12.1	12.0	12.3	East Asia
...	...	...	...	...	...	...	...	15.0	14.9	15.1	14.1**	13.9**	14.3**	Pacific
72**	71**	73**	1.02**	75**	75**	75**	1.00**	12.4	12.3	12.5	13.7**	13.4**	14.0**	Latin America and the Caribbean
...	...	...	...	...	...	...	...	10.1**	10.0**	10.0**	...	...	...	Caribbean
72**	71**	73**	1.02**	75**	75**	75**	1.00**	12.5	12.3	12.6	13.8**	13.5**	14.1**	Latin America
...	...	...	...	81**	81**	81**	1.00**	15.8	15.4**	16.3**	16.5**	16.0**	17.0**	North America and Western Europe
...	...	...	...	...	...	...	...	7.9**	8.8**	6.9**	10.3**	10.7**	9.9**	South and West Asia
34**	35**	33**	0.96**	57**	58**	56**	0.97**	6.7	7.3	6.0	9.1**	9.7	8.5**	Sub-Saharan Africa
49**	50**	47**	0.95**	66**	67**	65**	0.97**	6**	7**	6**	9.2**	9.7**	8.6**	Countries with low income
...	...	...	...	...	...	...	...	10**	10**	9**	11.4**	11.5**	11.2**	Countries with middle income
...	...	...	...	70**,z	72**,z	68**,z	0.94**,z	8**	9**	8**	10.5**	10.8**	10.1**	Lower middle
...	...	...	...	...	...	...	...	11**	11**	11**	12.8	12.5	13.1	Upper middle
...	...	...	...	78**	78**	78**	1.00**	15	15**	16**	16.2**	15.8**	16.6**	Countries with high income

6. Children can enter primary school at age 6 or 7.
7. Intake rates (either gross or net or both rates) for one or both of the two school years were not calculated due to lack of United Nations population data by age.
8. Data include French overseas departments and territories (DOM-TOM).
Data in bold are for the school year ending in 2011, those in italics are for 2000 and those in bold italics are for 2001.
(z) Data are for the school year ending in 2009.

(y) Data are for the school year ending in 2008.
(*) National estimate.
(**) For country level data: UIS partial estimate; for regional and other country-grouping sums and weighted averages: partial imputation due to incomplete country coverage (between 33% and 60% of population for the region or other country grouping).
(.) The category is not applicable or does not exist.
(. . .) No data available.

Table 5
Participation in primary education

Country or territory	Age group 2010	School-age population (000) 2010[1]	ENROLMENT IN PRIMARY EDUCATION — School year ending in 1999 Total (000)	% F	2010 Total (000)	% F	Enrolment in private institutions as % of total enrolment — School year ending in 1999	2010	GROSS ENROLMENT RATIO (GER) IN PRIMARY EDUCATION (%) — School year ending in 1999 Total	Male	Female	GPI (F/M)
Arab States												
1 Algeria	6-10	3 007	4 779	47	3 312	47	.	0.1	106	110	101	0.91
2 Bahrain[3]	6-11	...	76	49	91	49	19	31	107	107	107	1.00
3 Djibouti	6-10	103	38	41	61	47	9	12**	33	39	27	0.71
4 Egypt	6-11	9 939	8 086**	47**	10 004	48**	.	...	98**	102**	93**	0.91**
5 Iraq	6-11	5 087	3 604	44	...	...	.	...	97	105	88	0.83
6 Jordan	6-11	891	706	49	820	49	29	33	96	95	96	1.01
7 Kuwait[3]	6-10	...	140	49	214	49	32	39	106	105	107	1.02
8 Lebanon	6-11	441	414**	48**	462	48	67**	73	112**	115**	110**	0.96**
9 Libya	6-11	728	822	48	...	...	.	...	122	123	121	0.99
10 Mauritania	6-11	521	346	48	531	48	2	11	84	85	83	0.97
11 Morocco	6-11	3 543	3 462	44	**4 001**	**47**	4	12	87	95	78	0.82
12 Oman	6-11	283	316	48	302z	48z	5	19z	89	89	88	0.99
13 Palestine	6-9	444	368	49	403	48	9	12	100	100	100	1.00
14 Qatar	6-11	86	61	48	89	49	37	55	104	102	107	1.05
15 Saudi Arabia	6-11	3 132	...	...	3 321	49	...	9	...	...	...	...
16 Sudan (pre-secession)	6-11	6 668	2 513**	45**	4 744z	46z	2**	4z	48**	52**	44**	0.85**
17 Syrian Arab Republic	6-9	2 062	2 738	47	2 429	48	4	4	108	113	104	0.92
18 Tunisia	6-11	935	1 443	47	1 025z	48z	0.7	2z	115	119	111	0.93
19 United Arab Emirates[3]	6-10	...	270	48	327	49	44	72	93	94	93	0.99
20 Yemen	6-11	3 926	2 303	35	3 427	44	1	4	72	92	51	0.56
Central and Eastern Europe												
21 Albania	6-10	259	292	48	225	48	.	5	109	110	108	0.98
22 Belarus	6-9	357	*561*	*48*	358	49	*0.1*	0.1	*111*	*112*	*111*	*0.99*
23 Bosnia and Herzegovina	6-9	156	...	...	175	49	...	1	...	...	...	...
24 Bulgaria	7-10	254	412	48	260	48	0.3	0.8	104	106	103	0.97
25 Croatia	7-10	180	203	49	167	49	0.1	0.3	93	94	92	0.98
26 Czech Republic	6-10	438	655	49	460z	49z	0.8	1z	103	103	102	0.99
27 Estonia	7-12	74	127	48	74z	48z	1	4z	99	101	97	0.97
28 Hungary	7-10	382	503	48	390z	48z	5	8z	102	103	101	0.98
29 Latvia	7-12	113	141	48	114	48	1.0	1	95	97	94	0.97
30 Lithuania	7-10	128	220	48	122	48	0.4	0.8	101	102	100	0.98
31 Montenegro	7-10	33	...	...	35	48	...	.	...	...	...	...
32 Poland	7-12	2 266	3 434	48	2 294z	48z	...	3z	100	101	98	0.97
33 Republic of Moldova[4,5]	7-10	151*	*252*	*49*	141	48	...	0.9	*101*	*102*	*101*	*0.99*
34 Romania	7-10	878	1 285	49	842	48	–	0.3	96	97	95	0.98
35 Russian Federation[6]	7-10	5 166	6 743	49	5 015z	49z	...	0.6z	103	104	103	0.99
36 Serbia[4]	7-10	295*	387**	49**	283	49	...	0.1	112**	112**	111**	0.99**
37 Slovakia	6-9	210	317	49	212	49	4	6	99	99	98	0.98
38 Slovenia	6-11	109	92	48	107z	48z	0.1	0.3z	98	99	98	0.99
39 TFYR Macedonia	6-10	123	130	48	111	48	.	.z	102	103	101	0.98
40 Turkey	6-10	6 362	6 583	47	6 592z	49z	...	...	103	107	98	0.91
41 Ukraine	6-9	1 553	2 200	49	1 540	49	0.3	0.5	108	108	107	0.99
Central Asia												
42 Armenia	7-9	114	*176*	*49***	117	47	...	2	*102*	*102***	*102***	*1.00***
43 Azerbaijan[4,7]	6-9	514*	707	49	482	46	–	0.3	98	98	98	1.00
44 Georgia	6-11	266	302	49	289	47	0.5	9	94	94	94	0.99
45 Kazakhstan	7-10	863	*1 208*	*49*	**986**	**49**	0.5	**1.0**	*96*	*96*	*97*	*1.01*
46 Kyrgyzstan	7-10	392	470	49	391	49	0.2	0.8	96	97	96	0.99
47 Mongolia	6-10	224	251	50	274	49	0.5	5	96	95	96	1.01
48 Tajikistan	7-10	669	692	47	682	48	.	.y	*97*	*100*	*93*	*0.93*
49 Turkmenistan	7-9	285	...	...	...	...	.	...	...	...	...	...
50 Uzbekistan	7-10	2 093	2 570	49	**1 948**	**48**	...	.	98	98	98	1.00
East Asia and the Pacific												
51 Australia	5-11	1 918	1 885	49	2 015	49	27	31	101	101	101	1.00
52 Brunei Darussalam[3]	6-11	41	46	47	44	48	36	36	116	118	113	0.95
53 Cambodia	6-11	1 791	2 127	46	2 273	48	2	1	101	108	94	0.87
54 China[8]	7-11	90 811	*130 133*	*48*	101 019	46	...	5	*114*	*112*	*116*	*1.03*
55 Cook Islands[4]	5-10	2*	3	46	2	**49**	15	**23**	96	99	94	0.95
56 DPR Korea	6-9	1 518	...	...	...	...	...	...	...	...	...	...
57 Fiji	6-11	96	116	48	101z	48z	...	99y	104	104	103	0.99
58 Indonesia	7-12	25 686	*28 202***	*48***	30 342	50	*16***	17	*106***	*108***	*105***	*0.97***
59 Japan	6-11	6 904	7 692	49	7 099	49	0.9	1	101	101	101	1.00
60 Kiribati	6-11	14	14	49	16z	50z	...	...	108	108	109	1.01

GROSS ENROLMENT RATIO (GER) IN PRIMARY EDUCATION (%)				NET ENROLMENT RATIO (NER) IN PRIMARY EDUCATION (%)								OUT-OF-SCHOOL CHILDREN (000)[2]				
School year ending in				School year ending in								School year ending in				
2010				1999				2010				1999		2010		
Total	Male	Female	GPI (F/M)	Total	Male	Female	GPI (F/M)	Total	Male	Female	GPI (F/M)	Total	% F	Total	% F	
110	113	107	0.94	91	93	89	0.96	96	97	95	0.98	340	61	82	65	1
...	...	...	...	96	96	97	1.02	...	...	...	...	0.7	9.4	...	...	2
59	**62**	**56**	**0.90**	27	31	23	0.73	44**,z	47**,z	42**,z	0.90**,z	84**	53**	56**,z	52**,z	3
101	103**	98**	0.96**	90**	94**	87**	0.93**	94**	...	...	...	674**	70**	368**	...	4
...	...	...	...	89	95	82	0.87	...	...	...	...	423	76	...	...	5
92	92	92	1.00	89	88	89	1.01	91	91	91	1.00	57**	45**	83	49	6
...	...	...	...	91	91	92	1.01	...	...	...	...	2	30	...	...	7
105	106	103	0.97	92**	94**	90**	0.97**	92	92	91	0.99	22**	60**	30	51	8
...	...	...	...	...	...	...	...	...	...	...	...	...	...	...	...	9
102	99	105	1.05	61	62	60	0.97	74	72	76	1.04	161**	50**	134**	46**	10
114	**117**	**110**	**0.94**	71	76	65	0.86	**96**	**96**	**95**	**0.99**	1 157**	58**	**134**	**56**	11
105z	107z	104z	0.97z	79	78	79	1.02	94z	95z	92z	0.97z	70	45	5z	87z	12
91	92	90	0.98	92	92	92	1.00	87	87	86	0.98	23	48	48	52	13
103	103	103	1.00	91	87	95	1.10	92	92	92	1.01	3	2	3	43	14
106	106	106	0.99	...	...	...	...	90z	90z	89z	0.99z	...	...	318z	52z	15
73z	76z	69z	0.90z	40**	44**	36**	0.83**	...	...	...	...	2 989**	53**	...	...	16
118	119	116	0.98	94	97	90	0.93	93z	94z	92z	0.98z	87	...	19z	87z	17
109z	111z	107z	0.96z	94	96	92	0.96	98z	99z	98z	0.99z	64**	68**	5z	...	18
...	...	...	...	82	82	83	1.01	...	...	...	...	45	47	...	...	19
87	96	78	0.82	56	71	41	0.58	78	85	70	0.83	1 386	66	857	66	20
															Arab States	
87	87	87	0.99	99**	...	...	...	80	80	80	1.01	2**	...	52	47	21
100	100	100	1.00	*93***	...	...	...	92	...	...	...	*28***	...	29	...	22
112	111	113	1.02	...	...	...	...	87	86	88	1.02	...	...	20	45	23
103	103	102	1.00	96	97	95	0.98	98	98	98	1.00	6.3	74	1.3	26	24
93	93	93	1.00	86	87	85	0.98	87	87	87	0.99	16	53	7	36	25
106z	106z	106z	0.99z	96**	96**	96**	1.00**	...	...	...	...	26**	48**	...	...	26
99z	100z	98z	0.99z	94	95	93	0.98	94z	95z	93z	0.99z	2	51	3z	52z	27
102z	102z	101z	0.99z	88	88	87	0.99	92z	93z	92z	0.99z	15	48	8z	45z	28
101	101	100	0.99	92**	94**	91**	0.97**	95	94	96	1.02	9**	53**	5	38	29
96	96	95	0.99	94	94	93	0.99	93	93	92	0.99	7	47	5	47	30
107	107	106	0.98	...	...	...	...	83	...	...	...	...	...	6	...	31
97z	98z	97z	0.99z	97	98	97	0.99	96z	96z	96z	1.00z	91	55	94z	50z	32
94	94	93	1.00	*89*	*90*	*89*	*0.99*	88	88	87	1.00	*19*	*52***	15	48	33
96	96	95	0.99	89	89	88	0.99	88	88	87	0.99	99	50	109	50	34
99z	99z	99z	1.00z	...	...	...	...	93z	93z	93z	1.00z	...	...	221z	42z	35
96	96	96	0.99	...	...	...	...	93	93	92	0.99	...	...	16	50	36
101	101	101	0.99	...	...	...	...	...	...	...	...	...	...	...	...	37
98z	98z	97z	0.99z	94	95	94	0.99	97z	97z	97z	1.00z	3.4	51	3z	50z	38
90	89	91	1.01	95	96	94	0.98	88	87	89	1.01	6.3	59	2.2	22	39
102z	103z	101z	0.98z	94	98	90	0.92	97z	98z	97z	0.98z	374	82	162z	64z	40
99	99	100	1.01	...	...	...	...	91	90*	91*	1.01*	...	...	138	47*	41
														Central and Eastern Europe		
103	101	104	1.02	*91***	*90***	*91***	*1.01***	...	...	...	...	*12***	*45***	...	...	42
94	94	93	0.99	89	88*	89	1.01	84	85	84	0.99	82	46	78**	49**	43
109	107	111	1.03	...	...	...	...	100z	...	...	...	...	...	-z	...	44
111	**111**	**111**	**1.00**	86**	86**	87**	1.01**	**88**	**89**	**88**	0.99	75**	39**	**4**	**33**	45
100	100	99	0.99	87*	87*	86*	0.99*	87	88	87	0.99	34**	50**	18	51	46
122	123	121	0.98	87	87	88	1.01	99	99	98	0.99	27	46	2.1**	78**	47
102	104	100	0.96	*95*	*99*	*92*	*0.93*	97	99	95	0.96	*28*	*91*	15	88	48
...	...	...	...	...	...	...	...	...	...	...	...	...	...	...	...	49
95	**96**	**93**	**0.97**	...	...	...	...	**90**	**91**	**88**	**0.97**	...	...	**148**	**58**	50
														Central Asia		
105	105	105	0.99	94	94	95	1.01	97	97	97	1.01	103**	45**	54	43	51
108	107	109	1.01	...	...	...	...	...	...	...	...	...	...	...	...	52
127	130	124	0.95	87	92	81	0.88	96	96	95	0.99	274	70	73	55	53
111	110	113	1.03	...	...	...	...	...	...	...	...	...	...	...	...	54
111	**110**	**113**	**1.03**	85	87	83	0.96	94	94	95	1.00	0.4	54	0.03	23	55
...	...	...	...	...	...	...	...	...	...	...	...	...	...	...	...	56
105z	106z	104z	0.98z	94	94	95	1.01	97z	97z	97z	1.00z	6**	46**	0.9z	36z	57
118	117	119	1.02	*90***	*92***	*89***	*0.97***	96	95	97	1.02	*1 599***	*63***	236	...	58
103	103	103	1.00	100	...	...	...	100	...	...	...	0.5	...	2.0	...	59
113z	111z	115z	1.04z	99**	...	...	...	...	...	...	...	0.1**	...	...	...	60
														East Asia and the Pacific		

Table 5 (continued)

	Country or territory	Age group 2010	School-age population (000) 2010[1]	ENROLMENT IN PRIMARY EDUCATION				Enrolment in private institutions as % of total enrolment		GROSS ENROLMENT RATIO (GER) IN PRIMARY EDUCATION (%)			
				School year ending in 1999		School year ending in 2010		School year ending in 1999	School year ending in 2010	School year ending in 1999			
				Total (000)	% F	Total (000)	% F	1999	2010	Total	Male	Female	GPI (F/M)
61	Lao PDR	6-10	725	828	45	916	47	2	3	112	121	103	0.85
62	Macao, China	6-11	27	47	47	25	48	95**	97	100	101	100	0.99
63	Malaysia[3]	6-11	...	2 912	48	3 001ᶻ	48ᶻ	2	0.9ᶻ	95	96	95	0.98
64	Marshall Islands	6-11	8	8	48	**9**	**48**	25	**18**	90	90	89	0.99
65	Micronesia, F. S.	6-11	17	...	...	...	...	...	...	...	...	...	...
66	Myanmar	5-9	4 081	4 733	49	5 126	50	.	.	101	102	100	0.98
67	Nauru[4]	6-11	1*	2	53	1ʸ	50ʸ	...	...	99	86	115	1.33
68	New Zealand	5-10	344	361	49	348	49	...	12	100	101	100	1.00
69	Niue[4]	5-10	0.1*	0.3	46	...	...	...	...	99	99	98	1.00
70	Palau[4]	6-10	1*	2	47	...	...	18	...	114	118	109	0.93
71	Papua New Guinea	7-12	1 035	560	45	601ʸ	45ʸ	...	...	71	76	66	0.86
72	Philippines	6-11	13 131	12 503	49	13 687ᶻ	48ᶻ	8	8ᶻ	110	110	110	1.00
73	Republic of Korea	6-11	3 130	3 946	47	3 306	48	1	1	103	103	104	1.01
74	Samoa	5-10	29	27	48	31	48	16	16	98	98	97	0.98
75	Singapore[3]	6-11	...	...	...	295ᶻ	48ᶻ	...	8ᶻ	...	...	...	...
76	Solomon Islands	6-11	82	58	46	...	...	...	...	90	93	88	0.94
77	Thailand	6-11	5 889	6 120	48	5 371ᶻ	48ᶻ	13	18ᶻ	97	98	95	0.97
78	Timor-Leste	6-11	197	**189**	...	230	48	.	13	**125**	...	...	...
79	Tokelau[4]	5-10	0.2*	0.2	48	...	...	.	...	105	98	113	1.15
80	Tonga	5-10	16	17	46	...	...	7	...	112	115	109	0.95
81	Tuvalu[4]	6-11	1*	1	48	...	...	...	...	98	97	99	1.02
82	Vanuatu	6-11	36	34	48	42	47	...	28ᶻ	118	119	117	0.98
83	Viet Nam	6-10	6 517	10 250	47	6 923	47	0.3	0.6	111	115	106	0.93
	Latin America and the Caribbean												
84	Anguilla[9]	5-11	...	**1**	**49**	2	49	7	3	**104****	**105****	**104****	**0.98****
85	Antigua and Barbuda	5-11	11	13	...	11	47	38	52	124	...	...	...
86	Argentina	6-11	3 969	4 664	49	4 702ᶻ	49ᶻ	20	24ᶻ	113	113	112	0.99
87	Aruba	6-11	9	9	49	10	49	83	74	113	114	112	0.98
88	Bahamas	5-10	30	34	49	34	50	...	30	97	99	95	0.97
89	Barbados	5-10	19	25	49	23*	49*	...	11*	103	101	105	1.04
90	Belize	5-10	43	44	48	53	49	...	82	110	115	105	0.91
91	Bermuda	5-10	5	**5**	**50**	4	49**	**34**	37	**101**	**101**	**102**	**1.01**
92	Bolivia, P. S.	6-11	1 428	1 445	49	1 481ᶻ	49ᶻ	...	8ᶻ	114	115	113	0.98
93	Brazil[3]	7-10	...	20 939	48	16 893	47	8	14	155	159	150	0.94
94	British Virgin Islands[4]	5-11	3*	3	49	3	49	13	29	112	113	110	0.97
95	Cayman Islands	5-10	4	3	47	4ʸ	48ʸ	36	36ʸ	112	115	108	0.93
96	Chile	6-11	1 508	1 805	48	1 612ᶻ	48ᶻ	45	58ᶻ	101	102	99	0.97
97	Colombia	6-10	4 408	5 162	49	5 085	49	20	18	119	119	119	1.00
98	Costa Rica	6-11	474	570	48	521	48	7	8	112	113	112	0.99
99	Cuba	6-11	831	1 074	48	**828**	**48**	.	.	102	104	100	0.97
100	Dominica	5-11	7	12	48	8	49	26	35	120	119	121	1.02
101	Dominican Republic	6-11	1 215	1 315	49	1 318	46	14**	23	111	112	110	0.98
102	Ecuador	6-11	1 760	1 899	49	2 008ᶻ	49ᶻ	21	25ᶻ	114	114	114	1.00
103	El Salvador	7-12	824	**968**	**48**	940	48	**11**	10	**106**	**108**	**104**	**0.97**
104	Grenada	5-11	13	16	49	14	49	...	77	91	93	90	0.97
105	Guatemala	7-12	2 283	1 824	46	2 660	48	15	10	102	109	94	0.87
106	Guyana	6-11	117	107	49	99	49	1.0	5	107	107	107	1.01
107	Haiti	6-11	1 422	...	...	...	...	...	...	...	...	...	...
108	Honduras	6-11	1 102	1 095	50	1 275	49	...	9	107	107	108	1.01
109	Jamaica	6-11	337	316**	49**	299	49	4**	11	95**	95**	94**	0.99**
110	Mexico	6-11	13 063	14 698	49	14 906	49	7	8	110	112	109	0.98
111	Montserrat[9]	5-11	...	**0.4**	**45**	0.5ᶻ	49ᶻ	**35**	33ᶻ	**105**	**105**	**104**	**0.99**
112	Netherlands Antilles	6-11	17	25	48	...	...	74	...	135	138	131	0.95
113	Nicaragua	6-11	786	830	49	924	48	16	16	102	102	102	1.01
114	Panama	6-11	408	393	48	440	48	10	11	107	109	105	0.97
115	Paraguay	6-11	860	951**	48**	852ᶻ	48ᶻ	...	18ᶻ	119**	121**	117**	0.96**
116	Peru	6-11	3 482	4 350	49	3 763	49	13	22	124	125	123	0.99
117	Saint Kitts and Nevis	5-11	7	**7**	**50**	6	49	**18**	22	**109**	**108**	**110**	**1.02**
118	Saint Lucia	5-11	21	26	49	19	49	2**	5	104	106	101	0.95
119	Saint Vincent/Grenadines	5-11	14	19	48	14	48	4	5	118	121	115	0.95
120	Suriname	6-11	63	**65**	**49**	71ᶻ	48ᶻ	**48**	45ᶻ	**118**	**118**	**118**	**0.99**
121	Trinidad and Tobago	5-11	125	172	49	131	48	72**	72	97	97	96	0.99
122	Turks and Caicos Islands[9]	6-11	...	2	49	3ᶻ	49ᶻ	18	...	...	...	...	...
123	Uruguay	6-11	305	366	49	349ᶻ	48ᶻ	...	16ᶻ	111	112	111	0.99
124	Venezuela, B. R.	6-11	3 363	3 261	49	3 458	48	15	17	99	100	99	0.98

GROSS ENROLMENT RATIO (GER) IN PRIMARY EDUCATION (%)				NET ENROLMENT RATIO (NER) IN PRIMARY EDUCATION (%)								OUT-OF-SCHOOL CHILDREN (000)[2]				
School year ending in				School year ending in								School year ending in				
2010				1999				2010				1999		2010		
Total	Male	Female	GPI (F/M)	Total	Male	Female	GPI (F/M)	Total	Male	Female	GPI (F/M)	Total	% F	Total	% F	
126	131	122	0.93	77	81	74	0.92	97	98	95	0.97	168	57	23	70	61
94	94	93	1.00	85	84	87	1.05	82	81	84	1.04	7	41	5	43	62
...	...	...	...	95	96	94	0.99	...	...	...	...	148	56	...	...	63
102	**102**	**101**	**0.99**	...	...	...	...	**99**	...	...	...	...	...	**0.05**	...	64
...	...	...	...	...	...	...	...	...	...	...	...	...	...	...	...	65
126	126	126	1.00	...	...	...	...	...	...	...	...	...	...	...	...	66
93^y	90^y	96^y	1.06^y	...	...	...	...	...	...	...	...	...	...	...	...	67
101	101	101	1.00	99	99	99	1.00	99	99	99	1.00	2**	48**	1.8	33	68
...	...	...	...	99	99	98	1.00*	...	...	...	...	0.004	50	...	...	69
...	...	...	...	97**	99**	94**	0.94**	...	...	...	...	0.05**	91**	...	...	70
60^y	63^y	57^y	0.89^y	...	...	...	...	...	...	...	...	...	...	...	...	71
106^z	107^z	105^z	0.98^z	90	90	90	1.01	88^z	88^z	89^z	1.02^z	1 156	47	1 460^z	45^z	72
106	106	105	0.99	99	99	100	1.01	99	99	98	0.99	26	0.3	35**	70**	73
108	107	109	1.02	92	92	91	0.99	97	95	98	1.04	1.6	51	0.6	...	74
...	...	...	...	...	...	...	...	...	...	...	...	...	...	...	...	75
...	...	...	...	...	...	...	...	...	...	...	...	...	...	...	...	76
91^z	91^z	90^z	0.99^z	...	...	...	...	90^z	90^z	89^z	0.99^z	...	...	611^z	50^z	77
117	119	115	0.96	...	...	...	...	85	86	85	0.99	...	...	28	50	78
...	...	...	...	...	...	...	...	...	...	...	...	...	...	...	...	79
...	...	...	...	91	94	89	0.94	...	...	...	...	1.3	63	...	...	80
...	...	...	...	...	...	...	...	...	...	...	...	...	...	...	...	81
117	120	114	0.95	97	98	97	0.99	...	...	...	...	0.7**	62**	...	...	82
106	109	103	0.94	96	...	...	...	98	...	...	...	326**	...	121	...	83

Latin America and the Caribbean

...	106	97	0.92	*96***	*97***	*96***	*0.99***	...	...	...	...	*0.01***	*30***	...	...	84
102	106	97	0.92	...	...	...	...	87	89	84	0.94	...	...	1.3	63	85
118^z	118^z	117^z	0.99^z	99	100	99	0.99	...	...	...	...	24	80	...	...	86
114	116	112	0.97	98	98	99	1.01	100	100	100	1.00	0.1	29	0.03	19	87
114	113	115	1.02	91	92	90	0.98	98	...	...	...	3	54	0.7	...	88
120*	119*	122*	1.02*	95**	93**	98**	1.05**	95*,y	...	...	...	1.1**	21**	1*,y	...	89
121	127	116	0.91	88**	91**	85**	0.93**	95	...	...	...	4**	64**	1	...	90
92	92**	92**	1.00**	...	...	...	...	83**	83**	83**	0.99**	...	...	0.2**	...	91
105^z	105^z	104^z	0.99^z	95	95	95	1.00	...	...	...	...	52**	51**	...	...	92
...	...	...	...	91	...	...	...	...	...	...	...	1 039	...	...	...	93
100	103	97	0.94	96**	95**	97**	1.02**	87	88	85	0.96	0.04**	42**	0.3	56.8	94
90^y	91^y	89^y	0.97^y	96*	...	...	...	...	...	...	...	0.1*	...	...	...	95
106^z	108^z	103^z	0.95^z	...	...	...	...	94^z	94^z	93^z	1.00^z	...	...	94^z	51^z	96
115	116	114	0.98	93	93**	94**	1.01**	88	89	88	0.99	182	42**	374	50	97
110	110	109	0.99	...	...	...	...	...	...	...	...	...	...	...	...	98
101	**102**	**100**	**0.98**	97	98	97	0.99	**98**	**98**	**98**	**1.00**	13	59	**13**	**50**	99
112	113	111	0.98	95	94	96	*1.02*	94^z	94^z	95^z	1.01^z	*0.2*	...	0.1^z	...	100
108	115	102	0.88	83	82	83	1.01	90	93	87	0.93	191	47	85	67	101
114^z	114^z	115^z	1.01^z	98	97	98	1.01	97^z	96^z	98^z	1.03^z	13.5	8	27^z	...	102
114	117	111	0.95	*84*	*84*	*85*	*1.01*	94	94	94	1.00	*128*	*47*	38	48	103
103	103	103	1.00	*81***	*85***	*78***	*0.92***	87^z	87^z	87^z	0.99^z	3**	60**	0.3^z	14^z	104
116	119	114	0.96	83	86	79	0.91	97	98	96	0.98	289**	61**	32	86	105
85	83	86	1.04	...	...	...	...	81	79	82	1.04	...	...	19	42	106
...	...	...	...	...	...	...	...	...	...	...	...	...	...	...	...	107
116	116	116	1.00	*89*	*88*	*89*	*1.01*	96	95	97	1.02	*115*	48	31**	27**	108
89	91	87	0.95	90**	90**	90**	1.00**	82	83	81	0.97	30**	50**	59	53	109
114	115	113	0.99	97	97	97	1.00	98	98	98	1.00	59**	16**	58	13	110
...	...	...	...	*95***	*94***	*95***	*1.01***	...	...	...	...	*0.01*	...	...	...	111
...	...	...	...	...	...	...	...	...	...	...	...	...	...	...	...	112
118	119	116	0.98	78	77	78	1.01	92	92	93	1.01	153**	47**	48	44	113
108	109	106	0.97	95	96	95	0.99	98	99	97	0.99	14**	52**	5	67	114
100^z	101^z	98^z	0.97^z	96	96	97	1.00	85^z	85^z	85^z	1.00^z	26	46	123^z	49^z	115
108	108	108	1.00	98**	98**	97**	1.00**	95	95	96	1.01	4**	...	66	40	116
93	93	94	1.00	*93*	*92*	*94*	*1.02*	83	83	83	1.00	*0.1*	...	0.9*	49*	117
94	96	92	0.96	91**	93**	89**	0.96**	88	89	87	0.98	2**	61**	2**	52**	118
105	109	101	0.93	97**	...	...	...	94	96	91	0.95	*0.3***	...	0.2	...	119
113^z	116^z	111^z	0.95^z	*91***	*90***	*93***	*1.03***	91^z	91^z	91^z	1.00^z	*4***	*36***	6**,z	49**,z	120
105	107	103	0.97	88	88	88	1.00	94	94	94	0.99	14	47	3	56	121
...	...	...	...	...	...	...	...	...	...	...	...	...	...	...	...	122
113^z	115^z	111^z	0.97^z	...	...	...	...	99^z	99^z	99^z	0.99^z	...	...	1.6^z	78^z	123
103	104	101	0.97	85	85	86	1.01	93	93	92	1.00	439	47	171	47	124

Table 5 (continued)

				ENROLMENT IN PRIMARY EDUCATION				Enrolment in private institutions as % of total enrolment		GROSS ENROLMENT RATIO (GER) IN PRIMARY EDUCATION (%)			
				School year ending in				School year ending in		School year ending in			
		Age group	School-age population (000)	1999		2010		1999	2010	1999			
	Country or territory	2010	2010[1]	Total (000)	% F	Total (000)	% F			Total	Male	Female	GPI (F/M)
	North America and Western Europe												
125	Andorra	6-11	5	...	...	4	48	...	2	...	...	...	...
126	Austria	6-9	331	389	48	328	48	4	6	104	105	104	0.99
127	Belgium	6-11	706	763	49	732[z]	49[z]	55	54[z]	108	108	107	0.99
128	Canada	6-11	2 168	2 429	49	2 200[y]	49[y]	6	5[y]	100	100	100	1.00
129	Cyprus[4]	6-11	52*	64	48	55	49	4	8	97	98	97	1.00
130	Denmark	7-12	407	372	49	407[z]	49[z]	11	13[z]	101	101	101	1.00
131	Finland	7-12	351	383	49	347	49	1	1	101	101	100	1.00
132	France[10]	6-10	3 781	3 944	49	4 159	49	15	15	105	106	104	0.99
133	Germany	6-9	2 999	3 767	49	3 068	49	2	4	103	103	103	0.99
134	Greece	6-11	638	646	48	...	...	7	...	95	95	95	1.00
135	Iceland	6-12	30	30	48	30[z]	49[z]	1	2[z]	100	101	99	0.98
136	Ireland	5-12	469	457	49	506	49	0.9	0.7	102	102	102	0.99
137	Israel	6-11	774	662	49	786[z]	49[z]	.	[z]	105	105	104	0.99
138	Italy	6-10	2 773	2 876	48	2 822	48	7	7	105	105	104	0.99
139	Luxembourg	6-11	36	31	49	36[y]	49[y]	7	8[y]	99	99	100	1.01
140	Malta	5-10	25	35	49	25	49	36	41	100	100	101	1.00
141	Monaco[9]	6-10	...	2	50	2	51	31	22	...	...	...	...
142	Netherlands	6-11	1 201	1 268	48	1 294	49	68	...	109	110	108	0.98
143	Norway	6-12	428	412	49	424	49	1	2	101	101	101	1.00
144	Portugal	6-11	658	811	48	744[z]	48[z]	10	12[z]	122	125	119	0.96
145	San Marino[9]	6-10	2**	1	48	2	50	.	.	...	...	...	...
146	Spain	6-11	2 578	2 580	48	2 721	48	33	33	106	107	105	0.99
147	Sweden	7-12	568	763	49	576	49	3	9	110	108	112	1.03
148	Switzerland	7-12	480	530	49	493	48	3	5	106	106	105	0.99
149	United Kingdom	5-10	4 137	4 661	49	4 416[z]	49[z]	5	5[z]	101	101	101	1.00
150	United States	6-11	24 008	24 938	49	24 393	49	12	9	103	102	104	1.03
	South and West Asia												
151	Afghanistan	7-12	5 438	957	7	5 279	39	...	...	26	46	4	0.08
152	Bangladesh[3]	6-10	...	...	...	16 987*	51*	...	41*,[z]	...	...	...	...
153	Bhutan	6-12	99	81	46	**111**	**50**	2	**3**	75	81	68	0.85
154	India	6-10	123 619	113 613	44	143 310[y]	48[y]	17	...	94	102	85	0.84
155	Iran, Islamic Republic of	6-10	5 227	8 667	47	5 974	49	...	7	101	105	98	0.94
156	Maldives	6-12	40	74	49	42	48	3	4	131	130	131	1.01
157	Nepal[3]	5-9	...	3 588	42	4 952	50	...	12	114	129	99	0.77
158	Pakistan	5-9	19 755	14 205*	39*	18 756	44	...	31	71*	85*	57*	0.67*
159	Sri Lanka	5-9	1 742	1 768	49	1 721	49	-	3	108	109	107	0.99
	Sub-Saharan Africa												
160	Angola	6-11	3 433	...	...	4 273	45	...	2	...	...	...	...
161	Benin	6-11	1 421	872	39	1 788	46	7	13	83	102	65	0.64
162	Botswana	6-12	299	322	50	331[z]	49[z]	5	6[z]	103	103	103	1.00
163	Burkina Faso	6-11	2 709	816	40	**2 205**	**47**	11	**14**	42	49	34	0.70
164	Burundi	7-12	1 183	557	45	1 850	50	-	1	51	56	45	0.81
165	Cameroon	6-11	2 931	2 134	45	3 510	46	28	23	85	93	77	0.82
166	Cape Verde	6-11	65	92	49	71	48	-	0.4	125	129	122	0.95
167	Central African Republic	6-11	682	459*	41*	648	42	...	14	78*	93*	64*	0.68*
168	Chad	6-11	1 867	840	37	1 727	42	...	8	64	81	47	0.58
169	Comoros	6-11	115	83	45	111[y]	47[y]	12	15[y]	100	108	92	0.85
170	Congo	6-11	613	276	49	705	48	10	36	59	60	58	0.97
171	Côte d'Ivoire	6-11	3 074	1 911	43	**2 758**	**45**	12	**14**	74	85	63	0.74
172	D. R. Congo	6-11	11 285	4 022	47	10 572	46	...	83[z]	48	50	46	0.91
173	Equatorial Guinea	7-12	98	73	49**	85	49	...	50	108	110	105**	0.96**
174	Eritrea	7-11	641	262	45	286	45	11	8	52	57	47	0.83
175	Ethiopia	7-12	13 427	5 168	38	13 635	47	...	11	50	63	38	0.61
176	Gabon	6-10	174	265	50	**318**	**49**	17	**44**	140	140	140	1.00
177	Gambia	7-12	277	170	46	229	50	14	26	84	91	77	0.84
178	Ghana	6-11	3 517	2 377	47	**3 860**	**49**	13	**19****	81	83	77	0.93
179	Guinea	7-12	1 540	727	38	1 453	45	15	27	56	68	43	0.64
180	Guinea-Bissau	7-12	227	145**	40**	279	48	19	28	78**	93**	63**	0.67**
181	Kenya	6-11	6 511	4 782	49	7 150[z]	49[z]	...	11[z]	90	92	89	0.97
182	Lesotho	6-12	376	365	52	389	49	...	1	100	96	103	1.08

Table 5

GROSS ENROLMENT RATIO (GER) IN PRIMARY EDUCATION (%)				NET ENROLMENT RATIO (NER) IN PRIMARY EDUCATION (%)								OUT-OF-SCHOOL CHILDREN (000)[2]				
School year ending in				School year ending in								School year ending in				
2010				1999				2010				1999		2010		
Total	Male	Female	GPI (F/M)	Total	Male	Female	GPI (F/M)	Total	Male	Female	GPI (F/M)	Total	% F	Total	% F	
											North America and Western Europe					
84	84	85	1.01	...	...	...	...	77	77	78	1.01	...	...	1.1	47	125
99	100	99	0.99	...	...	...	...	...	...	...	...	...	...	...	...	126
105z	105z	104z	1.00z	99	99	99	1.00	99z	99z	99z	1.00z	6	43	7z	42z	127
99y	99y	98y	1.00y	100	100	100	1.00	...	...	...	...	6	16	...	...	128
106	106	105	0.99	95	95	95	1.00	99	99	99	1.00	1.3	49	0.5*	56	129
99z	99z	99z	1.00z	98	98	98	1.00	96z	95z	97z	1.02z	8	46	17z	35z	130
99	99	99	0.99	100	100	100	1.00	98	98	98	1.00	0.7	...	8	47	131
110	111	109	0.99	99	99	99	1.00	99	98	99	1.00	10	36	31	43	132
102	103	102	1.00	99**	99**	99**	1.00**	98**	98**	98**	1.00**	5**	...	7**	...	133
...	...	...	...	93	93	93	1.01	...	...	...	...	25	45	...	...	134
99z	99z	100z	1.00z	99	100	98	0.98	99z	99z	99z	1.00z	0.3	...	0.2z	38z	135
108	108	108	1.00	95	95	94	0.99	95	95	95	1.00	0.3	...	1.4	2	136
103z	103z	103z	1.01	98	98	97	1.00	97z	97z	97z	1.01z	15	53	23z	43z	137
102	102	101	0.99	99	99	99	1.00	97	98	97	0.99	3	...	25	80	138
100y	99y	100y	1.01y	96	95	97	1.02	95y	94y	96y	1.02y	1.0	34	1.1y	37y	139
101	101	101	1.01	94	93	94	1.01	94	93	94	1.01	2.2	43	2	45	140
...	...	...	...	...	...	...	...	...	...	...	...	...	...	...	...	141
108	108	107	0.99	99	100	99	0.99	100	100	100	1.00	7.4	99	0.3	...	142
99	99	99	1.00	100	100	100	1.00	99	99	99	1.00	0.9	72	4	43	143
114z	116z	112z	0.97z	97	...	...	...	99z	99z	99z	1.00z	20	...	4z	37z	144
94**	89**	101**	1.13**	...	...	...	...	92*,z	91*,z	93*,z	1.02*,z	...	...	0.1*,z	41*,z	145
106	106	105	0.99	100	100	100	1.00	100	100	100	1.00	7	76	6	33	146
101	102	101	0.99	100	...	...	...	99	100	99	0.99	2	...	4	75	147
103	103	102	1.00	96	96	96	1.00	94	94	94	1.00	3	29	4	33	148
106z	106z	106z	1.00z	100	100	100	1.00	100z	100z	100z	1.00z	1.7	30	8z	68z	149
102	102	101	0.99	96	96	96	1.00	95	94	95	1.00	743	47**	1 023	45	150
											South and West Asia					
97	114	79	0.69	...	...	...	...	...	...	...	...	...	...	...	...	151
...	...	...	...	...	...	...	...	...	...	...	...	...	...	...	...	152
111	**111**	**112**	**1.01**	56	59	52	0.88	**88**	**87**	**90**	**1.03**	48	54	**11**	**42**	153
116yz	116y	116y	1.00y	*79**	*86**	*72**	*0.84**	92y	93y	92y	0.99y	20 008**	70**	2 278**,y	62**,y	154
114	114	115	1.01	86**	88**	85**	0.96**	...	...	...	...	1 157**	55**	...	...	155
109	**111**	**107**	**0.96**	97	97	98	1.01	**96**	**96**	**96**	**1.00**	1.3	42	**1.3**	**48**	156
...	...	...	...	65*	73*	57*	0.78*	...	...	...	...	1 094*	60*	...	...	157
95	104	85	0.82	*58***	*69***	*46***	*0.67***	74*	81*	67*	0.82*	*8 399***	*62***	5 125*	63*	158
99	99	99	1.00	*100*	*99*	*100*	*1.00*	94	94	94	1.01	*3*	...	102	47	159
											Sub-Saharan Africa					
124	137	112	0.81	...	...	...	...	86*	93*	78*	0.84*	...	...	493**	76**	160
126	135	117	0.87	...	...	...	...	94	...	...	...	...	...	88	...	161
110	112z	108z	0.96z	80	78	81	1.04	87z	87z	88z	1.01z	64	46	38**,z	47**,z	162
79	**82**	**76**	**0.93**	33	39	27	0.70	**63**	**65**	**61**	**0.94**	1 310	54	**1 022**	**52**	163
156	157	155	0.99	37	41	34	0.84	...	...	...	...	687**	53**	...	...	164
120	129	111	0.86	...	...	...	...	92	99	86	0.87	...	...	179**	...	165
110	114	105	0.92	99**	...	...	...	93	94	92	0.98	1.0**	...	4	58	166
94	**109**	**79**	**0.73**	...	...	...	...	**69**	**78**	**59**	**0.76**	...	...	**214**	**66**	167
93	107	78	0.73	52	65	40	0.62	...	...	...	...	623	63	...	...	168
104y	109y	100y	0.92y	66	71	60	0.85	...	...	...	...	28**	57**	...	...	169
115	118	112	0.95	...	...	...	...	91*	92*	89*	0.97*	...	...	56*	58*	170
88	**96**	**80**	**0.83**	56	64	48	0.75	61z	67z	56z	0.83z	1 097**	59**	1 161z	57z	171
94	100	87	0.87	33	34	32	0.95	...	...	...	...	5 598**	50**	...	...	172
87	88	85	0.97	72**	...	...	...	56	57	56	0.99	*19***	...	43	50	173
45	48	41	0.84	33	35	31	0.86	33	36	31	0.87	338	52	418	51	174
102	106	97	0.91	36	43	30	0.69	81	84	79	0.94	6 509	55	2 390	57	175
182	**184**	**179**	**0.97**	...	...	...	...	...	...	...	...	...	...	...	...	176
83	82	84	1.02	69	74	64	0.87	66	64	67	1.03	61	58	85**	48**	177
107	**107**	**107**	**1.00**	61**	62**	60**	0.97**	**84**	**84**	**84**	**1.01**	1 138**	50**	**567**	**48**	178
94	103	86	0.87	43	51	35	0.69	77	83	70	0.85	739	56	355	63	179
123	127	119	0.94	50**	59**	42**	0.71**	74	75	72	0.96	92**	59**	57	53	180
113z	115z	112z	0.98z	62	62	62	1.01	83**,z	82**,z	83**,z	1.01**,z	1 980**	49**	1 010**,z	48**,z	181
103	104	102	0.98	56	53	59	1.12	73	72	75	1.04	160	46	99	47	182

Table 5 (continued)

	Country or territory	Age group 2010	School-age population (000) 2010[1]	ENROLMENT IN PRIMARY EDUCATION School year ending in 1999 Total (000)	% F	2010 Total (000)	% F	Enrolment in private institutions as % of total enrolment School year ending in 1999	2010	GROSS ENROLMENT RATIO (GER) IN PRIMARY EDUCATION (%) School year ending in 1999 Total	Male	Female	GPI (F/M)
183	Liberia	6-11	626	396	42	540[y]	47[y]	38	30[y]	94	107	80	0.75
184	Madagascar	6-10	2 856	2 012	49	4 242	49	22	18	97	98	95	0.97
185	Malawi	6-11	2 523	2 582	49	3 417	50	...	...	138	141	135	0.96
186	Mali	7-12	2 510	959	41	**2 115**	**46**	22	**35**	53	62	45	0.72
187	Mauritius	5-10	118	133	49	117	49	24	28	100	100	100	1.00
188	Mozambique	6-12	4 587	2 302	43	**5 254**	**47**	...	2	69	79	59	0.74
189	Namibia	7-13	380	383	50	407[z]	49[z]	4	5[z]	116	115	116	1.01
190	Niger	7-12	2 604	530	39	**1 910**	**44**	4	**4**	31	37	25	0.68
191	Nigeria[11]	6-11	24 835	17 907	44	20 682	47	...	8**	93	102	83	0.81
192	Rwanda	7-12	1 613	*1 476*	*50*	2 341	51	...	2	*106*	*106*	*105*	*0.99*
193	Sao Tome and Principe	6-11	26	24	49	**35**	49	-	0.5	110	112	108	0.97
194	Senegal	7-12	1 952	1 034	45	1 695	51	12	14	68	74	61	0.83
195	Seychelles	6-11	7	*10*	*49*	9	50	*4*	9	*112*	*112*	*112*	*1.00*
196	Sierra Leone	6-11	937	*443*	...	**1 195**	49	...	3	70	...	...	...
197	Somalia	6-11	1 533	...	...	...	...	...	...	...	...	...	...
198	South Africa	7-13	7 021	7 935	49	7 129[z]	49[z]	2	3[z]	113	114	111	0.97
199	South Sudan	...	...	...	...	...	...	...	...	...	...	...	...
200	Swaziland	6-12	208	213	49	241	48	-	0.2	94	96	92	0.96
201	Togo	6-11	921	954	43	1 287	47	36	34	126	144	108	0.75
202	Uganda	6-12	6 913	6 288	47	8 375	50	...	14	130	137	123	0.90
203	United Republic of Tanzania	7-13	8 232	4 190	50	8 419	50	0.2	2	67	67	67	1.00
204	Zambia	7-13	2 515	1 556	48	2 899	50	...	3	84	87	80	0.92
205	Zimbabwe	6-12	2 227	...	...	...	...	...	...	...	...	...	...

			Sum	Sum	% F	Sum	% F	Median		Weighted average			
I	World	...	651 781	651 249	47	690 665	48	7	9	99	103	95	0.92
II	Countries in transition	...	13 469	17 705	49	13 318**	49**	0.1	0.6	102	102	101	0.99
III	Developed countries	...	63 573	69 884	49	65 341	49	4	5	103	102	103	1.00
IV	Developing countries	...	574 739	563 660	46	612 007	48	11	13	98	103	94	0.91
V	Arab States	...	42 521	35 024	45	41 741	47	4	12	89	96	83	0.87
VI	Central and Eastern Europe	...	19 486	24 885	48	19 433**	49**	0.3	0.8	103	104	101	0.97
VII	Central Asia	...	5 420	6 838	49	5 461	48	0.3	0.9	97	97	97	0.99
VIII	East Asia and the Pacific	...	167 940	224 574**	48**	185 304	47	7	13	111**	111**	110**	0.99**
IX	East Asia	...	164 340	221 452**	48**	181 989	47	2	5	111**	111**	111**	0.99**
X	Pacific	...	3 600	3 122	48	3 314	48	...	...	95	96	93	0.97
XI	Latin America/Caribbean	...	58 256	69 978	48	66 413	48	16	18	121	123	119	0.97
XII	Caribbean	...	2 273	2 410**	49**	2 411**	49**	24	33	108**	108**	107**	0.98**
XIII	Latin America	...	55 984	67 569	48	64 002	48	14	16	122	123	120	0.97
XIV	N. America/W. Europe	...	49 604	52 822	49	51 140	49	7	7	103	103	104	1.01
XV	South and West Asia	...	176 942	155 075	44	188 366**	48**	...	7	89	97	81	0.83
XVI	Sub-Saharan Africa	...	131 612	82 053	46	132 809	48	11	12	80	87	74	0.85
XVII	Countries with low income	...	116 299	74 523	46	122 465	48	11	12	78	84	72	0.86
XVIII	Countries with middle income	...	464 940	500 470	46	495 538**	47**	5	8	102	106	98	0.92
XIX	Lower middle	...	281 032	246 203	45	293 373**	48**	4	9	93	100	86	0.86
XX	Upper middle	...	183 908	254 267**	48**	202 165	47	6	8	114**	115**	113**	0.99**
XXI	Countries with high income	...	70 542	76 256	49	72 663	49	7	9	102	102	102	1.00

Sources: UNESCO Institute for Statistics database (UIS, 2012). Enrolment ratios in the table are based on the United Nations Population Division estimates, revision 2010 (United Nations, 2011), median variant.
Note A: The country groupings by income level presented in the tables are as defined by the World Bank. They are based on the list of countries by income group as revised in July 2011.
Note B: The median values for 1999 and 2010 are not comparable since they are not necessarily based on the same number of countries.
1. Data are for 2010 except for countries with a split calendar school year, in which case data are for 2009.
2. Data reflect the actual number of children not enrolled at all, derived from the age-specific or adjusted net enrolment ratio (ANER) of primary school age children, which measures the proportion of those who are enrolled either in primary or in secondary schools.
3. Enrolment ratios for one or both of the two school years were not calculated due to inconsistencies in the population data.
4. National population data were used to calculate enrolment ratios.
5. Enrolment and population data exclude Transnistria.
6. In the Russian Federation two education structures existed in the past, both starting at age 7. The most common or widespread one lasted three years and was used to calculate indicators; the second one, in which about one-third of primary pupils were enrolled, had four grades. Since 2004, the four-grade structure has been extended all over the country.

Table 5

GROSS ENROLMENT RATIO (GER) IN PRIMARY EDUCATION (%)				NET ENROLMENT RATIO (NER) IN PRIMARY EDUCATION (%)								OUT-OF-SCHOOL CHILDREN (000)²				
School year ending in				School year ending in								School year ending in				
2010				1999				2010				1999		2010		
Total	Male	Female	GPI (F/M)	Total	Male	Female	GPI (F/M)	Total	Male	Female	GPI (F/M)	Total	% F	Total	% F	
96^y	101^y	91^y	0.91^y	46	52	40	0.78	...	...	...	...	226**	55**	...	...	183
149	150	147	0.98	65	65	66	1.01	...	...	...	...	715	50	...	...	184
135	133	138	1.04	99	99	98	0.98	97^z	94^z	99^z	1.05^z	17	...	62^z	...	185
82	**87**	**76**	**0.88**	42**	48**	35**	0.73**	**63**	**67**	**59**	**0.88**	1 038**	55**	850	56	186
99	99	100	1.01	92	92	92	1.01	93	92	94	1.02	11	47	8	41	187
111	**116**	**105**	**0.91**	52	58	46	0.79	**90**	**92**	**87**	**0.95**	1 598**	56**	482	61	188
107^z	108^z	107^z	0.99^z	87	84	90	1.07	85^z	83^z	88^z	1.05^z	39	36	52^z	40^z	189
71	**77**	**64**	**0.84**	26	31	21	0.68	**62**	**68**	**57**	**0.83**	1 254	52	**1 012**	**56**	190
83	87	79	0.91	61**	67**	56**	0.84**	58**	60**	55**	0.91**	7 444**	56	10 542**	52**	191
142	**140**	**143**	**1.03**	76**	75**	77**	1.03**	99	...	...	...	**337****	**48****	20	...	192
134	**136**	**132**	**0.97**	88	88	87	0.99	98	97	100	1.03	2**	51**	0.4	...	193
87	84	89	1.06	57	62	52	0.84	75	73	78	1.06	660	55	429	45	194
117	117	117	1.00	*92*	*91*	*92*	*1.01*	...	...	...	...	*0.7*	*45.6*	...	...	195
125	**129**	**120**	**0.93**	...	...	...	...	...	...	...	...	...	...	...	...	196
...	...	...	...	...	...	...	...	...	...	...	...	...	...	...	...	197
102^z	104^z	100^z	0.96^z	92	91	92	1.01	85**·^{z}	85**·^{z}	85**·^{z}	1.00**·^{z}	269**	33**	679**·^{z}	47**·^{z}	198
...	...	...	...	...	...	...	...	...	...	...	...	...	...	...	...	199
116	121	111	0.92	70	69	71	1.03	86	86	85	0.99	67	47	30	51	200
140	147	132	0.90	85	95	75	0.79	92^y	97^y	87^y	0.89^y	86	...	51^y	...	201
121	120	122	1.01	...	...	...	...	91	90	92	1.03	...	...	623	43	202
102	101	103	1.02	49	48	50	1.03	98^y	98^y	98^y	0.99^y	3 190	49	137^y	56^y	203
115	115	116	1.01	71	72	69	0.96	91	90	92	1.02	541**	52**	184**	41**	204
...	...	...	...	...	...	...	...	...	...	...	...	...	...	...	...	205
Weighted average				Weighted average				Weighted average				Sum	% F	Sum	% F	
106	107	105	0.97	82**	85**	79**	0.93**	89**	90**	88**	0.98**	107 614**	58**	60 684**	53**	I
99**	99**	99**	1.00**	90**	91**	90**	0.99**	91**	92**	91**	0.99**	1 365**	50**	824**	48**	II
103	103	102	0.99	97	97	97	1.00	97	97	97	1.00	1 322	49	1 586	45	III
106	108	105	0.97	80**	83**	77**	0.92**	88**	89**	87**	0.98**	104 927**	58**	58 274**	53**	IV
98	102	94	0.93	77	81	73	0.90	86**	89**	84**	0.94**	8 423	59	5 036**	61**	V
100**	100**	99**	0.99**	92**	93**	91**	0.98**	94**	94**	94**	0.99**	1 644**	57**	931**	49**	VI
101	102	100	0.98	91**	91**	90**	0.99**	90	91	89	0.98	439**	52**	317	54	VII
110	110	111	1.01	94**	94**	94**	0.99**	95**	95**	95**	1.00**	10 344**	51**	6 579**	44**	VIII
111	110	112	1.02	94**	95**	94**	0.99**	95**	95**	95**	1.00**	10 005**	51**	6 091**	44**	IX
92	93	91	0.98	90	90	89	0.98	86	88	85	0.97	339	52	488	54	X
114	116	112	0.97	92	93	91	0.98	94**	94**	94**	0.99**	3 607	55**	2 652**	50**	XI
106**	107**	105**	0.98**	72**	72**	72**	1.00**	69**	69**	69**	1.00**	612**	49**	681**	49**	XII
114	116	112	0.97	93	94	92	0.98	95**	95**	95**	0.99**	2 995	56	1 972**	51**	XIII
103	103	103	0.99	98	98	97	1.00	96	96	97	1.00	901	48	1 267	45	XIV
106**	108**	105**	0.98**	74**	80**	67**	0.83**	88**	89**	87**	0.98**	40 081**	64**	13 261**	55**	XV
101	105	97	0.93	58	62	54	0.87	76**	78**	74**	0.95**	42 174	54	30 641**	53**	XVI
105	108	102	0.95	58**	62**	55**	0.88**	80**	82**	78**	0.95**	39 163**	53**	22 244**	54**	XVII
107**	108**	105**	0.98**	85**	88**	81**	0.93**	90**	91**	89**	0.98**	66 192**	61**	36 592**	53**	XVIII
104**	106**	102**	0.96**	77**	82**	71**	0.86**	87**	88**	85**	0.97**	55 752**	62**	29 362**	54**	XIX
110	110	110	1.00	94**	95**	94**	0.99**	95**	95**	95**	1.00**	10 440**	52**	7 230**	48**	XX
103	103	103	0.99	96	96	96	1.00	97	96	97	1.00	2 259	48	1 848	46**	XXI

7. Enrolment and population data exclude the Nagorno-Karabakh region.
8. Children enter primary school at age 6 or 7. Since 7 is the most common entrance age, enrolment ratios were calculated using the 7–11 age group for population.
9. Enrolment ratios for one or both of the two school years were not calculated due to lack of United Nations population data by age.
10. Data include French overseas departments and territories (DOM-TOM).
11. Due to the continuing discrepancy in enrolment by single age, the net enrolment ratio in primary education is estimated using the age distribution from the 2007 MICS as from the school year ending in 2007.
Data in bold are for the school year ending in 2011, those in italics are for 2000 and those in bold italic are for 2001.

(z) Data are for the school year ending in 2009.
(y) Data are for the school year ending in 2008.
(*) National estimate.
(**) For country level data: UIS partial estimate; for regional and other country-grouping sums and weighted averages: partial imputation due to incomplete country coverage (between 33% and 60% of population for the region or other country grouping).
- Magnitude nil or negligible.
(.) The category is not applicable or does not exist.
(. . .) No data available.

ANNEX

Table 6
Internal efficiency in primary education: repetition, dropouts and completion

		Duration[1] of primary education	INTERNAL EFFICIENCY — REPETITION AND DROPOUTS											
			REPEATERS, ALL GRADES [%] — School year ending in						DROPOUTS, ALL GRADES [%] — School year ending in					
			1999			2010			1999			2009		
Country or territory		2010	Total	Male	Female	Total	Male	Female	Total	Male	Female	Total	Male	Femal
	Arab States													
1	Algeria	5	11.9	14.6	8.7	7.5	9.2	5.6	8.5	10.1	6.9	5.0	6.8	2.9
2	Bahrain	6	3.8	4.6	3.1	1.9^z	1.9^z	1.9^z	9.7	10.6	8.7	…	…	…
3	Djibouti	5	16.6	16.9**	16.1**	**9.6**	**9.9**	**9.4**	…	…	…	35.7**·^{y}	35.9**·^{y}	35.5**^{y}
4	Egypt	6	6.0**	7.1**	4.6**	3.7	…	…	…	…	…	…	…	…
5	Iraq	6	10.0	10.7	9.2	…	…	…	50.5**	48.5**	52.8**	…	…	…
6	Jordan	6	0.7	0.7	0.7	0.5	0.5	0.6	3.5	3.5	3.6	…	…	…
7	Kuwait	5	3.3	3.4	3.1	0.7	0.8	0.6	6.0	7.1	4.9	4.0	4.0	4.0
8	Lebanon	6	9.1**	10.4**	7.6**	8.1	9.4	6.7	…	…	…	8.2^y	9.7^y	6.7^y
9	Libya	6	…	…	…	…	…	…	…	…	…	…	…	…
10	Mauritania	6	*15.2***	*15.0***	*15.5***	3.5	3.4	3.5	**59.6**	**60.6**	**58.4**	29.3	29.1	29.6
11	Morocco	6	12.4	14.1	10.2	10.7	12.6	8.7	24.9	25.2	24.4	9.5	9.4	9.6
12	Oman	6	8.0	9.5	6.4	1.4^z	1.3^z	1.6^z	8.1	8.3	7.9	…	…	…
13	Palestine	4	2.1	2.2	2.0	-	-	-	1.3	0.7	1.9	…	…	…
14	Qatar	6	2.7**	3.5**	1.9**	0.5^z	0.5^z	0.5^z	…	…	…	6.4^x	9.3^x	3.2
15	Saudi Arabia	6	…	…	…	3.3^y	3.5^y	3.1^y	…	…	…	6.7*·^{x}	3.3*·^{x}	10*·
16	Sudan (pre-secession)	6	11.3**	10.9**	11.8**	3.7^z	3.8^z	3.5^z	22.9**	26.3**	18.5**	9.1^x	14.4^x	2.3^x
17	Syrian Arab Republic	4	6.5	7.2	5.6	7.6	8.6	6.5	13.1	12.9	13.2	5.4	5.7	5.1
18	Tunisia	6	18.3	20.0	16.4	6.8^z	8.4^z	5.1^z	12.8	13.9	11.7	5.3^y	6.1^y	4.5
19	United Arab Emirates	5	3.5	4.4	2.5	2.0	2.1	1.9	10.5	10.1	11.0	…	…	…
20	Yemen	6	10.6	11.7*	8.7*	6.5	7.1	5.7	**31.2****	**27.9****	**36.0****	…	…	…
	Central and Eastern Europe													
21	Albania	5	3.9**	4.6**	3.2**	1.0	1.1	0.8	9.9**	11.9**	7.7**	4.8	4.9	4.6
22	Belarus	4	0.5	0.5	0.5	0.0	…	…	0.8	1.0	0.6	0.3	…	…
23	Bosnia and Herzegovina	4	…	…	…	0.1	0.1	0.0	…	…	…	1.3	0.9	1.6
24	Bulgaria	4	3.2	3.7	2.7	0.6	0.7	0.5	7.1	7.4	6.7	2.6	2.4	2.9
25	Croatia	4	0.4	0.5	0.3	0.3	0.3	0.2	0.6	0.9	0.3	0.9	1.5	0.4
26	Czech Republic	5	1.2	1.5	1.0	0.6^z	0.7^z	0.5^z	1.7	2.0	1.4	0.4^y	0.6^y	0.2^y
27	Estonia	6	2.5	3.5	1.4	0.6^z	0.9^z	0.3^z	1.5	2.2	0.7	1.6^y	1.8^y	1.4^y
28	Hungary	4	2.2	2.1	2.2	2.0^z	2.4^z	1.6^z	3.6	4.6	2.4	2.3^y	2.5^y	2.1^y
29	Latvia	6	2.1	2.7**	1.3**	2.1	2.7	1.6	3.0	3.4	2.6	5.4	5.3	5.5
30	Lithuania	4	0.9	1.3	0.5	0.5	0.7	0.4	0.8	1.5	0.2	1.7	1.8	1.6
31	Montenegro	4	…	…	…	…	…	…	…	…	…	…	…	…
32	Poland	6	1.2	…	…	1.0^z	1.3^z	0.6^z	1.7	…	…	2.4^y	2.6^y	2.3^y
33	Republic of Moldova	4	0.9	0.9**	0.9**	0.1^z	0.1^z	0.1^z	10.5**	11.6**	9.3**	4.7	6.4	3.0
34	Romania	4	3.4	4.1	2.6	1.8	2.1	1.5	4.3	5.0	3.6	2.9	2.9	2.9
35	Russian Federation	4	1.4	…	…	0.4^z	…	…	5.2	…	…	3.9^y	…	…
36	Serbia	4	…	…	…	0.5	0.6	0.4	…	…	…	1.4	1.6	1.3
37	Slovakia	4	2.3	2.6	2.0	3.2	3.4	2.9	3.1	3.7	2.4	1.8	1.9	1.6
38	Slovenia	6	1.0	1.3	0.7	0.6^z	0.8^z	0.4^z	0.3	0.3	0.4	0.5^y	0.3^y	0.7^y
39	TFYR Macedonia	5	0.0	0.1	0.0	0.2	0.2	0.2	2.7	4.4	0.9	…	…	…
40	Turkey	5	…	…	…	1.8^z	1.7^z	1.9^z	…	…	…	8.2^y	9.3^y	7.0^y
41	Ukraine	4	0.8	0.8*	0.8*	0.1	0.1	0.1	3.3*	3.6*	3.0*	2.3	2.6	1.9
	Central Asia													
42	Armenia	3	*0.1***	*0.1***	*0.1***	0.2	0.2	0.2	…	…	…	…	…	…
43	Azerbaijan	4	0.4	0.4	0.4	0.3	0.3	0.2	3.7	4.7	2.6	3.6	4.6	2.5
44	Georgia	6	0.3	0.4**	0.3**	0.1	0.1	0.1	0.9	1.5	0.2	3.8	5.9	1.4
45	Kazakhstan	4	0.3	…	…	**0.1**	**0.1**	**0.0**	5.0**	2.6**	7.6**	**0.2**	**0.2**	**0.1**
46	Kyrgyzstan	4	0.3	0.4	0.2	0.1	0.1	0.1	5.5*	4.9*	6.1*	2.4	2.0	2.7
47	Mongolia	5	0.9	1.0	0.8	0.1	0.1	0.1	12.8	15.3	10.3	5.9	6.9	4.9
48	Tajikistan	4	0.5	0.5**	0.6**	0.3	0.3	0.3	4.2**	1.3**	7.3**	1.1	1.4	0.8
49	Turkmenistan	3	…	…	…	…	…	…	…	…	…	…	…	…
50	Uzbekistan	4	0.1	…	…	**0.0**	**0.0**	**0.0**	0.5**	…	…	**1.9**	**2.2**	**1.7**
	East Asia and the Pacific													
51	Australia	7	…	…	…	…	…	…	…	…	…	…	…	…
52	Brunei Darussalam	6	…	…	.	0.1	0.2	0.1	…	…	…	3.9	4.0	3.7
53	Cambodia	6	24.2	25.1	23.1	8.8	9.8	7.8	*45.3*	*43.9*	*46.9*	45.5^x	48.0^x	42.7
54	China	5	…	…	…	0.3	0.3	0.2	…	…	…	…	…	…
55	Cook Islands	6	2.6	…	…	-	-	-	…	…	…	…	…	…
56	DPR Korea	4	…	…	…	…	…	…	…	…	…	…	…	…
57	Fiji	6	.	.	.	1.1^z	1.3^z	0.8^z	17.9	17.8	18.0	9.1^y	6.6^y	11.7^y
58	Indonesia	6	*6.2*	*6.2*	*6.2*	3.3	3.9	2.7	*14.1*	*16.7*	*11.3*	20.0^x	22.6^x	17.2
59	Japan	6	…	…	…	-	-	-	…	…	…	0.0	0.0	0.1
60	Kiribati	6	.	.	.	.^{y}	.^{y}	.^{y}	*30.6*	*28.3*	*32.8*	…	…	…

INTERNAL EFFICIENCY															
PRIMARY EDUCATION COMPLETION															
SURVIVAL RATE TO GRADE 5 (%)						SURVIVAL RATE TO LAST GRADE (%)						PRIMARY COHORT COMPLETION RATE (%)			
School year ending in						School year ending in						School year ending in			
1999			2009			1999			2009			2009			
Total	Male	Female	Total	Male	Female	Total	Male	Female	Total	Male	Female	Total	Male	Female	
Arab States															
95	94	96	95	93	97	91	90	93	95	93	97	...	...	...	1
96	95	96	98[y]	98[y]	98[y]	90	89	91	...	...	...	...	...	...	2
...	...	...	64[**,y]	64[**,y]	64[**,y]	...	...	...	64[**,y]	64[**,y]	64[**,y]	...	...	...	3
...	...	...	97[**]	...	...	...	...	...	...	...	...	...	...	...	4
66[**]	67[**]	63[**]	...	...	...	49[**]	51[**]	47[**]	...	...	...	...	...	...	5
97	98	97	...	...	...	96	97	96	...	...	...	...	...	...	6
.	.	.	96	96	96	94	93	95	96	96	96	...	...	...	7
...	...	...	95[y]	94[y]	96[y]	...	...	...	92[y]	90[y]	93[y]	86	82	89	8
...	...	...	...	...	...	...	...	...	...	...	...	...	...	...	9
55	*54*	*56*	74	74	75	*40*	*39*	*42*	71	71	70	...	...	...	10
82	82	82	94	94	94	75	75	76	91	91	90	87	87	87	11
94	94	94	...	...	...	92	92	92	...	...	...	...	...	...	12
.	.	.	...	...	...	99	99	98	...	...	...	...	...	...	13
...	...	...	96	92[x]	99[x]	...	...	...	94[x]	91[x]	97[x]	...	...	...	14
...	...	...	94[*,x]	97[*,x]	91[*,x]	...	...	...	93[*,x]	97[*,x]	90[*,x]	93[*,x]	97[*,x]	89[*,x]	15
84[**]	81[**]	88[**]	94[x]	89[x]	100[x]	77[**]	74[**]	81[**]	91[x]	86[x]	98[x]	...	...	...	16
92	92	91	.	.	.	87	87	87	95	94	95	92	92	92	17
92	91	93	96[y]	95[y]	97	87	86	88	95[y]	94[y]	95[y]	90[y]	88[y]	92[y]	18
92	93	92	...	...	...	89	90	89	...	...	...	...	...	...	19
74[**]	*78[**]*	*70[**]*	...	...	...	*69[**]*	*72[**]*	*64[**]*	...	...	...	...	...	...	20
Central and Eastern Europe															
.[**]	.[**]	.[**]	95	95	95	90[**]	88[**]	92[**]	95	95	95	93	93	94	21
.	.	.	.	.	.	99	99	99	100	...	...	100	...	...	22
...	...	...	.	.	.	...	...	...	99	99	98	...	...	...	23
.	.	.	.	.	.	93	93	93	97	98	97	...	...	...	24
.	.	.	.	.	.	99	99	100	99	99	100	...	...	...	25
98	98	99	100[y]	99[y]	100[y]	98	98	99	100[y]	99[y]	100[y]	...	...	...	26
99	99	99	99[y]	99[y]	99[y]	98	98	99	98[y]	98[y]	99[y]	...	...	...	27
.	.	.	.[y]	.[y]	.[y]	96	95	98	98[y]	98[y]	98[y]	...	...	...	28
.	.	.	96	96	96	97	97	97	95	95	95	...	...	...	29
.	.	.	.	.	.	99	99	100	98	98	98	...	...	...	30
...	...	...	...	...	...	...	...	...	...	...	...	...	...	...	31
99	...	...	98[y]	98[y]	98[y]	98	...	...	98[y]	97[y]	98[y]	...	...	...	32
.[**]	.[**]	.[**]	.	.	.	*90[**]*	*88[**]*	*91[**]*	95	94	97	95	93	97	33
.	.	.	.	.	.	96	95	96	97	97	97	...	...	...	34
.	.	.	.[y]	.[y]	.[y]	95	...	...	96[y]	...	...	...	...	...	35
.	.	.	.	.	.	...	...	...	99	98	99	98	98	98	36
.	.	.	.	.	.	97	96	98	98	98	98	...	...	...	37
.	.	.	100[y]	100[y]	99[y]	100	100	100	100[y]	100[y]	99[y]	...	...	...	38
.	.	.	...	...	...	97	96	99	...	...	...	...	...	...	39
...	...	...	92[y]	91[y]	93[y]	...	...	...	92[y]	91[y]	93[y]	...	...	...	40
.*	.*	.*	.	.	.	97*	96*	97*	98	97	98	...	...	...	41
Central Asia															
.	.	.	...	...	...	96	95	97	...	...	...	...	...	...	42
.	.	.	...	...	...	99	99	100	96	95	98	94	91	98	43
.	.	.	96	94	99	99	99	100	96	94	99	96	94	99	44
.[**]	.[**]	.[**]	.	.	.	*95[**]*	*97[**]*	*92[**]*	**100**	**100**	**100**	98	99	98	45
.*	.*	.*	.	.	.	95*	95*	94*	98	98	97	96	97	94	46
.	.	.	94	93	95	87	85	90	94	93	95	...	...	...	47
.[**]	.[**]	.[**]	.	.	.	96[**]	99[**]	93[**]	99	99	99	91	92	91	48
...	...	...	.	.	.	...	...	...	...	...	...	...	...	...	49
.[**]	.	.	.	.	.	100[**]	...	...	**98**	**98**	**98**	**98**	**98**	**98**	50
East Asia and the Pacific															
...	...	...	98	97	99	...	...	...	96	96	96	87	85	89	51
...	...	...				...	...	...							52
63	*63*	*63*	62[x]	60[x]	65[x]	*55*	*56*	*53*	54[x]	52[x]	57	48[x]	46[x]	51[x]	53
...	...	...				...	...	...							54
...	...	...	**84**	**87**	**81**	...	...	...	...	...	...	...	...	...	55
...	...	...				...	...	...							56
87	89	86	94[y]	96[y]	92[y]	82	82	82	91[y]	93[y]	88[y]	91[y]	93[y]	88[y]	57
89	*87*	*92*	86[x]	83[x]	89	*86*	*83*	*89*	80[x]	77[x]	83[x]	...	...	...	58
...	...	...	100	100	100	...	...	...	100	100	100	...	...	...	59
72	*72*	*72*	...	...	...	*69*	*72*	*67*	...	...	...	...	...	...	60

357

Table 6 (continued)

Education for All Global Monitoring Report 2012

		Duration[1] of primary education	INTERNAL EFFICIENCY — REPETITION AND DROPOUTS											
			REPEATERS, ALL GRADES (%)						DROPOUTS, ALL GRADES (%)					
			School year ending in						School year ending in					
			1999			2010			1999			2009		
	Country or territory	2010	Total	Male	Female	Total	Male	Female	Total	Male	Female	Total	Male	Female
61	Lao PDR	5	20.9	22.4	19.1	14.0	15.2	12.8	45.4	44.7	46.2	33.0ˣ	33.8ˣ	32.2ˣ
62	Macao, China	6	6.3	7.3	5.1	5.7	6.9	4.3	...	...	...	1.9ʸ	2.4ʸ	1.5ʸ
63	Malaysia	6	.	.	.	.ᶻ	.ᶻ	.ᶻ	...	...	...	2.3ʸ	2.6ʸ	2.1ʸ
64	Marshall Islands	6	.	.	.	.	.	.	...	...	...	16.5ʸ	12.7ʸ	20.5ʸ
65	Micronesia, F. S.	6	...	...	...	.	.	.	...	...	...	...	...	...
66	Myanmar	5	1.7	1.7**	1.7**	0.3	0.3	0.3	44.8	44.7	44.8	25.2	27.8	22.5
67	Nauru	6	-	-	-	...	...	...	...	...	...	...	...	...
68	New Zealand	6	...	...	...	...	...	...	...	...	...	...	...	...
69	Niue	6	.	.	.	...	...	...	...	...	...	...	...	...
70	Palau	5	-	-	-	...	...	...	...	...	...	...	...	...
71	Papua New Guinea	6	-	-	-	.	.	.	...	...	...	...	...	...
72	Philippines	6	1.9	2.4	1.4	2.5ᶻ	3.2ᶻ	1.8ᶻ	**24.7**	**28.9**	**20.2**	24.2ʸ	28.0ʸ	20.0
73	Republic of Korea	6	-	-	-	0.0	0.0	0.0	0.8	0.6	0.9	0.7	0.8	0.7
74	Samoa	6	1.0	1.1	0.9	0.9	1.1	0.7	10.0*	11.5*	8.3*	...	...	...
75	Singapore	6	...	...	...	0.4ᶻ	0.4ᶻ	0.4ᶻ	...	...	...	1.3ʸ	1.5ʸ	1.2
76	Solomon Islands	6	...	...	...	...	...	...	...	...	...	...	...	...
77	Thailand	6	3.5	3.4	3.5	...	...	...	...	...	...	...	...	...
78	Timor-Leste	6		...	...	16.8	18.6	14.9	...	...	...	33.4	36.7	29.7
79	Tokelau	6	.	.	.	...	...	...	...	...	...	...	...	...
80	Tonga	6	8.8	8.5	9.2	...	...	...	...	...	...	...	...	...
81	Tuvalu	6	.	.	.	...	...	...	...	...	...	...	...	...
82	Vanuatu	6	10.6**	11.1**	9.9**	13.4	14.7	12.0	31.1	33.0	29.0	28.5ʸ	26.5ʸ	30.7ʸ
83	Viet Nam	5	3.8	4.2	3.2	...	...	...	17.2	20.1	13.8	...	...	...
	Latin America and the Caribbean													
84	Anguilla	7	0.3	0.4	0.3	-	-	-	...	...	...	...	...	...
85	Antigua and Barbuda	7	...	...	...	7.0*	8.2*	5.7*	...	...	...	...	...	...
86	Argentina	6	5.9	6.9	4.9	5.1ᶻ	6.1ᶻ	4.1ᶻ	11.3	13.8	8.7	6.2ʸ	6.4ʸ	5.9ʸ
87	Aruba	6	7.7	9.5	5.9	7.4	8.3	6.5	4.4	2.7	6.1	8.6ʸ	14.2ʸ	2.8ʸ
88	Bahamas	6	.	.	.	3.5	4.4	2.7	...	...	...	10.5	8.6	12.3
89	Barbados	6	.	.	.	.*	.*	.*	8.8	8.0	9.6	...	...	...
90	Belize	6	9.7	10.8	8.4	7.5	8.8	6.2	26.0	25.5	26.5	9.7	10.9	8.6
91	Bermuda	6	.	.	.	.	.**	.**	...	...	...	...	...	...
92	Bolivia, P. S.	6	2.4	2.6	2.3	0.8ʸ	0.8ʸ	0.7ʸ	20.2	17.9	22.6	16.3ˣ	15.1ˣ	17.6ˣ
93	Brazil	4	24.0	24.0	24.0	...	...	...	19.9**	23.9**	15.2**	...	...	...
94	British Virgin Islands	7	3.8**	4.1**	3.6**	5.6	6.9	4.3	...	...	...	...	...	...
95	Cayman Islands	6	0.2	0.2	0.1	-ʸ	-ʸ	-ʸ	...	...	...	...	...	...
96	Chile	6	2.4	2.9	1.9	1.0ᶻ	1.2ᶻ	0.7ᶻ	2.4	2.8	1.9	...	...	...
97	Colombia	5	5.2	5.8	4.6	1.9	2.2	1.6	33.4	36.0	30.7	15.5	16.0	14.9
98	Costa Rica	6	8.9	10.1	7.6	5.7	6.6	4.7	11.4	12.9	9.8	11.2	12.4	10.0
99	Cuba	6	1.9	2.6	1.1	**0.6**	**0.8**	**0.3**	5.3	6.2	4.3	**5.0**	**6.0**	**3.9**
100	Dominica	7	3.6	3.8	3.5	4.5	6.0	2.8	...	...	...	11.9	14.2	9.6
101	Dominican Republic	6	4.1	4.5	3.7	7.3	9.3	5.0	29.4	33.7	24.8	...	...	...
102	Ecuador	6	2.7	3.0	2.4	...	...	...	25.4	25.7	25.1	...	...	...
103	El Salvador	6	7.1**	7.7**	6.4**	5.7	6.8	4.6	37.5**	37.3**	37.8**	13.5	14.0	13.0
104	Grenada	7	6.5**	7.8**	5.1**	3.5	4.4	2.4	...	...	...	...	...	...
105	Guatemala	6	14.9	15.8	13.8	10.8	11.6	9.9	49.6	48.0	51.3	35.2ˣ	34.5ˣ	36.0ˣ
106	Guyana	6	3.1	3.6	2.5	0.5	0.6	0.4	34.9	38.5	31.1	16.5ʸ	14.6ʸ	18.4ʸ
107	Haiti	6	...	...	...	...	...	...	...	...	...	...	...	...
108	Honduras	6	...	...	...	0.8	0.9	0.7	...	...	...	23.8ˣ	26.2ˣ	21.2ˣ
109	Jamaica	6	5.1	6.6	3.5	2.4	2.7	2.1	**14.2**	**17.5**	**10.7**	4.8	5.8	3.8
110	Mexico	6	6.6	7.6	5.5	3.4	4.2	2.6	12.8	14.0	11.5	5.8	6.8	4.8
111	Montserrat	7	0.8	1.4	-	2.3ᶻ	2.4ᶻ	2.1ᶻ	...	...	...	...	...	...
112	Netherlands Antilles	6	12.0**	14.5**	9.3**	...	...	...	17.8**	23.8**	11.6**	...	...	...
113	Nicaragua	6	4.7	5.3	4.1	7.9	9.2	6.6	54.1	58.2	49.6	51.6ˣ	55.3ˣ	47.5ˣ
114	Panama	6	6.4	7.4	5.2	5.5	6.5	4.5	9.8	10.2	9.5	6.2	6.3	6.2
115	Paraguay	6	7.8**	8.8**	6.7**	5.0ᶻ	6.0ᶻ	3.9ᶻ	26.7**	28.9**	24.3**	21.9ʸ	23.9ʸ	19.7ʸ
116	Peru	6	10.2	10.5	9.9	6.2	6.5	5.9	16.9	15.6	18.2	9.6	10.2	9.0
117	Saint Kitts and Nevis	7	...	...	...	1.7	2.2	1.2	...	...	...	26.5	22.4	30.4
118	Saint Lucia	7	2.4**	2.8**	2.0**	2.6	3.0	2.1	...	...	...	7.9	6.5	9.4
119	Saint Vincent/Grenadines	7	**9.9****	**12.0****	**7.6****	4.7	5.8	3.4	...	...	...	...	...	...
120	Suriname	6	**11.3****	**9.1****	**13.6****	17.1ᶻ	19.5ᶻ	14.5ᶻ	...	...	...	9.7ʸ	18.1ʸ	0.4ʸ
121	Trinidad and Tobago	7	4.7	4.9	4.4	6.3	7.4	5.2	...	...	...	10.6*	13.1*	7.9*
122	Turks and Caicos Islands	6	8.4	8.7	8.0	1.8ᶻ	2.6ᶻ	1.0ᶻ	...	...	...	...	...	...
123	Uruguay	6	7.9	9.3	6.5	5.4ᶻ	6.5ᶻ	4.2	13.3	14.5	12.1	4.8ʸ	6.5ʸ	3.1ʸ
124	Venezuela, B. R.	6	7.0**	8.5**	5.5**	3.7	4.7	2.7ᶻ	11.9	15.8	7.9	7.9	9.9	5.8

INTERNAL EFFICIENCY															
PRIMARY EDUCATION COMPLETION															
SURVIVAL RATE TO GRADE 5 [%]						SURVIVAL RATE TO LAST GRADE [%]						PRIMARY COHORT COMPLETION RATE [%]			
School year ending in						School year ending in						School year ending in			
1999			2009			1999			2009			2009			
Total	Male	Female	Total	Male	Female	Total	Male	Female	Total	Male	Female	Total	Male	Female	
55	55	54	67[x]	66[x]	68[x]	55	55	54	67[x]	66[x]	68[x]	64[x]	63[x]	66[x]	61
...	...	...	99[y]	98[y]	100[y]	...	...	...	98[y]	98[y]	99[y]	96[y]	95[y]	97[y]	62
87	*87*	*87*	98[y]	98[y]	98[y]	...	...	...	98[y]	97[y]	98[y]	...	...	...	63
...	...	...	87[y]	92[y]	82[y]	...	...	...	83[y]	87[y]	80[y]	...	...	...	64
...	...	...	...	...	...	...	...	...	...	...	...	...	...	...	65
55	*55*	*55*	75	72	77	*55*	*55*	*55*	75	72	77	74	71	77	66
...	...	...	...	...	...	...	...	...	...	...	...	...	...	...	67
...	...	...	...	...	...	...	...	...	...	...	...	...	...	...	68
...	...	...	...	...	...	...	...	...	...	...	...	...	...	...	69
...	...	...	...	...	...	...	...	...	...	...	...	...	...	...	70
...	...	...	...	...	...	...	...	...	...	...	...	...	...	...	71
79	*76*	*83*	79[y]	75[y]	82[y]	*75*	*71*	*80*	76[y]	72[y]	80[y]	...	...	...	72
99	100	99	99	99	99	99	99	99	99	99	99	...	...	...	73
91*	89*	94*	96	94	99	90*	88*	92*	...	...	...	...	...	...	74
...	...	...	99[y]	99[y]	99[y]	...	...	...	99[y].	99[y]	99[y]	...	...	...	75
...	...	...	...	...	...	...	...	...	...	...	...	...	...	...	76
...	...	...	...	...	...	...	...	...	...	...	...	...	...	...	77
...	...	...	71	68	74	...	...	...	67	63	70	66	63	69	78
...	...	...	...	...	...	...	...	...	...	...	...	...	...	...	79
92	91	94	...	...	...	...	...	...	...	...	...	...	...	...	80
...	...	...	...	...	...	...	...	...	...	...	...	...	...	...	81
72	72	72	76[y]	78	74[y]	69	67	71	71[y]	74[y]	69[y]	...	...	...	82
83	80	86	...	...	...	83	80	86	...	...	...	...	...	...	83

Latin America and the Caribbean

Total	Male	Female	Total	Male	Female	Total	Male	Female	Total	Male	Female	Total	Male	Female	
*93**￼*	*91**￼*	*96*	...	...	...	...	...	...	...	...	...	...	...	...	84
...	...	...	94[x]	92[x]	95[x]	...	...	...	...	...	...	...	...	...	85
90	88	92	95[y]	96[y]	95[y]	89	86	91	94[y]	94[y]	94[y]	...	...	...	86
97	97	96	93[y]	87[y]	99[y]	96	97	94	91[y]	86[y]	97[y]	81[x]	80[x]	83[x]	87
...	...	...	91	93	90	...	...	...	89	91	88	...	...	...	88
92	93	90	92*,[y]	95*,[y]	90*,[y]	91	92	90	...	...	...	...	...	...	89
76	74	78	91	89	93	74	74	73	90	89	91	81	80	81	90
...	...	...	...	...	...	...	...	...	...	...	...	...	...	...	91
82	83	81	85[x]	86[x]	85[x]	80	82	77	84[x]	85[x]	82[x]	75[x]	75[x]	75[x]	92
.**	.**	.**	.	.	.	*80**￼*	*76**￼*	*85**￼*	...	...	...	...	...	...	93
...	...	...	...	...	...	...	...	...	...	...	...	...	...	...	94
93	*96*	*90*	...	...	...	...	...	...	...	...	...	...	...	...	95
98	98	98	...	...	...	98	97	98	...	...	...	...	...	...	96
67	64	69	85	84	85	67	64	69	85	84	85	80	80	80	97
91	90	93	91	90	92	89	87	90	89	88	90	83	81	85	98
96	95	96	**96**	**95**	**97**	95	94	96	**95**	**94**	**96**	**94**	**94**	**95**	99
86	87	85	90	86	94	...	...	...	88	86	90	81	73	90	100
75	71	79	...	...	...	71	66	75	...	...	...	...	...	...	101
77	77	77	...	...	...	75	74	75	...	...	...	...	...	...	102
65	64	66	89	89	90	62	63	62**	86	86	87	81	81	82	103
...	...	...	...	...	...	...	...	...	...	...	...	...	...	...	104
56	*58*	*54*	71[x]	71	70	*50*	*52*	*49*	65[x]	65[x]	64[x]	61[x]	62[x]	61[x]	105
77	71	84	87[y]	87[y]	86[y]	65	62	69	83[y]	85[y]	82[y]	...	...	...	106
...	...	...	...	...	...	...	...	...	...	...	...	...	...	...	107
...	...	...	78[x]	75[x]	80[x]	...	...	...	76[x]	74[x]	79[x]	76[x]	74[x]	79[x]	108
89	*87*	*91*	96	96	96	*86*	*83*	*89*	95	94	96	...	...	...	109
89	88	90	96	95	97	87	86	88	94	93	95	...	...	...	110
...	...	...	...	...	...	...	...	...	...	...	...	...	...	...	111
84**	80**	88**	...	...	...	82**	76**	88**	...	...	...	...	...	...	112
48	44	53	51[x]	48[x]	55[x]	46	42	50	48[x]	45[x]	52[x]	46[x]	42[x]	50[x]	113
92	92	92	95	95	94	90	90	91	94	94	94	86[y]	85[y]	87[y]	114
78**	76**	80**	82[y]	81[y]	84[y]	73**	71**	76**	78[y]	76[y]	80[y]	...	...	...	115
87	88	87	93	93	94	83	84	82	90	90	91	...	...	...	116
83	...	...	84	90	78	...	...	...	74	78	70	72	78	66	117
...	...	...	95	96	93	...	...	...	92	93	91	88*	85*	91*	118
...	...	...	...	...	...	...	...	...	...	...	...	...	...	...	119
...	...	...	94[y]	89[y]	100[y]	...	...	...	90[y]	82[y]	100[y]	82[y]	82[y]	83[y]	120
96	96	97	92*	90*	94*	...	...	...	89*	87*	92*	89*	85*	92*	121
...	...	...	...	...	...	...	...	...	...	...	...	...	...	...	122
89	*87*	*90*	95[y]	94[y]	97[y]	*87*	*85*	*88*	95[y]	94[y]	97[y]	...	...	...	123
91	88	94	94	93	95	88	84	92	92	90	94	90	88	92	124

Table 6 (continued)

Education for All Global Monitoring Report 2012

	Country or territory	Duration[1] of primary education 2010	REPEATERS, ALL GRADES (%) School year ending in						DROPOUTS, ALL GRADES (%) School year ending in					
			1999			2010			1999			2009		
			Total	Male	Female	Total	Male	Female	Total	Male	Female	Total	Male	Femal
	North America and Western Europe													
125	Andorra	6	…	…	…	2.4	2.5	2.3	…	…	…	…	…	…
126	Austria	4	1.5	1.8	1.3	-	-	-	…	…	…	3.0	4.2	1.8
127	Belgium	6	…	…	…	3.3ᶻ	3.4ᶻ	3.2ᶻ	…	…	…	6.6ʸ	7.8ʸ	5.3ˣ
128	Canada	6	-	-	-	-ʸ	-ʸ	-ʸ	1.4	1.7	1.1	…	…	…
129	Cyprus	6	0.4	0.5	0.3	0.2	0.2	0.1	5.1	6.4	3.7	4.7ˣ	6.1ˣ	3.2ˣ
130	Denmark	6	-	-	-	0.2ᶻ	0.2ᶻ	0.1ᶻ	0.1	0.1	0.1	0.5ʸ	0.6ʸ	0.5ˣ
131	Finland	6	0.4	0.6	0.3	0.4	0.5	0.3	0.6	0.5	0.7	0.3	0.5	0.1
132	France	5	4.2	…	…	…	…	…	2.0	…	…	…	…	…
133	Germany	4	1.7	1.9	1.5	0.5	0.5	0.5	0.9	1.2	0.6	3.8	4.3	3.2ˣ
134	Greece	6	-	-	-	…	…	…	…	…	…	…	…	…
135	Iceland	7	-	-	-	-ᶻ	-ᶻ	-ᶻ	*2.2*	*1.9*	*2.6*	…	…	…
136	Ireland	8	1.8	2.1	1.6	0.7	0.7	0.6	…	…	…	…	…	…
137	Israel	6	…	…	…	1.2ᶻ	1.5ᶻ	0.8ᶻ	*0.9*	*0.2*	*1.5*	1.1ʸ	-ʸ	2.3ˣ
138	Italy	5	0.4	0.5	0.3	0.3	0.4	0.2	*4.2*	*4.6*	*3.7*	0.4	0.5	0.2
139	Luxembourg	6	5.0	…	…	3.8ʸ	4.0ʸ	3.6ʸ	…	…	…	…	…	…
140	Malta	6	2.1	2.4	1.8	0.9	0.9	0.9	*2.1*	*2.4*	*1.7*	20.3ʸ	16.5ʸ	24.1ˣ
141	Monaco	5	-	-	-	-ᶻ	-ᶻ	-ᶻ	…	…	…	…	…	…
142	Netherlands	6	.	.	.	.	.	.	1.6	1.4	1.9	…	…	…
143	Norway	7	.	.	.	.	.	.	0.4	0.3	0.5	0.9	0.7	1.1
144	Portugal	6	…	…	…	…	…	…	…	…	…	…	…	…
145	San Marino	5	-	-	-	-	-	-	…	…	…	…	…	…
146	Spain	6	…	…	…	2.6	3.0	2.3	…	…	…	0.5ʸ	1.0ʸ	0.0ˣ
147	Sweden	6	-	-	-	-	-	-	1.7	1.5	1.9	0.6	0.7	0.4
148	Switzerland	6	1.8	1.9	1.6	1.4	1.5	1.3	…	…	…	…	…	…
149	United Kingdom	6	-	-	-	-ᶻ	-ᶻ	-ᶻ	…	…	…	…	…	…
150	United States	6	-**	-**	-**	-**	-**	-**	…	…	…	…	…	…
	South and West Asia													
151	Afghanistan	6	…	…	…	…	…	…	…	…	…	…	…	…
152	Bangladesh	5	…	…	…	12.5*	12.6*	12.3*	…	…	…	33.8*	38.1*	29.4*
153	Bhutan	7	12.1	12.5	11.7	**5.7**	**6.6**	**4.9**	18.5	22.0	14.2	**9.0**	**11.3**	**6.6**
154	India	5	4.0	4.0	4.1	3.4ʸ	3.5ʸ	3.4ʸ	38.0	36.7	39.6	…	…	…
155	Iran, Islamic Republic of	5	*5.4*	*6.6*	*4.1*	2.0ᶻ	2.4ᶻ	1.6ᶻ	*2.6*	*1.9*	*3.3*	5.7ʸ	5.8ʸ	5.5ˣ
156	Maldives	7	…	…	…	**3.8**	**4.1**	**3.5**	…	…	…	…	…	…
157	Nepal	5	22.9	22.2	23.8	**12.0**	**12.1**	**11.8**	41.0	43.4	37.5	38.3ˣ	40.2ˣ	36.3ˣ
158	Pakistan	5	…	…	…	4.3	4.5	4.1	…	…	…	38.5	36.3	41.1
159	Sri Lanka	5	*1.4*	*1.6*	*1.2*	0.7	0.8	0.6	…	…	…	…	…	…
	Sub-Saharan Africa													
160	Angola	6	…	…	…	10.8	10.2	11.7	…	…	…	68.1*	63.4*	73.1*
161	Benin	6	*19.9***	*20.0***	*19.8***	13.4**	13.4**	13.3**	*24.3*	*17.7*	*33.6*	…	…	…
162	Botswana	7	3.3	3.9	2.7	4.6**,ᶻ	5.5**,ᶻ	3.6**,ᶻ	18.0	21.4	14.5	7.0**,ʸ	8.7**,ʸ	5.3**ˣ
163	Burkina Faso	6	17.7	17.5	18.0	10.1	10.1	10.1	39.0	40.5	36.6	36.4	38.8	33.4
164	Burundi	6	25.4	25.5	25.2	33.7	33.5	33.9	46.2	46.0	46.4	43.8	48.2	38.9
165	Cameroon	6	26.7**	26.8**	26.5**	13.1	13.5	12.7	**55.2***	**56.2***	**54.0***	33.8	33.2	34.6
166	Cape Verde	6	11.6**	12.8**	10.3**	9.6	11.6	7.5	**11.7**	**13.7**	**9.5**	14.3ˣ	15.5ˣ	13.0ˣ
167	Central African Republic	6	…	…	…	22.6	22.0	23.5	…	…	…	53.5	51.4	56.1
168	Chad	6	25.9	25.7	26.3	22.4	22.0	22.9	52.2	48.9	58.0	72.2	71.7	73.0
169	Comoros	6	26.0	26.4	25.5	24.4ʸ	24.5ʸ	24.4ʸ	…	…	…	…	…	…
170	Congo	6	39.1	40.0	38.2	19.1	19.7	18.4	…	…	…	29.7**,ˣ	29.4**,ˣ	29.5**ˣ
171	Côte d'Ivoire	6	23.7	22.8**	24.9**	**16.6**	…	…	37.5	32.9	43.6	39.2ʸ	38.2ʸ	40.6ʸ
172	D. R. Congo	6	15.5	18.8	11.9	14.1	14.0	14.3	…	…	…	45.2	42.0	48.9
173	Equatorial Guinea	6	11.8	9.3	14.9	20.2	21.4	19.0	…	…	…	38.1	40.3	35.7
174	Eritrea	5	19.4	18.2	20.8	14.7	15.8	13.3	6.1	4.1	8.6	31.0	29.1	33.1
175	Ethiopia	6	10.6	9.8	11.9	3.9	3.7	4.2	49.1	50.6	46.0	52.5	52.6	52.5
176	Gabon	5	*36.5***	*37.3***	*35.7***	…	…	…	…	…	…	…	…	…
177	Gambia	6	9.2	9.2	9.1	5.5**	5.6**	5.3**	34.3**	34.7**	33.8**	38.9**	37.0**	40.6**
178	Ghana	6	4.2	4.3	4.1	**2.5**	**2.5**	**2.6**	*40.6*	*39.3*	*42.0*	27.8ʸ	24.3ʸ	31.3ʸ
179	Guinea	6	26.2	25.5	27.4	16.5	15.6	17.6	…	…	…	34.3	25.7	43.8
180	Guinea-Bissau	6	24.0**	23.6**	24.5**	14.1	13.9	14.2	…	…	…	…	…	…
181	Kenya	6	…	…	…	…	…	…	…	…	…	…	…	…
182	Lesotho	7	20.3	22.9	17.9	20.0	23.4	16.5	40.8	48.5	33.4	30.7	38.1	23.3

INTERNAL EFFICIENCY															
PRIMARY EDUCATION COMPLETION															
SURVIVAL RATE TO GRADE 5 [%]						SURVIVAL RATE TO LAST GRADE [%]						PRIMARY COHORT COMPLETION RATE [%]			
School year ending in						School year ending in						School year ending in			
1999			2009			1999			2009			2009			
Total	Male	Female	Total	Male	Female	Total	Male	Female	Total	Male	Female	Total	Male	Female	
North America and Western Europe															
...	...	...	94	93	96	...	...	...	...	...	...	...	...	...	125
·	·	·	·	·	·	...	...	...	97	96	98	...	...	...	126
...	...	...	97y	96y	97y	...	...	...	93y	92y	95y	...	...	...	127
99	98	99	...	...	...	99	98	99	...	...	...	...	...	...	128
95	94	96	95	94x	97x	95	94	96	95x	94x	97x	...	...	...	129
100	100	100	100	100y	100y	100	100	100	99y	99y	100y	...	...	...	130
99	100	99	100	100	100	99	100	99	100	100	100	...	...	...	131
98	...	...	...	...	...	98	...	...	...	...	...	...	...	...	132
·	·	·	·	·	·	99	99	99	96	96	97	...	...	...	133
...	...	...	...	...	...	...	...	...	...	...	...	...	...	...	134
98	*98*	*98*	99y	99y	99y	*98*	*98*	*97*	...	...	...	...	...	...	135
95	93	96	99	99	100	...	...	...	...	...	...	...	...	...	136
99	*100*	*99*	99y	100y	98y	*99*	*100*	*98*	99y	100y	98y	...	...	...	137
96	*95*	*96*	100	99	100	*96*	*95*	*96*	100	99	100	...	...	...	138
96	97	94	96x	95x	98x	...	...	...	...	...	...	...	...	...	139
98	98	98	83y	86y	81y	98	98	98	80y	83y	76y	...	...	...	140
...	...	...	...	...	...	...	...	...	...	...	...	...	...	...	141
100	100	100	99	98	100	98	99	98	...	...	...	...	...	...	142
100	100	100	99	99	100	100	100	99	99	99	99	...	...	...	143
...	...	...	...	...	...	...	...	...	...	...	...	...	...	...	144
...	...	...	...	...	...	...	...	...	...	...	...	...	...	...	145
...	...	...	100y	99y	100y	...	...	...	99y	99y	100y	99y	99y	100y	146
98	99	98	100	99	100	98	99	98	99	99	100	...	...	...	147
97	*97*	*96*	...	...	...	...	...	...	...	...	...	...	...	...	148
...	...	...	...	...	...	...	...	...	...	...	...	...	...	...	149
...	...	...	...	...	...	...	...	...	...	...	...	...	...	...	150
South and West Asia															
...	...	...	...	...	...	...	...	...	...	...	...	...	...	...	151
...	...	...	66*	62*	71*	...	...	...	66*	62*	71*	60*	56*	64*	152
90	89	92	**96**	**95**	**96**	82	78	86	**91**	**89**	**93**	84+1	84+1	85+1	153
62	63	60	...	...	...	62	63	60	...	...	...	...	...	...	154
97	98	97	94y	94y	94y	97	98	97	94y	94y	94y	...	...	...	155
...	...	...	...	...	...	...	...	...	...	...	...	...	...	...	156
59	57	63	62x	60x	64x	59	57	63	62x	60x	64x	...	...	...	157
...	...	...	62	64	59	...	...	...	62	64	59	45	47	43	158
...	...	...	...	...	...	...	...	...	...	...	...	...	...	...	159
Sub-Saharan Africa															
·	·	·	45*	53*	37*	...	...	...	32*	37*	27*	28*	33*	23*	160
84	*89*	*78*	60	62	59	76	82	66	...	...	...	...	...	...	161
87	84	89	97**,y	96**,y	97**,y	82	79	86	93**,y	91**,y	95**,y	...	...	...	162
68	67	70	75	73	78	61	60	63	64	61	67	53x	52x	55x	163
59	59	58	62	59	66	54	54	54	56	52	61	...	...	...	164
52*	***53****	***51****	76	76	77	***45****	***44****	***46****	66	67	65	49	48	49	165
91	**88**	**94**	90x	89x	91x	**88**	**86**	**90**	86x	85x	87x	...	...	...	166
...	...	...	55	58	51	...	...	...	46	49	44	...	...	...	167
56	59	51	37	36	37	48	51	42	28	28	27	...	...	...	168
...	...	...	...	...	...	...	...	...	...	...	...	...	...	...	169
...	...	...	77**,x	75**,x	79**,x	...	...	...	70**,x	71**,x	71**,x	...	...	...	170
69	73	65	66y	66y	66y	63	67	56	61y	62y	59y	...	...	...	171
...	...	...	60	62	58	...	...	...	55	58	51	51x	54x	48x	172
...	...	...	70	67	72	...	...	...	62	60	64	...	...	...	173
94	96	91	69	71	67	94	96	91	69	71	67	69	71	67	174
56	55	59	51	50	51	51	49	54	47	47	48	...	...	...	175
...	...	...	...	...	...	...	...	...	...	...	...	...	...	...	176
66**	65**	66**	65**	67**	63**	66**	65**	66**	61**	63**	59**	...	...	...	177
66	*67*	*65*	78y	80y	77y	*59*	*61*	*58*	72y	76y	69y	71y	73y	69y	178
...	...	...	69	74	62	...	...	...	66	74	56	43	47	38	179
...	...	...	...	...	...	...	...	...	...	...	...	...	...	...	180
...	...	...	...	...	...	...	...	...	...	...	...	...	...	...	181
75	68	81	80	76	85	59	52	67	69	62	77	67	...	...	182

Table 6 (continued)

			INTERNAL EFFICIENCY											
			REPETITION AND DROPOUTS											
			REPEATERS, ALL GRADES (%)						DROPOUTS, ALL GRADES (%)					
		Duration[1] of primary education	School year ending in						School year ending in					
			1999			2010			1999			2009		
	Country or territory	2010	Total	Male	Female	Total	Male	Female	Total	Male	Female	Total	Male	Female
183	Liberia	6	...	...	...	6.7[y]	6.5[y]	6.9[y]	...	...	...	54.4[x]	51.4[x]	57.4[x]
184	Madagascar	5	28.3**	27.7**	28.9**	19.9	21.0	18.8	47.6	47.8	47.3	65.4	66.2	64.6
185	Malawi	6	14.4	14.4	14.4	19.0	19.2	18.7	63.7	61.4	66.2	47.2	47.9	46.4
186	Mali	6	17.4	17.2	17.7	**12.9**	**12.8**	**12.9**	35.5**	33.7**	38.1**	**24.5**	**22.9**	**26.4**
187	Mauritius	6	3.8	4.1	3.5	3.5	4.1	2.8	1.5	1.0	2.2	2.2	1.5	3.0
188	Mozambique	7	23.8	23.2	24.7	**7.7**	**7.9**	**7.4**	70.6	68.2	73.4	**73.0**	**72.2**	**73.9**
189	Namibia	7	12.3	13.9	10.7	15.8[z]	18.1[z]	13.5[z]	17.7	19.7	15.8	17.4[y]	20.2[y]	14.7[y]
190	Niger	6	12.2	12.4	11.8	**3.7**	**3.6**	**3.8**	*30.9*	*29.6*	*33.0*	**30.7**	**28.6**	**33.1**
191	Nigeria	6	3.1**	3.0**	3.1**	.	.	.	...	...	...	20.1	22.7	17.0
192	Rwanda	6	29.1	29.2	29.0	13.8	14.1	13.5	68.9	68.8	69.0	63.0	65.0	61.0
193	Sao Tome and Principe	6	30.7	32.6	28.7	**12.4**	**13.5**	**11.2**	*41.2***	*47.2***	*34.7***	32.0**,[y]	38.0**,[y]	25.2**,[y]
194	Senegal	6	14.4	14.2	14.5	6.3	6.3	6.2	*37.1*	*33.5*	*41.2*	40.4	41.9	38.9
195	Seychelles	6	.	.	.	.	.	.	3.9	4.4	3.4	...	...	...
196	Sierra Leone	6	...	...	...	**15.6**	**15.2**	**16.1**	...	...	...	...	...	...
197	Somalia	6	...	...	...	...	...	...	...	...	...	...	...	...
198	South Africa	7	10.4	11.6	9.2	...	...	...	42.5	41.4	43.7	...	...	...
199	South Sudan	...	...	...	...	...	...	...	...	...	...	...	...	...
200	Swaziland	7	17.1	19.5	14.5	15.1	17.1	12.9	35.3	36.8	33.8	16.1	18.8	13.3
201	Togo	6	31.2	30.9	31.6	22.1	22.0	22.3	54.3	51.3	58.4	40.6	45.4	32.8
202	Uganda	7	***9.5***	***9.7***	***9.3***	10.8	11.0	10.5	*61.8*	*61.6*	*62.1*[+1]	68.2	68.3	68.1
203	United Republic of Tanzania	7	3.2	3.1	3.2	2.4	2.5	2.3	*26.1*	*28.6*	*23.5*[+1]	18.6	23.6	13.3
204	Zambia	7	6.1	6.4	5.8	6.0	6.4	5.7	33.7	29.5	38.0	46.9[y]	45.4[y]	48.4[x]
205	Zimbabwe	7	...	...	...	...	...	...	...	...	...	...	...	...
I	World[2]	...	3.8	4.2	3.2	2.5	2.5	2.6	12.8	14.6	11.0	9.1	14.4	2.3
II	Countries in transition	...	0.5	0.5	0.5	0.1	0.1	0.1	4.2	1.3	7.3	2.3	2.3	2.3
III	Developed countries	...	0.9	1.3	0.5	0.5	0.6	0.4	1.6	1.4	1.9	1.4	0.9	1.8
IV	Developing countries	...	6.5	7.4	5.6	5.1	6.1	4.1	24.9	25.7	24.3	18.6	23.6	13.3
V	Arab States	...	8.5	9.9	7.0	3.6	...	...	11.7	11.8	11.3	6.7	3.3	10.2
VI	Central and Eastern Europe	...	1.2	1.5	1.0	0.6	0.8	0.4	3.0	3.4	2.6	2.3	2.6	1.9
VII	Central Asia	...	0.3	...	...	0.1	0.1	0.1	4.2	1.3	7.3	2.4	2.0	2.7
VIII	East Asia and the Pacific	...	0.5	0.5	0.4	0.4	0.4	0.4	...	...	...	...	...	...
IX	East Asia	...	3.5	3.4	3.5	0.4	0.4	0.4	...	...	...	11.9	13.3	10.4
X	Pacific	...	.	.	.	...	...	...	...	...	...	...	...	...
XI	Latin America/Caribbean	...	5.1	6.2	4.1	3.7	4.7	2.7	17.4	19.7	14.9	10.5	13.1	9.4
XII	Caribbean	...	3.7	3.9	3.5	3.0	3.7	2.3	...	...	...	...	...	...
XIII	Latin America	...	6.5	7.5	5.4	5.1	6.1	4.1	18.4	19.8	16.7	11.2	12.4	10.0
XIV	N. America/W. Europe	...	-	-	-	0.2	0.2	0.1	1.6	1.4	1.9	...	...	...
XV	South and West Asia	...	5.4	6.6	4.1	4.1	4.3	3.8	...	...	...	33.8	38.1	29.4
XVI	Sub-Saharan Africa	...	17.2	18.4	16.1	13.3	13.5	13.0	38.2	33.2	42.4	38.1	40.3	35.7
XVII	Countries with low income	...	18.6	17.9	19.4	12.9	12.8	12.9	44.8	44.7	44.8	40.6	42.0	40.6
XVIII	Countries with middle income	...	4.2	4.4	3.9	3.4	3.5	3.4	16.9	15.6	18.2	9.5	9.4	9.6
XIX	Lower middle	...	6.1	6.3	6.0	4.3	4.5	4.1	28.6	28.6	28.6	21.9	23.9	20.0
XX	Upper middle	...	3.6	3.6	3.5	2.2	2.5	1.8	9.8	10.2	9.5	5.4	5.7	5.0
XXI	Countries with high income	...	1.2	...	...	0.6	0.8	0.4	...	...	...	1.9	2.4	1.5

Source: UNESCO Institute for Statistics database (UIS, 2012).
Note: The country groupings by income level presented in the tables are as defined by the World Bank. They are based on the list of countries by income group as revised in July 2011.
1. Duration in this table is defined according to ISCED97 and may differ from that reported nationally.
2. All values shown are medians. The median values for 1999, 2009 and 2010 are not comparable since they are not necessarily based on the same number of countries.

Data in bold are for the school year ending in 2010 for dropout, survival and primary cohort completion rates, and the school year ending in 2011 for percentage of repeaters (all grades). Those in italics are for 2000 and those in bold italic are for 2001.
(z) Data are for the school year ending in 2009.
(y) Data are for the school year ending in 2008.
(x) Data are for the school year ending in 2007.
(*) National estimate.
(**) UIS partial estimate.

INTERNAL EFFICIENCY															
PRIMARY EDUCATION COMPLETION															
SURVIVAL RATE TO GRADE 5 (%)						SURVIVAL RATE TO LAST GRADE (%)						PRIMARY COHORT COMPLETION RATE (%)			
School year ending in						School year ending in						School year ending in			
1999			2009			1999			2009			2009			
Total	Male	Female	Total	Male	Female	Total	Male	Female	Total	Male	Female	Total	Male	Female	
...	...	...	60ˣ	64ˣ	56ˣ	...	...	...	46ˣ	49ˣ	43ˣ	...	...	...	183
52	52	53	35	34	35	52	52	53	35	34	35	20	19	20	184
48	55	42	61	60	62	36	39	34	53	52	54	...	...	...	185
77**	78**	76**	**88**	**89**	**87**	65**	66**	62**	**75**	**77**	**74**	**44**	**47**	**41**	186
99	100	99	98	99	97	98	99	98	98	98	97	81	77	86	187
43	47	38	**44**	**45**	**43**	29	32	27	**27**	**28**	**26**	**22**	**23**	**22**	188
93	92	93	91ʸ	90ʸ	93ʸ	82	80	84	83ʸ	80ʸ	85ʸ	...	...	...	189
74	76	*71*	**71**	**74**	**69**	69	70	67	**69**	**71**	**67**	**37**	**39**	**34**	190
...	...	...	86	84	90	...	...	...	80	77	83	80	77	83	191
42	*41*	*43*	47	45	50	*31*	*31*	*31*	37	35	39	...	...	...	192
*62***	*59***	*65***	*77**·ʸ*	*74**·ʸ*	*81**·ʸ*	*59***	*53***	*65***	*68**·ʸ*	*62**·ʸ*	*75**·ʸ*	...	...	...	193
72	*75*	*69*	74	73	75	*63*	*67*	*59*	60	58	61	45ʸ	...	...	194
96	96	97	95ʸ	97ʸ	93ʸ	96	96	97	...	...	...	...	...	...	195
...	...	...	...	...	...	...	...	...	...	...	...	...	...	...	196
...	...	...	...	...	...	...	...	...	...	...	...	...	...	...	197
65	65	64	...	...	...	57	59	56	...	...	...	...	...	...	198
...	...	...	...	...	...	...	...	...	...	...	...	...	...	...	199
80	72	88	96	95	97	65	63	66	84	81	87	...	...	...	200
52	55	50	78	78	77	46	49	42	59	55	67	49	47	52	201
57	*56*	*58*	57	56	58	*38*	*38*	*38*	32	32	32	30ʸ	32ʸ	29ʸ	202
81	*80*	*83*	90	87	93	*74*	*71*	*77*	81	76	87	...	...	...	203
81	83	78	71ʸ	71ʸ	70ʸ	66	70	62	53ʸ	55ʸ	52ʸ	...	...	...	204
...	...	...	...	...	...	...	...	...	...	...	...	...	...	...	205
...	...	...	...	...	...	87	85	89	91	86	98	...	...	...	I
.	.	.	.	.	.	96	99	93	98	98	98	...	...	...	II
98	...	...	99	99	100	98	99	98	99	99	98	...	...	...	III
82	83	82	87	89	84	75	74	76	81	76	87	...	...	...	IV
92	92	92	95	...	...	88	88	89	93	97	90	...	...	...	V
.	.	.	.	.	.	97	97	97	98	97	98	...	...	...	VI
.	.	.	.	.	.	96	99	93	98	98	97	...	...	...	VII
...	...	...	87	92	82	...	...	...	...	...	...	...	...	...	VIII
81	78	85	92	90	94	...	...	...	88	87	90	...	...	...	IX
...	...	...	...	...	...	...	...	...	...	...	...	...	...	...	X
88	88	88	92	90	93	83	80	85	89	87	91	...	...	...	XI
89	87	91	92	90	94	...	...	...	...	...	...	...	...	...	XII
87	87	87	91	90	92	82	80	83	89	88	90	...	...	...	XIII
...	...	...	99	...	...	98	99	98	...	...	...	...	...	...	XIV
...	...	...	66	62	71	...	...	...	66	62	71	...	...	...	XV
69	70	68	71	71	70	62	67	58	62	60	64	...	...	...	XVI
59	59	58	62	60	64	55	55	55	59	58	59	...	...	...	XVII
...	...	...	91	...	...	83	84	82	91	91	90	...	...	...	XVIII
76	74	78	80	76	85	71	71	71	78	76	80	...	...	...	XIX
90	...	...	95	94	95	90	90	91	95	94	95	...	...	...	XX
96	95	96	...	...	...	...	...	...	98	98	99	...	...	...	XXI

- Magnitude nil or negligible.
(.) The category is not applicable or does not exist.
(. . .) No data available.

Table 7
Participation in secondary education[1]

Country or territory	Transition from primary to secondary general education (%) School year ending in 2009 — Total	Male	Female	Age group 2010	School-age population (000) 2010[3]	Total enrolment — School year ending in 1999 — Total (000)	% F	2010 — Total (000)	% F	Enrolment in private institutions as % of total enrolment Median — School year ending in 2010	Enrolment in technical and vocational education — School year ending in 2010 — Total (000)	% F	Lower secondary — School year ending in 2010 — Total	Male	Female	GPI (F/M)
Arab States																
1 Algeria	91ˣ	90ˣ	92ˣ	11-17	4 667	...	...	4 585ᶻ	49ᶻ	0.1ᶻ	446ᶻ	35ᶻ	133ᶻ	138ᶻ	127ᶻ	0.92ᶻ
2 Bahrain[4]	99ʸ	98ʸ	99ʸ	12-17	...	59	51	80	50	21	6	13	...	...	...	...
3 Djibouti	66ʸ	67ʸ	64ʸ	11-17	142	16	42	**51**	**44**	**10**	**2**	**41**	**44**	**49**	**40**	**0.82**
4 Egypt	...	...	...	12-17	9 444	7 671	47**	6 846	48	...	1 263**	43**	94	95	93	0.98
5 Iraq	...	...	...	12-17	4 203	1 105	38	...	...	...	...	...	...	...	...	...
6 Jordan	99**,ˣ	99**,ˣ	99	12-17	816	579	49	710	50	19	...	...	94	93	95	1.02
7 Kuwait[4]	99	99	99	11-17	...	235	49**	258	50	32	...	...	...	...	...	...
8 Lebanon	88	84	91	12-17	471	389	52**	383	52	60	57	42	90	86	94	1.10
9 Libya	...	...	...	12-17	654	...	...	...	...	...	...	...	...	...	...	...
10 Mauritania	34ʸ	38ʸ	31ʸ	12-17	456	63**	42**	111**	45**	27**	...	...	26**	27**	24**	0.87**
11 Morocco	**82**	**84**	**80**	12-17	3 756	1 470	43	...	...	...	...	...	82**	90**	73**	0.82**
12 Oman	...	...	...	12-17	306	229	49	322ᶻ	48ᶻ	8ᶻ	.ᶻ	.ᶻ	108ᶻ	111ᶻ	105ᶻ	0.95ᶻ
13 Palestine	97	96	98	10-17	827	444	50	711	51	5	9	35	88	87	90	1.04
14 Qatar	99ʸ	99ʸ	99ʸ	12-17	74	44	49	69	49	39	0.6	.	101	100	103	1.03
15 Saudi Arabia	94**,ʸ	91**,ʸ	97**,ʸ	12-17	3 019	...	...	3 036	48	12	-	.	106	107	106	0.99
16 Sudan (pre-secession)	94**,ʸ	96**,ʸ	92**,ʸ	12-16	4 840	966**	...	1 837ᶻ	46ᶻ	12ᶻ	28ᶻ	24ᶻ	54ᶻ	59ᶻ	49ᶻ	0.83ᶻ
17 Syrian Arab Republic	95	94	95	10-17	3 774	1 030	47	2 732	49	4	106	40	92	93	91	0.98
18 Tunisia	84ʸ	81ʸ	87ʸ	12-18	1 287	1 059	49	1 202ᶻ	50**,ᶻ	4**,ᶻ	143ᶻ	35**,ᶻ	116ᶻ	119ᶻ	113ᶻ	0.96ᶻ
19 United Arab Emirates[4]	96	94	99	11-17	...	202	50	337**	50**	56**	...	...	...	...	...	...
20 Yemen	...	...	...	12-17	3 542	1 042	26	1 562**	37**	...	...	...	54	65	42	0.64
Central and Eastern Europe																
21 Albania	97	97	97	11-17	400	364	48	356	48	6	20	31	95	94	95	1.01
22 Belarus	99	...	...	10-16	721	978	50	...	...	...	...	...	96	96	95	0.99
23 Bosnia and Herzegovina	84	84	83	10-17	354	...	...	323	49	2	109	45	99	98	99	1.00
24 Bulgaria	98	98	98	11-18	599	700	48	532	48	1	160	39	83	86	80	0.94
25 Croatia	100	100	99	11-18	406	416	49	389	50	1	144	49	105	103	106	1.03
26 Czech Republic	99ʸ	99ʸ	99ʸ	11-18	927	928	50	868ᶻ	49ᶻ	8ᶻ	341ᶻ	45ᶻ	93ᶻ	93ᶻ	92ᶻ	0.99ᶻ
27 Estonia	99ʸ	99ʸ	98ʸ	13-18	89	116	50	100ᶻ	49ᶻ	3ᶻ	19ᶻ	34ᶻ	105ᶻ	107ᶻ	102ᶻ	0.95ᶻ
28 Hungary	98ʸ	97ʸ	98ʸ	11-18	904	1 007	49	913ᶻ	49ᶻ	12ᶻ	131ᶻ	38ᶻ	99ᶻ	100ᶻ	97ᶻ	0.97ᶻ
29 Latvia	96	94	98	13-18	155	255	50	147	49	1	35	39	95	97	92	0.94
30 Lithuania	99	99	99	11-18	347	407	49	343	48	1	38	33	96	98	94	0.97
31 Montenegro	...	...	...	11-18	67	...	...	70	49	0.2	22	46	114	115	114	0.99
32 Poland	99ʸ	99ʸ	98ʸ	13-18	2 930	3 984	49	2 958ᶻ	49ᶻ	4ᶻ	816ᶻ	37ᶻ	97ᶻ	98ᶻ	96ᶻ	0.98ᶻ
33 Republic of Moldova[5,6]	98ʸ	99ʸ	98ʸ	11-17	350*	415	50	308	50	1	36	42	89	89	88	0.99
34 Romania	98	98	97	11-18	1 875	2 218	49	1 822	48	2	608	43	96	97	96	0.99
35 Russian Federation	100ʸ	...	...	11-17	10 141	15 863	...	9 614ᶻ	48ᶻ	0.7ᶻ	1 557ᶻ	37ᶻ	90ᶻ	89ᶻ	91ᶻ	1.01ᶻ
36 Serbia[5]	98	97	99	11-18	646*	737**	49**	591	49	0.5	218	47	99	99	98	1.00
37 Slovakia	97	98	97	10-18	608	674	50	550	49	10	195	45	92	93	91	0.98
38 Slovenia	99ʸ	99ʸ	98ʸ	12-18	142	220	49	142ᶻ	49ᶻ	1ᶻ	51ᶻ	41ᶻ	96ᶻ	96ᶻ	96ᶻ	1.00ᶻ
39 TFYR Macedonia	99	98	99	11-18	235	219	48	197	48	1	58	44	90	90	90	1.00
40 Turkey	99	98	99	11-17	9 172	5 523	40	7 101ᶻ	47ᶻ	...	1 419ᶻ	42ᶻ	96ᶻ	99ᶻ	93ᶻ	0.94ᶻ
41 Ukraine	100	100*	100*	10-16	3 278	5 214	50*	3 133	48*	0.4	242	36	104	104*	104*	1.00*
Central Asia																
42 Armenia	99ˣ	100ˣ	98	10-16	306	347	...	281	48	1	6	25	96	95	97	1.02
43 Azerbaijan[5,7]	98	98	99	10-17	1 255*	929	49	1 063	47	13	176	51	92	93	91	0.97
44 Georgia	100	100	100	12-17	371	442	49	342ᶻ	...	6ᶻ	5ᶻ	...	93ᶻ	95ᶻ	90ᶻ	0.95ᶻ
45 Kazakhstan	**100**	**100**	**100**	11-17	1 767	1 966	49	**1 680**	**48**	**0.9**	113	30	106	106	106	1.00
46 Kyrgyzstan	99	100	99	11-17	791	633	50	664*	49*	1*	23*	27*	94	94	93	0.99
47 Mongolia	97ˣ	96ˣ	98ˣ	11-16	309	205	55	276	51	7	28	47	89	87	91	1.04
48 Tajikistan	98	99	98	11-17	1 183	769	46	1 032	46	.ʸ	22	15	98	101	94	0.92
49 Turkmenistan	...	...	...	10-16	711	...	...	...	...		...	...	...	...	...	...
50 Uzbekistan	**99**	**100**	**98**	11-17	4 247	3 411	49	**4 370**	**49**	.	**1 623**	**48**	95	96	94	0.98
East Asia and the Pacific																
51 Australia[8]	...	...	...	12-17	1 739	2 491	49	2 282	47	33	749	42	113	115	111	0.97
52 Brunei Darussalam	100	99	100	12-18	44	34	51	49	49	14	4	41	79	79	80	1.01
53 Cambodia	80	80	81	12-17	2 056	316	34	949**	46**	...	...	...	60	61	58	0.95
54 China	...	...	...	12-17	122 223	77 436	...	99 218	47	10	20 419	45	92	89	94	1.06
55 Cook Islands[5]	**99**	**99**	**100**	11-17	2*	2	50	**2**	**52**	**14**	.	.	**98**	**93**	**103**	**1.11**
56 DPR Korea	...	...	...	10-15	2 499	...	...	...	...		...	...	...	...	...	...
57 Fiji	96ʸ	95ʸ	97	12-18	113	98	51	98ᶻ	51ᶻ	92ʸ	2ᶻ	31ᶻ	100	97	102ᶻ	1.05ᶻ
58 Indonesia	92ʸ	91ʸ	93	13-18	25 891	14 264**	48**	19 976	49	42	3 319	42	92	91	93	1.02
59 Japan	...	...	...	12-17	7 139	8 959	49	7 296	49	19	859	43	103	103	103	1.00
60 Kiribati	...	...	...	12-17	14	7	54	12ʸ	51ʸ	...	.ʸ	.ʸ	99	97	101ʸ	1.04ʸ

GROSS ENROLMENT RATIO (GER) IN SECONDARY EDUCATION (%)												OUT-OF-SCHOOL ADOLESCENTS (000)[2]						
Upper secondary				Total secondary								School year ending in Sum 1999			School year ending in 2010			
School year ending in 2010				School year ending in 1999				School year ending in 2010										
Total	Male	Female	GPI (F/M)	Total	Male	Female	GPI (F/M)	Total	Male	Female	GPI (F/M)	Total	Male	Female	Total	Male	Female	
																		Arab States
50ᶻ	42ᶻ	59ᶻ	1.42ᶻ	...	...	...	...	95ᶻ	94ᶻ	96ᶻ	1.02ᶻ	...	...	...	...	...	...	1
...	...	...	...	96	92	101	1.10	...	...	...	...	0.3	...	...	...	...	...	2
25	**29**	**22**	**0.75**	14	16	12	0.72	**36**	**40**	**32**	**0.80**	52**	25**	27**	49**,ʸ	22**,ʸ	27**,ʸ	3
51	53	49	0.92	80**	84**	76**	0.91**	72	74	71	0.96	...	...	...	214**	...	...	4
...	...	...	...	35	42	27	0.64	...	...	...	...	840	349	491	...	...	...	5
73	68	79	1.16	85	83	87	1.04	87	85	89	1.06	63**	37**	26**	101	85	17	6
...	...	...	...	109**	107**	111	1.03**	...	...	...	...	1**	...	...	2ʸ	...	...	7
73	67	78	1.16	77**	73**	80**	1.09**	81	77	86	1.12	...	...	...	32	17	14	8
...	...	...	...	...	...	...	...	...	...	...	...	...	...	...	...	...	...	9
22**	25**	19**	0.78**	18**	21**	15**	0.75**	24**	26**	22**	0.85**	...	...	...	...	...	...	10
...	...	...	...	37	41	32	0.78	...	...	...	...	968**	410**	558**	433**	171**	262**	11
93ᶻ	91ᶻ	94ᶻ	1.03ᶻ	71	71	72	1.01	100ᶻ	101ᶻ	100ᶻ	0.99ᶻ	35	17	17	4ᶻ	...	...	12
78	70	86	1.23	78	77	79	1.02	86	83	89	1.08	69	37	32	82	46	36	13
86	74	104	1.42	88	83	92	1.11	94	86	104	1.21	3	2	1.0	0.8	...	...	14
95	100	90	0.90	...	...	...	...	101	103	98	0.95	...	...	...	96	69	28	15
28ᶻ	29ᶻ	28ᶻ	0.95ᶻ	26**	...	...	...	39ᶻ	41ᶻ	36ᶻ	0.88ᶻ	...	...	...	...	...	...	16
37	35	39	1.11	44	46	42	0.92	72	72	73	1.01	448	202	245	280ᶻ	138ᶻ	142ᶻ	17
73ᶻ	67**,ᶻ	80**,ᶻ	1.18**,ᶻ	74	74	74	0.99	90ᶻ	88**,ᶻ	93**,ᶻ	1.06**,ᶻ	...	...	...	...	...	...	18
...	...	...	...	83	80	87	1.09	...	...	...	...	9	4	5	...	...	...	19
34**	42**	25**	0.59**	40	58	21	0.37	44**	54**	34**	0.62**	568	134	434	718**	262**	457**	20
																		Central and Eastern Europe
81	84	78	0.93	73	74	71	0.95	89	90	88	0.98	9**	3**	6**	...	...	...	21
...	...	...	...	85	83	87	1.05	...	...	...	...	...	...	...	24**	...	...	22
84	81	86	1.06	...	...	...	...	91	90	92	1.03	...	...	...	...	...	...	23
94	95	92	0.97	92	93	91	0.98	89	91	87	0.95	17	8	10	34	17	18	24
87	82	92	1.12	84	84	85	1.02	96	93	99	1.07	16	8	9	2	...	...	25
88ᶻ	87ᶻ	90ᶻ	1.03ᶻ	82	80	84	1.04	90ᶻ	90ᶻ	91ᶻ	1.01ᶻ	...	...	...	...	...	...	26
103ᶻ	99ᶻ	107ᶻ	1.08ᶻ	94	92	96	1.04	104ᶻ	103ᶻ	105ᶻ	1.02ᶻ	0.9	...	...	1.2ᶻ	0.7ᶻ	0.5ᶻ	27
98ᶻ	98ᶻ	98ᶻ	1.00ᶻ	93	92	94	1.01	98ᶻ	99ᶻ	98ᶻ	0.99ᶻ	15	7	8	6ᶻ	2ᶻ	4ᶻ	28
96	95	96	1.00	89	87	90	1.04	95	96	94	0.98	...	...	...	8	4	4	29
105	104	106	1.01	96	95	96	1.00	99	100	98	0.98	1	...	...	21	11	10	30
94	92	96	1.04	...	...	...	...	104	103	105	1.01	...	...	...	...	...	...	31
97ᶻ	97ᶻ	97ᶻ	1.00ᶻ	100	100	99	0.99	97ᶻ	98ᶻ	97ᶻ	0.99ᶻ	...	...	...	88ᶻ	46ᶻ	42ᶻ	32
86	82	91	1.11	83	84	82	0.98	88	87	89	1.02	...	...	...	29	14	15	33
98	99	97	0.99	81	81	82	1.01	97	98	97	0.99	43	21	22	52ᶻ	27ᶻ	24ᶻ	34
86ᶻ	90ᶻ	82ᶻ	0.91ᶻ	92	...	...	...	89ᶻ	90ᶻ	87ᶻ	0.98ᶻ	...	...	...	671ᶻ	380ᶻ	291ᶻ	35
85	83	87	1.05	93**	93**	94**	1.01**	91	91	92	1.02	...	...	...	8	4	4	36
89	87	90	1.04	84	83	85	1.02	90	90	91	1.01	...	...	...	...	...	...	37
98ᶻ	98ᶻ	97ᶻ	0.99ᶻ	100	98	101	1.03	97ᶻ	97ᶻ	97ᶻ	1.00ᶻ	5	3	2	1.3ᶻ	0.7ᶻ	0.6ᶻ	38
78	78	77	0.99	82	83	81	0.98	84	84	83	0.99	...	...	...	...	...	...	39
64ᶻ	68ᶻ	60ᶻ	0.89ᶻ	69	82	56	0.69	78ᶻ	81ᶻ	74ᶻ	0.91ᶻ	899**	275**	625**	181**,ᶻ	52**,ᶻ	129**,ᶻ	40
78	82*	75*	0.91*	98	97*	100*	1.03*	96	97*	94*	0.98*	...	...	...	92	49*	43*	41
																		Central Asia
85	83	86	1.04	92	...	...	...	92	91	93	1.02	...	...	...	...	...	...	42
75	75	75	0.99	78	79	78	0.99	85	85	84		119*	59*	60*	...	...	...	43
81ᶻ	...	...	...	79	80	78	0.98	86ᶻ	...	...	...	...	...	...	14	...	...	44
87	**91**	**82**	**0.91**	93	93	93	1.00	**100**	**101**	**98**	**0.97**	...	...	...	**0.1**	...	...	45
62*	62*	61*	0.98*	83	82	84	1.02	84*	85*	83*	0.99*	...	...	...	45*	22*	23*	46
90	84	96	1.13	61	54	68	1.26	89	86	92	1.07	57**	36**	20**	...	...	...	47
61	73	49	0.67	75	80	69	0.86	87	93	81	0.87	194	90	104	31	...	...	48
...	...	...	...	...	...	...	...	...	...	...	...	...	...	...	...	...	...	49
129	**131**	**128**	**0.97**	86	87	86	0.98	**106**	**107**	**104**	**0.98**	...	...	...	114ᶻ	47ᶻ	67ᶻ	50
																		East Asia and the Pacific
167	172	161	0.93	157	157	157	1.00	131	135	128	0.95	...	...	...	20	11	10	51
132	129	135	1.04	88	85	92	1.09	110	108	112	1.03	...	...	...	0.5**	...	...	52
...	...	...	...	16	20	11	0.53	46**	49**	44**	0.90**	947	463	484	...	...	...	53
71	71	72	1.02	61	...	...	...	81	80	83	1.04	...	...	...	...	...	...	54
62	**52**	**73**	**1.40**	60	58	63	1.08	**82**	**75**	**89**	**1.20**	0.01	...	...	**0.1**	...	...	55
...	...	...	...	...	...	...	...	...	...	...	...	...	...	...	...	...	...	56
69ᶻ	64ᶻ	75ᶻ	1.18ᶻ	78	74	83	1.11	86ᶻ	83ᶻ	91ᶻ	1.09ᶻ	3**	...	...	2**,ᶻ	...	...	57
63	63	62	0.98	53**	54**	51**	0.95**	77	77	77	1.00	4 795**	2 377**	2 418**	1 815	943	872	58
102	102	102	1.00	101	101	102	1.01	102	102	102	1.00	3	...	...	0.1	...	...	59
72ʸ	65ʸ	79ʸ	1.21ʸ	59	53	65	1.23	86ʸ	81ʸ	90ʸ	1.11ʸ	...	...	...	...	...	...	60

Table 7 (continued)

	Country or territory	Transition from primary to secondary general education (%) School year ending in 2009 — Total	Male	Female	Age group 2010	School-age population (000) 2010[3]	Total enrolment School year ending in 1999 — Total (000)	% F	Total enrolment 2010 — Total (000)	% F	Enrolment in private institutions as % of total enrolment Median 2010	Enrolment in technical and vocational education 2010 — Total (000)	% F	Lower secondary School year ending in 2010 — Total	Male	Female	GPI (F/M)
61	Lao PDR	79[x]	80[x]	77[x]	11-16	923	240	40	435	45	3	1	43	55	60	50	0.84
62	Macao, China	93	92	95	12-17	41	32	51	38	49	95	1	44	110	115	105	0.91
63	Malaysia[4]	100[y]	100[y]	99[y]	12-18	3 786	2 177	51	2 546[z]	51[z]	3[z]	158[z]	43[z]	91	90	92[z]	1.02[z]
64	Marshall Islands	91[y]	92[y]	90[y]	12-17	5	6	50	5[z]	50[z]	21[z]	...	...	110	109	112[z]	1.03[z]
65	Micronesia, F. S.	...	...	...	12-17	16	...	...	...	...	...	...	...	...	...	...	...
66	Myanmar	77	77	77	10-15	5 256	2 059	50	2 852	51	-	-	.	62	61	64	1.05
67	Nauru[5]	...	...	...	12-17	1*	0.7	54	0.8[y]	51[y]	...	...	.	...	...	...	...
68	New Zealand	...	...	...	11-17	430	437	50	512	50	19	79	49	104	105	104	0.99
69	Niue[5]	...	...	...	11-16	0.2*	0.3	54	...	...	...	...	...	...	...	...	...
70	Palau[5]	...	...	...	11-17	2*	2	49	...	...	...	...	...	...	...	...	...
71	Papua New Guinea	...	...	...	13-18	884	...	...	...	...	...	...	...	...	...	...	...
72	Philippines	98[y]	99[y]	97	12-15	8 088	5 117	51	6 767[z]	51[z]	20[z]	.[z]	.[z]	88[z]	85[z]	90[z]	1.05[z]
73	Republic of Korea	100[y]	100[y]	100	12-17	4 069	4 177	48	3 951	47	32	466	45	100	100	99	0.99
74	Samoa	99	99	99	11-17	31	22	50	26	51	...	...	...	105	105	105	1.00
75	Singapore[4]	89[y]	86[y]	92[y]	12-15	...	...	...	232[z]	48[z]	6[z]	27[z]	35[z]	...	...	...	...
76	Solomon Islands	...	...	...	12-18	82	17	41	...	...	...	...	...	...	...	...	...
77	Thailand	...	...	...	12-17	6 225	*4 072*	*49***	4 893	51	16	757	43	92	92	93	1.02
78	Timor-Leste	86	84	87	12-17	180	*40***	...	102	49	26	6	44	63	62	*64*	1.03
79	Tokelau[5]	...	...	...	11-15	0.1*	*0.2*	49	...	...	...	...	...	...	...	...	...
80	Tonga	...	...	...	11-16	14	15	50	...	...	...	...	...	...	...	...	...
81	Tuvalu[5]	...	...	...	12-17	1*	*0.9*	*46*	...	...	...	...	...	...	...	...	...
82	Vanuatu	79	79	79	12-18	37	9	45	20	49	...	2	39	65	63	66	1.05
83	Viet Nam	...	...	...	11-17	11 395	7 401	47	8 800	51	...	700	54	88	87	90	1.04
	Latin America and the Caribbean																
84	Anguilla[9]	95	...	...	12-16	...	*1.1***	*51***	1.0	50	.	0.0	25	...	...	...	...
85	Antigua and Barbuda	77	...	...	12-16	8	5	50	8	51	18	0.6	48	122	130	114	0.87
86	Argentina	96[y]	96[y]	97[y]	12-17	4 096	3 344	50	3 637[z]	52[z]	28[z]	287[z]	38[z]	109[z]	107[z]	112[z]	1.05[z]
87	Aruba	97[y]	99[y]	96[y]	12-17	8	6	51	7	50	92	1	37	106	111	102	0.92
88	Bahamas	98	99	98	11-16	36	27	49	34	51	30	.	.	101	100	103	1.03
89	Barbados	99*, x	...	...	11-15	19	22	51	19*	50*	6*	.	.	99*	97*	101*	1.04*
90	Belize[4]	92	89	94	11-16	...	22	51	33	52	63	1	50	...	...	...	...
91	Bermuda	...	...	...	11-17	6	*5*	*51*	4	53	45	.	.	87	81	93	1.15
92	Bolivia, P. S.	90[y]	89[y]	91	12-17	1 331	830	48	1 061[z]	49[z]	13[z]	.[z]	.[z]	94[z]	95[z]	93[z]	0.98[z]
93	Brazil[4]	...	...	...	11-17	...	24 983	52	23 539	51	14	1 324	57	...	...	...	...
94	British Virgin Islands[5]	...	...	...	12-16	2*	2	47	2	50	17	0.4	40	116	118	113	0.96
95	Cayman Islands	97[x]	...	...	11-16	4	2	48	3[y]	52[y]	29[y]	.[y]	.[y]	85[y]	81[y]	89[y]	1.10[y]
96	Chile	91[x]	84**, x	98**, x	12-17	1 699	1 305	50	1 528[z]	50[z]	57[z]	358[z]	48[z]	100[z]	101[z]	99[z]	0.98[z]
97	Colombia	97	97	96	11-16	5 271	3 589	52	5 080	51	21	386	54	105	102	108	1.06
98	Costa Rica	91	93	89	12-16	415	255	51	414	50	10	62	50	116	116	117	1.01
99	Cuba	**98**	**98**	**99**	12-17	905	740	50	**798**	**48**	.	215	38	96	98	95	**0.97**
100	Dominica	96	97	94	12-16	7	7	57	7	51	29	0.2	58	108	111	106	0.95
101	Dominican Republic	86	82	90	12-17	1 183	611	55	905	52	22	38	62	90	88	91	1.03
102	Ecuador	...	...	...	12-17	1 684	904	50	1 243**, y	50**, y	33**, y	277**, y	52**, y	85**, y	85**, y	84**, y	0.99**, y
103	El Salvador	95	95	94	13-18	888	406	49	577	50	16	105	52	86	86	86	1.00
104	Grenada	80[y]	76[y]	85[y]	12-16	11	...	...	12	50	62	0.5	32	121	125	117	0.94
105	Guatemala	91[x]	93[x]	90[x]	13-17	1 679	435	45	983	48	67	269	51	65	68	62	0.90
106	Guyana	95	93	97	12-16	89	66	50	81	51	6	5	43	99	95	103	1.09
107	Haiti	...	...	...	12-18	1 569	...	...	...	...	...	...	...	...	...	...	...
108	Honduras	...	...	...	12-16	892	...	...	655	54	25	...	...	75	70	80	1.14
109	Jamaica	91	92	91	12-16	286	231	50*,^	265	50	6	.	.	91	92	91	0.98
110	Mexico	95	95	94	12-17	13 158	8 722	50	11 682	51	14	1 870	56	117	113	122	1.08
111	Montserrat[9]	...	...	...	12-16	...	0.3	47	0.4[z]	48[z]	.[z]	.[z]	.[z]	...	...	...	...
112	Netherlands Antilles	...	...	...	12-17	15	15	54	...	...	...	...	...	...	...	...	...
113	Nicaragua	...	...	...	12-16	670	321**	54**	465	52	22	7	60	80	78	81	1.04
114	Panama	97	98	96	12-17	383	230	51	284	51	16	45	49	93	92	94	1.02
115	Paraguay	89[y]	89[y]	89[y]	12-17	827	425	50	549[z]	50[z]	22[z]	56[z]	50[z]	78[z]	77[z]	79[z]	1.03[z]
116	Peru	94	95	93	12-16	2 901	2 278	48	2 651	49	24	.	.	101	102	99	0.97
117	Saint Kitts and Nevis	95*	...	...	12-16	4	5	50	4	49	4	.	.	100	103	97	0.95
118	Saint Lucia	93	92	95	12-16	17	12	56	16	49	3	0.1	19	98	101	96	0.95
119	Saint Vincent/Grenadines	93[x]	...	...	12-16	11	*10***	*57***	11	50	24	...	...	119	123	114	0.93
120	Suriname	47[y]	40[y]	53[y]	12-18	64	*42*	*53*	47[z]	54[z]	18[z]	22[z]	47[z]	89[z]	85[z]	93[z]	1.09[z]
121	Trinidad and Tobago	88*	87*	89*	12-16	97	117	52	95**, y	51**, y	...	...	...	92*, y	90*, y	94*, y	1.05*, y
122	Turks and Caicos Islands[9]	...	...	...	12-16	...	1	51	2[z]	52[z]	...	.[z]	.[z]	...	...	...	...
123	Uruguay	81[y]	75[y]	87[y]	12-17	318	284	53	288[z]	...	14[z]	48[z]	...	113[z]	...	...	...
124	Venezuela, B. R.	97	96	97	12-16	2 733	1 439	54	2 255	51	29	122	50	90	87	92	1.06

GROSS ENROLMENT RATIO (GER) IN SECONDARY EDUCATION (%)

Upper secondary				Total secondary								OUT-OF-SCHOOL ADOLESCENTS (000)[2]						
School year ending in 2010				School year ending in 1999				School year ending in 2010				School year ending in Sum 1999			School year ending in 2010			
Total	Male	Female	GPI (F/M)	Total	Male	Female	GPI (F/M)	Total	Male	Female	GPI (F/M)	Total	Male	Female	Total	Male	Female	
32	35	29	0.82	33	39	27	0.70	47	51	43	0.83	97	36	62	174	76	97	61
78	80	77	0.96	80	78	82	1.05	92	96	89	0.93	1.8	0.8	1.0	2.0	0.9	1.1	62
50^z	46^z	54^z	1.16^z	66	64	69	1.08	68^z	66^z	71^z	1.07^z	98	57	40	159^z	91^z	68^z	63
92^z	90^z	93^z	1.03^z	68	66	70	1.06	99^z	97^z	100^z	1.03^z	...	...	...	...	...	...	64
...	...	...	...	...	...	...	...	...	...	...	...	...	...	...	...	...	...	65
38	36	41	1.13	36	36	36	1.00	54	53	56	1.06	...	...	...	...	...	...	66
...	...	...	...	47	43	51	1.17	63^y	58^y	69^y	1.20^y	...	...	...	...	...	...	67
137	131	145	1.11	111	108	114	1.05	119	116	122	1.05	...	...	...	0.8	...	...	68
...	...	...	...	98	93	103	1.10	...	...	...	...	0.01	0.00	0.01	...	...	...	69
...	...	...	...	101	98	105	1.07	...	...	...	...	...	...	...	...	...	...	70
...	...	...	...	...	...	...	...	...	...	...	...	...	...	...	...	...	...	71
76^z	69^z	83^z	1.20^z	74	71	78	1.10	85^z	82^z	88^z	1.08^z	1 262	675	587	332^z	202^z	130^z	72
94	95	94	0.98	100	100	99	1.00	97	98	96	0.99	77	44	33	9**	...	...	73
76	68	85	1.24	80	76	84	1.11	85	79	91	1.14	0.8	0.5	0.3	...	...	...	74
...	...	...	...	...	...	...	...	...	...	...	...	...	...	...	...	...	...	75
...	...	...	...	26	29	22	0.76	...	...	...	...	...	...	...	...	...	...	76
67	**61**	**72**	**1.18**	*62*	*63***	*62***	*0.98***	**79**	**76**	**82**	**1.08**	...	...	...	286^z	157^z	128^z	77
49	49	48	0.98	34**	...	...	...	56	56	56	1.01	...	...	...	34	17	17	78
...	...	...	...	92	92	93	1.01*	...	...	...	...	...	...	...	...	...	...	79
...	...	...	...	106	99	113	1.14	...	...	...	...	0.3	...	...	...	...	...	80
...	...	...	...	**80**	**76**	**84**	**1.10***	...	...	...	...	...	...	...	...	...	...	81
41	42	39	0.93	30	32	28	0.88	55	54	55	1.02	5**	2**	3**	...	...	...	82
65	60	71	1.17	61	64	58	0.90	77	74	81	1.09	1 221**	...	...	...	...	...	83
																	Latin America and the Caribbean	
...	...	...	...	107**	108**	106**	0.98**	...	...	...	...	0.0**	...	...	0.2**,^{y}	0.1**,^{y}	0.1**,^{y}	84
80	65	95	1.45	79	82	76	0.92	105	105	106	1.01	0.1**	...	...	0.1	...	...	85
68^z	60^z	76^z	1.26^z	85	83	87	1.05	89^z	83^z	94^z	1.12^z	...	...	...	35^z	...	...	86
79	75	82	1.10	99	96	102	1.06	90	89	90	1.01	0.0	...	...	0.4^z	0.2^z	0.2^z	87
90	87	94	1.08	78	78	77	0.99	96	93	98	1.05	1.4	0.6	0.8	1.1	0.7	0.4	88
103*	95*	111*	1.17*	108	103	115	1.12	101*	96*	105*	1.09*	0.4**	...	...	1.2*	0.9*	0.3*	89
50	48	52	1.09	62	60	64	1.07	...	...	...	...	3**	2**	2**	...	...	...	90
72	66	79	1.21	**79**	**77**	**82**	**1.07**	79	72	85	1.18	0.2**	...	...	0.2**	0.2**	0.1**	91
73^z	73^z	73^z	1.01^z	77	80	74	0.93	80^z	81^z	80^z	0.99^z	19**	4**	15**	...	...	...	92
...	...	...	...	99	94	104	1.11	...	...	...	...	...	...	...	...	...	...	93
82	74	90	1.22	99	103	94	0.91	102	100	104	1.03	0.05**	...	...	...	...	...	94
82^y	75^y	88^y	1.17^y	99	101	97	0.96	83^y	78^y	88^y	1.13^y	0.1**	0.1**	0.1**	0.3^y	0.1^y	0.1^y	95
82^z	80^z	85^z	1.06^z	79	78	81	1.04	88^z	87^z	89^z	1.03^z	...	...	...	30^z	14^z	16^z	96
80	73	87	1.19	73	69	77	1.11	96	92	101	1.10	...	...	...	221	121	100	97
75	69	82	1.18	62	59	65	1.10	100	97	103	1.06	...	...	...	...	...	...	98
84	**84**	**85**	**1.00**	80	77	82	1.06	**90**	**91**	**90**	**0.99**	18	11	7	**14**	**6**	**8**	99
84	71	99	1.39	100	86	115	1.33	98	94	103	1.09	0.4**	...	...	...	...	...	100
70	64	76	1.19	56	50	62	1.24	76	72	81	1.12	69	37	32	37	16	21	101
65**,^{y}	62**,^{y}	67**,^{y}	1.09**,^{y}	57	56	57	1.03	75**,^{y}	74**,^{y}	76**,^{y}	1.03**,^{y}	229	113	115	...	...	...	102
44	43	45	1.05	53	53	52	0.98	65	65	65	1.01	...	...	...	41	20	21	103
89	80	99	1.25	...	...	...	...	108	106	109	1.03	...	...	...	0.5^y	...	...	104
48	48	48	1.00	33	36	30	0.84	59	61	57	0.93	352**	143**	209**	233	93	140	105
78	73	83	1.14	88	89	88	0.99	91	87	96	1.11	...	...	...	5**,^{z}	3**,^{z}	2**,^{z}	106
...	...	...	...	...	...	...	...	...	...	...	...	...	...	...	...	...	...	107
71	60	83	1.39	...	...	...	...	73	66	81	1.23	...	...	...	...	...	...	108
95	90	100	1.11	88**	88**	88**	1.01**	93	91	94	1.03	8**	4**	4**	23	11	12	109
61	59	63	1.05	70	70	70	1.01	89	86	92	1.07	903**	385**	518**	272	142	130	110
...	...	...	...	183	212	158	0.75	...	...	...	...	0.02	...	...	...	...	...	111
...	...	...	...	91	84	97	1.15	...	...	...	...	0.1	...	...	...	...	...	112
54	49	60	1.23	52**	47**	56**	1.18**	69	66	73	1.10	...	...	...	69	36	33	113
54	50	59	1.17	67	65	69	1.07	74	72	77	1.07	35**	18**	18**	14	8	7	114
56^z	54^z	58^z	1.08^z	58	57	59	1.04	67^z	65^z	68^z	1.05^z	71	33	38	53^z	26^z	27^z	115
77	77	78	1.02	83	86	81	0.94	91	92	91	0.98	62**	20**	42**	36	19	17	116
93	90	97	1.07	97	95	99	1.04	97	98	97	0.99	0.0**	...	...	0.08*	0.04*	0.04*	117
93	91	96	1.05	71	62	79	1.26	96	97	96	0.99	3**	2**	1**	0.7**	0.3**	0.5**	118
91	81	101	1.24	82**	71**	95**	1.34**	107	106	109	1.02	1.2**	0.9**	0.3**	0.2^y	...	...	119
56^z	43	69^z	1.59^z	**73**	**67**	**80**	**1.19**	75^z	67^z	83^z	1.23^z	2**	...	...	8**,^{z}	4**,^{z}	4**,^{z}	120
87**,^{y}	84**,^{y}	91**,^{y}	1.09**,^{y}	78	74	81	1.09	90**,^{y}	87**,^{y}	93**,^{y}	1.07**,^{y}	11**	6**	5**	7	4	3	121
...	...	...	...	...	...	...	...	...	...	...	...	...	...	...	...	...	...	122
68^z	61^z	75^z	1.24^z	92	85	100	1.17	90^z	...	...	...	...	...	...	13^y	7^y	6^y	123
71	66	77	1.18	57	51	63	1.22	83	79	86	1.10	397	218	179	135	79	56	124

Table 7 (continued)

	Country or territory	TRANSITION FROM PRIMARY TO SECONDARY GENERAL EDUCATION [%] School year ending in 2009			Age group 2010	School-age population (000) 2010[3]	ENROLMENT IN SECONDARY EDUCATION Total enrolment School year ending in 1999		Total enrolment School year ending in 2010		Enrolment in private institutions as % of total enrolment Median School year ending in 2010	Enrolment in technical and vocational education School year ending in 2010		Lower secondary School year ending in 2010			
		Total	Male	Female			Total (000)	% F	Total (000)	% F		Total (000)	% F	Total	Male	Female	GPI (F/M)
	North America and Western Europe																
125	Andorra	...	...	...	12-17	5	...	...	4	48	2	0.4	50	88	90	86	0.96
126	Austria	100	100	100	10-17	752	748	48	744	48	10	294	44	102	102	102	1.00
127	Belgium	98[y]	...	...	12-17	729	1 033	51	810[z]	48[z]	69[z]	338[z]	44[z]	114[z]	117[z]	112[z]	0.95[z]
128	Canada	...	...	...	12-17	2 582	2 512	49	2 668[y]	48[y]	7[y]	.[y]	.[y]	99[y]	100[y]	99[y]	0.98[y]
129	Cyprus[5]	100	100	100	12-17	64*	63	49	64	49	17	4	16	102	102	102	1.00
130	Denmark	99[y]	99[y]	100	13-18	425	422	50	493[z]	49[z]	14[z]	128[z]	44[z]	116[z]	115[z]	117[z]	1.02[z]
131	Finland	100	100	100	13-18	397	480	51	427	50	8	131	47	99	100	99	0.99
132	France[10]	...	...	...	11-17	5 189	5 955	49	5 873	49	26	1 173	44	110	110	110	0.99
133	Germany	99[x]	99[x]	99[x]	10-18	7 417	8 185	48	7 664	47	8	1 557	39	101	102	100	0.99
134	Greece	...	...	...	12-17	655	771	49	...	...	...	...	...	...	...	...	...
135	Iceland	100[y]	100[y]	100[y]	13-19	33	32	50	35[z]	50[z]	12[z]	7[z]	42[z]	97[z]	96[z]	97[z]	1.01[z]
136	Ireland	...	...	...	13-17	278	346	50	336	50	0.7	63	53	110	109	110	1.01
137	Israel	99[y]	99[y]	99[y]	12-17	694	629	49	694[z]	49[z]	.[z]	129[z]	44[z]	94[z]	93[z]	95[z]	1.02[z]
138	Italy	100	100	100	11-18	4 608	4 450	49	4 626	48	8	1 709	40	107	107	106	0.99
139	Luxembourg	...	...	...	12-18	42	33	50	39[y]	50[y]	18[y]	12[y]	48[y]	110[y]	111[y]	110[y]	1.00[y]
140	Malta	99[x]	99[x]	99[x]	11-17	37	38	45	37	46	29	6	34	103	105	100	0.95
141	Monaco[9]	...	...	...	11-17	...	3	51	3	49	22	0.5	45	...	...	...	...
142	Netherlands	...	...	...	12-17	1 214	1 365	48	1 475	48	...	698	46	127	130	124	0.95
143	Norway	100	100	100	13-18	392	378	49	435	48	8	131	41	98	98	98	1.00
144	Portugal	...	...	...	12-17	661	847	51	710[z]	50[z]	16[z]	177[z]	43[z]	116[z]	118[z]	114[z]	0.97[z]
145	San Marino[9]	100	100	99	11-18	2**	1.0	49	2	48	.	0.5	32	99**	99**	99**	1.00**
146	Spain	94	93	95	12-17	2 554	3 299	50	3 185	49	28	533	47	120	121	120	0.99
147	Sweden	100	100	100	13-18	737	946	54	731	48	17	235	44	97	97	97	0.99
148	Switzerland	99	...	...	13-19	634	544	47	605	48	7	209	42	108	107	110	1.03
149	United Kingdom	...	...	...	11-17	5 258	5 202	49	5 430[z]	49[z]	27[z]	680[z]	48[z]	109[z]	111[z]	108[z]	0.97[z]
150	United States	...	...	...	12-17	25 190	22 445	...	24 193	49	8	.	.	103	102	103	1.01
	South and West Asia																
151	Afghanistan	...	...	...	13-18	4 489	*362*	–	2 044	32	...	...	...	62	79	43	0.54
152	Bangladesh	...	...	...	11-17	22 189	9 912	49	11 395	52	95	433	21	66	59	74	1.25
153	Bhutan	**96**	**95**	**97**	13-18	91	20	44	**63**	**50**	**11**	–	.	**84**	**80**	**88**	**1.09**
154	India	81[x]	81[x]	81[x]	11-17	170 352	67 090	39	107 687	46	...	...	...	81	83	79	0.95
155	Iran, Islamic Republic of	97[y]	96[y]	97[y]	11-17	8 934	9 727	47	8 120	45	7[y]	795	34	98	100	95	0.95
156	Maldives	86[y]	84[y]	89[y]	13-17	35	15	51	...	...	...	...	...	**128**	**123**	**133**	**1.08**
157	Nepal[4]	81[x]	81[x]	81[x]	10-16	...	1 265	40	2 305[y]	47[y]	14[y]	15[y]	...	...	...	...	...
158	Pakistan	74	73	74	10-16	28 293	...	...	9 685	42	32	412	42	44	50	39	0.77
159	Sri Lanka	96[y]	95[y]	97[y]	10-17	2 519	...	...	...	...	...	...	...	103	105	102	0.97
	Sub-Saharan Africa																
160	Angola	34[y]	26[y]	45[y]	12-17	2 716	300	43	850	41	11	363	33	39	45	34	0.76
161	Benin	...	...	...	12-18	1 370	213	31	...	...	...	...	...	...	...	...	...
162	Botswana	...	...	...	13-17	219	158	51	180**·[z]	51**·[z]	...	...	...	91[z]	89[z]	93[z]	1.05[z]
163	Burkina Faso	**52**	**43**	**62**	12-18	2 597	173	38	**604**	**43**	**41**	**26**	**46**	**31**	**34**	**28**	**0.82**
164	Burundi	36	41	31	13-19	1 362	*118***	*44***	338	42	9	15	36	34	38	29	0.76
165	Cameroon	43[y]	42[y]	45	12-18	3 041	643**	45**	1 283**	45**	22[z]	262**	37**	...	...	...	...
166	Cape Verde	89	86	93	12-17	70	*46*	51**	62	54	13	2	48	109	103	114	1.11
167	Central African Republic	44	43	45	12-18	685	*70***	...	**126**	**36**	13	**5**	**38**	**24**	**32**	**17**	**0.53**
168	Chad	71	76	64	12-18	1 747	123	21	430	29	15	6	38	29	40	18	0.45
169	Comoros	...	...	...	12-18	102	29	44	...	...	...	...	...	...	...	...	...
170	Congo	68	69	67	12-18	597	*173*	41	...	...	...	...	...	...	...	...	...
171	Côte d'Ivoire	46[y]	47[y]	45[y]	12-18	3 098	592**	35**	...	...	...	...	...	...	...	...	...
172	D. R. Congo	80*·[x]	83*·[x]	76*·[x]	12-17	9 238	1 235	34	3 484	36	16	687	33	48	58	37	0.65
173	Equatorial Guinea	...	...	...	13-19	101	20	27	...	...	...	...	...	...	...	...	...
174	Eritrea	82	82	82	12-18	777	115	41	248	43	5	1	45	44	49	39	0.80
175	Ethiopia	89	91	87	13-18	11 775	1 060	40	4 207	45	14	353	44	45	48	41	0.84
176	Gabon	...	...	...	11-17	243	87	46	...	...	...	...	...	...	...	...	...
177	Gambia	81**	80**	82**	13-18	230	...	...	124	49**	...	...	...	63	62	63	1.02
178	Ghana	91[y]	91[y]	92[y]	12-18	3 646	1 024	44	**2 148**	**46**	15**	72	44	**83**	**86**	**80**	**0.93**
179	Guinea	57	62	51	13-19	1 503	168**	26**	560**·[z]	36	23[y]	11**·[z]	44**·[z]	46[z]	57[z]	35[z]	0.61[z]
180	Guinea-Bissau	...	...	...	13-17	167	*26*	35	...	...	...	...	...	...	...	...	...
181	Kenya	...	...	...	12-17	5 420	1 822	49	3 204[z]	47[z]	13[z]	16[z]	58[z]	91[z]	94[z]	88[z]	0.93[z]
182	Lesotho	74**	75**	73	13-17	266	74	57	123	58	1.0	3	79	58	48	67	1.39

GROSS ENROLMENT RATIO (GER) IN SECONDARY EDUCATION (%)												OUT-OF-SCHOOL ADOLESCENTS (000)[2]						
Upper secondary				Total secondary								School year ending in Sum 1999			School year ending in 2010			
School year ending in 2010				School year ending in 1999				School year ending in 2010										
Total	Male	Female	GPI (F/M)	Total	Male	Female	GPI (F/M)	Total	Male	Female	GPI (F/M)	Total	Male	Female	Total	Male	Female	
North America and Western Europe																	
84	74	94	1.27	...	...	...	...	87	85	89	1.05	...	...	...	0.5	0.2	0.2	125
96	99	92	0.93	98	100	95	0.95	99	101	97	0.96	...	...	...	...	...	...	126
109[z]	110[z]	107[z]	0.98[z]	141	136	146	1.07	111[z]	112[z]	109[z]	0.97[z]	...	...	...	...	...	...	127
102[y]	104[y]	101[y]	0.98[y]	103	102	104	1.02	101[y]	102[y]	100[y]	0.98[y]	...	...	...	...	...	...	128
96	95	96	1.01	93	92	95	1.03	99	99	99	1.00	1.1	0.5	0.6	0.1	...	...	129
119[z]	118[z]	120[z]	1.02[z]	125	122	128	1.05	117[z]	116[z]	119[z]	1.02[z]	...	...	...	1.6[z]	1.0[z]	0.6[z]	130
115	110	121	1.09	121	116	126	1.09	108	105	110	1.05	0.2	...	...	4	2	2	131
117	116	119	1.03	109	109	109	1.00	113	113	114	1.01	95	54	40	2	...	...	132
107	114	100	0.88	98	99	97	0.98	103	106	100	0.95	...	...	...	...	...	...	133
...	...	...	...	91	89	93	1.04	...	...	...	...	40	23	17	...	...	...	134
115[z]	113[z]	118[z]	1.04[z]	109	106	112	1.05	107[z]	106[z]	109[z]	1.03[z]	0.7	0.5	0.3	0.4[z]	0.2[z]	0.2[z]	135
138	132	145	1.10	106	102	109	1.06	121	118	124	1.05	3	2	0.2	0.7	...	...	136
110[z]	109[z]	111[z]	1.02[z]	100	101	100	0.99	102[z]	101[z]	103[z]	1.02[z]	4	...	...	0.8[z]	...	...	137
97	98	96	0.99	92	93	92	0.99	100	101	100	0.99	14	...	...	9	...	...	138
88[y]	85[y]	90[y]	1.05[y]	98	95	100	1.05	98[y]	96[y]	99[y]	1.02[y]	1.0	0.6	0.4	0.5[y]	0.3[y]	0.2[y]	139
97	110	84	0.76	89	95	81	0.85	101	107	95	0.89	...	...	...	1.2	0.5	0.7	140
...	...	...	...	...	...	...	...	...	...	...	...	...	...	...	...	...	...	141
116	114	118	1.03	123	126	121	0.96	121	122	121	0.99	0.7	...	...	15	9	6	142
124	126	122	0.97	119	118	121	1.02	111	112	110	0.98	3	2	2	4	2	2	143
98[z]	92[z]	103[z]	1.12[z]	103	99	107	1.08	107[z]	105[z]	109[z]	1.04[z]	0.3	...	...	...	...	...	144
96**	95**	98**	1.03**	...	...	...	...	97**	96**	98**	1.02**	...	...	...	...	...	...	145
133	128	138	1.08	109	106	112	1.06	125	123	126	1.02	38	21	17	5	...	...	146
101	102	100	0.99	156	139	175	1.26	99	100	99	0.99	3	2	1	27	15	12	147
86	89	82	0.92	96	99	92	0.93	95	97	94	0.97	7	4	3	13	7	6	148
96[z]	94[z]	100[z]	1.06[z]	101	100	101	1.01	102[z]	101[z]	103[z]	1.02[z]	20	8	12	4[z]	...	...	149
90	89	91	1.01	94	...	...	...	96	96	97	1.01	462	...	...	122	...	...	150
South and West Asia																	
27	38	16	0.42	*11*	*22*	-	-	46	60	30	0.51	...	...	...	1 978*	1 415*	563*	151
40	40	40	0.99	47	47	47	0.99	51	48	55	1.13	...	...	...	...	...	...	152
44	**47**	**41**	**0.87**	37	41	33	0.80	**70**	**69**	**71**	**1.04**	13	6	7	**9**	**5**	**3**	153
50	53	47	0.88	43	51	36	0.70	63	66	60	0.92	...	...	...	...	...	...	154
87	96	77	0.80	79	82	76	0.93	91	98	84	0.86	...	...	...	88	...	...	155
...	...	...	...	41	40	43	1.08	...	...	...	...	2.0	1.1	0.9	...	...	...	156
...	...	...	...	34	39	28	0.70	...	...	...	...	...	...	...	...	...	...	157
26	30	22	0.74	...	...	...	...	34	39	29	0.76	...	...	...	7 207	3 342	3 865	158
...	...	...	...	...	...	...	...	...	...	...	...	...	...	...	...	...	...	159
Sub-Saharan Africa																	
22	28	16	0.56	13	15	11	0.75	31	37	25	0.69	...	...	...	172[z]	19[z]	153[z]	160
...	...	...	...	22	31	14	0.44	...	...	...	...	...	...	...	...	...	...	161
68**[z]	65**[z]	71**[z]	1.09**[z]	73	71	76	1.07	82**[z]	79[z]	84**[z]	1.06**[z]	11**	7**	4**	5**[z]	3**[z]	2**[z]	162
10	**12**	**7**	**0.60**	9	11	7	0.62	**23**	**25**	**20**	**0.78**	918	443	475	**873**	**418**	**455**	163
13	16	10	0.59	*11***	*12***	*10***	*0.79***	25	29	21	0.72	...	...	...	...	...	...	164
...	...	...	...	26**	28**	24**	0.84**	42**	46**	38**	0.83**	...	...	...	...	...	...	165
67	57	77	1.35	*68***	*66***	*69***	*1.04***	88	80	95	1.20	...	...	...	2.8	1.3	1.5	166
9	**11**	**7**	**0.63**	*12***	...	...	...	**18**	**23**	**13**	**0.55**	...	...	...	**224***	**88***	**136***	167
18	26	9	0.36	10	16	4	0.26	25	35	15	0.42	549	235	314	...	...	...	168
...	...	...	...	30	33	27	0.81	...	...	...	...	...	...	...	...	...	...	169
...	...	...	...	*36*	*42*	*29*	*0.70*	...	...	...	...	...	...	...	...	...	...	170
...	...	...	...	23**	30**	16**	0.54**	...	...	...	...	934**	...	...	...	...	...	171
32	42	22	0.52	19	25	13	0.53	38	48	28	0.58	...	...	...	...	...	...	172
...	...	...	...	33	48	18	0.37	...	...	...	...	...	...	...	...	...	...	173
22	26	18	0.71	22	26	18	0.68	32	36	28	0.76	113	52	61	201	93	107	174
16	19	13	0.69	13	16	11	0.67	36	39	32	0.82	3 599	1 521	2 078	3 134**	1 417**	1 717**	175
...	...	...	...	48	52	44	0.86	...	...	...	...	...	...	...	...	...	...	176
45**	48**	41**	0.85**	...	...	...	...	54**	56**	53**	0.95**	...	...	...	32**	16**	15**	177
39	**41**	**36**	**0.87**	40	44	36	0.81	**58**	**61**	**55**	**0.91**	507**	234**	273**	422**	206**	215**	178
26**[z]	34**[z]	18**[z]	0.53**[z]	14**	20**	7**	0.37**	38**[z]	48**[z]	28**[z]	0.59**[z]	507	215	292	445**[z]	187**[z]	258**[z]	179
...	...	...	...	*19*	*24*	*13*	*0.55*	...	...	...	...	42**	16**	26**	...	...	...	180
44[z]	47[z]	41[z]	0.87[z]	38	39	38	0.96	60[z]	63[z]	57[z]	0.90[z]	...	...	...	30**[z]	...	...	181
29	25	34	1.37	30	26	35	1.36	46	39	54	1.38	31**	22**	9**	40	23	17	182

Table 7 (continued)

ENROLMENT IN SECONDARY EDUCATION

Country or territory	Transition from primary to secondary general education (%) School year ending in 2009 Total	Male	Female	Age group 2010	School-age population (000) 2010[3]	Total enrolment School year ending in 1999 Total (000)	% F	Total enrolment 2010 Total (000)	% F	Enrolment in private institutions as % of total enrolment Median 2010	Enrolment in technical and vocational education 2010 Total (000)	% F	Lower secondary 2010 Total	Male	Female	GPI (F/M)
183 Liberia	62[x]	64[x]	60	12-17	509	114	39	...	...	...	...	...	...	...	...	...
184 Madagascar	64	65	63	11-17	3 399	...	...	1 022**,z	49**,z	40**,z	...	...	42[z]	43[z]	41[z]	0.96[z]
185 Malawi	77	78	76	12-17	2 155	556	41	692	47	-	.		40	41	39	0.94
186 Mali	73	74	72	13-18	2 010	218	34	**820**	**41**	**31**	**94**	**41**	**53**	**61**	**45**	**0.75**
187 Mauritius	70	65	76	11-17	148	104	49	133**	49**	54**	...	...	96	95	97	1.02
188 Mozambique	**50**	**49**	**52**	13-17	2 640	103	39	**716**	**46**	**13**	**34**	**34**	**35**	**38**	**33**	**0.87**
189 Namibia	81[y]	80[y]	83[y]	14-18	261	116	53	...	...	...	...	...	...	...	...	...
190 Niger	**62**	**63**	**59**	13-19	2 269	105	38	303	40	18	3	14	19	22	16	0.71
191 Nigeria	...	...	...	12-17	20 560	3 845	47	9 057	46	22	...	...	47	49	44	0.89
192 Rwanda	73	73	72	13-18	1 323	105	51	**486**	**52**	**21**	**59**	**50**	**47**	**45**	**49**	**1.09**
193 Sao Tome and Principe	**68**	**65**	**70**	12-16	20	...	...	**12**	**53**	**3**	**0.3**	**47**	**82**	**76**	**88**	**1.17**
194 Senegal	69	71	66	13-19	1 937	234	39	725	46	21	37	52	...	...	...	...
195 Seychelles	98	98	98	12-16	6	8	50	7	49	7	...	...	131	130	132	1.02
196 Sierra Leone	...	...	...	12-17	774	*156*	*42*	...	...	...	...	...	**58**	**65**	**52**	**0.79**
197 Somalia	...	...	...	12-17	1 200	...	...	...	...	...	...	...	...	...	...	...
198 South Africa	...	...	...	14-18	4 973	4 239	53	4 688[z]	51[z]	3[z]	269[z]	43[z]	96[z]	96[z]	97[z]	1.01[z]
199 South Sudan	...	...	...	...	...	...	...	...	...	...	...	...	...	...	...	...
200 Swaziland	91	90	92	13-17	153	62	50	89	50	2	-	.	67	67	67	1.00
201 Togo	70	73	67	12-18	949	232	29	...	...	...	...	...	62	...	...	...
202 Uganda	59	60	58	13-18	4 649	547	*43*	1 306**	46**	...	...	...	35**	37**	32**	0.87**
203 United Republic of Tanzania	41**	45**	37**	14-19	5 757	...	...	...	...	...	...	...	...	...	...	...
204 Zambia	66	65	68	14-18	1 451	...	...	...	...	...	...	...	72	76	68	0.90
205 Zimbabwe	...	...	...	13-18	1 949	...	...	...	...	...	...	...	...	...	...	...

	Median Total	Male	Female		Sum	Sum	% F	Sum	% F	Median	Sum	% F	Weighted average Total	Male	Female	GPI
I World	95	93	97	...	771 375	435 326	47	542 684	48	13	58 371	44	82	83	81	0.97
II Countries in transition	99	...	...	...	27 229	33 679	49**	25 206**	48**	1	4 226**	43**	95**	95**	95**	1.00**
III Developed countries	99	...	...	...	78 374	83 071	49	80 054	49	8	12 341	42	104	105	104	0.99
IV Developing countries	90	89	91	...	665 772	318 576	46	437 424	47	16	41 804	44	78	80	77	0.97
V Arab States	94	91	97	...	43 172	22 399	46	29 722**	47**	12	2 420**	40**	87	91	83	0.91
VI Central and Eastern Europe	98	99	98	...	34 347	40 699	48	30 347**	48**	1	6 072**	40**	95**	95**	94**	0.99**
VII Central Asia	99	100	98	...	10 939	9 218	49	10 443	48	1	1 947	47	97	98	96	0.98
VIII East Asia/Pacific	...	...	...	...	203 497	131 165	47**	163 268	48	19	27 740	45	90	88	92	1.04
X East Asia	92	91	93	...	200 124	127 907	47**	160 077	48	16	26 885	45	90	88	92	1.04
X Pacific	...	...	...	...	3 373	3 258	49	3 191	48	...	855	43	86	88	84	0.95
XI Latin America/Caribbean	94	95	93	...	66 986	52 555	51	60 074	51	21	5 806	53	102	100	103	1.03
XII Caribbean	94	93	96	...	2 299	1 062**	50**	...	...	18	...	...	75**	74**	75**	1.00**
XIII Latin America	94	95	93	...	64 686	51 493	51	58 679	51	22	5 768	53	103	101	104	1.03
XIV N. America/W. Europe	100	100	100	...	60 548	60 733	49	61 828	49	11	8 313	43	105	106	105	0.99
XV South and West Asia	86	84	89	...	241 825	97 762	41	143 351	46	14	2 560	30	75	77	73	0.95
XVI Sub-Saharan Africa	69	71	66	...	110 061	20 796	45	43 653	45	15	3 513**	40**	47	52	43	0.84
XVII Countries with low income	72	74	69	...	111 508	26 078	45	46 333	46	14	2 420	35	52	55	50	0.90
XVIII Countries with middle income	94	94	93	...	574 956	321 959	46	410 130	48	13	43 782**	45**	85	85	84	0.98
XIX Lower middle	91	90	92	...	333 858	138 688	43	204 343	46	13	11 088**	42**	76	78	73	0.94
XX Upper middle	96	97	94	...	241 098	183 271	48**	205 788	49	10	32 694	45	97	95	98	1.04
XXI Countries with high income	99	99	99	...	84 911	87 289	49	86 221	49	14	12 169	42	104	104	104	0.99

Source: UNESCO Institute for Statistics database (UIS, 2012). Enrolment ratios in the table are based on the United Nations Population Division estimates, revision 2010 (United Nations, 2011), median variant.
Note: The country groupings by income level presented in the tables are as defined by the World Bank. They are based on the list of countries by income group as revised in July 2011.
1. Refers to lower and upper secondary education (ISCED levels 2 and 3).
2. Data reflect the actual number of adolescents not enrolled at all, derived from the age-specific or adjusted net enrolment ratio (ANER) of lower secondary school age children, which measures the proportion of those who are enrolled either in primary or in secondary schools.

3. Data are for 2010 except for countries with a split calendar school year, in which case data are for 2009.
4. Enrolment ratios for one or both of the two school years were not calculated due to inconsistencies in the population data.
5. National population data were used to calculate enrolment ratios.
6. Enrolment and population data exclude Transnistria.
7. Enrolment and population data exclude the Nagorno-Karabakh region.
8. Enrolment data for upper secondary education include adult education (students over age 25), particularly in pre-vocational/vocational programmes, in which males are in the majority. This explains the high level of GER and the relatively low GPI.

GROSS ENROLMENT RATIO (GER) IN SECONDARY EDUCATION (%)

Upper secondary — School year ending in 2010				Total secondary — School year ending in 1999				Total secondary — School year ending in 2010				OUT-OF-SCHOOL ADOLESCENTS (000)[2] School year ending in Sum 1999			School year ending in 2010			
Total	Male	Female	GPI (F/M)	Total	Male	Female	GPI (F/M)	Total	Male	Female	GPI (F/M)	Total	Male	Female	Total	Male	Female	
...	...	...	...	31	38	24	0.65	...	...	...	...	...	...	...	...	...	...	183
15**,z	16**,z	14z	0.87**,z	...	...	...	...	31**,z	32**,z	30z	0.94**,z	...	...	...	...	...	...	184
15	17	13	0.74	38	45	32	0.70	32	34	31	0.91	68	...	...	319z	160z	159z	185
24	**30**	**18**	**0.62**	14	19	10	0.54	**39**	**46**	**33**	**0.71**	...	...	...	**557**	**243**	**314**	186
85**	86**	84**	0.98**	76	76	75	0.98	89**	89**	89**	1.00**	14**	7**	7**	...	...	...	187
12	**13**	**11**	**0.84**	5	6	4	0.63	**26**	**28**	**24**	**0.87**	730**	310**	420**	**606**	**256**	**350**	188
...	...	...	...	57	54	61	1.12	...	...	...	...	18**	11**	7**	...	...	...	189
4	6	2	0.44	7	9	5	0.59	13	16	11	0.66	787	375	412	1 011**,y	481**,y	530**,y	190
41	44	38	0.87	23	24	22	0.91	44	47	41	0.88	...	...	...	...	...	...	191
23	**23**	**22**	**0.96**	10	10	10	1.01	**36**	**35**	**37**	**1.05**	...	...	...	...	...	...	192
23	**23**	**24**	**1.06**	...	...	...	...	**59**	**55**	**63**	**1.15**	...	...	...	**0.5***	**0.4***	**0.2***	193
...	...	...	...	16	19	12	0.65	37	40	35	0.88	...	...	...	...	...	...	194
104	95	115	1.21	105	103	107	1.04	119	114	125	1.09	0.05	...	...	0.1z	...	...	195
...	...	...	...	*28*	*33***	*22***	*0.68***	...	...	...	...	...	...	...	...	...	...	196
...	...	...	...	...	...	...	...	...	...	...	...	...	...	...	...	...	...	197
92z	89z	95z	1.08z	88	83	94	1.13	94z	92z	96z	1.05z	161**	89**	72**	...	...	...	198
...	...	...	...	...	...	...	...	...	...	...	...	...	...	...	...	...	...	199
45	45	45	0.99	44	44	44	1.00	58	58	58	1.00	20	10	10	30	14	15	200
...	...	...	...	31	45	18	0.40	...	...	...	...	135	27	107	...	...	...	201
13**	15**	11**	0.75**	*16*	*19*	*14*	*0.76*	28**	30**	26**	0.85**	...	...	...	650**	305**	344**	202
...	...	...	...	...	...	...	...	...	...	...	...	...	...	...	...	...	...	203
...	...	...	...	...	...	...	...	...	...	...	...	...	...	...	...	...	...	204
...	...	...	...	...	...	...	...	...	...	...	...	...	...	...	...	...	...	205
Weighted average				Weighted average				Weighted average							Sum			
59	60	58	0.96	59	62	56	0.91	70	71	69	0.97	101 060**	46 456**	54 603**	70 570**	36 393**	34 177**	I
87**	90**	85**	0.95**	90	90**	90**	1.00**	93**	94**	92**	0.98**	2 732**	1 410**	1 322**	1 156**	603**	553**	II
100	100	100	1.00	100	99	101	1.02	102	102	102	1.00	1 357	870**	487**	834	357**	477**	III
53	55	52	0.95	52	55	48	0.88	66	67	64	0.96	96 971**	44 176**	52 794**	68 580**	35 433**	33 147**	IV
49**	49**	49**	0.99**	59	63	55	0.88	69**	71**	67**	0.94**	5 241**	2 177**	3 064**	3 732**	1 725**	2 007**	V
81**	83**	79**	0.95**	88	90	86	0.96	88**	90**	87**	0.97**	2 941**	1 371**	1 570**	1 281**	655**	626**	VI
92	94	90	0.96	84	85	84	0.99	95	97	94	0.97	905**	429**	475**	315**	133**	183**	VII
70	69	71	1.03	63	64**	61**	0.94**	80	79	82	1.03	25 039**	12 684**	12 355**	10 317**	7 143**	3 174**	VIII
70	69	71	1.03	62	64**	60**	0.94**	80	79	81	1.03	24 782**	12 552**	12 230**	9 990**	6 980**	3 009**	IX
110	112	109	0.97	109	109	109	1.00	95	97	93	0.96	258**	132**	126**	327	162**	165**	X
75	70	81	1.16	80	77	83	1.07	90	86	93	1.08	3 333**	1 630**	1 703**	1 749	871	878	XI
...	...	...	...	49**	50**	49**	0.99**	...	...	...	...	195**	103**	91**	200**	106**	94**	XII
76	71	82	1.16	81	78	84	1.07	91	87	94	1.08	3 138**	1 527**	1 612**	1 549	765	784	XIII
99	99	99	1.00	100	99	101	1.02	102	102	102	1.00	1 181	781**	400**	554	213**	341**	XIV
47	50	43	0.87	44	50	38	0.75	59	62	56	0.91	39 816**	17 471**	22 345**	30 946**	15 876**	15 070**	XV
31	34	27	0.79	25	27	22	0.82	40	44	36	0.82	22 604**	9 913**	12 690**	21 676**	9 777**	11 899**	XVI
29	33	26	0.79	29	32	26	0.83	42	45	39	0.87	21 812**	10 171**	11 641**	17 666**	8 534**	9 132**	XVII
58	59	58	0.97	58	61	54	0.90	71	72	71	0.98	77 580**	35 243**	42 338**	52 005**	27 452**	24 552**	XVIII
48	50	45	0.90	46	51	40	0.80	61	63	59	0.93	56 489**	24 739**	31 751**	43 214**	21 047**	22 167**	XIX
74	72	75	1.04	72	72**	71**	0.98**	85	84	87	1.04	21 091**	10 504**	10 587**	8 790**	6 405**	2 385**	XX
99	99	99	1.00	99	99	100	1.01	102	102	101	1.00	1 667	1 042**	624**	899	406**	493**	XXI

9. Enrolment ratios for one or both of the two school years were not calculated due to lack of United Nations population data by age.
10. Data include French overseas departments and territories (DOM-TOM).
Data in bold are for the school year ending in 2010 for transition rates, and the school year ending in 2011 for enrolment and enrolment ratios and others indicators in this table. Those in italics are for 2000 and those in bold italic are for 2001.
(z) Data are for the school year ending in 2009.
(y) Data are for the school year ending in 2008.
(x) Data are for the school year ending in 2007.

(*) National estimate.
(**) For country level data: UIS partial estimate; for regional and other country-grouping sums and weighted averages: partial imputation due to incomplete country coverage (between 33% and 60% of population for the region or other country grouping).
- Magnitude nil or negligible.
(.) The category is not applicable or does not exist.
(...) No data available.

Table 8
Teaching staff in pre-primary, primary and secondary education

Country or territory	PRE-PRIMARY EDUCATION						PRIMARY EDUCATION					
	Teaching staff				Pupil/teacher ratio[1]		Teaching staff				Pupil/teacher ratio[1]	
	School year ending in				School year ending in		School year ending in				School year ending in	
	1999		2010		1999	2010	1999		2010		1999	2010
	Total (000)	% F	Total (000)	% F			Total (000)	% F	Total (000)	% F		
Arab States												
Algeria	1	93	19	74	28	26	170	46	142	53	28	23
Bahrain	0.7	100	2	100	21	16	4**	72**	...	...	18**	...
Djibouti	0.01	100	0.1ᶻ	75ᶻ	29	16ᶻ	1.0	28	**2**	**24**	40	**35**
Egypt	*17***	*99***	33**,ᶻ	99**,ᶻ	*22***	25**,ᶻ	*353***	*53***	380	53	*22***	26
Iraq	*5*	*100*	...	...	*15*	...	*170*	*72*	...	...	*21*	...
Jordan	3	100	5	100	22	18	...	...	...	...	...	...
Kuwait	4	100	7	100	15	11	10	73	26	90	13	8
Lebanon	11**	95**	10	99	13**	16	29**	83**	33	86	14**	14
Libya	1	100	...	...	8	...	...	...	...	...	...	...
Mauritania	...	...	...	...	...	...	7	26	14	36	47	37
Morocco	40	40	**37**	**65**	20	**20**	123	39	**151**	**51**	28	**26**
Oman	...	...	2	99	...	23	12	52	26**,ᶻ	64**,ᶻ	25	12**,ᶻ
Palestine	3	100	5	100	29	19	10	54	14	69	38	28
Qatar	0.4**	96**	2ᶻ	99ᶻ	21**	15ᶻ	5	75	7	89	13	12
Saudi Arabia	...	...	19	100	...	10	...	...	298	50	...	11
Sudan (pre-secession)	*13*	*84*	21ᶻ	100ᶻ	*27*	30ᶻ	*117***	*52***	124**,ᶻ	61**,ᶻ	*24***	38**,ᶻ
Syrian Arab Republic	5	96	8	95	24	20	110	65**	132**,ʸ	66**,ʸ	25	18**,ʸ
Tunisia	4	95	...	...	20	...	60	50	60ᶻ	55ᶻ	24	17ᶻ
United Arab Emirates	3	100	7	98	19	19	17	73	19	86	16	17
Yemen	0.8	93	2	95	17	15	103**	20**	111	25	22**	31
Central and Eastern Europe												
Albania	4	100	4	100	20	18	13**	75**	11	82	23**	20
Belarus	54	...	44	98	5	6	32	99	24	99	20	15
Bosnia and Herzegovina	...	...	1	97	...	14	...	...	...	...	...	...
Bulgaria	19	...	18	100	11	12	23	...	15	94	18	17
Croatia	6	100	8	99	13	13	11	89	12	92	19	14
Czech Republic	17	100**	22ᶻ	100ᶻ	18	14ᶻ	36	85	25ᶻ	98ᶻ	18	19ᶻ
Estonia	7	100	9ᶻ	100ᶻ	8	6ᶻ	8	86**	6ᶻ	93ᶻ	16	12ᶻ
Hungary	32	100	30ᶻ	100ᶻ	12	11ᶻ	47	85	37ᶻ	96ᶻ	11	10ᶻ
Latvia	7	99	6	100	9	11	9	97	10	94	15	12
Lithuania	13	99	12	100	7	7	13	98	10	97	17	13
Montenegro	*0.6*	...	0.7	...	*20*	13	...	...	...	...	...	...
Poland	74	...	54ᶻ	98ᶻ	12	17ᶻ	*289*	*83*	239ᶻ	84ᶻ	*11*	10ᶻ
Republic of Moldova	*10*	*100*	12	100	9	10	12	96	9	98	21	16
Romania	37	100	38	100	17	17	69	86	52	86	19	16
Russian Federation	642	100*	607ᶻ	96ᶻ	7	8ᶻ	367	98	278ᶻ	98ᶻ	18	18ᶻ
Serbia	8	98**	11	99	21	14	...	...	17	90	...	16
Slovakia	16	100	11	100	10	12	17	93	14	89	19	15
Slovenia	5	99*	5ᶻ	98ᶻ	11	9ᶻ	6	96	6ᶻ	98ᶻ	14	17ᶻ
TFYR Macedonia	3	99	2	99	10	7	6	66	7	79	22	16
Turkey	17	...	29ᶻ	94ᶻ	15	27ᶻ	...	...	...	...	...	...
Ukraine	143	100	139ᶻ	99	8	9	107	98	98	99	20	16
Central Asia												
Armenia	8	...	5	99	7	10	*9***	*99***	...	...	*20***	...
Azerbaijan	12	100	10	100	7	9	37	83	44	88	19	11
Georgia	*7*	*100*	...	...	*11*	...	*18*	*95*	35*	86*	*17*	8*
Kazakhstan	19	...	**54**	**98**	9	**10**	65**	97**	**60**	**98**	19**	**16**
Kyrgyzstan	3	100	3	99	18	26	19	95	16	98	24	24
Mongolia	3	100	4	98	25	25	8	93	9	96	32	30
Tajikistan	*5*	*100*	5	100	*11*	12	*31*	*60*	27	64	*22*	25
Turkmenistan	...	...	...	...	...	...	...	...	...	...	...	...
Uzbekistan	66	96	**56**	**96**	9	**9**	123	84	**125**	**87**	21	**16**
East Asia and the Pacific												
Australia	...	...	...	...	...	...	105**	...	...	...	18**	...
Brunei Darussalam	0.6*	83*	0.7	97	20*	20	3*	66*	4	76	14*	11
Cambodia	*3*	*98*	4	92	*24*	28	*46*	*39*	47	46	*53*	48
China	875	94	1 106	97	27	24	*5 860*	*51*	5 997	58	*22*	17
Cook Islands	0.03	100	**0.03**	**97**	14	**16**	0.1	86	**0.1**	...	18	**16**
DPR Korea	...	...	...	...	...	...	...	...	...	...	...	...
Fiji	*0.3*	*99*	...	...	*21*	...	4	56	4ʸ	55ʸ	*28*	26ʸ
Indonesia	118**	98**	340ᶻ	97ᶻ	17**	12ᶻ	*1 290*	*52*	1 900	60	*22*	16
Japan	96	...	109	...	31	27	367	...	399	...	21	18
Kiribati	...	...	...	...	...	...	0.6	62	1ʸ	82ʸ	25	25ʸ

Teaching staff — Total secondary — School year ending in				Pupil/teacher ratio[1]						Country or territory
1999		2010		Lower secondary — School year ending in		Upper secondary — School year ending in		Total secondary — School year ending in		
Total (000)	% F	Total (000)	% F	1999	2010	1999	2010	1999	2010	
										Arab States
...	.z	...	...	...	...	...	...	...	...	Algeria
4**	52**	...	...	15**	...	13**	...	14**	...	Bahrain
0.7	22	**2**	...	26	**32**	16	**22**	23	**28**	Djibouti
*491***	*40***	506	42	*21***	19	*13***	9	*17***	14	Egypt
62	*69*	...	...	*22*	...	*16*	...	*20*	...	Iraq
...	...	...	...	...	...	17	12y	...	...	Jordan
22**	56**	32	55	12**	9	9**	7	11**	8	Kuwait
43**	52**	43	57	9**	11	8**	7	9**	9	Lebanon
...	...	...	...	...	...	...	...	...	...	Libya
2	10	...	...	28**	35**,y	24**	...	26**	...	Mauritania
88**	33**	...	...	19**	...	14**	...	17**	...	Morocco
13	50	22z	58z	19	12**,z	16	20z	18	15z	Oman
18	47	32	50	26	23	19	20	25	23	Palestine
4**	57**	7	55	13**	11	8**	9	10**	10	Qatar
...	...	311	52	...	9	...	11	...	10	Saudi Arabia
*52***	*49***	83**,z	55**,z	*24***	28**,z	**20**	17z	*22***	22**,z	Sudan (pre-secession)
54	...	...	...	...	18**,y	...	...	19	...	Syrian Arab Republic
56**	40**	87z	...	23**	16z	15**	12z	19**	14z	Tunisia
16	55	27**	65**	14	14	10	10**	12	12**	United Arab Emirates
48**	19**	...	...	22**	12	21	...	22**	...	Yemen
										Central and Eastern Europe
22	54	24	62	16	14	*18*	17	*16*	15	Albania
107	77	...	...	...	...	...	...	9	...	Belarus
...	...	...	...	...	...	...	13	...	...	Bosnia and Herzegovina
56	...	44	79	13	12	12	12	13	12	Bulgaria
33	64	48	69	14	9	11	7	12	8	Croatia
93	*66*	78z	66z	*13*	11z	*9*	11z	*11*	11z	Czech Republic
11	81**	11z	77z	11	9z	10	10z	10	9z	Estonia
100	71	88z	71z	11	10z	9	10z	10	10z	Hungary
25	80	16	83	10	8	10	10	10	9	Latvia
38	...	39	81	...	...	...	...	*11*	9	Lithuania
...	...	...	...	...	...	...	...	...	...	Montenegro
301	*66*	277z	70z	*11*	12z	*15*	10z	*13*	11z	Poland
33	72	29	77	13	10	12	12	13	10	Republic of Moldova
177	64	146	68	12	10	13	15	13	12	Romania
...	...	1 136z	81z	...	...	...	...	...	8z	Russian Federation
...	...	62	64	...	9	14	10	...	10	Serbia
54**	72**	46	75	13	12	12**	12	13**	12	Slovakia
17	69	16z	72z	14	7z	13	11z	13	9z	Slovenia
13	49	17	56	16	11	16	14	16	12	TFYR Macedonia
...	...	...	...	...	...	16	17z	...	...	Turkey
400	76	...	...	...	...	...	...	13	...	Ukraine
										Central Asia
...	...	42	84	...	...	...	...	...	7	Armenia
118	63	...	...	...	...	...	...	8	...	Azerbaijan
59	76	45*,z	86*,z	9	8*,z	5	8*,z	7	8*,z	Georgia
*177***	*83***	**189**	**85**	...	...	...	...	*11***	**9**	Kazakhstan
48	68	44	83	...	...	...	...	13	15*	Kyrgyzstan
11	69	19	73	19	...	17	...	19	14	Mongolia
47	43	60	59	...	...	...	...	16	17	Tajikistan
...	...	...	...	...	...	...	...	...	...	Turkmenistan
307	57	**329**	**62**	...	...	...	...	11	**13**	Uzbekistan
										East Asia and the Pacific
...	...	...	...	...	...	...	...	...	...	Australia
3	48	5z	63z	12*	...	10*	...	11	10z	Brunei Darussalam
20	**29**	...	...	**18**	24	**24**	...	**20**	...	Cambodia
4 763	*41***	6 417	48	*18*	15	*16*	16	*17*	15	China
0.1	...	**0.1**	**57**	...	...	...	...	*14*	**14**	Cook Islands
...	...	...	...	...	...	...	...	...	...	DPR Korea
*5***	*51***	5y	71y	...	20y	...	17y	*20***	19y	Fiji
1 040	*40*	1 641	48	*15*	13	*13*	11	*14*	12	Indonesia
630	...	614	...	16	14	13	11	14	12	Japan
0.4	*47*	0.7y	48y	...	17y	...	19y	**21**	17y	Kiribati

373

Table 8 (continued)

Country or territory	PRE-PRIMARY EDUCATION						PRIMARY EDUCATION					
	Teaching staff				Pupil/teacher ratio[1]		Teaching staff				Pupil/teacher ratio[1]	
	School year ending in				School year ending in		School year ending in				School year ending in	
	1999		2010		1999	2010	1999		2010		1999	2010
	Total (000)	% F	Total (000)	% F			Total (000)	% F	Total (000)	% F		
Lao PDR	2	100	5	97	18	18	27	43	32	51	31	29
Macao, China	0.5	100	0.6	99	31	17	1.5	87	2	88	31	16
Malaysia	21	100	43ᶻ	97ᶻ	27	18ᶻ	143	66	226ᶻ	69ᶻ	20	13ᶻ
Marshall Islands	0.1	…	…	…	11	…	0.6	…	…	…	15	…
Micronesia, F. S.	…	…	…	…	…	…	…	…	…	…	…	…
Myanmar	2	…	9	97	22	17	155	73	182	84	31	28
Nauru	0.1	98	0.04ʸ	98ʸ	13	16ʸ	0.1	92	0.1ʸ	93ʸ	21	22ʸ
New Zealand	7	98	10	98	15	11	20	82	24	84	18	14
Niue	0.01	100	…	…	11	…	0.02	100	…	…	16	…
Palau	0.1	98	…	…	10	…	0.1	82	…	…	15	…
Papua New Guinea	…	…	…	…	…	…	16**	39**	…	…	35**	…
Philippines	18	92**	…	…	33	…	360	87	435ᶻ	90ᶻ	35	31ᶻ
Republic of Korea	22	100	31ᶻ	99ᶻ	24	17ᶻ	122	67	158	78	32	21
Samoa	0.1**	94**	0.3	96	42**	12	1**	71**	1.0	77	24**	30
Singapore	…	…	…	…	…	…	…	…	16.9ᶻ	81ᶻ	…	17ᶻ
Solomon Islands	…	…	1ᶻ	…	…	15ᶻ	3.0	41	…	…	19	…
Thailand	111	79	**102**	**77**	25	**27**	298	63	**320**	**59**	21	…
Timor-Leste	…	…	…	…	…	…	4**	**30****	8	40	**51****	30
Tokelau	0.01	100	…	…	11	…	0.03	76	…	…	10	…
Tonga	0.1	100	…	…	18	…	0.8	67	…	…	21	…
Tuvalu	**0.0**	**100**	…	…	**18**	…	0.1	…	…	…	19	…
Vanuatu	**0.8**	**99**	0.8	94	**10**	14	1	49	2	54	24	22
Viet Nam	94	100	196	98	23	17	337	78	348	78	30	20
Latin America and the Caribbean												
Anguilla	0.03	100	0.04	100	18	14	0.1	87	0.1	93	22	14
Antigua and Barbuda	0.3	100	0.3	100	6	…	0.7	79	0.7	94	19	15
Argentina	50	96	72ʸ	96ʸ	24	20ʸ	221	88	289ʸ	87ʸ	21	16ʸ
Aruba	0.1	100	0.1	98	26	20	0.5	78	0.6	84	19	17
Bahamas	0.2	97	…	…	9	…	2.4	63	2	92	14	14
Barbados	0.3**	93**	0.4*	97*	18**	16*	1**	76**	2*	78*	18**	13*
Belize	0.2	98	0.4	98	19	17	2	64	2	73	23	22
Bermuda	…	…	…	…	…	…	**0.5**	**89**	0.6	90	**9**	7
Bolivia, P. S.	5	93	…	…	42	…	60	61**	…	…	25**	…
Brazil	304	98	384	97	19	18	807	93	762	91	26	22
British Virgin Islands	0.0**	100**	0.1ᶻ	100ᶻ	13**	13ᶻ	0.2	86	0.2	92	18	13
Cayman Islands	0.1	96	0.1ʸ	97ʸ	9	9ʸ	0.2	89	0.3ʸ	88ʸ	15	12ʸ
Chile	19	99	33ᶻ	97ᶻ	24	12ᶻ	56	77	70ᶻ	78ᶻ	32	23ᶻ
Colombia	59	94	49	96	18	27	215	77	181	78	24	28
Costa Rica	4	97	8	94	21	14	21	81	29	80	27	18
Cuba	26	98	**30**	**100**	19	**13**	91	79	**91**	**78**	12	**9**
Dominica	0.1	100	0.1	100	18	14	0.6	75	0.5	87	20	16
Dominican Republic	8	95	10	94	24	24	42	75	52	76	31	26
Ecuador	13	88	19**,ʸ	…	15	18**,ʸ	83	68	120*,ᶻ	63*,ᶻ	23	17*,ᶻ
El Salvador	…	…	9ᶻ	68ᶻ	…	23	…	…	31ᶻ	68ᶻ	…	31ᶻ
Grenada	0.2	96	0.2	100	18	14	0.8	76	0.9	79	20	16
Guatemala	12	…	24	91	26	24	48	…	95	65	38	28
Guyana	2	99	2	100	18	14	4	86	4	89	27	25
Haiti	…	…	…	…	…	…	…	…	…	…	…	…
Honduras	6	…	8ʸ	94ʸ	19	29ʸ	32	…	38ʸ	75ʸ	34	33ʸ
Jamaica	**6**	…	6	97	**24**	25	**10**	**87****	15	91	**34**	21
Mexico	150	94	182	96	22	25	540	62	530	67	27	28
Montserrat	0.01	100	0.01ᶻ	100ᶻ	12	9ᶻ	0.02	84	0.04ᶻ	97ᶻ	21	13ᶻ
Netherlands Antilles	0.3	99	…	…	21	…	1	86	…	…	20	…
Nicaragua	6	97	10	96	26	21	24	83	31	77	34	30
Panama	3	98	5	94	19	17	15	75	19	76	26	23
Paraguay	…	…	…	…	…	…	…	…	…	…	…	…
Peru	…	…	74	94ᶻ	…	19	150	62	191	66	29	20
Saint Kitts and Nevis	…	…	0.1	100	…	20	0.4	83	0.4	87	19	14
Saint Lucia	0.3**	100**	0.3	100	13**	10	**1**	**83**	1	87	**24**	19
Saint Vincent/Grenadines	…	…	0.4ᶻ	100ᶻ	…	8ᶻ	1**	71**	0.9	78	19**	16
Suriname	**0.7**	**99****	0.8ʸ	100ʸ	**22**	21ʸ	**3****	**82****	5ᶻ	93ᶻ	**20****	15ᶻ
Trinidad and Tobago	2**	100**	…	…	13**	…	8	76	7*	79*	21	18*
Turks and Caicos Islands	0.1**	92**	…	…	13**	…	0.1**	92**	…	…	18**	…
Uruguay	3	98**	5ᶻ	…	31	25ᶻ	18	92**	25ᶻ	…	20	14ᶻ
Venezuela, B. R.	…	…	…	…	…	…	…	…	…	…	…	…

				SECONDARY EDUCATION						
Teaching staff				Pupil/teacher ratio[1]						
Total secondary				Lower secondary		Upper secondary		Total secondary		
School year ending in				School year ending in		School year ending in		School year ending in		
1999		2010		1999	2010	1999	2010	1999	2010	
Total (000)	% F	Total (000)	% F							Country or territory
12	40	18^y	44^y	20	22^y	22	24^y	20	23^y	Lao PDR
1.4	56	2	59	24	17	21	16	23	16	Macao, China
120**	62**	186^z	67^z	18**	...	18**	...	18**	14^z	Malaysia
0.3	...	...	...	28	...	18	12^z	22	...	Marshall Islands
...	...	...	...	...	...	...	...	...	...	Micronesia, F. S.
68	76	84	85	28	36	38	28	30	34	Myanmar
0.04	39	...	...	...	...	...	...	17	...	Nauru
28	58	35	62	18	15	13	14	15	15	New Zealand^d
0.03	44	...	...	6	...	21	...	11	...	Niue
0.2	51	...	...	14	...	12	...	13	...	Palau
...	...	...	...	...	...	...	...	...	...	Papua New Guinea
150	76	194^z	76^z	41	39^z	21	25^z	34	35^z	Philippines
189	41	225	55	22	19	22	16	22	18	Republic of Korea
1**	57**	1	58	26**	24	17	20	20**	21	Samoa
...	...	16^z	66^z	...	15^z	...	15^z	...	15^z	Singapore
1	33	...	...	...	...	...	...	13	...	Solomon Islands
169**	**53****	**246**	**51**	**23****	**22**	**25****	**18**	**24****	**20**	Thailand
1**	...	4	29	**28****	26	**29****	20	**28****	23	Timor-Leste
0.01	64	...	...	...	...	...	...	16	...	Tokelau
1**	48**	...	...	15**	...	13**	...	15**	...	Tonga
...	...	...	...	**25**	...	...	...	...	...	Tuvalu
0.4	47	...	...	...	...	...	...	23	...	Vanuatu
284	65	474	...	28	17	29	22	28	19	Viet Nam
										Latin America and the Caribbean
0.1**	63**	...	...	...	...	...	...	15**	...	Anguilla
0.4	71	0.7	72	12	16	16	8	13	12	Antigua and Barbuda
311	69	324^y	68^y	11	14^y	12	8^y	11	11^y	Argentina
0.4	49	0.5	59	...	...	...	...	16	14	Aruba
1**	74**	3	76	23**	12	23**	12	23**	12	Bahamas
1**	58**	...	...	...	...	...	...	18**	...	Barbados
1.0	64	2	60	23	18	23	14	23	17	Belize
0.6	**67**	0.8	73	**8**	5	**7**	5	**7**	5	Bermuda
39**	52**	...	...	24**	...	20	...	21**	...	Bolivia, P. S.
1 104	79	1 413	67	23	18	21	15	23	17	Brazil
0.2	63	0.2	82	6	10	10	7	7	9	British Virgin Islands
0.2	46	0.4^y	61^y	11	...	7	...	9	9^y	Cayman Islands
45	62	68^z	63^z	32	22^z	27	22^z	29	22^z	Chile
200	49	187	50	...	30	...	22	18	27	Colombia
13	53	27	59	20	16	19	15	20	16	Costa Rica
65	60	**88**	**55**	12	**10**	10	**8**	11	**9**	Cuba
0.4**	68**	0.5	69	21**	15	15**	11	19**	13	Dominica
...	...	32	66	...	30	28	27	...	28	Dominican Republic
68**	49**	...	...	13**	...	14**	...	14**	...	Ecuador
...	...	23^z	68^z	...	25^z	...	23^z	...	24^z	El Salvador
...	...	0.7	62	...	...	...	...	...	15	Grenada
33	...	61	45	15	17	11	14	13	16	Guatemala
4**	63**	4	68	19**	22	19**	21	19**	21	Guyana
...	...	...	...	...	...	...	...	...	...	Haiti
...	...	...	...	...	...	...	11^y	...	...	Honduras
12**	...	18	73	18**	...	20**	...	19**	15	Jamaica
519	44	652	49	18	19	14	16	17	18	Mexico
0.0	62**	0.03^z	74^z	11**	15**.z	10**	11**.z	10	13^z	Montserrat
1	53	...	...	12	...	21	...	15	...	Netherlands Antilles
10*	56*	15	55	31*	...	31**	...	31**	31	Nicaragua
14	55	19	59	17	17	15	13	16	15	Panama
39	62	...	...	...	...	...	...	11	...	Paraguay
...	...	167	44	...	...	...	...	...	16	Peru
0.3	56	0.5	61	...	9	...	9	14	9	Saint Kitts and Nevis
0.7	**65**	1*	69*	...	16*	...	...	**17**	16*	Saint Lucia
0.4	57	0.7	64	24**	18	24**	15	24**	17	Saint Vincent/Grenadines
3**	**63****	4^z	69^z	**17****	15^z	**13****	11^z	**15****	13^z	Suriname
6**	59**	7**.y	63**.y	22**	14*.y	19**	14**.y	21**	14**.y	Trinidad and Tobago
0.1**	62**	...	...	9**	...	9**	...	9**	...	Turks and Caicos Islands
19	72**	23^z	...	12	11^z	23	15^z	15	12^z	Uruguay
...	...	...	...	...	...	...	...	...	...	Venezuela, B. R.

Table 8 (continued)

Country or territory	PRE-PRIMARY EDUCATION						PRIMARY EDUCATION					
	Teaching staff				Pupil/teacher ratio[1]		Teaching staff				Pupil/teacher ratio[1]	
	School year ending in				School year ending in		School year ending in				School year ending in	
	1999		2010		1999	2010	1999		2010		1999	2010
	Total (000)	% F	Total (000)	% F			Total (000)	% F	Total (000)	% F		
North America and Western Europe												
Andorra	...	...	0.2	89	...	13	...	...	0.5	80	...	10
Austria	14	99	19	99	16	12	29	89	30	90	13	11
Belgium	27	92	31^z	98^z	15	14^z	65**	78**	66^z	81^z	12**	11^z
Canada	30	68**	...	...	17	...	141	68**	...	...	17	...
Cyprus	1.0	99	1	100	19	17	4	67	4	83	18	14
Denmark	45	92	...	...	6	...	37	63	...	...	10	...
Finland	10	96	14	97	12	11	22	71	25	79	17	14
France	128	78	125	83	19	20	209	78	234	83	19	18
Germany	...	...	230	98	...	10	221	82	242	86	17	13
Greece	9	100**	...	...	16	...	48	57**	...	...	14	...
Iceland	3	98	2^z	96^z	4	6^z	...	...	...	...	...	...
Ireland	...	...	...	...	...	...	21	85	32	85	22	16
Israel	...	...	...	...	...	...	50**	85**	60**,z	84**,z	13**	13**,z
Italy	119	99	...	...	13	...	254	95	...	...	11	...
Luxembourg	0.9**	97**	1^y	98^y	15**	12^y	3	67	3^y	72^y	12	12^y
Malta	0.9	99	0.6	100	12	14	2	87	2	85	20	14
Monaco	0.04	100	...	...	25	...	0.1	87	...	...	22	...
Netherlands	...	...	...	...	...	...	...	...	...	...	...	...
Norway	...	...	...	...	...	...	...	...	...	...	...	...
Portugal	14	...	17^z	97^z	16	16^z	61	82	66^z	80^z	13	11^z
San Marino	0.1	99	0.1	98	8	7	0.2	91	0.2	93	5	6
Spain	68	93	149	94	17	12	172	68	219	75	15	12
Sweden	36	97	...	...	9	...	62	80	60	81	12	10
Switzerland	...	...	...	...	...	...	...	...	...	...	...	...
United Kingdom	51	95	60^z	92^z	23	19^z	249	81	246^z	81^z	19	18^z
United States	327	95	541	94	22	16	1 618	86	1 795	87	15	14
South and West Asia												
Afghanistan	...	...	...	...	...	...	...	...	119	31	...	44
Bangladesh	68	33	...	...	27	...	...	...	395	49	...	43*
Bhutan	0.01	31	0.1	100	22	12	2	32	4	41	42	25
India	504	...	...	...	35	...	3 135*	33*	...	...	35*	...
Iran, Islamic Republic of	9.5	98	...	...	23	...	315	54	278^z	57^z	25	20^z
Maldives	0.4	90	0.9	98	31	19	3	60	4	73	24	12
Nepal	11**	32**	41	90	24**	25	92	23	167	42	39	30
Pakistan	...	...	...	...	...	...	424**	45**	464	48	33**	40
Sri Lanka	...	...	...	...	...	...	67	...	72	85	26	24
Sub-Saharan Africa												
Angola	...	...	18**	40**	...	37**	...	...	93**	...	...	46**
Benin	0.6	61	3	71	28	33	16	23	39	19	53	46
Botswana	...	...	2^z	98^z	...	13^z	12	81	13^z	76^z	27	25^z
Burkina Faso	0.7**	66**	2	82	29**	23	19	23	46	37	47	48
Burundi	0.2**	99**	2	69	28**	34	12	54	37	53	46	51
Cameroon	4	97	15	97	23	22	41	36	77	48	52	46
Cape Verde	0.8**	100**	1	100	25**	20	3**	62**	3	68	29**	24
Central African Republic	...	...	0.5	88	...	44	...	...	8	18	...	81
Chad	...	...	0.6	79	...	35	12	9	28	15	68	62
Comoros	0.1**	94**	...	...	26**	...	2	26	4^y	37^y	35	30^y
Congo	0.6	100	2	96	10	23	7	37	14	53	60	49
Côte d'Ivoire	2	83	4	92	22	19	43	20	56	27	45	49
D. R. Congo	2**	88**	9	97	25**	25	155	21	286	27	26	37
Equatorial Guinea	0.4	36	2^y	87^y	43	24^y	1	28	3	36	57	27
Eritrea	0.3	97	1	98	36	35	6	35	8	41	47	38
Ethiopia	2	93	10	80	36	35	87	29	252	36	67	54
Gabon	0.5**	98**	...	...	30**	...	5	48	13	53	49	25
Gambia	0.8	55	...	...	37	...	5	32	6^z	33^z	37	37^z
Ghana	18**	92**	38**,z	85**,z	28**	35**,z	80	32	124	37	30	31
Guinea	...	...	4	53	...	34	16	25	34	29	47	42
Guinea-Bissau	0.2	73	0.3	69	21	29	3	20	5	22	44	52
Kenya	47**	64**	93^z	83^z	26**	21^z	148	42	153**,z	44**,z	32	47**,z
Lesotho	2	99	2	...	19	24	8	80	12	77	44	34

Teaching staff — Total secondary				Pupil/teacher ratio[1]						
				Lower secondary		Upper secondary		Total secondary		
School year ending in				School year ending in		School year ending in		School year ending in		
1999		2010		1999	2010	1999	2010	1999	2010	
Total (000)	% F	Total (000)	% F							Country or territory
North America and Western Europe										
...	...	...	...	...	7	...	...	...	...	Andorra
73	57	75	63	9	8	12	12	10	10	Austria
105	57	...	...	...	7^z	...	...	10	...	Belgium
139	68**	377^y	...	17	...	19	...	18	...	Canada
5	51	7	64	...	10	...	10	13	10	Cyprus
44	45	...	...	10	...	9	...	10	...	Denmark
39	64	43^z	64^z	10	10^z	14	10^z	12	10^z	Finland
495	57	463	59	13	14	11	11	12	13	France
533	51	594	59	15	12	16	15	15	13	Germany
75	56**	...	...	10	...	10	...	10	...	Greece
...	...	...	...	...	...	14	12^z	...	...	Iceland
...	...	...	...	...	...	...	...	...	...	Ireland
61**	70**	71**,z	73**,z	12**	11**,z	9	9^z	10**	10**,z	Israel
422	65	...	...	10	...	11	...	11	...	Italy
3	38	4^y	48^y	...	...	...	...	12	10^y	Luxembourg
4	48	4	60	9	8	38	15	11	9	Malta
0.3	59	0.5^y	68^y	15	...	8	...	10	6^y	Monaco
...	...	107	49	...	...	...	...	...	14	Netherlands
...	...	...	...	...	...	8	...	...	...	Norway
85	68	97^z	69^y	11	8^z	9	6^z	10	7^z	Portugal
...	...	0.2	78	5	...	...	...	...	14	San Marino
277	52	295	55	...	11	...	11	12	11	Spain
63	56	75	59	12	10	17	10	15	10	Sweden
...	...	...	...	...	...	...	...	...	...	Switzerland
355	56	375*,y	62*,y	16	15^y	14	14*,y	15	14*,y	United Kingdom
1 504	56	1 758	61	16	13	14	14	15	14	United States
South and West Asia										
...	...	...	...	...	44	...	...	...	...	Afghanistan
265	13	400	20	43	31	32	26	37	28	Bangladesh
0.6	32	**3**	**38**	35	**22**	27	**17**	32	**21**	Bhutan
1 995**	34**	4 252	40	...	31	...	21	34**	25	India
...	...	...	...	...	22^y	...	...	...	...	Iran, Islamic Republic of
0.9	25	...	...	18	**8**	9	...	17	...	Maldives
40	9	56^y	15^y	38	52^y	24	30^y	32	41^y	Nepal
...	...	...	...	...	...	...	...	...	...	Pakistan
...	...	...	...	*21*	17	...	...	...	...	Sri Lanka
Sub-Saharan Africa										
16**	33**	22**	...	...	37**	...	43**	18**	39**	Angola
10	*12*	...	...	27	...	15	...	*23*	...	Benin
9	45	...	...	...	...	...	...	18	...	Botswana
6**	...	**23**	**16**	29**	...	23**	...	28**	**26**	Burkina Faso
...	...	11	20	...	...	...	...	...	30	Burundi
28**	22**	...	...	...	...	...	...	23**	...	Cameroon
*2**	*36**	4	41	*29**	19	...	16	*25**	18	Cape Verde
...	...	**2**	**12**	...	...	...	...	...	**67**	Central African Republic
4	5	13	6	41	43	23	20	34	32	Chad
...	...	...	...	...	...	...	...	...	...	Comoros
...	...	...	...	...	...	...	...	...	...	Congo
20**	...	...	...	34**	...	21**	...	29**	...	Côte d'Ivoire
89	10	218	11	...	...	...	...	14	16	D. R. Congo
0.9	5	...	...	25	...	15	...	23	...	Equatorial Guinea
2	12	6	13	55	41	45	35	51	39	Eritrea
...	...	98	21	*28*	46	...	33	...	43	Ethiopia
3**	16**	...	...	28**	...	28**	...	28**	...	Gabon
...	...	...	...	24	27^z	...	...	...	...	Gambia
52	22	**115**	**24**	20	**16**	19	**25**	20	**19**	Ghana
...	...	18**,z	6**,z	31	36^z	...	25**,z	...	32**,z	Guinea
*2**	*7**	...	...	*17*	...	9**	...	*14**	...	Guinea-Bissau
...	...	108**,z	41**,z	...	33**,z	...	27^z	...	30**,z	Kenya
...	...	...	...	17	18**	...	...	...	...	Lesotho

377

Table 8 (continued)

Country or territory	PRE-PRIMARY EDUCATION						PRIMARY EDUCATION					
	Teaching staff				Pupil/teacher ratio[1]		Teaching staff				Pupil/teacher ratio[1]	
	School year ending in				School year ending in		School year ending in				School year ending in	
	1999		2010		1999	2010	1999		2010		1999	2010
	Total (000)	% F	Total (000)	% F			Total (000)	% F	Total (000)	% F		
Liberia	6	19	...	...	18	...	10	19	22y	12y	39	24
Madagascar	...	...	7	97	...	23	43	58	106	56	47	40
Malawi	...	...	...	...	...	...	...	...	43**	40**	...	79**
Mali	1**	73**	2	94	21**	44	15*	23*	44	28	62*	48
Mauritius	3	100	3	99	16	14	5	54	5	70	26	21
Mozambique	...	...	...	...	...	...	37	25	95	41	61	55
Namibia	1	88	...	...	27	...	12	67	14z	68z	32	30z
Niger	0.6	98	3	91	21	32	13	31	49	45	41	39
Nigeria	...	...	60**,y	65**,y	...	29**,y	432	48	574	48	41	36
Rwanda	0.5**	86**	3	80	35**	38	24	55	40	52	54	58
Sao Tome and Principe	0.1	95	0.3	94	28	19	0.7	...	1	56	36	30
Senegal	1	78	6	78	19	24	21	22	50	31	49	34
Seychelles	0.2	100	0.2	100	16	13	0.7	85	0.7	83	15	13
Sierra Leone	0.9	83	2	82	19	17	15	38	38	25	37	31
Somalia	...	...	...	...	...	...	...	...	...	...	...	...
South Africa	...	...	...	...	...	...	227	78	232z	77z	35	31z
South Sudan	...	...	...	...	...	...	...	...	...	...	...	...
Swaziland	...	...	2	95	...	11	6	75	7	71	33	32
Togo	0.6	97	2	79	17	26	23	13	32	14	41	41
Uganda	...	...	20	83	...	25	110	33	172	41	57	49
United Republic of Tanzania	...	...	16	54	...	57	106	45	166	50	46	51
Zambia	...	...	...	...	...	...	26**	49**	50**	51**	61**	58**
Zimbabwe	...	...	...	...	...	...	...	...	...	...	...	...

	Sum	% F	Sum	% F	Weighted average		Sum	% F	Sum	% F	Weighted average	
World	5 378	91	7 787**	94**	21	21**	24 809	58**	28 483	62	26	24
Countries in transition	1 000	100	996**	97**	7	9**	909	93	788**	94**	19	17**
Developed countries	1 408	94	1 885	94	18	15	4 444	81	4 678	82**	16	14
Developing countries	2 970	87	4 906**	93**	27	26**	19 456**	52**	23 017	57	29**	27
Arab States	118	77	193**	90**	20	20**	1 516	52	1 954	57	23	21
Central and Eastern Europe	1 119	100	1 086**	97**	8	10**	1 360**	83**	1 113**	82**	18**	17**
Central Asia	128	97	152**	97**	10	11**	331	86	323	90	21	17
East Asia and the Pacific	1 409	94	2 096	96	26	21	9 187**	55**	10 376	62	24**	18
East Asia	1 383	94	2 062	96	26	21	9 032**	54**	10 207	62	25**	18
Pacific	26**	89**	...	...	17**	...	155	72**	...	...	20	...
Latin America/Caribbean	759	96	1 028	96	21	20	2 714	77	3 020	78	26	22
Caribbean	15	99**	17	99	...	...	83**	54**	92**	59**	29**	26**
Latin America	745	96	1 011	96	21	20	2 631	78	2 928	78	26	22
N. America/W. Europe	1 064	92	1 545	94	18	14	3 418	82	3 741	83	15	14
South and West Asia	583**	69**	...	...	37**	...	4 327	36	4 853**	46**	36	39**
Sub-Saharan Africa	196**	70**	444**	76**	28**	27**	1 956	43	3 103	43	42	43
Countries with low income	213	59	384**	74	27**	24**	1 722**	38**	2 830	43	43**	43
Countries with middle income	3 776	92	5 504**	95	21	23**	18 343**	55**	20 461**	60**	27**	24**
Lower middle	1 179**	84**	...	...	26**	...	7 826	48	9 576**	55**	31	31**
Upper middle	2 597	96	3 152	96	19	19	10 516**	60**	10 885	65	24**	19
Countries with high income	1 390	93	1 899	94	18	15	4 745	79	5 193	80	16	14

Source: UNESCO Institute for Statistics database (UIS, 2012).
Note: The country groupings by income level presented in the tables are as defined by the World Bank. They are based on the list of countries by income group as revised in July 2011.
1. Based on headcounts of pupils and teachers.
Data in bold are for the school year ending in 2011, those in italics are for 2000 and those in bold italics are for 2001.
(z) Data are for the school year ending in 2009.
(y) Data are for the school year ending in 2008.

(*) National estimate.
(**) For country level data: UIS partial estimate; for regional and other country-grouping sums and weighted averages: partial imputation due to incomplete country coverage (between 33% and 60% of population for the region or other country grouping).
(. . .) No data available.

Table 8

SECONDARY EDUCATION										
Teaching staff				Pupil/teacher ratio[1]						
Total secondary				Lower secondary		Upper secondary		Total secondary		
School year ending in				School year ending in		School year ending in		School year ending in		
1999		2010		1999	2010	1999	2010	1999	2010	
Total (000)	% F	Total (000)	% F							Country or territory
7	16	…	…	17	…	18	…	17	…	Liberia
…	…	44^z	45^z	…	25^z	…	18**, z	…	23**, z	Madagascar
…	…	…	…	…	…	…	…	…	…	Malawi
8*	14*	**33**	…	31*	**38**	24	**13**	28*	**25**	Mali
5	47	8	58	…	…	…	…	20	16**	Mauritius
…	…	**21**	**19**	…	…	…	…	…	**34**	Mozambique
5	46	…	…	25	…	21	…	24	…	Namibia
4	18	10	18	34	34	12	15	24	30	Niger
129	36	274	46	…	31	…	36	30	33	Nigeria
6	*21*	**21**	**28**	…	…	…	…	*23*	**24**	Rwanda
…	…	**0.6**	**20****	…	**19**	…	**21**	…	**20**	Sao Tome and Principe
9	15	22	17	*31*	…	*20*	…	27	32	Senegal
0.6	54	0.6	60	14**	…	14**	…	14	12	Seychelles
6	*27*	…	…	*23*	19	*34*	…	*27*	…	Sierra Leone
…	…	…	…	…	…	…	…	…	…	Somalia
145	50	187^z	55^z	…	…	…	…	29	25^z	South Africa
…	…	…	…	…	…	…	…	…	…	South Sudan
3	…	5	48	…	…	…	…	*17*	18	Swaziland
7	13	…	…	44	…	20	…	35	…	Togo
31	*21*	71**, z	23**, z	…	…	…	…	*18*	18**, z	Uganda
…	…	…	…	…	…	…	…	…	…	United Republic of Tanzania
…	…	…	…	18**	32**, y	…	…	…	…	Zambia
…	…	…	…	…	…	…	…	…	…	Zimbabwe

Sum	% F	Sum	% F	Weighted average						
24 327**	52**	31 951	52	19**	18	16**	16	18**	17	World
3 220**	75**	2 496**	76**	…	…	…	…	10**	10**	Countries in transition
6 151	55	6 739	59**	14	12	13	12	14	12	Developed countries
14 956**	46**	22 717	47	22**	20	20**	18	21**	19	Developing countries
1 364	43	1 992**	46**	19**	17**	13**	12**	16	15**	Arab States
3 483**	73**	2 643**	72**	…	…	…	…	12**	11**	Central and Eastern Europe
850	66	920	71	…	…	…	…	11	11	Central Asia
7 605**	46**	10 459	50	18	16	15**	15	17**	16	East Asia and the Pacific
7 415**	45**	10 254	50	18	16	15**	15	17**	16	East Asia
…	…	…	…	…	…	…	…	…	…	Pacific
2 782	63	3 635	59	20	18	18	15	19	17	Latin America/Caribbean
51**	63**	76**	68**	21**	…	20**	…	21**	…	Caribbean
2 731	63	3 559	59	19	18	18	15	19	16	Latin America
4 486	56	5 204	61	14	12	13	12	14	12	N. America/W. Europe
2 925	35	5 376	39	36**	32	30**	22	33	27	South and West Asia
831	31	1 722**	30**	27**	26**	23**	24**	25	25**	Sub-Saharan Africa
969	30	1 787**	30**	29**	29**	23**	22**	27	26**	Countries with low income
17 022**	53**	22 949	52	20**	19	17**	17	19**	18	Countries with middle income
5 785	46	9 680	47	26**	24	21**	18	24	21	Lower middle
11 237**	57**	13 269	55	17	15	16**	16	16**	16	Upper middle
6 336	54	7 215	58	14	12	13	12	14	12	Countries with high income

Table 9
Financial commitment to education: public spending

Country or territory	Total public expenditure on education as % of GNP 1999	2010	Total public expenditure on education as % of total government expenditure 1999	2010	Public current expenditure on primary education as % of public current on education 1999	2010	Public current expenditure on primary education per pupil at PPP in constant 2009 US$ 1999	2010	Public current expenditure on secondary education as % of public current on education 1999	2010	Public current expenditure on secondary education per pupil at PPP in constant 2009 US$ 1999	2010
Arab States												
Algeria	...	4.4^y	...	20.3^y	...	...	...	...	...	...	...	...
Bahrain	...	3.1^y	...	11.7^y	...	...	...	...	...	...	...	...
Djibouti	7.5	7.6^x	...	22.8^x	...	...	...	...	...	...	...	...
Egypt	...	3.7^y	...	11.9^y	...	...	...	...	...	...	...	...
Iraq	...	...	...	...	...	...	...	...	...	...	...	...
Jordan	5.0	...	20.6	...	...	...	482	582^y	...	...	558	711^y
Kuwait	**5.6****	...	...	...	...	...	...	...	...	...	...	...
Lebanon	2.0	1.8^z	10.4	7.2^z	...	...	...	...	...	...	...	...
Libya	...	...	...	...	...	...	...	...	...	...	...	...
Mauritania	2.8**	4.3	...	15.2	...	45.8	...	216	...	24.4	...	551**
Morocco	5.5	5.5^z	25.7	25.7^y	39.1	...	510	682^y	43.5	...	1 337	1 536^x
Oman	4.2	4.7^z	21.3	...	**37.3**	32.7^z	1 905	3 122^z	**51.7**	39.9^z	3 705	3 573^z
Palestine	...	...	...	...	...	...	...	...	...	...	...	...
Qatar	...	2.4^y	...	8.2^y	...	...	...	5 621^z	...	...	...	5 969^z
Saudi Arabia	7.0	5.5^y	26.0	19.3^y	...	...	...	...	...	...	...	...
Sudan (pre-secession)	...	...	...	...	...	...	...	...	...	...	...	...
Syrian Arab Republic	...	5.0^x	...	16.7^x	...	...	387	692^z	...	...	668	597^z
Tunisia	6.5	6.6^y	17.4**	22.7^y	38.3**	...	923**	...	42.9**	...	1 326**	...
United Arab Emirates	**1.3***	1.0^z	22.2*	23.4^z	...	...	3 653	...	...	...	4 767	...
Yemen	10.5	5.6^y	32.8	16.0^y	...	...	...	...	...	...	...	...
Central and Eastern Europe												
Albania	...	...	...	...	...	...	...	...	...	...	...	...
Belarus	6.0	4.6^z	...	8.9^z	...	...	...	...	...	...	...	...
Bosnia and Herzegovina	...	...	...	...	...	...	...	...	...	...	...	...
Bulgaria	**3.5**	4.7^y	**8.8**	12.3^y	**20.8**	18.9^y	**1 393**	3 115^y	**46.6**	42.7^y	**1 679**	3 117^y
Croatia	...	4.5^z	...	...	...	...	...	...	...	...	...	...
Czech Republic	4.1	4.8^z	9.7	9.8^z	17.8**	15.8^z	1 897**	3 677^z	49.8**	47.3^z	3 740**	5 830^z
Estonia	6.8	6.0^y	15.4	14.2^y	...	25.3^y	...	5 441^y	...	40.8^y	...	6 185^y
Hungary	4.9	5.4^z	12.8	10.0^z	19.5**	17.4^z	2 629**	4 200^z	40.6**	41.7^z	2 736**	4 307^z
Latvia	5.8	5.2^z	14.4	12.8^z	...	...	...	...	...	...	...	...
Lithuania	**6.0**	5.6^z	**16.0**	12.9^z	...	12.9^z	...	3 127^z	...	52.6^z	...	4 596^z
Montenegro	...	...	...	...	...	...	...	...	...	...	...	...
Poland	4.7	5.3^z	11.4	11.4^z	...	30.4^z	...	4 611^z	...	37.0^z	...	4 341^z
Republic of Moldova	4.6	8.4	16.4	22.3	...	18.2	...	1 184	...	37.4	...	1 117
Romania	2.9	4.3^x	7.5	11.8^x	...	20.2^x	...	2 248^x	...	36.2^x	...	1 895^x
Russian Federation	3.0	4.2^y	10.6	11.9^y	...	...	...	...	...	...	...	...
Serbia	...	5.1^z	...	9.5^z	...	47.4^z	...	6 662^z	...	23.6^z	...	1 552^z
Slovakia	4.2	4.1	13.8	9.8	14.5	18.6^z	1 457	4 039^z	55.7	47.7^z	2 629	3 970^z
Slovenia	**5.9**	5.8	**12.4**	11.6^z	...	...	...	...	...	...	...	...
TFYR Macedonia	...	...	...	...	...	...	...	...	...	...	...	...
Turkey	3.0	...	...	...	...	...	...	...	...	...	...	...
Ukraine	3.7	5.4^x	13.6	20.2^x	...	...	...	...	...	...	...	...
Central Asia												
Armenia	2.2	3.1	12.8	13.0^z	...	...	...	...	...	...	...	...
Azerbaijan	4.3	3.5^z	24.4	10.9^z	...	...	...	...	...	...	...	...
Georgia	2.0	3.3*, ^{z}	10.3	7.7*, ^{z}	...	...	...	...	...	...	...	...
Kazakhstan	4.0	3.4^z	14.4	...	...	...	...	...	...	...	...	...
Kyrgyzstan	4.3	6.5^z	21.4	24.7^y	...	...	...	...	...	...	...	...
Mongolia	5.1	5.9	15.2	14.6^z	...	31.3	...	583	...	28.8	...	534
Tajikistan	2.1	4.1	11.8	14.7	...	...	...	...	...	...	...	...
Turkmenistan	...	...	...	...	...	...	...	...	...	...	...	...
Uzbekistan	...	...	...	...	...	...	...	...	...	...	...	...
East Asia and the Pacific												
Australia	5.1	5.2^z	13.8	12.9^y	32.9	34.5^z	5 257	6 946^z	39.5	37.3^z	4 782	6 644^z
Brunei Darussalam	4.9	2.0	9.3	**13.7**	...	28.7	...	2 512	...	46.8	...	3 800
Cambodia	1.0	2.7	8.7	12.4^x	61.7	...	59	...	**11.8**	...	**75**	...
China	1.9	...	13.0	...	34.3**	...	...	...	38.4**	...	303**	...
Cook Islands	...	...	13.1**	...	53.0	...	...	...	40.0	...	...	...
DPR Korea	...	...	...	...	...	...	...	...	...	...	...	...
Fiji	5.3	4.5^z	18.3	14.7^z	...	...	...	...	...	...	...	...
Indonesia	**2.8****	3.1	**11.5****	17.1	...	44.9	...	403	...	25.4	...	348
Japan	3.5	3.7	9.3	9.4^y	...	...	...	...	...	...	...	...
Kiribati	6.7	...	...	...	...	...	...	...	...	...	...	...

Education for All Global Monitoring Report 2 0 1 2

Table 9 (continued)

Country or territory	Total public expenditure on education as % of GNP		Total public expenditure on education as % of total government expenditure		Public current expenditure on primary education as % of public current on education		Public current expenditure on primary education per pupil at PPP in constant 2009 US$		Public current expenditure on secondary education as % of public current on education		Public current expenditure on secondary education per pupil at PPP in constant 2009 US$	
	1999	2010	1999	2010	1999	2010	1999	2010	1999	2010	1999	2010
Lao PDR	1.0	3.3	7.4	13.2	...	...	...	...	...	...	...	...
Macao, China	3.6	2.9^z	13.5	13.0^z	...	...	...	...	...	...	...	...
Malaysia	6.1	5.9^z	25.2	18.9^z	30.9**	35.5^z	1 063**	1 856^z	34.7**	42.1^z	1 639**	2 597^z
Marshall Islands	11.0	...	...	...	...	...	...	...	...	...	...	...
Micronesia, F. S.	6.2	...	...	...	...	...	...	...	...	...	...	...
Myanmar	0.6	...	8.1	...	...	...	...	...	**33.4**	...	...	...
Nauru	...	...	...	7.5*,^x	...	...	...	...	...	...	...	...
New Zealand	7.1	7.6	**16.1**	16.1^y	26.7**	23.3	4 423**	5 686	39.8**	38.0	5 432**	6 311
Niue	...	...	...	...	31.9	...	...	...	59.3	...	...	...
Palau	9.4**	...	...	...	...	...	...	...	...	...	...	...
Papua New Guinea	...	...	...	...	...	...	...	...	...	...	...	...
Philippines	3.3	2.7^z	13.9	15.0^z	59.5**	56.0^z	325**	302^y	22.0**	29.1^z	285**	300^y
Republic of Korea	3.8	5.0^z	13.1	15.8^y	43.5**	32.2^z	2 875**	5 179^z	38.3**	36.6^z	2 388**	5 148^z
Samoa	4.5	5.8^y	13.3	13.4^y	32.4**	...	282**	...	26.9**	...	298**	...
Singapore	**3.0**	3.3	...	10.3	**27.9**	20.2	...	5 057	**31.6**	24.3	...	7 712
Solomon Islands	2.3**	7.1^y	...	...	...	...	...	...	...	...	...	...
Thailand	5.1	3.9^y	28.1	22.3	**33.6****	47.8^z	**1 022****	1 889^z	**19.1****	15.9^z	**859****	709^z
Timor-Leste	...	3.6	...	11.7	...	...	...	...	...	...	...	...
Tokelau	...	...	11.2	...	...	...	...	...	...	...	...	...
Tonga	5.2**	...	16.5	...	...	...	...	...	...	...	...	...
Tuvalu	...	...	...	...	...	...	...	...	...	...	...	...
Vanuatu	6.3	5.4^z	17.4	23.7^z	38.9	55.3^z	428	732^z	51.9	30.4^z	2 181	872^z
Viet Nam	...	5.5^y	...	19.8^y	...	...	...	...	...	...	...	...
Latin America and the Caribbean												
Anguilla	...	3.4^y	...	10.7^y	...	...	...	...	...	...	...	...
Antigua and Barbuda	3.4	2.6^z	...	9.8^z	...	49.4^z	...	1 751^z	...	47.3^z	...	2 210^z
Argentina	4.6	6.2^z	13.3	14.0^z	36.7	32.6^z	1 416	2 373^z	35.4	40.5^z	1 903	3 815^z
Aruba	...	6.0^z	13.8	20.5^z	29.9	27.4^z	...	...	32.3	28.9^z	...	...
Bahamas	3.3**	...	19.7**	...	...	...	...	...	...	...	...	...
Barbados	5.3	7.5^z	15.4	14.3^z	21.5**	...	2 065**	...	31.3	29.0^z	3 419	5 235^z
Belize	5.7**	6.9^z	17.1**	18.7^y	61.7	45.3^z	896	1 151^z	32.0	39.9^z	898	1 683^z
Bermuda	...	1.9	...	13.4	...	30.9	...	...	...	45.3	...	...
Bolivia, P. S.	5.8	...	15.8	...	41.0**	...	433**	...	22.2**	...	409**	...
Brazil	4.0	5.8^z	10.5	16.8^z	33.3**	32.6^z	859**	2 026^z	36.1**	44.9^z	779**	2 063^z
British Virgin Islands	...	3.3^z	**9.0**	13.6	29.5	28.1	...	...	**33.6**	38.1	...	...
Cayman Islands	...	...	...	...	...	...	...	...	...	...	...	...
Chile	4.0	4.9^z	15.6	18.2^x	44.5	37.1^z	1 405	2 360^z	36.5	35.8^z	1 593	2 404^z
Colombia	4.5	5.0	16.9	14.9^y	...	38.4^z	...	1 132^z	...	35.0^z	...	1 096^z
Costa Rica	5.5	6.5^z	**21.1**	23.1^z	47.2	28.0^z	1 392	1 633^z	29.1	21.1^z	1 922	1 612^z
Cuba	6.9	13.6^z	13.7	18.3	35.5*	29.2	...	...	37.9*	28.9	...	...
Dominica	5.5**	3.7	...	9.3	...	55.4^y	...	1 557	...	44.4^y	...	1 686
Dominican Republic	2.0**	2.3^x	**13.1**	11.0^x	**54.7**	...	...	620	...	...	...	544
Ecuador	2.0	...	9.7	...	...	...	...	...	...	...	...	...
El Salvador	2.4**	3.3	17.1**	13.1*,^x	...	40.1^y	...	563^y	...	21.4^y	...	555^y
Grenada	...	...	...	...	...	...	...	...	...	...	...	...
Guatemala	...	3.3^y	...	...	...	57.6^y	...	430^y	...	14.0^y	...	289^y
Guyana	9.3**	...	18.4**	16.7	...	29.3	...	262	...	34.0	...	374
Haiti	...	...	...	...	...	...	...	...	...	...	...	...
Honduras	...	...	...	...	...	...	...	...	...	...	...	...
Jamaica	5.2	6.4**	10.8	11.5**	**30.2****	31.3^z	858	1 167^z	**34.5****	37.1^z	1 436*	1 629**
Mexico	4.5	5.4^z	22.6	21.6^x	40.8	36.8^z	1 494	1 950^z	...	30.4^z	...	2 086^z
Montserrat	...	6.3^z	10.7**	8.4^z	**20.3**	...	...	...	**29.3**	...	...	...
Netherlands Antilles	...	...	14.0	...	...	...	...	...	...	...	...	...
Nicaragua	4.0	...	17.8	...	...	...	...	...	...	...	...	...
Panama	5.1	4.1^y	**7.3**	...	...	...	1 149	967^x	...	...	1 638	1 268^x
Paraguay	5.1	4.1^x	8.8	11.9^x	47.9**	40.9^x	541**	475^x	29.7	35.6^x	730	695^x
Peru	3.4	2.9	21.1	17.1	40.4	40.6	421	632	28.4	33.3	565	735
Saint Kitts and Nevis	4.9	4.7^x	14.0	10.7^x	...	...	...	...	...	...	...	...
Saint Lucia	7.7	4.6*	21.3	10.9*	52.7**	41.9*	1 734**	1 640	32.6**	45.6*	2 319**	2 169*
Saint Vincent/Grenadines	7.2**	5.0	13.4**	10.2	49.0	...	1 273	1 399^x	25.8	...	1 332**	1 460^x
Suriname	...	...	...	...	...	...	...	...	...	...	...	...
Trinidad and Tobago	3.9	...	12.5**	...	39.8	...	1 532	3 249^z	31.1	...	1 760	3 019**,^y
Turks and Caicos Islands	...	...	17.4	...	29.7	...	...	...	39.6	...	...	...
Uruguay	2.4	...	11.8	...	32.4	...	708	...	36.9	...	1 040	...
Venezuela, B. R.	...	3.6	...	...	...	32.5^x	...	1 154^x	...	16.7^x	...	961^x

Table 9 (continued)

Country or territory	Total public expenditure on education as % of GNP		Total public expenditure on education as % of total government expenditure		Public current expenditure on primary education as % of public current on education		Public current expenditure on primary education per pupil at PPP in constant 2009 US$		Public current expenditure on secondary education as % of public current on education		Public current expenditure on secondary education per pupil at PPP in constant 2009 US$	
	1999	2010	1999	2010	1999	2010	1999	2010	1999	2010	1999	2010
North America and Western Europe												
Andorra	...	3.1z	...	...	...	28.7	...	...	...	20.8	...	...
Austria	6.4	5.5y	12.4	11.2y	19.0	18.1y	7 919	9 554y	45.1	47.1y	9 763	10 893y
Belgium	*5.9*	6.3y	*12.2*	12.9y	...	23.4y	...	8 020y	...	43.5y	...	13 384y
Canada	5.9	4.8y	*12.5*	...	...	...	...	...	...	...	...	...
Cyprus	5.3	8.1z	*14.5*	17.3z	33.9	27.2y	4 169	7 700y	52.5	43.0y	6 582	10 630y
Denmark	8.2	8.6z	14.9	15.1z	*21.4*	23.4z	8 397	9 944z	*34.6***	33.8z	13 235	11 849z
Finland	6.2	6.7z	12.5	12.1z	21.1	19.6z	4 902	6 766z	39.3	41.9z	7 284	11 859z
France	5.7	5.8z	11.5	10.4z	20.2**	20.2z	5 111	5 603z	49.8**	44.4z	8 356	8 727z
Germany	...	4.5y	...	10.4y	...	13.8y	...	5 915y	...	47.2y	...	8 246y
Greece	3.2	...	7.0	...	...	...	...	...	*38.1*	...	2 991	...
Iceland	6.7	9.7z	17.1	15.3z	34.2	31.6z	5 524	8 947z	34.1	32.2z	5 140	7 756z
Ireland	4.9	6.6y	13.2	13.3y	32.2	34.3y	3 400	6 933y	36.8	36.2y	5 118	11 214y
Israel	7.5	6.0z	13.9	13.6z	33.9	37.0z	4 749	5 327z	30.0	26.9z	4 418	4 393z
Italy	4.7	4.8z	9.6	9.1z	26.1**	25.9z	7 461**	7 935z	46.5**	43.3z	8 590**	8 183z
Luxembourg	*4.2*	...	*9.8*	...	...	...	...	10 787z	...	...	...	15 961y
Malta	...	6.0y	...	13.3y	...	22.8y	...	4 962y	...	52.6y	...	8 220y
Monaco	1.2	1.2z	5.1	6.4	17.7	15.1	...	...	50.9	38.0	...	...
Netherlands	4.8	6.1z	11.1	11.5z	...	...	...	...	...	...	...	...
Norway	7.2	7.4z	15.6	15.7z	...	24.8z	...	10 234z	...	34.2z	...	14 191z
Portugal	5.2**	5.1y	12.8**	10.9y	31.0**	29.2y	4 373**	5 040y	44.0**	42.0y	5 966**	7 904y
San Marino	...	...	...	...	...	...	...	...	...	...	...	...
Spain	4.4	5.1z	11.3	10.8z	28.1	26.3z	4 979	6 479z	47.5	38.5z	6 580	8 298z
Sweden	7.3	7.2z	13.6	13.2z	...	24.2y	7 687**	9 856z	...	37.1y	*8 642***	11 504z
Switzerland	5.0	5.7y	15.4	16.7y	31.6	25.0y	8 373	8 713y	40.5	45.5y	10 416	13 407y
United Kingdom	4.5	5.5z	11.4	11.3z	...	29.7z	...	7 916z	...	49.0z	...	10 644z
United States	5.0	5.4y	*17.1*	13.8y	...	...	...	...	...	...	...	...
South and West Asia												
Afghanistan	...	...	...	...	...	...	...	...	...	...	...	...
Bangladesh	2.3	2.1z	15.3	14.1z	38.9	42.7z	...	109z	42.0**	43.0z	80**	210
Bhutan	*6.2*	4.4	*13.8*	9.4	*26.9***	27.8	*200***	263	*47.9***	55.5	*1 434***	1 010
India	4.5	...	12.7	...	29.9**	...	206**	...	37.6**	...	429**	...
Iran, Islamic Republic of	4.5	4.7	18.7	19.8	*26.6***	25.9	*712***	1 468	*34.1*	50.0	*732*	2 089
Maldives	...	9.2z	...	16.0z	...	...	...	...	...	...	...	...
Nepal	2.9**	4.7	12.5**	20.2	52.7**	60.3z	67**	172z	28.9**	25.3z	105**	109y
Pakistan	2.6	2.3	...	9.9	...	...	...	...	...	...	...	...
Sri Lanka	...	2.1z	...	8.1z	...	31.4z	...	326z	...	52.1z	...	...
Sub-Saharan Africa												
Angola	3.4**	3.8	6.4**	8.5	...	...	...	...	...	...	...	...
Benin	3.0	4.5z	16.0	18.2z	*52.1***	59.1z	*147***	197z	*27.0***	22.0z	*310***	...
Botswana	...	8.2z	...	16.2z	...	19.2z	...	1 136z	...	31.3z	...	3 337**,z
Burkina Faso	...	4.0	...	20.8	...	56.6	...	191	...	20.2	...	260
Burundi	3.5	9.4	13.3	25.1	38.9	45.1	56	71	36.5	30.0	*252***	260
Cameroon	*2.1*	3.5	*9.8*	17.9	...	34.4	...	134	...	53.3	...	570**
Cape Verde	...	5.9	...	14.4	...	47.0z	...	590z	...	31.2z	...	474z
Central African Republic	1.6	1.2	14.5	12.0	...	55.0	...	34	...	21.8	...	99
Chad	3.2	3.1	17.1	10.1	44.6	53.1	69	94	33.3	27.0	348	192
Comoros	...	7.6y	...	...	...	...	...	...	...	...	...	...
Congo	...	...	...	...	...	...	...	...	...	...	...	...
Côte d'Ivoire	4.3	4.8y	20.6	24.6y	43.4**	...	281**	...	36.4**	...	763**	...
D. R. Congo	...	2.7	...	8.9	...	36.8	...	18	...	28.2	...	42
Equatorial Guinea	*1.0*	...	...	...	...	...	...	...	...	...	...	...
Eritrea	5.2	...	...	...	...	...	...	...	...	...	...	...
Ethiopia	*3.9*	4.7	*11.3*	25.4	...	64.8	...	104	...	10.5	...	55
Gabon	3.5**	...	...	...	...	...	...	...	...	...	...	...
Gambia	3.1	5.4	14.2	22.8	...	50.3	...	152	...	32.5	...	180**
Ghana	4.2**	5.6	...	24.4	*41.6*	34.8	*211*	173	*39.5*	...	*482*	348
Guinea	2.4	2.8y	14.7	19.2y	...	...	...	77y	...	...	...	68y
Guinea-Bissau	5.6	...	11.9	...	...	...	...	...	...	...	...	...
Kenya	5.4	6.7	*25.8*	17.2	68.3**	...	302**	...	17.6**	...	205**	...
Lesotho	10.9	10.3y	25.5	23.7y	42.8	35.7y	138	327y	24.4	20.8y	404	750**,y

Table 9 (continued)

Country or territory	Total public expenditure on education as % of GNP		Total public expenditure on education as % of total government expenditure		Public current expenditure on primary education as % of public current on education		Public current expenditure on primary education per pupil at PPP in constant 2009 US$		Public current expenditure on secondary education as % of public current on education		Public current expenditure on secondary education per pupil at PPP in constant 2009 US$	
	1999	2010	1999	2010	1999	2010	1999	2010	1999	2010	1999	2010
Liberia	…	3.5y	…	12.1y	…	…	…	…	…	…	…	…
Madagascar	2.8	3.2z	15.7	13.4y	…	47.2z	…	56z	…	20.1z	…	101**,z
Malawi	5.1	**5.9**	14.0	**14.7**	60.8	**36.6**	72	55	10.3	**28.7**	57	159
Mali	3.0**	4.6	11.4**	22.0	48.9**	39.9z	125**	107z	33.7**	40.7z	380**	306z
Mauritius	4.0	3.0z	17.7	11.4z	31.9	…	906	…	36.7	…	1 334	…
Mozambique	3.8	…	15.8	…	…	…	…	…	…	…	…	…
Namibia	7.9	8.1	22.3	22.4y	59.4	40.8	1 015	1 089	27.7	22.5	1 657	943y
Niger	3.3	3.9	18.7	16.9	56.0	60.4	204	136	26.6	22.0	491	283
Nigeria	…	…	…	…	…	…	…	…	…	…	…	…
Rwanda	4.3	**4.7**	21.9	**16.9**	47.7	**36.6**	68	**78**	18.5	**26.0**	324	**266**
Sao Tome and Principe	…	…	…	…	…	…	…	…	…	…	…	…
Senegal	3.2**	5.7	…	24.0z	…	40.1	…	292	…	27.7	…	470
Seychelles	5.5	…	…	…	…	…	…	…	…	…	…	…
Sierra Leone	5.1**	4.3z	…	18.1z	…	49.9z	…	…	…	32.6z	…	…
Somalia	…	…	…	…	…	…	…	…	…	…	…	…
South Africa	6.2	6.1	22.2	19.2	45.2	40.5z	1 145	1 685	33.7	31.4z	1 610	1 967
South Sudan	…	…	…	…	…	…	…	…	…	…	…	…
Swaziland	4.9	7.6	…	16.0	33.2	35.0y	390	634y	26.9	30.2y	1 087	1 534y
Togo	4.3	5.0	26.2	17.6z	36.8	49.1	73	91	33.6	27.3	273	157x
Uganda	2.5**	3.2z	…	15.0z	…	58.3z	…	78z	…	23.8z	…	216z
United Republic of Tanzania	2.0**	6.2	…	18.3	…	…	…	…	…	…	…	…
Zambia	2.0	1.5y	6.9	…	…	…	…	…	…	…	…	…
World[1]	4.5	4.8	13.8	14.0	…	…	…	…	…	…	…	…
Countries in transition	3.7	4.4	13.2	12.3	…	…	…	…	…	…	…	…
Developed countries	5.1	5.5	12.5	12.1	…	24.2	…	6 479	…	41.7	…	8 220
Developing countries	4.3	4.7	14.6	16.0	…	…	…	…	…	…	…	…
Arab States	5.5	4.5	…	16.7	…	…	…	…	…	…	…	…
Central and Eastern Europe	4.6	5.2	12.8	11.8	…	…	…	…	…	…	…	…
Central Asia	4.0	3.5	14.4	13.8	…	…	…	…	…	…	…	…
East Asia and the Pacific	4.7	3.9	13.2	13.7	…	…	…	…	…	…	…	…
East Asia	3.3	3.3	12.2	13.7	…	…	…	…	32.5	…	…	…
Pacific	6.2	…	…	…	…	…	…	…	…	…	…	…
Latin America/Caribbean	4.6	4.7	14.0	13.6	39.8	36.8	…	1 167	…	35.3	…	1 621
Caribbean	5.3	4.7	14.0	11.2	…	…	…	…	…	…	…	…
Latin America	4.3	4.5	14.6	16.8	40.8	36.9	1 004	1 132	…	31.8	…	1 096
N. America/W. Europe	5.2	5.8	12.5	12.9	28.1	24.9	5 111	7 916	42.2	42.0	6 933	10 644
South and West Asia	3.7	4.4	13.8	14.1	29.9	31.4	…	263	37.6	50.0	429	…
Sub-Saharan Africa	3.7	4.7	15.7	17.6	…	46.0	…	134	…	27.5	…	263
Countries with low income	3.2	4.3	14.5	17.1	…	50.3	…	92	…	26.0	…	…
Countries with middle income	4.5	4.8	14.4	14.8	…	…	…	…	…	…	…	…
Lower middle	4.5	4.7	…	15.6	…	…	…	…	…	…	…	…
Upper middle	4.6	4.8	14.4	12.8	…	…	…	…	…	…	…	…
Countries with high income	4.9	5.3	13.2	12.9	…	25.6	…	5 800	…	39.9	…	7 904

Source: UNESCO Institute for Statistics database (UIS, 2012).
Note: The country groupings by income level presented in the tables are as defined by the World Bank. They are based on the list of countries by income group as revised in July 2011.
1. All regional values shown are medians. The median values of 1999 and 2010 are not comparable since they are not necessarily based on the same number of countries.
Data in bold are for the school year ending in 2011, those in italics are for 2000 and those in bold italic are for 2001.
(z) Data are for the school year ending in 2009.
(y) Data are for the school year ending in 2008.
(x) Data are for 2007.
(*) National estimate.
(**) UIS partial estimate.
(…) No data available.

Table 10
Trends in basic or proxy indicators to measure EFA goals

		GOAL 1		GOAL 2		GOAL 3				GOAL 4			
		Early childhood care and education		Universal primary education		Learning needs of all youth and adults				Improving levels of adult literacy			
		GROSS ENROLMENT RATIO (GER) IN PRE-PRIMARY EDUCATION		NET ENROLMENT RATIO (NER) IN PRIMARY EDUCATION		YOUTH LITERACY RATE (15–24)				ADULT LITERACY RATE (15 and over)			
		School year ending in		School year ending in									
		1999	2010	1999	2010	1985–1994[1]		2005–2010[1]		1985–1994[1]		2005–2010[1]	
	Country or territory	Total (%)	Total (%)	Total (%)	Total (%)	Total (%)	GPI (F/M)	Total (%)	GPI (F/M)	Total (%)	GPI (F/M)	Total (%)	GPI (F/M)
	Arab States												
1	Algeria	2	77	91	96	74*	0.72*	92*	0.94*	50*	0.57*	73*	0.79*
2	Bahrain[3]	38	...	96	...	97*	0.99*	100	1.00	84*	0.87*	92	0.97
3	Djibouti	0.4	**4**	27	44**, z	...	...	...	...	...	...	...	...
4	Egypt	10	24z	90**	94**	63*	0.76*	88*	0.93*	44*	0.55*	72*	0.79*
5	Iraq	5	...	89	...	...	...	83	0.95	...	...	78*	0.82*
6	Jordan	29	32	89	91	...	...	99*	1.00*	...	...	93*	0.93*
7	Kuwait[3]	85	82y	91	92y	87*	0.93*	99*	1.00*	74*	0.88*	94*	0.97*
8	Lebanon	61**	81	92**	92	...	...	99*	1.01*	...	...	90*	0.92*
9	Libya	5	...	...	...	98	0.97	100	1.00	77	0.74	89	0.86
10	Mauritania	...	...	61	74	...	...	68	0.92	...	...	58	0.79
11	Morocco	62	**63**	71	**96**	58*	0.64*	79*	0.83*	42*	0.52*	56*	0.64*
12	Oman	...	45	79	94z	...	...	98*	1.00*	...	...	87*	0.90*
13	Palestine	35	39	92	87	...	...	99*	1.00*	...	...	95*	0.94*
14	Qatar	25	55z	91	92	90*	1.03*	97*	1.02*	76*	0.94*	96*	0.99*
15	Saudi Arabia	...	11	...	90z	88*	0.86*	98	0.98	71*	0.72*	87	0.90
16	Sudan (pre-secession)	19	27z	40**	...	...	...	87	0.93	...	...	71	0.77
17	Syrian Arab Republic	8	10	94	93z	...	...	95	0.97	...	...	83	0.86
18	Tunisia	14	...	94	98z	83	0.83	97*	0.98*	59	0.69	78*	0.82*
19	United Arab Emirates[3]	64	...	82	...	82*	1.04*	95*	1.04*	71*	0.95*	90*	1.02*
20	Yemen	0.7	1	56	78	60*	0.43*	85	0.77	37*	0.30*	64	0.58
	Central and Eastern Europe												
21	Albania	43	56	99**	80	...	...	99*	1.01*	...	...	96*	0.97*
22	Belarus	83	99	**93****	92	100*	1.00*	100*	1.00*	98*	0.97*	100*	1.00*
23	Bosnia and Herzegovina	...	17	...	87	...	...	100	1.00	...	...	98	0.97
24	Bulgaria	68	79	96	98	...	...	98*	1.00*	...	...	98*	0.99*
25	Croatia	39	61	86	87	100*	1.00*	100	1.00	97*	0.96*	99	0.99
26	Czech Republic	89	106z	96**	...	...	...	...	...	...	...	...	...
27	Estonia	93	96z	94	94z	100*	1.00*	100	1.00	100*	1.00*	100	1.00
28	Hungary	80	85z	88	92z	...	...	...	...	...	...	...	...
29	Latvia	56	84	92**	95	100*	1.00*	100	1.00	99*	0.99*	100	1.00
30	Lithuania	50	74	94	93	100*	1.00*	100	1.00	98*	0.99*	100	1.00
31	Montenegro	**34**	31	...	83	...	...	99	1.00	...	...	98	0.98
32	Poland	49	66z	97	96z	...	...	...	...	...	...	...	...
33	Republic of Moldova[4,5]	48	76	89	88	100*	1.00*	99	1.00	96*	0.96*	99	0.99
34	Romania	68	79	89	88	99*	1.00*	97	1.00	97*	0.96*	98	0.99
35	Russian Federation[6]	71	90z	...	93z	100*	1.00*	100	1.00	98*	0.97*	100	1.00
36	Serbia[4]	54	53	...	93	...	...	99	1.00	...	...	98	0.97
37	Slovakia	79	91	...	...	...	...	...	...	...	...	...	...
38	Slovenia	75	86z	94	97z	100*	1.00*	100	1.00	100*	1.00*	100	1.00
39	TFYR Macedonia	27	25	95	88	99*	0.99*	99	1.00	94*	0.94*	97	0.97
40	Turkey	7	22z	94	97z	93*	0.92*	98*	0.98*	79*	0.76*	91*	0.89*
41	Ukraine	50	97	...	91	...	...	100	1.00	...	...	100	1.00
	Central Asia												
42	Armenia	26	31	91**	...	100*	1.00*	100	1.00	99*	0.99*	100	1.00
43	Azerbaijan[4,7]	18	25	89	84	...	...	100*	1.00*	...	...	100*	1.00*
44	Georgia	35	58y	...	100z	...	...	100	1.00	...	...	100	1.00
45	Kazakhstan	15	**48**	86**	**88**	100*	1.00*	100	1.00	98*	0.97*	100	1.00
46	Kyrgyzstan	10	19	87*	87	...	...	100*	1.00*	...	...	99*	0.99*
47	Mongolia	26	77	87	99	...	...	96	1.03	...	...	97	1.01
48	Tajikistan	8	9	95	97	100*	1.00*	100	1.00	98*	0.98*	100	1.00
49	Turkmenistan	...	...	...	...	...	...	100	1.00	...	...	100	1.00
50	Uzbekistan	24	**26**	...	**90**	...	...	100	1.00	...	...	99	1.00
	East Asia and the Pacific												
51	Australia	**103**	78	94	97	...	...	...	...	...	...	...	...
52	Brunei Darussalam	81	88	...	...	98*	1.00*	100	1.00	88*	0.89*	95	0.97
53	Cambodia	5**	13	87	96	...	...	87*	0.97*	...	...	74*	0.80*
54	China[8]	37	54	...	...	94*	0.94*	99	1.00	78*	0.78*	94	0.94
55	Cook Islands[4]	86	**181**	85	94	...	...	...	...	...	...	...	...
56	DPR Korea	...	...	...	...	...	...	100*	1.00*	...	...	100*	1.00*
57	Fiji	15	18z	94	97z	...	...	...	...	...	...	...	...
58	Indonesia	23**	43	90**	96	96*	0.98*	99*	1.00*	82*	0.86*	93*	0.94*
59	Japan	83	88	100	100	...	...	...	...	...	...	...	...
60	Kiribati	...	...	99**	...	...	...	...	...	...	...	...	...

	GOAL 5								GOAL 6				
	Gender parity in primary education				Gender parity in secondary education				Educational quality				
	GROSS ENROLMENT RATIO (GER)				GROSS ENROLMENT RATIO (GER)				SURVIVAL RATE TO GRADE 5		PUPIL/TEACHER RATIO IN PRIMARY EDUCATION[2]		
	School year ending in				School year ending in				School year ending in		School year ending in		
	1999		2010		1999		2010		1999	2009	1999	2010	
	Total (%)	GPI (F/M)	Total (%)	GPI (F/M)	Total (%)	GPI (F/M)	Total (%)	GPI (F/M)	Total (%)	Total (%)			
													Arab States
106	0.91	110	0.94	...	...	95z	1.02z	95	95	28	23		1
107	1.00	...	...	96	1.10	...	...	96	98y	18**	...		2
33	0.71	**59**	**0.90**	14	0.72	**36**	**0.80**	...	64**,y	40	**35**		3
98**	0.91**	101	0.96**	80**	0.91**	72	0.96	...	97**	*22***	26		4
97	0.83	...	...	35	0.64	...	...	66**	...	*21*	...		5
96	1.01	92	1.00	85	1.04	87	1.06	97	...	...	...		6
106	1.02	...	...	109**	1.03**	...	...	.	96	13	8		7
112**	0.96**	105	0.97	77**	1.09**	81	1.12	.	95y	14**	14		8
122	0.99	...	...	...	...	...	...	...	...	...	...		9
84	0.97	102	1.05	18**	0.75**	24**	0.85**	**55**	74	47	37		10
87	0.82	**114**	**0.94**	37	0.78	...	...	82	94	28	**26**		11
89	0.99	105z	0.97z	71	1.01	100z	0.99z	94	...	25	12**,z		12
100	1.00	91	0.98	78	1.02	86	1.08	.	.	38	28		13
104	1.05	103	1.00	88	1.11	94	1.21	...	96x	13	12		14
...	...	106	0.99	...	...	101	0.95	...	94*,x	...	11		15
48**	0.85**	73z	0.90z	26**	...	39z	0.88z	84**	94x	*24***	38**,z		16
108	0.92	118	0.98	44	0.92	72	1.01	92	.	25	18**,y		17
115	0.93	109z	0.96z	74	0.99	90z	1.06**,z	92	96y	24	17z		18
93	0.99	...	...	83	1.09	...	...	92	...	16	17		19
72	0.56	87	0.82	40	0.37	44**	0.62**	**74***	...	22**	31		20
													Central and Eastern Europe
109	0.98	87	0.99	73	0.95	89	0.98	.**	95	23**	20		21
111	*0.99*	100	1.00	85	1.05	...	...	...	.	20	15		22
...	...	112	1.02	...	...	91	1.03	...	.	...	...		23
104	0.97	103	1.00	92	0.98	89	0.95	.	.	18	17		24
93	0.98	93	1.00	84	1.02	96	1.07	.	.	19	14		25
103	0.99	106z	0.99z	82	1.04	90z	1.01z	98	100y	18	19z		26
99	0.97	99z	0.99z	94	1.04	104z	1.02z	99	99y	16	12z		27
102	0.98	102z	0.99z	93	1.01	98z	0.99z	.	.y	11	10z		28
95	0.97	101	0.99	89	1.04	95	0.98	.	96	15	12		29
101	0.98	96	0.99	96	1.00	99	0.98	.	.	17	13		30
...	...	107	0.98	...	...	104	1.01	...	...	...	...		31
100	0.97	97z	0.99z	100	0.99	97z	0.99z	99	98y	*11*	10z		32
101	*0.99*	94	1.00	83	0.98	88	1.02	.**	.	21	16		33
96	0.98	96	0.99	81	1.01	97	0.99	.	.	19	16		34
103	0.99	99z	1.00z	92	...	89z	0.98z	.	.y	18	18z		35
112**	0.99**	96	0.99	93**	1.01**	91	1.02	...	.	...	16		36
99	0.98	101	0.99	84	1.02	90	1.01	.	.	19	15		37
98	0.99	98z	0.99z	100	1.03	97z	1.00z	.	100y	14	17z		38
102	0.98	90	1.01	82	0.98	84	0.99	.	.	22	16		39
103	0.91	102z	0.98z	69	0.69	78z	0.91z	...	92y	...	16		40
108	0.99	99	1.01	98	1.03*	96	0.98*	.*	.	20	16		41
													Central Asia
102	*1.00***	103	1.02	92	...	92	1.02	.	...	*20***	...		42
98	1.00	94	0.99	78	0.99	85	0.98	.	.	19	11		43
94	0.99	109	1.03	79	0.98	86z	...	.	96	*17*	8*		44
96	*1.01*	**111**	**1.00**	93	1.00	**100**	**0.97**	.**	.	*19***	**16**		45
96	0.99	100	0.99	83	1.02	84*	0.99*	.*	.	24	24		46
96	1.01	122	0.98	61	1.26	89	1.07	.	94	32	30		47
97	*0.93*	102	0.96	75	0.86	87	0.87	.**	.	*22*	25		48
...	...	...	...	...	...	...	...	...	...	...	...		49
98	1.00	**95**	**0.97**	86	0.98	**106**	**0.98**	.**	.	21	**16**		50
													East Asia and the Pacific
101	1.00	105	0.99	157	1.00	131	0.95	...	...	18**	...		51
116	0.95	108	1.01	88	1.09	110	1.03	...	98	14*	11		52
101	0.87	127	0.95	16	0.53	46**	0.90**	63	62x	*53*	48		53
114	*1.03*	111	1.03	61	...	81	1.04	...	...	*22*	17		54
96	0.95	**111**	**1.03**	60	1.08	**82**	**1.20**	...	84	18	**16**		55
...	...	...	...	...	...	...	...	...	...	...	...		56
104	0.99	105z	0.98z	78	1.11	86z	1.09z	87	94y	28	26y		57
106**	0.97**	118	1.02	53**	0.95**	77	1.00	**89**	86x	22	16		58
101	1.00	103	1.00	101	1.01	102	1.00	.	100	21	18		59
108	1.01	113z	1.04z	59	1.23	86y	1.11y	**72**	...	25	25y		60

Education for All Global Monitoring Report

Table 10 (continued)

	Country or territory	GOAL 1 Early childhood care and education — GROSS ENROLMENT RATIO (GER) IN PRE-PRIMARY EDUCATION — School year ending in 1999 Total [%]	2010 Total [%]	GOAL 2 Universal primary education — NET ENROLMENT RATIO (NER) IN PRIMARY EDUCATION — School year ending in 1999 Total [%]	2010 Total [%]	GOAL 3 Learning needs of all youth and adults — YOUTH LITERACY RATE (15–24) — 1985–1994[1] Total [%]	GPI [F/M]	2005–2010[1] Total [%]	GPI [F/M]	GOAL 4 Improving levels of adult literacy — ADULT LITERACY RATE (15 and over) — 1985–1994[1] Total [%]	GPI [F/M]	2005–2010[1] Total [%]	GPI [F/M]
61	Lao PDR	8	22	77	97	...	...	84*	0.88*	...	...	73*	0.77*
62	Macao, China	91	80	85	82	...	...	100*	1.00*	...	...	93*	0.94*
63	Malaysia[3]	54	67[z]	95	...	96*	0.99*	98*	1.00*	83*	0.87*	93*	0.95*
64	Marshall Islands	57	**46**	...	**99**	...	...	...	...	...	...	...	...
65	Micronesia, F. S.	37	...	...	...	...	...	...	...	...	...	...	...
66	Myanmar	2	10	...	...	...	...	96	0.99	...	...	92	0.95
67	Nauru[4]	74	94[y]	...	...	...	...	...	...	...	...	...	...
68	New Zealand	85	93	99	99	...	...	...	...	...	...	...	...
69	Niue[4]	154	...	99	...	...	...	...	...	...	...	...	...
70	Palau[4]	63	...	97**	...	...	...	...	...	...	...	...	...
71	Papua New Guinea	...	100[y]	...	...	...	...	68	1.11	...	...	61	0.90
72	Philippines	30	51[z]	90	88[z]	97*	1.01*	98*	1.02*	94*	0.99*	95*	1.01*
73	Republic of Korea	76	119	99	99	...	...	...	...	...	...	...	...
74	Samoa	53**	38	92	97	99*	1.00*	99	1.00	98*	0.99*	99	1.00
75	Singapore[3]	...	...	...	...	99*	1.00*	100*	1.00*	89*	0.87*	96*	0.96*
76	Solomon Islands	36**	49	...	...	...	...	...	...	...	...	...	...
77	Thailand	91	**100**	...	90[z]	...	...	98*	1.00*	...	...	94*	0.96*
78	Timor-Leste	...	...	...	85	...	...	80*	0.98*	...	...	58*	0.83*
79	Tokelau[4]	99	...	...	...	...	...	...	...	...	...	...	...
80	Tonga	29	...	91	...	...	...	99*	1.00*	...	...	99*	1.00*
81	Tuvalu[4]	**96**	...	...	...	...	...	...	...	...	...	...	...
82	Vanuatu	**53**	59	97	...	...	...	...	...	...	...	...	...
83	Viet Nam	40	82	96	98	94*	0.99*	97	0.99	88*	0.89*	93	0.96
	Latin America and the Caribbean												
84	Anguilla[9]	...	95**,y	**96***	...	...	...	...	...	...	...	...	...
85	Antigua and Barbuda	57	76[y]	...	87	...	...	...	...	...	...	99	1.01
86	Argentina	57	74[z]	99	...	98*	1.00*	99	1.00	96*	1.00*	98	1.00
87	Aruba	95	112	98	100	...	...	99*	1.00*	...	...	97*	1.00*
88	Bahamas	11	...	91	98	...	...	...	...	...	...	...	...
89	Barbados	75	108*	95**	95*,y	...	...	...	...	...	...	...	...
90	Belize	24	46	88**	95	76*	1.01*	...	...	70*	1.00*	...	...
91	Bermuda	...	...	...	83**	...	...	...	...	...	...	...	...
92	Bolivia, P. S.	44	45[z]	95	...	94*	0.95*	99*	0.99*	80*	0.82*	91*	0.91*
93	Brazil[3]	58	...	91	...	...	...	98*	1.01*	...	...	90*	1.00*
94	British Virgin Islands[4]	62	71**,z	96**	87	...	...	...	...	...	...	...	...
95	Cayman Islands	42	91[y]	96*	...	...	...	99*	0.99*	...	...	99*	1.00*
96	Chile	76	56[z]	...	94[z]	98*	1.01*	99*	1.00*	94*	0.99*	99*	1.00*
97	Colombia	39	49	93	88	91*	1.03*	98*	1.01*	81*	1.00*	93*	1.00*
98	Costa Rica	47	71	...	...	...	...	98	1.01	...	...	96	1.00
99	Cuba	105	104	97	**98**	...	...	100	1.00	...	...	100	1.00
100	Dominica	82	112	95	94[z]	...	...	...	...	...	...	...	...
101	Dominican Republic	32	38	83	90	...	...	97*	1.02*	...	...	90*	1.00*
102	Ecuador	65	112**,y	98	97[z]	96*	0.99*	99*	1.00*	88*	0.95*	92*	0.97*
103	El Salvador	41	64	**84***	94	85*	1.00*	96*	1.01*	74*	0.92*	84*	0.94*
104	Grenada	90	99	81**	87[z]	...	...	...	...	...	...	...	...
105	Guatemala	46	71	83	97	76*	0.87*	87	0.95	64*	0.80*	75	0.87
106	Guyana	101	76	...	81	...	...	...	...	...	...	...	...
107	Haiti	...	...	...	...	...	...	72*	0.95*	...	...	49	0.84
108	Honduras	22	44	89	96	...	...	95*	1.02*	...	...	85*	1.00*
109	Jamaica	79	113	90**	82	...	...	95	1.06	...	...	87	1.12
110	Mexico	73	101	97	98	95*	0.99*	98*	1.00*	88*	0.94*	93*	0.97*
111	Montserrat[9]	137	...	95**	...	...	...	...	...	...	...	...	...
112	Netherlands Antilles	112	...	...	...	97*	1.01*	98	1.00	95*	1.00*	96	1.00
113	Nicaragua	28	55	78	92	...	...	87*	1.04*	...	...	78*	1.00*
114	Panama	39	67	95	98	95*	0.99*	98*	0.99*	89*	0.99*	94*	0.99*
115	Paraguay	29	35[z]	96	85[z]	96*	0.99*	99*	1.00*	90*	0.96*	94*	0.98*
116	Peru	56	79	98**	95	95*	0.97*	97*	0.99*	87*	0.88*	90*	0.89*
117	Saint Kitts and Nevis	129	90	**93**	83	...	...	...	...	...	...	...	...
118	Saint Lucia	64**	60	91**	88	...	...	...	...	...	...	...	...
119	Saint Vincent/Grenadines	...	80[z]	97**	94	...	...	...	...	...	...	...	...
120	Suriname	**85**	85[z]	**91***	91[z]	...	...	98*	1.01*	...	...	95*	0.99*
121	Trinidad and Tobago	59**	...	88	94	99*	1.00*	100	1.00	97*	0.98*	99	0.99
122	Turks and Caicos Islands[9]	...	...	...	...	...	...	...	...	...	...	...	...
123	Uruguay	60	89[z]	...	99[z]	99*	1.01*	99*	1.01*	95*	1.01*	98*	1.01*
124	Venezuela, B. R.	45	73	85	93	95*	1.02*	99*	1.01*	90*	0.98*	96*	1.00*

	GOAL 5								GOAL 6			
	Gender parity in primary education				Gender parity in secondary education				Educational quality			
	GROSS ENROLMENT RATIO (GER)				GROSS ENROLMENT RATIO (GER)				SURVIVAL RATE TO GRADE 5		PUPIL/TEACHER RATIO IN PRIMARY EDUCATION[2]	
	School year ending in				School year ending in				School year ending in		School year ending in	
	1999		2010		1999		2010		1999	2009	1999	2010
	Total (%)	GPI (F/M)	Total (%)	GPI (F/M)	Total (%)	GPI (F/M)	Total (%)	GPI (F/M)	Total (%)	Total (%)		
61	112	0.85	126	0.93	33	0.70	47	0.83	55	67x	31	29
62	100	0.99	94	1.00	80	1.05	92	0.93	...	99y	31	16
63	95	0.98	...	...	66	1.08	68z	1.07z	87	98y	20	13z
64	90	0.99	**102**	**0.99**	68	1.06	99z	1.03z	...	87y	15	...
65	...	...	...	...	...	...	...	...	...	...	...	...
66	101	0.98	126	1.00	36	1.00	54	1.06	55	75	31	28
67	*99*	*1.33*	93y	1.06*,y	*47*	*1.17*	63y	1.20y	...	...	21	22y
68	100	1.00	101	1.00	111	1.05	119	1.05	...	...	18	14
69	99	1.00	...	...	98	1.10	...	...	...	...	16	...
70	114	0.93	...	...	101	1.07	...	...	...	...	15	...
71	*71*	*0.86*	60y	0.89y	...	...	...	...	...	...	*35***	...
72	110	1.00	106z	0.98z	74	1.10	85z	1.08z	**79**	79y	35	31z
73	103	1.01	106	0.99	100	1.00	97	0.99	99	99	32	21
74	98	0.98	108	1.02	80	1.11	85	1.14	91*	96	24**	30
75	...	...	...	...	...	...	...	...	...	99y	...	17z
76	90	0.94	...	...	26	0.76	...	...	...	...	19	...
77	97	0.97	91z	0.99z	**62**	**0.98***	**79**	**1.08**	...	...	21	...
78	**125**	...	117	0.96	**34***	...	56	1.01	...	71	**51***	30
79	*105*	*1.15*	...	...	*92*	*1.01*	...	...	...	...	*10*	...
80	112	0.95	...	...	106	1.14	...	...	92	...	21	...
81	98	1.02	...	...	**80**	**1.10**	...	...	...	...	19	...
82	118	0.98	117	0.95	30	0.88	55	1.02	72	76y	24	22
83	111	0.93	106	0.94	61	0.90	77	1.09	83	...	30	20
										Latin America and the Caribbean		
84	**104***	**0.98***	...	...	*107***	*0.98***	...	...	*93***	...	22	14
85	*124*	...	102	0.92	*79*	*0.92*	105	1.01	...	94x	*19*	15
86	113	0.99	118z	0.99z	85	1.05	89z	1.12z	90	95y	21	16y
87	113	0.98	114	0.97	99	1.06	90	1.01	97	93y	19	17
88	97	0.97	114	1.02	78	0.99	96	1.05	...	91	14	14
89	103	1.04	120*	1.02*	108	1.12	101*	1.09*	92	92*,y	18**	13*
90	110	0.91	121	0.91	62	1.07	...	...	76	91	23	22
91	**101**	**1.01**	92	1.00**	**79**	**1.07**	79	1.18	...	...	**9**	7
92	114	0.98	105z	0.99z	77	0.93	80z	0.99z	82	85x	25**	...
93	155	0.94	...	...	99	1.11	...	...	.**	.	26	22
94	112	0.97	100	0.94	99	0.91	102	1.03	...	...	18	13
95	112	0.93	90y	0.97y	99	0.96	83y	1.13y	93	...	15	12y
96	101	0.97	106z	0.95z	79	1.04	88z	1.03z	98	...	32	23z
97	119	1.00	115	0.98	73	1.11	96	1.10	67	85	24	28
98	112	0.99	110	0.99	62	1.10	100	1.06	91	91	27	18
99	102	0.97	**101**	**0.98**	80	1.06	**90**	**0.99**	96	**96**	12	**9**
100	120	1.02	112	0.98	100	1.33	98	1.09	86	90	20	16
101	111	0.98	108	0.88	56	1.24	76	1.12	75	...	31	26
102	114	1.00	114z	1.01z	57	1.03	75**,y	1.03**,y	77	...	23	17*,z
103	*106*	*0.97*	114	0.95	53	0.98	65	1.01	65	89	...	31z
104	*91*	*0.97*	103	1.00	...	...	108	1.03	...	...	*20*	16
105	102	0.87	116	0.96	33	0.84	59	0.93	*56*	71x	38	28
106	107	1.01	85	1.04	88	0.99	91	1.11	*77*	87y	27	25
107	...	...	...	...	...	...	...	...	...	...	...	...
108	*107*	*1.01*	116	1.00	...	...	73	1.23	...	78x	*34*	33y
109	95**	0.99**	89	0.95	88**	1.01**	93	1.03	**89**	96	**34**	21
110	110	0.98	114	0.99	70	1.01	89	1.07	89	96	27	28
111	**105**	**0.99**	...	...	183	0.75	...	...	...	...	21	13z
112	135	0.95	...	...	91	1.15	...	...	84**	...	20	...
113	102	1.01	118	0.98	52**	1.18**	69	1.10	48	51x	34	30
114	107	0.97	108	0.97	67	1.07	74	1.07	92	95	26	23
115	119**	0.96**	100z	0.97z	58	1.04	67z	1.05z	78**	82y	...	...
116	124	0.99	108	1.00	83	0.94	91	0.98	87	93	29	20
117	*109*	*1.02*	93	1.00	97	1.04	97	0.99	*83*	84	19	14
118	104	0.95	94	0.96	71	1.26	96	0.99	...	95	**24**	19
119	*118*	*0.95*	105	0.93	*82***	*1.34***	107	1.02	...	...	*19***	16
120	**118**	**0.99**	113z	0.95z	**73**	**1.19**	75z	1.23z	...	94y	**20***	15z
121	97	0.99	105	0.97	78	1.09	90**,y	1.07**,y	96	92*	21	18*
122	...	...	...	...	...	...	...	...	...	...	18**	...
123	111	0.99	113z	0.97z	92	1.17	90z	...	89	95y	20	14z
124	99	0.98	103	0.97	57	1.22	83	1.10	91	94	...	...

Table 10 (continued)

		GOAL 1		GOAL 2		GOAL 3				GOAL 4			
		Early childhood care and education		Universal primary education		Learning needs of all youth and adults				Improving levels of adult literacy			
		GROSS ENROLMENT RATIO (GER) IN PRE-PRIMARY EDUCATION		NET ENROLMENT RATIO (NER) IN PRIMARY EDUCATION		YOUTH LITERACY RATE (15–24)				ADULT LITERACY RATE (15 and over)			
		School year ending in		School year ending in		1985–1994[1]		2005–2010[1]		1985–1994[1]		2005–2010[1]	
	Country or territory	1999 Total [%]	2010 Total [%]	1999 Total [%]	2010 Total [%]	Total [%]	GPI (F/M)	Total [%]	GPI (F/M)	Total [%]	GPI (F/M)	Total [%]	GPI (F/M)
	North America and Western Europe												
125	Andorra	...	102	...	77	...	...	...	...	...	...	...	...
126	Austria	80	100	...	...	...	...	...	...	...	...	...	...
127	Belgium	114	118^z	99	99^z	...	...	...	...	...	...	...	...
128	Canada	63	71^y	100	...	...	...	...	...	...	...	...	...
129	Cyprus[4]	60	81	95	99	100*	1.00*	100	1.00	94*	0.93*	98	0.98
130	Denmark	90	96^z	98	96^z	...	...	...	...	...	...	...	...
131	Finland	47	68	100	98	...	...	...	...	...	...	...	...
132	France[10]	112	109	99	99	...	...	...	...	...	...	...	...
133	Germany	101	114	99**	98**	...	...	...	...	...	...	...	...
134	Greece	67	...	93	...	99*	1.00*	99	1.00	93*	0.93*	97	0.98
135	Iceland	86	97^z	99	99^z	...	...	...	...	...	...	...	...
136	Ireland	...	98	95	95	...	...	...	...	...	...	...	...
137	Israel	89	106^z	98	97^z	...	...	...	...	...	...	...	...
138	Italy	97	98	99	97	...	...	100	1.00	...	...	99	0.99
139	Luxembourg	72	87^y	96	95^y	...	...	...	...	...	...	...	...
140	Malta	100	117	94	94	98*	1.02*	98*	1.02*	88*	1.01*	92*	1.03*
141	Monaco[9]	...	...	...	...	...	...	...	...	...	...	...	...
142	Netherlands	97	93	99	100	...	...	...	...	...	...	...	...
143	Norway	75	99	100	99	...	...	...	...	...	...	...	...
144	Portugal	67	82^z	97	99^z	99*	1.00*	100	1.00	88*	0.92*	95	0.97
145	San Marino[9]	...	...	...	92*,^z	...	...	...	...	...	...	...	...
146	Spain	99	126	100	100	100*	1.00*	100*	1.00*	96*	0.97*	98*	0.98*
147	Sweden	76	95	100	99	...	...	...	...	...	...	...	...
148	Switzerland	92	99	96	94	...	...	...	...	...	...	...	...
149	United Kingdom	77	81^z	100	100^z	...	...	...	...	...	...	...	...
150	United States	59	69	96	95	...	...	...	...	...	...	...	...
	South and West Asia												
151	Afghanistan	...	...	...	...	...	...	...	...	...	...	...	...
152	Bangladesh[3]	19	13*	...	...	45*	0.73*	77	1.04	35*	0.58*	57	0.85
153	Bhutan	0.9	5	56	88	...	...	74*	0.85*	...	...	53*	0.59*
154	India	19	55	79*	92^y	62*	0.67*	81*	0.84*	48*	0.55*	63*	0.68*
155	Iran, Islamic Republic of	14	42	86**	...	87*	0.88*	99*	1.00*	66*	0.76*	85*	0.90*
156	Maldives	56	114	97	96	98*	1.00*	99*	1.00*	96*	1.00*	98*	1.00*
157	Nepal[3]	10*	...	65*	...	50*	0.48*	83	0.89	33*	0.35*	60	0.66
158	Pakistan	63*	...	58**	74*	...	...	71*	0.78*	...	...	55*	0.59*
159	Sri Lanka	...	...	100	94	...	...	98*	1.01*	...	...	91*	0.97*
	Sub-Saharan Africa												
160	Angola	27**	104	...	86*	...	...	73	0.82	...	...	70	0.70
161	Benin	4	18	...	94	40*	0.48*	55	0.68	27*	0.42*	42	0.55
162	Botswana	...	19^z	80	87^z	89*	1.07*	95	1.04	69*	1.09*	84	1.01
163	Burkina Faso	2	3	33	63	20*	0.53*	39*	0.71*	14*	0.42*	29*	0.59*
164	Burundi	0.8	9	37	...	54*	0.81*	78	1.00	37*	0.57*	67	0.85
165	Cameroon	11	28	...	92	...	...	83*	0.87*	...	...	71*	0.80*
166	Cape Verde	53**	70	99**	93	88*	0.96*	98	1.02	63*	0.71*	84	0.89
167	Central African Republic	...	6	...	69	48*	0.56*	65	0.80	34*	0.42*	56	0.62
168	Chad	...	2	52	...	17*	0.34*	47	0.76	11*	0.25*	34	0.54
169	Comoros	3	22^y	66	...	...	...	86	0.99	...	...	75	0.87
170	Congo	2	13	...	91*	...	...	80*	0.90*	...	...	...	...
171	Côte d'Ivoire	2	4	56	61^z	49*	0.63*	67	0.86	34*	0.53*	56	0.72
172	D. R. Congo	0.7**	3	33	...	...	...	65	0.90	...	...	67	0.74
173	Equatorial Guinea	27	55^y	72**	56	...	...	98	1.01	...	...	94	0.93
174	Eritrea	5	14	33	33	...	...	89	0.94	...	...	68	0.73
175	Ethiopia	1	5	36	81	34*	0.71*	55*	0.75*	27*	0.51*	39*	0.59*
176	Gabon	14**	42	...	...	93*	0.98*	98	0.98	72*	0.82*	88	0.92
177	Gambia	18	30	69	66	...	...	67	0.86	...	...	50	0.67
178	Ghana	31	69^z	61**	84	...	...	81	0.98	...	...	67	0.84
179	Guinea	...	14	43	77	...	...	63	0.82	...	...	41	0.58
180	Guinea-Bissau	4**	7	50**	74	...	...	72	0.83	...	...	54	0.60
181	Kenya	43	52^z	62	83**,^z	...	...	93	1.02	...	...	87	0.93
182	Lesotho	20**	33	56	73	...	...	92	1.14	...	...	90	1.15

	GOAL 5								GOAL 6				
	Gender parity in primary education				Gender parity in secondary education				Educational quality				
	GROSS ENROLMENT RATIO (GER)				GROSS ENROLMENT RATIO (GER)				SURVIVAL RATE TO GRADE 5		PUPIL/TEACHER RATIO IN PRIMARY EDUCATION[2]		
	School year ending in				School year ending in				School year ending in		School year ending in		
	1999		2010		1999		2010		1999	2009	1999	2010	
	Total [%]	GPI (F/M)	Total [%]	GPI (F/M)	Total [%]	GPI (F/M)	Total [%]	GPI (F/M)	Total [%]	Total [%]			
North America and Western Europe													
	...	...	84	1.01	...	...	87	1.05	...	94	...	10	125
	104	0.99	99	0.99	98	0.95	99	0.96	.	.	13	11	126
	108	0.99	105^z	1.00^z	141	1.07	111^z	0.97^z	...	97^y	12**	11^z	127
	100	1.00	99^y	1.00^y	103	1.02	101^y	0.98^y	99	...	17	...	128
	97	1.00	106	0.99	93	1.03	99	1.00	95	95^x	18	14	129
	101	1.00	99^z	1.00^z	125	1.05	117^z	1.02^z	100	100^y	10	...	130
	101	1.00	99	0.99	121	1.09	108	1.05	99	100	17	14	131
	105	0.99	110	0.99	109	1.00	113	1.01	98	...	19	18	132
	103	0.99	102	1.00	98	0.98	103	0.95	.	.	17	13	133
	95	1.00	...	...	91	1.04	...	...	...	...	14	...	134
	100	0.98	99^z	1.00^z	109	1.05	107^z	1.03^z	*98*	99^y	...	...	135
	102	0.99	108	1.00	106	1.06	121	1.05	95	99	22	16	136
	105	0.99	103^z	1.01^z	100	0.99	102^z	1.02^z	*99*	99^y	13**	13**,z	137
	105	0.99	102	0.99	92	0.99	100	0.99	*96*	100	11	...	138
	99	1.01	100^y	1.01^y	98	1.05	98^y	1.02^y	96	96^x	*12*	12^y	139
	100	1.00	101	1.01	89	0.85	101	0.89	98	83^y	20	14	140
	...	...	...	...	...	...	...	...	...	...	22	...	141
	109	0.98	108	0.99	123	0.96	121	0.99	100	99	...	...	142
	101	1.00	99	1.00	119	1.02	111	0.98	100	99	...	...	143
	122	*0.96*	114^z	0.97^z	103	1.08	107^z	1.04^z	...	...	13	11^z	144
	...	...	94**	1.13**	...	...	97**	1.02**	...	...	5	6	145
	106	0.99	106	0.99	109	1.06	125	1.02	...	100^y	15	12	146
	110	1.03	101	0.99	156	1.26	99	0.99	98	100	12	10	147
	106	0.99	103	1.00	96	0.93	95	0.97	97	...	...	...	148
	101	1.00	106^z	1.00^z	101	1.01	102^z	1.02^z	...	...	19	18^z	149
	103	1.03	102	0.99	94	...	96	1.01	...	...	15	14	150
South and West Asia													
	26	0.08	97	0.69	**11**	-	46	0.51	...	...	...	44	151
	...	...	47	0.99	51	1.13	...	...	...	66*	...	43*	152
	75	0.85	**111**	**1.01**	37	0.80	**70**	**1.04**	90	**96**	42	**25**	153
	94	*0.84*	116^y	1.00^y	43	0.70	63	0.92	62	...	35*	...	154
	101	0.94	114	1.01	79	0.93	91	0.86	97	94^y	*25*	20^z	155
	131	1.01	**109**	**0.96**	41	1.08	...	...	...	...	24	**12**	156
	114	0.77	...	...	34	0.70	...	...	59	62^x	39	30	157
	*71**	*0.67**	95	0.82	...	...	34	0.76	...	62	33**	40	158
	108	**0.99**	99	1.00	...	...	...	...	...	...	**26**	24	159
Sub-Saharan Africa													
	...	...	124	0.81	13	0.75	31	0.69	.	45*	...	46**	160
	83	0.64	126	0.87	22	0.44	...	...	84	60	53	46	161
	103	1.00	110^z	0.96^z	73	1.07	82**,z	1.06**,z	87	97**,y	27	25^z	162
	42	0.70	**79**	**0.93**	9	0.62	23	**0.78**	68	75	*47*	48	163
	51	0.81	156	0.99	**11***	**0.79***	25	0.72	*59*	62	46	51	164
	85	0.82	120	0.86	26**	0.84**	42**	0.83**	**52***	76	52	46	165
	125	0.95	110	0.92	**68***	**1.04***	88	1.20	**91**	90^x	29**	24	166
	*78**	*0.68**	**94**	**0.73**	*12***	...	**18**	**0.55**	...	55	...	**81**	167
	64	0.58	93	0.73	10	0.26	25	0.42	56	37	68	62	168
	100	0.85	104^y	0.92^y	30	0.81	...	...	...	...	35	30^y	169
	59	0.97	115	0.95	*36*	*0.70*	...	...	...	77**,x	*60*	49	170
	74	0.74	**88**	**0.83**	23**	0.54**	...	...	69	66^y	45	**49**	171
	48	0.91	94	0.87	19	0.53	38	0.58	...	60	26	37	172
	108	*0.96***	87	0.97	33	0.37	...	...	...	70	57	27	173
	52	0.83	45	0.84	22	0.68	32	0.76	94	69	47	38	174
	50	0.61	102	0.91	13	0.67	36	0.82	56	51	67	54	175
	140	1.00	**182**	**0.97**	48	0.86	...	...	...	...	*49*	25	176
	84	0.84	83	1.02	...	...	54**	0.95**	66**	65**	*37*	37^z	177
	81	0.93	**107**	**1.00**	40	0.81	**58**	**0.91**	66	78^y	30	**31**	178
	56	0.64	94	0.84	14**	0.37**	38**,z	0.59**,z	...	69	47	42	179
	78**	0.67**	123	0.94	*19*	*0.55*	...	...	...	...	44	52	180
	90	0.97	113^z	0.98^z	38	0.96	60^z	0.90^z	...	...	32	47**,z	181
	100	1.08	103	0.98	30	1.36	46	1.38	75	80	44	34	182

Table 10 (continued)

		GOAL 1		GOAL 2		GOAL 3				GOAL 4			
		Early childhood care and education		Universal primary education		Learning needs of all youth and adults				Improving levels of adult literacy			
		GROSS ENROLMENT RATIO (GER) IN PRE-PRIMARY EDUCATION		NET ENROLMENT RATIO (NER) IN PRIMARY EDUCATION		YOUTH LITERACY RATE (15–24)				ADULT LITERACY RATE (15 and over)			
		School year ending in		School year ending in									
		1999	2010	1999	2010	1985–1994[1]		2005–2010[1]		1985–1994[1]		2005–2010[1]	
	Country or territory	Total (%)	Total (%)	Total (%)	Total (%)	Total (%)	GPI (F/M)	Total (%)	GPI (F/M)	Total (%)	GPI (F/M)	Total (%)	GPI (F/M)
183	Liberia	47	...	46	...	60	0.82	77	1.16	43	0.58	61	0.88
184	Madagascar	3**	9	65	...	...	...	65*	0.97*	...	...	64	0.91
185	Malawi	...	...	99	97^z	59*	0.70*	87	1.00	49*	0.51*	75	0.84
186	Mali	1	**3**	42**	**63**	...	...	44*	0.60*	...	...	31*	0.47*
187	Mauritius	95	96	92	93	91*	1.01*	97	1.02	80*	0.88*	89	0.95
188	Mozambique	...	...	52	**90**	...	...	72	0.83	...	...	56	0.61
189	Namibia	33	...	87	85^z	88*	1.06*	93	1.04	76*	0.95*	89	0.99
190	Niger	1	**6**	26	**62**	...	...	37*	0.44*	...	...	29*	0.35*
191	Nigeria[11]	*8*	14	61**	58**	71*	0.77*	72	0.85	55*	0.65*	61	0.70
192	Rwanda	3**	11	**76****	99	75	...	77	1.01	58	...	71	0.90
193	Sao Tome and Principe	24	**62**	88	98	94*	0.96*	95	1.01	73*	0.73*	89	0.90
194	Senegal	3	13	57	75	38*	0.57*	65*	0.76*	27*	0.48*	50*	0.63*
195	Seychelles	110	102	*92*	...	99*	1.01*	99	1.01	88*	1.02*	92	1.01
196	Sierra Leone	4	**7**	...	...	...	...	59	0.73	...	...	42	0.59
197	Somalia	...	...	...	...	...	...	...	...	...	...	...	...
198	South Africa	21	65^z	92	85**,^z	...	...	98*	1.01*	...	...	89	0.96*
199	South Sudan	...	...	...	...	...	...	...	...	...	...	...	...
200	Swaziland	...	23	70	86	84*	1.01*	94	1.03	67*	0.94*	87	0.99
201	Togo	3	9	85	92^y	...	...	82*	0.85*	...	...	57	0.61*
202	Uganda	...	14	...	91	70*	0.82*	87*	0.95*	56*	0.66*	73*	0.78*
203	United Republic of Tanzania	...	33	49	98^y	82*	0.90*	77	0.98	59*	0.67*	73	0.85
204	Zambia	...	...	71	91	66*	0.97*	74	0.82	65*	0.79*	71	0.77
205	Zimbabwe	...	...	...	...	95*	0.98*	99	1.01	84*	0.88*	92	0.95
						Weighted average				Weighted average			
I	World	32	48	82**	89**	83	0.90	90	0.95	76	0.85	84	0.90
II	Countries in transition	46	64**	90**	91**	100	1.00	100	1.00	98	0.97	99	1.00
III	Developed countries	75	85	97	97	...	...	...	...	...	...	...	...
IV	Developing countries	27	43	80**	88**	80	0.88	88	0.93	67	0.77	80	0.86
V	Arab States	15	22**	77	86**	74	0.78	89	0.93	55	0.62	75	0.79
VI	Central and Eastern Europe	51	69**	92**	94**	98	0.98	99	1.00	96	0.96	98	0.98
VII	Central Asia	19	30	91**	90	100**	1.00**	100	1.00	98**	0.98**	99	1.00
VIII	East Asia and the Pacific	39	57	94**	95**	95	0.96	99	1.00	82	0.84	94	0.95
IX	East Asia	39	57	94**	95**	95	0.96	99	1.00	82	0.84	94	0.95
X	Pacific	67**	78	90	86	...	...	...	...	...	...	...	...
XI	Latin America/Caribbean	54	70	92	94**	93**	1.01**	97	1.00	86**	0.97**	91	0.98
XII	Caribbean	...	...	72**	69**	...	...	81	0.98	...	...	69	0.96
XIII	Latin America	55	72	93	95**	93**	1.01**	98**	1.00**	86**	0.97**	92	0.98
XIV	N. America/W. Europe	76	85	98	96	...	...	...	...	...	...	...	...
XV	South and West Asia	21	48	74**	88**	60	0.70	81	0.86	47	0.57	63	0.70
XVI	Sub-Saharan Africa	10**	17	58	76**	66**	0.80**	72	0.87	53**	0.68**	63	0.76
XVII	Countries with low income	11**	15	58**	80**	60**	0.79**	74	0.93	51**	0.69**	63	0.81
XVIII	Countries with middle income	32	52	85**	90**	84	0.89	91	0.94	72	0.80	83	0.88
XIX	Lower middle	22	45	77**	87**	71	0.80	84	0.89	59	0.71	71	0.78
XX	Upper middle	43	62	94**	95**	94	0.96	99	1.00	82	0.86	94	0.95
XXI	Countries with high income	72	82	96	97	...	...	...	...	...	...	...	...

Sources: UNESCO Institute for Statistics database (UIS, 2012). Enrolment ratios in the table are based on the United Nations Population Division estimates, revision 2010 (United Nations, 2011), median variant.
Note A: The country groupings by income level presented in the tables are as defined by the World Bank. They are based on the list of countries by income group as revised in July 2011.
Note B: The median values for 1999 and 2009 are not comparable since they are not necessarily based on the same number of countries.
1. Data are for the most recent year available during the period specified. See the web version of the introduction to the statistical tables for a broader explanation of national literacy definitions, assessment methods, and sources and years of data. For countries indicated with (*), national observed literacy data are used. For all others, UIS literacy estimates are used. The estimates were generated using the UIS Global Age-specific Literacy Projections model. Those in the most recent period are for 2010 and are based on the most recent observed data available for each country.

2. Based on headcounts of pupils and teachers.
3. Enrolment ratios for one or both of the two school years were not calculated due to inconsistencies in the population data.
4. National population data were used to calculate enrolment ratios.
5. Enrolment and population data used to calculate enrolment rates exclude Transnistria.
6. In the Russian Federation two education structures existed in the past, both starting at age 7. The most common or widespread one lasted three years and was used to calculate indicators; the second one, in which about one-third of primary pupils were enrolled, had four grades. Since 2004, the four-grade structure has been extended all over the country.
7. Enrolment and population data exclude the Nagorno-Karabakh region.
8. Children enter primary school at age 6 or 7. Since 7 is the most common entrance age, enrolment ratios were calculated using the 7–11 age group for both enrolment and population.

	GOAL 5								GOAL 6			
	Gender parity in primary education				Gender parity in secondary education				Educational quality			
	GROSS ENROLMENT RATIO (GER)				GROSS ENROLMENT RATIO (GER)				SURVIVAL RATE TO GRADE 5		PUPIL/TEACHER RATIO IN PRIMARY EDUCATION[2]	
	School year ending in				School year ending in				School year ending in		School year ending in	
	1999		2010		1999		2010		1999	2009	1999	2010
	Total (%)	GPI (F/M)	Total (%)	GPI (F/M)	Total (%)	GPI (F/M)	Total (%)	GPI (F/M)	Total (%)	Total (%)	Total (%)	Total (%)
183	94	0.75	96^y	0.91^y	31	0.65	...	...	...	60^x	39	24^y
184	97	0.97	149	0.98	...	...	31**,z	0.94**,z	52	35	47	40
185	138	0.96	135	1.04	38	0.70	32	0.91	48	61	...	79**
186	53	0.72	**82**	**0.88**	14	0.54	**39**	**0.71**	77**	**88**	62*	**48**
187	100	1.00	99	1.01	76	0.98	89**	1.00**	99	98	26	21
188	69	0.74	**111**	**0.91**	5	0.63	**26**	**0.87**	43	**44**	61	**55**
189	116	1.01	107^z	0.99^z	57	1.12	...	...	93	91^y	32	30^z
190	31	0.68	**71**	**0.84**	7	0.59	13	0.66	*74*	**71**	41	**39**
191	93	0.81	83	0.91	23	0.91	44	0.88	...	86	41	36
192	*106*	*0.99*	142	1.03	10	1.01	**36**	**1.05**	*42*	47	54	**58**
193	110	0.97	**134**	**0.97**	...	...	**59**	**1.15**	*62***	77**,y	36	**30**
194	68	0.83	87	1.06	16	0.65	37	0.88	72	74	49	34
195	*112*	*1.00*	117	1.00	105	1.04	119	1.09	96	95^y	15	13
196	*70*	...	**125**	**0.93**	*28*	*0.68***	...	...	...	...	*37*	**31**
197	...	...	...	...	...	...	...	...	...	...	...	...
198	113	0.97	102^z	0.96^z	88	1.13	94^z	1.05^z	65	...	35	31^z
199	...	...	...	...	...	...	...	...	...	...	...	...
200	94	0.96	116	0.92	44	1.00	58	1.00	80	96	33	32
201	126	0.75	140	0.90	31	0.40	...	...	52	78	41	41
202	130	0.90	121	1.01	*16*	*0.76*	28**	0.85**	*57*	57	57	49
203	67	1.00	102	1.02	...	...	...	...	*81*	90	*46*	51
204	84	0.92	115	1.01	...	...	...	...	81	71^y	61**	58**
205	...	...	...	...	...	...	...	...	...	...	...	...

	Total (%)	GPI (F/M)	Total (%)	GPI (F/M)	Total (%)	GPI (F/M)	Total (%)	GPI (F/M)	Median		Weighted average	
I	99	0.92	106	0.97	59	0.91	70	0.97	...	...	26	24
II	102	0.99	99**	1.00**	90	1.00**	93**	0.98**	.	.	19	17**
III	103	1.00	103	0.99	100	1.02	102	1.00	98	99	16	14
IV	98	0.91	106	0.97	52	0.88	66	0.96	82	87	29**	27
V	89	0.87	98	0.93	59	0.88	69**	0.94**	92	95	23	21
VI	103	0.97	100**	0.99**	88	0.96	88**	0.97**	.	.	18**	17**
VII	97	0.99	101	0.98	84	0.99	95	0.97	.	.	21	17
VIII	111**	0.99**	110	1.01	63	0.94**	80	1.03	...	87	24**	18
IX	111**	0.99**	111	1.02	62	0.94**	80	1.03	81	92	25**	18
X	95	0.97	92	0.98	109	1.00	95	0.96	.	.	20	...
XI	121	0.97	114	0.97	80	1.07	90	1.08	88	92	26	22
XII	108**	0.98**	106**	0.98**	49**	0.99**	...	...	89	92	29**	26**
XIII	122	0.97	114	0.97	81	1.07	91	1.08	87	91	26	22
XIV	103	1.01	103	0.99	100	1.02	102	1.00	...	99	15	14
XV	89	0.83	106**	0.98**	44	0.75	59	0.91	...	66	36	39**
XVI	80	0.85	101	0.93	25	0.82	40	0.82	69	71	42	43
XVII	78	0.86	105	0.95	29	0.83	42	0.87	59	62	43**	43
XVIII	102	0.92	107**	0.98**	58	0.90	71	0.98	...	91	27**	24**
XIX	93	0.86	104**	0.96**	46	0.80	61	0.93	76	80	31	31**
XX	114**	0.99**	110	1.00	72	0.98**	85	1.04	90	95	24**	19
XXI	102	1.00	103	0.99	99	1.01	102	1.00	96	...	16	14

9. Enrolment ratios for one or both of the two school years were not calculated due to lack of United Nations population data by age.
10. Data include French overseas departments and territories (DOM-TOM).
11. Due to the continuing discrepancy in enrolment by single age, the net enrolment ratio in primary education is estimated using the age distribution from the 2007 MICS as from the school year ending in 2007.
Data in bold are for the school year ending in 2010 for survival rates, and the school year ending in 2011 for enrolment and pupil/teacher ratios. Those in italics are for 2000 and those in bold italic are for 2001.
(z) Data are for the school year ending in 2009.
(y) Data are for the school year ending in 2008.
(x) Data are for the school year ending in 2007.

(*) National estimate.
(**) For country level data: UIS partial estimate; for regional and other country-grouping weighted averages: partial imputation due to incomplete country coverage (between 33% and 60% of population for the region or other country grouping).
(.) The category is not applicable or does not exist.
(...) No data available.

Young people on a tailoring course at
St Anthony Vocational Training Centre in Musoma,
United Republic of Tanzania. The course is
supported by the NGO Terre des Hommes.

Aid tables

Introduction[1]

The data on aid used in this Report are derived from the OECD International Development Statistics (IDS) databases, which record information provided annually by all member countries of the OECD Development Assistance Committee (DAC), as well as a growing number of donors that are not members of the committee. The IDS databases are the DAC database, which provides aggregate data, and the Creditor Reporting System (CRS), which provides project- and activity-level data. In this Report, total figures for official development assistance (ODA) come from the DAC database while those for sector-allocable aid and aid to education come from the CRS. Both are available at www.oecd.org/dac/stats/idsonline

Official development assistance are public funds provided to developing countries to promote their economic and social development. It is concessional; that is, it takes the form either of a grant or of a loan carrying a lower rate of interest than is available on the market and, usually, a longer repayment period.

A more extensive version of the aid tables including total ODA per recipient is available on the Report's website, www.efareport.unesco.org

Aid recipients and donors

Developing countries are those in Part I of the DAC List of Aid Recipients: all low and middle income countries except twelve Central and Eastern European countries and a few more advanced developing countries.

Bilateral donors are countries that provide development assistance directly to recipient countries. Most are members of the DAC, a forum of major bilateral donors established to promote aid and its effectiveness. Non-DAC bilateral donors include Brazil, China, India and some Arab states. Bilateral donors also contribute substantially to the financing of multilateral donors through contributions recorded as multilateral ODA.

Multilateral donors are international institutions with government membership that conduct all or a significant part of their activities in favour of developing countries. They include multilateral development banks (e.g. the World Bank and the Inter-American Development Bank), United Nations agencies and regional groupings (e.g. the European Commission). The development banks also make non-concessional loans to several middle and higher income countries; these are not counted as part of ODA.

Types of aid

Total ODA: bilateral and multilateral aid for all sectors, as well as aid that is not allocable by sector, such as general budget support and debt relief. In Table 1, total ODA from bilateral donors is bilateral aid only, while aid as percentage of gross national income (GNI) is bilateral and multilateral ODA.

Sector-allocable ODA: aid allocated to a specific sector, such as education or health. It does not include aid for general development purposes (e.g. general budget support), balance-of-payments support, debt relief or emergency assistance.

Debt relief: includes debt forgiveness, i.e. the extinction of a loan by agreement between the creditor (donor) and the debtor (aid recipient), and other action on debt, including debt swaps, buy-backs and refinancing. In the DAC database, debt forgiveness is reported as a grant and therefore counts as ODA.

Country programmable aid: defined by subtracting from total ODA aid that:

- is unpredictable by nature (humanitarian aid and debt relief);

- entails no cross-border flows (administrative costs, imputed student costs, and costs related to promotion of development awareness, research in donor countries and refugees in donor countries);

- is not part of cooperation agreements between governments (food aid and aid from local governments);

- is not country programmable by the donor (core funding of NGOs).

Country programmable aid is not included in the aid tables, but is used in a few places in the Report.

---

1. A full set of statistics and indicators related to this introduction is posted in Excel format on the EFA Global Monitoring Report website at www.efareport.unesco.org

Education aid

Direct aid to education: aid to education reported in the CRS database as direct allocations to the education sector. It is the total of direct aid, as defined by the DAC, to:

- **basic education**, defined by the DAC as covering primary education, basic life skills for youth and adults, and early childhood education;

- **secondary education**, both general secondary education and vocational training;

- **post-secondary education**, including advanced technical and managerial training;

- **education, 'level unspecified'**, which refers to any activity that cannot be attributed solely to the development of a particular level of education, such as education research and teacher training. General education programme support is often reported within this subcategory.

Total aid to education: direct aid to education plus 20% of general budget support (aid provided to governments without being earmarked for specific projects or sectors) to represent the estimated 15% to 25% of budget support that typically benefits.

Total aid to basic education: direct aid to basic education, plus 10% of general budget support, plus 50% of education, 'level unspecified'.

Commitments and disbursements: A commitment is a firm obligation by a donor, expressed in writing and backed by the necessary funds, to provide specified assistance to a country or multilateral organization. Disbursements record the actual international transfer of financial resources or of goods or services. Starting with the 2011 Report, disbursement figures are used in the text and the aid tables, while in previous years commitments were reported. As the aid committed in a given year can be disbursed later, sometimes over several years, the annual aid figures based on commitments cannot be directly compared to disbursements. Reliable figures on aid disbursements have only been available since 2002, which consequently is used as the base year.

Current and constant prices: aid figures in the DAC databases are expressed in US dollars. When comparing aid figures between years, adjustment is required to compensate for inflation and changes in exchange rates. Such adjustments result in aid being expressed in constant dollars, i.e. in dollars fixed at the value they held in a given reference year, including their external value in terms of other currencies. This Report presents most aid data in constant 2010 US dollars.

Source: OECD-DAC, 2012a, 2012b.

Table 1: Bilateral and multilateral ODA

	Total ODA Constant 2010 US$ millions				ODA as % of GNI				Sector-allocable ODA Constant 2010 US$ millions			Debt relief and other actions relating to debt Constant 2010 US$ millions		
	2002–2003 annual average	2009	2010	2011[1]	2002–2003 annual average	2009	2010	2011[1]	2002–2003 annual average	2009	2010	2002–2003 annual average	2009	2010
Australia	1 799	2 859	3 241	3 441	0.26	0.29	0.32	0.35	1 234	2 222	2 631	12	4	8
Austria	443	490	612	450	0.23	0.30	0.32	0.27	206	302	328	54	57	155
Belgium	1 579	1 535	2 051	1 490	0.52	0.55	0.64	0.53	702	1 126	1 128	703	105	556
Canada	2 489	3 581	3 926	3 771	0.26	0.30	0.34	0.31	1 062	2 415	2 645	13	55	57
Denmark	1 592	1 874	2 109	2 072	0.90	0.88	0.91	0.86	520	997	1 468	0	-	47
Finland	390	755	839	773	0.35	0.54	0.55	0.52	266	469	520	0	-	-
France	6 368	6 891	7 787	7 975	0.39	0.47	0.50	0.46	2 939	5 045	5 370	3 369	1 829	1 709
Germany	5 044	6 790	8 036	8 440	0.28	0.35	0.39	0.40	3 811	6 940	8 227	1 741	145	216
Greece	261	287	212	56	0.21	0.19	0.17	0.11	226	214	146	-	-	-
Ireland	404	643	585	588	0.40	0.54	0.52	0.52	286	456	406	-	-	0
Italy	1 541	835	759	1 492	0.19	0.16	0.15	0.19	201	536	554	909	170	275
Japan	8 231	6 417	7 337	5 804	0.22	0.18	0.20	0.18	4 156	9 707	12 520	772	112	190
Kuwait[2]	88	222	211	...	...	...	...	...	...	...	612	-	-	-
Luxembourg	225	265	262	262	0.82	1.04	1.05	0.99	...	182	204	-	-	-
Netherlands	3 765	4 623	4 644	3 948	0.81	0.82	0.81	0.75	1 657	3 430	3 233	447	42	499
New Zealand	186	267	271	288	0.23	0.28	0.26	0.28	121	168	185	-	-	-
Norway	2 300	3 507	3 561	3 190	0.91	1.06	1.10	1.00	1 153	2 246	2 426	26	18	16
Portugal	278	266	396	419	0.25	0.23	0.29	0.29	242	212	264	-	2	3
Republic of Korea	283	665	901	912	0.06	0.10	0.12	0.12	...	646	862	-	-	2
Spain	1 688	4 272	3 999	2 187	0.25	0.46	0.43	0.29	987	3 162	3 206	174	193	433
Sweden	2 118	3 236	2 915	3 274	0.82	1.12	0.97	1.02	1 001	1 981	1 694	107	22	-
Switzerland	1 282	1 821	1 712	1 992	0.35	0.45	0.40	0.46	680	851	787	26	169	32
United Arab Emirates[2]	1 002	841	380	...	...	0.35	0.16	...	...	701	347	-	-	-
United Kingdom	4 369	7 515	8 017	7 562	0.33	0.51	0.57	0.56	1 795	5 684	6 314	436	43	183
United States	15 004	25 463	26 587	26 524	0.14	0.21	0.21	0.20	8 377	17 853	18 914	1 775	259	186
Total bilaterals	62 728	85 921	91 350	86 909	0.24	0.31	0.32	0.31	31 621	67 545	74 990	10 562	3 225	4 568
African Development Fund	966	3 420	2 345	...	...	...	...	...	691	2 284	1 477	151	726	561
Arab Fund for Economic and Social Development	...	893	1 028	...	...	...	...	...	...	881	1 021	-	-	-
Asian Development Bank Special Funds	...	...	1 930	...	...	...	...	...	...	...	1 850	-	-	1
Asian Development Fund[3]	...	...	...	...	...	...	...	...	...	...	...	...	...	...
EU institutions	2 437	12 473	12 570	...	...	...	...	...	1 460	8 379	8 201	4	154	23
World Bank (IDA)	10 248	12 912	12 123	...	...	...	...	...	9 735	11 206	9 967	512	1 555	2 002
Inter-American Development Bank Special Fund	...	1 034	1 204	...	...	...	...	...	...	596	714	-	424	484
International Monetary Fund (Concessional Trust Funds)	2 509	2 629	2 973	...	...	...	...	...	...	...	...	473	119	1 627
OPEC Fund for International Development	...	329	327	...	...	...	...	...	...	290	310	-	-	14
UNDP	...	636	613	...	...	...	...	...	...	581	552	-	-	-
UNICEF	819	1 114	1 050	...	...	...	...	...	493	756	770	-	-	-
UN Peacebuilding Fund	...	43	51	...	...	...	...	...	...	43	47	-	-	-
UN Relief and Works Agency for Palestine Refugees	...	477	545	...	...	...	...	...	...	388	429	-	-	-
World Food Programme	...	295	244	...	...	...	...	...	...	88	94	-	-	-
Total multilaterals[4]	17 943	40 371	42 033	...	...	...	...	...	13 216	29 375	30 226	1 267	3 153	4 874
Total	80 671	126 292	133 383	...	...	...	...	...	44 837	96 920	105 216	11 829	6 378	9 442

Notes:
1. Preliminary data.
2. Kuwait and the United Arab Emirates are not part of the DAC but are included in its Creditor Reporting System (CRS) database from 2009 onwards.
3. The Asian Development Fund is a donor to education but does not report to the OECD on disbursements.
4. The total includes ODA from other multilaterals not listed above.
(...) indicates that data are not available, (-) represents a nil value.
Total ODA represents net disbursements. Sector-allocable ODA and debt relief and other actions relating to debt represent gross disbursements.
Total ODA from DAC donors is bilateral ODA only, while ODA as % of GNI includes multilateral ODA.
Source: OECD-DAC (2012a, 2012b).

Table 2: Bilateral and multilateral aid to education

	Total aid to education Constant 2010 US$ millions			Total aid to basic education Constant 2010 US$ millions			Direct aid to education Constant 2010 US$ millions			Direct aid to basic education Constant 2010 US$ millions			Direct aid to secondary education Constant 2010 US$ millions		
	2002–2003 annual average	2009	2010	2002–2003 annual average	2009	2010	2002–2003 annual average	2009	2010	2002–2003 annual average	2009	2010	2002–2003 annual average	2009	2010
Australia	189	347	279	61	135	133	186	340	262	41	88	83	29	138	54
Austria	65	126	131	5	5	5	65	125	130	3	3	3	3	16	18
Belgium	146	237	221	28	43	37	141	237	219	15	17	21	17	28	26
Canada	257	418	483	107	219	237	253	400	471	74	122	150	11	35	40
Denmark	50	83	161	28	43	85	46	70	147	10	15	35	2	12	9
Finland	38	47	57	21	25	30	37	40	50	8	9	8	2	2	2
France	1 397	1 786	1 825	179	342	381	1 353	1 736	1 739	24	234	225	36	297	248
Germany	1 103	1 664	1 701	126	278	320	1 103	1 638	1 681	97	141	187	68	106	97
Greece	61	94	86	30	12	9	61	93	86	25	8	6	21	9	6
Ireland	69	88	70	40	54	40	63	82	64	15	30	15	1	6	3
Italy	45	114	71	17	53	25	43	112	69	1	24	10	2	9	19
Japan	611	1 104	1 094	173	322	329	546	907	1 001	99	85	133	45	72	59
Kuwait[1]	...	...	20	...	...	2	...	...	20	...	...	-	...	...	-
Luxembourg	...	32	39	...	11	10	...	32	39	...	9	7	...	19	27
Netherlands	318	565	570	210	331	321	288	525	541	175	273	266	1	28	30
New Zealand	79	58	60	22	26	29	77	55	57	9	22	26	9	2	1
Norway	185	339	301	108	226	197	172	300	265	84	182	153	9	12	9
Portugal	73	73	74	11	13	13	73	72	73	7	5	1	8	6	5
Republic of Korea	...	86	150	...	20	23	...	86	150	...	13	11	...	29	67
Spain	198	365	369	66	203	207	198	358	364	43	145	140	45	57	48
Sweden	104	135	144	68	95	111	86	104	120	42	72	88	3	6	6
Switzerland	64	68	54	30	27	16	58	61	48	23	15	7	26	12	12
United Arab Emirates[1]	...	24	35	...	10	17	...	22	18	...	0	-	...	1	0
United Kingdom	263	941	881	181	601	500	162	831	751	108	334	268	7	15	53
United States	403	887	889	255	671	644	226	801	889	156	525	586	0	3	11
Total bilaterals	**5 718**	**9 681**	**9 765**	**1 764**	**3 766**	**3 721**	**5 237**	**9 029**	**9 254**	**1 058**	**2 371**	**2 431**	**346**	**920**	**853**
African Development Fund	94	192	182	51	95	91	72	110	120	11	16	...	2	15	...
Arab Fund for Economic and Social Development	...	25	8	...	9	1	...	25	8	...	1	...	...	6	5
Asian Development Bank Special Funds	-	-	210	-	-	102	-	-	210	...	...	89	...	...	90
Asian Development Fund[2]	...	...	...	...	...	...	...	...	...	...	...	...	...	...	...
EU institutions	210	1 072	1 236	100	435	574	74	845	925	24	151	242	13	123	77
World Bank (IDA)	1 114	1 487	1 280	748	808	679	1 114	1 480	1 277	624	527	437	101	131	236
Inter-American Development Bank Special Fund	...	21	35	...	9	22	...	21	35	...	1	20	...	4	9
International Monetary Fund (Concessional Trust Funds)	407	502	269	204	251	135	-	-	-	-	-	-	-	-	-
OPEC Fund for International Development	...	34	23	...	12	12	...	34	23	...	12	11	...	11	3
UNDP	...	6	6	...	5	5	...	6	6	...	4	5	...	1	1
UNICEF	72	66	68	72	65	66	72	66	68	72	63	64	0	0	0
UN Peacebuilding Fund	...	1	6	...	-	0	...	1	6	...	...	...	...	1	5
UN Relief and Works Agency for Palestine Refugees	...	300	330	...	300	330	...	300	330	...	300	330	...	-	-
World Food Programme	...	37	51	...	37	51	...	37	51	...	37	51	...	-	-
Total multilaterals	**1 898**	**3 744**	**3 703**	**1 175**	**2 025**	**2 068**	**1 333**	**2 926**	**3 059**	**731**	**1 111**	**1 249**	**117**	**292**	**426**
Total	**7 616**	**13 425**	**13 468**	**2 939**	**5 791**	**5 789**	**6 571**	**11 955**	**12 313**	**1 789**	**3 483**	**3 680**	**463**	**1 212**	**1 279**

Notes:
1. Kuwait and the United Arab Emirates are not part of the DAC but are included in its Creditor Reporting System (CRS) database from 2009 on.
2. The Asian Development Fund is a donor to education but does not report to the OECD on disbursements.
Aid from France, the United Kingdom and New Zealand includes funds disbursed to overseas territories (see Table 3).
(...) indicates that data are not available, (-) represents a nil value.
All data represent gross disbursements.
Source: OECD-DAC (2012a, 2012b).

Direct aid to post-secondary education (Constant 2010 US$ millions)			Education, level unspecified (Constant 2010 US$ millions)			Share of education in total ODA (%)			Share of direct aid to education in total sector-allocable ODA (%)			Share of basic education in total aid to education (%)			
2002–2003 annual average	2009	2010	2002–2003 annual average	2009	2010	2002–2003 annual average	2009	2010	2002–2003 annual average	2009	2010	2002–2003 annual average	2009	2010	
79	27	42	37	89	83	11	12	9	15	15	10	32	39	48	Australia
55	103	105	4	3	3	15	26	21	32	42	40	8	4	4	Austria
87	140	142	22	52	30	9	15	11	20	21	19	19	18	17	Belgium
106	66	119	62	176	161	10	12	12	24	17	18	42	52	49	Canada
2	1	17	32	43	85	3	4	8	9	7	10	56	51	53	Denmark
2	4	4	25	24	35	10	6	7	14	9	10	56	53	52	Finland
1 028	1 039	1 039	265	165	227	22	26	23	46	34	32	13	19	21	France
881	1 143	1 149	57	248	248	22	25	21	29	24	20	11	17	19	Germany
4	68	69	11	9	5	23	33	41	27	43	59	49	13	10	Greece
4	3	3	42	43	44	17	14	12	22	18	16	57	62	56	Ireland
10	23	14	30	55	27	3	14	9	21	21	12	38	46	34	Italy
319	474	509	84	276	299	7	17	15	13	9	8	28	29	30	Japan
...	...	16	...	...	5	...	...	10	...	...	3	...	...	11	Kuwait[1]
...	0	0	...	4	5	...	12	15	...	18	19	...	34	25	Luxembourg
72	149	164	39	75	81	8	12	12	17	15	17	66	59	56	Netherlands
35	26	27	24	5	3	42	22	22	64	33	31	28	45	48	New Zealand
44	57	49	35	49	53	8	10	8	15	13	11	58	67	66	Norway
50	45	44	9	17	22	26	28	19	30	34	28	15	18	17	Portugal
...	30	49	...	14	23	...	13	17	...	13	17	...	24	15	Republic of Korea
65	46	46	45	109	129	12	9	9	20	11	11	33	56	56	Spain
8	10	4	34	16	23	5	4	5	9	5	7	65	71	77	Sweden
2	17	17	8	17	11	5	4	3	8	7	6	47	39	29	Switzerland
...	2	0	...	19	17	...	3	9	...	3	...	...	...	49	United Arab Emirates[1]
1	59	97	46	424	333	6	13	11	9	15	12	69	64	57	United Kingdom
50	68	176	21	204	117	3	3	3	3	4	5	63	76	72	United States
2 903	3 601	3 901	931	2 137	2 069	9	11	11	17	13	12	31	39	38	Total bilaterals
0	2	...	59	77	120	10	6	8	10	5	8	54	50	50	African Development Fund
...	1	1	...	17	2	...	3	1	...	3	1	...	36	14	Arab Fund for Economic and Social Development
...	...	5	...	...	27	...	...	11	...	...	11	...	...	49	Asian Development Bank Special Funds
...	...	...	...	...	...	...	...	...	...	...	...	...	...	...	Asian Development Fund[2]
21	230	252	16	341	354	9	9	10	5	10	11	48	41	46	EU institutions
140	268	122	249	555	482	11	12	11	11	13	13	67	54	53	World Bank (IDA)
...	-	2	...	16	4	...	2	3	...	...	...	...	42	62	Inter-American Development Bank Special Fund
-	-	-	-	-	-	16	19	9	...	...	...	50	50	50	International Monetary Fund (Concessional Trust Funds)
...	11	8	...	...	1	...	10	7	...	12	7	...	36	52	OPEC Fund for International Development
...	0	...	...	0	0	...	1	1	...	1	1	...	82	87	UNDP
0	-	-	...	3	4	9	6	6	15	9	9	99	98	97	UNICEF
...	-	-	...	...	0	...	3	11	...	3	12	...	-	2	UN Peacebuilding Fund
...	-	-	...	-	-	...	63	61	...	77	77	...	100	100	UN Relief and Works Agency for Palestine Refugees
...	-	-	...	0	0	...	13	21	...	42	54	...	100	100	World Food Programme
161	513	389	324	1 010	995	11	9	9	10	10	10	62	54	56	Total multilaterals
3 064	4 115	4 290	1 256	3 147	3 064	9	11	10	15	12	12	39	43	43	Total

Education for All Global Monitoring Report

Table 3: Recipients of aid to education

	Total aid to education (Constant 2010 US$ millions)			Total aid to basic education (Constant 2010 US$ millions)			Total aid to basic education per primary school-age child (Constant 2010 US$)			Direct aid to education (Constant 2010 US$ millions)			Direct aid to basic education (Constant 2010 US$ millions)		
	2002–2003 annual average	2009	2010	2002–2003 annual average	2009	2010	2002–2003 annual average	2009	2010	2002–2003 annual average	2009	2010	2002–2003 annual average	2009	2010
Arab States	1 056	1 983	1 824	211	853	779	6	23	21	920	1 860	1 764	106	600	613
Unallocated within the region	*4*	*40*	*55*	*3*	*4*	*10*	...	...	...	*4*	*40*	*55*	*2*	*2*	*8*
Algeria	132	136	148	1	5	16	0	2	5	132	136	148	0	2	14
Bahrain	0	–	–	0	–	–	0	–	–	0	–	–	–	–	–
Djibouti	29	22	30	7	10	13	60	101	125	27	16	24	5	6	5
Egypt	108	245	137	53	120	48	7	12	5	91	208	137	43	64	40
Iraq	10	94	103	1	38	40	0	8	8	10	94	103	1	3	8
Jordan	134	211	186	56	146	142	76	168	159	27	165	186	0	101	126
Lebanon	42	132	115	1	55	50	3	121	113	42	131	115	0	46	47
Libya	–	7	9	–	0	1	–	0	1	–	7	9	–	0	1
Mauritania	34	28	33	13	10	11	29	20	21	30	28	25	8	7	4
Morocco	300	322	270	17	78	61	4	22	17	300	322	270	6	42	44
Oman	1	2	4	0	0	1	0	2	5	1	2	2	0	0	0
Palestine	48	262	321	20	216	236	47	491	533	48	237	293	14	188	203
Saudi Arabia	3	–	–	0	–	–	0	–	–	3	–	–	–	–	–
Sudan[1]	25	89	75	11	52	45	...	...	...	21	88	75	7	43	32
Syrian Arab Republic	38	110	113	2	34	37	1	17	18	38	110	113	1	33	29
Tunisia	103	178	133	2	10	5	2	10	5	103	171	128	1	1	1
Yemen	44	107	92	23	73	63	6	19	16	43	107	82	16	63	53
Central and Eastern Europe	325	496	537	85	60	75	8	6	8	290	481	488	41	25	21
Unallocated within the region	*20*	*40*	*54*	*5*	*5*	*9*	...	...	...	*18*	*40*	*54*	*1*	*2*	*3*
Albania	78	70	71	37	6	4	152	24	16	76	70	71	25	4	2
Belarus	–	23	24	–	1	2	–	4	4	–	23	24	–	0	1
Bosnia and Herzegovina	35	37	35	11	3	3	64	16	15	35	37	35	6	1	0
Croatia	12	20	18	0	2	2	1	9	9	12	20	18	–	0	0
Montenegro	–	5	6	–	1	1	...	44	43	–	5	6	–	0	0
Republic of Moldova	10	16	50	2	1	18	9	4	122	8	16	14	0	0	0
Serbia	41	58	63	9	14	13	28	48	46	39	45	50	3	4	3
TFYR Macedonia	13	26	21	4	11	8	35	88	65	10	24	21	2	9	7
Turkey	117	124	119	17	11	9	3	2	1	93	124	119	3	4	3
Ukraine	–	76	75	–	4	4	–	3	3	–	76	75	–	1	1
Central Asia	139	231	311	40	57	93	6	10	17	102	212	272	16	33	49
Unallocated within the region	–	*17*	*23*	–	*1*	*9*	...	...	...	–	*17*	*23*	–	*1*	*9*
Armenia	18	23	45	7	6	13	42	53	112	9	23	34	1	3	1
Azerbaijan	13	10	12	4	1	1	6	2	3	7	10	12	1	1	0
Georgia	31	42	42	6	9	10	23	33	37	26	37	33	3	5	4
Kazakhstan	8	22	22	1	3	2	1	3	2	8	22	22	1	0	0
Kyrgyzstan	12	28	29	4	9	9	9	22	24	5	22	21	0	4	3
Mongolia	34	29	46	10	6	17	45	24	74	31	29	46	8	4	10
Tajikistan	9	28	29	4	17	17	6	25	25	3	20	17	1	12	9
Turkmenistan	1	3	3	0	0	1	1	1	2	1	3	3	0	0	0
Uzbekistan	14	30	59	2	6	14	1	3	7	13	30	59	1	3	12
East Asia and the Pacific	1 147	2 305	2 140	231	671	636	1	4	4	1 065	2 092	1 989	116	310	371
Unallocated within the region	*14*	*47*	*37*	*3*	*7*	*18*	...	...	...	*14*	*47*	*36*	*2*	*5*	*16*
Cambodia	48	45	51	18	20	20	8	11	11	39	45	51	6	14	13
China	449	814	800	17	57	29	0	1	0	449	814	800	10	6	5
Cook Islands	3	3	4	1	1	3	459	558	2 034	3	3	4	0	–	3
DPR Korea	2	2	3	0	1	2	0	1	2	2	2	3	0	1	2

Note:
1. Refers to the former Sudan, before the separation of the South in 2011.

Direct aid to secondary education			Direct aid to post-secondary education			Education, level unspecified			Share of education in total ODA [%]			Share of direct aid to education in sector-allocable ODA [%]			Share of basic education in total aid to education [%]		
Constant 2010 US$ millions			Constant 2010 US$ millions			Constant 2010 US$ millions												
2002–2003 annual average	2009	2010	2002–2003 annual average	2009	2010	2002–2003 annual average	2009	2010	2002–2003 annual average	2009	2010	2002–2003 annual average	2009	2010	2002–2003 annual average	2009	2010
61	202	128	679	676	751	74	382	271	14	13	13	22	16	15	20	43	43
0	*2*	*2*	*1*	*32*	*41*	*1*	*4*	*4*	*4*	*10*	*13*	*10*	*16*	*15*	*66*	*9*	*18*
1	10	9	129	120	123	2	5	3	52	37	52	80	41	61	1	3	10
0	-	-	0	-	-	0	-	-	55	...	...	59	...	...	1	...	...
6	1	1	14	6	8	2	2	11	31	14	21	35	17	26	25	48	42
12	25	22	33	44	59	3	75	16	7	15	9	9	16	10	49	49	35
1	5	11	8	15	19	0	70	64	1	3	5	1	4	5	14	40	39
3	3	4	19	18	24	6	43	32	13	23	17	9	27	18	42	69	76
2	14	13	38	52	48	2	18	7	31	22	23	42	25	28	3	42	44
-	0	1	-	6	6	-	0	1	...	15	21	...	16	22	...	4	12
2	3	2	14	12	12	6	7	8	9	8	9	16	9	8	38	37	34
4	43	30	267	164	161	22	73	35	38	23	19	58	24	19	6	24	23
0	0	0	0	1	1	0	1	0	10	1	11	10	1	7	23	22	32
7	6	12	14	12	40	12	31	39	8	10	13	11	13	16	42	82	74
1	-	-	2	-	-	0	-	-	52	...	...	54	...	...	5	...	...
1	17	3	10	10	14	3	18	26	6	4	4	21	9	7	43	59	60
0	7	3	36	66	64	1	4	16	32	26	36	48	39	42	4	31	33
16	61	12	85	99	113	2	10	2	23	23	15	36	24	16	2	5	4
6	5	3	9	19	17	12	19	9	13	16	12	19	23	14	51	68	68
31	36	37	165	365	371	54	54	58	7	10	10	12	10	10	26	12	14
1	*3*	*2*	*10*	*29*	*37*	*6*	*7*	*12*	*3*	*6*	*6*	*6*	*8*	*8*	*25*	*14*	*17*
21	8	8	9	53	56	21	5	4	20	19	19	26	20	20	47	9	6
-	0	0	-	21	21	-	2	2	...	30	20	...	32	22	...	6	6
1	3	5	18	28	25	10	5	5	7	9	7	10	10	7	31	9	9
0	1	1	11	16	14	0	3	3	9	11	11	13	11	11	1	8	9
-	1	1	-	2	3	-	3	2	-	7	10	-	8	10	...	27	22
0	3	1	6	13	12	2	1	0	7	7	11	8	7	5	20	4	37
3	6	7	23	28	32	10	7	8	2	10	9	5	9	8	23	24	21
1	0	1	5	12	12	2	1	2	5	13	13	4	14	13	33	44	38
3	11	11	83	95	93	4	14	13	22	7	8	37	7	9	14	9	8
-	1	1	-	68	66	-	6	7	...	12	13	...	13	13	...	6	6
8	33	47	67	118	127	11	29	48	7	7	11	8	8	11	29	25	30
-	*2*	*2*	*-*	*14*	*12*	*-*	*0*	*0*	*...*	*5*	*12*	*...*	*5*	*13*	*...*	*7*	*40*
0	6	2	5	9	18	3	6	12	6	5	12	4	5	11	37	25	28
0	0	0	5	8	10	1	1	2	3	5	7	4	5	7	34	9	11
3	4	2	19	25	24	1	3	3	9	5	7	11	6	6	20	21	23
0	2	3	6	15	15	1	5	4	3	9	11	5	9	12	17	12	10
1	4	3	3	10	10	1	5	4	6	11	9	4	11	9	36	32	32
0	2	4	20	20	20	2	3	13	15	9	14	20	10	14	31	20	36
0	4	3	1	3	2	0	1	4	5	9	7	4	9	5	49	60	57
0	0	0	1	2	2	0	0	1	4	12	12	8	12	12	28	13	19
3	9	28	7	13	14	2	5	5	7	17	24	11	18	24	15	19	24
92	204	186	709	1 068	1 053	147	510	379	10	15	14	16	16	14	20	29	30
1	*31*	*13*	*10*	*8*	*5*	*1*	*3*	*2*	*9*	*11*	*8*	*15*	*15*	*10*	*19*	*14*	*48*
2	5	10	17	15	14	13	12	14	10	7	7	11	7	7	37	44	40
22	7	11	403	699	735	14	101	49	17	29	31	23	29	32	4	7	4
0	0	0	1	1	1	1	2	-0	40	33	29	42	25	37	32	38	82
1	0	-	1	1	1	0	0	0	1	3	4	3	6	7	13	48	68

Table 3 (continued)

	Total aid to education (Constant 2010 US$ millions)			Total aid to basic education (Constant 2010 US$ millions)			Total aid to basic education per primary school-age child (Constant 2010 US$)			Direct aid to education (Constant 2010 US$ millions)			Direct aid to basic education (Constant 2010 US$ millions)		
	2002–2003 annual average	2009	2010	2002–2003 annual average	2009	2010	2002–2003 annual average	2009	2010	2002–2003 annual average	2009	2010	2002–2003 annual average	2009	2010
Fiji	10	31	27	3	15	11	27	161	114	10	31	27	2	1	2
Indonesia	160	438	420	48	176	205	2	7	8	151	397	379	32	104	96
Kiribati	9	4	5	3	1	1	223	76	89	9	4	5	0	0	0
Lao PDR	30	51	59	8	22	31	11	31	43	24	46	58	4	9	22
Malaysia	18	39	45	1	2	2	0	1	1	18	39	45	0	0	0
Marshall Islands	11	16	1	5	8	1	759	980	85	1	16	1	0	0	0
Micronesia, F. S.	23	31	1	11	16	0	674	930	22	2	31	1	0	0	0
Myanmar	12	27	31	6	16	19	1	4	5	12	27	31	5	15	18
Nauru	0	3	3	0	1	1	14	915	939	0	3	3	-	-	0
Niue	4	1	2	2	0	1	11 390	3 187	4 960	3	1	1	0	0	0
Palau	4	3	1	2	1	0	1 059	1 041	328	1	1	1	0	0	0
Papua New Guinea	84	67	74	38	47	43	45	46	41	84	66	74	23	33	33
Philippines	37	91	106	9	44	61	1	3	5	36	71	53	5	16	29
Samoa	11	12	28	4	5	15	140	171	520	11	11	26	1	2	11
Solomon Islands	7	17	23	2	13	14	29	163	167	6	17	17	0	12	9
Thailand	34	37	39	2	4	5	0	1	1	34	37	39	0	1	2
Timor-Leste	19	35	38	4	16	16	26	82	80	16	33	36	2	7	4
Tonga	7	6	9	2	2	5	114	142	295	7	6	8	1	1	4
Tuvalu	2	1	3	1	0	0	547	224	241	2	1	2	0	0	0
Vanuatu	16	14	19	3	5	8	102	152	221	16	14	17	0	3	4
Viet Nam	131	470	313	39	189	124	4	29	19	115	331	271	19	78	95
Latin America and the Caribbean	**547**	**983**	**1 039**	**212**	**385**	**413**	**4**	**7**	**7**	**526**	**920**	**960**	**159**	**203**	**227**
Unallocated within the region	*10*	*28*	*53*	*4*	*8*	*24*	*...*	*...*	*...*	*10*	*28*	*53*	*1*	*4*	*20*
Antigua and Barbuda	0	0	3	0	0	1	6	4	112	0	0	0	-	0	0
Argentina	20	33	34	2	9	9	1	2	2	20	33	34	1	3	4
Aruba	-	-	-	-	-	-	-	-	-	-	-	-	-	-	-
Barbados	0	0	0	-	0	0	-	4	6	0	0	0	-	0	0
Belize	0	1	2	0	1	1	5	12	19	0	1	2	0	0	0
Bolivia, P. S.	85	74	74	53	35	33	39	24	23	81	74	74	44	23	17
Brazil	44	96	108	4	22	21	0	2	2	44	96	108	2	5	5
Chile	15	29	31	1	6	7	1	4	5	15	29	31	0	2	3
Colombia	34	68	65	5	17	17	1	4	4	34	68	65	2	12	10
Costa Rica	4	9	9	0	3	3	1	5	6	4	9	9	0	1	1
Cuba	12	12	8	3	2	2	3	3	2	12	12	8	3	1	2
Dominica	1	1	2	0	1	1	33	87	166	0	0	0	-	0	0
Dominican Republic	20	35	55	13	18	29	11	15	24	20	30	48	12	7	9
Ecuador	18	70	36	3	29	13	2	16	7	18	70	36	2	7	4
El Salvador	9	25	48	3	14	17	3	17	20	9	25	48	2	9	10
Grenada	0	6	4	-	2	2	-	173	132	0	1	1	-	0	0
Guatemala	30	40	44	15	19	27	8	9	12	29	40	44	12	12	19
Guyana	16	8	1	6	4	0	51	34	4	14	6	1	3	0	0
Haiti	23	96	164	12	60	98	9	42	69	23	79	119	9	42	70
Honduras	36	42	33	27	23	16	25	21	15	35	42	29	23	19	12
Jamaica	12	13	13	9	8	8	25	22	24	8	5	5	6	4	4
Mexico	34	60	56	2	10	9	0	1	1	34	60	56	1	3	3
Nicaragua	58	81	62	33	42	23	39	53	29	49	74	57	22	27	14
Panama	5	6	5	0	1	1	1	3	3	5	6	5	0	1	1
Paraguay	8	30	39	4	16	21	5	19	24	8	29	39	3	7	6
Peru	35	71	54	9	21	19	3	6	5	35	67	54	7	12	12
Saint Kitts and Nevis	0	0	1	0	0	1	2	15	86	0	0	0	-	0	-
Saint Lucia	1	3	3	0	1	2	11	63	93	1	1	3	0	0	1
Saint Vincent and the Grenadines	0	3	5	0	1	2	5	105	151	0	2	5	0	0	0

Direct aid to secondary education			Direct aid to post-secondary education			Education, level unspecified			Share of education in total ODA			Share of direct aid to education in sector-allocable ODA			Share of basic education in total aid to education		
Constant 2010 US$ millions			Constant 2010 US$ millions			Constant 2010 US$ millions			[%]			[%]			[%]		
2002–2003 annual average	2009	2010	2002–2003 annual average	2009	2010	2002–2003 annual average	2009	2010	2002–2003 annual average	2009	2010	2002–2003 annual average	2009	2010	2002–2003 annual average	2009	2010
0	0	5	6	1	2	3	29	17	19	38	33	25	43	35	28	50	41
21	114	45	75	75	61	23	104	177	7	13	12	16	14	13	30	40	49
0	0	0	3	2	3	6	2	2	34	14	23	34	17	25	33	27	23
2	7	7	15	7	11	2	22	18	10	13	13	10	14	14	28	44	53
4	2	2	12	33	40	2	4	3	8	13	23	35	13	23	5	6	4
0	0	0	0	0	0	0	15	1	18	25	2	10	27	2	47	50	50
0	0	0	1	0	0	0	31	0	18	25	0	7	26	0	48	50	68
0	1	1	5	9	9	1	2	2	10	7	8	16	15	12	49	60	62
-	-	-	0	0	0	0	2	2	0	10	11	1	11	11	46	46	43
-	0	0	1	1	0	2	0	-	41	17	12	63	14	7	45	32	39
0	0	0	1	0	0	0	0	0	13	9	3	7	4	3	46	48	70
7	1	9	25	4	13	29	28	19	18	13	13	19	14	14	45	71	58
5	6	2	21	12	10	5	37	12	3	7	7	8	7	5	23	48	58
1	0	4	4	4	4	5	4	7	22	16	18	22	18	20	36	40	54
1	0	1	2	3	3	2	1	4	7	7	7	7	7	5	29	76	60
2	2	2	28	29	29	4	6	7	4	13	9	8	15	10	6	10	13
6	3	7	7	5	4	2	18	20	8	15	13	7	16	13	22	47	41
1	1	1	3	2	2	2	1	1	22	15	12	24	16	12	27	36	52
0	0	1	1	1	1	1	0	0	17	9	19	18	9	27	36	21	13
5	2	4	5	4	3	6	4	6	33	12	17	36	13	17	20	38	43
10	21	60	64	150	100	22	82	15	8	13	9	10	11	8	29	40	40
73	**118**	**123**	**209**	**297**	**316**	**86**	**302**	**294**	**8**	**10**	**8**	**12**	**12**	**10**	**39**	**39**	**40**
1	*0*	*2*	*3*	*16*	*24*	*5*	*8*	*7*	*4*	*5*	*7*	*5*	*6*	*8*	*35*	*28*	*45*
-	0	0	0	0	0	0	0	0	2	10	13	2	10	3	39	11	47
1	3	3	16	15	17	3	13	10	18	24	23	29	25	23	11	28	26
-	-	-	-	-	-	-	-	-	...	...	...	...	...	...	...	...	...
-	-	-	0	0	0	-	0	0	4	4	2	5	4	3	-	18	29
0	0	0	0	0	0	0	1	1	4	5	7	5	6	7	55	48	49
15	18	18	7	10	8	15	22	32	8	10	9	14	11	11	63	47	44
4	4	6	34	54	65	4	32	32	10	16	13	19	17	14	9	22	19
1	1	2	12	18	17	2	8	8	21	28	15	23	29	19	8	20	24
3	8	6	23	38	34	6	10	15	4	7	7	5	8	8	15	25	26
0	1	0	3	5	4	0	3	4	6	7	6	8	7	7	10	27	31
1	1	1	7	7	5	0	3	1	16	11	7	19	13	7	25	20	24
0	0	-	0	0	0	-	0	0	7	4	7	4	1	1	29	49	50
3	3	3	2	3	2	2	17	34	10	17	22	16	18	24	67	52	53
5	7	5	10	13	10	2	43	17	6	26	15	8	28	15	17	40	36
2	2	21	3	3	4	2	11	14	4	8	12	7	8	13	37	58	35
0	1	1	0	0	0	-	0	0	2	17	14	2	12	7	-	42	40
6	7	5	6	8	4	4	13	16	9	10	10	12	11	12	50	47	61
6	0	-	1	0	0	4	6	1	19	5	1	25	4	1	35	50	48
1	9	8	7	9	30	6	19	10	12	5	4	17	10	11	52	63	60
2	4	8	2	10	4	8	9	5	8	9	6	15	10	5	76	56	49
0	0	0	0	1	0	2	1	0	11	7	7	12	4	4	74	61	64
6	5	4	25	38	35	2	15	14	15	23	9	16	24	9	5	16	17
3	17	14	13	7	17	12	22	13	9	11	10	14	11	10	56	52	37
3	2	0	1	3	2	0	1	1	11	8	3	14	8	3	9	19	27
1	3	2	2	2	1	2	17	30	8	14	23	14	14	23	48	53	53
6	21	9	18	20	18	5	14	14	5	10	7	9	11	7	25	30	36
-	0	0	0	0	0	0	0	0	1	5	12	1	5	1	28	39	48
0	0	1	0	0	0	0	0	1	4	8	8	4	3	9	34	46	61
0	0	1	0	0	0	0	1	4	5	12	35	7	9	36	25	48	41

Table 3 (continued)

| | Total aid to education | | | Total aid to basic education | | | Total aid to basic education per primary school-age child | | | Direct aid to education | | | Direct aid to basic education | | |
| | Constant 2010 US$ millions | | | Constant 2010 US$ millions | | | Constant 2010 US$ | | | Constant 2010 US$ millions | | | Constant 2010 US$ millions | | |
	2002–2003 annual average	2009	2010	2002–2003 annual average	2009	2010	2002–2003 annual average	2009	2010	2002–2003 annual average	2009	2010	2002–2003 annual average	2009	2010
Suriname	3	15	3	1	7	1	21	106	9	3	6	3	1	0	0
Trinidad and Tobago	1	1	1	0	0	-	0	1	-	1	1	1	-	0	0
Uruguay	3	7	8	1	2	3	2	7	11	3	7	8	0	0	1
Venezuela, B. R.	10	17	13	1	3	2	0	1	1	10	17	13	1	1	1
South and West Asia	**949**	**2 172**	**2 127**	**561**	**1 379**	**1 228**	**3**	**8**	**7**	**769**	**2 147**	**2 100**	**431**	**1 071**	**936**
Unallocated within the region	-	*2*	*8*	-	*0*	*6*	...	...	...	-	*2*	*8*	-	*0*	*6*
Afghanistan	42	290	398	25	165	273	6	31	50	34	280	391	15	110	226
Bangladesh	144	227	343	92	166	237	6	10	15	135	227	343	84	149	216
Bhutan	9	17	11	5	4	3	45	38	27	9	16	9	3	2	1
India	365	772	543	262	601	363	2	5	3	347	771	543	244	538	316
Iran, Islamic Republic of	58	63	62	1	1	1	0	0	0	58	63	62	1	0	1
Maldives	9	5	5	3	1	1	62	19	29	9	5	4	3	0	1
Nepal	58	171	141	36	129	70	10	35	19	55	171	132	24	111	44
Pakistan	214	568	541	122	291	254	6	14	13	78	556	532	46	148	119
Sri Lanka	51	56	76	17	21	20	11	12	12	44	56	76	12	13	6
Sub-Saharan Africa	**2 689**	**3 865**	**3 718**	**1 400**	**1 890**	**1 781**	**13**	**15**	**14**	**2 141**	**2 859**	**2 996**	**876**	**862**	**878**
Unallocated within the region	*87*	*160*	*220*	*61*	*93*	*145*	...	...	...	*86*	*134*	*200*	*48*	*65*	*117*
Angola	42	31	26	24	14	9	13	4	3	42	31	26	18	12	6
Benin	43	75	70	16	33	33	13	24	23	38	52	53	11	17	17
Botswana	3	24	35	0	9	17	1	30	58	3	24	35	0	0	0
Burkina Faso	87	180	132	52	101	74	24	40	27	61	131	89	34	47	42
Burundi	13	44	45	6	21	21	5	18	18	9	28	29	2	8	9
Cameroon	122	127	110	20	23	13	7	8	5	110	97	106	12	5	5
Cape Verde	37	41	41	4	2	4	60	36	59	34	38	34	2	0	0
Central African Republic	9	21	17	1	9	7	2	13	10	9	8	10	1	2	2
Chad	27	19	15	13	11	8	9	6	5	18	19	15	5	8	7
Comoros	13	12	15	4	3	4	46	27	35	13	8	12	4	0	0
Congo	26	19	21	2	3	4	5	4	6	26	18	21	1	2	3
Côte d'Ivoire	91	99	72	32	41	26	12	14	9	54	31	59	8	7	17
D. R. Congo	120	184	145	54	101	88	6	9	8	30	127	107	5	42	60
Equatorial Guinea	9	10	10	5	4	5	64	44	50	9	10	10	3	0	2
Eritrea	18	20	18	8	10	9	15	16	14	18	20	18	4	2	3
Ethiopia	103	360	308	55	185	156	5	14	12	79	326	275	30	48	37
Gabon	31	27	30	5	1	1	25	6	5	29	27	30	4	1	1
Gambia	9	9	7	6	5	3	26	19	10	8	5	7	4	2	2
Ghana	123	174	167	76	91	91	24	26	26	78	95	93	44	31	34
Guinea	45	38	38	26	10	7	19	7	4	41	37	38	22	7	3
Guinea-Bissau	10	16	22	4	7	10	20	33	43	10	9	18	4	4	1
Kenya	84	144	48	53	75	23	10	12	4	80	102	48	47	31	18
Lesotho	23	15	21	12	11	12	31	30	31	20	15	7	7	9	3
Liberia	3	27	50	2	22	37	4	37	59	3	23	46	2	19	28
Madagascar	81	52	51	35	25	23	15	9	8	64	52	51	20	24	19
Malawi	73	76	152	43	51	100	20	21	39	69	66	97	30	38	56
Mali	98	166	156	53	108	91	27	45	36	76	147	132	30	77	64
Mauritius	17	37	27	0	13	8	3	112	65	17	14	14	0	1	1
Mozambique	152	295	259	85	179	139	23	40	30	111	203	177	46	98	51
Namibia	26	29	21	13	18	9	37	47	23	26	29	21	11	13	2
Niger	55	43	48	28	26	14	14	10	5	34	40	46	8	19	9
Nigeria	35	133	165	16	43	72	1	2	3	34	133	165	12	20	25
Rwanda	60	114	104	27	60	38	19	38	24	43	81	79	5	34	13
Sao Tome and Principe	6	9	7	1	2	0	46	59	12	6	8	7	1	1	0
Senegal	115	181	172	37	65	62	22	34	32	110	150	158	20	26	30

Direct aid to secondary education (Constant 2010 US$ millions)			Direct aid to post-secondary education (Constant 2010 US$ millions)			Education, level unspecified (Constant 2010 US$ millions)			Share of education in total ODA (%)			Share of direct aid to education in sector-allocable ODA (%)			Share of basic education in total aid to education (%)		
2002–2003 annual average	2009	2010	2002–2003 annual average	2009	2010	2002–2003 annual average	2009	2010	2002–2003 annual average	2009	2010	2002–2003 annual average	2009	2010	2002–2003 annual average	2009	2010
0	-	-	1	2	2	0	4	1	7	10	3	7	6	3	42	43	18
0	-	0	1	1	1	0	0	-	16	16	13	16	18	15	1	9	-
0	1	1	2	2	2	1	3	5	20	10	13	23	13	13	16	29	41
1	2	1	8	10	8	1	5	3	13	31	28	17	33	30	9	18	18
53	**125**	**196**	**205**	**359**	**410**	**80**	**593**	**558**	**8**	**13**	**11**	**12**	**15**	**13**	**59**	**64**	**58**
-	*0*	*0*	-	*1*	*1*	-	*0*	*0*	...	*1*	*8*	...	*3*	*15*	...	*20*	*80*
1	24	27	6	46	51	12	100	87	3	5	6	5	6	7	60	57	69
23	26	58	21	18	27	7	35	41	10	15	17	12	18	19	64	73	69
1	8	4	1	3	3	3	2	1	15	17	8	17	18	8	53	23	25
13	39	47	73	70	85	18	124	95	11	18	12	13	18	12	72	78	67
1	1	2	56	60	58	0	2	1	40	64	52	59	74	68	1	2	2
2	3	1	3	1	2	1	1	1	40	11	4	57	18	5	37	16	24
3	3	19	9	20	27	20	38	42	12	22	15	14	26	16	61	75	50
1	6	18	15	128	134	16	275	261	6	19	15	7	25	25	57	51	47
7	14	20	22	13	22	3	17	29	7	5	7	11	7	9	33	37	26
131	**258**	**355**	**635**	**688**	**678**	**499**	**1 051**	**1 084**	**10**	**9**	**8**	**15**	**10**	**10**	**52**	**49**	**48**
3	*5*	*9*	*9*	*33*	*39*	*26*	*31*	*35*	*5*	*3*	*6*	*8*	*4*	*7*	*71*	*58*	*66*
1	9	8	11	6	5	12	5	8	8	11	9	19	11	9	57	45	36
3	3	3	19	22	17	4	10	15	12	11	10	16	10	9	36	44	47
1	4	0	1	2	0	1	18	34	6	9	21	8	9	22	14	38	49
7	5	5	10	18	21	11	60	21	13	17	13	15	18	12	60	56	56
0	6	7	3	4	5	4	11	8	5	2	7	8	8	6	43	48	47
2	3	4	93	84	84	3	5	14	11	17	17	33	24	23	16	18	12
3	12	13	27	25	20	2	1	0	27	20	12	31	22	13	12	6	9
1	1	1	7	3	4	1	1	2	13	2	6	18	6	8	12	43	40
1	1	1	5	5	4	7	6	3	8	3	3	7	8	7	47	56	55
1	0	0	8	6	7	0	2	4	36	21	21	40	30	24	31	25	27
0	2	3	22	14	14	3	1	1	24	6	1	43	23	18	9	13	17
2	4	15	34	19	20	10	2	7	8	4	8	18	6	10	35	42	37
4	8	13	14	17	15	8	60	19	3	7	2	5	9	8	45	55	61
1	0	1	1	1	1	4	8	6	28	29	11	35	33	32	49	43	49
3	1	1	3	1	1	7	16	12	6	16	12	11	22	15	45	49	52
4	10	17	17	27	16	28	242	204	6	9	9	8	12	12	54	51	51
2	3	4	22	22	24	1	0	0	20	25	23	40	36	26	17	4	3
1	1	3	1	1	0	1	2	2	13	8	7	14	6	7	63	56	40
2	7	7	12	16	12	19	40	40	11	10	10	13	8	7	62	52	54
4	2	2	11	23	27	3	6	6	13	15	16	18	21	18	58	27	17
1	2	1	5	3	2	0	1	14	7	10	7	17	9	18	41	46	45
5	7	5	21	18	14	7	45	12	13	7	3	16	8	3	62	52	48
5	0	1	2	0	0	6	5	3	21	11	8	23	12	4	50	78	56
0	2	3	0	0	1	1	1	14	3	5	3	15	7	11	70	81	74
2	4	4	29	22	20	13	2	7	12	12	11	15	14	13	44	48	45
16	8	4	2	5	5	22	15	33	13	10	15	17	10	15	58	66	66
6	9	20	17	18	19	23	43	30	14	17	14	16	18	15	54	65	58
-	2	2	16	10	10	0	0	0	35	22	18	37	26	17	2	36	29
4	12	14	25	24	18	36	69	93	7	15	13	11	15	13	56	61	54
7	4	4	4	2	1	4	10	14	18	10	8	20	10	8	51	62	42
3	3	2	4	8	26	19	11	9	11	9	7	13	11	10	51	60	30
2	14	16	12	52	30	8	47	95	9	8	8	10	8	8	47	33	44
5	14	7	7	13	33	25	20	26	13	12	10	16	11	9	44	53	37
1	1	2	3	5	4	0	2	0	14	31	15	19	34	24	18	21	4
3	19	18	58	57	60	29	47	50	17	18	18	21	19	20	32	36	36

ANNEX

Table 3 (continued)

	Total aid to education (Constant 2010 US$ millions)			Total aid to basic education (Constant 2010 US$ millions)			Total aid to basic education per primary school-age child (Constant 2010 US$)			Direct aid to education (Constant 2010 US$ millions)			Direct aid to basic education (Constant 2010 US$ millions)		
	2002–2003 annual average	2009	2010	2002–2003 annual average	2009	2010	2002–2003 annual average	2009	2010	2002–2003 annual average	2009	2010	2002–2003 annual average	2009	2010
Seychelles	1	3	5	0	1	2	50	182	307	1	1	1	-	0	0
Sierra Leone	23	36	35	14	25	17	20	27	18	11	20	18	7	16	4
Somalia	4	27	37	3	23	28	3	16	18	4	27	36	3	23	23
South Africa	114	73	108	52	32	67	7	5	10	114	73	108	42	24	57
Swaziland	3	6	12	2	4	7	7	18	34	3	6	12	0	2	5
Togo	15	30	33	1	11	13	2	12	14	15	19	17	1	4	4
Uganda	211	127	188	148	58	84	27	9	12	182	102	161	104	26	54
U. R. Tanzania	284	338	323	217	147	129	32	18	16	216	152	233	170	24	26
Zambia	127	194	109	79	102	59	39	41	23	87	101	57	43	19	13
Zimbabwe	13	21	21	6	10	11	2	5	5	13	21	21	4	5	5
Overseas territories[1]	237	402	491	118	166	229	...	...	...	233	397	485	1	99	126
Anguilla (UK)	1	0	0	0	0	0	74	...	...	1	0	0	-	0	-
Mayotte (France)	167	330	420	83	142	204	...	...	...	167	330	416	-	87	114
Montserrat (UK)	4	1	1	2	0	0	5 577	...	...	0	1	1	-	0	-
Saint Helena (UK)	0	4	1	0	2	0	...	...	...	0	1	1	-	-	-
Tokelau (New Zealand)	5	2	2	2	1	1	11 215	5 774	5 282	4	0	1	0	-	0
Turks and Caicos Islands (UK)	0	-	-	0	-	-	413	...	...	0	-	-	0	-	-
Wallis and Futuna (France)	59	65	67	30	21	23	...	...	...	59	65	67	-	12	12
Unallocated by region or country	*525*	*988*	*1 281*	*81*	*329*	*556*	...	...	...	*524*	*988*	*1 258*	*43*	*281*	*458*
Total	**7 616**	**13 425**	**13 468**	**2 939**	**5 791**	**5 789**	**5**	**10**	**10**	**6 571**	**11 955**	**12 313**	**1 789**	**3 483**	**3 680**
Low income countries	2 002	3 386	3 528	1 154	1 899	1 913	11	17	17	1 562	2 697	2 941	747	1 081	1 160
Lower middle income countries	2 933	5 550	5 054	1 205	2 704	2 315	5	10	8	2 491	4 933	4 589	787	1 668	1 420
Upper middle income countries	1 917	3 079	3 080	381	714	759	2	4	4	1 764	2 947	3 017	153	367	448
High income countries	28	34	33	6	7	8	1	2	2	28	34	31	3	1	2
Unallocated by income	735	1 377	1 773	193	467	793	...	...	...	726	1 344	1 735	99	366	650
Total	**7 616**	**13 425**	**13 468**	**2 939**	**5 791**	**5 789**	**5**	**10**	**10**	**6 571**	**11 955**	**12 313**	**1 789**	**3 483**	**3 680**
Arab States	1 056	1 983	1 824	211	853	779	6	23	21	920	1 860	1 764	106	600	613
Central and Eastern Europe	325	496	537	85	60	75	8	6	8	290	481	488	41	25	21
Central Asia	139	231	311	40	57	93	6	10	17	102	212	272	16	33	49
East Asia and the Pacific	1 147	2 305	2 140	231	671	636	1	4	4	1 065	2 092	1 989	116	310	371
Latin America and the Carribbean	547	983	1 039	212	385	413	4	7	7	526	920	960	159	203	227
South and West Asia	949	2 172	2 127	561	1 379	1 228	3	8	7	769	2 147	2 100	431	1 071	936
Sub-Saharan Africa	2 689	3 865	3 718	1 400	1 890	1 781	13	15	14	2 141	2 859	2 996	876	862	878
Overseas territories	237	402	491	118	166	229	...	...	...	233	397	485	1	99	126
Unallocated by region or country	525	988	1 281	81	329	556	...	...	...	524	988	1 258	43	281	458
Total	**7 616**	**13 425**	**13 468**	**2 939**	**5 791**	**5 789**	**5**	**10**	**10**	**6 571**	**11 955**	**12 313**	**1 789**	**3 483**	**3 680**

Notes:
1. As defined on the OECD-DAC list of ODA recipients.
(...) indicates that data are not available, (-) represents a nil value.
The share of education in total ODA does not match that in Table 2 because the DAC database is used for donors and the CRS database for recipients in total ODA figures.
Malta and Slovenia are not listed in the table because they were removed from the OECD-DAC list of ODA recipients in 2005. However, the aid they received in 2002–2003 is included in the totals.
The classification by income is based on the World Bank list as of July 2011.
All data represent gross disbursements.
Source: OECD-DAC database (2012a, 2012b).

Table 3

Direct aid to secondary education			Direct aid to post-secondary education			Education, level unspecified			Share of education in total ODA (%)			Share of direct aid to education in sector-allocable ODA (%)			Share of basic education in total aid to education (%)		
Constant 2010 US$ millions			Constant 2010 US$ millions			Constant 2010 US$ millions												
2002–2003 annual average	2009	2010	2002–2003 annual average	2009	2010	2002–2003 annual average	2009	2010	2002–2003 annual average	2009	2010	2002–2003 annual average	2009	2010	2002–2003 annual average	2009	2010
0	-	-	0	0	1	1	0	0	18	11	7	18	4	9	37	50	45
1	1	4	1	1	1	2	2	9	5	8	8	6	6	5	61	69	48
-	3	2	0	0	2	1	0	9	2	4	8	9	16	16	78	87	76
9	11	10	43	21	21	21	17	19	22	7	10	25	7	10	46	45	62
0	0	2	0	0	0	3	3	5	10	9	12	14	9	13	46	67	60
0	2	1	13	10	10	1	2	2	19	6	6	27	11	11	8	37	40
6	17	60	13	20	15	59	40	31	19	7	11	25	7	11	70	45	45
7	28	51	14	40	38	25	60	118	15	12	11	21	8	10	76	44	40
4	4	2	8	6	3	31	72	39	10	15	12	15	14	9	62	52	54
0	0	1	5	5	3	4	12	12	6	3	3	10	6	4	44	49	53
1	168	158	1	1	2	230	129	200	65	54	58	69	56	60	50	41	47
0	-	-	0	0	0	0	0	0	22	2	2	22	2	2	18	19	0
-	132	125	0	0	0	167	111	176	76	63	69	77	63	70	50	43	49
-	0	0	0	1	0	-0	0	0	10	2	2	1	2	2	52	8	9
0	0	0	-	0	0	0	1	0	7	10	2	7	4	2	6	49	19
-	-	-	0	0	1	3	0	-	52	17	14	67	10	8	49	46	38
-	-	-	-	-	-	-	-	-	19	...	...	19	...	...	100	...	...
-	36	32	0	0	1	59	17	23	75	57	52	75	57	54	50	32	35
13	*68*	*48*	*394*	*542*	*581*	*74*	*98*	*171*	*5*	*4*	*4*	*11*	*7*	*8*	*15*	*33*	*43*
463	1 212	1 279	3 064	4 115	4 290	1 256	3 147	3 064	9	10	9	15	12	12	39	43	43
115	227	363	325	442	498	375	947	919	9	9	8	13	11	10	58	56	54
187	496	530	1 123	1 313	1 313	394	1 456	1 327	9	12	11	15	14	12	41	49	46
138	351	282	1 171	1 667	1 727	303	562	560	13	18	18	20	19	19	20	23	25
3	1	2	17	20	18	5	12	9	15	7	11	20	8	13	20	19	24
20	136	102	428	673	734	180	169	249	5	4	5	11	7	8	26	34	45
463	1 212	1 279	3 064	4 115	4 290	1 256	3 147	3 064	9	10	9	15	12	12	39	43	43
61	202	128	679	676	751	74	382	271	14	13	13	22	16	15	20	43	43
31	36	37	165	365	371	54	54	58	7	10	10	12	10	10	26	12	14
8	33	47	67	118	127	11	29	48	7	7	11	8	8	11	29	25	30
92	204	186	709	1 068	1 053	147	510	379	10	15	14	16	16	14	20	29	30
73	118	123	209	297	316	86	302	294	8	10	8	12	12	10	39	39	40
53	125	196	205	359	410	80	593	558	8	13	11	12	15	13	59	64	58
131	258	355	635	688	678	499	1 051	1 084	10	9	8	15	10	10	52	49	48
1	168	158	1	1	2	230	129	200	65	54	58	69	56	60	50	41	47
13	68	48	394	542	581	74	98	171	5	4	4	11	7	8	15	33	43
463	1 212	1 279	3 064	4 115	4 290	1 256	3 147	3 064	9	10	9	15	12	12	39	43	43

Glossary

Adult literacy rate. Number of literate persons aged 15 and above, expressed as a percentage of the total population in that age group.

Age-specific enrolment ratio (ASER). Enrolment of a given age or age group, regardless of the level of education in which pupils or students are enrolled, expressed as a percentage of the population of the same age or age group.

Child or under-5 mortality rate. Probability of dying between birth and the fifth birthday, expressed per 1,000 live births.

Constant prices. Prices of a particular item adjusted to remove the overall effect of general price changes (inflation) since a given baseline year.

Dropout rate by grade. Percentage of students who drop out of a given grade in a given school year.

Early childhood care and education (ECCE). Services and programmes that support children's survival, growth, development and learning – including health, nutrition and hygiene, and cognitive, social, emotional and physical development – from birth to entry into primary school.

EFA Development Index (EDI). Composite index aimed at measuring overall progress towards EFA. At present, the EDI incorporates four of the most easily quantifiable EFA goals – universal primary education as measured by the primary adjusted net enrolment ratio; adult literacy as measured by the adult literacy rate; gender parity as measured by the gender-specific EFA index; and quality of education as measured by the survival rate to grade 5. Its value is the arithmetic mean of the observed values of these four indicators.

Gender parity index (GPI). Ratio of female to male values of a given indicator. A GPI between 0.97 and 1.03 indicates parity between the genders. A GPI below 0.97 indicates a disparity in favour of males. A GPI above 1.03 indicates a disparity in favour of females.

Gross domestic product (GDP). The value of all final goods and services produced in a country in one year (see also Gross national product).

Gross enrolment ratio (GER). Total enrolment in a specific level of education, regardless of age, expressed as a percentage of the population in the official age group corresponding to this level of education. The GER can exceed 100% because of early or late entry and/or grade repetition.

Gross intake rate (GIR). Total number of new entrants to a given grade of primary education, regardless of age, expressed as a percentage of the population at the official school entrance age for that grade.

Gross national income (GNI). The value of all final goods and services produced in a country in one year (gross domestic product) plus income that residents have received from abroad, minus income claimed by non-residents.

Gross national product (GNP). Former denomination of gross national income.

Infant mortality rate. Probability of dying between birth and the first birthday, expressed as deaths per 1,000 live births.

International Standard Classification of Education (ISCED). Classification system designed to serve as an instrument for assembling, compiling and presenting comparable indicators and statistics of education both within countries and internationally. The system, introduced in 1976, was revised in 1997 and 2011.

Literacy. According to UNESCO's 1958 definition, the term refers to the ability of an individual to read and write with understanding a simple short statement related to his/her everyday life. The concept of literacy has since evolved to embrace several skill domains, each conceived on a scale of different mastery levels and serving different purposes.

Net attendance rate (NAR). Number of pupils in the official age group for a given level of education who attend school at that level, expressed as a percentage of the population in that age group.

Net enrolment ratio (NER). Enrolment of the official age group for a given level of education, expressed as a percentage of the population in that age group.

Net intake rate (NIR). New entrants to the first grade of primary education who are of the official primary school entrance age, expressed as a percentage of the population of that age.

New entrants. Pupils entering a given level of education for the first time; the difference between enrolment and repeaters in the first grade of the level.

Out-of-school adolescents. Those of lower secondary school age who are not enrolled in either primary or secondary school.

Out-of-school children. Children in the official primary school age range who are not enrolled in either primary or secondary school.

Pre-primary education (ISCED level 0). Programmes at the initial stage of organized instruction, primarily designed to introduce very young children, aged at least 3 years, to a school-type environment and provide a bridge between home and school. Variously referred to as infant education, nursery education, pre-school education, kindergarten or early childhood education, such programmes are the more formal component of ECCE. Upon completion of these programmes, children continue their education at ISCED 1 (primary education).

Primary adjusted net enrolment ratio (ANER). Enrolment of children of the official primary school age group in either primary or secondary schools, expressed as a percentage of the population in that age group.

Primary cohort completion rate. Proxy measure of primary school completion. It focuses on children who have access to school, measuring how many successfully complete it. The primary cohort completion rate is the product of the survival rate to the last grade and the percentage of those in the last grade who successfully graduate.

Primary education (ISCED level 1). Programmes generally designed to give pupils a sound basic education in reading, writing and mathematics, and an elementary understanding of subjects such as history, geography, natural sciences, social sciences, art and music.

Private institutions. Institutions that are not operated by public authorities but are controlled and managed, whether for profit or not, by private bodies such as non-governmental organizations, religious bodies, special interest groups, foundations or business enterprises.

Public expenditure on education. Total current and capital expenditure on education by local, regional and national governments, including municipalities. Household contributions are excluded. The term covers public expenditure for both public and private institutions.

Pupil/teacher ratio (PTR). Average number of pupils per teacher at a specific level of education.

Purchasing power parity (PPP). An exchange rate adjustment that accounts for price differences between countries, allowing international comparisons of real output and income.

Repetition rate by grade. Number of repeaters in a given grade in a given school year, expressed as a percentage of enrolment in that grade the previous school year.

School age population. Population of the age group officially corresponding to a given level of education, whether enrolled in school or not.

School life expectancy (SLE). Number of years a child of school entrance age is expected to spend in school or university, including years spent on repetition. It is the sum of the age-specific enrolment ratios for primary, secondary, post-secondary non-tertiary and tertiary education. A school life expectancy can be calculated for each level of education, including pre-primary education.

Secondary education (ISCED levels 2 and 3). Programme made up of two stages: lower and upper secondary. Lower secondary education (ISCED 2) is generally designed to continue the basic programmes of the primary level but the teaching is typically more subject-focused, requiring more specialized teachers for each subject area. The end of this level often coincides with the end of compulsory education. In upper secondary education (ISCED.3), the final stage of secondary education in most countries, instruction is often organized even more along subject lines and teachers typically need a higher or more subject-specific qualification than at ISCED level 2.

Stunting rate. Proportion of children in a given age group whose height for their age is between two and three standard deviations (moderate stunting) or three or more standard deviations (severe stunting) below the reference median established by the National Center for Health Statistics and the World Health Organization. Low height for age is a basic indicator of malnutrition.

Survival rate by grade. Percentage of a cohort of students who are enrolled in the first grade of an education cycle in a given school year and are expected to reach a specified grade, regardless of repetition.

Technical and vocational education and training (TVET). Programmes designed mainly to prepare students for direct entry into a particular occupation or trade (or class of occupations or trades).

Tertiary or higher education (ISCED levels 5 and 6). Programmes with an educational content more advanced than what is offered at ISCED levels 3 and 4. The first stage of tertiary education, ISCED level 5, includes level 5A, composed of largely theoretically based programmes intended to provide sufficient qualifications for gaining entry to advanced research programmes and professions with high skill requirements;

and level 5B, where programmes are generally more practical, technical and/or occupationally specific. The second stage of tertiary education, ISCED level 6, comprises programmes devoted to advanced study and original research, and leading to the award of an advanced research qualification.

Transition rate to secondary education. New entrants to the first grade of secondary education in a given year, expressed as a percentage of the number of pupils enrolled in the final grade of primary education in the previous year. The indicator measures transition to secondary general education only.

Youth literacy rate. Number of literate persons aged 15 to 24, expressed as a percentage of the total population in that age group.

Abbreviations

AIDS   Acquired immunodeficiency syndrome

ALL   Adult Literacy and Life Skills

ANER   Adjusted net enrolment ratio

BCG   Bacillus Calmette-Guérin (tuberculosis vaccine)

BRAC   (formerly) Bangladesh Rural Advancement Committee

BRICS   Brazil, Russia, India, China, South Africa

CEI   Centro de Educación Inicial (Peru)

CRS   Creditor Reporting System (OECD)

DAC   Development Assistance Committee (OECD)

DFID   Department for International Development (United Kingdom)

DPT3   Diphtheria toxoid, tetanus toxoid and pertussis vaccine (third dose)

ECCE   Early childhood care and education

EDI   EFA Development Index

EFA   Education for All

EITI   Extractive Industries Transparency Initiative

EPDC   Education Policy and Data Center

EU   European Union

Eurostat   European statistics

F/M   Female/male

FTI   Fast Track Initiative

G8   Group of Eight (Canada, France, Germany, Italy, Japan, the Russian Federation, the United Kingdom and the United States, plus EU representatives)

G20   Group of Twenty Finance Ministers and Central Bank Governors

GALP   Global Age-Specific Literacy Projections Model

GAVI   Global Alliance for Vaccines and Immunisation

GDP   Gross domestic product

GEI   Gender-specific EFA Index

GER   Gross enrolment ratio

GIR   Gross intake rate

GNI   Gross national income

GNP   Gross national product

GPI   Gender parity index

HepB3   Hepatitis B vaccine (third dose)

HIV   Human immunodeficiency virus

IBE	International Bureau of Education (UNESCO)
ICT	Information and communication technology
IDA	International Development Association (World Bank)
IDS	International Development Statistics (OECD)
IIEP	International Institute for Educational Planning (UNESCO)
ILO	International Labour Office/Organization
IMF	International Monetary Fund
ISCED	International Standard Classification of Education
IT	Information technology
LAMP	Literacy Assessment and Monitoring Programme (UIS)
MDG	Millennium Development Goal
NER	Net enrolment ratio
NGO	Non-government organization
NIR	Net intake rate
NSDC	National Skill Development Corporation (India)
ODA	Official development assistance
OECD	Organisation for Economic Co-operation and Development
OREALC	UNESCO Regional Bureau of Education for Latin America and the Caribbean
PASEC	Programme on the Analysis of Education Systems of the CONFEMEN (Conference of Education Ministers of Countries Using French as a Common Language)
PIACC	Programme for the International Assessment of Adult Competencies (OECD)
PIRLS	Progress in International Reading Literacy Study
PISA	Programme for International Student Assessment (OECD)
Polio3	Polio vaccine (third dose)
PPP	Purchasing power parity
PROJoven	Programa de Capacitación Laboral Juvenil/Youth Labour Training Programme (Peru)
PRONOEI	Programa no Escolarizados de Educación Inicia (Peru)
SACMEQ	Southern and Eastern Africa Consortium for Monitoring Educational Quality
SENA	Servicio Nacional de Aprendizaje (Colombia)
SENAI	Serviço Nacional de Aprendizagem Industrial (Brazil)
SERCE	Segundo Estudio Regional Comparativo y Explicativo
SEWA	Self-Employed Women's Association (India)
STEP	Skills Toward Employment and Productivity (World Bank)
SYEP	Summer Youth Employment Program (New York City)
TIMSS	Trends in International Mathematics and Science Study
TREE	Training for Rural Economic Empowerment (ILO)
TVE(T)	Technical and vocational education (and training)

UIL	UNESCO Institute for Lifelong Learning
UIS	UNESCO Institute for Statistics
UK	United Kingdom of Great Britain and Northern Ireland
UN	United Nations
UNAIDS	Joint United Nations Programme on HIV/AIDS
UNDP	United Nations Development Programme
UNESCO	United Nations Educational, Scientific and Cultural Organization
UNGASS	United Nations General Assembly Special Session
UN-HABITAT	United Nations Human Settlements Programme
UNHCR	United Nations High Commissioner for Refugees (Office of the)
UNICEF	United Nations Children's Fund
UNPD	United Nations Population Division
UNRWA	United Nations Relief and Works Agency for Palestine Refugees in the Near East
UOE	UIS/OECD/Eurostat
UPE	Universal Primary Education
US	United States of America
USAID	United States Agency for International Development
WEI	World Education Indicators (UNESCO)
WFP	World Food Programme (United Nations)
WHO	World Health Organization (United Nations)
YAIP	Young Adult Internship Program (New York City)

References*

Part I. Monitoring progress towards the EFA goals

Abadzi, H. 2010. *Reading Fluency Measurements in EFA FTI Partner Countries: Outcomes and Improvement Prospects (Update December 2010)*. Washington, DC, Education for All Fast Track Initiative Secretariat. (Working Paper Series.)

Aboud, F. E. and Hossain, K. 2011. The impact of preprimary school on primary school achievement in Bangladesh. *Early Childhood Research Quarterly,* Vol. 26, No. 2, pp. 237–46.

ABS and AIHW. 2011. *The Health and Welfare of Australia's Aboriginal and Torres Strait Islander Peoples*. Canberra, Australian Bureau of Statistics/Australian Institute of Health and Welfare. http://www.abs.gov.au/AUSSTATS/abs@.nsfookup/4704.0Main+Features1Oct%202010?OpenDocument (Accessed 24 January 2012.)

ACCES. 2011. *Evidence-Based Answers*. Tempe, AZ, American Council for CoEducational Schooling, School of Social and Family Dynamics, Arizona State University. http://lives.clas.asu.edu/acces/faq.html (Accessed 18 May 2012.)

Acosta, A. M. 2011. *Analysing Success in the Fight Against Malnutrition in Peru*. Brighton, United Kingdom, Institute of Development Studies. (Working Paper, 367.)

ActionAid. 2011. *Real Aid: Ending Aid Dependency*. London, ActionAid.

___. 2012. *How Tax Dodging Affects Rwanda*. London, ActionAid. http://www.actionaid.org.uk/102040/the_rwanda_revenue_authority.html (Accessed 17 July 2012.)

ADB. 2010. *Report and Recommendation of the President to the Board of Directors: Proposed Loan, Technical Assistance Grant, and Administration of Technical Assistance Grant, Republic of the Philippines: Social Protection Support Project*. Manila, Asian Development Bank.

Ade, A., Gupta, S., Maliye, C., Deshmukh, P. and Garg, B. 2010. Effect of improvement of pre-school education through *Anganwadi* center on intelligence and development quotient of children. *Indian Journal of Pediatrics,* Vol. 77, No. 5, pp. 541–46.

Akaguri, L. and Akyeampong, K. 2010. *Public and Private Schooling in Rural Ghana: Are the Poor Being Served?* Brighton, United Kingdom, Consortium for Research on Educational Access, Transitions and Equity, University of Sussex. (CREATE Ghana Policy Brief, 3.)

Akyeampong, K. 2003. *Teacher Training in Ghana – Does it Count? Multi-Site Teacher Education Research Project (MUSTER). Country Report One*. London, United Kingdom, Department for International Development. (Educational Papers.)

___. 2011. *(Re)Assessing the Impact of School Capitation Grants on Educational Access in Ghana*. Brighton, United Kingdom, Consortium for Research on Educational Access, Transitions and Equity, University of Sussex. (CREATE Pathways to Access Research Monograph, 71.)

Akyeampong, K., Pryor, J., Westbrook, J. and Lussier, K. 2011. *Teacher Preparation and Continuing Professional Development in Africa: Learning to Teach Early Reading and Mathematics*. Brighton, United Kingdom, Centre for International Education, University of Sussex.

Altinok, N. 2012a. A new international database on the distribution of student achievement. Background paper for *EFA Global Monitoring Report 2012*.

___. 2012b. Performance differences between subpopulations in PISA 2009+. Background paper for *EFA Global Monitoring Report 2012*.

American Red Cross. 2010. *Together We Can: Youth HIV Prevention Peer Education Program*. Washington, DC, American National Red Cross. (Fact Sheet.)

___. 2012. *Together We Can*. Washington, DC, American National Red Cross. http://www.redcross.org/portal/site/en/menuitem.d229a5f06620c6052b1ecfbf43181aa0/?vgnextoid=5ded9891353ab110VgnVCM10000089f0870aRCRD&cpsextcurrchannel=1 (Accessed 6 February 2012.)

ANLCI. 2008. *Illiteracy: The Statistics — Analysis by the National Agency to Fight Illiteracy of the IVQ Survey Conducted in 2004–2005 by INSEE*. Lyon, Agence nationale de lutte contre l'illettrisme.

Antoninis, M. and Mia, A. 2011. Bangladesh Country Study — Global Initiative on Out-of-School Children. Dhaka, UNICEF Bangladesh. (Unpublished.)

*All background papers for *EFA Global Monitoring Reports* are available at www.efareport.unesco.org

Armenia Government. 2008. *Strategic Program for 2008–2015 Reforms in Preschool Education of the Republic of Armenia*. Yerevan, Government of the Republic of Armenia.

Arnold, C., Bartlett, K., Gowani, S. and Merali, R. 2006. Is everybody ready? Readiness, transition and continuity: lessons, reflections and moving forward. Background paper for *EFA Global Monitoring Report 2007*.

Asadullah, M. N. and Chaudhury, N. 2009. Reverse gender gap in schooling in Bangladesh: insights from urban and rural households. *Journal of Development Studies,* Vol. 45, No. 8, pp. 1360–80.

Attanasio, O., Meghir, C. and Santiago, A. 2012. Education choices in Mexico: using a structural model and a randomized experiment to evaluate Progresa. *Review of Economic Studies,* Vol. 79, No. 1, pp. 37–66.

Auty, R. 2006. Mining enclave to economic catalyst: large mineral projects in developing countries. *Brown Journal of World Affairs,* Vol. 13, No. 1, pp. 135–45.

Avenstrup, R., Liang, X. and Nellemann, S. 2004. *Kenya, Lesotho, Malawi and Uganda: Universal Primary Education and Poverty Reduction*. Washington, DC, World Bank.

Aviva. 2011. *Corporate Responsibility Report*. London, Aviva.

Ayogu, M. and Lewis, Z. 2011. Conflict minerals: an assessment of the Dodd-Frank Act. *Opinion,* Washington, DC, Brookings Institution, 3 October. http://www.brookings.edu/opinions/2011/1003_conflict_minerals_ayogu. aspx (Accessed 25 July 2012.)

Ayyar, R. and Bashir, S. 2004. District Primary Education Programme. *Journal of Educational Planning and Administration,* Vol. 19, No. 1, pp. 49–65.

Azam, M. and Kingdon, G. G. 2011. *Are Girls the Fairer Sex in India? Revisiting Intra-household Allocation of Education Expenditure*. London, Department of Quantitative Social Science, Institute of Education. (DoQSS Working Paper, 11-03.)

Azim Premji Foundation. 2012. *Azim Premji Foundation*. Bangalore, India, Azim Premji Foundation. http://www.azimpremjifoundation.org/ (Accessed 1 May 2012.)

Baer, J., Kutner, M. and Sabatini, J. 2009. *Basic Reading Skills and the Literacy of America's Least Literate Adults — Results from the 2003 National Assessment of Adult Literacy (NAAL) Supplemental Studies*. Washington, DC, National Center for Education Statistics, Institute of Education Sciences/US Department of Education. (NCES 2009–481.)

Bajaj, V. 2011. Skipping rote memorization in Indian schools. *New York Times,* 17 February 2011.

Bakaroudis, M. 2011. Sister 2 Sister Initiative: Life Skills PLUS Extracurricular Peer Educator Training Package for Young Women 15–19 Years Old in Malawi. Lilongwe. (Debrief Presentation of Consultancy Mission and Summary of Proof of Concept Validation Study; Unpublished.)

Banco Santander. 2012. *Sustainability Report*. Madrid, Banco Santander.

Banerjee, A., Banerji, R., Duflo, E. and Walton, M. 2012. *Read India: Helping Primary School Students in India Acquire Basic Reading and Math Skills*. Boston, MA, Abdul Latif Jameel Poverty Action Lab, Massachusetts Institute of Technology. http://www.povertyactionlab.org/evaluation/read-india-helping-primary-school-students-india-acquire-basic-reading-and-math-skills (Accessed 29 February 2012.)

Bangladesh Ministry of Education. 2010. *National Education Policy 2010*. Dhaka, Ministry of Education.

Bangladesh NIPORT. 2010. *Bangladesh Demographic and Health Survey 2011 – Preliminary Report*. Dhaka/Calverton, MD, National Institute of Population Research and Training/Mitra and Associates/ICF International.

Barma, N. H., Kaiser, K., Le, T. M. and Vinuela, L. 2012. *Rents to Riches? The Political Economy of Natural Resource-led Development*. Washington, DC, World Bank.

Barrera-Osorio, F., Bertrand, M., Linden, L. L. and Perez-Calle, F. 2011. Improving the design of conditional transfer programs: evidence from a randomized education experiment in Colombia. *American Economic Journal: Applied Economics,* Vol. 3, No. 2, pp. 167–95.

Bathmaker, A.-M. 2007. The impact of Skills for Life on adult basic skills in England: how should we interpret trends in participation and achievement? *International Journal of Lifelong Education,* Vol. 26, No. 3, pp. 295–313.

Beltrán, A. C. and Seinfeld, J. N. 2010. *La heterogeneidad del impacto de la educación inicial sobre el rendimiento escolar en el Perú [The Heterogeneity of the Impact of Preschool on School Performance in Peru]*. Lima, Centro de Investigación de la Universidad del Pacífico.

Bennell, P. 2011. A UPE15 emergency programme for primary school teachers. Background paper for *EFA Global Monitoring Report 2012*.

Bennell, P. and Akyeampong, K. 2007. *Teacher Motivation in Sub-Saharan Africa and South Asia*. London, United Kingdom Department for International Development. (Researching the Issues, 71.)

Berlinski, S., Galiani, S. and Gertler, P. 2009. The effect of pre-primary education on primary school performance. *Journal of Public Economics,* Vol. 93, No. 1–2, pp. 219–34.

Berlinski, S., Galiani, S. and Manacorda, M. 2008. Giving children a better start: preschool attendance and school-age profiles. *Journal of Public Economics,* Vol. 92, No. 5–6, pp. 1416–40.

Bhutta, Z. A., Ahmed, T., Black, R. E., Cousens, S., Dewey, K., Giugliani, E., Haider, B. A., Kirkwood, B., Morris, S. S., Sachdev, H. P. S. and Shekar, M. 2008. What works? Interventions for maternal and child undernutrition and survival. *The Lancet,* Vol. 371, No. 9610, pp. 417–40.

Biersteker, L. 2010. *Scaling-Up Early Child Development in South Africa: Introducing a Reception Year (Grade R) for Children Aged Five Years as the First Year of Schooling.* Washington, DC, Brookings Institution.

Biersteker, L., Ngaruiya, S., Sebatane, E. and Gudyanga, S. 2008. Introducing preprimary classes in Africa: opportunities and challenges. Garcia, M., Pence, A. and Evans, J. L. (eds), *Africa's Future, Africa's Challenge: Early Childhood Care and Development in Sub-Saharan Africa.* Washington, DC, World Bank, pp. 227–48.

Birdsall, N. and Perakis, R. 2012. *Cash on Delivery: Implementation of a Pilot in Ethiopia.* Washington, DC, Center for Global Development.

Blössner, M. and de Onis, M. 2005. *Malnutrition: Quantifying the Health Impact at National and Local Levels.* Geneva, Switzerland, World Health Organization. (WHO Environmental Burden of Disease Series, 12.)

BMZ. 2011. *10 Objectives for Education: BMZ Education Strategy.* Bonn, Germany, Bundesministerium für wirtschaftliche Zusammenarbeit und Entwicklung.

Boadway, R. and Keen, M. 2010. Theoretical perspectives on resource tax design. Daniel, P., Keen, M. and McPherson, C. (eds), *The Taxation of Petroleum and Minerals: Principles, Problems and Practice.* New York, Routledge/International Monetary Fund.

Botcheva, L. and Huffman, L. 2004. *GRS HIV/AIDS Education Program: An Intervention in Zimbabwe — Evaluation Report.* Palo Alto, CA, The Children's Health Council.

Bräutigam, D. 2011. Aid 'with Chinese characteristics': Chinese foreign aid and development finance meet the OECD-DAC aid regime. *Journal of International Development,* Vol. 23, No. 5, pp. 752–64.

Bray, M. 2009. *Confronting the Shadow Education System: What Government Policies for What Private Tutoring?* Paris, UNESCO — International Institute for Educational Planning.

Brown, G. 2012. *Out of Wedlock, Into School: Combating Child Marriage Through Education.* London, Office of Sarah and Gordon Brown.

Bruns, B., Evans, D. and Luque, J. 2012. *Achieving World-Class Education in Brazil.* Washington, DC, World Bank.

Burde, D. and Linden, L. L. 2009. *The Effect of Proximity on School Enrollment: Evidence from a RCT in Afghanistan.* Washington, DC, Center for Global Development. (Draft.)

Busan Partnership for Effective Development Co-operation. 2011. *Fourth High Level Forum on Aid Effectiveness.* Paper presented at the 4th High Level Forum on Aid Effectiveness, Busan, Republic of Korea, 29 November–1 December 2011.

Cambridge Education, Mokoro and OPM. 2010. *Mid-Term Evaluation of the EFA Fast Track Initiative. Final Synthesis Report. Volume 1 – Main Report.* Cambridge/Oxford, Cambridge Education/Mokoro Ltd/Oxford Policy Management.

Cameron, L. 2009. Can a public scholarship program successfully reduce school dropouts in a time of economic crisis? Evidence from Indonesia. *Economics of Education Review,* Vol. 28, No. 3, pp. 308–17.

Canada Council of Ministers of Education. 2008. *The Development and State of the Art of Adult Learning and Education (ALE) — Report for Canada.* Toronto, Canada, Council of Ministers of Education.

Canada Ministry of Finance. 2012. *Jobs, Growth and Long-Term Prosperity.* Ottawa, Ministry of Finance.

Carnegie Corporation of New York. 2011. *Annual Report.* New York, Carnegie Corporation of New York.

Carpentieri, J., Fairfax-Cholmeley, K., Litster, J. and Vorhaus, J. 2011. *Family Literacy in Europe: Using Parental Support Initiatives to Enhance Early Literacy Development.* London, National Research and Development Centre for Adult Literacy and Numeracy. (EAC/16/2009.)

Cassen, R. and Kingdon, G. 2007. *Tackling Low Educational Achievement.* York, United Kingdom, Joseph Rowntree Foundation.

Center for Global Prosperity. 2012. *The Index of Global Philanthropy and Remittances.* Washington, DC, Hudson Institute.

Center for Universal Education. 2011. *A Global Compact on Learning: Taking Action on Education in Developing Countries.* Washington, DC, Center for Universal Education at Brookings Institution.

Centre for Strategy and Evaluation Services. 2011. *Evaluation of ESF Support for Enhancing Access to the Labour Market and the Social Inclusion of Migrants and Ethnic Minorities — Roma Thematic Report*. Brussels, European Commission Directorate General for DG Employment, Social Affairs and Equal Opportunities.

Christian Aid. 2010. *A First for Children First in Jamaica*. http://www.christianaid.org.uk/whatwedo/partnerfocus/children-first-award.aspx (Accessed 20 January 2012.)

CINOP. 2011. *Opbrengsten in beeld. Rapportage Aanvalsplan Laaggeletterdheid 2006–2010 [Focusing on Results — Report on the Plan of Attack Against Illiteracy 2006–2010]*. 's-Hertogenbosch, the Netherlands, CINOP.

Citigroup. 2011. *Global Citizenship Report 2010*. New York, Citigroup.

Clarke, D. J. and Aggleton, P. 2012. Life skills-based HIV education and Education for All. Background paper for *EFA Global Monitoring Report 2012*.

Clarke, P. 2011. The status of girls' education in Education for All Fast Track Initiative partner countries. *Prospects,* Vol. 41, No. 4, pp. 479–90.

Claussen, J. and Assad, M. J. 2010. *Public Expenditure Tracking Survey for Primary and Secondary Education in Mainland Tanzania*. Dar es Salaam, United Republic of Tanzania Government.

Collier, P., van der Ploeg, F. and Venables, A. J. 2009. *Managing Resource Revenues in Developing Economies*. Oxford, United Kingdom, Oxford Centre for the Analysis of Resource Rich Economies/Centre for the Study of African Economies.

Comings, J. and Soricone, L. 2005. Massachusetts: a case study of improvement and growth of adult education services. Comings, J., Garner, B. and Smith, C. (eds), *Review of Adult Learning and Literacy*, Vol. 5. Boston, MA, Lawrence Erlbaum Associates, Inc., pp. 85–123.

Corden, W. M. 1984. Booming sectors and Dutch disease economics: survey and consolidation. *Oxford Economic Papers,* Vol. 36, No. 3, pp. 359–80.

Côrtes Neri, M., Gustafsson-Wright, E., Sedlacek, G. and Orazem, P. F. 2005. *The Responses of Child Labor, School Enrollment, and Grade Repetition to the Loss of Parental Earnings in Brazil, 1982–1999*. Washington, DC, World Bank. (Social Protection Discussion Paper Series, 0512.)

Cunningham, W., McGinnis, L., Verdú, R. G., Tesliuc, C. and Verner, D. 2008. *Youth at Risk in Latin America and the Caribbean: Understanding the Causes, Realizing the Potential*. Washington, DC, World Bank.

Das, N. C. and Shams, R. 2011. *Asset Transfer Programme for the Ultra Poor: A Randomized Control Trial Evaluation*. Dhaka, Research and Evaluation Division, BRAC. (CFPR Working Paper, 22.)

Dawson, M. 2011. Supplementary education in Cambodia. *The Newsletter,* 56.

de Onis, M. and Blössner, M. 1997. *WHO Global Database on Child Growth and Malnutrition*. Geneva, Switzerland, World Health Organization.

de Onis, M., Blössner, M. and Borghi, E. 2012. Prevalence and trends of stunting among pre-school children, 1990–2020. *Public Health Nutrition,* Vol. 15, No. 1, pp. 142–8.

de Walque, D. 2009. Does education affect HIV status? Evidence from five African countries. *The World Bank Economic Review,* Vol. 23, No. 2, pp. 209–33.

Deininger, K. 2003. Does cost of schooling affect enrollment by the poor? Universal primary education in Uganda. *Economics of Education Review,* Vol. 22, No. 3, pp. 291–305.

Delpiano, P. V. and Vega, M. C. 2011. Success factors in an integrated early childhood development policy. Moreno, T. (ed.), *Early Learning: Lessons from Scaling Up*. The Hague, Bernard van Leer Foundation, pp. 12–16. (Early Childhood Matters.)

Delprato, M. 2012. Schooling profiles: between and within country differences. Educational dataset prepared for the GMR 2012 based on DHS household surveys. Background paper for *EFA Global Monitoring Report 2012*.

Deming, D. 2009. Early childhood intervention and life-cycle skill development: evidence from Head Start. *American Economic Journal: Applied Economics,* Vol. 1, No. 3, pp. 111–34.

Diaz, J.-J. 2006. *Pre-school Education and Schooling Outcomes in Peru*. Lima, Niños del Milenio (Young Lives).

Dolata, S. 2011. *Are There Any Disparities Between Girls and Boys in the Response of the Education Sector of HIV and AIDS? Assessment of Educational HIV/AIDS Prevention Programmes Applied by SACMEQ III Countries*. Conference paper for Gender Equality in Education: Looking Beyond Parity — An IIEP Evidence-Based Policy Forum, Paris, UNESCO—International Institute for Educational Planning.

Dolata, S. and Ross, K. N. 2010. *How Successful are HIV-AIDS Prevention Education Programmes?* Paris, Southern and Eastern Africa Consortium for Monitoring Educational Quality. (SACMEQ Policy Issues Series, 3.)

D. R. Congo Ministry of Planning and Reconstruction and UNICEF. 2002. *Enquête Nationale sur la Situation des Enfants et des Femmes MICS2/2001: Rapport d'Analyse [National Survey on the Situation of Children and Women MICS2/2001: Analytical Report]*. Kinshasa, Democratic Republic of the Congo Ministry of Planning and Reconstruction/UNICEF.

D. R. Congo National Institute of Statistics and UNICEF. 2011. *Enquête par Grappes à Indicateurs Multiples en République Démocratique du Congo (MICS-RDC 2010): Rapport Final [Multiple Indicator Cluster Survey in the Democratic Republic of the Congo (DRC MICS-2010): Final Report]*. Kinshasa, Democratic Republic of the Congo National Institute of Statistics/UNICEF.

DuBois, D. L., Holloway, B. E., Valentine, J. C. and Cooper, H. 2002. Effectiveness of mentoring programs for youth: a meta-analytic review. *American Journal of Community Psychology,* Vol. 30, No. 2, pp. 157–97.

Duflo, E., Dupas, P. and Kremer, M. 2011. *Education, HIV and Early Fertility: Experimental Evidence from Kenya*. New Haven, CT, Innovations for Poverty Action.

Duncan, G. J., Dowsett, C. J., Claessens, A., Magnuson, K., Huston, A. C., Klebanov, P., Pagani, L. S., Feinstein, L., Engel, M., Brooks-Gunn, J., Sexton, H., Duckworth, K. and Japel, C. 2007. School readiness and later achievement. *Developmental Psychology,* Vol. 43, No. 6, pp. 1428–46.

Dupas, P. 2011. Do teenagers respond to HIV risk information? Evidence from a field experiment in Kenya. *American Economic Journal: Applied Economics,* Vol. 3, No. 1, pp. 1–34.

Duryea, S., Lam, D. and Levison, D. 2007. Effects of economic shocks on children's employment and schooling in Brazil. *Journal of Development Economics,* Vol. 84, No. 1, pp. 188–214.

Economic Times. 2010. Centre, states to share RTE expenses in 68:32 ratio. *The Economic Times,* 30 July 2010.

Education Development Center. 2012. *Living: Skills for Life, Botswana's Window of Hope*. Waltham, MA, Education Development Center. http://www.hhd.org/resources/publications/living-skills-life-botswana-s-window-hope (Accessed 8 February 2012.)

EFA-FTI. 2004. *Framework*. Washington, DC, Education for All-Fast Track Initiative.

EFA-FTI and Brookings Institution. 2011. *Prospects for Bilateral Aid to Basic Education Put Students at Risk*. Washington, DC, Education for All-Fast Track Initiative/Brookings Institution.

EITI. 2009. *EITI Case Study — Addressing the Roots of Liberia's Conflict through EITI*. Oslo, Extractive Industries Transparency Initiative.

___. 2012. *What is the EITI?* Oslo, Extractive Industries Transparency Initiative. http://eiti.org/eiti (Accessed 5 February 2012.)

El-Zanaty, F. and Gorin, S. 2007. *Egypt Household Education Survey 2005–06*. Cairo/Calverton, MD, El-Zanaty and Associates/Macro International.

El-Zanaty, F. and Way, A. 2009. *Egypt Demographic and Health Survey 2008*. Cairo/Calverton, MD, Egypt Ministry of Health/El-Zanaty and Associates/Macro International.

Eliot, L. 2011. The trouble with sex differences. *Neuron,* Vol. 72, No. 6, pp. 895–8.

England, A. 2011. Zambia to double mine royalties. *Financial Times,* London, 11 November.

Engle, P. L., Fernald, L. C. H., Alderman, H., Behrman, J., O'Gara, C., Yousafzai, A., de Mello, M. C., Hidrobo, M., Ulkuer, N., Ertem, I. and Iltus, S. 2011. Strategies for reducing inequalities and improving developmental outcomes for young children in low-income and middle-income countries. *The Lancet,* Vol. 378, No. 9799, pp. 1339–53.

EPDC (Education Policy and Data Center) and UNESCO. 2009. Estimating the costs of reaching Education for All in low-income countries. Background paper for *EFA Global Monitoring Report 2010*.

ESSPIN. 2011. *Teacher Development Needs Analysis — Kano State, Nigeria*. Abuja, Education Sector Support Programme in Nigeria.

Ethiopia Central Statistical Agency and ICF International. 2012. *Ethiopia Demographic and Health Survey 2011*. Addis Ababa/Calverton, MA, Central Statistical Agency/ICF International.

European Commission. 2011a. Commission launches high-level expert group on literacy chaired by Princess Laurentien of the Netherlands. Brussels, European Commission. (Press release, 01/02/2011.)

___. 2011b. *Education and Training for a Smart, Sustainable and Inclusive Europe: Analysis of the Implementation of the Strategic Framework for European Cooperation in Education and Training (ET2020) at the European and National Levels*. Brussels, European Commission. (Commission Staff Working Document.)

European Parliament and European Council. 2006. Recommendation of the European Parliament and of the Council of 18 December 2006 on key competences for lifelong learning. *Official Journal of the European Union,* Vol. L 394, pp. 10–18.

European Union Agency for Fundamental Rights. 2009. *EU-MIDIS European Union Minorities and Discrimination Survey: Data in Focus Report 1 — The Roma*. Vienna, European Union Agency for Fundamental Rights.

Eurostat. 2011. *Lifelong Learning Statistics*. Luxembourg, Eurostat. http://epp.eurostat.ec.europa.eu/statistics_explained/index.php/Lifelong_learning_statistics (Accessed 17 May 2012.)

Evans, D., Kremer, M. and Ngatia, M. 2011. *The Impact of Distributing School Uniforms on Children's Education in Kenya*. New Haven, CT, Yale University.

ExxonMobil. 2011. *Corporate Citizenship Report*. Irving, TX, ExxonMobil.

FAO. 2011. *The State of Food Insecurity in the World. How Does International Price Volatility Affect Domestic Economies and Food Security?* Rome, Food and Agriculture Organization of the United Nations.

Fernandez, L. and Olfindo, R. 2011. *Overview of the Philippines' Conditional Cash Transfer Program: The Pantawid Pamilyang Pilipino Program (Pantawid Pamilya)*. Manila, World Bank. (Philippine Social Protection Note.)

Ferreira, F. H. G. and Gignoux, J. 2011. *The Measurement of Educational Inequality: Achievement and Opportunity*. Washington, DC, World Bank. (Policy Research Working Paper, 5873.)

Figueroa, M. 2010. Coming to terms with boys at risk in Jamaica and the rest of the Caribbean. Jones-Parry, R. and Green, R. (eds), *Commonwealth Education Partnerships, 2010/11*. Cambridge, United Kingdom, Commonwealth Secretariat/Nexus Strategic Partnerships, pp. 66–68.

Fishman, S. A., Caulfield, L. E., De Onis, M., Blössner, M., Hyder, A. A., Mullany, L. and Black, R. E. 2004. Childhood and maternal underweight. Ezzati, M., Lopez, A. D., Rodgers, A. and Murray, C. J. L. (eds), *Comparative Quantification of Health Risks: Global and Regional Burden of Disease Attributable to Selected Major Risk Factors*, Vol. 1. Geneva, Switzerland, World Health Organization.

Fiszbein, A., Schady, N., Ferreira, F. H. G., Grosh, M., Kelleher, N., Olinto, P. and Skoufias, E. 2009. *Conditional Cash Transfers: Reducing Present and Future Poverty*. Washington, DC, World Bank.

Foko, B., Tiyab, B. K. and Husson, G. 2012. *Household Education Spending: An Analytical and Comparative Perspective for 15 African Countries*. Dakar, Pôle de Dakar, UNESCO-BREDA.

Ford Foundation. 2011. *2010 Annual Report*. New York, Ford Foundation.

Frank, C. and Guesnet, L. 2009. *"We Were Promised Development and All We Got is Misery" — The Influence of Petroleum on Conflict Dynamics in Chad*. Bonn, Germany, Bonn International Center for Conversion. (Brief, 41.)

G8. 2011. *G8 Declaration: Renewed Commitment for Freedom and Democracy*. G8 Summit of Deauville, France, 26–27 May 2011.

G20. 2010. *Annex II: Multi-Year Action Plan on Development*. Toronto, Canada, Munk School of Global Affairs, University of Toronto. http://www.g20.utoronto.ca/2010/g20seoul-development.html (Accessed 23 July 2012.)

Gakidou, E., Cowling, K., Lozano, R. and Murray, C. J. L. 2010. Increased educational attainment and its effect on child mortality in 175 countries between 1970 and 2009: a systematic analysis. *The Lancet,* Vol. 376, No. 9745, pp. 959–74.

Garcia, M. and Moore, C. M. T. 2012. *The Cash Dividend: The Rise of Cash Transfer Programs in Sub-Saharan Africa*. Washington, DC, World Bank.

Gavas, M. 2012. *The European Commission's Legislative Proposals for Financing EU Development Cooperation*. London, Overseas Development Institute (Background Note, February.)

Gazette of India. 2009. *The Right of Children to Free and Compulsory Education Act*. New Delhi, Government of India.

George, J., Quamina-Aiyejina, L., Cain, M. and Mohammed, C. 2009. *Gender Issues in Education and Intervention Strategies to Increase Participation of Boys*. Port of Spain, Trinidad and Tobago Ministry of Education.

George, N. and Murray, T. S. 2012. Strengthening adult literacy among indigenous populations in Canada and other OECD countries. Background paper for *EFA Global Monitoring Report 2012*.

Georgia State Office of the Governor. 2011. *Report on the 2009 Criterion Referenced Competency Test*. Atlanta, GA, Special Investigations, Office of the Governor.

Ghana Education Service. 2010. *Open and Distance Learning (ODL) Teacher Education to Support Teacher Development in Ghana — Evaluation Report*. Accra, Teacher Education Division, Ghana Education Service.

Ghana Ministry of Finance and Economic Planning. 2010. *Petroleum Revenue Management Act, 2010*. Accra, Ministry of Finance and Economic Planning.

Gitter, S. R. and Barham, B. L. 2007. Credit, natural disasters, coffee, and educational attainment in rural Honduras. *World Development,* Vol. 35, No. 3, pp. 498–511.

Givaudan, M., Leenen, I., Van De Vijver, F. J. R., Poortinga, Y. H. and Pick, S. 2007. Longitudinal study of a school based HIV/AIDS early prevention program for Mexican adolescents. *Psychology, Health & Medicine,* Vol. 13, No. 1, pp. 98–110.

Glewwe, P. and Kassouf, A. L. 2012. The impact of the Bolsa Escola/Familia conditional cash transfer program on enrollment, dropout rates and grade promotion in Brazil. *Journal of Development Economics,* Vol. 97, No. 2, pp. 505–17.

Glick, P. and Sahn, D. 2010. Early academic performance, grade repetition and school attainment in Senegal: a panel data analysis. *World Bank Economic Review,* Vol. 24, No. 1, pp. 93–120.

Global Campaign for Education. 2012. President Obama's 2013 budget gets a failing grade on international education. Washington, DC, Global Campaign for Education US Chapter. (Press release, 12 March 2012.)

Global Fund. 2012. *Pledges and Contributions Geneva, Switzerland, Global Fund to fight AIDS, Tuberculosis and Malaria.* http://www.theglobalfund.org/en/ (Accessed 6 August 2012.)

Global Partnership for Education. 2011a. *Pledging Conference Summary Report.* Conference paper for Global Partnership for Education 2011 Pledging Conference, Copenhagen, Global Partnership for Education, November 8, 2011.

___. 2011b. *Statement from Pearson at the Global Partnership for Education Pledging Conference.* Copenhagen, Global Partnership for Education.

___. 2011c. *Substitution of Financing in the Context of the Global Partnership for Education.* Copenhagen, Global Partnership for Education. (Meeting of the Board of Directors, 9–10 November 2011.)

___. 2012a. *Conflict-affected and Fragile States.* Washington, DC, Global Partnership for Education. http://www.globalpartnership.org/who-we-are/strategy/fragile-states/ (Accessed 25 July 2012.)

___. 2012b. *EFA-FTI Catalytic Fund: 2012 Quarterly Financial Update for the Quarter Ending in June 2012.* Washington, DC, Global Partnership for Education.

___. 2012c. *Report of the Strategic Plan Working Group.* Berlin, Global Partnership for Education. (Report of the Board of Directors, 6 June 2012.)

___. 2012d. *Results Report.* Washington, DC, Global Partnership for Education. (Draft.)

Global Witness. 2009. *"Faced With a Gun, What Can You Do?" War and the Militarization of Mining in Eastern Congo.* London, Global Witness.

Gonzales, P., Williams, T., Jocelyn, L., Roey, S., Kastberg, D. and Brenwald, S. 2009. *Highlights from TIMSS 2007: Mathematics and Science Achievement of U.S. Fourth and Eighth-Grade Students in an International Context.* Washington, DC, National Center for Education Statistics, US Department of Education. (NCES 2009-001 Revised.)

Goswami, U. A. 2011. Pre-school education likely to come under Right to Education Act's ambit. *Economic Times,* 22 July 2011. http://economictimes.indiatimes.com/news/politics/nation/pre-school-education-likely-to-come-under-right-to-education-acts-ambit/articleshow/9318380.cms (Accessed 23 May 2012.)

Gove, A. and Cvelich, P. 2011. *Early Reading: Igniting Education for All. A Report by the Early Grade Learning Community of Practice. Revised Edition.* Research Triangle Park, NC, Research Triangle Institute.

Grassroot Soccer. 2012. *Grassroot Soccer.* http://www.grassrootsoccer.org/ (Accessed 8 February 2012.)

Grotlüschen, A. and Riekmann, W. 2011. *leo. – Level One Study: Literacy of Adults at the Lower Rungs of the Ladder.* Hamburg, Germany, Universität Hamburg. (Press brochure.)

Guadalupe, C. and Cardoso, M. 2011. Measuring the continuum of literacy skills among adults: educational testing and the LAMP experience. *International Review of Education,* Vol. 57, No. 1–2, pp. 199–217.

Guarcello, L., Henschel, B., Lyon, S., Rosati, F. and Valdivia, C. 2006. *Child Labour in the Latin America and Caribbean Region: A Gender-Based Analysis.* Geneva, Switzerland, International Labour Office.

Haldre, K., Part, K. and Ketting, E. 2012. Forthcoming. Sexuality education and the improvement of youth sexual health in Estonia. *The European Journal of Contraception and Reproductive Health Care.*

Halpern, D. F., Eliot, L., Bigler, R. S., Fabes, R. A., Hanish, L. D., Hyde, J., Liben, L. S. and Martin, C. L. 2011. The pseudoscience of single-sex schooling. *Science,* Vol. 333, No. 6050, pp. 1706–7.

Harding, C., Romanou, E., Williams, J., Peters, M., Winkley, J., Burke, P., Hamer, J., Jeram, K., Nelson, N., Rainbow, B., Bond, B. and Shay, M. 2011. *2011 Skills for Life Survey: Headline Findings.* London, United Kingdom Department for Business, Innovation and Skills. (BIS Research Paper, 57.)

Härmä, J. 2010. *School Choice for the Poor? The Limits of Marketisation of Primary Education in Rural India.* Brighton, United Kingdom, Consortium for Research on Educational Access, Transitions and Equity, University of Sussex. (CREATE Pathways to Access Research Monograph, 23.)

___. 2011a. *Household Survey on Private Education in Lagos.* Abuja, Education Sector Support Programme in Nigeria. (Report, LG 503.)

___. 2011b. *Lagos Private School Census 2010/2011 Report.* Abuja, Education Sector Support Programme in Nigeria. (Report, LG 501.)

Hart Nurse Ltd. 2011. *Validation of the Extractive Industry Transparency Initiative in Zambia.* Lusaka, Extractive Industry Transparency Initiative. (Report to the Zambia EITI Council.)

Hartmann, S. 2008. *The Informal Market of Education in Egypt. Private Tutoring and Its Implications.* Mainz, Germany, Department of Anthropology and African Studies, University of Mainz. (Arbeitspapiere/Working Papers, 88.)

Heuty, A. and Aristi, J. 2010. *Fool's Gold: Assessing the Performance of Alternative Fiscal Instruments*. New York, Revenue Watch Institute. (Boom, Bust and Better Policy: Crisis Lessons for Resource Rich Countries.)

Hoffman, J. V., Beretvas, N., Pearson, P. D., Hugo, C. and Mathee, B. 2004. Improving literacy instruction in South African schools: the Business Trust's Learning for Living Project. *Thinking Classroom,* Vol. 5, No. 2, pp. 27–33.

Human Resources and Skills Development Canada and Statistics Canada. 2005. *Building on our Competencies: Canadian Results of the International Adult Literacy and Skills Survey*. Ottawa, Canada Minister of Industry.

Hungi, N., Makuwa, D., Ross, K., Saito, M., Dolata, S., van Cappelle, F., Paviot, L. and Vellien, J. 2010. *SACMEQ III Project Results: Pupil Achievement Levels in Reading and Mathematics*. Paris, Southern and Eastern Africa Consortium for Monitoring Educational Quality. (Working Document, 1.)

___. 2011. *SACMEQ III Project Results: Levels and Trends in School Resources among SACMEQ School Systems*. Paris, Southern and Eastern Africa Consortium for Monitoring Educational Quality. (Working Document, 2.)

Hussain, S. 2010. *Adult Literacy in Norway: An Overview on the Strategies and Policies*. Bonn, Germany, German Institute for Adult Education — Leibniz Centre for Lifelong Learning.

Hyde, J. S. 2005. The gender similarities hypothesis. *American Psychologist,* Vol. 60, No. 6, pp. 581–92.

IAG-TVET. 2012. *Proposed Indicators for Assessing Technical and Vocational Education and Training*. Paris, Inter-Agency Working Group on Technical and Vocational Education and Training Indicators.

IASC. 2012. *2012 Strategic Document — Version 2: Response plan addressing the food and nutrition crisis in the Sahel*. Dakar, Food Security and Nutrition Working Group, Inter-Agency Standing Committee.

IGME. 2011. *Levels & Trends in Child Mortality: Report 2011 — Estimates Developed by the UN Inter-Agency Group for Child Mortality Estimation*. New York/Geneva, Switzerland/Washington, DC, United Nations Inter-Agency Group for Child Mortality Estimation (UNICEF/WHO/The World Bank/UN Population Division).

IKEA. 2012. *Education is a Basic Right*. Delft, the Netherlands, Ikea. http://en.wikipedia.org/wiki/IKEA (Accessed 7 August 2012.)

IMF. 2007. *Guide on Resource Revenue Transparency*. Washington, DC, International Monetary Fund.

___. 2011a. *Chad: 2011 Article iV Consultation*. Washington, DC, International Monetary Fund.

___. 2011b. South Sudan Faces Hurdles as World's Newest Country. *IMF Survey online,* Washington, DC, 18 July 2011. http://www.imf.org/external/pubs/ft/survey/so/2011/car071811a.htm (Accessed 18 July 2012.)

___. 2011c. *Zambia: Sixth Review Under the Three-Year Arrangement Under the Extended Credit Facility*. Washington, DC, International Monetary Fund.

___. 2012a. *Ghana: Fifth Review Under the Three-Year Arrangement Under the Extended Credit Facility and Request for Modification of Performance Criteria — Staff Report*. Washington, DC, International Monetary Fund.

___. 2012b. *Indices of Primary Commodity Prices, 2002–2012*. Washington, DC, International Monetary Fund. http://www.imf.org/external/np/res/commod/Table1.pdf. (Accessed 23 May 2012.)

Independent Evaluation Group. 2009. *The World Bank Group Program of Support for the Chad–Cameroon Petroleum Development and Pipeline Construction — Program Performance Assessment Report*. Washington, DC, World Bank. (Report, 50315.)

India Ministry of External Affairs. 2012. *Ministry of External Affairs Annual Report 2011–2012*. New Delhi, Ministry of External Affairs.

ING. 2012. *Sustainability Report*. Amsterdam, ING.

Intel. 2011. *2010 Corporate Responsibility Report*. Santa Clara, CA, Intel.

___. 2012. *Intel in Education: Transforming Education for a World of Opportunity*. Santa Clara, CA, Intel.

International Institute for Population Sciences and Macro International Inc. 2007. *National Family Health Survey (NFHS-3) 2005–06 India*. Mumbai, India, International Institute for Population Sciences.

Isaac, A. 2012. Two Years of Right of Children to Free and Compulsory Education. *Times of India,* 2 April 2012.

Jackson, C. K. 2011. *Single-Sex Schools, Student Achievement, and Course Selection: Evidence from Rule-Based Student Assignments in Trinidad and Tobago*. Cambridge, MA, National Bureau of Economic Research. (NBER Working Paper Series, 16817.)

Jacob, B. A. and Levitt, S. D. 2003. Rotten apples: an investigation of the prevalence and predictors of teacher cheating. *Quarterly Journal of Economics,* Vol. 118, No. 3, pp. 843–77.

Japan Ministry of Finance. 2011. *Highlights of the Budget for FY2012*. Tokyo, Ministry of Finance.

Jenkins, A., Ackerman, R., Frumkin, L., Salter, E. and Vorhaus, J. 2011. *Literacy, Numeracy and Disadvantage Among Older Adults in England: Final Report for Nuffield Foundation*. London, National Research and Development Centre for Adult Literacy and Numeracy.

Jensen, B. 2012. *Catching Up: Learning From the Best School Systems in East Asia*. Carlton, Australia, Grattan Institute. (Report, 2012-3.)

Jewkes, R., Nduna, M., Levin, J., Jama, N., Dunkle, K., Wood, K., Koss, M., Puren, A. and Duvvury, N. 2007. *Evaluation of Stepping Stones: A Gender Transformative HIV Prevention Intervention*. Pretoria, Medical Research Council South Africa. (Policy Brief.)

Jha, J., Bakshi, S. and Martins Faria, E. 2012. Understanding and challenging boys' disadvantage in secondary education in developing countries. Background paper for *EFA Global Monitoring Report 2012*.

Jha, J. and Kelleher, F. 2006. *Boys' Underachievement in Education — An Exploration in Selected Commonwealth Countries*. London/Vancouver, Canada, Commonwealth Secretariat/Commonwealth of Learning.

Jones-Parry, R. and Green, R. 2010. *Commonwealth Education Partnerships, 2010/11*. Cambridge, UK, Commonwealth Secretariat/Nexus Strategic Partnerships.

Kaga, Y., Bennett, J. and Moss, P. 2010. *Caring and Learning Together — A Cross-National Study on the Integration of Early Childhood Care and Education within Education*. Paris, UNESCO.

Kagan, S. L., Karnati, R., Friedlander, J. and Tarrant, K. 2010. *A Compendium of Transition Initiatives in the Early Years — A Resource Guide to Alignment and Continuity Efforts in the United States and other Countries*. New York, National Center for Children and Families.

Kagitcibasi, C., Sunar, D., Bekman, S., Baydar, N. and Cemalcilar, Z. 2009. Continuing effects of early enrichment in adult life: The Turkish Early Enrichment Project 22 years later. *Journal of Applied Developmental Psychology*, Vol. 30, No. 6, pp. 764–79.

Kane, J. M. and Mertz, J. E. 2012. Debunking myths about gender and mathematics performance. *Notices of the American Mathematical Society*, Vol. 59, No. 1, pp. 10–21.

Karl, T. L. 2007. Ensuring fairness: the case for a transparent fiscal social contract. Humphreys, M., Sachs, J. D. and Stiglitz, J. E. (eds), *Escaping the Resource Curse*. New York, Columbia University Press.

Kaufman, Z., Perez, K., Adams, L. V., Khanda, M., Ndlovu, M. and Holmer, H. 2010. *Long-Term Behavioral Impact of a Soccer-Themed, School-Based HIV Prevention Program in Zimbabwe and Botswana*. Vienna. (Poster Presentation at the XVIII International HIV and AIDS Conference, 18–23 July 2010.)

Kenya CT-OVC Evaluation Team. 2012. The impact of Kenya's Cash Transfer for Orphans and Vulnerable Children on human capital. *Journal of Development Effectiveness*, Vol. 4, No. 1, pp. 38–49.

Keogh, H. 2009. *The State and Development of Adult Learning and Education in Europe, North America and Israel — Regional Synthesis Report*. Hamburg, Germany, UNESCO Institute for Lifelong Learning.

Kholowa, F. 2011. Can We Afford to Lose the Investment in Transit?: Exploring Linkages between Community Based Child Care Centres (CBCCs) and Early Primary School — Key Issues from Research in Malawi. Zomba, Malawi, University of Malawi. (Unpublished.)

Kirby, D. B., Laris, B. A. and Rolleri, L. A. 2007. Sex and HIV education programs: their impact on sexual behaviors of young people throughout the world. *Journal of Adolescent Health*, Vol. 40, No. 3, pp. 206–17.

Kirsch, I. S., Jungeblut, A., Jenkins, L. and Kolstad, A. 2002. *Adult Literacy in America: A First Look at the Findings of the National Adult Literacy Survey*. Washington, DC, National Center for Education Statistics/Institute of Education Sciences/U.S. Department of Education.

Kivela, J., Ketting, E. and Baltussen, R. 2011. *Cost and Cost-Effectiveness Analysis of School-Based Sexuality Education Programmes in Six Countries*. Paris, UNESCO.

Kojo, N. C. 2010. *Diamonds Are Not Forever: Botswana Medium-term Fiscal Sustainability*. Washington, DC, World Bank. (Policy Research Working Paper, 5480.)

Koutrouba, K. 2008. *Η επιμόρφωση ως παράγοντας ενίσχυσης της παιδαγωγικής κατάρτισης και της διδακτικής αποτελεσματικότητας των εκπαιδευτικών στα Σχολεία Δεύτερης Ευκαιρίας [Professional training as a factor strengthening pedagogical skills and teaching effectiveness of teachers in the Second Chance Schools]*. Conference paper for Lifelong Learning for Growth, Employment and Social Cohesion, Volos, Greece, General Secretariat for Adult Education and Institute of Adult Continuing Education, 31 March–2 April 2006.

Koutrouba, K., Vamvakari, M., Margara, T. and Anagnou, E. 2011. Adult student assessment in second chance schools in Greece: teachers' views. *International Journal of Lifelong Education*, Vol. 30, No. 2, pp. 249–70.

Kruidenier, J. R., MacArthur, C. A. and Wrigley, H. S. 2010. *Adult Education Literacy Instruction: A Review of the Research*. Washington, DC, National Institute for Literacy.

Kutner, M., Greenberg, E., Jin, Y., Boyle, B., Hsu, Y., Dunleavy, E. and White, S. 2007. *Literacy in Everyday Life — Results From the 2003 National Assessment of Adult Literacy*. Washington, DC, National Center for Education Statistics, US Department of Education. (NCES 2007-480.)

Lange, G.-M. and Wright, M. 2002. *Sustainable Development in Mineral Economies: the Example of Botswana*. Pretoria, Centre for Environmental Economics and Policy in Africa, University of Pretoria. (CEEPA Discussion Paper Series 3.)

Leerlooijer, J., Ruiter, R., Reinders, J., Darwisyah, W., Kok, G. and Bartholomew, L. 2011. The World Starts With Me: using intervention mapping for the systematic adaptation and transfer of school-based sexuality education from Uganda to Indonesia. *Translational Behavioral Medicine,* Vol. 1, No. 2, pp. 331–40.

Levy, D. and Ohls, J. 2007. *Evaluation of Jamaica's PATH Program: Final Report.* Washington, DC, Mathematica Policy Research, Inc.

Lewin, K. M. 2007. *Improving Access, Equity and Transitions in Education: Creating a Research Agenda.* Brighton, UK, Consortium for Research on Educational Access, Transitions and Equity, University of Sussex. (CREATE Pathways to Access Research Monograph, 1.)

Lewin, K. M. and Stuart, J. S. 2003. *Researching Teacher Education: New Perspectives on Practice, Performance and Policy. Multi-Site Teacher Education Research Project (MUSTER) Synthesis Report.* London, Department for International Development. (Educational Papers, 49.)

Li, H., Wong, J.M.S. and Wang, X.C. 2010. Affordability, accessibility, and accountability: Perceived impacts of the Pre-primary Education Vouchers in Hong Kong. *Early Childhood Research Quarterly,* Vol. 25, No. 1, pp 125–38.

Liddell, C. and Rae, G. 2001. Predicting early grade retention: a longitudinal investigation of primary school progress in a sample of rural South African children. *British Journal of Educational Psychology,* Vol. 71, No. 3, pp. 413–28.

Lim, S. S., Stein, D. B., Charrow, A. and Murray, C. J. L. 2008. Tracking progress towards universal childhood immunisation and the impact of global initiatives: a systematic analysis of three-dose diphtheria, tetanus, and pertussis immunisation coverage. *The Lancet,* Vol. 372, No. 9655, pp. 2031–46.

Little, A. W. 2010. *Access to Elementary Education in India: Politics, Policies and Progress.* Brighton, UK, Consortium for Research on Educational Access, Transitions and Equity, University of Sussex. (CREATE Pathways to Access Research Monograph, 44.)

Luo, R., Zhang, L., Liu, C., Zhao, Q., Shi, Y., Rozelle, S. and Sharbono, B. 2011. *Behind Before They Begin: The Challenge of Early Childhood Education in Rural China.* Stanford, CA, Rural Education Action Project, Stanford University.

Machin, S. and McNally, S. 2008. The literacy hour. *Journal of Public Economics,* Vol. 92, No. 5–6, pp. 1441–62.

Magnani, R., MacIntyre, K., Karim, A. M., Brown, L., Hutchinson, P., Kaufman, C., Rutenburg, N., Hallman, K., May, J. and Dallimore, A. 2005. The impact of life skills education on adolescent sexual risk behaviors in KwaZulu-Natal, South Africa. *Journal of Adolescent Health,* Vol. 36, No. 4, pp. 289–304.

Malmberg, L.-E., Mwaura, P. and Sylva, K. 2011. Effects of a preschool intervention on cognitive development among East-African preschool children: a flexibly time-coded growth model. *Early Childhood Research Quarterly,* Vol. 26, No. 1, pp. 124–33.

Manasan, R. G. 2011. *Pantawid Pamilyang Pilipino Program and School Attendance: Early Indications of Success.* Manila, Philippine Institute for Development Studies. (Policy Notes, 2011–19.)

Martinez, S., Naudeau, S. and Pereira, V. 2012. *The Promise of Preschool in Africa: A Randomized Impact Evaluation of Early Childhood Development in Rural Mozambique.* Washington, DC/Westport, CT, World Bank/Save the Children.

MasterCard Foundation. 2010. *Financial Statements.* Toronto, Canada, MasterCard Foundation.

McBride, R. 2005. *Maldives: Preschools 'Built Back Better' Than Before Tsunami.* New York, UNICEF. http://www.unicef.org/infobycountry/index_30061.html (Accessed 23 May 2012.)

McManus, A. and Dhar, L. 2008. Study of knowledge, perception and attitude of adolescent girls towards STIs/HIV, safer sex and sex education: (A cross sectional survey of urban adolescent school girls in South Delhi, India). *BMC Women's Health,* Vol. 8, No. 12, pp. 1–6.

Mehrotra, S. 2012. The cost and financing of the right to education in India: can we fill the financing gap? *International Journal of Educational Development,* Vol. 32, No. 1, pp. 65–71.

Meier, V. and Schütz, G. 2007. *The Economics of Tracking and Non-Tracking.* Munich, Germany, Ifo Institute for Economic Research. (Working Paper, 50.)

Mingat, A. and Seurat, A. 2011. *Développement des enfants de 0 à 6 ans et pratiques parentales à Madagascar [Development of Children Aged 0 to 6 and Parenting Practices in Madagascar].* Antananarivo, UNICEF Madagascar.

Monteiro, C. A., D'Aquino Benicio, M. H., Konno, S. C., Feldenheimer da Silva, A. C., Lovadino de Lima, A. L. and Lisboa Conde, W. 2009. Causes for the decline in child under-nutrition in Brazil, 1996–2007. *Revista de Saúde Pública,* Vol. 43, No. 1, pp. 35–43.

Montenegro, L. 2011. Realities and perspectives arising from professional development to improve the teaching and learning of reading and writing: the CETT Project in the Dominican Republic. Townsend, T. and MacBeath, J. (eds), *International Handbook of Leadership for Learning.* Dordrecht, the Netherlands, Springer, pp. 817–28.

Moss, T. 2011. *Oil to Cash: Fighting the Resource Curse through Cash Transfers*. Washington, DC, Centre for Global Development. (Working Paper, 237.)

MSI. 2005. *A Gender Analysis of the Educational Achievement of Boys and Girls in the Jamaican Educational System*. Washington, DC, Management Systems International. (Prepared for US Agency for International Development.)

Mtahabwa, L. and Rao, N. 2010. Pre-primary education in Tanzania: observations from urban and rural classrooms. *International Journal of Educational Development,* Vol. 30, No. 3, pp. 227–35.

Mulkeen, A. 2010. *Teachers in Anglophone Africa: Issues in Teacher Supply, Training and Management*. Washington, DC, World Bank.

Mullis, I. V. S., Martin, M. O., Kennedy, A. M. and Foy, P. 2007. *IEA's Progress in International Reading Literacy Study in Primary School in 40 Countries*. Chestnut Hill, MA, TIMSS & PIRLS International Study Center, Boston College.

Mullola, S., Ravaja, N., Lipsanen, J., Alatupa, S., Hintsanen, M., Jokela, M. and Keltikangas-Järvinen, L. 2012. Gender differences in teachers' perceptions of students' temperament, educational competence, and teachability. *British Journal of Educational Psychology,* Vol. 82, No. 2, pp. 185–206.

Munns, G., Arthur, L., Downes, T., Gregson, R., Power, A., Sawyer, W., Singh, M., Thistleton-Martin, J. and Steele, F. 2006. *Motivation and Engagement of Boys: Evidence-Based Teaching Practices*. Canberra, Australia Government Department of Education, Science and Training.

Muyanga, M., Olwande, J., Mueni, E. and Wambugu, S. 2010. Free primary education in Kenya: an impact evaluation using propensity score methods. Cockburn, J. and Kabubo-Mariara, J. (eds), *Child Welfare in Developing Countries*. New York, Springer.

Myers, S. L. 2011. Foreign aid set to take a hit in U.S. budget crisis. *New York Times,* 3 October 2011.

Naandi Foundation. 2011. *HUNGaMA: Fighting Hunger and Malnutrition. The HUNGaMA Survey Report – 2011*. Hyderabad, India, Naandi Foundation.

Nath, S. R. and Chowdhury, A. M. R. 2009. *Education Watch 2008: State of primary education in Bangladesh — progress made, challenges remained*. Dhaka, Campaign for Popular Education.

National Adult Literacy Agency. 2011. *A Literature Review of International Adult Literacy Policies*. Dublin, National Adult Literacy Agency.

National Panel on First Nation Elementary and Secondary Education for Students on Reserve. 2012. *Nurturing the Learning Spirit of First Nation Students: The Report of the National Panel on First Nation Elementary and Secondary Education for Students on Reserve*. Ottawa, National Panel on First Nation Elementary and Secondary Education for Students on Reserve.

NEPAD. 2011. *Africa-India Forum Summit*. Johannesburg, South Africa, New Partnership for Africa's Development. (Press release, 26 May 2011.)

Nepal Ministry of Health and Population, New ERA and Inc., I. I. 2012. *Nepal Demographic and Health Survey 2011*. Kathmandu/Calverton, MA, Ministry of Health and Population/New ERA/ICF International Inc.

Netherlands Ministry of Foreign Affairs. 2011a. *Education matters: policy review of the Dutch contribution to basic education 1999–2009*. The Hague, Ministry of Foreign Affairs.

___. 2011b. *Letter to the House of Representatives Presenting the Spearheads of Development Cooperation Policy*. The Hague, Ministry of Foreign Affairs.

___. 2012. *Vaststelling van de begrotingsotaten van het Ministerie van Buitenlandse Zaken voor het jaar 2012* (Adoption of the budget of the Ministry of Foreign Affairs for the year 2012). the Hague, Homogene Groep Internationale Samenwerking (HGIS)/Ministry of Foreign Affairs.

New Zealand Ministry of Education. 2008. *Development and State of Adult Learning and Education — National Report of New Zealand*. Hamburg, Germany, UNESCO Institute for Lifelong Learning. (Prepared for CONFINTEA VI.)

New Zealand Tertiary Education Commission. 2008. *Literacy, Language and Numeracy Action Plan 2008–2012 — Raising the Literacy, Language and Numeracy Skills of the Workforce*. Wellington, Tertiary Education Commission — Te Amorangi Mātauranga Matua.

___. 2011. *Annual Report for the Year Ended 30 June 2011*. Wellington, Tertiary Education Commission — Te Amorangi Mātauranga Matua.

___. 2012. *Workplace Literacy*. Wellington, Tertiary Education Commission — Te Amorangi Mātauranga Matua. http://www.tec.govt.nz/Learners-Organisations/Employers/Workplace-literacy/ (Accessed 23 May 2012.)

Ngorosho, D. 2011. Reading and writing ability in relation to home environment: a study in primary education in rural Tanzania. *Child Indicators Research,* Vol. 4, No. 3, pp. 369–88.

Ngware, M., Oketch, M., Mutisya, M. and Abuya, B. 2010. *Classroom Observation Study: A Report on the Quality and Learning in Primary Schools in Kenya*. Nairobi, African Population and Health Research Center.

Niger National Institute of Statistics and Macro International Inc. 2007. *Enquête Démographique et de Santé et à Indicateurs Multiples du Niger 2006 [Niger Demographic, Health and Multiple Indicator Survey, 2006]*. Niamey/Calverton, MA, National Institute of Statistics/Macro International Inc.

Nigeria Federal Ministry of Education. 2011. *Fact Sheet on HIV/AIDS in Nigeria's Education Sector*. Abuja, Federal Ministry of Education.

Nigeria National Population Commission and RTI International. 2011. *Nigeria DHS EdData Survey 2010: Education Data for Decision-Making*. Washington, DC, National Population Commission/RTI International.

Noboa-Hidalgo, G. E. and Urzúa, S. S. 2012. The effects of participation in public child care centers: evidence from Chile. *Journal of Human Capital*, Vol. 6, No. 1, pp. 1–34.

Nonoyama-Tarumi, Y. and Bredenberg, K. 2009. Impact of school readiness program interventions on children's learning in Cambodia. *International Journal of Educational Development*, Vol. 29, No. 1, pp. 39–45.

Nonoyama-Tarumi, Y. and Ota, Y. 2010. Early childhood development in developing countries: pre-primary education, parenting, and health care. Background paper for *EFA Global Monitoring Report 2011*.

Nordstrum, L. E. 2012a. Incentives to exclude: the political economy constraining school fee abolition in South Africa. *Journal of Education Policy*, Vol. 27, No. 1, pp. 67–88.

___. 2012b. Private educational expenditure, cost-reduction strategies and the financial barriers that remain after fee abolition: assessing patterns of household primary spending in 12 low- and middle-income countries, and policy implications for Education For All. Background paper for *EFA Global Monitoring Report 2012*.

Nores, M. and Barnett, W. S. 2010. Benefits of early childhood interventions across the world: (under) investing in the very young. *Economics of Education Review*, Vol. 29, No. 2, pp. 271–82.

Norway Ministry of Foreign Affairs. 2011. Greater focus on climate change and renewable energy in poor countries. Oslo, Ministry of Foreign Affairs. (Press release, 06 October 2011.)

Obanya, P. 2011. *Politics and the Dilemma of Meaningful Access to Education: The Nigerian Story*. Brighton, UK, Consortium for Research on Educational Access, Transitions and Equity, University of Sussex. (CREATE Pathways to Access Research Monograph, 56.)

OCHA. 2011a. *Kenya 2012+ Emergency Humanitarian Response Plan*. New York/Geneva, Switzerland, United Nations Office for the Coordination of Humanitarian Affairs.

___. 2011b. *Somalia 2012 Consolidated Appeal*. New York/Geneva, Switzerland, United Nations Office for the Coordination of Humanitarian Affairs.

OECD-DAC. 2011. *Aid Effectiveness 2005–2010: Progress in Implementing the Paris Declaration*. Paris, Organisation for Economic Co-operation and Development.

___. 2012a. *Canada: Development Assistance Committee Peer Review 2012*. Paris, Organisation for Economic Co-operation and Development.

___. 2012b. *International Development Statistics: Creditor Reporting System*. Paris, Organisation for Economic Co-operation and Development. http://stats.oecd.org/Index.aspx?datasetcode=CRS1. (Accessed 20 April 2012.)

___. 2012c. *International Development Statistics: DAC Annual Aggregates*. Paris, Organisation for Economic Co-operation and Development. http://www.oecd.org/document/33/0,2340, en_2649_34447_36661793_1_1_1_1,00.html. (Accessed 20 April 2012.)

___. 2012d. *Outlook on Aid: Preliminary Findings from the OECD DAC Survey on Donors' Forward Spending Plans 2012–2015*. Paris, Organisation for Economic Co-operation and Development.

OECD. 2004. *Learning for Tomorrow's World — First Results from PISA 2003*. Paris, Organisation for Economic Co-operation and Development.

___. 2005. *The Definition and Selection of Key Competencies: Executive Summary*. Paris, Organisation for Economic Co-operation and Development.

___. 2007. *PISA 2006 Science Competencies for Tomorrow's World — Volume 2: Data*. Paris, Organisation for Economic Co-operation and Development.

___. 2010a. *PISA 2009 Results: Learning Trends — Changes in student performance since 2000 (Volume V)*. Paris, Organisation for Economic Co-operation and Development.

___. 2010b. *PISA 2009 Results: Overcoming Social Background. Equity in Learning Opportunities and Outcomes (Volume II)*. Paris, Organisation for Economic Co-operation and Development.

___. 2010c. *PISA 2009 Results: What Makes a School Successful? Resources, Policies and Practices (Volume IV)*. Paris, Organisation for Economic Co-operation and Development.

___. 2010d. *PISA 2009 Results: What Students Know and Can Do — Student performance in reading, mathematics and science (Volume I)*. Paris, Organisation for Economic Co-operation and Development.

___. 2011a. *Against the Odds: Disadvantaged Students Who Succeed in School*. Paris, Organisation for Economic Co-operation and Development.

___. 2011b. *Does Participation in Pre-Primary Education Translate into Better Learning Outcomes at School?* Paris, Organisation for Economic Co-operation and Development. (PISA In Focus, 2011/1 February.)

___. 2012a. *Literacy, Numeracy and Problem Solving in Technology-Rich Environments: Framework for the OECD Survey of Adult Skills*. Paris, Organisation for Economic Co-operation and Development.

___. 2012b. *OECD Economic Outlook, May 2012*. Paris, Organisation for Economic Co-operation and Development.

OECD and Statistics Canada. 2000. *Literacy in the Information Age: Final Report of the International Adult Literacy Survey*. Paris/Ottawa, Organisation for Economic Co-operation and Development/Statistics Canada.

___. 2011. *Literacy for Life: Further Results from the Adult Literacy and Life Skills Survey*. Paris/Ottawa, Organisation for Economic Co-operation and Development/Canada Minister of Industry.

OECD and World Bank. forthcoming. *Developing Indicators of Skills for Employment and Productivity: An Initial Draft Framework and Approach for Low-Income Countries*. Paris, Organisation for Economic Cooperation and Development.

Oliva, A. 2011. Sintesi del Quaderno N. 9 [Summary of Quaderno no. 9]. *Quaderno*, Vol. 9, No. 2 — Il lifelong learning e l'educazione degli adulti in Italia e in Europa [Lifelong learning and adult education in Italy and Europe], pp. 13–26.

Orlando, M. B. and Lundwall, J. 2010. *Boys at Risk: A Gender Issue in the Caribbean Requiring a Multi-Faceted and Cross-Sectoral Approach*. Washington, DC, World Bank. (en breve, Special Series: Doing Gender in LAC, 158.)

OSISA, Third World Network Africa, Tax Justice Network Africa, ActionAid International and Christian Aid. 2009. *Breaking the Curse: How Transparent Taxation and Fair Taxes Can Turn Africa's Mineral Wealth into Development*. Johannesburg/Accra/Nairobi/London, Open Society Institute of Southern Africa/Third World Network Africa/Tax Justice Network Africa/ActionAid International/Christian Aid.

Page, E. and Jha, J. (eds). 2009. *Exploring the Bias: Gender and Stereotyping in Secondary Schools*. London, Commonwealth Secretariat.

Parsons, S. and Bynner, J. 2007. *Illuminating Disadvantage: Profiling the Experiences of Adults with Entry Level Literacy or Numeracy Over the Lifecourse*. London, National Research and Development Centre for Adult Literacy and Numeracy.

Pearson. 2012. New Pearson investment fund to enhance education opportunity among the world's poorest. London, Pearson plc. (Press release, 2 July 2012.)

Perova, E. and Vakis, R. 2009. *Welfare Impacts of the "Juntos" Program in Peru: Evidence from a Non-Experimental Evaluation*. Washington, DC, World Bank.

Philippines Presidential Communications Operations Office. 2012. Aquino to formally announce enactment of Kindergarten Law. Manila, Presidential Communications Operations Office. (Press release, 26 February 2012.)

Pohan, M. N., Hinduan, Z. R., Riyanti, E., Mukaromah, E., Mutiara, T., Tasya, I. A., Sumintardja, E. N., Pinxten, W. J. L. and Hospers, H. J. 2011. HIV-AIDS prevention through a life-skills school based program in Bandung, West Java, Indonesia: evidence of empowerment and partnership in education. *Procedia — Social and Behavioral Sciences*, Vol. 15, pp. 526–30.

Pôle de Dakar. 2009. *La scolarisation primaire universelle en Afrique : le défi enseignant [Universal Primary Education in Africa: The Teacher Challenge]*. Dakar, Pôle de Dakar, UNESCO-BREDA.

Ponera, G., Mhonyiwa, J. and Mrutu, A. 2011. *Pupil and Teacher Knowledge about HIV and AIDS in Tanzania*. Paris, Southern and Eastern Africa Consortium for Monitoring Educational Quality (Policy Brief, 5.)

Punjab Education Foundation. 2012a. *Education Voucher Scheme (PEF-EVS)*. Lahore, Punjab Education Foundation. http://www.pef.edu.pk/pef-departments-evs-overview.html (Accessed 8 June 2012.)

___. 2012b. *Personal Communication with the Director of the Education Voucher Scheme*. Lahore, Pakistan.

Rao, N. and Li, H. 2009. Quality matters: early childhood education policy in Hong Kong. *Early Child Development and Care*, Vol. 179, No. 3, pp. 233–45.

Rao, N. and Sun, J. 2010. *Early Childhood Care and Education Regional Report — Asia and the Pacific*. Paris, UNESCO. (Prepared for the World Conference on Early Childhood Care and Education, Moscow, 27–29 September 2010.)

Rao, N., Sun, J., Zhou, J. and Zhang, L. 2012. Early achievement in rural China: the role of preschool experience. *Early Childhood Research Quarterly*, Vol. 27, No. 1, pp. 66–76.

READ Trust Fund. 2012. *READ Annual Report 2011*. Washington, DC, Russia Education Aid for Development Trust Fund.

Revenue Watch Institute. 2011. Disclosure rules: U.S. and EU Standards. New York, http://www.revenuewatch.org/training/resource_center/disclosure-rules-us-and-eu-standards (Accessed 23 May 2012.)

Reynolds, A. J., Temple, J. A. and Ou, S.-R. 2010. Preschool education, educational attainment, and crime prevention: contributions of cognitive and non-cognitive skills. *Children and Youth Services Review,* Vol. 32, No. 8, pp. 1054–63.

Rivera, J. A., Irizarry, L. M. and Gonzalez-de Cossio, T. 2009. Overview of the nutritional status of the Mexican population in the last two decades. *Salud Pública de México,* Vol. 51, Suppl. 4, pp. S645–56.

Rodrigues, C. G., Pinto, C. X. C. and Santos, D. D. 2011. *The Impact of Daycare Attendance on Math Test Scores for a Cohort of 4th Graders in Brazil.* São Paulo, Brazil, Escola de Economia de São Paulo da Fundação Getulio Vargas. (CMicro Working Paper 10.)

Rodríguez Alvariño, M. 2008. Evolución de la oferta educativa para adultos: de la Educación a Distancia a los Centros de Segunda Oportunidad [Evolution of Educational Provision for Adults: From Distance Education to Second Chance Centres]. *CEE Participación Educativa,* Vol. 9, pp. 30–52.

Romano, E., Babchishin, L., Pagani, L. S. and Kohen, D. 2010. School readiness and later achievement: replication and extension using a nationwide Canadian survey. *Developmental Psychology,* Vol. 46, No. 5, pp. 995–1007.

Room to Read. 2012. *Reading and Writing Instruction.* San Francisco, CA, Room to Read. http://www.roomtoread.org/page.aspx?pid=285 (Accessed 27 March 2012.)

RTI International. 2011. *Northern Nigeria Education Initiative (NEI): Results of the Early Grade Reading Assessment (EGRA) in Hausa.* Research Triangle Park, NC, Research Triangle Institute. (Prepared for US Agency for International Development/Nigeria.)

Sachs, J. D. 2007. How to handle the macroeconomics of oil wealth. Humphreys, M., Sachs, J. D. and Stiglitz, J. E. (eds), *Escaping the Resource Curse.* New York, Columbia University Press.

Sachs, J. D. and Warner, A. 1997. *Natural Resource Abundance and Economic Growth.* Cambridge, MA, Center for International Development/Harvard Institute for International Development.

Saito, M. 2010. *Has Gender Equality in Reading and Mathematics Achievement Improved?* Paris, Southern and Eastern Africa Consortium for Monitoring Educational Quality. (SACMEQ Policy Issues Series, 4.)

Sala-i-Martin, X. and Subramanian, A. 2003. *Addressing the Natural Resource Curse: An Illustration from Nigeria.* Cambridge, MA, National Bureau of Economic Research.

Samuels, F. 2012. Life-skills education in the context of HIV and AIDS. Background paper for *EFA Global Monitoring Report 2012.*

Samuels, F., Kivela, J., Chetty, D., Herat, J., Castle, C., Ketting, E. and Baltussen, R. forthcoming. Advocacy for school-based sexuality education: lessons from India and Nigeria. *Sex Education.*

Sanchez Puerta, M. L. and Valerio, A. 2012. *STEP Skills Measurement Study.* Washington, DC, World Bank.

Satherley, P. and Lawes, E. 2009. *Literacy and Life Skills for Māori Adults: Results from the Adult Literacy and Life Skills (ALL) Survey.* Wellington, Comparative Education Research Unit, Research Division, New Zealand Ministry of Education.

Save the Children. 2008. *The Child Development Index.* London, Save the Children.

___. 2012. *State of the World's Mothers 2012.* Westport, CT/London, Save the Children.

Schollar, E. 2008. *The Learning for Living Project, 2000–2004: A Book-Based Approach to the Learning of Language in South African Primary Schools.* Cape Town, South Africa, Centre for Social Science Research, University of Cape Town. (Working Paper, 233.)

Segal, P. 2010. Resource rents, redistribution, and halving global poverty: the resource dividend. *World Development,* Vol. 39, No. 4, pp. 475–89.

Sentebale. 2011. *Herd Boy Night School.* London, Sentebale. http://www.sentebale.org/home/06035934.html (Accessed 28 November 2011.)

Smith, C. A. and Stormont, M. A. 2011. Building an effective school-based mentoring program. *Intervention in School and Clinic,* Vol. 47, No. 1, pp. 14–21.

Smith, E. and Rosenblum, P. 2011. *Enforcing the Rules: Government and Citizen Oversight of Mining.* New York, Revenue Watch Institute.

Smith, K., Fordelone, T. Y. and Zimmermann, F. 2010. *Beyond the DAC: Welcome Role of Other Providers of Development Co-operation.* Paris, OECD Development Co-operation Directorate. (DCD Issues Brief, May 2010.)

Smith, L. C., Ruel, M. T. and Ndiaye, A. 2005. Why is child malnutrition lower in urban than in rural areas? Evidence from 36 developing countries. *World Development,* Vol. 33, No. 8, pp. 1285–305.

South Africa Department of Education. 2003. *Report to the Minister: Review of the Financing, Resourcing and Costs of Education in Public Schools.* Pretoria, Department of Education.

Spain Ministry of Education Culture and Sport. 2012. *Las cifras de la educación en España. Curso 2009–2010 (Edición 2012) [The Figures in Education in Spain, 2009–2010 (2012 Edition)]*. Madrid, Ministry of Education, Culture and Sport. http://www.educacion.gob.es/horizontales/estadisticas/indicadores-publicaciones-sintesis/cifras-educacion-espana/2012.html. (Accessed 29 March 2012.)

Sparrow, R. 2007. Protecting education for the poor in times of crisis: an evaluation of a scholarship programme in Indonesia. *Oxford Bulletin of Economics and Statistics*, Vol. 69, No. 1, pp. 99–122.

St. Clair, R., Tett, L. and Maclachlan, K. 2010. *Scottish Survey of Adult Literacies 2009: Report of Findings*. Edinburgh, UK, Scottish Government Social Research.

Statistics Canada and OECD. 2005. *Learning a Living: First Results of the Adult Literacy and Life Skills Survey*. Ottawa/Paris, Statistics Canada/Organisation for Economic Co-operation and Development.

Statistics New Zealand. 2007. *QuickStats About Māori*. Auckland, New Zealand, Statistics New Zealand.

Stiglitz, J. E. 2007. What is the role of the state? Humphreys, M., Sachs, J. D. and Stiglitz, J. E. (eds), *Escaping the Resource Curse*. New York, Columbia University Press.

Streuli, N., Vennam, U. and Woodhead, M. 2011. *Increasing Choice or Inequality? Pathways Through Early Education in Andhra Pradesh, India*. The Hague, Bernard van Leer Foundation. (Working papers in Early Childhood Development, 58.)

Svedberg, P. 2009. Child malnutrition in India and China: a comparison. von Braun, J., Vargas Hill, R. and Pandya-Lorch, R. (eds), *The Poorest and Hungry: Assessments, Analyses, and Actions*. Washington, DC, International Food Policy Research Institute.

Taneja, A., Sachdeva, S. and Malur, V. 2012. *Status of Implementation of the Right of Children to Free and Compulsory Education Act, 2009: Year Two*. New Delhi, RTE Forum.

TARSHI. 2008. *A Review of the Revised Sexuality Education Curriculum in India*. New Delhi, Talking About Reproductive and Sexual Health Issues.

The Times of India. 2010. Azim Premji pledges $2bn to foundation. *The Times of India,* 2 December 2010.

Thomson, S., De Bortoli, L., Nicholas, M., Hillman, K. and Buckley, S. 2011. *Challenges for Australian Education: Results from PISA 2009 — The PISA 2009 Assessment of Students' Reading, Mathematical and Scientific Literacy*. Melbourne, Australia, Australian Council for Educational Research.

Tooley, J. and Dixon, P. 2006. '*De facto*' privatisation of education and the poor: implications of a study from sub-Saharan Africa and India. *Compare,* Vol. 36, No. 4, pp. 443–62.

Transparency International. 2007. *National Integrity Systems: Country Study Report, Botswana*. Berlin, Transparency International.

Trudell, B., Dowd, A. J., Piper, B. and Bloch, C. 2012. *Early Grade Literacy in African Classrooms: Lessons Learned and Future Directions*. Conference paper for Triennale on Education and Training in Africa, Ouagadougou, 12–17 February 2012.

Truth and Reconciliation Commission of Canada. 2012. *About the Commission*. Winnipeg, Canada, Indian Residential Schools Truth and Reconciliation Commission. http://www.trc.ca/websites/trcinstitution/index.php?p=39 (Accessed 24 April 2012.)

UBS. 2009. *Grant Area: Education and Child Protection*. Zurich, Switzerland, UBS.

Uganda Bureau of Statistics and Macro International Inc. 2007. *Uganda Demographic and Health Survey 2006*. Kampala/Calverton, MA, Bureau of Statistics/Macro International Inc.

UIL. 2011. *Effective Literacy Practices*. Hamburg, Germany, UNESCO Institute for Lifelong Learning. http://www.unesco.org/uil/litbase/?menu=1. (Accessed 24 April 2012.)

UIS. 2008. *A Typology of Out-of-School Children to Improve Policies that Address Exclusion*. Conference paper for International Conference on Education, Forty-Eighth Session, Geneva, Switzerland, 25–28 November 2008. Montreal, Canada, UNESCO Institute for Statistics.

___. 2011. *The Global Demand for Primary Teachers — 2011 Update*. Montreal, Canada, UNESCO Institute for Statistics. (Information Sheet, 6.)

___. 2012. Current status of youth employment programmes. Background paper for *EFA Global Monitoring Report 2012*.

UNAIDS. 2000. *Report on the Global HIV/AIDS Epidemic*. Geneva, Switzerland, Joint United Nations Programme on HIV/AIDS.

___. 2010. *Global Report. UNAIDS Report on the Global AIDS Epidemic 2010*. Geneva, Switzerland, Joint United Nations Programme on HIV/AIDS.

___. 2011a. *AIDS at 30: Nations at the Crossroads*. Geneva, Switzerland, Joint United Nations Programme on HIV/AIDS.

___. 2011b. *Securing the Future Today — Synthesis of Strategic Information on HIV and Young People*. Geneva, Switzerland, Joint United Nations Programme on HIV/AIDS.

UNDP. 2012. *Caribbean Human Development Report 2012 — Human Development and the Shift to Better Citizen Security*. New York, United Nations Development Program.

UNESCO-IBE. 2009. *Assessment of the Pre- and In-Service Teacher Training on Health and Family Life Education in Guyana*. Geneva, Switzerland, UNESCO International Bureau of Education. (IBE/2009/RP/HV01.)

___. 2011. *World Data on Education — Seventh Edition 2010/11*. Geneva, Switzerland, UNESCO International Bureau of Education. http://www.ibe.unesco.org/en/services/online-materials/world-data-on-education/seventh-edition-2010-11.html. (Accessed 23 May 2012.)

UNESCO-OREALC. 2008. *Student Achievement in Latin America and the Caribbean: Results of the Second Regional Comparative and Explanatory Study — Executive Summary*. Santiago, Latin American Laboratory for Assessment of the Quality of Education, Regional Bureau for Education in Latin America and the Caribbean, UNESCO.

UNESCO. 2000. *The Dakar Framework for Action: Education for All — Meeting our Collective Commitments (Including Six Regional Frameworks for Action)*. Adopted by the World Education Forum. Dakar, 26–28 April 2000, UNESCO.

___. 2005. *EFA Global Monitoring Report 2006: Literacy for Life*. Paris, UNESCO.

___. 2006. *EFA Global Monitoring Report 2007: Strong Foundations: Early Childhood Care and Education*. Paris, UNESCO.

___. 2009. *EFA Global Monitoring Report 2009: Overcoming Inequality — Why Governance Matters*. Paris, UNESCO.

___. 2010a. *Early Childhood Care and Education Regional Report: Africa*. Dakar, UNESCO-BREDA.

___. 2010b. *EFA Global Monitoring Report 2010: Reaching the Marginalized*. Paris, UNESCO.

___. 2011a. *Beyond Busan: Strengthening Aid to Improve Education Outcomes*. Paris, Education for All Global Monitoring Report. (EFA GMR Policy Paper, 02.)

___. 2011b. *Building a Better Future: Education for an Independent South Sudan*. Paris, UNESCO. (EFA GMR Policy Paper.)

___. 2011c. *EFA Global Monitoring Report 2011: The Hidden Crisis — Armed Conflict and Education*. Paris, UNESCO.

___. 2011d. *Pre-service Teacher Training*. Paris, UNESCO. (Good Policy and Practice in HIV & AIDS Education, Booklet 6.)

___. 2011e. *School-Based Sexuality Education Programmes: A Cost and Cost-effectiveness Analysis in Six Countries*. Paris, UNESCO.

___. 2012a. *Holistic Early Childhood Development Index*. Paris, UNESCO (Accessed 5 July 2012.)

___. 2012b. *Untangling Aid in National Education Budgets*. Technical note for *EFA Global Monitoring Report 2012*.

___. 2012c. *World Inequality Database on Education (WIDE). The State of Education in Developing Countries*. Data set prepared for *EFA Global Monitoring Report 2012*. Paris, UNESCO.

UNFPA. 2009. *Report of the Expert Group Consultation on the Cultural Relevance of Adolescence Education*. New Delhi, United Nations Population Fund/UNESCO/UNICEF.

___. 2011. *Concurrent Evaluation of the Adolescent Health Education Programme (2010–11). Executive Summary*. New York, United Nations Population Fund.

UNHCR. 2012. *Summary: 2012–2016 Education Strategy*. Geneva, Switzerland, United Nations High Commissioner for Refugees.

UNICEF. 2009. *Strengthening Health and Family Life Education in the Region. The Implementation, Monitoring and Evaluation of HFLE in Four CARICOM Countries*. Bridgetown, UNICEF.

___. 2010a. *Getting Ready for School: A Child-to-Child Approach, Programme Evaluation for Year One*. New York, UNICEF.

___. 2010b. *Progress for Children – Achieving the MDGs with Equity*. New York, UNICEF. (Number 9.)

___. 2011a. *Child Poverty and Disparities in Mozambique 2010*. Maputo, UNICEF.

___. 2011b. *Opportunity in Crisis: Preventing HIV from Early Adolescence to Early Adulthood*. New York, UNICEF.

___. 2011c. *The State of the World's Children 2011: Adolescence – An Age of Opportunity*. New York, UNICEF.

___. 2012. *The State of the World's Children: Children in an Urban World*. New York, UNICEF.

UNICEF. n.d. *Child-friendly Education Goes Digital to Reach All 20 Atolls*. Malé, UNICEF. http://www.unicef.org/maldives/children_3451.htm (Accessed 23 May 2012.)

United Kingdom Public Accounts Committee. 2009. *Skills for Life: Progress in Improving Adult Literacy and Numeracy — Third Report of Session 2008–09. Report, Together With Formal Minutes, Oral and Written Evidence*. London, The Stationery Office Limited for the UK House of Commons. (HC 154.)

United Nations. 2001. *Declaration of Commitment on HIV/AIDS "Global Crisis — Global Action"*. New York, United Nations General Assembly Special Session on HIV/AIDS. (A/RES/S-26/2.)

Urzúa, S. and Veramandi, G. 2011. *The Impact of Out-of-Home Childcare Centers on Early Childhood Development*. Washington, DC, Inter-American Development Bank. (IDB Working Paper Series, 240.)

USAID. 2011a. *Centers for Excellence in Teacher Training (CETT): Two-Year Impact Study Report (2008–2009)*. Washington, DC, US Agency for International Development.

___. 2011b. *Education: Opportunity Through Learning*. Washington, DC, US Agency for International Development.

Uwazi. 2010. *Capitation Grant for Education: When Will it Make a Difference?* Dar es Salaam, Uwazi. (Policy brief, TZ.08/2010E.)

Uwezo. 2011. *Are Our Children Learning? Numeracy and Literacy across East Africa*. Nairobi, Uwezo.

van Fleet, J. W. 2011. *A Global Education Challenge: Harnessing Corporate Philanthropy to Educate the World's Poor*. Washington, DC, Brookings Institution.

___. 2012. Private philanthropy and social investment in support of Education for All. Background paper for *EFA Global Monitoring Report 2012*.

Varly, P. 2010. *The Monitoring of Learning Outcomes in Mali: Language of Instruction and Teachers' Methods in Mali Grade 2 Curriculum Classrooms*. Research Triangle Park, NC, RTI International.

Vegas, E. and Santibáñez, L. 2010. *The Promise of Early Childhood Development in Latin America and the Caribbean*. Washington, DC, World Bank.

Velunta, L. 2012. Conditional cash transfer program to aid 5 million families by 2014. *Philippine Online Chronicles,* 28 March 2012.

Victor, D. G., Hults, D. R. and Thurber, M. 2012. *Oil and Governance: State-owned Enterprises and the World Energy Supply*. Cambridge, UK, Cambridge University Press.

Victora, C. G., Aquino, E. M. L., do Carmo Leal, M., Monteiro, C. A., Barros, F. C. and Szwarcwald, C. L. 2011. Maternal and child health in Brazil: progress and challenges. *The Lancet,* Vol. 377, No. 9780, pp. 1863–76.

Viet Nam General Statistics Office. 2007. *Viet Nam Multiple Indicator Cluster Survey 2006 — MICS3*. Ha Noi, General Statistics Office/UNICEF/Committee for Population, Family and Children.

Vox. 2012. *The Basic Competence in Working Life Programme*. Oslo, Vox (Norwegian Agency for Lifelong Learning), Norway Ministry of Education and Research. www.vox.no/no/global-meny/English/Basic-skills/Basic-Competences-in-Working-Life/ (Accessed 29 March 2012.)

Walker, M. 2011. *PISA 2009 Plus Results: Performance of 15-year-olds in Reading, Mathematics and Science for 10 Additional Participants*. Melbourne, Australia, Australian Council for Educational Research.

Walton, M. and Banerji, R. 2011. *What Helps Children to Learn? Evaluation of Pratham's Read India Program in Bihar and Uttarakhand*. Cambridge, MA, Abdul Latif Jameel Poverty Action Lab.

Whitman, I. 2011. *Early childhood education: an international development issue*. Paris, Organisation for Economic Co-operation and Development. http://oecdeducationtoday.blogspot.com/2011/11/early-childhood-education-international.html (Accessed 20 November 2011.)

WHO. 2012. *WHO Global Database on Child Growth and Malnutrition*. Geneva, Switzerland, World Health Organization. http://www.who.int/nutgrowthdb/en/. (Accessed 20 April 2012.)

Widyanti, W. and Suryahadi, A. 2008. *The State of Local Governance and Public Services in the Decentralized Indonesia in 2006: Findings from the Governance and Decentralization Survey 2 (GDS2)*. Jakarta, SMERU Research Institute.

Wildeman, R. A. 2008. *Reviewing Eight Years of the Implementation of the School Funding Norms, 2000 to 2008*. Pretoria, IDASA. (IDASA Economic Governance Programme Research Paper.)

William and Flora Hewlett Foundation. 2010. *Global Development Program Report to the Board*. Menlo Park, CA, The William and Flora Hewlett Foundation.

Wolf, A. 2008. *Adult Learning in the Workplace: Creating Formal Provision with Impact*. London, Teaching and Learning Research Programme, Institute of Education. (Teaching and Learning Research Briefing, 59.)

Wood, B., Betts, J., Etta, F., Gayfer, J., Kabell, D., Ngwira, N., Sagasti, F. and Samaranayake, M. 2011. *The Evaluation of the Paris Declaration. Phase 2. Final report*. Copenhagen, Danish Institute of International Studies.

Woodhead, M. 2009. *Pathways Through Early Childhood Education in Ethiopia, India and Peru: Rights, Equity and Diversity*. Oxford, UK, Young Lives, Department of International Development, University of Oxford. (Working Paper, 54.)

Woodhead, M., Ames, P., Vennam, U., Abebe, W. and Streuli, N. 2009. *Equity and Quality? Challenges for Early Childhood and Primary Education in Ethiopia, India and Peru*. The Hague, Bernard van Leer Foundation. (Working Papers in Early Childhood Development, 55.)

World Bank. 2003. *Timor-Leste Poverty Assessment: Poverty in a New Nation — Analysis for Action*. Washington, DC, World Bank. (25662-TP.)

___. 2008. *Project Appraisal Document on a Proposed Credit in the Amount of SDR 80.3 million (US$130.7 million equivalent) to the People's Republic of Bangladesh for a Secondary Education Quality and Access Enhancement Project*. Washington, DC, World Bank. (43955-BD.)

___. 2011a. *Accelerating Progress Toward the Education MDGs*. Washington, DC, World Bank. http://go.worldbank.org/V4Y8DXVXG0 (Accessed 13 January 2012.)

___. 2011b. *Caribbean Initiative Focuses on Youth at Risk*. Washington, World Bank. http://go.worldbank.org/VUHTMM37V0 (Accessed 3 July 2012.)

___. 2011c. *Early Childhood Development and Education in China: Breaking the Cycle of Poverty and Improving Future Competitiveness*. Washington, DC, World Bank. (China Policy Note, 53746-CN.)

___. 2011d. *A New Instrument to Advance Development Effectiveness: Program-for-Results Financing*. Washington, DC, World Bank.

___. 2011e. *Republic of Chad — Public Expenditure Review Update: Using Public Resources for Economic Growth and Poverty Reduction*. Washington, DC, World Bank.

___. 2012. *World Development Indicators Online*. Washington, DC, World Bank. http://databank.worldbank.org/ddp/home.do?Step=3&id=4. (Accessed 23 May 2012.)

___. forthcoming. *STEP Skills Measurement Study: Data Analysis*. Washington, DC, World Bank.

World Bank and Commonwealth Secretariat. 2009. *Boys Out of Risk*. Conference paper for Regional Caribbean Conference on Keeping Boys Out of Risk, Montego Bay, Jamaica, 5–7 May 2009.

World Bank and UNICEF. 2009. *Abolishing School Fees in Africa: Lessons from Ethiopia, Ghana, Kenya, Malawi and Mozambique*. Washington, DC, World Bank/UNICEF.

Yankah, E. and Aggleton, P. 2008. Effects and effectiveness of life skills education for HIV prevention in young people. *AIDS Education and Prevention,* Vol. 20, No. 6, pp. 465–85.

Yarnell, V., Lambson, T. and Pfannenstiel, J. 2010. *2009 Study of the BIE Family and Child Education Program*. Overland Park, KS, Research & Training Associates, Inc. (Prepared for the Bureau of Indian Education, Bureau of Indian Affairs, US Department of the Interior.)

Younger, M., Warrington, M., Gray, J., Rudduck, J., McLellan, R., Bearne, E., Kershner, R. and Bricheno, P. 2005. *Raising Boys' Achievement*. Norwich, UK, Department for Education and Skills. (Research Report, 636.)

Zimmermann, L. 2012. Reconsidering gender bias in intra-household allocation in India. *Journal of Development Studies,* Vol. 48, No. 1, pp. 151–63.

Part II. Putting education to work

Abed, F. H. 2009. Microfinance interventions to enable the poorest to improve their asset base. von Braun, J., Vargas Hill, R. and Pandya-Lorch, R. (eds), *The Poorest and Hungry: Assessments, Analyses, and Actions*. Washington, DC, International Food Policy Research Institute, pp. 339–44.

Aboagye, A., Ali, S., Ishii, M., Lalni, N. and Ragland, R. 2012. Financing skills development for disadvantaged groups: an analysis of equity training funds. Background paper for *EFA Global Monitoring Report 2012*.

Abriac, D., Rathelot, R. and Sanchez, R. 2009. L'apprentissage, entre formation et insertion professionnelles [Apprenticeship, between training and professional integration]. INSEE (ed.), *Formations et emploi — Édition 2009*. Paris, Institut national de la statistique et des études économiques, pp. 57–74.

Adams, A. V. 2007. *The Role of Youth Skills Development in the Transition to Work: A Global Review*. Washington, DC, World Bank.

___. 2008. Skills Development in the Informal Sector of Sub-Saharan Africa. Washington, DC, World Bank. (Unpublished.)

___. 2010. *The Mubarak Kohl Initiative — Dual System in Egypt: An Assessment of Its Impact on the School to Work Transition*. Eschborn, Germany, Deutsche Gesellschaft für Internationale Zusammenarbeit.

Adams, A. V., Johansson, R., de Silva, S. and Razmara, S. forthcoming. *Improving Skills Development in the Informal Sector: Skills for Sub-Saharan Africa*. Washington, DC, World Bank.

ADB. 2005. *Project Performance Audit Report on Basic Skills Project in Cambodia*. Manila, Asian Development Bank.

___. 2008. *Papua New Guinea: Employment-Oriented Skills Development Project*. Manila, Asian Development Bank. (Completion Report.)

___. 2009a. *PHI: Secondary Education Development and Improvement Project*. Manila, Asian Development Bank.

___. 2009b. *Proposed Asian Development Fund Grant for the Kingdom of Cambodia: Strengthening Technical and Vocational Education and Training Project*. Manila, Asian Development Bank.

ADB, ILO and IDB. 2010. *Indonesia: Critical Development Constraints*. Manila/Geneva/Jeddah, Asian Development Bank/International Labour Organization/Islamic Development Bank.

Addae-Mensah, I., Djangmah, J. and Agbenyega, C. 1973. *Family Background and Educational Opportunities in Ghana*. Accra, Ghana University Press.

Advocates for Youth. 2012. *Women's Centre of Jamaica Foundation Programme for Adolescent Mothers*. Washington, DC, Advocates for Youth. http://www.advocatesforyouth.org/publications/publications-a-z/1330-womens-centre-of-jamaica-foundation-programme-for-adolescent-mothers. (Accessed 6 June 2012.)

AfDB. 2011. *Tunisia: Social Inclusion and Transition Support Program*. Tunis, African Development Bank. (Appraisal Report.)

African Union. 2006. *Second Decade of Education for Africa (2006–2015): Plan of Action*. Addis Ababa, African Union.

___. 2007. *Strategy to Revitalize Technical and Vocational Education and Training (TVET) in Africa*. Addis Ababa, African Union.

Agrawal, S. 2012. Technical training, curriculum support and education initiatives: an assesment of India's overseas aid in skills development. Background paper for *EFA Global Monitoring Report 2012*.

Agriculture for Impact. 2012. *Growth With Resilience: Opportunities in African Agriculture*. London, Agriculture for Impact.

AidData. 2012. *AidData Raw*. Washington, DC, AidData. http://www.aiddata.org/content/index/AidData-Raw. (Accessed 3 July 2012.)

Akyeampong, A. K. 2005. Vocationalisation of secondary education in Ghana. Lauglo, J. and Maclean, R. (eds), *Vocationalisation of Secondary Education Revisited: Technical and Vocational Education and Training — Issues, Concerns and Prospects*. Dordrecht, The Netherlands, Springer, pp. 149–226.

___. 2010. *50 Years of Educational Progress and Challenge in Ghana*. Brighton, UK, University of Sussex. (CREATE Pathways to Access Research Monograph, 33.)

Allais, S. 2010. *The Implementation and Impact of National Qualifications Frameworks: Report of a Study in 16 Countries*. Geneva, Switzerland, International Labour Office.

Allais, S., Raffe, D. and Young, M. 2009. *Researching NQFs: Some Conceptual Issues*. Geneva, Switzerland, International Labour Office. (Employment Working Paper, 44.)

Almeida, R. K. and Aterido, R. 2010. *The Investment in Job Training: Why Are SMEs Lagging So Much Behind?* Washington, DC, World Bank. (Social Protection Discussion Paper, 1004.)

Altinok, N. 2012. General versus vocational education: some new evidence from PISA 2009. Background paper for *EFA Global Monitoring Report 2012*.

Amer, M. 2012. *The School-To-Work Transition of Jordanian Youth*. Giza, Egypt, Economic Research Forum. (Working Paper, 686.)

Angel-Urdinola, D. F., Semlali, A. and Brodmann, S. 2010. *Non-public Provision of Active Labour Market Programs in Arab-Mediterranean Countries: An Inventory of Youth Programs*. Washington, DC, World Bank.

Annie E. Casey Foundation. 2012. *Kids Count Data Center*. Baltimore, MD, Annie E. Casey Foundation. http://datacenter.kidscount.org/ (Accessed 3 July 2012.)

Asankha, P. and Takashi, Y. 2011. Impacts of universal secondary education policy on secondary school enrollments in Uganda. *Journal of Accounting, Finance and Economics,* Vol. 1, No. 1, pp. 16–30.

Ashe, J. and Parrott, L. 2001. *Impact Evaluation: PACT's Women's Empowerment Program in Nepal*. Boston, MA, Brandeis University.

Ashton, D., Green, F., James, D. and Sung, J. 1999. *Education and Training for Development in East Asia: The Political Economy of Skill Formation in East Asian Newly Industrialised Economies*. London, Routledge.

Ashton, D., Green, F., Sung, J. and James, D. 2002. The evolution of education and training strategies in Singapore, Taiwan and South Korea: a development model of skill formation. *Journal of Education and Work,* Vol. 15, No. 1, pp. 5–30.

Aslam, M., Kingdon, G., De, A. and Kumar, R. 2010. *Economic Returns to Schooling and Skills — An Analysis of India and Pakistan*. Cambridge, UK, Research Consortium on Educational Outcomes and Poverty, University of Cambridge. (RECOUP Working Paper, 38.)

Assaad, R. and Barsoum, G. 2007. *Youth Exclusion in Egypt: In Search of "Second Chances"*. Washington, DC/Dubai, United Arab Emirates, Wolfensohn Center for Development/Dubai School of Government. (Middle East Youth Initiative Working Paper, 2.)

Atchoarena, D. and Esquieu, P. 2002. *Private Technical and Vocational Education in Sub-Saharan Africa: Provision Patterns and Policy Issues*. Paris, UNESCO — International Institute for Educational Planning.

Attanasio, O., Kugler, A. and Meghir, C. 2011. Subsidizing vocational training for disadvantaged youth in Colombia: evidence from a randomized trial. *American Economic Journal: Applied Economics,* Vol. 3, No. 3, pp. 188–220.

Baird, S., McIntosh, C. and Özler, B. 2009. *Designing Cost-Effective Cash Transfer Programs to Boost Schooling among Young Women in sub-Saharan Africa*. Washington, DC, World Bank. (Policy Research Working Paper, 5090.)

Baker, J. and Reichardt, I. 2007. *A Review of Urban Development Issues in Poverty Reduction Strategies*. Washington, DC, World Bank. (Urban Papers, 3.)

Balasubramanian, K., Thamizoli, P., Umar, A. and Kanwar, A. 2010. Using mobile phones to promote lifelong learning among rural women in southern India. *Distance Education,* Vol. 31, No. 2, pp. 193–209.

Bandiera, O., Buehren, N., Burgess, R., Rasul, I. and Sulaiman, M. 2011. *Initial Findings from Impact Evaluation of BRAC's Programme for Adolescent Girls in Uganda*. Dhaka/London/Washington, DC, BRAC/London School of Economics/University College London/World Bank.

Banerjee, A., Duflo, E., Glennerster, R. and Kinnan, C. 2010. The Miracle of Microfinance? Evidence from a Randomized Evaluation. Cambridge, MA, Massachusetts Institute of Technology. (Unpublished.)

Bangladesh Planning Commission. 2008. *Moving Ahead: National Strategy for Accelerated Poverty Reduction II (FY 2009–11)*. Dhaka, General Economics Division/Planning Commission/Government of the People's Republic of Bangladesh.

Baradai, F. 2012. An evaluation of acquired skills through measurements of potential earning returns to education institution types. Background paper for *EFA Global Monitoring Report 2012*.

Barnett, B., Eggleston, E., Jackson, J. and Hardee, K. 1996. *Case Study of the Women's Center of Jamaica Foundation, Program for Adolescent Mothers*. Research Triangle Park, NC, Family Health International.

Barua, D. 2012. *Pioneer and Expanding Green Energy for the Rural People: Experience of Grameen Shakti, Bangladesh*. Dhaka, Bright Green Energy Foundation. http://www.greenenergybd.com/Pioneer.html (Accessed 15 May 2012.)

Barwa, S. D. 2003. *Impact of Start Your Business (SYB) Training on Women Entrepreneurs in Vietnam*. Ho Chi Minh City, Vietnam, International Labour Office.

Bennell, P., Bulwani, G. and Musikanga, M. 2005. *Cost and Financing of Secondary Education in Zambia: A Situational Analysis*. Brighton, UK, University of Sussex. (Case study report for Lewin, K. M.2008. *Seeking Secondary Schooling in sub-Saharan Africa: Strategies for Sustainable Financing*. Washington, DC, World Bank.)

Betcherman, G., Godfrey, M., Puerto, S., Rother, F. and Stavreska, A. 2007. *A Review of Interventions to Support Young Workers: Findings of the Youth Employment Inventory*. Washington, DC, World Bank. (Social Protection Discussion Paper, 0715.)

Bhatti, F., Malik, R. and Naveed, A. 2011. *Educational Outcomes and Poverty: Insights from a Quantitative Survey in Punjab and Khyber Pakhtunkhwa*. Cambridge, UK, Research Consortium on Educational Outcomes and Poverty, University of Cambridge. (RECOUP Working Paper, 39.)

Bhowmik, S. K. 2005. Street vendors in Asia: a review. *Economic and Political Weekly,* Vol. 40, No. 22, pp. 2256–64.

BIBB. 2011. *Datenreport zum Berufsbildungsbericht 2011 [Data Report for Professional Education and Training Report 2011]*. Bonn, Germany, Bundesinstitut für Berufsbildung.

Boeha, B., Brady, P., Gorham, A. and Johanson, R. 2007. *Technical-Vocational Skills Development in Papua New Guinea*. Suva, Pacific Islands Forum Secretariat.

BRAC. 2011a. *Adolescent Development Programme*. Dhaka, BRAC. http://www.brac.net/content/adolescent-development-programme (Accessed 9 May 2012.)

___. 2011b. *Where We Work: Uganda — Empowerment and Livelihoods for Adolescents*. Dhaka, BRAC. http://www.brac.net/content/where-we-work-uganda-empowerment-and-livelihoods-adolescents (Accessed 1 May 2012.)

Brady, M., Assaad, R., Ibrahim, B., Salem, A., Salem, R. and Zibani, N. 2007. *Providing New Opportunities to Adolescent Girls in Socially Conservative Settings: The Ishraq Program in Rural Upper Egypt*. New York, Population Council.

Braun, A. and Duveskog, D. 2008. *The Farmer Field School Approach — History, Global Assessment and Success Stories*. Rome, International Fund for Agricultural Development. (Background Paper for the *IFAD Rural Poverty Report 2010*.)

Braun, P. and Islam, F. 2012. *ICT-Enabled Knowledge Brokering for Farmers in Coastal Areas of Bangladesh*. Manchester, UK, Centre for Development Informatics, University of Manchester.

Brilleau, A., Roubaud, F. and Torelli, C. 2004. *L'emploi, le chômage et les conditions d'activité dans les principales agglomérations de sept Etats membres de l'UEMOA. Principaux résultats de la phase 1 de l'enquête 1-2-3 de 2001–2002 [Employment, Unemployment and Working Conditions in the Main Agglomerations of the Seven Member States of WAEMU]*. Paris, Développement, Institutions et Analyses de Long Terme. (Document de travail, DT/2004/06.)

Brinton, M. C. 1998. From high school to work in Japan: lessons for the United States? *Social Science Review,* Vol. 72, No. 4, pp. 442–51.

Brixiova, Z. and Asaminew, E. 2010. *Unlocking Productive Entrepreneurship in Ethiopia: Which Incentives Matter?* Tunis, African Development Bank. (Working paper, 116.)

Brown, G. 2012. *Out of Wedlock, into School: Combating Child Marriage through Education*. London, Office of Sarah and Gordon Brown.

Bruhn, M., Karlan, D. and Schoar, A. 2010. What capital is missing in developing countries? *American Economic Review: Papers and Proceedings,* Vol. 100, No. 2, pp. 629–33.

Bruhn, M. and Zia, B. 2011. *Stimulating Managerial Capital in Emerging Markets: The Impact of Business and Financial Literacy for Young Entrepreneurs*. Washington, DC, World Bank. (Policy Research Working Paper, 5642.)

Cahn, M. and Liu, M. 2008. Women and rural livelihood training: a case study from Papua New Guinea. *Gender and Development,* Vol. 16, No. 1, pp. 133–46.

Caillods, F. 2010. *Access to Secondary Education*. Bangkok, UNESCO. (Asia-Pacific Secondary Education System Review Series, 2.)

Calderon, G., Cunha, J. and de Giorgi, G. 2011. *Business Literacy and Development: Evidence from a Randomized Trial in Rural Mexico*. Stanford, CA/Monterey, CA, Stanford University/Naval Postgraduate School.

Calvès, A.-E. and Schoumaker, B. 2004. Deteriorating economic context and changing patterns of youth employment in urban Burkina Faso: 1980–2000. *World Development,* Vol. 32, No. 8, pp. 1341–54.

CAP Foundation. 2011. *Basic Employability Skills Training (BEST)*. Hyderabad, India, CAP Foundation. http://www.capfoundation.in/?p=358 (Accessed 9 August 2012.)

Card, D., Ibarrarán, P., Regalia, F., Rosas, D. and Soares, Y. 2011. The labor market impacts of youth training in the Dominican Republic: evidence from a randomized evaluation. *Journal of Labor Economics,* Vol. 29, No. 2, pp. 267–300.

Cárdenas, M., de Hoyos, R. and Székely, M. 2011. *Idle Youth in Latin America: A Persistent Problem in a Decade of Prosperity*. Washington, DC, Brookings Institution.

Carneiro, P., Galasso, E. and Ginja, R. 2009. *The Impact of Providing Psycho-Social Support to Indigent Families and Increasing their Access to Social Services: Evaluating Chile Solidario*. London, University College London.

CEDEFOP. 2011. *Empowering the Young of Europe to Meet Labour Market Challenges. Findings from Study Visits 2009/10*. Thessaloniki, Greece, European Centre for the Development of Vocational Training.

CEDPA. 2001. *Adolescent Girls in India Choose a Better Future: An Impact Assessment*. Washington, DC, Centre for Development and Population Activities.

Chakroun, B. 2010. National qualifications frameworks: from policy borrowing to policy learning. *European Journal of Education,* Vol. 45, No. 2, pp. 199–216.

Chand, R., Prasanna, P. A. L. and Singh, A. 2011. Farm size and productivity: understanding the strengths of smallholders and improving their livelihoods. *Economic and Political Weekly,* Vol. 46, No. 26–27, pp. 5–11.

Charmes, J. 2009. Concepts, measurement and trends. Jütting, J. P. and de Laiglesia, J. R. (eds), *Is Informal Normal? Towards More and Better Jobs in Developing Countries*. Paris, Organisation for Economic Co-operation and Development, pp. 27–62.

Chaudhury, D. R. 2011. India gives $5 billion aid to Africa. *India Today, 25* May 2011.

Chen, M., Mirani, N. and Parikh, M. 2006. *Self Employed Women: A Profile of SEWA's Membership*. Ahmedabad, India, Self Employed Women's Association.

Chiang, Y., Hannum, E. C. and Kao, G. 2011. *Who Goes, Who Stays, and Who Studies? Gender, Migration, and Educational Decisions among Rural Youth in China*. Philadelphia, PA, University of Pennsylvania. (Gansu Survey of Children and Families Papers.)

China Information Office of the State Council. 2011. *China's Foreign Aid: White Paper*. Beijing, Information Office of the State Council.

China Ministry of Education. 2009. *Outline of China's National Plan for Medium and Long-term Education Reform and Development*. Beijing, Ministry of Education of the People's Republic of China.

Chowdhury, S. 2011. Employment in India: what does the latest data show? *Economic and Political Weekly,* Vol. 46, No. 32, pp. 23–26.

Chuhan-Pole, P., Angwafo, M., Buitano, M., Dennis, A., Korman, V. and Fox, M. L. 2011. *Africa's Pulse*. Washington, DC, World Bank. (Africa's Pulse, 4.)

Chun, H.-M., Munyi, E. N. and Lee, H. 2010. South Korea as an emerging donor: challenges and changes on its entering OECD/DAC. *Journal of International Development,* Vol. 22, No. 6, pp. 788–802.

Clement, U. 2012. Aid for skills development: Germany case study. Background paper for *EFA Global Monitoring Report 2012*.

Coduras Martínez, A., Levie, J., Kelley, D. J., Sæmundsson, R. J. and Schøtt, T. 2010. *Global Entrepreneurship Monitor Special Report: A Global Perspective on Entrepreneurship Education and Training*. London, Global Entrepreneurship Research Association, London Business School.

Colclough, C., Kingdon, G. and Patrinos, H. 2010. The changing pattern of wage returns to education and its implications. *Development Policy Review,* Vol. 28, No. 6, pp. 733–47.

Collett, K. 2010. *Skills for Agriculture*. London, City and Guilds Centre for Skills Development. (Series Briefing Notes, 24.)

Collett, K. and Gale, C. 2009. *Training for Rural Development: Agricultural and Enterprise Skills for Women Smallholders*. London, City and Guilds Centre for Skills Development.

Coneus, K., Gernandt, J. and Saam, M. 2009. *Noncognitive Skills, School Achievements and Educational Dropout*. Berlin, Deutsches Institut für Wirtschaftsforschung, German Socio-Economic Panel Study. (SOEP Papers on Multidiscipliny Panel Data Research, 176.)

Coneval. 2011. *Informe de la Evaluación Específica de Desempeño 2010–2011. Valoración de la Información contenida en el Sistema de Evaluación del Desempeño (SED) [Report on the Special Assessment of Performance 2010–2011: Valuation of the Information Contained in the Performance Assessment System]*. México City, Consejo Nacional de Evaluación de la Política de Desarrollo Social.

Cortés, R. and Giacometti, C. 2010. *Políticas de educación y su impacto sobre la superación de la pobreza infantil [Education Policies and their Impact on Overcoming Child Poverty]*. Santiago, Chile, Economic Commission for Latin America. (Políticas sociales, 157.)

Costa Vaz, A. and Aoki Inoue, C. Y. 2007. *Emerging Donors in International Development Assistance: The Brazil Case*. Ottawa, International Development Research Centre.

Creed, C. and Perraton, H. 2001. *Distance Education in the E9 Countries*. Paris, UNESCO.

Cristia, J. P., Ibarrarán, P., Cueto, S., Santiago, A. and Severín, E. 2012. *Technology and Child Development: Evidence from the One Laptop per Child Program*. Washington, DC, Inter-American Development Bank. (IDB Working Paper, 304.)

Danida. 2004. *Danida Evaluation: Farm Women in Development — Impact Study of Four Training Projects in India*. Copenhagen, Ministry of Foreign Affairs of Denmark, Danida.

Daniels, J. 2010. *Mega-schools, Technology and Teachers: Achieving Education for All*. London/New York, Routledge.

Davis, B., Winters, P., Carletto, G., Covarrubias, K., Quinones, E., Zezza, A., Stamoulis, K., Bonomi, G. and Di Giuseppe, S. 2007. *Rural Income Generating Activities: A Cross Country Comparison*. Rome, Food and Agriculture Organization of the United Nations. (ESA Working Paper 07-16.)

Davis, K., Nkonya, E., Kato, E., Mekonnen, D. A., Odendo, M., Miiro, R. and Nkuba, J. 2010. *Impact of Farmer Field Schools on Agricultural Productivity and Poverty in East Africa*. Washington, DC, International Food Policy Research Institute.

Dawson, N. and Hosie, A. 2005. *The Education of Pregnant Young Women and Young Mothers in England*. Bristol, UK, University of Bristol.

De Moura Castro, C., Wolff, L. and García, N. 1999. Bringing education by television to rural areas: Mexico's Telesecundaria. *TechKnowLogia*, Vol. 1, No. 1, pp. 29–33.

De Witte, K. and Cabus, S. J. 2010. *Dropout Prevention Measures in The Netherlands, an Evaluation*. Leuven, Belgium, Katholieke Universiteit Leuven.

DeStefano, J., Schuh Moore, A.-M., Balwanz, D. and Hartwell, A. 2007. *Reaching the Underserved: Complementary Models of Effective Schooling*. Washington, DC, US Agency for International Development.

Devenish, A. and Skinner, C. 2004. *Organising Workers in the Informal Economy: The Experience of the Self Employed Women's Union, 1994–2004*. Durban, South Africa, School of Development Studies, University of KwaZulu-Natal.

di Gropello, E., Kruse, A. and Tandon, P. 2011. *Skills for the Labor Market in Indonesia: Trends in Demand, Gaps, and Supply*. Washington, DC, World Bank.

di Gropello, E., Tan, H. and Tandon, P. 2010. *Skills for the Labor Market in the Philippines*. Washington, DC, World Bank.

DIAL. 2007. *Youth and Labour Markets in Africa: A Critical Review of Literature*. Paris, Développement Institutions et Analyses de Long Terme. (Document de travail, DT/2007-02.)

Díaz, J. J. and Jaramillo, M. 2006. *An Evaluation of the Peruvian «Youth Labor Training Program» — PROJOVEN*. Washington, DC, Inter-American Development Bank. (Office of Evaluation and Oversight Working Papers, 1006.)

Diop, N. 2010. *Knowledge and Innovation for Growth and Job Creation in Tunisia.* Conference paper for: 'Beyond Recovery — Tunisia's Knowledge Approach to Long Term Growth and Job Creation', Washington, DC, World Bank, 6 October 2010.

Drayton, C., Montgomery, S. B., Modeste, N. N., Frye Anderson, B. A. and McNeil, P. 2000. The impact of the Women's Centre of Jamaica Foundation programme for adolescent mothers on repeat pregnancies. *West Indian Medical Journal,* Vol. 49, No. 4, pp. 316–26.

Drexler, A., Fischer, G. and Schoar, A. 2011. *Keeping it Simple: Financial Literacy and Rules of Thumb*. Cambridge, MA, Poverty Action Lab.

Drydakis, N. and Vlassis, M. 2007. Ethnic Discrimination in the Greek Labour Market: Occupational Access, Insurance Coverage, and Wage Offers. Rethymnon, Greece, University of Crete. (Unpublished.)

Eastwood, R., Lipton, M. and Newell, A. 2004. *Farm Size*. Brighton, UK, University of Sussex.

ECLAC. 2007. Teenage motherhood in Latin America and the Caribbean Trends, problems and challenges. *Challenges: Newsletter on Progress towards the Millennium Development Goals from a Child Rights Perspective*, No. 4, pp. 1–12.

ECOTEC. 2009. *Addressing Inequality in Apprenticeships: Learners' Views*. Coventry, UK, Learning and Skills Council.

Education Development Center. 2009. *Rwanda Youth Employment Assessment Report*. Washington, DC, US Agency for International Development. (EQUIP3.)

Edukans Foundation. 2009. *Technical Vocational Education and Training Mapping in Ethiopia*. Amersfoort, The Netherlands, Edukans Foundation. (Learn4Work. Schokland Programme on TVET.)

Eide, A. H. 2012. Education, employment and barriers for young people with disabilities in Southern Africa. Background paper for *EFA Global Monitoring Report 2012*.

El-Zanety and Associates. 2007. *School-to-work Transition: Evidence from Egypt*. Geneva, Switzerland, International Labour Office. (Employment Policy Papers, 2007/2.)

Engel, J. 2012. Review of policies to strengthen skills-employment linkages for marginalised young people. Background paper for *EFA Global Monitoring Report 2012*.

EPDC and UNESCO. 2009. Estimating the costs of achieving Education for All in low-income countries. Background paper for *EFA Global Monitoring Report 2010*.

Esquivel, V. 2010. *The Informal Economy in Greater Buenos Aires: A Statistical Profile*. Cambridge, MA, Harvard University. (Urban Policies Research Report, 9.)

ETF. 2012. *In Lebanon, Entrepreneurial Learning Goes National*. Turin, European Training Foundation. http://www. etf.europa.eu/web.nsf/pages/In_Lebanon_Entrepreneurship_Education_Goes_National_EN (Accessed 6 June 2012.)

Ethiopia Ministry of Education. 2005. *Education Sector Development Program III (2005/2006 – 2010/2011): Program Action Plan*. Addis Ababa, Ministry of Education.

___. 2008. *National Technical and Vocational Education and Training Strategy*. Addis Ababa, Ministry of Education.

Ethiopia MoARD. 2010. *Ethiopia's Agricultural Sector Policy and Investment Framework (PIF) 2010–2020*. Addis Ababa, Ministry of Agriculture and Rural Development.

Ethiopia MoFED. 2010. *Growth and Transformation Plan (2010/11-2014/15)*. Addis Ababa, Ministry of Finance and Economic Development.

European Commission. 2006. *Briefing Note on Gender Equality and Technical and Vocational Training (TVET)*. Brussels, European Commission.

___. 2010. *Reducing Early School Leaving. Accompanying Document to the Proposal for a Council Recommendation on Policies to Reduce Early School Leaving*. Brussels, European Commission.

European Youth Forum. 2008. *The Sunshine Report on Non-Formal Education*. Brussels, European Youth Forum.

___. 2011. *Interns Revealed. A Survey on Internship Quality in Europe*. Brussels, European Youth Forum.

Eurostat. 2010. *EU Labour Force Survey*. Kirchberg, Luxembourg, Eurostat. http://epp.eurostat.ec.europa.eu/portal/page/portal/structural_indicators/indicators/social_cohesion. (Accessed 6 June 2012.)

Falter, J.-M. and Wendelspiess Chavez Juarez, F. 2011. Professional Matura as Inequality Reducing Measure? Geneva, Switzerland, Institute of Applied Economics, University of Geneva. (Unpublished.)

FAO, IFAD and ILO. 2010. *Gender Dimensions of Agricultural and Rural Employment: Differentiated Pathways Out of Poverty*. Rome, Food and Agricultural Organization of the United Nations/International Fund for Agricultural Development/International Labour Office.

FAWE. 2004. *Re-entry for Adolescent School-girl Mothers, Zambia*. Nairobi, Forum for African Women Educationalists.

Feder, G., Murgai, R. and Quizon, J. B. 2004. Sending farmers back to school: the impact of farmer field schools in Indonesia. *Review of Agricultural Economics*, Vol. 26 No. 1, pp. 45–62.

Fernández-Macías, E., Antón, J.-I., Muñoz de Bustillo, R. and Braña, F.-J. forthcoming. Early school leaving in Spain: evolution, intensity and determinants. *European Journal of Education*.

Field, S., Kuczera, M. and Pont, B. 2007. *No More Failure: Ten Steps to Equity in Education*. Paris, Organisation for Economic Co-operation and Development

Findley, M. G., Hawkins, D., Hicks, R. L., Nielson, D. L., Parks, B. C., Powers, R. M., Roberts, J. T., Tierney, M. J. and Wilson, S. 2009. *AidData: Tracking Development Finance*. Conference paper for PLAID Data Vetting Workshop, September 2009.

Fluitman, F. 2009. *Skills Development for the Informal Economy: Issues and Options in Vocational Education and Training in the Southern Partner Countries of the European Neighbourhood Policy*. Hemel Hempstead, UK, HTSPE Limited/European Commission.

___. 2010. *A World of Skills at Work: A Global Training Strategy*. Geneva, Switzerland, International Labour Office.

FOCAC. 2009. *Implementation of the Follow-up Actions of the Beijing Summit of the Forum on China-Africa Cooperation*. Beijing, Forum on China-Africa Cooperation. http://www.focac.org/eng/ltda/dsjbzjhy/hywj/t627504.htm (Accessed 10 August 2012.)

France DARES. 2011. *L'apprentissage en 2010 : des entrées presque aussi nombreuses qu'en 2009 et des contrats plus longs [Apprenticeships in 2010: Almost as Many People Starting as in 2009 and on Longer Contracts]*. Paris, Direction de l'animation de la recherche, des études et des statistiques, Ministère du travail, de l'emploi et de la santé. (DARES analyse, 89.)

Freedman, D. H. 2008. *Improving Skills and Productivity of Disadvantaged Youth*. Geneva, Switzerland, International Labour Office. (Employment Working Paper, 7.)

Gaidzanwa, R. B. 2008. *Gender Issues in Technical and Vocational Education and Training*. Conference paper for Association for the Development of Education in Africa Biennale on Education in Africa *(Maputo, Mozambique, 5–9 May 2008)*.

Garcia, M. and Fares, J. (eds). 2008. *Youth in Africa's Labor Market*. Washington, DC, World Bank.

Genda, Y. and Kurosawa, M. 2001. Transition from school to work in Japan. *Journal of Japanese and International Economics*, Vol. 15, No. 4, pp. 465–88.

Germany Ministry of Education. 2011. *Dual Training at a Glance*. Bonn, Germany, Federal Ministry of Education and Research.

GHK. 2005. *Study on Access to Education and Training, Basic Skills and Early School Leavers (Ref. DG EAC 38/04): Lot 3 — Early School Leavers, Final Report, European Commission DG EAC*. London, GHK Consulting Ltd.

___. 2012. Recognition of prior learning and experiences as a means to support youth policies: country examples. Background paper for *EFA Global Monitoring Report 2012*.

Global Partnership for Education. 2011. *Rwanda*. Washington, DC, Global Partnership for Education. (Success Stories Series.)

Gonon, P. 2004. *Challenges in the Swiss VET-System: bwp@, No. 7*, http://www.bwpat.de/7eu/gonon_ch_bwpat7_draft.pdf (Accessed 5 June 2012.)

Gorak-Sosnowska, K. 2009. *Studies on Youth Policies in the Mediterranean Partner Countries: Jordan*. Brussels, Euromed Youth Technical Assistance Unit.

Grameen Creative Lab. 2011. *Grameen Shakti: A Case Study*. London, HULT International Business School.

Grameen Shakti. 2009. *Diversification and Scaling Up GS Activities Through Entrepreneur Development*. Dhaka, Grameen Shakti. http://www.gshakti.org/index.php?option=com_content&view=section&layout=blog&id=6&Itemid=57 (Accessed 15 May 2012.)

Grant, U. 2012. Urbanization and the employment opportunities of youth in developing countries. Background paper for *EFA Global Monitoring Report 2012*.

Granville, G. 2005. *The National Qualification Framework and the Shaping of a New South Africa: Indications of the Impact of the NQF in Practice*. Pretoria, South African Qualifications Authority. (SAQA Bulletin, 1.)

Guarcello, L., Lyon, S. and Rosati, F. 2006. *The Twin Challenges of Child Labor and Youth Employment in Ethiopia*. Rome, Understanding Children's Work. (Working Paper.)

Hanushek, E. A. and Woessmann, L. 2005. *Does Educational Tracking Affect Performance and Inequality? Differences-in-Differences - Evidence across Countries*. Bonn, Germany, Institute for the Study of Labour. (IZA Discussion Paper, 1901.)

___. 2011. GDP projections for low-income countries based on education quality. Background paper for *EFA Global Monitoring Report 2012*.

Hanushek, E. A., Woessmann, L. and Zhang, L. 2011. *General Education, Vocational Education, and Labor-Market Outcomes Over the Life-Cycle*. Bonn, Germany, Institute for the Study of Labour. (IZA Discussion Paper, 6083.)

Hattie, J. 2009. *Visible Learning: A Synthesis of Over 800 Meta-Analyses Relating to Achievement*. London/New York, Routledge.

Haughey, M., Murphy, E. and Muirhead, B. 2008. Open schooling. Evans, T., Haughey, M. and Murphy, D. (eds), *International Handbook of Distance Education*. Bingley, UK, Emerald, pp. 147–66.

Heckman, J. J., Stixrud, J. and Urzua, S. 2006. The effects of cognitive and noncognitive abilities on labor market outcomes and social behaviour. *Journal of Labor Economics,* Vol. 24, No. 3, pp. 411–82.

Heitmann, W. 2010. *Background Report for Round Table Discussions on Key Milestones for the Creation of National Qualifications Fameworks*. Conference paper for AFD/GTZ Regional Workshop: Towards Sustainable Skills Development, Tunis, Deutsche Gesellschaft für Internationale Zusammenarbeit, 18–19 October.

Heitmann, W. and Schröter, H.-G. 2009. *South Africa. They All Profit from the Transformation of the Vocational Education and Training System in South Africa: the People — the Economy — the Government*. Eschborn, Germany, Deutsche Gesellschaft für Internationale Zusammenarbeit.

Helvetas. 2011. *Nepal Employment Fund: Half Annual Report*. Kathmandu, Employment Fund Secretariat/Helvetas Swiss Intercooperation Nepal.

Hippach-Schneider, U. and Toth, B. 2009. *The German Vocational Education and Training (VET) System*. Thessaloniki, Greece, European Centre for the Development of Vocational Training. (ReferNet-Country Report.)

Hofmann, C. 2011. Apprenticeship Laws in Africa. Geneva, Switzerland, Skills and Employability Department, International Labour Office. (Unpublished.)

Holder, M. 2010. *Unemployment in New York City during the Recession and Early Recovery. Young Black Men Hit the Hardest*. New York, Community Service Society of New York.

Hollande, F. 2012. *Election présidentielle 22 avril 2012 : Le changement, c'est maintenant — Mes 60 engagements pour la France [Presidential Election 22nd April 2012: Change Comes Now — My 60 Promises for France]*. Paris, Parti Socialiste.

Hoppers, W. (ed.). 2008. *Post-Primary Education in Africa: Challenges and Approaches for Expanding Learning Opportunities: Synthesis Prepared for and Lessons Learned from the* Association for the Development of Education in Africa Biennale on Education in Africa *(Maputo, Mozambique, 5–9 May 2008)*. Tunis, Association for the Development of Education in Africa.

Hori, Y. 2010. School to work transition and employment of youth in non-metropolitan areas. *Japan Labor Review,* Vol. 7, No. 3, pp. 127–43.

Hubbard, D. 2008. *School Policy on Learner Pregnancy in Namibia: Background to Reform*. Windhoek, Gender Research and Advocacy Project/Legal Assistance Centre/Ministry of Education.

Hunt, F. 2012. Mapping donors' skills development strategies and programmes. Background paper for *EFA Global Monitoring Report 2012*.

Ibarrarán, P. and Rosas Shady, D. 2009. Evaluating the impact of job training programmes in Latin America: evidence from IDB funded operations. *Journal of Development Effectiveness*, Vol. 1, No. 2, pp. 195–216.

IFAD. 2010. *Rural Poverty Report 2011: New Realities, New Challenges: New Opportunities for Tomorrow's Generation*. Rome, International Fund for Agricultural Development.

IFAD, WFP and FAO. 2011. *State of Food Insecurity in the World 2011*. Rome, Food and Agriculture Organization of the United Nations.

ILO. 2005. *Evaluation: Training for Rural Economic Empowerment (TREE) Project*. Geneva, Switzerland, International Labour Office. (Evaluation Summaries.)

___. 2008. *Apprenticeship in the Informal Economy in Africa: Workshop Report — Geneva, 3–4 May 2007*. Geneva, Switzerland, International Labour Office, Skills and Employability Department. (Employment Report, 1.)

___. 2009a. *Guide to the New Millennium Development Goals Employment Indicators Including the Full Set of Decent Work Indicators*. Geneva, Switzerland, International Labour Office.

___. 2009b. *Rural Skills Training: A Generic Manual on Training for Rural Economic Empowerment*. Geneva, Switzerland, International Labour Office.

___. 2010a. *Accelerating Action Against Child Labour: Global Report Under the Follow-up to the ILO Declaration on Fundamental Principles and Rights at Work*. Geneva, Switzerland, International Labour Office.

___. 2010b. *Global Employment Trends*. Geneva, Switzerland, International Labour Office.

___. 2011a. *Global Employment Trends 2011: The Challenge of a Jobs Recovery*. Geneva, Switzerland, International Labour Office.

___. 2011b. *Key Indicators of the Labour Market*. Geneva, Switzerland, International Labour Office. http://kilm.ilo.org/kilmnet/. (Seventh Edition, accessed 4 June 2012.)

___. 2011c. *School-To-Work Transition Survey (SWTS) Micro Data Files*. Geneva, Switzerland, International Labour Office. http://www.ilo.org/employment/areas/WCMS_159352/lang--en/index.htm. (Accessed 5 June 2012.)

___. 2011d. *Statistical Update on Employment in the Informal Economy*. Geneva, Switzerland, International Labour Office.

___. 2012a. *Global Employment Trends 2012: Preventing a Deeper Jobs Crisis*. Geneva, Switzerland, International Labour Office.

___. 2012b. *World of Work Report 2012: Better Jobs for a Better Economy*. Geneva, Switzerland, International Labour Office, International Institute for Labour Studies.

___. 2012c. *The Youth Employment Crisis: A Call for Action*. Geneva, Switzerland, International Labour Office.

ILO Nepal. 2005. *Dalits and Labour in Nepal: Discrimination and Forced Labour*. Kathmandu, International Labour Office Nepal. (Decent Work for All Women and Men in Nepal, 5.)

Improving Institutions for Pro-Poor Growth. 2011. *Can You Successfully Teach People How to Run a Small Business?* Oxford, UK, Improving Institutions for Pro-Poor Growth, University of Oxford. (Briefing Paper, 14.)

India Department of Agriculture and Cooperation. 2012. *Department of Agriculture and Cooperation Looks for Public Private Partnerships for Integrated Agricultural Development (PPP-IAD)*. New Delhi, Department of Agriculture and Cooperation.

India MHUPA. 2006. *National Policy on Urban Street Vendors: Report and Recommendations*. New Delhi, Ministry of Housing and Urban Poverty Alleviation.

India NCEUS. 2009. *Skill Formation and Employment Assurance in the Unorganised Sector*. New Delhi, National Commission for Enterprises in the Unorganised Sector.

India NSDC. 2011. *Concept Paper on Labour Market Information System. An Indian Perspective*. New Delhi, National Skills Development Corporation.

___. n.d. *Human Resource and Skill Requirements in the Unorganised Sector: Study on Mapping of Human Resource Skill Gaps in India till 2022*. New Delhi, National Skill Development Corporation. (NSDC Skill Gap Analysis Reports.)

Indonesia Coordinating Ministry for Economic Affairs. 2011. *Masterplan: Acceleration and Expansion of Indonesia Economic Development 2011–2025*. Jakarta, Coordinating Ministry for Economic Affairs.

INJAZ Jordan. 2012. *Fact Sheet 2010–2011*. Amman, INJAZ Jordan. http://www.injaz.org.jo (Accessed 15 May 2012.)

International Youth Foundation. 2011. *Equipping Youth Who Are Harder to Hire for the Labour Market: Results from Entra21*. Baltimore, MD, International Youth Foundation. (Learning Series, 8.)

___. 2012. *Education and Employment Alliance*. Baltimore, MD, International Youth Foundation. http://www.iyfnet. org/EEA (Accessed 1 February 2012.)

Ishraq. 2010. *A Second Chance Program for Marginalized Rural Girls in Upper Egypt*. New York, Population Council.

Janjua, S. and Naveed, A. 2009. *Skill Acquisition and the Significance of Informal Training System in Pakistan — Some Policy Implications*. Cambridge, UK, Research Consortium on Educational Outcomes and Poverty, University of Cambridge. (RECOUP Policy Brief, 7.)

Jansen, S. 2010. *Managing the Risks of Mobile Money: The Banking Agent Reform in Kenya — A Scenario-Based Policy Analysis*. Boston, MA, Harvard University, Harvard Center for International Development. (Working Paper, 45.)

JASSO. 2011. *Scholarships for International Students in Japan 2011–2012*. Tokyo, Japan Student Service Organization.

Jere, K. 2012. Alternative approaches to education provision for out-of-school youth in Malawi. Background paper for *EFA Global Monitoring Report 2012*.

Jhabvala, R., Desai, S. and Dave, J. n.d. *Empowering Women in an Insecure World: Joining SEWA Makes a Difference*. Ahmedabad, India, Self-Employed Women's Association.

Johanson, R. 2002. *Sub-Sahara Africa (SSA): Regional Response to Bank TVET Policy in the 1990s — Part II: Case Studies*. Washington, DC, World Bank. (Report, 31509.)

___. 2009. *A Review of National Training Funds*. Washington, DC, World Bank. (Social Protection Discussion Paper, 0922.)

Johanson, R. and Adams, A. V. 2004. *Skills Development in Sub-Saharan Africa*. Washington, DC, World Bank.

Kaas, L. and Manger, C. 2010. *Ethnic Discrimination in Germany's Labour Market: A Field Experiment*. Bonn, Germany, Institute for the Study of Labour. (IZA Discussion Paper, 4741.)

Kabbani, N. and Kothari, E. 2005. *Youth Employment in the MENA Region: A Situational Assessment*. Washington, DC, World Bank. (Social Protection Discussion Paper, 0534.)

Kabeer, N., Anh, T. T. V. and Loi, V. M. 2005. *Preparing For the Future: Forward-Looking Strategies to Promote Gender Equity in Viet Nam*. Ha Noi, United Nations/World Bank. (Thematic Discussion Paper.)

Kahyarara, G. and Teal, F. 2008. The returns to vocational training and academic education: evidence from Tanzania. *World Development,* Vol. 36, No. 11, pp. 2223–42.

Kamano, P. J., Rakotomalala, R., Bernard, J.-M., Husson, G. and Reuge, N. 2010. *Les défis du système éducatif burkinabé en appui à la croissance* économicque *[Challenges for Burkina Faso's Educational System in Support of Economic Growth]*. Washington, DC, World Bank. (African Human Development, 196.)

Karlan, D. and Valdivia, M. 2006. Teaching Entrepreneurship: Impact of Business Training on Microfinance Clients and Institutions. New Haven, CT, Yale University. (Unpublished.)

Kasonka, C. and Mutelo, N. 2011. *Financial Education for Young Women in Rural Areas of Zambia End of Project Evaluation Report*. Cambridge, UK, Campaign for Female Education.

Kasumuni, L. 2011. *Delivering Video by Mobile Phone to Classrooms in Tanzania*, e-Learning in Africa News Portal. www.elearning-africa.com/eLA_Newsportal/delivering-video-by-mobile-phone-to-classrooms-in-tanzania (Accessed 6 June 2012.)

Kemple, J. J. 2004. *Career Academies: Impacts on Labour Market Outcomes and Educational Attainment*. New York, MDRC.

Kenya Ministry of Education. 2005. *Kenya Education Sector Support Programme 2005–2010. Delivering Quality Education and Training to All Kenyans*. Nairobi, Ministry of Education, Science and Technology.

Kenya NCADP. 2008. *Kenya National Survey for Persons with Disabilities: Preliminary Report*. Nairobi, National Coordinating Agency for Population and Development.

Kenyon, P. 2009. *Partnerships for Youth Employment*. Geneva, Switzerland, International Labour Office. (Employment Working Paper, 33.)

Kett, M. 2012. Skills development for youth living with disabilities in four developing countries. Background paper for *EFA Global Monitoring Report 2012*.

King, K. 2010. China's cooperation in education and training with Kenya: a different model? *International Journal of Educational Development,* Vol. 30, No. 5, pp. 488–96.

King, K. and Palmer, R. 2010. *Planning for Technical and Vocational Skills Development*. Paris, UNESCO — International Institute for Educational Planning. (Fundamentals of Educational Planning, 94.)

Kolev, A. and Robles, P. S. 2010. Exploring the gender pay gap through different age cohorts: the case of Ethiopia. Arbache, J. S., Kolev, A. and Filipiak, E. (eds), *Gender Disparities in Africa's Labor Market*. Washington, DC, World Bank, pp. 57–86.

Kondylis, F. and Manacorda, M. 2008. Youth in the labor market and the transition from school to work in Tanzania. Garcia, M. and Fares, J. (eds), *Youth in Africa's Labor Market*. Washington, DC, World Bank, pp. 225–61.

Krishna, A., Poghosyan, M. and Das, N. 2010. *How Much Can Asset Transfers Help the Poorest? The Five Cs of Community-Level Development and BRAC's Ultra-Poor Programme*. Manchester, UK, University of Manchester, Brooks World Poverty Institute.

Krishnan, P. and Krutikova, S. 2012. *Non-cognitive Skill Formation in Poor Neighbourhoods of Urban India*. Cambridge, UK, University of Cambridge. (Cambridge Working Papers in Economics, 1010.)

Kuepie, M., Nordman, C. J. and Roubaud, F. 2006. *Education and Labour Market Outcomes in Sub-Saharan West Africa*. Paris, Développement, Institutions et Analyses de Long Terme. (Document de travail, DT/2006-16.)

Laabs, V., Amelung, W., Pinto, A., Wantzen, M., da Silva, C. and Zech, W. 2001. Pesticides in surface water, sediment and rainfall of the northeastern Pantanal Basin, Brazil. *Journal of Environmental Quality*, Vol. 31, No. 5, pp. 1636–48.

Lakwo, A. 2006. *Microfinance, Rural Livelihoods, and Women's Empowerment in Uganda*. Leiden, The Netherlands, Leiden University. (Research Report, 85/2006.)

Lall, A. and Sakellariou, C. 2010. Evolution of education premiums in Cambodia: 1997–2007. *Asian Economic Journal*, Vol. 24, No. 4, pp. 333–54.

Lamb, S. 2011. School dropout and inequality. Lamb, S., Markussen, E., Teese, R., Polesel, J. and Sandberg, N. (eds), *School Dropout and Completion: International Comparative Studies in Theory and Policy*. Dordrecht, The Netherlands, Springer, pp. 369–90.

Larsen, K., Kim, R. and Theus, F. (eds). 2009. *Agribusiness and Innovation Systems in Africa*. Washington, DC, World Bank.

Lasida, J. and Rodriguez, E. 2006. *Entering the World of Work: Results from Six Entra21 Youth Employment Projects*. Baltimore, MD, International Youth Foundation. (Learning Series, 2.)

Lassibille, G. and Tan, J.-P. 2005. The returns to education in Rwanda. *Journal of African Economies*, Vol. 14, No. 1, pp. 92–116.

Lauglo, J. 2005. Vocationalised secondary education revisited. Lauglo, J. and Maclean, R. (eds), *Vocationalisation of Secondary Education Revisited*. Dordrecht, The Netherlands, Springer, pp. 3–51.

Law, S. S. 2011. Case study on 'national policies linking TVET with economic expansion: lessons from Singapore'. Background paper for *EFA Global Monitoring Report 2012*.

Learning and Skills Council. 2008. *Research Into Expanding Apprenticeships — Final Report*. Coventry, UK, Learning and Skills Council.

Lee, K. W. 2006. Effectiveness of government's occupational skills development strategies for small- and medium-scale enterprises: a case study of Korea. *International Journal of Educational Development*, Vol. 26, No. 3, pp. 278–94.

Lefresne, F. 2011. Lutte contre l'exclusion et insertion par l'emploi : bilan des politiques en France au regard de certaines expériences étrangères [The fight against exclusion and integration through employment: assessment of policies in France paralleled with certain foreign experiences]. *Informations sociales*, No. 165–166, pp. 136–44.

Livanos, I. and Núñez, I. 2012. Young workers' employability and higher education in Europe in the aftermath of the financial crisis: an initial assessment. *Intereconomics: Review of European Economic Policy*, Vol. 47, No. 1, pp. 10–16.

Lustig, N., Lopez-Calva, L. F. and Ortiz-Juarez, E. 2011. *The Decline in Inequality in Latin America: How Much, Since When and Why*. New Orleans, LA, Tulane University, Department of Economics. (Tulane Economics Working Paper, 1118.)

Lyche, C. 2010. *Taking on the Completion Challenge: A Literature Review on Policies to Prevent Dropout and Early School Leaving*. Paris, Organisation for Economic Co-operation and Development. (OECD Education Working Papers, 53.)

Lynd, M. 2010. *Assessment Report and Proposal for an Education Strategy*. Washington, DC, US Agency for International Development.

Maes, J. P. and Reed, L. R. 2012. *State of the Microcredit Summit Campaign Report 2012*. Washington, DC, Microcredit Summit Campaign.

Mak, J., Vassall, A., Kiss, L., Vyas, S. and Watts, C. 2010. *Exploring the Costs and Outcomes of Camfed's Seed Money Scheme (SMS) in Zimbabwe and Tanzania*. London, London School of Hygiene and Tropical Medicine.

Mano, Y., Iddrisu, A., Yoshino, Y. and Sonobe, T. 2011. *How Can Micro and Small Enterprises in Sub-Saharan Africa Become More Productive? The Impacts of Experimental Basic Managerial Training*. Washington, DC, World Bank. (Policy Research Working Paper, 5755.)

Markussen, E. and Sandberg, N. 2011. Policies to reduce school dropout and increase completion. Lamb, S., Markussen, E., Teese, R., Polesel, J. and Sandberg, N. (eds), *School Dropout and Completion: International Comparative Studies in Theory and Policy*. Dordrecht, The Netherlands, Springer, pp. 391–406.

Martins, P. S. 2010. *Can Targeted, Non-Cognitive Skills Programs Improve Achievement? Evidence from EPIS*. Bonn, Germany, Institute for the Study of Labour. (IZA Discussion Paper, 5266.)

MasterCard Foundation. 2011. *Education for Employment and the MasterCard Foundation Partner to Increase Youth Employment in Morocco*. Toronto, Canada, MasterCard Foundation. http://mastercardfdn.org/newsroom/press/education-for-employment-and-the-mastercard-foundation-partner-to-increase-youth-employment-in-morocco (Accessed 12 June 2012.)

___. 2012a. *Philanthropic Groups Partner to Increase Participation in Secondary Education in Developing Countries*. Toronto, Canada, MasterCard Foundation. http://mastercardfdn.org/newsroom/press/philanthropic-groups-partner-to-increase-participation-in-secondary-education-in-developing-countries (Accessed 9 August 2012.)

___. 2012b. *Youth Learning: Camfed*. Toronto, Canada, MasterCard Foundation. http://mastercardfdn.org/Projects/camfed (Accessed 9 August 2012.)

___. 2012c. *Youth Learning: Swisscontact*. Toronto, Canada, MasterCard Foundation. http://mastercardfdn.org/Projects/swisscontact (Accessed 9 August 2012.)

Matsumoto, M. and Elder, S. 2010. *Characterizing the School-To-Work Transitions of Young Men and Women: Evidence from ILO School-To-Work Transition Surveys*. Geneva, Switzerland, International Labour Office. (Employment Working Paper, 51.)

Mawathe, A. 2008. Kenya's expensive free education. *BBC News,* 31 July 2008.

McCord, A. 2005. A critical evaluation of training within the South African National Public Works Programme. *Journal of Vocational and Educational Training,* Vol. 57, No. 4, pp. 563–86.

___. 2012. Skills development as part of social protection programmes. Background paper for *EFA Global Monitoring Report 2012*.

McGrath, S. 2009. Lifelong learning in South Africa: critical reflections on developments since 1994. *International Journal of Continuing Education and Lifelong Learning,* Vol. 1, No. 2, pp. 52–53.

Measure DHS. 2012. *Demographic and Health Surveys*. Calverton, MD, ICF International. http://www.measuredhs.com/. (Accessed 5 June 2012.)

Meth, C. 2011. *Employer of Last Resort? South Africa's Expanded Public Works Programme (EPWP)*. Cape Town, South Africa, Southern Africa Labour and Development Research Unit, University of Cape Town. (Working Paper, 58.)

Mitullah, W. V. 2004. *A Review of Street Trade in Africa*. Nairobi, Institute for Development Studies, University of Nairobi.

Moussa, B., Otoo, M., Fulton, J. and Lowenberg-DeBoer, J. 2011. Effectiveness of alternative extension methods through radio broadcasting in West Africa. *Journal of Agricultural Education and Extension,* Vol. 17, No. 4, pp. 355–69.

Mugisha, S. 2012. 12-YBE to cost over Rwf 13bn. *The New Times,* 17 September 2012.

Mugo, J. K., Oranga, J. and Singal, N. 2010. *Testing Youth Transitions in Kenya: Are Young People with Disabilities Falling Through the Cracks?* Cambridge, UK, Research Consortium on Educational Outcomes and Poverty, University of Cambridge. (RECOUP Working Paper, 34.)

Mujahid-Mukhtar, E. 2008. *Poverty and Economic Vulnerability in South Asia: Does It Impact Girls' Education?* New York, UNICEF.

Murphy-Graham, E., Vega de Rovelo, A. L., Del Gatto, F., Gijsbers, I. and Richards, S. 2002. *Final Evaluation of DFID Tutorial Learning System (SAT) Rural Education Project on the North Coast of Honduras 1997–2002*. London, UK Department for International Development.

Mwinzi, D. C. and Kelemba, J. K. 2010. Access to and retention of early school leavers in basic technical education in Kenya. Zeelen, J., Van der Linden, J., Nampota, D. and Ngabirano, M. (eds), *The Burden of Educational Exclusion: Understanding and Challenging Early School Leaving in Africa*. Rotterdam, The Netherlands, Sense Publishers, pp. 241–56.

Näslund-Hadley, E. and Binstock, G. 2010. *The Miseducation of Latin American Girls: Poor Schooling Makes Pregnancy a Rational Choice*. Washington, DC, Inter-American Development Bank. (Technical Notes, 204.)

New York City DYCD. 2012a. *Summer Youth Employment*. New York, New York City Department of Youth and Community Development. http://www.nyc.gov/html/dycd/html/jobs/summer_youth_employment.shtml (Accessed 9 August 2012.)

___. 2012b. *Young Adult Internship Program*. New York, New York City Department of Youth and Community Development. http://www.nyc.gov/html/dycd/html/jobs/young_adult_internship_program.shtml (Accessed 9 August 2012.)

NYC Department of Education (2012). *Mayor Bloomberg and Chancellor Walcott Announce that Record Number of Students Graduated from High School in 2011*. New York, New York City Department of Education. http://schools.nyc.gov/Offices/mediarelations/NewsandSpeeches/2011-2012/Grad_Rates_20120611.htm (Accessed 8 August 2012.)

Newby, L. 2012. ICT and skills development: new opportunities for using ICT to extend skills development programs to marginalized young people. Background paper for *EFA Global Monitoring Report 2012*.

Ng, P. T. 2008. Educational reform in Singapore: from quantity to quality. *Educational Research for Policy and Practice,* Vol. 7, pp. 5–15.

Nicholson, S. 2007. *Accelerated Learning in Post Conflict Settings*. Westport, CT, Save the Children US.

Njoroge, J. K. and Kerei, K. O. 2012. Free day secondary schooling in Kenya: an audit from cost perspective. *International Journal of Current Research,* Vol. 4, No. 3, pp. 160–63.

Nkutu, A., Bang, T. and Tooman, D. 2010. *Protecting Children's Right to Education. Evaluation of Norwegian Refugee Council's Accelerated Learning Programme in Liberia*. Oslo, Norwegian Refugee Council.

Nordman, C. J. and Pasquier-Doumer, L. 2012. Vocational education, on-the-job training and labour market integration of young workers in urban West Africa. Background paper for *EFA Global Monitoring Report 2012*.

Nsowah-Nuamah, N., Teal, F. and Awoonor, W. W. 2012. Jobs, skills and incomes in Ghana: how was poverty halved? *Comparative Education,* Vol. 48, No. 2, pp. 231–48.

Nübler, I., Hofmann, C. and Greiner, C. 2009. *Understanding Informal Apprenticeship: Findings from Empirical Research in Tanzania*. Geneva, Switzerland, International Labour Office. (Employment Report, 32.)

Nyerere, J. 2009. *Technical and Vocational Education and Training Sector Mapping in Kenya for the Dutch Shoklands TVET Programme, Edukans Foundation*. Amersfoort, The Netherlands, Edukans Foundation.

ODI. 2006. *National Employment Fund: Tunisia*. London, Overseas Development Institute. (Policy brief, 7.)

OECD-DAC. 2012. *International Development Statistics: Creditor Reporting System*. Paris, Organisation for Economic Co-operation and Development. http://stats.oecd.org/Index.aspx?datasetcode=CRS1. (Accessed 20 April 2012.)

OECD. 2006. *ICT and Learning. Supporting Out-of-school Youth and Adults*. Paris, Organisation for Economic Co-operation and Development.

___. 2008. *OECD Employment Outlook: 2008*. Paris, Organisation for Economic Co-operation and Development.

___. 2010a. *Learning for Jobs*. Paris, Organisation for Economic Co-operation and Development.

___. 2010b. *PISA 2009 Results: What Makes a School Successful? Resources, Policies and Practices (Volume IV)*. Paris, Organisation for Economic Co-operation and Development.

___. 2011. *PISA 2009 Results: Students on Line. Digital Technologies and Performance (Volume VI)*. Paris, Organisation for Economic Co-operation and Development.

___. 2012a. *Better Skills, Better Jobs, Better Lives: A Strategic Approach to Skills Policies*. Paris, Organisation for Economic Co-operation and Development.

___. 2012b. *Equity and Quality in Education: Supporting Disadvantaged Students and Schools*. Paris, Organisation for Economic Co-operation and Development.

OECD and Statistics Canada. 2011. *Literacy for Life: Further Results from the Adult Literacy and Life Skills Survey*. Paris/Ottawa, Organisation for Economic Co-operation and Development/Statistics Canada.

OECD Development Centre. 2012. *African Economic Outlook 2012: Promoting Youth Employment*. Paris, African Development Bank/Organisation for Economic Co-operation and Development/United Nations Development Programme/United Nations Economic Commission for Africa.

Ohba, A. 2009. *Does Free Secondary Education Enable the Poor to Gain Access? A Study from Rural Kenya*. Brighton, UK, University of Sussex. (CREATE Pathways to Access Research Monograph, 21.)

Oketch, M. and Mutisya, M. 2012. Education, training and work amongst youth living in slums of Nairobi, Kenya. Background paper for *EFA Global Monitoring Report 2012*.

Onsomu, E. N., Muthaka, D., Ngware, M. and Kosimbei, G. 2006. *Financing of Secondary Education in Kenya: Costs and Options*. Nairobi, Kenya Institute for Public Policy Research and Analysis. (KIPPRA Discussion Paper, 55.)

Orlando, J. 2011. ICT, constructivist teaching and 21st century learning. *Curriculum Leadership,* Melbourne, Australia, Vol. 9, No. 11, http://www.curriculum.edu.au/leader/ict,_constructivist_teaching_and_21st_century_lear,33278.html?issueID=12401 (Accessed 5 June 2012).

Oyaro, K. 2008. Free secondary schooling policy faces testing times. *Inter Press Service News Agency,* 26 March 2008.

Paciello, M. C. 2011. *Tunisia: Changes and Challenges of Political Transition*. Brussels, Centre for European Policy Studies (MEDPRO Technical Paper, 3.)

Palmer, R. 2007. *Skills Development, the Enabling Environment and Informal Micro-Enterprise in Ghana*. Edinburgh, UK, University of Edinburgh.

Panta, T. R. and Pokhrel, Y. R. 2011. *Financing Education in Federal Republic of Nepal — Priority, Trend and Transformation.* Conference paper for Regional Policy Seminar 2011. Towards Quality Learning for All in Asia and the Pacific Region, Seoul, 28–30 July 2011.

Pantuliano, S., Buchanan-Smith, M., Metcalfe, V., Pavanello, S. and Martin, E. 2011. *City Limits: Urbanisation and Vulnerability in Sudan — Synthesis Report*. London, Overseas Development Institute, Humanitarian Policy Group.

Pastore, F. 2012. Marginalization of young people in education and work: findings from the School-To-Work Transition Surveys. Background paper for *EFA Global Monitoring Report 2012*.

Patrinos, H. A., Ridao-Cano, C. and Sakellariou, C. N. 2006. *Estimating the Returns to Education: Accounting for Heterogeneity in Ability*. Washington, DC, World Bank. (Policy Research Working Paper, 4040.)

Paudyal, B. 2008. *The Way Paved by TfE*. Lalitpur, Nepal, Training for Employment Project/Nepal Alliance for Social Mobilization/Swiss Agency for Development and Cooperation Nepal.

Peeters, P., Cunningham, W., Acharya, G. and Adams, A. V. 2009. *Youth Employment in Sierra Leone: Sustainable Livelihood Opportunities in a Post-Conflict Setting*. Washington, DC, World Bank.

Pezzullo, S. 2006. *Preparing youth for 21st century jobs: 'Entra21' across Latin America and the Caribbean*. Washington, DC/Baltimore, MD, World Bank/International Youth Foundation. (Youth Development Notes, Vol. 2, No. 2.)

___. 2009. *Final Report of the Entra21 Program Phase I: 2001–2007*. Washington, DC/Baltimore, MD, Inter-American Development Bank/International Youth Foundation.

___. 2011. *Program in Focus: Entra21*. Baltimore, MD, International Youth Foundation.

Qiang, L., de Brauw, A., Rozelle, S. and Linxiu, Z. 2005. Labor market emergence and returns to education in rural China. *Review of Agricultural Economics,* Vol. 27, No. 3, pp. 418–24.

Questscope. 2012. *Education in Jordan: Second Chances for At-Risk Youth in Jordan — Education, a Job, and a Future*. Amman/Washington, DC/London, Questscope. www.questscope.org/education (Accessed 10 May 2012.)

Quintini, G. 2011. *Over-Qualified or Under-Skilled: A Review of Existing Literature*. Paris, Organisation for Economic Co-operation and Development. (OECD Social, Employment and Migration Working Papers, 121.)

Rakodi, C. 2004. Livelihood Choices in Downtown Kingston — a Partnership Sharing and Research Initiative. Birmingham, UK, International Development Department, University of Birmingham. (Unpublished.)

Ravallion, M. 2009. Are there lessons for Africa from China's success against poverty? *World Development,* Vol. 37, No. 2, pp. 303–13.

Riley, T. A. and Steel, W. F. 2000. Kenya voucher programme for training and business development services. Levitsky, J. (ed.), *Business Development Services: A Review of International Experience*. London, Intermediate Technology Publications, pp. 165–75.

Robles, P. S. 2010. Gender disparities in time allocation, time poverty, and labor allocation across employment sectors in Ethiopia. Arbache, J. S., Kolev, A. and Filipiak, E. (eds), *Gender Disparities in Africa's Labor Market*. Washington, DC, World Bank, pp. 299–332.

Roegiers, X. 2008. L'approche par les compétences dans le monde : entre uniformisation et différenciation, entre équité et inéquité [The approach through proficiencies in the world: between standardisation and differentiation and between equity and inequity]. *inDIRECT. Les clés de la gestion scolaire*, No. 10, pp. 61–77.

Rolleston, C. and James, Z. 2012. The role of schooling in skill development: evidence from Young Lives in Ethiopia, India, Peru and Vietnam. Background paper for *EFA Global Monitoring Report 2012*.

Rumble, G. and Koul, B. N. 2007. *Open Schooling for Secondary and Higher Secondary Education: Costs and Effectiveness in India and Namibia.* Vancouver, Canada, Commonwealth of Learning

Rural Poverty Portal. 2012a. *Rural Poverty in Bangladesh*. Rome, International Fund for Agricultural Development. http://www.ruralpovertyportal.org/web/guest/country/home/tags/bangladesh (Accessed 9 May 2012.)

___. 2012b. *Rural Poverty in Uganda*. Rome, International Fund for Agricultural Development. http://www.ruralpovertyportal.org/web/guest/country/home/tags/uganda (Accessed 9 May 2012.)

Rwanda Ministry of Education. 2012. *Progress Report on the Implementation of 12 YBE and Quality of Education*. Kigali, Ministry of Education.

Sabry, S. 2010. How poverty is underestimated in Greater Cairo, Egypt. *Environment and Urbanization,* Vol. 22, No. 2, pp. 523–41.

Salehi-Isfahani, D., Tunali, I. and Assad, R. 2009. Education and earnings in the Middle East: a comparative study of returns to schooling in Egypt, Iran, and Turkey. *Middle East Development Journal,* Vol. 1, No. 2, pp. 145–87.

Sánchez, J. and Salinas, A. 2008. ICT and learning in Chilean schools: lessons learned. *Computers and Education,* Vol. 51, No. 4, pp. 1621–33.

Sang-Duk, C. 2010. *Lessons from Economic Growth and Human Capital Formation Policies in South Korea.* Seoul, Korean Educational Development Institute.

Sawiris Foundation for Social Development. 2012. *Sawiris Foundation for Social Development.* Cairo, Sawiris Foundation for Social Development. http://www.sawirisfoundation.org/sawiris/index.php?option=com_content&view=frontpage&Itemid=1&lang=en (Accessed 1 February 2012.)

Schmidt, D. 2007. Decent employment and the Millennium Development Goals: description and analysis of a new target. ILO (ed.), *Key Indicators of the Labour Market, Fifth Edition.* Geneva, Switzerland, International Labour Office.

Schweisfurth, M. 2011. Learner-centred education in developing country contexts: from solution to problem? *International Journal of Educational Development,* Vol. 31, No. 5, pp. 425–32.

Senegal METFP. 2007. *Projet PAO/sfp, Intégration de l'apprentissage traditionnel dans les métiers de l'automobile au sein du dispositif global de la formation professionnelle technique. Rapport final de l'étude d'opportunité [PAO/sfp Project: Integration of traditional apprenticeship in Jobs in the Automobile Industry, as Part of the Overall System of Professional Technical Training. Final report of the opportunity study].* Dakar, Ministère de l'Enseignement technique et de la formation professionnelle.

Severo, L. 2012. Youth and skills in Latin America: strategies, programmes and best practices. Background paper for *EFA Global Monitoring Report 2012.*

SEWA. 2008. *Annual Report 2008.* Ahmedabad, India, Self Employed Women's Association.

Shanthy, T. R. and Thiagarajan, R. 2011. Interactive multimedia instruction versus traditional training programmes: analysis of their effectiveness and perception. *Journal of Agricultural Education and Extension,* Vol. 17, No. 5, pp. 459–72.

Slater, R., Ashley, S., Tefera, M., Buta, M. and Esubalew, D. 2006. *PSNP Policy, Programme and Institutional Linkages.* London/Bristol, UK/Addis Ababa, Overseas Development Institute/IDL Group/Indak.

Slavin, R. E. 2009. *Can Financial Incentives Enhance Educational Outcomes? Evidence from International Experiments.* York, UK, Institute for Effective Education, University of York.

Solotaroff, J., Hashimi, N. and Olesen, A. 2009. *Increasing Women's Employment Opportunities Through TVET.* Washington, DC, World Bank. (Afghanistan Gender Mainstreaming Implementation Note, 4.)

Somerset, A. 2009. Universalising primary education in Kenya: the elusive goal. *Comparative Education,* Vol. 45, No. 2, pp. 233–50.

South Africa Government. 2007. *Accelerated and Shared Growth Initiative-South Africa (ASGISA).* Pretoria, Office of the Presidency.

___. 2009a. *Human Resource Development Strategy for South Africa (HRD-SA) 2010–2030.* Pretoria, Department of Education.

___. 2009b. *National Youth Policy (2009–2014).* Pretoria, National Youth Commission.

___. 2010a. *Strategic Plan 2010–2013.* Pretoria, Department of Basic Education.

___. 2010b. *Strategic Plan 2010/11 to 2014/15 and Operational Plans for the 2010/11 Financial Year.* Pretoria, Department of Higher Education and Training.

___. 2011a. *Framework for the National Skills Development Strategy 2011/12-2015/16.* Pretoria, Department of Higher Education and Training.

___. 2011b. *Strategic Plan for the Department of Labour 2011–2016.* Pretoria, Department of Labour.

South Africa National Treasury. 2011. *Confronting Youth Unemployment: Policy Options for South Africa.* Pretoria, National Treasury.

South Sudan Ministry of Education. 2012. *Republic of South Sudan Education Sector Strategic Plan 2012/3-2016/7.* Juba, Ministry of Education, Science and Technology/Ministry of General Education and Instruction/Ministry of Higher Education, Science and Technology.

South Sudan National Bureau of Statistics. 2010. *Key Indicators for Southern Sudan.* Juba, National Bureau of Statistics.

SouthAfrica.info. 2011. *IDC's R8.4bn Investment in Job Creation.* Johannesburg, South Africa, Brand South Africa. http://www.southafrica.info/business/economy/development/idc-010711.htm (Accessed 20 February 2012.)

Sparreboom, T. and Powell, M. 2009. *Labour Market Information and Analysis for Skills Development.* Geneva, Switzerland, International Labour Office. (Employment Sector Working Paper, 27.)

Statistics Indonesia. 2012. *Hari Statistik*. Jakarta, Badan Pusat Statistik-Statistics Indonesia. http://www.bps.go.id/ (Accessed 29 May 2012.)

Subrahmanyam, G. 2011. *Tackling Youth Unemployment in the Maghreb*. Tunis, African Development Bank. (Economic Brief.)

Sudarshan, R. M. 2012. National skills development strategies and the urban informal sector: the case of India. Background paper for *EFA Global Monitoring Report 2012*.

Sumra, S. and Rajani, R. 2006. *Secondary Education in Tanzania: Key Policy Challenges*. Dar es Salaam, HakiElimu.

Tabulawa, R. T. 2009. Education reform in Botswana: reflections on policy contradictions and paradoxes. *Comparative Education*, Vol. 45, No. 1, pp. 87–107.

Tacoli, C. and Mabala, R. 2010. Exploring mobility and migration in the context of rural-urban linkages: why gender and generation matter. *Environment and Urbanization*, Vol. 22, No. 2, pp. 389–95.

te Lintelo, D. 2011. *Youth and Policy Processes*. Brighton, UK, Future Agricultures Consortium. (Working Paper, 025.)

Tehio, V. 2009. *Politiques publiques en éducation: l'exemple des réformes curriculaires. Actes du séminaire final de l'étude sur les réformes curriculaires par l'approche par compétences en Afrique, 10–12 juin 2009 [Public Policies in Education: the Example of Curriculum Reforms — Proceedings of the Final Seminar on Curriculum Reforms Through Competencies in Africa]*. Sèvres, France, Centre International d'Etudes Pédagogiques.

Thiéba, D. and Ndiaye, A. 2004. Étude d'impact de la formation professionnelle de type dual du PAA *[Study of the Impact of the PAA Dual Vocational Training Programme]*. Bamako, Swiss Development Cooperation.

Tippelt, R. 2010. Bildung in Entwicklungslaendern und internationale Bildungsarbeit [Training in developing countries and international educational work]. Tippelt, R. (ed.), *Handbuch Bildungsforschung*. Wiesbaden, Germany, VS Verlag für Sozialwissenschaften, pp. 249–73.

Tomlinson, R. 2011. Budget cut leaves pregnant teens in the cold: women's centre hit by government expenditure cuts. *Jamaica Observer*, 16 August 2011.

Treschan, L., Richie-Baggage, M., and Spriano-Vasquez, S. (2011). *Missed Opportunity: How New York City Can Do a Better Job of Reconnecting Youth on Public Assistance to Education and Jobs*. New York, Community Service Society of New York.

Trucano, M. 2005. *Knowledge Maps: ICT in Education — What Do We Know About the Effective Uses of Information and Communication Technologies in Education in Developing Countries?* Washington, DC, Information for Development Program/World Bank. (ICT and Education Series.)

TUC and YWCA. 2010. *Apprenticeships and Gender*. London, Trade Union Congress/Young Women's Christian Association.

UIS. 2012a. *Educational Attainment Amongst 15–24 Year Olds*. Data set prepared for *EFA Global Monitoring Report 2012*. Montreal, Canada, UNESCO Institute for Statistics.

___. 2012b. Taking stock of youth employment programmes in developing countries. Background paper for *EFA Global Monitoring Report 2012*.

UK Office for National Statistics. 2012. *Conceptions in England and Wales 2010*. London, Office for National Statistics.

UN-HABITAT. 2008. *State of the World's Cities 2010/2011: Bridging the Urban Divide*. Nairobi, United Nations Human Settlements Programme.

UN ECOSOC. 2008. *Trends in South-South and Triangular Development Cooperation*. New York, United Nations Economic and Social Council. (Background Study for the Development Cooperation Forum.)

UN Population Division. 2010. *World Population Prospects: The 2010 Revision*. New York, United Nations Department of Economic and Social Affairs, Population Division. http://esa.un.org/unpd/wpp/index.htm. (Accessed 4 June 2012.)

Understanding Children's Work. 2012. Youth disadvantage in the labour market: empirical evidence from nine developing countries. Background paper for *EFA Global Monitoring Report 2012*.

UNDESA. 2012. *Building a Better Tomorrow: The Voices of Young People with Disabilities*. New York, United Nations Department of Economic and Social Affairs.

UNEP, ILO, IOE and ITUC. 2008. *Green Jobs: Towards Decent Work in a Sustainable, Low-Carbon World*. Nairobi, United Nations Environment Programme.

UNESCO-IBE. 2010. *Botswana*. Geneva, Switzerland, UNESCO International Bureau of Education. (World Data on Education.)

___. 2011. *Zambia*. Geneva, Switzerland, UNESCO International Bureau of Education. (World Data on Education.)

UNESCO. 2012a. *Shanghai Consensus: Recommendations of the Third International Congress on Technical and Vocational Education and Training 'Transforming TVET — Building skills for work and life'* Shanghai, People's Republic of China, 14–16 May 2012. Paris, UNESCO.

___. 2012b. *World Inequality Database on Education (WIDE). The State of Education in Developing Countries.* Data set prepared for *EFA Global Monitoring Report 2012.* Paris, UNESCO.

UNICEF. 2011a. *Adolescence in Tanzania.* Dar es Salaam, UNICEF.

___. 2011b. *Multiple Indicator Cluster Surveys.* New York, UNICEF. http://www.childinfo.org/mics.html. (Accessed 5 June 2012.)

United Nations. 2011a. *Millennium Development Goals Indicators.* New York, United Nations. http://mdgs.un.org/unsd/mdg/Data.aspx. (Accessed 15 January 2012.)

___. 2011b. *The Millennium Development Goals Report 2011.* New York, United Nations.

United Nations, World Bank, GDC, IFAD and EU. 2010. *Strategies and Lessons Learned on Sustainable Reintegration and Job Creation: A Joint Presentation by UN, World Bank, GDC, IFAD and EU Based on the Practical Experience in Sierra Leone.* New York, United Nations/World Bank/German Development Cooperation/International Fund for Agriculture Development/European Union.

USAID. 2012. *Productive Safety Net Program (PSNP).* Addis Ababa, US Agency for International Development. http://ethiopia.usaid.gov/programs/feed-future-initiative/projects/productive-safety-net-program-psnp (Accessed 1 May 2012.)

Van den Berg, H. and Jiggins, J. 2007. Investing in farmers — the impacts of farmer field schools in relation to integrated pest managements. *World Development,* Vol. 35, No. 4, pp. 663–86.

van Fleet, J. W. 2012. Private philanthropy and social investment in support of Education for All. Background paper for *EFA Global Monitoring Report 2012.*

Wally, N. 2012. Youth, skills and productive work: analysis report on the Middle East and North Africa region. Background paper for *EFA Global Monitoring Report 2012.*

Walther, R. 2006a. *La formation professionnelle en secteur informel. Rapport sur l'enquête terrain en Ethiopie [Vocational Training in the Informal Sector: Report on the Field Survey in Ethiopia].* Paris, Agence française de développement. (Document de travail, 34.)

___. 2006b. *Vocational Training in the Informal Sector. Issue Paper.* Paris, Agence française de développement. (Working Paper, 15.)

___. 2011. Building skills in the informal sector. Background paper for *EFA Global Monitoring Report 2012.*

Walther, R. and Filipiak, E. 2007a. *Nouvelles formes d'apprentissage en Afrique de l'Ouest: vers une meilleure insertion professionnelle des jeunes [New Forms of Apprenticeship in West Africa: Towards Better Youth Professional Integration].* Paris, Agence française de développement.

___. 2007b. *Vocational Training in the Informal Sector or How to Stimulate the Economies of Developing Countries? Conclusions of a Field Survey in Seven African Countries.* Paris, Agence française de développement.

Walther, R. and Gauron, A. 2006. *Le financement de la formation professionnelle en Afrique: étude de cas sur cinq fonds de la formation [Financing of Vocational Training in Africa: Case Studies on Five Training Funds].* Paris, Ministère des Affaires Etrangères, Direction Générale de la Coopération Internationale et du Développement.

Walther, R. and Savadogo, B. 2010. *Les coûts de formation et d'insertion professionnelles. Les conclusions d'une enquête terrain au Burkina Faso [Cost of Training and Professional Integration: Conclusions of a Field Survey in Burkina Faso].* Paris, Agence française de développement. (Document de travail, 98.)

Walther, R., with Filipiak, E. and Uhder, C. 2006a. *La formation en secteur informel. Rapport sur l'enquête en Afrique du Sud [Training in the Informal Sector: Report on the South African Survey Case].* Paris, Agence française de développement. (Document de travail, 30.)

___. 2006b. *La formation professionnelle en secteur informel. Rapport sur l'enquête terrain au Cameroun [Vocational Training in the Informal Sector: Report on the Cameroon Survey].* Paris, Agence française de développement. (Document de travail, 17.)

Wardany, Y. 2012. The Mubarak regime's failed youth policies and the January uprising. *IDS Bulletin,* Vol. 43, No. 1, pp. 37–46.

Watts, A. G. and Fretwell, D. H. 2004. *Public Policies for Career Development: Case Studies and Emerging Issues for Designing Career Information and Guidance Systems in Developing and Transition Economies.* Washington, DC, World Bank.

Wedig, K. 2010a. *Labour Market Information in Solo, Indonesia.* Bonn, Germany, Deutsche Gesellschaft für Internationale Zusammenarbeit.

___. 2010b. *Linking Labour Organisation and Vocational Training in Uganda: Lessons for Rural Poverty Reduction.* Paris, Agence française de développement. (Focales, 3.)

___. 2012. *Economic Organisation Under Adverse Conditions: Small Producers and Casual Labourers in Uganda*. London, School of Oriental and African Studies. (Unpublished doctoral thesis.)

WESTAT (2009). *Evaluation of the Young Adult Internship Program (YAIP): Analysis of Existing Participant Data*. New York, New York City Center for Economic Opportunity.

WFP. 2004. *A Report from the Office of Evaluation: Full Report of the Evaluation of AFGHANISTAN PRRO 10233*. Rome, World Food Programme. (OEDE/2005/1.)

Williams, J. and Bentrovato, D. 2010. *Education and Fragility in Liberia*. Paris, UNESCO — International Institute for Educational Planning /Inter-agency Network on Education in Emergencies. (IIEP Research Paper.)

Winthrop, R. and Smith, M. S. 2012. *A New Face of Education: Bringing Technology into the Classroom in the Developing World*. Washington, DC, Brookings Institution. (Brooke Shearer Working Paper, 1.)

Wiśniewski , J. 2007. *Secondary Education in Poland: 18 Years of Changes*. Conference paper for Fourth ECA Education Conference, Tirana, 24–26 October 2007.

Woessmann, L. 2009. *International Evidence on School Tracking: A Review*. Munich, Germany, CESifo. (CESifo DICE Report, 1.)

Wolf, A. 2011. *Review of Vocational Education: The Wolf Report*. London, UK Department for Education.

Women in Development. 2003. *Independent External Evaluation of EMPOWER Program for USAID/Ethiopia*. Washington, DC, US Agency for International Development.

Woods, M., Hales, J., Purdon, S., Sejersen, T. and Hayllar, O. 2009. *A Test for Racial Discrimination in Recruitment Practice in British Cities*. Norwich, UK, UK Department for Work and Pensions. (Research Report, 607.)

World Bank. 2003. *Implementation Completion Report (IDA-26370) on a loan to Cote d'Ivoire for a Labour Force Training Project*. Washington, DC, World Bank.

___. 2006a. *Burundi: diagnostic et perspectives pour une nouvelle politique burundais dans le contexte de l'éducation gratuite pour tous (Burundi: Diagnosis and Perspectives for a New Burundian Policy in the Context of Free Education For All)*. Washington, DC, World Bank.

___. 2006b. *The Rural Investment Climate: It Differs and It Matters*. Washington, DC, World Bank.

___. 2006c. *Zambia: Education Sector Public Expenditure Review*. Washington, DC, World Bank. (Report, 36552-ZM.)

___. 2007a. *Le système éducatif tchadien: éléments de diagnostic pour une politique éducative nouvelle et une meilleure efficacité de la dépense publique [The Educational System in Chad: Elements of the Diagnosis for a New Educational Policy and a More Efficient Public Spending]*. Washington, DC, World Bank. (Document de travail de la Banque mondiale, 110.)

___. 2007b. *World Development Report 2007: Development and the Next Generation*. Washington, DC, World Bank.

___. 2008a. *Curricula, Examinations, and Assessment in Secondary Education in sub-Saharan Africa*. Washington, DC, World Bank. (Working Paper, 128.)

___. 2008b. *Czech Republic: Improving Employment Chances of the Roma*. Washington, DC, World Bank. (Report, 46120 CZ.)

___. 2008c. *Le système éducatif centrafricain: contraintes et marges de manoeuvre pour la reconstruction du système éducatif dans la perspective de la réduction de la pauvreté [The Central African Educational System: Constraints and Republic's Opportunities for the Reconstruction of the Educational System from of a Poverty Reduction Perspective]*. Washington, DC, World Bank. (Document de travail de la Banque mondiale, 144.)

___. 2008d. *World Development Report 2008: Agriculture for Development*. Washington, DC, World Bank.

___. 2009a. *Are Skills Constraining Growth in Bosnia and Herzegovina?* Washington, DC, World Bank. (Report, 54901-BA.)

___. 2009b. *Gender in Bolivian Production: Reducing Differences in Formality and Productivity of Firms*. Washington, DC, World Bank. (World Bank Country Study.)

___. 2010a. *Indonesia Jobs Report: Towards Better Jobs and Security for All*. Washington, DC, World Bank.

___. 2010b. *Project Appraisal Document on a Proposed Grant from the Global Environmental Facility Trust Fund in the Amount of US$ 4.0 Million to the Republic of Yemen for an Agro-Biodiversity and Climate Adaptation Project*. Washington, DC, World Bank.

___. 2010c. *Ready for Work: Increasing Economic Opportunity for Adolescent Girls and Young Women*. Washington, DC, World Bank.

___. 2011a. *Accelerating Catch-up: Tertiary Education for Growth in sub-Saharan Africa*. Washington, DC, World Bank.

___. 2011b. *Project Performance Assessment Report: Ethiopia Productive Safety Net Project*. Washington, DC, World Bank. (Report, 62549.)

___. 2011c. *Republic of Ghana: Tackling Poverty in Northern Ghana*. Washington, DC, World Bank.

___. 2011d. *Rwanda: Toward Quality Enhancement and Achievement of Universal Nine Year Basic Education — An Education System in Transition, a Nation in Transition*. Washington, DC, World Bank.

___. 2011e. *Strengthening Skills and Employability in Peru*. Washington, DC, World Bank.

___. 2011f. *World Development Report 2013: Jobs — Outline*. Washington, DC, World Bank.

___. 2012a. *Africa's Pulse: an analysis of issues shaping Africa's economic future*. Washington, DC, World Bank.

___. 2012b. *Kingdom of Morocco: Promoting Youth Opportunities and Participation*. Washington, DC, World Bank.

___. 2012c. *World Development Indicators*. Washington, DC, World Bank. http://data.worldbank.org/data-catalog/world-development-indicators. (Accessed 9 August 2012.)

World Bank and IPEA. 2012. *Bridging the Atlantic: Brazil and Sub-Saharan Africa — South-South Partnering for Growth*. Washington, DC/Rio de Janeiro, Brazil, World Bank/Institute for Applied Economic Research.

World Economic Forum, World Bank and African Development Bank. 2011. *Africa Competitiveness Report 2011*. Geneva, Switzerland/Washington, DC/Tunis, World Economic Forum/World Bank/African Development Bank.

Yoshida, K. and Yamada, S. 2012. Aid to skills development: case study on Japan's foreign aid program. Background paper for *EFA Global Monitoring Report 2012*.

Youth Employment Network. 2009. *Joining Forces With Young People: A Practical Guide to Collaboration for Youth Employment*. Geneva, Switzerland, International Labour Office, Youth Employment Network.

Zambia MoFNP. 2011. *Sixth National Development Plan (2011–2015)*. Lusaka, Ministry of Finance and National Planning.

Ziderman, A. 2003. *Financing Vocational Training in Sub-Saharan Africa*. Washington, DC, World Bank. (Africa Region Human Development Series.)

Zossou, E., Van Mele, P., Vodouhe, S. D. and Wanvoeke, J. 2009. Comparing farmer-to-farmer video with workshops to train rural women in improved rice parboiling in central Benin. *Journal of Agricultural Education and Extension,* Vol. 15, No. 4, pp. 329–39.

Annex

Eurydice. 2011. *National System Overview on Education Systems in Europe*. Brussels, European Commission.

OECD-DAC. 2012a. International Development Statistics: Creditor Reporting System. Paris, Organisation for Economic Co-operation and Development. http://stats.oecd.org/Index.aspx?datasetcode=CRS1. (Accessed 20 April 2012.)

___. 2012b. *International Development Statistics: DAC Annual Aggregates*. Paris, Organisation for Economic Co-operation and Development. http://www.oecd.org/document/33/0.2340.en_2649_34447_36661793_1_1_1_1.00.html. (Accessed 20 April 2012.)

UNDP. 2011. *Human Development Report 2011: Sustainability and Equity — A Better Future for All*. New York, United Nations Development Programme.

UNESCO-IBE. 2011. *World Data on Education: Seventh Edition 2010/11*. Geneva, Switzerland, UNESCO International Bureau of Education. http://www.ibe.unesco.org/en/services/online-materials/world-data-on-education/seventh-edition-2010-11.html. (Accessed 23 May 2012.)

UNICEF. 2012. *The State of the World's Children 2012: Children in an Urban World*. New York, UNICEF.

United Nations. 2011. *World Population Prospects: The 2010 Revision,*CD-Rom edn. New York, United Nations.

World Bank. 2011. *World Development Indicators 2011*. Washington, DC, World Bank

Index

Note: *Italic* page numbers refer to figures and tables; those in **bold** refer to material in boxes and panels; ***bold italics*** indicates a figure or table in a box or panel.

Education for All Global Monitoring Report 2 0 1 2

Education for All Global Monitoring Report